Addison-Wesley

Elements of CALCULUS and Analytic Geometry

Solution Manual

Addison-Wesley

Elements of CALCULUS and Analytic Geometry

Solution Manual

George B. Thomas, Jr.
Massachusetts Institute of Technology

Ross L. Finney
Massachusetts Institute of Technology

Prepared by
Alexia B. Latimer
Benita H. Albert
Judith Broadwin

Addison-Wesley Publishing Company
Menlo Park, California • Reading, Massachusetts • New York
Don Mills, Ontario • Wokingham, England • Amsterdam
Bonn • Sydney • Singapore • Tokyo • Madrid • Bogotá
Santiago • San Juan

About the Authors

Dr. Alexia Latimer is Chairwoman of the Mathematics Department at Eastside High School in Taylors, South Carolina. She was a recipient of the Presidential Award for Excellence in Mathematics Teaching in 1985. She is a reader for Advanced Placement Calculus Examinations and a consultant for the College Board, Southern Region.

Benita Albert is Chairwoman of the Oak Ridge High School Mathematics Department in Oak Ridge, Tennessee. She serves as a consultant for the College Board, Southeastern Region, and is the author of the Teacher's Guide for Advanced Placement Mathematics.

Judith Broadwin is a mathematics teacher at Jericho High School in Jericho, New York. She is a governor of the Mathematics Association of America, a member of the Advanced Placement Test Development Committee, Educational Testing Service, and chairs the Academic Advisory Panel for the College Board, Middle States Region.

Printed in the United States of America. Published simultaneously in Canada.

ISBN 0-201-22303-1

6 7 8 9 10 - ML - 95

Contents

CHAPTER 1

THE RATE OF CHANGE OF A FUNCTION

1.1 COORDINATES FOR THE PLANE

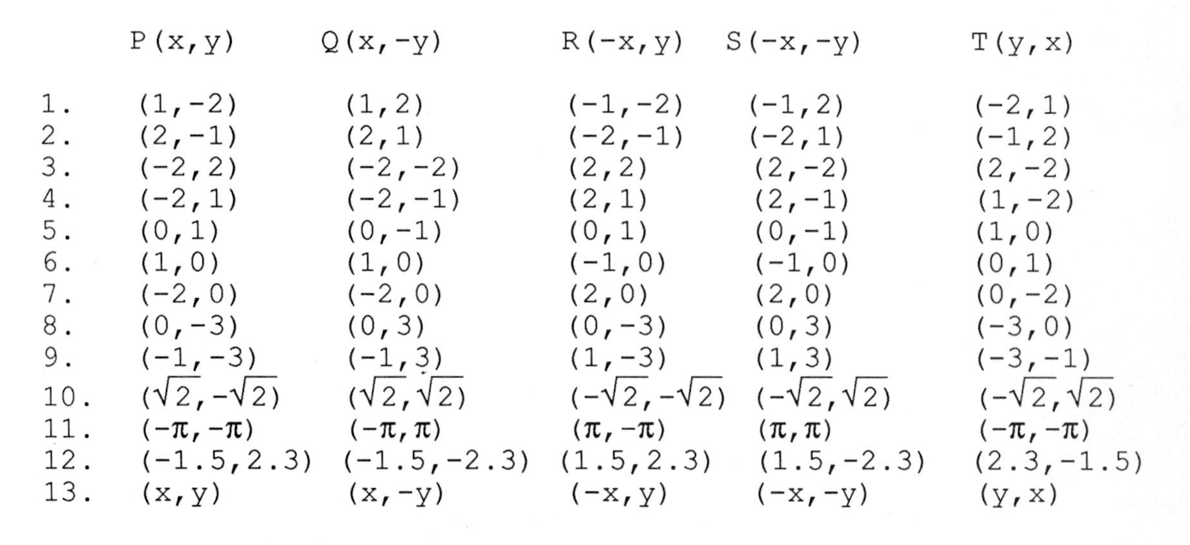

	P(x,y)	Q(x,-y)	R(-x,y)	S(-x,-y)	T(y,x)
1.	(1,-2)	(1,2)	(-1,-2)	(-1,2)	(-2,1)
2.	(2,-1)	(2,1)	(-2,-1)	(-2,1)	(-1,2)
3.	(-2,2)	(-2,-2)	(2,2)	(2,-2)	(2,-2)
4.	(-2,1)	(-2,-1)	(2,1)	(2,-1)	(1,-2)
5.	(0,1)	(0,-1)	(0,1)	(0,-1)	(1,0)
6.	(1,0)	(1,0)	(-1,0)	(-1,0)	(0,1)
7.	(-2,0)	(-2,0)	(2,0)	(2,0)	(0,-2)
8.	(0,-3)	(0,3)	(0,-3)	(0,3)	(-3,0)
9.	(-1,-3)	(-1,3)	(1,-3)	(1,3)	(-3,-1)
10.	$(\sqrt{2},-\sqrt{2})$	$(\sqrt{2},\sqrt{2})$	$(-\sqrt{2},-\sqrt{2})$	$(-\sqrt{2},\sqrt{2})$	$(-\sqrt{2},\sqrt{2})$
11.	$(-\pi,-\pi)$	$(-\pi,\pi)$	$(\pi,-\pi)$	(π,π)	$(-\pi,-\pi)$
12.	(-1.5,2.3)	(-1.5,-2.3)	(1.5,2.3)	(1.5,-2.3)	(2.3,-1.5)
13.	(x,y)	(x,-y)	(-x,y)	(-x,-y)	(y,x)

14. The angle is 45°, or $\frac{\pi}{4}$ radians.

15.

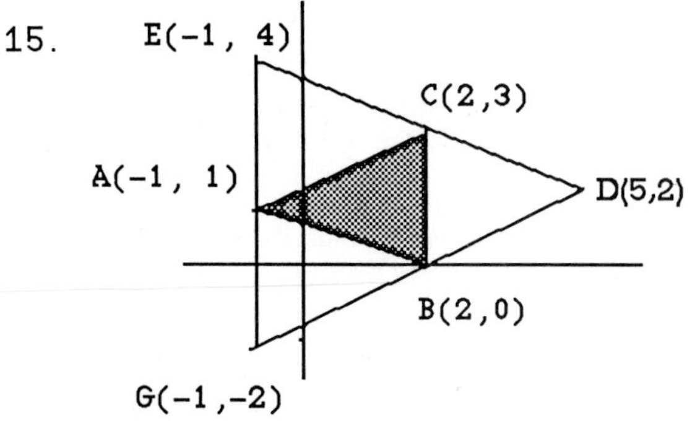

BC = 3 units.

In ▱ACBG, G(−1, 1 − 3) = G(−1, −2)

and in ▱ABCE, E(−1, 1 + 3) = E(−1, 4).

$m_{AD} = \frac{-1}{3}$.

In ▱ABDC, D(3 − 1, 2 + 3) = D(5, 2)

16. (a) The missing vertices are (3,-7) and (-4,-2).
    (b) The length is 7, the height is 5, so the area is 35.

17. l = 3w and 2l + 2w = 56. Therefore, l = 21 and w = 7. The coordinates are A(-12,2), B(-12,-5) and C(9,-5).

18. (a) It meets the x-axis at (-3,0).
    (b) It has center (-3,3).

19. b = 2

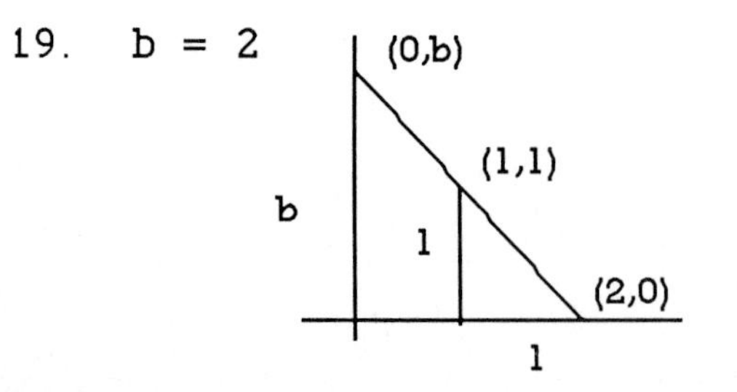

20. A 90°-rotation takes the point (x,y) into $((-y,x)$

(a) $(4,1) \to (-1,4)$ (b) $(-2,-3) \to (3,-2)$

(c) $(2,-5) \to (5,2)$ (d) $(x,0) \to (0,x)$

(e) $(0,y) \to (-y,0)$ (f) $(x,y) \to (-y,x)$

(g) $(3,-10) \to (10,3)$

1.2 THE SLOPE OF A LINE

1. $\Delta x = 1 - (-1) = 2$ $\Delta y = 2 - 1 = 1$

2. $\Delta x = -1 -1 = -2$ $\Delta y = -1 -2 = -3$

3. $\Delta x = -1 - (-3) = 2$ $\Delta y = -2 - 2 = -4$

4. $\Delta x = -3 - (-1) = -2$ $\Delta y = 2 - (-2) = 4$

5. $\Delta x = -8 - (-3) = -5$ $\Delta y = 1 - 1 = 0$

6. $\Delta x = 0 - 0 = 0$ $\Delta y = -2 -4 = -6$

7. (a) $\Delta x = 57 - 0 = 57$, $\Delta y = 22 - 32 = -10$ (b) $\Delta x = 26 - 28 = -2$, $\Delta y = 6 - 18 = -12$ (c) $\Delta x = 40 - 39 = 1$, $\Delta y = 4 - 18 = -14$

8. $\Delta x = 40 - 57 = -17$ $\Delta y = 4 - 22 = -18$

9. right, above 10. right 11. left 12. above

13. right, below 14. left,below 15. below 16. left

17. $m = \dfrac{-1-2}{1-2} = 3;\ m_\perp = -\dfrac{1}{3}$

18. $m = \dfrac{-1-2}{-2-(-1)} = 3;\ m_\perp = -\dfrac{1}{3}$

19. $m = \dfrac{-1-(-2)}{-2-1} = -\dfrac{1}{3};\ m_\perp = 3$

20. $m = \dfrac{1-(-1)}{-2-2} = -\dfrac{1}{2};\ m_\perp = 2$

21. $m = \dfrac{0-1}{1-0} = -1;\ m_\perp = 1$

22. $m = \dfrac{0-0}{1-(-1)} = 0;\ m_\perp$ is undefined

23. $m = \dfrac{3-3}{2-(-1)} = 0;\ m_\perp$ is undefined

24. $m = \dfrac{-3-3}{2-0} = -3;\ m_\perp = \dfrac{1}{3}$

25. $m = \dfrac{-2-0}{0-(-2)} = -1;\ m_\perp = 1$

26. $m = \dfrac{-3-2}{1-1}$ is undefined; $m_\perp = 0$

27. $m = \dfrac{-4-0}{-2-0} = 2$; $m_\perp = -\dfrac{1}{2}$

28. $m = \dfrac{-\frac{1}{3} - 0}{0 - \frac{1}{2}} = \dfrac{2}{3}$; $m_\perp = -\dfrac{3}{2}$

29. $m = \dfrac{y-0}{x-0} = \dfrac{y}{x}$; $m_\perp = \dfrac{x}{y}$ if $y \neq 0$, undefined if $y = 0$

30. $m = \dfrac{0-0}{x-0} = 0$; $m_\perp$ is undefined

31. m is undefined; $m_\perp = 0$

32. $m = \dfrac{b-0}{0-a} = -\dfrac{b}{a}$; $m_\perp = \dfrac{a}{b}$

33. $\tan\alpha = \dfrac{5}{16} \Rightarrow \alpha = 17.35^0$; $\tan\beta = \dfrac{9}{8} \Rightarrow \beta = 48.37^0$

34. $\tan 40^0 = \dfrac{R}{T} \Rightarrow 0.8391 = \dfrac{R}{9} \Rightarrow R = 7.55$ in

35. $\tan 40^0 = 0.8391$

36. (a) $\dfrac{-1}{0.35 \text{ in}} = -2.9^0/\text{in}$ (b) $\dfrac{-58}{3.6} = -16.1^0/\text{in}$ (c) $\dfrac{-5}{0.7} \approx -7.1^0/\text{in}$

37. Fiberglass is the best with $-16^0/\text{in}$

Gypsum is the poorest with $-3^0/\text{in}$

38. (a) A(0,1); B(1,2); C(2,1), D(1,0)

$m_{AB} = 1$; $m_{DC} = 1$; $M_{AD} = -1$; $M_{BC} = -1$ ∴ parallelogram

(b) A(3,1); B(2,2); C(0,1); D(1,0)

$m_{AB} = -1$; $m_{DC} = -1$; $M_{AD} = \frac{1}{2}$; $M_{BC} = \frac{1}{2}$ ∴ parallelogram

(c) A(-1,-2); B(2,-1); C(2,1); D(1,0)

$m_{AB} = \frac{1}{3}$; $m_{DC} = 1$; ∴ not a parallelogram

(d) A(-2,2); B(1,3); C(2,0); D(-1,-1)

$m_{AB} = \frac{1}{3}$; $m_{DC} = \frac{1}{3}$; $M_{AD} = -3$; $M_{BC} = -3$ ∴ parallelogram

(e) A(-1,0); B(0,-1); C(2,0); D(0,2)

$m_{BC} = \frac{1}{2}$; $m_{AD} = 2$ ∴ not a parallelogram

39. (a) A(1,0); B(0,1); C(2,1)

$m_{AB} = -1$; $m_{AC} = 1$ ∴ not collinear

(b) A(-2,1); B(0,5); C(-1,2)

$m_{AB} = \frac{4}{2} = 2;\ m_{AC} = \frac{1}{1} = 1 \therefore$ not collinear

(c) A(-2,1); B(-1,1); C(0,1); D(1,0)

$m_{AB} = 0;\ m_{BC} = 2;\ m_{CD} = 2;\ m_{BD} = \frac{6}{3} = 2 \therefore$ B,C,D collinear

(d) A(-2,3); B(0,2); C(2,0)

$m_{AB} = \frac{1}{-2};\ m_{BC} = -1 \therefore$ A,B,C not collinear

(e) A(-3,-2); B(-2,0); C(-1,2); D(1,6)

$m_{AB} = \frac{-2}{-1} = 2;\ m_{BC} = \frac{2}{1} = 2;\ m_{CD} = \frac{4}{2} = 2 \therefore$ A,B,C,D collinear

40. All of the triangles would have the same altitude - a line through the origin perpendicular to the line of motion. Since the triangles all have the same base length - constant velocity for $\Delta t = 1$ - they will all have the same area.

41. A(-2,3): $x = -2 + \Delta x = -2 + 5 = 3;\ y = 3 - \Delta x = 3 - 6 = -3$
New position is P(3,-3)

42. A(6,0): $x = 6 + (-6) = 0;\ y = 0 + 0 = 0$. New position is P(0,0).

43. Moves from A(x,y) to B(3,-3) with $\Delta x = 5$ and $\Delta y = 6$
Original $x = 3 - 5 = -2$; original $y = -3 - 6 = -9$

44. $\Delta x = 0$ and $\Delta y = 0$.

1.3 EQUATIONS FOR LINES

1. Vertical: $x = 2$ Horizontal: $y = 3$

2. Vertical: $x = -7$ Horizontal: $y = -7$

3. Vertical: $x = 0$ Horizontal: $y = 0$

4. Vertical: $x = 0$ Horizontal: $y = -4$

5. Vertical: $x = -4$ Horizontal: $y = 0$

6. Vertical: $x = a$ Horizontal: $y = 0$

7. Vertical: $x = 0$ Horizontal: $y = b$

8. Vertical: $x = x_1$ Horizontal: $y = y_1$

9. $y - 1 = x - 2 \Rightarrow y = x$

10. $y + 1 = -1(x - 1) \Rightarrow y + x = 0$

11. $y - 1 = x + 1 \Rightarrow y = x + 2$

12. $y - 1 = -1(x + 1) \Rightarrow y + x = 0$

13. $y - b = 2x \Rightarrow y = 2x + b$

14. $y = -2(x - a) \quad \Rightarrow \quad y + 2x = 2a$

15. $m = \frac{3}{2}; \quad y = \frac{3}{2}x$

16. $y = 1$

17. $x = 1$

18. $m = \frac{-2 - 1}{2 - (-2)} = -\frac{3}{4}; \quad y - 1 = -\frac{3}{4}(x + 2) \quad \Rightarrow 3x + 4y = -2$

19. $x = -2$

20. $m = \frac{1 - 3}{3 - 1} = -1; \; y - 3 = -1(x - 1) \quad \Rightarrow \quad x + y = 4$

21. $m = \frac{-F_o}{T} \quad y = \frac{-F_o}{T}(x - T) \Rightarrow Ty = -F_o x + TF_o$
$F_o x + Ty = TF_o$

22. $m = \frac{0 - 0}{1 - 0} = 0; \quad y = 0$

23. $x = 0$

24. $m = \frac{3 + 1}{-2 - 2} = -1; \quad y + 1 = -(x - 2) \quad \Rightarrow \quad x + y = 1$

25. $m = \frac{.7}{-2.1} = \frac{-1}{3} \quad \Rightarrow y - 1.5 = \frac{-1}{3}(x + 7) \quad \Rightarrow 15y = -5x + 19$

26. $m = \frac{\sqrt{5} - \sqrt{2}}{\sqrt{5} - \sqrt{2}} = 1; \quad y - \sqrt{2} = x - \sqrt{2} \quad \Rightarrow x - y = 0$

27. $m = \frac{y_1 - y_o}{x_1 - x_0} \qquad y - y_1 = \frac{y_1 - y_0}{x_1 - x_0}(x - x_1)$

28. $m = \frac{25000}{1.5} = \frac{50000}{3}; \quad y = 35000 = \frac{50000}{3}(x - 2)$
$3y - 50{,}000x = 5{,}000$

29. $y = 3x - 2$

30. $y = -x + 2$

31. $y = x + \sqrt{2}$

32. $y = -\frac{1}{2}x - 3$

33. $y = -5x + 2.5$

34. $y = \frac{1}{3}x - 1$

35. $y = 3x + 5$: $(-\frac{5}{3},0)$ $(0,5)$; $m = 3$

36. $2y = 3x + 5$: $(-\frac{5}{3},0)$ $(0,\frac{5}{2})$; $m = \frac{3}{2}$

37. $x + y = 2$: $(2,0)$ $(0,2)$; $m = -1$

38. $2x - y = 4$: $(2,0)$ $(0,-4)$; $m = 2$

39. $x - 2y = 4$: $(4,0)$ $(0,-2)$; $m = \frac{1}{2}$

40. $3x + 4y = 12$: $(4,0)$ $(0,3)$; $m = -\frac{3}{4}$

41. $4x - 3y = 12$: $(3,0)$ $(0,-4)$; $m = \frac{4}{3}$

42. $x = 2y - 5$: $(-5,0)$ $(0,\frac{5}{2})$; $m = \frac{1}{2}$

43. $\frac{x}{3} + \frac{y}{4} = 1$: $(3,0)$ $(0,4)$; $m = \frac{-4}{3}$

44. $\frac{2x}{5} - \frac{y}{3} = 1$: $(\frac{5}{2},0)$ $(0,-3)$; $m = \frac{6}{5}$

45. $\frac{x}{2} - \frac{y}{3} = 1$; $(-2,0)$ $(0,3)$; $m = \frac{3}{2}$

46. $\frac{x}{3} + \frac{y}{1} = -1$: $(-3,0)$ $(0,-1)$; $m = -\frac{1}{3}$

47. $1.05x - 0.35y = 7 \Rightarrow 105x - 700 = 35y \Rightarrow 3x - 20 = y$

$(0,-20)$ $(\frac{20}{3},0)$ $m = \dfrac{20}{\frac{20}{3}} = 3$

48. $0.98x + 1.96y = 9.8 \Rightarrow 196y = -98x + 980 \Rightarrow y = -\frac{1}{2}x + 5$

$(10,0)$ $(0,5)$ $m = -\frac{1}{2}$

49. $\frac{x}{a} + \frac{y}{b} = 1$ $(0,b)$ $(a,0)$ $m = \frac{-b}{a}$

50. $m = 3$, $P(1,2) \Rightarrow y - 2 = 3(x - 1)$ or $3x - y = 1$

51. $m = \frac{-\sqrt{3}}{3}$; $y - 1 = -\frac{\sqrt{3}}{3}x \Rightarrow 3y - 3 = -x\sqrt{3} \Rightarrow 3y - 3 = -x\sqrt{3}$

52. (a) L_1: $m = \dfrac{\frac{1}{2}}{1}$; $y = \frac{1}{2}x$ L_2: $m = 1$; $y = x$

L_3: $m = 2$; $y = 2x$ L_4: $m = 3$; $y = 3x$

(b) L_1: $m = \dfrac{\frac{1}{2}}{-1}$; $y = -\frac{1}{2}x$ L_2: $m = -1$; $y = -x$

L_3: $m = -2$; $y = -2x$ L_4: $m = -3$; $y = -3x$

(c) $y = mx$; $(1,m)$

53. $P(2,1)$, L: $y = x + 2$

$\parallel$: $y - 1 = x - 2 \Rightarrow y = x - 1$

$\perp$: $y - 1 = -(x - 2) \Rightarrow y = -x + 3$

$$d = \frac{|2 - 1 + 2|}{\sqrt{2}} = \frac{3}{\sqrt{2}}$$

54. $P(0,0)$, L: $y = -x + 2$

$\parallel$: $y = -x$

$\perp$: $y = x$

$$d = \frac{|0 + 0 - 2|}{\sqrt{2}} = \sqrt{2}$$

55. $P(0,0)$, L: $y\sqrt{3} = -x + 3 \Rightarrow y = -\frac{1}{\sqrt{3}}x + \sqrt{3}$

$\parallel$: $y = \frac{-1}{\sqrt{3}}x$

$\perp$: $y = x\sqrt{3}$

$$d = \frac{|-3|}{\sqrt{1 + 3}} = \frac{3}{2}$$

56. $P(1,2)$, L: $x + 2y = 3$

$\parallel$: $y - 2 = -\frac{1}{2}(x - 2)$ or $x + 2y = 5$

$\perp$: $y - 2 = 2(x - 1)$ or $2x - y = 0$

$$d = \frac{|1 + 2(2) - 3|}{\sqrt{5}} = \frac{2}{\sqrt{5}}$$

57. $P(-2,2)$, L: $y = -2x + 4$

$\parallel$: $y - 2 = -2(x + 2) \Rightarrow y = -2x - 2$

$\perp$: $y - 2 = \frac{1}{2}(x + 2) \Rightarrow y = \frac{1}{2}x + 3$

$2y = x + 6$

$-6 = x - 2y$

$$d = \frac{|2 - 4 - 4|}{\sqrt{1 + 4}} = \frac{6}{\sqrt{5}}$$

58. $P(3,6)$, L: $x + y = 3$

$\parallel$: $y - 6 = -(x - 3)$ or $x + y = 9$

$\perp$: $y - 6 = x - 3$ or $x - y = -3$

$$d = \frac{|3 + 6 - 3|}{\sqrt{2}} = 3\sqrt{2}$$

59. $P(1,0)$, L: $2x - y = -2 \Rightarrow 2x + 2 = y$

$\parallel$: $y = 2(x - 1) \Rightarrow y = 2x - 2$

$\perp$: $y = \frac{-1}{2}(x - 1) \Rightarrow x + 2y = 1$

$$d = \frac{|2 + 2|}{\sqrt{5}} = \frac{4}{\sqrt{5}}$$

60. $P(-2,4)$, L: $x = 5$

$\parallel$: $x = -2$

$\perp$: $y = 4$

$d = |5 - (-2)| = 7$

61. P(3,2), L: $x = -5$

$\parallel$: $x = 3$ $\perp$: $y = 2$ $d = 8$

62. P(3,2), L: $y = -4$

$\parallel$: $y = 2$

$\perp$: $x = 3$

$d = |-4 - 2| = 6$

63. P(a,b), L: $x = -1$

$\parallel$: $x = a$ $\perp$: $y = b$ $d = |a + 1|$

64. P(3,-h), L: $y = 4$ $(h > 0)$

$\parallel$: $y = -h$

$\perp$: $x = 3$

$d = |4 - (-h)| = 4 + h$

65. P(4,6), L: $3y = -4x + 12 \Rightarrow y = \frac{-4}{3}x + 4$

$\parallel$: $y - 6 = \frac{-4}{3}(x - 4) \Rightarrow y = \frac{-4}{3}x + \frac{34}{3}$

$\perp$: $y - 6 = \frac{3}{4}(x - 4) \Rightarrow y = \frac{3}{4}x + 3$

$d = \frac{|16 + 18 - 12|}{5} = \frac{22}{5}$

66. $P(\frac{2}{\sqrt{3}}, -1)$, L: $\sqrt{3}x + y = -3$

$\parallel$: $y + 1 = -\sqrt{3}\,(x - \frac{2}{\sqrt{3}})$ or $y + \sqrt{3}x = 1$

$\perp$: $y + 1 = \frac{\sqrt{3}}{3}(x - \frac{2}{\sqrt{3}})$ or $\sqrt{3}x - 3y = 5$

$d = \frac{|2 - 1 + 3|}{2} = 2$

67. $y = x + 2$; $m = 1 \Rightarrow \phi = 45^\circ = \frac{\pi}{4}$ radians

68. $y = -x + 2$; $m = -1 \Rightarrow \phi = 135^\circ = \frac{3\pi}{4}$ radians

69. $y\sqrt{3} = -x + 3$

$y = \frac{-1}{\sqrt{3}}x + \sqrt{3}$, $m = \frac{-1}{\sqrt{3}} \Rightarrow \phi = 150^\circ = \frac{5\pi}{6}$ radians

70. $x + 2y = 3$; $m = -\frac{1}{2} \Rightarrow \phi \approx 153.4^\circ \approx 2.59$ radians

71. $y = -2x + 4$; $m = -2 = \tan\phi \Rightarrow \phi = 180^\circ - \tan^{-1} 2$ or 116.6°

72. $2x - y = -2$; $m = 2 \Rightarrow \phi \approx 63.4^\circ \approx 1.11$ radians

73. $3y = -4x + 12$; $m = \frac{-4}{3}$; $\phi \approx 180^\circ - \text{Arctan}\,\frac{4}{3}$ or 126.9°

74. $\sqrt{3}x + y = -3$; $m = -\sqrt{3}$, $\phi = 120^\circ = \frac{2\pi}{3}$ radians.

75. $m = \tan\phi = \sqrt{3} \Rightarrow y - 4 = \sqrt{3}(x - 1)$ or $y = x\sqrt{3} + (4 - \sqrt{3})$

76. $\tan 135^\circ = -1 \Rightarrow y + 1 = -(x + 1)$ or $x + y = -2$

77. $x = -2$

78. $\tan 0^\circ = 0 \Rightarrow y + 2 = 0(x - 3)$ or $y = -2$

79. $p = kd + 1$

$d = 100 \Rightarrow p = 10.94$ so $10.94 = 100k + 1$ or $k = \frac{9.94}{100}$

$k = .0994$
$p = (.0994)d + 1$
$p = (.0994)(50) + 1 \approx 5.97$ atm

80. $\angle\alpha = 45^\circ \Rightarrow \angle\beta = 45^\circ$. $\therefore \tan\beta = 1$. The x-intercept is $(1,0)$

so $y - 0 = (x - 1)$ or $x - y = 1$.

81. $m = \frac{35 - 35.16}{65 - 135} = \frac{-.16}{-70} = \frac{.16}{70}$

$s - 35 = \frac{.16}{70}(t - 65)$
$70s - 2450 = .16t - 10.4$
$70s = .16t + 2439.6$
$s = 0.0023t + 34.85$

82. (a) $m = \frac{212 - 32}{100-0} = \frac{9}{5}$; $F - 32 = \frac{9}{5}C$ or $F = \frac{9}{5}C + 32$

(b) $F = C$ when $C - 32 = \frac{9}{5}C$ or when $C = -40$.

83. $\sin 37.1 = \frac{14}{z} \Rightarrow z = \frac{14}{\sin 37.1} \approx 23$ ft

1.4 FUNCTIONS AND GRAPHS

1. $y = 2\sqrt{x}$ D: $x \geq 0$ R: $y \geq 0$
2. $y = 1 + \sqrt{x}$ D: $x \geq 0$ R: $y \geq 1$
3. $y = -\sqrt{x}$ D: $x \geq 0$ R: $y \leq 0$
4. $y = \sqrt{-x}$ D: $x \leq 0$ R: $y \geq 0$
5. $y = \sqrt{x + 4}$ D: $x \geq -4$ R: $y \leq 0$
6. $y = \sqrt{x - 2}$ D: $x \geq 2$ R: $y \geq 0$
7. $y = \frac{1}{x - 2}$ D: $x \in R$, $x \neq 2$ R: $y \neq 0$
8. $y = \frac{1}{x + 2}$ D: $x \in R$, $x \neq -2$ R: $y \neq 0$
9. $y = 2\cos x$ D: $x \in R$ R: $-2 \leq y \leq 2$
10. $y = -\cos x$ D: $x \in R$ R: $-1 \leq y \leq 1$
11. $y = -3\sin x$ D: $x \in R$ R: $-3 \leq y \leq 3$
12. $y = 2\sin 4x$ D: $x \in R$ R: $-2 \leq y \leq 2$

13. $y = x^2 + 1$
(a) D: $x \in R$
(b) R: $y \geq 1$

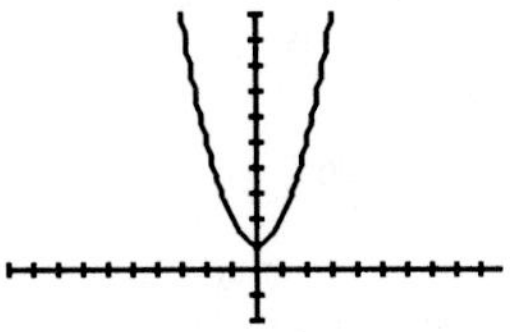

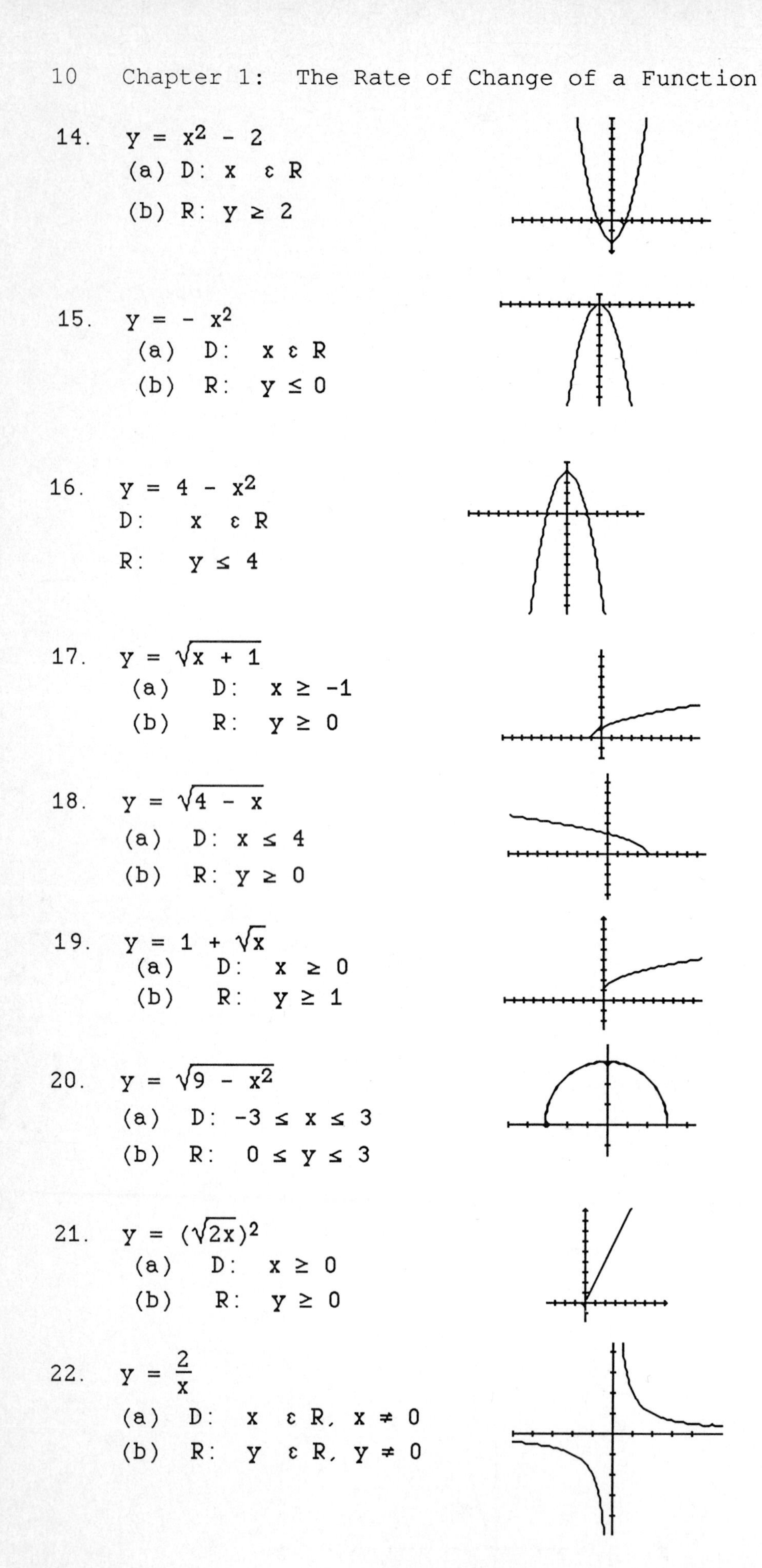

14. $y = x^2 - 2$
(a) D: $x \in R$
(b) R: $y \geq 2$

15. $y = -x^2$
(a) D: $x \in R$
(b) R: $y \leq 0$

16. $y = 4 - x^2$
D: $x \in R$
R: $y \leq 4$

17. $y = \sqrt{x + 1}$
(a) D: $x \geq -1$
(b) R: $y \geq 0$

18. $y = \sqrt{4 - x}$
(a) D: $x \leq 4$
(b) R: $y \geq 0$

19. $y = 1 + \sqrt{x}$
(a) D: $x \geq 0$
(b) R: $y \geq 1$

20. $y = \sqrt{9 - x^2}$
(a) D: $-3 \leq x \leq 3$
(b) R: $0 \leq y \leq 3$

21. $y = (\sqrt{2x})^2$
(a) D: $x \geq 0$
(b) R: $y \geq 0$

22. $y = \frac{2}{x}$
(a) D: $x \in R,\ x \neq 0$
(b) R: $y \in R,\ y \neq 0$

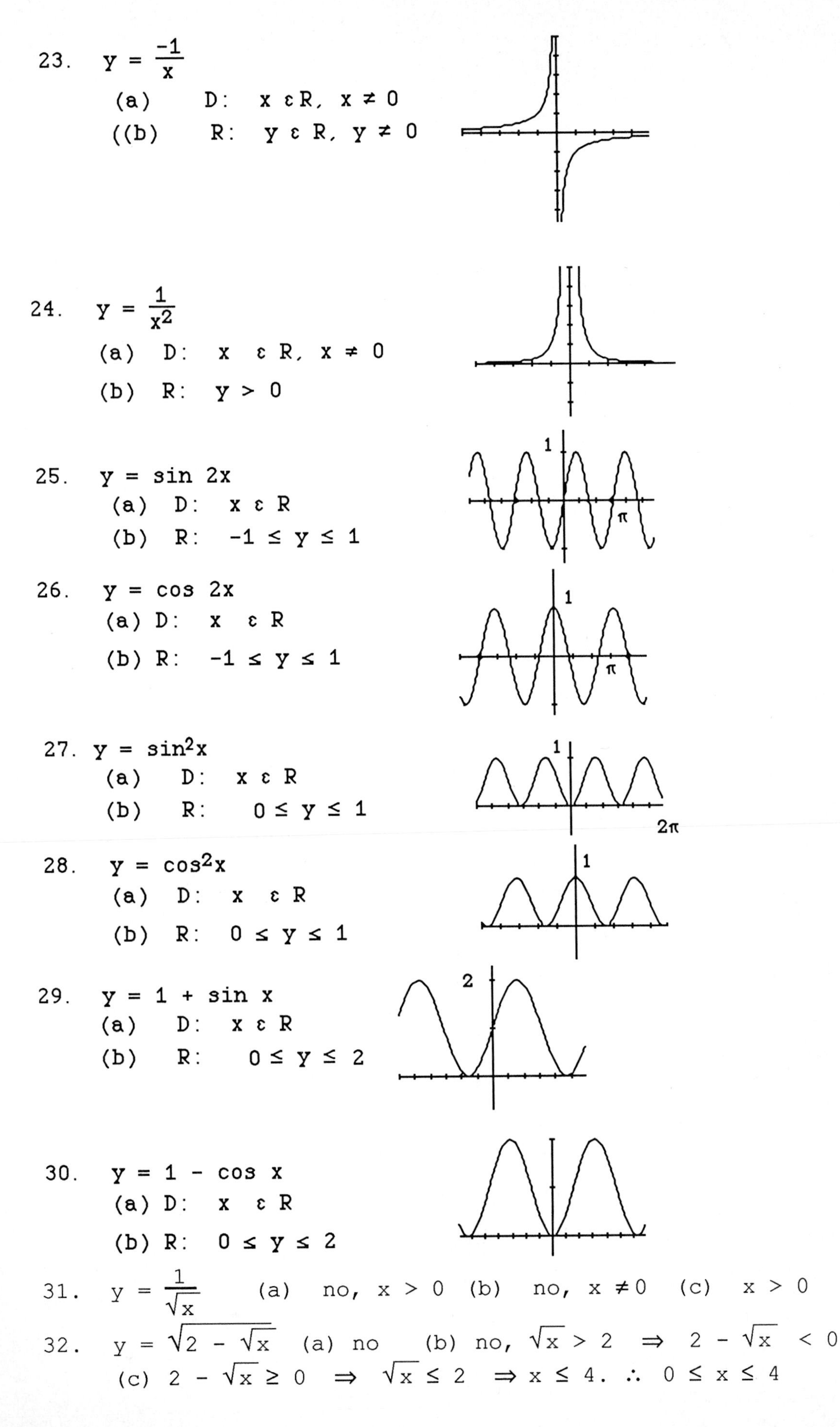

23. $y = \frac{-1}{x}$

 (a) D: $x \in R,\ x \neq 0$

 ((b) R: $y \in R,\ y \neq 0$

24. $y = \frac{1}{x^2}$

 (a) D: $x \in R,\ x \neq 0$

 (b) R: $y > 0$

25. $y = \sin 2x$

 (a) D: $x \in R$

 (b) R: $-1 \leq y \leq 1$

26. $y = \cos 2x$

 (a) D: $x \in R$

 (b) R: $-1 \leq y \leq 1$

27. $y = \sin^2 x$

 (a) D: $x \in R$

 (b) R: $0 \leq y \leq 1$

28. $y = \cos^2 x$

 (a) D: $x \in R$

 (b) R: $0 \leq y \leq 1$

29. $y = 1 + \sin x$

 (a) D: $x \in R$

 (b) R: $0 \leq y \leq 2$

30. $y = 1 - \cos x$

 (a) D: $x \in R$

 (b) R: $0 \leq y \leq 2$

31. $y = \frac{1}{\sqrt{x}}$ (a) no, $x > 0$ (b) no, $x \neq 0$ (c) $x > 0$

32. $y = \sqrt{2 - \sqrt{x}}$ (a) no (b) no, $\sqrt{x} > 2 \Rightarrow 2 - \sqrt{x} < 0$

 (c) $2 - \sqrt{x} \geq 0 \Rightarrow \sqrt{x} \leq 2 \Rightarrow x \leq 4.\ \therefore\ 0 \leq x \leq 4$

33. $f(x) = \sqrt{\frac{1}{x} - 1}$

$\frac{1}{x} - 1 \geq 0 \Leftrightarrow \frac{1-x}{x} \geq 0$

(a) no (b) no (c) no (d) $0 < x \leq 1$

34. $y = \sqrt{\frac{1 + \cos 2x}{2}}$ (a) yes (b) $|\cos 2x| \leq 1$

(c) If $\cos 2x = 1$, $\frac{1 + \cos 2x}{2} = \frac{1+1}{2} = 1$;

If $\cos 2x = -1$, $\frac{1 + \cos 2x}{2} = \frac{1-1}{2} = 0$

(d) D: all reals; R: $0 \leq y \leq 1$

35. $y = \tan \frac{x}{2}$

(a) $\frac{x}{2} \neq \pm \frac{\pi}{2}, \pm \frac{3\pi}{2}, \ldots, \pm \frac{(2n-1)\pi}{2}$, n a positive integer

(b) $x \neq \pm\pi, \pm 3\pi, \pm 5\pi, \ldots, \pm (2n-1)\pi$, n a positive integer

(c) $-\infty < y < \infty$

(d) D: $x \neq \pm\pi, \pm 3\pi, \ldots, \pm(2n-1)\pi$ R: $-\infty < y < \infty$

36. (a) The correct graph is (i), since $x = 0 \Rightarrow y = -1$

(b) The correct graph is (iv), since $x = 1 \Rightarrow y = 0$

37. $y = 4x^2$. Since $y \geq 0$ it is not (i); $f(0) = 0$ so cannot be (iii) or (iv)

38. $y^2 = x \Rightarrow y = \pm\sqrt{x}$. Let $y_1 = \sqrt{x}$ and $y_2 = -\sqrt{x}$.

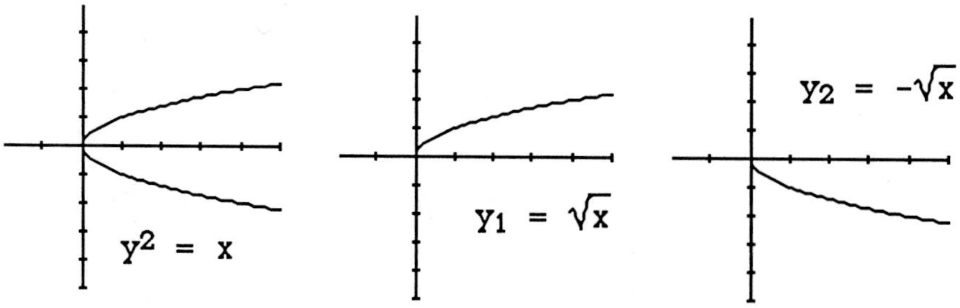

$y^2 = x$ $y_1 = \sqrt{x}$ $y_2 = -\sqrt{x}$

39.

x	f(x)
0	0
1	1
2	0

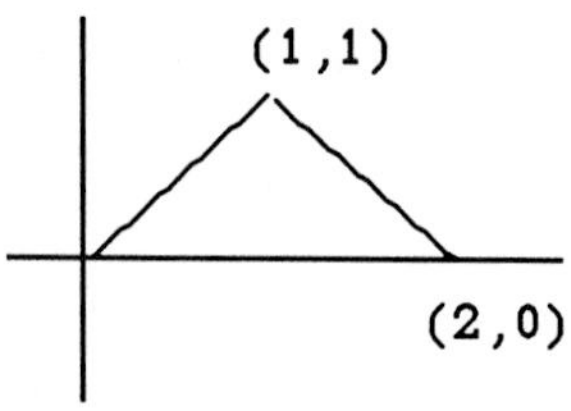

(1,1) (2,0)

40. $y = \begin{cases} 3 - x & \text{if } x \leq 1 \\ 2x & x > 1 \end{cases}$

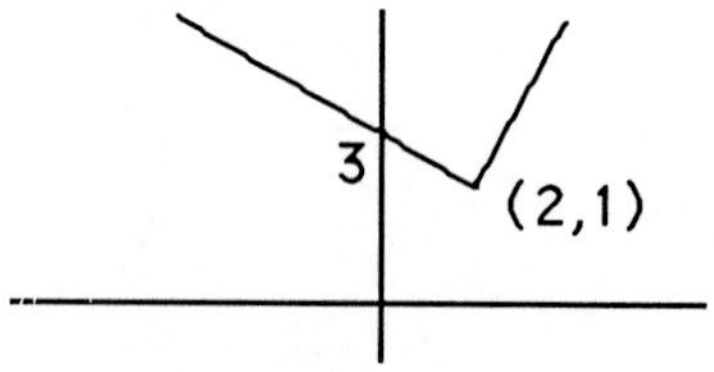

3 (2,1)

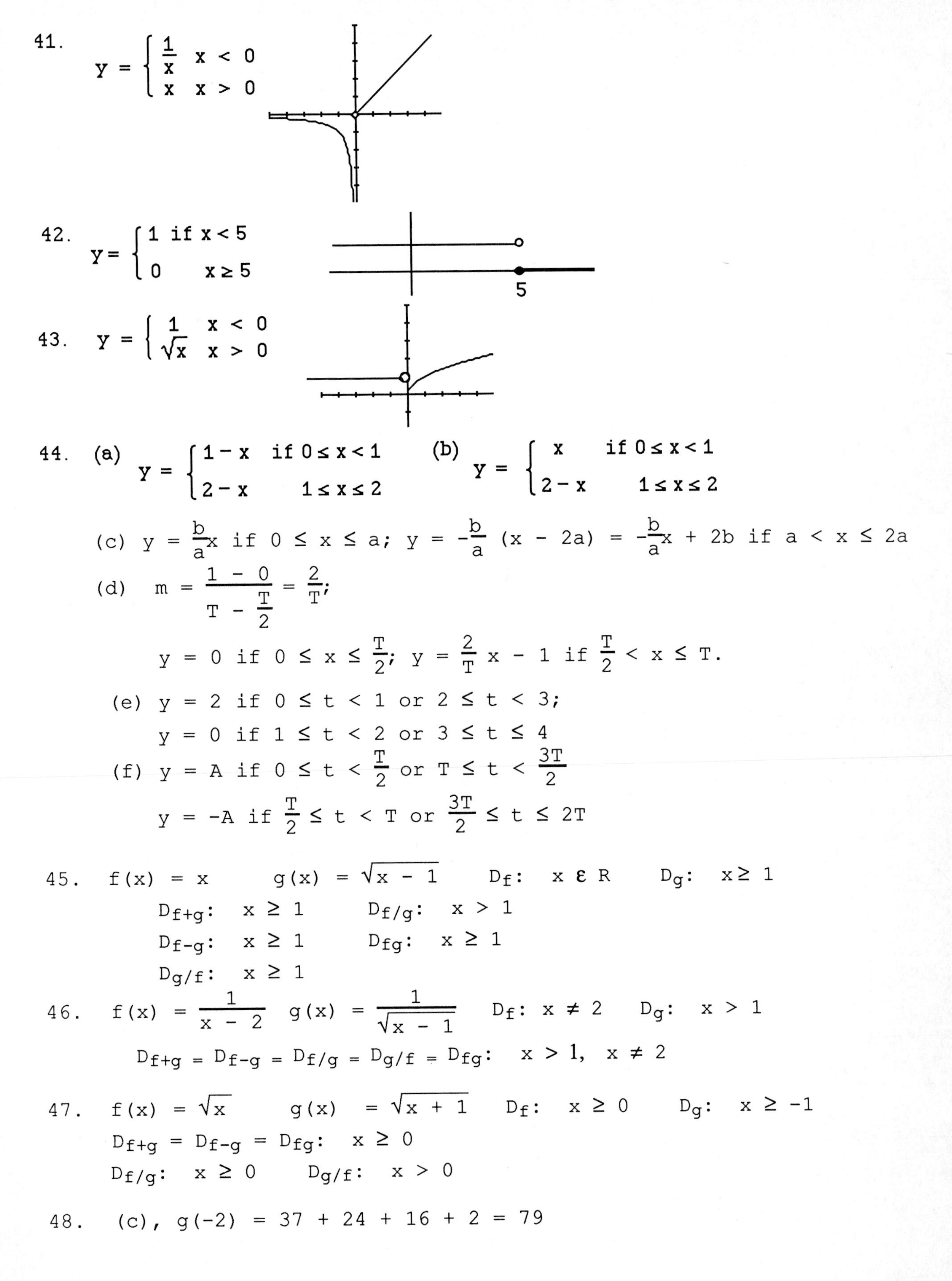

41. $y = \begin{cases} \frac{1}{x} & x < 0 \\ x & x > 0 \end{cases}$

42. $y = \begin{cases} 1 \text{ if } x < 5 \\ 0 \quad x \geq 5 \end{cases}$

43. $y = \begin{cases} 1 & x < 0 \\ \sqrt{x} & x > 0 \end{cases}$

44. (a) $y = \begin{cases} 1 - x & \text{if } 0 \leq x < 1 \\ 2 - x & 1 \leq x \leq 2 \end{cases}$ (b) $y = \begin{cases} x & \text{if } 0 \leq x < 1 \\ 2 - x & 1 \leq x \leq 2 \end{cases}$

(c) $y = \frac{b}{a}x$ if $0 \leq x \leq a$; $y = -\frac{b}{a}(x - 2a) = -\frac{b}{a}x + 2b$ if $a < x \leq 2a$

(d) $m = \dfrac{1 - 0}{T - \frac{T}{2}} = \frac{2}{T}$;

$y = 0$ if $0 \leq x \leq \frac{T}{2}$; $y = \frac{2}{T}x - 1$ if $\frac{T}{2} < x \leq T$.

(e) $y = 2$ if $0 \leq t < 1$ or $2 \leq t < 3$;

$y = 0$ if $1 \leq t < 2$ or $3 \leq t \leq 4$

(f) $y = A$ if $0 \leq t < \frac{T}{2}$ or $T \leq t < \frac{3T}{2}$

$y = -A$ if $\frac{T}{2} \leq t < T$ or $\frac{3T}{2} \leq t \leq 2T$

45. $f(x) = x$ $g(x) = \sqrt{x - 1}$ D_f: $x \in R$ D_g: $x \geq 1$

D_{f+g}: $x \geq 1$ $D_{f/g}$: $x > 1$

D_{f-g}: $x \geq 1$ D_{fg}: $x \geq 1$

$D_{g/f}$: $x \geq 1$

46. $f(x) = \dfrac{1}{x - 2}$ $g(x) = \dfrac{1}{\sqrt{x - 1}}$ D_f: $x \neq 2$ D_g: $x > 1$

$D_{f+g} = D_{f-g} = D_{f/g} = D_{g/f} = D_{fg}$: $x > 1$, $x \neq 2$

47. $f(x) = \sqrt{x}$ $g(x) = \sqrt{x + 1}$ D_f: $x \geq 0$ D_g: $x \geq -1$

$D_{f+g} = D_{f-g} = D_{fg}$: $x \geq 0$

$D_{f/g}$: $x \geq 0$ $D_{g/f}$: $x > 0$

48. (c), $g(-2) = 37 + 24 + 16 + 2 = 79$

49. $h = 1 + \frac{5}{x}$

(a) $h(-1) = -4$ (b) $h(\frac{1}{2}) = 11$ (c) $h(5) = 2$

(d) $h(5x) = 1 + \frac{1}{x}$ (e) $h(10x) = 1 + \frac{1}{2x}$

(f) $h(\frac{1}{x}) = 1 + 5x,\ x \neq 0$

50. (a) $g(f(0)) = g(5) = 22$

(b) $f(g(0) = f(-3) = 2$

(c) $g(f(x)) = (x + 5)^2 - 3 = x^2 + 10x + 22$

(d) $f(g(x)) = x^2 - 3 + 5 = x^2 + 2$

(e) $f(f(-50 = f(0) = 5$

(f) $g(g(2)) = g(10 = -2$

(g) $f(f(x)) = f(x + 5) = x + 5 + 5 = x + 10$

(h) $g(g(x)) = g(x^2 - 3) = (x^2 - 3)^2 - 3 = x^4 - 6x^2 + 6$

51. $f(x) = \frac{x - 1}{x}$ $f(1 - x) = \frac{-x}{1 - x}$

$f(x) \cdot f(1 - x) = \frac{x - 1}{x} \cdot \frac{-x}{1 - x} = 1$

52. $f(x) = \frac{1}{x}$

(a) $f(2) = \frac{1}{2}$

(b) $f(x + 2) = \frac{1}{x + 2}$

(c) $\frac{f(x + 2) - f(2)}{2} = \frac{\frac{1}{x + 2} - \frac{1}{2}}{2} = \frac{-x}{4(x + 2)}$

53. $F(t) = 4t - 3$

$\frac{F(t + h) - F(t)}{h} = \frac{4(t + h) - 3 - 4t + 3}{h} = \frac{4h}{h} = 4$

54. (a) $g \circ f(x) = \sqrt{x - 7}$

(b) $g \circ f(x) = 3(x + 2) = 3x + 6$

(c) $f(x) = x^2$ if $g \circ f(x) = \sqrt{x^2 - 7}$

(d) $g \circ f(x) = \frac{\frac{x}{x - 1}}{\frac{x}{x - 1} - 1} = x$

(e) $f(x) = \frac{1}{x - 1}$ if $g \circ f(x) = x$

(f) $g(x) = \frac{1}{x}$ if $g \circ f(x) = x$

1.5 ABSOLUTE VALUES

1. $|-3| = 3$

2. $|2 - 7| = 5$

3. $|-2 + 7| = 5$

4. $|1.1 - 5.2| = 4.1$

5. $|x| = 2 \Rightarrow x = \pm 2$

6. $|x - 3| = 7 \Rightarrow x - 3 = \pm 7 \Rightarrow x = 10$ or -4

7. $|2x + 5| = 4 \Rightarrow 2x + 5 = \pm 4 \Rightarrow 2x = -1$ or $2x = -9 \Rightarrow x = -\frac{1}{2}$ or $-\frac{9}{2}$

8. $|1 - x| = 1 \Rightarrow 1 - x = \pm 1 \Rightarrow x = 0$ or 2

9. $|8 - 3x| = 9 \Rightarrow 8 - 3x = \pm 9 \Rightarrow 17 = 3x$ or $-1 = 3x \Rightarrow x = \frac{17}{3}$ or $\frac{-1}{3}$

10. $|\frac{x}{2} - 1| = 1 \Rightarrow \frac{x}{2} - 1 = \pm 1 \Rightarrow \frac{x}{2} = 2$ or $0 \Rightarrow x = 4$ or 0

11. $|x| < 4 \Rightarrow -4 < x < 4$, f

12. $|x + 3| \le 1 \Rightarrow -1 < x + 3 < 1 \Rightarrow -4 < x < -2$, g

13. $|x - 5| < 2 \Rightarrow -2 < x - 5 < 2 \Rightarrow 3 < x < 7$, c

14. $|\frac{x}{2}| < 1 \Rightarrow -1 < \frac{x}{2} < 1 \Rightarrow -2 < x < 2$, e

15. $|1 - x| < 2 \Rightarrow -2 < 1 - x < 2 \Rightarrow -3 < -x < 1 \Rightarrow -1 < x < 3$, b

16. $|2x - 5| \le 1 \Rightarrow -1 \le 2x - 5 \le 1 \Rightarrow 4 \le 2x \le 6 \Rightarrow 2 \le x \le 3$, h

17. $|2x + 4| < 1 \Rightarrow -1 < 2x + 4 < 1 \Rightarrow -5 < 2x < -3 \Rightarrow \frac{-5}{2} < x < \frac{-3}{2}$, d

18. $|\frac{x - 1}{2}| < 1 \Rightarrow -1 < \frac{x - 1}{2} < 1 \Rightarrow -2 < x - 1 < 2 \Rightarrow -1 < x < 3$, b

19. $|\frac{2x + 1}{3}| < 1 \Rightarrow -3 < 2x + 1 < 3 \Rightarrow -4 < 2x < 2 \Rightarrow -2 < x < 1$, a

20. $|x^2 - 2| \le 2 \Rightarrow -2 \le x^2 - 2 \le 2 \Rightarrow 0 \le x^2 \le 4 \Rightarrow -2 \le x \le 2$, i

21. $|x| < 2 \Rightarrow -2 < x < 2$

22. $|x| \le 2 \Rightarrow -2 \le x \le 2$

23. $|x - 1| \le 2 \Rightarrow -2 \le x - 1 \le 2 \Rightarrow -1 \le x \le 3$

24. $|x - 1| < 2 \Rightarrow -2 < x - 1 < 2 \Rightarrow -1 < x < 3$

25. $|x + 1| < 3 \Rightarrow -3 < x + 1 < 3 \Rightarrow -4 < x < 2$

26. $|x + 2| \le 1 \Rightarrow -1 \le x + 2 \le 1 \Rightarrow -3 \le x \le -1$

27. $|2x + 2| < 1 \Rightarrow -1 < 2x + 2 < 1 \Rightarrow -3 < 2x < -1 \Rightarrow \frac{-3}{2} < x < \frac{-1}{2}$

28. $|1 - x| < 1 \Rightarrow -1 < 1 - x < 1 \Rightarrow -2 < -x < 0 \Rightarrow 2 > x > 0$

29. $|1 - 2x| \le 1 \Rightarrow -1 \le 1 - 2x \le 1 \Rightarrow -2 \le -2x \le 0 \Rightarrow 0 \le x \le 1$

30. $|3x - 6| < 1 \Rightarrow -1 < 3x - 6 < 1 \Rightarrow 5 < 3x < 7 \Rightarrow \frac{5}{3} < x < \frac{7}{3}$

31. $\frac{1}{|x|} \le 1 \Rightarrow 1 \le |x| \Rightarrow x \ge 1$ or $x \le -1$

32. $|\frac{x}{2} - 1| \le 1 \Rightarrow -1 \le \frac{x}{2} \le 1 \Rightarrow 0 \le \frac{x}{2} \le 2 \Rightarrow 0 \le x \le 4$

33. $|x| < 8$

34. $-3 < y < 5$; the midpoint is 1; the distance to either endpoint is 4; the interval is open; thus $|y - 1| < 4$.

35. $-5 < x < 1$; the midpoint of the segment is -2; the distance to either endpoint is 3; the interval is open. $\therefore$ $|x + 2| < 3$

36. $1 < y < 7$; the midpoint is 4; the radius is 3; the interval is open; thus $|y - 4| < 3$

37. $-a < y < a \Rightarrow |y| < a$

38. $-1 < x < 2$; the midpoint is $\frac{1}{2}$; the radius is $\frac{3}{2}$; the interval is open; thus $|x - \frac{1}{2}| < \frac{3}{2}$

39. $L - \varepsilon < y < L + \varepsilon \Rightarrow -\varepsilon < y - L < \varepsilon \Rightarrow |y - L| < \varepsilon$

40. $1 - \delta < x < 1 + \delta \Rightarrow -\delta < x - 1 < \delta \Rightarrow |x - 1| < \delta$

41. $|x - x_0| < 5$

42. (a) $|-a| \neq a$ for any negative a; i.e. $|-(-4)| \neq -4$

(b) $|-a| = a$ for any $a \geq 0$; i.e. $|-4| = 4$

43. $|1 - x| = 1 - x$ when $x \leq 1$; $|1 - x| = x - 1$ when $x \geq 1$

44. (iii) since $y \geq 0$, and $x = 3 \Rightarrow y = 0$

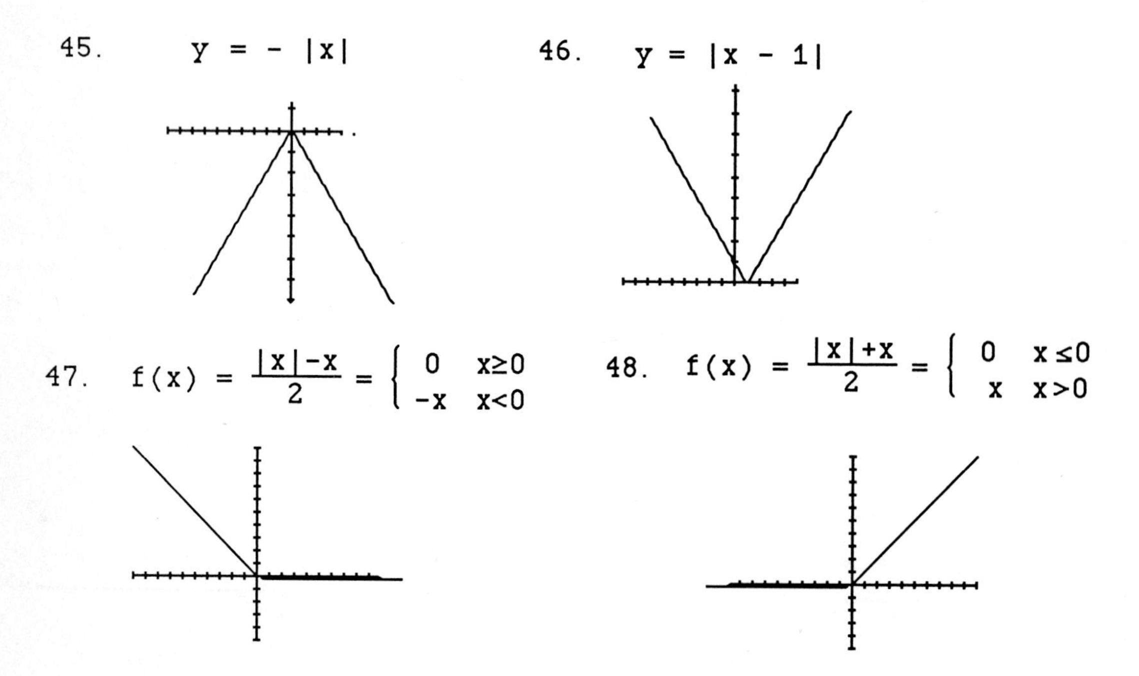

49. $y = \sqrt{x^2} = |x|$ has domain D: $x \in R$ and range R: $y \geq 0$
$y = (\sqrt{x})^2 = x,\ x \geq 0$ has domain D: $x \geq 0$ and range R: $y \geq 0$

50. $g(f(x)) = |x| \Rightarrow \sqrt{f(x)} = |x| \Rightarrow f(x) = x^2$.

51. $f(x) = x^2 + 2x + 1 = (x + 1)^2$ and $g(f(x)) = |x + 1|$ $\therefore$ $g(x) = \sqrt{x}$

52. Let $f(x) = x^2$ and $g(x) = |\sin\sqrt{x}|$.

53. (a) $y = x - [x],\ -3 \le x \le 3$

This function may be expressesed:

$$f(x) = \begin{cases} 3 & \text{if } x = 3 \\ x - 2 & 2 \le x \le 3 \\ x - 1 & 1 \le x < 2 \\ x & 0 \le x < 1 \\ x + 1 & -1 \le x < 0 \\ x + 2 & -3 \le x < -2 \\ -3 & x = -3 \end{cases}$$

(b) $y = [\frac{x}{2}],\ -3 \le x \le 3$

$$f(x) = \begin{cases} -2 & \text{if } -3 \le x < 2 \\ -1 & -2 \le x < 0 \\ 0 & 0 \le x < 2 \\ 1 & 2 \le x \le 3 \end{cases}$$

(c) $y = [2x] - 2[x]$

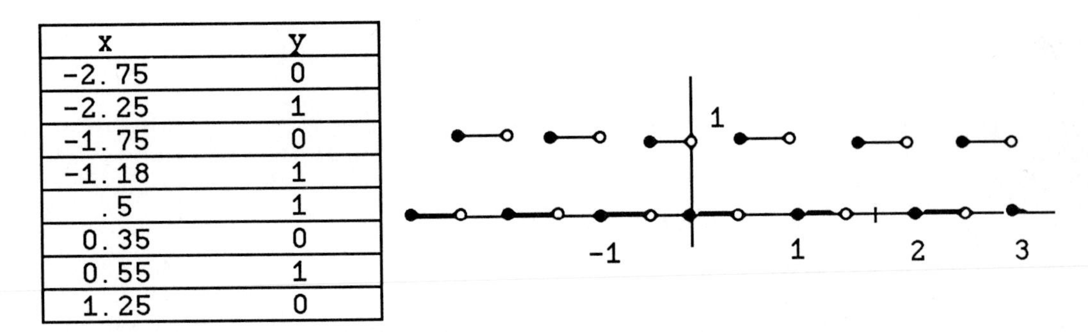

x	y
-2.75	0
-2.25	1
-1.75	0
-1.18	1
.5	1
0.35	0
0.55	1
1.25	0

(d) $y = \frac{1}{2}([x] + x)$

$$f(x) = \begin{cases} \frac{1}{2}(x - 3) & \text{if } -3 \le x < -2 \\ \frac{1}{2}(x - 2) & -2 \le x < -1 \\ \frac{1}{2}(x - 1) & -1 \le x < 0 \\ \frac{1}{2}x & 0 \le x < 1 \\ \frac{1}{2}(x + 1) & 1 \le x < 2 \\ \frac{1}{2}(x + 2) & 2 \le x < 3 \\ 3 & x = 3 \end{cases}$$

54. $[x] = 0$ when $0 \le x < 1$.

55. If $x < 0$ is not an integer, then $[x]$ is one less that the integer part of the decimal representation of x.

1.6 TANGENT LINES, SLOPES OF QUADRATIC AND CUBIC CURVES

1. $\frac{\Delta F}{\Delta t} = \frac{140}{40} = 3.5$ flies/day

2. (a)

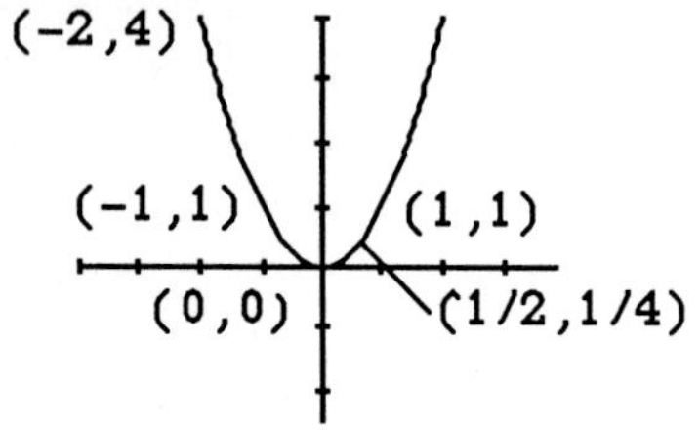

(-2,4) (-1,1) (1,1) (0,0) (1/2,1/4)

(b) $m_{sec} = \frac{(x+\Delta x)^2 - x^2}{\Delta x} = \frac{x^2 + 2x\Delta x + \Delta x^2 - x^2}{\Delta x} = 2x + \Delta x$

$m_{tan} = 2x$. At $(1,1)$, $m_{tan} = 2(1) = 2$

$y - 1 = 2(x-1)$ or $y = 2x - 1$

(c) $m_{sec} = \frac{1-4}{1+2} = -1$ $\quad m_{sec} = \frac{1-1}{1+1} = 0$

$m_{sec} = \frac{1-0}{1-0} = 1$ $\quad m_{sec} = \frac{1-\frac{1}{4}}{1-\frac{1}{2}} = \frac{3}{2}$

(d) $m_{PQ} = \frac{1-(1-\Delta x)^2}{1-(1-\Delta x)} = \frac{2\Delta x - \Delta x^2}{\Delta x} = 2 - \Delta x$

$\lim_{\Delta x \to 0} (2 - \Delta x) = 2$, which is the slope of the tangent at $(1,1)$.

3. $y = x^3 - 3x + 3$ $\quad Q(h, h^3 - 3h + 3)$

(a) $m_{sec} = \frac{f(h) - f(0)}{h - 0} = \frac{h^3 - 3h + 3 - 3}{h} = \frac{h(h^2 - 3)}{h} = h^2 - 3$

(b) $\lim_{h \to 0} (h^2 - 3) = -3$

(c) $y - 3 = -3x$ or $y + 3x = 3$

4. (a) $m = 3x^2 - 3 = 3(3)^2 - 3 = 24$

$y - 21 = 24(x-3)$ or $y = 24x - 51$

(b) $m = 3(-3)^2 - 3 = 24$

$y + 15 = 24(x+3)$ or $y = 24x + 57$

(c) $m = 3(\sqrt{2})^2 - 3 = 3$

$y - (3 - \sqrt{2}) = 3(x - \sqrt{2})$ or $y = 3x - 4\sqrt{2} + 3$

5. $y = x^2 + 1$, $P(2,5)$

(a) $m_{sec} = \dfrac{[(x+\Delta x)^2 + 1] - (x^2 + 1)]}{\Delta x} = \dfrac{2x\Delta x + (\Delta x)^2}{\Delta x} = 2x + \Delta x$

$m_{tan} = 2x$

(b) $x = 2 \Rightarrow m = 4$. $\therefore y - 5 = 4(x - 2)$ or $y = 4x - 3$

(c) $2x = 0 \Leftrightarrow x = 0$

6. $y = -x^2$, $P(1,-1)$

(a) $m_{sec} = \dfrac{-(x+\Delta x)^2 - (-x^2)}{\Delta x} = \dfrac{-2x\,\Delta x - \Delta x^2}{\Delta x} = -2x - \Delta x$

$m_{tan} = -2x$

(b) $x = 1 \Rightarrow m = -2$. $\therefore y + 1 = -2(x - 1)$ or $y = -2x + 1$

(c) $-2x = 0 \Leftrightarrow x = 0$ $(0,0)$

7. $y = 4 - x^2$, $P(-1,3)$

(a) $m_{sec} = \dfrac{[4 - (x+\Delta x)^2] - [4 - x^2]}{\Delta x} = \dfrac{-2x\,\Delta x - (\Delta x)^2}{\Delta x} = -2x - \Delta x$

$m_{tan} = -2x$

(b) $x = -1 \Rightarrow m = 2$. $\therefore y - 3 = 2(x + 1)$ or $y = 2x + 5$

(c) $-2x = 0 \Leftrightarrow x = 0$ $(0,4)$

8. $y = x^2 - 4x$, $P(4,0)$

(a) $m_{sec} = \dfrac{(x+\Delta x)^2 - 4(x+\Delta x) - x^2 + 4x}{\Delta x} = \dfrac{2x\,\Delta x + \Delta x^2 - 4\Delta x}{\Delta x} = 2x + \Delta x - 4$

$m_{tan} = 2x - 4$

(b) $x = 4 \Rightarrow m = 4$. $\therefore y = 4(x - 4)$ or $y = 4x - 16$

(c) $2x - 4 = 0 \Leftrightarrow x = 2$ $(2,-4)$

9. $y = x^2 + 3x + 2$, $P(-1,0)$

(a) $m_{sec} = \dfrac{[(x+\Delta x)^2 + 3(x+\Delta x) + 2] - [x^2 + 3x + 2]}{\Delta x}$

$= \dfrac{2x\,\Delta x + (\Delta x)^2 + 3\Delta x}{\Delta x} = 2x + \Delta x + 3$; $m_{tan} = 2x + 3$

(b) $x = -1 \Rightarrow m = 1$ $\therefore y = x + 1$

(c) $2x + 3 = 0 \Leftrightarrow x = -\dfrac{3}{2}$. $\left(-\dfrac{3}{2}, -\dfrac{1}{4}\right)$

10. $y = x^2 - 2x - 3$, $P(0,-3)$

(a) $m_{sec} = \dfrac{(x+\Delta x)^2 - 2(x+\Delta x) - 3 - x^2 + 2x + 3}{\Delta x}$

$= \dfrac{2x\,\Delta x + \Delta x^2 - 2\Delta x}{\Delta x} = 2x + \Delta x - 2;\quad m_{tan} = 2x - 2$

(b) $x = 0 \Rightarrow m = -2$. $\therefore\ y + 3 = -2x$ or $y = -2x - 3$

(c) $2x - 2 = 0 \Leftrightarrow x = 1\quad (1,-4)$

11. $y = x^2 + 4x + 4$, $P(-2,0)$

(a) $m_{sec} = \dfrac{[(x+\Delta x)^2 + 4(x+\Delta x) + 4] - [x^2 + 4x + 4]}{\Delta x}$

$= \dfrac{2x\,\Delta x + (\Delta x)^2 + 4\Delta x}{\Delta x} = 2x + \Delta x + 4;\quad m_{tan} = 2x + 4$

(b) $x = -2 \Rightarrow m = 0\quad \therefore\ y = 0$

(c) $2x + 4 = 0 \Leftrightarrow x = -2\quad (-2,0)$

12. $y = 6 + 4x - x^2$, $P(2,10)$

(a) $m_{sec} = \dfrac{6 + 4(x+\Delta x) - (x+\Delta x)^2 - 6 - 4x + x^2}{\Delta x}$

$= \dfrac{4\Delta x - 2x\,\Delta x - \Delta x^2}{\Delta x} = 4 - 2x - \Delta x;\quad m_{tan} = 4 - 2x$

(b) $x = 2 \Rightarrow m = 0$. $\therefore\ y = 10$

(c) $4 - 2x = 0 \Leftrightarrow x = 2\quad (2,10)$

13. $y = x^2 - 4x + 4$, $P(1,1)$

(a) $m_{sec} = \dfrac{[(x+\Delta x)^2 - 4(x+\Delta x) + 4] - [x^2 - 4x + 4]}{\Delta x}$

$= \dfrac{2x\,\Delta x + (\Delta x)^2 - 4\Delta x}{\Delta x} = 2x + \Delta x - 4;\quad m_{tan} = 2x - 4$

(b) $x = 1 \Rightarrow m = -2\ \therefore\ y - 1 = -2(x - 1)$ or $y = -2x + 3$

(c) $2x - 4 = 0 \Leftrightarrow x = 2\quad (2,0)$

14. $y = 2 - x - x^2$, $P(1,0)$

(a) $m_{sec} = \dfrac{2 - (x + \Delta x) - (x + \Delta x)^2 - 2 + x + x^2}{\Delta x}$

$= \dfrac{-\Delta x \ -2x\,\Delta x - \Delta x^2}{\Delta x} = -1 - 2x - \Delta x;$ $\quad m_{tan} = -1 - 2x$

(b) $x = 1 \Rightarrow m = -3.$ $\therefore$ $y = -3(x - 1)$ or $y = -3x + 3$

(c) $-1 - 2x = 0 \Leftrightarrow x = -\dfrac{1}{2}$ $\quad \left(-\dfrac{1}{2}, \dfrac{9}{4}\right)$

15. $y = x^3$, $P(1,1)$

(a) $m_{sec} = \dfrac{(x + \Delta x)^3 - x^3}{\Delta x} = \dfrac{x^3 + 3x^2\Delta x + 3x(\Delta x)^2 + (\Delta x)^3 - x^3}{\Delta x}$

$= 3x^2 + 3x\Delta x + (\Delta x)^2$; $\quad m_{tan} = \ = 3x^2$

(b) $x = 1 \Rightarrow m = 3$ $\therefore$ $y - 1 = 3(x - 1)$ or $y = 3x - 2$

(c) $3x^2 = 0 \Leftrightarrow x = 0$ $\quad (0,0)$

16. $y = x^3 - 12x$, $P(0,0)$

(a) $m_{sec} = \dfrac{(x + \Delta x)^3 - 12(x + \Delta x) \ -x^3 + 12x}{\Delta x}$

$= \dfrac{x^3 + 3x^2\Delta x + 3x(\Delta x)^2 + (\Delta x)^3 - 12x - 12\Delta x - x^3 + 12x}{\Delta x}$

$= 3x^2 + 3x\Delta x + (\Delta x)^2 - 12;$ $\quad m_{tan} = \ 3x^2 - 12$

(b) $x = 0 \Rightarrow m = -12$ $\quad \therefore$ $y = -12x$

(c) $3x^2 - 12 = 0 \Leftrightarrow x = \pm 2.$ $(2,-16)$ and $(-2,16)$

17. $y = x^3 - 3x$, $P(-1,2)$

(a) $m_{sec} = \dfrac{(x + \Delta x)^3 - 3(x + \Delta x) \ -x^3 + 3x}{\Delta x}$

$= \dfrac{x^3 + 3x^2\Delta x + 3x(\Delta x)^2 + (\Delta x)^3 - 3x - 3\Delta x - x^3 + 3x}{\Delta x}$

$= 3x^2 + 3x\Delta x + (\Delta x)^2 - 3;$ $\quad m_{tan} = \ 3x^2 - 3$

(b) $x = -1 \Rightarrow m = 0$ $\therefore$ $y = 2$

(c) $3x^2 - 3 = 0 \Leftrightarrow x = \pm 1.$ $(1,-2)$ and $(-1,2)$

18. $y = 4x^3 + 6x^2 + 1$, $P(-1, 3)$

(a) $$m_{sec} = \frac{4(x+\Delta x)^3 + 6(x+\Delta x)^2 + 1 - 4x^3 - 6x^2 - 1}{\Delta x}$$

$$= \frac{4x^3 + 12x^2\Delta x + 12x(\Delta x)^2 + 4(\Delta x)^3 + 6x^2 + 12x\Delta x + 6(\Delta x)^2 + 1 - 4x^3 - 6x^2 - 1}{\Delta x}$$

$$= 12x^2 + 12x\Delta x + 4(\Delta x)^2 + 12x + 6\Delta x; \quad m_{tan} = \; = 12x^2 + 12x$$

(b) $x = -1 \Rightarrow m = 0 \;\therefore\; y = 3$

(c) $12x^2 + 12x = 0 \;\Leftrightarrow x = 0$ or -1 $(0, 1)$ and $(-1, 3)$

19. $y = x^3 - 3x^2 + 4$, $P(1, 2)$

(a) $$m_{sec} = \frac{(x+\Delta x)^3 - 3(x+\Delta x)^2 + 4 - x^3 + 3x^2 - 4}{\Delta x}$$

$$= \frac{x^3 + 3x^2\Delta x + 3x(\Delta x)^2 + (\Delta x)^3 - 3x^2 - 6x\Delta x - 3(\Delta x)^2 - x^3 + 3x^2 - 4}{\Delta x}$$

$$= 3x^2 + 3x\Delta x + (\Delta x)^2 - 6x - 3\Delta x; \quad m_{tan} = \; = 3x^2 - 6x$$

(b) $x = 1 \Rightarrow m = -3 \;\therefore\; y - 2 = -3(x - 1)$ or $y = -3x + 5$

(c) $3x^2 - 6x = 0 \;\Leftrightarrow x = 0$ or 2 $(0, 4)$ and $(2, 0)$

20. $y = 2x^3 + 3x^2 - 12x$, $P(2, 4)$

(a) $$m_{sec} = \frac{2(x+\Delta x)^3 + 3(x+\Delta x)^2 - 12(x+\Delta x) - 2x^3 - 3x^2 + 12x}{\Delta x}$$

$$= \frac{2x^3 + 6x^2\Delta x + 6x(\Delta x)^2 + 2(\Delta x)^3 + 3x^2 + 6x\Delta x + 2(\Delta x)^2 - 12x - 12\Delta x - 2x^3 - 3x^2 + 12x}{\Delta x}$$

$$= 6x^2 + 6x\Delta x + 2(\Delta x)^2 + 6x + 3\Delta x - 12; \quad m_{tan} = \; = 6x^2 + 6x - 12$$

(b) $x = 2 \Rightarrow m = 24 \quad \therefore\; y - 4 = 24(x - 2)$ or $y = 24x - 44$

(c) $6x^2 + 6x - 12 = 0 \;\Leftrightarrow x = 1$ or -2 $(1, -7)$ and $(-2, 20)$

1.7 THE SLOPE OF THE CURVE y = f(x). DERIVATIVES

1. $f(x) = x^2$

$$f'(x) = \lim_{h\to 0} \frac{f(x+h) - f(x)}{h} = \lim_{h\to 0} \frac{(x+h)^2 - x^2}{h}$$

$$= \lim_{h\to 0} \frac{2xh + h^2}{h} = \lim_{h\to 0} 2x + h = 2x$$

$f'(3) = 6;$ $f(3) = 9;$ $y - 9 = 6x - 18$ or $y = 6x - 9$

2. $f(x) = x^3$

$$f'(x) = \lim_{h\to 0}\frac{f(x+h)-f(x)}{h} = \lim_{h\to 0}\frac{(x+h)^3 - x^3}{h} =$$

$$\lim_{h\to 0}\frac{x^3 + 3x^2h + 3xh^2 + h^3 - x^3}{h} = \lim_{h\to 0}(3x^2 + 3xh + h^2) = 3x^2$$

$f'(3) = 27;\ f(3) = 27;\ y - 27 = 27(x-3)$ or $y = 27x - 54$

3. $f(x) = 2x + 3$

$$f'(x) = \lim_{h\to 0}\frac{f(x+h) - f(x)}{h} = \lim_{h\to 0}\frac{2(x+h) + 3 - 2x - 3}{h}$$

$$= \lim_{h\to 0}\frac{2h}{h} = 2$$

$f(3) = 9;\ y - 9 = 2(x - 3)$ or $y = 2x + 3$

4. $f(x) = x^2 - x + 1$

$$f'(x) = \lim_{h\to 0}\frac{f(x+h)-f(x)}{h} = \lim_{h\to 0}\frac{(x+h)^2 - (x+h) + 1 - x^2 + x - 1}{h} =$$

$$\lim_{h\to 0}\frac{x^2 + 2xh + h^2 - x - h + 1 - x^2 + x - 1}{h} = \lim_{h\to 0}(2x + h - 1) = 2x - 1$$

$f'(3) = 5;\ f(3) = 7;\ y - 7 = 5(x-3)$ or $y = 5x - 8$

5. $f(x) = 1 + \sqrt{x}$

$$f'(x) = \lim_{h\to 0}\frac{f(x+h)-f(x)}{h} = \lim_{h\to 0}\frac{1 + \sqrt{x+h} - (1+\sqrt{x})}{h} =$$

$$\lim_{h\to 0}\frac{\sqrt{x+h} - \sqrt{x}}{h}\cdot\frac{\sqrt{x+h}+\sqrt{x}}{\sqrt{x+h}+\sqrt{x}} = \lim_{h\to 0}\frac{1}{\sqrt{x+h}+\sqrt{x}} = \frac{1}{2\sqrt{x}}$$

$f'(3) = \frac{1}{2\sqrt{3}};\ f(3) = 1 + \sqrt{3};\ y - (1+\sqrt{3}) = \frac{1}{2\sqrt{3}}(x-3)$ or $x - 2\sqrt{3}y = -(3 + 2\sqrt{3})$

6. $f(x) = \frac{1}{x^2}$

$$f'(x) = \lim_{h\to 0}\frac{f(x+h)-f(x)}{h} = \lim_{h\to 0}\frac{\frac{1}{(x+h)^2} - \frac{1}{x^2}}{h}$$

$$\lim_{h\to 0}\frac{x^2 - (x+h)^2}{h\,x^2(x+h)^2} = \lim_{h\to 0}\frac{-2x-h}{x^2(x+h)^2} = -\frac{2}{x^3}$$

$f'(3) = -\frac{2}{27};\ f(3) = \frac{1}{9};\ y - \frac{1}{9} = -\frac{2}{27}(x-3)$ or $27y + 2x = 9$

7. $f(x) = \dfrac{1}{2x + 1}$

$$f(x + h) - f(x) = \frac{1}{2x + 2h + 1} - \frac{1}{2x + 1}$$
$$= \frac{-2h}{(2x + 2h + 1)(2x + 1)}$$
$$\frac{f(x + h) - f(x)}{h} = \frac{-2}{(2x + 2h + 1)(2x + 1)}$$

$$f'(x) = \lim_{h \to 0} \frac{-2}{(2x + 2h + 1)(2x + 1)} = \left.\frac{-2}{(2x + 1)^2}\right|_{x=3} = \frac{-2}{49}$$

$f(3) = \frac{1}{7}$; $y - \frac{1}{7} = \frac{-2}{49}(x - 3)$ or $49y + 2x = 13$

8. $f(x) = \dfrac{x}{x+1}$

$$f'(x) = \lim_{h \to 0} \frac{f(x+h) - f(x)}{h} = \lim_{h \to 0} \frac{\dfrac{x+h}{x+h+1} - \dfrac{x}{x+1}}{h}$$

$$\lim_{h \to 0} \frac{(x+h)(x+1) - x(x+h+1)}{h(x+1)(x+h+1)} = \lim_{h \to 0} \frac{1}{(x+h+1)(x+1)} = \frac{1}{(x+1)^2}$$

$f'(3) = \frac{1}{16}$; $f(3) = \frac{3}{4}$; $y - \frac{3}{4} = \frac{1}{16}(x - 3)$ or $16y - x = 9$

9. $f(x) = 2x^2 - x + 5$

$$f'(x) = \lim_{h \to 0} \frac{f(x+h) - f(x)}{h} = \lim_{h \to 0} \frac{2(x+h)^2 - (x+h) + 5 - 2x^2 + x - 5}{h}$$

$$= \lim_{h \to 0} \frac{4xh + 2h^2 - h}{h} = \lim_{h \to 0}(4x + 2h - 1) = 4x - 1$$

$f'(3) = 11$; $f(3) = 20$

$y - 20 = 11(x - 3)$ or $y = 11x - 13$

10. $f(x) = x^3 - 12x + 11$

$$f'(x) = \lim_{h \to 0} \frac{f(x+h) - f(x)}{h} = \lim_{h \to 0} \frac{(x+h)^3 - 12(x+h) + 11 - x^3 + 12x - 11}{h}$$

$$= \lim_{h \to 0} \frac{x^3 + 3x^2h + 3xh^2 + h^3 - 12x - 12h + 11 - x^3 + 12x - 11}{h}$$

$$= \lim_{h \to 0} 3x^2 + 3xh - 12 = 3x^2 - 12$$

$f'(3) = 15$; $f(3) = 2$; $y - 2 = 15(x - 3)$ or $y - 15x = -43$

11. $f(x) = x^4$; $f'(x) = \lim_{h\to 0} \dfrac{f(x+h) - f(x)}{h} = \lim_{h\to 0} \dfrac{x^4 + 4x^3h + 6x^2h^2 + 4xh^3 + h^4 - x^4}{h}$

$= \lim_{h\to 0} (4x^3 + 6x^2h + 4xh^2 + h^3) = 4x^3\Big]_{x=3} = 108$

$f(3) = 81$; $y - 81 = 108(x - 3)$ or $y = 108x - 243$

12. $f(x) = ax^2 + bx + c$

$f'(x) = \lim_{h\to 0} \dfrac{f(x+h) - f(x)}{h} = \lim_{h\to 0} \dfrac{a(x+h)^2 + b(x+h) + c - ax^2 - bx - c}{h}$

$= \lim_{h\to 0} \dfrac{ax^2 + 2axh + ah^2 + bx + bh + c - ax^2 - bx - c}{h}$

$= \lim_{h\to 0} 2ax + ah + b = 2ax + b$

$f'(3) = 6a + b$; $f(3) = 9a^2 + 3b + c$;

$y - (9a^2 + 3b + c) = (6a + b)(x - 3)$ or $y = (6a + b)x + 9a^2 - 18a + c$

13. $f(x) = x - \dfrac{1}{x}$

$f(x + h) = x + h - \dfrac{1}{x + h}$

$f(x + h) - f(x) = h - \dfrac{1}{x + h} + \dfrac{1}{x} = h + \dfrac{-x + x + h}{x(x + h)}$

$f'(x) = \lim_{h\to 0} \dfrac{f(x + h) - f(x)}{h} = \lim_{h\to 0} 1 + \dfrac{1}{x(x + h)} = 1 + \dfrac{1}{x^2}\Big|_{x=3} = \dfrac{10}{9}$

$f(3) = \dfrac{8}{3}$; $y - \dfrac{8}{3} = \dfrac{10}{9}(x - 3)$ or $10x - 6 = 9y$

14. $f(x) = ax + \dfrac{b}{x}$

$f'(x) = \lim_{h\to 0} \dfrac{f(x+h) - f(x)}{h} = \lim_{h\to 0} \dfrac{1}{h}\left[a(x+h) - ax + \dfrac{b}{x+h} - \dfrac{b}{x}\right]$

$= \lim_{h\to 0} \dfrac{1}{h}\left[ah + \dfrac{bx - b(x+h)}{x(x+h)}\right] = a - \dfrac{b}{x^2}$

$f'(3) = a - \dfrac{b}{9}$; $f(3) = 3a + \dfrac{b}{3}$

$y - \left(3a + \dfrac{b}{3}\right) = \left(a - \dfrac{b}{9}\right)(x - 3)$ or $y = \dfrac{9a - b}{9}(x - 3) + \dfrac{9a + b}{3}$

15. $f(x) = \sqrt{2x}$

$$f'(x) = \lim_{h\to 0} \frac{f(x+h) - f(x)}{h} = \lim_{h\to 0} \frac{\sqrt{2x+2h} - \sqrt{2x}}{h}$$

$$= \lim_{h\to 0} \frac{\sqrt{2x+2h} - \sqrt{2x}}{h} \cdot \frac{\sqrt{2x+2h} + \sqrt{2x}}{\sqrt{2x+2h} + \sqrt{2x}}$$

$$= \lim_{h\to 0} \frac{2}{\sqrt{2x+2h} + \sqrt{2x}} = \frac{1}{\sqrt{2x}}$$

$f'(3) = \frac{1}{\sqrt{6}}$; $f(3) = \sqrt{6}$

$y - \sqrt{6} = \frac{1}{\sqrt{6}}(x - 3)$

$y = \frac{1}{\sqrt{6}}x - \frac{3}{\sqrt{6}}\frac{\sqrt{6}}{\sqrt{6}} + \sqrt{6} = \frac{1}{\sqrt{6}}x + \frac{1}{2}\sqrt{6}$

$y\sqrt{6} = x + 3$

16. $f(x) = \sqrt{x+1}$

$$f'(x) = \lim_{h\to 0} \frac{f(x+h) - f(x)}{h} = \lim_{h\to 0} \frac{\sqrt{x+h+1} - \sqrt{x+1}}{h} \cdot \frac{\sqrt{x+h+1} + \sqrt{x+1}}{\sqrt{x+h+1} + \sqrt{x+1}}$$

$$= \lim_{h\to 0} \frac{x+h+1-x-1}{h(\sqrt{x+h+1} + \sqrt{x+1})} = \frac{1}{2\sqrt{x+1}}$$

$f'(3) = \frac{1}{4}$; $f(3) = 2$

$y - 2 = \frac{1}{4}(x - 3)$ or $4y = x + 5$

17. $f(x) = \sqrt{2x+3}$

$$f'(x) = \lim_{h\to 0} \frac{f(x+h) - f(x)}{h}$$

$$= \lim_{h\to 0} \frac{\sqrt{2x+2h+3} - \sqrt{2x+3}}{h} \cdot \frac{\sqrt{2x+2h+3} + \sqrt{2x+3}}{\sqrt{2x+2h+3} + \sqrt{2x+3}}$$

$$= \lim_{h\to 0} \frac{2}{\sqrt{2x+2h+3} + \sqrt{2x+3}} = \frac{2}{2\sqrt{2x+3}} = \frac{1}{\sqrt{2x+3}}$$

$f'(3) = \frac{1}{3}$; $f(3) = 3$

$y - 3 = \frac{1}{3}(x - 3)$ or $y = \frac{1}{3}x + 2$

18. $f(x) = \frac{1}{\sqrt{x}}$

$$f'(x) = \lim_{h\to 0} \frac{f(x+h) - f(x)}{h} = \lim_{h\to 0} \frac{1}{h}\left(\frac{1}{\sqrt{x+h}} - \frac{1}{\sqrt{x}}\right)$$

$$= \lim_{h\to 0} \frac{\sqrt{x} - \sqrt{x+h}}{h\sqrt{x}\sqrt{x+h}} \cdot \frac{\sqrt{x} + \sqrt{x+h}}{\sqrt{x} + \sqrt{x+h}} = \lim_{h\to 0} \frac{x - x - h}{h\sqrt{x}\sqrt{x+h}(\sqrt{x} + \sqrt{x+h})}$$

$$= -\frac{1}{2x^{3/2}};\quad f'(3) = -\frac{\sqrt{3}}{18};\quad f(3) = \frac{\sqrt{3}}{3}$$

$$y - \frac{\sqrt{3}}{3} = -\frac{\sqrt{3}}{18}(x - 3) \quad \text{or } y = -\frac{\sqrt{3}}{18}x + \frac{\sqrt{3}}{2}$$

19. $f(x) = \frac{1}{\sqrt{2x + 3}}$

$$f'(x) = \lim_{h\to 0} \frac{f(x + h) - f(x)}{h} = \lim_{h\to 0} \frac{\frac{1}{\sqrt{2x + 2h + 3}} - \frac{1}{\sqrt{2x + 3}}}{h}$$

$$= \lim_{h\to 0} \frac{\sqrt{2x + 3} - \sqrt{2x + 2h + 3}}{h\sqrt{(2x + 3)(2x + 2h + 3)}} \cdot \frac{\sqrt{2x + 3} + \sqrt{2x + 2h + 3}}{\sqrt{2x + 3} + \sqrt{2x + 2h + 3}}$$

$$= \lim_{h\to 0} \frac{-2}{h\sqrt{(2x + 3)(2x + 2h + 3)}\ \sqrt{2x + 3} + \sqrt{2x + 2h + 3}}$$

$$= \frac{-2}{(2x + 3)(2\sqrt{2x + 3})} = \left.\frac{-1}{(2x + 3)^{3/2}}\right|_{x=3} = \frac{-1}{27}$$

$$f(3) = \frac{1}{3};\quad y - \frac{1}{3} = \frac{-1}{27}(x - 3) \quad \text{or} \quad y = \frac{-1}{27}x + \frac{4}{9}$$

20. $f(x) = \sqrt{x^2 + 1}$

$$f'(x) = \lim_{h\to 0} \frac{f(x+h) - f(x)}{h} = \lim_{h\to 0} \frac{\sqrt{(x+h)^2 + 1} - \sqrt{x^2 + 1}}{h} \cdot \frac{\sqrt{(x+h)^2 + 1} + \sqrt{x^2 + 1}}{\sqrt{(x+h)^2 + 1} + \sqrt{x^2 + 1}}$$

$$= \lim_{h\to 0} \frac{2xh + h^2}{h\left(\sqrt{(x+h)^2 + 1} + \sqrt{x^2 + 1}\right)} = \frac{x}{\sqrt{x^2 + 1}}$$

$$f'(3) = \frac{3}{\sqrt{10}};\quad f(3) = \sqrt{10};\quad y - \sqrt{10} = \frac{3}{\sqrt{10}}(x - 3) \quad \text{or } \sqrt{10}\,y = 3x + 1$$

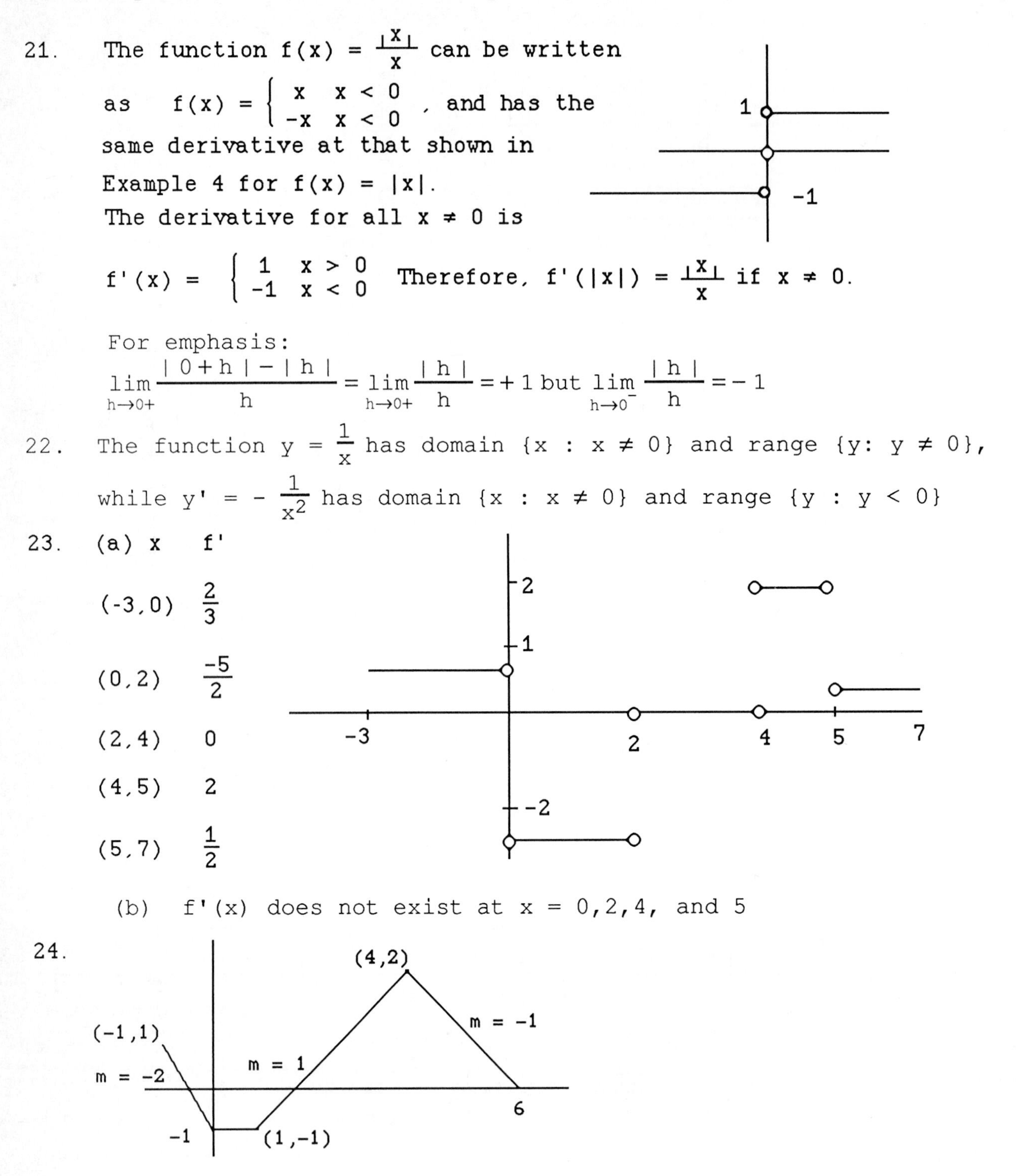

21. The function $f(x) = \frac{|x|}{x}$ can be written as $f(x) = \begin{cases} x & x < 0 \\ -x & x < 0 \end{cases}$, and has the same derivative at that shown in Example 4 for $f(x) = |x|$.
The derivative for all $x \neq 0$ is

$f'(x) = \begin{cases} 1 & x > 0 \\ -1 & x < 0 \end{cases}$ Therefore, $f'(|x|) = \frac{|x|}{x}$ if $x \neq 0$.

For emphasis:

$$\lim_{h \to 0+} \frac{|0+h| - |h|}{h} = \lim_{h \to 0+} \frac{|h|}{h} = +1 \text{ but } \lim_{h \to 0^-} \frac{|h|}{h} = -1$$

22. The function $y = \frac{1}{x}$ has domain $\{x : x \neq 0\}$ and range $\{y : y \neq 0\}$, while $y' = -\frac{1}{x^2}$ has domain $\{x : x \neq 0\}$ and range $\{y : y < 0\}$

23. (a)

x	f'
(-3,0)	$\frac{2}{3}$
(0,2)	$\frac{-5}{2}$
(2,4)	0
(4,5)	2
(5,7)	$\frac{1}{2}$

(b) $f'(x)$ does not exist at $x = 0, 2, 4,$ and 5

24.

25. When the number of rabbits is the largest ($t = 40$ days), the derivative is zero. When the number of rabbits is the smallest ($t \geq 135$ days), the derivative is zero.

26. The largest: 1700; the smallest: 1200

27. foxes/day

28. (a)

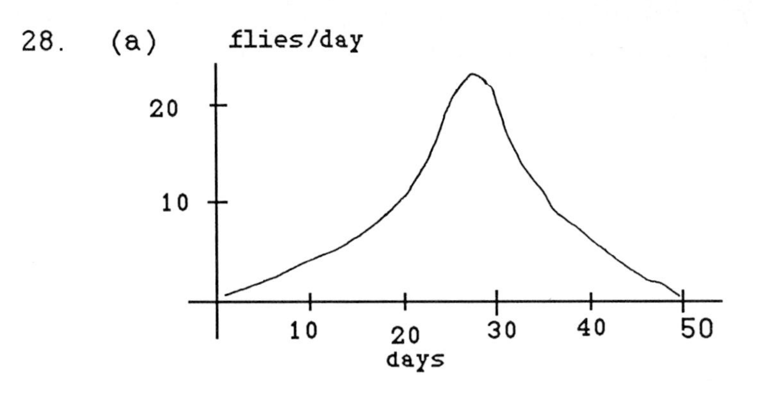

(b) fastest growth for $20 < t < 30$, app. $t = 25$ days.

(c) slowest growth for $0 \le t \le 5$ or $45 \le t \le 50$ days.

1.8 VELOCITY AND OTHER RATES OF CHANGE

1. $F(t + \Delta t) = a(t + \Delta t)^2 + b(t + \Delta t) + c$

$$\frac{f(t + \Delta t) - f(t)}{\Delta t} = \frac{a(2t\Delta t + \Delta t^2) + b\Delta t}{\Delta t} = 2at + a\Delta t + b$$

$$\lim_{\Delta t \to 0} (2at + a\Delta t + b) = 2at + b$$

2. $s = 4.9t^2$

(a) $s(0) = 0$ $s(2) = 19.6$, $\Delta s = 19.6 - 0 - 19.6$, $\dfrac{\Delta s}{\Delta t} = \dfrac{19.6}{2} = 9.8$

(b) $\dfrac{ds}{dt} = 2at + b = 2(4.9)t = 9.8t$

(c) $\left.\dfrac{ds}{dt}\right|_{t=2} = 19.6$

3. $s = .8t^2$

(a) $s(0) = 0$ $s(2) = 3.2$

$\Delta s = s(2) - s(0) = 3.2$, $\dfrac{\Delta s}{\Delta t} = \dfrac{3.2}{2} = 1.6$

(b) $\dfrac{ds}{dt} = 2at + b = 1.6t$

(c) $\left.\dfrac{ds}{dt}\right|_{t=2} = 3.2$

4. $s = 1.86t^2$

(a) $s(0) = 0$ $s(2) = 7.44$, $\Delta s = 7.44 - 0 = 7.44$, $\dfrac{\Delta s}{\Delta t} = \dfrac{7.44}{2} = 3.72$

(b) $\dfrac{ds}{dt} = 2at + b = 2(1.86)t = 3.72t$

(c) $\left.\dfrac{ds}{dt}\right|_{t=2} = 7.44$

5. $s = 2t^2 + 5t - 3$

(a) $s(0) = -3$, $s(2) = 15$, $\Delta s = 18$, $\frac{\Delta s}{\Delta t} = \frac{18}{2} = 9$

(b) $\frac{ds}{dt} = 4t + 5$

(c) $\frac{ds}{dt}\Big|_{t=2} = 13$

6. $s = t^2 - 3t + 2$

(a) $s(0) = 2$ $s(2) = 0$, $\Delta s = 0 - 2 = -2$, $\frac{\Delta s}{\Delta t} = \frac{-2}{2} = -1$

(b) $\frac{ds}{dt} = 2at + b = 2t - 3$

(c) $\frac{ds}{dt}\Big|_{t=2} = 4 - 3 = 1$

7. $s = 4 - 2t - t^2$

(a) $s(0) = 4$, $s(2) = -4$, $\Delta s = -8$, $\frac{\Delta s}{\Delta t} = -4$

(b) $\frac{ds}{dt} = -2t - 2$

(c) $\frac{ds}{dt}\Big|_{t=2} = -6$

8. $s = 3 - 2t^2$

(a) $s(0) = 3$ $s(2) = -5$, $\Delta s = -5 - 3 = -8$, $\frac{\Delta s}{\Delta t} = \frac{-8}{2} = -4$

(b) $\frac{ds}{dt} = 2at + b = -4t$

(c) $\frac{ds}{dt}\Big|_{t=2} = -8$

9. $s = 4t + 3$

(a) $s(0) = 3$, $s(2) = 11$, $\Delta s = 8$, $\frac{\Delta s}{\Delta t} = 4$

(b) $\frac{ds}{dt} = 4$

(c) $\frac{ds}{dt}\Big|_{t=2} = 4$

10. $s = \frac{1}{2}gt^2 + v_0t + s_0$

(a) $s(0) = s_0 \quad s(2) = 2g + 2v_0 + s_0$

$\Delta s = 2g + 2v_0, \quad \frac{\Delta s}{\Delta t} = \frac{2g + 2v_0}{2} = g + v_0$

(b) $\frac{ds}{dt} = gt + v_0$

(c) $\left.\frac{ds}{dt}\right|_{t=2} = 2g + v_0$

11. (a) $s = 490t^2, \quad v = 980t$

(b) $160 = 490t^2 \quad \Rightarrow \frac{16}{49} = t^2 \quad \Rightarrow t = \frac{4}{7}$ sec

$$V_{av} = \frac{s(\frac{4}{7}) - s(0)}{\frac{4}{7}} = \frac{160}{\frac{4}{7}} = 280 \text{ cm/sec}$$

(c) $\frac{\frac{4}{7}}{17} = \frac{4}{119} \approx 0.034$ sec/flash

12. (a) Average velocity $\approx \frac{170}{10} = 17$ m/sec

(b) Reading $\approx \frac{250}{7.5} \approx 33.3$ m/sec

13.

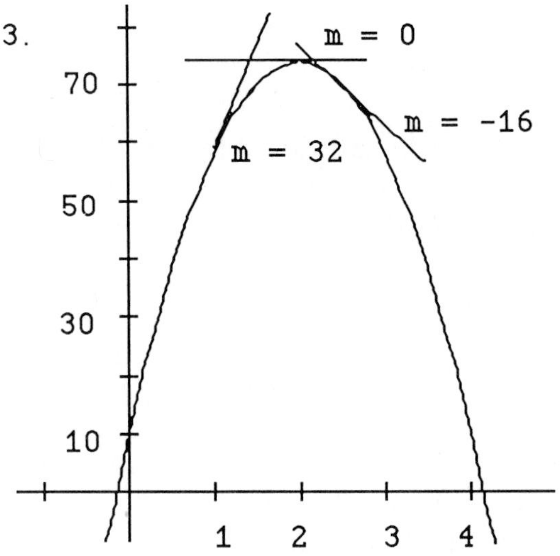

m = 0
m = -16
m = 32
70
50
30
10
1 2 3 4

14. (a) Average $= \frac{57.1 - 44.8}{20 - 10} = \frac{12.3}{10} = 1.23$ moles/min

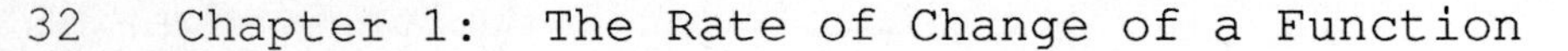

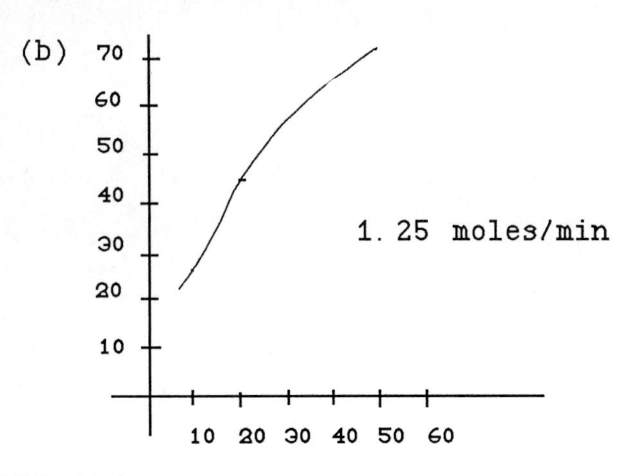

15. 190 ft/sec

16. From $t = 0$ to $t = 2$ seconds.

17. Rocket was at maximum height at $t = 8$ sec. ($v > 0$ means rocket is rising). The velocity was equal to 0 then.

18. At 10.8 seconds; 90 ft/sec.

19. 2.8 sec

20. $b(t) = 10^6 + 10^4 t - 10^3 t^2$; $a = -10^3$, $b = 10^4$, $c = 10^6$

(a) $\frac{db}{dt}\Big|_{t=0} = 10{,}000$

(b) $\frac{db}{dt}\Big|_{t=5} = 2(-10^3)(5) + 10^4 = 0$

(c) $\frac{db}{dt}\Big|_{t=10} = 2((-10^3)(10) + 10^4 = -10{,}000$

21. $Q = 200(30 - t)^2$

(a) $\frac{dQ}{dt} = -400(30 - t)\Big|_{t=10} = -400(20) = -8000$ gal/min

(b) $Q(10) = 200(400) = 80000$; $Q(0) = 200(900) = 180000$

$$\frac{Q(10) - Q(0)}{10} = \frac{-100000}{10} = -10000 \text{ gal/min}$$

22. (a) distance is shown on the bottom graph, since it is not constant anywhere.

(b) velocity is shown on the middle graph

(c) acceleration is shown on the top graph, since it shows values of 0 over the interval $55 \le t \le 80$ where the middle graph shows a contant value of roughly 35 mph.

(d) Maximum acceleration is slightly less than 2 m/s^2, and the minimum acceleration is -2 m/s^2.

23. $f(x) = 2000 + 100x - 0.1x^2$

(a) $f(100) = 11,000;\ f(0) = 2000$

$$\frac{f(100) - f(0)}{100} = \frac{9000}{100} = \$90/\text{machine}$$

(b) $f' = 100 - .2(x)\big|_{x=100}$
$f' = 100 - 20 = \$80/\text{machine}$, marginal cost

(c) $f(101) = 2000 + (100)(101) - .1(101)^2 = 11,080$
$f(101) - f(100) = \$80.$

1.9 LIMITS

1. $\lim_{x\to 2} 2x = 4$ 2. $\lim_{x\to 0} 2x = 0$ 3. $\lim_{x\to 4} 4 = 4$ 4. $\lim_{x\to -2} 4 = 4$

5. $\lim_{x\to 1} (3x-1) = 2$ 6. $\lim_{x\to \frac{1}{3}} (3x-1) = 0$ 7. $\lim_{x\to 5} x^2 = 25$

8. $\lim_{x\to 2} x(2-x) = 2(0) = 0$ 9. $\lim_{x\to 0} (x^2 - 2x + 1) = 1$

10. $\lim_{x\to 5} (x^2 - 3x - 18) = 25 - 15 - 18 = -8$

11. $\lim_{\Delta x\to 0} (2x + \Delta x) = 2x$

12. $\lim_{t\to 2} t^2 = (2)^2 = 4$

13. $\lim_{x\to 1} |x - 1| = 0$

14. $\lim_{x\to -3} |x| = |-3| = 3$

15. $\lim_{x\to 0} 5(2x - 1) = -5$

16. $\lim_{x\to 1} x(2x-1) = 1$

17. $\lim_{x\to 2} 3x(2x - 1) = 6(3) = 18$

18. $\lim_{x\to 2} 3(2x-1)(x+1) = 3(3)(3) = 27$

19. $\lim_{x\to 2} 3x^2(2x - 1) = (12)(3) = 36$

20. $\lim_{x\to 2} 3(2x-1)(x+1)^2 = 3(3)(9) = 81$

21. $\lim_{x\to -1} (x + 3) = 2$

22. $\lim_{x\to -1} (x+3)^2 = 2^2 = 4$

23. $\lim_{x\to -1} (x^2 + 6x + 9) = 1 - 6 + 9 = 4$

24. $\lim_{x \to -2} (x+3)^{171} = 1$

25. $\lim_{x \to -4} (x + 3)^{1984} = 1$

26. $\lim_{x \to 1} (x^3 + 3x^2 - 2x - 17) = 1 + 3 - 2 - 17 = -15$

27. If $\lim_{x \to c} f(x) = 5$ and $\lim_{x \to c} g(x) = -2$, then:

(a) $\lim_{x \to c} f(x) \cdot g(x) = 5(-2) = -10$

(b) $\lim_{x \to 0} 2\, f(x)\, g(x) = 2\,(5)\,(-2) = -20$

28. $\lim_{x \to b} [f(x) + g(x)] = 7 + (-3) = 4$

29. If $\lim_{x \to b} f(x) = 7$ and $\lim_{x \to b} g(x) = -3$, then:

(a) $\lim_{x \to b} (f(x) + g(x)) = 7 - 3 = 4$

(b) $\lim_{x \to b} f(x) \cdot g(x) = (7)(-3) = -21$

(c) $\lim_{x \to b} 4g(x) = 4(-3) = -12$

(d) $\lim_{x \to b} \frac{f(x)}{g(x)} = \frac{7}{-3} = -\frac{7}{3}$

30. (a) $\lim_{x \to -2} [p(x) + r(x) + s(x)] = 4 + 0 + (-3) = 1$

(b) $\lim_{x \to -2} p(x)\, r(x)\, s(x) = (4)\,(0)\,(-3) = 0$

31. $\lim_{t \to 2} \frac{t + 3}{t + 2} = \frac{5}{4}$

32. $\lim_{x \to 5} \frac{x^2 - 25}{x - 5} = \lim_{x \to 5} (x + 5) = 10$

33. $\lim_{x \to 5} \frac{x^2 - 25}{x + 5} = \lim_{x \to 5} (x - 5) = 0$

34. $\lim_{x \to 5} \frac{x - 5}{x^2 - 25} = \lim_{x \to 5} \frac{1}{x + 5} = \frac{1}{10}$

35. $\lim_{x \to 5} \frac{x + 5}{x^2 - 25} = \lim_{x \to 5} \frac{1}{x - 5}$ does not exist

36. $\lim_{x \to 1} \frac{x^2 - x - 2}{x^2 - 1} = \lim_{x \to 1} \frac{(x-2)(x+1)}{(x+1)(x-1)} = \lim_{x \to 1} \frac{x - 2}{x - 1}$ does not exist.

37. $\lim_{x \to 0} \frac{x^2 (5x + 8)}{x^2 (3x^2 - 16)} = \lim_{x \to 0} \frac{5x + 8}{3x^2 - 16} = -\frac{1}{2}$

38. $\lim_{y \to 2} \frac{y^2 + 5y + 6}{y + 2} = \frac{20}{4} = 5$

39. $\lim_{x\to 2} \frac{(y-2)(y-3)}{y-2} = \lim_{x\to 2} (y-3) = -1$

40. $\lim_{x\to -5} \frac{x^2+3x-10}{x+5} = \lim_{x\to -5} \frac{(x+5)(x-2)}{x+5} = -5-2 = -7$

41. $\lim_{x\to 4} \frac{x-4}{(x-4)(x-1)} = \lim_{x\to 4} \frac{1}{x-1} = \frac{1}{3}$

42. $\lim_{t\to 3} \frac{t^2-3t+2}{t^2-1} = \lim_{t\to 3} \frac{(t-2)(t-1)}{(t+1)(t-1)} = \frac{1}{4}$

43. $\lim_{t\to 1} \frac{(t-2)(t-1)}{(t-1)(t+1)} = \lim_{t\to 1} \frac{t-2}{t+1} = -\frac{1}{2}$

44. $\lim_{x\to 2} \frac{x-2}{x^2-6x+8} = \lim_{x\to 2} \frac{x-2}{(x-4)(x-2)} = -\frac{1}{2}$

45. $\lim_{x\to -3} \frac{x^2+4x+3}{x-3} = \frac{0}{-6} = 0$

46. $\lim_{x\to -3} \frac{x+3}{x^2+4x+3} = \lim_{x\to -3} \frac{x+3}{(x+3)(x+1)} = -\frac{1}{2}$

47. $\lim_{x\to -2} \frac{(x+2)(x-1)}{(x+2)(x-2)} = \lim_{x\to -2} \frac{x-1}{x-2} = \frac{3}{4}$

48. $\lim_{x\to 1} \frac{x^2+x-2}{x-2} = \lim_{x\to 1} \frac{(x+2)(x-1)}{x-2} = \frac{0}{-1} = 0$

49. $\lim_{x\to 2} \frac{x^2-7x+10}{x-2} = \lim_{x\to 2} \frac{(x-2)(x-5)}{x-2} = \lim_{x\to 2} (x-5) = -3$

50. $\lim_{t\to 1} \frac{t^3-1}{t-1} = \lim_{t\to 1} \frac{(t-1)(t^2+t+1)}{t-1} = 3$

51. $\lim_{x\to a} \frac{x^3-a^3}{x^4-a^4} = \lim_{x\to a} \frac{(x-a)(x^2+ax+a^2)}{(x-a)(x+a)x^2+a^2)} = \frac{3a^2}{2a\,(2a^2)} = \frac{3}{4a}$

52. Since $x^n - 1 = (x-1)(x^{n-1} + x^{n-2} + \ldots + x^2 + x + 1)$,

$$\lim_{x\to 1} \frac{x^n-1}{x-1} = \lim_{x\to 1} (x^{n-1} + x^{n-2} + \ldots + x^2 + x + 1) = n\,(1) = n$$

53. Let $f(x) = \begin{cases} \frac{1}{x} & x \neq 0 \\ 0 & x=0 \end{cases}$ and $g(x) = \begin{cases} \frac{-1}{x} & x \neq 0 \\ 0 & x=0 \end{cases}$

Then the limits of $f(x)$ and $g(x)$ do not exist as $x\to 0$ but $f(x)+g(x) = \frac{1}{x} - \frac{1}{x} = 0$ and $\lim_{x\to 0} [f(x)+g(x)] = \lim_{x\to 0} 0 = 0$

54. Let $f(x) = \begin{cases} 1 & x \geq 0 \\ -1 & x < 0 \end{cases}$ and $g(x) = \begin{cases} -1 & x \geq 0 \\ 1 & x < 0 \end{cases}$

Then the limits of $f(x)$ and $g(x)$ do not exist as $x\to 0$ but $\lim f(x)g(x) = \lim (-1) = -1$ as $x\to 0$.

55. Let $f(x) = \frac{1}{x}$ and $g(x) = \frac{1}{x^2}$. Then neither the limit of $f(x)$ nor $g(x)$ exists as $x\to 0$ but

$$\lim \frac{f(x)}{g(x)} = \lim \frac{\frac{1}{x}}{\frac{1}{x^2}} = \lim x = 0 \text{ as } x \to 0.$$

56. This is the derivative of $f(x) = (1 + x)^2$ at $x = 0$.

57. If $\lim\limits_{h \to o} \dfrac{|-1+h| - |-1|}{h} = f'(0)$, then $f(x) = |x - 1|$.

58. All are true except (b) and (c), since the limit of $f(x)$ at $x = 2$ is 1.

59. $f(x) = \begin{cases} \sqrt{1-x^2} & 0 \le x < 1 \\ 1 & 1 \le x < 2 \\ 2 & x = 2 \end{cases}$

(a) $0 < c < 1$
$1 < c < 2$
(b) $c = 2$
(c) $c = 0$

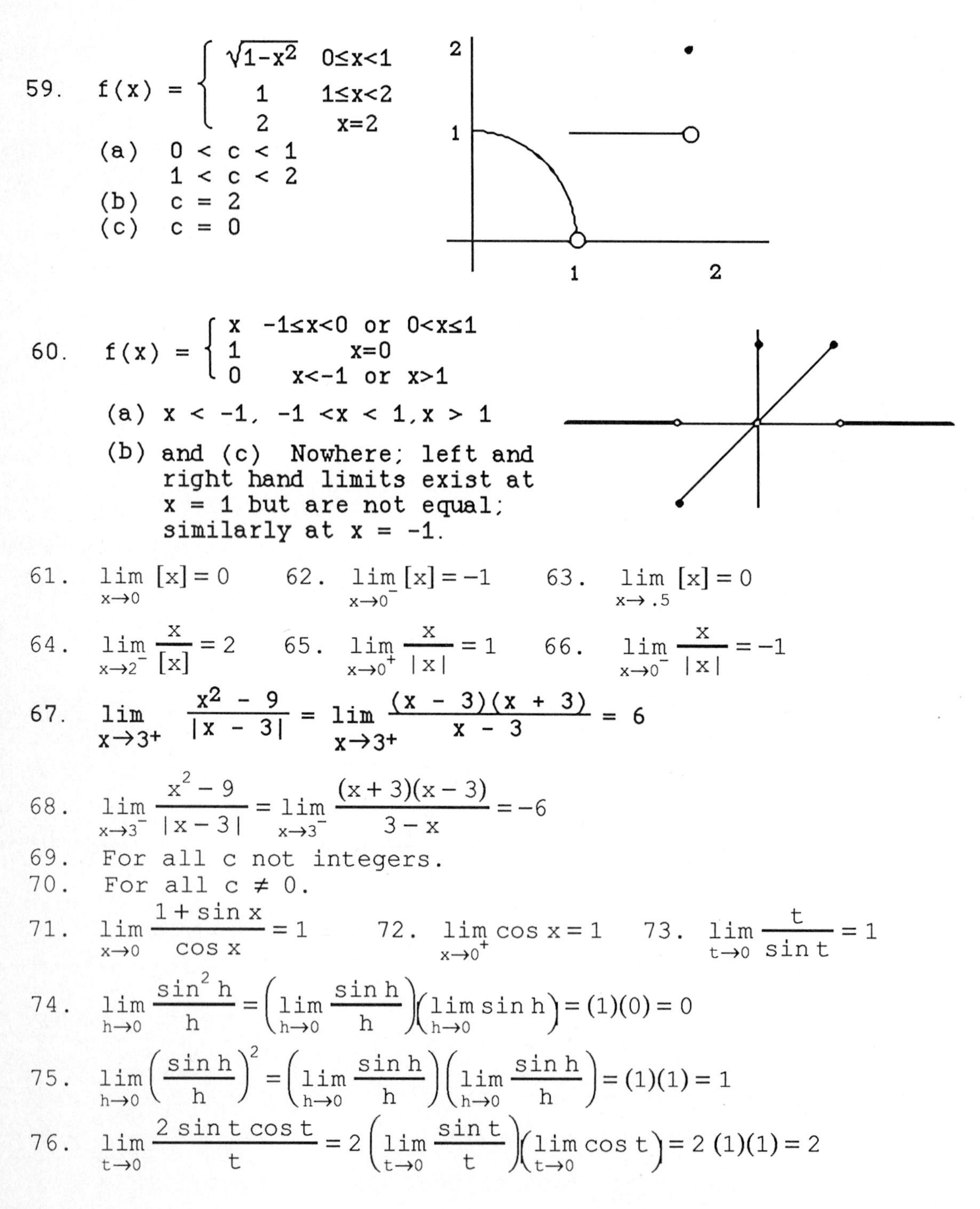

60. $f(x) = \begin{cases} x & -1 \le x < 0 \text{ or } 0 < x \le 1 \\ 1 & x = 0 \\ 0 & x < -1 \text{ or } x > 1 \end{cases}$

(a) $x < -1$, $-1 < x < 1$, $x > 1$

(b) and (c) Nowhere; left and right hand limits exist at $x = 1$ but are not equal; similarly at $x = -1$.

61. $\lim\limits_{x \to 0} [x] = 0$ 62. $\lim\limits_{x \to 0^-} [x] = -1$ 63. $\lim\limits_{x \to .5} [x] = 0$

64. $\lim\limits_{x \to 2^-} \dfrac{x}{[x]} = 2$ 65. $\lim\limits_{x \to 0^+} \dfrac{x}{|x|} = 1$ 66. $\lim\limits_{x \to 0^-} \dfrac{x}{|x|} = -1$

67. $\lim\limits_{x \to 3+} \dfrac{x^2 - 9}{|x - 3|} = \lim\limits_{x \to 3+} \dfrac{(x - 3)(x + 3)}{x - 3} = 6$

68. $\lim\limits_{x \to 3^-} \dfrac{x^2 - 9}{|x - 3|} = \lim\limits_{x \to 3^-} \dfrac{(x+3)(x-3)}{3 - x} = -6$

69. For all c not integers.

70. For all $c \neq 0$.

71. $\lim\limits_{x \to 0} \dfrac{1 + \sin x}{\cos x} = 1$ 72. $\lim\limits_{x \to 0^+} \cos x = 1$ 73. $\lim\limits_{t \to 0} \dfrac{t}{\sin t} = 1$

74. $\lim\limits_{h \to 0} \dfrac{\sin^2 h}{h} = \left(\lim\limits_{h \to 0} \dfrac{\sin h}{h}\right)\left(\lim\limits_{h \to 0} \sin h\right) = (1)(0) = 0$

75. $\lim\limits_{h \to 0} \left(\dfrac{\sin h}{h}\right)^2 = \left(\lim\limits_{h \to 0} \dfrac{\sin h}{h}\right)\left(\lim\limits_{h \to 0} \dfrac{\sin h}{h}\right) = (1)(1) = 1$

76. $\lim\limits_{t \to 0} \dfrac{2 \sin t \cos t}{t} = 2\left(\lim\limits_{t \to 0} \dfrac{\sin t}{t}\right)\left(\lim\limits_{t \to 0} \cos t\right) = 2\,(1)(1) = 2$

77. $\lim_{x\to 0} \tan x = 0$

78. $\lim_{\theta\to 0} \frac{\tan\theta}{\theta} = \lim_{\theta\to 0} \frac{\sin\theta}{\theta\cos\theta} = \lim_{\theta\to 0}\left(\frac{\sin\theta}{\theta}\right)\left(\frac{1}{\cos\theta}\right) = 1$

79. $\lim_{x\to 0^-} \sin x = 0$

80. $\lim_{x\to 0^+} \frac{\sin x}{|x|} = \lim_{x\to 0^+} \frac{\sin x}{x} = 1$

81. $\lim_{x\to 0^-} \frac{\sin x}{-x} = -\lim_{x\to 0^-} \frac{\sin x}{x} = -1$

82. $\lim_{x\to 0} x\cos x = 0\,(1) = 0$

83. $\lim_{x\to 0} \frac{\sin 2x}{x} = \lim_{x\to 0} \frac{2\sin 2x}{2x} = 2\,(1) = 2$

84. $\lim_{x\to 0} \frac{\sin 5x}{\sin 3x} = \lim_{x\to 0}\left(\frac{5x}{5x}\right)\left(\frac{3x}{3x}\right)\left(\frac{\sin 5x}{\sin 3x}\right) = \lim_{x\to 0}\left(\frac{5x}{3x}\right)\left(\frac{\sin 5x}{5x}\right)\left(\frac{3x}{\sin 3x}\right) = \frac{5}{3}$

85. $\lim_{y\to 0} \frac{\tan 2y}{3y} = \lim_{y\to 0}\left(\frac{2}{3}\right)\left(\frac{\sin 2y}{2y}\right)\left(\frac{1}{\cos 2y}\right) = \frac{2}{3}$

86. $\lim_{x\to 0} \frac{\sin 2x}{2x^2 + x} = \lim_{x\to 0} \frac{\sin 2x}{2x\left(x + \frac{1}{2}\right)} = \lim_{x\to 0}\left(\frac{\sin 2x}{2x}\right)\left(\frac{1}{x + \frac{1}{2}}\right) = 2$

87. (a) $|\sin \frac{1}{x}| \le 1 \Rightarrow -1 \le \sin \frac{1}{x} \le 1$. If $x > 0$, then $-x \le x \sin \frac{1}{x} \le x$. If $x < 0$, then $x \le x \sin \frac{1}{x} \le -x$. Therefore, we must have $-|x| \le x \sin \frac{1}{x} \le |x|$.

(b) From the results in (a), $\lim_{x\to 0} -|x| = \lim_{x\to 0} x \sin \frac{1}{x} \le \lim_{x\to 0} |x|$

Since $\lim_{x\to 0} |x| = 0$, we must have, by the Sandwich Theorem, that $\lim_{x\to 0} x \sin \frac{1}{x} = 0$

88. $1 - \frac{x^2}{6} < \frac{\sin x}{x} < 1 \Rightarrow \lim_{x\to 0} 1 - \frac{x^2}{6} \le \lim_{x\to 0} \frac{\sin x}{x} \le \lim_{x\to 0} 1$.

Therefore, $1 \le \lim_{x\to 0} \frac{\sin x}{x} \le 1 \Rightarrow \lim_{x\to 0} \frac{\sin x}{x} = 1$

89. (a) $F(t) = 2t + 3$, $c = 1$

$\lim_{t\to 1} (2t + 3) = 5$ if there exists $\delta > 0$ for which $|(2t + 3) - 5| < \varepsilon$ whenever $0 < |t - 1| < \delta$. But $|2t + 3 - 5| < \varepsilon \Leftrightarrow 0 < |2t - 2| < \varepsilon \Leftrightarrow 0 < |t - 1| < \frac{\varepsilon}{2}$.

Therefore, choose $\delta \le \frac{\varepsilon}{2}$.

(b) $F(t) = 2t - 3$, $c = 1$

$\lim_{t \to 1} (2t - 3) = -1$ if there exists $\delta > 0$ for which $|(2t - 3) + 1| < \varepsilon$ whenever $0 < |x - 1| < \delta$. But

$|2t - 3) + 1| < \varepsilon \Leftrightarrow 2|t - 1| < \varepsilon \Leftrightarrow 0 < |t - 1| < \frac{\varepsilon}{2}$.

Therefore, choose choose $\delta \le \frac{\varepsilon}{2}$

(c) $F(t) = 5 - 3t$, $c = 2$

$\lim_{t \to 2} (5 - 3t) = -1$ if there exists $\delta > 0$ for which $|5 - 3t + 1| < \varepsilon$ whenever $0 < |x - 2| < \delta$. But

$|-3t + 6| < \varepsilon \Leftrightarrow 3|t - 2| < \varepsilon \Leftrightarrow 0 < |t - 2| < \frac{\varepsilon}{3}$.

Choose $\delta \le \frac{\varepsilon}{3}$.

(d) $F(t) = 7$, $c = -1$.

Since $|7 - 7| = 0 < \varepsilon$, choose any $\delta > 0$. Then $\lim_{t \to -1} 7 = 7$.

(e) $F(t) = \frac{t^2 - 4}{t - 2}$, $c = 2$

$\lim_{t \to 2} (t + 2) = 4$ if there exists $\delta > 0$ for which

$|t + 2 - 4| < \varepsilon$ whenever $0 < |t - 2| < \delta$. Since

$|t + 2 - 4| = |t - 2| < \varepsilon$, choose $\delta \le \varepsilon$.

(f) $F(t) = \frac{t^2 + 6t + 5}{t + 5}$, $c = -3$

$\lim_{t \to 5} \frac{t^2 + 6t + 5}{t + 5} = \frac{60}{10} = 6$ if there exists $\delta > 0$ for which

$\left|\frac{t^2 + 6t + 5}{t + 5} - 6\right| < \varepsilon$ whenever $0 < |t + 3| < \delta$. Since

$\left|\frac{t^2 + 6t + 5}{t + 5} - 6\right| = \left|\frac{(t + 5)(t + 1)}{t + 5} - 6\right| = |t + 1 - 6| =$

$|t - 5| < \varepsilon$, choose $\delta \le \varepsilon$

(g) $F(t) = \frac{3t^2 + 8t - 3}{2t + 6}$, $c = -3$

$\lim_{t\to -3} \frac{(t + 3)(3t - 1)}{2(t + 3)} = \frac{-10}{2} = -5$ if there exists $\delta > 0$ for which

$\left|\frac{3t^2 + 8t - 3}{2t + 6} + 5\right| < \varepsilon$ whenever $0 < |t - 2| < \delta$. Since

$\left|\frac{3t^2 + 8t - 3}{2t + 6} + 5\right| = \left|\frac{(t + 3)(3t - 1)}{2(t + 3)} + 5\right| = \left|\frac{3t - 1}{2} + 5\right| =$

$\left|\frac{3t - 1 + 10}{2}\right| = \left|\frac{3t + 9}{2}\right| = \frac{3}{2}|t + 3| < \varepsilon$ if $|t + 3| < \frac{2\varepsilon}{3}$,

choose $\delta \le \frac{2\varepsilon}{3}$.

(h) $F(t) = \frac{4}{t}$, $c = 2$

$\lim_{t\to 2} \frac{4}{t} = 2$ if there exists $\delta > 0$ for which

$\left|\frac{4}{t} - 2\right| < \varepsilon$ whenever $0 < |t - 2| < \delta$. But $\left|\frac{4}{t} - 2\right| = \left|\frac{4 - 2t}{t}\right|$.

$= \frac{|4 - 2t|}{|t|}$. First we restrict the size of $|t|$. Choose $\delta = 1$

$|t - 2| < 1 \Rightarrow 1 < t < 3$ and $\frac{|4 - 2t|}{|t|} < \frac{|4 - 2t|}{1}$. Then

$|4 - 2t| < 3\varepsilon \Leftrightarrow 2|t - 2| < 3\varepsilon \Leftrightarrow |t - 2| < \frac{3\varepsilon}{2}$.

Choose $\delta \le \min\left(\frac{3\varepsilon}{2}, 1\right)$

(i) $F(t) = \frac{\frac{1}{t} - \frac{1}{3}}{t - 3}$, $c = 3$

$\lim_{t\to 3} \frac{\frac{1}{t} - \frac{1}{3}}{t - 3} = \frac{3 - t}{3t} \cdot \frac{1}{t - 3} = \frac{-1}{9}$ if there exists $\delta > 0$ for which

$\left|\frac{\frac{1}{t} - \frac{1}{3}}{t - 3} - \frac{-1}{9}\right| = \left|\frac{-1}{3t} + \frac{1}{9}\right| = \frac{1}{3}\left|\frac{1}{t} - \frac{1}{3}\right| = \frac{1}{3}\left|\frac{t - 3}{3t}\right|$.

Choose $\delta = 1$ so that $|t - 3| < 1 \Rightarrow 2 < t < 4 \Rightarrow 6 < 3t < 12$.

Then $\frac{1}{3}\left|\frac{3 - t}{3t}\right| < \frac{1}{3}\left|\frac{3 - t}{6}\right| < \varepsilon \Rightarrow |t - 3| < 18\varepsilon$.

Choose $\delta \le \min(18\varepsilon, 1)$.

90. $f(t) = t^2$; $\lim_{t\to 3} t^2 = 9$

(a) $|t^2 - 9| < \frac{1}{10} \Leftrightarrow |(t + 3)(t - 3)| < \frac{1}{10}$.

Choose $\delta = 1$ so that $|t - 3| < 1 \Rightarrow 2 < t < 4$. Then

$|t + 3| < 7$, and $|(t + 3)(t - 3)| < 7|t - 3| < \frac{1}{10}$ if $|t - 3| < \frac{1}{70}$. Choose $\delta \le \frac{1}{70}$. (We know that $\frac{1}{70} < 1$).

(b) Choose $\delta \le \frac{1}{700}$

(c) Choose $\delta \le \min\left(\frac{\varepsilon}{7}, 1\right)$

91. $f(t) = t^2 + t$; $\lim_{t \to 3} (t^2 + t) = 12$

(a) $|t^2 + t - 12| < \frac{1}{10} \Leftrightarrow |(t + 4)(t - 3)| < \frac{1}{10}$.

Choose $\delta = 1$ so that $|t - 3| < 1 \Rightarrow 2 < t < 4$. Then $|(t + 4)(t - 3)| < 8|t - 3| < \frac{1}{10}$ if $|t - 3| < \frac{1}{80}$.

Choose $\delta \le \frac{1}{80}$. (We know that $\frac{1}{80} < 1$)

(b) Choose $\delta \le \frac{1}{800}$

(c) Choose $\delta \le \min\left(\frac{\varepsilon}{8}, 1\right)$

92. (a) Your values should be close to $\frac{1}{4}$, since

$$\lim_{h \to 0} \frac{\sqrt{4+h} - 2}{h} = \lim_{h \to 0} \frac{\sqrt{4+h} - 2}{h} \cdot \frac{\sqrt{4+h} + 2}{\sqrt{4+h} + 2} = \lim_{h \to 0} \frac{1}{\sqrt{4+h} + 2} = \frac{1}{4}.$$

(b) This limit is the derivative of $f(x) = \sqrt{x}$ at $x = 4$.

93. $f(x) = \sqrt{9 - x^2}$

$$\frac{f(\Delta x) - f(0)}{\Delta x} = \frac{\sqrt{9 - (\Delta x)^2} - 3}{\Delta x}$$

Δx	$\frac{\sqrt{9 - (\Delta x)^2} - 3}{\Delta x}$
0.1	-0.0166713
0.01	-0.0016667
0.001	-0.0001666...
-0.1	0.0166713
-0.01	0.001666...
-0.001	0.0001666...

1.10 INFINITY AS A LIMIT

1. $$\lim_{x \to \infty} \frac{2x + 3}{5x + 7} = \lim_{x \to \infty} \frac{2 + \frac{3}{x}}{5 + \frac{7}{x}} = \frac{2}{5}$$

2. $$\lim_{t\to\infty} \frac{t^3+7}{t^4} = \lim_{t\to\infty} \frac{\frac{1}{t}+\frac{7}{t^4}}{1} = \frac{0}{1} = 0$$

3. $$\lim_{x\to\infty} \frac{x+1}{x^2+3} = \lim_{x\to\infty} \frac{\frac{1}{x}+\frac{1}{x^2}}{1+\frac{3}{x^2}} = 0$$

4. $$\lim_{x\to\infty} \frac{3x^2-6x}{4x-8} = \lim_{x\to\infty} \frac{3x(x-2)}{4(x-2)} = \lim_{x\to\infty} \frac{3x}{4} = \infty$$

5. $$\lim_{y\to\infty} \frac{3y+7}{y^2-2} = \lim_{y\to\infty} \frac{\frac{3}{y}+\frac{7}{y^2}}{1-\frac{2}{y^2}} = 0.$$

6. $$\lim_{x\to\infty} \frac{7x-28}{x^3} = \lim_{x\to\infty} \frac{\frac{7}{x^2}-\frac{28}{x^3}}{1} = \frac{0}{1} = 0$$

7. $$\lim_{t\to\infty} \frac{t^2-2t+3}{2t^2+5t-3} = \lim_{t\to\infty} \frac{1-\frac{2}{t}+\frac{3}{t^2}}{2+\frac{5}{t}-\frac{3}{t^2}} = \frac{1}{2}$$

8. $$\lim_{t\to\infty} \frac{t^2+1}{t+1} = \lim_{t\to\infty} \frac{1+\frac{1}{t^2}}{\frac{1}{t}+\frac{1}{t^2}} = \infty$$

9. $$\lim_{x\to\infty} \frac{x}{x-1} = \lim_{x\to\infty} \frac{1}{1-\frac{1}{x}} = 1$$

10. $$\lim_{x\to\infty} [x] = \infty$$

11. $$\lim_{x\to-\infty} |x| = \infty$$

12. $$\lim_{x\to-\infty} \frac{1}{|x|} = 0$$

13. $$\lim_{a\to\infty} \frac{|a|}{|a|+1} = \lim_{a\to\infty} \frac{1}{1+\frac{1}{|a|}} = 1$$

14. $$\lim_{t\to-\infty} \frac{t}{t+1} = \lim_{t\to-\infty} \frac{1}{1+\frac{1}{t}} = 1$$

15. $$\lim_{x\to\infty} \frac{3x^3+5x^2-7}{10x^3-11x+5} = \lim_{x\to\infty} \frac{3+\frac{5}{x}-\frac{7}{x^3}}{10-\frac{11}{x^2}+\frac{5}{x^3}} = \frac{3}{10}$$

16. $\lim\limits_{x\to\infty}\left(\frac{1}{x}+1\right)\left(\frac{5x^2-1}{x^2}\right)\lim\limits_{x\to\infty}\left(\frac{1}{x}+1\right)\left(\frac{5-\frac{1}{x^2}}{1}\right)=5$

17. $\lim\limits_{s\to\infty}\left(\frac{s}{s+1}\right)\left(\frac{s^2}{5+s^2}\right)=\lim\limits_{s\to\infty}\left(\frac{1}{1+\frac{1}{s}}\right)\left(\frac{1}{\frac{5}{s^2}+1}\right)=1$

18. $\lim\limits_{x\to\infty}\frac{8x^{23}-7x^2+5}{2x^{23}+x^{22}}=\lim\limits_{x\to\infty}\frac{8-\frac{7}{x^{21}}+\frac{5}{x^{23}}}{2+\frac{1}{x}}=4$

19. $\lim\limits_{r\to-\infty}\frac{8r^2+7r}{4r^2}=\lim\limits_{r\to-\infty}\frac{8+\frac{7}{r}}{4}=2$

20. $\lim\limits_{x\to\infty}\frac{7x^3}{x^3-3x^2+6x}=\lim\limits_{x\to\infty}\frac{7}{1-\frac{3}{x}+\frac{6}{x^2}}=7$

21. $\lim\limits_{y\to\infty}\frac{y^4}{y^4-7y^3+7y^2+9}=\lim\limits_{y\to\infty}\frac{1}{1-\frac{7}{y}+\frac{7}{y^2}+\frac{9}{y^4}}=1$

22. $\lim\limits_{x\to\infty}\frac{5x^3-6x+2}{10x^3+5}=\lim\limits_{x\to\infty}\frac{5-\frac{6}{x^2}+\frac{2}{x^3}}{10+\frac{5}{x^3}}=\frac{5}{10}=\frac{1}{2}$

23. $\lim\limits_{x\to\infty}\frac{x-3}{x^2-5x+4}=\lim\limits_{x\to\infty}\frac{\frac{1}{x}-\frac{3}{x^2}}{1-\frac{5}{x}+\frac{4}{x^2}}=0$

24. $\lim\limits_{x\to\infty}\frac{9x^4+x}{2x^4+4x^2-x+6}=\lim\limits_{x\to\infty}\frac{9+\frac{1}{x^3}}{2+\frac{4}{x^2}-\frac{1}{x^3}+\frac{6}{x^4}}=\frac{9}{2}$

25. $\lim\limits_{x\to\infty}\frac{-2x^3-2x+3}{3x^3+3x^2-5x}=\lim\limits_{x\to\infty}\frac{-2-\frac{2}{x^2}+\frac{3}{x^3}}{3+\frac{3}{x}-\frac{5}{x^2}}=-\frac{2}{3}$

26. $\lim\limits_{x\to-\infty}\frac{-2x^3-2x+3}{3x^3+3x^2-5x}=-\frac{2}{3}$ (See Problem 25)

27. $\lim\limits_{x\to\infty}\frac{x+\sin x}{x+\cos x}=\lim\limits_{x\to\infty}\frac{1+\frac{\sin x}{x}}{1+\frac{\cos x}{x}}=1$

28. $\lim_{x\to-\infty} \frac{1-x^2}{1+2x^2} = \lim_{x\to-\infty} \frac{\frac{1}{x^2}-1}{\frac{1}{x^2}+2} = -\frac{1}{2}$

29. $\lim_{x\to\infty} \left(\frac{1}{x^4}+\frac{1}{x}\right) = 0$

30. $\lim_{x\to\infty} \frac{\sin 2x}{x} = 0$ (Pinching Theorem, since $|\sin 2x| \le 1$)

31. $\lim_{x\to\infty} \left(\cos\frac{1}{x}+1\right) = \lim_{y\to0} (\cos y + 1) = 2$

32. $\lim_{y\to\infty} \frac{1}{y^2+5} = 0$

33. $\lim_{x\to0^+} \frac{1}{3x} = \infty$

34. $\lim_{x\to0^-} \frac{2}{x} = -\infty$

35. $\lim_{x\to0^+} \frac{5}{2x} = \infty$

36. $\lim_{t\to2^+} \frac{t^2+4}{t-2} = \infty$

37. $\lim_{t\to2} \frac{t^2-4}{t-2} = \lim_{t\to2} (t+2) = 4$

38. $\lim_{x\to2^-} \frac{x}{x-2} = -\infty$

39. $\lim_{x\to1+} \frac{x}{x-1} = \infty$

40. $\lim_{x\to0} \frac{|x|}{|x|+1} = 0$

41. $\lim_{x\to1^-} \frac{1}{x+1} = -\infty$

42. $\lim_{x\to0} \frac{1}{|x|} = \infty$

43. $\lim_{x\to-2+} \frac{1}{x+2} = \infty$

44. $\lim_{x\to3^-} \frac{x^2}{x-3} = -\infty$

45. $\lim_{x\to3} \frac{x-3}{x^2} = \frac{0}{9} = 0$

46. $\lim_{x\to1^+} \frac{2}{x^2-1} = \infty$

47. $\lim_{x\to2^-} \frac{x^2+5}{x-2} = -\infty$

48. $\lim_{x\to2} \frac{x-2}{x^2+5} = 0$

49. $\lim_{x \to -5} \frac{x^2 + 3x - 10}{x + 5} = \lim_{x \to -5} \frac{(x+5)(x-2)}{x+5} = -7$

50. $\lim_{x \to 1^+} \frac{x + 4}{x^2 + 2x - 3} = \lim_{x \to 1^+} \frac{x+4}{(x+3)(x-1)} = \infty$

51. (a) $\lim_{x \to 0} \frac{x - 1}{2x^2 - 7x + 5} = -\frac{1}{5}$

(b) $\lim_{x \to \infty} \frac{x - 1}{2x^2 - 7x + 5} = 0$

(c) $\lim_{x \to 1} \frac{x - 1}{2x^2 - 7x + 5} = -\frac{1}{3}$

52. Domain: $\frac{1}{x} - 1 \geq 0 \Rightarrow \frac{1}{x} \geq 1$ so $0 < x \leq 1$

Range: $y \geq 0$

53. $f(x) = \frac{1}{x - 2}$ has a vertical asymptote at $x = 2$ because $\lim_{x \to 2^+} f(x) = +\infty$ and $\lim_{x \to 2^-} f(x) = -\infty$.

f has a horizontal asymptote at $y = 0$ because $\lim_{x \to \infty} f(x) = 0$.

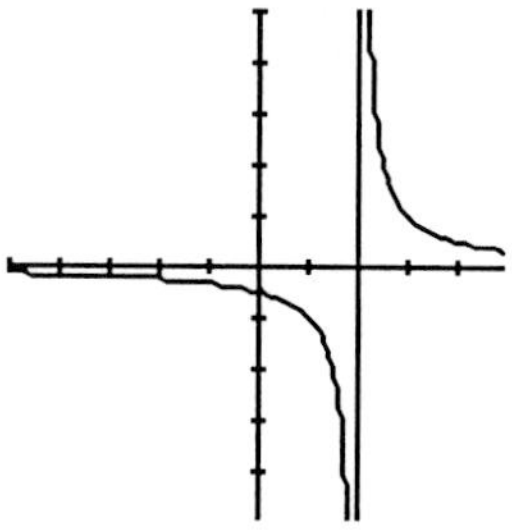

54. $f(x) = \frac{1}{x + 1}$ has a vertical asymptote at $x = -1$ because $\lim_{x \to -1^+} f(x) = \infty$ and $\lim_{x \to -1^-} f(x) = -\infty$.

f has a horizontal asymptote at $y = 0$ because $\lim_{x \to \infty} f(x) = 0$.

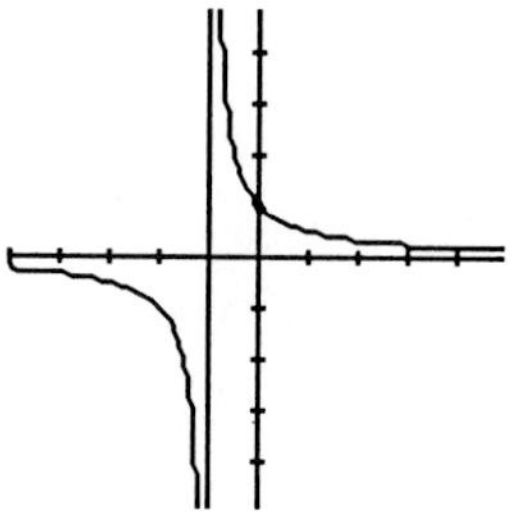

55. $f(x) = 1 + \frac{1}{x}$ has a vertical asymptote at $x = 0$ because $\lim_{x \to 0^+} f(x) = +\infty$ and $\lim_{x \to 0^-} f(x) = -\infty$.

f has a horizontal asymptote at $y = 1$ because $\lim_{x \to \infty} f(x) = 1$.

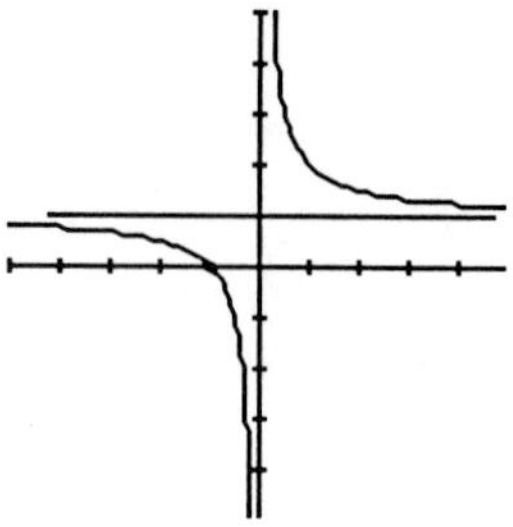

56. $f(x) = \frac{1}{|x|}$ has a vertical asymptote at $x = 0$ because $\lim_{x \to 0} f(x) = \infty$.

f has a horizontal asymptote at $y = 0$ because $\lim_{x \to \infty} f(x) = 0$.

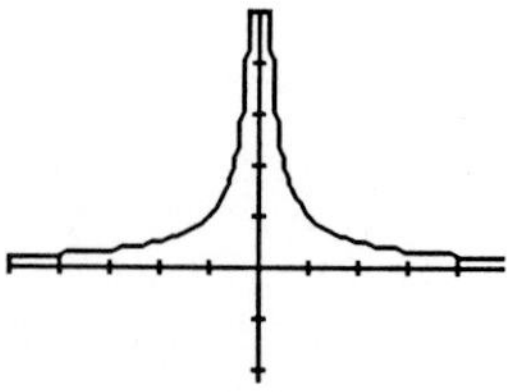

57. $\frac{2x-3}{x} < f(x) < \frac{2x^2+5x}{x^2} \Rightarrow \lim_{x\to\infty} \frac{2x-3}{x} < \lim_{x\to\infty} f(x) < \lim_{x\to\infty} \frac{2x^2+5x}{x^2}$.

Since $\lim_{x\to\infty} \frac{2x-3}{x} = 2$ and $\lim_{x\to\infty} \frac{2x^2+5x}{x^2} = 2$,

by the Squeeze Theorem, $\lim_{x\to\infty} f(x) = 2$.

58. $\lim_{x\to\infty} \frac{a_n x^n + a_{n-1}x^{n-1} + \ldots + a_0}{b_m x^m + b_{m-1}x^{m-1} + \ldots + b_0} = \lim_{x\to\infty} \frac{a_n x^{n-m} + a_{n-1}x^{n-m-1} + \ldots + a^{-m}}{b_m + b_{m-1}x^{-1} + \ldots + b_0 x^{-m}}$

Case I: If $m = n$, then $x^{n-m} = x^0 = 1$ and all other exponents are negative. Since $\lim_{x\to\infty} \frac{c}{x^k} = 0$, $\lim_{x\to\infty} \frac{f(x)}{g(x)} = \frac{a_n}{b_m}$.

Case II: If $m > n$, all exponents are negative and $\lim_{x\to\infty} \frac{f(x)}{g(x)} = 0$.

Case III: If $m < n$, then $n - m > 0$ and $\lim_{x\to\infty} \frac{f(x)}{g(x)} = \infty$.

1.11 CONTINUITY

1.
(a) $f(-1) = 0$ yes
(b) $\lim_{x\to -1^+} f(x) = 0$ yes
(c) $\lim_{x\to -1^+} f(x) = f(-1)$ yes
(d) f is continuous at $x = -1$

2.
(a) $f(1) = 1$ yes
(b) $\lim_{x\to 1} f(x) = 2$ yes
(c) $f(1) = 1$ no
(d) $\lim_{x\to 1} f(x) \neq f(1)$ no

3.
(a) $f(2)$ does not exist no
(b) f is NOT continuous at $x = 2$ no

4. For $-1 \le x < 0$, $0 < x < 1$, $1 < x < 2$ or $2 < x \le 3$.

5.
(a) $\lim_{x\to 2} f(x) = 0$
(b) $f(2) = 0$

6. $f(1) = 2$, since the limit equals 2 at $x = 1$.

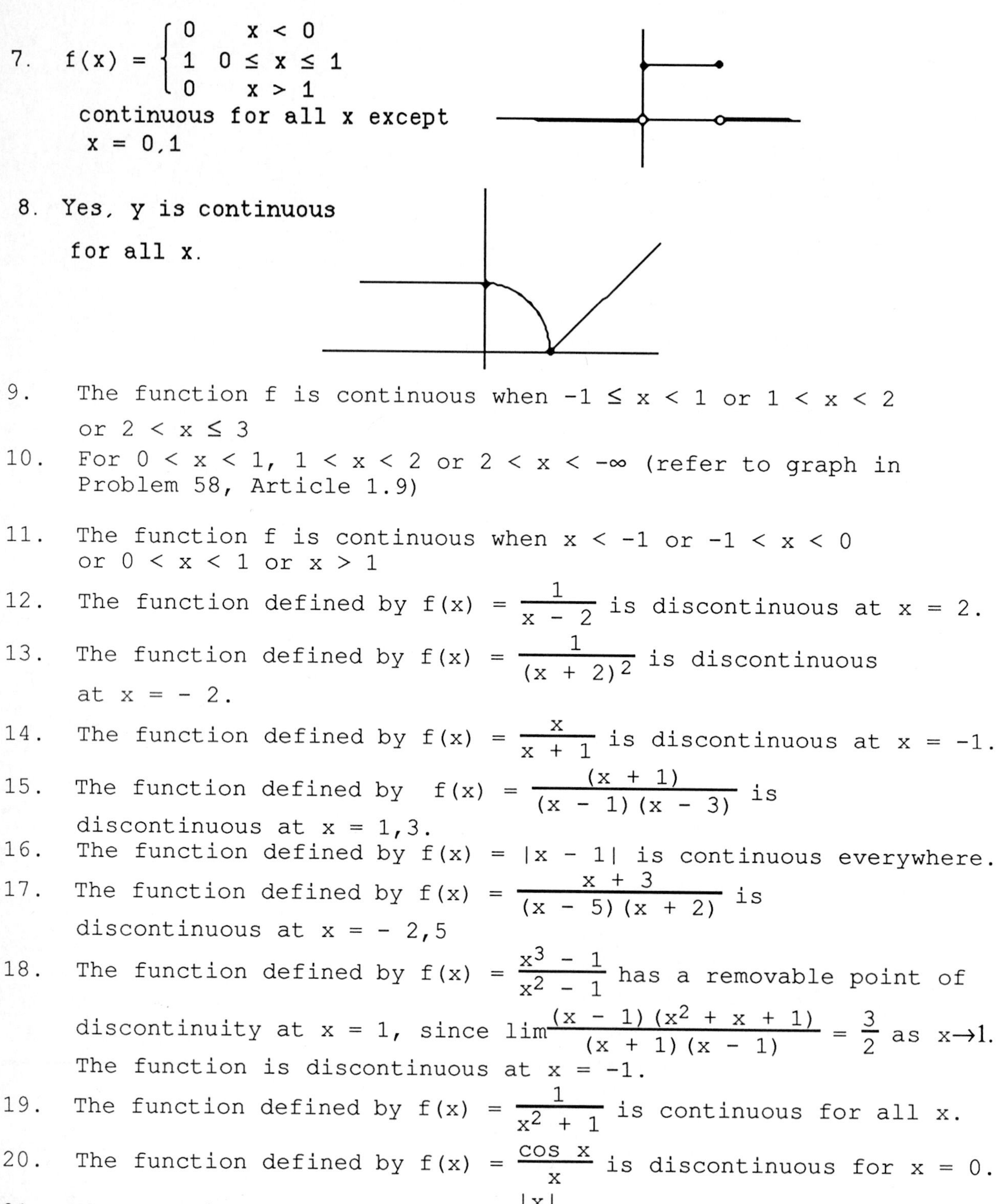

7. $f(x) = \begin{cases} 0 & x < 0 \\ 1 & 0 \le x \le 1 \\ 0 & x > 1 \end{cases}$

continuous for all x except $x = 0, 1$

8. Yes, y is continuous for all x.

9. The function f is continuous when $-1 \le x < 1$ or $1 < x < 2$ or $2 < x \le 3$

10. For $0 < x < 1$, $1 < x < 2$ or $2 < x < -\infty$ (refer to graph in Problem 58, Article 1.9)

11. The function f is continuous when $x < -1$ or $-1 < x < 0$ or $0 < x < 1$ or $x > 1$

12. The function defined by $f(x) = \dfrac{1}{x - 2}$ is discontinuous at $x = 2$.

13. The function defined by $f(x) = \dfrac{1}{(x + 2)^2}$ is discontinuous at $x = -2$.

14. The function defined by $f(x) = \dfrac{x}{x + 1}$ is discontinuous at $x = -1$.

15. The function defined by $f(x) = \dfrac{(x + 1)}{(x - 1)(x - 3)}$ is discontinuous at $x = 1, 3$.

16. The function defined by $f(x) = |x - 1|$ is continuous everywhere.

17. The function defined by $f(x) = \dfrac{x + 3}{(x - 5)(x + 2)}$ is discontinuous at $x = -2, 5$

18. The function defined by $f(x) = \dfrac{x^3 - 1}{x^2 - 1}$ has a removable point of discontinuity at $x = 1$, since $\lim \dfrac{(x - 1)(x^2 + x + 1)}{(x + 1)(x - 1)} = \dfrac{3}{2}$ as $x \to 1$. The function is discontinuous at $x = -1$.

19. The function defined by $f(x) = \dfrac{1}{x^2 + 1}$ is continuous for all x.

20. The function defined by $f(x) = \dfrac{\cos x}{x}$ is discontinuous for $x = 0$.

21. The function defined by $f(x) = \dfrac{|x|}{x}$ is discontinuous at $x = 0$.

22. $\lim \dfrac{x^2 - 1}{x - 1} = \lim (x + 1) = 2$ as $x \to 1$ and $f(1) = 2$, so f is continuous at $x = 1$.

23. $\lim\limits_{x \to 3} \dfrac{x^2 - 9}{x - 3} = \lim\limits_{x \to 3} (x + 3) = 6$ so define $g(3) = 6$.

24. As $x \to 2$, $\lim \dfrac{x^2 + 3x - 10}{x - 2} = \lim (x + 5) = 7$ so define $h(2) = 7$.

25. $f(x) = \frac{x^3 - 1}{x^2 - 1} = \frac{(x - 1)(x^2 + x + 1)}{(x - 1)(x + 1)} = \frac{x^2 + x + 1}{x + 1}$

$\lim_{x \to 1} \frac{x^2 + x + 1}{x + 1} = \frac{3}{2}$ so define $f(1) = \frac{3}{2}$.

26. $g(x) = \frac{x^2 - 16}{x^2 - 3x + 4} = \frac{(x + 4)(x - 4)}{(x - 4)(x + 1)}$, so $g(x)$ has limit $\frac{8}{5}$ as $x \to 4$. Define $g(4) = \frac{8}{5}$.

27. (a) $f(x) = \begin{cases} x & 0 \le x \le 1 \\ 2 - x & 1 < x \le 2 \end{cases}$

(1,1)

(b) $\lim_{x \to 1^+} x = 1$; $\lim_{x \to 1^-} (2 - x) = 1$

$f(1) = 1$, so f is continuous at $x = 1$.

(c) $f'(x) = \begin{cases} 1 & 0 \le x < 1 \\ -1 & 1 < x \le 2 \end{cases}$

Therefore, $f'(1)$ does not exist

28. Define $f(2) = 1$.

29. $\lim_{x \to 3^+} (x^2 - 1) = 8$; $\lim_{x \to 3^-} 2ax = 8$. Therefore, $2a(3) = 6a = 8$ so $a = \frac{4}{3}$.

30. The $\lim_{x \to \frac{1-}{2}} x^3 = \frac{1}{8}$ and $\lim_{x \to \frac{1+}{2}} bx^2 = \frac{b}{4}$. Therefore, $\frac{b}{4} = \frac{1}{8}$ or $b = \frac{1}{2}$.

31. $\lim_{x \to 0} \frac{1 + \cos x}{2} = \frac{2}{2} = 1$

32. $\lim_{x \to 0} \cos\left(1 - \frac{\sin x}{x}\right) = \cos 0 = 1$

33. $\lim_{x \to 0} \tan x = 0$

34. $\lim_{x \to 0} \sin\left(\frac{\pi}{2}\cos(\tan x)\right) = \sin\left(\frac{\pi}{2}\cos\left(\lim_{x \to 0}(\tan x)\right)\right) = \sin\left(\frac{\pi}{2}\cos 0\right) = \sin\frac{\pi}{2} = 1$

35. $f(x) = |x| = \begin{cases} x & 0 \le x \le 1 \\ -x & -1 \le x < 0 \end{cases}$ has a maximum value of 1 and a minimum value of 0.

36. The maximum value occurs at $x = 2$ and $x = 3$. There is no minimum value, since $f(x) > 0$ but $f(x) \neq 0$ for any x.

37. The function $f(x) = x^2$ has no maximum on $-1 < x < 1$ because the interval is open, but there is a minimum value of 0 at $x = 0$.

38. No, continuity on a closed interval is sufficient for a maximum and/or a minimum, but not necessary.

39. If $f(0) < 0$ and $f(1) > 0$, then there exists at least one

value of x, say $x = c$, $0 < x < 1$, such that $f(c) = 0$ by the Intermediate Value Theorem.

40. The function defined by $f(x) = \cos x - x$ is continuous, $f(0) = 1$ and $f(\frac{\pi}{2}) = -\frac{\pi}{2}$. Therefore, by the Intermediate Value Theorem, there exists a value somewhere between 0 and $\frac{\pi}{2}$ for which $f(x) = 0$.

41. $\lim_{x\to 0} f(x)$ does not exist. Therefore $f(x)$ is not continuous at $x = 0$ and does not have the Intermediate Value property.

Also, if $f(x)$ is to be the derivative of a function, $F(x)$, then

$F'(0) = \lim_{\Delta x\to 0} \frac{f(\Delta x) - f(0)}{\Delta x}$ must exist but $\lim_{\Delta x\to 0^+} \frac{1 - 1}{\Delta x} = 0$ and $\lim_{\Delta x\to 0^-} \frac{-1 - 1}{\Delta x} = \infty$ so $F'(0)$ does not exist.

1.M MISCELLANEOUS PROBLEMS

1. If the particle ends at the point $B(u,v)$ after traveling $\Delta x = h$ and $\Delta y = k$ units, then it must have begun at the point $A(u - h, v - k)$.

2. Since $-2 + \Delta x = 0 \Rightarrow \Delta x = 2$, $\Delta y = 3\Delta x = 6$. Then $5 + 6 = 11$ and the new point is $(0,11)$.

3. On the curve $y = x^2$ between $A(1,1)$ and $B(a,a^2)$,
$\frac{\Delta y}{\Delta x} = \frac{a^2 - 1}{a - 1} = a + 1$, $a \neq 1$.

4. (b) $m_{AB} = \frac{1-10}{8-2} = -\frac{3}{2}$ $\quad m_{BC} = \frac{6-10}{-4-2} = \frac{2}{3}$

$m_{CD} = \frac{-3-6}{2-(-4)} = -\frac{3}{2}$ $\quad m_{DA} = \frac{-3-1}{2-8} = \frac{2}{3}$

$m_{CE} = \frac{6-6}{\frac{14}{3}-(-4)} = 0$ $\quad m_{BD} = \frac{-3-10}{2-2} =$ undefined

(c) $AB \parallel CD$ and $BC \parallel DA$, so ABCD is a ▱.

(d) $m_{BE} = \frac{6-10}{\frac{14}{3}-2} = -\frac{3}{2}$, so A, B and E are collinear.

(e) Line CD has equation $y = -\frac{3}{2}x$, and contains $(0,0)$.

(f) AB: $y - 1 = -\frac{3}{2}(x - 8)$ or $3x + 2y = 26$.

CD: $y - 6 = -\frac{3}{2}(x + 4)$ or $3x + 2y = 0$.

AD: $y - 1 = \frac{2}{3}(x - 8)$ or $2x - 3y = 13$.

CE: $y - 6 = 0$ or $y = 6$

BD: $x - 2 = 0$ or $x = 2$

(g) AB: $\left(-\frac{26}{3}, 0\right)$ and $(0, 13)$

CD: $(0, 0)$

AD: $\left(\frac{13}{2}, 0\right)$ and $\left(0, -\frac{13}{3}\right)$

CE: $(0, 6)$, no x-intercept

BD: $(2, 0)$, no y intercept

5. (a) $2y = 3x + 4$ or $y = \frac{3}{2}x + 2$. Therefore the line through $P(1, -3)$ perpendicular to $L: 2y - 3x = 4$ would have slope $m_{\perp} = -\frac{2}{3}$. Thus $y + 3 = \frac{-2}{3}(x - 1)$ or

$$2x + 3y = -7 \text{ is the required line.}$$

(b) $$d = \frac{|-3 - 6 - 4|}{\sqrt{9 + 4}} = \frac{13}{\sqrt{13}} = \sqrt{13}$$

6. (a) $m_{AB} = \frac{-3 - 4}{4 - 6} = \frac{7}{2}$, $m_{BC} = \frac{3 - (-3)}{-2 - 4} = -1$, $m_{AC} = \frac{3 - 4}{-2 - 6} = \frac{1}{8}$

None are negative reciprocals.

(b) $L(AB) = \sqrt{(6 - 4)^2 + (4 + 3)^2} = \sqrt{53}$

$L(AC) = \sqrt{(6 + 2)^2 + (4 - 3)^2} = \sqrt{65}$

$L(BC) = \sqrt{(4 + 2)^2 + (-3 - 3)^2} = \sqrt{72}$; none are equal

(c) Line BC: $y - (-3) = -(x - 4)$ or $y = -x + 1$

$0 < 0 + 1$ so $(0, 0)$ is below the line.

(d) $m_{BC'} = \frac{y + 3}{-2 - 4} = -\frac{2}{7} \Rightarrow 7y + 21 = 12$ or $y = -\frac{9}{7}$

7. The equation of the circle is $(y - 1)^2 + (x - 2)^2 = 4$. Therefore the circle is tangent to the y-axis and one tangent line is $x = 0$. Let $P(x_1, y_1)$ be the other point of tangency. Then

(i) the slope between the center $(2, 1)$ and P is $\frac{y_1 - 1}{x_1 - 2}$

and the slope between the origin and P is $\frac{y_1}{x_1}$;

(ii) these slopes are negative reciprocals, so

$$\frac{y_1 - 1}{x_1 - 2} \cdot \frac{y_1}{x_1} = -1 \Rightarrow y_1^2 - y_1 = -x_1^2 + 2x_1 \text{ or}$$

$$x_1^2 + y_1^2 - 2x_1 - y_1 = 0$$

(iii) The point P also satisfies the equation of the circle, so substituting and solving the two equations simultaneously,

$$\begin{aligned} x_1^2 + y_1^2 - 2x_1 - y_1 &= 0 \\ x_1^2 + y_1^2 - 4x_1 - 2y_1 &= -1 \end{aligned}$$

$$\begin{aligned} 2x_1 + y_1 &= 1 \\ y_1 &= -2x_1 + 1 \\ (-2x_1)^2 + x_1^2 - 4x_1 + 4 &= 4 \\ 4x_1^2 + x_1^2 - 4x_1 &= 0 \\ x_1(5x_1 - 4) &= 0 \quad \text{or} \quad x_1 = \frac{4}{5} \\ y_1 &= -\frac{8}{5} + 1 = -\frac{3}{5} \end{aligned}$$

(iv) The slope between the point $(\frac{4}{5}, \frac{-3}{5})$ and $(0,0)$ is

$$m = \frac{-\frac{3}{5}}{\frac{4}{5}} = -\frac{3}{4}$$

The required line is $y + \frac{3}{5} = -\frac{3}{4}(x - \frac{4}{5})$

or $y = -\frac{3}{4}x$

8. $x_m = \frac{x_1 + x_2}{2}$; $y_m = \frac{y_1 + y_2}{2}$

9. $Ax + By = C \Rightarrow By = -Ax + C$ or $y = \frac{-A}{B}x + \frac{C}{B}$

(a) $m = -\frac{A}{B}$

(b) y-intercept is $\frac{C}{B}$

(c) x-intercept is $\frac{C}{A}$

(d) $m_{\perp} = \frac{B}{A}$. Therefore $y = \frac{-A}{B}x + \frac{C}{B}$ or $Bx - Ay = 0$.

10.

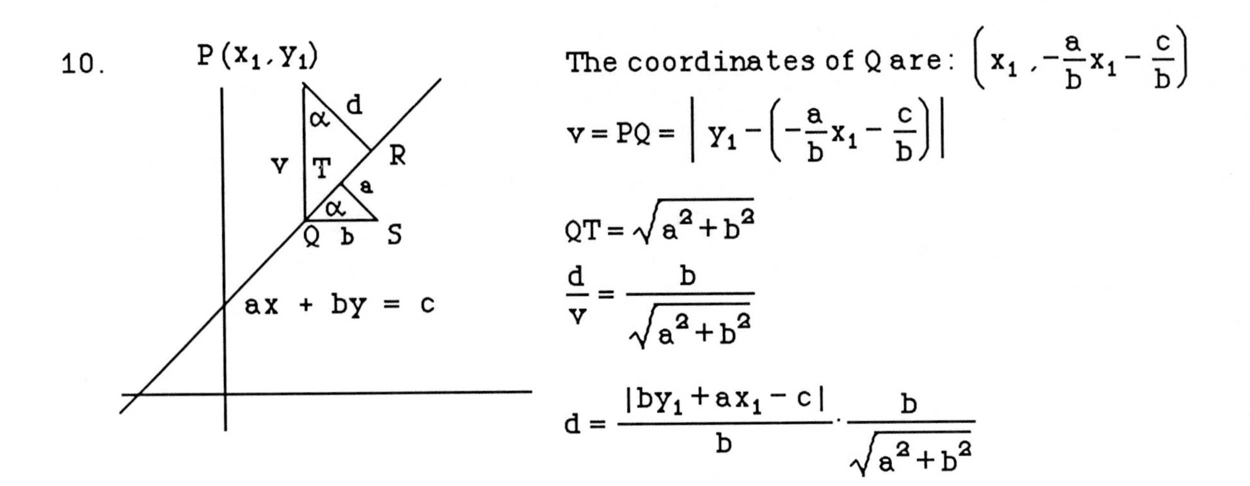

The coordinates of Q are: $\left(x_1, -\frac{a}{b}x_1 - \frac{c}{b}\right)$

$$v = PQ = \left| y_1 - \left(-\frac{a}{b}x_1 - \frac{c}{b}\right)\right|$$

$$QT = \sqrt{a^2+b^2}$$

$$\frac{d}{v} = \frac{b}{\sqrt{a^2+b^2}}$$

$$d = \frac{|by_1 + ax_1 - c|}{b} \cdot \frac{b}{\sqrt{a^2+b^2}}$$

11. $x = p\cos\alpha$ and $y = p\sin\alpha$

$$m_{ON} = \frac{y}{x} \text{ and } m_l = -\frac{x}{y} = \frac{-\cos\alpha}{\sin\alpha}$$

$$y - p\sin\alpha = -\frac{\cos\alpha}{\sin\alpha}(x - p\cos\alpha)$$

$$y\sin\alpha - p\sin^2\alpha = -x\cos\alpha + p\cos^2\alpha$$

$$x\cos\alpha + y\sin\alpha = p$$

12. Let L_1: $Ax + By = C$ and L_2: $Ax + By = C'$. Then $m_{L_1} = -\frac{A}{B} = m_{L_2}$

so that $L_1 \parallel L_2$. Moreover, if $C = C'$ the lines are coincident.

Let L_3: $Bx - Ay = C'$. Then $m_{L_3} = \frac{B}{A}$. Then $L_3 \perp L_1$ since their

slopes are negative reciprocals.

13. Let $P(x_1, y_1)$ be the center of one such circle. If the circle is to be tangent to the lines $x + y - 1 = 0$, $x - y + 1 = 0$, and $x - 3y - 1 = 0$ then P must be equidistant from each. That is,

$$\frac{|x_1+y_1-1|}{\sqrt{2}} = \frac{|x_1-y_1+1|}{\sqrt{2}} = \frac{|x_1-3y_1-1|}{\sqrt{10}}.$$ We separate these into four cases and solve the resulting systems.

Case I: $x_1 + y_1 - 1 = +(x_1 - y_1 + 1) \Rightarrow 2y_1 = 2$ or $y_1 = 1$

$$\sqrt{5}(x_1 - y_1 + 1) = +(x_1 - 3y_1 - 1) \text{ and } y_1 = 1 \Rightarrow$$

$$\sqrt{5}x_1 = x_1 - 3 - 1 \text{ or } x_1(\sqrt{5} - 1) = -4$$

$$x_1 = \frac{4}{1-\sqrt{5}} \cdot \frac{1+\sqrt{5}}{1+\sqrt{5}} = -1 - \sqrt{5}$$

The radius is $r = \frac{|-1-\sqrt{5}+1-1|}{\sqrt{2}} = \frac{1+\sqrt{5}}{\sqrt{2}} \cdot \frac{\sqrt{2}}{\sqrt{2}} = \frac{\sqrt{2}+\sqrt{10}}{2}$

Case II: $x_1 + y_1 - 1 = -(x_1 - y_1 + 1) = -x_1 + y_1 - 1$

$$2x_1 = 0 \text{ or } x_1 = 0$$

$$\sqrt{5}(x_1 + y_1 - 1) = -(x_1 - 3y_1 - 1) = -x_1 + 3y_1 + 1 \text{ and } -x_1 + 3y_1 + 1$$

$$y_1\sqrt{5} - \sqrt{5} = 3y_1 + 1 \text{ or } -1 - \sqrt{5} = y_1(3 - \sqrt{5})$$

$$y_1 = \frac{1+\sqrt{5}}{\sqrt{5}-3} = \frac{1+\sqrt{5}}{\sqrt{5}-3}\cdot\frac{\sqrt{5}+3}{\sqrt{5}+3} = \sqrt{5} - 2$$

The radius is $r = \dfrac{|-2-\sqrt{5}-1|}{\sqrt{2}} = \dfrac{3 + \sqrt{5}}{\sqrt{2}}\cdot\dfrac{\sqrt{2}}{\sqrt{2}} = \dfrac{3\sqrt{2} + \sqrt{10}}{2}$

Case III: $\sqrt{5}(x_1 + y_1 - 1) = x_1 - 3y_1 - 1$

$$y_1\sqrt{5} - \sqrt{5} = -3y_1 - 1 \Rightarrow y_1(\sqrt{5} + 3) = \sqrt{5} - 1$$

$$y_1 = \frac{\sqrt{5}-1}{3+\sqrt{5}}\cdot\frac{3-\sqrt{5}}{3-\sqrt{5}}$$

$$y_1 = \frac{3\sqrt{5} - 3 - 5 + \sqrt{5}}{4} = \frac{4\sqrt{5} - 8}{4} = -2 + \sqrt{5}$$

The radius is $r = \dfrac{|-2 + \sqrt{5} - 1|}{\sqrt{2}} = \dfrac{3 - \sqrt{5}}{\sqrt{2}}\cdot\dfrac{\sqrt{2}}{\sqrt{2}} = \dfrac{3\sqrt{2} - \sqrt{10}}{2}$

Case IV: $\sqrt{5}(x_1 - y_1 + 1) = -x_1 + 3y_1 + 1$ and $y_1 = 1$

$$\sqrt{5}(x_1) = -x_1 + 4 \quad \Rightarrow \quad x_1(1 + \sqrt{5}) = 4$$

$$x_1 = \frac{4}{1+\sqrt{5}}\cdot\frac{1-\sqrt{5}}{1-\sqrt{5}} = \frac{4 - 4\sqrt{5}}{-4} = \sqrt{5} - 1$$

The radius is $r = \dfrac{|\sqrt{5}-1+1-1|}{\sqrt{2}} = \dfrac{|\sqrt{5}-1|}{\sqrt{2}} = \dfrac{\sqrt{10} - \sqrt{2}}{2}$

14. We will find the distance from the point $(0,b')$ on line $y = mx + b'$ to the line $y - mx - b = 0$.

$$d = \frac{|b' - m(0) - b|}{\sqrt{m^2 + 1}} = \frac{|b' - b|}{\sqrt{m^2 + 1}}$$

15. Let L_1: $a_1x + b_1y + c_1 = 0$ and L_2: $a_2x + b_2y + c_2 = 0$ be two lines. If L_1 not parallel to L_2 then

$$L_3: \quad a_1x + b_1y + c_1 + k(a_2x + b_2y + c_2) = 0$$

is the family of all lines through the point of intersection of L_1 and L_2. The reason is that if $P(x_1, y_1)$ is the point of intersection of L_1 and L_2 then the coordinates of P satisfy both equations (i.e. make them equal to zero) and $0 + k \cdot 0 = 0$. If $L_1 \parallel L_2$, then L_3 is the family of all lines $\parallel$ to L_1 and L_2.

16. Let $(x, y) = (x, 3x + 1)$ be a point on $y = 3x + 1$. Then

$$\sqrt{(x+3)^2 + (3x-3)^2} = \sqrt{x^2 + (3x+1)^2} \Rightarrow 10x^2 - 12x + 18 = 10x^2 + 6x + 1$$

$-18x = -17$ or $x = \frac{17}{18}$. Then $y = 3\left(\frac{17}{18}\right) + 1 = \frac{23}{6}$.

The point is $\left(\frac{17}{18}, \frac{23}{6}\right)$.

17. The line $5x - y = 1$ has slope $m = 5$. Then $m_\perp = -\frac{1}{5}$.

There are two such lines:

$$\frac{b}{-a} = -\frac{1}{5} \text{ and } \frac{1}{2}ab = 5 \Rightarrow 5b = a \text{ and } \frac{1}{2}(5b) \cdot b = 5$$

Then $b^2 = 2$ or $b = \pm\sqrt{2}$.

L_1: $(5\sqrt{2}, \sqrt{2})$

$$y - \sqrt{2} = \frac{-1}{5}(x - 5\sqrt{2})$$
$$5y - 5\sqrt{2} = -x + 5\sqrt{2}$$
$$x + 5y = 10\sqrt{2}$$

L_2: $(-5\sqrt{2}, \sqrt{2})$

$$y + \sqrt{2} = \frac{-1}{5}(x + 5\sqrt{2})$$
$$5y + 5\sqrt{2} = -x - 5\sqrt{2}$$
$$x + 5y = -10\sqrt{2}$$

18. $y = \dfrac{x^2 + 2}{x^2 - 1} \Rightarrow yx^2 - y = x^2 + 2 \Rightarrow yx^2 - x^2 = 2 + y \Rightarrow$

$$x^2(y - 1) = y + 2 \text{ or } x = \pm\sqrt{\frac{y+2}{y-1}}.$$

x is real when $\frac{y+2}{y-1} \geq 0$ or if $y > 1$ or $y \leq -2$.

19. $A = \pi r^2 \Rightarrow \frac{A}{\pi} = r^2$ or $r = \sqrt{\frac{A}{\pi}}$

$C = 2\pi r \Rightarrow r = \frac{C}{2\pi}$

$$\sqrt{\frac{A}{\pi}} = \frac{C}{2\pi} \Rightarrow \frac{A}{\pi} = \frac{C^2}{4\pi^2} \text{ or } A = \frac{C^2}{4\pi}$$

20. If $f(x) = x - \frac{1}{x}$, then $f\left(\frac{1}{x}\right) = \frac{1}{x} - \frac{1}{\frac{1}{x}} = \frac{1}{x} - x = -f(x)$.

$f(-x) = -x - \frac{1}{(-x)} = \frac{1}{x} - x = -f(x)$. $\therefore f(x) = f(-x) = f\left(\frac{1}{x}\right)$.

21. $y = \frac{1}{1+x}$ D: $x \neq -1$ R: $y \neq 0$

22. $y = \frac{1}{1+x^2}$ D: all reals R: $0 < y \leq 1$

23. $y = \frac{1}{1+\sqrt{x}}$ has domain D: $x \geq 0$. To find the range, we solve for x in terms of y:

$1 + \sqrt{x} = \frac{1}{y} \Rightarrow \sqrt{x} = \frac{1}{y} - 1 = \frac{1-y}{y}$

$\frac{1-y}{y} \geq 0$ if $0 < y \leq 1$. Therefore the range is R: $0 < y \leq 1$.

24. $y = \frac{1}{\sqrt{3-x}}$ D: $x < 3$ R: $y > 0$

25. If $f(x) = ax + b$ and $g(x) = cx + d$, then

$f(g(x)) = a(cx + d) + b$ and $g(f(x)) = c(ax + b) + d$.
Therefore, we must have $acx + ad + b = acx + bc + d$
or $ad + b = bc + d$.

26. Let $f(x) = \frac{ax+b}{cx-a}$. Then $f(f(x)) = \frac{a\left(\frac{ax+b}{cx-a}\right)+b}{c\left(\frac{ax+b}{cx-a}\right)-a} =$

$$\frac{a(ax+b)+b(cx-a)}{c(ax+b)-a(cx-a)} = \frac{a^2x+ab+bcx-ab}{acx+bc-acx+a^2} = \frac{(a^2+bc)x}{a^2+bc} = x.$$

27. (a) $f\left(\frac{1}{x}\right) = \frac{\frac{1}{x}}{\frac{1-x}{x}} = \frac{1}{1-x}$, $x \neq 0$

(b) $f(-x) = \frac{-x}{-x-1} = \frac{x}{x+1}$, $x \neq -1$

(c) $f(f(x)) = \frac{\frac{x}{x-1}}{\frac{x}{x-1} - 1} = \frac{\frac{x}{x-1}}{\frac{x-x+1}{x-1}} = x$, $x \neq 1$

(d) $f\left(\frac{1}{f(x)}\right) = \frac{\frac{x-1}{x}}{\frac{x-1}{x} - 1} = \frac{\frac{x-1}{x}}{\frac{x-1-x}{x}} = \frac{x-1}{-1} = 1 - x$, $x \neq 0, 1$

28. $|x + 1| < 4 \Rightarrow -4 < x + 1 < 4 \Rightarrow -5 < x < 3$

29. $|x| + |y| = 1$

In Quadrant I, $x \geq 0$, $y \geq 0$ and $x + y = 1$ or $y = 1 - x$
In Quadrant II, $x \leq 0$, $y \geq 0$ and $-x + y = 1$ or $y = x + 1$
In Quadrant III, $x \leq 0$, $y \leq 0$ and $-x - y = 1$ or $y = -x - 1$
In Quadrant IV, $x \geq 0$, $y \leq 0$ and $x - y = 1$ or $y = x - 1$.
The graph is the intersection of these four lines.

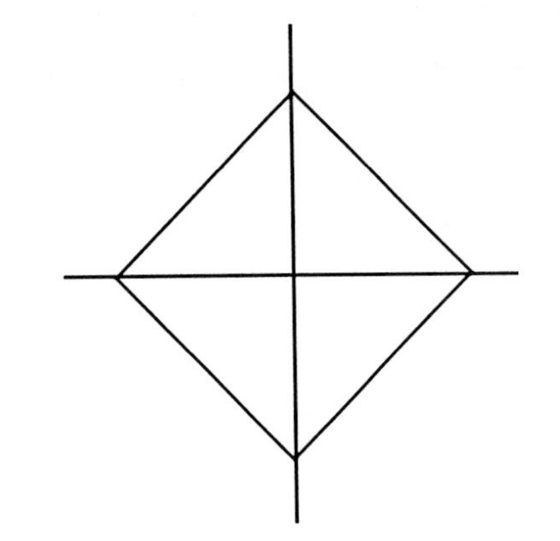

30.

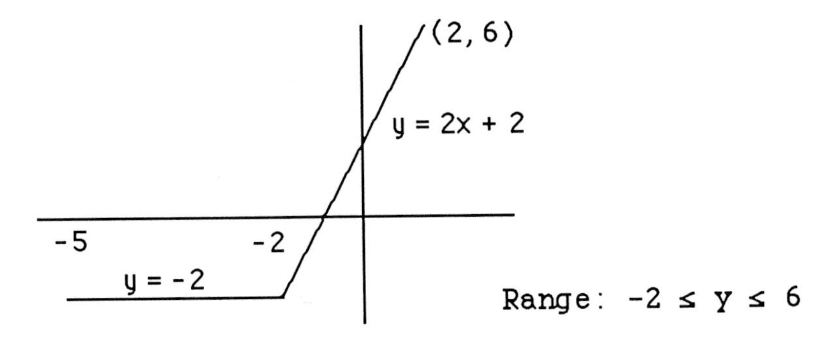

Range: $-2 \leq y \leq 6$

31. $M(a,b) = \dfrac{a + b}{2} + \dfrac{|a - b|}{2}$. If $a \geq b$,

$M = \dfrac{a+b}{2} + \dfrac{a-b}{2} = \dfrac{2a}{a} = a$; if $a \leq b$, $M = \dfrac{a+b}{2} + \dfrac{b-a}{2} = \dfrac{2b}{b} = b$.

The expression $M(a,b) = \dfrac{a+b}{2} - \dfrac{|a-b|}{2}$ gives the smaller, because when $a \leq b$ $m = \dfrac{a+b}{2} - \dfrac{b-a}{2} = a$ and when $b \geq a$ $m = \dfrac{a+b}{2} - \dfrac{a-b}{2} = b$

32. (a) $f(x) = (x - 2)(x + 1)$

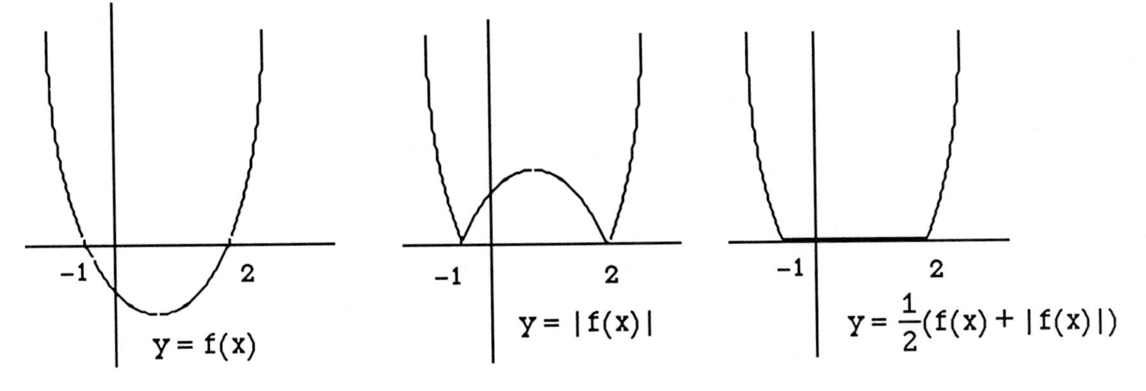

(b) All three graphs are the same as $f(x) = x^2$

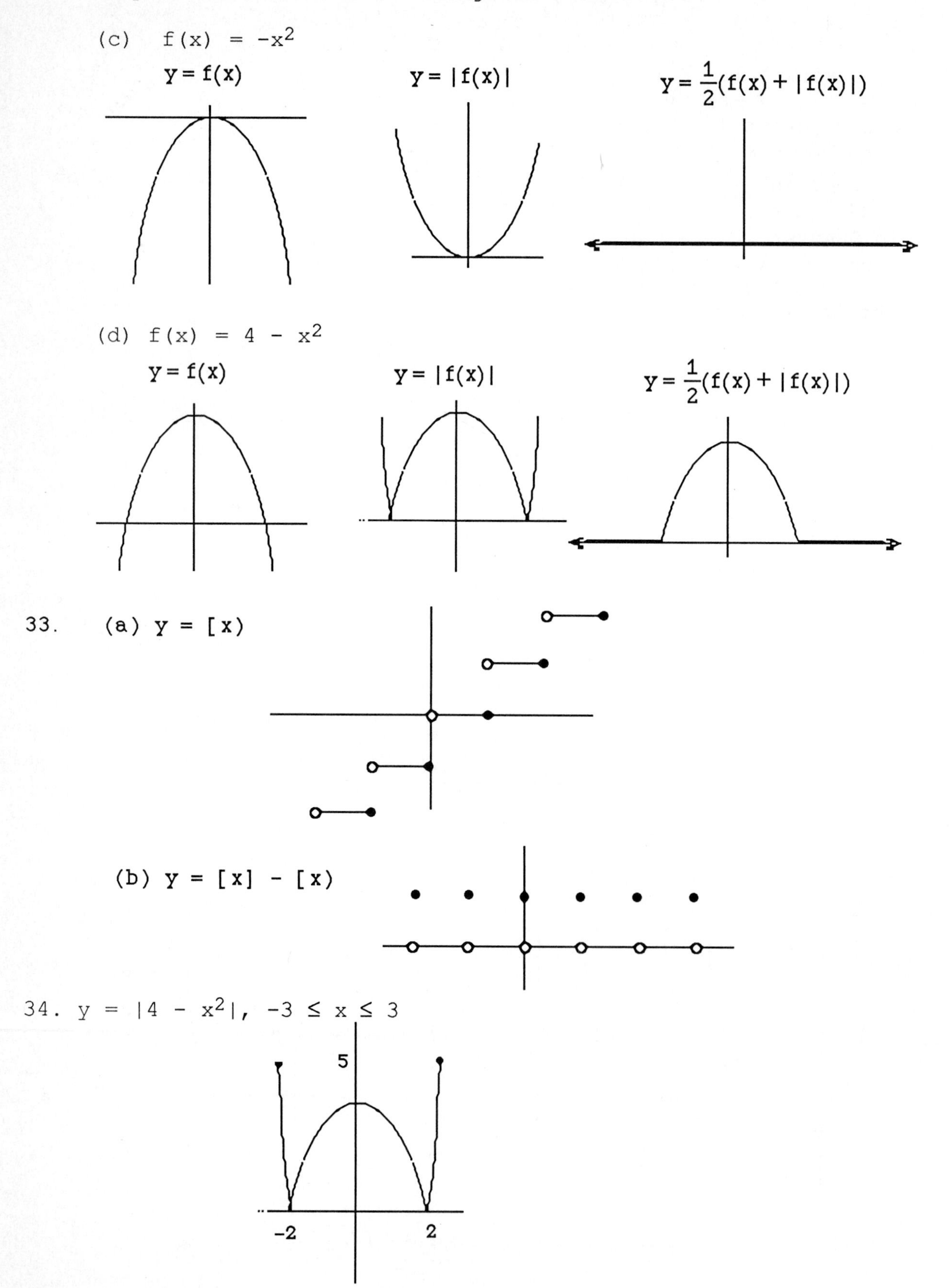
(c) f(x) = -x2
y = f(x)
y = |f(x)|
y = 1/2(f(x) + |f(x)|)
(d) f(x) = 4 - x2
y = f(x)
y = |f(x)|
y = 1/2(f(x) + |f(x)|)
33. (a) y = [x)
(b) y = [x] - [x)
34. y = |4 - x2|, -3 ≤ x ≤ 3
5
-2
2

35. (a) $f(x) = \dfrac{x-1}{x+1}$

$$f'(x) = \lim_{h\to 0} \frac{\dfrac{x+h-1}{x+h+1} - \dfrac{x-1}{x+1}}{h} = \lim_{h\to 0} \frac{2h}{h(x+h+1)(x+1)}$$

$$= \lim_{h\to 0} \frac{2}{(x+h+1)(x+1)} = \frac{2}{(x+1)^2}$$

(b) $f(x) = x^{3/2}$

$$\frac{f(x+h)-f(x)}{h} = \frac{(x+h)^{3/2}-x^{3/2}}{h}$$

$$= \frac{(x+h)^3-x^3}{h[(x+h)^{3/2} + x^{3/2}]}$$

$$= \frac{3x^2h + 3xh^2 + h^2}{h[(x+h)^{3/2} + x^{3/2}]}$$

$$f'(x) = \lim_{h\to 0} \frac{3x^2 + 3xh + h^2}{(x+h)^{3/2} + x^{3/2}} = \frac{3}{2}x^{1/2}$$

(c) $f(x) = x^{1/3}$

$$\frac{f(x+h)-f(x)}{h} = \frac{(x+h)^{1/3} - x^{1/3}}{h}$$

$$= \frac{1}{(x+h)^{2/3} + (x+h)^{1/3}x^{1/3} + x^{2/3}}$$

$$f'(x) = \lim_{h\to 0} \frac{1}{(x+h)^{2/3} + (x+h)^{1/3}x^{1/3} + x^{2/3}} = \frac{1}{3x^{2/3}}$$

36. (a) $f'(x) = \lim_{h\to 0} \dfrac{(x+h)^2 - 3(x+h) - 4 - x^2 + 3x + 4}{h}$

$$= \lim_{h\to 0} \frac{x^2 + 2xh + h^2 - 3x - 3h - 4 - x^2 + 3x + 4}{h}$$

$$\lim_{h\to 0} \frac{2xh + h^2 - 3h}{h} = \lim_{h\to 0} (2x + h - 3) = 2x - 3$$

(b) $\dfrac{dy}{dx} = \lim_{h\to 0} \dfrac{\dfrac{1}{3(x+h)} + 2(x+h) - \dfrac{1}{3x} - 2x}{h}$

$$= \lim_{h\to 0} \frac{\dfrac{x-x-h}{3x(x+h)} + 2h}{h} = \lim_{h\to 0}\left[\frac{-h}{3xh(x+h)} + \frac{2h}{h}\right] = -\frac{1}{3x^2} + 2$$

(c) $f'(t) = \lim_{h\to 0} \frac{\sqrt{(t+h)-4} - \sqrt{t-4}}{h} \cdot \frac{\sqrt{(t+h)-4} + \sqrt{t-4}}{\sqrt{(t+h)-4} + \sqrt{t-4}}$

$= \lim_{h\to 0} \frac{t+h-4-t+4}{h(\sqrt{(t+h)-4} + \sqrt{t-4})} = \frac{1}{2\sqrt{t-4}}$

37. (a) $y = 2x^3 + 2 = 2(x^3 + 1)$

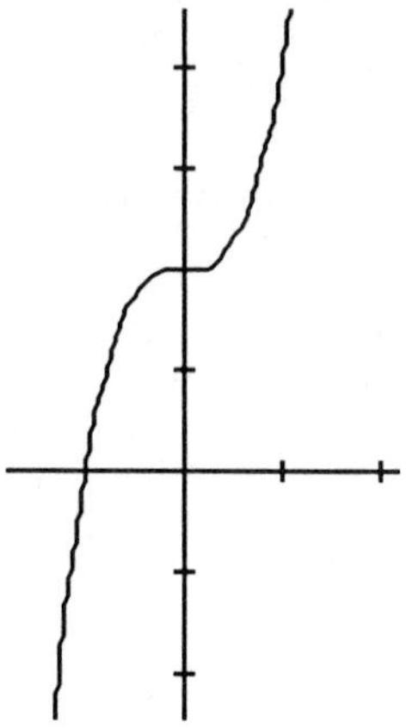

$\Delta y = 2(x^3 + 1) - 2(x + \Delta x)^3 + 2$

$\frac{\Delta y}{\Delta x} = \frac{2(3x^2\Delta x + 3x\Delta x^2 + \Delta x^3)}{\Delta x}$

$= 6x^2 + 6x\Delta x + 2\Delta x^2$

$f'(x) = \lim_{\Delta x\to 0} (6x^2 + 6x\Delta x + 2\Delta x^2)$

$= 6x^2 \big|_{x=1} = 6$

(b) $6x^2 = 0 \Leftrightarrow x = 0$

when $x = 0$ tangent is parallel to the x-axis.

38. Let $f(x) = \frac{2x}{x-1}$

(a) $f(0) = 0$; $f(-1) = \frac{-2}{-2} = 1$; $f\left(\frac{1}{x}\right) = \frac{2\left(\frac{1}{x}\right)}{\frac{1}{x} - 1} = \frac{2}{1-x}$

(b) $\Delta f(x) = f(x + \Delta x) - f(x) = \frac{2(x + \Delta x)}{(x + \Delta x) - 1} - \frac{2x}{x-1}$

$= \frac{2(x + \Delta x)(x-1) - 2x(x + \Delta x - 1)}{(x-1)(x + \Delta x - 1)}$

$= \frac{2x^2 + 2x\Delta x - 2x - 2\Delta x - 2x^2 - 2x\Delta x + 2x}{(x-1)(x + \Delta x - 1)} = \frac{-2\Delta x}{(x-1)(x + \Delta x - 1)}$

(c) $f'(x) = \lim_{\Delta x\to 0} \frac{\Delta f(x)}{\Delta x} = \lim_{\Delta x\to 0} \frac{-2\Delta x}{(x-1)(x+\Delta x-1)} = \frac{-2}{(x-1)^2}$

39. $y = 180x - 16x^2 = 4x(45 - 4x)$

$$f'(x_1) = \lim_{h\to 0} \frac{f(x_1+h) - f(x_1)}{h}$$

$$= \lim_{h\to 0} \frac{180(x_1 + h) - 16(x_1 + h)^2 - 180x_1 + 16x_1^2}{h}$$

$$= \frac{180h - 16(x_1^2 + 2x_1h + h^2) + 16x_1^2}{h}$$

$$= \frac{180h - 32x_1h - 16h^2}{h}$$

$$= 180 - 32x_1 - 16h$$

$$\left.\frac{dy}{dx}\right|_{x=x1} = 180 - 32x_1$$

$180 - 32x_1 = 0$ when $x_1 = \frac{45}{8}$

$$f(\tfrac{45}{8}) = 180\cdot\frac{45}{8} - 16(\tfrac{45}{8})^2 = \frac{8100}{8} - 16\cdot\frac{2045}{648} = \frac{2025}{4}.$$

Therefore, horizontal tangent occurs at $(\frac{45}{8}, \frac{2025}{4})$.

40. We use the formula derived in Article 1.8, Prob. 1

If $s = 180t - 16t^2$, then $v = 180 - 32t$. $v = 0$ when $t = \frac{180}{32} = \frac{45}{8}$.

41. $s = 32t - 16t^2$; $s' = 32 - 32t = 0$ when $t = 1$. $s(1) = 16$

42. (a) $$\frac{\Delta P}{\Delta V} = \frac{\frac{1}{V+\Delta V} - \frac{1}{V}}{\Delta V} = \frac{V - V - \Delta V}{V\Delta V\,(V+\Delta V)} = \frac{-1}{V\,(V+\Delta V)}$$

(b) $$P' = \lim_{\Delta V\to 0} \frac{-1}{V\,(V+\Delta V)} = \frac{-1}{V^2};\quad P'(2) = -\frac{1}{4}$$

43. $$\lim_{x\to\infty} \frac{\sin x}{x} = 0$$

44. Since $0 \le \left|\frac{\sin x}{2x+5}\right| \le \left|\frac{1}{2x+5}\right|$, by the Sandwich Theorem,

$$0 \le \lim_{x\to\infty} \left|\frac{\sin x}{2x+5}\right| \le \lim_{x\to\infty} \left|\frac{1}{2x+5}\right| = 0, \text{ so } \lim_{x\to\infty} \left|\frac{\sin x}{2x+5}\right| = 0$$

$$\lim_{x\to\infty} \frac{x + \sin x}{2x+5} = \lim_{x\to\infty} \left(\frac{x}{2x+5} + \frac{\sin x}{2x+5}\right) = \frac{1}{2} + 0 = \frac{1}{2}$$

45. $$\lim_{x\to\infty} \frac{1 + \sin x}{x} = 0$$

46. $$\lim_{x\to 1} \frac{x^2 - 4}{x^3 - 8} = \lim_{x\to 1} \frac{(x+2)(x-2)}{(x-2)(x^2+2x+4)} = \frac{3}{7}$$

47. $$\lim_{x\to 0} \frac{x}{\tan 3x} = \lim_{x\to 0} \frac{x\cos 3x}{\sin 3x} = \lim_{x\to 0} \frac{3x}{\sin 3x}\cdot\frac{\cos 3x}{3} = \frac{1}{3}$$

48. Let $x = n\pi$. Then $\lim_{x\to\infty} \frac{x \sin x}{x + \sin x} = \lim_{n\to\infty} \frac{n\pi \sin n\pi}{n\pi + \sin n\pi} = \frac{0}{n\pi} = 0$.

Now let $x = (2n+1)\frac{\pi}{2}$. $\lim_{n\to\infty} \frac{(2n+1)\frac{\pi}{2} \sin (2n+1)\frac{\pi}{2}}{(2n+1)\frac{\pi}{2} + \sin (2n+1)\frac{\pi}{2}} = 1$.

$\therefore \lim_{x\to\infty} \frac{x \sin x}{x + \sin x}$ does not exist.

49. $\lim_{x\to a} \frac{x^2 - a^2}{x - a} = \lim_{x\to a} (x + a) = 2a$

50. $\lim_{x\to a} \frac{x^2 - a^2}{x + a} = \lim_{x\to a} (x - a) = 0$

51. $\lim_{h\to 0} \frac{(x+h)^2 - x^2}{h} = \lim_{h\to 0} \frac{x^2 + 2xh + h^2 - x^2}{h} = \lim_{h\to 0} \frac{2xh + h^2}{h} = 2x$

52. $\lim_{h\to 0} \frac{\sqrt{x+h} - \sqrt{x}}{h} \cdot \frac{\sqrt{x+h} + \sqrt{x}}{\sqrt{x+h} + \sqrt{x}} = \lim_{h\to 0} \frac{x + h - x}{h(\sqrt{x+h} + \sqrt{x})}$

$\lim_{h\to 0} \frac{1}{\sqrt{x+h} + \sqrt{x}} = \frac{1}{2\sqrt{x}}$

53. $\lim_{\Delta x\to 0} \frac{\frac{1}{x+\Delta x} - \frac{1}{x}}{\Delta x} = \lim_{\Delta x\to 0} \frac{x - x - \Delta x}{(\Delta x)(x)(x+\Delta x)} = \lim_{\Delta x\to 0} \frac{-1}{x(x+\Delta x)} = -\frac{1}{x^2}$

54. $\lim_{x\to 0^+} \frac{1}{x} = \infty$

55. $\lim_{x\to 1} \frac{1-\sqrt{x}}{1-x} = \lim_{x\to 1} \frac{1-\sqrt{x}}{1-x} \cdot \frac{1+\sqrt{x}}{1+\sqrt{x}} = \lim_{x\to 0} \frac{1}{1+\sqrt{x}} = 1$

56. $\lim_{x\to 0^+} \frac{(2x-3)(\sqrt{x}-1)}{2x^2 + x - 3} = \lim_{x\to 0^+} \frac{(2x-3)(\sqrt{x}-1)}{(2x+3)(x-1)} = \lim_{x\to 0^+} \frac{2x-3}{(2x+3)(\sqrt{x}+1)} = -\frac{1}{10}$

57. $\lim_{x\to\infty} (1 - x\cos x)$ does not exist.

58. $\lim_{x\to 1} \frac{\sqrt{x+1} - \sqrt{2x}}{x(x-1)} \cdot \frac{\sqrt{x+1} + \sqrt{2x}}{\sqrt{x+1} + \sqrt{2x}} = \lim_{x\to 1} \frac{1-x}{x(x-1)(\sqrt{x+1} + \sqrt{2x})} = \frac{-1}{2\sqrt{2}}$

59. $\lim_{x\to 0^+} \frac{|x|}{x} = 1$

60. $\lim_{x\to 0^-} \frac{|x|}{x} = \lim_{x\to 0^-} \frac{-x}{x} = -1$

61. $\lim_{x\to 4^-} ([x] - x) = 3 - 4 = -1$

62. $\lim_{x\to 1^+} ([x] - x) = 0$

63. $\lim_{x\to 3^+} \frac{[x]^2 - 9}{x^2 - 9} = 0$

64. $\lim_{x\to 3^-} \frac{[x]^2 - 9}{x^2 - 9} = \lim_{x\to 3^-} \frac{4 - 9}{x^2 - 9} = \infty$

65. $\lim_{x\to 0} x[x] = 0$

66. $\lim_{x\to 0^+} \dfrac{\sqrt{x}}{\sqrt{4+\sqrt{x}}-2} = \lim_{x\to 0^+} \dfrac{\sqrt{x}}{\sqrt{4+\sqrt{x}}-2} \cdot \dfrac{\sqrt{4+\sqrt{x}}+2}{\sqrt{4+\sqrt{x}}+2}$

$= \lim_{x\to 0^+} \dfrac{\sqrt{x}\left(\sqrt{4+\sqrt{x}}+2\right)}{4+\sqrt{x}-4} = \lim_{x\to 0^+} \sqrt{4+\sqrt{x}}+2 = 4$

67. $f(x) = \dfrac{x-1}{2x^2-7x+5}$

(a) $\lim_{x\to\infty} \dfrac{x-1}{2x^2-7x+5} = 0$

(b) $\lim_{x\to 1} \dfrac{x-1}{(x-1)(2x-5)} = \lim_{x\to 1} \dfrac{1}{2x-5} = \dfrac{-1}{3}$

(c) $f\left(\frac{-1}{x}\right) = \dfrac{\frac{-1}{x}-1}{\frac{2}{x^2}+\frac{7}{x}+5} = \dfrac{-1-x}{\frac{2+7x+5x^2}{x}} = \dfrac{-x(x+1)}{5x^2+7x+2}$

$f(0) = \dfrac{-1}{5}$

$\dfrac{1}{f(x)} = \dfrac{2x^2-7x+5}{x-1} = 2x-5,\ x \neq 1, 5/2$

68. $3x+5y=1 \Rightarrow 3c^2x+5c^2y=c^2$. Subtracting $(2+c)x+5c^2y=1$ from this gives $(3c^2-c-2)x = c^2-1$ or $x=\dfrac{c+1}{3c+2}$.

$y=\dfrac{1}{5}\left(1-3\left(\dfrac{c+1}{3c+2}\right)\right)=\dfrac{-1}{5(3c+2)}$. $\lim_{c\to 1}\left(\dfrac{c+1}{3c+2}, \dfrac{-1}{5(3c+2)}\right)=\left(\dfrac{2}{5},-\dfrac{1}{25}\right)$

69. (a) $\lim_{n\to\infty} \sqrt{n^2+1}-h = \lim_{n\to\infty} \sqrt{n^2+1}-h \cdot \dfrac{\sqrt{n^2+1}+n}{\sqrt{n^2+1}+n}$

$= \lim_{n\to\infty} \dfrac{n^2+1-n^2}{\sqrt{n^2+1}+n} = \lim_{n\to\infty} \dfrac{1}{\sqrt{n^2+1}+n} = 0$

(b) $\lim_{n\to\infty} \sqrt{n^2+n}-n = \lim_{n\to\infty} \sqrt{n^2+n}-n \cdot \dfrac{\sqrt{n^2+n}+n}{\sqrt{n^2+n}+n}$

$= \lim_{n\to\infty} \dfrac{n^2+n-n^2}{\sqrt{n^2+n}+n} = \lim_{n\to\infty} \dfrac{1}{\sqrt{1+\frac{1}{n}}+1} = \dfrac{1}{2}$

70. We must find a $\delta > 0$ so that any $0 < |t-1| < \delta$ makes $\sqrt{t^2-1} < \varepsilon$ or equivalently $|t^2-1| = |(t+1)(t-1)| < \varepsilon^2$. First choose $\delta_1 \le 1$. Then, $|t-1| < 1 \Rightarrow 0 < t < 2$ or $1 < t+1 < 3$. Thus,

$$0 < |t-1| < \delta_1 \Rightarrow |(t+1)(t-1)| \le 3|t-1|.$$

Choose $\delta = \text{minimum}\ \{1, \frac{\varepsilon^2}{3}\}$.

71. We must find M such that $\left|\frac{t^2 + t}{t^2 - 1} - 1\right| = \left|\frac{t^2 + t - t^2 + 1}{t^2 - 1}\right| =$
$\left|\frac{t + 1}{t^2 - 1}\right| = \frac{1}{|t - 1|} < \varepsilon$ for all $t > M$. Let $t > 1$. Then
$t - 1 > \frac{1}{\varepsilon}$ or $t > \frac{1}{\varepsilon} + 1$. Let $M = \frac{1}{\varepsilon} + 1$.

72. (a) $f(x) = x^3 - 3x^2 - 4x + 12 = x^2(x - 3) - 4(x - 3) = (x^2 - 4)(x - 3)$.

Thus $h(x) = \frac{f(x)}{x - 3} = 0$ when $x^2 - 4 = 0$ or when $x = \pm 2$.

(b) $\lim_{x \to 3} (x^2 - 4) = 5 = k$

(c) Since $h(-x) = h(x)$, h is an even function.

73. We are given that $F(t) \le M$ and that $F(t) \to L$ as $t \to c$. Suppose that $L > M$ and take $\varepsilon = \frac{L - M}{2}$. There exists $\delta > 0$ for which $0 < |t - c| < \delta \Rightarrow |F(t) - L| < \frac{L - M}{2}$. But then we have $F(t) - L > L - \frac{L - M}{2} = \frac{L}{2} + \frac{M}{2} > \frac{M}{2} + \frac{M}{2} > M$, which is a contradiction. Therefore, $L \le M$.

74. Let f be a function with the properties:

(i) $f(x + h) = f(x) \cdot f(h)$ for all x, h

(ii) $f(0) \neq 0$

(a) Let $x = h = 0$. Then $f(0 + 0) = f(0) \cdot f(0)$. Since $f(0) \neq 0$,
$f(0) = 1$.

(b) $$f'(x) = \lim_{h \to 0} \frac{f(x + h) - f(x)}{h} = \lim_{h \to 0} \frac{f(x)f(h) - f(x)}{h}$$

$$= \lim_{h \to 0} f(x)\frac{f(h) - 1}{h} = f(x)\lim_{h \to 0} \frac{f(0 + h) - f(0)}{h} = f(x)f'(0)$$

75. $f(x) = \frac{x^2 - 16}{|x - 4|}$

$$\lim_{x \to 4^+} \frac{x^2 - 16}{|x - 4|} = \lim_{x \to 4^+} \frac{x^2 - 16}{x - 4} = \lim_{x \to 4^+} (x + 4) = 8$$

$$\lim_{x \to 4^-} \frac{x^2 - 16}{4 - x} = \lim_{x \to 4^-} - \frac{(16 - x^2)}{4 - x} = \lim_{x \to 4^-} - (4 + x) = -8$$

f x) cannot be defined so as to make f continuous at since $\lim_{x \to 4} f(x)$ does not exist

76. As $x \to 0$, $\frac{1}{x} \to \infty$. Since the period of the sine function is only 2π units, $y = \sin\frac{1}{x}$ will oscillate infinitely often in any

neighborhood of 0. That is, for any $\delta > 0$, there are values of x, $|x| < \delta$ for which $\sin \frac{1}{x}$ takes on any value between -1 and 1. Therefore let L, $|L| \le 1$, be any proposed limit.
It would be impossible to find $\delta > 0$ for $|\sin \frac{1}{x} - L| < \varepsilon$ for any ε. Therefore, f(0) cannot be defined in such a way to make $f(x) = \sin \frac{1}{x}$ continuous at x = 0.

77. $y = \frac{1}{[x]}$ is discontinuous when $0 \le x < 1$ and at every integer.

78. Let $p(x) = a_n x^n + a_{n-1}x^{n-1} + \ldots + a_1 x + a_0$ be a polynomial of odd degree. Without loss of generality, we may assume that $a_n > 0$. Then $\lim_{x\to\infty} p(x) = +\infty$ and $\lim_{x\to-\infty} p(x) = -\infty$. There must be some values x_1 and x_2 for which $p(x_1) < 0$ and $p(x_2) > 0$. By the Intermediate Value Theorem, there must exist $x_1 < c < x_2$ for which $p(c) = 0$.

79. The function $f(x) = |x|$ is continuous at $x = 0 \Rightarrow$ $\lim_{x\to 0} |x| = 0 \Rightarrow ||x| - 0|$ can be made to be as small as needed. In particular, $||x| - 0| = |x| = |x - 0| < \varepsilon$. Therefore, take $\delta \le \varepsilon$.

80. (a)

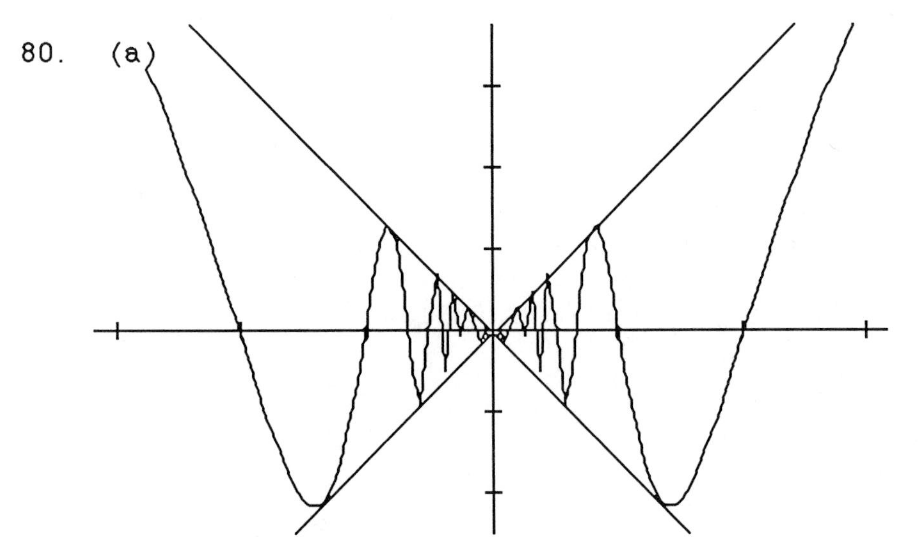

(b) Choose $\delta = \varepsilon$. Since $|\sin \frac{1}{x}| \le 1$, $|x \sin \frac{1}{x}| \le |x|$. Therefore, whenever $0 < |x| < \delta$, we have $|x \sin \frac{1}{x}| < e$, which says that f is continuous at x = 0.

81. Let f be a continuous function and suppose that $f(c) > 0$. Take $\varepsilon = \frac{f(c)}{2}$. Since the limit of $f(x) = f(c)$ as $x \to c$, there

is $\delta > 0$ for which $|x - c| < \delta \Rightarrow |f(x) - f(c)| < \frac{f(c)}{2}$.

But then we have $\frac{f(c)}{2} < f(x) < \frac{3f(c)}{2}$.

82. (a) If $a < b$, then $b - a > 0$. Observe that
$b - a = (b + c) - (a + c)$ and
$b - a = (b - c) - (a - c)$. Therefore,
$(b + c) - (a + c) > 0 \Rightarrow a + c < b + c$, and
$(b - c) - (a - c) > 0 \Rightarrow a - c < b - c$.

(b) No, $4 < 10$ and $-2 < 11$ but $4 - (-2) = 6 > 10 - 11 = 1$.

(c) If $a < b$ then $b - a > 0$. Now $\frac{1}{a} - \frac{1}{b} = \frac{b - a}{ab}$. Therefore, if either both a and b are negative, or both a and b are positive, then $ab > 0$. Therefore,
$\frac{1}{a} - \frac{1}{b} > 0$, or $\frac{1}{b} < \frac{1}{a}$.

(d) $a < 0 \Rightarrow \frac{1}{a} < 0$, and $b > 0 \Rightarrow \frac{1}{b} > 0$. Therefore $\frac{1}{b} > \frac{1}{a}$.

(e) $a < b \Rightarrow b - a > 0$. Thus $c > 0 \Rightarrow$
$c(b - a) = cb - ca > 0$, so $ac < bc$.

(f) $a < b \Rightarrow b - a > 0$. Thus $c > 0 \Rightarrow -c > 0$, so
$-c(b - a) = -cb + ca > 0$, so $bc < ac$.

83. (a) $a^2 < b^2 \Rightarrow b^2 - a^2 > 0$. But
$b^2 - a^2 = (|b| + |a|)(|b| - |a|)$
and $|b| + |a|$ is positive. Therefore $b^2 - a^2 > 0$
$\Leftrightarrow |b| - |a| > 0$ or $|b| > |a|$.

(b) $|a + b| < (|a| + |b|) \Leftrightarrow (a + b)^2 < (|a| + |b|)^2$, from part (a). But

$(|a| + |b|)^2 = |a|^2 + |b|^2 + 2|a||b|$ and
$(a + b)^2 = a^2 + b^2 + 2ab$.
Since $2|a||b| > 2ab$, the result follows.

(c) Since $a = b + (a - b)$, $|a| = |b + (a - b)| \leq |b| + |a - b|$,
so $|a| - |b| \leq |a - b|$. This is true for all a,b so
$|b| - |a| \leq |b - a| = |a - b|$. Together, these imply
$||a| - |b|| \leq |a - b|$.

(d) From part (b), $|a_1 + a_2| \leq |a_1| + |a_2|$. Suppose that
$|a_1 + a_2 + \ldots + a_k| \leq |a_1| + |a_2| + \ldots + |a_k|$.
Then $|(a_1 + a_2 + \ldots + a_k) + a_{k+1}| \leq$
$|(a_1 + a_2 + \ldots + a_k)| + |a_{k+1}| \leq$
$|a_1| + |a_2| + \ldots + |a_k| + |a_{k+1}|$.

84. $$(fg)'(x_0) = \lim_{x\to x_0} \frac{f(x)g(x) - f(x_0)g(x_0)}{x - x_0}$$

$$= \lim_{x\to x_0} \frac{f(x)g(x) - f(x_0)g(x) + f(x_0)g(x) - f(x_0)g(x_0)}{x - x_0}$$

$$= \lim_{x\to x_0} \frac{g(x)[f(x) - f(x_0)]}{x - x_0} + \lim_{x\to x_0} \frac{f(x_0)[g(x) - g(x_0)]}{x - x_0}$$

$$= g(x_0)f'(x_0) + f(x_0)\lim_{x\to x_0} \frac{g(x) - g(x_0)}{x - x_0}$$

$$= g(x_0)f'(x_0) \text{ if } f(x_0) = 0.$$

85. Let $\Phi_i(x) = K_i(x - x_1)\ldots(x - x_{i-1})(x - x_{i+1})\ldots(x - x_n)$.

To find K, let $\Phi_i(x_i) = 1$. Then

$$K = \frac{1}{(x_i - x_1)\ldots(x_i - x_{i-1})(x_i - x_{i+1})\ldots(x_i - x_n)}.$$ Thus,

$$\Phi_i(x) = \frac{(x - x_1)\ldots(x - x_{i-1})(x - x_{i+1})\ldots(x - x_n)}{(x_i - x_1)\ldots(x_i - x_{i-1})(x_i - x_{i+1})\ldots(x_i - x_n)}$$

CHAPTER 2

DERIVATIVES

2.1 POLYNOMIAL FUNCTIONS AND THEIR DERIVATIVES

1. $y = x \Rightarrow \frac{dy}{dx} = 1$ and $\frac{d^2y}{dx^2} = 0$

2. $y = -x \Rightarrow \frac{dy}{dx} = -1$ and $\frac{d^2y}{dx^2} = 0$

3. $y = x^2 \Rightarrow \frac{dy}{dx} = 2x$ and $\frac{d^2y}{dx^2} = 2$

4. $y = -10x^2 \Rightarrow \frac{dy}{dx} = -20x$ and $\frac{d^2y}{dx^2} = -20$

5. $y = -x^2 + 3 \Rightarrow \frac{dy}{dx} = -2x$ and $\frac{d^2y}{dx^2} = -2$

6. $y = \frac{x^3}{3} - x \Rightarrow \frac{dy}{dx} = x^2 - 1$ and $\frac{d^2y}{dx^2} = 2x$

7. $y = 2x + 1 \Rightarrow \frac{dy}{dx} = 2$ and $\frac{d^2y}{dx^2} = 0$

8. $y = x^2 + x + 1 \Rightarrow \frac{dy}{dx} = 2x + 1$ and $\frac{d^2y}{dx^2} = 2$

9. $y = \frac{x^3}{3} + \frac{x^2}{2} + x \Rightarrow \frac{dy}{dx} = x^2 + x + 1$ and $\frac{d^2y}{dx^2} = 2x + 1$

10. $y = 1 - x + x^2 - x^3 \Rightarrow \frac{dy}{dx} = -1 + 2x - 3x^2$ and $\frac{d^2y}{dx^2} = 2 - 6x$

11. $s = 16t^2 + 3 \Rightarrow v = \frac{ds}{dt} = 32\,t$ and $a = \frac{d^2s}{dt^2} = 32$

12. $s = 832t - 16t^2 \Rightarrow \frac{ds}{dt} = 832 - 32t$ and $\frac{d^2s}{dt^2} = -32$

13. $s = 16t^2 - 60t \Rightarrow v = \frac{ds}{dt} = 32\,t - 60$ and $a = \frac{d^2s}{dt^2} = 32$

14. $s = 6 + 50t - 16t^2 \Rightarrow \frac{ds}{dt} = 50 - 32t$ and $\frac{d^2s}{dt^2} = -32$

15. $s = \frac{gt^2}{2} + v_0t + s_0$ $(g, v_0, s_0$ constants$) \Rightarrow v = \frac{ds}{dt} = gt + v_0$ and $a = \frac{d^2s}{dt^2} = g$

16. $y = x^4 - 7x^3 + 2x^2 + 15 \Rightarrow \frac{dy}{dx} = 4x^3 - 21x^2 + 4x$ and $\frac{d^2y}{dx^2} = 12x^2 - 42x + 4$

17. $y = 5x^3 - 3x^5 \Rightarrow \frac{dy}{dx} = 15x^2 - 15x^4 \Rightarrow \frac{d^2y}{dx^2} = 30x - 60x^3$

18. $y = 4x^2 - 8x + 1 \Rightarrow \frac{dy}{dx} = 8x - 8$ and $\frac{d^2y}{dx^2} = 8$

19. $y = \frac{x^4}{4} - \frac{x^3}{3} + \frac{x^2}{2} - x + 3 \Rightarrow \frac{dy}{dx} = x^3 - x^2 + x - 1$ and $\frac{d^2y}{dx^2} = 3x^2 - 2x + 1$

20. $y = 2x^4 - 4x^2 - 8 \Rightarrow \frac{dy}{dx} = 8x^3 - 8x$ and $\frac{d^2y}{dx^2} = 24x^2 - 8$

21. $12y = 6x^4 - 18x^2 - 12x \Rightarrow y = \frac{1}{2}x^4 - \frac{3}{2}x^2 - x$, so

$\frac{dy}{dx} = 2x^3 - 3x - 1$ and $\frac{d^2y}{dx^2} = 6x^2 - 3$

22. $y = 3x^7 - 7x^3 + 21x^2 \Rightarrow \frac{dy}{dx} = 21x^6 - 21x^2 + 42x$ and $\frac{d^2y}{dx^2} = 126x^5 - 42x + 42$

23. $y = x^2(x^3 - 1) = x^5 - x^2 \Rightarrow \frac{dy}{dx} = 5x^4 - 2x$ and $\frac{d^2y}{dx^2} = 20x^3 - 2$

24. $y = (x - 2)(x + 3) = x^2 + x - 6 \Rightarrow \frac{dy}{dx} = 2x + 1$ and $\frac{d^2y}{dx^2} = 2$

25. $y = (3x - 1)(2x + 5) = 6x^2 + 13x - 5 \Rightarrow \frac{dy}{dx} = 12x + 13$ and $\frac{d^2y}{dx^2} = 12$

26. (a) $y = x^3 \Rightarrow \left.\frac{dy}{dx} = 3x^2\right]_{x=2} = 12$. The tangent line is:

$y - 8 = 12(x - 2)$ or $y - 12x = -16$

(b) $y = 2x^2 + 4x - 3 \Rightarrow \left.\frac{dy}{dx} = 4x + 4\right]_{x=1} = 8$. The tangent line is:

$y - 3 = 8(x - 1)$ or $y - 8x = -5$

(c) $y = x^3 - 6x^2 + 5x \Rightarrow \left.\frac{dy}{dx} = 3x^2 - 12x + 5\right]_{x=0} = 5$. The tangent line is:

$y - 0 = 5(x - 0)$ or $y = 5x$.

27. (c) If $y = x^2 + 5x$, then $y' = 2x + 5$ and $y'(3) = 11$

28. (c), because $3x - 2y + 12 = 0 \Rightarrow y = \frac{3}{2}x + 6$, so slope is $\frac{3}{2}$.

29. $y = x^3 - 3x + 1 \Rightarrow y' = 3x^2 - 3$. The slope of tangent is $y'(2) = 9$.
$m_\perp = -\frac{1}{9}$. At (2,3) the normal is $y - 3 = -\frac{1}{9}(x - 2)$ or $9y + x = 29$.

30. The slope of $y = x$ is $m = 1$. If $y = x^2 + c$, then $y' = 2x$. Equating, $2x = 1$ if $x = \frac{1}{2}$. Then $y = \frac{1}{2}$, and
$\frac{1}{2} = \frac{1}{4} + c \quad \Rightarrow \quad c = \frac{1}{4}$

31. $y = x^3 + x \Rightarrow y' = 3x^2 + 1$. Since the slope is 4, we have $3x^2 + 1 = 4 \Leftrightarrow 3x^2 = 4 \Leftrightarrow x = \pm 1$. To find the points, find $y(1) = 2$ and $y(-1) = -2$. $\therefore$ Tangent line at $(1,2)$ with slope 4 is: $y - 2 = 4(x - 1)$ or $y = 4x - 2$

The tangent line at $(-1,-2)$ with slope 4 is: $y + 2 = 4(x + 1)$ or $y = 4x + 2$. Since $y = 3x^2 + 1$ is an upward opening parabola the smallest value will occur at the vertex $(0,1)$. Thus the smallest slope is 1 and this occurs when $x = 0$.

32. If $y = 2x^3 - 3x^2 - 12x + 20$, then $y' = 6x^2 - 6x - 12$. We need the points where $y' = 0$, since to be parallel to the x-axis requires 0 slope.

$6x^2 - 6x - 12 = 6(x^2 - x - 2) = 6(x - 2)(x + 1) = 0 \Leftrightarrow x = 2$ or -1.

$y(2) = 0$ and $y(-1) = 27$. The points are $(2,0)$ and $(-1,27)$.

33. $y = x^3 \Rightarrow y' = 3x^2$. $y'(-2) = 12$. Tangent at $(-2,-8)$ is:

$y + 8 = 12(x + 2)$ or $y = 12x + 16$. $x = 0 \Rightarrow y = 16$.

y-intercept is $(0,16)$. $y = 0 \Rightarrow x = -\frac{4}{3}$. x-intercept is $\left(-\frac{4}{3}, 0\right)$.

34. If $y = x^3 - x$, then $y' = 3x^2 - 1$ and $y'(-1) = 2$. The equation of the tangent line is $y - 0 = 2(x + 1)$ or $y = 2x + 2$. This intersects the curve where $2x + 2 = x^3 - x$ or where $x^3 - 3x - 2 = 0$. One root is clearly $x = -1$. Dividing we have $x^3 - 3x - 2 = (x + 1)(x^2 - x - 2) = (x + 1)(x - 2)(x + 1)$. If $x = 2$, $y(2) = 6$ and the other point is $(2,6)$.

35. The curve $y = ax^2 + bx + c$ is tangent to $y = x$ at the origin $\Rightarrow (0,0)$ is a point on the curve. $\therefore 0 = 0a + 0b + c$ or $c = 0$. If $y = ax^2 + bx$, then $y' = 2ax + b$ measures the slope of the tangent to the curve at any point. In particular, $y = x$

has slope 1 at $x = 0$. $\therefore 1 = 2a(0) + b \Rightarrow b = 1$ and $y = ax^2 + 1$. Since the point $(1,2)$ is also given on the curve, $2 = (1)^2 a + 1$ or $a = 1$. $\therefore$ The equation is $y = x^2 + x$.

36. If $(1,0)$ is a point on $y = x^2 + ax + b$, then $a + b = -1$. If $(1,0)$ is a point on $y = cx - x^2$, then $c = 1$. The slopes of the two curves are $y' = 2x + a$ and $y' = c - 2x$. These are equal at $x = 1$, so $2 + a = c - 2$. Then, $a - 1 = -4$ or $a = -3$ and $b = 2$.

37. Mars: $s = 1.86t^2$ m Jupiter: $s = 11.44t^2$ m

$v = 3.72t$ m/sec $v = 22.88t$ m/sec

$3.72t = 16.6$ $22.88t = 16.6$

$t = 4.46$ sec $t = .73$ sec

38. Given that $s = 24t - 0.8t^2$.

(a) $v = 24 - 1.6t$ and $a = -1.6$.

(b) $v = 0$ when $24 - 1.6t = t$ or when $t = 15$ sec.

(c) $s(15) = 24(15) - 0.8(15)^2 = 180$ m.

(d) $24t - 0.8t^2 = 90$ if $8t^2 - 240t + 900 = 0$ or if

$$t = \frac{240 \pm \sqrt{240^2 - 4(8)(900)}}{16}$$

$$= \frac{240 \pm 120\sqrt{2}}{16} = 15 \pm \frac{15\sqrt{2}}{2} \text{ seconds.}$$

(e) For a total of $15 + 15 = 30$ seconds.

39. $s = 24t - 4.9t^2$ m $\Rightarrow v = 24 - 9.8t$ m/sec. The maximum height will occur when the rock ceases to rise, i.e. when the velocity is zero. $\therefore 24 - 9.8t = 0$ when $t = 2.45$ sec. $s(2.45) = 24(2.45) - 4.9(2.45)^2 = 29.39$ m.

40. On the moon, $832t - 2.6t^2 = 0$ when $2.6t(320 - t) = 0$, or $t = 320$ seconds. On the earth, $832t - 16t^2 = 0$ when $16t(52 - t) = 0$ or $t = 52$ seconds.

41. $s = t^3 - 4t^2 - 3t \Rightarrow v = 3t^2 - 8t - 3$.

$3t^2 - 8t - 3 = 0 \Leftrightarrow (3t + 1)(t - 3) = 0 \Leftrightarrow t = -\frac{1}{3}$ or 3

$a = 6t - 8$. $\therefore$ $a(3) = 10$ and $a(-\frac{1}{3}) = -10$.

42. The slope of $y = x^2$ is $y = 2x$. The equation of the tangent line at a point (x_0, y_0) is $y - x_0^2 = 2x_0(x - x_0)$. The x- intercept of this line, i.e. $y = 0$, is $2x_0x - 2x_0^2 = -x_0^2$ or $x = \dfrac{x_0^2}{2x_0} = \dfrac{x_0}{2}$.

43. $y = x^n \Rightarrow y' = nx^{n-1}$. Therefore $y'(x_1) = nx_1^{n-1}$ is the slope of the tangent at $P(x_1, y_1)$. Since this tangent contains the point $T(t,0)$, its slope is also given by $m = \dfrac{y_1 - 0}{x_1 - t}$. Equating the two expressions for slope, we have

$$nx_1^{n-1} = \frac{y_1}{x_1 - t} \Leftrightarrow nx_1^{n-1} = \frac{x_1^n}{x_1 - t} \Leftrightarrow x_1 - t = \frac{x_1^n}{nx_1^{n-1}} \Leftrightarrow$$

$$x_1 - t = \frac{1}{n} x_1^{n-n+1} \Leftrightarrow t = x_1 - \frac{1}{n} x_1 = x_1(1 - \frac{1}{n}).$$

$\therefore$ The tangent to any other point $Q(x_2, y_2)$ has x-intercept $T(x_2(1-\frac{1}{n}), 0)$. To construct this tangent, connect these two points.

2.2 PRODUCTS, POWERS AND QUOTIENTS

1. $y = \dfrac{x^3}{3} - \dfrac{x^2}{2} + x - 1 \Rightarrow \dfrac{dy}{dx} = x^2 - x + 1$

2. $y = (x-1)^3 (x+2)^4 \Rightarrow \dfrac{dy}{dx} = (x-1)^3 \dfrac{d}{dx}(x+2)^4 + (x+2)^4 \dfrac{d}{dx}(x-1)^3$

$$= (x-1)^3 [4(x+2)^3] + (x+2)^4 [3(x-1)^2]$$

$$= (x-1)^2 (x+2)^3 [4(x-1) + 3(x+2)] = (x-1)^2 (x+2)^3 (7x+2)$$

3. $y = (x^2 + 1)^5$

$$\frac{dy}{dx} = 5(x^2+1)^4 \frac{d}{dx}(x^2+1) = 5(x^2+1)(2x) = 10x\,(x^2+1)^4$$

4. $y = (x^3 - 3x)^4 \Rightarrow \dfrac{dy}{dx} = 4(x^3-3x)^3 \dfrac{d}{dx}(x^3 - 3x) = 4(x^3-3x)^3(3x^2-3)$

$$= 12(x^3 - 3x)^3 (x^2 - 1)$$

5. $y = (x+1)^2 (x^2+1)^{-3}$

$$\frac{dy}{dx} = (x+1)^2 \left[-3(x^2+1)^{-4} \frac{d}{dx}(x^2+1)\right] + (x^2+1)^{-3} [2(x+1)]$$

$$= (x+1)^2 (-6x)(x^2+1)^{-4} + 2(x+1)(x^2+1)^{-3}$$

$$= -2(x+1)(x^2+1)^{-4}(2x^2 + 3x - 1)$$

6. $y = \frac{2x+1}{x^2-1} \Rightarrow \frac{dy}{dx} = \frac{(x^2-1)\frac{d}{dx}(2x+1) - (2x+1)\frac{d}{dx}(x^2-1)}{(x^2-1)^2}$

$= \frac{2(x^2-1) - 2x(2x+1)}{(x^2-1)^2} = \frac{-2x^2-2x-2}{(x^2-1)^2}$

7. $y = \frac{2x+5}{3x-2}$

$\frac{dy}{dx} = \frac{(3x-2)\frac{d}{dx}(2x+5) - (2x+5)\frac{d}{dx}(3x-2)}{(3x-2)^2}$

$= \frac{2(3x-2) - 3(2x+5)}{(3x-2)^2}$

$= \frac{-19}{(3x-2)^2}$

8. $y = \left(\frac{x+1}{x-1}\right)^2 = \frac{x^2+2x+1}{x^2-2x+1}$

$\frac{dy}{dx} = \frac{(x^2-2x+1)\frac{d}{dx}(x^2+2x+1) - (x^2+2x+1)\frac{d}{dx}(x^2-2x+1)}{(x^2-2x+1)^2}$

$= \frac{(2x+2)(x^2-2x+1) - (2x-2)(x^2+2x+1)}{(x^2-2x+1)^2} = -\frac{4(x+1)}{(x-1)^3}$

9. $y = (1-x)(1+x^2)^{-1}$

$\frac{dy}{dx} = (1-x)\left[-(1+x^2)^{-2}(2x)\right] + (1+x^2)^{-1}(-1)$

$= (1+x^2)^{-2}\left[-2x(1-x) - (1+x^2)\right]$

$= (1+x^2)^{-2}(x^2-2x-1)$

10. $y = (x+1)^2(x^2+2x)^{-2}$

$\frac{dy}{dx} = 2(x+1)(x^2+2x)^{-2} + (x+1)^2\left[-2(x^2+2x)^{-3}(2x+2)\right]$

$= 2(x+1)(x^2+2x)^{-3}\left[x^2+2x-2(x+1)^2\right]$

$= -2(x+1)(x^2+2x)^{-3}(x^2+2x+2)$

11. $y = \frac{5}{(2x-3)^4} = 5(2x-3)^{-4} \Rightarrow \frac{dy}{dx} = -20(2x-3)^{-5}(2) = -40(2x-3)^{-5}$

12. $y = (x-1)^3(x+2) \Rightarrow \frac{dy}{dx} = (x-1)^3 + (x+2)(3)(x-1)^2$

$= (x-1)^2(x-1+3x+6) = (x-1)^2(4x+5)$

13. $y = (5 - x)(4 - 2x) \Rightarrow \frac{dy}{dx} = -2\,(5 - x) - (4 - 2x) = 4x - 14$

14. $y = [\,(5 - x)(4 - 2x)]^2 = (5 - x)^2\,(4 - 2x)^2$

$\frac{dy}{dx} = (5 - x)^2\,[2\,(4 - 2x)(-2)] + (4 - 2x)^2\,[2\,(5 - x)(-1)]$

$= -2\,(5 - x)(4 - 2x)[2\,(5 - x) + 4 - 2x] = -4\,(5 - x)(4 - 2x)(7 - 2x)$

15. $y = (2x - 1)^3(x + 7)^{-3}$

$\frac{dy}{dx} = (2x - 1)^3\left[-3(x + 7)^{-4}\right] + (x + 7)^{-3}\left[3(2x - 1)^2(2)\right]$

$= (2x - 1)^2(x + 7)^{-4}\left[-3(2x - 1) + 6(x + 7)\right]$

$= 45(2x - 1)^2(x + 7)^{-4}$

16. $y = \frac{x^3 + 7}{x} = x^2 + 7x^{-1} \Rightarrow \frac{dy}{dx} = 2x - 7x^{-2}$

17. $y = (2x^3 - 3x^2 + 6x)^{-5} \Rightarrow \frac{dy}{dx} = -5\,(2x^3 - 3x^2 + 6x)^{-6}\,(6x^2 - 6x + 6)$

18. $y = \frac{x^2}{(x - 1)^2} \Rightarrow \frac{dy}{dx} = \frac{2x\,(x - 1)^2 - 2x^2(x - 1)}{(x - 1)^4} = \frac{-2x}{(x - 1)^3}$

19. $y = \frac{(x - 1)^2}{x^2} = \frac{x^2 - 2x + 1}{x^2} = 1 - 2x^{-1} + x^{-2} \Rightarrow \frac{dy}{dx} = 2x^{-2} - 2x^{-3}$

20. $y = \frac{-1}{15\,(5x - 1)^3} = -\frac{1}{15}\,(5x - 1)^{-3} \Rightarrow \frac{dy}{dx} = \frac{1}{5}(5x - 1)^{-4}\,(5) = (5x - 1)^{-4}$

21. $y = \frac{12}{x} - \frac{4}{x^3} + \frac{3}{x^4} = 12x^{-1} - 4x^{-3} + 3x^{-4}$

$\frac{dy}{dx} = -12x^{-2} + 12x^{-4} - 12x^{-5}$

22. $y = \frac{(x - 1)(x^2 + x + 1)}{x^3} = \frac{x^3 - 1}{x^3} = 1 - x^{-3} \Rightarrow \frac{dy}{dx} = 3x^{-4}$

23. $y = \frac{x^2 - 1}{x^2 + x - 2} = \frac{(x + 1)(x - 1)}{(x + 2)(x - 1)} = \frac{x + 1}{x + 2} \Rightarrow \frac{dy}{dx} = \frac{x + 2 - x - 1}{(x + 2)^2} = \frac{1}{(x + 2)^2}$

24. $y = \frac{(x^2 + x)(x^2 - x + 1)}{x^4} = \frac{x\,(x^3 + 1)}{x^4} = \frac{x^3 + 1}{x^3} = 1 + x^{-3} \Rightarrow \frac{dy}{dx} = -3x^{-4}$

25. $s = \frac{t}{t^2 + 1} \Rightarrow \frac{ds}{dt} = \frac{t^2 + 1 - t\,(2t)}{(t^2 + 1)^2} = \frac{1 - t^2}{(t^2 + 1)^2}$

26. $s = (2t + 3)^3 \Rightarrow \frac{ds}{dt} = 3\,(2t + 3)^2\,(2) = 6\,(2t + 3)^2$

27. $s = (t^2 - t)^{-2} \Rightarrow \frac{ds}{dt} = -2(t^2 - t)^{-3}(2t - 1) = \frac{2 - 4t}{(t^2 - t)^3}$

28. $s = t^2(t+1)^{-1} \Rightarrow \frac{ds}{dt} = t^2[-(t+1)^{-2}] + (t+1)^{-1}(2t) = t(t+2)(t+1)^{-2}$

29. $s = \frac{2t}{3t^2+1} \Rightarrow \frac{ds}{dt} = \frac{2(3t^2+1) - 2t(6t)}{(3t^2+1)^2} = \frac{2-6t^2}{(3t^2+1)^2}$

30. $s = (t+t^{-1})^2 = t^2 + 2 + t^{-2} \Rightarrow \frac{ds}{dt} = 2t - 2t^{-3}$

31. $s = (t^2+3t)^3 \Rightarrow \frac{ds}{dt} = 3(t^2+3t)^2(2t+3)$

32. $s = \frac{(t^2-7t)(5-2t^3+t^4)}{t^3} = (t-7)(5t^{-2} - 2t + t^2)$

$\frac{ds}{dt} = (t-7)(-10t^{-3} - 2 + 2t) + (5t^{-2} - 2t + t^2)$

$= -10t^{-2} - 2t + 2t^2 + 70t^{-3} + 14 - 14t + 5t^{-2} - 2t + t^2$

$= 70t^{-3} - 5t^{-2} + 14 - 18t + 3t^2$

33. Each of the following is evaluated at $x = 0$:

(a) $\frac{d}{dx}(uv) = uv' + vu' = (5)(2)+(-1)(-3) = 13$

(b) $\frac{d}{dx}(\frac{u}{v}) = \frac{vu'-uv'}{v^2} = \frac{(-1)(-3)-(5)(2)}{(-1)^2} = -7$

(c) $\frac{d}{dx}(\frac{v}{u}) = \frac{uv'-vu'}{u^2} = \frac{(5)(2)-(-1)(-3)}{5^2} = \frac{7}{25}$

(d) $\frac{d}{dx}(7v-2u) = 7v'-2u' = 7(2) - 2(-3) = 20$

(e) $\frac{d}{dx}(u^3) = 3u^2u' = 3(5)^2(-3) = -225$

(f) $\frac{d}{dx}(5v^{-3}) = -3(5)(v^{-4})v' = -15(-1)^{-4}(2) = -30$

34. $y = \frac{x}{x^2+1} \Rightarrow \frac{dy}{dx} = \frac{x^2+1-2x^2}{(x^2+1)^2} = \left.\frac{-x^2+1}{(x^2+1)^2}\right]_{x=o} = 1.$

The tangent line is $y = x$.

35. $y = x + \frac{1}{x} = x + x^{-1} \Rightarrow y' = 1 - x^{-2}$. When $x = 2$,

$y = 2 + \frac{1}{2} = \frac{5}{2}$ and $y' = 1 - \frac{1}{4} = \frac{3}{4}$.

$\therefore\ y - \frac{5}{2} = \frac{3}{4}(x-2)$ or $4y - 3x = 4$.

36. $f(x) = (x^2 + 3x + 1)^3 \Rightarrow \frac{df}{dx} = 3(x^2 + 3x + 1)^2 (2x + 3)$ and

$$\frac{d^2f}{dx^2} = 6(x^2 + 3x + 1)^2 + 6(2x + 3)(x^2 + 3x + 1)(2x + 3)$$

$$= 6(x^2 + 3x + 1)[x^2 + 3x + 1 + 4x^2 + 12x + 9]$$

$$= 30(x^2 + 3x + 1)(x^2 + 3x + 2)$$

37. $y = (3-2x)^{-1} \Rightarrow \frac{dy}{dx} = -(3-2x)^{-2}(-2) = 2(3-2x)^{-2}$

$$\frac{d^2y}{dx^2} = -4(3-2x)^{-3}(-2) = 8(3-2x)^{-3}$$

38. $x = \frac{5y}{y+1} \Rightarrow \frac{dx}{dy} = \frac{5(y+1) - 5y}{(y+1)^2} = \frac{5}{(y+1)^2}$

39. $y = x(x-1)(x+1)$

$$\frac{dy}{dx} = x(x-1)\frac{d}{dx}(x+1) + x(x+1)\frac{d}{dx}(x-1) + (x+1)(x-1)\frac{d}{dx}(x)$$

$$= x(x-1) + x(x+1) + (x+1)(x-1) = 3x^2 - 1$$

Alternatively, $y = x(x^2 - 1) = x^3 - x \Rightarrow \frac{dy}{dx} = 3x^2 - 1$

40. $y = (x-1)(x+1)(x^2+1) = x^4 - 1 \Rightarrow \frac{dy}{dx} = 4x^3$. By the Product Rule,

$$\frac{dy}{dx} = (x+1)(x^2+1) + (x-1)(x^2+1) + 2x(x-1)(x+1)$$

$$= (x^2+1)(x+1+x-1) + 2x(x^2-1) = 2x(x^2+1+x^2-1) = 4x^3$$

41. $y = (1-x)(x+1)(3-x^2)$

$$\frac{dy}{dx} = (1-x)(x+1)\frac{d}{dx}(3-x^2) + (1-x)(3-x^2)\frac{d}{dx}(x+1) + (x+1)(3-x^2)\frac{d}{dx}(1-x)$$

$$= (1-x^2)(-2x) + (3-3x-x^2+x^3) + (3+3x-x^2-x^3)(-1) = 4x^3 - 8x$$

42. $y = x^2(x-1)(x^2+x+1) = x^2(x^3-1) = x^5 - x^2 \Rightarrow \frac{dy}{dx} = 5x^4 - 2x$.

By the Product Rule,

$$\frac{dy}{dx} = x^2(x^2+x+1) + x^2(x-1)(2x+1) + 2x(x-1)(x^2+x+1)$$

$$= x^4 + x^3 + x^2 + 2x^4 - x^3 - x^2 + 2x^4 - 2x = 5x^4 - 2x.$$

43. If $y = uv$ then $\frac{dy}{dt} = u\frac{dv}{dt} + v\frac{du}{dt} = u(.05v) + v(.04u) = .09uv = .09y$

44. Increasing by 1%, since $0.03uv - 0.02\,uv = 0.01\,uv = 0.01\,y$

45. $p(t) = \frac{a^2 kt}{akt + 1} \Rightarrow \frac{dp}{dt} = \frac{(akt + 1)(a^2 k) - (a^2 kt)(ak)}{(akt + 1)^2}$

$= \frac{a^2 k}{(akt + 1)^2}$. Since the numerator is constant and the denominator is increasing, $\frac{dp}{dt}$ is decreasing. $\therefore$ The largest value will occur when $t = 0$.

$\therefore$ The maximum value is $\frac{dp}{dt} = a^2 k$.

46. $\frac{d}{dx}(cu) = u\frac{dc}{dx} + c\frac{du}{dx} = 0 + c\frac{du}{dx} = c\frac{du}{dx}$

47. If $y = u_1 u_2 u_3 \ldots u_n$, then

$\frac{dy}{dx} = u_2 u_3 \ldots u_n \frac{d}{dx}(u_1) + \ldots\ldots\ldots + u_1 u_2 \ldots u_{n-1} \frac{d}{dx}(u_n)$

Let $u = u_1 = u_2 = \ldots = u_n$. Then $y = u^n$ and

$\frac{dy}{dx} = uu..u\frac{du}{dx} + \ldots\ldots\ldots + uu\ldots u\frac{du}{dx}$

$= u^{n-1}\frac{du}{dx} + \ldots + u^{n-1}\frac{du}{dx} = n\,u^{n-1}\frac{du}{dx}$.

2.3 IMPLICIT DIFFERENTIATION AND FRACTIONAL POWERS

1. $x^2 + y^2 = 1 \Rightarrow 2x + 2y\frac{dy}{dx} = 0 \Rightarrow 2y\frac{dy}{dx} = -2x \Rightarrow \frac{dy}{dx} = -\frac{x}{y}$

2. $y^2 = \frac{x-1}{x+1} \Rightarrow 2y\frac{dy}{dx} = \frac{x+1-x+1}{(x+1)^2} = \frac{2}{(x+1)^2} \Rightarrow \frac{dy}{dx} = \frac{1}{y(x+1)^2}$.

3. $x^2 - xy = 2 \Rightarrow 2x - x\frac{dy}{dx} - y = 0 \Rightarrow -x\frac{dy}{dx} = y - 2x \Rightarrow$

$\frac{dy}{dx} = \frac{y-2x}{x}$

4. $x^2 y + xy^2 = 6 \Rightarrow x^2\frac{dy}{dx} + 2xy + y^2 + 2xy\frac{dy}{dx} = 0$

$(x^2 + 2xy)\frac{dy}{dx} = -2xy - y^2 \Rightarrow \frac{dy}{dx} = -\frac{2xy + y^2}{2xy + x^2}$.

5. $y^2 = x^3 \Rightarrow 2y\frac{dy}{dx} = 3x^2 \Rightarrow \frac{dy}{dx} = \frac{3x^2}{2y}$

6. $x^{2/3} + y^{2/3} = 1 \Rightarrow \frac{2}{3} y^{-1/3} \frac{dy}{dx} + \frac{2}{3} x^{-1/3} = 0$

$y^{-1/3} \frac{dy}{dx} = -x^{-1/3} \Rightarrow \frac{dy}{dx} = -x^{-1/3} y^{1/3}$

7. $x^{\frac{1}{2}} + y^{\frac{1}{2}} = 1 \Rightarrow \frac{1}{2} x^{-\frac{1}{2}} + \frac{1}{2} y^{-\frac{1}{2}} \frac{dy}{dx} = 0$

$y^{-\frac{1}{2}} \frac{dy}{dx} = -x^{-\frac{1}{2}} \Rightarrow \frac{dy}{dx} = -x^{-\frac{1}{2}} y^{\frac{1}{2}} = -\sqrt{\frac{y}{x}}$

8. $x^3 - xy + y^3 = 1 \Rightarrow 3x^2 - x\frac{dy}{dx} - y + 3y^2 \frac{dy}{dx} = 0 \Rightarrow \frac{dy}{dx} = \frac{y - 3x^2}{3y^2 - x}$

9. $x^2 = \frac{x-y}{x+y} \Rightarrow x^3 + x^2 y = x - y \Rightarrow 3x^2 + x^2 \frac{dy}{dx} + 2xy = 1 - \frac{dy}{dx}$

$(x^2 + 1)\frac{dy}{dx} = 1 - 2xy - 3x^2 \Rightarrow \frac{dy}{dx} = \frac{1 - 2xy - 3x^2}{x^2 + 1}$

10. $y = \frac{x}{\sqrt{x^2 + 1}} = x(x^2 + 1)^{-1/2} \Rightarrow \frac{dy}{dx} = (x^2 + 1)^{-1/2} + x\left[-\frac{1}{2}(x^2 + 1)^{-3/2}(2x)\right]$

$= (x^2 + 1)^{-3/2}[x^2 + 1 - x^2] = (x^2 + 1)^{-3/2}.$

11. $y = x\sqrt{x^2 + 1} = x(x^2 + 1)^{\frac{1}{2}}$

$\frac{dy}{dx} = (x^2 + 1)^{\frac{1}{2}} + x\left[\frac{1}{2}(x^2 + 1)^{-\frac{1}{2}}(2x)\right] = \frac{\sqrt{x^2 + 1}}{1} + \frac{x^2}{\sqrt{x^2 + 1}} = \frac{2x^2 + 1}{\sqrt{x^2 + 1}}$

12. $y^2 = x^2 + \frac{1}{x^2} \Rightarrow 2y\frac{dy}{dx} = 2x - \frac{2}{x^3} \Rightarrow \frac{dy}{dx} = \frac{1}{y}\left(x - \frac{1}{x^3}\right)$

13. $2xy + y^2 = x + y \Rightarrow 2x\frac{dy}{dx} + 2y + 2y\frac{dy}{dx} = 1 + \frac{dy}{dx}$

$2x\frac{dy}{dx} + 2y\frac{dy}{dx} - \frac{dy}{dx} = 1 - 2y$

$\frac{dy}{dx} = \frac{1 - 2y}{2x + 2y - 1}$

14. $y = \sqrt{x} + \sqrt[3]{x} + \sqrt[4]{x} \Rightarrow \frac{dy}{dx} = \frac{1}{2}x^{-1/2} + \frac{1}{3}x^{-2/3} + \frac{1}{4}x^{-3/4}$

15. $y^2 = \dfrac{x^2 - 1}{x^2 + 1} \Rightarrow 2y\dfrac{dy}{dx} = \dfrac{(x^2 + 1)(2x) - (x^2 - 1)(2x)}{(x^2 + 1)^2}$

$2y\dfrac{dy}{dx} = \dfrac{2x^3 + 2x - 2x^3 + 2x}{(x^2 + 1)^2} = \dfrac{4x}{(x^2 + 1)^2} \Rightarrow \dfrac{dy}{dx} = \dfrac{2x}{y(x^2 + 1)^2}$

16. $(x + y)^3 + (x - y)^3 = x^4 + y^4 \Rightarrow$

$3(x + y)^2\left(1 + \dfrac{dy}{dx}\right) + 3(x - y)^2\left(1 - \dfrac{dy}{dx}\right) = 4x^3 + 4y^3\dfrac{dy}{dx}$

$[3(x + y)^2 - 3(x - y)^2 - 4y^3]\dfrac{dy}{dx} = 4x^3 - 3(x + y)^2 - 3(x - y)^2$

$\dfrac{dy}{dx} = \dfrac{4x^3 - 3(x + y)^2 - 3(x - y)^2}{3(x + y)^2 - 3(x - y)^2 - 4y^3}$

17. $(3x + 7)^5 = 2y^3 \Rightarrow 5(3x + 7)^4(3) = 6y^2\dfrac{dy}{dx}$

$\dfrac{dy}{dx} = \dfrac{5(3x + 7)^4}{2y^2}$

18. $y = (x + 5)^4(x^2 - 2)^3$

$\dfrac{dy}{dx} = (x + 5)^4[3(x^2 - 2)^2(2x)] + (x^2 - 2)^3[4(x + 5)^3]$

$= 2(x + 5)^3(x^2 - 2)^2[3x(x + 5) + 2(x^2 - 2)]$

$= 2(x + 5)^3(x^2 - 2)^2(5x^2 + 15x - 4)$

19. $\dfrac{1}{x} + \dfrac{1}{y} = 1 \Rightarrow x^{-1} + y^{-1} = 1 \Rightarrow -x^{-2} - y^{-2}\dfrac{dy}{dx} = 0$

$\therefore \dfrac{dy}{dx} = -x^{-2}y^2 = -[\dfrac{y}{x}]^2$

20. $y = (x^2 + 5x)^3 \Rightarrow \dfrac{dy}{dx} = 3(x^2 + 5x)^2(2x + 5)$

21. $y^2 = x^2 - x \Rightarrow 2y\dfrac{dy}{dx} = 2x - 1 \Rightarrow \dfrac{dy}{dx} = \dfrac{2x - 1}{2y}$

22. $x^2y^2 = x^2 + y^2$

$2x^2y\dfrac{dy}{dx} + 2xy^2 = 2x + 2y\dfrac{dy}{dx}$

$(2x^2y - 2y)\dfrac{dy}{dx} = 2x - 2xy^2 \Rightarrow \dfrac{dy}{dx} = \dfrac{x - xy^2}{x^2y - y}$

23. $y = \dfrac{\sqrt[3]{x^2+3}}{x} = \dfrac{(x^2+3)^{\frac{1}{3}}}{x} \Rightarrow \dfrac{dy}{dx} = \dfrac{x\left[\frac{1}{3}(x^2+3)^{-\frac{2}{3}}(2x)\right] - (x^2+3)^{\frac{1}{3}}}{x^2}$

$= \dfrac{\frac{2}{3}x^2(x^2+3)^{-\frac{2}{3}} - (x^2+3)^{\frac{1}{3}}}{x^2} = \dfrac{2x^2 - 3(x^2+3)}{3x^2(x^2+3)^{\frac{2}{3}}} = \dfrac{-x^2-9}{3x^2(x^2+3)^{\frac{2}{3}}}$

24. $y = x^2\sqrt{1-x^2} \Rightarrow \dfrac{dy}{dx} = x^2\left[\frac{1}{2}(1-x^2)^{-1/2}(-2x)\right] + 2x(1-x^2)^{1/2}$

$= -\dfrac{x^3}{\sqrt{1-x^2}} + 2x\sqrt{1-x^2} = \dfrac{2x-3x^3}{\sqrt{1-x^2}}$

25. $x^3 + y^3 = 18xy \Rightarrow 3x^2 + 3y^2\dfrac{dy}{dx} = 18\left(x\dfrac{dy}{dx} + y\right)$

$y^2\dfrac{dy}{dx} - 6x\dfrac{dy}{dx} = 6y - x^2 \Rightarrow \dfrac{dy}{dx} = \dfrac{6y-x^2}{y^2-6x}$

26. $y = (3x^2+5x+1)^{3/2} \Rightarrow \dfrac{dy}{dx} = \dfrac{3}{2}(3x^2+5x+1)^{1/2}(6x+5)$

27. $y = (2x+5)^{-\frac{1}{5}} \Rightarrow \dfrac{dy}{dx} = -\dfrac{2}{5}(2x+5)^{-\frac{6}{5}}$

28. $y = 3(2x^{-1/2}+1)^{-1/3} \Rightarrow \dfrac{dy}{dx} = -(2x^{-1/2}+1)^{-4/3}(-x^{-3/2})$

29. $y = \sqrt{1-\sqrt{x}} = (1-x^{\frac{1}{2}})^{\frac{1}{2}} \Rightarrow \dfrac{dy}{dx} = \dfrac{1}{2}(1-x^{\frac{1}{2}})^{-\frac{1}{2}}\dfrac{d}{dx}(1-x^{\frac{1}{2}})$

$= \dfrac{1}{2}(1-x^{\frac{1}{2}})^{-\frac{1}{2}}\left(-\dfrac{1}{2}x^{-\frac{1}{2}}\right) = \dfrac{-1}{4\sqrt{x}\sqrt{1-\sqrt{x}}} = \dfrac{-1}{4\sqrt{x-x\sqrt{x}}}$

30. $T^2 = \dfrac{4\pi^2 L}{g} = \left(\dfrac{4\pi^2}{g}\right)L \Rightarrow 2T\dfrac{dT}{dL} = \left(\dfrac{4\pi^2}{g}\right) \Rightarrow \dfrac{dT}{dL} = \dfrac{2\pi^2 g}{T}$

31. $y = x^{\frac{1}{2}} \Rightarrow y' = \dfrac{1}{2}x^{-\frac{1}{2}}$; $y(4) = 2$ and $y'(4) = \dfrac{1}{4}$.

∴ Tangent line is: $y - 2 = \dfrac{1}{4}(x-4)$ or $4y - x = 4$.

The x-intercept is (-4,0) and y-intercept is (0,1).

32. (b) since if $u = x^{5/3}$, $\dfrac{du}{dx} = \dfrac{5}{3}x^{2/3}$ and $\dfrac{d^2u}{dx^2} = \dfrac{10}{9}x^{-1/3}$.

33. $b = a^{\frac{2}{3}} \Rightarrow \dfrac{db}{da} = \dfrac{2}{3}a^{-\frac{1}{3}}$. $\dfrac{db}{da}$ does not exist if $a = 0$.

34. (a) $x^2 - y^2 = 1 \Rightarrow 2x - 2y\frac{dy}{dx} = 0 \Rightarrow \frac{dy}{dx} = \frac{x}{y}$

(b) $\frac{d^2y}{dx^2} = \frac{y - x\frac{dy}{dx}}{y^2} = \frac{y - x\left(\frac{x}{y}\right)}{y^2} = \frac{y^2 - x^2}{y^3} = -\frac{1}{y^3}$

35. $x^2 + y^2 = 1 \Rightarrow 2x + 2y\frac{dy}{dx} = 0 \Rightarrow \frac{dy}{dx} = -\frac{x}{y}$

$$\frac{d^2y}{dx^2} = -\frac{y - x\frac{dy}{dx}}{y^2} = -\frac{y - x\left(-\frac{x}{y}\right)}{y^2} = -\frac{y^2 + x^2}{y^3} = -\frac{1}{y^3}$$

36. $x^3 + y^3 = 1 \Rightarrow 3x^2 + 3y^2\frac{dy}{dx} = 0 \Rightarrow \frac{dy}{dx} = -\frac{x^2}{y^2}$

$$\frac{d^2y}{dx^2} = -\frac{y^2(2x) - (x^2)\left(2y\frac{dy}{dx}\right)}{y^4} = -\frac{2xy^2 - 2x^2y\left(-\frac{x^2}{y^2}\right)}{y^4} = -\frac{2xy^3 + 2x^4}{y^5}$$

37. $x^{\frac{2}{3}} + y^{\frac{2}{3}} = 1 \Rightarrow \frac{2}{3}x^{-\frac{1}{3}} + \frac{2}{3}y^{-\frac{1}{3}}\frac{dy}{dx} = 0 \Rightarrow \frac{dy}{dx} = -x^{-\frac{1}{3}}y^{\frac{1}{3}} = -\left(\frac{y}{x}\right)^{\frac{1}{3}}$

$$\frac{d^2y}{dx^2} = -\left[x^{-\frac{1}{3}}\left(\frac{1}{3}y^{-\frac{2}{3}}\frac{dy}{dx}\right) + y^{\frac{1}{3}}\left(-\frac{1}{3}x^{-\frac{4}{3}}\right)\right] =$$

$$-\frac{1}{3}[(x^{-\frac{1}{3}}y^{-\frac{2}{3}})(-x^{-\frac{1}{3}}y^{\frac{1}{3}}) - y^{\frac{1}{3}}x^{-\frac{4}{3}}] = \frac{1}{3}x^{-\frac{4}{3}}y^{-\frac{1}{3}}$$

38. $y^2 = x^2 + 2x \Rightarrow 2y\frac{dy}{dx} = 2x + 2 \Rightarrow \frac{dy}{dx} = \frac{x+1}{y}$

$$\frac{d^2y}{dx^2} = \frac{y - (x+1)\frac{dy}{dx}}{y^2} = \frac{y - (x+1)\left(\frac{x+1}{y}\right)}{y^2} = \frac{y^2 - (x+1)^2}{y^3}$$

39. $y^2 + 2y = 2x + 1 \Rightarrow 2y\frac{dy}{dx} + 2\frac{dy}{dx} = 2 \Rightarrow \frac{dy}{dx} = \frac{1}{y+1}$

$$\frac{d^2y}{dx^2} = -(y+1)^{-2}\frac{dy}{dx} = -\frac{1}{(y+1)^2}\cdot\frac{1}{y+1} = -\frac{1}{(y+1)^3}$$

40. $y^2 = 1 - \frac{2}{x} \Rightarrow 2y\frac{dy}{dx} = \frac{2}{x^2} \Rightarrow \frac{dy}{dx} = x^{-2}y^{-1}$

$$\frac{d^2y}{dx^2} = -x^{-2}y^{-2}\frac{dy}{dx} - 2y^{-1}x^{-3} = -x^{-2}y^{-2}(x^{-2}y^{-1}) - 2y^{-1}x^{-3}$$

$$= -\left(\frac{1}{x^4y^3} + \frac{2}{x^3y}\right)$$

41. $y + 2\sqrt{y} = x \Rightarrow \frac{dy}{dx} + 2(\frac{1}{2}y^{-\frac{1}{2}})\frac{dy}{dx} = 1 \Rightarrow \frac{dy}{dx} + \frac{1}{\sqrt{y}}\frac{dy}{dx} = 1$

$$\frac{dy}{dx} = \frac{1}{1 + \frac{1}{\sqrt{y}}} = (1 + y^{-\frac{1}{2}})^{-1}$$

$$\frac{d^2y}{dx^2} = -(1+y^{-1/2})^{-2}\left(-\frac{1}{2}y^{-3/2}\frac{dy}{dx}\right) = \frac{1}{2}y^{-3/2}(1+y^{-1/2})^{-2}(1+y^{-1/2})^{-1}$$

$$= \frac{1}{2}y^{-3/2}(1+y^{-1/2})^{-3} = \frac{1}{2}[y^{1/2}(1+y^{-1/2})]^{-3} = \frac{1}{2}(\sqrt{y}+1)^{-3}$$

42. $xy + y^2 = 1 \Rightarrow x\frac{dy}{dx} + y + 2y\frac{dy}{dx} = 0 \Rightarrow \frac{dy}{dx} = -\frac{y}{x+2y}$

$$\frac{d^2y}{dx^2} = -\frac{(x+2y)\frac{dy}{dx} - y\left(1 + 2\frac{dy}{dx}\right)}{(x+2y)^2} = -\frac{(x+2y)\left(-\frac{y}{x+2y}\right) - y\left(1 - \frac{2y}{x+2y}\right)}{(x+2y)^2}$$

$$= \frac{y(x+2y) + xy}{(x+2y)^3} = \frac{2xy + 2y^2}{(x+2y)^3}$$

43. $x^2 + xy - y^2 = 1 \Rightarrow 2x + x\frac{dy}{dx} + y - 2y\frac{dy}{dx} = 0.$

At P(2,3): $4 + 2\frac{dy}{dx} + 3 - 6\frac{dy}{dx} = 0$ or $\frac{dy}{dx} = \frac{7}{4}$

Slope of normal is $m = -\frac{4}{7}$

(a) $y - 3 = \frac{7}{4}(x - 2) \Rightarrow 4y - 7x = -2$

(b) $y - 3 = -\frac{4}{7}(x - 2) \Rightarrow 7y + 4x = 29$

44. $x^2 + y^2 = 25 \Rightarrow 2x + 2y\frac{dy}{dx} = 0 \Rightarrow \frac{dy}{dx} = -\frac{x}{y}\Big]_{(x,y)=(3,-4)} = \frac{3}{4}$

Tangent: $y + 4 = \frac{3}{4}(x - 3) \Rightarrow 4y - 3x = -25$

Normal: $y + 4 = -\frac{4}{3}(x - 3) \Rightarrow 3y + 4x = 0$

45. $x^2y^2 = 9 \Rightarrow 2x^2y\frac{dy}{dx} + 2xy^2 = 0$. At P(−1, 3),

$2(-1)^2(3)\frac{dy}{dx} + 2(-1)(3)^2 = 0 \Rightarrow \frac{dy}{dx} = 3$

(a) Tangent: $y - 3 = 3(x+1) \Rightarrow y - 3x = 6$

(b) Normal: $y - 3 = -\frac{1}{3}(x+1) \Rightarrow 3y + x = 8$.

46. $\frac{x-y}{x-2y} = 2 \Rightarrow x - y = 2x - 4y \Rightarrow 3y = x$. $\therefore \frac{dy}{dx} = \frac{1}{3}$

Tangent: $y - 1 = \frac{1}{3}(x-3) \Rightarrow 3y - x = 0$

Normal: $y - 1 = -3(x-3) \Rightarrow y + 3x = 10$

47. $y^2 - 2x - 4y - 1 = 0 \Rightarrow 2y\frac{dy}{dx} - 2 - 4\frac{dy}{dx} = 0$. At P(−2, 1)

$2\frac{dy}{dx} - 2 - 4\frac{dy}{dx} = 0 \Rightarrow \frac{dy}{dx} = -1$

(a) tangent: $y - 1 = -(x+2) \Rightarrow y + x = -1$

(b) normal: $y - 1 = x + 2 \Rightarrow y - x = 3$

48. $xy + 2x - 5y = 2 \Rightarrow x\frac{dy}{dx} + y + 2 - 5\frac{dy}{dx} = 0 \Rightarrow \frac{dy}{dx} = -\left.\frac{y+2}{x-5}\right]_{(x,y)=(3,2)} = 2$

Tangent: $y - 2 = 2(x-3) \Rightarrow y - 2x = -4$

Normal: $y - 2 = -\frac{1}{2}(x-3) \Rightarrow 2y + x = 7$

49. $xy + 2x - y = 0 \Rightarrow x\frac{dy}{dx} + y + 2 - \frac{dy}{dx} = 0 \Rightarrow \frac{dy}{dx} = \frac{y+2}{1-x}$. The line $2x + y = 0$ has slope $m = -2$. To be parallel, the normal lines must also have slope $m = -2$. Since a normal is perpendicular to a tangent, the tangent line must have slope $m = \frac{1}{2}$. $\therefore$

$\frac{y+2}{1-x} = \frac{1}{2} \Leftrightarrow 2y + 4 = 1 - x \Leftrightarrow x = -3 - 2y$. Substituting,

$y(-3-2y) + 2(-3-2y) - y = 0 \Leftrightarrow y^2 + 4y + 3 = 0 \Rightarrow y = -3, -1$

$y = -3 \Rightarrow x = 3$ and $y + 3 = -2(x-3) \Rightarrow y + 2x = 3$

$y = -1 \Rightarrow x = -1$ and $y + 1 = -2(x+1) \Rightarrow y + 2x = -3$

50. $y^2 = x \Rightarrow \frac{dy}{dx} = \frac{1}{2y}$. If a normal is drawn from $(a, 0)$ to (x_1, y_1),

$\frac{y_1 - 0}{x_1 - a} = -2y_1 \Rightarrow y_1 = -2y_1(x_1 - a)$ or $a = x_1 + \frac{1}{2}$. Since $x_1 \geq 0$,

we must have that $a \geq \frac{1}{2}$. The two points on the parabola are

$\left(x_1, \sqrt{x_1}\right)$ and $\left(x_1, -\sqrt{x_1}\right)$. To be perpendicular,

$(-2y)(2y) = -1 \Rightarrow y = \pm\frac{1}{2}$ and $x = \frac{1}{4}$. $\therefore \left(\frac{1}{4}, \pm\frac{1}{2}\right)$ and $a = \frac{3}{4}$.

51. $y = x^2 + 2x - 3 \Rightarrow \frac{dy}{dx} = 2x + 2$. At $P(1, 0)$, $\frac{dy}{dx} = 4$. $\therefore$ Normal has equation $y = -\frac{1}{4}(x - 1) = -\frac{1}{4}x + \frac{1}{4}$. To find point of intersection, equate $-\frac{1}{4}x + \frac{1}{4} = x^2 + 2x - 3 \Rightarrow$

$4x^2 + 9x - 13 = 0 \Rightarrow x = 1, -\frac{13}{4}$.

$y(-\frac{13}{4}) = -\frac{1}{4}(-\frac{13}{4}) + \frac{1}{4} = \frac{17}{16}$. $\therefore (-\frac{13}{4}, \frac{17}{16})$

52. $x^2 + y^2 = a^2 \Rightarrow 2x + 2y\frac{dy}{dx} = 0$ or $\frac{dy}{dx} = -\frac{x}{y}$. A normal at any point (x_0, y_0)

would have slope $m = \frac{y_0}{x_0}$ and equation $y - y_0 = \frac{y_0}{x_0}(x - x_0)$.

Simplifying gives $y = \frac{y_0}{x_0}x$, so the normal passes through $(0, 0)$.

53. $x^2 + xy + y^2 = 7$ crosses the x-axis when $y = 0$, i.e. when $x = \pm\sqrt{7}$

$2x + x\frac{dy}{dx} + y + 2y\frac{dy}{dx} = 0 \Rightarrow \frac{dy}{dx} = \frac{-2x - y}{x + 2y}$

At the points $(\pm\sqrt{7}, 0)$, $\frac{dy}{dx} = -2 \Rightarrow$ the tangents are parallel.

54. $x^2 + xy + y^2 = 7 \Rightarrow 2x + x\frac{dy}{dx} + y + 2y\frac{dy}{dx} = 0$ or $\frac{dy}{dx} = -\frac{2x+y}{x+2y}$.

(a) $\|$ to x–axis $\Rightarrow -\frac{2x+y}{x+2y} = 0$ or $2x + y = 0$. Substituting,

$$x^2 + x(-2x) + (-2x)^2 = 7 \Rightarrow x = \pm\sqrt{\frac{7}{3}}.$$

The points are $\left(\sqrt{\frac{7}{3}}, -2\sqrt{\frac{7}{3}}\right)$ and $\left(-\sqrt{\frac{7}{3}}, 2\sqrt{\frac{7}{3}}\right)$.

(b) $\|$ to y–axis $\Rightarrow -\frac{2x+y}{x+2y}$ is undefined $\Rightarrow x + 2y = 0$. Substituting,

$$(-2y)^2 + y(-2y) + y^2 = 7 \Rightarrow y = \pm\sqrt{\frac{7}{3}}.$$

The points are $\left(2\sqrt{\frac{7}{3}}, -\sqrt{\frac{7}{3}}\right)$ and $\left(-2\sqrt{\frac{7}{3}}, \sqrt{\frac{7}{3}}\right)$.

55. $s(t) = \sqrt{1 + 4t} \Rightarrow v(t) = \frac{1}{2}(1 + 4t)^{-\frac{1}{2}}(4) = \frac{2}{\sqrt{1 + 4t}}$

$v(6) = \frac{2}{\sqrt{25}} = \frac{2}{5}$ m/s

$a(t) = 2\left[-\frac{1}{2}(1 + 4t)^{-\frac{3}{2}}(4)\right] = \frac{-4}{(1 + 4t)^{\frac{3}{2}}}$

$a(6) = \frac{-4}{(25)^{\frac{3}{2}}} = -\frac{4}{125}$ m/s^2

56. $y = \sqrt{x} \Rightarrow \frac{dy}{dx} = \frac{1}{2\sqrt{x}} = 1$ if $x = \frac{1}{4}$ and $y = \frac{1}{2}$

57. $2x^2 + 3y^2 = 5 \Rightarrow 4x + 6y\frac{dy}{dx} = 0 \Rightarrow \frac{dy}{dx} = -\frac{2x}{3y}$.

$y^2 = x^3 \Rightarrow \frac{dy}{dx} = \frac{3x^2}{2y}$.

At $(1,1)$, $m_1 = -\frac{2}{3}$ and $m_2 = \frac{3}{2} \Rightarrow$ tangents are orthogonal

At $(1,-1)$, $m_1 = \frac{2}{3}$ and $m_2 = -\frac{3}{2} \Rightarrow$ tangents are orthogonal.

58. $m(v^2 - v_0^2) = k(x_0^2 - x^2) \Rightarrow m\left(2v\frac{dv}{dt}\right) = k\left(-2x\frac{dx}{dt}\right)$

$m\frac{dv}{dt} = -\frac{k}{v}x\frac{dx}{dt} = \left(-\frac{k}{v}\right)(xv) = -kx.$

2.4 LINEAR APPROXIMATIONS

1. $f(x) = x^4$; $f'(x) = 4x^3$; $f'(1) = 4$ and $f(1) = 1$

   $L(x) = 1 + 4(x - 1) = 4x - 3$

   $L(1.01) = 4(1.01) - 3 = 1.04$

   By calculator, $f(1.01) = 1.04060$ to five decimal places.

2. $f(x) = x^2 + 2x$; $f'(x) = 2x + 2$; $f'(0) = 2$ and $f(0) = 0$

   $L(x) = 0 + 2x = 2x$

   $L(0.1) = 0.2$

   By calculator, $f(0.1) = 0.21$

3. $f(x) = x^{-1} \Rightarrow f'(x) = -x^{-2}$; $f'(2) = -\frac{1}{4}$ and $f(2) = \frac{1}{2}$

   $L(x) = \frac{1}{2} - \frac{1}{4}(x - 2) = -\frac{1}{4}x + 1.$

   $L(2.1) = -\frac{1}{4}(2.1) + 1 = 0.475$. By calculator, $f(2.1) = 0.47619$

4. $f(x) = x^{-1} \Rightarrow f'(x) = -x^{-2}$; $f'(0.5) = -4$ and $f(0.5) = 2$

   $L(x) = 2 - 4\left(x - \frac{1}{2}\right) = -4x + 4$

   $L(0.6) = -4(0.6) + 4 = 1.6$. By calculator, $f(0.6) = 1.667$

5. $f(x) = x^3 - x \Rightarrow f'(x) = 3x^2 - 1$; $f(1) = 0$ and $f'(1) = 2$

   $L(x) = 0 + 2(x-1) = 2x - 2$. $L(1.1) = 2.2 - 2 = .2$

   By calculator, $f(1.1) = (1.1)^3 - 1.1 = 0.231$

6. $f(x) = 2x^2 + 4x - 3 \Rightarrow f'(x) = 4x + 4$; $f'(-1) = 0$ and $f(-1) = -5$

   $L(x) = -5$

   $L(-0.9) = -5$. By calculator, $f(-0.9) = -4.98$

7. $f(x) = x^3 - 2x + 3 \Rightarrow f'(x) = 3x^2 - 2$; $f(2) = 7$ and $f'(2) = 10$

   $L(x) = 7 + 10(x - 2) = 10x - 13$; $L(1.9) = 6$

   By calculator, $f(1.9) = 6.059$

8. $f(x) = \sqrt{1+x} \Rightarrow f'(x) = \dfrac{1}{2\sqrt{1+x}}$; $f'(8) = \dfrac{1}{6}$ and $f(8) = 3$

$L(x) = 3 + \dfrac{1}{6}(x-8) = \dfrac{1}{6}x + \dfrac{5}{3}$

$L(9.1) = 3.183$. By calculator, $f(9.1) = 3.178$

9. $f(x) = \sqrt{x} \Rightarrow f'(x) = \dfrac{1}{2}x^{-\frac{1}{2}}$; $f(4) = 2$ and $f'(4) = \dfrac{1}{4}$.

$L(x) = 2 + \dfrac{1}{4}(x-4) = \dfrac{1}{4}x + 1$. $L(4.1) = 2.025$.

By calculator, $f(4.1) = 2.02485$

10. $f(x) = x^{1/3} \Rightarrow f'(x) = \dfrac{1}{3}x^{-2/3}$; $f'(8) = \dfrac{1}{12}$ and $f(8) = 2$

$L(x) = 2 + \dfrac{1}{12}(x-8) = \dfrac{1}{12}x + \dfrac{4}{3}$

$L(8.5) = 2.042$. By calculator, $f(8.5) = 2.041$

11. $f(x) = \sqrt{x^2+9} \Rightarrow f'(x) = \dfrac{1}{2}(x^2+9)^{-\frac{1}{2}}(2x) = \dfrac{x}{\sqrt{x^2+9}}$

$L(x) = 5 - \dfrac{4}{5}(x+4) = -\dfrac{4}{5}x + \dfrac{9}{5}$

$L(-4.2) = 5 - \dfrac{4}{5}(-4.2+4) = 5.16$

By calculator, $f(-4.2) = 5.16140$

12. $f(x) = \dfrac{x}{x+1} \Rightarrow f'(x) = \dfrac{1}{(x+1)^2}$; $f'(1) = \dfrac{1}{4}$ and $f(1) = \dfrac{1}{2}$

$L(x) = \dfrac{1}{2} + \dfrac{1}{4}(x-1) = \dfrac{1}{4}x + \dfrac{1}{4}$

$L(1.3) = 0.575$. By calculator, $f(1.3) = 0.5652$

13. $(1+x)^2 \approx 1 + 2x$

14. $(1+x)^3 \approx 1 + 3x$

15. $(1+x)^{-5} \approx 1 - 5x$

16. $4(1+x)^{-2} \approx 4(1-2x) = 4 - 8x$

17. $2(1-x)^{-4} \approx 2(1+4x) = 2 + 8x$

18. $(1-x)^6 \approx 1 - 6x$

19. $2(1+x)^{1/2} \approx 2\left(1+\frac{1}{2}x\right) = x+2$

20. $3(1+x)^{1/3} \approx 3\left(1+\frac{1}{3}x\right) = x+3$

21. $(1+x)^{-1} \approx 1-x$

22. $(1+x)^{-1/2} \approx 1-\frac{1}{2}x$

23. (a) $(1.0002)^{100} = (1 + .0002)^{100} \approx 1 + 100(.0002) = 1.02$

(b) $\sqrt[3]{1.009} = (1 + .009)^{\frac{1}{3}} \approx 1 + \frac{1}{3}(.009) = 1.003$

(c) $\frac{1}{0.999} = (.999)^{-1} = (1 - .001)^{-1} \approx 1 - (-.001) = 1.001$

24. This is a calculator problem that requires no solution key.

25. $f(x) = x^2 + 2x$, $a = 0$, $\Delta x = 0.1$

$\Delta y = f(0.1) - f(0) = [(.1)^2 + 2(.1)] - 0 = .21$

$dy = f'(0)\Delta x = [2(0) + 2](.1) = .2$

$\text{Error} = \Delta y - dy = .21 - .2 = .01$

26. $f(x) = 2x^2 + 4x - 3$, $a = -1$, $\Delta x = 0.1$

$\Delta y = f(-1 + 0.1) - f(-1) = 0.02$

$dy = f'(-1)\,\Delta x = (4x + 4)\,\Delta x = 0$

$\text{Error} = \Delta y - dy = 0.02$

27. $f(x) = x^3 - x$, $a = 1$, $\Delta x = 0.1$

$\Delta y = f(1.1) - f(1) = [(1.1)^3 - 1] - 0 = .231$

$dy = f'(1)\Delta x = [3(1)^2 - 1](.1) = 0.2$

$\text{Error} = \Delta y - dy = 0.231 - 0.2 = 0.031$

28. $f(x) = x^4$, $a = 1$, $\Delta x = 0.1$

$\Delta y = f(1.1) - f(1) = 0.4641$

$dy = f'(1)\,\Delta x = 4x^3\,\Delta x = 0.4$

$\text{Error} = \Delta y - dy = 0.4641 - 0.4 = 0.0641$

29. $f(x) = x^{-1}$, $a = .5$, $\Delta x = .1$

$\Delta y = f(.6) - f(.5) = (.6)^{-1} - (.5)^{-1} = -.\overline{3}$

$dy = f'(.5)\Delta x = -(.5)^{-2}(.1) = -.4$

$\text{Error} = \Delta y - dy = -.\overline{3} - (-.4) = .0\overline{6}$

30. $f(x) = x^3 - 2x + 3$, $a = 2$, $\Delta x = 0.1$

$\Delta y = f(2.1) - f(2) = 1.061$

$dy = f'(2)\,\Delta x = (3x^2 - 2)\,\Delta x = 1.0$

$\text{Error} = \Delta y - dy = 1.061 - 1 = 0.061$

31. $V = \frac{4}{3}\pi r^3 \Rightarrow dV = 4\pi r^2\,dr$

32. $S = 4\pi r^2 \Rightarrow dS = 8\pi r\,dr$

33. $V = x^3 \Rightarrow dV = 3x^2\,dx$

34. $S = 6x^2 \Rightarrow dS = 12x\,dx$

35. $V = \pi r^2 h$ and h constant $\Rightarrow dV = 2\pi rh dr$

36. $s = 2\pi rh$ and r constant $\Rightarrow dS = 2\pi r\,dh$

37. $V = \frac{1}{3}\pi r^2 h$ and h constant $\Rightarrow dV = \frac{2}{3}\pi rh\,dr$

38. $S = \pi r\sqrt{r^2 + h^2}$ and r constant $\Rightarrow dS = \dfrac{\pi rh\,dh}{\sqrt{r^2 + h^2}}$

39. $A = \pi r^2$, $dr = 0.02$, $r = 2$

(a) $dA = 2\pi r dr$. If $r = 2$ and $dr = 0.02$, $dA = 0.08\pi$

(b) % error $= \dfrac{dA}{A} \times 100 = \dfrac{.08\pi}{16\pi} \times 100 = 2\%$

40. $C = 2\pi r \Rightarrow dC = 2\pi dr$. $dC = 2$ in $\Rightarrow dr = \dfrac{2}{2\pi} = \dfrac{1}{\pi}$. The diameter

grew about $\frac{2}{\pi}$ in. $A = \pi r^2 \Rightarrow dA = 2\pi r\,dr \Rightarrow dA = 2\pi(5)\left(\frac{1}{\pi}\right) = 10\text{ in}^2$.

41. If $x = 10$ cm, then $dx = (.01)(10) = .1$ cm.

$V = x^3 \Rightarrow dV = 3x^2 dx = 3(10)^2(.1) = 30\text{ cm}^3$.

$\dfrac{dV}{V} = \dfrac{30}{1000} = .03$. $\therefore$ Error $= 3\%$

42. $V = \frac{4}{3}\pi r^3 \Rightarrow dV = 4\pi r^2\,dr$. Since $dr = \pm 0.5$ cm,

$dV = 4\pi(50)^2(\pm 0.5) = 5000\pi\text{ cm}^3$.

Percent error $= \dfrac{dV}{V} \times 100 = \dfrac{5000\pi}{\frac{4}{3}\pi(50)^3} \times 100 = 3\%$

43. $A = x^2$. For A to be within 2% of true value, we need

$|\Delta A| \le .02A = .02x^2$. $\Delta A \approx dA = (\frac{dA}{dx})dx = 2xdx$.

$\therefore\ |2xdx| \le .02x^2 \Leftrightarrow |dx| \le \frac{.02x^2}{2x} = .01x$.

The side x must be measured to within 1% of its true value.

44. (a) $S = 6x^2 \Rightarrow dS = 12x\,dx$. To be within 2% of the surface area, we need

$\frac{12\,x\,|dx|}{6x^2} < 0.02 \Leftrightarrow \frac{|dx|}{x} < 0.01$. The edge must be measured to within 1% of its true value.

(b) $V = x^3 \Rightarrow dV = 3x^2\,dx < 3x^2(0.01x) = 0.03\,x^3$. The error in the volume will be less than 3%.

45. $V = \frac{1}{3}\pi h^3$. We need $|\Delta V| \le .01V$. Since $\Delta V \approx dV$ and $dV = \pi h^2 dh$,

$\pi h^2 |dh| \le .01V \Rightarrow$

$$|dh| \le \frac{.01(\frac{1}{3}\pi h^3)}{\pi h^2} = \frac{.01h}{3} = \frac{1}{3}\%\text{ of the true height.}$$

46. (a) $C = 2\pi r \Rightarrow dC = 2\pi\,dr$ so $0.4 = 2\pi\,dr \Rightarrow dr = \frac{.2}{\pi} = \frac{1}{5\pi}$

$r = \frac{C}{2\pi} = \frac{5}{\pi}$, so $\frac{dr}{r} \times 100 = \frac{1}{5\pi}\cdot\frac{\pi}{5} \times 100 = 4\%$

(b) $S = 4\pi r^2 \Rightarrow dS = 8\pi\,r\,dr$ so $dS = 8\pi\left(\frac{5}{\pi}\right)\left(\frac{1}{5\pi}\right) = \frac{8}{\pi}$

$S = 4\pi\left(\frac{5}{\pi}\right)^2 = \frac{100}{\pi}$, so $\frac{dS}{S} \times 100 = \frac{8}{\pi} \times \frac{\pi}{100} \times 100 = 8\%$

(c) $V = \frac{4}{3}\pi r^3 \Rightarrow dV = 4\pi\,r^2\,dr$, so $dV = 4\pi\left(\frac{5}{\pi}\right)^2\left(\frac{1}{5\pi}\right) = \frac{20}{\pi^2}$

$V = \frac{4}{3}\pi\left(\frac{5}{\pi}\right)^3 = \frac{500}{3\pi^2}$, so $\frac{dV}{V} \times 100 = \left(\frac{20}{\pi^2}\right)\left(\frac{3\pi^2}{500}\right)(100) = 12\%$

47. $r = \frac{D}{2} \Rightarrow V = \frac{1}{3}\pi r^3 = \frac{1}{6}\pi D^3$. $\Delta V \approx dv = \frac{1}{2}\pi D^2 dD$. To be within 3% of the Volume, we need $\frac{dV}{V} \le .03. \Rightarrow$

$\frac{\frac{1}{2}\pi D^2 dD}{\frac{1}{6}\pi D^3} \le .03 \Leftrightarrow \frac{dD}{D} \le .01$. The diameter needs to be within 1%.

48. (a) $V = 10\pi r^2 = 10\pi\left(\frac{D}{2}\right)^2 = \frac{5\pi D^2}{2} \Rightarrow dV = 5\pi D\, dD$. To be within 1% of the true volume, we need $\frac{dV}{V} \le 0.01$ or $\frac{5\pi D\, dD}{\frac{5\pi D^2}{2}} \le 0.01 \Rightarrow \frac{dD}{D} \le 0.005$.

The diameter must be measured to within $\frac{1}{2}$% of its true value.

(b) $S = 10\pi D \Rightarrow dS = 10\pi\, dD$. $\frac{10\pi\, dD}{10\pi D} \le 0.05$ if $\frac{dD}{D} \le 0.05$, or the exterior diameter must be measured to within 5%.

49. $W = kV = k\pi r^2 h = Kr^2$ where $K = k\pi h$ is constant.

We need $|\Delta W| \le .001W$. $\Delta W \approx dW = 2Krdr$. $\therefore\ 2Kr|dr| \le .001Kr^2 \Rightarrow$

$2|dr| \le .001r \Rightarrow |dr| \le .0005r$ or to within .05% of true value.

50. (a) $1 = \frac{4\pi^2 L}{32.2} \Rightarrow L = \frac{32.2}{4\pi^2} \approx 0.8156$ ft.

(b) $T^2 = \frac{4\pi^2 L}{32.2} \Rightarrow 2T\, dt = \frac{4\pi^2}{32.2} dL$, so $2(1)\, dT = \frac{4\pi^2}{32.2}(0.01)$ or

$dT \approx 0.000621\pi^2 \approx 0.00195\pi$ sec.

(c) $0.00195\pi \times 3600 \times 24 = 529.2$ sec

51. $y = x^3 + \Delta y = (x + \Delta x)^3 = x^3 + 3x^2\Delta x + 3x\Delta x^2 + \Delta x^3$

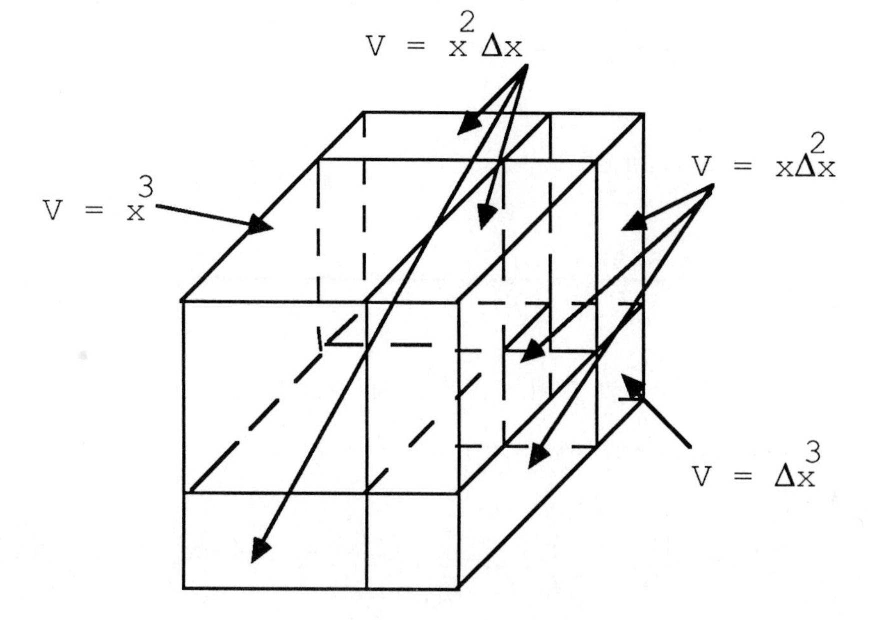

52. (a) If $g(x) = \sqrt{x} + \sqrt{1+x} - 4$, then $g(4) = 2 + \sqrt{5} - 4 = \sqrt{2} - 2 > 0$ and $g(3) = \sqrt{3} + 2 - 4 = \sqrt{3} - 2 < 0$. Therefore, by the Intermediate Value Theorem, there is a value $3 < x < 4$ for which $g(x) = 0$.

(b) $\sqrt{x} \approx \sqrt{3} + \dfrac{1}{2\sqrt{3}}(x-3)$

$\sqrt{1+x} \approx 2 + \dfrac{1}{4}(x-3)$

$\sqrt{3} + \dfrac{1}{2\sqrt{3}}(x-3) + 2 + \dfrac{1}{4}(x-3) - 4 = 0$

$\left(\dfrac{1}{2\sqrt{3}} + \dfrac{1}{4}\right)(x-3) = 2 - \sqrt{3}$ or $x = 28\sqrt{3} - 45 \approx 3.4974$

(c) $g(28\sqrt{3} - 45) = -0.0091$

53. $f(x) = \dfrac{2}{1-x} + \sqrt{1+x} - 3.1$

(a) $f(0) = 2 + 1 - 3.1 = -.1$

$f(\frac{1}{2}) = \dfrac{2}{1-\frac{1}{2}} + \sqrt{1+\frac{1}{2}} - 3.1 = 4 + \sqrt{\frac{3}{2}} - 3.1 > 0$

$\therefore \exists\ x_1,\ 0 < x_1 < \frac{1}{2}$ for which $f(x_1) = 0$ (Intermediate Value Thm)

(b) Let $L_1(x) = 2 + 2x$ and $L_2(x) = 1 + \frac{1}{2}x$ be the linearizations of $f_1(x) = \dfrac{2}{1-x}$ and $f_2(x) = \sqrt{1+x}$ respectively.

Then $f(x) \approx L_1(x) + L_2(x) - 3.1 = 2 + 2x + 1 + \frac{1}{2}x - 3.1$

$= \frac{5}{2}x - .1 = 0 \Leftrightarrow x = .04$

(c) $f(0.04) = \dfrac{2}{1-.04} + \sqrt{1+.04} - 3.1 \approx 0.003137$

54. $f(0) = 1$ and $f'(0) = k$, so $L(x) = 1 + k(x-0) = 1 + kx$.

55. $M = \dfrac{M_o}{\sqrt{1 - (\frac{v}{c})^2}} = M_o\left[1 - (\frac{v}{c})^2\right]^{-\frac{1}{2}}$. The linearization of M is

$L(M) = M_o\left[1 + \frac{1}{2}(\frac{1}{c})^2 v^2\right] = M_o + \dfrac{M_o}{2c^2}v^2$. $\Delta M_o = M - M_o = \dfrac{M_o}{2c^2}v^2$.

$\therefore \dfrac{\Delta M_o}{M_o} = \dfrac{\frac{M_o v^2}{2c^2}}{M_o} = \dfrac{1}{2c^2}v^2$ will be equal to 1% = .01

$\Leftrightarrow v^2 = .02c^2 \Leftrightarrow v = c\sqrt{.02} = .14c.$ $\therefore$ an increase of velocity of 14% the speed of light is needed.

2.5 THE CHAIN RULE

1. $y = x^2 \Rightarrow \frac{dy}{dx} = 2x \qquad x = 2t - 5 \Rightarrow \frac{dx}{dt} = 2$

$\frac{dy}{dt} = \frac{dy}{dx} \bullet \frac{dx}{dt} = 2x(2) = 4x = 4(2t - 5) = 8t - 20$

2. $y = x^4 \Rightarrow \frac{dy}{dx} = 4x^3 \qquad x = t^{1/3} \Rightarrow \frac{dx}{dt} = \frac{1}{3}t^{-2/3}$

$\frac{dy}{dt} = \frac{dy}{dx} \cdot \frac{dx}{dt} = 4x^3\left(\frac{1}{3}t^{-2/3}\right) = 4(t^{1/3})^3\left(\frac{1}{3}t^{-2/3}\right) = \frac{4}{3}t^{1/3}$

3. $y = 8 - \frac{x}{3} \Rightarrow \frac{dy}{dx} = -\frac{1}{3}$ and $x = t^3 \Rightarrow \frac{dx}{dt} = 3t^2.$

$\frac{dy}{dt} = \frac{dy}{dx} \bullet \frac{dx}{dt} = -\frac{1}{3}(3t^2) = -t^2.$

4. $y + 4x^2 = 7 \Rightarrow \frac{dy}{dx} = -8x \qquad x + \frac{5}{4}t = 3 \Rightarrow \frac{dx}{dt} = -\frac{5}{4}$

$\frac{dy}{dt} = \frac{dy}{dx} \cdot \frac{dx}{dt} = -8x\left(-\frac{5}{4}\right) = 10x = 10\left(3 - \frac{5}{4}t\right) = 30 - \frac{25}{2}t$

5. $2x - 3y = 9 \Rightarrow 2 - 3\frac{dy}{dx} = 0 \Rightarrow \frac{dy}{dx} = \frac{2}{3}.$

$2x + \frac{t}{3} = 1 \Rightarrow 2\frac{dx}{dt} + \frac{1}{3} = 0 \Rightarrow \frac{dx}{dt} = -\frac{1}{6}.$

$\frac{dy}{dt} = \frac{dy}{dx} \bullet \frac{dx}{dt} = \frac{2}{3}(-\frac{1}{6}) = -\frac{1}{9}.$

6. $y = x^{-1} \Rightarrow \frac{dy}{dx} = -x^{-2} \qquad x = t^2 - 3t + 8 \Rightarrow \frac{dx}{dt} = 2t - 3$

$\frac{dy}{dt} = \frac{dy}{dx} \cdot \frac{dx}{dt} = -x^{-2}(2t - 3) = -\frac{2t - 3}{(t^2 - 3t + 8)^2}$

7. $y = \sqrt{x + 2} \Rightarrow \frac{dy}{dx} = \frac{1}{2}(x + 2)^{-\frac{1}{2}}$

$x = \frac{2}{t} \Rightarrow \frac{dx}{dt} = -\frac{2}{t^2}$

$\frac{dy}{dt} = \frac{1}{2}(x + 2)^{-\frac{1}{2}}\left(\frac{-2}{t^2}\right) = -t^{-2}(2t^{-1} + 2)^{-\frac{1}{2}}$

8. $y = \frac{x^2}{x^2+1} \Rightarrow \frac{dy}{dx} = \frac{2x(x^2+1) - 2x(x^2)}{(x^2+1)^2} = \frac{2x}{(x^2+1)^2}$

$x = \sqrt{2t+1} \Rightarrow \frac{dx}{dt} = \frac{1}{\sqrt{2t+1}}$

$\frac{dy}{dt} = \frac{dy}{dx}\cdot\frac{dx}{dt} = \left(\frac{2x}{(x^2+1)^2}\right)\left(\frac{1}{\sqrt{2t+1}}\right) = \left(\frac{2\sqrt{2t+1}}{(2t+1+1)^2}\right)\left(\frac{1}{\sqrt{2t+1}}\right)$

$= \frac{1}{2(t+1)^2}$

9. $y = x^2 + 3x - 7 \Rightarrow \frac{dy}{dx} = 2x + 3.$ $x = 2t + 1 \Rightarrow \frac{dx}{dt} = 2$

$\frac{dy}{dt} = 2(2x + 3) = 2[2(2t + 1) + 3] = 8t + 10$

10. $y = x^{2/3} \Rightarrow \frac{dy}{dx} = \frac{2}{3}x^{-1/3}$ $x = t^2 + 1 \Rightarrow \frac{dx}{dt} = 2t$

$\frac{dy}{dt} = \frac{dy}{dx}\cdot\frac{dx}{dt} = \left(\frac{2}{3}x^{-1/3}\right)(2t) = \frac{4}{3}t(t^2+1)^{-1/3}$

11. $z = w^2 - w^{-1} \Rightarrow \frac{dz}{dw} = 2w + w^{-2}.$ $w = 3x \Rightarrow \frac{dw}{dx} = 3.$

$\frac{dz}{dx} = \frac{dz}{dw} \bullet \frac{dw}{dx} = 3(2w + w^{-2}) = 3[6x + (3x)^{-2}] = 18x + \frac{1}{3x^2}$

12. $y = 2v^3 + 2v^{-3} \Rightarrow \frac{dy}{dv} = 6v^2 - 6v^{-4}$

$v = (3x+2)^{2/3} \Rightarrow \frac{dv}{dx} = 2(3x+2)^{-1/3}$

$\frac{dy}{dx} = \frac{dy}{dv}\cdot\frac{dv}{dx} = 2(6v^2 - 6v^{-4})(3x+2)^{-1/3}$

$= 12([(3x+2)^{2/3}]^2 - [(3x+2)^{2/3}]^{-4})(3x+2)^{-1/3}$

$= 12[(3x+2) - (3x+2)^{-3}]$

13. $r = (s + 1)^{\frac{1}{2}} \Rightarrow \frac{dr}{ds} = \frac{1}{2}(s + 1)^{-\frac{1}{2}}.$ $s = 16t^2 - 20t \Rightarrow$

$\frac{ds}{dt} = 32t - 20.$ $\frac{dr}{dt} = \frac{dr}{ds}\cdot\frac{ds}{dt} = \frac{1}{2}(s + 1)^{-\frac{1}{2}}(32t - 20) =$

$(16t^2 - 20t + 1)^{-\frac{1}{2}}(16t - 10)$

14. $a = 7r^3 - 2 \Rightarrow \frac{da}{dr} = 21r^2$ $r = 1 - \frac{1}{b} \Rightarrow \frac{dr}{db} = \frac{1}{b^2}$

$\frac{da}{db} = \frac{da}{dr}\cdot\frac{dr}{db} = 21r^2\left(\frac{1}{b^2}\right) = 21\left(\frac{b-1}{b}\right)^2\left(\frac{1}{b^2}\right) = \frac{21(b-1)^2}{b^4}$

15. $u = t + \frac{1}{t} \Rightarrow \frac{du}{dt} = 1 - t^{-2}$. $t = 1 - \frac{1}{v} \Rightarrow \frac{dt}{dv} = v^{-2}$

$\frac{du}{dv} = \frac{du}{dt} \bullet \frac{dt}{dv} = (1 - t^{-2})(v^{-2}) = \left[1 - (1 - \frac{1}{v})^{-2}\right] v^{-2} =$

$\left[1 - (\frac{v}{v - 1})^{2}\right]\left[\frac{1}{v^2}\right] = \frac{(v - 1)^2 - v^2}{(v - 1)^2} \bullet \frac{1}{v^2} = \frac{1 - 2v}{v^2 (v - 1)^2}$

16. $y = u^5 \Rightarrow \frac{dy}{du} = 5u^4$ $u = 3x^2 - 7x + 5 \Rightarrow \frac{du}{dx} = 6x - 7$

$\frac{dy}{dx} = \frac{dy}{du} \cdot \frac{du}{dx} = 5u^4 (6x - 7) = 5(3x^2 - 7x + 5)^4 (6x - 7)$

17. $y = 3x^{\frac{2}{3}} \Rightarrow \frac{dy}{dx} = 2x^{-\frac{1}{3}}$. $x = 8t^3 \Rightarrow \frac{dx}{dt} = 24t^2$.

$\frac{dy}{dt} = (2x^{-\frac{1}{3}})(24t^2) = 48t^2 [8t^3]^{-\frac{1}{3}} = 24t$. By substitution,

$y = 3(8t^3)^{\frac{2}{3}} = 3(2t)^2 = 12t^2$ and $\frac{dy}{dt} = 24t$.

18. $y = x^2 - 1 \Rightarrow \frac{dy}{dx} = 2x$ $x = \sqrt{t + 1} \Rightarrow \frac{dx}{dt} = \frac{1}{2\sqrt{t + 1}}$

$\frac{dy}{dt} = \frac{dy}{dx} \cdot \frac{dx}{dt} = 2x\left(\frac{1}{2\sqrt{t + 1}}\right) = 2\sqrt{t + 1}\left(\frac{1}{2\sqrt{t + 1}}\right) = 1$.

By substitution, $y = (\sqrt{t + 1})^2 - 1 = t \Rightarrow \frac{dy}{dt} = 1$

19. $y = \frac{1}{x^2 + 1} \Rightarrow \frac{dy}{dx} = -2x(x^2 + 1)^{-2}$. $x = \sqrt{4t - 1} = (4t - 1)^{\frac{1}{2}}$

$\Rightarrow \frac{dx}{dt} = \frac{1}{2}(4t - 1)^{-\frac{1}{2}}(4) = 2(4t - 1)^{-\frac{1}{2}}$.

$\frac{dy}{dt} = \left[-2x(x^2 + 1)^{-2}\right]\left[2(4t - 1)^{-\frac{1}{2}}\right] =$

$= \left[-2\sqrt{4t - 1}(4t - 1 + 1)^{-2}\right]\left[\frac{2}{\sqrt{4t - 1}}\right] =$

$= -4(\frac{1}{16t^2}) = -\frac{1}{4t^2}$. By substitution, $y = \frac{1}{(\sqrt{4t - 1})^2 + 1} =$

$(4t)^{-1}$ and $\frac{dy}{dt} = -(4t)^{-2}(4) = -\frac{1}{4t^2}$.

20. $y = 1 - \frac{1}{x} \Rightarrow \frac{dy}{dx} = \frac{1}{x^2}$ $\quad x = \frac{1}{1-t} \Rightarrow \frac{dx}{dt} = \frac{1}{(1-t)^2}$

$$\frac{dy}{dt} = \frac{dy}{dx} \cdot \frac{dx}{dt} = \frac{1}{x^2}\left(\frac{1}{(1-t)^2}\right) = (1-t)^2 \frac{1}{(1-t)^2} = 1$$

By substitution, $y = 1 - (1-t) = t \Rightarrow \frac{dy}{dt} = 1$

21. $g(x) = x^2 + 1 \Rightarrow g'(x) = 2x.$ $\quad x = f(t) = \sqrt{t+1} \Rightarrow$

$f'(t) = \frac{1}{2}(t+1)^{-\frac{1}{2}}.$ $\quad t = 0 \Rightarrow f(0) = 1$ and $f'(0) = \frac{1}{2}.$

$$\frac{d}{dt}(g \circ f)\bigg|_{x=0} = g'(f(0))f'(0) = g'(1)f'(0) = (2)\left(\frac{1}{2}\right) = 1$$

22. $g(x) = \sqrt{x+5} \Rightarrow g'(x) = \frac{1}{2\sqrt{x+5}}.$ $\quad x = f(t) = 10\sqrt{t} \Rightarrow f'(t) = \frac{5}{\sqrt{t}}$

$t = 4 \Rightarrow f(4) = 20$ and $f'(4) = \frac{5}{2}.$

$$\frac{d}{dt}(g \circ f)\bigg|_{x=4} = g'(f(4))f'(4) = g'(20)f'(4) = \frac{1}{10} \cdot \frac{5}{2} = \frac{1}{4}$$

23. $g(x) = \sqrt{1 + x^3} \Rightarrow g'(x) = \frac{1}{2}(1 + x^3)^{-\frac{1}{2}}(3x^2).$ $\quad x = f(t) = t^{\frac{1}{3}} \Rightarrow$

$f'(t) = \frac{1}{3}t^{-\frac{2}{3}}.$ $\quad t = 1 \Rightarrow f(1) = 1$ and $f'(1) = \frac{1}{3}.$

$$\frac{d}{dt}(g \circ f)\bigg|_{t=1} = g'(f(1))f'(1) = g'(1)f'(1) = \frac{3}{2\sqrt{2}} \bullet \frac{1}{3} = \frac{\sqrt{2}}{4}$$

24. $g(x) = 1 - \frac{1}{x} \Rightarrow g'(x) = \frac{1}{x^2}.$ $\quad x = f(t) = \frac{1}{1-t} \Rightarrow f'(t) = \frac{1}{(1-t)^2}$

$t = -1 \Rightarrow f(-1) = \frac{1}{2}$ and $f'(-1) = \frac{1}{4}$

$$\frac{d}{dt}(g \circ f)\bigg|_{t=-1} = g'(f(-1))f'(-1) = g'\left(\frac{1}{2}\right)f'(-1) = 4\left(\frac{1}{4}\right) = 1$$

25. $g(x) = \frac{2x}{x^2 + 1} \Rightarrow g'(x) = \frac{(x^2 + 1)(2) - 2x(2x)}{(x^2 + 1)^2} = \frac{2 - 2x^2}{(x^2 + 1)^2}$

$x = f(t) = 10t^2 + t + 1 \Rightarrow f'(t) = 20t + 1.$

$$\frac{d}{dt}(g \circ f)|_{t=0} = g'(f(0))f'(0) = g'(1)f'(0) = 0$$

26. $g(x) = \left(\frac{x-1}{x+1}\right)^2 \Rightarrow g'(x) = \frac{4(x-1)}{(x+1)^3}$. $x = f(t) = \frac{1}{t^2} - 1 \Rightarrow f'(t) = -\frac{2}{t^3}$

$t = -1 \Rightarrow f(-1) = 0$ and $f'(-1) = 2$

$$\left.\frac{d}{dt}(g \circ f)\right|_{t=-1} = g'(f(-1))f'(-1) = g'(0)f'(-1) = -8$$

27. $v = k\sqrt{s}$ m/sec $\Rightarrow a = \frac{dv}{dt} = \frac{1}{2}ks^{-\frac{1}{2}}\frac{ds}{dt} = \frac{1}{2}ks^{-\frac{1}{2}} \bullet ks^{\frac{1}{2}} = \frac{1}{2}k^2 = K$

28. Let $h(x) = f(g(x))$, where $f(x) = x^2$ and $g(x) = |x|$. Then $h(x) = (|x|)^2 = x^2$ so $h'(x) = 2x$ and $h'(0) = 0$. Similarly, let $H(x) = g(f(x))$. Then $H(x) = |x^2| = x^2$, $H'(x) = 2x$ and $H'(0) = 0$. The function $g(x) = |x|$ is not differentiable at $x = 0$ and thus does not satisfy the hypothesis of the Chain Rule, and hence does not contradict it.

29. $T = 2\pi\sqrt{\frac{L}{g}} \Rightarrow \frac{dT}{dL} = 2\pi\left[\frac{1}{2}\left(\frac{L}{g}\right)^{-\frac{1}{2}}\frac{1}{g}\right]$. $\frac{dT}{d\theta} = \frac{dT}{dL} \bullet \frac{dL}{d\theta} = \pi\left(\frac{L}{g}\right)^{-\frac{1}{2}}\frac{1}{g}KL = \pi K\sqrt{\frac{L}{g}} = \frac{KT}{2}$

30. (a) $T = 2\pi\left(\frac{L}{g}\right)^{1/2} \Rightarrow dT = 2\pi\sqrt{L}\left(-\frac{1}{2}g^{-3/2}\right)dg = -\pi\sqrt{L}\,g^{-3/2}\,dg$

(b) If g increases, then $dg > 0 \Rightarrow dT < 0$. Then both the pendulum speed and clock speed increase.

(c) $0.001 = -\pi\sqrt{100}\,(980^{-3/2})\,dg \Rightarrow dg = -0.976$ cm/sec^2.

2.6 A BRIEF REVIEW OF TRIGONOMETRY

1. $y = 2\sin x$ 2. $y = 5\sin 2x$

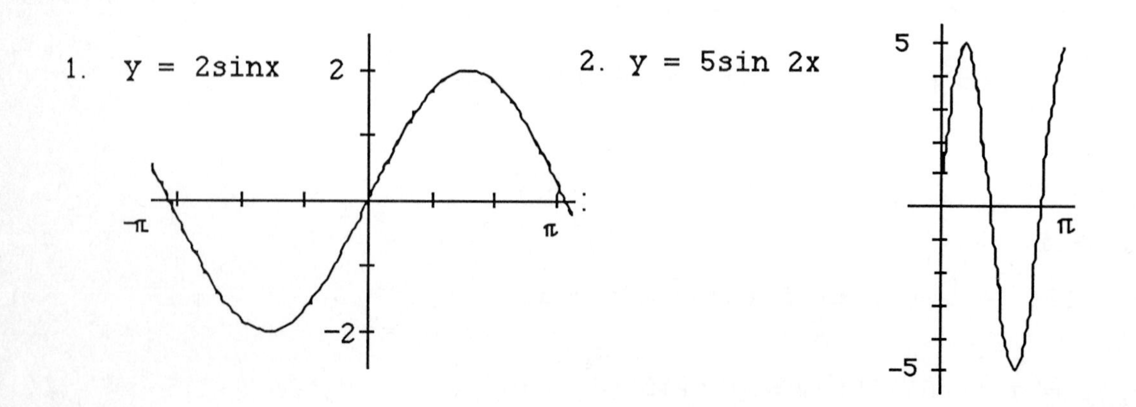

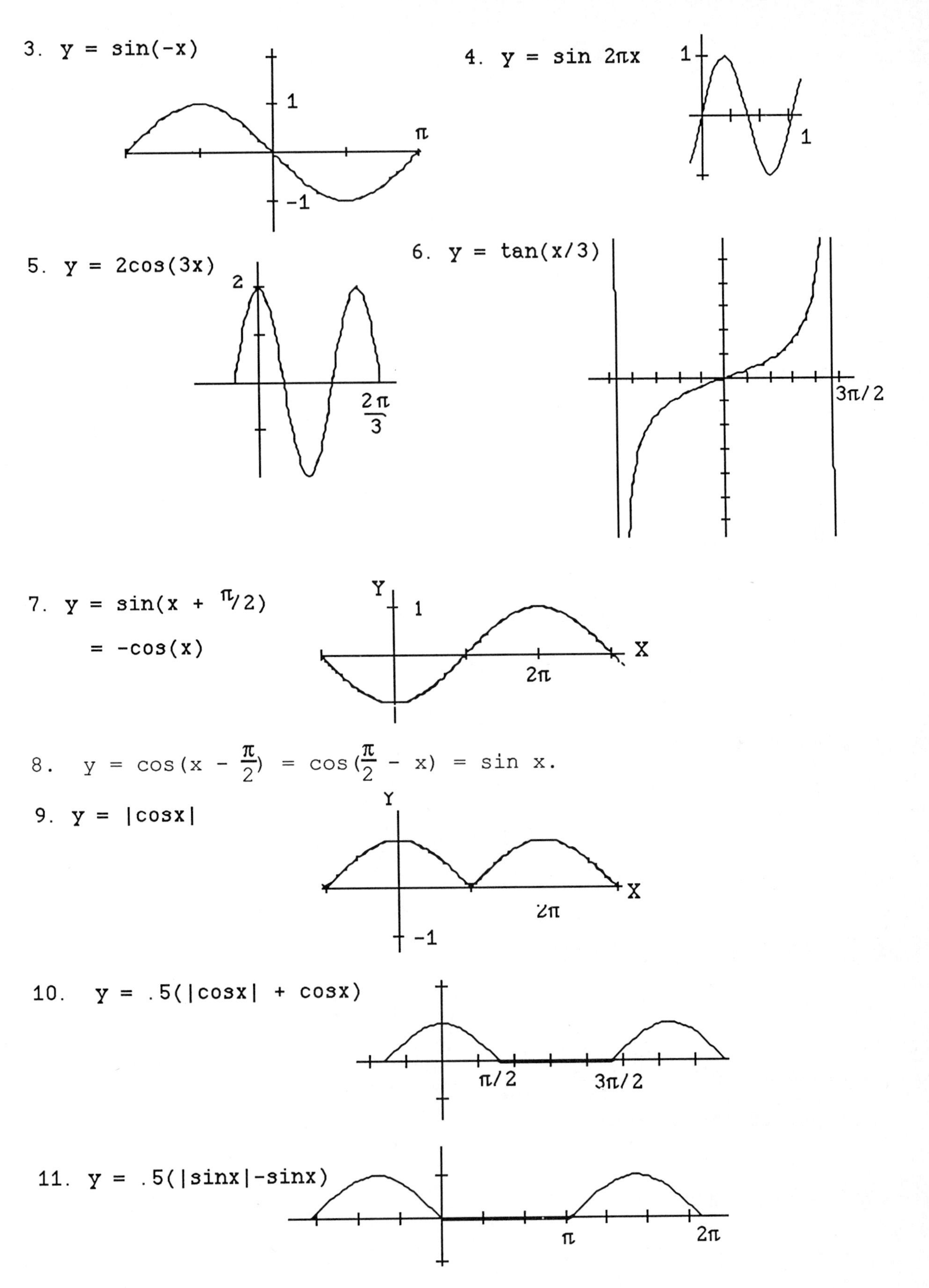

3. y = sin(-x)
1
π
-1
4. y = sin 2πx
1
1
5. y = 2cos(3x)
2
2π/3
6. y = tan(x/3)
3π/2
7. y = sin(x + π/2)
= -cos(x)
Y
1
X
2π
8. y = cos(x - π/2) = cos(π/2 - x) = sin x.
9. y = |cosx|
Y
X
2π
-1
10. y = .5(|cosx| + cosx)
π/2
3π/2
11. y = .5(|sinx|-sinx)
π
2π

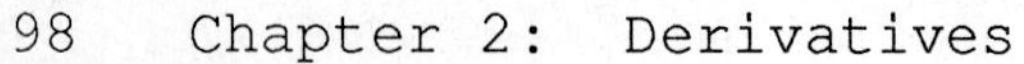

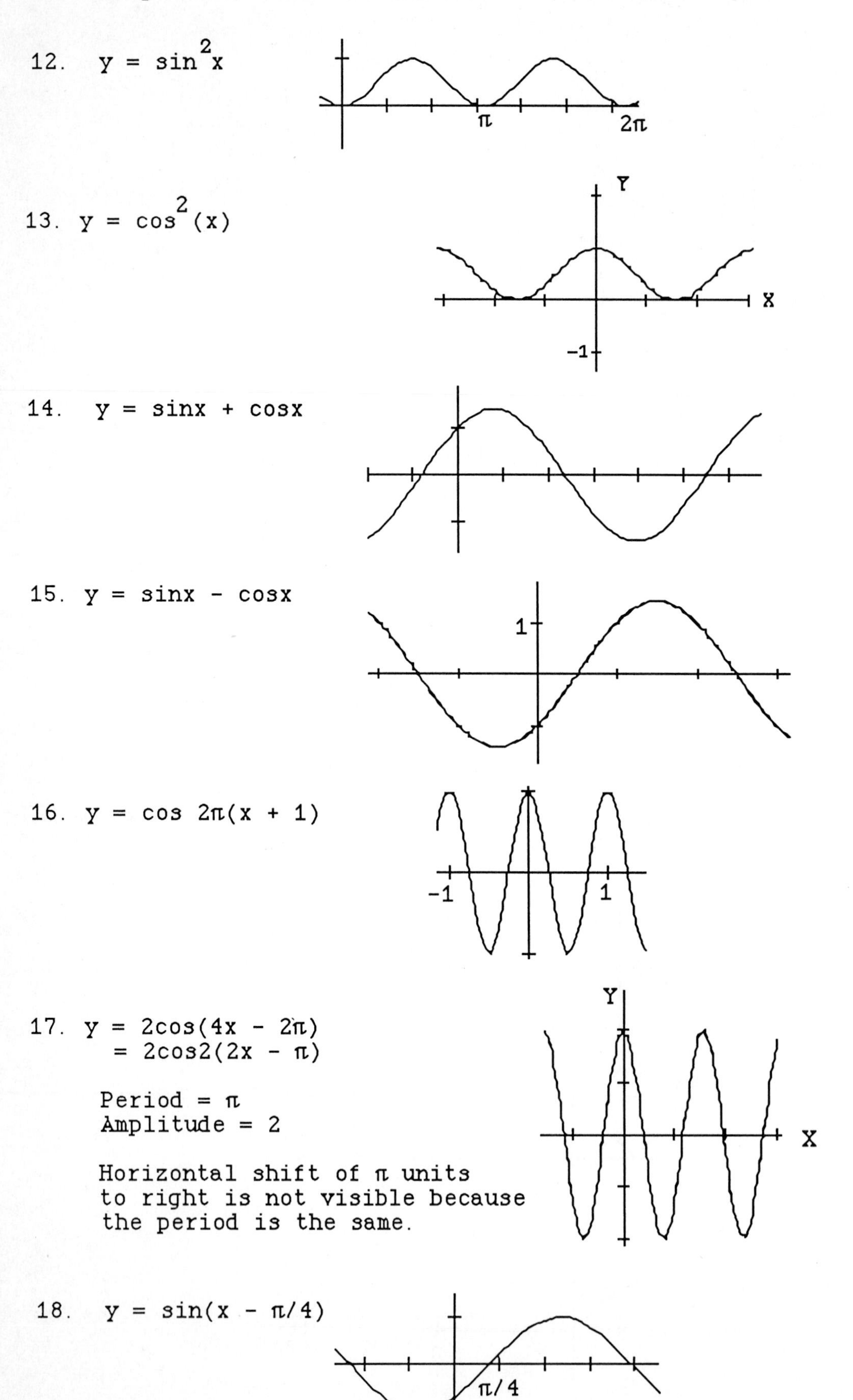

12. $y = \sin^2 x$

13. $y = \cos^2(x)$

14. $y = \sin x + \cos x$

15. $y = \sin x - \cos x$

16. $y = \cos 2\pi(x + 1)$

17. $y = 2\cos(4x - 2\pi)$
$= 2\cos 2(2x - \pi)$

Period = π
Amplitude = 2

Horizontal shift of π units to right is not visible because the period is the same.

18. $y = \sin(x - \pi/4)$

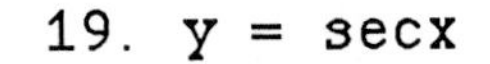

19. $y = \sec x$

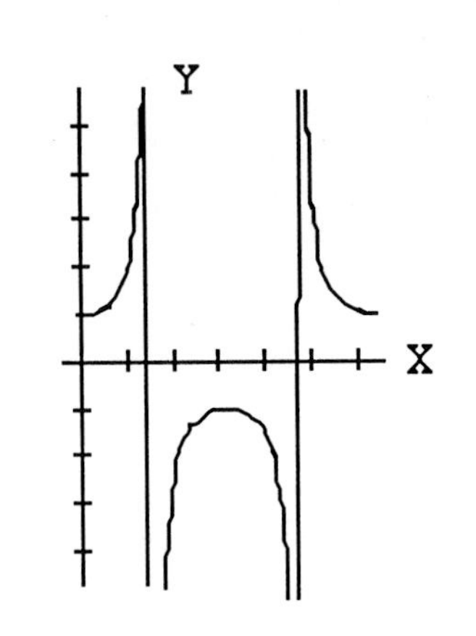

20.

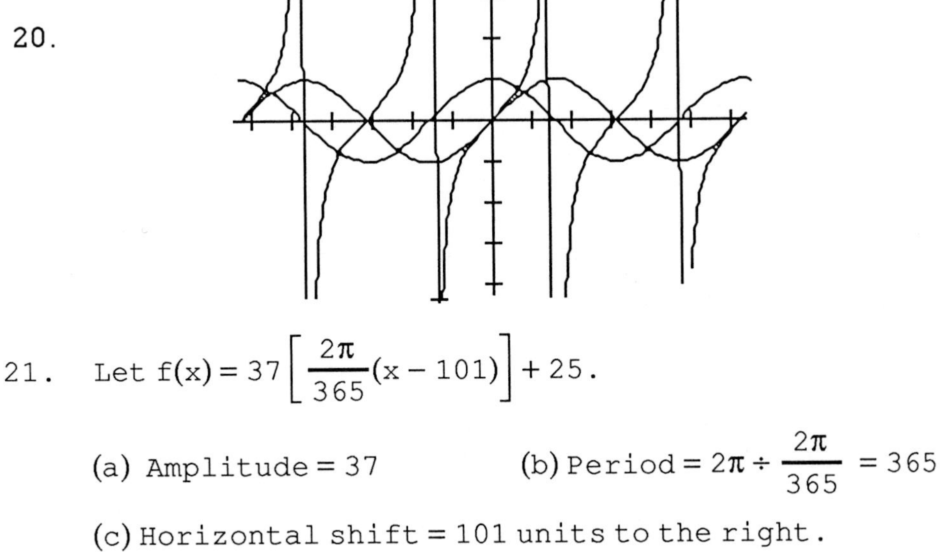

21. Let $f(x) = 37\left[\frac{2\pi}{365}(x - 101)\right] + 25.$

(a) Amplitude $= 37$ (b) Period $= 2\pi \div \frac{2\pi}{365} = 365$

(c) Horizontal shift $= 101$ units to the right.

(d) Vertical shift $= 25$ units upward.

22. (a) $(37 + 25)^\circ = 62^\circ$
(b) $(-37 + 25)^\circ = -12^\circ$

(c) 25°; if A = amplitude and V = vertical shift, the the maximum = V + A and the minimum = V - A, so the average is $\frac{1}{2}(V + A + V - A) = V$.

23. $$\lim_{h\to 0} \frac{(\sin h)(1 - \cos h)}{h^2} = \lim_{h\to 0} \frac{\sin h}{h} \bullet \frac{1 - \cos h}{h} = (1)(0) = 0$$

24. $$\lim_{x\to 0} \frac{1 - \cos x}{x^2} \cdot \frac{1 + \cos x}{1 + \cos x} = \lim_{x\to 0} \frac{\sin^2 x}{x^2 (1 + \cos x)} = \lim_{x\to 0} \left(\frac{\sin x}{x}\right)^2 \left(\frac{1}{1 + \cos x}\right) = \frac{1}{2}$$

25. $\lim_{x\to 0} \frac{1 - \cos x}{\sin x} = \lim_{x\to 0} \frac{x}{x} \cdot \frac{1-\cos x}{\sin x} = \lim_{x\to 0} \frac{1-\cos x}{x} \cdot \frac{x}{\sin x} = 0$

26. $\lim_{x\to 0} x \cot x = \lim_{x\to 0} (\cos x)\left(\frac{x}{\sin x}\right) = 1$

27. In the formula (11d), let B = A. We then have

$\cos(A-A) = \cos A \cos A + \sin A \sin A$ or $\cos^2 A + \sin^2 A = \cos 0 = 1.$

28. cos x and sec x are even, the rest are odd.

29. $\sin(x-\frac{\pi}{2}) = (\sin x)(\cos\frac{\pi}{2}) - (\cos x)(\sin\frac{\pi}{2}) = (\sin x)(0) - (\cos x)(1) = -\cos x$

30. $\sin\left(x+\frac{\pi}{2}\right) = \sin x \cos\frac{\pi}{2} + \cos x \sin\frac{\pi}{2} = \sin x(0) + \cos x(1) = \cos x$

31. $\cos(x-\frac{\pi}{2}) = (\cos x)(\cos\frac{\pi}{2}) + (\sin x)(\sin\frac{\pi}{2}) = (\cos x)(0) + (\sin x)(1) = \sin x$

32. $\cos\left(x+\frac{\pi}{2}\right) = \cos x \cos\frac{\pi}{2} - \sin x \sin\frac{\pi}{2} = \cos x(0) - \sin x(1) = -\sin x$

33. $\sin(\pi-x) = (\sin\pi)(\cos x) - (\cos\pi)(\sin x) = (0)(\cos x) - (-1)(\sin x) = \sin x$

34. $\cos(\pi - x) = \cos\pi \cos x - \sin\pi \sin x = \cos x(-1) - \sin x(0) = -\cos x$

35. $\tan(A+B) = \frac{\sin(A+B)}{\cos(A+B)} = \frac{\sin A\cos B + \cos A\sin B}{\cos A\cos B - \sin A\sin B} \cdot \frac{\frac{1}{\cos A\cos B}}{\frac{1}{\cos A\cos B}}$

$$\frac{\frac{\sin A\cos B}{\cos A\cos B} + \frac{\cos A\sin B}{\cos A\cos B}}{\frac{\cos A\cos B}{\cos A\cos B} - \frac{\sin A\sin B}{\cos A\cos B}} = \frac{\tan A + \tan B}{1 - \tan A\tan B}$$

$$\tan(A-B) = \tan(A+(-B)) = \frac{\tan A + \tan(-B)}{1 - \tan A\tan(-B)} = \frac{\tan A - \tan B}{1 + \tan A\tan B}$$

2.7 DERIVATIVES OF TRIGONOMETRIC FUNCTIONS

1. $y = \sin(x + 1) \Rightarrow y' = \cos(x + 1)$
2. $y = -\cos x \Rightarrow y' = \sin x$
3. $y = \sin(\frac{x}{2}) \Rightarrow y' = \frac{1}{2}\cos(\frac{x}{2})$
4. $y = \sin(-x) = -\sin x \Rightarrow y' = -\cos x$
5. $y = \cos 5x \Rightarrow y' = -5\sin 5x$
6. $y = \cos(-x) = \cos x \Rightarrow y' = -\sin x$
7. $y = \cos(-2x) = \cos(2x) \Rightarrow y' = -\sin(2x)(2) = -2\sin(2x)$
8. $y = \sin 7x \Rightarrow y' = 7\cos 7x$
9. $y = \sin(3x + 4) \Rightarrow y' = 3\cos(3x + 4)$
10. $y = \cos(2-x) \Rightarrow y' = -\sin(2-x)(-1) = \sin(2-x)$

11. $y = x\sin x \Rightarrow y' = x\cos x + \sin x$

12. $y = \sin 5(x-1) \Rightarrow y' = 5\cos 5(x-1)$

13. $y = x\sin x + \cos x \Rightarrow y' = x\cos x + \sin x - \sin x = x\cos x$

14. $y = \dfrac{1}{\sin x} = \csc x \Rightarrow y' = -\cot x\csc x$

15. $y = \dfrac{1}{\cos x} = \sec x \Rightarrow y' = \sec x\tan x$

16. $y = \dfrac{\sin x}{\cos x} = \tan x \Rightarrow y' = \sec^2 x$

17. $y = \sec(x - 1) \Rightarrow y' = \sec(x - 1)\tan(x - 1)$

18. $y = \cot x \Rightarrow y' = -\csc^2 x$

19. $y = \sec(1 - x) \Rightarrow y' = -\sec(1 - x)\tan(1 - x)$

20. $y = \dfrac{2}{\cos 3x} = 2\sec 3x \Rightarrow y' = 6\sec 3x\tan 3x$

21. $y = \tan 2x \Rightarrow y' = 2\sec^2 2x$

22. $y = \cos(ax + b) \Rightarrow y' = -a\sin(ax + b)$

23. $y = \sin^2 x \Rightarrow y' = 2\sin x\cos x = \sin 2x$

24. $y = \sin^2 x + \cos^2 x = 1 \Rightarrow y' = 0$

25. $y = \cos^2 5x \Rightarrow y' = 2\cos 5x(-\sin 5x)(5) = -10\cos 5x\sin 5x = -5\sin 10x$

26. $y = \cot^2 x \Rightarrow y' = 2\cot x(-\csc^2 x) = -2\cot x\csc^2 x$

27. $y = \tan(5x - 1) \Rightarrow y' = 5\sec^2(5x - 1)$

28. $y = \sin x - x\cos x \Rightarrow y' = \cos x - \cos x + x\sin x = x\sin x$

29. $y = 2\sin x\cos x = \sin 2x \Rightarrow y' = 2\cos 2x$

30. $y = \sec(x^2 + 1) \Rightarrow y' = 2x\sec(x^2 + 1)\tan(x^2 + 1)$

31. $y = \sqrt{2 + \cos 2x} \Rightarrow y' = \dfrac{1}{2}(2 + \cos 2x)^{-1/2}(-2\sin 2x) = \dfrac{-\sin 2x}{\sqrt{2 + \cos 2x}}$

32. $y = \sin(1-x^2) \Rightarrow y' = -2x\cos(1-x^2)$

33. $y = \cos\sqrt{x} \Rightarrow \dfrac{dy}{dx} = -\sin\sqrt{x}\left(\dfrac{1}{2}x^{-1/2}\right) = -\dfrac{\sin\sqrt{x}}{2\sqrt{x}}$

34. $y = \sec^2 x - \tan^2 x = 1 \Rightarrow y' = 0$

35. $y = \sqrt{\dfrac{1 + \cos 2x}{2}} = \sqrt{\cos^2 x} = |\cos x| \Rightarrow \dfrac{dy}{dx} = -\sin x$ if $\cos x > 0$

and $\sin x$ if $\cos x < 0$.

36. $y = \sin^2(x^2) \Rightarrow y' = 4x\sin(x^2)\cos(x^2)$

37. $x = \tan y \Rightarrow 1 = \sec^2 y\dfrac{dy}{dx} \Rightarrow \dfrac{dy}{dx} = \dfrac{1}{\sec^2 y} = \cos^2 y$

38. $x = \sin y \Rightarrow 1 = \cos y\dfrac{dy}{dx} \Rightarrow \dfrac{dy}{dx} = \dfrac{1}{\cos y} = \sec y = \sec(\sin^{-1} x) = \dfrac{1}{\sqrt{1 - x^2}}$

39. $y^2 = \sin^4 2x + \cos^4 2x \Rightarrow$

$$2y\frac{dy}{dx} = 4(\sin^3 2x)(\cos 2x)(2) + 4(\cos^3 2x)(-\sin 2x)(2)$$

$$= 8\sin 2x\cos 2x(\sin^2 2x - \cos^2 2x) = 4\sin 4x(-\cos 4x) = -2\sin 8x$$

$$\frac{dy}{dx} = -\frac{\sin 8x}{y}$$

40. $x + \sin y = xy \Rightarrow 1 + \cos y\frac{dy}{dx} = x\frac{dy}{dx} + y$

$$(\cos y - x)\frac{dy}{dx} = y - 1 \quad \text{or} \quad \frac{dy}{dx} = \frac{y-1}{\cos y - x}$$

41. $x + \tan(xy) = 0 \Rightarrow 1 + \sec^2(xy)\left[y + x\frac{dy}{dx}\right] = 0$

$$1 + y\sec^2(xy) = -x\sec^2(xy)\frac{dy}{dx}$$

$$\frac{dy}{dx} = \frac{-(1 + y\sec^2(xy))}{x\sec^2(xy)}$$

or $\frac{dy}{dx} = -\frac{1}{x}\left[\cos^2(xy) + y\right]$

42. $2xy + \pi\sin y = 2\pi \Rightarrow 2x\frac{dy}{dx} + 2y + \pi\cos y\frac{dy}{dx} = 0$. When $x = 1$ and $y = \frac{\pi}{2}$,

$$2(1)\frac{dy}{dx} + 2\left(\frac{\pi}{2}\right) + \pi\cos\frac{\pi}{2}\frac{dy}{dx} = 0 \Rightarrow \frac{dy}{dx} = -\frac{\pi}{2}.$$

43. $x\sin 2y = y\cos 2x \Rightarrow 2x\cos 2y\frac{dy}{dx} + \sin 2y = -2y\sin 2x + \cos 2x\frac{dy}{dx}$

Evaluating at $(\frac{\pi}{4}, \frac{\pi}{2})$:

$$2(\frac{\pi}{4})(\cos\pi)\frac{dy}{dx} + \sin\pi = -2(\frac{\pi}{2})\sin\frac{\pi}{2} + (\cos\frac{\pi}{2})\frac{dy}{dx}$$

$$-\frac{\pi}{2}\frac{dy}{dx} = -\pi \Rightarrow \frac{dy}{dx} = 2$$

$y - \frac{\pi}{2} = 2(x - \frac{\pi}{4}) \Rightarrow y = 2x$ is the equation of the tangent.

44. $\lim_{x\to 2}\sin\left(\frac{1}{x} - \frac{1}{2}\right) = 0$

45. $\lim_{x\to\frac{\pi}{4}}\frac{\sin x}{\cos x} = \lim_{x\to\frac{\pi}{4}}\tan x = 1$

46. $\lim_{x\to-\pi}\cos^2 x = (-1)^2 = 1$

47. $\lim_{x\to\pi}\sec(1 + \cos x) = \sec(1 - 1) = \sec 0 = 1$

48. $\lim_{x\to 0}(\sec x + \tan x) = 1 + 0 = 1$

49. $\lim_{x\to 0}x\csc x = \lim_{x\to 0}\frac{x}{\sin x} = 1$

50. $\lim_{h\to 0}\frac{\sin(a+h) - \sin a}{h} = f'(a)$ where $f(x) = \sin x$. $\therefore f'(a) = \cos a$.

51. $\lim_{h \to 0} \dfrac{\cos(a+h) - \cos a}{h} = \dfrac{d}{dx}(\cos x)\Big|_{x=a} = -\sin a$

52. $y = \sin mx \Rightarrow y' = m \cos mx$. $y(0) = 0$ and $y'(0) = m$.

$y - 0 = m(x - 0)$ or $y = mx$.

53. $y = \tan x$ and the linearization $L(x) = x$.

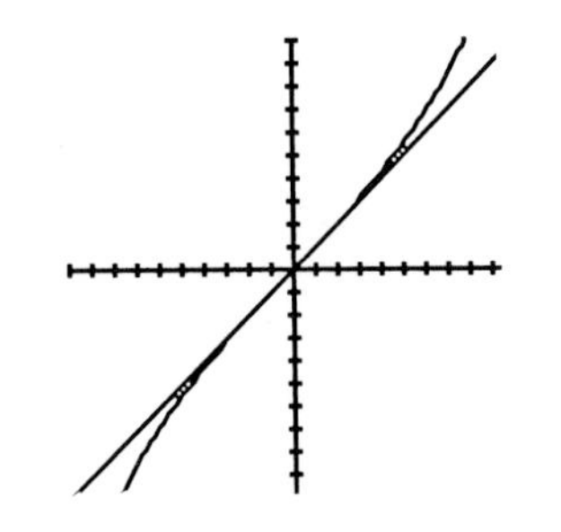

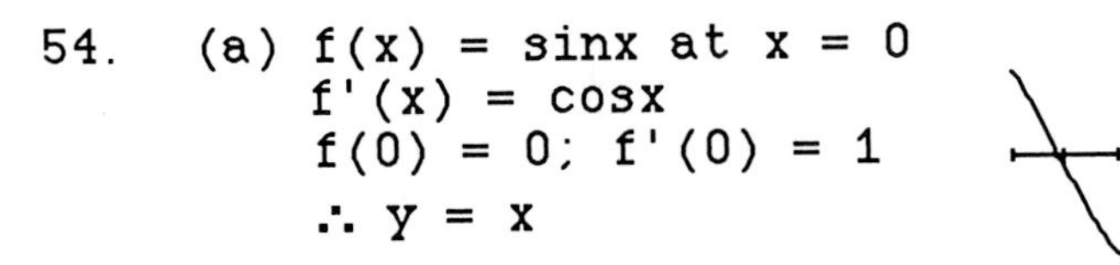

54. (a) $f(x) = \sin x$ at $x = 0$

$f'(x) = \cos x$

$f(0) = 0$; $f'(0) = 1$

$\therefore y = x$

(b) $f(x) = \sin x$ at $x = \pi$

$f(\pi) = 0$; $f'(\pi) = -1$

$\therefore y = -1(x-\pi) = \pi - x$

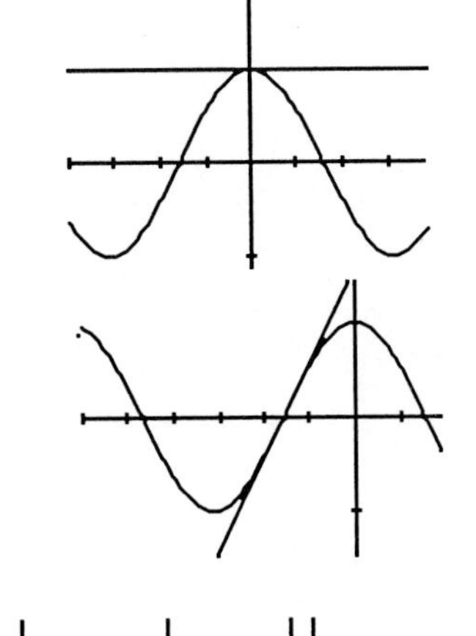

(c) $f(x) = \cos x$ at $x = 0$

$f'(x) = -\sin x$; $f(0) = 1$

$f'(0) = 0$

$\therefore y = 1$

(d) $f(x) = \cos x$ at $x = -\frac{\pi}{2}$

$f(-\frac{\pi}{2}) = 0$; $f'(-\frac{\pi}{2}) = 1$

$\therefore y = x + \frac{\pi}{2}$

(e) $f(x) = \tan x$ at $x = \frac{\pi}{4}$

$f'(x) = \sec^2 x$

$f(\frac{\pi}{4}) = 1$; $f'(\frac{\pi}{4}) = 2$

$y = 1 - \frac{\pi}{2} + 2x$

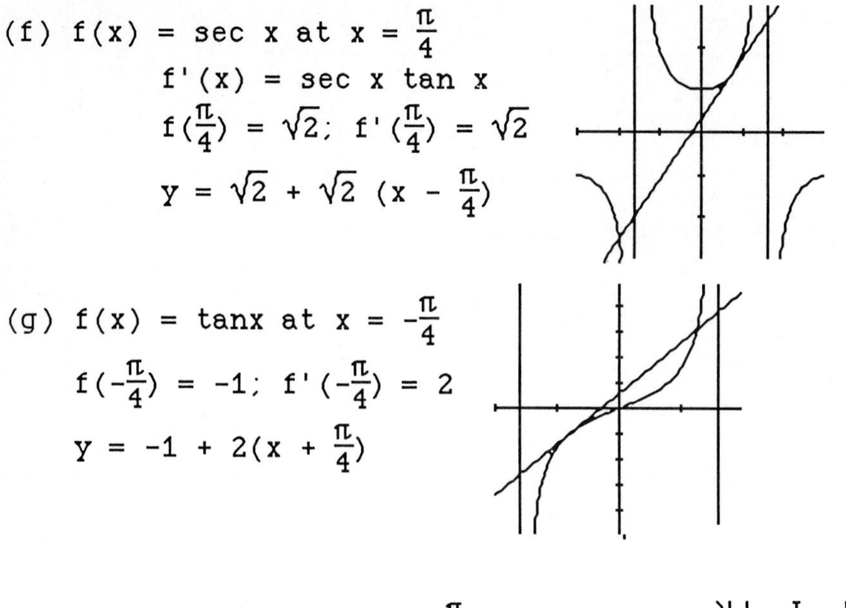

(f) $f(x) = \sec x$ at $x = \frac{\pi}{4}$

$f'(x) = \sec x \tan x$

$f(\frac{\pi}{4}) = \sqrt{2}$; $f'(\frac{\pi}{4}) = \sqrt{2}$

$y = \sqrt{2} + \sqrt{2}\,(x - \frac{\pi}{4})$

(g) $f(x) = \tan x$ at $x = -\frac{\pi}{4}$

$f(-\frac{\pi}{4}) = -1$; $f'(-\frac{\pi}{4}) = 2$

$y = -1 + 2(x + \frac{\pi}{4})$

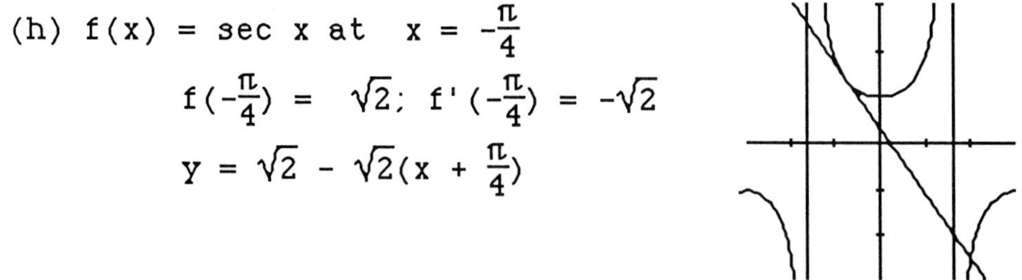

(h) $f(x) = \sec x$ at $x = -\frac{\pi}{4}$

$f(-\frac{\pi}{4}) = \sqrt{2}$; $f'(-\frac{\pi}{4}) = -\sqrt{2}$

$y = \sqrt{2} - \sqrt{2}(x + \frac{\pi}{4})$

55. If $b = 1$, then the left and right hand limits of $f(x)$ at $x=0$ both exist and equal 1. Since $f(0)=1$, the function is continuous at $x = 0$.

56. (a) $\tan\theta = x$

(b) $\sec^2\theta \frac{d\theta}{dt} = \frac{dx}{dt} \Rightarrow \left(-\frac{3}{5}\right)\sec^2\theta = \frac{dx}{dt}$

(c) $\frac{dx}{dt} = \left(-\frac{3}{5}\right)(\sec 0)^2 = -\frac{3}{5}$

(d) $.6$ rad/sec $= 36$ rad/min $= \frac{36}{2\pi} = \frac{18}{\pi}$ rev/min

57. $f(x) = \sqrt{1 + x} + \sin x \Rightarrow f'(x) = \frac{1}{2}(1 + x)^{-\frac{1}{2}} + \cos x.$

$f(x) \approx L(0) = f(0) + f'(0)x = 1 + \frac{3}{2}x.$

$\sqrt{1 + x} \approx L_1(0) = 1 + \frac{1}{2}x$ and $\sin x \approx L_2(0) = x$

Observe that $L(0) = L_1(0) + L_2(0)$.

58. (a) Let $f(x) = 2\cos x - \sqrt{1+x}$. Then $f(0) = 2 - 1 > 0$ and

$f\left(\frac{\pi}{2}\right) = -\sqrt{1+\frac{\pi}{2}} < 0$, so there is $0 < x < \frac{\pi}{2}$ for which $f(x) = 0$

by the Intermediate Value Theorem.

(b) $\cos x \approx \cos\left(\frac{\pi}{4}\right) - \sin\left(\frac{\pi}{4}\right)\left(x - \frac{\pi}{4}\right) = -\frac{1}{\sqrt{2}}x + \frac{1}{\sqrt{2}}\left(\frac{\pi}{4} + 1\right)$

$\sqrt{1+x} \approx \sqrt{1+.69} + \frac{1}{\sqrt{1+.69}}(x - .69) = 1.3 + \frac{1}{2.6}(x - .69)$

(c) $2\left[-\frac{1}{\sqrt{2}}x + \frac{1}{\sqrt{2}}\left(\frac{\pi}{4} + 1\right)\right] = 1.3 + \frac{1}{2.6}(x - .69)$

$\left(-\sqrt{2} - \frac{1}{2.6}\right)x = -\sqrt{2}\left(\frac{\pi}{4} + 1\right) + 1.3 - \frac{0.69}{2.6}$

$-1.79883\,x = -1.49032 \Rightarrow x \approx 0.8285$

Checking, $f(0.8285) \approx 0.0034$

59. $\frac{d}{dx}(\sec u) = \frac{d}{dx}\left(\frac{1}{\cos u}\right) = \frac{-(-\sin u)}{\cos^2 u}\cdot\frac{du}{dx} = \tan u \sec u\cdot\frac{du}{dx}$

60. $\frac{d}{dx}(\csc u) = \frac{d}{dx}\left(\frac{1}{\sin u}\right) = \frac{-\cos u}{\sin^2 u}\cdot\frac{du}{dx} = -\csc u \cot u\cdot\frac{du}{dx}$

61. $\frac{d}{dx}(\cot u) = \frac{d}{dx}\left(\frac{\cos u}{\sin u}\right) = \frac{\sin u(-\sin u) - \cos u(\cos u)}{\sin^2 u}\cdot\frac{du}{dx}$

$= -\frac{\sin^2 u + \cos^2 u}{\sin^2 u}\cdot\frac{du}{dx} = -\frac{1}{\sin^2 u}\cdot\frac{du}{dx} = -\csc^2 u\cdot\frac{du}{dx}$

2.8 PARAMETRIC EQUATIONS

1. $x = \cos t$, $y = \sin t$, $0 \le t \le 2\pi$. The path is the unit circle, since $x^2 = \cos^2 t$, $y^2 = \sin^2 t \Rightarrow x^2 + y^2 = \cos^2 t + \sin^2 t = 1$. The particle begins at the point $P(\cos 0, \sin 0) = P(1,0)$ and travels in a counterclockwise direction to end at the point $Q(\cos 2\pi, \sin 2\pi) = Q(1,0) = P(1,0)$.

2. $x = \cos t$, $y = \sin t$, $0 \le t \le \pi$. The path is the top half of the unit circle. The particle begins at $P(1,0)$ and travels in a counterclockwise direction to point $Q(-1,0)$.

3. $x = \cos 2\pi t$, $y = \sin 2\pi t$, $0 \le t \le 1$, is the same path as that of problem 1 above.

4. $x = \cos(\pi - t)$, $y = \sin(\pi - t)$, $0 \le t \le \pi$. The path is the top half of the unit circle traversed in a clockwise direction from P(-1,0) to Q(1,0).

5. $x = 3\cos t$, $y = 3\sin t$, $0 \le t \le 2\pi$, is a circle with center at the origin and radius 3, since

$x^2 + y^2 = 9\cos^2 t + 9\sin^2 t = 9$. The particle starts and stops at the point P(3,0) and travels in a counterclockwise direction.

6. $x = \cos t$, $y = -\sin t$, $0 \le t \le 2\pi$. The path is the entire unit circle traversed in a clockwise direction, begininng and ending at the point P(1,0).

7. $x = \cos^2 t$, $y = \sin^2 t$, $0 \le t \le \frac{\pi}{2}$. Since $x + y = 1$, the particle travels along a line, starting at P(1,0) and stopping at Q(0,1), in the direction from P to Q.

8. $x = \tan^2 t$, $y = \sec^2 t$, $-\frac{\pi}{3} \le t \le \frac{\pi}{3}$. Since $\tan^2 t + 1 = \sec^2 t$, the path is part of the line $y = x + 1$. The path begins at the point P(3,4), travels towards Q(1,0) and back to the point P(3,4).

9. (a) clockwise: $x = 2\cos t$, $y = -2\sin t$, $0 \le t \le 2\pi$

(b) counterclockwise: $x = 2\cos t$, $y = 2\sin t$, $0 \le t \le 2\pi$

10. (a) For the domain $0 \le t \le \pi$:

clockwise: $x = 2\cos 2t$, $y = -2\sin 2t$

counterclockwise: $x = 2\cos 2t$, $y = 2\sin 2t$

(b) For the domain $0 \le t \le 1$:

clockwise: $x = 2\cos 2\pi t$, $y = -2\sin 2\pi t$

counterclockwise: $x = 2\cos 2\pi t$, $y = 2\sin 2\pi t$.

11. $x = 2t - 5 \Rightarrow t = \frac{x+5}{2}$

$y = 4t - 7 = 4\left(\frac{x+5}{2}\right) - 7$

$= 2x + 3$

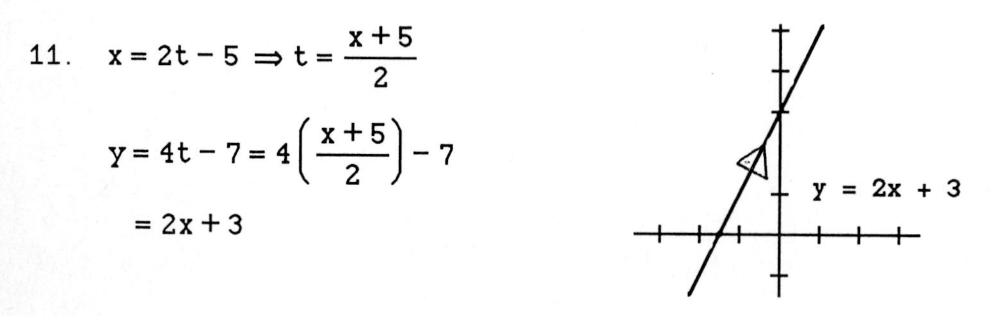

12. $x = 1 - t \Rightarrow t = 1 - x$

$y = 1 + t = 1 + 1 - x$

$= 2 - x$

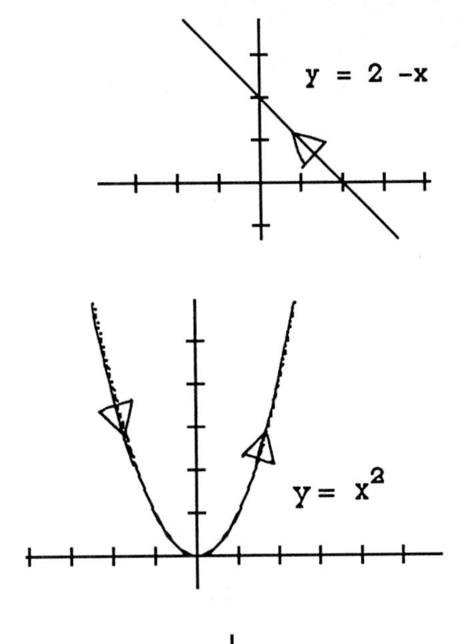

13. $x = 3t,\ y = 9t^2 \Rightarrow$

$y = (3t)^2 = x^2$

14. $x = t,\ y = \sqrt{1 - t^2}$

$y = \sqrt{1 - x^2},\ -1 \le x \le 1$

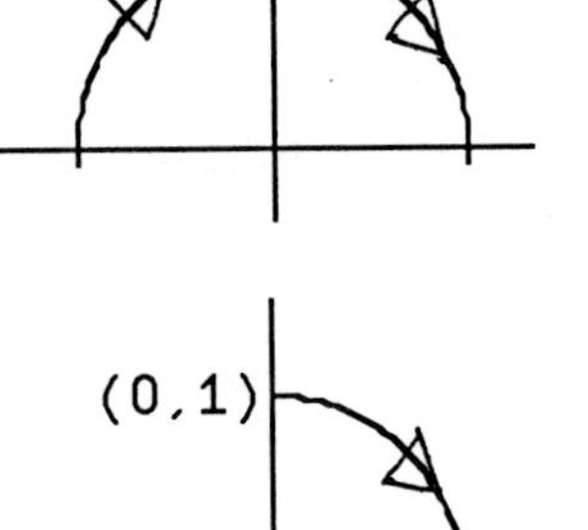

15. $x = t,\ y = \sqrt{1 - t^2} \Rightarrow$

$y = \sqrt{1 - x^2}$.

(0,1)

(1,0)

16. $x = -\sqrt{t},\ y = t = -\sqrt{x}$

$y = x^2,\ x \le 0$

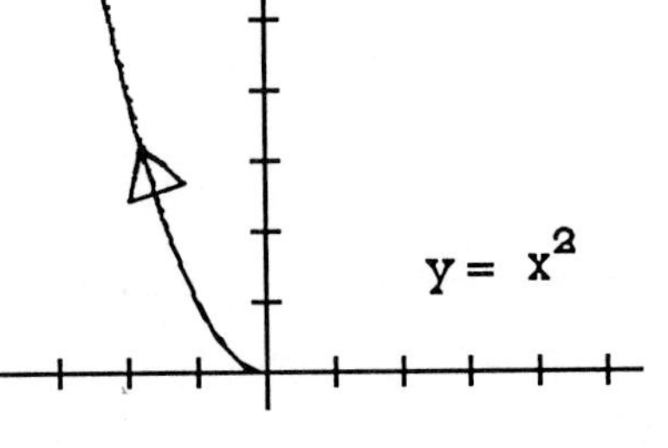

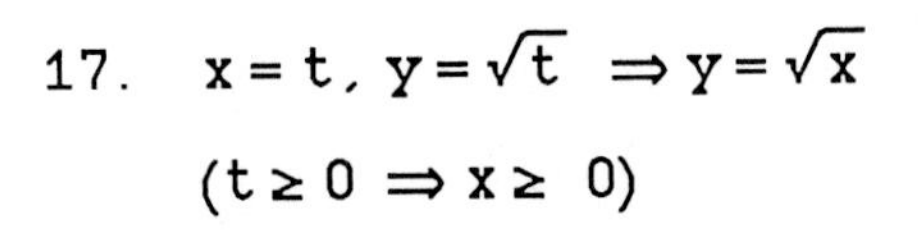

17. $x = t,\ y = \sqrt{t} \Rightarrow y = \sqrt{x}$

$(t \ge 0 \Rightarrow x \ge 0)$

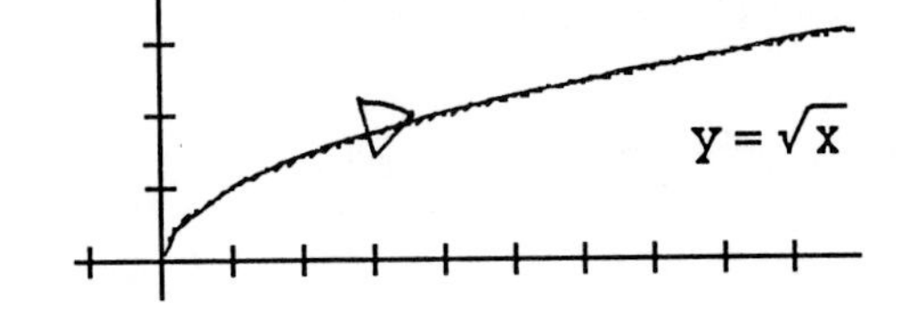

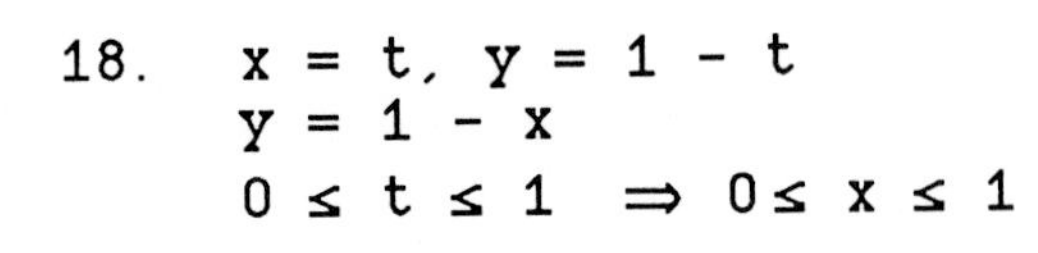

18. $x = t,\ y = 1 - t$

$y = 1 - x$

$0 \le t \le 1 \Rightarrow 0 \le x \le 1$

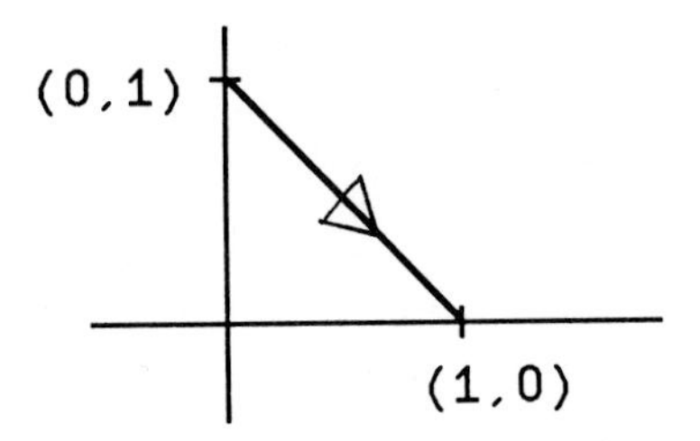

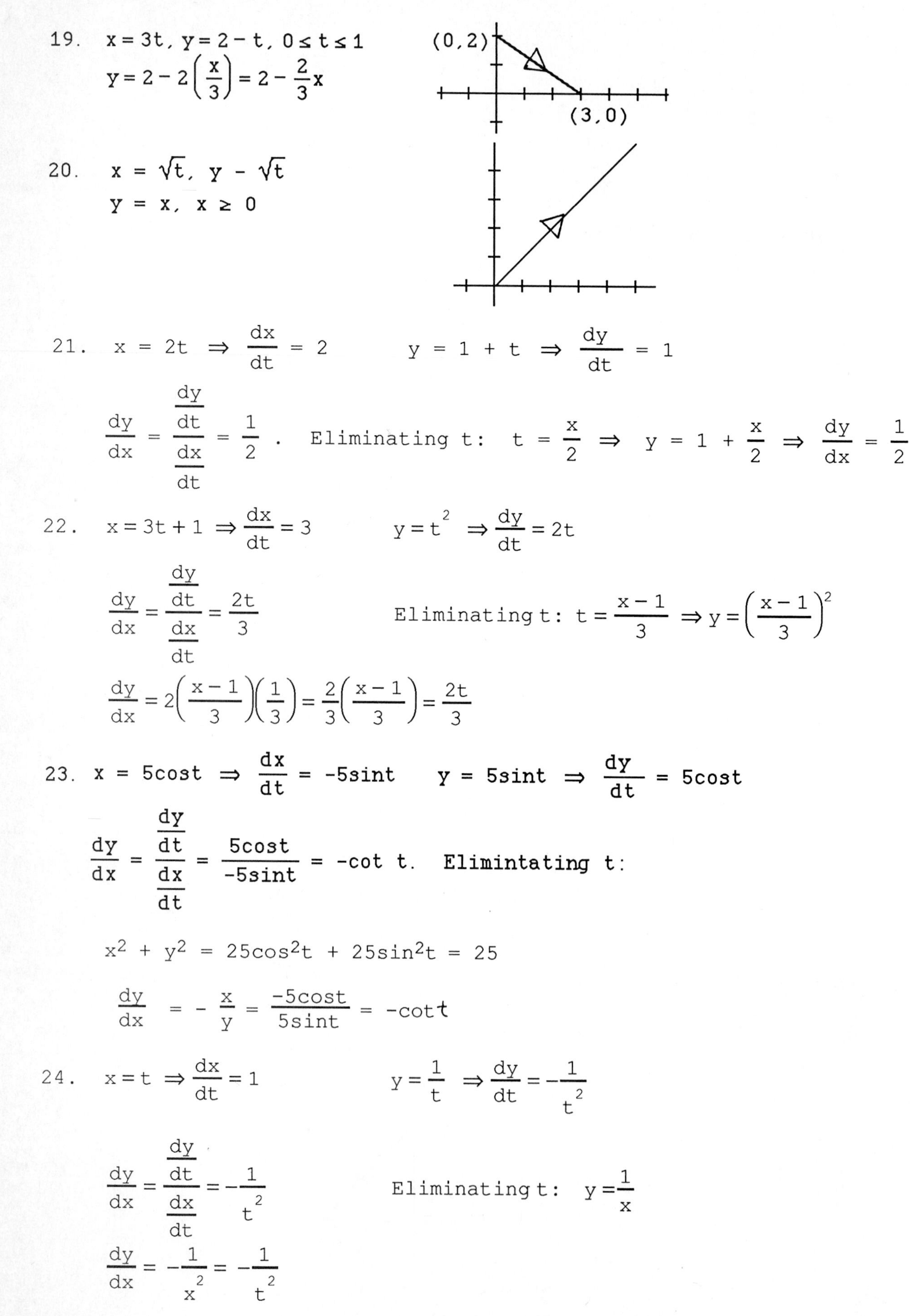

19. $x = 3t,\ y = 2 - t,\ 0 \le t \le 1$

$$y = 2 - 2\left(\frac{x}{3}\right) = 2 - \frac{2}{3}x$$

20. $x = \sqrt{t},\ y - \sqrt{t}$

$y = x,\ x \ge 0$

21. $x = 2t \Rightarrow \frac{dx}{dt} = 2 \qquad y = 1 + t \Rightarrow \frac{dy}{dt} = 1$

$$\frac{dy}{dx} = \frac{\frac{dy}{dt}}{\frac{dx}{dt}} = \frac{1}{2}.$$ Eliminating t: $t = \frac{x}{2} \Rightarrow y = 1 + \frac{x}{2} \Rightarrow \frac{dy}{dx} = \frac{1}{2}$

22. $x = 3t + 1 \Rightarrow \frac{dx}{dt} = 3 \qquad y = t^2 \Rightarrow \frac{dy}{dt} = 2t$

$$\frac{dy}{dx} = \frac{\frac{dy}{dt}}{\frac{dx}{dt}} = \frac{2t}{3}$$ Eliminating t: $t = \frac{x-1}{3} \Rightarrow y = \left(\frac{x-1}{3}\right)^2$

$$\frac{dy}{dx} = 2\left(\frac{x-1}{3}\right)\left(\frac{1}{3}\right) = \frac{2}{3}\left(\frac{x-1}{3}\right) = \frac{2t}{3}$$

23. $x = 5\cos t \Rightarrow \frac{dx}{dt} = -5\sin t \qquad y = 5\sin t \Rightarrow \frac{dy}{dt} = 5\cos t$

$$\frac{dy}{dx} = \frac{\frac{dy}{dt}}{\frac{dx}{dt}} = \frac{5\cos t}{-5\sin t} = -\cot t.$$ Elimintating t:

$$x^2 + y^2 = 25\cos^2 t + 25\sin^2 t = 25$$

$$\frac{dy}{dx} = -\frac{x}{y} = \frac{-5\cos t}{5\sin t} = -\cot t$$

24. $x = t \Rightarrow \frac{dx}{dt} = 1 \qquad y = \frac{1}{t} \Rightarrow \frac{dy}{dt} = -\frac{1}{t^2}$

$$\frac{dy}{dx} = \frac{\frac{dy}{dt}}{\frac{dx}{dt}} = -\frac{1}{t^2}$$ Eliminating t: $y = \frac{1}{x}$

$$\frac{dy}{dx} = -\frac{1}{x^2} = -\frac{1}{t^2}$$

25. $x = t^2 - \frac{\pi}{2}$. $y = \sin(t^2) = \sin(\frac{\pi}{2} + x) = \cos x$. $\frac{dy}{dx} = -\sin x$.
$\frac{dx}{dt} = 2t$ and $\frac{dy}{dt} = 2t\cos(t^2) \Rightarrow \frac{dy}{dx} = \frac{2t\cos(t^2)}{2t} = \cos(t^2) =$

$\cos(\frac{\pi}{2} + x) = -\sin x$.

26. $x = t^2 \Rightarrow \frac{dx}{dt} = 2t$ $\qquad y = t^3 \Rightarrow \frac{dy}{dt} = 3t^2$

$$\frac{dy}{dx} = \frac{\frac{dy}{dt}}{\frac{dx}{dt}} = \frac{3t^2}{2t} = \frac{3}{2}t$$

Eliminating t: $t = x^{1/2} \Rightarrow y = x^{3/2}$

$$\frac{dy}{dx} = \frac{3}{2}x^{1/2} = \frac{3}{2}t$$

27. $x = \cos t \Rightarrow \frac{dx}{dt} = -\sin t$. $y = 1 + \sin t \Rightarrow \frac{dy}{dt} = \cos t$.

$$\frac{dy}{dx} = \frac{\frac{dy}{dt}}{\frac{dx}{dt}} = \frac{\cos t}{-\sin t} = -\cot t.$$

Eliminating t: $y - 1 = \sin t$

and $x = \cos t \Rightarrow (y-1)^2 + x^2 = \sin^2 t + \cos^2 t = 1$. $2(y-1)\frac{dy}{dx} + 2x = 0$

or $\frac{dy}{dx} = -\frac{x}{y-1} = -\cot t$.

28. $x = \cos t \Rightarrow \frac{dx}{dt} = -\sin t$ $\qquad y = 1 - \sin^2 t \Rightarrow \frac{dy}{dt} = -2\sin t\cos t$

$$\frac{dy}{dx} = \frac{\frac{dy}{dt}}{\frac{dx}{dt}} = \frac{-2\sin t\cos t}{-\sin t} = 2\cos t.$$

Eliminating t:

$y = 1 - \sin^2 t = \cos^2 t = x^2$. $\frac{dy}{dx} = 2x = 2\cos t$

29. (c)
$x = 4t - 5 \Rightarrow \frac{dx}{dt} = 4$. $\qquad y = t^2 \Rightarrow \frac{dy}{dt} = 2t$.

$$\frac{dy}{dx} = \frac{\frac{dy}{dt}}{\frac{dx}{dt}} = \frac{2t}{4}\Big|_{t=2} = 1.$$

30. (b) $x = 3t^2 + 2 \Rightarrow \frac{dx}{dt} = 6t$ $y = 2t^4 - 1 \Rightarrow \frac{dy}{dt} = 8t^3$

$$\frac{dy}{dx} = \frac{\frac{dy}{dt}}{\frac{dx}{dt}} = \frac{8t}{6t} = \frac{4}{3}$$

31. $x = t + \frac{1}{t} \Rightarrow \frac{dx}{dt} = 1 - \frac{1}{t^2}\Big|_{t=2} = \frac{3}{4}$.

$y = t - \frac{1}{t} \Rightarrow \frac{dy}{dt} = 1 + \frac{1}{t^2}\Big|_{t=2} = \frac{5}{4} \therefore \frac{dy}{dx} = \frac{\frac{5}{4}}{\frac{3}{4}} = \frac{5}{3}$.

$y(2) = \frac{3}{2}$ and $x(2) = \frac{5}{2}$. Tangent line: $y - \frac{3}{2} = \frac{5}{3}(x - \frac{5}{2})$

$\Rightarrow 6y - 9 = 10x - 25 \Rightarrow 3y - 5x + 8 = 0$.

32. $x = \sqrt{2t^2 + 1} \Rightarrow \frac{dx}{dt} = \frac{2t}{\sqrt{2t^2 + 1}}\Big|_{t=2} = \frac{4}{3}$

$y = (2t + 1)^2 \Rightarrow \frac{dy}{dt} = 4(2t + 1)\Big|_{t=2} = 20 \therefore \frac{dy}{dx} = \frac{20}{\frac{4}{3}} = 15$

$y(2) = 25$ and $x(2) = 3$. Tangent line: $y - 25 = 15(x - 3)$ or $y - 15x = -20$.

33. $x = t\sqrt{2t + 5} \Rightarrow \frac{dx}{dt} = (2t + 5)^{\frac{1}{2}} + t\left[\frac{1}{2}(2t + 5)^{-\frac{1}{2}}(2)\right]$

$\frac{dx}{dt}\Big|_{t=2} = \sqrt{9} + \frac{2}{\sqrt{9}} = \frac{11}{3}$. $y = (4t)^{\frac{1}{3}} \Rightarrow \frac{dy}{dt} = \frac{1}{3}(4t)^{-\frac{2}{3}}(4)$.

$\frac{dy}{dt}\Big|_{t=2} = \frac{1}{3}$. $\frac{dy}{dx} = \frac{\frac{1}{3}}{\frac{11}{3}} = \frac{1}{11}$. $x(2) = 6$ and $y(2) = 2$.

$y - 2 = \frac{1}{11}(x - 6) \Rightarrow 11y - x = 16$.

34. $x = \frac{t - 1}{t + 1} \Rightarrow \frac{dx}{dt} = \frac{2}{(t + 1)^2}\Big|_{t=2} = \frac{2}{9}$

$y = \frac{t + 1}{t - 1} \Rightarrow \frac{dy}{dt} = \frac{-2}{(t - 1)^2}\Big|_{t=2} = -2 \therefore \frac{dy}{dx} = -9$

$y(2) = 3$ and $x(2) = \frac{1}{3}$. Tangent line: $y - 3 = -9\left(x - \frac{1}{3}\right)$ or $y + 9x = 6$

35. $x = t^{-2} \Rightarrow \frac{dx}{dt} = -2t^{-3}\Big|_{t=2} = -\frac{1}{4}$. $y = \sqrt{t^2 + 12} \Rightarrow$

$\frac{dy}{dt} = \frac{1}{2}(t^2 + 12)^{-\frac{1}{2}}(2t)\Big|_{t=2} = \frac{1}{2}$. $x(2) = \frac{1}{4}$ and $y(2) = 4$.

$\frac{dy}{dx} = \frac{\frac{1}{2}}{\frac{-1}{4}} = -2$. Tangent line: $y - 4 = -2(x - \frac{1}{4}) \Rightarrow 2y + 4x = 9$.

36. $x = \frac{1}{t} + t^2 \Rightarrow \frac{dx}{dt} = -\frac{1}{t^2} + 2t = \frac{2t^3 - 1}{t^2}\Big|_{t=1} = 1$

$y = t^2 - t + 1 \Rightarrow \frac{dy}{dt} = 2t - 1\Big|_{t=1} = 1 \quad \therefore \frac{dy}{dx} = 1$

Tangent line: $y - 1 = x - 2$ or $y - x = -1$

37. $x = 80t \Rightarrow \frac{dx}{dt} = 80$. $y = 64t - 16t^2 \Rightarrow \frac{dy}{dt} = 64 - 32t$.

$\frac{dy}{dx} = \frac{64 - 32t}{80} = 0 \Leftrightarrow 64 - 32t = 0 \Rightarrow t = 2$.

38. $x^2 y^3 = 27 \Rightarrow 2xy^3 \frac{dx}{dt} + 3y^2 x^2 \frac{dy}{dt} = 0$. When P is at (1,3), $\frac{dy}{dt} = 10$.

$\therefore 2(27)\frac{dx}{dt} + 3(9)(10) = 0 \Rightarrow \frac{dx}{dt} = -5$.

39. $x^2 + y^2 = 25 \Rightarrow 2x\frac{dy}{dx} + 2y = 0$

$(3)(4) + (4)\frac{dy}{dx} = 0$ or $\frac{dy}{dx} = -3$

40. $x = \cos^2 t \Rightarrow \frac{dx}{dt} = -2\cos t \sin t$. $y = \sin^2 t \Rightarrow \frac{dy}{dt} = 2\sin t \cos t$. $\frac{dy}{dx} = -1$

$$\frac{d^2y}{dx^2} = \frac{\frac{dy'}{dt}}{\frac{dx}{dt}} = \frac{\frac{d}{dt}\left(\frac{dy}{dx}\right)}{\frac{dx}{dt}} = \frac{0}{-2\cos t \sin t} = 0$$

41. $x = 2t - 5 \Rightarrow \frac{dx}{dt} = 2$. $y = 4t - 7 \Rightarrow \frac{dy}{dt} = 4$. $\frac{dy}{dx} = \frac{4}{2} = 2$.

$$\frac{d^2y}{dx^2} = \frac{\frac{dy'}{dt}}{\frac{dx}{dt}} = \frac{\frac{d}{dt}\left(\frac{dy}{dx}\right)}{\frac{dx}{dt}} = \frac{0}{2} = 0.$$

42. $x = 3t \Rightarrow \frac{dx}{dt} = 3$. $y = 9t^2 \Rightarrow \frac{dy}{dt} = 18t$. $\frac{dy}{dx} = 6t$

$$\frac{d^2y}{dx^2} = \frac{\frac{dy'}{dt}}{\frac{dx}{dt}} = \frac{\frac{d}{dt}\left(\frac{dy}{dx}\right)}{\frac{dx}{dt}} = \frac{6}{3} = 2.$$

43. $x = t \Rightarrow \frac{dx}{dt} = 1$. $y = \sqrt{t} \Rightarrow \frac{dy}{dt} = \frac{1}{2\sqrt{t}}$. $\frac{dy}{dx} = \frac{1}{2\sqrt{t}}$.

$$\frac{d^2y}{dx^2} = \frac{\frac{dy'}{dt}}{\frac{dx}{dt}} = \frac{\frac{d}{dt}\left(\frac{dy}{dx}\right)}{\frac{dx}{dt}} = \frac{-\frac{1}{4}t^{-3/2}}{1} = -\frac{1}{4}t^{-3/2}.$$

44. $x = 5\cos t \Rightarrow \frac{dx}{dt} = -5\sin t$. $y = 5\sin t \Rightarrow \frac{dy}{dt} = 5\cos t$. $\frac{dy}{dx} = -\cot t$

$$\frac{d^2y}{dx^2} = \frac{\frac{dy'}{dt}}{\frac{dx}{dt}} = \frac{\frac{d}{dt}\left(\frac{dy}{dx}\right)}{\frac{dx}{dt}} = \frac{\csc^2 t}{-5\sin t} = -\frac{1}{5}\csc^3 t$$

45. $x = t,\ y = t^{-1} \Rightarrow \frac{dx}{dt} = 1$ and $\frac{dy}{dt} = -t^{-2}$

$$\frac{dy}{dx} = \frac{\frac{dy}{dt}}{\frac{dx}{dt}} = \frac{-t^{-2}}{1}. \quad \frac{d^2y}{dx^2} = \frac{\frac{dy'}{dt}}{\frac{dx}{dt}} = \frac{2t^{-3}}{1}.$$

46. $x = t^2 - \frac{\pi}{2} \Rightarrow \frac{dx}{dt} = 2t$. $y = \sin(t^2) \Rightarrow \frac{dy}{dt} = 2t\cos(t^2)$. $\frac{dy}{dx} = \cos(t^2)$

$$\frac{d^2y}{dx^2} = \frac{\frac{dy'}{dt}}{\frac{dx}{dt}} = \frac{\frac{d}{dt}\left(\frac{dy}{dx}\right)}{\frac{dx}{dt}} = \frac{-2t\sin(t^2)}{2t} = -\sin(t^2)$$

47. $x = \cos t \Rightarrow \frac{dx}{dt} = -\sin t$. $y = 1 + \sin t \Rightarrow \frac{dy}{dt} = \cos t$.

$$\frac{dy}{dx} = -\cot t. \quad \frac{d^2y}{dx^2} = \frac{\frac{dy'}{dt}}{\frac{dx}{dt}} = \frac{\frac{d}{dt}\left(\frac{dy}{dx}\right)}{\frac{dx}{dt}} = \frac{\csc^2 t}{-\sin t} = -\frac{1}{\sin^3 t} = -(1 - x^2)^{3/2}$$

48. $x = \cos t \Rightarrow \frac{dx}{dt} = -\sin t$. $y = 1 - \sin^2 t \Rightarrow \frac{dy}{dt} = -2\sin t\cos t$.

$$\frac{dy}{dx} = 2\cos t. \quad \frac{d^2y}{dx^2} = \frac{\frac{dy'}{dt}}{\frac{dx}{dt}} = \frac{\frac{d}{dt}\left(\frac{dy}{dx}\right)}{\frac{dx}{dt}} = \frac{-2\sin t}{-\sin t} = 2$$

49. $x = 80t \Rightarrow \frac{dx}{dt} = 80$. $y = 64t = 16t^2 \Rightarrow \frac{dy}{dt} = 64 - 32t$.

$$\frac{dy}{dx} = \frac{4}{5} - \frac{2}{5}t. \quad \frac{d^2y}{dx^2} = \frac{\frac{dy'}{dt}}{\frac{dx}{dt}} = \frac{\frac{d}{dt}\left(\frac{dy}{dx}\right)}{\frac{dx}{dt}} = \frac{-\frac{2}{5}}{80} = -\frac{1}{200}$$

50. $x = \cos 2t \Rightarrow \frac{dx}{dt} = -2\sin 2t.\ \frac{dy}{dx} = \sqrt{4 - \sin^2 t} \Rightarrow$

$$\frac{d}{dt}\left(\frac{dy}{dx}\right) = \frac{-\sin t \cos t}{\sqrt{4 - \sin^2 t}}\ .\ \frac{d^2y}{dx^2} = \frac{-\sin t \cos t}{\sqrt{4 - \sin^2 t}} \cdot \frac{-1}{2 \sin 2t} = \frac{1}{4\sqrt{4 - \sin^2 t}}$$

51. $\frac{d^2y}{dx^2} = \frac{\frac{dy'}{dt}}{\frac{dx}{dt}} = \frac{3t^2 + 3}{\frac{dx}{dt}} = t^2 + 1 \Leftrightarrow \frac{dx}{dt} = \frac{3t^2 + 3}{t^2 + 1} = 3.$

52.

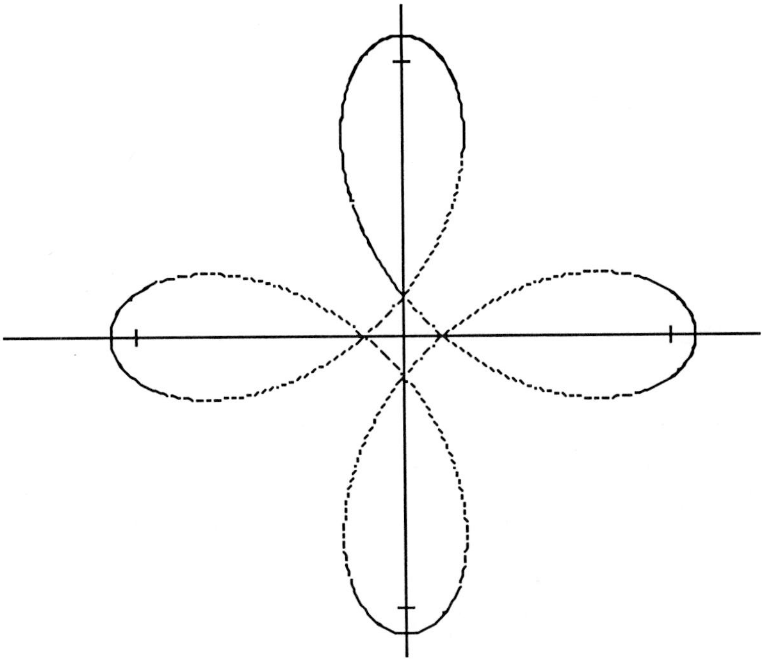

2.9 NEWTON'S METHOD FOR APPROXIMATING SOLUTIONS OF EQUATIONS

1. $f(x) = x^2 + x - 1$. $f(0) = -1$ and $f(1) = 1$. Take $x_1 = .5$.
$f'(x) = 2x + 1$. $x_2 = .5 - \frac{f'(.5)}{f(.5)} = 0.625000$. Similarly,
$x_3 = 0.618056$, $x_4 = 0.618034$. The root is 0.618.

2. $f(x) = x^3 + x - 1$. $f(0) = -1$ and $f(1) = 1$. Take $x_1 = 0.5$.

$f'(x) = 3x^2 + 1$. $x_2 = 0.5 - \frac{f'(0.5)}{f(0.5)} = 0.7142857$. Similarly,

$x_3 = 0.6831797$, $x_4 = 0.6823284$, $x_5 = 0.6823278$. The root is 0.682.

3. $f(x) = x^4 + x - 3$. $f(1) = -1$ and $f(2) = 15$. The root is much closer to 1. Take $x_1 = 1$. $f'(x) = 4x^3 + 1$. $x_2 = 1 - \frac{f'(1)}{f(1)} =$ 1.20000, $x_3 = 1.165420$, $x_4 = 1.164037$, $x_5 = 1.164035$.

The root is 1.164.

4. $f(x) = x^4 - 2$. $f(1) = -1$ and $f(2) = 15$. Take $x_1 = 1.75$.

$f'(x) = 4x^3$. $x_2 = 1.75 - \frac{f'(1.75)}{f(1.75)} = 1.4057944$. Similarly,

$x_3 = 1.2343176$, $x_4 = 1.191620$, $x_5 = 1.1892144$, $x_6 = 1.1892071$.

The root is 1.189.

5. $f(x) = 2 - x^4$. $f(-2) = -14$ and $f(-1) = 1$. Take $x_1 = -1$.
$f'(x) = -4x^3$. $x_2 = -1 - \frac{f(-1)}{f'(-1)} = -1.250000$. $x_3 = -1.193500$.
$x_4 = -1.189230$. $x_5 = -1.189207$. The root is -1.189

6. $f(x) = \sqrt{2x + 1} - \sqrt{x + 4}$. $f(2) = -0.2$, $f(3) = 0.17$, one guesses $x = 3$ and observes that $f(3) = 0$.

7. If $f(x_o) = 0$ then $x_1 = x_o - \frac{f(x_o)}{f'(x_o)} = x_o - \frac{0}{f'(x_o)} = x_o$.

If $f(x_n) = 0$ then $x_{n+1} = x_n - \frac{f(x_n)}{f'(x_n)} = x_n$. The iterations are constant.

8. You cannot start with $x_o = 0$ or π, since $f'(x) = 0$.

9. $f(x) = x^3 + 2x - 4$. $f(1) = -1$ and $f(2) = 8$. Take $x_1 = 1$.
$f'(x) = 3x^2 + 2$. $x_2 = -1 - \frac{f(-1)}{f'(-1)} = 1.20000000$. $x_3 = 1.1797468$.
$x_4 = 1.17950906$. $x_5 = 1.17950902$. The root is 1.179509

10. $f(x) = x^4 - x^3 - 75$. $f(3) = -21$ and $f(4) = 117$. Take $x_1 = 3.2$.

$f'(x) = 4x^3 - 3x^2$. $x_2 = 3.22900$, $x_3 = 3.2285773$, $x_4 = 3.2285772$.

The root is 3.22858

11. (i) $\Rightarrow$ (ii) A root of the equation would be such that

$x^3 - 3x - 1 = 0 \Rightarrow x^3 = 3x + 1$

(ii) $\Rightarrow$ (iii) If $x^3 = 3x + 1$ then $x^3 - 3x = 1$

(iii) $\Rightarrow$ (iv) If $x^3 - 3x = 1$ then $g'(x) = 0$ since

$g(x) = \frac{1}{4}x^4 - \frac{3}{2}x^2 - x + 5 \Rightarrow g'(x) = x^3 - 3x - 1$

(iv) $\Rightarrow$ (i) $g'(x) = f(x)$

(b)

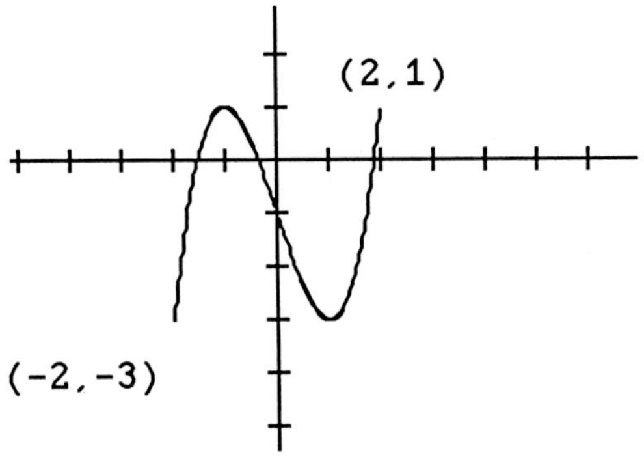

(2,1)

(-2,-3)

(c) 1.87939

(d) -0.34730, -1.53209

12. $f(x) = \tan x$. Take $x_1 = 3.0$. $f'(x) = \sec^2 x = (\cos x)^{-2}$

$x_2 = 3.139707$ and $x_3 = 3.141592$.

13. The point of intersection of y = cos x with y = x is value of x for which cos x = x and hence a root of cos x - x = 0. The two graphs cross between x = 0 and $x = \frac{\pi}{2}$. Take $x_1 = 1$.

$f(x) = \cos x - x$ and $f'(x) = -\sin x - 1$. $x_2 = 1 - \frac{\cos(1) - 1}{-\sin(1) - 1} =$ 0.7503639. $x_3 = 0.7391129$. $x_4 = 0.7390851$. $x_5 = 0.73908513$.

The root is 0.73909.

14. $f(x) = x - 1 - \frac{1}{2}\sin x$. Take $x_1 = 1.5$. $f'(x) = 1 - \frac{1}{2}\cos x$

$x_2 = 1.49870$.

15. Divide $f(x) = x^4 - 2x^3 - x^2 - 2x + 2$ synthetically by successive integers until a sign change of the remainder indicates a root. The work is arranged in a table:

	1	-2	-1	-2	2
-2	1	-4	7	-16	34
-1	1	-3	2	-4	6
0	1	-2	-1	-2	2
1	1	-1	-2	-4	-2
2	1	0	-1	-4	-6
3	1	1	2	4	14

Between 0 and 1
and
between 2 and 3

$f'(x) = 3x^3 - 6x^2 - 2x - 2$. Let $x_1 = .5$. $x_2 = 0.64062500$.

$x_3 = 0.63017159$. $x_4 = 0.63011540$. $x_5 = 0.63011540$. The root between 0 and 1 is 0.630115. For the second root, let $x_1 = 2.5$. $x_2 = 2.5798611$. $x_3 = 2.5733190$. $x_4 = 2.5732719$. $x_5 = 2.5732719$. The root between 2 and 3 is 2.573272.

16. $f(x) = \dfrac{1}{x^2+1} - x$. $f(0) = 1$ and $f(1) = -\dfrac{1}{2}$. Take $x_1 = .5$.

$f'(x) = -\dfrac{2x}{(x^2+1)^2} - 1$. $x_2 = 0.682926$, $x_3 = 0.6823277$, $x_4 = 0.6823278$. The root is 0.68233.

17.

$$f(x) = \sqrt{x - r} \text{ if } x \geq r \Rightarrow f'(x) = \frac{1}{2}(x - r)^{-\frac{1}{2}}$$

$$f(x) = \sqrt{r - x} \text{ if } x \leq r \Rightarrow f'(x) = \frac{1}{2}(r - x)^{-\frac{1}{2}}.$$

If $x_o = r + h$, then $x_1 = r + h - \dfrac{\sqrt{r+h-r}}{\dfrac{1}{2\sqrt{r+h-r}}} = r + h - 2h = r - h$

If $x_o = r - h$. then $x_1 = r - h - \dfrac{\sqrt{r-(r-h)}}{\dfrac{1}{2\sqrt{r-(r-h)}}} = r - h + 2h = r + h$

Thus, if $x_o \neq r$, successive iterations will alternate between $r + h$ and $r - h$ and will never converge to the root.

18. Let $f(x) = \begin{cases} (x-r)^{1/3} & \text{if } x \geq r \\ -(r-x)^{1/3} & \text{if } x \leq r \end{cases}$. Then $f'(x) = \begin{cases} \frac{1}{3}(x-r)^{-2/3} & \text{if } x \geq r \\ \frac{1}{3}(r-x)^{-2/3} & \text{if } x \leq r \end{cases}$

If $x \geq r$, then $x_{n+1} = x_n - \dfrac{(x_n - r)^{1/3}}{\frac{1}{3}(x_n - r)^{-2/3}} = 3r - 2x_n$. A similar calculation for $x \leq r$ gives the same result, i.e. $x_{n+1} = 3r - 2x_n$ for all x.

Take $x_0 = r - h$. Then $x_1 = 3r - 2(r - h) = r + 2h$, $x_2 = 3r - 2(r + 2h) = r - 4h$, and in general $x_n = r \pm (2^n)h$. If $x_0 = r + h$, the same result istrue. Thus, successive iterations are farther away from the root.

2.10 DERIVATIVE FORMULAS IN DIFFERENTIAL NOTATION

1. $y = x^3 - 3x \Rightarrow dy = (3x^2 - 3)\,dx$

2. $y = x\sqrt{1-x^2} \Rightarrow dy = \left[\sqrt{1-x^2} + \frac{1}{2}x\,(1-x^2)^{-1/2}(-2x)\right]dx = \frac{1-2x^2}{\sqrt{1-x^2}}dx$

3. $y = \frac{2x}{1+x^2} \Rightarrow dy = \left[\frac{2\,(1+x^2) - 2x\,(2x)}{(1+x^2)^2}\right]dx = \frac{2-2x^2}{(1+x^2)^2}\,dx$

4. $y = (3x^2-1)^{3/2} \Rightarrow dy = \frac{3}{2}(3x^2-1)^{1/2}(6x)\,dx = 9x(3x^2-1)^{1/2}\,dx$

5. $y + xy - x = 0 \Rightarrow dy + xdy + ydx - dx = 0$

$(1 + x)dy = (1 - y)dx$

$$dy = \frac{1-y}{1+x}\,dx$$

6. $xy^2 + x^2y - 4 = 0 \Rightarrow y^2\,dx + 2xy\,dy + x^2\,dy + 2xy\,dx = 0$

$2xy\,dy + x^2\,dy = -y^2\,dx - 2xy\,dx$

$(2xy + x^2)dy = -(y^2 + 2xy)\,dx \Rightarrow dy = -\frac{y^2+2xy}{2xy+x^2}\,dx$

7. $y = \sin 5x \Rightarrow dy = 5\cos 5x\,dx$

8. $y = \cos(x^2) \Rightarrow dy = -2x\sin(x^2)\,dx$

9. $y = 4\tan\frac{x}{2} \Rightarrow dy = 2\sec^2\frac{x}{2}\,dx$

10. $y = \sec(x^2-1) \Rightarrow dy = 2x\sec(x^2-1)\tan(x^2-1)\,dx$

11. $y = 3\csc\left(1-\frac{x}{3}\right) \Rightarrow dy = \csc\left(1-\frac{x}{3}\right)\cot\left(1-\frac{x}{3}\right)dx$

12. $y = 2\cot\sqrt{x} \Rightarrow dy = -\frac{1}{\sqrt{x}}\csc^2\sqrt{x}\,dx$

13. $x = t + 1 \Rightarrow dx = dt.\; y = t + \frac{t^2}{2} \Rightarrow dy = (1+t)\,dt.$

$$\frac{dy}{dx} = \frac{(1+t)\,dt}{dt} = 1 + t$$

14. $x = 1 + \frac{1}{t} \Rightarrow dx = -\frac{1}{t^2}dt.\; y = t - \frac{1}{t} \Rightarrow dy = \left(1 + \frac{1}{t^2}\right)dt.$

$$\frac{dy}{dx} = \frac{\frac{t^2+1}{t^2}dt}{-\frac{1}{t^2}dt} = -(t^2+1)$$

15. $x = \cos t \Rightarrow dx = -\sin t\, dt$. $y = 1 + \sin t \Rightarrow dy = \cos t\, dt$.

$$\frac{dy}{dx} = \frac{\cos t\, dt}{-\sin t\, dt} = -\cot t$$

16. $x = t - \sin t \Rightarrow dx = (1 - \cos t)\, dt$. $y = 1 - \cos t \Rightarrow dy = \sin t\, dt$.

$$\frac{dy}{dx} = \frac{\sin t\, dt}{(1 - \cos t)\, dt} = \frac{\sin t}{1 - \cos t}$$

2.M MISCELLANEOUS PROBLEMS

1. $$y = \frac{x}{\sqrt{x^2 - 4}} = x(x^2 - 4)^{-\frac{1}{2}} \Rightarrow$$

$$\frac{dy}{dx} = (x^2 - 4)^{-\frac{1}{2}} + x\left[-\frac{1}{2}(x^2 - 4)^{-\frac{3}{2}}(2x)\right] = -4(x^2 - 4)^{-\frac{3}{2}}$$

2. $$x^2 + xy + y^2 - 5x = 2 \Rightarrow 2x + x\frac{dy}{dx} + y + 2y\frac{dy}{dx} - 5 = 0$$

$$(x + 2y)\frac{dy}{dx} = -y - 2x + 5 \text{ or } \frac{dy}{dx} = -\frac{y + 2x - 5}{x + 2y}$$

3. $$xy + y^2 = 1 \Rightarrow x\frac{dy}{dx} + y + 2y\frac{dy}{dx} = 0 \Rightarrow \frac{dy}{dx} = -\frac{y}{x + 2y}.$$

4. $$x^3 + 4xy - 3y^3 = 2 \Rightarrow 3x^2 + 4x\frac{dy}{dx} + 4y - 9y^2\frac{dy}{dx} = 0$$

$$(4x - 9y^2)\frac{dy}{dx} = -3x^2 - 4y \text{ or } \frac{dy}{dx} = \frac{3x^2 + 4y}{9y^2 - 4x}$$

5. $$x^2y + xy^2 = 10 \Rightarrow x^2\frac{dy}{dx} + 2xy + 2xy\frac{dy}{dx} + y^2 = 0$$

$$(x^2 + 2xy)\frac{dy}{dx} = -2xy - y^2 \Rightarrow \frac{dy}{dx} = -\frac{2xy + y^2}{2xy + x^2}$$

6. $$y = (x + 1)^2(x^2 + 2x)^{-2} \Rightarrow$$

$$\frac{dy}{dx} = (x + 1)^2[-2(x^2 + 2x)^{-3}(2x + 2)] + (x^2 + 2x)^{-2}[2(x + 1)]$$

$$= 2(x + 1)(x^2 + 2x)^{-3}[-2(x + 1)^2 + x^2 + 2x]$$

$$= -2(x + 1)(x^2 + 2x)^{-3}(x^2 + 2x + 2)$$

7. $$y = \cos(1 - 2x) \Rightarrow \frac{dy}{dx} = (-\sin(1 - 2x))(-2) = 2\sin(1 - 2x)$$

8. $$y = \frac{\cos x}{\sin x} = \cot x \Rightarrow \frac{dy}{dx} = -\csc^2 x$$

9. $y = \frac{x}{x+1} = x(x+1)^{-1} \Rightarrow \frac{dy}{dx} = (x+1)^{-1} - x(x+1)^{-2} = \frac{1}{(x+1)^2}$

10. $y = \sqrt{2x+1} \Rightarrow \frac{dy}{dx} = \frac{1}{2}(2x+1)^{-1/2}(2) = \frac{1}{\sqrt{2x+1}}$

11. $y = x^2\sqrt{x^2 - a^2} = x^2(x^2 - a^2)^{\frac{1}{2}}$

$$\frac{dy}{dx} = 2x(x^2 - a^2)^{\frac{1}{2}} + x^2\left[\frac{1}{2}(x^2 - a^2)^{-\frac{1}{2}}(2x)\right]$$

$$= 2x\sqrt{x^2 - a^2} + \frac{x^3}{\sqrt{x^2 - a^2}} = \frac{3x^3 - 2xa^2}{\sqrt{x^2 - a^2}}$$

12. $y = \frac{2x+1}{2x-1} \Rightarrow \frac{dy}{dx} = \frac{2(2x-1) - 2(2x+1)}{(2x-1)^2} = -\frac{4}{(2x-1)^2}$

13. $y = \frac{x^2}{1-x^2} \Rightarrow \frac{dy}{dx} = \frac{(1-x^2)(2x) - x^2(-2x)}{(1-x^2)^2} = \frac{2x}{(1-x^2)^2}$

14. $y = (x^2 + x + 1)^3 \Rightarrow \frac{dy}{dx} = 3(x^2 + x + 1)^2(2x+1)$

15. $y = \sec^2(5x) \Rightarrow \frac{dy}{dx} = 2(\sec 5x)(\sec 5x \tan 5x)(5) = 10\sec^2 5x \tan 5x$

16. $y^3 = \sin^3 x + \cos^3 x \Rightarrow 3y^2\frac{dy}{dx} = 3\sin^2 x \cos x - 3\cos^2 x \sin x$

$$\frac{dy}{dx} = \frac{1}{3y^2}(3\sin x \cos x)(\sin^2 x - \cos^2 x)$$

$$= -\frac{1}{2y^2}(2\sin x \cos x)(\cos^2 x - \sin^2 x) = -\frac{\sin 2x \cos 2x}{2y^2} = -\frac{\sin 4x}{4y^2}$$

17. $y = \frac{(2x^2 + 5x)^{\frac{3}{2}}}{3} \Rightarrow \frac{dy}{dx} = \frac{1}{3}\left(\frac{3}{2}\right)(2x^2 + 5x)^{\frac{1}{2}}(4x + 5) =$

$$\frac{(4x + 5)\sqrt{2x^2 + 5x}}{2}$$

18. $y = 3(2x^2 + 5x)^{-3/2} \Rightarrow \frac{dy}{dx} = -\frac{9}{2}(2x^2 + 5x)^{-5/2}(4x + 5)$

19. $xy^2 + \sqrt{xy} = 2 \Rightarrow y^2 + 2xy\frac{dy}{dx} + x^{\frac{1}{2}}[\frac{1}{2}y^{-\frac{1}{2}}\frac{dy}{dx}] + \frac{1}{2}x^{-\frac{1}{2}}y^{\frac{1}{2}}$

$(2xy + \frac{\sqrt{x}}{2\sqrt{y}})\frac{dy}{dx} = -y^2 - \frac{\sqrt{y}}{2\sqrt{x}}$

$$\frac{dy}{dx} = \frac{\dfrac{-2y^2\sqrt{x} - \sqrt{y}}{2\sqrt{x}}}{\dfrac{4xy\sqrt{y} + \sqrt{x}}{2\sqrt{y}}} = \frac{-2y^2\sqrt{xy.} - y}{4xy\sqrt{xy} + x}$$

20. $x^2 - y^2 = xy \Rightarrow 2x - 2y\frac{dy}{dx} = x\frac{dy}{dx} + y$

$(x + 2y)\frac{dy}{dx} = 2x - y$ or $\frac{dy}{dx} = \frac{2x - y}{x + 2y}$

21. $x^{\frac{2}{3}} + y^{\frac{2}{3}} = a^{\frac{2}{3}} \Rightarrow \frac{2}{3}x^{-\frac{1}{3}} + \frac{2}{3}y^{-\frac{1}{3}}\frac{dy}{dx} = 0 \Rightarrow \frac{dy}{dx} = -\sqrt[3]{\frac{y}{x}}$

22. $x^{1/2} + y^{1/2} = a^{1/2} \Rightarrow \frac{1}{2}x^{-1/2} + \frac{1}{2}y^{-1/2}\frac{dy}{dx} = 0$

$\frac{dy}{dx} = -x^{-1/2}y^{1/2} = -\left(\frac{y}{x}\right)^{1/2}$

23. $xy = 1 \Rightarrow x\frac{dy}{dx} + y = 0 \Rightarrow \frac{dy}{dx} = -\frac{y}{x}$

24. $x^{1/2}y^{1/2} = 1 \Rightarrow \frac{1}{2}x^{-1/2}y^{1/2} + \frac{1}{2}x^{1/2}y^{-1/2}\frac{dy}{dx} = 0$

$x^{1/2}y^{-1/2}\frac{dy}{dx} = -x^{-1/2}y^{1/2}$ or $\frac{dy}{dx} = -x^{-1}y = -\frac{y}{x}$

25. $(x + 2y)^2 + 2xy^2 = 6 \Rightarrow 2(x + 2y)(1 + 2\frac{dy}{dx}) + 2y^2 + 4xy\frac{dy}{dx} = 0$

$4(x + 2y)\frac{dy}{dx} + 4xy\frac{dy}{dx} = -2x - 4y - 2y^2$

$\frac{dy}{dx} = -\frac{x + 2y + y^2}{2x + 4y + 2xy}$

26. $y = \sqrt{\frac{1 - x}{1 + x^2}} \Rightarrow \frac{dy}{dx} = \frac{1}{2}\left(\frac{1 - x}{1 + x^2}\right)^{-1/2}\left(\frac{-(1 + x^2) - 2x(1 - x)}{(1 + x^2)^2}\right)$

$= \frac{1}{2}\left(\frac{1 + x^2}{1 - x}\right)^{1/2}\left(\frac{x^2 - 2x - 1}{(1 + x^2)^2}\right) = \frac{x^2 - 2x - 1}{2(1 - x)^{1/2}(1 + x^2)^{3/2}}$

27. $y^2 = \frac{x}{x+1} \Rightarrow 2y\frac{dy}{dx} = \frac{x+1-x}{(x+1)^2} \Rightarrow \frac{dy}{dx} = \frac{1}{2y(x+1)^2}$

28. $x^2y + xy^2 = 6(x^2+y^2) \Rightarrow 2xy + x^2\frac{dy}{dx} + y^2 + 2xy\frac{dy}{dx} = 12\left(x + y\frac{dy}{dx}\right)$

$(x^2 + 2xy - 12y)\frac{dy}{dx} = -2xy - y^2 + 12x$

$\frac{dy}{dx} = \frac{12x - 2xy - y^2}{x^2 + 2xy - 12y}$

29. $xy + 2x + 3y = 1 \Rightarrow x\frac{dy}{dx} + y + 2 + 3\frac{dy}{dx} = 0$

$(x+3)\frac{dy}{dx} = -y - 2 \Rightarrow \frac{dy}{dx} = -\frac{y+2}{x+3}$

30. $x^2 + xy + y^2 + x + y + 1 = 0 \Rightarrow 2x + x\frac{dy}{dx} + y + 2y\frac{dy}{dx} + 1 + \frac{dy}{dx} = 0$

$(x + 2y + 1)\frac{dy}{dx} = -2x - y - 1$ or $\frac{dy}{dx} = -\frac{2x+y+1}{x+2y+1}$

31. $x^3 - xy + y^3 = 1 \Rightarrow 3x^2 - x\frac{dy}{dx} - y + 3y^2\frac{dy}{dx} = 0$

$(3y^2 - x)\frac{dy}{dx} = y - 3x^2 \Rightarrow \frac{dy}{dx} = \frac{y - 3x^2}{3y^2 - x}$

32. $xy^3 + 3x^2y^2 = 7 \Rightarrow y^3 + 3y^2x\frac{dy}{dx} + 6xy^2 + 6x^2y\frac{dy}{dx} = 0$

$(3y^2x + 6x^2y)\frac{dy}{dx} = -y^3 - 6xy^2$ or $\frac{dy}{dx} = -\frac{y^2 + 6xy}{3xy + 6x^2}$

33. $y = \sqrt{\frac{1+x}{1-x}} \Rightarrow \frac{dy}{dx} = \frac{1}{2}\left(\frac{1+x}{1-x}\right)^{-\frac{1}{2}}\frac{d}{dx}\left(\frac{1+x}{1-x}\right)$

$= \frac{1}{2}\sqrt{\frac{1-x}{1+x}} \bullet \frac{1-x+1+x}{(1-x)^2} = \sqrt{\frac{1-x}{1+x}} \bullet \frac{1}{(1-x)^2}$

$= \frac{1}{(1+x)^{\frac{1}{2}}(1-x)^{\frac{3}{2}}}$

34. $y = \sqrt{x} + 1 + \frac{1}{\sqrt{x}} \Rightarrow \frac{dy}{dx} = \frac{1}{2\sqrt{x}} - \frac{1}{2x\sqrt{x}}$

35. $y = (x^3+1)^{1/3} \Rightarrow \frac{dy}{dx} = \frac{1}{3}(x^3+1)^{-2/3}(3x^2) = x^2(x^3+1)^{-2/3}$

36. $y = x^2\sin^5 2x \Rightarrow \frac{dy}{dx} = x^2(10\sin^4 2x\cos 2x) + 2x\sin^5 2x$

$= 2x\sin^4 2x(5x\cos 2x + \sin 2x)$

37. $y = \cot 2x \Rightarrow \frac{dy}{dx} = -2\csc^2 2x$

38. $y = \sin^2(1+3x) \Rightarrow \frac{dy}{dx} = 6\sin(1+3x)\cos(1+3x)$

39. $y = \frac{\sin x}{\cos^2 x} \Rightarrow \frac{dy}{dx} = \frac{\cos^2 x(\cos x) - \sin x(2\cos x)(-\sin x)}{\cos^4 x}$

$= \frac{\cos^3 x + 2\sin^2 x\cos x}{\cos^4 x} = \frac{\cos^2 x + 2\sin^2 x}{\cos^3 x}$

(Also: $\sec x + 2\tan^2 x\sec x$)

40. $y = \sin^3 2x \Rightarrow \frac{dy}{dx} = 6\sin^2 2x\cos 2x$

41. $y = x^2\cos 8x \Rightarrow \frac{dy}{dx} = -8x^2\sin 8x + 2x\cos 8x$

42. $y = \sin(\cos^2 x) \Rightarrow \frac{dy}{dx} = \cos(\cos^2 x)(2\cos x)(-\sin x) = -\sin 2x\cos(\cos^2 x)$

43. $y = \frac{\sin x}{1+\cos x} \Rightarrow \frac{dy}{dx} = \frac{(1+\cos x)(\cos x) - \sin x(-\sin x)}{(1+\cos x)^2} =$

$\frac{\cos x + \cos^2 x + \sin^2 x}{(1+\cos x)^2} = \frac{1+\cos x}{(1+\cos x)^2} = \frac{1}{1+\cos x}$

44. $y = \frac{\sin^2 x}{\cos x} = \tan x\sin x \Rightarrow \frac{dy}{dx} = \tan x\cos x + \sin x\sec^2 x$

45. $y = \csc x \Rightarrow \frac{dy}{dx} = -\csc x\cot x$

46. $y = \cot x^2 \Rightarrow \frac{dy}{dx} = -2x\csc x^2$

47. $y = \cos(\sin^2 x) \Rightarrow \frac{dy}{dx} = -\sin(\sin^2 x)\frac{d}{dx}(\sin^2 x)$

$= -\sin(\sin^2 x)(2\sin x\cos x) = -2\sin x\cos x\sin(\sin^2 x)$

48. $y = \frac{\sin x}{x} \Rightarrow \frac{dy}{dx} = \frac{x\cos x - \sin x}{x^2}$

49. $y = \sec^2 x \Rightarrow \frac{dy}{dx} = 2\sec x\sec x\tan x = 2\sec^2 x\tan x$

50. $y = \sec x\sin x = \tan x \Rightarrow \frac{dy}{dx} = \sec^2 x$

51. $y = \cos(\sin^2 3x) \Rightarrow \frac{dy}{dx} = -\sin(\sin^2 3x)(2\sin 3x)(\cos 3x)(3)$

$= -3\sin 6x\sin(\sin^2 3x)$ $[2\sin 3x\cos 3x = \sin 6x]$

52. $y = u^2 - 1 \Rightarrow \frac{dy}{du} = 2u$ $x = u^2 + 1 \Rightarrow \frac{dx}{du} = 2u$

$\frac{dy}{dx} = \frac{dy}{du}\cdot\frac{du}{dx} = \frac{dy}{du}\cdot\frac{1}{\frac{dx}{du}} = 2u\left(\frac{1}{2u}\right) = 1$

53. $y = \sqrt{2t + t^2} \Rightarrow \dfrac{dy}{dt} = \dfrac{1}{2}(2t + t^2)^{-\frac{1}{2}}(2 + 2t)$

$t = 2x + 3 \Rightarrow \dfrac{dt}{dx} = 2.\quad \dfrac{dy}{dx} = \dfrac{dy}{dt} \bullet \dfrac{dt}{dx} = \dfrac{2(1 + t)}{\sqrt{2t + t^2}}$

54. $x = \dfrac{t}{1+t^2} \Rightarrow \dfrac{dx}{dt} = \dfrac{1+t^2-2t^2}{(1+t^2)^2} \qquad y = 1+t^2 \Rightarrow \dfrac{dy}{dt} = 2t$

$\dfrac{dy}{dx} = \dfrac{\frac{dy}{dt}}{\frac{dx}{dt}} = \dfrac{2t\,(1+t^2)^2}{1-t^2} = \dfrac{2xy^3}{1-x^2y^2}$ (Note that $xy = t$)

55. $t = \dfrac{x}{1 + x^2},\ y = x^2 + t^2 \Rightarrow y = x^2 + \left(\dfrac{x}{1+ x^2}\right)^2$

$\dfrac{dy}{dx} = 2x + 2\left(\dfrac{x}{1 + x^2}\right)\left[\dfrac{1 + x^2 - x(2x)}{(1 + x^2)^2}\right] = 2x + \dfrac{2x(1 - x^2)}{(1 + x^2)^3}$

56. $x = t^2 - 1 \Rightarrow \dfrac{dx}{dt} = 2t \qquad y = 3t^4 - t^2 \Rightarrow \dfrac{dy}{dt} = 12t^3 - 2t$

$\dfrac{dy}{dx} = \dfrac{\frac{dy}{dt}}{\frac{dx}{dt}} = \dfrac{12t^3 - 2t}{2t} = 6t^2 - 1 = 6(x+1) - 1 = 6x + 5$

57. $x = t^2 + t \Rightarrow \dfrac{dx}{dt} = 2t + 1 \qquad y = t^3 - 1 \Rightarrow \dfrac{dy}{dt} = 3t^2$

$\dfrac{dy}{dx} = \dfrac{\frac{dy}{dt}}{\frac{dx}{dt}} = \dfrac{3t^2}{2t + t}$

58. $x = \cos 3t \Rightarrow \dfrac{dx}{dt} = -3\sin 3t \qquad y = \sin(t^2 + 1) \Rightarrow \dfrac{dy}{dt} = 2t\cos(t^2 + 1)$

$\dfrac{dy}{dx} = \dfrac{\frac{dy}{dt}}{\frac{dx}{dt}} = -\dfrac{2t\cos(t^2 + 1)}{3\sin 3t}$

59. $y = \dfrac{x}{x^2 + 1} \Rightarrow \dfrac{dy}{dx} = \dfrac{x^2 + 1 - 2x^2}{(x^2 + 1)^2} = \dfrac{1 - x^2}{(x^2 + 1)^2}$

$\left.\dfrac{dy}{dx}\right|_{x=0} = 1.\quad y(0) = 0.\quad \therefore$ Tangent line is $y = x$.

60. $x^2 - 2xy + y^2 + 2x + y - 6 = 0 \Rightarrow 2x - 2x\frac{dy}{dx} - 2y + 2y\frac{dy}{dx} + 2 + \frac{dy}{dx} = 0$

$(2y - 2x + 1)\frac{dy}{dx} = 2y - 2x - 2 \Rightarrow \frac{dy}{dx} = \frac{2y - 2x - 2}{2y - 2x + 1}\Big]_{(x,y)=(2,2)} = -2$

Therefore, tangent line is: $y - 2 = -2(x - 2)$ or $y + 2x = 6$

61. $y = 2x^2 - 6x + 3 \Rightarrow y' = 4x - 6$. $y(2) = -1$, $y'(2) = 2$.

Tangent line is: $y + 1 = 2(x - 2)$ or $y - 2x = -5$

62. $y = 2x^3 - 3x^2 - 12x + 20 \Rightarrow \frac{dy}{dx} = 6x^2 - 6x - 12$

$6x^2 - 6x - 12 = 6(x^2 - x - 2) = 6(x - 2)(x + 1) = 0$ if $x = 2$ or -1.

Tangent at $(2, 0)$ and $(-1, 27)$ are parallel to x-axis.

63. $V = \pi[10 - \frac{x}{3}]x^2 = \pi[10x^2 - \frac{x^3}{3}] \Rightarrow \frac{dV}{dx} = \pi(20x - x^2)$

64. $r = px = x\left(3 - \frac{x}{40}\right)^2 \Rightarrow \frac{dr}{dx} = \left(3 - \frac{x}{40}\right)^2 + 2x\left(3 - \frac{x}{40}\right)\left(-\frac{1}{40}\right)$

$= \left(3 - \frac{x}{40}\right)\left(3 - \frac{x}{40} - \frac{2x}{40}\right) = 0$ if $3 - \frac{x}{40} = 0$ or $3 - \frac{3x}{40} = 0$,

or if $x = 1200$ or 40. The bus only holds 60 people. If $x = 40$, $p = \$4.00$.

65. $s = at - 16t^2 \Rightarrow v = \frac{ds}{dt} = a - 32t$. Maximum height will occur when $v = 0$, i.e. $a - 32t = 0$ or $t = \frac{a}{32}$. At this moment, $s=49$. That is, $a(\frac{a}{32}) - 16(\frac{a}{32})^2 = 49 \Rightarrow a = 56$ ft/sec.

66. (a)

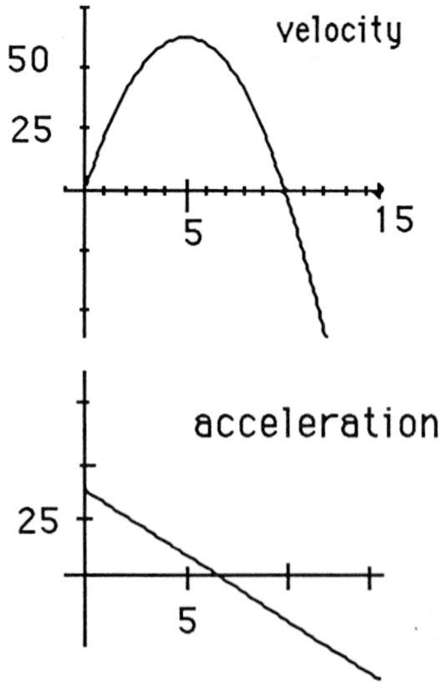

(b) The graphs are the same.

67. $$\lim_{\Delta x \to 0} \frac{[2 - 3(x + \Delta x)]^2 - [2 - 3x]^2}{\Delta x} =$$

$$\lim_{\Delta x \to 0} \frac{4 - 12(x + \Delta x) + 9(x + \Delta x)^2 - 4 + 12x - 9x^2}{\Delta x} =$$

$$\lim_{\Delta x \to 0} \frac{-12x - 12\Delta x + 9x^2 + 18x\Delta x + 9\Delta x^2 + 12x - 9x^2}{\Delta x} =$$

$$\lim_{\Delta x \to 0} \frac{-12\Delta x + 18x\Delta x + 9\Delta x^2}{\Delta x} = -12 + 18x.$$

This is the derivative of $f(x) = (2 - 3x)^2$

68. Let $u = y^2$ and $v = x^2$, where $y = x - x^2$.

Then $y^2 = (x - x^2)^2 = x^2 - 2x^3 + x^4$, so $u = v - 2v^{3/2} + v^2$.

$\frac{du}{dv} = 1 - 3v^{1/2} + 2v = 1 - 3x + 2x^2$.

69. $x^2y + xy^2 = 6 \Rightarrow x^2\frac{dy}{dx} + 2xy + y^2 + 2xy\frac{dy}{dx} = 0$. At $P(1,2)$,

$$(1)^2\frac{dy}{dx} + 2(1)(2) + (2)^2 + 2(1)(2)\frac{dy}{dx} = 0$$

$$5\frac{dy}{dx} + 8 = 0 \Rightarrow \frac{dy}{dx} = -\frac{8}{5}.$$

70. $y = x\sqrt{2x - 3} \Rightarrow \frac{dy}{dx} = \sqrt{2x - 3} + \frac{x}{\sqrt{2x - 3}}$

$$\frac{d^2y}{dx^2} = \frac{1}{\sqrt{2x - 3}} + \frac{1}{\sqrt{2x - 3}} - \frac{x}{\sqrt{(2x - 3)^3}} = \frac{2(2x - 3) - x}{\sqrt{(2x - 3)^3}} = \frac{3(x - 2)}{\sqrt{(2x - 3)^3}}$$

71. $y^3 + y = x \Rightarrow 3y^2\frac{dy}{dx} + \frac{dy}{dx} = 1$. At $P(2,1)$, $3(1)^2\frac{dy}{dx} + \frac{dy}{dx} = 1$

$4\frac{dy}{dx} = 1 \Rightarrow \frac{dy}{dx} = \frac{1}{4}$. To find the $\frac{d^2y}{dx^2}$:

$(3y^2)\frac{d^2y}{dx^2} + \frac{dy}{dx} \bullet 6y\frac{dy}{dx} + \frac{d^2y}{dx^2} = 0$. Evaluating at $P(2,1)$ and $\frac{dy}{dx} = \frac{1}{4}$:

$$3(1)^2\frac{d^2y}{dx^2} + 6(1)\left(\frac{1}{4}\right)^2 + \frac{d^2y}{dx^2} = 0 \Rightarrow \frac{d^2y}{dx^2} = -\frac{3}{32}.$$

72. $y = \frac{2}{\sqrt{x-1}} \Rightarrow \frac{dy}{dx} = -\frac{1}{\sqrt{(x-1)^3}}\Big]_{x=10} = -\frac{1}{27}$; $y(10) = \frac{2}{3}$

Tangent line is: $y - \frac{2}{3} = -\frac{1}{27}(x - 10)$ or $27y + x = 28$

73. $x^2 = 4y \Rightarrow 2x = 4\frac{dy}{dx} \Rightarrow \frac{dy}{dx} = \frac{x}{2}$. At $(2,1)$, $\frac{dy}{dx} = 1$, so the slope of the normal is -1. The normal is: $y - 1 = -(x - 2)$ or $y + x = 3$.

74. $$\frac{dy}{dx} = \lim_{h\to 0} \frac{\sqrt{2(x+h)+3} - \sqrt{2x+3}}{h} \cdot \frac{\sqrt{2(x+h)+3} + \sqrt{2x+3}}{\sqrt{2(x+h)+3} + \sqrt{2x+3}}$$

$$= \lim_{h\to 0} \frac{2x + 2h + 3 - 2x - 3}{h(\sqrt{2(x+h)+3} + \sqrt{2x+3})} = \frac{2}{2\sqrt{2x+3}} = \frac{1}{\sqrt{2x+3}}.$$

By the Power Rule, $\frac{dy}{dx} = \frac{1}{2}(2x+3)^{-1/2}(2) = \frac{1}{\sqrt{2x+3}}$

75. (a) $y = \sqrt{2x - 1} \Rightarrow \frac{dy}{dx} = \frac{1}{2}(2x - 1)^{-\frac{1}{2}}(2) = (2x - 1)^{-\frac{1}{2}}$

$$\frac{d^2y}{dx^2} = -\frac{1}{2}(2x - 1)^{-\frac{3}{2}}(2) = -(2x - 1)^{-\frac{3}{2}}$$

$$\frac{d^3y}{dx^3} = \frac{3}{2}(2x - 1)^{-\frac{5}{2}}(2) = 3(2x - 1)^{-\frac{5}{2}}$$

(b) $y = (3x + 2)^{-1} \Rightarrow \frac{dy}{dx} = -(3x + 2)^{-2}(3) = -3(3x + 2)^{-2}$

$$\frac{d^2y}{dx^2} = 6(3x + 2)^{-3}(3) = 18(3x + 2)^{-3}$$

$$\frac{d^3y}{dx^3} = -54(3x + 2)^{-4}(3) = -162(3x + 2)^{-4}$$

(c) $y = ax^3 + bx^2 + cx + d$ $\quad y' = 3ax^2 + 2bx + c$

$y'' = 6ax + 2b$ $\quad y''' = 6a$

76. The line through (0, 3) and (5, −2) has slope $m = \frac{3+2}{0-5} = -1$ and has equation $y = -x + 3$. The curve and the line share a common point, i.e. $-x + 3 = \frac{c}{x+1}$, and equal tangents.

If $y = \frac{c}{x+1}$, then $\frac{dy}{dx} = \frac{-c}{(x+1)^2}$. Thus $\frac{c}{(x+1)^2} = 1 \Rightarrow$

$\frac{c}{x+1} = x + 1 \Rightarrow -x + 3 = x + 1$ or $x = 1$. Then $y = 2$ and

$2 = \frac{c}{1+1} \Rightarrow c = 4$.

77. $y = x^3 \Rightarrow y' = 3x^2$. $y'(a) = 3a^2$. The tangent line through (a, a^3) with slope $3a^2$ is: $y - a^3 = 3a^2(x - a)$ or $y = 3a^2x - 2a^3$.

To find points of intersection with $y = x^3$, equate these:

$x^3 = 3a^2x - 2a^3$. Since we know $x = a$ is one root:

a |	1	0	$-3a^2$	$2a^3$
		a	a^2	$-2a^3$
	1	a	$-2a^2$	

a |	1	a	$-2a^2$
		a	$2a^2$
	1	2a	

$x = -2a$

Observe that $y'(-2a) = 12a^2$ is 4 times the slope at $y'(a) = 3a^2$.

78. $(y - x)^2 = 2x + 4 \Rightarrow 2(y - x)\left(\frac{dy}{dx} - 1\right) = 2$. At (6, 2),

$2(2 - 6)\left(\frac{dy}{dx} - 1\right) = 2 \Rightarrow \frac{dy}{dx} = \frac{3}{4}$.

Tangent: $y - 2 = \frac{3}{4}(x - 6)$ or $4y - 3x = -10$

Normal: $y - 2 = -\frac{4}{3}(x - 6)$ or $3y + 4x = 30$

79. (a) The circle $(x - h)^2 + (y - k)^2 = a^2$ is tangent to $y = x^2 + 1$ at (1, 2)

$\Rightarrow$ there is a mutual tangent line there. We find the equation of this tangent: $y' = 2x$ and $y'(1) = 2$ so $y = 2x$. This tangent is $\perp$ the radius through (h, k) and (1, 2). Therefore

$\frac{k-2}{h-1} = -\frac{1}{2} \Rightarrow h = 5 - 2k$. ∴ The locus is $\{(h, k) \mid h + 2k = 5\}$

(b) $(x-h)^2+(y-k)^2=a^2 \Rightarrow (y-k)\frac{dy}{dx}=-x+h$ or $\frac{dy}{dx}=\frac{h-x}{y-k}$.

$$\frac{d^2y}{dx^2}=\left.\frac{(y-k)(-1)-(h-x)\frac{dy}{dx}}{(y-k)^2}\right]_{(x,y)=(1,2)}=\frac{-(2-k)-2(h-1)}{(2-k)^2}.$$

Since $\frac{d^2y}{dx^2}=2$ for the parabola, we have $\frac{-(2-k)-2(h-1)}{(2-k)^2}=2$

or $k-2h=2(2-k)^2$. Substituting $h=5-2k$ from part (a),

we have $2k^2-13k+18=0$ or $k=\frac{9}{2}$ or 2. If $k=\frac{9}{2}$, $h=-4$

and the circle is $(x+4)^2+\left(y-\frac{9}{2}\right)^2=a^2$. Substituting the point

$(1,2)$ gives $a^2=\frac{125}{4}$, so $a=\frac{5\sqrt{5}}{2}$.

80. (d), I and III, since $f(x)=\frac{9}{28}x^{7/3}+9 \Rightarrow f'(x)=\frac{3}{4}x^{4/3} \Rightarrow f''(x)=x^{1/3}$

81. $x^2y+xy^2=6 \Rightarrow x^2\frac{dy}{dx}+2xy+y^2+2xy\frac{dy}{dx}=0$ or $\frac{dy}{dx}=-\frac{2xy+y^2}{x^2+2xy}$.

If $x=1$, then $y^2+y-6=0$ or $y=-3$, 2. At $(1,2)$, $\frac{dy}{dx}=-\frac{8}{5}$ and

the tangent line is $y-2=-\frac{8}{5}(x-1)$ or $5y+8x=18$. At $(1,-3)$,

$\frac{dy}{dx}=\frac{3}{5}$ and the tangent line is $y+3=\frac{3}{5}(x-1)$ or $5y-3x=-18$.

82. (a) $x^2+2y^2=9 \Rightarrow 2x+4y\frac{dy}{dx}=0 \Rightarrow \frac{dy}{dx}=-\left.\frac{x}{2y}\right|_{(x,y)=(1,2)}=-\frac{1}{4}$

$\therefore\ y-2=-\frac{1}{4}(x-1)$ or $4y+x=9$

(b) $x^3+y^2=2 \Rightarrow 3x^2+2y\frac{dy}{dx}=0 \Rightarrow \frac{dy}{dx}=-\left.\frac{3x^2}{2y}\right|_{(x,y)=(1,1)}=-\frac{3}{2}$

$\therefore\ y-1=-\frac{3}{2}(x-1)$ or $2y+3x=5$

83. Let the coordinates of the upper right-hand corner of the gondola be the point P(x,y). Observe that x is one-half the width of the gondola. Since the radius of the balloon is 15 ft. plus 8 ft. makes y = -23.

$x^2 + y^2 = 225 \Rightarrow 2x + 2y\frac{dy}{dx} = 0 \Rightarrow \frac{dy}{dx} = -\frac{x}{y}$. At (12,-9)

$\frac{dy}{dx} = -\frac{12}{-9} = \frac{4}{3}$. The slope of the tangent line through

(x,-23) and (12,-9) must have slope $\frac{4}{3}$. Therefore

$$\frac{-23 - (-9)}{x - 12} = \frac{4}{3} \Rightarrow x = \frac{3}{2}.$$

The width of the gondola is then 3 feet.

84. $V = 6\pi r^2 \Rightarrow dV = 12\pi r\, dr$ and $\Delta V = 6\pi (r + \Delta r)^2 - 6\pi r^2$

$\Delta V - dV = 6\pi [r^2 + 2r\Delta r + \Delta r^2 - r^2] - 12\pi r\, dr = 6\pi\ \Delta r^2$.

ΔV is the volume of a shell of thickness Δr, around the cylinder. $dV = \Delta V - 6\pi\ \Delta r^2$ is what is left of the volume of that shell after a cylinder of radius Δr has been removed.

85. $y = 2x^2 - 3x + 5$. $\Delta y = y(3.1) - y(3) = 14.92 - 14 = .92$

$dy = f'(x)\Delta x = (4x - 3)\Delta x$. At $x = 3$, $dy = (9)(.1) = .9$

86. $\frac{h}{20 + a} = \frac{6}{a} \Rightarrow h = \frac{6}{a}(20 + a) = \frac{120}{a} + 6$. $a = 15 \Rightarrow h = 14$.

$dh = -\frac{120}{a^2}\, da$ so $dh = -\frac{120}{(15)^2}\cdot\frac{1}{12} = -\frac{2}{45}$. The lampost is 14 feet with a possible error of $-\frac{2}{45}$ feet or 4%.

87. $\frac{d}{dt}(f(g(t)) = f'(g(t))g'(t)$. For $t = 1$,

$$= f'(g(1))g'(1) = f'(3)g'(1) = (5)(6) = 30$$

88. $y = x^2 + 1$ and $u = \sqrt{x^2 + 1} \Rightarrow y = u^2$ so $\frac{dy}{du} = 2u$.

89. $x = y^2 + y \Rightarrow \frac{dx}{dy} = 2y + 1$. $u = (x^2 + x)^{3/2} \Rightarrow \frac{du}{dx} = \frac{3}{2}(x^2 + x)^{1/2}(2x + 1)$

$$\frac{dy}{du} = \frac{1}{\frac{du}{dy}} = \frac{1}{\frac{dx}{dy}\cdot\frac{du}{dx}} = \frac{2}{3(2x + 1)(2y + 1)\sqrt{x^2 + x}}$$

90. $y = f(x^2) \Rightarrow \frac{dy}{dx} = 2x\, f'(x^2) = 2x\sqrt{3(x^2)^2 - 1} = 2x\sqrt{3x^4 - 1}$

91. $f'(x) = \sin(x^2)$ and $y = f\left(\frac{2x - 1}{x + 1}\right)$.

$$\frac{dy}{dx} = f'\left(\frac{2x - 1}{x + 1}\right) \bullet \frac{d}{dx}\left(\frac{2x - 1}{x + 1}\right) = \sin\left(\frac{2x - 1}{x + 1}\right)^2 \bullet \frac{2(x + 1) - 2x + 1}{(x + 1)^2} =$$

$$\frac{3}{(x + 1)^2} \sin\left(\frac{2x - 1}{x + 1}\right)^2$$

92. $y = 3 \sin 2x$ and $x = u^2 + \pi \Rightarrow y = 3 \sin 2(u^2 + \pi)$.

$\frac{dy}{du} = 12 u \cos 2(u^2 + \pi) = 0$ when $u = 0$.

93. $y = \sqrt{x^2 + 16} \Rightarrow \frac{dy}{dx} = \frac{1}{2}(x^2 + 16)^{-\frac{1}{2}}(2x) = \frac{x}{\sqrt{x^2 + 16}}$

$$t = \frac{x}{x - 1} \Rightarrow \frac{dt}{dx} = \frac{x - 1 - x}{(x - 1)^2} = \frac{-1}{(x - 1)^2}$$

$$\frac{dy}{dt} = \frac{\frac{dy}{dx}}{\frac{dt}{dx}} = \frac{x}{\sqrt{x^2 + 16}} \bullet \frac{(x - 1)^2}{-1}.$$ At $x=3$, $\frac{dy}{dt} = \frac{3}{5}(-4) = -\frac{12}{5}$

94. $f(x) = x^{2/3}$ and $g(x) = x^3$. If $h(x) = f(g(x))$ then $h(x) = (x^3)^{2/3} = x^2$ and $h'(x) = 2x$ is defined at $x = 0$. If $H(x) = g(f(x)) = (x^{2/3})^3 = x^2$ and $H'(x) = 2x$ is also defined at $x = 0$. The function f is not differentiable at $x = 0$ and hence does not satisfy the hypotheses of the Chain Rule. Consequently, the Chain Rule is not contradicted.

95. Differentiate $\cos y = y \sin z$ with respect to z:

$$(-\sin y - \sin z)\frac{dy}{dz} = y \cos z$$

$$\frac{dy}{dz} = \frac{-y \cos z}{\sin y + \sin z}$$

Differentiate $z = x \sin y - y^2$ with respect to z:

$$1 = \sin y \frac{dx}{dz} + x \cos y \frac{dy}{dz} - 2y \frac{dy}{dz}$$

$$\sin y \frac{dx}{dz} = 1 - x \cos y \frac{dy}{dz} + 2y \frac{dy}{dz}$$

$$\sin y \frac{dx}{dz} = 1 - (x \cos y - 2y)\left(\frac{-y \cos z}{\sin y + \sin z}\right)$$

$$\frac{dx}{dz} = \frac{\sin y + \sin z + x y \cos y \cos z - 2y^2 \cos z}{\sin y (\sin y + \sin z)}$$

96. Yes, if $\sin(x+a) = \sin x \cos a + \cos x \sin a$, then differentiating both sides gives $\cos(x+a) = \cos x \cos x - \sin x \sin a$, which is an identity. The principle does not apply to $x^2 - 2x - 8 = 0$ because this is not an identity, but is true only for $x = 4$ or $x = -2$.

97. $f(x) = (1 + \tan x)^{-1} \Rightarrow f'(x) = -(1 + \tan x)^{-2}(\sec^2 x)$.

$f(0) = 1$ and $f'(0) = -1$. $L(x) = f(0) + f'(0)x = 1 - x$

98. (a) $f(x) = \sqrt{1+x} + \sin x - 0.5$; $f\left(-\frac{\pi}{4}\right) = \sqrt{1 - \frac{\pi}{4}} - \frac{1}{\sqrt{2}} - 0.5 \approx -0.743$

$f(0) = 1 - 0.5 = 0.5 \Rightarrow$ there is at least one solution between $-\frac{\pi}{4}$ and 0

(b) $\sqrt{1+x} + \sin x - 0.5 \approx 1 + \frac{1}{2}x + x - \frac{1}{2} = 0$ if $x = -\frac{1}{3}$

(c) $f\left(-\frac{1}{3}\right) \approx -0.0107$

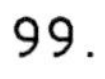

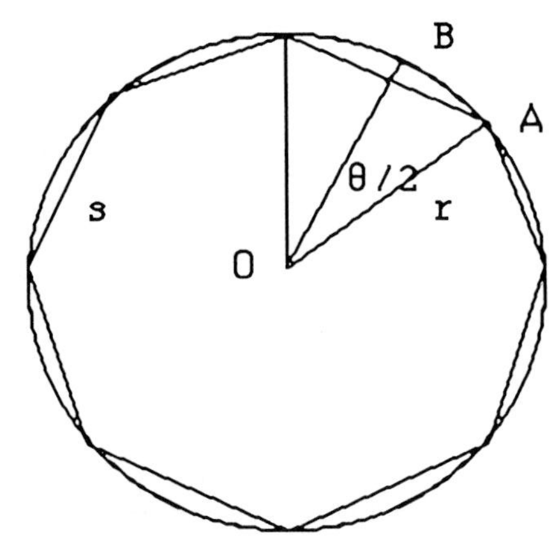

$$\theta = \frac{2\pi}{n} \Rightarrow \frac{\theta}{2} = \frac{\pi}{2}$$

$$\sin\frac{\theta}{2} = \frac{s/2}{r}$$

$$s = 2r\sin\frac{\pi}{n}$$

$$P = ns = 2nr\sin\frac{\pi}{n}$$

$$\lim_{n\to\infty} 2rn\sin\frac{\pi}{n} = \lim_{n\to\infty} 2r\,\frac{\sin\frac{\pi}{n}}{\frac{1}{n}}.$$ Let $t = \frac{1}{n}$ so that $n \to\infty \Rightarrow t \to 0$.

We have then

$$\lim_{t\to 0} 2r\,\frac{\sin\pi t}{t} \cdot \frac{\pi}{\pi} = 2\pi r \lim_{t\to 0}\frac{\sin\pi t}{\pi t} = (2\pi r)(1) = 2\pi r.$$

100. (a) $x = \cos^2 t$ and $y = \sin^2 t \Rightarrow x + y = 1$. $\therefore \dfrac{dy}{dx} = -1$

(b) $x = \cos^3 t \Rightarrow \dfrac{dx}{dt} = -3\cos^2 t \sin t$.

$$y = \sin^3 t \Rightarrow \frac{dy}{dt} = 3\sin^2 t \cos t. \quad \frac{dy}{dx} = \frac{-3\cos^2 t \sin t}{3\sin^2 t \cos t}$$

$$= -\tan t \Big|_{t=\frac{\pi}{4}} = -1.$$

(c) $x = \tan^2 t \Rightarrow \dfrac{dx}{dt} = 2\tan t \sec^2 t$.

$$y = \sin 2t \Rightarrow \frac{dy}{dt} = 2\cos 2t. \quad \frac{dy}{dx} = \frac{2\cos 2t}{2\tan t \sec^2 t}\Bigg|_{x=\frac{\pi}{4}} = 0.$$

101. $x = \cos 3t \Rightarrow \dfrac{dx}{dt} = -3\sin 3t$. $y = \sin^2 3t \Rightarrow \dfrac{dy}{dt} = 6\sin 3t\cos 3t$

$$\frac{dy}{dx} = \frac{\frac{dy}{dt}}{\frac{dx}{dt}} = \frac{6\sin 3t\cos 3t}{-3\sin 3t} = -2\cos 3t.$$

$$\frac{d^2y}{dx^2} = \frac{\frac{d}{dt}(\frac{dt}{dx})}{\frac{dx}{dt}} = \frac{6\sin 3t}{-3\sin 3t} = -2.$$

102. $x = 3t + 1 \Rightarrow \dfrac{dx}{dt} = 3 \quad y = t^2 + t \Rightarrow \dfrac{dy}{dt} = 2t + 1$.

$$\frac{dy}{dx} = \frac{2t+1}{3}. \text{ Eliminating } t\text{: } t = \frac{x-1}{3} \Rightarrow y = \left(\frac{x-1}{3}\right)^2 + \frac{x-1}{3}.$$

$$\frac{dy}{dx} = 2\left(\frac{x-1}{3}\right)\left(\frac{1}{3}\right) + \frac{1}{3} = \frac{2x+1}{9}. \text{ Checking, } \frac{2(3t+1)+1}{9} = \frac{6t+3}{9} = \frac{2t+1}{3}.$$

103. $x = t - t^2 \Rightarrow \dfrac{dx}{dt} = 1 - 2t \quad y = t - t^3 \Rightarrow \dfrac{dy}{dt} = 1 - 3t^2$

$$\frac{dy}{dx} = \frac{\frac{dy}{dt}}{\frac{dx}{dt}} = \frac{1-3t^2}{1-2t}\Bigg|_{t=1} = 2.$$

$$\frac{d}{dt}\left(\frac{dy}{dx}\right) = \frac{(1-2t)^2(-6t)-(1-3t^2)(-2)}{(1-2t)^2} = \frac{6t^2-6t+3}{(1-2t)^2}\Bigg|_{t=1} = 2$$

$$\frac{d^2y}{dx^2} = \frac{\frac{d}{dt}(\frac{dt}{dx})}{\frac{dx}{dt}}\Bigg|_{t=1} = \frac{2}{-1} = -2$$

104. $[x(t)]^2 + [y(t)]^2 = \left(\frac{1-t^2}{1+t^2}\right)^2 + \left(\frac{2t}{1+t^2}\right)^2 = \frac{1-2t^2+t^4+4t^2}{(1+t^2)^2} = 1$.

$(x, y) = (0, -1)$ when $t = -1$; $(x, y) = (1, 0)$ when $t = 0$;

$(x, y) = (0, 1)$ when $t = 1$. $(-1, 0)$ is not on the trace. The direction of motion is counterclockwise.

105. Let $y = u_1 u_2 ... u_n$. We want to prove that

$$\frac{dy}{dx} = \frac{du_1}{dx} u_2 u_3 .... u_n + u_1 \frac{du_2}{dx} ... u_n + ... + u_1 u_2 ... u_{n-1} \frac{du_n}{dx}$$

The statement is true for $n = 1$, since

$$\frac{dy}{dx} = \frac{du_1}{dx} \text{ is true if } y = u_1$$

Assume, for $n = k$, that $\frac{dy}{dx} = \frac{du_1}{dx} u_2 ... u_k + u_1 \frac{du_2}{dx} .. u_k + .. + u_1 .. u_{k-1} \frac{du_k}{dx}$.

Then, for $n = k+1$, $y = u_1 u_2 .. u_k u_{k+1} = (u_1 u_2 .. u_k) u_{k+1}$ and

$$\frac{dy}{dx} = \frac{d}{dx}(u_1 u_2 .. u_k) u_{k+1} + u_1 u_2 .. u_k \frac{d}{dx}(u_{k+1})$$

106. If $f(x) = (x-a)^n g(x)$ then $f(a) = (a-a)^n g(a) = 0$.

$f'(x) = n(x-a)^{n-1} g(x) + g'(x)(x-a)^n$ so $f'(a) = 0$.

$f''(x) = n(n-1)(x-a)^{n-2} g(x) + 2n(x-a)^{n-1} g'(x) + (x-a)^n g''(x)$ so $f''(a) = 0$.

It can be seen that all of the terms of $f^{(3)}, ..., f^{(n-1)}(x)$ will contain a factor of $(x-a)$ to some power, so that $f^{(3)}(a) = .. = f^{(n-1)}(a) = 0$, but that one term of $f^{(n)}(x)$ will be $n(n-1)..(3)(2)(1)(x-a)^0 g(x) = n!\, g(x)$ so that $f^{(n)}(a) \neq 0$.

107. (a) $\frac{d^2}{dx^2}(uv) = \frac{d}{dx}\left(\frac{d}{dx}(uv)\right) = \frac{d}{dx}\left[u\frac{dv}{dx} + v\frac{du}{dx}\right] =$

$\frac{d}{dx}\left[u\frac{dv}{dx}\right] + \frac{d}{dx}\left[v\frac{du}{dx}\right] = u\frac{d^2v}{dx^2} + \frac{dv}{dx}\bullet\frac{du}{dx} + \frac{dv}{dx}\bullet\frac{du}{dx} + v\frac{d^2u}{dx^2} =$

$u\frac{d^2v}{dx^2} + 2\frac{dv}{dx}\bullet\frac{du}{dx} + v\frac{d^2u}{dx^2}$

(b) $\frac{d^3}{dx^3}(uv) = \frac{d}{dx}\left(\frac{d^2}{dx^2}(uv)\right) = \frac{d}{dx}\left[u\frac{d^2v}{dx^2} + 2\frac{dv}{dx}\bullet\frac{du}{dx} + v\frac{d^2u}{dx^2}\right]$

$= \frac{d}{dx}\left(u\frac{d^2v}{dx^2}\right) + 2\,\frac{d}{dx}\left(\frac{dv}{dx}\bullet\frac{du}{dx}\right) + \frac{d}{dx}\left(v\frac{d^2u}{dx^2}\right)$

$= \frac{du}{dx}\bullet\frac{d^2v}{dx^2} + u\frac{d^3v}{dx^3} + 2\left[\frac{dv}{dx}\bullet\frac{d^2u}{dx^2} + \frac{d^2v}{dx^2}\bullet\frac{du}{dx}\right] + \frac{dv}{dx}\bullet\frac{d^2u}{dx^2} + v\frac{d^3u}{dx^3}$

$= u\frac{d^3v}{dx^3} + 3\frac{du}{dx}\bullet\frac{d^2v}{dx^2} + 3\frac{d^2u}{dx^2}\bullet\frac{dv}{dx} + v\frac{d^3u}{dx^3}$

(c) We prove this by mathematical induction. The case for n = 2 is proved in part (a). We also need the fact that

$$\binom{m}{k} + \binom{m}{k+1} = \frac{m!}{k!(m-k)!} + \frac{m!}{(k+1)(m-k-1)!}$$

Assume the truth of the statement for n = m, that is:

$$\frac{d^m(uv)}{dx^m} = \frac{d^mu}{dx^m}v + m\frac{d^{m-1}u}{dx^{m-1}}\frac{dv}{dx} + \binom{m}{2}\frac{d^{m-2}u}{dx^{m-2}}\frac{dv^2}{dx^2} = \ldots + \binom{m}{m-1}\frac{du}{dx}\frac{d^{m-1}v}{dx^{m-1}} + u\frac{d^mv}{dx^m}$$

$$\frac{d^{m+1}(uv)}{dx^{m+1}} = \frac{d}{dx}\left(\frac{d^m(uv)}{dx^m}\right) = \left[v\frac{d^{m+1}u}{dx^{m+1}} + \frac{d^mu}{dx^m}\frac{dv}{dx}\right] + \left[m\frac{d^mu}{dx^m}\frac{dv}{dx} + m\frac{d^{m-1}u}{dx^{m-1}}\frac{d^2v}{dx^2}\right] + \ldots +$$

$$\left[\binom{m}{m-1}\frac{d^2u}{dx^2}\frac{d^{m-1}v}{dx^{m-1}} + \binom{m}{m-1}\frac{du}{dx}\frac{d^mu}{dx^m}v\right] + u\frac{d^{m+1}v}{dx^{m+1}}$$

$$= v\frac{d^{m+1}u}{dx^{m+1}} + \left[\frac{d^mu}{dx^m}\frac{dv}{dx} + m\frac{d^mu}{dx^m}\frac{dv}{dx}\right] + \left[m\frac{d^{m-1}u}{dx^{m-1}}\frac{d^2v}{dx^2} + \binom{m}{2}\frac{d^{m-1}u}{dx^{m-1}}\frac{d^2v}{dx^2}\right] + \ldots + u\frac{d^{m+1}v}{dx^{m+1}}$$

$$= v\frac{d^{m+1}u}{dx^{m+1}} + (m+1)\frac{d^mu}{dx^m}\frac{dv}{dx} + \binom{m+1}{2}\frac{d^{m-1}u}{dx^{m-1}}\frac{d^2v}{dx^2} + \ldots + u\frac{d^{m+1}v}{dx^{m+1}}$$

108. (a) $f'(x) = \lim_{h\to 0} \frac{f(x+h)-f(x)}{h} = \lim_{h\to 0} \frac{f(x)\,f(h)-f(x)}{h}$ (By (i))

$$= \lim_{h\to 0}\left[f(x)\cdot\frac{f(h)-1}{h}\right] = \lim_{h\to 0}\left[f(x)\frac{h\,g(h)}{h}\right] \quad \text{(By (ii))}$$

$$= f(x)\lim_{h\to 0} g(h) = f(x)\,(1) = f(x)$$

(b) $f'(x) = f(x)$ by part (a)

109. (a) To be continuous at $x = \pi$ requires that $y(\pi) = \lim_{x\to\pi} y\,(x)$.

From the right, $\lim_{x\to\pi^+} (mx+b) = m\pi + b = y(\pi)$. From the left, $\lim_{x\to\pi^-} \sin x = 0$. We require that $m\pi + b = 0$ or $m = -\frac{b}{\pi}$.

(b) $y' = \begin{cases} \cos x & \text{if } x<\pi \\ m & \text{if } x>\pi \end{cases}$. $y'(\pi) = m \Rightarrow \lim_{x\to\pi^-} \cos x = m$. Since $\cos\pi = -1$, we have $m = -1$. Then $b = \pi$.

110. $f'(0) = \lim_{x\to 0} \frac{f(x)-f(0)}{x-0} = \lim_{x\to 0} \frac{\frac{1-\cos x}{x} - 0}{x} = \lim_{x\to 0} \frac{1-\cos x}{x^2}\cdot\frac{1+\cos x}{1+\cos x}$

$$= \lim_{x\to 0}\left(\frac{\sin x}{x}\right)^2\cdot\frac{1}{1+\cos x} = \frac{1}{2}.$$ Hence $f'(0)$ exists.

111. (a) $f'(0) = \lim_{h\to 0} \frac{f(0+h)-f(0)}{h} = \lim_{h\to 0} \frac{h^2 \sin \frac{1}{h}}{h} = \lim_{h\to 0} h\sin\frac{1}{h} = 0$ since $|\sin\frac{1}{h}| \le$

(b) $f'(x) = x^2 \cos\frac{1}{x}\left(-\frac{1}{x^2}\right) + 2x\sin\frac{1}{x} = 2x\sin\frac{1}{x} - \cos\frac{1}{x}$

(c) No, $\lim_{x\to 0} \cos\frac{1}{x}$ does not exist.

112. (a) $h(x) = |x| \sin x$ is differentiable at $x = 0$ because $g(x) = |x|$ is continuous at $x = 0$, and $f(x) = \sin x$ is such that $f(0) = 0$ and $f'(0)$ exists.

(b) $h(x) = x^{2/3} \sin x$ is differentiable at $x = 0$ because $g(x) = x^{2/3}$ is continuous at $x = 0$, and $f(x) = \sin x$ is such that $f(0) = 0$ and $f'(0)$ exists.

(c) $h(x) = x^{1/3}(1 - \cos x)$ is differentiable at $x = 0$ because $g(x) = x^{1/3}$ is continuous at $x = 0$, and $f(x) = 1 - \cos x$ is such that $f(0) = 0$ and $f'(0)$ exists.

113. Define $g(x) = m(x - a) + c$, m and c constants.

$$e(x) = f(x) - g(x).$$

Further suppose that (1) $e(a) = 0$

(2) $\lim_{x \to 0} \dfrac{e(x)}{x - a} = 0.$

$e(a) = 0 \Rightarrow f(a) = g(a)$. But $g(a) = c$. $\therefore$ $f(a) = c$.

$$0 = \lim_{x \to a} \frac{e(x)}{x - a} = \lim_{x \to a} \frac{f(x) - g(x)}{x - a} = \lim_{x \to a} \frac{f(x) - f(a) + f(a) - g(x)}{x - a}$$

$$= \lim_{x \to a} \frac{f(x) - f(a)}{x - a} + \lim_{x \to a} \frac{g(a) - g(x)}{x - a} \quad \text{(since } f(a) = g(a)\text{)}$$

$$= f'(a) - g'(a) = f'(a) - m \Rightarrow f'(a) = m.$$

$\therefore$ $g(x) = f(a) + f'(a)(x - a)$.

114. If $f(x) = x^q - a$, then $f'(x) = qx^{q-1}$ and $x_1 = x_0 - \dfrac{x_0^q - a}{qx_0^{q-1}} =$

$x_0 - \dfrac{1}{q}x_0 + \dfrac{1}{q}\left(\dfrac{a}{x_0^{q-1}}\right) = \left(1 - \dfrac{1}{q}\right)x_0 + \dfrac{1}{q}\left(\dfrac{a}{x_0^{q-1}}\right)$. Take $m_0 = 1 - \dfrac{1}{q}$

and $m_1 = \dfrac{1}{q}$. If $x_0 = \dfrac{a}{x_0^{q-1}}$ then $x_0^q = a$ so that $x_0 = a^{1/q}$. In

that case $x_1 = m_0 x_0 + m_1 x_0 = (m_0 + m_1)x_0 = x_0$.

CHAPTER 3

APPLICATIONS OF DERIVATIVES

3.1 CURVE SKETCHING WITH THE FIRST DERIVATIVE

1. $y = x^2 - x + 1$

   $y' = 2x - 1$

   $2x - 1 = 0 \Leftrightarrow x = \frac{1}{2}$

   f decreases on $(-\infty, \frac{1}{2})$

   f increases on $(\frac{1}{2}, \infty)$

   $f(\frac{1}{2}) = \frac{3}{4}$ is local minimum

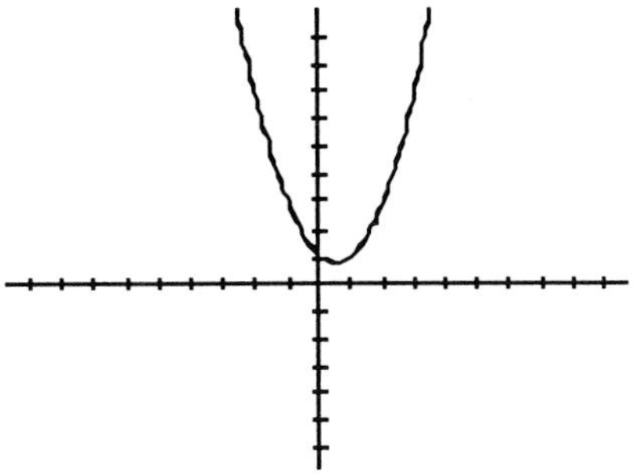

2. $y = 12 - 12x + 2x^2$

   $y' = 4x - 12 = 4(x - 3)$

   $4(x - 3) = 0 \Leftrightarrow x = 3$

   f decreases on $(-\infty, 3)$

   f increases on $(3, \infty)$

   $f(3) = -6$ is local minimum

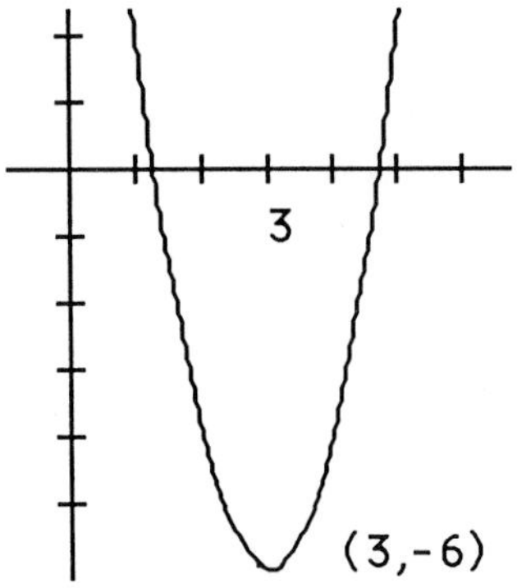

3. $y = \frac{x^3}{3} - \frac{x^2}{2} - 2x + \frac{1}{3}$

   $y' = x^2 - x - 2$

   $(x - 2)(x + 1) = 0 \Leftrightarrow x = 2$ or $x = -1$

   f increases on $(-\infty, -1) \cup (2, \infty)$

   f decreases on $(-1, 2)$

   $f(-1) = \frac{3}{2}$ is local maximum

   $f(2) = -3$ is local minimum

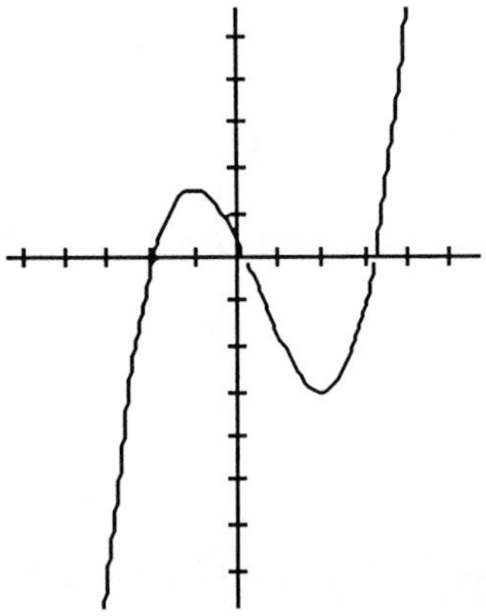

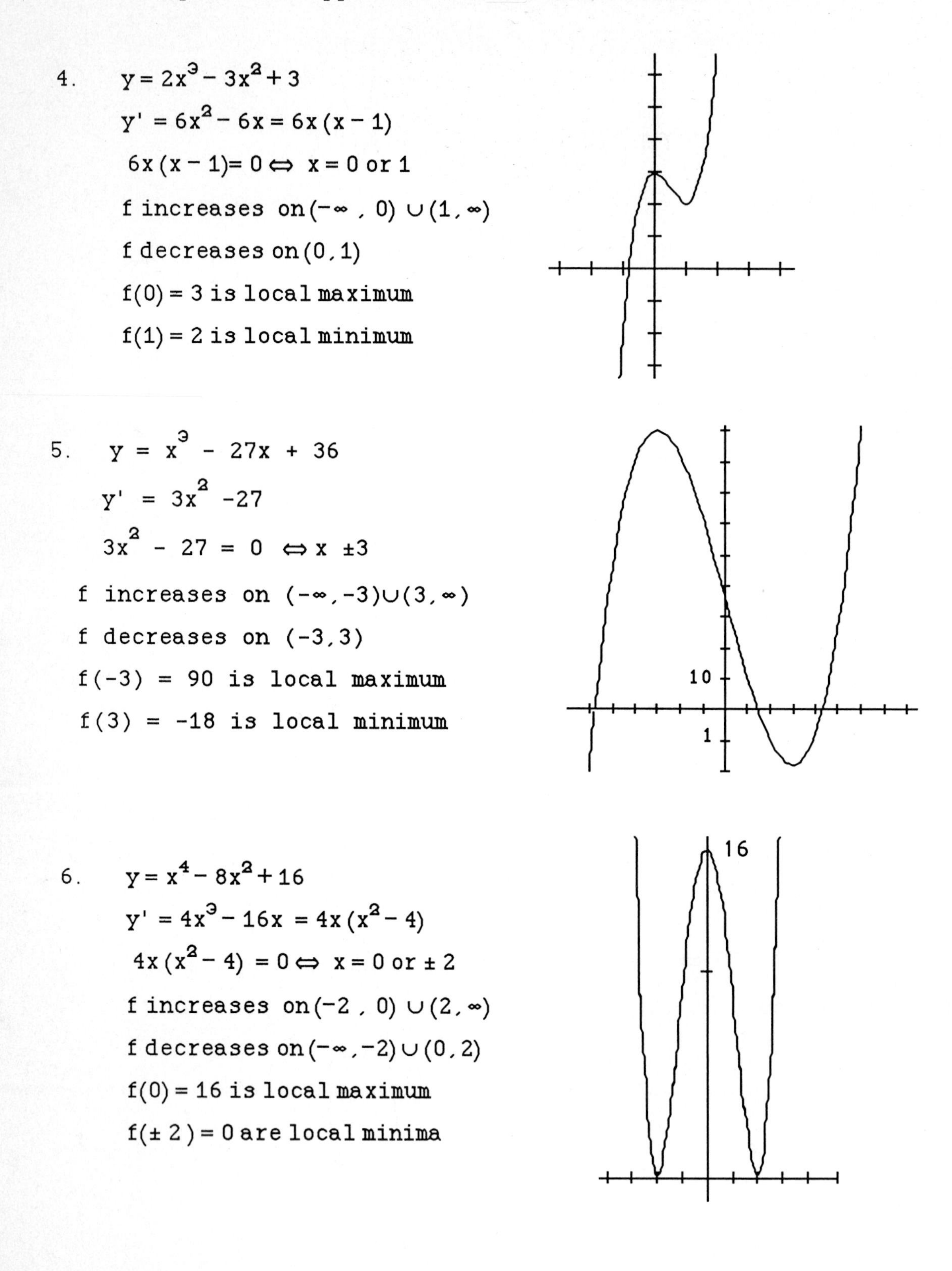

4. $y = 2x^3 - 3x^2 + 3$

$y' = 6x^2 - 6x = 6x(x - 1)$

$6x(x - 1) = 0 \Leftrightarrow x = 0 \text{ or } 1$

f increases on $(-\infty, 0) \cup (1, \infty)$

f decreases on $(0, 1)$

$f(0) = 3$ is local maximum

$f(1) = 2$ is local minimum

5. $y = x^3 - 27x + 36$

$y' = 3x^2 - 27$

$3x^2 - 27 = 0 \Leftrightarrow x \pm 3$

f increases on $(-\infty, -3) \cup (3, \infty)$

f decreases on $(-3, 3)$

$f(-3) = 90$ is local maximum

$f(3) = -18$ is local minimum

6. $y = x^4 - 8x^2 + 16$

$y' = 4x^3 - 16x = 4x(x^2 - 4)$

$4x(x^2 - 4) = 0 \Leftrightarrow x = 0 \text{ or } \pm 2$

f increases on $(-2, 0) \cup (2, \infty)$

f decreases on $(-\infty, -2) \cup (0, 2)$

$f(0) = 16$ is local maximum

$f(\pm 2) = 0$ are local minima

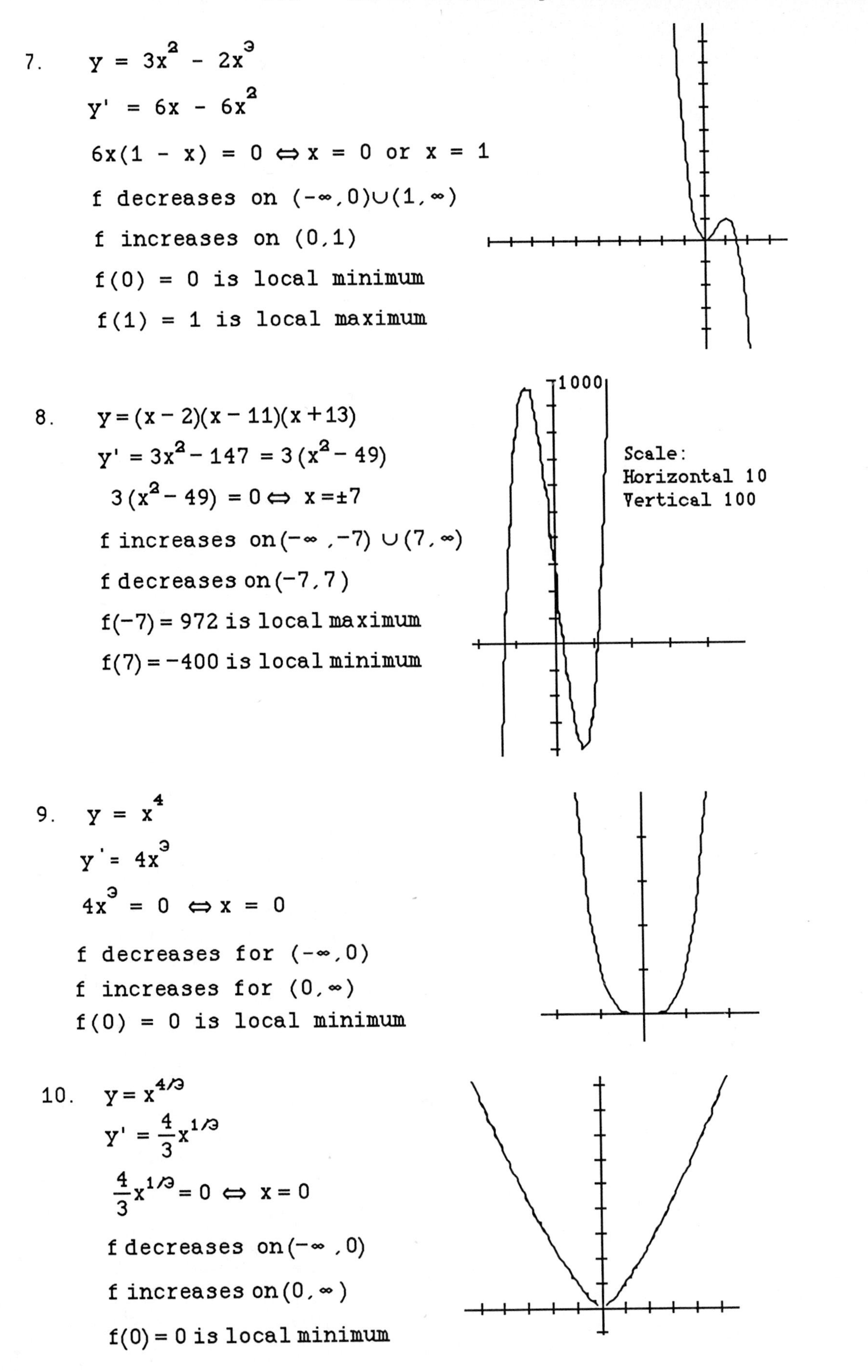

7. $y = 3x^2 - 2x^3$

$y' = 6x - 6x^2$

$6x(1 - x) = 0 \Leftrightarrow x = 0$ or $x = 1$

f decreases on $(-\infty, 0) \cup (1, \infty)$

f increases on $(0, 1)$

$f(0) = 0$ is local minimum

$f(1) = 1$ is local maximum

8. $y = (x - 2)(x - 11)(x + 13)$

$y' = 3x^2 - 147 = 3(x^2 - 49)$

$3(x^2 - 49) = 0 \Leftrightarrow x = \pm 7$

f increases on $(-\infty, -7) \cup (7, \infty)$

f decreases on $(-7, 7)$

$f(-7) = 972$ is local maximum

$f(7) = -400$ is local minimum

9. $y = x^4$

$y' = 4x^3$

$4x^3 = 0 \Leftrightarrow x = 0$

f decreases for $(-\infty, 0)$

f increases for $(0, \infty)$

$f(0) = 0$ is local minimum

10. $y = x^{4/3}$

$y' = \frac{4}{3}x^{1/3}$

$\frac{4}{3}x^{1/3} = 0 \Leftrightarrow x = 0$

f decreases on $(-\infty, 0)$

f increases on $(0, \infty)$

$f(0) = 0$ is local minimum

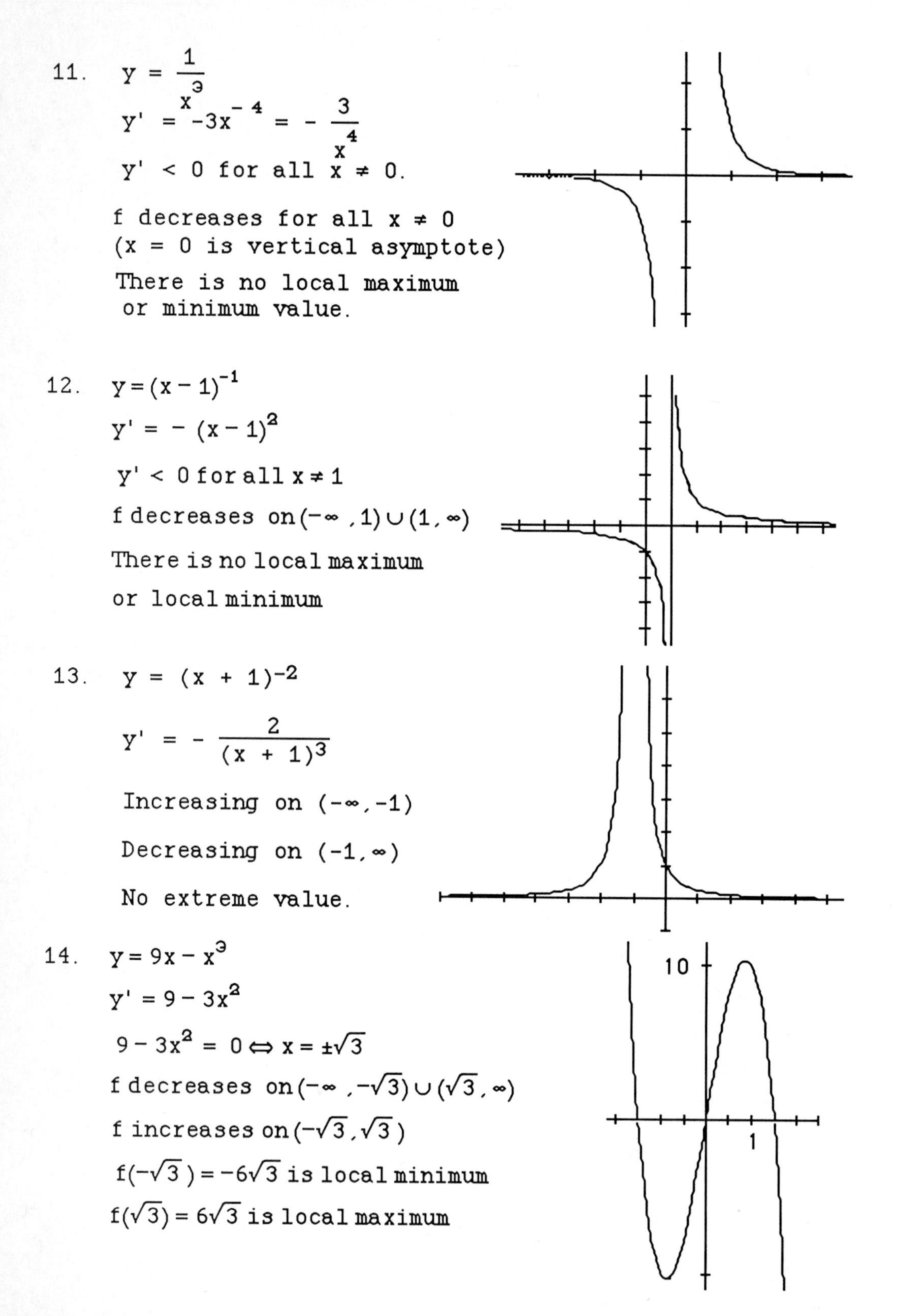

11. $y = \frac{1}{x^3}$

$y' = -3x^{-4} = -\frac{3}{x^4}$

$y' < 0$ for all $x \neq 0$.

f decreases for all $x \neq 0$
($x = 0$ is vertical asymptote)

There is no local maximum
or minimum value.

12. $y = (x - 1)^{-1}$

$y' = -(x - 1)^2$

$y' < 0$ for all $x \neq 1$

f decreases on $(-\infty, 1) \cup (1, \infty)$

There is no local maximum
or local minimum

13. $y = (x + 1)^{-2}$

$y' = -\frac{2}{(x + 1)^3}$

Increasing on $(-\infty, -1)$

Decreasing on $(-1, \infty)$

No extreme value.

14. $y = 9x - x^3$

$y' = 9 - 3x^2$

$9 - 3x^2 = 0 \Leftrightarrow x = \pm\sqrt{3}$

f decreases on $(-\infty, -\sqrt{3}) \cup (\sqrt{3}, \infty)$

f increases on $(-\sqrt{3}, \sqrt{3})$

$f(-\sqrt{3}) = -6\sqrt{3}$ is local minimum

$f(\sqrt{3}) = 6\sqrt{3}$ is local maximum

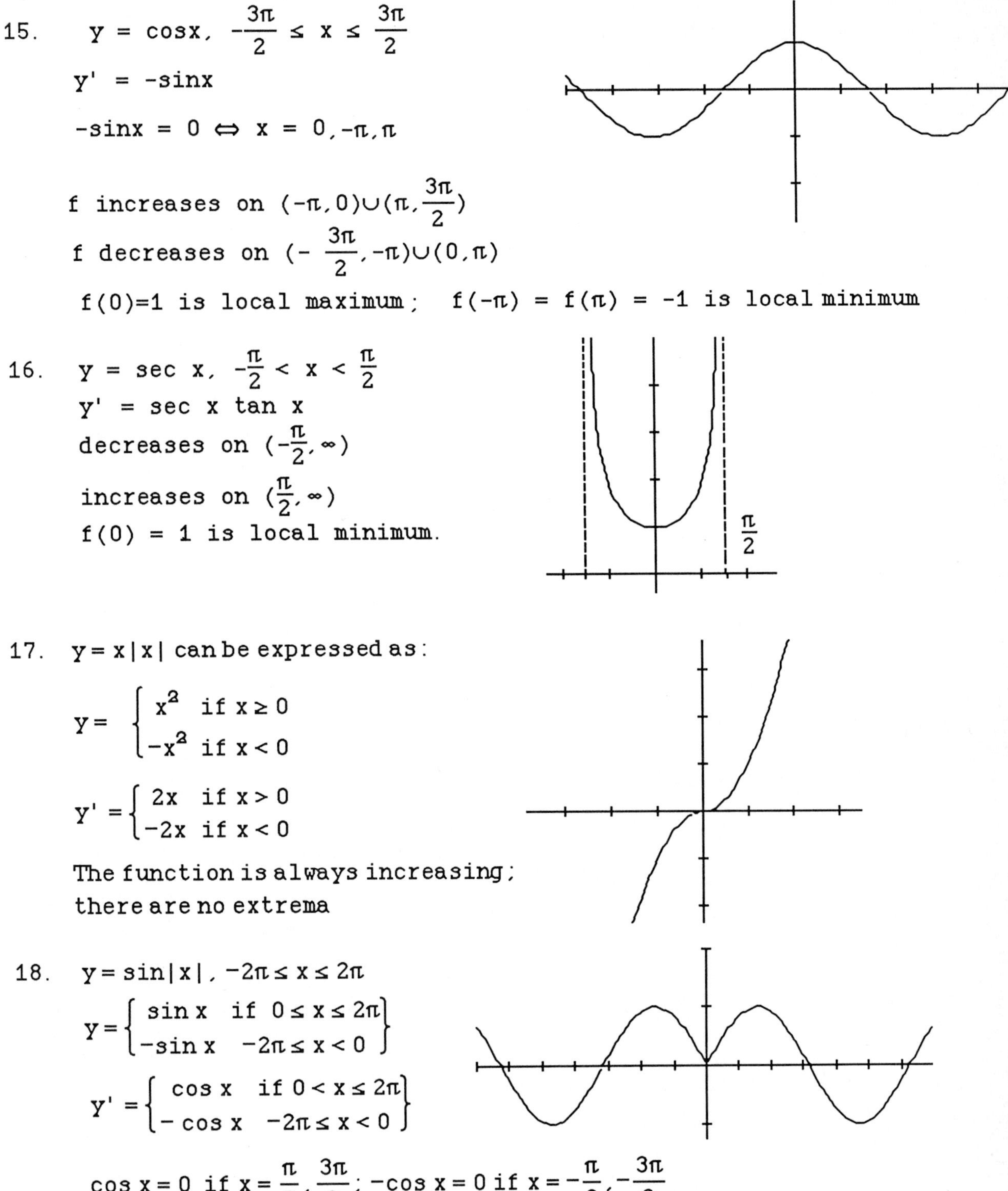

15. $y = \cos x, \ -\frac{3\pi}{2} \le x \le \frac{3\pi}{2}$

$y' = -\sin x$

$-\sin x = 0 \Leftrightarrow x = 0, -\pi, \pi$

f increases on $(-\pi, 0) \cup (\pi, \frac{3\pi}{2})$

f decreases on $(-\frac{3\pi}{2}, -\pi) \cup (0, \pi)$

$f(0)=1$ is local maximum; $f(-\pi) = f(\pi) = -1$ is local minimum

16. $y = \sec x, \ -\frac{\pi}{2} < x < \frac{\pi}{2}$

$y' = \sec x \tan x$

decreases on $(-\frac{\pi}{2}, \infty)$

increases on $(\frac{\pi}{2}, \infty)$

$f(0) = 1$ is local minimum.

17. $y = x|x|$ can be expressed as:

$$y = \begin{cases} x^2 & \text{if } x \ge 0 \\ -x^2 & \text{if } x < 0 \end{cases}$$

$$y' = \begin{cases} 2x & \text{if } x > 0 \\ -2x & \text{if } x < 0 \end{cases}$$

The function is always increasing; there are no extrema

18. $y = \sin|x|, \ -2\pi \le x \le 2\pi$

$$y = \begin{cases} \sin x & \text{if } 0 \le x \le 2\pi \\ -\sin x & -2\pi \le x < 0 \end{cases}$$

$$y' = \begin{cases} \cos x & \text{if } 0 < x \le 2\pi \\ -\cos x & -2\pi \le x < 0 \end{cases}$$

$\cos x = 0$ if $x = \frac{\pi}{2}, \frac{3\pi}{2}$; $-\cos x = 0$ if $x = -\frac{\pi}{2}, -\frac{3\pi}{2}$

$\cos x = 0$ if $x = \frac{\pi}{2}, \frac{3\pi}{2}$; $-\cos x = 0$ if $x = -\frac{\pi}{2}, -\frac{3\pi}{2}$

Decreases on $\left(-2\pi, -\frac{3\pi}{2}\right) \cup \left(-\frac{\pi}{2}, 0\right) \cup \left(\frac{\pi}{2}, \frac{3\pi}{2}\right)$

Increases on $\left(-\frac{3\pi}{2}, -\frac{\pi}{2}\right) \cup \left(0, \frac{\pi}{2}\right) \cup \left(\frac{3\pi}{2}, 2\pi\right)$

Local minima at $\left(\pm\frac{3\pi}{2}, -1\right)$; lo cal maxima at $\left(\pm\frac{\pi}{2}, 1\right)$

Note: there is also a local minimum at (0, 0) where y' does not exist.

19. Since $f(x) = \cos x$ is an even function, $\cos|x| = \cos x$. Therefore, this problem is very similar to problem 15.

20. $y = \frac{1}{2}(|\sin x| + \sin x)$, $0 \le x \le 2\pi$

$$y = \begin{cases} \sin x & \text{if } 0 \le x \le \pi \\ 0 & \pi \le x \le 2\pi \end{cases}$$

π 2π

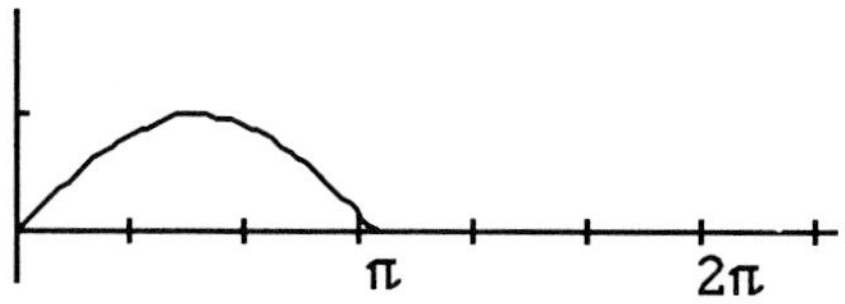

$$y' = \begin{cases} \cos x & \text{if } 0 \le x < \pi \\ 0 & \pi < x \le 2\pi \end{cases}$$

$y' = 0$ if $x = \frac{\pi}{2}$ or $\pi < x \le 2\pi$

$f\left(\frac{\pi}{2}\right) = 1$ is local maximum; local minima $= 0$ for all x in $(\pi, 2\pi]$.

21. $y = \frac{x}{x+1} \Rightarrow y' = \frac{x+1-x}{(x+1)^2} = \frac{1}{(x+1)^2}$. Since $y' > 0$ for all x,

the functions increases on every interval in its domain.

22. No, consider $f(x) = x^3$. $f'(x) = 3x^2 = 0$ for $x = 0$, but $f'(x) \ge 0$ for all x. Therefore, f is always increasing for $x \ne 0$ and has no local extreme values.

23. There is no unique answer to this problem. Any function with properties like the one below is correct.

$$f(x) = \begin{cases} 1 - x & \text{if } x \le 0 \\ 1 - 2x & \text{if } x > 0 \end{cases} \qquad f'(x) = \begin{cases} -1 & \text{if } x < 0 \\ -2 & \text{if } x > 0 \end{cases}$$

24. (a) $\lim_{x \to 1^-} (mx + b) = m + b$ and $f(1) = 2$. Therefore f will be continuous for all value of m and b such that $m + b = 2$.

(b) For $x > 1$, $f'(x) = 2x$ so that $f'(1)$ would have to be equal to 2. For $x < 1$, $f'(x) = m$. Therefore $m = 2$ and $b = 0$.

25. $y = x - 2\sin x$

$y' = 1 - 2\cos x$

$1 - 2\cos x = 0$

$\cos x = \frac{1}{2}$

$x = \frac{\pi}{3}$

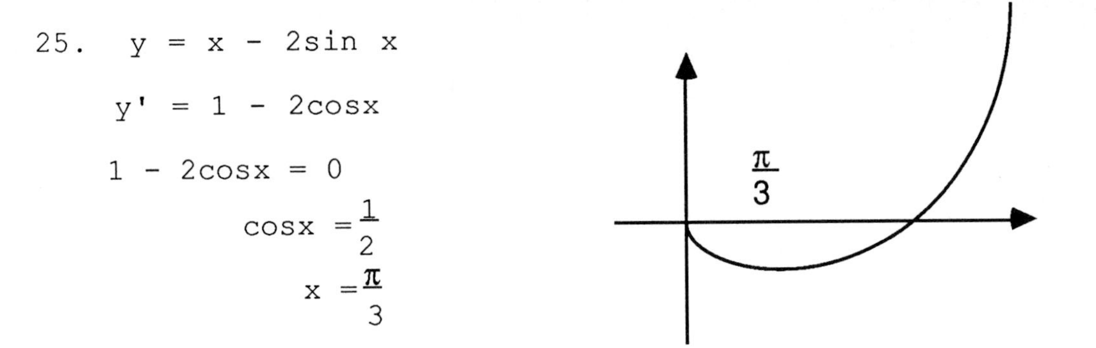

Use Newton's Method: $f(\pi) = \pi$ and $f(\frac{\pi}{2}) = \frac{\pi}{2} - 2 < 0 \Rightarrow$ there is a root r_1 such that $\frac{\pi}{2} < r_1 < \pi$. Take $x_0 = 1.5 \approx \frac{\pi}{2}$. Using the iterative formula

$$x_{n+1} = x_n - \frac{f(x_n)}{f'(x_n)},$$

we have $x_1 = 2.0765$, $x_2 = 1.9105$, $x_3 = 1.8956$, $x_4 = 1.8954$.

To two decimal places, $r_1 = 1.90$.

26. (a) Let $n = 2k > 0$. Then $\frac{d}{dx}(x^{2k}) = (2k)x^{2k-1}$, where $2k - 1$ is odd.

Thus $\frac{dy}{dx} < 0$ when $x < 0$ and $\frac{dy}{dx} > 0$ when $x > 0$, so y increases when $x > 0$ and decreases when $x < 0$.

(b) Let $n = 2k + 1$. Then $\frac{d}{dx}(x^{2k+1}) = (2k + 1)x^{2k}$, where $2k$ is even.

Thus $\frac{dy}{dx} > 0$ for all $x \neq 0$, and y increases for all $x \neq 0$.

(b) f' negative and f" positive state that the curve is decreasing and concave up. <u>Point P.</u>

3.2 CONCAVITY AND POINTS OF INFLECTION

1. $y = x^2 - 4x + 3$

$y' = 2x - 4 \qquad y'' = 2$

$y' = 0 \Leftrightarrow x = 2$

curve rises for $(2, \infty)$
curve falls for $(-\infty, 2)$
everywhere concave up

no inflection points
$f(2) = -1$ is minimum .

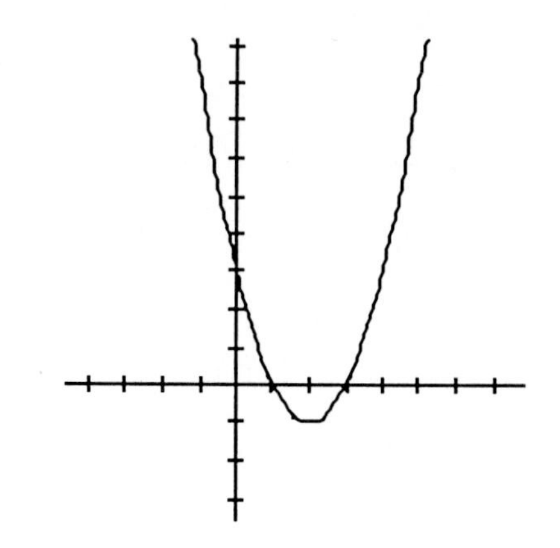

2. $y = 20x - x^2$

$y' = 20 - 2x \qquad y'' = -2$

$y' = 0 \Leftrightarrow x = 10$

curve rises for $(-\infty, 10)$

curve falls for $(10, \infty)$

everywhere concave down

no inflection points

$f(10) = 100$ is maximum

3. $y = x^{\frac{5}{3}}$

$y' = \frac{5}{3}x^{\frac{2}{3}} \qquad y'' = \frac{10}{9}x^{-\frac{1}{3}}$

$y' = 0 \Leftrightarrow x = 0$

curve always rising ($y' > 0$)
concave down for $(-\infty, 0)$
concave up for $(0, \infty)$
$(0,0)$ is inflection point

no local extreme points

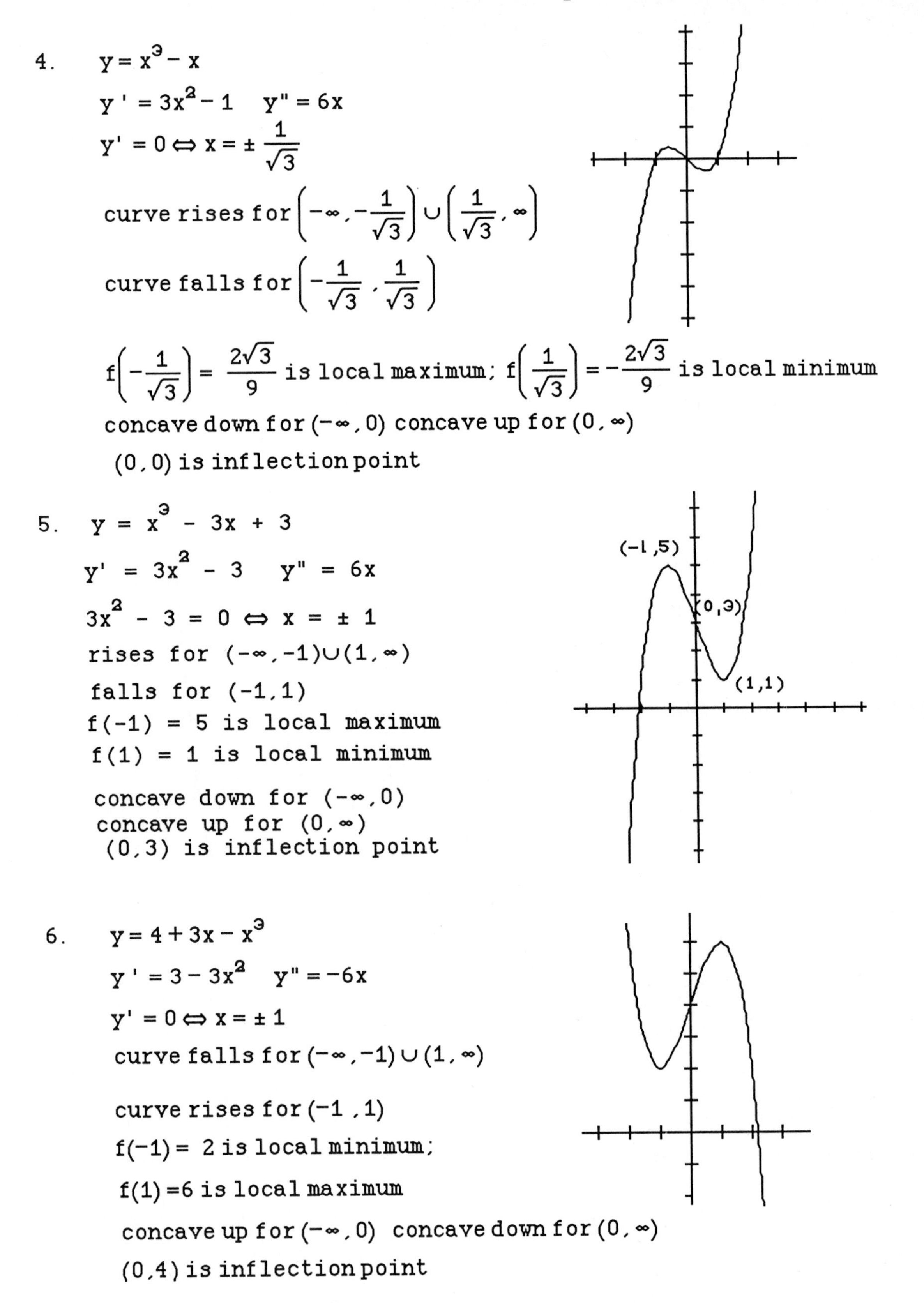

4. $y = x^3 - x$

$y' = 3x^2 - 1 \quad y'' = 6x$

$y' = 0 \Leftrightarrow x = \pm \dfrac{1}{\sqrt{3}}$

curve rises for $\left(-\infty, -\dfrac{1}{\sqrt{3}}\right) \cup \left(\dfrac{1}{\sqrt{3}}, \infty\right)$

curve falls for $\left(-\dfrac{1}{\sqrt{3}}, \dfrac{1}{\sqrt{3}}\right)$

$f\left(-\dfrac{1}{\sqrt{3}}\right) = \dfrac{2\sqrt{3}}{9}$ is local maximum; $f\left(\dfrac{1}{\sqrt{3}}\right) = -\dfrac{2\sqrt{3}}{9}$ is local minimum

concave down for $(-\infty, 0)$ concave up for $(0, \infty)$

$(0, 0)$ is inflection point

5. $y = x^3 - 3x + 3$

$y' = 3x^2 - 3 \quad y'' = 6x$

$3x^2 - 3 = 0 \Leftrightarrow x = \pm 1$

rises for $(-\infty, -1) \cup (1, \infty)$

falls for $(-1, 1)$

$f(-1) = 5$ is local maximum

$f(1) = 1$ is local minimum

concave down for $(-\infty, 0)$

concave up for $(0, \infty)$

$(0, 3)$ is inflection point

6. $y = 4 + 3x - x^3$

$y' = 3 - 3x^2 \quad y'' = -6x$

$y' = 0 \Leftrightarrow x = \pm 1$

curve falls for $(-\infty, -1) \cup (1, \infty)$

curve rises for $(-1, 1)$

$f(-1) = 2$ is local minimum;

$f(1) = 6$ is local maximum

concave up for $(-\infty, 0)$ concave down for $(0, \infty)$

$(0, 4)$ is inflection point

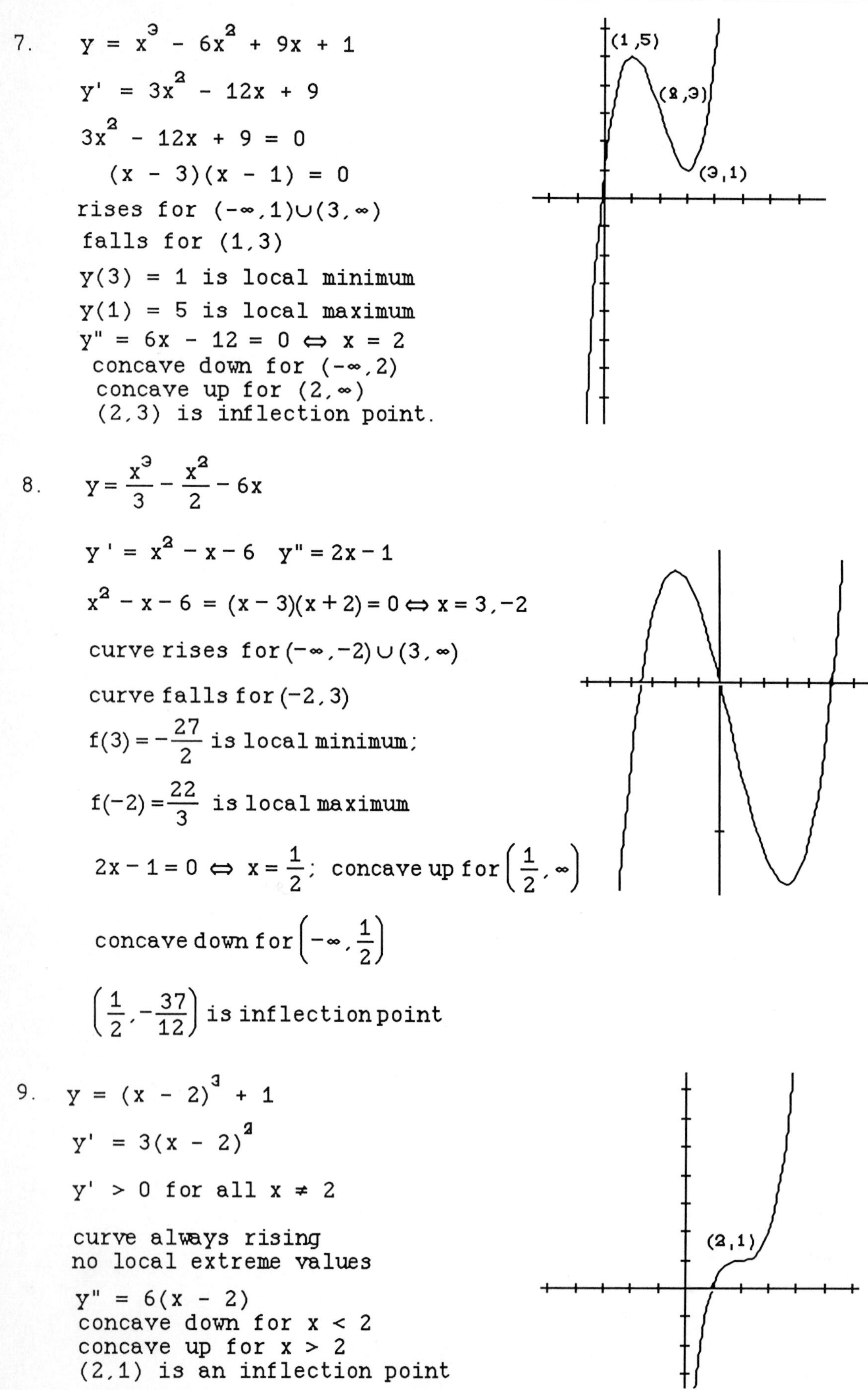

7. $y = x^3 - 6x^2 + 9x + 1$

$y' = 3x^2 - 12x + 9$

$3x^2 - 12x + 9 = 0$

$(x - 3)(x - 1) = 0$

rises for $(-\infty,1)\cup(3,\infty)$

falls for $(1,3)$

$y(3) = 1$ is local minimum

$y(1) = 5$ is local maximum

$y'' = 6x - 12 = 0 \Leftrightarrow x = 2$

concave down for $(-\infty,2)$

concave up for $(2,\infty)$

$(2,3)$ is inflection point.

8. $y = \frac{x^3}{3} - \frac{x^2}{2} - 6x$

$y' = x^2 - x - 6 \quad y'' = 2x - 1$

$x^2 - x - 6 = (x - 3)(x + 2) = 0 \Leftrightarrow x = 3, -2$

curve rises for $(-\infty,-2)\cup(3,\infty)$

curve falls for $(-2,3)$

$f(3) = -\frac{27}{2}$ is local minimum;

$f(-2) = \frac{22}{3}$ is local maximum

$2x - 1 = 0 \Leftrightarrow x = \frac{1}{2}$; concave up for $\left(\frac{1}{2},\infty\right)$

concave down for $\left(-\infty,\frac{1}{2}\right)$

$\left(\frac{1}{2},-\frac{37}{12}\right)$ is inflection point

9. $y = (x - 2)^3 + 1$

$y' = 3(x - 2)^2$

$y' > 0$ for all $x \neq 2$

curve always rising
no local extreme values

$y'' = 6(x - 2)$

concave down for $x < 2$

concave up for $x > 2$

$(2,1)$ is an inflection point

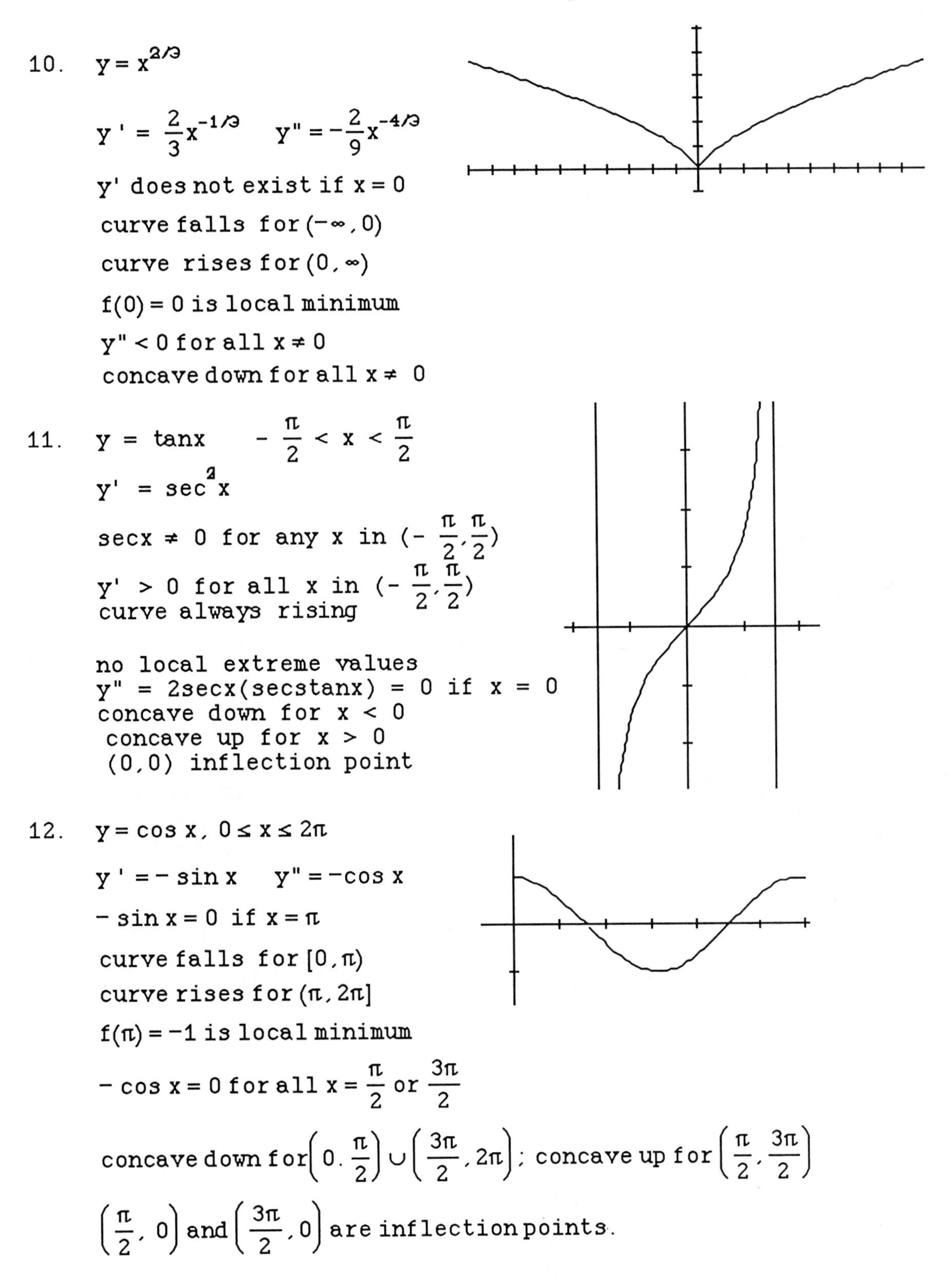

10. $y = x^{2/3}$

$y' = \frac{2}{3}x^{-1/3}$ $y'' = -\frac{2}{9}x^{-4/3}$

y' does not exist if $x = 0$

curve falls for $(-\infty, 0)$

curve rises for $(0, \infty)$

$f(0) = 0$ is local minimum

$y'' < 0$ for all $x \neq 0$

concave down for all $x \neq 0$

11. $y = \tan x$ $-\frac{\pi}{2} < x < \frac{\pi}{2}$

$y' = \sec^2 x$

$\sec x \neq 0$ for any x in $(-\frac{\pi}{2}, \frac{\pi}{2})$

$y' > 0$ for all x in $(-\frac{\pi}{2}, \frac{\pi}{2})$
curve always rising

no local extreme values
$y'' = 2\sec x(\sec x \tan x) = 0$ if $x = 0$
concave down for $x < 0$
concave up for $x > 0$
(0,0) inflection point

12. $y = \cos x$, $0 \leq x \leq 2\pi$

$y' = -\sin x$ $y'' = -\cos x$

$-\sin x = 0$ if $x = \pi$

curve falls for $[0, \pi)$

curve rises for $(\pi, 2\pi]$

$f(\pi) = -1$ is local minimum

$-\cos x = 0$ for all $x = \frac{\pi}{2}$ or $\frac{3\pi}{2}$

concave down for $\left(0, \frac{\pi}{2}\right) \cup \left(\frac{3\pi}{2}, 2\pi\right)$; concave up for $\left(\frac{\pi}{2}, \frac{3\pi}{2}\right)$

$\left(\frac{\pi}{2}, 0\right)$ and $\left(\frac{3\pi}{2}, 0\right)$ are inflection points.

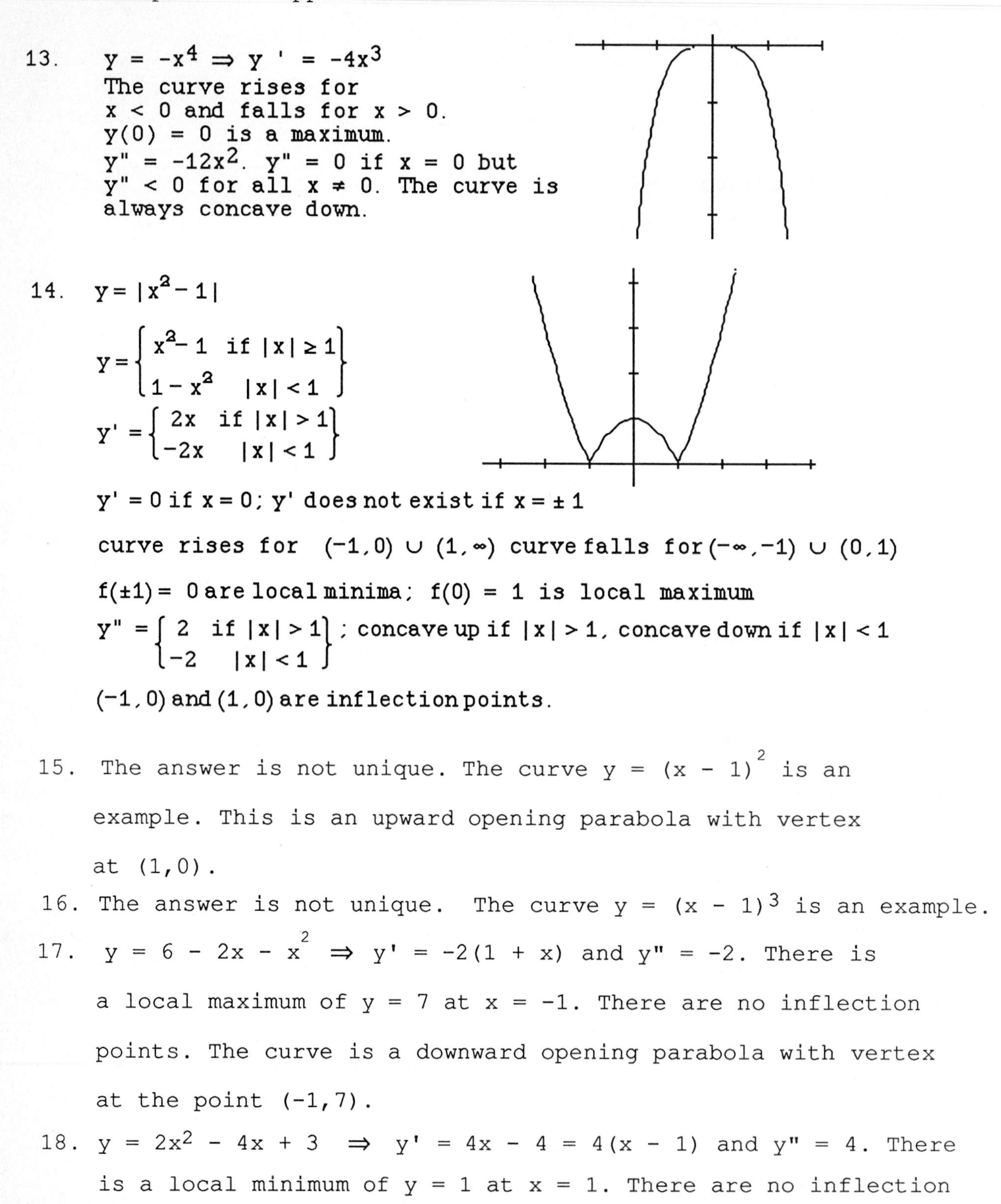

13. $y = -x^4 \Rightarrow y' = -4x^3$
The curve rises for $x < 0$ and falls for $x > 0$.
$y(0) = 0$ is a maximum.
$y'' = -12x^2$. $y'' = 0$ if $x = 0$ but $y'' < 0$ for all $x \neq 0$. The curve is always concave down.

14. $y = |x^2 - 1|$

$$y = \begin{cases} x^2 - 1 & \text{if } |x| \geq 1 \\ 1 - x^2 & |x| < 1 \end{cases}$$

$$y' = \begin{cases} 2x & \text{if } |x| > 1 \\ -2x & |x| < 1 \end{cases}$$

$y' = 0$ if $x = 0$; y' does not exist if $x = \pm 1$

curve rises for $(-1, 0) \cup (1, \infty)$ curve falls for $(-\infty, -1) \cup (0, 1)$

$f(\pm 1) = 0$ are local minima; $f(0) = 1$ is local maximum

$$y'' = \begin{cases} 2 & \text{if } |x| > 1 \\ -2 & |x| < 1 \end{cases}$$; concave up if $|x| > 1$, concave down if $|x| < 1$

$(-1, 0)$ and $(1, 0)$ are inflection points.

15. The answer is not unique. The curve $y = (x - 1)^2$ is an example. This is an upward opening parabola with vertex at $(1,0)$.

16. The answer is not unique. The curve $y = (x - 1)^3$ is an example.

17. $y = 6 - 2x - x^2 \Rightarrow y' = -2(1 + x)$ and $y'' = -2$. There is a local maximum of $y = 7$ at $x = -1$. There are no inflection points. The curve is a downward opening parabola with vertex at the point $(-1,7)$.

18. $y = 2x^2 - 4x + 3 \Rightarrow y' = 4x - 4 = 4(x - 1)$ and $y'' = 4$. There is a local minimum of $y = 1$ at $x = 1$. There are no inflection points. The curve is an upward opening parabola with vertex at the point $(1,1)$.

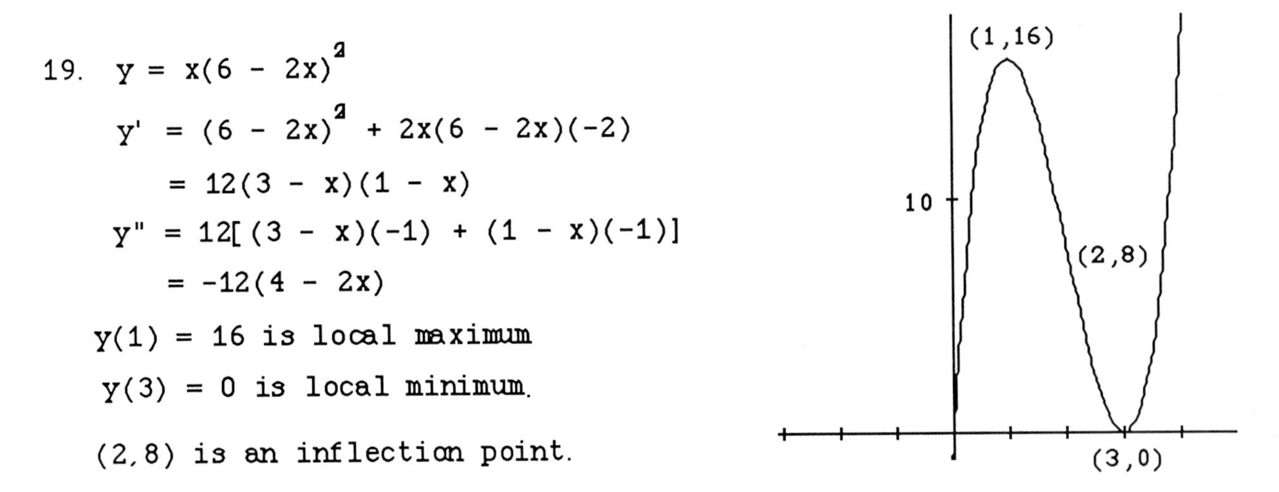

19. $y = x(6 - 2x)^2$

$y' = (6 - 2x)^2 + 2x(6 - 2x)(-2)$

$= 12(3 - x)(1 - x)$

$y'' = 12[(3 - x)(-1) + (1 - x)(-1)]$

$= -12(4 - 2x)$

$y(1) = 16$ is local maximum

$y(3) = 0$ is local minimum.

(2, 8) is an inflection point.

20. $y = (x - 1)^2(x + 2) \Rightarrow y' = (x - 1)^2 + 2(x - 1)(x + 2) = (x - 1)(x - 1 + 2x + 4) = 3(x - 1)(x + 1) = 0$ if $x = \pm 1$. $y(-1) = 4$ is local maximum, $y(1) = 0$ is local minimum. $y'' = 6x = 0$ if $x = 0$. $y(0) = 2$ is inflection point. The graph is similar to Problem 5.

21. $y = 12 - 12x + x^3 \Rightarrow y' = -12 + 3x^2$ and $y'' = 6x$. $y' = 0$ if $x = \pm 2$. $y(-2) = 28$ is local maximum; $y(2) = 4$ is local minimum. The point (0,12) is an inflection point. The graph is similar to that of Problem 5 or 7.

22. $y = x^3 - 3x^2 + 2 \Rightarrow y' = 3x^2 - 6x = 3x(x - 2) = 0$ if $x = 0$ or $x = 2$. $y(0) = 2$ is local maximum and $y(2) = -2$ is local minimum. $y'' = 6x - 6 = 6(x - 1) = 0$ if $x = 1$. $y(1) = 0$ is inflection point. The graph is similar to Problem 5 or 7.

23. $y = x^3 + 3x^2 + 3x + 2 \Rightarrow y' = 3x^2 + 6x + 3 = 3(x + 1)^2$.

$y' > 0$ for all $x \neq -1$ so the graph is always rising. There is no maximum or minimum at $x = -1$ because the derivative does not change sign there. $y'' = 6(x + 1)$.

The point (-1,1) is an inflection point. The graph is similar to Problem 9.

24. $y = x^3 + 3x^2 - 9x - 11 \Rightarrow y' = 3x^2 + 6x - 9 = 3(x + 3)(x - 1)$. $y' = 0$ if $x = -3$ or 1. $y(-3) = 16$ is local maximum, and $y(1) = -16$ is local minimum. $y'' = 6x - 6 = 0$ if $x = -1$.

$y(-1) = 0$ is point of inflection. The graph is similar to the other cubics, as in Problem 5.

25. $y = x^3 - 6x^2 - 135x \Rightarrow y' = 3x^2 - 12x - 135 = 3(x - 9)(x + 5)$.

$y(-5) = 400$ is local maximum and $y(9) = -972$ is local minimum. $y'' = 3(2x - 4)$. The point $(2,-286)$ is an inflection point. The graph is similar in shape to the other cubics but greatly elongated.

26. $y = x^3 - 33x^2 + 216x \Rightarrow y' = 3x^2 - 66x + 216 = 3(x - 4)(x - 18)$.

$y' = 0$ if $x = 4$ or 18. $y(4) = 400$ is local maximum and $y(18) = -972$ is local minimum. $y'' = 6x - 66 = 0$ if $x = 11$.

$y(11) = -286$ is point of inflection. The graph is similar in shape to the other cubics but greatly elongated.

27. $y = x^4 - 2x^2 \;\; 2 \Rightarrow y' = 4x^3 - 4x = 4(x^2 - 1)$. The graph decreases on $(-\infty,-1)$, increases on $(-1,0)$, decreases on $(0,1)$ and increases on $(1,\infty)$. $y(-1) = y(1) = 1$ are local minimum values. $y(0) = 2$ is a local maximum.

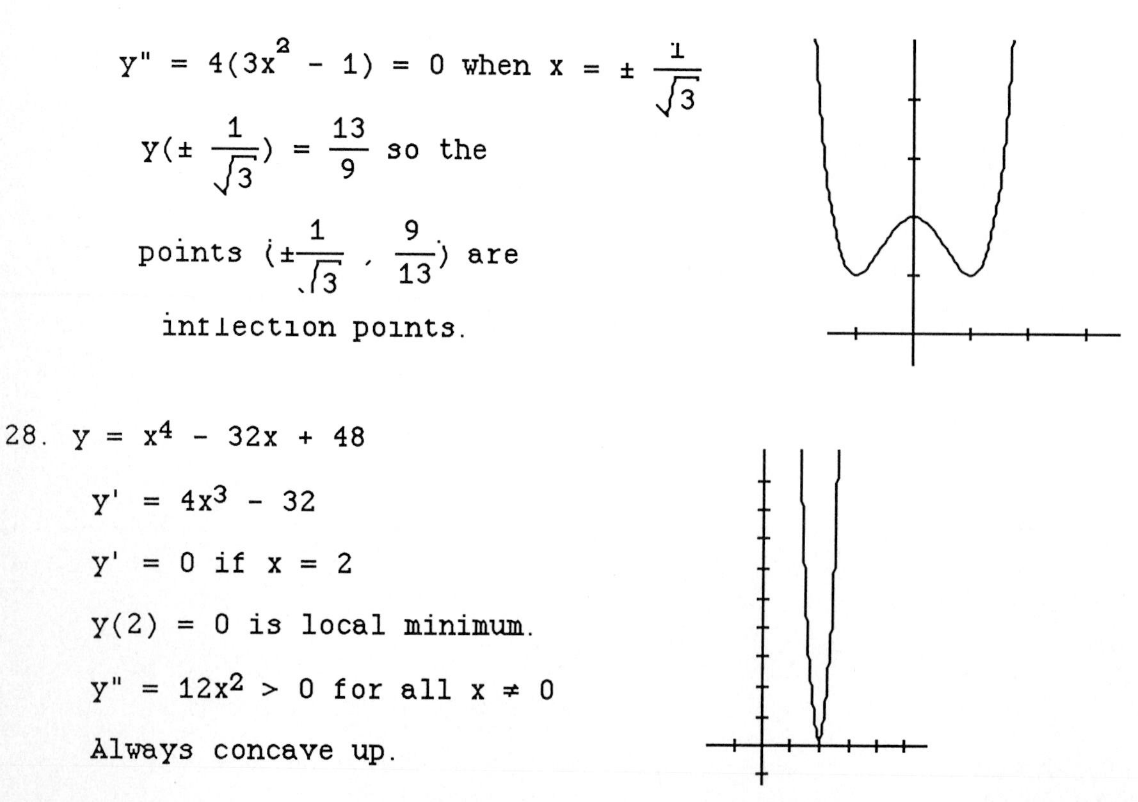

$y'' = 4(3x^2 - 1) = 0$ when $x = \pm \frac{1}{\sqrt{3}}$

$y(\pm \frac{1}{\sqrt{3}}) = \frac{13}{9}$ so the points $(\pm\frac{1}{\sqrt{3}}, \frac{9}{13})$ are inflection points.

28. $y = x^4 - 32x + 48$

$y' = 4x^3 - 32$

$y' = 0$ if $x = 2$

$y(2) = 0$ is local minimum.

$y'' = 12x^2 > 0$ for all $x \neq 0$

Always concave up.

29. $y = 3x^4 - 4x^3 \Rightarrow y' = 12x^3 - 12x^2 = 12x^2(x - 1)$. $y' < 0$ for $x < 1$ and $y' > 0$ for $x > 1 \Rightarrow y(1) = -1$ is a local minimum. There is no local extreme value at $x = 0$ because y' does not change sign there. $y'' = 36x^2 - 24x = 12x(3x - 2)$.

$y'' > 0$ for $x < 0$ and $x > \frac{2}{3}$, but $y'' < 0$ for $0 < x < \frac{2}{3}$. $(0,0)$ and $(\frac{2}{3}, -\frac{16}{27})$ are inflection points.

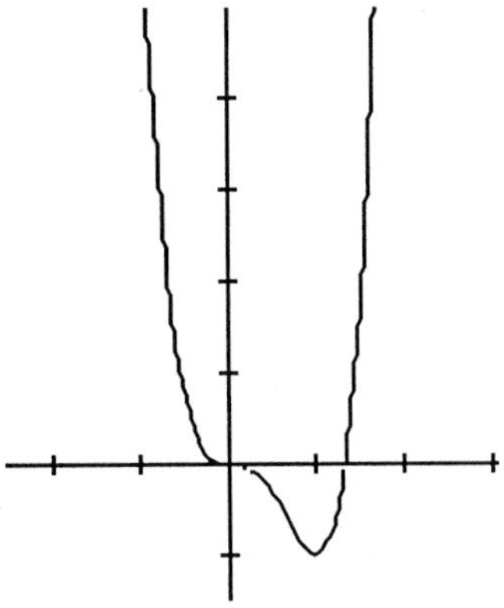

30. $y = x + \sin 2x$

$y' = 1 + 2\cos 2x$

$1 + 2\cos 2x = 0$ if

$x = \frac{\pi}{3} + k\pi$ or $\frac{2\pi}{3} + k\pi$, k an integer.

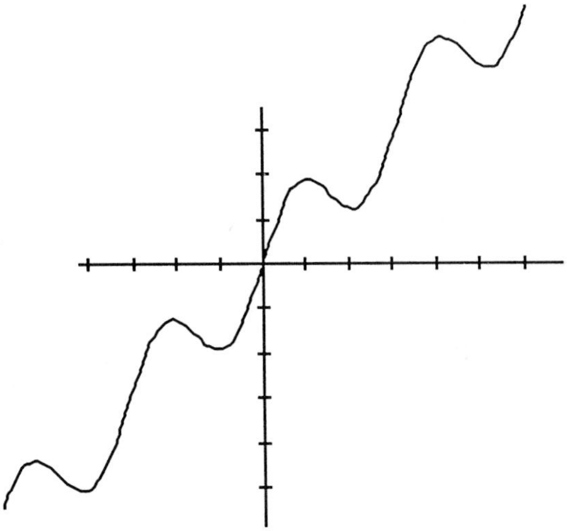

$$y\left(\frac{\pi}{3} + k\pi\right) = \left(\frac{\pi}{3} + k\pi\right) + \sin 2\left(\frac{\pi}{3} + k\pi\right)$$

$$= \left(\frac{\pi}{3} + k\pi\right) + \sin\frac{2\pi}{3}$$

$$= \left(\frac{\pi}{3} + k\pi\right) + \frac{\sqrt{3}}{2}$$ are local maxima.

$$y\left(\frac{2\pi}{3} + k\pi\right) = \left(\frac{2\pi}{3} + k\pi\right) + \sin 2\left(\frac{2\pi}{3} + k\pi\right)$$

$$= \left(\frac{2\pi}{3} + k\pi\right) + \sin\frac{4\pi}{3} = \left(\frac{2\pi}{3} + k\pi\right) - \frac{\sqrt{3}}{2}$$ are local minima.

$y'' = -2\sin 2x = 0$ if $x = \frac{k\pi}{2}$. Inflection points at each $\left(\frac{k\pi}{2}, \frac{k\pi}{2}\right)$.

31. $y = \sin x + \cos x \Rightarrow y' = \cos x - \sin x$. $y' = 0$ if $\sin x = \cos x$. This occurs when $x = \frac{\pi}{4}, \frac{5\pi}{4}, -\frac{3\pi}{4}, -\frac{7\pi}{4}, \ldots$ The values $y(\frac{\pi}{4}) = y(-\frac{7\pi}{4}) = \ldots = \sqrt{2}$ are local maxima. The values

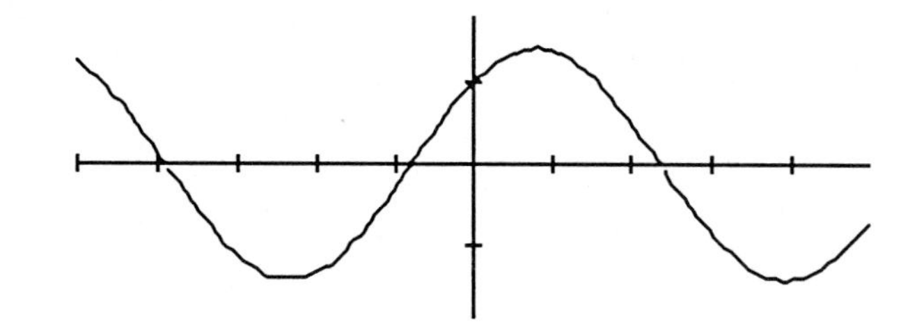

$y(\frac{5\pi}{4}) = y(-\frac{3\pi}{4}) = \ldots. = -\sqrt{2}$ are local minima

$y'' = -\sin x - \cos x = 0$ when $y = 0$. This occurs when $x = \frac{3\pi}{4}, -\frac{5\pi}{4}, \frac{7\pi}{4}, \ldots.$ Thus there are inflection points at each x-intercept.

32. $y = |x^3 - x|$

$$y = \begin{cases} x^3 - x & \text{if } -1 \le x \le 0 \text{ or } x \ge 1 \\ x - x^3 & x < -1 \text{ or } 0 < x < 1 \end{cases}$$

$$y' = \begin{cases} 3x^2 - 1 & \text{if } -1 < x < 0 \text{ or } x > 1 \\ 1 - 3x^2 & x < -1 \text{ or } 0 < x < 1 \end{cases}$$

y' does not exist at $x = \pm 1, 0$; $y' = 0$ if $x = \pm \frac{1}{\sqrt{3}}$

$y(\pm 1) = y(0) = 0$ are local minina; $y\left(\pm \frac{1}{\sqrt{3}}\right) = \frac{2\sqrt{3}}{9}$ are local maxima.

$$y'' = \begin{cases} 6x & \text{if } -1 < x < 0 \text{ or } x > 1 \\ -6x & x < -1 \text{ or } 0 < x < 1 \end{cases}.$$ Inflection points at $(\pm 1, 0)$

33. (a) f' and f" both negative state that the curve is both decreasing and concave down. Point T

(b) f' negative and f" positive state that the curve is decreasing and concave up. Point P.

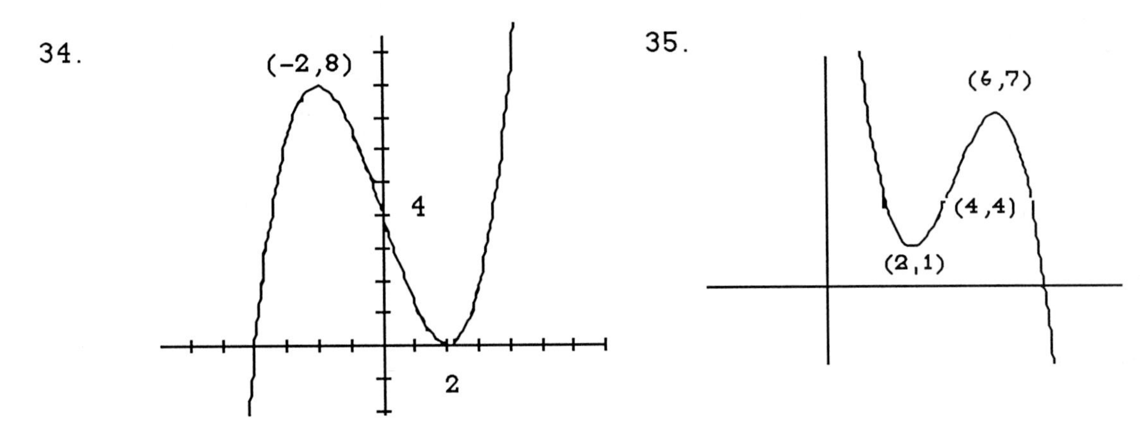

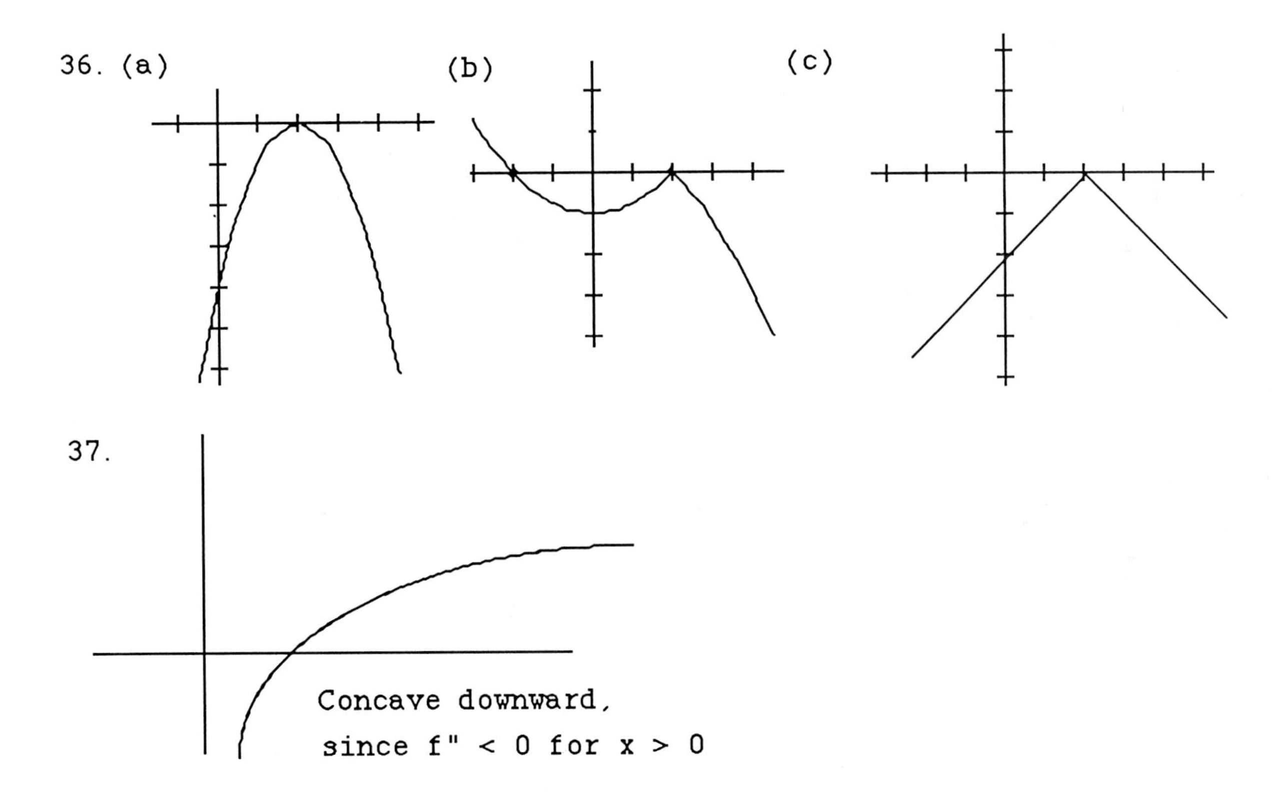

38. (d), since $y = x^3 + bx^2 + cx + d \Rightarrow y' = 3x^2 + 2bx + c$ and $y'' = 6x + 2b$. For there to be a point of inflection at $x = 1$, it is necessary for $y''(1) = 0$, so $0 = 6 + 2b$, or $b = -3$. To guarantee a point of inflection, y'' must also change sign at $x = 1$, which it will since y'' is linear.

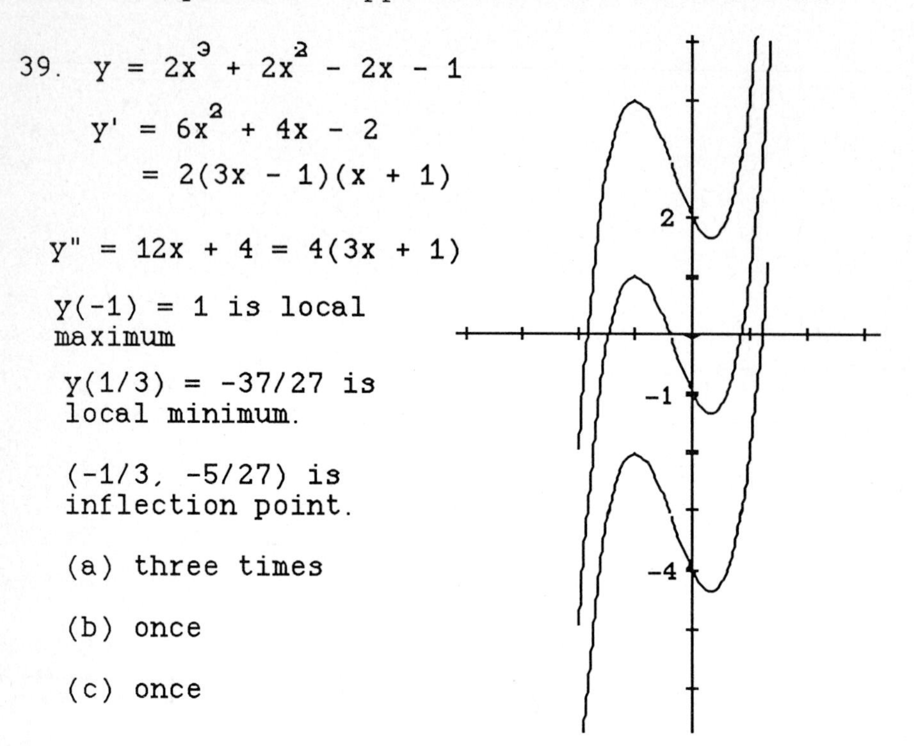

39. $y = 2x^3 + 2x^2 - 2x - 1$

$y' = 6x^2 + 4x - 2$
$= 2(3x - 1)(x + 1)$

$y'' = 12x + 4 = 4(3x + 1)$

$y(-1) = 1$ is local maximum

$y(1/3) = -37/27$ is local minimum.

$(-1/3, -5/27)$ is inflection point.

(a) three times

(b) once

(c) once

40. $y = x + \sin x \Rightarrow$
$\frac{dy}{dx} = 1 + \cos x \geq 0$ for all x
since $|\cos x| \leq 1$. Thus
y is always increasing and
cannot attain local maximum
or local minimum values.
$\frac{dy}{dx} = 0$ when $x = (2k + 1)\pi$,
so that there are horizontal
tangents at these points.

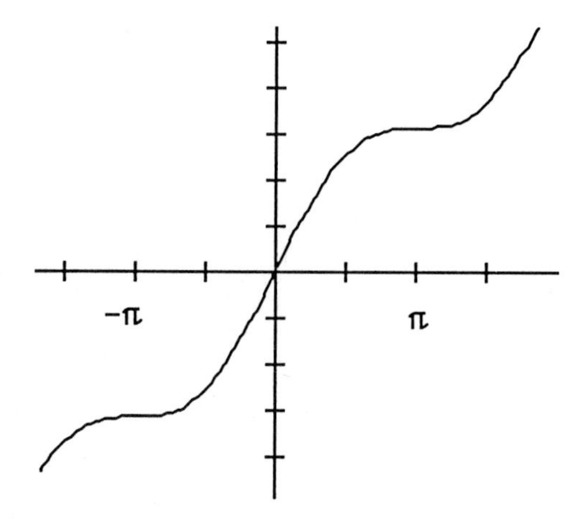

41. $y = x^4 + 8x^3 - 270x^2 \Rightarrow y' = 4x^3 + 24x^2 - 540x =$

$4x(x - 9)(x + 15)$. $y'' = 12x^2 + 48x - 540 = 12(x + 9)(x - 5)$.

x	y	curve
$x < -15$		falling, concave up
-15	$-37,125$	local minimum
$-15 < x < -9$		rising, convave up
-9	$-21,141$	inflection point
$-9 < x < 0$		rising, concave down,
0	0	local maximum
$0 < x < 5$		falling, concave down
5	$-5,125$	inflection point
$5 < x < 9$		falling, concave up
9	$-9,477$	local minimum
$9 < x$		rising, concave up

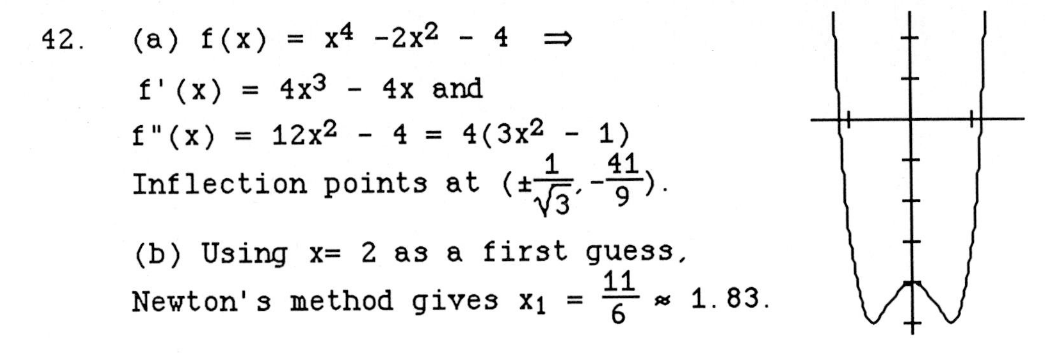

42. (a) $f(x) = x^4 - 2x^2 - 4 \Rightarrow$

$f'(x) = 4x^3 - 4x$ and

$f''(x) = 12x^2 - 4 = 4(3x^2 - 1)$

Inflection points at $(\pm\frac{1}{\sqrt{3}}, -\frac{41}{9})$.

(b) Using x= 2 as a first guess, Newton's method gives $x_1 = \frac{11}{6} \approx 1.83$.

43. (a) At x = 2 because y' changes from positive to negative.

(b) At x = 4 because y' changes from negative to positive.

3.3 ASYMPTOTES AND SYMMETRY

1. Odd. 2. Even 3. Odd 4. Even 5. Neither

6. Neither 7. Even 8. Odd 9. Even 10. Neither

11. Odd. $f(-x) = \frac{-x}{(-x)^2 - 1} = \frac{-x}{x^2 - 1} = -\frac{x}{x^2 - 1} = -f(x)$

12. Even

13. $y = \frac{1}{2x - 3}$

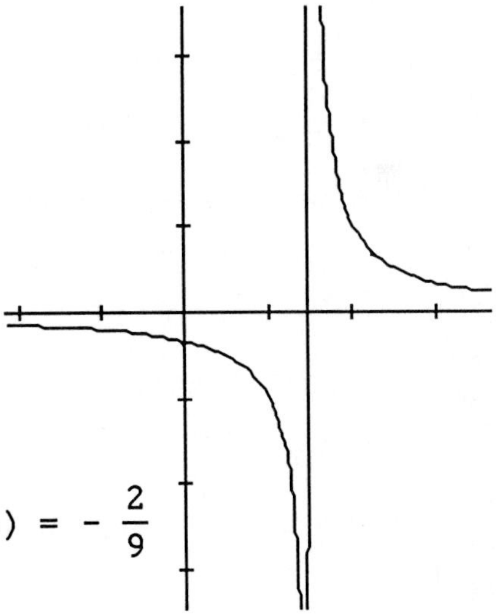

(a) No symmetry

(b) $x = 0 \Rightarrow y = -\frac{1}{3}$.

No x-intercept because y cannot be zero.

(c) $x = \frac{3}{2}$ is vertical asymptote

$y = 0$ is horizontal asymptote

(d) $y' = -(2x - 3)^{-2}(2) = \frac{-2}{(2x - 3)^2}$. $y'(0) = -\frac{2}{9}$

(e) $y' < 0$ for all $x \neq \frac{3}{2} \Rightarrow$ graph always falling.

(f) $y'' = 2(2x - 3)^{-3}2 = \frac{8}{(2x - 3)^3}$. Concave down for x in $(-\infty, \frac{3}{2})$ and concave up for x in $(\frac{3}{2}, \infty)$.

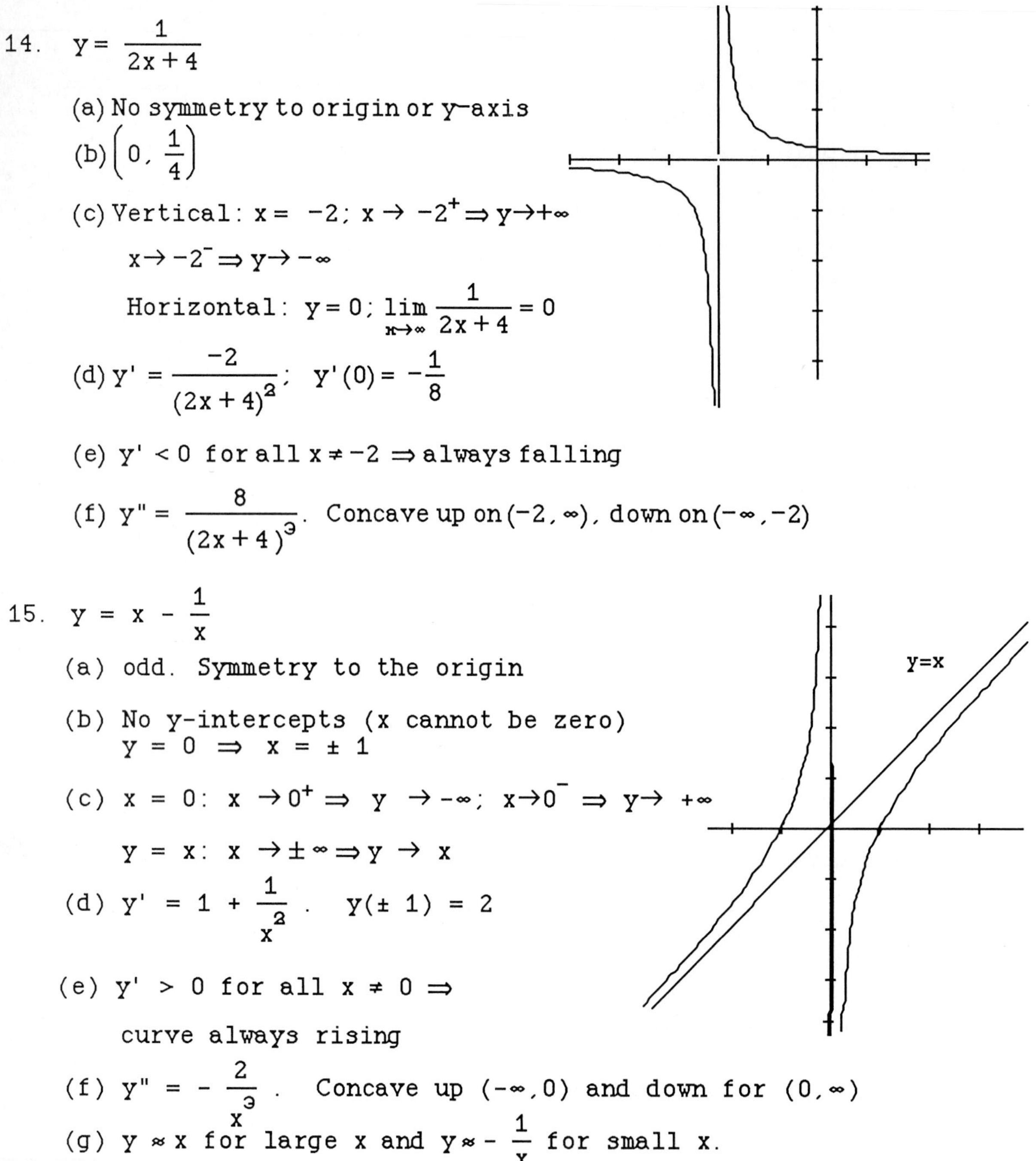

14. $y = \dfrac{1}{2x+4}$

(a) No symmetry to origin or y-axis

(b) $\left(0, \dfrac{1}{4}\right)$

(c) Vertical: $x = -2$; $x \to -2^+ \Rightarrow y \to +\infty$

$x \to -2^- \Rightarrow y \to -\infty$

Horizontal: $y = 0$; $\lim\limits_{x\to\infty} \dfrac{1}{2x+4} = 0$

(d) $y' = \dfrac{-2}{(2x+4)^2}$; $y'(0) = -\dfrac{1}{8}$

(e) $y' < 0$ for all $x \neq -2 \Rightarrow$ always falling

(f) $y'' = \dfrac{8}{(2x+4)^3}$. Concave up on $(-2, \infty)$, down on $(-\infty, -2)$

15. $y = x - \dfrac{1}{x}$

(a) odd. Symmetry to the origin

(b) No y-intercepts (x cannot be zero)
$y = 0 \Rightarrow x = \pm 1$

(c) $x = 0$: $x \to 0^+ \Rightarrow y \to -\infty$; $x \to 0^- \Rightarrow y \to +\infty$

$y = x$: $x \to \pm\infty \Rightarrow y \to x$

(d) $y' = 1 + \dfrac{1}{x^2}$. $y(\pm 1) = 2$

(e) $y' > 0$ for all $x \neq 0 \Rightarrow$

curve always rising

(f) $y'' = -\dfrac{2}{x^3}$. Concave up $(-\infty, 0)$ and down for $(0, \infty)$

(g) $y \approx x$ for large x and $y \approx -\dfrac{1}{x}$ for small x.

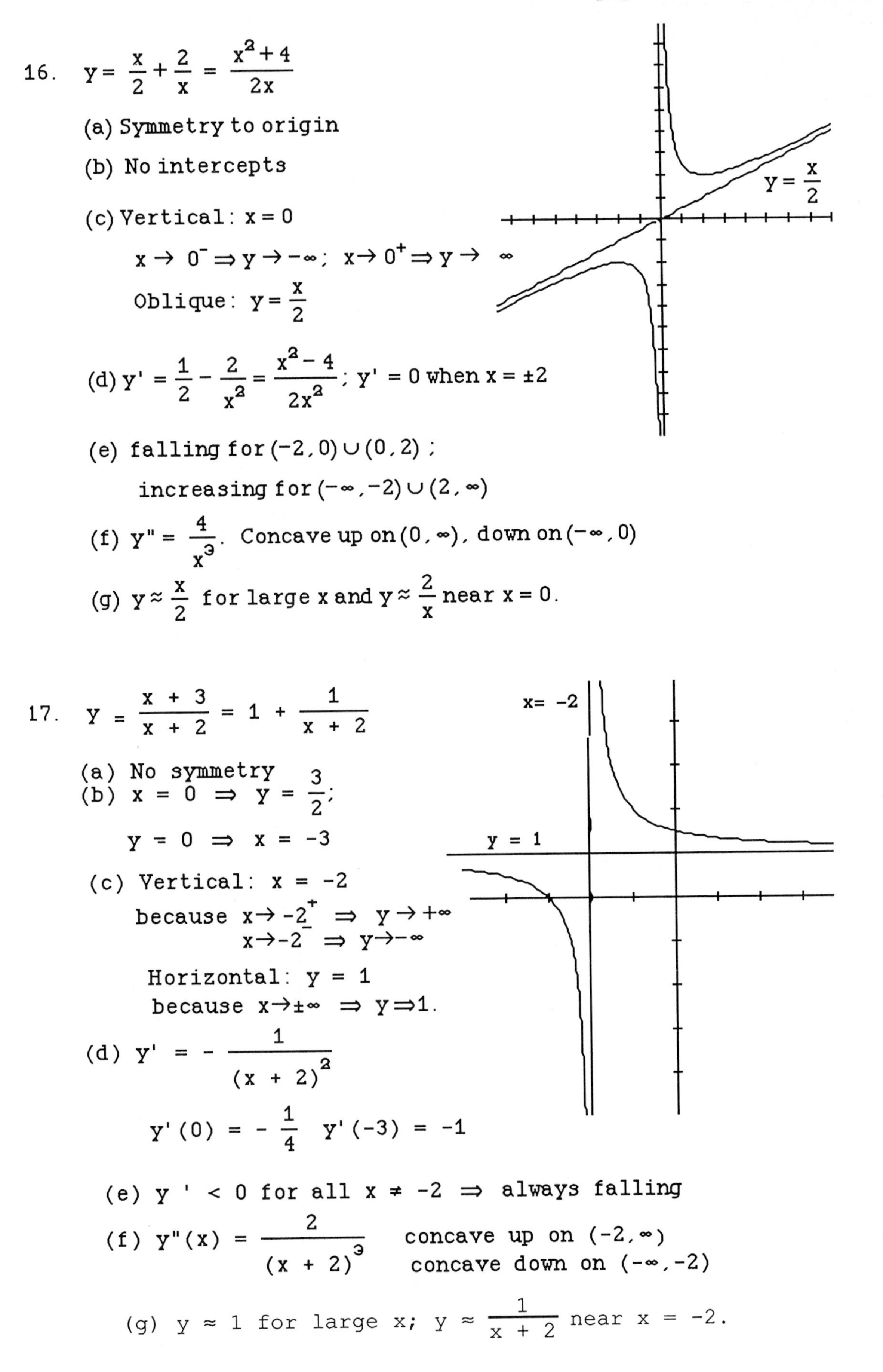

16. $y = \frac{x}{2} + \frac{2}{x} = \frac{x^2+4}{2x}$

(a) Symmetry to origin

(b) No intercepts

(c) Vertical: $x = 0$

$x \to 0^- \Rightarrow y \to -\infty$; $x \to 0^+ \Rightarrow y \to \infty$

Oblique: $y = \frac{x}{2}$

(d) $y' = \frac{1}{2} - \frac{2}{x^2} = \frac{x^2-4}{2x^2}$; $y' = 0$ when $x = \pm 2$

(e) falling for $(-2,0) \cup (0,2)$;

increasing for $(-\infty,-2) \cup (2,\infty)$

(f) $y'' = \frac{4}{x^3}$. Concave up on $(0,\infty)$, down on $(-\infty,0)$

(g) $y \approx \frac{x}{2}$ for large x and $y \approx \frac{2}{x}$ near $x = 0$.

17. $y = \frac{x+3}{x+2} = 1 + \frac{1}{x+2}$

(a) No symmetry

(b) $x = 0 \Rightarrow y = \frac{3}{2}$;

$y = 0 \Rightarrow x = -3$

(c) Vertical: $x = -2$

because $x \to -2^+ \Rightarrow y \to +\infty$
$x \to -2^- \Rightarrow y \to -\infty$

Horizontal: $y = 1$
because $x \to \pm\infty \Rightarrow y \Rightarrow 1$.

(d) $y' = -\frac{1}{(x+2)^2}$

$y'(0) = -\frac{1}{4}$ $y'(-3) = -1$

(e) $y' < 0$ for all $x \neq -2 \Rightarrow$ always falling

(f) $y''(x) = \frac{2}{(x+2)^3}$ concave up on $(-2,\infty)$
concave down on $(-\infty,-2)$

(g) $y \approx 1$ for large x; $y \approx \frac{1}{x+2}$ near $x = -2$.

18. $y = \frac{x}{x+1} = 1 - \frac{1}{x+1}$

(a) No symmetry to origin or y-axis

(b) Intercept is (0, 0)

(c) Vertical: $x = -1$

$x \to -1^+ \Rightarrow y \to -\infty$; $x \to -1^- \Rightarrow y \to \infty$

Horizontal: $y = 1$

(d) $y' = \frac{1}{(x+1)^2}$; $y'(0) = 1$

(e) $y' > 0$ for all $x \Rightarrow$ always rising

(f) $y'' = \frac{-2}{(x+1)^3}$. Concave up on $-\infty, -1)$,

down on $(-1, \infty)$

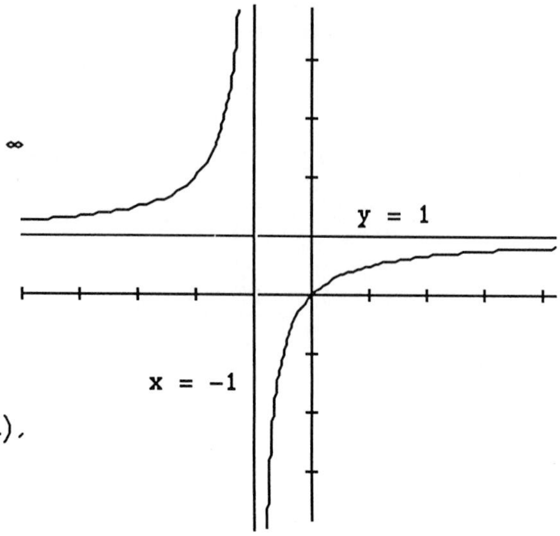

y = 1

x = -1

(g) $y \approx 1$ for large x and $y \approx \frac{1}{x+1}$ near $x = -1$

19. $y = \frac{x+1}{x-1} = 1 + \frac{2}{x-1}$

(a) No symmetry

(b) $x = 0 \Rightarrow y = -1$ $y = 0 \Rightarrow x = -1$

(c) $x = 1$: $x \to 1^+ \Rightarrow y \to +\infty$

$x \to 1^- \to y \to -\infty$

$y = 1$: $x \to \infty \Rightarrow y \to 1$

(d) $y'(x) = -\frac{2}{(x-1)^2} < 0$ for all x.

$y'(0) = -2$; $y'(-1) = -\frac{1}{2}$

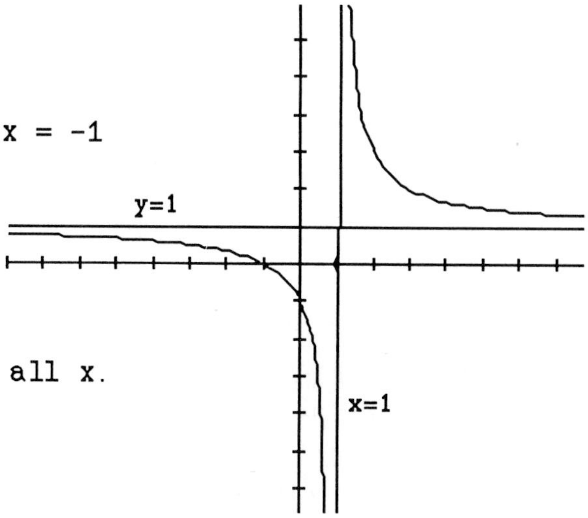

y=1

x=1

(e) graph is always falling.

(f) $y''(x) = \frac{4}{(x-1)^3}$ Convave up for $(1, \infty)$

Concave down for $(-\infty, 1)$

(g) $y \approx 1$ for large x; $y \approx \frac{2}{x-1}$ near $x = 1$.

20. $y = \dfrac{x-4}{x-5} = 1 + \dfrac{1}{x-5}$

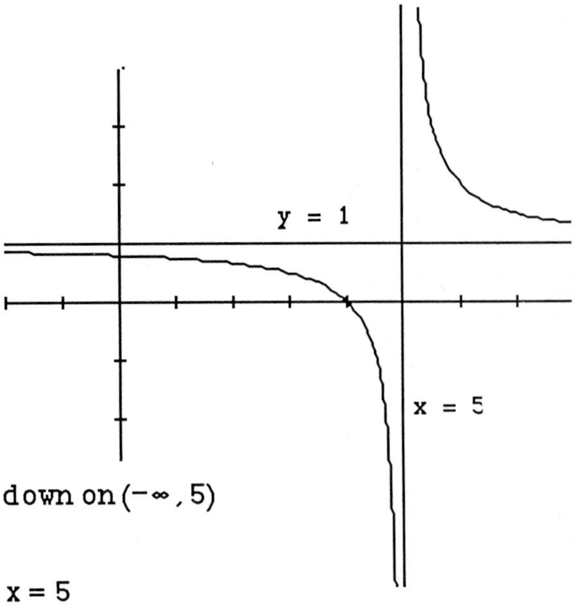

(a) No symmetry to origin or y-axis

(b) $\left(0, \dfrac{4}{5}\right)$ and $(4, 0)$

(c) Vertical: $x = 5$

$x \to 5^- \Rightarrow y \to -\infty$; $x \to 5^+ \Rightarrow y \to \infty$

Horizontal: $y = 1$

(d) $y' = -\dfrac{1}{(x-5)^2}$; $y'(0) = -\dfrac{1}{25}$; $y'(4) = -1$

(e) $y' < 0$ for all $x \Rightarrow$ always falling

(f) $y'' = \dfrac{2}{(x-5)^3}$. Concave up on $(5, \infty)$, down on $(-\infty, 5)$

(g) $y \approx 1$ for large x and $y \approx \dfrac{1}{x-5}$ near $x = 5$

21. $y = \dfrac{1}{x^2+1} = (x^2+1)^{-1}$

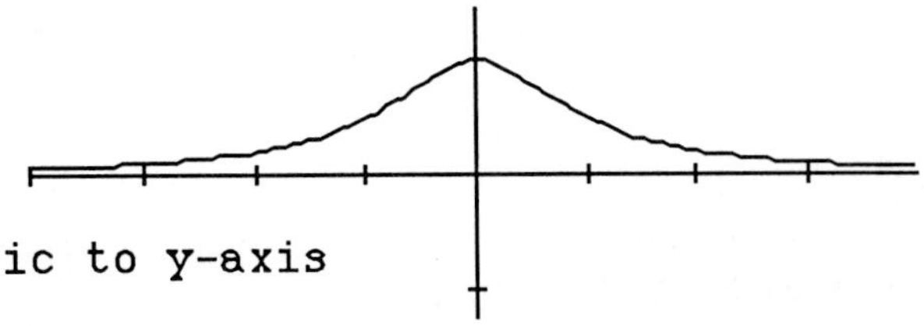

(a) even function - symmetric to y-axis

(b) $x = 0 \Rightarrow y = 1$. No x-intercept (y cannot be zero)

(c) No vertical asymptote. Horizontal: $y = 0$ since $x \to \pm\infty \Rightarrow y \to 0$

(d) $y'(x) + -(x^2+1)^{-2}(2x) = \dfrac{-2x}{(x^2+1)^2}$ $y'(0) = 0$

(e) $y' > 0$ if $x < 0$ rising
$y' < 0$ if $x > 0$ falling
$y(0) = 1$ is local maximum

(f) $y''(x) = (-2)(x^2+1)^{-2} + -2x[-2(x^2+1)^{-3}(2x)]$

$= \dfrac{2(3x^2-1)}{(x^2+1)^3}$. $y'' = 0 \Leftrightarrow x = \pm\dfrac{1}{\sqrt{3}}$.

concave up for $(-\infty, \dfrac{-1}{\sqrt{3}}) \cup (\dfrac{1}{\sqrt{3}}, \infty)$ concave down $(-\dfrac{1}{\sqrt{3}}, \dfrac{1}{\sqrt{3}})$

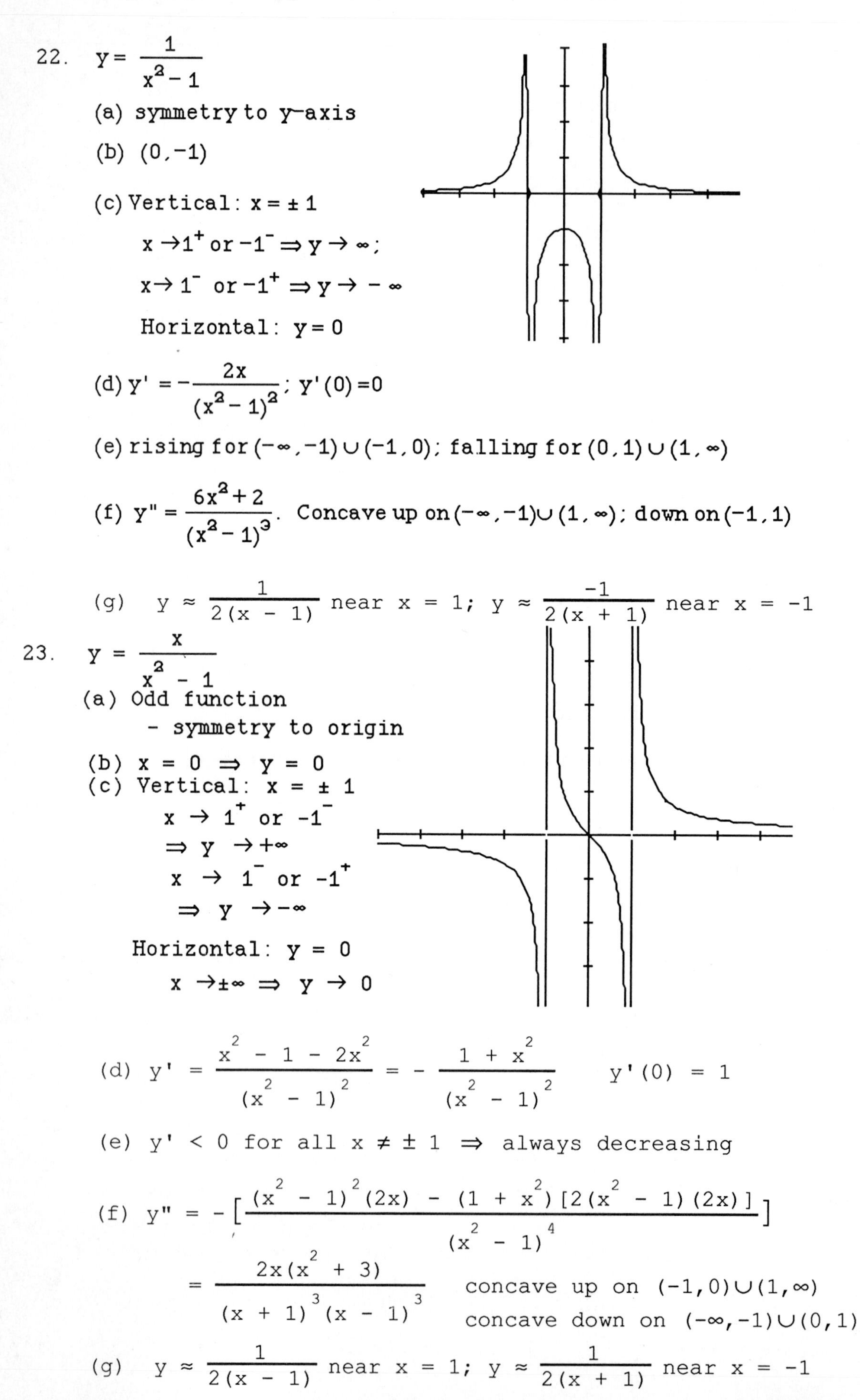

22. $y = \dfrac{1}{x^2 - 1}$

(a) symmetry to y-axis

(b) (0,−1)

(c) Vertical: $x = \pm 1$

$x \to 1^+$ or $-1^- \Rightarrow y \to \infty$;

$x \to 1^-$ or $-1^+ \Rightarrow y \to -\infty$

Horizontal: $y = 0$

(d) $y' = -\dfrac{2x}{(x^2 - 1)^2}$; $y'(0) = 0$

(e) rising for $(-\infty, -1) \cup (-1, 0)$; falling for $(0, 1) \cup (1, \infty)$

(f) $y'' = \dfrac{6x^2 + 2}{(x^2 - 1)^3}$. Concave up on $(-\infty, -1) \cup (1, \infty)$; down on $(-1, 1)$

(g) $y \approx \dfrac{1}{2(x - 1)}$ near $x = 1$; $y \approx \dfrac{-1}{2(x + 1)}$ near $x = -1$

23. $y = \dfrac{x}{x^2 - 1}$

(a) Odd function

- symmetry to origin

(b) $x = 0 \Rightarrow y = 0$

(c) Vertical: $x = \pm 1$

$x \to 1^+$ or -1^-

$\Rightarrow y \to +\infty$

$x \to 1^-$ or -1^+

$\Rightarrow y \to -\infty$

Horizontal: $y = 0$

$x \to \pm\infty \Rightarrow y \to 0$

(d) $y' = \dfrac{x^2 - 1 - 2x^2}{(x^2 - 1)^2} = -\dfrac{1 + x^2}{(x^2 - 1)^2}$ $\quad y'(0) = 1$

(e) $y' < 0$ for all $x \neq \pm 1 \Rightarrow$ always decreasing

(f) $y'' = -\left[\dfrac{(x^2 - 1)^2(2x) - (1 + x^2)[2(x^2 - 1)(2x)]}{(x^2 - 1)^4}\right]$

$= \dfrac{2x(x^2 + 3)}{(x + 1)^3(x - 1)^3}$ concave up on $(-1, 0) \cup (1, \infty)$
concave down on $(-\infty, -1) \cup (0, 1)$

(g) $y \approx \dfrac{1}{2(x - 1)}$ near $x = 1$; $y \approx \dfrac{1}{2(x + 1)}$ near $x = -1$

24. $y = \dfrac{x^2}{x-1} = x + 1 + \dfrac{1}{x-1}$

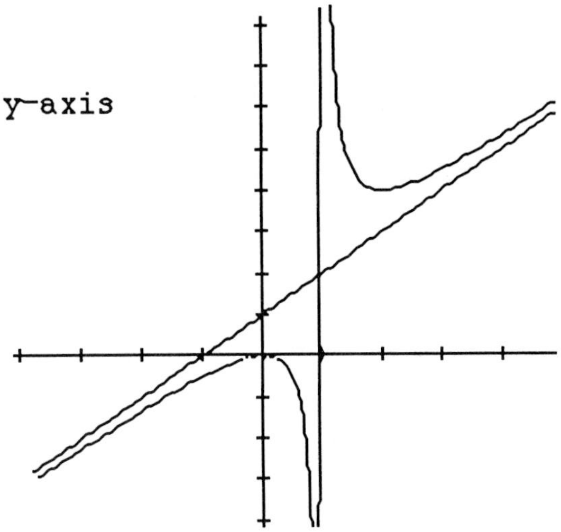

(a) No symmetry to origin or y-axis

(b) (0, 0)

(c) Vertical: $x = 1$

$x \to 1^+ \Rightarrow y \to \infty$;

$x \to 1^- \Rightarrow y \to -\infty$

Oblique: $y = x + 1$

(d) $y' = \dfrac{x^2 - 2x}{(x-1)^2}$; $y'(0) = 0$

(e) rising for $(-\infty, 0) \cup (2, \infty)$; falling for $(0, 1) \cup (1, 2)$

(f) $y'' = \dfrac{2}{(x-1)^3}$. Concave down on $(-\infty, 1)$; up on $(1, \infty)$

(g) $y \approx x + 1$ for large x and $y \approx \dfrac{1}{x-1}$ near $x = 1$

25. $y = \dfrac{x^2}{x^2 - 1} = 1 + \dfrac{1}{x^2 - 1}$

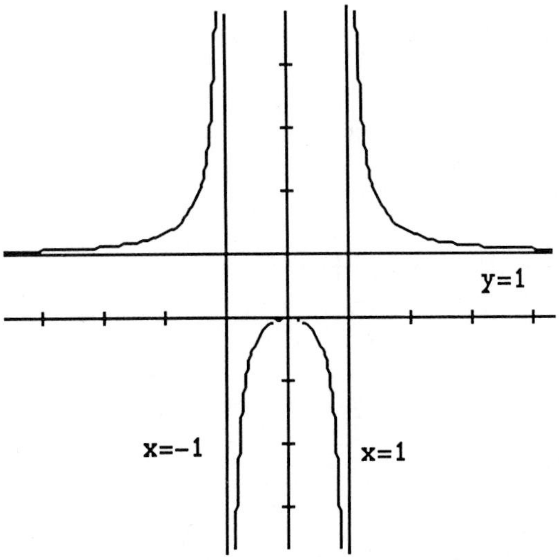

(a) Even - symmetric to y-axis

(b) $x = 0 \Rightarrow y = 0$

(c) Vertical: $x = \pm 1$

$x \to 1^+$ or $-1^- \Rightarrow y \to -\infty$

$x \to 1^-$ or $-1^+ \Rightarrow y \to +\infty$

Horizontal: $y = 1$

$x \to \pm\infty \Rightarrow y \to 1$

(d) $y' = \dfrac{-2x}{(x^2 - 1)^2}$ $y'(0) = 0$

(e) rising on $(-\infty, 0)$ and falling on $(0, \infty)$ $y(0) = 0$ local max

(f) $y'' = \dfrac{(x^2 - 1)^2(-2) + 2x(2)(x^2 - 1)(2x)}{(x^2 - 1)^4} = \dfrac{2(1 + 3x^2)}{(x^2 - 1)^3}$

y'' does not exist at $x = \pm 1$, and changes sign there.
concave down $(-1, 1)$ and concave up on $(-\infty, -1) \cup (1, \infty)$

(g) $y \approx 1$ for x large; $y \approx \dfrac{1}{2(x - 1)}$ near $x = 1$;

$y \approx \dfrac{1}{2(x + 1)}$ near $x = -1$.

$y \approx \frac{1}{2(x+1)}$ near $x = -1$.

26. $y = \frac{x^2+1}{x-1} = x + 1 + \frac{2}{x-1}$

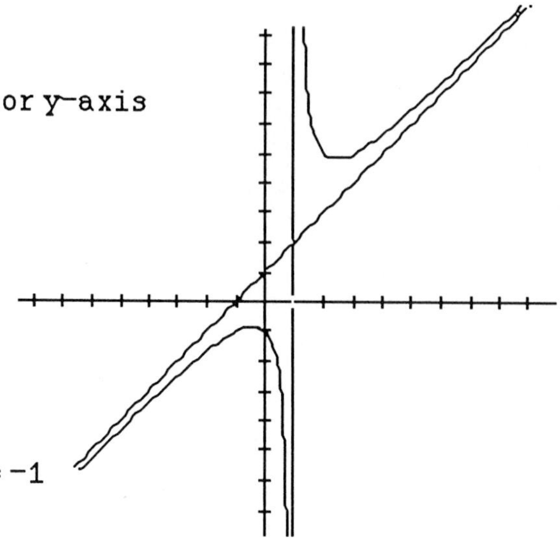

(a) No symmetry to origin or y-axis

(b) $(0, -1)$

(c) Vertical: $x = 1$

$x \to 1^+ \Rightarrow y \to \infty$;

$x \to 1^- \Rightarrow y \to -\infty$

Oblique: $y = x + 1$

(d) $y' = \frac{x^2 - 2x - 1}{(x-1)^2}$; $y'(0) = -1$

(e) rising for $(-\infty, 1-\sqrt{2}) \cup (1+\sqrt{2}, \infty)$; falling for $(1-\sqrt{2}, 1) \cup (1, 1+\sqrt{2})$

(f) $y'' = \frac{4}{(x-1)^3}$; Concave down on $(-\infty, 1)$; up on $(1, \infty)$

(g) $y \approx x + 1$ for large x and $y \approx \frac{2}{x-1}$ near $x = 1$

27. $y = \frac{x^2 - 4}{x - 1} = x + 1 - \frac{3}{x-1}$

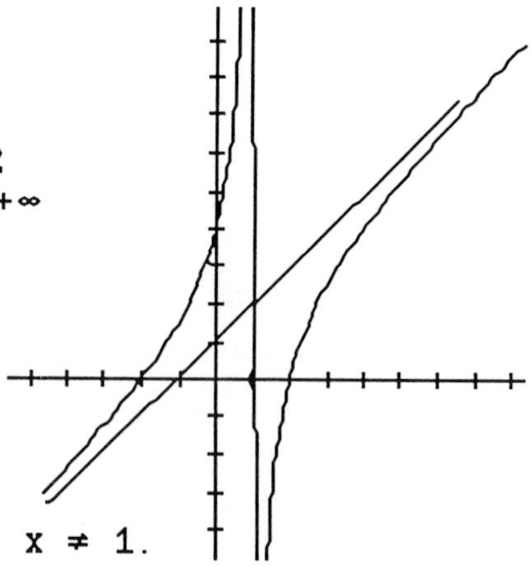

(a) No symmetry

(b) $x = 0 \Rightarrow y = 4$ $\quad y = 0 \Rightarrow x = \pm 2$

(c) Vertical: $x = 1$ $\quad x \to 1^+ \Rightarrow y \to +\infty$

$x \to 1^- \Rightarrow y \to -\infty$

Slant: $y \to x + 1$ as $x \to \infty$

(d) $y' = 1 + \frac{3}{(x-1)^2}$

$y'(0) = 4$; $y'(2) = 4$; $y'(-2) = \frac{4}{3}$

(e) Always rising since $y' > 0$ for all $x \neq 1$.

(f) $y'' = \frac{-6}{(x-1)^3}$ $\quad$ concave up $(-\infty, 1)$ and concave down $(1, \infty)$

(g) x large $\Rightarrow y \approx x + 1$.

$y \approx -\frac{3}{x-1}$ near $x = 1$

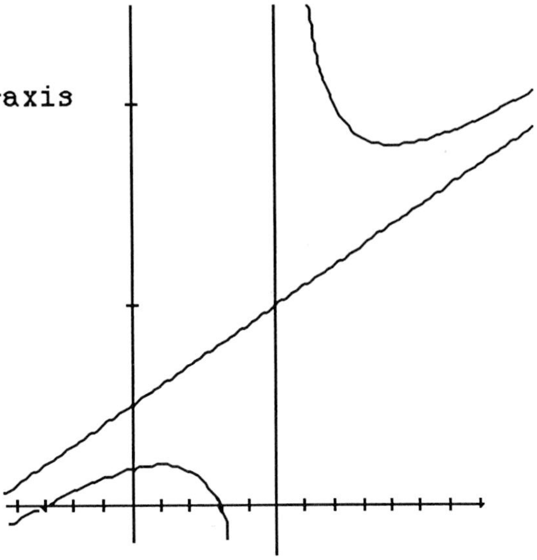

28. $y = \dfrac{x^2 - 9}{x - 5} = x + 5 + \dfrac{16}{x - 5}$

(a) No symmetry to origin or y-axis

(b) $\left(0, \dfrac{9}{5}\right)$, $(\pm 3, 0)$

(c) Vertical: $x = 5$

$x \to 5^+ \Rightarrow y \to \infty$;

$x \to 5^- \Rightarrow y \to -\infty$

Oblique: $y = x + 5$

(d) $y' = 1 - \dfrac{16}{(x - 5)^2}$; $y'(0) = \dfrac{9}{25}$;

$y'(3) = -3$; $y'(-3) = \dfrac{3}{4}$

(e) rising for $(-\infty, 1) \cup (9, \infty)$; falling for $1, 5) \cup (5, 9)$

(f) $y'' = \dfrac{32}{(x - 5)^3}$. Concave down on $(-\infty, 5)$; up on $(5, \infty)$

(g) $y \approx x + 5$ for large x and $y \approx \dfrac{14}{x - 5}$ near $x = 5$

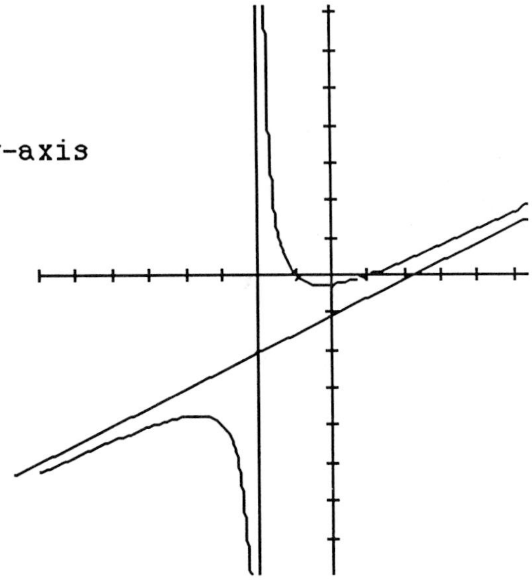

29. $y = \dfrac{x^2 - 1}{2x + 4} = \dfrac{1}{2}x - 1 + \dfrac{3}{2x + 4}$

(a) no symmetry to origin or y-axis

(b) $(0, -\dfrac{1}{4})$ $(\pm 1, 0)$

(c) vertical: $x = -2$

$x \to -2^+ \Rightarrow y \to \infty$
$x \to -2^- \Rightarrow y \to -\infty$

slant: $y = \dfrac{1}{2}x - 1$

(d) $y' = \dfrac{1}{2} - \dfrac{3}{2(x + 2)^2}$

$y'(1) = \dfrac{1}{3}$; $y'(-1) = -1$; $y'(0) = \dfrac{1}{8}$

(e) $y' = 0 \Leftrightarrow x = -2 \pm \sqrt{3}$. rising on $(-\infty, -2-\sqrt{3}) \cup (-2+\sqrt{3}\ \infty)$
falling on $(-2-\sqrt{3}, -2) \cup (-2, -2+\sqrt{3})$

(f) $y' = \dfrac{3}{(x + 2)^3}$ concave up $(-2, \infty)$ concave down $(-\infty, -2)$

(g) $y \approx \dfrac{1}{2}x - 1$ for x large; $y \approx \dfrac{3}{2x + 4}$ near $x = -2$

30. $y = \frac{x^2 + x - 2}{x - 2} = x + 3 + \frac{4}{x - 2}$

(a) No symmetry to y-axis or origin

(b) (0, 1), (1, 0) and (−2, 0)

(c) Vertical : $x = 2$

$x \to 2^- \Rightarrow y \to -\infty$

$x \to 2^+ \Rightarrow y \to \infty$

Oblique: $y = x + 3$

(d) $y' = 1 - \frac{4}{(x - 2)^2}$ $y'(0) = 0$;

$y'(-2) = \frac{3}{4}$; $y'(1) = -3$

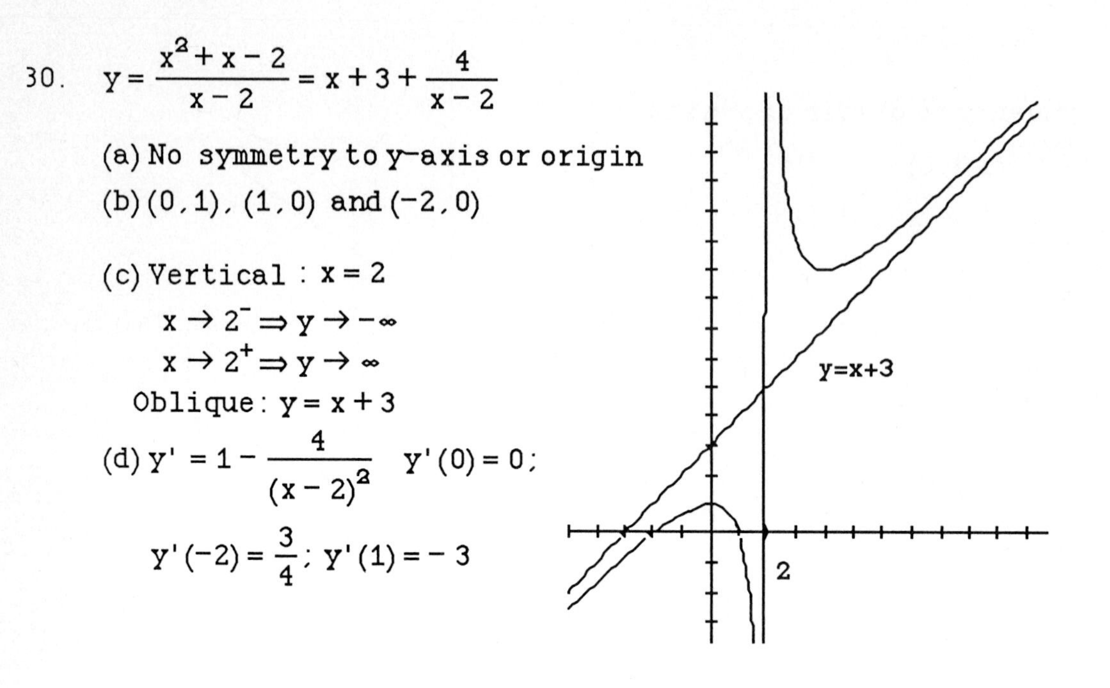

(e) rising on $(-\infty, 0) \cup (4, \infty)$; falling on $(0, 2) \cup (2, 4)$

(f) $y'' = \frac{8}{(x - 2)^3}$. Concave down on $(-\infty, 2)$

Concave up on $(2, \infty)$

(g) $y \approx x + 3$ for x large; $y \approx \frac{4}{x - 2}$ near $x = 2$

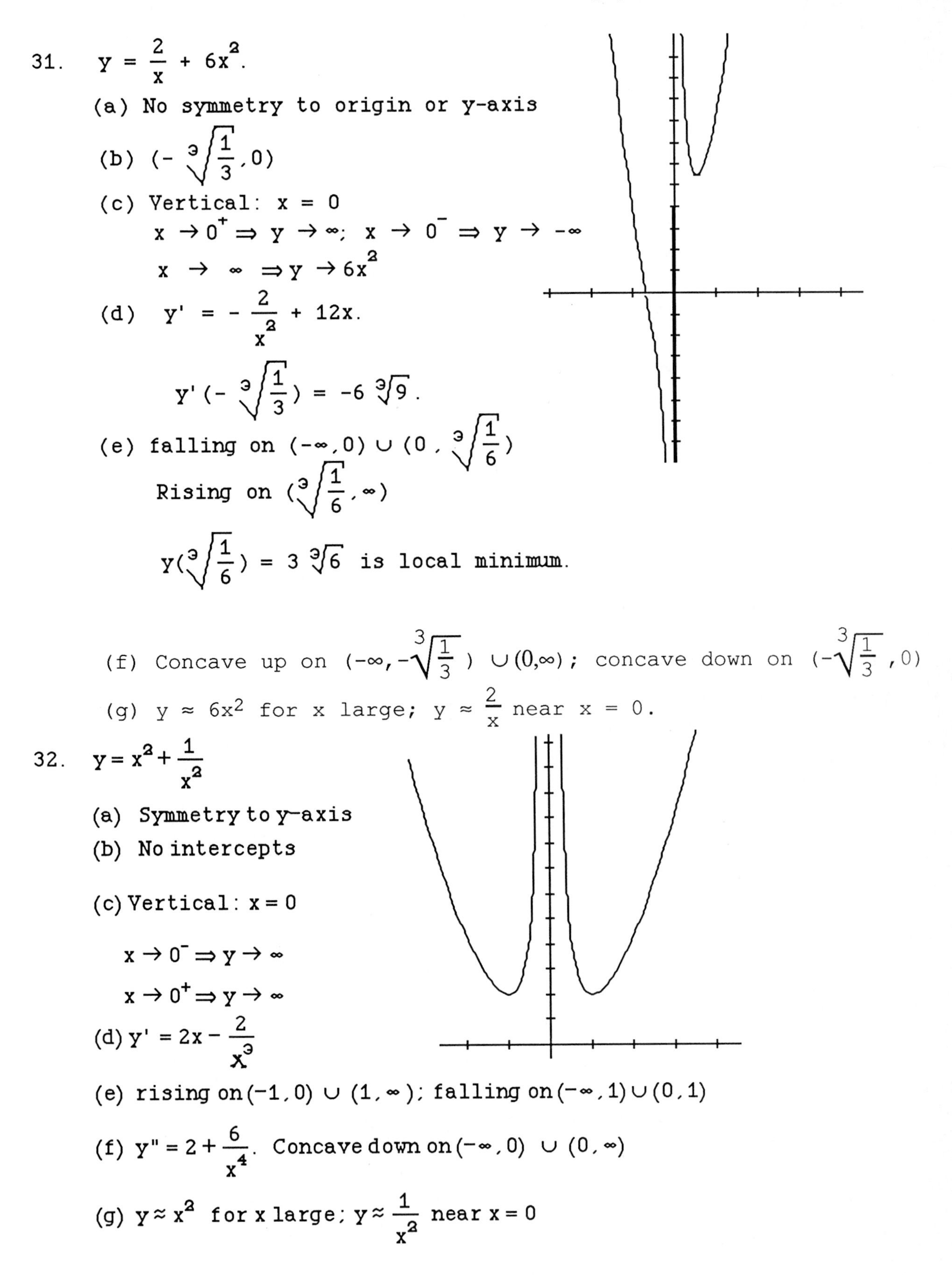

31. $y = \frac{2}{x} + 6x^2$.

(a) No symmetry to origin or y-axis

(b) $(-\sqrt[3]{\frac{1}{3}}, 0)$

(c) Vertical: $x = 0$

$x \to 0^+ \Rightarrow y \to \infty$; $x \to 0^- \Rightarrow y \to -\infty$

$x \to \infty \Rightarrow y \to 6x^2$

(d) $y' = -\frac{2}{x^2} + 12x$.

$y'(-\sqrt[3]{\frac{1}{3}}) = -6\sqrt[3]{9}$.

(e) falling on $(-\infty, 0) \cup (0, \sqrt[3]{\frac{1}{6}})$

Rising on $(\sqrt[3]{\frac{1}{6}}, \infty)$

$y(\sqrt[3]{\frac{1}{6}}) = 3\sqrt[3]{6}$ is local minimum.

(f) Concave up on $(-\infty, -\sqrt[3]{\frac{1}{3}}) \cup (0, \infty)$; concave down on $(-\sqrt[3]{\frac{1}{3}}, 0)$

(g) $y \approx 6x^2$ for x large; $y \approx \frac{2}{x}$ near $x = 0$.

32. $y = x^2 + \frac{1}{x^2}$

(a) Symmetry to y-axis

(b) No intercepts

(c) Vertical: $x = 0$

$x \to 0^- \Rightarrow y \to \infty$

$x \to 0^+ \Rightarrow y \to \infty$

(d) $y' = 2x - \frac{2}{x^3}$

(e) rising on $(-1, 0) \cup (1, \infty)$; falling on $(-\infty, 1) \cup (0, 1)$

(f) $y'' = 2 + \frac{6}{x^4}$. Concave down on $(-\infty, 0) \cup (0, \infty)$

(g) $y \approx x^2$ for x large; $y \approx \frac{1}{x^2}$ near $x = 0$

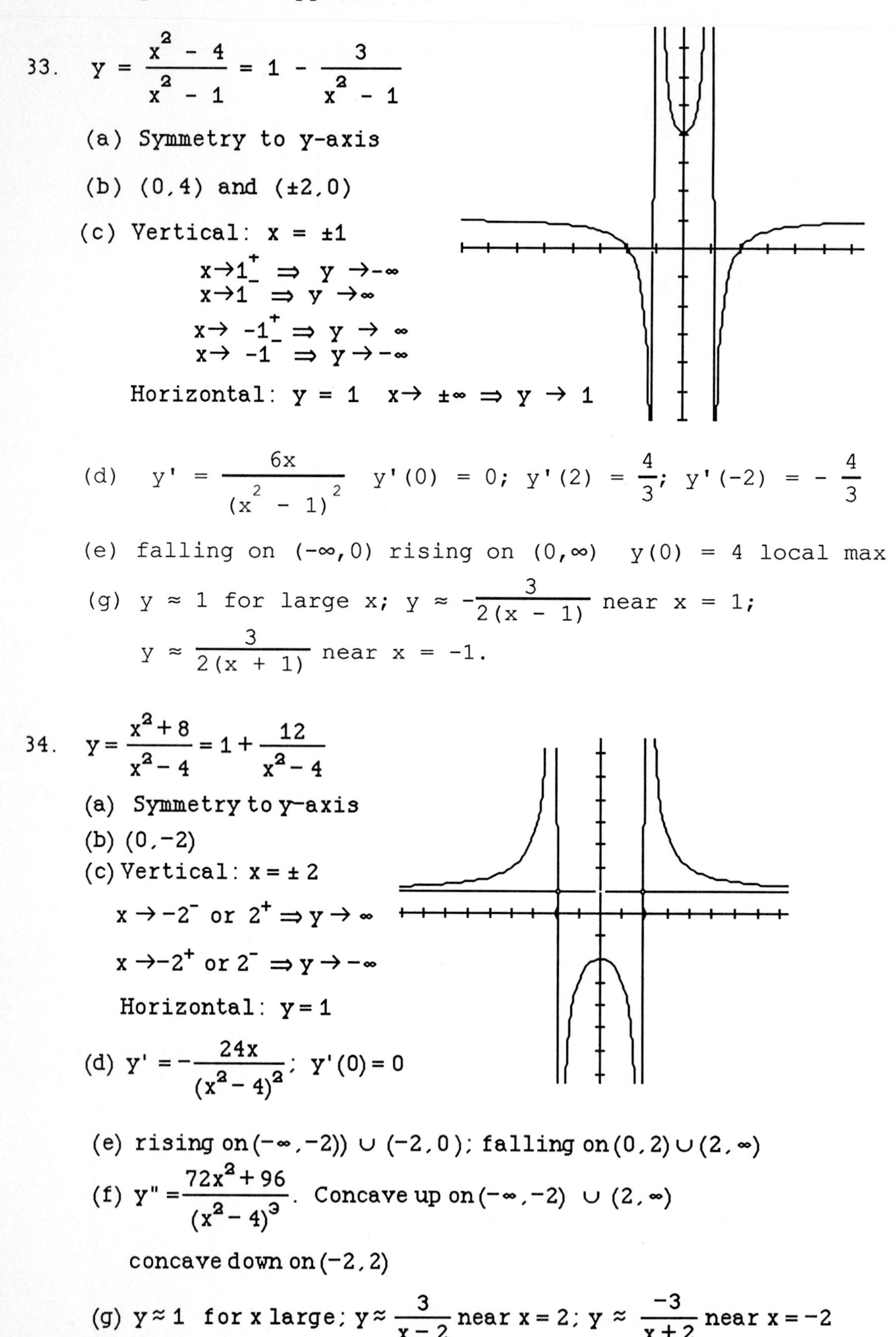

33. $y = \dfrac{x^2 - 4}{x^2 - 1} = 1 - \dfrac{3}{x^2 - 1}$

(a) Symmetry to y-axis

(b) (0,4) and (±2,0)

(c) Vertical: $x = \pm 1$

$x \to 1^+ \Rightarrow y \to -\infty$
$x \to 1^- \Rightarrow y \to \infty$

$x \to -1^+ \Rightarrow y \to \infty$
$x \to -1^- \Rightarrow y \to -\infty$

Horizontal: $y = 1$ $x \to \pm\infty \Rightarrow y \to 1$

(d) $y' = \dfrac{6x}{(x^2 - 1)^2}$ $y'(0) = 0$; $y'(2) = \dfrac{4}{3}$; $y'(-2) = -\dfrac{4}{3}$

(e) falling on $(-\infty, 0)$ rising on $(0, \infty)$ $y(0) = 4$ local max

(g) $y \approx 1$ for large x; $y \approx -\dfrac{3}{2(x - 1)}$ near $x = 1$;

$y \approx \dfrac{3}{2(x + 1)}$ near $x = -1$.

34. $y = \dfrac{x^2 + 8}{x^2 - 4} = 1 + \dfrac{12}{x^2 - 4}$

(a) Symmetry to y-axis

(b) (0,−2)

(c) Vertical: $x = \pm 2$

$x \to -2^- \text{ or } 2^+ \Rightarrow y \to \infty$

$x \to -2^+ \text{ or } 2^- \Rightarrow y \to -\infty$

Horizontal: $y = 1$

(d) $y' = -\dfrac{24x}{(x^2 - 4)^2}$; $y'(0) = 0$

(e) rising on $(-\infty, -2)) \cup (-2, 0)$; falling on $(0, 2) \cup (2, \infty)$

(f) $y'' = \dfrac{72x^2 + 96}{(x^2 - 4)^3}$. Concave up on $(-\infty, -2) \cup (2, \infty)$

concave down on $(-2, 2)$

(g) $y \approx 1$ for x large; $y \approx \dfrac{3}{x - 2}$ near $x = 2$; $y \approx \dfrac{-3}{x + 2}$ near $x = -2$

35. $y = \dfrac{x^2+1}{x^2-4x+3} = 1 + \dfrac{4x-2}{x^2-4x+3}$

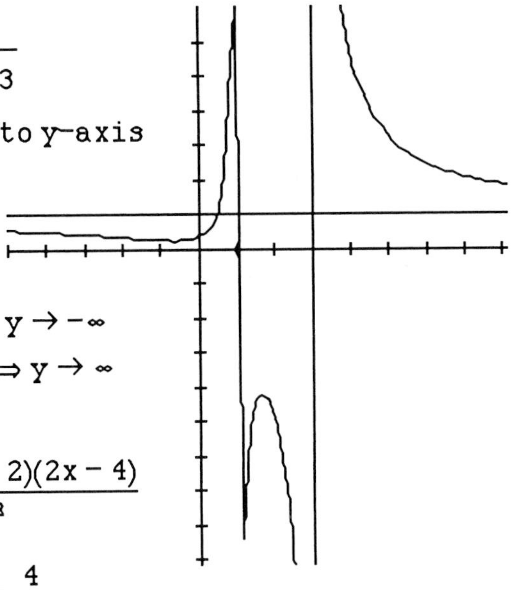

(a) No symmetry to origin or to y-axis

(b) $\left(0, \frac{1}{3}\right)$

(c) Horizontal: $x = 3,\ x = 1$

$x \to 3^+ \Rightarrow y \to \infty;\ x \to 3^- \Rightarrow y \to -\infty$

$x \to 1^+ \Rightarrow y \to -\infty,\ x \to 1^- \Rightarrow y \to \infty$

Vertical: $y = 1$

(d) $y' = \dfrac{(x^2-4x+1)(4)-(4x-2)(2x-4)}{(x^2-4x+3)^2}$

$= \dfrac{-4(x^2-x-1)}{(x^2-4x+3)^2};\ y'(0) = \dfrac{4}{9}$

(e) $y' = 0 \Leftrightarrow x = \dfrac{1 \pm \sqrt{5}}{2}$. Rising on $\left(\dfrac{1-\sqrt{5}}{2}, \dfrac{1+\sqrt{5}}{2}\right) \approx (-.6, 1.6)$

Falling on $(-\infty, -.6) \cup (1.6, \infty)$. $y(1.6) = -4.24$ local maximum

$y(-.6) = .24$ local minimum

(f) $y'' = \dfrac{4(2x^3-3x^2+6x+11)}{(x^2-4x+3)^3}$. y'' changes sign at $x = 1,\ x = 3$

and $x = -1$

Concave down on $(-\infty, -1)$, concave up $(-1, 1)$, concave down on $(1, 3)$

and concave up on $(3, \infty)$

36. $y = \dfrac{1}{x} - \dfrac{1}{x^2}$

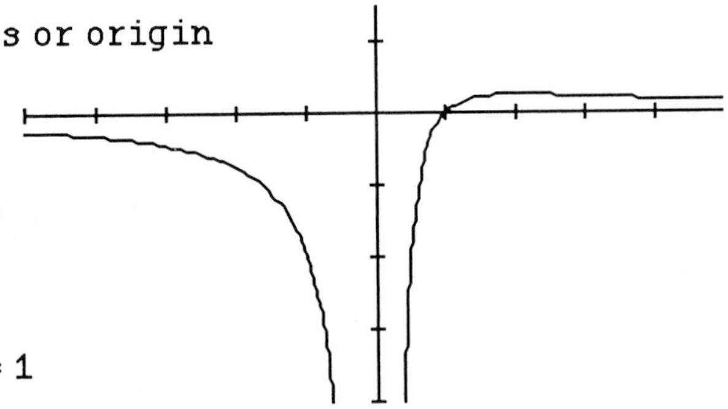

(a) No symmetry to y-axis or origin

(b) (1, 0)

(c) Vertical: $x = 0$

$x \to 0^+$ or $0^- \Rightarrow y \to -\infty$

Horizontal: $y = 0$

(d) $y' = -\dfrac{1}{x^2} + \dfrac{2}{x^3};\ y'(1) = 1$

(e) falling on $(-\infty, 0) \cup (2, \infty)$; rising on $(0, 2)$

(f) $y'' = \frac{2}{x^3} - \frac{6}{x^4}$. Concave up on $(3, \infty)$

concave down on $(-\infty, 0) \cup (0, 3)$

37. $y = \frac{x-1}{x^2(x-2)}$

(a) No symmetry to origin or y-axis

(b) (1, 0)

(c) Vertical: $x = 0$, $x = 2$

$x \to 2^+ \Rightarrow y \to \infty$

$x \to 2^- \Rightarrow y \to -\infty$

$x \to 0 \Rightarrow y \to \infty$

Horizontal: $y = 0$

(d) $y' = \frac{(x^3 - 2x^2) - (x-1)(3x^2 - 4x)}{[x^2(x-2)]^2} = -\frac{2x^2 - 5x + 4}{x^3(x-2)^2}$. $y'(1) = -1$

(e) zeros of numerator are complex and do not affect signs.

Rising on $(-\infty, 0)$ and falling on $(0, 2) \cup (2, \infty)$

(f) $y'' = -\frac{x^3(x-2)^2 - (2x^2 - 5x + 4)[2x^3(x-2) + 3x^2(x-2)^2]}{[x^3(x-2)^2]^2}$

$= \frac{2(3x^3 - 12x^2 + 20x - 12)}{x^4(x-2)^3}$. The numerator has a zero

between $x = 1$ and $x = 2$ (specifically at $x = 1.22$).

The graph is concave up on $(-\infty, 0) \cup (0, 1.22)$,

concave down on $(1,22, 2)$ and concave up on $(2, \infty)$.

38. $y = \frac{x^2 + 1}{x^3 - 4x}$

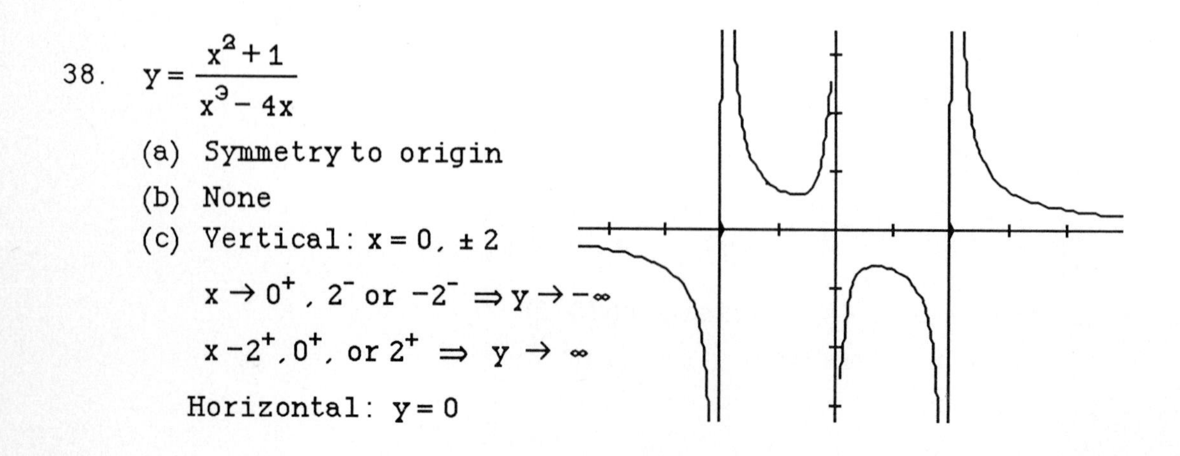

(a) Symmetry to origin

(b) None

(c) Vertical: $x = 0, \pm 2$

$x \to 0^+, 2^-$ or $-2^- \Rightarrow y \to -\infty$

$x -2^+, 0^+$, or $2^+ \Rightarrow y \to \infty$

Horizontal: $y = 0$

(d) $y' = -\dfrac{x^4 - 7x^2 + 4}{(x^3 - 4x)^2}$; $y' = 0$ if $x = \pm\sqrt{\dfrac{-7+\sqrt{65}}{2}} \approx \pm 0.7$

(e) falling on $(-\infty,-2) \cup (-2,-0.7) \cup (0.7,2) \cup (2,\infty)$;

rising on $(-0.7,0) \cup (0,0.7)$

(f) $y'' = \dfrac{2(x^6 + 18x^4 - 12x^2 + 16)}{(x^3 - 4x)^3}$. Concave up on $(-2,0) \cup (2,\infty)$

concave down on $(-\infty,-2) \cup (0,2)$

39. If $f(x) = 2 + \dfrac{\sin x}{x}$, $x > 0$, then $f'(x) = \dfrac{\cos x}{x} - \dfrac{\sin x}{x^2}$.

$\lim\limits_{x\to\infty} \dfrac{\cos x}{x} - \dfrac{\sin x}{x^2} = 0 =$ slope of line $y = 2$.

40. (a) $\lim\limits_{x\to 0} \dfrac{x^3 - 4x}{x^3 - x} = \lim\limits_{x\to 0} \dfrac{x^2 - 4}{x^2 - 1} = 4$

$\lim\limits_{x\to \pm\infty} \dfrac{x^3 - 4x}{x^3 - x} = 1$

(b) $f(0) = 4$

(c) $x = \pm 1$, $y = 1$

(d) Symmetric to y-axis

(e)

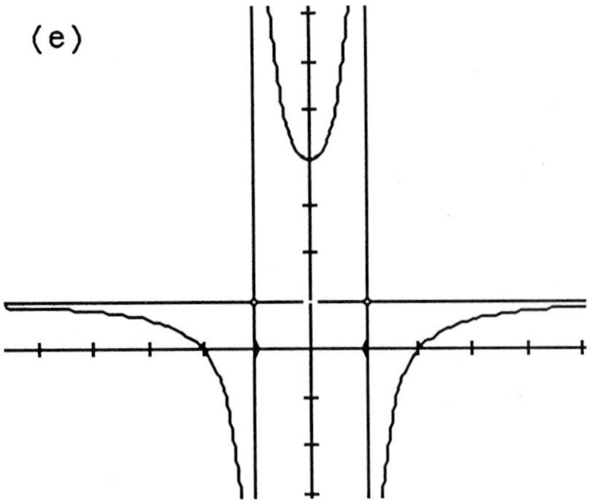

41. odd 42. even

43. even - is the reciprocal of an even function

44. odd 45. odd 46. odd 47. odd

48. even 49. even - it is squared 50. even

51. odd - the product of an odd function with an even one

52. even

53. even - the product of two odd functions (see 59 d)

54. odd 55. neither 56. odd

57. (a) even (b) even

58. Let u and v be even functions, i.e. $u(-x) = u(x)$ and $v(-x) = v(x)$.

(a) $(u + v)(-x) = u(-x) + v(-x) = u(x) + v(x) = (u + v)(x)$

Therefore $u + v$ is even.

(b) $(u-v)(-x) = u(-x) - v(-x) = u(x) - v(x) = (u-v)(x)$

Therefore $u-v$ is even.

(c) $\left(\frac{u}{v}\right)(-x) = \frac{u(-x)}{v(-x)} = \frac{u(x)}{v(x)} = \left(\frac{u}{v}\right)(x)$

Therefore $\frac{u}{v}$ is even.

(d) $(u\,v)(-x) = u(-x)\,v(-x) = u(x)\,v(x) = (u\ v)(x)$

Therefore $u\,v$ is even.

59. Let u and v be odd functions, i.e. $u(-x) = -u(x)$ and $v(-x) = -v(x)$.

(a) $(u+v)(-x) = u(-x) + v(-x) = -u(x) - v(x) = -[u(x) + v(x)]$

$= -(u+v)(x)$. Therefore, $u+v$ is odd.

(b) $(u-v)(-x) = u(-x) - v(-x) = -u(x) + v(x) = -[u(x) - v(x)]$

$= -(u-v)(x)$. Therefore, $u-v$ is odd.

(c) $\left(\frac{u}{v}\right)(-x) = \frac{u(-x)}{v(-x)} = \frac{-u(x)}{-v(x)} = \left(\frac{u}{v}\right)(x)$. Therefore u/v is even.

(d) $(uv)(-x) = u(-x)v(-x) = (-u(x))(-v(x)) = u(x)v(x) = uv(x)$.

Therefore uv is even.

60. Let be an even function and v be an odd function.

(a) $(uv)(-x) = u(-x)v(-x) = u(x)(-v(x)) = -u(x)v(x) = -uv(x)$.

Therefore uv is odd.

(b) $\left(\frac{u}{v}\right)(-x) = \frac{u(-x)}{v(-x)} = \frac{u(x)}{-v(x)} = \left(-\frac{u}{v}\right)(x)$

Therefore $\frac{u}{v}$ is odd.

(c) odd by the same argument as in (b).

61. (a) It must be increasing because of the symmetry about the origin.

(b) It must be decreasing because of the symmetry about the y-axis.

(c) Concave down, as in part (a).

(d) Concave down, as in part (b).

3.4 MAXIMA AND MINIMA: THEORY

1. $y = x - x^2$ on $[0, 1]$. $y' = 1 - 2x$. $y' = 0 \Leftrightarrow x = \frac{1}{2}$. $y' > 0$ if $x < \frac{1}{2}$ and $y' < 0$ if $x > \frac{1}{2} \Rightarrow y\left(\frac{1}{2}\right) = \frac{1}{4}$ is local maximum which absolute, since $y(0) = 0$ and $y(1) = 0$ are absolute minimimum values.

2. $y = x - x^3$, $-\infty < x < \infty$. $y' = 1 - 3x^2$. $y' = 0 \Leftrightarrow x = \pm\frac{1}{\sqrt{3}}$. $y' < 0$ if $x < -\frac{1}{\sqrt{3}}$, $y' > 0$ if $-\frac{1}{\sqrt{3}} < x < \frac{1}{\sqrt{3}}$ and $y' < 0$ if $x > \frac{1}{\sqrt{3}}$. Therefore, $y\left(\frac{1}{\sqrt{3}}\right) = \frac{2\sqrt{3}}{9}$ is a local maximum and $y\left(-\frac{1}{\sqrt{3}}\right) = -\frac{2\sqrt{3}}{9}$ is a local minimum. There are no absolute extrema.

3. $y = x - x^3$ on $[0, 1]$. $y' = 1 - 3x^2$. $y' = 0 \Leftrightarrow x = \pm\frac{1}{\sqrt{3}}$. The value $x = -\frac{1}{\sqrt{3}}$ is out of the domain. $y\left(\frac{1}{\sqrt{3}}\right) = \frac{2\sqrt{3}}{9}$ is local maximum which is absolute, since $y(0) = 0$ and $y(1) = 0$ are absolute minimum values.

4. $y = x^3 - 3x^2 + 2$, $-\infty$, $x < \infty$. $y' = 3x^2 - 6x$. $y' = 0 \Leftrightarrow x = 0$ or 2. $y' > 0$ if $x < 0$, $y' < 0$ if $0 < x < 2$ and $y' > 0$ if $x > 2$. Therefore, $y(0) = 2$ is a local maximum and $y(2) = -2$ is a local minimum. There are no absolute extrema.

5. $y = x^3 - 147x$ on $(-\infty, \infty)$. $y' = 3x^2 - 147$. $y' = 0 \Leftrightarrow x = \pm 7$. $y' > 0$ if $x < -7$, $y' < 0$ if $-7 < x < 7$, and $y' > 0$ if $x > 7$. Therefore, $y(-7) = 686$ is local maximum, and $y(7) = -686$ is local minimum. There are no absolute extrema.

6. $y = x^3 - 2x^2 + x$ on $[-1, 2]$. $y' = 3x^2 - 4x + 1$. $y' = 0 \Leftrightarrow x = \frac{1}{3}$ or 1. $y' > 0$ if $x < \frac{1}{3}$, $y' < 0$ if $\frac{1}{3} < x < 1$ and $y' > 0$ if $x > 1$. Therefore, $y\left(\frac{1}{3}\right) = \frac{4}{27}$ is a local maximum and $y(1) = 0$ is a local minimum. There is an absolute maximum at $y(2) = 2$ and an absolute minimum at $y(-1) = -4$.

7. $y = x^2 - 4x + 3$ on $(0, 3)$. $y' = 2x - 4$. $y' = 0 \Rightarrow x = 2$. $y'' = 2$ $\Rightarrow y(2) = -1$ is absolute minimum. No absolute maximum values since the domain interval is open.

8. $y = x^3 - 6x$ on $[0, 2]$.. $y' = 3x^2 - 6$. $y' = 0 \Leftrightarrow x = \pm\sqrt{2}$.

$y' < 0$ if $0 \le x < \sqrt{2}$, $y' > 0$ if $\sqrt{2} < x \le 2$. $\therefore$ $y\sqrt{2}) = -4\sqrt{2}$ is a local minimum which is absolute since $y(2) = -4$. There is an absolute maximum at $y(0) = 0$.

9. $y = x - x^2$ on $(0, 1)$. $y' = 1 - 2x$. $y' = 0 \Leftrightarrow x = \frac{1}{2}$. $y'' = -2 \Rightarrow$ $y\left(\frac{1}{2}\right) = \frac{1}{4}$ is a local maximum which is absolute. There are no other extrema since the domain interval is open.

10. $y = \dfrac{1}{x - 2}$ on $(1, 3)$.. $y' = -\dfrac{1}{(x - 2)^2}$. $y' < 0$ for all $x \ne 2$.

There are no critical points, since $x = 2$ is not in the domain. There are no absolute extrema since the interval is open.

11. $y = 2x$ on $[0, 3]$. $y'' = 2 \ne 0 \Rightarrow$ no local extrema. $y(0) = 0$ is absolute minimum and $y(3) = 6$ is absolute maximum.

12. $y = \dfrac{1}{3 - x}$ on $[0, 4]$. $y' = \dfrac{1}{(3 - x)^2}$. $y' > 0$ for all $x \ne 3$.

There are no critical points, and there are no absolute extrema because of the vertical asymptote at $x = 3$.

13. $y = x^2 + \dfrac{2}{x}$, $x > 0$. $y' = 2x - \dfrac{2}{x^2}$. $y' = 0 \Leftrightarrow x = 1$.

$y'' = 2 + \dfrac{4}{x^3} > 0$ if $x = 1 \Rightarrow y(1) = 3$ is local minimum which is absolute on $x > 0$. There are no other extreme values.

14. $y = \dfrac{x}{1 + x}$ on $[0, 1]$. $y' = \dfrac{1}{(1 + x)^2}$. $y' > 0$ for all x in $[0, 1]$.

There are no critical points. $y(0) = 0$ is absolute minimum and $y(1) = \dfrac{1}{2}$ is absolute maximum.

15. $y = x^3 + 3x^2 + 3x + 2$, $-\infty < x < \infty$. $y' = 3x^2 + 6x + 3$. $y' = 0 \Leftrightarrow$ $3(x + 1)^2 = 0 \Leftrightarrow x = -1$. There is no sign change in y'. Therefore there are no extreme values.

15. $y = x^3 + 3x^2 + 3x + 2$, $-\infty < x < \infty$. $y' = 3x^2 + 6x + 3$. $y' = 0 \Leftrightarrow$ $3(x+1)^2 = 0 \Leftrightarrow x = -1$. There is no sign change in y'. Therefore there are no extreme values.

16. $y = -x^2 + 4x$, $x \geq 0$. $y' = -2x + 4$. $y' = 0$ $x = 2$. $y'' = -2 < 0 \Rightarrow y(2) = 4$ is local maximum which is absolute. There is no absolute minimum.

17. $y = \sqrt{x} - x$, $x \geq 0$. $y' = \frac{1}{2\sqrt{x}} - 1$. $y' = 0 \Leftrightarrow 1 - 2\sqrt{x} = 0$ or $x = \frac{1}{4}$.

$y'' = -\frac{1}{4}x^{-\frac{3}{2}} < 0 \Rightarrow y\left(\frac{1}{4}\right) = \frac{1}{4}$ is local maximum which is absolute since $y(0) = 0$ is absolute minimum.

18. $y = \sqrt{4 - x^2}$ on $[-2,2]$. $y' = \frac{-x}{4 - x^2}$. $y' = 0$ if $x = 0$.

$y' > 0$ if $x < 0$ and $y' < 0$ if $x > 0 \Rightarrow y(0) = 2$ is a local maximum which is absolute. $y(\pm 2) = 0$ are absolute minimum values .

19. $y = x^4 - 4x$ on $[0,2]$. $y' = 4x^3 - 4$. $y' = 0 \Leftrightarrow x = 1$.

$y'' = 12x^2$. $y''(1) > 0 \Rightarrow y(1) = -3$ is a local minimum. $y(0) = 0$ and $y(2) = 8$. Therefore 8 is the absolute maximum, and -3 is an absolute minimum.

20. $y = x^4 - x^2$ on $[-1,1]$. $y' = 4x^3 - 2x$. $y' = 0 \Leftrightarrow x = 0$ or $\pm\frac{1}{\sqrt{2}}$.

$y'' = 12x^2 - 2$. $y''(0) = -2 \Rightarrow y(0) = 0$ is alocal maximum.

$y''\left(\pm\frac{1}{\sqrt{2}}\right) > 0 \Rightarrow y\left(\pm\frac{1}{\sqrt{2}}\right) = -\frac{1}{4}$ are local minimum which are absolute. $y(\pm 1) = 0$ so 0 is an absolute maximum also.

21. $y = \tan x$ on $\left[0, \frac{\pi}{2}\right)$. $y' = \sec^2 x > 0$. Therefore $y = \tan x$ is always rising; $y(0) = 0$ is absolute minimum, and there is no maximum.

22. $y = \sec x$ on $\left(-\frac{\pi}{2}, \frac{\pi}{2}\right)$. $y' = \sec x \tan x = 0$ if $x = 0$. $y' < 0$ if $x < 0$ and $y' > 0$ if $x > 0$; $y(0) = 1$ is a local minimum which is absolute, and there is no absolute maximum.

23. $y = 2\sin x + \cos 2x$ on $\left[0, \frac{\pi}{2}\right]$. $y' = 2\cos x - 2\sin 2x$
$= 2\cos x - 4\sin x\cos x = 2\cos x(1 - 2\sin x)$. $y' = 0 \Leftrightarrow \cos x = 0$
or $\sin x = \frac{1}{2} \Leftrightarrow x = \frac{\pi}{2}$ or $\frac{\pi}{6}$. $y'' = -2\sin x - 4\cos 2x$. $y''\left(\frac{\pi}{6}\right) =$
$-2\left(\frac{1}{2}\right) - 4\left(\frac{1}{2}\right) < 0 \Rightarrow y\left(\frac{\pi}{6}\right) = 2\left(\frac{1}{2}\right) + \frac{1}{2} = \frac{3}{2}$ = local maximum.
$y(0) = 1$ and $y\left(\frac{\pi}{2}\right) = 1$ are absolute minima, and the local maximum becomes absolute.

24. $y = x^4 - 2x^2 + 2$ on $[-1, 2]$. $y' = 4x^3 - 4x = 0$ if $x = 0$ or ± 1.
$y' > 0$ if $-1 \le x > 0$ or $1 < x \le 2$ and $y' < 0$ if $0 < x < 1 \Rightarrow y(0) = 2$ is a local maximum and $y(\pm 1) = 1$ are local minimum values which are absolute. $y(2) = 10$ is absolute maximum.

25. $y = x^4 - 8x^3 - 270x^2$ on $-\infty < x < \infty$. $y' = 4x^3 - 24x^2 - 540x$. $y' = 0 \Leftrightarrow$
$4x(x - 15)(x + 9) = 0 \Leftrightarrow x = -9, 0, 15$. $y(-9) = -9477$ is a local minimum and $y(15) = -37125$ is an absolute minimum. $y(0) = 0$ is a local maximum.

26. $y = x^4 - \frac{x^3}{3} - 2x^2 + x - 1$, $-\infty < x < \infty$. $y' = 4x^3 - x^2 - 4x + 1 =$
$(x - 1)(4x - 1)(x + 1) = 0$ if $x = \pm 1$ or $\frac{1}{4}$. $y' < 0$ if $x < -1$, $y' > 0$ if
if $-1 < x < \frac{1}{4}$, $y' < 0$ if $\frac{1}{4} < x < 1$ and $y' > 0$ if $x > 1$. Therefore
$y(1) = -\frac{4}{3}$ and $y\left(\frac{1}{4}\right) = \frac{673}{768}$ are local maximum. $y(-1) = -\frac{8}{3}$ is a local minimum which is absolute. There are no absolute maximum.

27. $y = (x - x^2)^{-1}$ on $(0, 1)$. $y' = -\frac{1 - 2x}{(x - x^2)^2}$. $y' = 0 \Leftrightarrow x = \frac{1}{2}$. $y' < 0$ if $x < \frac{1}{2}$
and $y' > 0$ if $x > \frac{1}{2} \Rightarrow y\left(\frac{1}{2}\right) = 4$ is a local minimum which is absolute on $(0, 1)$. $y \to \infty$ if $x \to 0^-$ or $x \to 1^+ \Rightarrow$ no maximum values.

28. $y = |x^3|$ on $[-2, 3]$. There is a critical point at $x = 0$ and $y(0) = 0$ is a local and absolute minimum. The absolute maximum is $y(3) = 27$. If the interval were $[-2, 3)$ there would be no absolute maximum.

29. $y = \begin{cases} -x & \text{for } x \le 0 \\ 2x - x^2 & \text{for } x > 0 \end{cases}$ $y' = \begin{cases} -1 & \text{for } x < 0 \\ 2 - 2x & \text{for } x > 0 \end{cases}$

$y' = 0 \Leftrightarrow 2 - 2x = 0 \Leftrightarrow x = 1$. For $x = 1$, $y'' = -2 \Rightarrow y(1) = 1$ is a local maximum. y' is undefined if $x = 0$, $y' < 0$ if $x < 0$ and $y' > 0$ if $x > 0 \Rightarrow y(0) = 0$ is alocal minimum.

30. $y(0) = 3$, $y(2) = 1$ is absolute minimum and $y(3) = \frac{9}{2}$ is absolute maximum.

31. $y = \frac{x}{1 + |x|}$ can be expressed as

$y = \begin{cases} \frac{x}{1 - x} & \text{for } x \le 0 \\ \frac{x}{1 + x} & \text{for } x > 0 \end{cases}$. Then $y' = \begin{cases} \frac{1}{(1 - x)^2} & \text{for } x \le 0 \\ \frac{1}{(1 + x)^2} & \text{for } x > 0 \end{cases}$

Note that each point for which y' does not exist is not in the domain of that piece. Therefore, $y' > 0$ always $\Rightarrow$ there are no extreme values.

32. $y = \begin{cases} \frac{x}{1 + x} & \text{if } x \ge 0 \\ \frac{-x}{1 - x} & x < 0 \end{cases}$ $y' = \begin{cases} \frac{1}{(1 + x)^2} & \text{if } x > 0 \\ \frac{-1}{(1 - x)^2} & \text{if } x < 0 \end{cases}$. $x = 0$ is only critical point.

$y(0) = 0$ is absolute minimum. There is no absolute maximum.

33. $y = \sin|x|$, $-2\pi \le x \le 2\pi$.

$y = \begin{cases} \sin x & \text{for } 0 \le x \le 2\pi \\ -\sin x & -2\pi \le x < 0 \end{cases}$ $y' = \begin{cases} \cos x & \text{for } 0 < x \le 2\pi \\ -\cos x & \text{for } -2\pi \le x < 0 \end{cases}$

$x \to 0^+ \Rightarrow y' \to 1$ and $x \to 0^- \Rightarrow y' \to -1$. Therefore, $y'(0)$ does not exist and 0 is a critical point of y.

$\cos x = 0$ for $x = \frac{\pi}{2}$ and $\frac{3\pi}{2}$ in $(0, 2\pi]$ and $-\cos x = 0$ for

$x = -\frac{\pi}{2}$ and $-\frac{3\pi}{2}$ in $[-2\pi, 0)$. $y(0) = 0$ is local minimum.

$y\left(\pm\frac{\pi}{2}\right) = 1$ are absolute maximum values. $y\left(\pm\frac{3\pi}{2}\right) = -1$

are absolute minimum values.

34. $y = \frac{|x|}{x} = \begin{cases} 1 & \text{if } x > 0 \\ -1 & \text{if } x < 0 \end{cases}$. The absolute maximum is 1 and

the absolute minimum is -1.

35. $y = |x^2 - 1|, -1 \le x \le 2.$

$$y = \begin{cases} 1 - x^2 & \text{for } -1 \le x \le 1 \\ x^2 - 1 & \text{for } 1 < x \le 2 \end{cases} \qquad y' = \begin{cases} -2x & \text{for } -1 < x < 1 \\ 2x & \text{for } 1 < x \le 2 \end{cases}$$

$y' = 0 \Leftrightarrow -2x = 0 \Leftrightarrow x = 0$. $y'' = -2 < 0 \Rightarrow y(0) = 1$ is local maximum.

y' does not exist if $x = 1$. $y(-1) = 0$, $y(1) = 0$ are absolute minimum values. $y(2) = 3$ is absolute maximum.

36. $$y = |x - x^2|,\ x \ge 0 = \begin{cases} x - x^2 & \text{if } 0 \le x \le 1 \\ x^2 - x & x > 1 \end{cases}. \quad y' = \begin{cases} 1 - 2x & 0 \le x < 1 \\ 2x - 1 & x > 1 \end{cases}$$

$y' > 0$ if $0 < x < \frac{1}{2}$, $y' < 0$ if $\frac{1}{2} < x < 1$ and $y' > 0$ if $x > 1$.

There is an absolute minimum at $(0, 0)$ and $(1, 0)$, and no absolute maximum.

37. $(x - 1)^2 \ge 0 \Leftrightarrow x^2 - 2x + 1 \ge 0 \Leftrightarrow x^2 + 1 \ge 2x$. If $x > 0$, then $x + \frac{1}{x} \ge 2$

38. $y = x^3 \Rightarrow y' = 3x^2$ and $y'' = 6x$. $y''(0) = 0$ and the graph has an inflection point at $(0, 0)$. $y = x^4 \Rightarrow y' = 4x^3$ and $y'' = 12x^2$. $y''(0) = 0$ and the graph has an absolute minimum at $(0, 0)$. $y = -x^4 \Rightarrow y' = -4x^3$ and $y'' = -12x^2$. $y''(0) = 0$ and the graph has an absolute maximum at $(0, 0)$.

39. $y = \dfrac{x}{x^2 + 1}$. $y' = \dfrac{(x^2 + 1) - x(2x)}{(x^2 + 1)^2} = \dfrac{1 - x^2}{(x^2 + 1)^2}$.

$y' = 0 \Leftrightarrow x = \pm 1$. $y' < 0$ if $x < -1$ or $x > 1$.

$y' >$ if $-1 < x < 1$.

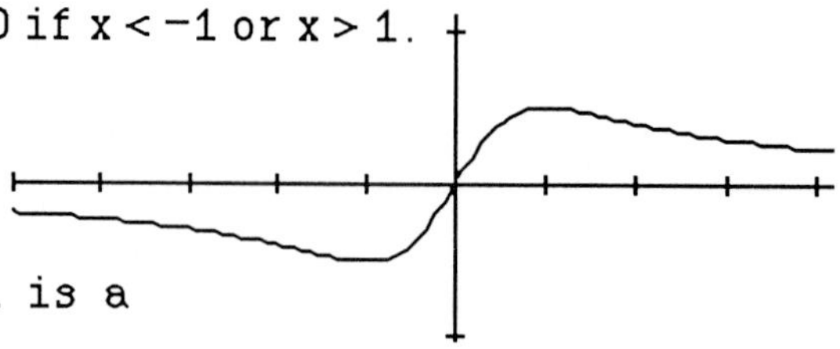

Therefore, $y(-1) = -\frac{1}{2}$ is a local minimum and $y(1) = \frac{1}{2}$ is a local maximum.

$y = 0$ is a horizontal asymptote. $y'' = \dfrac{2x(x^2-3)}{(x^2+1)3}$.

$y'' > 0$ if $x > \sqrt{3}$, $y'' < 0$ if $0 < x < \sqrt{3}$, $y'' > 0$ if $-\sqrt{3} < x < 0$ and $y'' < 0$ if $x < -\sqrt{3}$. Therefore inflection points are $\left(-\sqrt{3}, -\frac{\sqrt{3}}{4}\right)$, $(0, 0)$ and $\left(\sqrt{3}, \frac{\sqrt{3}}{4}\right)$

40. $y = \frac{x^3}{6} + \frac{x^2}{2} - 1 + \cos x \Rightarrow y' = \frac{x^2}{2} + x - \sin x = 0$ if $x = 0$.

$y' < 0$ if $x < 0$ and $y' > 0$ if $x > 0 \Rightarrow y(0) = 0$ is local minimum.

41. (b), f' must change sign at $x = c$, since it exists. The function $f(x) = x^2$ serves as a counterexample for (a) and (c).

42. $y = 4\sin x - 3\cos x \Rightarrow y' = 4\cos x + 3\sin x = 0$ if $\tan x = -\frac{4}{3}$.

There are two possibilities: $\sin x = \frac{4}{5}$ and $\cos x = -\frac{3}{5}$, or $\sin x = -\frac{4}{5}$ and $\cos x = \frac{3}{5}$. The first gives $y = 5$ which is the maximum height. (The second gives $y = -5$.)

43. $y = 4\sin^2 x - 3\cos^2 x$. $y' = 8\sin x\cos x + 6\cos x\sin x = 14\sin x\cos x$. $y' = 0 \Leftrightarrow \sin x = 0$ or $\cos x = 0 \Leftrightarrow$ $x = 0, \pm\frac{\pi}{2}, \pm\pi, \pm\frac{3\pi}{2}, \ldots$. $y(0) = y(\pm\pi) = \ldots = -3$.

$y\left(\pm\frac{\pi}{2}\right) = y\left(\pm\frac{3\pi}{2}\right) = \ldots = 4$. Maximum height is 4 units.

44. (a) $y = 2x^3 + bx + c \Rightarrow y' = 6x^2 + b$. For there to be a local minimum at $x = 1$, $y'(1) = 0$ or $0 = 6 + b \Rightarrow b = -6$. $y' < 0$ if $x < 1$ and $y' > 0$ if $x > 1 \Rightarrow$ this is minimum.

(b) $y'' = 12x > 0$ at $x = 1$ so graph is concave up and there cannot be a maximum there.

3.5 MAXIMA AND MINIMA: PROBLEMS

1. (a) Let x and $20 - x$ represent the numbers. Then the expression to be maximized is

$$f(x) = x^2 + (20 - x)^2, \quad 0 \le x \le 20.$$
$$f'(x) = 4x - 40 = 0 \text{ if } x = 10.$$
$$f''(x) = 4 \Rightarrow f(10) = 200 \text{ is a minimum.}$$

Therefore, the maximum must occur at the endpoints, or when the numbers are 0 and 20, with maximum of 400.

(b) $f(x) = x^3(20 - x)^2 = x^3(400 - 40x + x^2) = 400x^3 - 40x^4 + x^5$.

$f'(x) = 1200x^2 - 160x^3 + 5x^4$. $f'(x) = 0 \Leftrightarrow 5x^2(x - 20)(x - 12) = 0$

$\Leftrightarrow x = 12$ or 8. $f''(x) = 2400x - 480x^2 + 20x^3$. $f''(20) = 207920$

$f''(12) = -5760$. Therefore 12 and 8 give maximum.

(c) $g(x) = 20 - x + \sqrt{x}$. $g'(x) = -1 + \dfrac{1}{2\sqrt{x}}$. $g'(x) = 0 \Leftrightarrow x = \dfrac{1}{4}$.

$g''(x) = -\dfrac{1}{4}x^{-\frac{3}{2}}$. $g''\left(\dfrac{1}{4}\right) < 0 \Rightarrow g\left(\dfrac{1}{4}\right)$ is a maximum.

2. Let x and y be the legs of the triangle. Then $A = \dfrac{1}{2}xy$.

Since $x^2 + y^2 = 25$, we have $A(x) = \dfrac{1}{2}x\sqrt{25 - x^2}$. Then

$A'(x) = \dfrac{-2x^2 + 25}{2\sqrt{25 - x^2}}$. $A'(x) = 0 \Leftrightarrow x = \dfrac{5}{\sqrt{2}}$. $A'(x) > 0$ if

$x > \dfrac{5}{\sqrt{2}}$ and $A'(x) < 0$ if $x < \dfrac{5}{\sqrt{2}} \Rightarrow A\left(\dfrac{5}{\sqrt{2}}\right) = \dfrac{25}{4}$ is a maximum area.

3. Let l = length and w = width. Then $lw = 16 \Rightarrow l = 16w^{-1}$.

$p = 2l + 2w = 2(16w^{-1}) + 2w$. $p' = -32w^{-2} + 2$. $p' = 0 \Leftrightarrow$

$w = 4$. $p'' = 64w^{-3}$. $p''(4) > 0 \Rightarrow p(4) = 16$ is a minimum.

4. If $f(x) = \sin x + \cos x$, $0 \le x \le \dfrac{\pi}{2}$, then $f'(x) = \cos x - \sin x$. $f'(x) = 0$

if $\cos x = \sin x$, or if $x = \dfrac{\pi}{4}$. $f\left(\dfrac{\pi}{4}\right) = \sqrt{2}$, $f(0) = 1$ and $f\left(\dfrac{\pi}{2}\right) = 1$.

Therefore, the sum is smallest at $x = 0$ or $\dfrac{\pi}{2}$.

5. $d = \sqrt{(1 - \cos t)^2 + (\sqrt{3} - \sin t)^2}$. It is sufficient to minimize the expression under the radical.

$D = 1 - 2\cos t + \cos^2 t + 3 - 2\sqrt{3}\sin t + \sin^2 t = 5 - 2\cos t - 2\sqrt{3}\sin t$.

$D' = 2\sin t - 2\sqrt{3}\cos t$. $D' = 0 \Leftrightarrow 2\sin t = 2\sqrt{3}\cos t \Leftrightarrow \tan t = \sqrt{3}$.

$\Leftrightarrow t = \dfrac{\pi}{3}$. $D'' = 2\cos t + 2\sqrt{3}\sin t$. $D''\left(\dfrac{\pi}{3}\right) > 0 \Rightarrow \left(\cos\dfrac{\pi}{3}, \sin\dfrac{\pi}{3}\right) =$

$\left(\dfrac{1}{2}, \dfrac{\sqrt{3}}{2}\right)$ is closest point.

6. (a) The slope of line AB $= -1$. $\therefore$ $y - 1 = -(x - 0)$ or $y = -x + 1$.

(b) $A = 2xy = 2x(1 - x)$

(c) $A'(x) = 2 - 4x = 0$ if $x = \frac{1}{2}$. $A' > 0$ if $x < \frac{1}{2}$ and $A' < 0$ if $x > \frac{1}{2}$ $\Rightarrow$

$A\left(\frac{1}{2}\right) = \frac{1}{2}$ is the maximum area.

7. Let (x, y) be a point on the parabola. Then $A = 2xy =$

$2x(12 - x^2)$. $A' = 24 - 6x^2$. $A' = 0 \Leftrightarrow x = 2$. $A'' = -12 < 0$

so $A(2) = 32$ is largest area.

8. $V(x) = x(8 - 2x)(15 - 2x) = 120x - 46x^2 + 4x^3$, $0 \le x \le 4$.

$V'(x) = 120 - 92x + 12x^2 = 4(3x - 5)(x - 6) = 0$ if $x = \frac{5}{3}$ or 6.

$x = 6$ is out of the domain. $V(0) = V(4) = 0$ is a minimum volume.

$V\left(\frac{5}{3}\right)$ is a maximum. $\therefore$ Dimensions are $\frac{5}{3} \times \frac{14}{3} \times \frac{35}{3}$.

9. Let y = dimension parallel to river and x the other two

sides. Then $2x + y = 800 \Rightarrow y = 800 - 2x$. $A = xy$ $x(800 - 2x) =$

$800x - 2x^2$. $A' = 800 - 4x$. $A' = 0 \Leftrightarrow x = 200$ m.

$A'' = -4 < 0 \Rightarrow A(200) = 200(400) = 80{,}000\ \text{m}^2$ is maximum area.

10. Let x and y be the dimensions of the rectangle, so that $A = xy$

and $P = 2x + 2y$. Then $y = \frac{1}{2}(P - 2x) \Rightarrow A = \frac{1}{2}x(P - 2x)$.

$A' = \frac{P}{2} - 2x = 0$ if $x = \frac{P}{4}$. $A' > 0$ if $x < \frac{P}{4}$ and $A' < 0$ if $x > \frac{P}{4}$ $\Rightarrow$

$A\left(\frac{P}{4}\right)$ is a maximum. If $x = \frac{P}{4}$ then $y = \frac{P}{4}$, so the rectangle is a square.

11. Let x be the base dimension and y the side. Then

$x^2 + 4xy = 108 \Rightarrow y = \dfrac{108 - x^2}{4x} = 27x^{-1} - \frac{1}{4}x$. $V = x^2 y =$

$x^2\left(27x^{-1} - \frac{1}{4}x\right) = 27x - \frac{1}{4}x^3$. $V' = 27 - \frac{3}{4}x^2$. $V' = 0 \Leftrightarrow$

$x = 6$. $V'' = -\frac{3}{2}x$. $V''(6) = -9 < 0 \Rightarrow V(6)$ is maximum. The

dimensions are 6 by 6 by 3.

12. Let x be the base dimensions and y be the height of the box. Then

$V = x^2 y = 32\ \text{ft}^3 \Rightarrow y = 32x^{-2}$. $S = x^2 + 4xy = x^2 + 4x(32x^{-2}) \Rightarrow$

$S' = 2x - \dfrac{128}{x^2}$. $S' = 0$ if $x = 4$. $S' < 0$ if $x < 4$ and $S' > 0$ if $x > 4$ $\Rightarrow$

$S(4)$ is a minimum. The dimensions are $4 \times 4 \times 2$ feet.

13. $A = \frac{1}{2}ab$, where $a^2 + b^2 = 20^2$. $A = \frac{1}{2}a\sqrt{20^2 - a^2}$.

$$A' = \frac{1}{2}\left[(20^2 - a^2)^{\frac{1}{2}} + \frac{1}{2}a(20^2 - a^2)^{-\frac{1}{2}}(-2a)\right] = \frac{20^2 - 2a^2}{2\sqrt{20^2 - a^2}}.$$

$A' = 0 \Leftrightarrow a = 10\sqrt{2}$. $A' > 0$ if $a < 10\sqrt{2}$ and $A' < 0$ if $a > 10\sqrt{2}$

$\Rightarrow A(10\sqrt{2})$ is a maximum. Then $b = 20^2 - 200 = 10\sqrt{2} = a$.

14. (a) If $y = mx + b$, then $mx = y - b \Rightarrow m = \frac{y - b}{x}$. At $(2, 1)$ $m = \frac{1-b}{2}$.

(b) We have $y = \left(\frac{1 - b}{2}\right)x + b$. If $y = 0$, $x = -b\left(\frac{2}{1 - b}\right) = \frac{-2b}{1 - b}$.

(c) $A(b) = \frac{1}{2}b\left(\frac{-2b}{1 - b}\right) = \frac{-b^2}{1 - b}$, $b > 0$.

(d) $A' = \frac{b^2 - 2b}{(1 - b)^2} = 0$ if $b = 0$ or 2. $A' < 0$ if $b < 2$ and $A' > 0$ if $b > 2$

so $A(b)$ is a minimum. If $b = 2$, $m = -\frac{1}{2}$ and $y = -\frac{1}{2}x + 2$.

15. $x = (t - 1)(t - 4)^4$. $x'(t) = (t - 1)^4 + 4(t - 1)(t - 4)^3$

$= (t - 4)^3(t - 4 + 4t - 4) = (t - 4)^3(5t - 8)$.

(a) The particle is at rest when $t = 4$ or $t = \frac{8}{5}$.

(b) The particle moves to the left for t in $\left(\frac{8}{5}, 4\right)$.

(c) $a(t) = x''(t) = 5(t - 4)^3 + 3(5t - 8)(t - 4)^2 = 4(t - 4)^2(5t - 11)$.

$a < 0$ for $\frac{8}{5} < t < \frac{11}{5}$. Since v and a have the same sign,

the velocity is increasing. $a > 0$ for $\frac{11}{5} < t < 4$. Since

v and a have opposite signs, the velocity is decreasing.

Therefore, the maximum velocity occurs when $t = \frac{11}{5}$,

and is $v\left(\frac{11}{5}\right) = -\frac{2187}{125}$.

16. $x = \frac{1}{t} \Rightarrow \frac{dx}{dt} = -\frac{1}{t^2}$. $y = \frac{t^3}{3} - 4t,\ t > 0 \Rightarrow \frac{dy}{dt} = t^2 - 4$.

$\therefore \frac{dy}{dx} = \frac{t^2 - 4}{-\frac{1}{t^2}} = -t^4 + 4t^2$. We are required to maximize the

slope. $\frac{d^2y}{dx^2} = 4t^5 - 8t^3 = 0$ if $t = \sqrt{2}$. $\frac{d^2y}{dx^2} > 0$ if $t < \sqrt{2}$ and

$\frac{d^2y}{dx^2} < 0$ if $t > \sqrt{2} \Rightarrow$ maximum value at $t = \sqrt{2}$. $\frac{dy}{dx}(\sqrt{2}) = 4$.

17. Let x and y be the dimensions of the written material. Then $xy = 50 \Rightarrow y = 50x^{-1}$. The total area is $A = (8 + x)(4 + y)$ $= 32 + 4x + 400x^{-1} + 50$. $A' = 4 - 400x^{-2}$. $A' = 0 \Leftrightarrow x = 10$. $A'' = 800x^{-3}$. $A''(10) > 0 \Rightarrow$ maximum area. Overall dimensions are 18 in. by 9 in.

18. (a) $s = -16t^2 + 96t + 112 \Rightarrow v = -32t + 96$. $v(0) = 96$ ft/sec.

(b) $-32t + 96 = 0$ when $t = 3$. Maximum height is $s(3) = 256$ feet.

(c) $-16t^2 + 96t + 112$ when $t = 7$. $v(7) = -128$ ft/sec.

19. Let x and y be the dimensions. Then $xy = 216 \Rightarrow y = 216x^{-1}$. $p = 3x + 2y = 3x + 432x^{-1}$. $p' = 3 - 432x^{-2}$. $p' = 0 \Leftrightarrow x = 12$. $p'' = 864x^{-3}$. $p''(12) > 0 \Rightarrow$ minimum. The dimensions are 12 by 18.

20. $A = \frac{1}{2}ab\sin\theta \Rightarrow A' = \frac{1}{2}ab\cos\theta = 0$ when $\theta = \frac{\pi}{2}$. $A' > 0$ when $\theta < \frac{\pi}{2}$ and $A' < 0$ when $\theta > \frac{\pi}{2} \Rightarrow$ maximum area is $A = \frac{1}{2}ab$.

21. $V = \pi r^2 h$. $\pi r^2 h = 1000 \Rightarrow h = \frac{1000}{\pi} r^{-2}$. $S = \pi r^2 + 2\pi rh =$

$\pi r^2 + 2\pi r\left(\frac{1000}{\pi r^2}\right) = \pi r^2 + 2000r^{-1}$. $S' = 2\pi r - 2000r^{-2}$.

$S' = 0 \Leftrightarrow 2\pi r = 2000r^{-2} \Leftrightarrow r^3 = \frac{2000}{2\pi} \Leftrightarrow r = \frac{10}{\sqrt[3]{\pi}}$.

$S'' = 2\pi + 6000r^{-3} > 0$ for $r > 0 \Rightarrow$ minimum. $h = \frac{10}{\sqrt[3]{\pi}}$.

22. Let $S = 2x + y$. Since $x^2 + y^2 = 5$, $y = \sqrt{5 - x^2}$ and $S(x) = 2x + \sqrt{5 - x^2}$.

$$S' = 2 - \frac{x}{\sqrt{5 - x^2}} = 0 \text{ if } \frac{x^2}{5 - x^2} = 4, \text{ or if } x = 2. \ S' > 0 \text{ if } x < 2$$

and $S' < 0$ if $x > 2 \Rightarrow s(2) = 5$ is a maximum value.

23. Let x and y be the other dimensions. Then $xy = 2 \Rightarrow y = 2x^{-1}$.

The cost is $C = 10x + 5(2y) + 5(2xy) = 10x + 20x^{-1} + 20$.

$C' = 10 - 20x^{-2}$. $C' = 0 \Leftrightarrow x = \sqrt{2}$. $C'' = 40x^{-3}$. $C''(\sqrt{2}) > 0$

$\Rightarrow$ cost is minimum. Dimensions are $\sqrt{2}$ by $\sqrt{2}$ by 1.

24. We will maximize the volume. $V = Lx^2$, where $4x + L = 108$.

$\therefore V = x^2(108 - 4x) \Rightarrow V' = 216x - 12x^2$. $V' = 0$ if $x = 18$.

$V' > 0$ if $x < 18$ and $V' < 0$ if $x > 18 \Rightarrow$ a maximum value.

If $x = 18$ the dimensions are $18 \times 18 \times 36$ inches.

25. Let $D = (x - 2)^2 + \left(x + \frac{1}{2}\right)^2$. $D' = 2(x - 2) + 2\left(x + \frac{1}{2}\right)(2x)$.

$= 4(x^3 + x - 1)$. $D' = 0 \Leftrightarrow x^3 + x - 1 = 0 \Leftrightarrow x(x^2 + 1) = 1 \Leftrightarrow$

$\frac{1}{x^2 + 1} = x$. $D'' = 4(3x^2 + 1) > 0 \Rightarrow$ minimum value.

26. (a) $2x + 2y = 36 \Rightarrow y = 18 - x$. The circumference of the base

is $x = 2\pi r \Rightarrow r = \frac{x}{2\pi}$. Therefore the volume is

$$V = \pi r^2 h = \pi\left(\frac{x}{2\pi}\right)^2 y = \pi\left(\frac{x}{2\pi}\right)^2 (18 - x) = \frac{1}{4\pi}x^2(18 - x).$$

$V' = \frac{1}{4\pi}(36x - 3x^2) = 0$ if $x = 12$. $V' > 0$ if $x < 12$ and $V' < 0$ if

$x > 12 \Rightarrow V(12) = \frac{216}{\pi}$ is a maximum volume.

(b) $V = \pi x^2 y = \pi x^2(18 - x) \Rightarrow V' = \pi(36x - 3x^2) = 0$ if $x = 12$.

$V' > 0$ if $x < 12$ and $V' < 0$ if $x > 12 \Rightarrow V(12) = 864\pi$ is a maximum volume.

27. Let x and y be the legs of the right triangle, and H be the fixed hypotenuse. Then $x^2 + y^2 = H^2$. $V = \frac{1}{3}\pi x^2 y =$

$\frac{\pi}{3}y(H^2 - y^2) = \frac{\pi H^2}{3}y - \frac{\pi}{3}y^3$. $V' = \frac{\pi H^2}{3} - \pi y^2$. $V' = 0 \Leftrightarrow$

$\pi y^2 = \frac{\pi H^2}{3} \Leftrightarrow y = \sqrt{\frac{H^2}{3}} = \frac{H}{\sqrt{3}}$. $V'' = -2\pi y < 0 \Rightarrow$ maximum.

$x^2 = H^2 - \frac{H^2}{3} = \frac{2H^2}{3} \Rightarrow x = \sqrt{\frac{2}{3}}\,H$.

28. The profit $p = nx - nc = n(x - c) = \left[\frac{a}{x - c} + b(100 - x)\right](x - c)$.

$p' = 100b - 2bx + bc = 0$ if $x = 50 + \frac{c}{2}$. $p'' = -2b < 0 \Rightarrow$ the maximum selling price is $x = 50 + \frac{c}{2}$.

29. $F(x) = x^2 + \frac{a}{x} \Rightarrow f'(x)$

(a) For a local minimum at $x = 2$, we need $f'(2) = 0$ or $4 - \frac{a}{4} = 0$ or $a = 16$.

(b) For a local minimum at $x = -3$, we need $f'(-3) = 0$ or $-6 - \frac{a}{9} = 0$ or $a = -54$

(c) $f''(x) = 2 + \frac{2a}{x^3}$. For an inflection point at $x = 1$ we need $f''(1) = 0$, or $2 + 2a = 0$ or $a = -1$.

(d) $f'(x) = 0$ if $2x^3 - a = 0$ or if $x = \left(\frac{a}{2}\right)^{\frac{1}{3}}$. For this value of x, $f'' = 2 + \frac{2a}{\frac{a}{2}} = 6 > 0$ for all values of a. Therefore, there are no local maximum values.

30. (a) $f(x) = x^3 + ax^2 + bx + c \Rightarrow f'(x) = 3x^2 + 2ax + b$. A local maximum at $x = -1 \Rightarrow f'(-1) = 0$ or $3 - 2a + b = 0$.

A local minimum at $x = 3 \Rightarrow f'(3) = 0$ or $27 + 6a + b = 0$.

Solving these equations simultaneously gives $a = -3$ and $b = -9$.

(b) A local minimum at $x = 4 \Rightarrow f'(4) = 0$ or $48 + 8a + b = 0$.

$f''(x) = 6x + 2a$. An inflection point at $x = 1 \Rightarrow$

$f''(1) = 0$ or $6 + 2a = 0$. Solving these equations

simultaneously gives $a = -3$ and $b = 24$.

31. Let x be a side of the square and y be a side of the triangle.

(a) Then $4x + 3y = L \Rightarrow y = \frac{L - 4x}{3}$. $A = x^2 + \frac{y^2\sqrt{3}}{4} = x^2 + \frac{\sqrt{3}}{4}\left(\frac{L - 4x}{3}\right)^2$.

$A' = 2x + 2\left(\frac{L - 4x}{3}\right)\left(-\frac{4}{3}\right)\left(\frac{\sqrt{3}}{4}\right)$. $A' = 0 \Leftrightarrow 2x - \frac{2\sqrt{3}}{3}\left(\frac{L - 4x}{3}\right) = 0$

$\Leftrightarrow 2x + \frac{8\sqrt{3}}{9}x = \frac{2L\sqrt{3}}{9} \Leftrightarrow x = \frac{L}{3\sqrt{3} + 4}$. $A''(x) = 2 + \frac{8\sqrt{3}}{9} > 0 \Rightarrow$

local minimum value. Cut piece $\frac{4L}{3\sqrt{3} + 4}$ for square.

(b) If $y = 0$, $x = \frac{L}{4}$ and $a = \frac{L^2}{16}$. If $x = 0$, $y = \frac{L}{3}$ and $A = \frac{L^2}{12\sqrt{3}}$.

The maximum occurs if all of the area is in the square.

32. Let $P(x, \sqrt{x})$ be the point nearest to $(c, 0)$. The distance is

given by $d = \sqrt{(x - c)^2 + (\sqrt{x})^2}$ but it is sufficient to minimize the

square of the distance, $D = (x - c)^2 + x$. $D' = 2(x - c) + 1 = 0$

if $x = c - \frac{1}{2}$. $f''(x) = 2 > 0 \Rightarrow$ any critical point will be a

minimum.

(a) If $c \geq \frac{1}{2}$, then $f'(x) = 0$ at $x = c - \frac{1}{2}$ and the nearest point

is the point $\left(c - \frac{1}{2}, \sqrt{c - \frac{1}{2}}\right)$.

(b) If $c < \frac{1}{2}$, then $f' \neq 0$ for any value $x \geq 0$. Therefore,

the minimum distance will occur at the endpoint $(0, 0)$.

33. $V=\frac{1}{3}\pi x^2(y+r)=\frac{1}{3}\pi(r^2-y^2)(r+y)=\frac{\pi}{3}(r^3-ry^2+r^2y-y^3)$

$V'=\frac{\pi}{3}(-2ry+r^2-3y^2)$. $V'=0 \Leftrightarrow r^2-2ry-3y^2=0 \Leftrightarrow$

$(r-3y)(r+y)=0 \Leftrightarrow y=\frac{r}{3}$. $V''=\frac{\pi}{3}(-2r-6y)$. $V''\left(\frac{r}{3}\right)<0$

$\Rightarrow V$ is a maximum. $V=\frac{32\pi r^3}{81}$.

34. Let r and h be the radius and height of the cylinder. Then

$r^2+\left(\frac{h}{2}\right)^2=R^2$, where R is the radius of the sphere. The volume

of the cylinder is $V=\pi r^2h=\pi\left(R^2-\frac{h^2}{4}\right)h \Rightarrow V'=\pi\left(R^2-\frac{3h^2}{4}\right)$.

$V'=0$ if $h=\frac{2R}{\sqrt{3}}$. $V''=\frac{-6\pi h}{4}<0 \Rightarrow$ a maximum volume $=\frac{4\sqrt{3}\pi R^3}{9}$.

35. Let x = radius and y = height of inscribed cylinder.

Then $\frac{h}{r}=\frac{y}{r-x} \Rightarrow y=\frac{hr-hx}{r}$. $V_{cyl}=\pi x^2y=\pi x^2\left(\frac{hr-hx}{r}\right)=$

$\frac{\pi h}{r}(rx^2-x^3)$. $V'=\frac{\pi h}{r}(2rx-3x^2)$. $V'=0 \Leftrightarrow 2rx-3x^2=0$

$\Leftrightarrow x=0$ or $x=\frac{2r}{3}$. $V''=2r-6x$. $V''\left(\frac{2r}{3}\right)=2r-4r<0 \Rightarrow$

maximum value. $y=\frac{hr-h\left(\frac{2r}{3}\right)}{r}=\frac{h}{3}$. $V_{cyl}=\pi\left(\frac{2r}{3}\right)^2\left(\frac{h}{3}\right)=$

$\frac{4\pi r^2h}{27}$. $V_{cone}=\frac{\pi}{3}r^2h$. $\frac{V_{cyl}}{V_{cone}}=\frac{\frac{4\pi r^2h}{27}}{\frac{\pi r^2h}{3}}=\frac{4}{9}$.

36. $S=kwd^2=kw(4r^2-w^2) \Rightarrow S'=4kr^2-3kw^2$. $W'=0$ if $w=\frac{2r}{\sqrt{3}}$.

$S''=-6kw \Rightarrow$ a maximum value. The dimensions are $w=\frac{2r}{\sqrt{3}}$ and $d=\frac{2\sqrt{6}r}{3}$.

37. Let x and y be the dimensions of the beam. Then $S = Kxy^3$.

$x^2 + y^2 = D^2 \Rightarrow S = Ky^3(D^2 - y^2)^{\frac{1}{2}}$.

$$S' = \frac{1}{2}Ky^3(D^2 - y^2)^{-\frac{1}{2}}(-2y) + 3Ky^2(D^2 - y^2)^{\frac{1}{2}} = \frac{3D^2Ky^2 - 4Ky^4}{\sqrt{D^2 - y^2}}.$$

$S' = 0 \Leftrightarrow Ky^2(3D^2 - 4y^2) = 0 \Leftrightarrow y = 0$ or $y = \frac{\sqrt{3}}{2}D$. $S' < 0$ if

$y > \frac{\sqrt{3}}{2}D$ and $S' > 0$ if $y < \frac{\sqrt{3}}{2}D \Rightarrow$ stiffness is maximum if

$y = \frac{\sqrt{3}}{2}D$ and $x = D^2 - y^2 = \frac{1}{2}D$.

38. Let x = distance from source a and $c-x$ = distance from source b.

Then $l = l_1 + l_2 = \frac{ka}{x^2} + \frac{kb}{(c-x)^2} \Rightarrow l' = \frac{-2ka}{x^3} + \frac{2kb}{(c-x)^3} = 0$

if $(c-x)^3 = \frac{b}{a}x^3$ or $x = \frac{ca^{1/3}}{a^{1/3} + b^{1/3}}$. $l'' = \frac{6ka}{x^4} + \frac{6kb}{(c-x)^4} > 0$

so a minimum value occurs at this position.

39. Let $2x$ and y be the dimensions of the rectangle. Then

$p = 2y + 2x + \pi x$. $2\frac{dy}{dx} + 2 + \pi = 0 \Rightarrow \frac{dy}{dx} = -\frac{2+\pi}{2}$.

$$L = \frac{1}{2}\left(\frac{\pi x^2}{2}\right) + 2xy. \quad L' = \frac{\pi x}{2} + 2x\frac{dy}{dx} + 2y = \frac{\pi x}{2} + 2x\left(-\frac{2+\pi}{2}\right) + 2y.$$

$$L' = 0 \Leftrightarrow \frac{\pi x}{2} - 2x - \pi x + 2y = 0 \Leftrightarrow x\left(\frac{\pi}{2} + 2\right) = 2y \Leftrightarrow \frac{x}{y} = \frac{4}{4+\pi}.$$

$$L'' = \frac{\pi}{2} + 2x\frac{d^2y}{dx^2} + 2\frac{dy}{dx} + 2\frac{dy}{dx} = \frac{\pi}{2} + 0 + 4\left(-\frac{2+\pi}{2}\right) = -4 - \frac{3\pi}{2} < 0$$

$\Rightarrow$ Light is maximum when $\frac{2x}{y} = \frac{8}{4+\pi}$.

40. $V = \pi r^2 h \Rightarrow h = \frac{V}{\pi r^2}$. $A = 8r^2 + 2\pi rh = 8r^2 + 2\pi r\left(\frac{V}{\pi r^2}\right) = 8r^2 + \frac{2V}{r} \Rightarrow$

$A' = 16r - \frac{2V}{r^2} = 0$ if $\frac{V}{r^3} = 8$. $A'' = 16 + \frac{4V}{r^3} > 0 \Rightarrow$ a minimum.

41. $S = \pi r^2 + 2\pi rh + 2\pi r^2 = 3\pi r^2 + 2\pi rh$. $h = \dfrac{S - 3\pi r^2}{2\pi r}$.

$$V = \pi r^2 h + \frac{2}{3}\pi r^3 = \pi r^2\left(\frac{S - 3\pi r^2}{2\pi r}\right) + \frac{2\pi r^3}{3} = \frac{rS}{2} - \frac{5\pi r^3}{6}.$$

$V' = \dfrac{S}{2} - \dfrac{5\pi r^2}{2} = 0 \Leftrightarrow r = \sqrt{\dfrac{S}{5\pi}}$. $V'' = -5\pi r < 0$ for $r > 0 \Rightarrow$ maximum value.

$h = \dfrac{S - 3\pi\left(\dfrac{S}{5\pi}\right)}{2\pi\sqrt{\dfrac{S}{5\pi}}} = \dfrac{\dfrac{S}{5}}{\pi\sqrt{\dfrac{S}{5\pi}}} = \sqrt{\dfrac{S}{5\pi}}$. Maximum occurs when $r = h$

42. $2\pi r + 4x = L \Rightarrow x = \dfrac{L}{4} - \dfrac{\pi r}{2}$. $A = \pi r^2 + x^2 = \pi r^2 + \left(\dfrac{L}{4} - \dfrac{\pi r}{2}\right)^2$.

$A' = 2\pi r - \pi\left(\dfrac{L}{4} - \dfrac{\pi r}{2}\right) = 0$ if $r = \dfrac{L}{2(4+\pi)}$. $A'' = 2\pi + \dfrac{\pi}{2} > 0$

so this gives a minimum value. If $r = \dfrac{L}{2(4+\pi)}$, then $x = \dfrac{L}{4+\pi}$.

43. (a) $f(x) = x^2 - x + 1$ is never negative, because $f'(x) = 2x - 1$ $= 0$ if $x = \dfrac{1}{2}$. $f''(x) = 2 \Rightarrow f\left(\dfrac{1}{2}\right) = \dfrac{3}{4}$ is a local minimum

which is absolute since there are no other critical points.

(b) $f(x) = 3 + 4\cos x + \cos 2x$ is never negative because

$f'(x) = -4\sin x - 2\sin 2x = -4\sin x - 4\sin x\cos x = 0 \Leftrightarrow$

$\sin x(1 + \cos x) = 0 \Leftrightarrow \sin x = 0$ or $\cos x = -1 \Leftrightarrow x = 0$ or π

(over one period). $f(0) = 8$ and $f(\pi) = 0$.

44. Let t be the other base of the trapezoid, and h be its height.

Then $h = \cos\theta$ and $t = 2\sin\theta + 1$.

(a) $V = Bl = 20B = 20\left[\dfrac{1}{2}h(1+t)\right] = 20\left[\dfrac{1}{2}(1 + 1 + 2\sin\theta)\cos\theta\right]$

$= 20\cos\theta + 10\sin 2\theta$

(b) $V' = -20\sin\theta + 20\cos 2\theta = 0$ if

$-20(\sin\theta - 1 + 2\sin^2\theta) = 0$, or if $\sin\theta = \dfrac{1}{2}$.

$V'' = -20\cos\theta - 40\sin 2\theta$, and $V''\left(\dfrac{\pi}{6}\right) < 0 \Rightarrow$ maximum.

$V\left(\dfrac{\pi}{6}\right) = 10(2+1)\dfrac{\sqrt{3}}{2} = 15\sqrt{3}$ ft^3.

45. If $y = \sin x + \cos x$, then $y' = \cos x - \sin x$ and $y' = 0 \Leftrightarrow \cos x = \sin x$ or

$x = \frac{\pi}{4}$ or $\frac{5\pi}{4}$. $y\left(\frac{\pi}{4}\right) = \frac{\sqrt{2}}{2} + \frac{\sqrt{2}}{2} = \sqrt{2}$ is a maximum and

$y\left(\frac{5\pi}{4}\right) = -\frac{\sqrt{2}}{2} - \frac{\sqrt{2}}{2} = -\sqrt{2}$ is a minimum value.

46. Draw AQ, and let F be the point of intersection with DP.

Note that DP is the $\perp$-bisector of AQ. Let the length of AQ and QB be denoted by m and z respectively. Now

$$\frac{AF}{AP} = \frac{AB}{AQ}, \text{ or } \frac{m/2}{x} = \frac{8.5}{m} \Rightarrow m^2 = 17x.$$

$$\frac{QB}{AQ} = \frac{AP}{DP}, \text{ or } \frac{z}{m} = \frac{x}{L} \Rightarrow L = \frac{xm}{z}. \quad \text{Then}$$

$$L^2 = \frac{x^2m^2}{z^2} = \frac{x^2(17x)}{m^2 - (8.5)^2} = \frac{17x^3}{17x - \left(\frac{17}{2}\right)^2} = \frac{2x^3}{2x - 8.5}, \quad 4.25 < x < 8.5$$

(b) Let $f(x) = L^2$, then $f' = \frac{8x^3 - 51x^2}{(2x - 8.5)^2} = 0$ if $x = \frac{51}{8}$. $f' < 0$ for

$x < \frac{51}{8}$ and $f' > 0$ for $x > \frac{51}{8} \Rightarrow$ a minimum value of $L^2 = \frac{(17)^2(27)}{64} \approx 11.04$

47. Let $x =$ the radius of the hemisphere, and $y =$ height of the cylinder. Then

$V = \pi x^2 y + \frac{2}{3}\pi x^3 \Rightarrow y = \frac{V}{\pi x^2} - \frac{2x}{3}$. $C = 2\pi xy + 2(2\pi x^2)$

$$= 2\pi x\left(\frac{V}{\pi x^2} - \frac{2x}{3}\right) + 4\pi x^2 = \frac{2V}{x} + \frac{8\pi}{3}x^2.$$

$$C' = -2Vx^{-2} + \frac{16\pi}{3}x = 0 \Leftrightarrow x^3 = \frac{3V}{8\pi} \text{ or } x = \left(\frac{3V}{8\pi}\right)^{\frac{1}{3}}.$$

$C'' = 4Vx^{-3} + \frac{16\pi}{3} > 0$ for $x > 0 \Rightarrow$ this gives a minimum value.

If $x = \left(\frac{3V}{8\pi}\right)^{\frac{1}{3}}$ then $y = \left(\frac{3V}{\pi}\right)^{\frac{1}{3}}$.

48. Let A = fixed total surface area, V = total volume, r = radius of sphere, and x = edge of cube. Then $A = 4\pi r^2 + 6x^2 \Rightarrow 0 = 8\pi r + 12x\frac{dx}{dr} \Rightarrow$

$$\frac{dx}{dr} = -\frac{2\pi r}{3x}. \quad V = \frac{4}{3}\pi r^3 + x^3 \Rightarrow \frac{dV}{dr} = 4\pi r^2 + 3x^2\frac{dx}{dr} = 4\pi r^2 + 3x^2\left(-\frac{2\pi r}{3x}\right) = 0$$

if $4\pi r^2 - 2\pi rx = 0$ or if $x = 2r$ or 0.

(a) $\frac{d^2V}{dr^2} = 8\pi r - 2\pi x + \frac{4\pi^2 r^2}{3x}$ and at $x = 2r$, $\frac{d^2V}{dr^2} = 2\pi\left(2 + \frac{\pi}{3}\right)r > 0$

so the volume is a minimum when $x = 2r$ or $\frac{x}{2r} = 1$.

(b) The maximum volume is when $x = 0$, or when the shpere gets it all.

Then $r = \sqrt{\frac{A}{4\pi}}$ or $2r = \sqrt{\frac{A}{\pi}}$.

49. $(x + y)^2 + (b - a)^2 = c^2 \Rightarrow 2(x + y)\left(1 + \frac{dy}{dx}\right) = 0 \Rightarrow \frac{dy}{dx} = -1$

$d_1 = (x^2 + b^2)^{\frac{1}{2}}$ and $d_2 = (y^2 + a^2)^{\frac{1}{2}}$. Then $t = d_1 + d_2$ is the distance to be minimized.

$$\frac{dt}{dx} = \frac{1}{2}(x^2 + b^2)^{-\frac{1}{2}}(2x) + \frac{1}{2}(y^2 + a^2)^{-\frac{1}{2}}(2y)\left(\frac{dy}{dx}\right)$$

$$= x(x^2 + b^2)^{-\frac{1}{2}} - y(y^2 + a^2)^{-\frac{1}{2}}$$

$$\frac{dt}{dx} = 0 \Leftrightarrow x(y^2 + a^2)^{-\frac{1}{2}} = y(x^2 + b^2)^{-\frac{1}{2}} \Leftrightarrow x^2(y^2 + a^2) = y^2(x^2 + b^2)$$

$$\Leftrightarrow x^2a^2 = y^2b^2 \Leftrightarrow y = \frac{a}{b}x.$$

$$\frac{d^2t}{dx^2} = (x^2 + b^2)^{-\frac{1}{2}} - \frac{x}{2}(x^2 + b^2)^{-\frac{3}{2}}(2x) - (y^2 + b^2)^{-\frac{1}{2}}\frac{dy}{dx} - + \frac{y}{2}(y^2 + a^2)^{-\frac{3}{2}}(2y)\frac{dy}{dx}$$

$$= \frac{x^2 + b^2 - x^2}{(x^2 + b^2)^{\frac{3}{2}}} + \frac{y^2 + b^2 - y^2}{(y^2 + b^2)^{\frac{3}{2}}} > 0 \Rightarrow \text{minimum distance.}$$

$$t = \sqrt{x^2 + b^2} + \sqrt{\frac{a^2x^2}{b^2} + a^2} = \left(1 + \frac{a}{b}\right)\sqrt{x^2 + b^2}.$$

To get x in terms of c we use: $c^2 = (b - a)^2 + \left(x + \frac{ax}{b}\right)^2 =$

$$(b - a)^2 + x^2\left(1 + \frac{a}{b}\right)^2 \Rightarrow x^2 = \frac{c^2 - (b - a)^2}{\left(1 + \frac{a}{b}\right)^2}.$$

$$t = \left(1 + \frac{a}{b}\right)\sqrt{\frac{c^2 - (b - a)^2 + b^2\,\frac{(b + a)^2}{b^2}}{\left(1 + \frac{a}{b}\right)^2}} = \sqrt{c^2 + 4ab}$$

50. Let $f(x) = (a^2 + x^2)^{1/2} + [(c - x)^2 + b^2]^{1/2}$ be the total distance that the light travels. Then

$$f'(x) = \frac{x}{(a^2 + x^2)^{1/2}} + \frac{-(c - x)}{[(c - x)^2 + b^2]^{1/2}} = 0$$

if $\frac{x^2}{a^2 + x^2} = \frac{(c - x)^2}{(c - x)^2 + b^2}$ or if $\frac{x}{a} = \frac{c - x}{b}$. Thus $\Delta OAT \approx \Delta CBT$, so $\theta_1 = \theta_2$.

51. The distance between the graphs is $D(x) = f(x) - g(x)$.
$D'(x) = f'(x) - g'(x) = 0 \Leftrightarrow f'(x) = g'(x)$.
$D''(x) = f''(x) - g''(x) < 0$ since, from the graph, $f''(x) < 0$ and $g''(x) > 0$ for $a < x < b$. Therefore, the critical point occurs where $f'(c) = g'(c)$, so that the tangent lines are parallel.

52. Let x = number of additional persons above 50. Then
$P = (50 + x)(200 - 2x) - [6000 + 32(50 + x)] = 2400 + 68x - 2x^2$.
$P' = 68 - 4x = 0$ if $x = 17$. $P'' = -4 \Rightarrow x = 17$ gives maximum.
$P(50) = \$10{,}000$, $P(80) = \$11{,}760$ and $P(67) = \$19{,}266$. $\therefore$ 67 people will maximize the profit.

53. Marginal cost $= \frac{dy}{dx}$. Let the revenue be $R = xP$, so that

$$\frac{dR}{dx} = x\frac{dP}{dx} + P.$$

(a) Profit $T = xP - y = R - y$ would be maximized at a point where $\frac{dT}{dx} = \frac{dR}{dx} - \frac{dy}{dx} = 0$ or where $\frac{dR}{dx} = \frac{dy}{dx}$.

(b) For T to be maximal, $\frac{d^2T}{dx^2} < 0$, or $\frac{d^2R}{dx^2} - \frac{d^2y}{dx^2} < 0$ or $\frac{d^2y}{dx^2} > \frac{d^2R}{dx^2}$.

54. $\frac{8}{x} = \frac{y}{x+27} \Rightarrow y = 8 + \frac{216}{x}$.

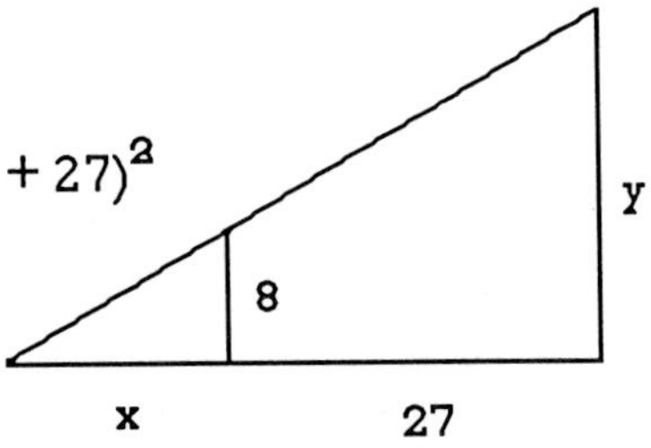

$$L^2 = y^2 + (x+27)^2 = \left(8 + \frac{216}{x}\right)^2 + (x+27)^2$$

Let $f(x) = L^2(x)$. Then

$$f'(x) = 2\left(8 + \frac{216}{x}\right)\left(-\frac{216}{x^2}\right) + 2(x+27) = 0$$

if $x = 12$. $f'(x) < 0$ if $x < 12$ and $f'(x) > 0$ if $x > 12 \Rightarrow L(12) = 46.87$ is minimum.

55. $v = kx(a-x) = kax - kx^2 \Rightarrow \frac{dv}{dx} = ka - 2kx$.

$\frac{dv}{dx} = 0$ if $x = \frac{a}{2}$. $\frac{d^2v}{dx^2} = -2k < 0 \Rightarrow$ a maximum of

$v\left(\frac{a}{2}\right) = \frac{ka^2}{4}$ occurs.

3.6 RELATED RATES OF CHANGE

1. $A = \pi r^2 \Rightarrow \frac{dA}{dt} = 2\pi r\frac{dr}{dt}$

2. $S = 4\pi r^2 \Rightarrow \frac{dS}{dt} = 8\pi r\frac{dr}{dt}$

3. $V = s^3 \Rightarrow \frac{dV}{dt} = 3s^2\frac{ds}{dt}$

4. $A = \pi r^2 \Rightarrow \frac{dA}{dt} = 2\pi r\frac{dr}{dt}$. When $r = 50$ cm and $\frac{dr}{dt} = 0.01$ cm/min,

$\frac{dA}{dt} = 2\pi(50)(0.01) = \pi$ cm^2/min.

5. $V = IR \Rightarrow$ (a) $\frac{dV}{dt} = 1$ (b) $\frac{dI}{dt} = -\frac{1}{3}$

(c) $R = VI^{-1} \Rightarrow \frac{dR}{dt} = I^{-1}\frac{dV}{dt} + V(-I^{-2}\frac{dI}{dt})$

(d) $\frac{dR}{dt} = \frac{1}{2}(1) - (\frac{12}{4})(-\frac{1}{3}) = \frac{3}{2}$

6. $\frac{dl}{dt} = -2$ cm/sec, $\frac{dw}{dt} = 2$ cm/sec. When $l = 12$ cm and $w = 5$ cm,

(a) $A = lw \Rightarrow \frac{dA}{dt} = l\frac{dw}{dt} + w\frac{dl}{dt} = (12)(2) + (5)(-2) = 14$ cm^2/sec and is increasing.

(b) $p = 2w + 2l \Rightarrow \frac{dp}{dt} = 2\frac{dw}{dt} + 2\frac{dl}{dt} = 2(2) + 2(-2) = 0$ (not changing)

(c) $D^2 = l^2 + w^2 \Rightarrow 2D\frac{dD}{dt} = 2l\frac{dl}{dt} + 2w\frac{dw}{dt} \Rightarrow$

$$\frac{dD}{dt} = \frac{(12)(-2) + (5)(2)}{\sqrt{12^2 + 5^2}} = -\frac{14}{13} \text{ cm/sec (decreasing)}$$

7. Let x = distance from 2nd base

y = distance from 3rd base.

Then $y = \sqrt{x^2 + 90^2} = \sqrt{60^2 + 90^2} = 30\sqrt{13}$

$y^2 = x^2 + 90^2 \Rightarrow 2y\frac{dy}{dt} = 2x\frac{dx}{dt}$. Now $\frac{dx}{dt} = -16$ ft/s so

$30\sqrt{13}\frac{dy}{dt} = (60)(-16) \Rightarrow \frac{dy}{dt} = -\frac{32}{\sqrt{13}}$ ft/s

8. $V = 5\pi r^2 \Rightarrow \frac{dV}{dr} = 10\pi r = 30\pi$ when $r = 3$.

$S = 2\pi r^2 + 10\pi r \Rightarrow \frac{dS}{dr} = 4\pi r + 10\pi = 22\pi$ when $r = 3$.

$$\therefore \quad \frac{dV}{dS} = \frac{\frac{dv}{dr}}{\frac{dS}{dr}} = \frac{30\pi}{22\pi} = \frac{15}{11}.$$

9. $A=\frac{1}{2}xy \Rightarrow \frac{dA}{dt}=\frac{1}{2}\left(x\frac{dy}{dt}+y\frac{dx}{dt}\right)$. From Example 3, When $x=10$, $y=24$ and $\frac{dy}{dt}=-\frac{5}{3}$. $\therefore \frac{dA}{dt}=\frac{1}{2}\left[(10)\left(-\frac{5}{3}\right)+(24)(4)\right]=\frac{119}{3}$.

$$A=\frac{1}{2}x\sqrt{26^2-x^2} \Rightarrow \frac{dA}{dt}=\frac{1}{2}\sqrt{26^2-x^2}+\frac{-x^2}{2\sqrt{26^2-x^2}}$$

$$=\frac{26^2-2x^2}{2\sqrt{26^2-x^2}}=0 \text{ if } t=\frac{x}{4}=\frac{13\sqrt{2}}{4}\text{ sec. Since } \frac{dA}{dx}>0 \text{ for } 0<x<13\sqrt{2}$$

and $\frac{dA}{dx}<0$ for $13\sqrt{3}<x<26$, this gives a maximum value.

10. $V=\frac{1}{3}\pi r^2 h = \frac{1}{3}\pi\left(\frac{h}{2}\right)^2 h = \frac{1}{12}\pi h^3 \Rightarrow \frac{dV}{dt}=\frac{\pi}{4}h^2\frac{dh}{dt}$.

$\frac{dV}{dt}=10$, and when $h=5$, $10=\frac{25\pi}{4}\frac{dh}{dt} \Rightarrow \frac{dh}{dt}=\frac{8}{5\pi}$.

11. An accumulation of moisture is a change in volume. $\therefore \frac{dV}{dt}=kS$, where k is the constant of proportionality. $V=\frac{4}{3}\pi r^3 \Rightarrow \frac{dV}{dt}=4\pi r^2\frac{dr}{dt}$.

Equating, $4\pi r^2\frac{dr}{dt}=kS=k(4\pi r^2) \Rightarrow \frac{dr}{dt}=k$.

12. $D^2=x^2+y^2 \Rightarrow 2D\frac{dD}{dt}=2x\frac{dx}{dt}+2y\frac{dy}{dt}$. $\therefore \frac{dD}{dt}=\frac{x\frac{dx}{dt}+y\frac{dy}{dt}}{\sqrt{x^2+y^2}}=\frac{ax+by}{\sqrt{x^2+y^2}}$.

13. $V=\frac{4}{3}\pi r^3 \Rightarrow \frac{dV}{dt}=4\pi r^2\frac{dr}{dt}$. $\therefore 100=4\pi(3)^2\frac{dr}{dt} \Rightarrow \frac{dr}{dt}=\frac{25}{9\pi}$ ft/min.

Since $S=4\pi r^2$, $\frac{dS}{dt}=8\pi r\frac{dr}{dt}=8\pi(3)\frac{25}{9\pi}=\frac{200}{30}$ ft^2/min.

14. $r^2=16+x^2 \Rightarrow 2r\frac{dr}{dt}=2x\frac{dx}{dt} \Rightarrow 10(-2)=(2\sqrt{21})\frac{dx}{dt}$ or $\frac{dx}{dt}=-\frac{10}{\sqrt{21}}$

15. $s^2=x^2+(200+y)^2 \Rightarrow 2s\frac{ds}{dt}=2x\frac{dx}{dt}+2(200+y)\frac{dy}{dt} \Rightarrow$

$$\frac{ds}{dt}=\frac{(66)(66)+(215)(15)}{\sqrt{215^2+66^2}}\approx 33.7 \text{ ft/sec}$$

16. $\frac{r}{h}=\frac{4}{10} \Rightarrow r=\frac{2}{5}h$. $V=\frac{1}{3}\pi r^2 h=\frac{1}{3}\pi\left(\frac{2h}{5}\right)^2 h=\frac{4\pi h^3}{75}$.

$\frac{dV}{dt}=\frac{4\pi}{25}h^2\frac{dh}{dt}$. $\therefore 5=\frac{4\pi}{25}(6)^2\frac{dh}{dt} \Rightarrow \frac{dh}{dt}\ \frac{125}{144\pi}$

17. (a) $3x^2 - y^2 = 12 \Rightarrow 6x\frac{dx}{dt} - 2y\frac{dy}{dt} = 0 \Rightarrow \frac{dx}{dt} = \frac{y}{3x}\frac{dy}{dt}$

$\therefore \left.\frac{dx}{dt}\right|_{x=4} = \left(\frac{\pm 6}{12}\right)(6) = \pm 3$

(b) $\frac{dy}{dx} = \frac{\frac{dy}{dt}}{\frac{dx}{dt}} = \frac{6}{\pm 3} = \pm 2$

18. $x^2 + y^2 = 1 \Rightarrow 2x\frac{dx}{dt} + 2y\frac{dy}{dt} = 0$. $\frac{dx}{dt} = y \Rightarrow xy + y\frac{dy}{dt} = 0$ or $\frac{dy}{dt} = -x$. When $x > 0$ and $y > 0$, $\frac{dx}{dt} = y > 0 \Rightarrow$ clockwise movement.

19. $\frac{dx}{dt} = 10$ m/sec. $\tan\theta = \frac{y}{x} = \frac{x^2}{x} = x$. $\sec^2\theta\,\frac{d\theta}{dt} = \frac{dx}{dt}$.

$x = 3 \Rightarrow \sec^2\theta = 1 + \tan^2\theta = 10$ and $\frac{d\theta}{dt} = 1$.

$x = 103 \Rightarrow \sec^2\theta = 1 + 103^2 = 10610$ and $\frac{d\theta}{dt} = \frac{10}{10610} \approx 0.00094$

20. We parametize $x^2 + y^2 = 1$ as $x = \cos\theta$, $y = \sin\theta$, $0 \le \theta < 2\pi$.

$\frac{d\theta}{dt} = 1$ rev/sec $= 2\pi$ rad/sec. $\frac{dx}{dt} = -\sin\theta\,\frac{d\theta}{dt}$. At the moment when it passes through $(0, 1)$, $\theta = \frac{\pi}{2}$ and $\frac{dx}{dt} = -2\pi$.

21. (a) Length of shadow: $\frac{6}{y} = \frac{16}{y+z} \Rightarrow y = \frac{3}{5}z$

$\frac{dy}{dt} = \frac{3}{5}\frac{dz}{dt} = \frac{3}{5}(5) = 3$ ft/sec.

(b) Tip of shadow: $\frac{6}{y} = \frac{16}{x} \Rightarrow x = \frac{8}{3}y \Rightarrow \frac{dx}{dt} = \frac{8}{3}\frac{dy}{dt} = \frac{8}{3}(3) = 8$ ft/sec.

22. $\frac{x}{30} = \frac{50 - s}{s} \Rightarrow x = 1500\,s^{-1} - 1$. $\therefore \frac{dx}{dt} = -1500s^{-2}\frac{ds}{dt}$. Since $s = 16t^2$, $s = 4$ and $\frac{ds}{dt} = 32\left(\frac{1}{2}\right) = 16$ when $t = \frac{1}{2}$.

Thus $\frac{dx}{dt} = -1500\,(4)^{-2}\,(16) = -1500$ ft/sec.

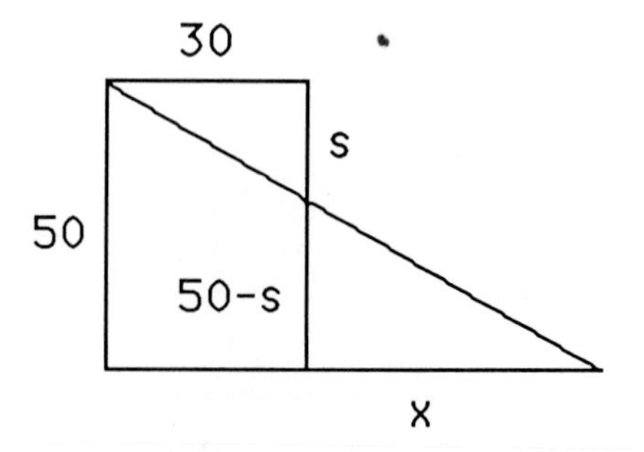

23. $s^2 = x^2 + 300^2 \Rightarrow 2s\dfrac{ds}{dt} = 2x\dfrac{dx}{dt}$. When $s = 500$, $x = 400$.

$$\frac{ds}{dt} = \frac{(400)(25)}{500} = 20 \text{ ft/sec.}$$

24. $V = \dfrac{4}{3}\pi r^3 \Rightarrow \dfrac{dV}{dt} = 4\pi r^2\dfrac{dr}{dt}$. The diameter is 8 in. and the ice is 2 in. so $r = 6$. $10 = 4\pi(6)^2\dfrac{dr}{dt} \Rightarrow \dfrac{dr}{dt} = \dfrac{10}{144\pi} = \dfrac{5}{72\pi}$ in/min.

$$S = 4\pi r^2 \Rightarrow \frac{dS}{dt} = 8\pi r\frac{dr}{dt} = 8\pi(6)\left(\frac{5}{72\pi}\right) = \frac{10}{3} \text{ in}^2\text{/min.}$$

25. $s^2 = 1 + (x - z)^2 \Rightarrow 2s\dfrac{ds}{dt} = 2(x - z)\left(\dfrac{dx}{dt} - \dfrac{dz}{dt}\right)$

$$(1.5)(-136) = \frac{\sqrt{5}}{2}\left(\frac{dx}{dt} - 120\right) \Rightarrow \frac{dx}{dt} = 62.4 \text{ miles per hour.}$$

26. $0.25 \text{ deg/min} = \dfrac{\pi}{720}$ rad/min. If x is the length of the shadow,

then $x = 80\tan\theta \Rightarrow \dfrac{dx}{dt} = 80\sec^2\theta\,\dfrac{d\theta}{dt}$

$$= 80\left(\frac{5}{3}\right)^2\frac{\pi}{720} = \frac{25\pi}{81} \text{ ft/min} \approx 11.6 \text{ in/min}$$

27. (a) At noon, ship A is due north of ship B $\Rightarrow x = s \Rightarrow \dfrac{ds}{dt} = 12$.

(b) At 1 p.m. ship B is due east of ship B $\Rightarrow y = s \Rightarrow \dfrac{ds}{dt} = 8$.

(c) $s^2 = x^2 + y^2$, $x = 12 - 12t$ and $y = 8t$.

$\therefore s^2 = (12 - 12t)^2 + (8t)^2 \Rightarrow 2s\dfrac{ds}{dt} = 2(12 - 12t)(-12) + 128t$

$= 0 \Leftrightarrow t = \dfrac{9}{13}$. Then $x = \dfrac{48}{13}$, $y = \dfrac{72}{13}$ and $s \approx 6.5$.

The minimum distance is greater than 5, and the ships do not see each other.

28. $s^2 = x^2 + y^2 - 2xy\cos 120^\circ = x^2 + y^2 + xy$

$2s\dfrac{ds}{dt} = 2x\dfrac{dx}{dt} + 2y\dfrac{dy}{dt} + x\dfrac{dy}{dt} + y\dfrac{dx}{dt}$

$2\sqrt{148}\dfrac{ds}{dt} = 28(20) + 26(30) + 8(30) + 6(20) = \dfrac{260}{\sqrt{37}}$ m/hr.

3.7 THE MEAN VALUE THEOREM

1. $f(x) = x^4 + 3x + 1$, $[-2, -1]$. $f(-2) = 11$ and $f(-1) = -1 \Rightarrow$ by the Intermediate Value Theorem that f has at least one root between -2 and -1. $f'(x) = 4x^3 + 3 = 0 \Leftrightarrow x = -\left(\frac{3}{4}\right)^{\frac{1}{3}} > -1$.
$\therefore$ f' has no zero between -2 and -1, so f has exactly one root.

2. $f(x) = x^4 + 2x^3 - 2$, $[0, 1]$. $f(-1) = 1$, $f(0) = -2$, $f(1) = 1 \Rightarrow$ by The Intermediate Value Theorem that f has at least one root between 0 and 1. $f'(x) = 4x^3 + 6x^2 = 2x^2(2x + 3)$.
$f'(x) = 0$ if $x = 0$ or $-\frac{3}{2}$. $\therefore$ f has exactly one root on $[0, 1]$.

3. $f(x) = 2x^3 - 3x^2 - 12x - 6$, $[-1, 0]$. $f(-1) = 1$, $f(0) = -6 \Rightarrow$ by The Intermediate Value Theorem that f has at least one root between -1 and 0. $f'(x) = 6x^2 - 6x - 12 = 6(x - 2)(x + 1)$.
$f'(x) = 0$ if $x = 2$ or -1. $\therefore$ f has exactly one root on $[-1, 0]$.

4. Let c_1, c_2 and c_3 in (a, b) be such that $f(c_1) = f(c_2) = f(c_3) = 0$. Since f is continuous and differentiable on $[a, b]$, there is, by Rolle's Theorem, at least one z_1 in (c_1, c_2) and at least one z_2 in (c_2, c_3) for which $f'(z_1) = f'(z_2) = 0$. But Rolle's Theorem again implies that there is at least one z_3 in (z_1, z_2) for which $f'(z_3) = 0$. To generalize, let f and its first n derivatives be continuous on $[a, b]$. If f has $n + 1$ zeros in this interval, then $f^{(n)}(x)$ has at least one zero between a and b.

5.(a) (i) $y = x^2 - 4 = 0 \Leftrightarrow x = \pm 2$. $y' = 2x = 0 \Leftrightarrow x = 0$. Note $-2 < 0 < 2$.

(ii) $y = x^2 + 8x + 15 = (x + 3)(x + 5) = 0 \Leftrightarrow x = -3$ or -5.
$y' = 2x + 4 = 0 \Leftrightarrow x = -4$. Note $-5 < -4 < -3$.

(iii) $y = (x + 1)(x - 2)^2 = 0 \Leftrightarrow x = -1$ or $x = 2$. $y' = 3x(x - 2) = 0$ $\Leftrightarrow x = 0$ or $x = 2$. Note that $x = 2$ is a double root of y and that y' has a zero at $x = 2$ also.

(iv) $y = x(x - 9)(x - 24) = 0 \Leftrightarrow x = 0$, 9 or 24. $y' = 3(x - 4)(x - 18)$ $= 0 \Leftrightarrow x = 4$ or $x = 18$. Note that $0 < 4 < 9$ and $9 < 18 < 24$.

(b) Let r_1 and r_2 be zeros of the polynomial $p(x) = x^n + a_{n-1}x^{n-1} + \ldots + a_1x + a_0$. Then $p(r_1) = p(r_2) = 0$. Since polynomials are everywhere continuous and differentiable, by Rolle's Theorem, $p'(r) = 0$ for some $r_1 < r < r_2$. But $p'(x) = nx^{n-1} + (n-1)a_{n-1}x^{n-2} + \ldots + a_1$.

6. This function is not continuous on the closed interval $[0,1]$. Specifically, it is discontinuous at $x = 1$.

7. $f(x) = x^2 + 2x - 1$, $a = 0$, $b = 1$. $f'(x) = 2x + 2$

$$2c + 2 = \frac{f(1) - f(0)}{1 - 0} \Rightarrow 2c + 2 = 3 \Leftrightarrow c = \frac{1}{2}$$

8. This function is discontinuous at $x = 1$ and so does not satisy the hypotheses of Rolle's Theorem.

9. $f(x) = x + \frac{1}{x}$, $a = \frac{1}{2}$, $b = 2$. $f'(x) = 1 - x^{-2}$.

$$1 - \frac{1}{c^2} = \frac{f(2) - f\left(\frac{1}{2}\right)}{2 - \frac{1}{2}} \Rightarrow 1 - \frac{1}{c^2} = 0 \Leftrightarrow c = \pm 1. \therefore c = 1$$

10. $f(x) = \sqrt{x - 1}$, $a = 1$, $b = 3$. $f'(x) = \frac{1}{2\sqrt{x-1}}$.

$$\frac{1}{2\sqrt{c-1}} = \frac{f(3) - f(1)}{3 - 1} \Rightarrow \sqrt{c-1} = \frac{1}{\sqrt{2}} \Leftrightarrow c - 1 = \frac{1}{2}. \therefore c = \frac{3}{2}$$

11. By Mean Value Theorem, $\exists\ a < c < x$ for which $f'(c) = \frac{f(x) - f(a)}{x - a}$

Since $|f'(c)| \le 1$, $\left|\frac{f(x) - f(a)}{x - a}\right| = \frac{|f(x) - f(a)|}{|x - a|} \le 1 \Rightarrow |f(x) - f(a)| \le |x - a|$.

12. Suppose $f(a) = f(b) = C$. Define the function g by the equation $g(x) = f(x) - C$. Then g is continuous on $[a,b]$ and $g'(x) = f'(x)$ for all x in (a,b). Since $g(a) = g(b) = 0$, by Rolle's Theorem there is at least one c in (a,b) for which $g'(c) = 0$. But then $f'(c) = 0$ and this is a contradiction.

13. Let $f(x) = \sin x$. Then f is continuous on $[a,b]$ and differentiable on $(a,b) \Rightarrow \exists\ c$ for which $f'(c) = \cos c = \frac{\sin b - \sin a}{b - a}$.

Since $|\cos c| \le 1$, $\frac{|\sin b - \sin a|}{|b - a|} \le 1 \Rightarrow |\sin b - \sin a| \le |b - a|$.

14. $y = x$ is continuous on $[0,1]$ and $y' = 1$ for all x in $(0,1)$. Therefore c could be any value in $(0,1)$.

15. There is no contradiction. The converse of the Mean Value Theorem is not true. The theorem states sufficient conditions for there to be a horizontal tangent line, but not necessary

16. If $f(x) = \tan x$, then $f'(x) = \sec^2 x > 0$ for all x except for x such that $\cos x = 0$. Therefore $f(x) = \tan x$ increases for all x such that $\cos x \neq 0$.

17. The function $f(x) = [x]$ is continuous on $[0,1)$ but not continuous on $[0,1]$ as the theorem requires.

18. This function satisfies the hypotheses of the Mean Value Theorem. Therefore there must exist at least on c in $(0,1)$ for which $f'(c) = \frac{f(1) - f(0)}{1-0} = 1$.

19. This is precisely what the Mean Value Theorem asserts. The expression on the right side is the average value of a function on an interval (in this case from 0 miles to 30 miles in 1 hour). The expression on the left is the instantaneous rate of change at some moment. The Mean Value

20. $f(x) \approx f(0) + f'(0)x$ so $f\left(\frac{\pi}{2}\right) \approx 3 + \frac{1}{2}\left(\frac{\pi}{2}\right) \approx 3.785$

21. Consider the given function on $[-3,0]$ and $[0,3]$.

On $[-3,0]$, we have $\frac{f(0) - f(-3)}{0-(-3)} \leq 1 \Rightarrow f(0) + 3 \leq 3 \Rightarrow f(0) \leq 0$

On $[0,3]$, we have $\frac{f(3) - f(0)}{3-0} \leq 1 \Rightarrow 3 - f(0) \leq 3 \Rightarrow f(0) \geq 0$.

Since f is differentiable for all x, f must be continuous for all x, so $f(0) = 0$.

22. By the Mean Value Theorem, there exists c in (a,b) such that

$f'(c) = \frac{f(b) - f(a)}{b-a} > 0$ since $f(b) > f(a)$.

23. No. Corollary 3 states that functions with the same derivatives differ from each other by at most a constant. Therefore, the family of functions $f(x) = 3x + b$ describes all functions for which $f'(x) = 3$.

24. Let $f(x) = \frac{x}{x+1}$ and $g(x) = -\frac{1}{x+1}$. Observe that $\frac{x}{x+1} = 1 - \frac{1}{x+1}$ so that $\frac{d}{dx}\left(\frac{x}{x+1}\right) = \frac{d}{dx}\left(-\frac{1}{x+1}\right)$. Since $f(x) = 1 - g(x)$, f and g differ by a constant and there is no contradiction.

25. Let x_1 and x_2 be any two values such that $a \le x_1 < x_2 \le b$.

By Mean Value Theorem, $\exists$ c for which $x_1 < c < x_2$ and

$\dfrac{f(x_2) - f(x_1)}{x_2 - x_1} = f'(c)$. Since $f'(x) = 0$ for all x in (a,b),

$f(x_2) - f(x_1) = 0 \Rightarrow f(x_2) = f(x_1)$. $\therefore$ f(x) is constant on (a,b).

26. Define the function h be $h(x) = F_1(x) - F_2(x)$. Then

$h'(x) = F_1'(x) - F_2'(x) = 0$ so by Corollary 2, $h(x) = C$.

Then $F_1(x) - F_2(x) = C$.

3.8 INDETERMINATE FORMS AND L'HOPITAL'S RULE

1. $\lim\limits_{x\to 2} \dfrac{x-2}{x^2-4} = \lim\limits_{x\to 2} \dfrac{1}{2x} = \dfrac{1}{4}$

2. $\lim\limits_{t\to\infty} \dfrac{6t+5}{3t-8} = \lim\limits_{t\to\infty} \dfrac{6}{3} = 2$

3. $\lim\limits_{x\to\infty} \dfrac{5x^2-3x}{7x^2+1} = \lim\limits_{x\to\infty} \dfrac{10x-3}{14x} = \lim\limits_{x\to\infty} \dfrac{10}{14} = \dfrac{5}{7}$

4. $\lim\limits_{x\to 1} \dfrac{x^3-1}{4x^3-x-3} = \lim\limits_{x\to 1} \dfrac{3x^2}{12x^2-1} = \dfrac{3}{11}$

5. $\lim\limits_{t\to 0} \dfrac{\sin t^2}{t} = \lim\limits_{t\to 0} \dfrac{2\sin t\cos t}{1} = 0$

6. $\lim\limits_{x\to\frac{\pi}{2}} \dfrac{2x-\pi}{\cos x} = \lim\limits_{x\to\frac{\pi}{2}} \dfrac{2}{-\sin x} = -2$

7. $\lim\limits_{x\to 0} \dfrac{\sin 5x}{x} = \lim\limits_{x\to 0} \dfrac{5\cos 5x}{1} = 5$

8. $\lim\limits_{t\to 0} \dfrac{\cos t - 1}{t^2} = \lim\limits_{t\to 0} \dfrac{-\sin t}{2t} = \lim\limits_{t\to 0} \dfrac{-\cos t}{2} = -\dfrac{1}{2}$

9. $\lim_{\theta\to\pi} \frac{\sin\theta}{\pi-\theta} = \lim_{\theta\to\pi} \frac{\cos\theta}{-1} = \frac{-1}{-1} = 1$

10. $\lim_{x\to\frac{\pi}{2}} \frac{1-\sin x}{1+\cos 2x} = \lim_{x\to\frac{\pi}{2}} \frac{-\cos x}{-2\sin 2x} = \lim_{x\to\frac{\pi}{2}} \frac{1}{4\sin x} = \frac{1}{4}$

11. $\lim_{x\to\frac{\pi}{4}} \frac{\sin x - \cos x}{x-\frac{\pi}{4}} = \lim_{x\to\frac{\pi}{4}} \frac{\cos x + \sin x}{1} = \sqrt{2}$

12. $\lim_{x\to\frac{\pi}{3}} \frac{\cos x - 0.5}{x-\frac{\pi}{3}} = \lim_{x\to\frac{\pi}{3}} \frac{-\sin x}{1} = -\frac{\sqrt{3}}{2}$

13. $\lim_{x\to\frac{\pi}{2}} \left[-\left(x-\frac{\pi}{2}\right)\tan x\right] = \lim_{x\to\frac{\pi}{2}} \left[\frac{-\left(x-\frac{\pi}{2}\right)}{\cot x}\right] = \lim_{x\to\frac{\pi}{2}} \left(\frac{-1}{-\csc^2 x}\right) = 1$

14. $\lim_{x\to 0} \frac{2x}{x+7\sqrt{x}} = \lim_{x\to 0} \frac{2}{1+\frac{7}{2\sqrt{x}}} = \lim_{x\to 0} \frac{4\sqrt{x}}{2\sqrt{x}+7} = 0$

15. $\lim_{x\to 1} \frac{2x^2-(3x+1)\sqrt{x}+2}{x-1} = \lim_{x\to 1} \frac{4x-3\sqrt{x}-\frac{3x+1}{2\sqrt{x}}}{1} = -1$

16. $\lim_{x\to 2} \frac{\sqrt{x^2+5}-3}{x^2-4} = \lim_{x\to 2} \frac{\frac{1}{\sqrt{x^2+5}}}{2} = \frac{1}{6}$

17. $\lim_{x\to 0} \frac{\sqrt{a(a+x)}-a}{x} = \lim_{x\to 0} \frac{\frac{1}{2}[a(a+x)]^{-\frac{1}{2}}(a)}{1} = \frac{1}{2}$

18. $\lim_{t\to 0} \frac{10(\sin t - t)}{t^3} = \lim_{t\to 0} \frac{10\cos t - 10}{3t^2} = \lim_{t\to 0} \frac{-10\sin t}{6t} = \lim_{t\to 0} \frac{-10\cos t}{6} = -\frac{5}{3}$

19. $\lim_{x\to 0} \frac{x(\cos x - 1)}{\sin x - x} = \lim_{x\to 0} \frac{-x\sin x + \cos x - 1}{\cos x - 1} =$

$\lim_{x\to 0} \frac{-x\cos x - \sin x - \sin x}{-\sin x} = \lim_{x\to 0} \frac{x\sin x - \cos x - 2\cos x}{-\cos x} = 3$

20. $\lim_{h\to 0} \frac{\sin(a+h)-\sin a}{h} = \lim_{h\to 0} \frac{\cos(a+h)}{1} = \cos a$

21. $\lim_{r\to 1} \frac{a(r^n-1)}{r-1}$ (n a positive integer) $= \lim_{r\to 1} \frac{nar^{n-1}}{1} = na$

22. $\lim_{x\to 0^+} \left(\frac{1}{x}-\frac{1}{\sqrt{x}}\right) = \lim_{x\to 0^+} \frac{1-\sqrt{x}}{x} = \infty$ (L'Hopital's Rule does not apply)

23. $\lim_{x\to\infty}\left(x-\sqrt{x^2+x}\right)=\lim_{x\to\infty}\frac{x-\sqrt{x^2+x}}{1}\cdot\frac{x+\sqrt{x^2+x}}{x+\sqrt{x^2+x}}$

$$\lim_{x\to\infty}\frac{-x}{x+\sqrt{x^2+x}}=\lim_{x\to\infty}\frac{-\frac{x}{x}}{\frac{x}{x}+\sqrt{\frac{x^2}{x^2}+\frac{x}{x^2}}}=\lim_{x\to\infty}\frac{-1}{1+\sqrt{1+\frac{1}{x}}}=-\frac{1}{2}$$

24. (b) is correct. L'Hopital's Rule does not apply in (a) since the denominator is not zero.

25. $\lim_{x\to\infty}\frac{\sqrt{10x+1}}{\sqrt{x+1}}=\lim_{x\to\infty}\frac{\sqrt{10+\frac{1}{x}}}{\sqrt{1+\frac{1}{x}}}=\sqrt{10}$

26. $\lim_{x\to\frac{\pi}{2}}\frac{\sec x}{\tan x}=\lim_{x\to\frac{\pi}{2}}\frac{\cos x}{\sin x\cos x}=1$

27. (a) $y=\sec x+\tan x,\ -\frac{\pi}{2}<x<\frac{\pi}{2}$. $y=\frac{1+\sin x}{\cos x}\geq 0$

since $|\sin x|\leq 1\Rightarrow 1+\sin x>0$, and $\cos x>0$ for $-\frac{\pi}{2}<x<\frac{\pi}{2}$.

$\therefore\ y'=\sec x\tan x+\sec^2 x=\frac{\sin x+1}{\cos^2 x}\geq 0$ also.

$y''=\sec x(\sec^2 x)+\tan x(\sec x\tan x)+2\sec x(\sec x\tan x)$

$=\frac{1}{\cos^3 x}+\frac{\sin^2 x}{\cos^3 x}+\frac{2\sin x}{\cos^3 x}=\frac{(1+\sin x)^2}{\cos^3 x}\geq 0.$

(b) $\lim_{x\to\left(-\frac{\pi}{2}\right)^-}(\sec x+\tan x)=\lim_{x\to\left(-\frac{\pi}{2}\right)^-}\frac{1+\sin x}{\cos x}=\lim_{x\to\left(-\frac{\pi}{2}\right)^-}\frac{\cos x}{-\sin x}=0$

(c)

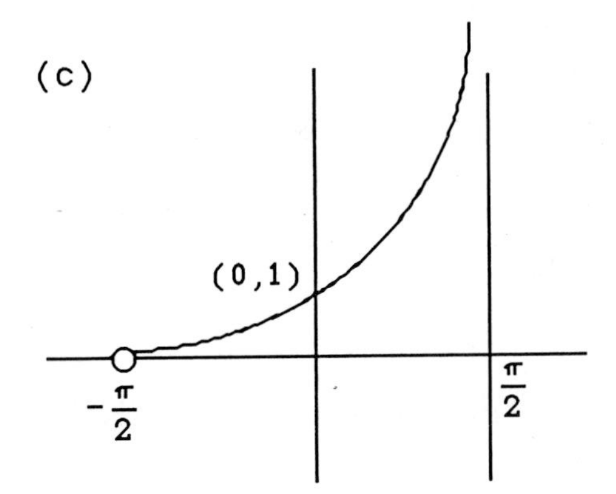

28. (a) $\frac{PA}{PD} = \frac{AB}{CD}$ or $\frac{PA}{PA - (1 - \cos\theta)} = \frac{\theta}{\sin\theta}$.

$PA \sin\theta = PA\,\theta - \theta(1 - \cos\theta)$

$PA(\theta - \sin\theta) = \theta(1 - \cos\theta)$

$PA = 1 - x = \frac{\theta(1 - \cos\theta)}{\theta - \sin\theta}$

(b) $\lim_{\theta\to 0} \frac{\theta(1 - \cos\theta)}{\theta - \sin\theta} = \lim_{\theta\to 0} \frac{1 - \cos\theta + \theta\sin\theta}{1 - \cos\theta}$

$= \lim_{\theta\to 0} \frac{\sin\theta + \sin\theta + \theta\cos\theta}{\sin\theta} = 2 + \lim_{\theta\to 0} \frac{\theta}{\sin\theta}\cos\theta = 3$

(c) $\lim_{\theta\to\infty} [(1 - x) - (1 - \cos\theta)] = \lim_{\theta\to\infty} \left[\frac{\theta(1 - \cos\theta)}{\theta - \sin\theta} - (1 - \cos\theta)\right]$

$= \lim_{\theta\to\infty} \left[(1 - \cos\theta)\left(\frac{\theta - \theta + \sin\theta}{\theta - \sin\theta}\right)\right]$

$= \lim_{\theta\to\infty} \left[\frac{\frac{\sin\theta}{\theta} - \frac{\sin\theta\cos\theta}{\theta}}{1 - \frac{\sin\theta}{\theta}}\right] = \frac{0}{1} = 0$

29. (a) $\lim_{\theta\to\frac{\pi}{2}} r - y = \lim_{\theta\to\frac{\pi}{2}} (r - r\sin\theta) = 0$

(b) $\lim_{\theta\to\frac{\pi}{2}} (r^2 - y^2) = \lim_{\theta\to\frac{\pi}{2}} 1 = 1$

(c) $\lim_{\theta\to\frac{\pi}{2}} (r^3 - y^3) = \lim_{\theta\to\frac{\pi}{2}} (\sec^3\theta - \tan^3\theta) = \lim_{\theta\to\frac{\pi}{2}} \left(\frac{1 - \sin^3\theta}{\cos^3\theta}\right)$

$= \lim_{\theta\to\frac{\pi}{2}} \frac{-3\sin^2\theta\cos\theta}{-3\cos^2\theta\sin\theta} = \lim_{\theta\to\frac{\pi}{2}} \tan\theta = \infty$

30. $\lim_{x\to 0} \frac{f(x)}{g(x)} = \lim_{x\to 0} \frac{x + 2}{x + 1} = 2$, but $\lim_{x\to 0} \frac{f'(x)}{g'(x)} = 1$. Since f and g are neither continuous nor differentiable at $x = 0$, there is no contradiction to L'Hopital's Rule.

3.9 QUADRATIC APPROXIMATIONS AND APPROXIMATION ERRORS

1. $\sin x \approx x \Rightarrow x \sin x \approx x^2$

2. $\sqrt{1 + \sin x} \approx (1 + x)^{1/2} \approx 1 + \frac{1}{2}x - \frac{1}{8}x^2$

3. $\cos x \approx 1 - \frac{x^2}{2} \Rightarrow \cos\sqrt{1 + x} \approx 1 - \frac{1 + x}{2} = \frac{1}{2} - \frac{1}{2}x$ since

$\sqrt{1+x} \approx 0$ if $x \approx -1$.

4. $\sec x = \dfrac{1}{\cos x} \approx (1-x^2)^{-1} \approx 1 + x^2$; $\dfrac{1}{1-x} = (1-x)^{-1} \approx 1 + x + x^2$

$\therefore \dfrac{\sec x}{1-x} \approx (1+x^2)(1+x+x^2) = 1 + x + 2x^2$

5. $\sqrt{x} = \sqrt{1 + (x-1)} \approx 1 + \dfrac{x-1}{2} - \dfrac{(x-1)^2}{8} = \dfrac{3}{8} + \dfrac{3}{4}x - \dfrac{1}{8}x^2$.

6. $\sec x = \dfrac{1}{\cos x} \approx (1-x^2)^{-1} \approx 1 + x^2$; $\tan x \approx x$ (See Problem 9)

$\therefore \sec x + \tan x \approx 1 + x + x^2$

7. (a) $\sqrt{1+x} \approx 1 + \dfrac{x}{2} \Rightarrow f''(x) = \dfrac{1}{4}(1+x)^{-3/2}$ which, for $|x| \le 0.1$,

attains its maximum when $x = -0.1$. Therefore,

$$|e_1(x)| \le \frac{1}{2}\left(\frac{1}{4(.9)^{3/2}}\right)(.1)^2 < 0.00146$$

(b) $|f''(x)| \le 1$ so take $M = 1$. $|e_1(x)| < \dfrac{1}{2}(.1)^2 < 0.005$

8. (a) $f(x) = \sqrt{1+x}$ and $f(0) = 1$; $f'(x) = \dfrac{1}{2}(1+x)^{-1/2}$ and $f'(0) = \dfrac{1}{2}$.

$f''(x) = -\dfrac{1}{4}(1+x)^{-3/2}$ and $f''(0) = -\dfrac{1}{4}$. $f'''(x) = \dfrac{3}{8}(1+x)^{-5/2}$

$\therefore \sqrt{1+x} \approx 1 + \dfrac{1}{2}x - \dfrac{1}{8}x^2$.

(b) $|e_2(x)| \le \dfrac{1}{6}\left(\dfrac{3}{8}\right)(1-0.1)^{-5/2}(0.1)^3 \approx 0.0000813$

9. $y = \tan x$, $y' = \sec^2 x$ and $y'' = 2\sec^2 x \tan x$. $y(0) = 0$, $y'(0) = 1$ and $y''(0) = 0$. Therefore, $\tan x \approx x$. $f'''(x) = 4\sec^2 x \tan^2 x + 2\sec^4 x$. If one takes $x = \dfrac{\pi}{6}$, then $|e_2(x)| \le \dfrac{1}{6}\left(\dfrac{48}{9}\right)(0.1)^3 \approx 0.00089$.

If one uses a calculator and $x = 0.1$, $|e_2(x)| \le 0.0003$

10. (a) $f(x) = \cos x$ and $f(0) = 1$; $f'(x) = -\sin x$ and $f'(0) = 0$.

$f''(x) = -\cos x$ and $f''(0) = -1$. $f'''(x) = \sin x$

$\therefore \cos x \approx 1 - \dfrac{1}{2}x^2$.

(b) $|e_2(x)| \le \dfrac{1}{6}(1)(0.1)^3 \approx 0.000167$

11. $f(x) = \sin x$ and $f\left(\frac{\pi}{2}\right) = 1$; $f'(x) = \cos x$ and $f'\left(\frac{\pi}{2}\right) = 0$.

$f''(x) = -\sin x$ and $f''\left(\frac{\pi}{2}\right) = -1$. Therefore, $\sin x \approx 1 - \frac{1}{2}\left(x - \frac{\pi}{2}\right)^2$.

$|e_2(x)| \leq \frac{1}{6}(0.1)^3 \approx 0.000167$

12. (a) $f(x) = \sin x$ and $f(\pi) = 0$; $f'(x) = \cos x$ and $f'(\pi) = -1$.

$f''(x) = -\sin x$ and $f''(\pi) = 0$. $f'''(x) = -\cos x$

$\therefore \sin x \approx -1(x - \pi) = \pi - x$

(b) $|e_2(x)| \leq \frac{1}{6}(1)(0.1)^3 \approx 0.000167$

13. $f(x) = \cos x$ and $f\left(\frac{\pi}{2}\right) = 0$; $f'(x) = -\sin x$ and $f'\left(\frac{\pi}{2}\right) = -1$.

$f''(x) = -\cos x$ and $f''\left(\frac{\pi}{2}\right) = 0$. Therefore, $\cos x \approx -\left(x - \frac{\pi}{2}\right)$

$|e_2(x)| \leq \frac{1}{6}(0.1)^3 \approx 0.000167$

14. (a) $f(x) = \cos x$ and $f(\pi) = 1$; $f'(x) = -\sin x$ and $f'(\pi) = 0$.

$f''(x) = -\cos x$ and $f''(\pi) = 1$. $f'''(x) = \sin x$

$\therefore \cos x \approx -1 + \frac{1}{2}(x - \pi)^2$.

(b) $|e_2(x)| \leq \frac{1}{6}(1)(0.1)^3 \approx 0.000167$

15. $|e_2(x)| \leq \max\left|\frac{f'''(x)}{6}\right| x^3 = \frac{1}{6}x^3$. Therefore,

(a) $\frac{1}{6}x^3 \leq 0.01 \Leftrightarrow |x| \leq \left(\frac{6}{100}\right)^{1/3} \approx 0.391$

(b) $\frac{1}{6}x^3 \leq 0.01\,|x| \Leftrightarrow |x| \leq \left(\frac{6}{100}\right)^{1/2} \approx 0.245$

16. $|e_2(x)| \leq \max\left|\frac{f'''(x)}{6}\right| x^3 = \frac{1}{6}x^3$. Therefore,

(a) $\frac{1}{6}x^3 \leq 0.01 \Leftrightarrow |x| \leq \left(\frac{6}{100}\right)^{1/3} \approx 0.391$

(b) $\frac{1}{6}x^3 \leq 0.01\,|x| \Leftrightarrow |x| \leq \left(\frac{6}{100}\right)^{1/2} \approx 0.245$

17. If $y = (1 + x)^k$, then $y' = k(1 + x)^{k-1}$ and $y'' = k(k - 1)(1 + x)^{k-2}$.

Therefore, $y(0) = 1$, $y'(0) = k$ and $y''(0) = k(k - 1)$, and

$y \approx 1 + kx + \frac{k(k-1)}{2}x^2$.

18. $f(x) = 3x^2 + 2x + 4$, $f'(x) = 6x + 2$, and $f''(x) = 6$.

$f(1) = 9$, $f'(1) = 8$, and $f''(1) = 6$. Therefore

$$f(x) = 9 + 8(x-1) + \frac{6}{2}(x-1)^2 = 3x^2 + 2x + 4 = f(x).$$

19. $f(x) = x^3 + 5x - 7$, $f'(x) = 3x^2 + 5$, $f''(x) = 6x$, and $f'''(x) = 6$.

$f(1) = -1$, $f'(1) = 8$, $f''(1) = 6$ and $f'''(1) = 6$. Therefore

$$f(x) = -1 + 8(x-1) + \frac{6}{2}(x-1)^2 + \frac{6}{6}(x-1)^3 = x^3 + 5x - 7 = f(x).$$

20. (a) Let $(a-h, a+h)$ be an interval in which $f''(x) \le 0$.

If $f'(a) = 0$, then $f(x) = f(a) + \dfrac{f''(c_2)}{2}(x-a)^2$ where

we can write this equation for $a < c_2 < x < a+h$ or for

$a - h < x < c_2 < a$. Then $f(x) < f(a)$ because $f''(c_2) \le 0$

for all x in some interval and $f(a)$ is a local maximum.

(b) Let $(a-h, a+h)$ be an interval in which $f''(x) \ge 0$.

If $f'(a) = 0$, then $f(x) = f(a) + \dfrac{f''(c_2)}{2}(x-a)^2$ where

we can write this equation for $a < c_2 < x < a+h$ or for

$a - h < x < c_2 < a$. Then $f(x) > f(a)$ because $f''(c_2) \ge 0$

for all x in some interval and $f(a)$ is a local minimum.

3.M MISCELLANEOUS

1. $y = 9x - x^2$; $y' = 9 - 2x$; $y'' = -2$

(a) y increases on $\left(-\infty, \frac{9}{2}\right)$

(b) y decreases on $\left(\frac{9}{2}, \infty\right)$

(c) never concave up

(d) always concave down

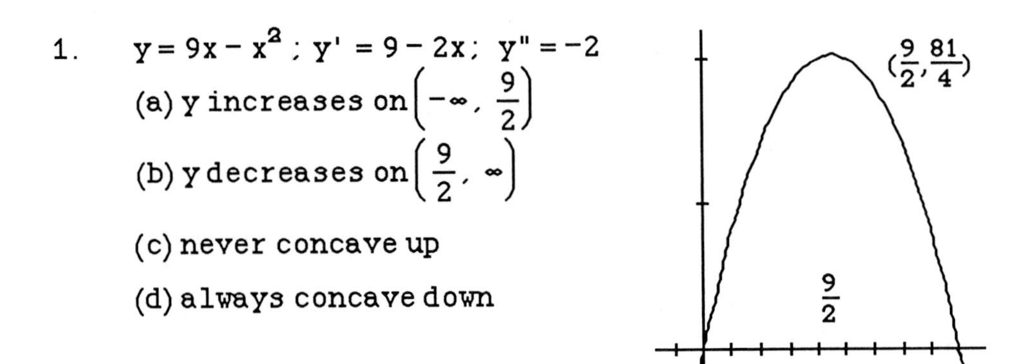

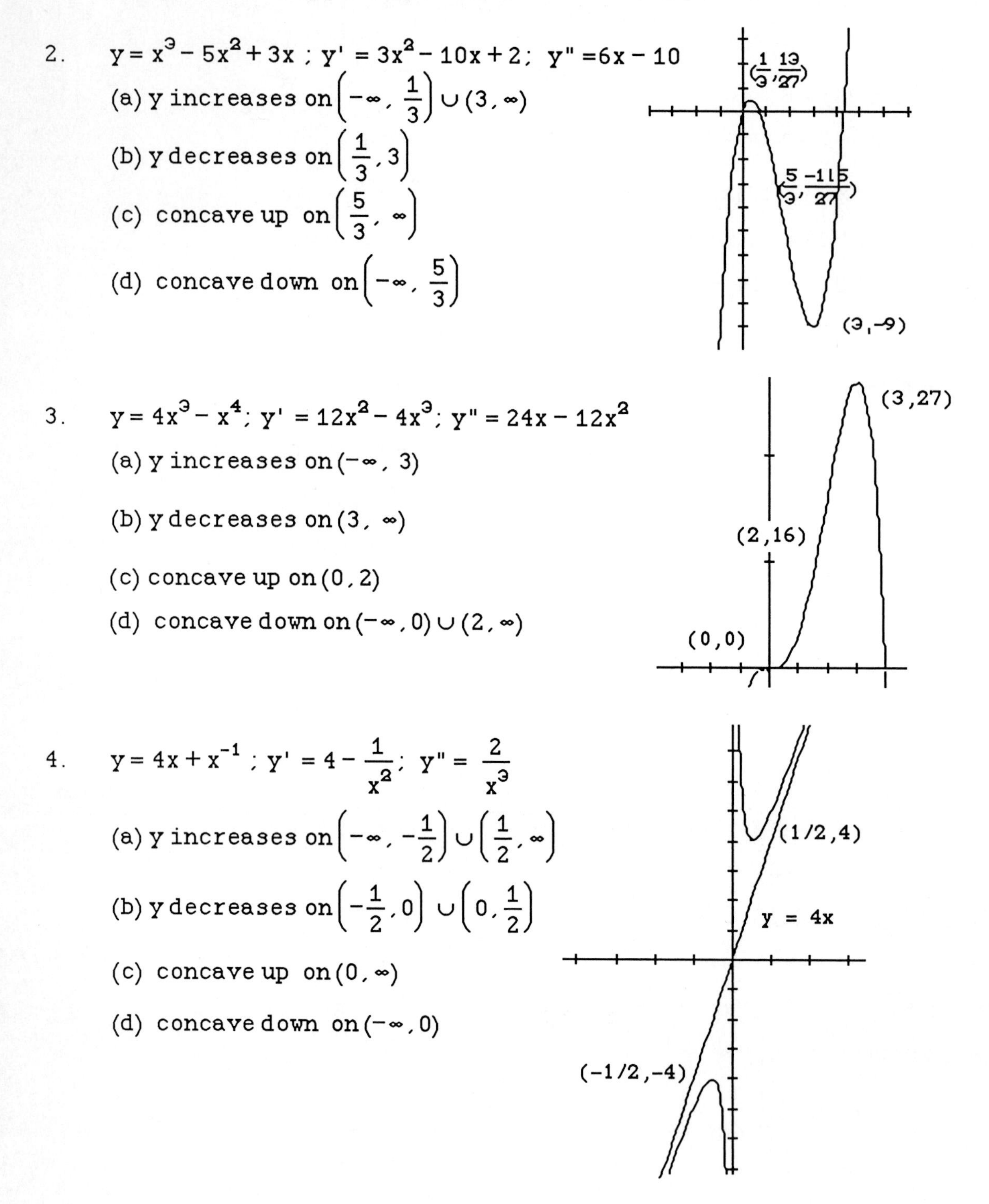

2. $y = x^3 - 5x^2 + 3x$; $y' = 3x^2 - 10x + 2$; $y'' = 6x - 10$

(a) y increases on $\left(-\infty, \frac{1}{3}\right) \cup (3, \infty)$

(b) y decreases on $\left(\frac{1}{3}, 3\right)$

(c) concave up on $\left(\frac{5}{3}, \infty\right)$

(d) concave down on $\left(-\infty, \frac{5}{3}\right)$

3. $y = 4x^3 - x^4$; $y' = 12x^2 - 4x^3$; $y'' = 24x - 12x^2$

(a) y increases on $(-\infty, 3)$

(b) y decreases on $(3, \infty)$

(c) concave up on $(0, 2)$

(d) concave down on $(-\infty, 0) \cup (2, \infty)$

4. $y = 4x + x^{-1}$; $y' = 4 - \frac{1}{x^2}$; $y'' = \frac{2}{x^3}$

(a) y increases on $\left(-\infty, -\frac{1}{2}\right) \cup \left(\frac{1}{2}, \infty\right)$

(b) y decreases on $\left(-\frac{1}{2}, 0\right) \cup \left(0, \frac{1}{2}\right)$

(c) concave up on $(0, \infty)$

(d) concave down on $(-\infty, 0)$

5. $y = x^2 + 4x^{-1}$; $y; = 2x - 4x^{-2}$; $y'' = 2 + 8x^{-3}$

(a) y increases on $(\sqrt[3]{2}, \infty)$

(b) y decreases on $(-\infty, \sqrt[3]{2})$

(c) concave up on $(-\infty, -\sqrt[3]{4}) \cup (0, \infty)$

(d) concave down on $(-\sqrt[3]{4}, 0)$

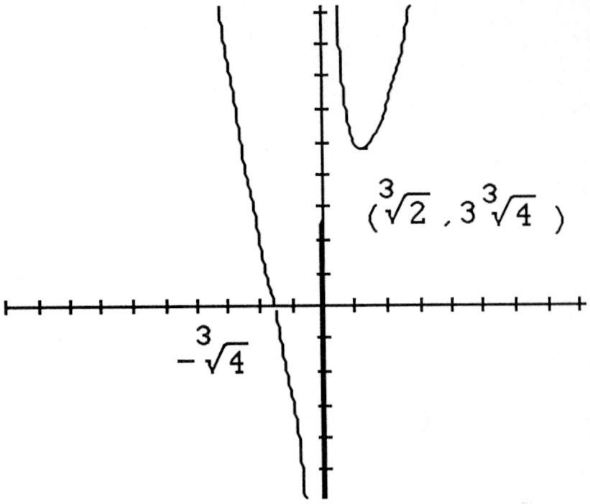

$(\sqrt[3]{2}, 3\sqrt[3]{4})$

$-\sqrt[3]{4}$

6. $y = x + 4x^{-2}$; $y' = 1 - \dfrac{8}{x^3}$; $y'' = \dfrac{24}{x^4}$

(a) y increases on $(-\infty, 0) \cup (2, \infty)$

(b) y decreases on $(0, 2)$

(c) concave up on $(-\infty, 0) \cup (0, \infty)$

(d) never concave down

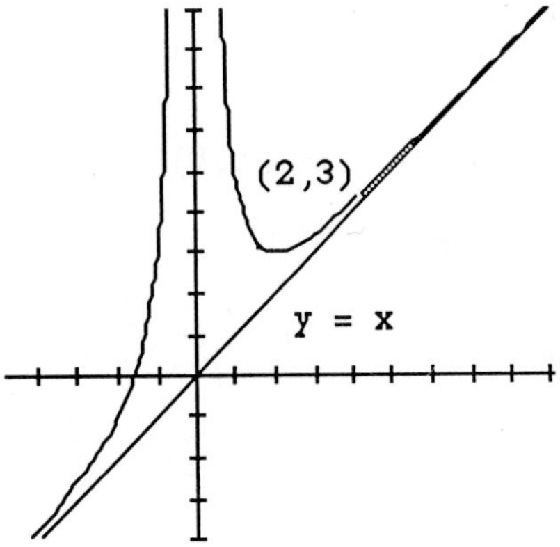

(2,3)

y = x

7. $y = 5 - x^{2/3}$; $y' = -\frac{2}{3}x^{-1/3}$; $y'' = \frac{1}{9}x^{-4/3}$

(a) y increases on $(-\infty, 0)$

(b) y decreases on $(0, \infty)$

(c) concave up on for all $x \neq 0$

(d) for no x

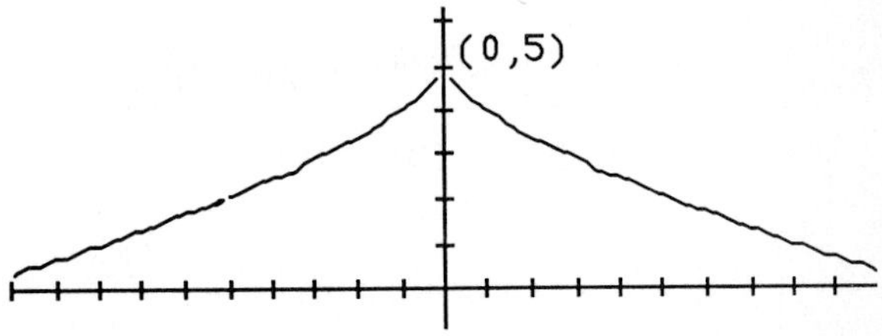

(0,5)

8. $y = \dfrac{x-1}{x+1} = 1 - \dfrac{2}{x+1}$; $y' = \dfrac{2}{(x+1)^2}$; $y'' = \dfrac{-4}{(x+1)^3}$

(a) y increases on $(-\infty, 1) \cup (1, \infty)$

(b) y never decreases

(c) concave up on $(-\infty, -1)$

(d) concave down on $(-1, \infty)$

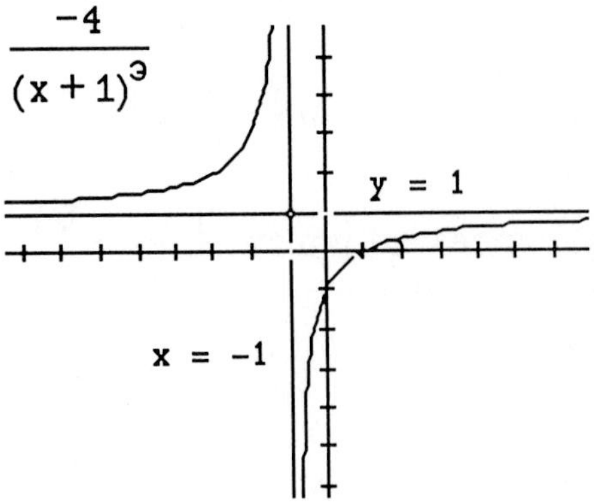

y = 1

x = -1

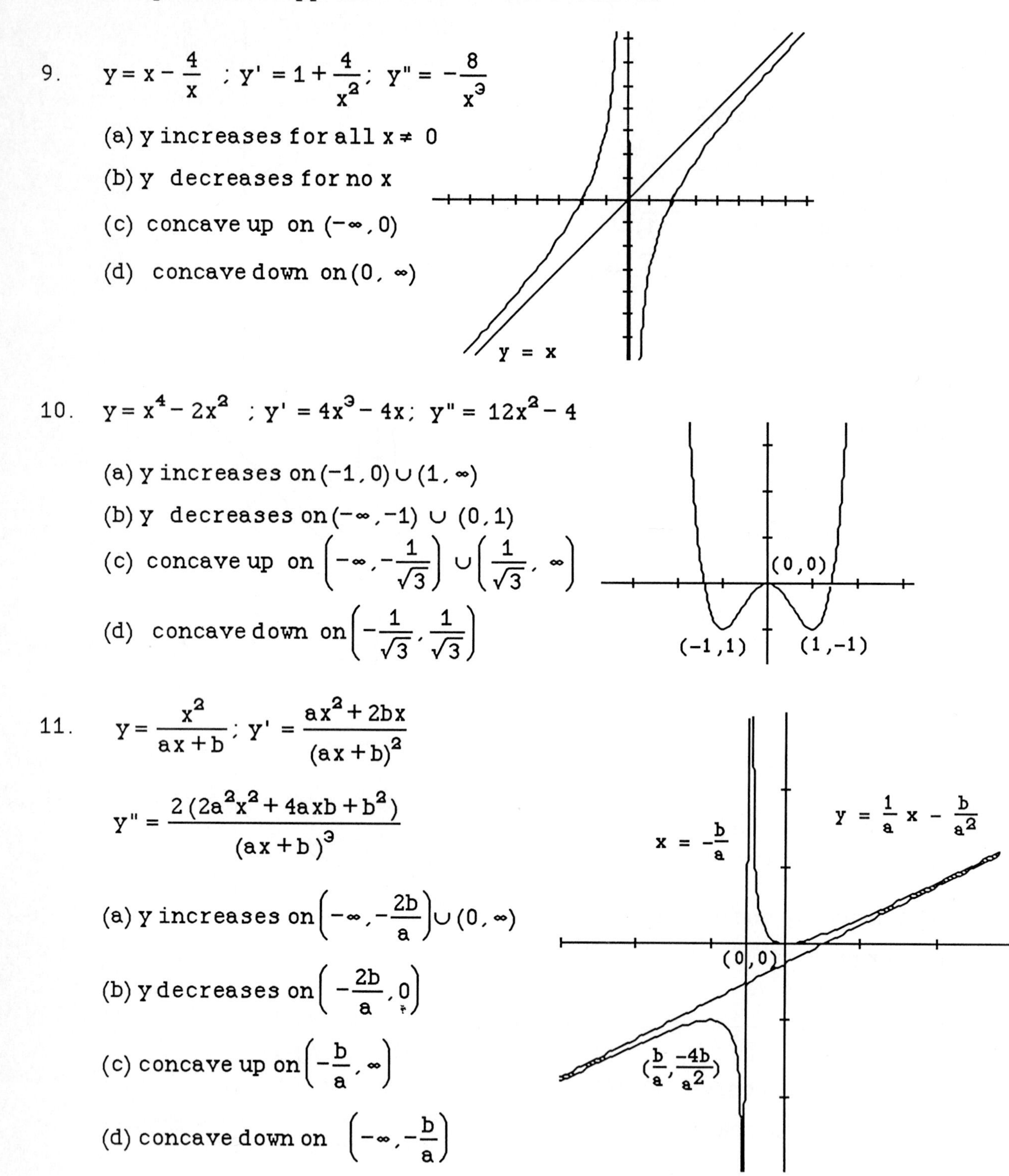

9. $y = x - \frac{4}{x}$; $y' = 1 + \frac{4}{x^2}$; $y'' = -\frac{8}{x^3}$

(a) y increases for all $x \neq 0$

(b) y decreases for no x

(c) concave up on $(-\infty, 0)$

(d) concave down on $(0, \infty)$

10. $y = x^4 - 2x^2$; $y' = 4x^3 - 4x$; $y'' = 12x^2 - 4$

(a) y increases on $(-1, 0) \cup (1, \infty)$

(b) y decreases on $(-\infty, -1) \cup (0, 1)$

(c) concave up on $\left(-\infty, -\frac{1}{\sqrt{3}}\right) \cup \left(\frac{1}{\sqrt{3}}, \infty\right)$

(d) concave down on $\left(-\frac{1}{\sqrt{3}}, \frac{1}{\sqrt{3}}\right)$

11. $y = \frac{x^2}{ax+b}$; $y' = \frac{ax^2 + 2bx}{(ax+b)^2}$

$$y'' = \frac{2(2a^2x^2 + 4axb + b^2)}{(ax+b)^3}$$

(a) y increases on $\left(-\infty, -\frac{2b}{a}\right) \cup (0, \infty)$

(b) y decreases on $\left(-\frac{2b}{a}, 0\right)$

(c) concave up on $\left(-\frac{b}{a}, \infty\right)$

(d) concave down on $\left(-\infty, -\frac{b}{a}\right)$

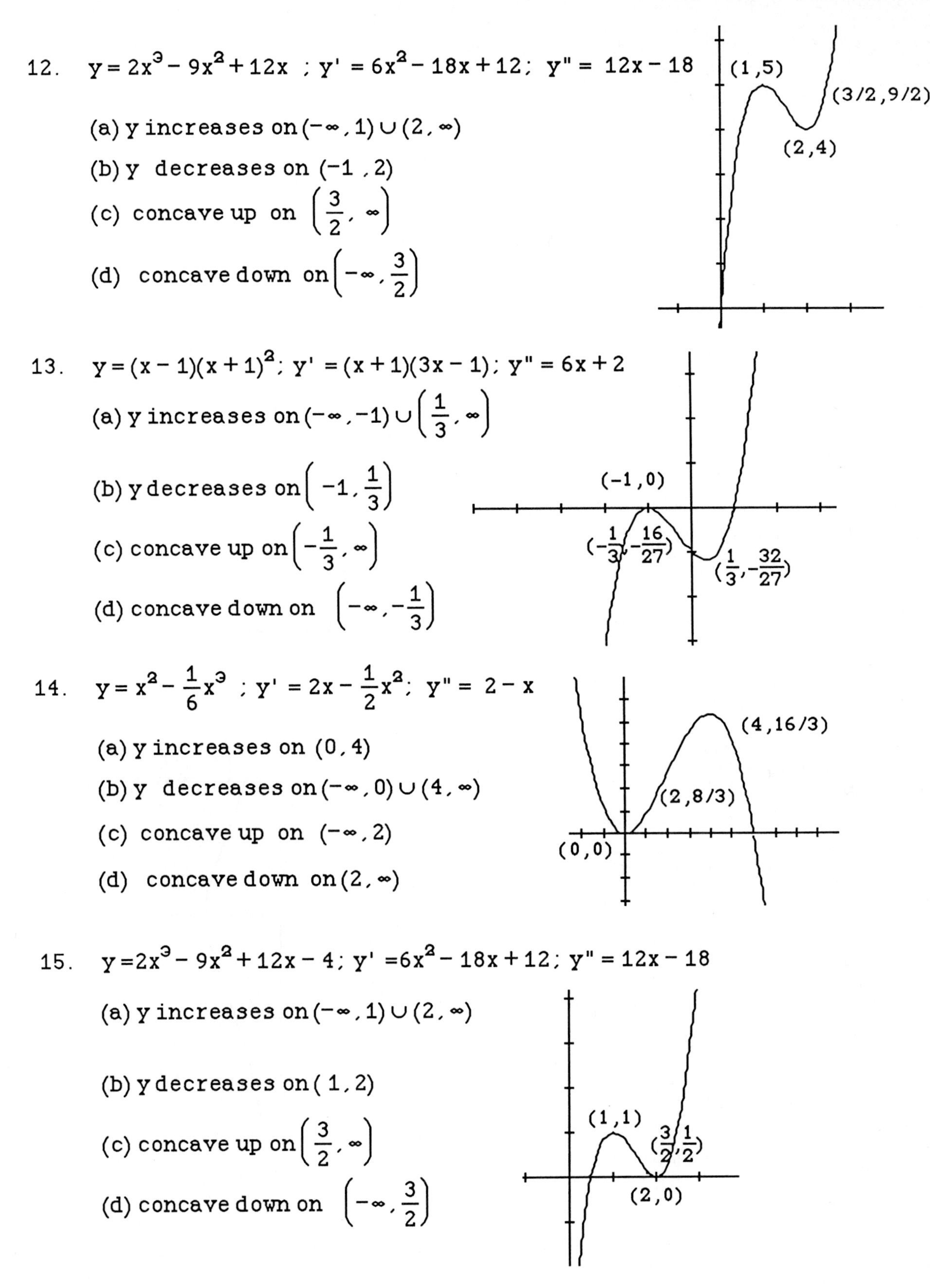

12. $y = 2x^3 - 9x^2 + 12x$; $y' = 6x^2 - 18x + 12$; $y'' = 12x - 18$

(a) y increases on $(-\infty, 1) \cup (2, \infty)$

(b) y decreases on $(-1, 2)$

(c) concave up on $\left(\frac{3}{2}, \infty\right)$

(d) concave down on $\left(-\infty, \frac{3}{2}\right)$

13. $y = (x - 1)(x + 1)^2$; $y' = (x + 1)(3x - 1)$; $y'' = 6x + 2$

(a) y increases on $(-\infty, -1) \cup \left(\frac{1}{3}, \infty\right)$

(b) y decreases on $\left(-1, \frac{1}{3}\right)$

(c) concave up on $\left(-\frac{1}{3}, \infty\right)$

(d) concave down on $\left(-\infty, -\frac{1}{3}\right)$

14. $y = x^2 - \frac{1}{6}x^3$; $y' = 2x - \frac{1}{2}x^2$; $y'' = 2 - x$

(a) y increases on $(0, 4)$

(b) y decreases on $(-\infty, 0) \cup (4, \infty)$

(c) concave up on $(-\infty, 2)$

(d) concave down on $(2, \infty)$

15. $y = 2x^3 - 9x^2 + 12x - 4$; $y' = 6x^2 - 18x + 12$; $y'' = 12x - 18$

(a) y increases on $(-\infty, 1) \cup (2, \infty)$

(b) y decreases on $(1, 2)$

(c) concave up on $\left(\frac{3}{2}, \infty\right)$

(d) concave down on $\left(-\infty, \frac{3}{2}\right)$

16. $y = 3x(x-1)(x+1)^2$; $y' = 3(x+1)(4x^2 - x - 1)$

$y'' = 6(6x^2 + 3x - 1)$

(a) $y' = 0$ if $x = \dfrac{1 \pm \sqrt{17}}{8}$ or $x = 1$.

y increases for $\left(-1, \dfrac{1-\sqrt{17}}{8}\right) \cup \left(\dfrac{1+\sqrt{17}}{8}, \infty\right)$

(b) y decreases for $(-\infty, -1) \cup \left(\dfrac{1-\sqrt{17}}{8}, \dfrac{1+\sqrt{17}}{8}\right)$

(c) $y'' = 0$ if $x = \dfrac{-3 \pm \sqrt{33}}{12}$

concave up for $\left(-\infty, \dfrac{-3-\sqrt{33}}{12}\right) \cup \left(\dfrac{-3+\sqrt{33}}{12}, \infty\right)$

(d) concave down for $\left(\dfrac{-3-\sqrt{33}}{12}, \dfrac{-3+\sqrt{33}}{12}\right)$

17. The relation $xy^2 = 3(1-x)$ is symmetric to the x-axis, and not a function. We will solve it for y, graph the top half, and reflect this about the y-axis for the bottom half.

$$y = \pm\sqrt{\frac{3(1-x)}{x}}$$

$$y' = -\frac{3}{2x^2}\sqrt{\frac{x}{3(1-x)}}$$

$$y'' = \frac{\sqrt{3}}{4}x^{-5/2}(1-x)^{-3/2}(3-4x)$$

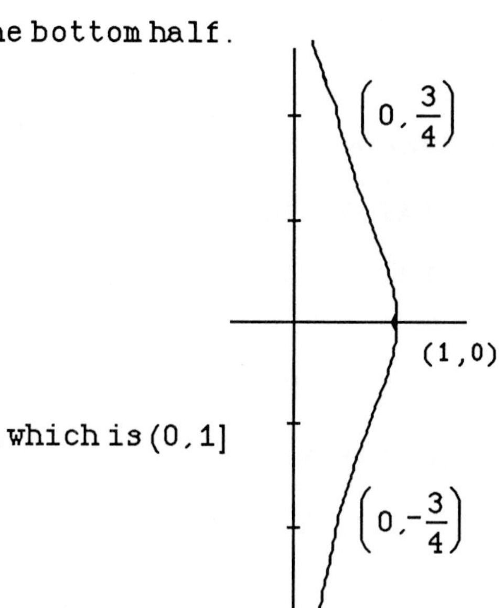

(a) y does not increase on its domain which is (0, 1]

(b) y decreases on (0, 1]

(c) concave up on $\left(0, \dfrac{3}{4}\right)$

(d) concave down on $\left(\dfrac{3}{4}, 1\right]$

18. $y = 2\cos x + \cos^2 x$; $y' = -2\sin x - 2\cos x \sin x$;

$y'' = -2\cos x - 2\cos^2 x + 2\sin^2 x = -2\cos x - 2\cos$;

(a) $y' = -\sin x(1 + \cos x)$. $y' > 0$ when $\sin x < 0$.

y increases for $\pi + 2k\pi < x < 2\pi + 2k\pi$

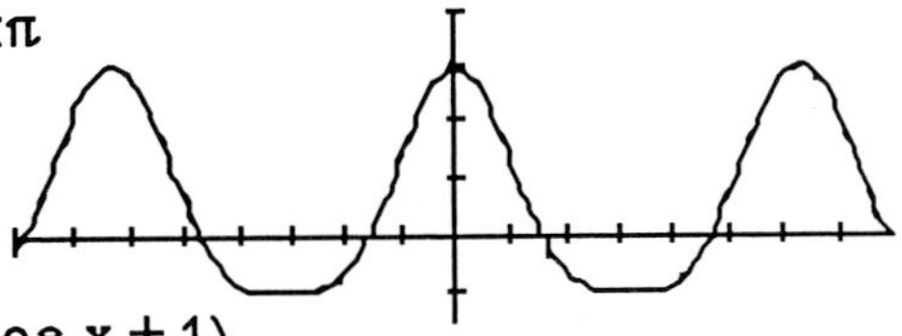

(b) $y' < 0$ when $\sin x > 0$

y decreases for $2k\pi < x < \pi + 2k\pi$

(c) $y'' = -2(2\cos^2 x - 1) = -2(2\cos x - 1)(\cos x + 1)$

$y'' > 0$ when $2\cos x - 1 < 0$

concave up when $\frac{\pi}{3} + 2k\pi < x < \frac{5\pi}{3} + 2k\pi$

(d) $y'' < 0$ when $2\cos x - 1 > 0$

concave down when $-\frac{\pi}{3} + 2k\pi < x < \frac{\pi}{3} + 2k\pi$

19 (a). $y = \frac{x+1}{x^2+1}$; Domain is all reals

(a) No symmetry to origin or y-axis

(b) (0, 1) and (−1, 0)

(c) No vertical asymptote

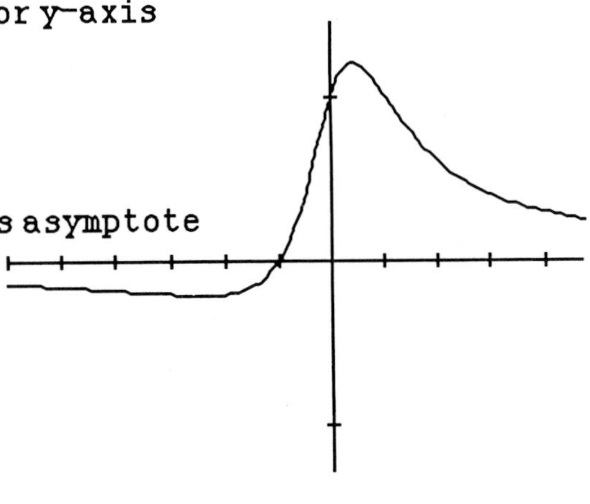

$\lim_{x\to\pm\infty} \frac{x+1}{x^2+1} = 0 \Rightarrow$ x-axis asymptote

(d) $y' = \frac{1 - 2x - x^2}{(x^2+1)^2}$

$y'(-1) = \frac{1}{2}$; $y'(0) = 1$

(e) rising for x in $(-1-\sqrt{2}, -1+\sqrt{2})$

falling for x in $(-\infty, -1-\sqrt{2}) \cup (-1+\sqrt{2}, \infty)$

(f) $y'' = \frac{2(x^3 + 3x^2 - 3x - 1)}{(x^2+1)^3}$; $x^3 + 3x^2 - 3x - 1 = (x-1)x^2 + 4x + 1)$

$y'' = 0$ if $x = 1, -2 \pm \sqrt{3}$.

Concave down if x in $(-\infty, -2-\sqrt{3}) \cup (-2+\sqrt{3}, 1)$

Concave up if x in $(-2-\sqrt{3}, -2+\sqrt{3}) \cup (1, \infty)$

19(b). $y = \frac{x^2+1}{x+1} = x - 1 + \frac{2}{x+1}$; Domain is all $x \neq -1$

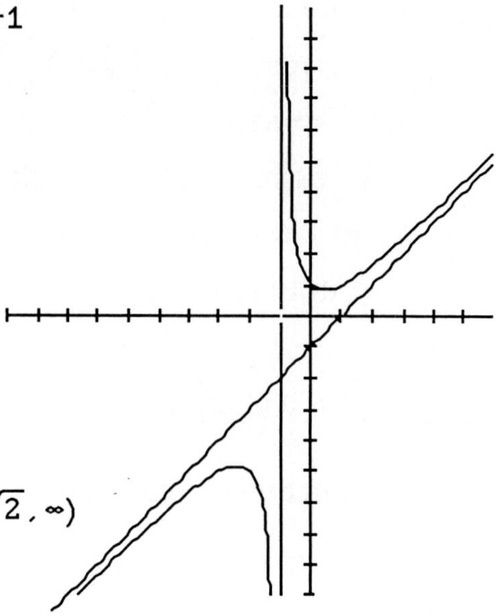

(a) No symmetry to origin or y-axis

(b) (0, 1)

(c) Vertical asymptote: $x = -1$

slant asymptote: $y = x - 1$

(d) $y' = 1 - \frac{2}{(x+1)^2}$; $y'(0) = -1$

(e) falling for x in $(-1-\sqrt{2}, -1+\sqrt{2})$

rising for x in $(-\infty, -1-\sqrt{2}) \cup (-1+\sqrt{2}, \infty)$

(f) $y'' = \frac{4}{(x+1)^3}$

Concave down if x in $(-\infty, -1)$; concave up if x in $(-1, \infty)$

20. (a) $y = x + \frac{1}{x^2}$; Domain is all $x \neq 0$

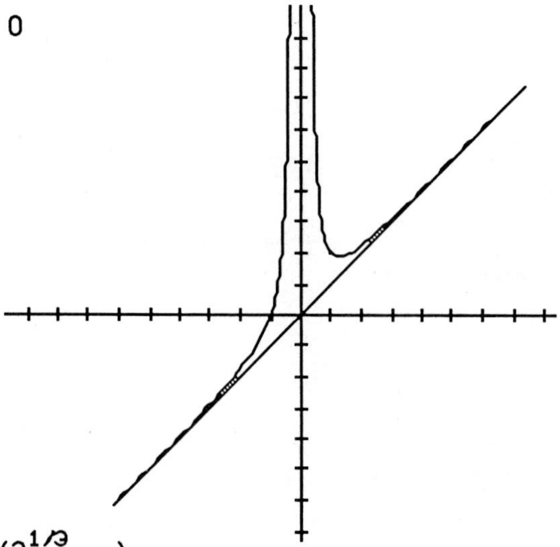

(a) No symmetry

(b) (−1, 0)

(c) vertical: $x = 0$

oblique: $y = x$

(d) $y' = 1 - \frac{2}{x^3}$

$y'(-1) = 3$

(e) falling for x in $(0, 2^{1/3})$

rising for x in $(-\infty, 0) \cup (2^{1/3}, \infty)$

(f) $y'' = \frac{6}{x^4}$

Concave up if x in $(-\infty, 0) \cup (0, \infty)$

(g) $y \approx x$ for $x \to \pm\infty$; $y \approx \frac{1}{x^2}$ for x near 0.

(b) $y = x^2 + \frac{1}{x^2}$; Domain is all $x \neq 0$

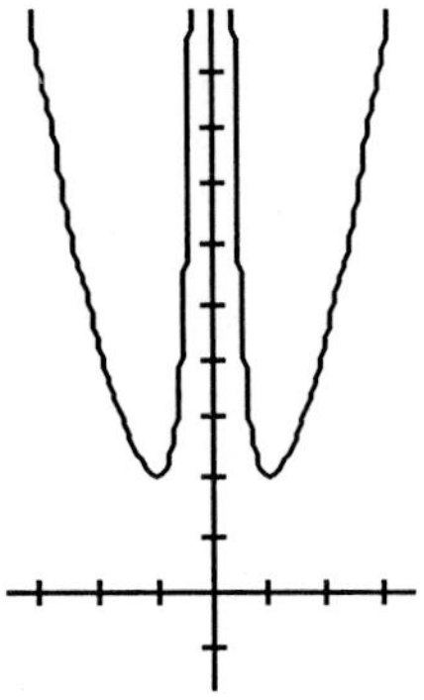

(a) Symmetry to y-axis

(b) no intercepts

(c) vertical: $x = 0$

(d) $y' = 2x - \frac{2}{x^3} = 0$ if $x = \pm 1$

$y'(\pm 1) = 0$

(e) rising for x in $(-1, 0) \cup (1, \infty)$

falling for x in $(-\infty, -1) \cup (0, 1)$

(f) $y'' = 2 + \frac{6}{x^4}$

Concave up if x in $(-\infty, 0) \cup (0, \infty)$

(g) $y \approx x^2$ for $x \to \pm\infty$; $y \approx \frac{1}{x^2}$ for x near 0.

21. $y = x(x+1)(x-2)$; Domain is all x

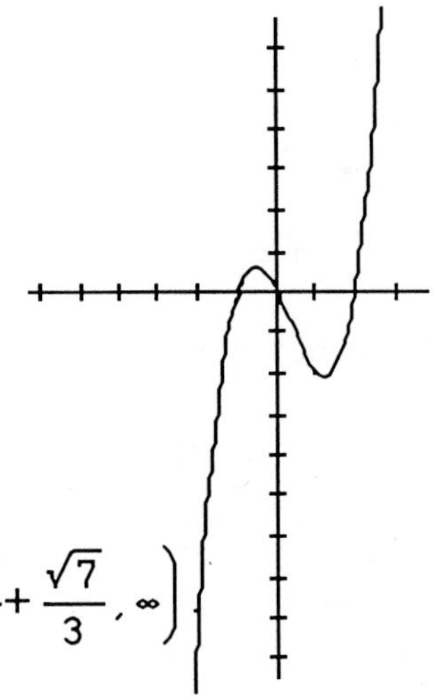

(a) No symmetry to origin or y-axis

(b) $(0, 0)$, $(-1, 0)$ and $(2, 0)$

(c) no asymptotes

(d) $y' = 3x^2 - 2x - 2$

$y'(0) = -2$; $y'(-1) = 3'$ $y'(2) = 6$

(e) falling for x in $\left(\frac{1}{3} - \frac{\sqrt{7}}{3}, \frac{1}{3} + \frac{\sqrt{7}}{3}\right)$

rising for x in $\left(-\infty, \frac{1}{3} - \frac{\sqrt{7}}{3}\right) \cup \left(\frac{1}{3} + \frac{\sqrt{7}}{3}, \infty\right)$

(f) $y'' = 6x - 2$

Concave down if x in $\left(-\infty, \frac{1}{3}\right)$; concave up if x in $\left(\frac{1}{3}, \infty\right)$

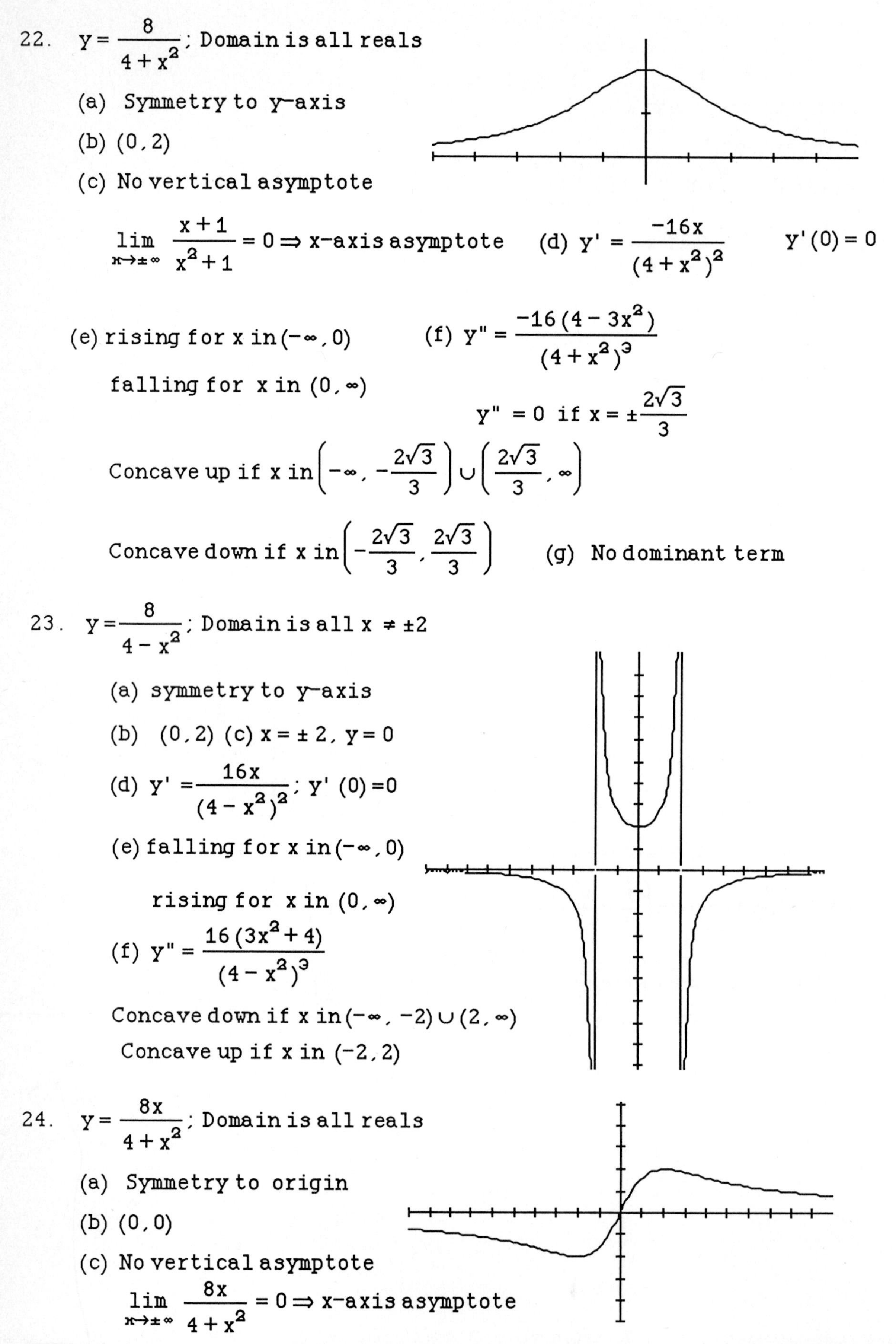

22. $y = \dfrac{8}{4+x^2}$; Domain is all reals

(a) Symmetry to y-axis

(b) (0, 2)

(c) No vertical asymptote

$\lim\limits_{x\to\pm\infty} \dfrac{x+1}{x^2+1} = 0 \Rightarrow$ x-axis asymptote (d) $y' = \dfrac{-16x}{(4+x^2)^2}$ $y'(0) = 0$

(e) rising for x in $(-\infty, 0)$

falling for x in $(0, \infty)$

(f) $y'' = \dfrac{-16(4-3x^2)}{(4+x^2)^3}$

$y'' = 0$ if $x = \pm\dfrac{2\sqrt{3}}{3}$

Concave up if x in $\left(-\infty, -\dfrac{2\sqrt{3}}{3}\right) \cup \left(\dfrac{2\sqrt{3}}{3}, \infty\right)$

Concave down if x in $\left(-\dfrac{2\sqrt{3}}{3}, \dfrac{2\sqrt{3}}{3}\right)$ (g) No dominant term

23. $y = \dfrac{8}{4-x^2}$; Domain is all $x \neq \pm 2$

(a) symmetry to y-axis

(b) (0, 2) (c) $x = \pm 2$, $y = 0$

(d) $y' = \dfrac{16x}{(4-x^2)^2}$; $y'(0) = 0$

(e) falling for x in $(-\infty, 0)$

rising for x in $(0, \infty)$

(f) $y'' = \dfrac{16(3x^2+4)}{(4-x^2)^3}$

Concave down if x in $(-\infty, -2) \cup (2, \infty)$

Concave up if x in $(-2, 2)$

24. $y = \dfrac{8x}{4+x^2}$; Domain is all reals

(a) Symmetry to origin

(b) (0, 0)

(c) No vertical asymptote

$\lim\limits_{x\to\pm\infty} \dfrac{8x}{4+x^2} = 0 \Rightarrow$ x-axis asymptote

(d) $y' = \dfrac{-8(x^2-4)}{(4+x^2)^2}$ $y'(0)=2$

(e) rising for x in $(-2, 2)$

falling for x in $(-\infty, -2) \cup (2, \infty)$

(f) $y'' = \dfrac{4x(4x^2-48)}{(4+x^2)^3}$ $y''=0$ if $x = \pm 2\sqrt{3}$

Concave down if x in $(-\infty, -2\sqrt{3}) \cup (0, 2\sqrt{3})$

Concave up if x in $(-2\sqrt{3}, 0) \cup (2\sqrt{3}, \infty)$

(g) No dominant term

25. $x^2y - y = 4(x-2) \Rightarrow y = \dfrac{4(x-2)}{x^2-1}$; Domain is all $x \neq \pm 1$

(a) No symmetry

(b) $(2, 0)$, $(0, 8)$ (c) $x = \pm 1$, $y = 0$

(d) $y' = \dfrac{-4(x^2-4x+1)}{(x^2-1)^2}$; $y'(2) = \dfrac{4}{3}$; $y'(0) = -4$

(e) falling for x in $(-\infty, 2-\sqrt{3}) \cup (2+\sqrt{3}, \infty)$

rising for x in $(2-\sqrt{3}, 2+\sqrt{3})$

(f) $y'' = \dfrac{8(x^3-6x^2+3x-2)}{(x^2-1)^3}$

Concave down if x in $(-\infty, -1) \cup (1, 5.5)$

Concave up if x in $(-1, 1) \cup (5.5, \infty)$

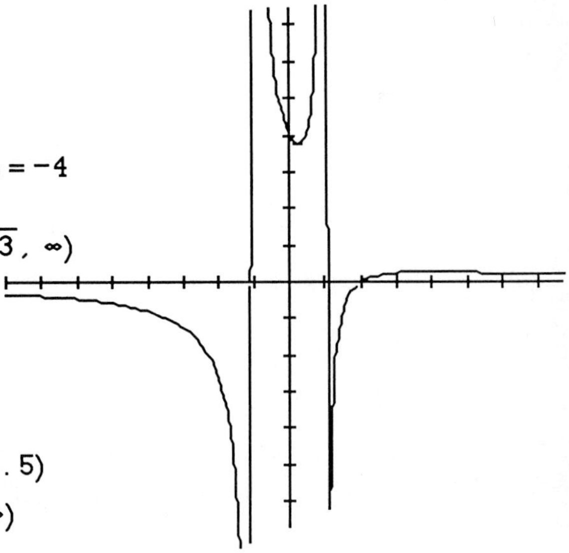

26. $y = \dfrac{x^2+1}{x^2-1} = 1 + \dfrac{2}{x^2-1}$; Domain is all $x \neq \pm 1$

(a) Symmetry to y axis

(b) $(0, -1)$

(c) vertical: $x = \pm 1$

$\lim\limits_{x \to \pm\infty} \dfrac{x^2+1}{x^2+1} = 1 \Rightarrow y = 1$

(d) $y' = \dfrac{-4x}{(x^2-1)^2}$

$y'(0) = 0$

(e) falling for x in $(0, 1) \cup (1, \infty)$

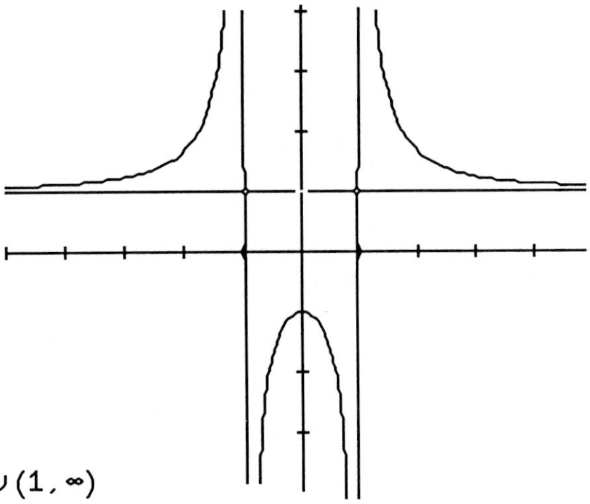

rising for x in $(-\infty,-1)\cup(-1,0)$

(f) $y'' = \dfrac{4(3x^2+1)}{(x^2-1)^3}$

Concave down if x in $(-1,1)$

Concave up if x in $(-\infty,-1)\cup(1,\infty)$

(g) $y \approx 1$ for $x \to \pm\infty$; $y \approx -\dfrac{1}{x+1}$ for x near -1; $y \approx \dfrac{1}{x-1}$ for x near 1.

27. $y = \dfrac{ax+b}{cx^2+dx+e}$, a, b, c, d, and e are either 0 or 1.

(1) If there is no y − intercept, then $x \neq 0 \Rightarrow e = 0$

(2) x–axis an asymptote $\Rightarrow \lim\limits_{x\to\infty} \dfrac{ax+b}{cx^2+dx+e} = 0 \Rightarrow c \neq 0$ so $c = 1$

(3) x–intercept is $(-1,0) \Rightarrow 0 = \dfrac{-a+b}{c-d} \Rightarrow a = b$. If $a = b = 0$, the funtion is $y = 0$. Therefore $a = b = 1$. The value of d must be 0, because otherwise the function is $y = \dfrac{1}{x}$.

28. Symmetry to the y–axis means that:

(x, y) belongs to graph $\Rightarrow$ $(-x, y)$ belongs to graph.

Symmetry to the origin would then mean that:

$(-x, y)$ belongs to graph $\Rightarrow$ $(x, -y)$ belongs to graph.

Putting the two together would state that:

(x, y) belongs to graph $\Rightarrow$ $(x, -y)$ belongs to graph.

This is precisely the condition we need for symmetry to the x–axis.

29. If $\dfrac{dy}{dx} = 6(x-1)(x-2)^2(x-3)^3(x-4)^4$, then $\dfrac{dy}{dx}$ can only change signs at $x = 1$ and $x = 4$. Moreover, there is a local maximum at $x = 1$ because the change is from positive to negative, and a local minimum at $x = 3$ because the change is from negative to positive.

30. Let x and $20 - x$ be the two parts. Then $P(x) = x^2(20-x) = 20x^2 - x^3$. $P'(x) = 40x - 3x^2 = 0$ if $x = 0$ or $\dfrac{40}{3}$. $P' > 0$ if $x < \dfrac{40}{3}$ and $P' < 0$ if $x > \dfrac{40}{3}$ $\Rightarrow$ a maximum value. The two parts are $\dfrac{40}{3}$ and $\dfrac{20}{3}$.

31. $f(x) = 4x^3 - 8x^2 + 5x \Rightarrow f'(x) = 12x^2 - 16x + 5 = (2x - 1)(6x - 5)$

$f'(x) = 0 \Leftrightarrow x = \frac{1}{2}$ or $x = \frac{5}{6}$. We check $\{0, \frac{1}{2}, \frac{5}{6}, 2\}$.

$f(0) = 0 \quad f(\frac{1}{2}) = 1 \quad f(\frac{5}{6}) = \frac{25}{27} \quad f(2) = 10$. The largest value of f on $[0,2]$ is 10.

32. Let x and $36 - x$ be the numbers. Then $p(x) = x(36 - x) = 36x - x^2$, $x > 0$.

$p'(x) = 36 - 2x = 0$ if $x = 18$ or 0. $x = 0$ is out of the domain.

$p''(x) = -2 \Rightarrow$ a maximum. There is no minimum value.

33. $y = ax^3 + bx^2 + cx + d \Rightarrow f'(x) = 3ax^2 + 2bx + c$ and

$f''(x) = 6ax + 2b$.

Inflection pt. at $(1,-6) \Rightarrow f''(1) = 0 \Rightarrow \quad 6a + 2b = 0$
Local maximum at $(-1,10) \Rightarrow f'(-1) = 10 \Rightarrow \quad 3a - 2b + c = 10$
$(1,-6)$ on curve $\Rightarrow f(1) = -6 \Rightarrow \quad a + b + c + d = -6$

$(-1,10)$ on curve $\Rightarrow f(-1) = 10 \Rightarrow \quad -a + b - c + d = 10$

$6a + 2b = 0 \Rightarrow b = -3a$. Substituting into second equation:

$3a - 2(-3a) + c = 0 \Rightarrow c = -9a$. Substituting for b and c:

$-a - 3a + 9a + d = 10 \Rightarrow 5a + d = 10 \Rightarrow d = 10 - 5a$

$a + (-3a) + (-9a) + (10 - 5a) = -6 \Rightarrow a = 1$.

Then $b = -3$, $c = -9$, $d = 5$ and $y = x^3 - 3x^2 - 9x + 5$

34. Let $D = x - x^2$. Then $D' = 1 - 2x = 0$ if $x = \frac{1}{2}$. $D'' = -2 \Rightarrow$ maximum difference occurs if $x = \frac{1}{2}$ and $x^2 = \frac{1}{4}$.

35. $p = 2r + s \Rightarrow 2r + s = 100 \Rightarrow s = 100 - 2r$

$A = \frac{1}{2}rs = \frac{1}{2}r(100 - 2r) = 50r - r^2$. $A' = 50 - 2r = 0$

if $r = 25$ ft. $A'' = -2 \Rightarrow$ maximum area.

36. $s = 32t - 16t^2 \Rightarrow v = \frac{ds}{dt} = 32 - 32t$. The ball will reach its maximum height when $v = 0$ or when $t = 1$ sec. At this moment, it will have risen $s(1) = 16$ feet.

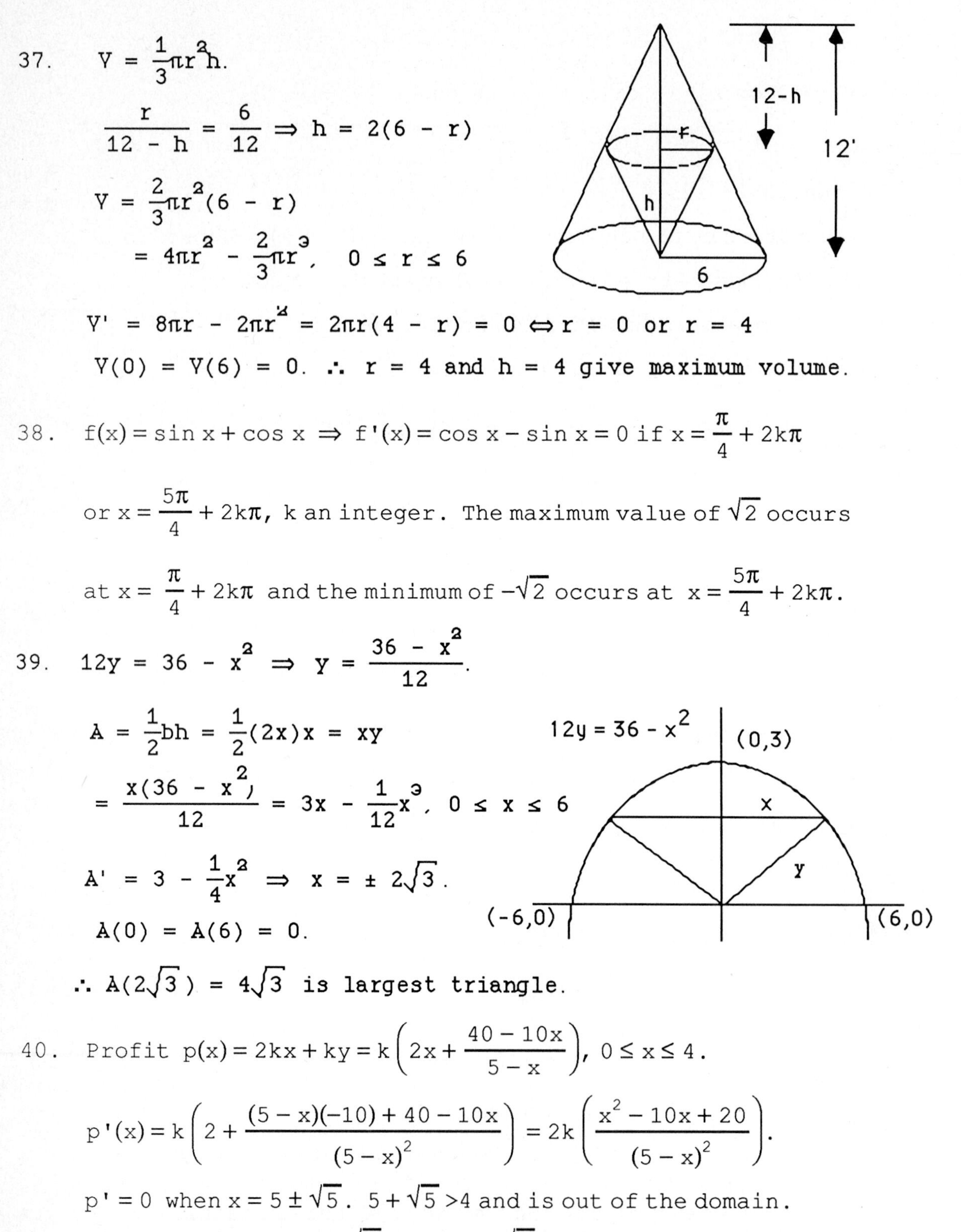

37. $V = \frac{1}{3}\pi r^2 h.$

$$\frac{r}{12 - h} = \frac{6}{12} \Rightarrow h = 2(6 - r)$$

$$V = \frac{2}{3}\pi r^2 (6 - r)$$

$$= 4\pi r^2 - \frac{2}{3}\pi r^3, \quad 0 \le r \le 6$$

$$V' = 8\pi r - 2\pi r^2 = 2\pi r(4 - r) = 0 \Leftrightarrow r = 0 \text{ or } r = 4$$

$V(0) = V(6) = 0.$ ∴ $r = 4$ and $h = 4$ give maximum volume.

38. $f(x) = \sin x + \cos x \Rightarrow f'(x) = \cos x - \sin x = 0$ if $x = \frac{\pi}{4} + 2k\pi$

or $x = \frac{5\pi}{4} + 2k\pi$, k an integer. The maximum value of $\sqrt{2}$ occurs

at $x = \frac{\pi}{4} + 2k\pi$ and the minimum of $-\sqrt{2}$ occurs at $x = \frac{5\pi}{4} + 2k\pi$.

39. $12y = 36 - x^2 \Rightarrow y = \frac{36 - x^2}{12}.$

$$A = \frac{1}{2}bh = \frac{1}{2}(2x)x = xy$$

$$= \frac{x(36 - x^2)}{12} = 3x - \frac{1}{12}x^3, \quad 0 \le x \le 6$$

$$A' = 3 - \frac{1}{4}x^2 \Rightarrow x = \pm 2\sqrt{3}.$$

$A(0) = A(6) = 0.$

∴ $A(2\sqrt{3}) = 4\sqrt{3}$ is largest triangle.

40. Profit $p(x) = 2kx + ky = k\left(2x + \frac{40 - 10x}{5 - x}\right)$, $0 \le x \le 4$.

$$p'(x) = k\left(2 + \frac{(5 - x)(-10) + 40 - 10x}{(5 - x)^2}\right) = 2k\left(\frac{x^2 - 10x + 20}{(5 - x)^2}\right).$$

$p' = 0$ when $x = 5 \pm \sqrt{5}$. $5 + \sqrt{5} > 4$ and is out of the domain.

$p(0) = p(4) = 8k$. $p(5 - \sqrt{5}) = 4k(5 - \sqrt{5}) \approx 11.1k$ is maximum.

41. $x^2 - y^2 = 1$ is a hyperbola with vertices $(\pm 1, 0)$. A restraint on x is that $|x| \geq 1$. Let s be the distance from the point (x,y) to the point P(a,0). Then we have

$$s = \sqrt{(x - a)^2 + y^2} = \sqrt{(x - a)^2 + (x^2 - 1)}.$$

$$\frac{ds}{dx} = \frac{1}{2}[(x - a)^2 + (x^2 - 1)]^{-\frac{1}{2}} (2(x - a) + 2x) =$$

$$\frac{4x - 2a}{2\sqrt{(x - a)^2 + (x^2 - 1)}}. \quad \frac{ds}{dx} = 0 \Leftrightarrow x = \frac{a}{2}.$$

(a) If a = 4 then x = 2 and $y = \pm\sqrt{3}$. $\frac{ds}{dx} > 0$ if $x > 2$ and $\frac{ds}{dx} < 0$ if $x < 2$ $\Rightarrow$ distance is a minimum.

(b) If a = 2 then x = 1 and y = 0, which is the vertex and hence the closest.

(c) If $a = \sqrt{2}$ then $x = \frac{\sqrt{2}}{2} < 1$ (not on hyperbola) so again the vertex (1,0) is closest

42. (a) $t = \frac{\sqrt{25 + x^2}}{15} + \frac{5 - x}{39} \Rightarrow t' = \frac{x}{15\sqrt{25 + x^2}} - \frac{1}{39} = 0$ if

$39x = 15\sqrt{25 + x^2}$ or if $x = \frac{25}{12}$.

$t' < 0$ if $x < \frac{25}{12}$ and $t' > 0$ if $x > \frac{25}{12}$

so $t\left(\frac{25}{12}\right)$ is minimum.

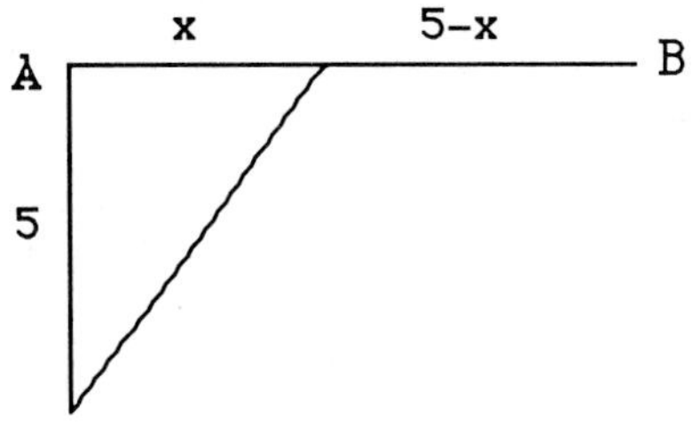

x
5-x
A
B
5

(b) $t = \frac{\sqrt{25 + x^2}}{15} + \frac{10 - x}{39}$ has the same derivative and same answer.

(c) The critical point is now not between 0 and 1, so the extrema occur at the endpoints. In this case the shortest time occurs if the drive is straight across the desert to B.

43. $C = ly + w\sqrt{a^2 + (b-y)^2} \Rightarrow C' = l + \dfrac{-w(b-y)}{\sqrt{a^2 + (b-y)^2}} = 0 \Leftrightarrow$

$l\sqrt{a^2 + (b-y)^2} = w(b-y) \Leftrightarrow l^2[a^2 + (b-y)^2] = w^2(b-y)^2 \Leftrightarrow$

$(l^2 - w^2)(b-y)^2 = -l^2a^2 \Leftrightarrow (b-y)^2 = \dfrac{-l^2a^2}{l^2 - w^2} \Leftrightarrow b - y = \dfrac{la}{\sqrt{w^2 - l^2}}.$

Thus $y = b - \dfrac{la}{\sqrt{w^2 - l^2}}$ and $x = \dfrac{wa}{\sqrt{w^2 - l^2}}$. $C'' = \dfrac{wa^2}{[a^2 + (b-y)^2]^{3/2}} > 0$

so these values give a minimum cost.

44. Let x and y be the sides of the triangle, and r be the radius of the circle. Then $x^2 + y^2 = r^2 \Rightarrow 2x + 2y\dfrac{dy}{dx} = 0 \Rightarrow \dfrac{dy}{dx} = -\dfrac{x}{y}$. Also

$A = \dfrac{1}{2}xy \Rightarrow \dfrac{dA}{dx} = \dfrac{1}{2}\left(y + x\dfrac{dy}{dx}\right) = \dfrac{1}{2}\left(y + x\left(-\dfrac{x}{y}\right)\right) = 0$ if

$y + x\left(-\dfrac{x}{y}\right) = 0$ or if $x = y$. Since $x = 0$ or $y = 0 \Rightarrow A = 0$, this

critical point gives a maximum. ∴ (a) is true and (b) is false.

$P = x + y + 2r \Rightarrow \dfrac{dP}{dx} = 1 + \dfrac{dy}{dx} = 1 - \dfrac{x}{y} = 0$ when $x = y$ and this

also must be a maximum. ∴ (c) is true and (d) is false.

45. Let k and p be the fixed base and perimeter of the triangle.

Let x and y denote the other two sides. Then $p = x + y + k$ and $s = \dfrac{p}{2}$. $A = \sqrt{s(s-x)(s-y)(s-k)} = \sqrt{\dfrac{p}{2}(\dfrac{p}{2}-x)(\dfrac{p}{2}-y)(\dfrac{p}{2}-k)} =$

$\dfrac{1}{4}\sqrt{p(p-2x)(p-2y)(p-2k)} = \dfrac{\sqrt{p(p-2k)}}{4}\sqrt{(p-2x)(p-2(p-x-k))} =$

$K\sqrt{(p-2x)(2x+2k-p)}$.

$A' = \dfrac{K}{2} \cdot \dfrac{2(p-2x) - 2(2x+2k-p)}{\sqrt{(p-2x)(2x+2k-p)}} = K\dfrac{2p - 4x - 2k}{\sqrt{(p-2x)(2x+2k-p)}}.$

$A' = 0 \Leftrightarrow 2p - 4x - 2k = 0 \Leftrightarrow x = \dfrac{p-k}{2} \Rightarrow y = \dfrac{p-k}{2}.$

$0 < x < \dfrac{p-k}{2} \Rightarrow A' > 0$ and $\dfrac{p-k}{2} < x \Rightarrow$ maximum area

46. $A = \frac{1}{2}bh \Rightarrow h = \frac{2A}{b}$. Since $b = h\cot\beta + h\cot\alpha \Rightarrow$

$\cot\beta + \cot\alpha = \frac{b}{h}$.

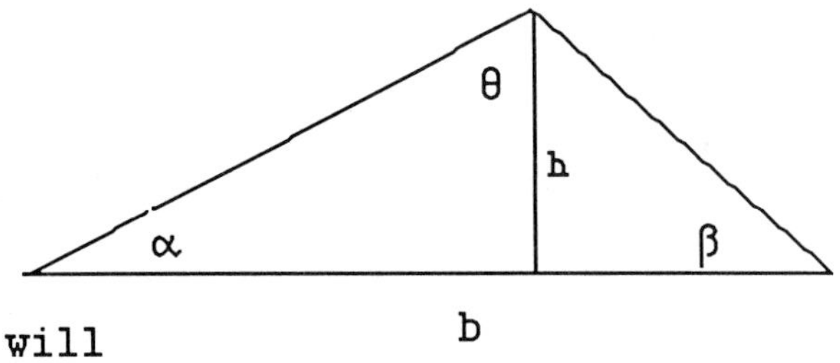

$-\csc^2\beta\,\frac{d\beta}{d\alpha} - \csc^2\alpha = 0 \Rightarrow$

θ

h

α

β

b

$\frac{d\beta}{d\alpha} = -\frac{\csc^2\alpha}{\csc^2\beta} = -\frac{\sin^2\beta}{\sin^2\alpha}$. We will

minimize $S = \alpha + \beta$. $\frac{dS}{d\alpha} = 1 + \frac{d\beta}{d\alpha} = 1 - \frac{\sin^2\beta}{\sin^2\alpha} = 0 \Rightarrow \sin\alpha = \sin\beta \Rightarrow \alpha = \beta$.

Then $b = 2h\cot\beta \Rightarrow \beta = \cot^{-1}\left(\frac{b}{2h}\right) = \tan^{-1}\left(\frac{2h}{b}\right) = \tan^{-1}\left(\frac{4A}{b^2}\right)$.

47. $|PQ| = \sqrt{|OP|^2 + |OQ|^2} = \sqrt{x^2 + y^2} = \sqrt{x^2 + \left(\frac{bx}{x-a}\right)^2}$

$$d'(x) = \frac{1}{2}\left(x^2 + \frac{b^2x^2}{(x-a)^2}\right)^{-\frac{1}{2}}\left[2x + 2\left(\frac{bx}{x-a}\right)\left(\frac{b(x-a) - bx}{(x-a)^2}\right)\right]$$

$$= \frac{1}{2\sqrt{\frac{x^2(x-a)^2 + b^2x^2}{(x-a)^2}}} \bullet \frac{2x(x-a)^3 - 2ab^2x}{(x-a)^3}$$

$$= \frac{x[(x-a)^3 - ab^2]}{\sqrt{x^2(x-a)^2 + b^2x^2}} = 0 \Leftrightarrow x = 0 \text{ or } (x-a)^3 - ab^2 = 0$$

$$(x-a)^3 = ab^2$$

$$x = a + (ab^2)^{\frac{1}{3}}.$$

$x = 0$ is out of the domain. $d' > 0$ for values to the right and negative for values to the left of this root, giving a minimum value. Then

$$y = b + \frac{ab}{x-a} = b + \frac{ab}{a + (ab^2)^{\frac{1}{3}} - a} = b + (a^2b)^{\frac{1}{3}}.$$

$x^2 = a^2 + 2a(ab^2)^{\frac{1}{3}} + (ab^2)^{\frac{2}{3}}$ and $y^2 = b^2 + 2b(a^2b)^{\frac{1}{3}} + (a^2b)^{\frac{2}{3}}$

$a^2 + 2a^{\frac{4}{3}}b^{\frac{2}{3}} + a^{\frac{2}{3}}b^{\frac{4}{3}}$ $\qquad$ $b^2 + 2b^{\frac{4}{3}}a^{\frac{2}{3}} + a^{\frac{4}{3}}b^{\frac{2}{3}}$

$$x^2 + y^2 = a^2 + 3a^{\frac{4}{3}}b^{\frac{2}{3}} + 3a^{\frac{2}{3}}b^{\frac{4}{3}} + b^2 = (a^{\frac{2}{3}} + b^{\frac{2}{3}})^{\frac{3}{2}}.$$

(b) $|OP| + |OQ| = x + y = x + \dfrac{bx}{x - a} = s(x)$.

$$s'(x) = 1 + \frac{b(x - a) - bx}{(x - a)^2} = \frac{(x - a)^2 - ab}{(x - a)^2} = 0 \text{ if } x = a + \sqrt{ab}.$$

$y = b + \dfrac{ab}{a + \sqrt{ab} - a} = b + \sqrt{ab}$. y' changes from negative to positive $\Rightarrow$ this is a minimum.

Then $x + y = a + 2\sqrt{ab} + b = (\sqrt{a} + \sqrt{b})^2$

(c) $|OP||OQ| = xy = x\left(\dfrac{bx}{x - a}\right) = \dfrac{bx^2}{x - a} = p(x)$.

$$p'(x) = \frac{(x - a)(2bx) - bx^2}{(x - a)^2} = \frac{2bx^2 - 2abx - bx^2}{(x - a)^2} = \frac{bx(x - 2a)}{(x - a)^2} = 0$$

if $x = 2a$. y' changes from negative to positive $\Rightarrow$ minimum.

$y = b + \dfrac{ab}{2a - a} = 2b$. $xy = 4ab$.

48. Let $f(x) = mx - 1 + \dfrac{1}{x}$. First, if $x > 0$ then $f(x) \geq 0$ only if

$m \geq 0$. If $m = 0$, then $-1 + \dfrac{1}{x} \geq 0$ only if $x \geq 1$. $\therefore$ $m > 0$.

Then $f'(x) = m - \dfrac{1}{x^2} = 0$ if $x = \dfrac{1}{\sqrt{m}} \Rightarrow \sqrt{m} - 1 + \sqrt{m} \geq 0 \Rightarrow m \geq \dfrac{1}{4}$.

$\therefore$ The smallest value is $m = \dfrac{1}{4}$.

49. Let $S = (x_1 - x)^2 + (y_1 - y)^2$ be the square of the distance between $P_1(x_1, y_1)$ and any point $Q(x, y)$ on line L. Then

$$\frac{dS}{dx} = -2\ (x_1 - x) - 2(y_1 - y)\frac{dy}{dx}.$$ Since P is on the line

$y = -\dfrac{a}{b}x - \dfrac{c}{b}$, $\dfrac{dy}{dx} = -\dfrac{a}{b}$ so that $\dfrac{dS}{dx} = -2\ (x_1 - x) + 2(y_1 - y)\dfrac{a}{b}$. Now,

let $P(x_0, y_0)$ be the point on L closest to P_1, so that $\dfrac{dS}{dx} = 0$.

Then $2(y_1 - y_0)\dfrac{a}{b} = 2(x_1 - x_0)$ or $\dfrac{y_1 - y_0}{x_1 - x_0} = \dfrac{b}{a}$. Thus, the slope of

PP_1 is the negative reciprocal of the slope of L, and $PP_1 \perp L$.

(b) $S = (x_1 - x_0)^2 + (y_1 - y_0)^2 = (x_1 - x_0)^2 + \frac{b^2}{a^2}(x_1 - x_0)^2$

$= (x_1 - x_0)^2\left(\frac{a^2 + b^2}{a^2}\right)$. Now $P(x_0, y_0)$ satisfies both the equation of L: $ax_0 + by_0 + c = 0$ and PP_1: $y_1 - y_0 = \frac{b}{a}(x_1 - x_0)$.

Substituting, $ax_0 + b\left[y_1 - \frac{b}{a}(x_1 - x_0)\right] + c = 0 \Rightarrow$

$a^2x_0 + [a^2x_1 - a^2x_1] + aby_1 - b^2(x_1 - x_0) + ac = 0 \Rightarrow$

$-a^2(x_1 - x_0) + a(ax_1 + by_1 + c) - b^2(x_1 - x_0) = 0 \Rightarrow$

$(a^2 + b^2)(x_1 - x_0) = a(ax_1 + by_1 + c)$. Hence

$S = \frac{a^2 + b^2}{a^2}\left[\frac{a(ax_1 + by_1 + c)}{a^2 + b^2}\right]^2 = \frac{ax_1 + by_1 + c}{a^2 + b^2}$. Since $S = d^2$,

$$d = \frac{|ax_1 + by_1 + c|}{\sqrt{a^2 + b^2}}.$$

50. $400 = 2x + 2\pi y \Rightarrow y = \frac{200 - x}{\pi}$. Then $A = 2xy = 2x\left(\frac{200 - x}{\pi}\right)$.

$A' = \frac{2}{\pi}(200 - 2x) = 0$ if $x = 100$. $A' > 0$ if $x < 100$ and $A' < 0$ if $x < 100 \Rightarrow$ maximum value occurs if $x = 100$. Then $y = \frac{100}{\pi}$.

51. Given that $ax + \frac{b}{x} \geq c$ where a,b, and c are positive constants.

Let $f(x) = ax + \frac{b}{x} \Rightarrow f'(x) = a - \frac{b}{x^2}$ and $f''(x) = \frac{2b}{x^3}$.

$f'(x) = 0 \Leftrightarrow x = \sqrt{\frac{b}{a}}$. $f'' > 0$ for $x > 0$ so this value gives a minimum, that is

$f\left(\sqrt{\frac{b}{a}}\right) > ax + \frac{b}{x} \geq c \Rightarrow a\sqrt{\frac{b}{a}} + b\sqrt{\frac{a}{b}} \geq c \Rightarrow 2\sqrt{ab} \geq c \Rightarrow$

$4ab \geq c^2 \Rightarrow ab \geq \frac{c^2}{4}$.

52. Let $f(x) = ax^2 + \frac{b}{x}$. Then $f'(x) = 2ax - \frac{b}{x^2} = 0$ if $x = \left(\frac{b}{2a}\right)^{1/3}$.

$f''(x) = 2a + \frac{2b}{x^3} > 0$ so that $f(x) \geq f\left(\left(\frac{b}{2a}\right)^{1/3}\right) \geq c$. Then

$$a\left(\left(\frac{b}{2a}\right)^{1/3}\right)^2 + b\left(\frac{2a}{b}\right)^{1/3} \geq c \Rightarrow 2^{-2/3}a^{1/3}b^{2/3} + 2^{1/3}b^{2/3}a^{1/3} \geq c$$

$$\left[\left(\frac{1}{4}\right)^{1/3} + 2^{1/3}\right]a^{1/3}b^{2/3} \geq c \Rightarrow \frac{27}{4}ab^2 \geq c^3 \text{ or } 27ab^2 \geq 4c^3.$$

53. If $f(x) = ax^2 + 2bx + c$, then $f'(x) = 2ax + 2b = 0 \Leftrightarrow x = -\frac{b}{a}$. If $a > 0$, then $f'(x) = 2a > 0$ and there is a minimum value at $x = -\frac{b}{a}$.

Therefore, for any x, $f(x) \geq f\left(-\frac{b}{a}\right) = a\left(-\frac{b}{a}\right)^2 + 2b\left(-\frac{b}{a}\right) + c =$
$-b^2 + ac \geq 0 \Rightarrow b^2 - ac \leq 0$.

54. If $f(x) = (a_1x + b_1)^2 + \ldots + (a_nx + b_n)^2$, then define $F(x) = Ax^2 + Bx + C$,

where $A = \sum_{i=1}^{n} a_i^2$, $B = \sum_{i=1}^{n} a_ib_i$, and $C = \sum_{i=1}^{n} b_i^2$. By problem 53,

$$B^2 \leq AC \text{ or } \left(\sum_{i=1}^{n} a_ib_i\right)^2 \leq \left(\sum_{i=1}^{n} a_i^2\right)\left(\sum_{i=1}^{n} b_i^2\right).$$

55. $B^2 = AC$ only if $F(x_0) = 0$ for some x_0, where $F(x)$ is as in Problem 54. Then $f(x_0) = (a_1x_0 + b_1)^2 + \ldots + (a_nx_0 + b_n)^2 = 0$, so that $ax_i + b_i = 0$ for each i.

56. Let $f(x) = x^m - 1 - m(x - 1)$. Then $f'(x) = mx^{m-1} - m = 0$ if $x = 1$. $f''(x) = m(m-1)x^{m-2} > 0$ if $x > 0$ so $f(1)$ is a minimum. Then $f(x) \geq f(1) = 1^m - 1 - m(1 - 1) = 0$.

57. By similar triangles, $\frac{12 - y}{12} = \frac{x}{36}$, where y is the height of the rectangle and x is the length of theside which lies on the base of the triangle. Then $A = xy = x\left(12 - \frac{1}{3}x\right)$, and $A' = 12 - \frac{2}{3}x$.

$A' = 0$ if $x = 18$. $A'' = -\frac{2}{3} < 0 \Rightarrow A(18)$ is maximum.

The dimensions and 18 by 6.

58. Let the other base $b = 2x + 12$. Then

$$A = \frac{1}{2}h(b + 12) = \frac{1}{2}(12 + 12 + 2x)\sqrt{36 - x^2} = (12 + x)\sqrt{36 - x^2}.$$

$$A' = \frac{2x^2 + 12x - 36}{\sqrt{36 - x^2}} = 0 \text{ if } x = -3 \pm 3\sqrt{3}. \text{ x cannot be } -3 - 3\sqrt{3} < 0.$$

$A' > 0$ if $x < 3 + 3\sqrt{3}$ and $A' < 0$ if $x > 3 + 3\sqrt{3}$ $\Rightarrow$ a maximum occurs here.

The base is $12 + 2(-3 + 3\sqrt{3}) = 6 + 6\sqrt{3}$.

59. If $d = \left|\sin t - \sin\left(t + \frac{\pi}{3}\right)\right|$, then $d = 0$ when $t = \frac{\pi}{3}, \frac{4\pi}{3}, \ldots$

Otherwise, $d' = \cos t - \cos\left(t + \frac{\pi}{3}\right) = 0$ when $t = -\frac{\pi}{6}, \frac{5\pi}{6}, \ldots$

and for these values, $d = 1$.

60. Let d = distance traveled. Then $C = t(a + bv^n) = \frac{d}{v}(a + bv^n)$

$$C' = \frac{d}{v}(bnv^{n-1}) - \frac{d}{v^2}(a + bv^n) = 0 \text{ if}$$

$$v(bnv^{n-1}) = a + bv^n \text{ or if } v = \left(\frac{a}{b(n-1)}\right)^{1/n}.$$

61. $A = \frac{1}{2}r^2\theta$ and $p = r\theta + 2r = \frac{2A}{r} + 2r$. $p' = -\frac{2A}{r^2} + 2 = 0 \Leftrightarrow$

$r = \sqrt{A}$. $p'' = \frac{4A}{r^3} > 0 \Rightarrow$ minimum value. If $= \sqrt{A}$, $\theta = 2$ radians.

62. $$I = \frac{k\cos\theta}{h^2 + r^2} = \frac{k\left(\frac{h}{\sqrt{h^2 + r^2}}\right)}{h^2 + r^2} = kh(h^2 + r^2)^{-3/2}$$

$$I' = k(h^2 + r^2)^{-3/2} + kh\left[-\frac{3}{2}(h^2 + r^2)^{-5/2}(2h)\right]$$

$$= k(h^2 + r^2)^{-5/2}(h^2 + r^2 - 3h^2) = 0 \text{ if } 2h^2 = r^2 \text{ or } h = \frac{r}{\sqrt{2}}.$$

$I' > 0$ if $h > \frac{r}{\sqrt{2}}$ and $I' < 0$ if $h < \frac{r}{\sqrt{2}}$ $\Rightarrow$ a maximum value.

63. (a) $A = \pi(r_2^2 - r_1^2) \Rightarrow \dfrac{dA}{dt} = 2\pi\left(r_2 \dfrac{dr_2}{dt} - r_1 \dfrac{dr_1}{dt}\right) = 2\pi[6(.01) - 4(.02)] = -0.04\pi$

(b) $r_1 = 3 + at$, $r_2 = 5 + bt$ and we want t for which $\dfrac{dA}{dt} = 0$.

$2\pi[(5 + bt)(b) - (3 + at)(a)] = 0 \Leftrightarrow (b^2 - a^2)t = 3a - 5b$ or

$t = \dfrac{3a - 5b}{b^2 - a^2}$. $\dfrac{d^2A}{dt^2} = b^2 - a^2 < 0$ since $\dfrac{3}{5}a < b < a \Rightarrow$ a maximum value.

64. $r_1 = r + at$ and $r_2 = R + bt$. $V = \dfrac{4}{3}\pi(r_2^3 - r_1^3) = \dfrac{4}{3}\pi[(R + bt)^3 - (r + at)^3]$

$\dfrac{dV}{dt} = \dfrac{4}{3}\pi[3b(R + bt)^2 - 3a(r + at)^2] = 0$ if $b(R + bt)^2 = a(r + at)^2 \Rightarrow$

$\sqrt{a}(r + at) = \sqrt{b}(R + bt) \Rightarrow (a^{3/2} - b^{3/2})t = R\sqrt{b} - r\sqrt{a}$ or

$t = \dfrac{R\sqrt{b} - r\sqrt{a}}{a^{3/2} - b^{3/2}}$ when the volume is largest.

65. $s(t) = at - (1 + a^4)t^2 \Rightarrow \dfrac{ds}{dt} = a - 2t(1 + a^4) = 0 \Leftrightarrow t = \dfrac{a}{2(1 + a^4)}$.

For this t, $s = a\left(\dfrac{a}{2(1 + a^4)}\right) - (1 + t^4)\left(\dfrac{a}{2(1 + a^4)}\right)^2 = \dfrac{a^2}{4(1 + a^4)} > 0$.

For $t > \dfrac{a}{2(1 + a^4)}$, $\dfrac{ds}{dt} < 0$ and the particle moves back. If you

consider $s(a) = \dfrac{a^2}{4(1 + a^4)}$, then $\dfrac{ds}{da} = \dfrac{2a(1 + a^4) - 4a^5}{4(1 + a^4)^2} = 0 \Leftrightarrow$

$2a - 2a^5 = 0 \Leftrightarrow a(1 - a^4) = 0 \Leftrightarrow a = \pm 1, 0$ and $s(1) = \dfrac{1}{8}$.

66. (a) $h(x) = f(x)g(x) \Rightarrow h'(x) = f'(x)g(x) + g'(x)f(x)$

$h(a) = f'(a)g(a) + g'(a)f(a) = 0$ since $f'(a) = g'(a) = 0$.

We are given that f and g are positive functions, and

f' and g' change from positive to negative at $x = a$.

Therefore, $h'(x) > 0$ if $x < a$ and $h'(x) < 0$ if $x > a$ and h has

a local maximum at $x = a$.

(b) No, consider $f(x) = x^{1/3}$ and $g(x) = x^{1/3}$ which have a point

of inflection at $x = 0$, but $h(x) = x^{2/3}$ does not.

67. If $f(x) = (c_1 - x)^2 + (c_2 - x)^2 + \ldots + (c_n - x)^2$, then

$f'(x) = -2(c_1 - x) - 2(c_2 - x) - \ldots - 2(c_n - x) = 0 \Leftrightarrow$

$nx = c_1 + c_2 + \ldots + c_n$ or $x = \dfrac{1}{n}(c_1 + c_2 + \ldots + c_n)$. $f''(x) = 2n$

$\Rightarrow$ minimum value. Notice that this is just the arithmetic mean.

68. $S = \left(-\frac{1}{2} + 2m - 1\right)^2 + (1 - 0 - 1)^2 + (2 - m - 1)^2 + (3 - 3m - 1)^2$

$= \left(-\frac{3}{2} + 2m\right)^2 + (1 - m)^2 +) + (2 - 3m)^2$

$S' = 4\left(-\frac{3}{2} + 2m\right) -2(1 - m) - 6(2 - 3m) = -20 + 28m = 0$ if $m = \frac{5}{7}$.

$S'' = 28 > 0$ so the sum is a minimum if $m = \frac{5}{7}$.

69. Let $M = a_1 a_2 \ldots a_{n-1}$ and $N = a_1 + a_2 + \ldots + a_{n-1}$.

Define $f(x) = \dfrac{\frac{N + x}{n}}{Mx^{\frac{1}{n}}} = \dfrac{N + x}{Mn} x^{-\frac{1}{n}} = \dfrac{N}{Mn} x^{-\frac{1}{n}} + \dfrac{1}{Mn} x^{1 - \frac{1}{n}}$.

$f'(x) = \frac{1}{Mn}\left[-\frac{N}{n} x^{-\frac{1}{n} - 1} + \left(1 - \frac{1}{n}\right) x^{-\frac{1}{n}}\right] = \frac{1}{Mn^2} x^{-\frac{1}{n} - 1}\left[-N + (n-1)x\right]$

$f'(x) = 0$ if $-N + (n-1)x = 0 \Leftrightarrow x = \frac{N}{n-1}$.

That is, x is the arithmetic mean.

70. (a) $PL(x) = (c - ex)x - (a + bx) = -ex^2 + (c - b)x - a$

$PL'(x) = -2ex + c - b = 0$ if $x = \frac{c - b}{2e}$. $PL'' = -2 \Rightarrow$ maximum.

(b) $P = c - e\left(\frac{c - b}{2e}\right) = \frac{b + c}{2}$

(c) $PL = -e\left(\frac{c - b}{2e}\right)^2 + (c - b)\left(\frac{c - b}{2e}\right) - a = \frac{(c - b)^2}{4e} - a$

(d) Price $- t = (c - t) - ex$. The new price is $\frac{b + c - t}{2} = \frac{b + c}{2} - \frac{t}{2}$.

The tax is split evenly between the consumer and firm.

71. $V = \frac{dx}{dt} = f(x) \Rightarrow \frac{dv}{dx} = f'(x)$.

$a = \frac{d^2x}{dt^2} = \frac{dv}{dt}$. Since $\frac{dv}{dt} = \frac{dv}{dx} \bullet \frac{dx}{dt}$, we have $a = f'(x)f(x)$

72. $v = \frac{k}{\sqrt{s}} = ks^{-1/2}$. $a = \frac{dv}{dt} = ks^{-3/2}\frac{ds}{dt} = ks^{-3/2}(v) = (ks^{-3/2})(ks^{-1/2})$

$= k^2 s^{-2} = \frac{K}{s^2}$

73. $V = x^3 \Rightarrow \frac{dV}{dx} = 3x^2 \frac{dx}{dt}$. $300 = 3(20)^2 \frac{dx}{dt} \Rightarrow \frac{dx}{dt} = \frac{1}{4}$ in/min.

74. $V = \frac{1}{3}\pi r^2 h = \frac{1}{3}\pi (2h)^2 h = \frac{4}{3}\pi h^3$. $\frac{dV}{dt} = 4\pi h^2 \frac{dh}{dt}$ so

$3 = 4\pi (100) \frac{dh}{dt}$ or $\frac{dh}{dt} = \frac{3}{400\pi}$ ft/min.

75. (a) $V = \frac{4}{3}\pi r^3 \Rightarrow \frac{dV}{dt} = 4\pi r^2 \frac{dr}{dt}$. $\frac{dr}{dt} = \frac{-12\pi}{4\pi(20)^2} = -\frac{3}{400}$ ft/min

$S = 4\pi r^2 \Rightarrow \frac{dS}{dt} = 8\pi r \frac{dr}{dt}$. $\frac{dS}{dt} = 8\pi(20)(-\frac{3}{400}) = -\frac{6\pi}{5}\frac{ft^2}{min}$

If $f(x) \geq 0$ for all x then $f(-\frac{b}{a}) \geq 0$. Conversely, suppose $b^2 - c \leq 0 \Rightarrow -b^2 + c \geq 0$. Then $f(x) \geq f(-\frac{b}{a}) \geq 0$.

(b) $\Delta r \approx dr = \frac{dr}{dt}\Delta r = -\frac{3}{400}\frac{ft}{min} \bullet \frac{6\ sec}{1} \bullet \frac{1\ min}{60\ sec} = -\frac{3}{4000}$ ft

$\Delta S \approx \frac{dS}{dt}\Delta t = -\frac{6\pi}{5}\frac{ft^2}{min} \bullet \frac{6\ sec}{1} \bullet \frac{1\ min}{60\ sec} = -\frac{3\pi}{25} ft^2$

76. (a) $s^2 = x^2 + y^2 - 2xy\cos 60^\circ = x^2 + y^2 - xy$.

$2s\frac{ds}{dt} = 2x\frac{dx}{dt} + 2y\frac{dy}{dt} - x\frac{dy}{dt} - y\frac{dx}{dt}$. At the moment in question,

$y = 4$, $x = 2 \Rightarrow s = 2\sqrt{3}$, so $4\sqrt{3}\frac{ds}{dt} = 4200$ or $\frac{ds}{dt} = 350\sqrt{3}$ mi/hr

(b) $y = 4 - 700t$ and $x = 2 - 400t$. Therefore,

$2s\frac{ds}{dt} = 500(2x - y) + 700(2y - x) = 300x + 900y$

$\frac{ds}{dt} = \frac{150x + 450y}{s} = \frac{150(2 - 400t) + 450(4 - 700t)}{s} = 0$

if $2100 - 390000t = 0$ or if $t = \frac{7}{300}$ sec. At this moment,

$x = -\frac{9}{13}$, $y = \frac{3}{13}$ and $s = \frac{\sqrt{117}}{13} \approx 0.83$ miles.

77. Let $s = \sqrt{x^2 + y^2} = \sqrt{x^2 + x^3}$. $\frac{ds}{dt} = \frac{1}{2}(x^2 + x^3)^{-\frac{1}{2}}(2x + 3x^2)\frac{dx}{dt}$

$\frac{dx}{dt}(2^2 + 3(2)^2)^{-\frac{1}{2}}(\frac{1}{2})(4 + 8) = 2$ $\quad \frac{8}{\sqrt{12}}\frac{dx}{dt} = 2$ $\quad \frac{dx}{dt} = \frac{\sqrt{3}}{2}$.

78. $A = \frac{1}{2}xy \Rightarrow \frac{dA}{dt} = \frac{1}{2}\left(x\frac{dy}{dt} + y\frac{dx}{dt}\right)$. When $x = 17\sqrt{2}$, $y^2 = 26^2 - (17\sqrt{2})^2 = 98$, so $y = 7\sqrt{2}$. $x^2 + y^2 = 26^2 \Rightarrow 2x\frac{dx}{dt} + 2y\frac{dy}{dt} = 0 \Rightarrow (17\sqrt{2})(4) + 7\sqrt{2}\frac{dy}{dt} = 0$

or $\frac{dy}{dt} = -\frac{68}{7}$. Then $\frac{da}{dt} = \frac{1}{2}(17\sqrt{2})\left(-\frac{68}{7}\right) + (7\sqrt{2})(4)$

$= -\frac{480\sqrt{2}}{7}$ ft^2/sec ≈ -96.7 ft^2/sec

79. By similar triangles, $\frac{x}{y} = \frac{5}{10}$ or $y = \frac{1}{2}x$. The volume is then $V = \frac{1}{3}\pi x^2 y = \frac{1}{12}\pi y^3$ and $\frac{dV}{dt} = \frac{\pi}{4}y^2\frac{dy}{dt}$. The net change in volume is $\frac{dV}{dt} = c - 0.08\sqrt{y}$ ft^3/min. At the moment when $y = \frac{25}{4}$ and $\frac{dy}{dt} = .02$ ft/min,

$\frac{\pi}{4}\left(\frac{25}{4}\right)^2(.02) = c - .08\sqrt{\frac{25}{4}}$ or $c = \frac{25\pi}{128} + \frac{1}{5} \approx 0.8$. For $0 \le y \le 10$, $\frac{dV}{dt} > 0$, so the tank will fill.

80. $v = \sqrt{v_0^2 - 2gR\left[1 - \frac{R}{s}\right]} \Rightarrow \frac{dv}{ds} = \frac{1}{2}\left(v_0^2 - 2gR\left[1 - \frac{R}{s}\right]\right)^{-1/2}\left(-2g\frac{R^2}{s^2}\right)$

$= -\frac{gR^2}{vs^2}$. Now acceleration is $a = \frac{dv}{dt} = \frac{dv}{ds}\cdot\frac{ds}{dt} = v\frac{dv}{ds}$.

$\therefore\ a = v\left(-\frac{gR^2}{vs^2}\right) = \frac{K}{s^2}$ where $K = -gR^2$.

81. Let the altitude fromA to BC = h, and $|BC| = a$. Let K = area of BCED. Then $K = \frac{1}{2}x(y - a)$. By similar triangles, $\frac{y}{h - x} = \frac{a}{h}$, so $y = \frac{a}{h}(h - x)$ and $K = \frac{1}{2}x\left(\frac{a}{h}(h - x) - a\right) = \frac{a}{2h}(2hx - x^2)$.

Then $\frac{dK}{dx} = \frac{a}{2h}(2h - 2x) = y$.

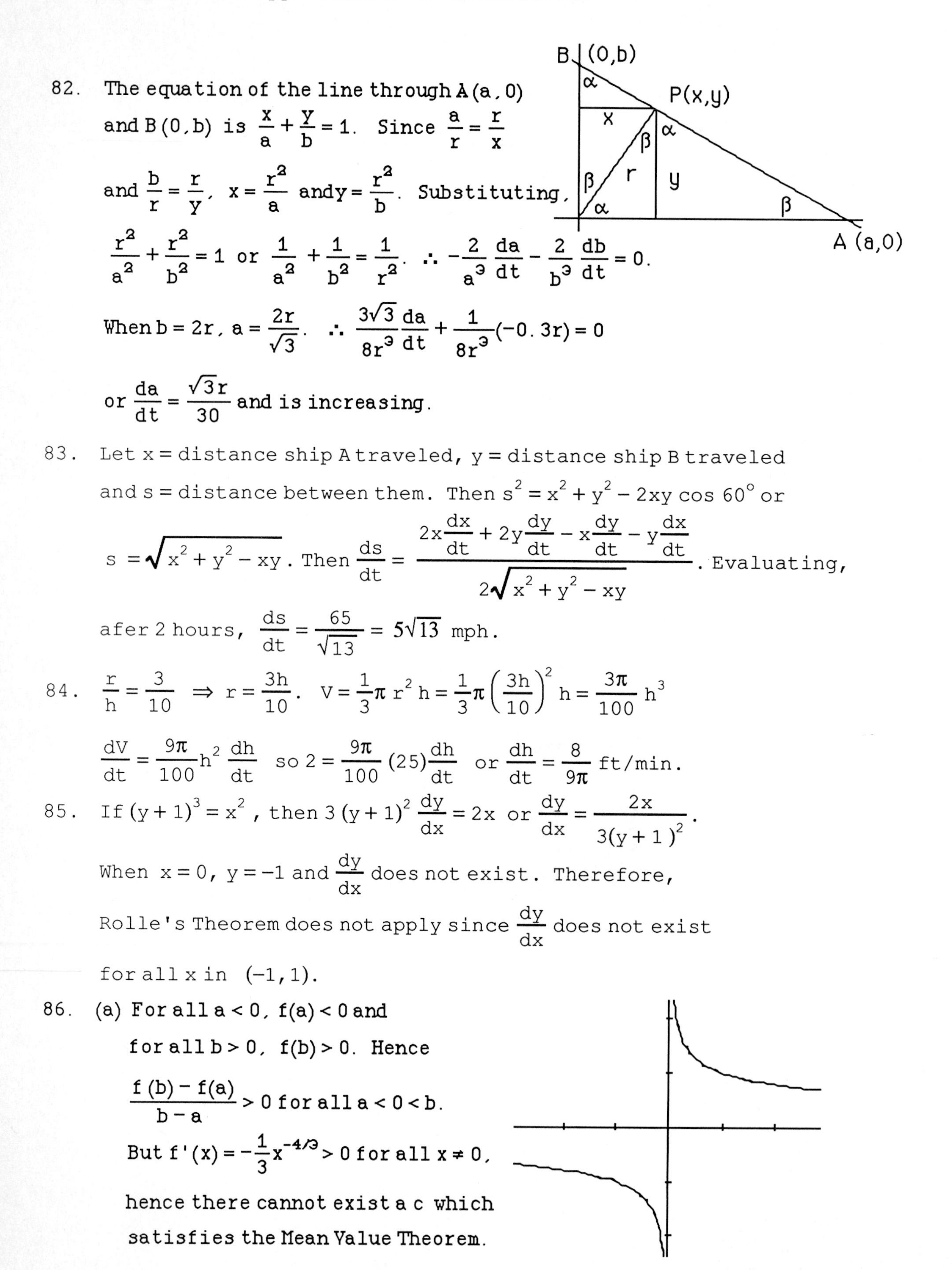

82. The equation of the line through A(a, 0) and B(0, b) is $\frac{x}{a} + \frac{y}{b} = 1$. Since $\frac{a}{r} = \frac{r}{x}$ and $\frac{b}{r} = \frac{r}{y}$, $x = \frac{r^2}{a}$ and $y = \frac{r^2}{b}$. Substituting, $\frac{r^2}{a^2} + \frac{r^2}{b^2} = 1$ or $\frac{1}{a^2} + \frac{1}{b^2} = \frac{1}{r^2}$. $\therefore -\frac{2}{a^3}\frac{da}{dt} - \frac{2}{b^3}\frac{db}{dt} = 0$.

When $b = 2r$, $a = \frac{2r}{\sqrt{3}}$. $\therefore \frac{3\sqrt{3}}{8r^3}\frac{da}{dt} + \frac{1}{8r^3}(-0.3r) = 0$

or $\frac{da}{dt} = \frac{\sqrt{3}r}{30}$ and is increasing.

83. Let x = distance ship A traveled, y = distance ship B traveled and s = distance between them. Then $s^2 = x^2 + y^2 - 2xy\cos 60^\circ$ or $s = \sqrt{x^2 + y^2 - xy}$. Then $\frac{ds}{dt} = \frac{2x\frac{dx}{dt} + 2y\frac{dy}{dt} - x\frac{dy}{dt} - y\frac{dx}{dt}}{2\sqrt{x^2 + y^2 - xy}}$. Evaluating, afer 2 hours, $\frac{ds}{dt} = \frac{65}{\sqrt{13}} = 5\sqrt{13}$ mph.

84. $\frac{r}{h} = \frac{3}{10} \Rightarrow r = \frac{3h}{10}$. $V = \frac{1}{3}\pi r^2 h = \frac{1}{3}\pi\left(\frac{3h}{10}\right)^2 h = \frac{3\pi}{100}h^3$

$\frac{dV}{dt} = \frac{9\pi}{100}h^2\frac{dh}{dt}$ so $2 = \frac{9\pi}{100}(25)\frac{dh}{dt}$ or $\frac{dh}{dt} = \frac{8}{9\pi}$ ft/min.

85. If $(y+1)^3 = x^2$, then $3(y+1)^2\frac{dy}{dx} = 2x$ or $\frac{dy}{dx} = \frac{2x}{3(y+1)^2}$.

When $x = 0$, $y = -1$ and $\frac{dy}{dx}$ does not exist. Therefore, Rolle's Theorem does not apply since $\frac{dy}{dx}$ does not exist for all x in $(-1, 1)$.

86. (a) For all $a < 0$, $f(a) < 0$ and for all $b > 0$, $f(b) > 0$. Hence $\frac{f(b) - f(a)}{b - a} > 0$ for all $a < 0 < b$. But $f'(x) = -\frac{1}{3}x^{-4/3} > 0$ for all $x \neq 0$, hence there cannot exist a c which satisfies the Mean Value Theorem.

(b) We will prove the existence of such a c by finding it. $f'(x) = \frac{1}{3}x^{-2/3}$.

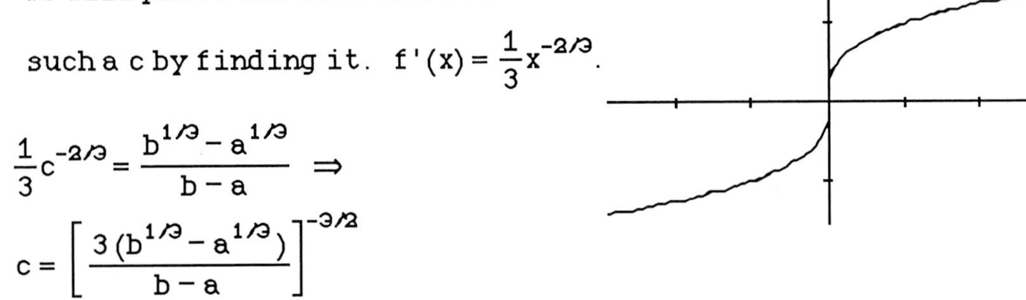

$$\frac{1}{3}c^{-2/3} = \frac{b^{1/3} - a^{1/3}}{b - a} \Rightarrow$$

$$c = \left[\frac{3(b^{1/3} - a^{1/3})}{b - a}\right]^{-3/2}$$

87. If $y = \sin x \sin(x+2) - \sin^2(x+1)$, $-\pi \le x \le \pi$, then

$$\frac{dy}{dx} = [\sin x \cos(x+2) + \sin(x+2)\cos x] - 2\sin(x+1)\cos(x+1)$$

$$= \sin(x+x+2) - \sin 2(x+1) = 0.$$ Therefore y is a constant

function and the graph is a horizontal line. If $x = \pi$, $y \approx 0.7$.

88. For $f(x) = 2x^3 - 3x^2 + 6x + 6$, $f(-1) = -5$ and $f(0) = 6$. Therefore, By the Intermediate Value Theorem, f has at least one root between 0 and -1. $f'(x) = 6x^2 - 6x + 6 = 6(x^2 - x + 1) > 0$ for all x $\left(\text{it has an absolute minimum value of } \frac{9}{2} \text{ at } x = \frac{1}{2}\right)$ and has no real roots.

If f had two roots between -1 and 0 then f' would have to have a root there by Rolle's Theorem. Thus f has exactly one such root.

To find it, we use Newton's method with $x_0 = -0.5$. Then

$x_1 = -0.690476190$, $x_2 = -0.672672504$, $x_3 = -0.672495828$,

and $x_4 = -0.672495811$.

89. By the Mean Value Theorem, $\frac{f(6) - f(0)}{6} = f'(c)$ for some c in $(0, 6)$ or

$f(6) - f(0) = 6f'(c) \le 6(2) = 12$.

90. Let z_1 be any point in $[a, c)$. By the Mean Value Theorem, $\exists$ c_1 in (z_1, c) for

which $f'(c_1) = \frac{f(c) - f(z_1)}{c - z_1} \le 0$ by hypothesis. Since $c - z_1 > 0$,

$f(c) - f(z_1) \le 0$. Since z_1 was any point, $f(x) \le f(c)$ for all x in $[a, c)$.

Similarly, if z_2 is any point in $(c, b]$, $\exists$ c_2 for which

$f'(c_2) = \frac{f(z_2) - f(c)}{z_2 - c} \ge 0$. Since $z_2 - c > 0$, $f(z_2) \ge f(c)$.

Thus $f(x) \ge f(c)$ for all x in $[a, b]$.

91. (a) $(x+1)^2 \ge 0 \Rightarrow x^2+1 \ge -2x \Rightarrow 1 \ge -2\left(\frac{x}{x^2+1}\right) \Rightarrow -\frac{1}{2} \le \frac{x}{x^2+1}$.

$(x-1)^2 \ge 0 \Rightarrow x^2+1 \ge 2x \Rightarrow 1 \ge 2\left(\frac{x}{x^2+1}\right) \Rightarrow \frac{x}{x^2+1} \le \frac{1}{2}$

(b) By the Mean Value Theorem, $|f(b)-f(a)| \le |f'(c)|\,|(b-a)|$ for some c in [a,b]. By part (a), $f'(c) = \frac{c}{c^2+1} \le \frac{1}{2}$.

Therefore, $|f(b)-f(a)| \le \frac{1}{2}|b-a|$

92. (a) $\lim_{x\to 0} \frac{2 \sin 5x}{3x} = \lim_{x\to 0} \frac{10 \cos 5x}{3} = \frac{10}{3}$

(b) $\lim_{x\to 0} \sin 5x \cot 3x = \lim_{x\to 0} \frac{\sin 5x}{\tan 3x} = \lim_{x\to 0} \frac{5 \cos 5x}{3 \sec^2 3x} = \frac{5}{3}$

(c) $\lim_{x\to 0} x \csc^2 \sqrt{2x} = \lim_{x\to 0} \frac{x}{\sin^2 \sqrt{2x}} = \lim_{x\to 0} \frac{\sqrt{2x}}{2 \sin \sqrt{2x} \cos \sqrt{2x}} = \frac{1}{2}$

(d) $\lim_{x\to \frac{\pi}{2}} (\sec x - \tan x) = \lim_{x\to \frac{\pi}{2}} \frac{1-\sin x}{\cos x} = \lim_{x\to \frac{\pi}{2}} \frac{-\cos x}{-\sin x} = 0$

(e) $\lim_{x\to 0} \frac{x-\sin x}{x-\tan x} = \lim_{x\to 0} \frac{1-\cos x}{1-\sec^2 x} = \lim_{x\to 0} \frac{\sin x}{-2 \sec^2 x \tan x}$

$= \lim_{x\to 0} -\frac{\cos^3 x}{2} = -\frac{1}{2}$

(f) $\lim_{x\to 0} \frac{\sin x^2}{x \sin x} = \lim_{x\to 0} \frac{2x \cos x^2}{\sin x + x \cos x} = \lim_{x\to 0} \frac{2 \cos x^2 - 4x^2 \sin x^2}{-x \sin x + \cos x + \cos x} = 1$

(g) $\lim_{x\to 0} \frac{\sec x - 1}{x^2} = \lim_{x\to 0} \frac{\sec x \tan x}{2x} = \lim_{x\to 0} \frac{\sec^3 x + \sec x \tan^2 x}{2} = \frac{1}{2}$

(h) $\lim_{x\to 2} \frac{x^3-8}{x^2-4} = \lim_{x\to 2} \frac{3x^2}{2x} = 3$

93. (a) $\lim_{x\to\infty} \frac{\sqrt{x+5}}{\sqrt{x}+5} = \lim_{x\to\infty} \frac{\sqrt{1+\frac{5}{x}}}{1+\frac{5}{\sqrt{x}}} = 1$

(b) $\lim_{x\to\infty} \frac{2x}{x+7\sqrt{x}} = \lim_{x\to\infty} \frac{2}{1+\frac{7}{\sqrt{x}}} = 2$

94. Let $\varepsilon = \frac{1}{2}|f''(c)|$. Since $\lim_{h\to 0} \frac{f'(c+h) - f'(c)}{h} = f''(c)$, there exists $\delta > 0$ for which $0 < |h| < \delta \Rightarrow \left| \frac{f'(c+h) - f'(c)}{h} - f''(c) \right| < \frac{1}{2}|f''(c)|$. Since $f'(c) = 0$, we have $f''(c) - \frac{1}{2}|f''(c)| < \frac{f'(c+h)}{h} < f''(c) + \frac{1}{2}|f''(c)|$.

Thus $f''(c) < 0 \Rightarrow \frac{f'(c+h)}{h} < 0$ and $f''(c) > 0 \Rightarrow \frac{f'(c+h)}{h} > 0$.

Case I: $f''(c) < 0$. Then $-\delta < h < 0 \Rightarrow f'(c+h) > 0$ and $0 < h < \delta$ $f'(c+h) < 0$ so $f(c)$ is a local maximum.

Case II: $f''(c) > 0$. Then $-\delta < h < 0 \Rightarrow f'(c+h) < 0$ and $0 < h < \delta \Rightarrow$ $f'(c+h) > 0$ so $f(c)$ is a local minimum.

95. (a) $F(b) = 0$ by definition of k. Direct substitution shows that $F(a) = f(a) - f(a) - (a-1)f'(a) - \ldots - k(a-a)^{n+1} = 0$

(b) $F^{(k)}(a) = f^{(k)}(a) - f^{(k)}(a) - f^{(k+1)}(a-a) - \ldots - k(n+1)(n)(n-1)\ldots(a-a)^{n+1-k}$ $= 0$, $k = 1, 2, \ldots, n$.

(c) Since $F(a) = F(b) = 0$, by Rolle's Theorem there exists a c_1 such that $a < c_1 < b$ and $F'(c_1) = 0$. Since $F'(a) = F'(c_1) = 0$, there exists a c_2 such that $a < c_2 < c_1$ and $F''(c_2) = 0$. In a there exists $c_3, c_4, \ldots, c_n$, $a < c_{n+1} < c_n < c_{n-1} < \ldots < c_1 < b$ such that $0 = F''(c_1) = F''(c_2) = \ldots = F^{(n+1)}(c_{n+1})$.

(d) $F^{(n+1)}(x) = f^{(n+1)}(x) - k(n+1)!$. Since $0 = F^{(n+1)}(c_{n+1})$, $f^{(n+1)}(c_{n+1}) - k(n+1)!$, and $k = \frac{f^{(n+1)}(c_{n+1})}{(n+1)!}$.

96. $f(x) = f(a) + f'(a)(x-a) + \frac{f''(a)}{2}(x-a)^2 + \ldots + \frac{f^{(n)}(a)}{n!}(x-a)^n + \frac{f^{(n+1)}(a)}{(n+1)!}(x-a)^{n+1}$

$f(x) = \frac{1}{1-x} \Rightarrow f(0) = 1$; $f'(x) = \frac{1}{(1-x)^2} \Rightarrow f'(0) = 1$;

$f''(x) = \frac{2}{(1-x)^3} \Rightarrow f''(0) = 2$; $f'''(x) = \frac{6}{(1-x)^4} \Rightarrow f'''(0) = 6$;

$f^{(4)}(x) = \frac{24}{(1-x)^5}$. $\therefore \frac{1}{1-x} \approx 1 + x + x^2 + x^3$.

The error $e_3(x) \le \frac{\max f^{(4)}(x)}{4!} x^4 < \frac{24}{4!}(0.1)^4 = 0.0001$

97. (a) $x_{n+1} = x_n - \frac{f(x_n)}{f'(x_n)} = x_n - \frac{\frac{1}{x_n} - a}{-\left(\frac{1}{x_n}\right)^2} = x_n + x_n - ax_n^2 = x_n(2 - ax_n)$

(b) $x_1 = x_0(2 - ax_0) = ax_1\left(\frac{2}{a} - x_0\right)$. Therefore,

$x_0 > \frac{2}{a}$ would make $x_1 < 0$ and

$0 < x_0 < \frac{2}{a} \Rightarrow x_1 > 0$. Equality would

make all of all of the iterations zero.

The appropriate interval is $0 < x_0 < \frac{2}{a}$.

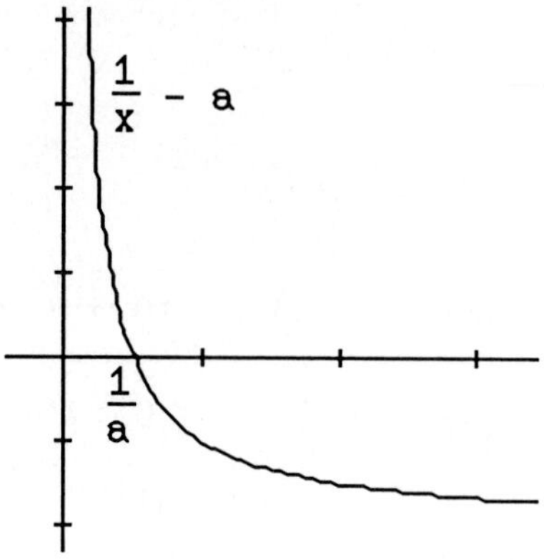

$\frac{1}{x} - a$

$\frac{1}{a}$

CHAPTER 4

INTEGRATION

4.1 INDEFINITE INTEGRALS

1. (a) $\int 2x\,dx = x^2 + C$ (b) $\int 3\,dx = 3x + C$ (c) $\int (2x + 3)dx = x^2 + 3x + C$

2. (a) $\int 6x\,dx = 3x^2 + C$ (b) $\int -2\,dx = -2x + C$ (c) $\int (6x - 2)dx = 3x^2 - 2x + C$

3. (a) $\int 3x^2dx = x^3 + C$ (b) $\int x^2dx = \frac{1}{3}x^3 + C$ (c) $\int (x^2 + 2x)dx = \frac{1}{3}x^3 + x^2 + C$

4. (a) $\int 8x^7dx = x^8 + C$ (b) $\int x^7dx = \frac{1}{8}x^8 + C$ (c) $\int (x^7 - 6x)dx = \frac{1}{8}x^3 - 3x^2 + C$

5. (a) $\int -3x^{-4}dx = x^{-3} + C$ (b) $\int x^{-4}dx = -\frac{1}{3}x^{-3} + C$

   (c) $\int (x^{-4} + 2x + 3)dx = -\frac{1}{3}x^{-3} + x^2 + 3x + C$

6. (a) $\int \frac{1}{x^2}dx = -x^{-1} + C$ (b) $\int \frac{-5}{x^2}dx = 5x^{-1} + C$ (c) $\int \left(2 - \frac{5}{x^2}\right)dx = 2x + 5x^{-1} + C$

7. (a) $\int \frac{3}{2}\sqrt{x}\,dx = x^{\frac{3}{2}} + C$ (b) $\int 4\sqrt{x}\,dx = \frac{8}{3}x^{\frac{3}{2}} + C$

   (c) $\int (x^2 - 4\sqrt{x}\,)dx = \frac{1}{3}x^3 - \frac{8}{3}x^{\frac{3}{2}} + C$

8. (a) $\int \frac{3}{2}\sqrt{x + 1}\,dx = (x + 1)^{3/2} + C$ (b) $\int \sqrt{x + 1}\,dx = \frac{2}{3}(x + 1)^{3/2} + C$

   (c) $\int \sqrt{5x + 1}\,dx = \frac{2}{15}(5x + 1)^{3/2} + C$

9. (a) $\int (2x - 1)dx = x^2 - x + C$ (b) $\int (2x - 1)^2dx = \frac{1}{6}(2x - 1)^3 + C$

   (c) $\int (2x - 1)^3dx = \frac{1}{8}(2x - 1)^4 + C$

10. (a) $\int 5\,(x - 2)^4\,dx = (x - 2)^5 + C$ (b) $\int (x - 2)^4\,dx = \frac{1}{5}(x - 2)^5 + C$

    (c) $\int 2\,(x - 2)^4\,dx = \frac{2}{5}(x - 2)^5 + C$

11. (a) $\int (x^2 - 3)\,2x\,dx = (x^2 - 3)^2 + C$ (b) $\int (x^2 - 3)\ x\,dx = \frac{1}{4}(x^2 - 3) + C$

12. (a) $\int 2\,(2x^3 + 1)\,6x^2\,dx = (2x^3 + 1)^2 + C$ (b) $\int (2x^3 + 1)\,x^2\,dx = \frac{1}{12}(2x^3 + 1)^2 + C$

13. $\frac{dy}{dx} = 2x - 7 \Rightarrow y = \int (2x - 7)dx = x^2 - 7x + C$

14. $\frac{dy}{dx} = 7 - 2x \Rightarrow y = \int (7 - 2x)\,dx = 7x - x^2 + C$

15. $\frac{dy}{dx} = x^2 + 1 \Rightarrow y = \int (x^2 + 1)dx = \frac{1}{3}x^3 + x + C$

16. $\frac{dy}{dx} = \frac{1}{x^2}$, $x > 0 \Rightarrow y = \int \frac{1}{x^2}\, dx = -\frac{1}{x} + C$

17. $\frac{dy}{dx} = \frac{-5}{x^2}$, $x > 0$, $\Rightarrow y = \int \frac{-5}{x^2}\, dx = 5x^{-1} + C$

18. $\frac{dy}{dx} = 3x^2 - 2x + 5 \Rightarrow y = \int (3x^2 - 2x + 5)\, dx = x^3 - x^2 + 5x + C$

19. $\frac{dy}{dx} = (x-2)^4 \Rightarrow y = \int (x-2)^4\, dx = \frac{1}{5}(x-2)^5 + C$

20. $\frac{dy}{dx} = (5x-2)^4 \Rightarrow y = \int (5x-2)^4\, dx = \frac{1}{25}(5x-2)^5 + C$

21. $\frac{dy}{dx} = \frac{1}{x^2} + x$, $x > 0 \Rightarrow y = \int (x^{-2} + x)dx = -x^{-1} + \frac{1}{2}x^2 + C$

22. $\frac{dy}{dx} = x + \sqrt{2x} \Rightarrow y = \int (x + \sqrt{2x})\, dx = \frac{1}{2}x^2 + \frac{1}{3}(2x)^{3/2} + C$

23. $\frac{dy}{dx} = \frac{x}{y}$, $y > 0 \Rightarrow ydy = xdx \Rightarrow \int ydy = \int xdx \Rightarrow \frac{1}{2}y^2 = \frac{1}{2}x^2 + C_1$

$y^2 = x^2 + C$ or $y = \sqrt{x^2 + C}$, $y > 0$

24. $\frac{dy}{dx} = \sqrt{\frac{x}{y}}$, $y > 0 \Rightarrow \int y^{1/2}\, dy = \int x^{1/2}\, dx$

$\frac{2}{3}y^{3/2} = \frac{2}{3}x^{3/2} + C \Rightarrow y^{3/2} = x^{3/2} + C$

25. $\frac{dy}{dx} = \frac{x+1}{y-1}$, $y > 1 \Rightarrow \int (y-1)\, dy = \int (x+1)\, dx \Rightarrow$

$\frac{1}{2}(y-1)^2 = \frac{1}{2}(x+1)^2 + C_1 \Rightarrow (y-1)^2 = (x+1)^2 + C$

26. $\frac{dy}{dx} = \frac{\sqrt{x+1}}{\sqrt{y-1}}$, $y > 1 \Rightarrow \int (y-1)^{1/2}\, dy = \int (x+1)^{1/2}\, dx$

$\frac{2}{3}(y-1)^{3/2} = \frac{2}{3}(x+1)^{3/2} + C \Rightarrow (y-1)^{3/2} = (x+1)^{3/2} + C$

27. $\frac{dy}{dx} = \sqrt{xy}$, $x > 0$, $y > 0 \Rightarrow \int y^{-\frac{1}{2}}\, dy = \int x^{\frac{1}{2}}\, dx \Rightarrow$

$2y^{\frac{1}{2}} = \frac{2}{3}x^{\frac{3}{2}} + C_1 \Rightarrow y^{\frac{1}{2}} = \frac{1}{3}x^{\frac{3}{2}} + C$

28. $\frac{dy}{dx} = x\sqrt{x^2+1} \Rightarrow y = \int x(x^2+1)^{1/2}\, dx = \frac{1}{6}(x^2+1)^{3/2} + C$

29. $\frac{dy}{dx} = 2xy^2$, $y > 0 \Rightarrow y^{-2}\, dy = 2x\, dx \Rightarrow -y^{-1} = x^2 + C$ or $y = -\frac{1}{x^2 + C}$

30. $\frac{dy}{dx} = \left(\frac{y}{x}\right)^{1/3}$, $x > 0$, $y > 0 \Rightarrow \int y^{-1/3}\, dy = \int x^{-1/3}\, dx$

$\frac{3}{2}y^{2/3} = \frac{3}{2}x^{2/3} + C \Rightarrow y^{2/3} = x^{2/3} + C$

31. $x^3 \frac{dy}{dx} = -2,\ x > 0 \Rightarrow dy = -2x^{-3}\,dx \Rightarrow y = x^{-2} + C$

32. $x^2 \frac{dy}{dx} = \frac{1}{y^2 + \sqrt{y}},\ x > 0,\ y > 0 \Rightarrow \int (y^2 + \sqrt{y})\,dy = \int x^{-2}\,dx$

$$\frac{1}{3}y^3 + \frac{2}{3}y^{3/2} = -\frac{1}{x} + C$$

33. $\frac{ds}{dt} = 3t^2 + 4t - 6 \Rightarrow \int ds = \int (3t^2 + 4t - 6)dt \Rightarrow s = t^3 + 2t^2 - 6t + C$

34. $\frac{dx}{dt} = 8\sqrt{x},\ x > 0 \Rightarrow \int x^{-1/2}\,dx = \int 8\,dt \Rightarrow 2x^{1/2} = 8t + C$

35. $\frac{dy}{dt} = (2t + t^{-1})^2,\ t > 0 \Rightarrow \int dy = \int (4t^2 + 4 + t^{-2})\,dt \Rightarrow$

$$y = \frac{4}{3}t^3 + 4t - t^{-1} + C$$

36. Observe that $(z^2 - z^{-2})^2 + 4 = z^4 - 2 - z^{-4} + 4 = (z^2 + z^{-2})^2$

$$\frac{dy}{dz} = \sqrt{(z^2 - z^{-2})^2 + 4} = \sqrt{(z^2 + z^{-2})^2} = z^2 + z^{-2} \quad (\text{since } z > 0)$$

$$y = \frac{1}{3}z^3 - \frac{1}{z} + C$$

37. $a = \frac{dv}{dt} = 1.6\ \text{m/sec}^2 \Rightarrow v = \int 1.6dt = 1.6t + C.\ v_o = 0 \Rightarrow C = 0.$

$v(30) = 1.6(30) = 48$ m/sec.

38. $a = 20\ \text{m/s}^2 \Rightarrow v = 20t + C$. The initial velocity is 0, so $C = 0$. Therefore $v(1\ \text{min}) = v(60\ \text{sec}) = 20(60) = 1200$ m/sec.

4.2 SELECTING A VALUE FOR THE CONSTANT OF INTEGRATION

1. $v = 3t^2,\ s_o = 4 \Rightarrow s = t^3 + C.\ 4 = 0 + C \Rightarrow C = 4.\ \therefore s = t^3 + 4$

2. $v = 2t + 1,\ s_0 = 0 \Rightarrow s = t^2 + t + C.\ 0 = 0 + C \Rightarrow C = 0.\ \therefore s = t^2 + t$

3. $v = (t + 1)^2,\ s_o = 0 \Rightarrow s = \frac{1}{3}(t + 1)^3 + C.\ 0 = \frac{1}{3}(1)^3 + C \Rightarrow C = -\frac{1}{3}.$

$$\therefore s = \frac{1}{3}(t + 1)^3 - \frac{1}{3}$$

4. $v = t^2 + 1,\ s_0 = 1 \Rightarrow s = \frac{1}{3}t^3 + t + C.\ 1 = 0 + C \Rightarrow C = 1.\ \therefore s = \frac{1}{3}t^3 + t + 1$

5. $v = (t + 1)^{-2},\ s_o = -5 \Rightarrow s = -(t + 1)^{-1} + C.\ -5 = -(-1)^{-1} + C \Rightarrow C = -4$

$$\therefore s = -(t + 1)^{-1} - 4$$

6. $v = \frac{ds}{dt} = 8\sqrt{s},\ s_0 = 9 \Rightarrow \int s^{-1/2}\,ds = \int 8\,dt \Rightarrow 2s^{1/2} = 8t + C$

$2(9)^{1/2} = 8(0) + C \Rightarrow C = 6.\ \therefore 2\sqrt{s} = 8t + 6 \Rightarrow s = (4t + 3)^2$

7. $a = 9.8$, $v_o = 20$, $s_o = 0$. $a = \frac{dv}{dt} \Rightarrow v = 9.8t + C_1$. $20 = 0 + C_1 \Rightarrow$

$C_1 = 20$ and $v = \frac{ds}{dt} = 9.8t + 20$. $s = 4.9t^2 + 20t + C_2$.

$0 = 0 + C_2 \Rightarrow C_2 = 0$. $\therefore s = 4.9t^2 + 20t$.

8. $a = 9.8$, $v_0 = 0$, $s_0 = 20$. $a = \frac{dv}{dt} \Rightarrow v = 9.8t + C_1$. $0 = 0 + C_1 \Rightarrow C_1 = 0$.

$v = \frac{ds}{dt} = 9.8t \Rightarrow s = 4.9t^2 + C_2$. $20 = 0 + C_2 \Rightarrow C_2 = 20$. $\therefore s = 4.9t^2 + 20$.

9. $a = 2t$, $v_o = 1$, $s_o = 1$. $a = \frac{dv}{dt} \Rightarrow v = t^2 + C_1$. $1 = 0 + C_1 \Rightarrow$

$C_1 = 1$ and $v = \frac{ds}{dt} = t^2 + 1$. $s = \frac{1}{3}t^3 + t + C_2$.

$1 = 0 + C_2 \Rightarrow C_2 = 1$. $\therefore s = \frac{1}{3}t^3 + t + 1$.

10. $a = 6t$, $v_0 = 0$, $s_0 = 5$. $a = \frac{dv}{dt} \Rightarrow v = 3t^2 + C_1$. $0 = 0 + C_1 \Rightarrow C_1 = 0$.

$v = \frac{ds}{dt} = 3t^2 \Rightarrow s = t^3 + C_2$. $5 = 0 + C_2 \Rightarrow C_2 = 5$. $\therefore s = t^3 + 5$.

11. $a = 2t + 2$, $v_0 = 1$, $s_0 = 0$. $v = t^2 + 2t + C_1$. $1 = 0 + C_1 \Rightarrow C_1 = 1$.

$v = t^2 + 2t + 1 \Rightarrow s = \frac{1}{3}t^3 + t^2 + t + C_2$. $0 = 0 + C_2 \Rightarrow C_2 = 0$.

$\therefore s = \frac{1}{3}t^3 + t^2 + t$.

12. $a = \frac{4}{v}$, $v_0 = 0$, $s_0 = 25$. $\int v\,dv = \int 4\,dt \Rightarrow \frac{1}{2}v^2 = 4t + C_1$. $0 = 0 + C_1 \Rightarrow C_1 = 0$.

$v = \frac{ds}{dt} = \sqrt{8t} \Rightarrow s = \frac{1}{12}(8t)^{3/2} + C_2$. $25 = 0 + C_2 \Rightarrow C_2 = 25$.

$\therefore s = \frac{1}{12}(8t)^{3/2} + 25$.

13. $\frac{dy}{dx} = 3x^2 + 2x + 1$, $y = 0$ when $x = 1$. $y = x^3 + x^2 + x\ C$.

$0 = 1 + 1 + 1 + C \Rightarrow C = -3$. $\therefore y = x^3 + x^2 + x - 3$

14. $\frac{dy}{dx} = 9x^2 - 4x + 5$, $y = 0$ when $x = -1$. $y = 3x^3 - 2x^2 + 5x + C$.

$0 = -3 - 2 - 5 + C \Rightarrow C = 10$. $\therefore y = 3x^3 - 2x^2 + 5x + 10$.

15. $\frac{dy}{dx} = 4(x - 7)^3$, $y = 10$ when $x = 8$. $y = (x - 7)^4 + C$

$10 = 1 + C \Rightarrow C = 9$. $\therefore y = (x - 7)^4 + 9$

16. $\frac{dy}{dx} = x^{1/2} + x^{1/4}$, $y = -2$ when $x = 0$. $y = \frac{2}{3}x^{3/2} + \frac{4}{5}x^{5/4} + C$.

$-2 = 0 + C \Rightarrow C = -2$ $\therefore$ $y = \frac{2}{3}x^{3/2} + \frac{4}{5}x^{5/4} - 2$.

17. $\frac{dy}{dx} = x\sqrt{y}$, $y = 1$ when $x = 0$. $y^{-\frac{1}{2}}\,dy = xdx \Rightarrow 2y^{\frac{1}{2}} = \frac{1}{2}x^2 + C$

$2 = 0 + C \Rightarrow C = 2$. $\therefore 2\,y^{\frac{1}{2}} = \frac{1}{2}x^2 + 2$ or $y = \left(\frac{x^2}{4} + 1\right)^2$

18. $\frac{dy}{dx} = \frac{x^2 + 1}{x^2} = 1 + x^{-2}$, $y = 1$ when $x = 1$. $y = x - x^{-1} + C$.

$1 = 1 - 1 + C \Rightarrow C = 1$ $\therefore$ $y = x - x^{-1} + 1$.

19. $\frac{dy}{dx} = 2xy^2$, $y = 1$ when $x = 1 \Rightarrow y^{-2}\,dy = 2xdx \Rightarrow -y^{-1} = x^2 + C$

$-1 = 1 + C \Rightarrow C = -2$ $\therefore$ $\frac{1}{y} = 2 - x^2$ or $y = \frac{1}{2 - x^2}$

20. $\frac{dy}{dx} = (x + x^{-1})^2 = x^2 + 2 + x^{-2}$, $y = 1$ when $x = 1$. $y = \frac{1}{3}x^3 + 2x - \frac{1}{x} + C$.

$1 = \frac{1}{3} + 2 - 1 + C \Rightarrow C = -\frac{1}{3}$ $\therefore$ $y = \frac{1}{3}x^3 + 2x - \frac{1}{x} - \frac{1}{3}$.

21. $\frac{d^2y}{dx^2} = 2 - 6x$, $y = 1$, $\frac{dy}{dx} = 4$ when $x = 0$.

$\frac{dy}{dx} = 2x - 3x^2 + C$. $4 = 0 - 0 + C \Rightarrow C = 4$. $\frac{dy}{dx} = 2x - 3x^2 + 4$.

$y = x^2 - x^3 + 4x + C$. $1 = 0 + C \Rightarrow C = 1$. $y = x^2 - x^3 + 4x + 1$.

22. $\frac{d^3y}{dx^3} = 6$, $y = 5$, $\frac{dy}{dx} = 0$, $\frac{d^2y}{dx^2} = -8$ when $x = 0$.

$\frac{d^3y}{dx^3} = 6 \Rightarrow \frac{d^2y}{dx^2} = 6x + C_3$. $-8 = 6(0) + C_3 \Rightarrow C_3 = -8$.

$\frac{d^2y}{dx^2} = 6x - 8 \Rightarrow \frac{dy}{dx} = 3x^2 - 8x + C_2$. $0 = 0 + C_2 \Rightarrow C_2 = 0$.

$\frac{dy}{dx} = 3x^2 - 8x \Rightarrow y = x^3 - 4x^2 + C_1$. $5 = 0 + C_1 \Rightarrow C_1 = 5$.

$\therefore$ $y = x^3 - 4x^2 + 5$

23. $\dfrac{d^2y}{dx^2} = \dfrac{3x}{8}$, through (4,4) with slope 3.

$\dfrac{dy}{dx} = \dfrac{3}{16}x^2 + C$. $3 = \dfrac{3}{16}(4)^2 + C \Rightarrow C = 0$. $\dfrac{dy}{dx} = \dfrac{3}{16}x^2$.

$y = \dfrac{1}{16}x^3 + C$. $4 = \dfrac{4^3}{16} + C \Rightarrow C = 0$. $y = \dfrac{1}{16}x^3$.

24. $\dfrac{d^2y}{dx^2} = 2x - 3x^2 + 1$, (0,0) and (1,1) belong to graph of y.

$\dfrac{d^2y}{dx^2} = 2x - 3x^2 + 1 \Rightarrow \dfrac{dy}{dx} = x^2 - x^3 + x + C_2 \Rightarrow$

$y = \dfrac{1}{3}x^3 - \dfrac{1}{4}x^4 + \dfrac{1}{2}x^2 + C_2 x + C_1$. $y(0) = 0 \Rightarrow C_1 = 0$.

$y(1) = 1 \Rightarrow 1 = \dfrac{1}{3} - \dfrac{1}{4} + \dfrac{1}{2} + C_2 \Rightarrow C_2 = \dfrac{5}{12}$.

$\therefore\ y = \dfrac{1}{3}x^3 - \dfrac{2}{3}x^4 + \dfrac{1}{2}x^2 + \dfrac{5}{12}x$

25. $\dfrac{dy}{dx} = 3\sqrt{x} \Rightarrow y = 2x^{\frac{3}{2}} + C$. (9,4) belongs to graph so

$4 = 2\,(9)^{\frac{3}{2}} + C \Rightarrow C = -50$ and $f(x) = 2x^{\frac{3}{2}} - 50$.

26. $\dfrac{dy}{dx} = \dfrac{2x}{y^2}$, $y = 3$ when $x = 3$.

$\int y^2\,dy = \int 2x\,dx \Rightarrow \dfrac{1}{3}y^3 = x^2 + C$. $\dfrac{1}{3}(3)^3 = 3^2 + C \Rightarrow C = 0$.

$\dfrac{1}{3}y^3 = (1)^2 \Rightarrow y^3 = 3 \Rightarrow y = \sqrt[3]{3}$.

27. $a = \dfrac{dv}{dt} = 9.8 \Rightarrow v = 9.8t + C$. $v_0 = 0 \Rightarrow C = 0$.

$v = \dfrac{ds}{dt} = 9.8t \Rightarrow s = 4.9t^2 + C$. $s_0 = 0 \Rightarrow C = 0$. He will enter

the water when $4.9t^2 = 30$, or when $t = 2.47$ sec. His velocity at that time is $v(2.47) = 24.25$ m/s.

28. $a = \dfrac{dv}{dt} = -3.72\ \text{m/s}^2 \Rightarrow v = -3.72\,t + C$. $v(0) = 23 \Rightarrow C = 23$.

$\therefore\ v = \dfrac{ds}{dt} = -3.72t + 23 \Rightarrow s = -1.86t^2 + 23t + C$. $s(0) = 0 \Rightarrow C = 0$.

$v = 0$ when $t = \dfrac{23}{3.72} \approx 6.18$ s, and $s(6.18) \approx 71.1$ meters.

29. It cannot be choice (a) because $y(1) \neq 0$. The slope of tangent through $(1,1)$ and $\left(\frac{1}{2}, 0\right)$ is 2. In (b) and (c), $y'(1) \neq 2$, so it cannot be either of these. It is (d), because $y = x^2 + C$ and $1 = 1 + C \Rightarrow C = 0$.

30. (a) $\dfrac{dy}{dt} = -k\sqrt{y} \Rightarrow \int y^{-1/2}\,dy = \int -k\,dt \Rightarrow 2\sqrt{y} = -kt + C \Rightarrow$

$4y = (C - kt)^2 \Rightarrow y = \dfrac{1}{4}(C - kt)^2$

(b) $9 = \dfrac{1}{4}(C - 0)^2 \Rightarrow C = 6$. $\therefore\ y = \dfrac{1}{4}\left(6 - \dfrac{1}{10}t\right)^2$.

(c) $\dfrac{1}{4}\left(6 - \dfrac{1}{10}t\right)^2 = 0$ when $t = 60$ minutes.

31. $a = v\dfrac{dv}{ds}$ and $F = ma \Rightarrow -\dfrac{mgR^2}{s^2} = mv\dfrac{dv}{ds}$. Then

$v\,dv = -\dfrac{gR^2}{s^2}\,ds$ or $\dfrac{1}{2}v^2 = \dfrac{gR^2}{s} + C$. At the surface of the earth,

$s = R$ and $v_0 = \sqrt{2gR}$. So $\dfrac{2gR}{2} = \dfrac{gR^2}{R} + C \Rightarrow C = 0$. Then

$v = \sqrt{\dfrac{2gR^2}{s}} = \sqrt{2gR}\sqrt{\dfrac{R}{s}} = v_0\sqrt{\dfrac{R}{s}}$. Since $\dfrac{ds}{dt} = v_0\sqrt{\dfrac{R}{s}}$,

$\sqrt{s}\,ds = v_0\sqrt{R}\,dt$ or $\dfrac{2}{3}s^{\frac{3}{2}} = v_0\sqrt{R}\,t + C$. $s(0) = R \Rightarrow C = \dfrac{2}{3}R^{\frac{3}{2}}$.

Then $s^{\frac{3}{2}} = \dfrac{3}{2}v_0\sqrt{R}\,t + R^{\frac{3}{2}} = R^{\frac{3}{2}}\left(1 + \dfrac{3v_0 t}{2R}\right)$.

4.3 SUBSTITUTION METHOD OF INTEGRATION

1. $\int (x-1)^{243}\,dx = \dfrac{1}{244}(x-1)^{244} + C$

2. $\int \sqrt{1-x}\,dx = -\int \sqrt{u}\,du = -\dfrac{2}{3}u^{3/2} + C = -\dfrac{2}{3}(1-x)^{3/2} + C$

Let $u = 1 - x \Rightarrow du = -dx$

3. $\int \dfrac{1}{\sqrt{1-x}}\,dx = \int -u^{-\frac{1}{2}}\,du = -2u^{\frac{1}{2}} + C = -2(1-x)^{\frac{1}{2}} + C$

Let $u = 1 - x \Rightarrow du = -dx$

4. $\int 2x\sqrt{x^2-1}\,dx = \int \sqrt{u}\,du = \frac{2}{3}u^{3/2} + C = \frac{2}{3}(x^2-1)^{3/2} + C$

Let $u = x^2 - 1 \Rightarrow du = 2x\,dx$

5. $\int x\sqrt{2x^2-1}\,dx = \int u^{\frac{1}{2}}\left(\frac{1}{4}\,du\right) = \frac{1}{4}\left(\frac{2}{3}u^{\frac{3}{2}}\right) + C = \frac{1}{6}(2x^2-1)^{\frac{3}{2}} + C$

Let $u = 2x^2 - 1 \Rightarrow du = 4x\,dx \Rightarrow x\,dx = \frac{1}{4}\,du$

6. $\int (3x-1)^5\,dx = \frac{1}{3}\int u^5\,du = \frac{1}{3}\left(\frac{1}{6}u^6\right) + C = \frac{1}{18}(3x-1)^6 + C$

Let $u = 3x - 1 \Rightarrow du = 3\,dx \Rightarrow dx = \frac{1}{3}du$

7. $\int (2-t)^{\frac{2}{3}}\,dt = \int -u^{\frac{2}{3}}\,du = -\frac{3}{5}u^{\frac{5}{3}} + C = -\frac{3}{5}(2-t)^{\frac{5}{3}} + C$

8. $\int x^2\sqrt{1+x^3}\,dx = \frac{1}{3}\int u^{1/2}\,du = \frac{1}{3}\left(\frac{2}{3}u^{3/2}\right) + C = \frac{2}{9}(1+x^3)^{3/2} + C$

Let $u = 1 + x^3 \Rightarrow du = 3\,x^2\,dx \Rightarrow x^2\,dx = \frac{1}{3}du$

9. $\int (1+x^3)^2\,dx = \int (1 + 2x^3 + x^6)\,dx = x + \frac{1}{2}x^4 + \frac{1}{7}x^7 + C$

10. $\int (1+x^3)^2\,3x^2\,dx = \int u^2\,du = \frac{1}{3}u^3 + C = \frac{1}{3}(1+x^3)^3 + C$

Let $u = 1 + x^3 \Rightarrow du = 3x^2\,dx$

11. $\int x\,(x^2+1)^{10}\,dx = \int u^{10}\left(\frac{1}{2}du\right) = \frac{1}{2}\left(\frac{1}{11}u^{11}\right) + C = \frac{1}{22}(x^2+1)^{11} + C$

Let $u = x^2 + 1 \Rightarrow du = 2x\,dx \Rightarrow x\,dx = \frac{1}{2}du$

12. $\int \frac{dt}{2\sqrt{1+t}} = \int \frac{1}{2}u^{-1/2}\,du = \frac{1}{2}(2u^{1/2}) + C = \sqrt{1+t} + C$

Let $u = 1 + t \Rightarrow du = dt$

13. $\int \frac{x^2}{\sqrt{1+x^3}}\,dx = \int u^{-1/2}\left(\frac{1}{3}du\right) = \frac{1}{3}(2u^{1/2}) + C = \frac{2}{3}(1+x^3)^{1/2} + C$

Let $u = 1 + x^3 \Rightarrow du = 3x^2\,dx \Rightarrow x^2\,dx = \frac{1}{3}du$

14. $\int \sqrt{2+5y}\,dy = \frac{1}{5}\int u^{1/2}\,du = \frac{1}{5}\left(\frac{2}{3}u^{3/2}\right) + C = \frac{2}{15}(2+5y)^{3/2} + C$

Let $u = 2 + 5y \Rightarrow du = 5\,dy \Rightarrow dy = \frac{1}{5}\,du$

15. $\int \frac{dx}{(3x+2)^2} = \int u^{-2}\left(\frac{1}{3}du\right) = -\frac{1}{3}u^{-1} + C = -\frac{1}{3}(3x+2)^{-1} + C$

Let $u = 3x + 2 \Rightarrow du = 3\,dx \Rightarrow dx = \frac{1}{3}\,du$

16. $\int 5r\sqrt{1-r^2}\,dr = -\frac{5}{2}\int u^{1/2}\,du = -\frac{5}{2}\left(\frac{2}{3}u^{3/2}\right) + C = -\frac{5}{3}(1-r^2)^{3/2} + C$

Let $u = 1 - r^2 \Rightarrow du = -2\,r\,dr \Rightarrow r\,dr = -\frac{1}{2}\,du$

17. $\int \frac{3r\,dr}{\sqrt{1-r^2}} = 3\int u^{-\frac{1}{2}}\left(-\frac{1}{2}du\right) = -\frac{3}{2}(2u^{\frac{1}{2}}) + C = -3\sqrt{1-r^2} + C$

Let $u = 1 - r^2 \Rightarrow du = -2r\,dr \Rightarrow r\,dr = -\frac{1}{2}\,du$

18. $\int \frac{y\,dy}{\sqrt{2y^2+1}} = -\frac{1}{4}\int u^{-1/2}\,du = \frac{1}{4}(2u^{1/2}) + C = \frac{1}{2}(2y^2+1)^{1/2} + C$

Let $u = 2y^2 + 1 \Rightarrow du = 4y\,dy \Rightarrow y\,dy = \frac{1}{4}\,du$

19. $\int x^4(7-x^5)^3\,dx = -\frac{1}{5}\int u^3\,du = -\frac{1}{5}\left(\frac{1}{4}u^4\right) + C = -\frac{1}{20}(7-x^5)^4 + C$

Let $u = 7 - x^5 \Rightarrow du = -5x^4\,dx \Rightarrow x^4\,dx = -\frac{1}{5}\,du$

20. $\int \frac{x^3\,dx}{\sqrt[4]{1+x^4}} = \frac{1}{4}\int u^{-1/4}\,du = \frac{1}{4}\left(\frac{4}{3}u^{3/4}\right) + C = \frac{1}{3}(1+x^4)^{3/4} + C$

Let $u = 1 + x^4 \Rightarrow du = 4x^3\,dx \Rightarrow x^3\,dx = \frac{1}{4}\,du$

21. $\int \frac{ds}{(s+1)^3} = \int (s+1)^{-3}\,ds = -\frac{1}{2}(s+1)^{-2} + C$

22. $\int \frac{s\,ds}{(s^2+1)^2} = \frac{1}{2}\int u^{-2}\,du = \frac{1}{2}(-u^{-1}) + C = -\frac{1}{2(s^2+1)} + C$

Let $u = s^2 + 1 \Rightarrow du = 2s\,ds \Rightarrow s\,ds = \frac{1}{2}\,du$

23. $\int \frac{1}{x^2+4x+4}\,dx = \int (x+2)^{-2}\,dx = -(x+2)^{-1} + C$

24. $\int \frac{dy}{y^2-2y+1} = \int \frac{dy}{(y-1)^2} = \int u^{-2}\,du = -u^{-1} + C = -\frac{1}{y-1} + C$

25. $\int \frac{x+1}{2\sqrt{x+1}}\,dx = \frac{1}{2}\int \frac{u}{\sqrt{u}}\,du = \frac{1}{2}\int u^{\frac{1}{2}}\,du = \frac{1}{3}u^{\frac{3}{2}} + C = \frac{1}{3}(x+1)^{\frac{3}{2}} + C$

Let $u = x + 1 \Rightarrow du = dx$

26. $\int x\sqrt{a^2-x^2}\,dx = -\frac{1}{2}\int u^{1/2}\,du = -\frac{1}{2}\left(\frac{2}{3}u^{3/2}\right) + C = -\frac{1}{3}(a^2-x^2)^{3/2} + C$

Let $u = a^2 - x^2 \Rightarrow du = -2x\,dx \Rightarrow x\,dx = -\frac{1}{2}du$

27. $\int (y^3 + 6y^2 + 12y + 8)(y^2 + 4y + 4)\,dy = \int (y+2)^3 (y+2)^2\,dy$

$= \int (y+2)^5\,dy = \frac{1}{6}(y+2)^6 + C$

28. $\int \frac{(z+1)\,dz}{\sqrt[3]{z^2 + 2z + 2}} = \frac{1}{2}\int u^{-1/3}\,du = \frac{1}{2}\left(\frac{3}{2}u^{2/3}\right) + C = \frac{3}{4}(z^2 + 2z + 2)^{2/3} + C$

Let $u = z^2 + 2z + 2 \Rightarrow du = (2z+2)\,dz \Rightarrow (z+1)\,dz = \frac{1}{2}du$

29. $\int \frac{1}{\sqrt{x}\,(1+\sqrt{x})^2}\,dx = \int \frac{1}{u^2}\cdot 2du = \int 2u^{-2}\,du = -2u^{-1} + C = -2(1+\sqrt{x})^{-1} + C$

Let $u = 1 + \sqrt{x} \Rightarrow du = \frac{1}{2\sqrt{x}}\,dx \Rightarrow \frac{dx}{\sqrt{x}} = 2du$

30. $\int (y^4 + 4y^2 + 1)^2 (y^3 + 2y)\,dy = \int (y^8 + 8y^4 + 1)(y^3 + 2y)\,dy =$

$\int (y^{11} + 2y^9 + 8y^7 + 16y^5 + y^3 + 2y)\,dy = \frac{1}{12}y^{12} + \frac{1}{5}y^{10} + y^8 + \frac{8}{3}y^6 + \frac{1}{4}y^4 + y^2 + C$

31. $\frac{dy}{dx} = x\sqrt{1+x^2}$, $y = 0$ when $x = 0$. $y = \int x\sqrt{1+x^2}\,dx$

$= \frac{1}{3}(1+x^2)^{3/2} + C$. $0 = \frac{1}{3}(1)^{3/2} + C \Rightarrow C = -\frac{1}{3}$. $\therefore y = \frac{1}{3}(1+x^2)^{3/2} - \frac{1}{3}$.

32. $\frac{dy}{dx} = 3x^2\sqrt{1+x^3}$, $y = 1$ when $x = 0$. $y = \int 3x^2\sqrt{1+x^3}\,dx$

$= \frac{2}{3}(1+x^3)^{3/2} + C$. $1 = \frac{2}{3}(1)^{3/2} + C \Rightarrow C = \frac{1}{3}$. $\therefore y = \frac{2}{3}(1+x^3)^{3/2} + \frac{1}{3}$.

33. $\frac{dr}{dz} = 24z\,(3z^2 - 1)^3$, $r = -3$ when $z = 0$. $r = \int 24z\,(3z^2 - 1)^3\,dz$

$= (3z^2 - 1)^4 + C$. $-3 = (-1)^4 + C \Rightarrow C = -4$. $\therefore r = (3z^2 - 1)^4 - 4$.

34. $\frac{dy}{dx} = 4x\,(x^2 - 8)^{-1/3}$, $y = 0$ when $x = 0$. $y = \int 4x\,(x^2 - 8)^{-1/3}\,dx$

$= 3(x^2 - 8)^{2/3} + C$. $0 = 3(-8)^{2/3} + C \Rightarrow C = -12$. $\therefore y = 3(x^2 - 8)^{2/3} - 12$.

35. $2y\frac{dy}{dx} = 3x\sqrt{x^2+1}\sqrt{y^2+1}$, $y = 0$ when $x = 0$.

$[(y^2+1)^{-\frac{1}{2}}\,y]\,dy = \frac{3}{2}x\sqrt{x^2+1}\,dx \Rightarrow (y^2+1)^{\frac{1}{2}} = \frac{1}{2}(x^2+1)^{\frac{3}{2}} + C$.

$(1)^{\frac{1}{2}} = \frac{1}{2}(1)^{\frac{3}{2}} + C \Rightarrow C = \frac{1}{2}$. $\therefore\ 2(y^2+1)^{\frac{1}{2}} = (x^2+1)^{\frac{3}{2}} + 1$

36. $\frac{dy}{dx} = \frac{4\sqrt{(1+y^2)^3}}{y}$, y = 0 when x = 0.

$$\int \frac{y\,dy}{\sqrt{(1+y^2)^3}} = \int 4\,dx \Rightarrow -(1+y^2)^{-1/2} = 4x + C$$

$$-(1)^{-1/2} = 0 + C \Rightarrow C = -1 \;.\; \therefore\; (1+y^2)^{-1/2} = 1 - 4x$$

37. Only (a) and (c). You are never allowed to factor a variable term out of the integal sign.

4.4 INTEGRALS OF TRIGONOMETRIC FUNCTIONS

1. $\int \sin 3x\,dx = -\frac{1}{3}\cos 3x + C$

2. $\int \cos(2x+4)\,dx = \frac{1}{2}\sin(2x+4) + C$

3. $\int \sec^2(x+2)\,dx = \tan(x+2) + C$

4. $\int \sec 2x \operatorname{tax} 2x\,dx = \frac{1}{2}\sec 2x + C$

5. $\int \csc\left(x+\frac{\pi}{2}\right)\cot\left(x+\frac{\pi}{2}\right)dx = -\csc\left(x+\frac{\pi}{2}\right) + C$

6. $\int \csc^2(2x-3)\,dx = -\frac{1}{2}\cot(2x-3) + C$

7. $\int x\sin(2x^2)\,dx = \frac{1}{4}\int \sin u\,du = -\frac{1}{4}\cos u + C = -\frac{1}{4}\cos(2x^2) + C$

   Let $u = 2x^2\,dx \Rightarrow du = 4x\,dx \Rightarrow x\,dx = \frac{1}{4}du$

8. $\int (\cos\sqrt{x})\frac{dx}{\sqrt{x}} = 2\sin\sqrt{x} + C$

9. $\int \sin 2t\,dt = -\frac{1}{2}\cos 2t + C$

10. $\int \cos(3\theta-1)\,d\theta = \frac{1}{3}\sin(3\theta-1) + C$

11. $\int 4\cos 3y\,dy = \frac{4}{3}\sin 3y + C$

12. $\int 2\sin z\cos z\,dz = \int \sin 2z\,dz = -\frac{1}{2}\cos 2z + C$ or

    $\int 2\sin z\cos z\,dz = \sin^2 z + C$ or $-\cos^2 z + C$

13. $\int \sin^2 x\cos x\,dx = \int u^2\,du = \frac{1}{3}u^3 + C = \frac{1}{3}\sin^3 x + C$

    Let $u = \sin x \Rightarrow du = \cos x\,dx$

14. $\int \cos^2 2y \sin 2y\, dy = -\frac{1}{2}\int u^2\, du = -\frac{1}{2}\left(\frac{1}{3}u^3\right) + C = -\frac{1}{6}\cos^3 2y + C$

Let $u = \cos 2y \Rightarrow du = -2 \sin 2y\, dy$

15. $\int \sec^2 2\theta\, d\theta = \frac{1}{2} \tan 2\theta + C$

16. $\int \sec^3 x \tan x\, dx = \int \sec^2 x\,(\sec x \tan x)\, dx = \frac{1}{3}\sec^3 x + C$

17. $\int \sec \frac{x}{2} \tan \frac{x}{2}\, dx = 2 \sec \frac{x}{2} + C$

18. $\int \frac{d\theta}{\cos^2\theta} = \int \sec^2 \theta\, d\theta = \tan \theta + C$

19. $\int \frac{d\theta}{\sin^2\theta} = \int \csc^2\theta\, d\theta = -\cot \theta + C$

20. $\int \csc^2 5\theta \cot 5\theta\, d\theta = -\frac{1}{10}\cot^2 5\theta + C$ or $-\frac{1}{10}\csc^2 5\theta + C$

21. $\int \cos^2 y\, dy = \int\left(\frac{1}{2} + \frac{1}{2}\cos 2y\right) dy = \frac{1}{2}y + \frac{1}{4}\sin 2y + C$

22. $\int \sin^2 \frac{x}{2}\, dx = \int\left(\frac{1}{2} - \frac{1}{2}\cos x\right)dx = \frac{1}{2}x - \frac{1}{2}\sin x + C$

23. $\int (1 - \sin^2 3t)\cos 3t\, dt = \int \cos 3t\, dt - \int \sin^2 3t \cos 3t\, dt = \frac{1}{3}\sin 3t - \frac{1}{9}\sin^3 3t + C$

24. $\int \frac{\sin x\, dx}{\cos^2 x} = \int \sec x \tan x\, dx = \sec x + C$

25. $\int \frac{\cos x\, dx}{\sin^2 x} = \int \cot x \csc x\, dx = -\csc x + C$

26. $\int \sqrt{2 + \sin 3t}\, \cos 3t\, dt = \frac{2}{9}(2 + \sin 3t)^{3/2} + C$

27. $\int \frac{\sin 2t\, dt}{\sqrt{2 - \cos 2t}} = \int (2 - \cos 2t)^{-\frac{1}{2}} \sin 2t\, dt = (2 - \cos 2t)^{\frac{1}{2}} + C$

28. $\int \sin^3 \frac{y}{2} \cos \frac{y}{2}\, dy = \frac{1}{2} \sin^4 \frac{y}{2} + C$

29. $\int \cos^2 \frac{2x}{3} \sin \frac{2x}{3}\, dx = -\frac{1}{2} \cos^3 \frac{2x}{3} + C$

30. $\int \frac{\sec^2 u\, du}{\tan^2 u} = \int \csc^2 u\, du = -\cot u + C$

31. $\int \sec\theta\,(\sec\theta + \tan\theta)\, d\theta = \int (\sec^2\theta + \sec\theta\tan\theta)\, d\theta = \tan\theta + \sec\theta + C$

32. $\int (1 + \tan^2\theta)\, d\theta = \int \sec^2\theta\, d\theta = \tan\theta + C$

33. $\int (\sec^2 y + \csc^2 y)\, dy = \tan y - \cot y + C$

34. $\int (1 + \sin 2t)^{3/2} \cos 2t\, dt = \frac{1}{5}(1 + \sin 2t)^{5/2} + C$

35. $\int (3\sin 2x + 4\cos 3x)dx = -\frac{3}{2}\cos 2x + \frac{4}{3}\sin 3x + C$

36. $\int \sin t \cos t (\sin t + \cos t)\, dt = \int \sin^2 t \cos t\, dt + \int \cos^2 t \sin t\, dt$

$\frac{1}{3}\sin^3 t - \frac{1}{3}\cos^3 t + C$

37. $\int \tan^2 x \sec^2 x\, dx = \frac{1}{3}\tan^3 x + C$

38. $\int \tan^3 5x \sec^2 5x\, dx = \frac{1}{20}\tan^4 5x + C$

39. $\int \cot^3 x \csc^2 x\, dx = -\frac{1}{4}\cot^4 x + C$

40. $\int \sin^4 x \cos^3 x\, dx = \int \sin^4 x (1 - \sin^2 x)\cos x\, dx =$

$\int \sin^4 x \cos x\, dx - \int \sin^6 x \cos x\, dx = \frac{1}{5}\sin^5 x - \frac{1}{7}\sin^7 x + C$

41. $\int \sqrt{\tan x}\, \sec^2 x\, dx = \frac{2}{3}\tan^{\frac{3}{2}} x + C$

42. $\int \sec^{3/2} x \tan x\, dx = \int \sec^{1/2} x (\sec x \tan x)dx = \frac{2}{3}\sec^{3/2} x + C$

43. $\int (\sin x)^{\frac{3}{2}} \cos x\, dx = \frac{2}{5}\sin^{\frac{5}{2}} x + C$

44. $\int x^2 \cos (x^3 + 1)\, dx = \frac{1}{3}\sin (x^3 + 1) + C$

45. $\int \cos^3 x\, dx = \int (\cos^2 x)\cos x\, dx = \int (1 - \sin^2 x) \cos x\, dx =$

$\int \cos x\, dx - \int \sin^2 x \cos x\, dx = \sin x - \frac{1}{3}\sin^3 x + C.$

46. $\int \tan^2 4x\, dx = \int (\sec^2 4x - 1)\, dx = \frac{1}{4}\tan 4x - x + C$

47. $\int \cos^5 x\, dx = \int (\cos^2 x)^2 \cos x\, dx = \int (1 - \sin^2 x)^2 \cos x\, dx =$

$\int (1 - 2\sin^2 x + \sin^4 x) \cos x\, dx = \sin x - \frac{2}{3}\sin^3 x + \frac{1}{5}\sin^5 x + C.$

48. $\int \sin^{-3} 5x \cos 5x\, dx = -\frac{1}{10}\sin^{-2} 5x + C$

49. $\int \cos^{-4} 2x \sin 2x\, dx = \frac{1}{6}\cos^{-3} 2x + C$

50. $\int \frac{\cos\sqrt{x}\,dx}{\sqrt{x}\sin^2\sqrt{x}} = \int \cot\sqrt{x}\ \csc\sqrt{x}\ \frac{dx}{\sqrt{x}} = -2\csc\sqrt{x} + C$

51. $\int \frac{\tan^2\sqrt{x}}{\sqrt{x}}\,dx = 2\int \tan^2 u\,du = 2\int (\sec^2 u - 1)\,du = 2\tan u - 2u + C$

$= 2\tan\sqrt{x} - 2\sqrt{x} + C$

Let $u = \sqrt{x} \Rightarrow du = \frac{1}{2\sqrt{x}}dx \Rightarrow \frac{1}{\sqrt{x}}\,dx = 2\,du$

52. $\int \frac{1}{x^2}\sin\frac{1}{x}\cos\frac{1}{x}\,dx = -\frac{1}{2}\sin^2\frac{1}{x} + C$

53. $\int \frac{x\ \mathrm{cox}\sqrt{3x^2-6}}{\sqrt{3x^2-6}}\,dx = \frac{1}{3}\int \cos u\,du = \frac{1}{3}\sin u\,du + C = \frac{1}{3}\sin\sqrt{3x^2-6} + C$

Let $u = \sqrt{3x^2-6} \Rightarrow du = \frac{3x\,dx}{\sqrt{3x^2-6}}\,dx$

54. $\int \frac{\sin\frac{z-1}{3}\,dz}{\cos^2\left(\frac{z-1}{3}\right)} = \int \tan\frac{z-1}{3}\sec\frac{z-1}{3}dz = 3\sec\frac{z-1}{3} + C$

55. (d) because $\frac{d}{dx}\left(\sec x - \frac{\pi}{4}\right) = \sec x\tan x$

56. (b) and (d), since $\frac{d}{dx}(-\cot x + C) = -(-\csc^2 x) = \csc^2 x$

57. $2y\frac{dy}{dx} = 5x - 3\sin x$, $y = 0$ when $x = 0$.

$2y\,dy = (5x - 3\sin x)\,dx \Rightarrow y^2 = \frac{5}{2}x^2 + 3\cos x + C$. $0 = 0 + 3 + C \Rightarrow C = -3$.

$\therefore\ y^2 = \frac{5}{2}x^2 + 3\cos x - 3$.

58. $\frac{dy}{dx} = \frac{\sqrt{y^2+1}}{y}\cos x$, $y = \sqrt{3}$ when $x = \pi$.

$\int \frac{y\,dy}{\sqrt{y^2+1}} = \int \cos\ dx \Rightarrow \sqrt{y^2+1} = \sin x + C$.

$2 = \sin\pi + C \Rightarrow C = 2$. $\therefore \sqrt{y^2+1} = -\sin x + 2$.

59. $\dfrac{dy}{dx} = \dfrac{\pi \cos \pi x}{\sqrt{y}}$, $y = 1$ when $x = \dfrac{1}{2}$

$\sqrt{y}\, dy = \pi \cos \pi x\, dx \Rightarrow \dfrac{2}{3}y^{\frac{3}{2}} = \sin \pi x + C$. $\dfrac{2}{3} - \sin\dfrac{\pi}{2} + C \Rightarrow C = -\dfrac{1}{3}$

$2y^{\frac{3}{2}} = 3 \sin \pi x - 1$ or $y = \left(\dfrac{3\sin \pi x - 1}{2}\right)^{\frac{2}{3}}$

60. $y^{(4)} = \cos x$, $y = 3$, $y' = 2$, $y'' = 1$, and $y''' = 0$ when $x = 0$.

$y''' = \displaystyle\int \cos x\, dx = \sin x + C_4$, and $y''' = 0$ when $x = 0 \Rightarrow C_4 = 0$.

$y'' = \displaystyle\int \sin x\, dx = -\cos x + C_3$, and $y'' = 1$ when $x = 0 \Rightarrow C_3 = 2$

$y' = \displaystyle\int (-\cos x + 2)\, dx = -\sin x + 2x + C_2$, and $y' = 2$ when $x = 0 \Rightarrow C_2 = 2$.

$y = \displaystyle\int (-\sin x + 2x + 2)\, dx = \cos x + x^2 + 2x + C_1$,

and $y = 3$ when $x = 0 \Rightarrow C_1 = 2$. $\therefore y = \cos x + x^2 + 2x + 2$

61. $v = \dfrac{ds}{dt} = 6 \sin 2t$, $s = 0$ when $t = 0$. $s = \displaystyle\int 6 \sin 2t\, dt =$

$-3 \cos 2t + C$. $0 = -3 \cos 0 + C \Rightarrow C = 3 \Rightarrow s = -3 \cos 2t + 3$.

$s\left(\dfrac{\pi}{2}\right) = -3 \cos \pi + 3 = 6$ m.

62. $a = \pi^2 \cos \pi t$, and $s = 0$, $v = 8$ when $t = 0$.

$v = \displaystyle\int \pi^2 \cos \pi t\, dt = \pi \sin \pi t + C$, and $v = 8$ when $t = 0 \Rightarrow C = 8$.

$s = \displaystyle\int (\pi \sin \pi t + 8)\, dt = -\cos \pi t + 8t + C$, and $s = 0$ when $t = 0 \Rightarrow C = 1$.

$s(t) = -\cos \pi t + 8t + 1 \Rightarrow s(1) = 10$.

63. All three are correct. The double-angle cosine formulas

$$\frac{1}{2} - \frac{1}{2}\cos 2x = \sin^2 x \text{ and } \frac{1}{2} + \frac{1}{2}\cos 2x = \cos^2 x$$

state that $\cos 2x$, $\sin^2 x$ and $\cos^2 x$ differ from each other by a constant.

64. Both are correct, since the formula $1 + \tan^2 x = \sec^2 x \Rightarrow$ $\frac{1}{2} + \frac{1}{2}\tan^2 x = \frac{1}{2}\sec^2 x$, so that these antiderivatives differ from each other by a constant.

65. (a) Let $u = x - 1$ and $du = dx$. Then

$$\int \sqrt{1 + \sin^2(x-1)}\sin(x-1)\cos(x-1)\,dx = \int \sqrt{1+\sin^2 u}\,\sin u \cos u\,du.$$

Let $v = \sin u$ and $dv = \cos u\,du$. Then

$$\int \sqrt{1+\sin^2 u}\,\sin u\cos u\,du = \int \sqrt{1+v^2}\;v\,dv.$$

Let $w = 1 + v^2$ and $dw = 2v\,dv$ or $v\,dv = \frac{1}{2}dw$. Then

$$\int \sqrt{1+v^2}\;v\,dv = \int \frac{1}{2}\sqrt{w}\,dw = \frac{1}{3}w^{\frac{3}{2}} + C = \frac{1}{3}(1+v^2)^{\frac{3}{2}} + C$$

$$= \frac{1}{3}(1+\sin^2 u)^{\frac{3}{2}} + C = \frac{1}{3}[1+\sin^2(x-1)]^{\frac{3}{2}} + C.$$

(b) Let $v = \sin(x-1)$ and $dv = \cos(x-1)\,dx$. Then

$$\int \sqrt{1+\sin^2(x-1)}\sin(x-1)\cos(x-1)\,dx = \int\sqrt{1+v^2}\;v\,dv.$$

Let $w = 1 + v^2$ and $dw = 2v\,dv$ or $v\,dv = \frac{1}{2}dw$. Then

$$\int \sqrt{1+v^2}\;v\,dv = \int \frac{1}{2}\sqrt{w}\,dw = \frac{1}{3}w^{\frac{3}{2}} + C = \frac{1}{3}(1+v^2)^{\frac{3}{2}} + C$$

$$= \frac{1}{3}[1+\sin^2(x-1)]^{\frac{3}{2}} + C.$$

4.5 DEFINITE INTEGRALS: THE AREA UNDER A CURVE

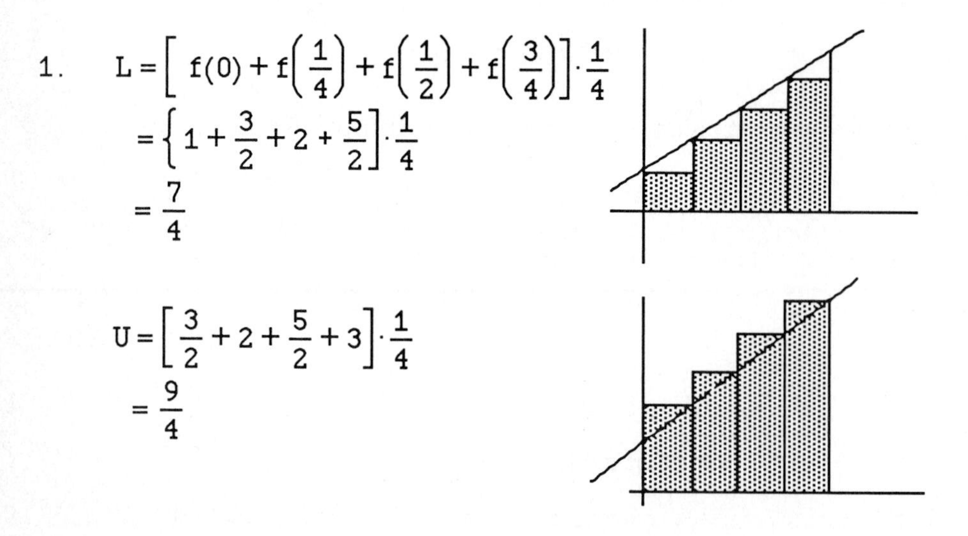

1. $$L = \left[f(0) + f\left(\frac{1}{4}\right) + f\left(\frac{1}{2}\right) + f\left(\frac{3}{4}\right)\right]\cdot\frac{1}{4}$$

$$= \left\{1 + \frac{3}{2} + 2 + \frac{5}{2}\right]\cdot\frac{1}{4}$$

$$= \frac{7}{4}$$

$$U = \left[\frac{3}{2} + 2 + \frac{5}{2} + 3\right]\cdot\frac{1}{4}$$

$$= \frac{9}{4}$$

2. $L = \left[\left(-\frac{1}{2}\right)^2 + 0^2 + 0^2 + \left(\frac{1}{2}\right)^2\right]\cdot\frac{1}{2}$

$= \left(\frac{1}{4} + \frac{1}{4}\right)\cdot\frac{1}{2} = \frac{1}{4}$

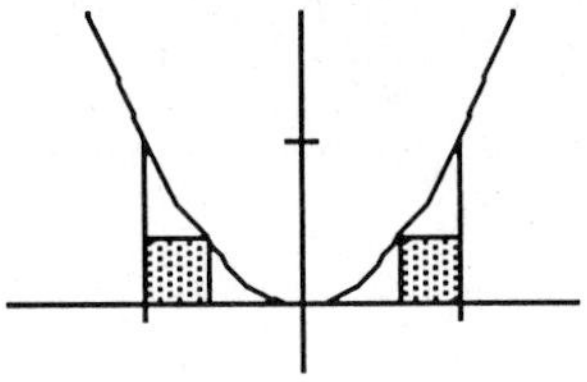

$U = \left[(-1)^2 + \left(-\frac{1}{2}\right)^2 + 0^2 + \left(\frac{1}{2}\right)^2 + 1^2\right]\cdot\frac{1}{2}$

$= \left(1 + \frac{1}{4} + \frac{1}{4} + 1\right)\cdot\frac{1}{2} = \frac{5}{4}$

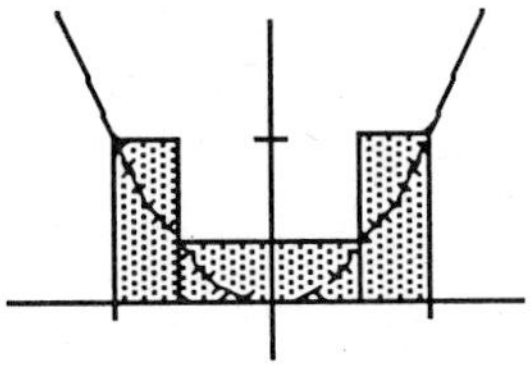

3. $L = \left(\sin 0 + \sin\frac{\pi}{4} + \sin\frac{3\pi}{4} + \sin\pi\right)\cdot\frac{\pi}{4}$

$= \left(\frac{\sqrt{2}}{2} + \frac{\sqrt{2}}{2}\right)\cdot\frac{\pi}{4} = \frac{\pi\sqrt{2}}{4}$

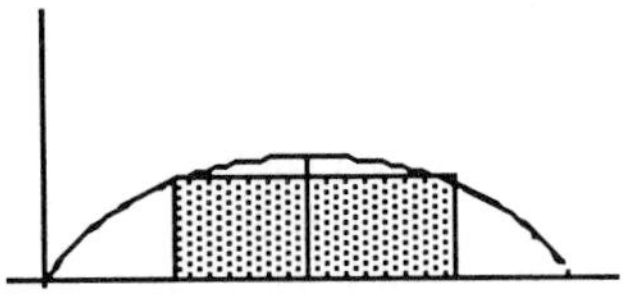

$U = \left(\sin\frac{\pi}{4} + \sin\frac{\pi}{2} + \sin\frac{\pi}{2} + \sin\frac{3\pi}{4}\right)\cdot\frac{\pi}{4}$

$= \frac{(2+\sqrt{2})\pi}{4}$

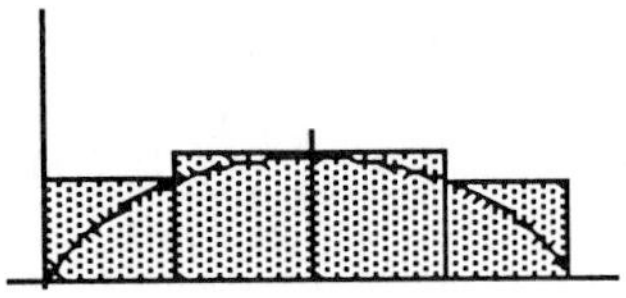

4. $L = \left[1 + \frac{4}{5} + \frac{2}{3} + \frac{4}{7}\right]\cdot\frac{1}{4}$

$= \frac{319}{420} \approx 0.752$

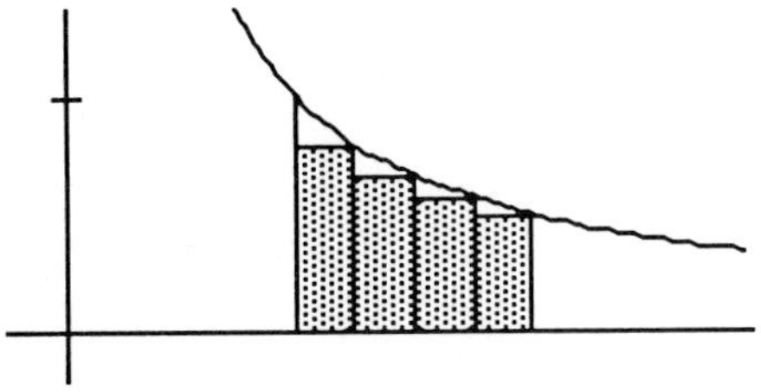

$U = \left[\frac{4}{5} + \frac{2}{3} + \frac{4}{7} + \frac{1}{2}\right]\cdot\frac{1}{4}$

$= \frac{533}{840} \approx 0.635$

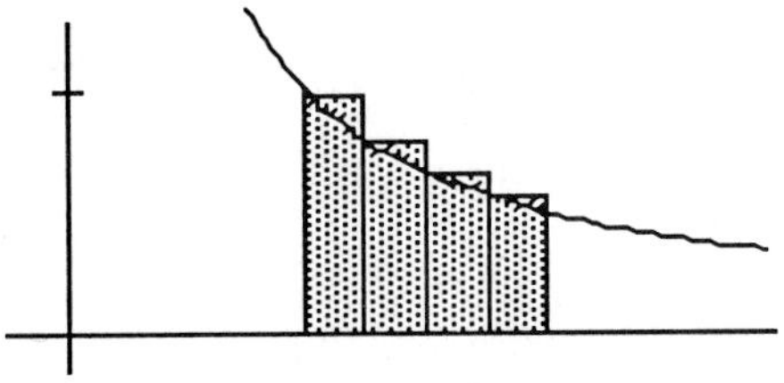

5. $L = (\sqrt{0} + \sqrt{1} + \sqrt{2} + \sqrt{3})(1)$

≈ 4.15

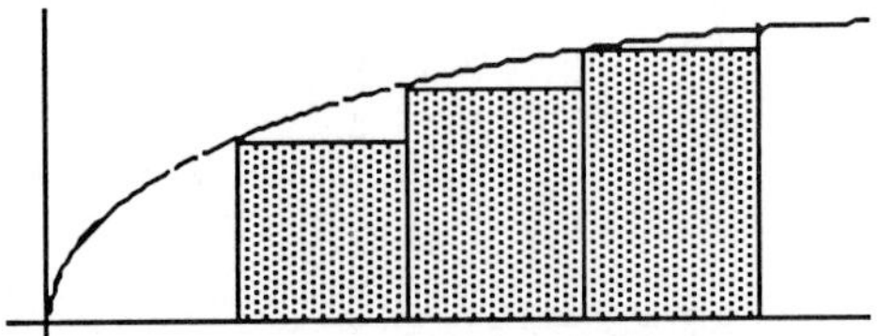

$U = (\sqrt{1} + \sqrt{2} + \sqrt{3} + \sqrt{4})(1)$

≈ 6.15

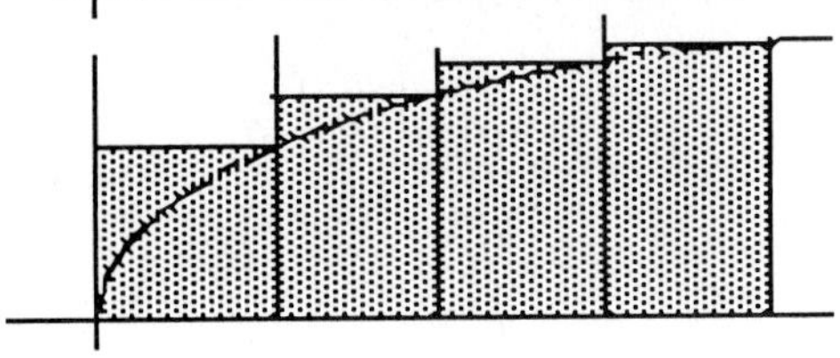

6. $\sum_{k=1}^{5} \frac{1}{k} = 1 + \frac{1}{2} + \frac{1}{3} + \frac{1}{4} + \frac{1}{5}$

7. $\sum_{i=-1}^{3} 2^{i} = 2^{-1} + 2^{0} + 2^{1} + 2^{2} + 2^{3} = \frac{1}{2} + 1 + 2 + 4 + 8$

8. $\sum_{n=1}^{4} \cos n\pi x = \cos \pi x + \cos 2\pi x + \cos 3\pi x + \cos 4\pi x$

9. $\sum_{n=0}^{4} \frac{n}{4} = \frac{0}{4} + \frac{1}{4} + \frac{2}{4} + \frac{3}{4} + \frac{4}{4} = \frac{5}{2}$

10. $\sum_{k=1}^{3} \frac{k-1}{k} = 0 + \frac{2-1}{2} + \frac{3-1}{3} = \frac{1}{2} + \frac{2}{3} = \frac{7}{6}$

11. $\sum_{m=0}^{5} \sin\frac{m\pi}{2} = \sin 0 + \sin\frac{\pi}{2} + \sin \pi + \sin\frac{3\pi}{2} + \sin 2\pi + \sin\frac{5\pi}{2} = 1$

12. $\sum_{i=1}^{4} (i^{2} - 1) = 0 + (4-1) + (9-1) + (16-1) = 26$

13. $\sum_{i=0}^{3} (i^{2} + 5) = 5 + 6 + 9 + 14 = 34$

14. $\sum_{k=0}^{5} \frac{1}{2^{k}} = 1 + \frac{1}{2} + \frac{1}{4} + \frac{1}{8} + \frac{1}{16} + \frac{1}{32} = \frac{63}{32}$

15. (a) $\sum_{j=2}^{7} 2^{j-2} = 2^{0} + 2^{1} + 2^{2} + 2^{3} + 2^{4} + 2^{5}$ (c) $\sum_{j=0}^{5} 2^{j} = 2^{0} + 2^{1} + 2^{2} + 2^{3} + 2^{4} + 2^{5}$

(b) $\sum_{k=0}^{5} 2^{k} = 2^{0} + 2^{1} + 2^{2} + 2^{3} + 2^{4} + 2^{5}$ (d) $\sum_{j=1}^{6} 2^{j-1} = 2^{0} + 2^{1} + 2^{2} + 2^{3} + 2^{4} + 2^{5}$

Therefore, all express the same sum.

16. (a) $\int_{1}^{5} f(x)\,dx = \int_{1}^{2} f(x)\,dx + \int_{2}^{5} f(x)\,dx = -4 + 6 = 2$

(b) $\int_{5}^{1} -4f(x)\,dx = 4\int_{1}^{5} f(x)\,dx = 4\,(2) = 8$ by part (a)

(c) $\int_{1}^{5} [4\,f(x) - 2\,g(x)]\,dx = 4\int_{1}^{5} f(x)\,dx - 2\int_{1}^{5} g(x)\,dx = 4(2) - 2(8) = -8$

17. (a) $\int_{1}^{9} -2f(x)\,dx = -2\int_{1}^{9} f(x)\,dx = -2\left(\int_{1}^{7} f(x)\,dx + \int_{7}^{9} f(x)\,dx\right) = -2\,(-1 + 5) = -8$

(b) $\int_{7}^{9} [\,2f(x) - h\,(x)\,]\,dx = 2\int_{7}^{9} f(x)\,dx - \int_{7}^{9} h\,(x)\,dx = 2\,(5) - 4 = 6$

(c) $\int_{9}^{7} f(x)\,dx = -\int_{7}^{9} f(x)\,dx = -5$ (d) $\int_{7}^{7} [f(x) + h(x)]\,dx = 0$

18. $\int_3^4 f(y)\,dy = \int_3^0 f(y)\,dy + \int_0^4 f(y)\,dy = -\int_0^3 f(y)\,dy + \int_0^4 f(y)\,dy = -3 + 7 = 4$

19. On each subinterval $[x_{i-1}, x_i]$, let $L_i = f(x_{i-1})\,\Delta x$ and $U_i = f(x_i)\,\Delta x$.

Then $U_i - L_i = [\,f(x_i) - f(x_{i-1})]\Delta x$ and $U - L = \sum_{i=0}^{n} [\,f(x_i) - f(x_{i-1})]\Delta x$

$= [f(x_n) - f(x_0)]\,\Delta x = [f(b) - f(a)\,]\,\Delta x$

20. Using the notation of problem 19, $U - L = [f(a) - f(b)]\Delta x$

21. Use the notation of problem 19, and assume that f is increasing.

Then $U_i - L_i = [\,f(x_i) - f(x_{i-1})]\Delta x_i$ and $U - L = \sum_{i=0}^{n} [\,f(x_i) - f(x_{i-1})]\Delta x_i$

$\le \sum_{i=0}^{n} [\,f(x_i) - f(x_{i-1})]\Delta x_{max} = [f(x_n) - f(x_0)]\,\Delta x_{max} = [f(b) - f(a)\,]\,\Delta x_{max}$.

If f is decreasing, we have $L - U \le [f(b) - f(a)\,]\,\Delta x_{max}$. Therefore,

$|\,U - L\,| \le [f(b) - f(a)\,]\,\Delta x_{max}$.

4.6 CALCULATING DEFINITE INTEGRALS BY SUMMATION

1. Verify $\sum_{k=1}^{n} k^3 = \left(\frac{n\,(n+1)}{2}\right)^2$. For $n = 1$, $1^3 = \left(\frac{1\cdot 2}{2}\right)^2 = 1$.

For $n = 2$, $9 = 1^3 + 2^3 = \left(\frac{2\cdot 3}{2}\right)^2 = 9$. For $n = 3$, $36 = 1^3 + 2^3 + 3^3 = \left(\frac{3\cdot 4}{2}\right)^2 = 36$.

In general, $1^3 + 2^3 + \,.\,. + (n+1\,)^3 = \left(\frac{n(n+1)}{2}\right)^2 + (n+1\,)^3 =$

$\left(\frac{n(n+1)}{2}\right)^2 + \frac{4(\,n+1\,)^3}{4} = \frac{(\,n+1\,)^2}{4}[n^2 + 4\,(\,n+1)] = \left(\frac{(n+1)(n+2)}{2}\right)^2$.

2. $S_n = \left[\left(\frac{b}{n}\right)^3 + \left(\frac{2b}{n}\right)^3 + \ldots + \left(\frac{b\,(n-1)}{n}\right)^3\right]\cdot\frac{b}{n}$

$= [1^3 + 2^3 + 3^3 + \ldots + (n-1)^3\,]\cdot\left(\frac{b}{n}\right)^4 = \left[\frac{n\,(n-1)}{2}\right]^2\cdot\left(\frac{b}{n}\right)^4$

$A = \int_0^b x^3\,dx = \lim_{n\to\infty}\left[\frac{n\,(n-1)}{2}\right]^2\cdot\left(\frac{b}{n}\right)^4 = \lim_{n\to\infty}\left[\frac{n\,(n-1)}{n^2}\right]^2\cdot\frac{b^4}{4} = \frac{b^4}{4}$

3. $U = [\,m(a+\Delta x) + m(a+2\Delta x) + \ldots + m(a+n\Delta x)$

$$= m[na + (1+2+\ldots+n)]\,\Delta x = m\left[\,na + \frac{n(n-1)}{2}\,\right]\Delta x$$

$$= m\left[\,a + \frac{n-1}{2}\,\right]n\Delta x = m\left[\,a + \frac{n-1}{2}\cdot\frac{b-a}{n}\,\right](b-a).$$

$$\int_a^b mx\,dx = \lim_{n\to\infty} m\left[\,a + \frac{n-1}{n}\cdot\frac{b-a}{2}\,\right](b-a) = m\left(\frac{b^2-a^2}{2}\right).$$

4. $S_n = [1^2 + 2^2 + 3^2 + \ldots + n^2]\left(\frac{b}{n}\right)^3 = \frac{n(n+1)(2n+1)}{6}\cdot\left(\frac{b}{n}\right)^3$

$$A = \int_0^b x^2\,dx = \lim_{n\to\infty}\frac{n(n+1)(2n+1)}{6}\cdot\left(\frac{b}{n}\right)^3 = \lim_{n\to\infty}\frac{b^3}{6}\left(1+\frac{1}{n}\right)\left(2+\frac{1}{n}\right) = \frac{b^3}{6}$$

5. Let $\Delta x = \frac{b}{n}$, $x_i = \frac{ib}{n}$, and $f(x_i) = \frac{i^3b^3}{n^3}$. Then $\sum_{i=1}^{n}\frac{i^3b^3}{n^3}\cdot\frac{ib}{n}$

$$= \frac{b^4}{n^4}\sum_{i=1}^{n} i^3 = \frac{b^4}{n^4}\left(\frac{n(n+1)}{2}\right)^2.\ \lim_{n\to\infty}\frac{b^4}{n^4}\left(\frac{n(n+1)}{2}\right)^2$$

$$= \frac{b^4}{4}\lim_{n\to\infty}\frac{n^4+2n^3+n^2}{n^4} = \frac{b^4}{4}.$$

6. Prove that $\sum_{k=1}^{n}(2k-1) = n^2$. If $n = 1$, then $2(1) = 1 = 1^2$.

$$\sum_{k=1}^{n+1}(2k-1) = \sum_{k=1}^{n}(2k-1) + 2(n+1) - 1 = n^2 + 2n + 1 = (n+1)^2.$$

7. Prove that $\sum_{k=1}^{n}\frac{1}{k(k+1)} = \frac{n}{n+1}$. If $n = 1$, then $\frac{1}{1\cdot 2} = \frac{1}{1+1}$.

$$\sum_{k=1}^{n+1}\frac{1}{k(k+1)} = \sum_{k=1}^{n}\frac{1}{k(k+1)} + \frac{1}{(n+1)(n+2)} = \frac{n}{n+1} + \frac{1}{(n+1)(n+2)}$$

$$= \frac{n(n+2)+1}{(n+1)(n+2)} = \frac{(n+1)^2}{(n+1)(n+2)} = \frac{n+1}{n+2}.$$

8. (a) $\int_0^2 3x\,dx = 3\int_0^2 x\,dx = 3\left(\frac{2^2}{2}\right) = 6$

(b) $\int_2^3 4x\,dx = 4\left[\int_2^0 x\,dx + \int_0^3 x\,dx\right] = 4\left[-\int_0^2 x\,dx + \int_0^3 x\,dx\right] = 4\left[-\frac{2^2}{2} + \frac{3^2}{2}\right] = 10$

(c) $\int_0^2 x^2\,dx = \frac{1}{3}(2)^3 = \frac{8}{3}$

(d) $\int_0^2 (x^2 - 5x)\,dx = \int_0^2 x^2\,dx - 5\int_0^2 x\,dx = \frac{8}{3} - 5(2) = -\frac{22}{3}$

(e) $\int_0^1 x^2\,dx = \frac{1}{3}(1)^3 = \frac{1}{3}$

(f) $\int_1^2 x^2\,dx = \int_1^0 x^2\,dx + \int_0^2 x^2\,dx = -\int_0^1 x^2\,dx + \int_0^2 x^2\,dx = -\frac{1}{3} + \frac{8}{3} = \frac{7}{3}$

(g) $\int_1^3 x^2\,dx = \int_1^0 x^2\,dx + \int_0^3 x^2\,dx = -\int_1^0 x^2\,dx + \int_0^3 x^2\,dx = -\frac{1}{3} + 9 = \frac{26}{3}$

(h) $\int_2^3 x^2\,dx = \int_2^0 x^2\,dx + \int_0^3 x^2\,dx = -\int_0^2 x^2\,dx + \int_0^3 x^2\,dx = -\frac{8}{3} + 9 = \frac{19}{3}$

9. $\int_0^1 (1 + x^2)\,dx = \int_0^1 1\,dx + \int_0^1 x^2\,dx = 1 + \frac{1}{3} = \frac{4}{3}$

10. $\lim_{n\to\infty} S_n = \lim_{n\to\infty}\left(\frac{1}{n}\left[\frac{1}{n} + \frac{2}{n} + \frac{3}{n} + \ldots + \frac{n-1}{n}\right]\right) = \int_0^1 x\,dx = \frac{1}{2}$

11. Let $f(x) = x^2$ on $[0, 1]$. Let $\Delta x = \frac{1-0}{n} = \frac{1}{n}$. Then

$S_n = \frac{1}{n}\left[\left(\frac{1}{n}\right)^2 + \left(\frac{2}{n}\right)^2 + \ldots + \left(\frac{n-1}{n}\right)^2\right]$ is a lower sum and hence

$\lim_{n\to\infty} S_n = \int_0^1 x^2\,dx = \frac{1}{3}$.

12. (a) $U = \frac{\pi}{2n}\left[\sin\frac{\pi}{2n} + \sin\frac{2\pi}{2n} + \sin\frac{3\pi}{2n} + \ldots + \sin\frac{n\pi}{2n}\right]$

$$= \frac{\pi}{2n}\left[\frac{\cos\frac{\pi}{4n} - \cos\left(n + \frac{1}{2}\right)\frac{\pi}{2n}}{2\sin\frac{\pi}{4n}}\right]$$

(b) $\lim_{n\to\infty} \frac{\frac{\pi}{2n}}{2\sin\frac{\pi}{4n}}\left[\cos\frac{\pi}{4n} - \cos\left(n + \frac{1}{2}\right)\frac{\pi}{2n}\right] = 1\left[\cos 0 - \cos\frac{\pi}{2}\right] = 1$

4.7 THE FUNDAMENTAL THEOREM OF INTEGRAL CALCULUS

1. $\int_0^3 y\,dx = \int_0^3 (x^2 + 1)\,dx = \frac{1}{3}x^3 + x\Big]_0^3 = 9 + 3 = 12$

2. $\int_0^1 (2x+3)\,dx = x^2 + 3x\,]_0^1 = 4$

3. $\int_0^4 \sqrt{2x+1}\,dx = \frac{1}{3}(2x+1)^{3/2}\Big]_0^4 = \frac{26}{3}$

4. $\int_0^4 \frac{1}{\sqrt{2x+1}}\,dx = \sqrt{2x+1}\Big]_0^4 = 3 - 1 = 2$

5. $\int_1^2 (2x+1)^{-2}\,dx = -\frac{1}{2}(2x+1)^{-1}\Big]_1^2 = \frac{1}{15}$

6. $\int_{-1}^3 (2x+1)^2\,dx = \frac{1}{6}(2x+1)^3\Big]_{-1}^3 = \frac{1}{6}[7^3 - (-1)^3] = \frac{172}{3}$

7. $\int_0^2 (x^3 + 2x + 1)\,dx = \frac{1}{4}x^4 + x^2 + x\Big]_0^2 = 10$

8. $\int_0^2 x\sqrt{2x^2+1}\,dx = \frac{1}{6}(2x^2+1)^{3/2}\Big]_0^2 = \frac{1}{6}[9^{3/2} - 1] = \frac{13}{3}$

9. $\int_0^2 \frac{x\,dx}{\sqrt{2x^2+1}} = \frac{1}{2}\sqrt{2x^2+1}\Big]_0^2 = 1$

10. $\int_0^2 \frac{x}{(2x^2+1)^2}\,dx = -\frac{1}{4}(2x^2+1)^{-1}\Big]_0^2 = -\frac{1}{4}\left(\frac{1}{9} - 1\right) = \frac{2}{9}$

11. $\int_0^1 (1-x)\,dx = x - \frac{1}{2}x^2\Big]_0^1 = \frac{1}{2}$

12. $\int_1^4 \frac{1}{\sqrt{x}}\,dx = 2\sqrt{x}\Big]_1^4 = 2(2-1) = 2$

13. $\int_0^1 \sqrt{1-x}\,dx = -\frac{2}{3}(1-x)^{\frac{3}{2}}\Big]_0^1 = \frac{2}{3}$

14. $A = 2\int_0^{\frac{\pi}{6}} \cos 3x\,dx = \frac{2}{3}\sin 3x\Big]_0^{\frac{\pi}{6}} = \frac{2}{3}$

15. $\int_{-1}^1 (1-y^2)\,dy = 2\left(y - \frac{1}{3}y^3\right)\Big]_0^1 = \frac{4}{3}$

16. $A = \int_0^{\frac{\pi}{a}} \sin ax\,dx = -\frac{1}{a}\cos ax\Big]_0^{\frac{\pi}{a}} = -\frac{1}{a}(-1-1) = \frac{2}{a}$

17. $\sin^2 3x = 0 \Leftrightarrow 3x = 0 \text{ or } \pi \Rightarrow x = 0 \text{ or } \frac{\pi}{3}$.

$$A = \int_0^{\frac{\pi}{3}} \sin^2 3x\,dx = \int_0^{\frac{\pi}{3}} \left(\frac{1}{2} - \frac{1}{2}\cos 6x\right)dx = \frac{1}{2}x - \frac{1}{12}\sin 6x\Big]_0^{\frac{\pi}{3}} = \frac{\pi}{6}$$

18. (a) $\int_{-3}^{2}(6-x-x^2)\,dx = 6x-\frac{1}{2}x^2-\frac{1}{3}x^3\Big]_{-3}^{2} = \frac{125}{6}$

(b) $y' = -1-2x = 0$ if $x = -\frac{1}{2}$. $y\left(-\frac{1}{2}\right) = 6+\frac{1}{2}-\frac{1}{4} = \frac{25}{4}$

(c) $\frac{25}{4}[2-(-3)] = \frac{125}{4}$ and $\frac{2}{3}\cdot\frac{125}{4} = \frac{125}{6}$

19. $2-x = x^2 \Leftrightarrow (x+2)(x-1) = 0 \Leftrightarrow x = 1$ or -2.

The point of intersection for the 'vertex' of the region is (1,1). Therefore,

$$A = \int_0^1 [(2-y)-\sqrt{y}\,]\,dy = 2y-\frac{1}{2}y^2-\frac{2}{3}y^{\frac{3}{2}}\Big]_0^1 = \frac{5}{6}$$

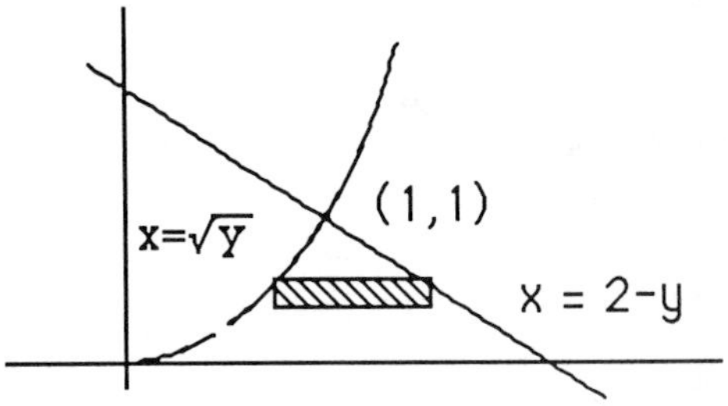

$x=\sqrt{y}$ (1,1) $x = 2-y$

20. (a) $\int_{-a}^{a}\sqrt{a^2-x^2}\,dx = \frac{1}{2}(\text{area of circle}) = \frac{1}{2}(\pi a^2)$

(b) $\int_{0}^{a}\sqrt{a^2-x^2}\,dx = \frac{1}{4}(\text{area of circle}) = \frac{1}{4}(\pi a^2)$

21. $\int_1^2 (2x+5)\,dx = x^2+5x\Big]_1^2 = 8$

22. $\int_0^1 (x^2-2x+3)\,dx = \frac{1}{3}x^3 - x^2 + 3x\Big] = \frac{7}{3}$

23. $\int_{-1}^{1} (x+1)^2\,dx = \frac{1}{3}(x+1)^3\Big]_{-1}^{1} = \frac{8}{3}$

24. $\int_0^2 \sqrt{4x+1}\,dx = \frac{1}{6}(4x+1)^{3/2}\Big]_0^2 = \frac{13}{3}$

25. $\int_0^{\pi} \sin x\,dx = -\cos x\Big]_0^{\pi} = 2$

26. $\int_0^{\pi} \cos x\,dx = \sin x\Big]_0^{\pi} = 0$

27. $\int_{\frac{\pi}{4}}^{\frac{\pi}{2}} \frac{\cos x\,dx}{\sin^2 x} = -(\sin x)^{-1}\Big]_{\frac{\pi}{4}}^{\frac{\pi}{2}} = \sqrt{2}-1$

28. $\int_0^{\frac{\pi}{6}} \frac{\sin 2x\,dx}{\cos^2 2x} = \int_0^{\frac{\pi}{6}} \sec 2x \tan 2x\,dx = \frac{1}{2}\sec 2x\Big]_0^{\frac{\pi}{6}} = \frac{1}{2}$

29. $\int_0^{\pi} \sin^2 x\,dx = \int_0^{\pi}\left(\frac{1}{2}-\frac{1}{2}\cos 2x\right)dx = \frac{1}{2}x-\frac{1}{4}\sin 2x\Big]_0^{\pi} = \frac{\pi}{2}$

30. $\int_0^{\frac{2\pi}{\omega}} \cos^2(\omega t)\,dt = \int_0^{\frac{2\pi}{\omega}}\left(\frac{1}{2}+\frac{1}{2}\cos 2\omega t\right)dt = \frac{1}{2}t+\frac{1}{4\omega}\sin 2\omega t\Big]_0^{\frac{2\pi}{\omega}} = \frac{\pi}{\omega}$

31. $$\int_0^1 \frac{dx}{(2x+1)^3} = -\frac{1}{4}(2x+1)^{-2}\Big]_0^1 = \frac{2}{9}$$

32. $$\int_{-1}^0 x\sqrt{1-x^2}\, dx = -\frac{1}{3}(1-x^2)^{3/2}\Big]_{-1}^0 = -\frac{1}{3}$$

33. $$\int_0^1 \sqrt{5x+4}\, dx = \frac{2}{15}(5x+4)^{\frac{3}{2}}\Big]_0^1 = \frac{38}{15}$$

34. $$\int_{-2}^0 (4-w)^2\, dw = -\frac{1}{3}(4-w)^3\Big]_{-2}^0 = -\frac{1}{3}(64-216) = \frac{152}{3}$$

35. $$\int_{-1}^0 \left(\frac{x^7}{2} - x^{15}\right) dx = \frac{1}{16}x^8 - \frac{1}{16}x^{16}\Big]_{-1}^0 = 0$$

36. $$\int_0^2 (t+1)(t^2+4)\, dt = \int_0^2 (t^3+t^2+4t+4)\, dt = \frac{1}{4}t^4 + \frac{1}{3}t^3 + 2t^2 + 4t\Big]_0^2 = \frac{68}{3}$$

37. $$\int_1^2 \frac{x^2+1}{x^2}\, dx = \int_1^2 \left(1 + \frac{1}{x^2}\right) dx = x - \frac{1}{x}\Big]_1^2 = \frac{3}{2}$$

38. $$\int_9^4 \frac{1-\sqrt{u}}{\sqrt{u}}\, du = \int_9^4 (u^{-1/2} - 1)\, du = 2\sqrt{u} - u\Big]_9^4 = 3$$

39. $$\int_{\frac{\pi}{6}}^{\frac{\pi}{2}} \cos^2\theta \sin\theta\, d\theta = -\frac{1}{3}\cos^3\theta\Big]_{\frac{\pi}{6}}^{\frac{\pi}{2}} = \frac{\sqrt{3}}{8}$$

40. $$\int_0^\pi x\cos\left(2x - \frac{\pi}{2}\right) dx = \int_0^\pi x\sin 2x\, dx = -\frac{1}{2}x\cos 2x + \frac{1}{4}\sin 2x\Big]_0^\pi = -\frac{\pi}{2}$$

41. $$\int_{-4}^4 |x|\, dx = \int_{-4}^0 (-x)\, dx + \int_0^4 x\, dx = -\frac{1}{2}x^2\Big]_{-4}^0 + \frac{1}{2}x^2\Big]_0^4 = 16$$

42. $$\int_0^\pi \frac{1}{2}(\cos x + |\cos x|)\, dx = \int_0^{\frac{\pi}{2}} \frac{1}{2}(\cos x + \cos x) + \int_{\frac{\pi}{2}}^\pi \frac{1}{2}(\cos x - \cos x)\, dx$$

$$= \int_0^{\frac{\pi}{2}} \cos x\, dx = \sin x\Big]_0^{\frac{\pi}{2}} = 1$$

43. $$\int_0^b \left(-\frac{h}{b}x + h\right) dx = -\frac{h}{b}\left(\frac{x^2}{2}\right) + hx\Big]_0^b = \frac{1}{2}bh$$

44. By evaluating the integral, $\int_0^x \cos t\, dt = \sin t\Big]_0^x = \sin x$

and $\frac{d}{dx}(\sin x) = \cos x$. By Fundamental Theorem, $\frac{d}{dx}\int_0^x \cos t\, dt = \cos x$.

45. $$\frac{d}{dx}\int_0^x \sqrt{1+t^2}\, dt = \sqrt{1+x^2}$$

46. $\dfrac{d}{dx}\displaystyle\int_1^x \frac{dt}{t} = \frac{1}{x}$

47. $\dfrac{d}{dx}\displaystyle\int_x^1 \sqrt{1-t^2}\,dt = -\frac{d}{dx}\int_1^x \sqrt{1-t^2}\,dt = -\sqrt{1-x^2}$

48. $\dfrac{d}{dx}\displaystyle\int_1^x \frac{dt}{1+t^2} = \frac{1}{1+x^2}$

49. $\dfrac{d}{dx}\displaystyle\int_1^{2x} \cos(t^2)\,dt = \left(\frac{d}{du}\int_1^u \cos(t^2)\,dt\right)\left(\frac{du}{dx}\right)$, where $u = 2x$,

$= \cos(u^2)(2) = 2\cos(2x)^2 = 2\cos 4x^2$

50. $\dfrac{d}{dx}\displaystyle\int_1^{x^2} \frac{dt}{1+\sqrt{1-t}} = \frac{1}{1+\sqrt{1-x^2}}\frac{d}{dx}(x^2) = \frac{2x}{1+\sqrt{1-x^2}}$

51. $\dfrac{d}{dx}\displaystyle\int_{\sin x}^0 \frac{dt}{2+t} = -\frac{d}{dx}\int_0^{\sin x} \frac{dt}{2+t} = -\frac{1}{2+\sin x}\cdot\frac{d}{dx}(\sin x) = \frac{-\cos x}{2+\sin x}$

52. $\displaystyle\int_{1/x}^1 \frac{1}{t}\,dt = -\int_1^{1/x} \frac{1}{t}dt = -\left(\frac{1}{1/x}\right)\frac{d}{dx}\left(\frac{1}{x}\right) = -x\left(-\frac{1}{x^2}\right) = \frac{1}{x}$

53. $\dfrac{d}{dx}\displaystyle\int_{\cos x}^0 \frac{1}{1-t^2}\,dt = -\frac{d}{dx}\int_0^{\cos x} \frac{1}{1-t^2}\,dt = \frac{-1}{1-\cos^2 x}\cdot\frac{d}{dx}(\cos x)$

$= \dfrac{\sin x}{1-\cos^2 x} = \dfrac{1}{\sin x} = \csc x$

54. $\displaystyle\int_{\sqrt{x}}^{10} \sin t^2\,dt = -\int_{10}^{\sqrt{x}} \sin t^2\,dt = -\sin(\sqrt{x})^2\,\frac{d}{dx}\sqrt{x} = -\frac{\sin x}{2\sqrt{x}}$

55. If $F(x) = \displaystyle\int_0^x f(t)\,dt = \sin x$, then $F'(x) = f(x) = \cos x$.

56. $\displaystyle\lim_{x\to 0}\frac{1}{x^3}\int_0^x \frac{t^2}{t^4+1}\,dt = \lim_{x\to 0}\frac{\frac{x^2}{x^4+1}}{3x^2} = \frac{1}{3}$

57. (a) If $f(x) = 2 + \displaystyle\int_0^x \frac{10}{1+t}dt$, then $f(0) = 2$ and $f'(x) = \dfrac{10}{1+x}$

so $f'(0) = 10$ and $L(x) = 2 + 10x$.

(b) $f''(x) = -\dfrac{10}{(1+x)^2}$ and $f'(0) = -10$. Therefore $Q(x) = 2 + 10x - 5x^2$.

58. (a) True, by Fundamental Theorem, since f must be continuous if it is differentiable.

(b) True, since y is differentiable.

(c) True, since $\frac{dy}{dx} = f(x)$ and $f(1) = 0$.

(d) False, $f'(x) > 0$ for all x so $\frac{d^2y}{dx^2} > 0$ for all x, so the graph of y is concave up at $x = 1$.

(e) True, by the reasoning in (d).

(f) False, $\frac{d^2y}{dx^2} \neq 0$ at $x = 1$.

(g) True, by (c)

59. (a) Let $F(x) = \int_0^x f(t)\,dt = x\cos\pi x$. Then

$F'(x) = f(x) = \cos\pi x - \pi x\sin\pi x$ so $f(4) = \cos 4\pi - 4\pi\sin 4\pi = 1$.

(b) Let $F(x) = \int_0^{x^2} f(t)\,dt = x\cos\pi x$. Then

$F'(x) = 2x\,f(x^2) = \cos\pi x - \pi x\sin\pi x$. When $x = 2$,

$4f(4) = = \cos 2\pi - 2\pi\sin 2\pi = 1$ so $f(4) = \frac{1}{4}$.

(c) If $\int_0^{f(x)} t^2\,dt = x\cos\pi x$, then $\left.\frac{1}{3}t^3\right]_0^{f(x)} = x\cos\pi x$. Thus,

$\frac{1}{3}f^3(x) = x\cos\pi x$, $f(x) = (3x\cos\pi x)^{\frac{1}{3}}$, and $f(4) = (12)^{\frac{1}{3}}$.

60. If $F(x) = \frac{x^2}{2} + \frac{x}{2}\sin x + \frac{\pi}{2}\cos x$, then $F'(x) = f(x) = x + \frac{x}{2}\cos x - \frac{\pi}{2}\sin x$, and $f\left(\frac{\pi}{2}\right) = \frac{1}{2}$.

4.8 SUBSTITUTION IN DEFINITE INTEGRALS

1. (a) $\int_0^3 \sqrt{y+1}\,dy = \int_1^4 \sqrt{u}\,du = \left.\frac{2}{3}u^{\frac{3}{2}}\right]_1^4 = \frac{14}{3}$

(b) $\int_{-1}^0 \sqrt{y+1}\,dy = \int_0^1 \sqrt{u}\,du = \left.\frac{2}{3}u^{\frac{3}{2}}\right]_0^1 = \frac{2}{3}$

Let $u = y + 1 \Rightarrow du = dy$. In (a) $y = 0 \Rightarrow u = 1$, $y = 3 \Rightarrow u = 4$.

In (b) $y = -1 \Rightarrow u = 0$, $y = 0 \Rightarrow u = 1$

2. (a) $\int_0^1 r\sqrt{1-r^2}\,dr = -\frac{1}{2}\int_1^0 u^{1/2}\,du = -\frac{1}{2}\left(\frac{2}{3}u^{3/2}\right]_1^0 = \frac{1}{3}$

(b) $\int_{-1}^1 r\sqrt{1-r^2}\,dr = 0$

Let $u = 1 - r^2 \Rightarrow du = -2r\,dr$, $r = 0 \Rightarrow u = 1$, $r = 1 \Rightarrow u = 0$

3. (a) $\int_0^{\frac{\pi}{4}} \tan x \sec^2 x\,dx = \int_0^1 u\,du = \frac{1}{2}u^2\Big]_0^1 = \frac{1}{2}$

(b) $\int_{-\frac{\pi}{4}}^0 \tan x \sec^2 x\,dx = \int_{-1}^0 u\,du = \frac{1}{2}u^2\Big]_{-1}^0 = -\frac{1}{2}$

Let $u = \tan x \Rightarrow du = \sec^2 x\,dx \Rightarrow$. Then in (a), $x = 0 \Rightarrow u = 0$,

$x = \frac{\pi}{4} \Rightarrow u = 1$, and in (b) $x = -\frac{\pi}{4} \Rightarrow u = -1$, $x = 0 \Rightarrow u = 0$.

4. (a) $\int_0^1 x^3(1+x^4)^3\,dx = \frac{1}{16}(1+x^4)^4\Big]_0^1 = \frac{15}{16}$

(b) $\int_{-1}^1 x^3(1+x^4)^3\,dx = \frac{1}{16}(1+x^4)^4\Big]_{-1}^1 = 0$

5. (a) $\int_0^1 \frac{x^3}{\sqrt{x^4+9}}\,dx = \int_9^{10} \frac{1}{4}u^{-\frac{1}{2}}\,du = \frac{1}{2}u^{\frac{1}{2}}\Big]_9^{10} = \frac{\sqrt{10}-3}{2}$

(b) $\int_{-1}^0 \frac{x^3}{\sqrt{x^4+9}}\,dx = \int_{10}^9 \frac{1}{4}u^{-\frac{1}{2}}\,du = \frac{1}{2}u^{\frac{1}{2}}\Big]_{10}^9 = \frac{3-\sqrt{10}}{2}$

Let $u = x^4 + 9 \Rightarrow du = 4x^3\,dx \Rightarrow x^3\,dx = \frac{1}{4}\,du$. Then in (a), $x = 0 \Rightarrow u = 9$,

$x = 1 \Rightarrow u = 10$, , and in (b) $x = -1 \Rightarrow u = 10$, $x = 0 \Rightarrow u = 9$.

6. (a) $\int_{-1}^1 \frac{x}{(1+x^2)^2}\,dx = -\frac{1}{2(1+x^2)}\Big]_{-1}^1 = 0$

(b) $\int_0^1 \frac{x}{(1+x^2)^2}\,dx = -\frac{1}{2(1+x^2)}\Big]_0^1 = \frac{1}{4}$

7. (a) $\int_0^{\sqrt{7}} x(x^2+1)^{\frac{1}{3}}\,dx = \int_1^8 \frac{1}{2}u^{\frac{1}{3}}\,du = \frac{3}{8}u^{\frac{4}{3}}\Big]_1^8 = \frac{45}{8}$

(b) $\int_{-\sqrt{7}}^{0} x(x^2+1)^{\frac{1}{3}}\,dx = \int_8^1 \frac{1}{2}u^{\frac{1}{3}}\,du = \frac{3}{8}u^{\frac{4}{3}}\Big]_8^1 = -\frac{45}{8}$ }

Let $u = x^2 + 1 \Rightarrow du = 2x\,dx \Rightarrow x\,dx = \frac{1}{2}\,du$. Then in (a), $x = 0 \Rightarrow u = 1$, $x = \sqrt{7} \Rightarrow u = 8$, and in (b) $x = -\sqrt{7} \Rightarrow u = 8$, $x = 0 \Rightarrow u = 1$.

8. (a) $\int_0^{\pi} 3\cos^2 x \sin x\,dx = -\cos^3 x\Big]_0^{\pi} = 2$

(b) $\int_{2\pi}^{3\pi} 3\cos^2 x \sin x\,dx = -\cos^3 x\Big]_{2\pi}^{3\pi} = 2$

9. (a) $\int_0^{\frac{\pi}{6}} (1-\cos 3x)\sin 3x\,dx = \int_0^1 \frac{1}{3}u\,du = \frac{1}{6}u^2\Big]_0^1 = \frac{1}{6}$

(b) $\int_{\frac{\pi}{6}}^{\frac{\pi}{3}} (1-\cos 3x)\sin 3x\,dx = \int_1^2 \frac{1}{3}u\,du = \frac{1}{6}u^2\Big]_1^2 = \frac{1}{2}$

Let $u = 1 - \cos 3x \Rightarrow du = 3\sin 3x\,dx \Rightarrow \sin 3x\,dx = \frac{1}{3}\,u\,du$

Then in (a), $x = 0 \Rightarrow u = 0$, $x = \frac{\pi}{6} \Rightarrow u = 1$, and in (b) $x = \frac{\pi}{3} \Rightarrow u = 2$.

10. (a) $\int_0^{\sqrt{3}} \frac{4x}{\sqrt{x^2+1}}\,dx = 2\int_1^4 u^{-1/2}\,du = 4\sqrt{u}\Big]_1^4 = 4$

(b) $\int_{-\sqrt{3}}^{\sqrt{3}} \frac{4x}{\sqrt{x^2+1}}\,dx = 0$

11. (a) $\int_0^{2\pi} \frac{\cos x\,dx}{\sqrt{2+\sin x}} = 2\sqrt{2+\sin x}\Big]_0^{2\pi} = 0$

(b) $\int_{-\pi}^{\pi} \frac{\cos x\,dx}{\sqrt{2+\sin x}} = 2\sqrt{2+\sin x}\Big]_{-\pi}^{\pi} = 0$

12. (a) $\int_{-\pi/2}^{0} \frac{\sin x}{(3+\cos x)^2}\,dx = (3+\cos x)^{-1}\Big]_{-\pi/2}^{0} = -\frac{1}{12}$

(b) $\int_0^{\pi/2} \frac{\sin x}{(3+\cos x)^2}\,dx = (3+\cos x)^{-1}\Big]_0^{\pi/2} = \frac{1}{12}$

13. (a) $\int_{-\pi}^{\pi} x \cos(2x^2)\, dx = \frac{1}{4} \sin(2x^2)\Big]_{-\pi}^{\pi} = 0$

(b) $\int_{-\pi}^{0} x \cos(2x^2)\, dx = \frac{1}{4} \sin(2x^2)\Big]_{-\pi}^{0} = -\frac{1}{4}\sin(2\pi^2)$

14. $\int_{\pi^2/9}^{\pi^2/4} \frac{\cos\sqrt{x}}{\sqrt{x}}\, dx = 2 \sin\sqrt{x}\Big]_{\pi^2/9}^{\pi^2/4} = 2 - \sqrt{3}$

15. $\int_0^1 \sqrt{t^5 + 2t}\,(5t^4 + 2)\, dt = \frac{2}{3}(t^5 + 2t)^{\frac{3}{2}}\Big]_0^1 = 2\sqrt{3}$

16. $\int_1^4 \frac{dy}{2\sqrt{y}\,(1 + \sqrt{y})^2} = \int_2^3 u^{-2} du = -\frac{1}{u}\Big]_2^3 = \frac{1}{6}$

Let $u = 1 + \sqrt{y} \Rightarrow du = \frac{dy}{2\sqrt{y}}$, $y = 1 \Rightarrow u = 2$, $y = 4 \Rightarrow u = 3$

17. $\int_0^{\frac{\pi}{2}} \cos^3 2x \sin 2x\, dx = \int_1^{-1} -\frac{1}{2} u^3\, du = -\frac{1}{8} u^4\Big]_1^{-1} = 0$

Let $u = \cos 2x \Rightarrow du = -2 \sin 2x\, dx \Rightarrow \sin 2x\, dx = -\frac{1}{2} du$.

Then $x = 0 \Rightarrow u = 1$, $x = \frac{\pi}{2} \Rightarrow u = -1$.

18. $\int_{-\pi/4}^{\pi/4} \tan^2 x \sec^2 x\, dx = \frac{1}{3} \tan^3 x\Big]_{-\pi/4}^{\pi/4} = \frac{2}{3}$

19. (a)

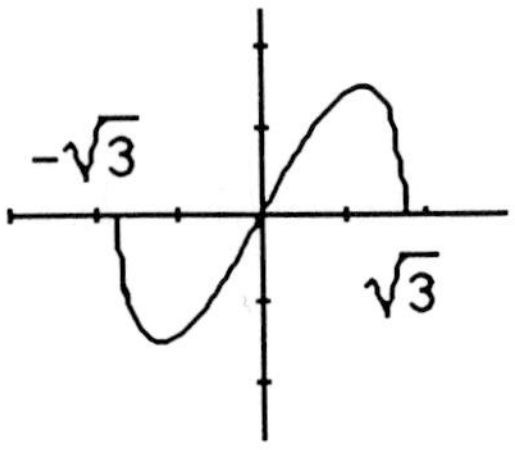

$-\sqrt{3}$

$\sqrt{3}$

(b) $2\int_0^{\sqrt{3}} x\sqrt{3 - x^2}\, dx = -\frac{2}{3}(3 - x^2)^{3/2}\Big]_0^{\sqrt{3}} = 2\sqrt{3}$

20. $\int_0^{2\pi} |\cos x|\, dx = 4\int_0^{\pi/2} \cos x\, dx = 4 \sin x\Big]_0^{\pi/2} = 4$

21. $\int_1^3 \frac{\sin 2x}{x}\, dx = 2\int_1^3 \frac{\sin 2x}{2x} dx = \int_2^6 \frac{\sin u}{u}\, du$, where we let

$u = 2x \Rightarrow \frac{1}{2} du = dx$ and $x = 1 \Rightarrow u = 2$, $x = 3 \Rightarrow u = 6$.

Therefore, $\int_1^3 \frac{\sin 2x}{x}\, dx = F(6) - F(2)$.

22. (a) If f is odd, the graph of f is symmetrical with respect to the origin. Therefore,

$$\int_{-1}^{0} f(x)\,dx = -3 \text{ if } \int_{0}^{1} f(x)\,dx = 3$$

(b) If f is even, the graph of f is symmetrical with respect to the y-axis. Therefore,

$$\int_{-1}^{0} f(x)\,dx = 3 \text{ if } \int_{0}^{1} f(x)\,dx = 3$$

23. (a) Let $F(x) = h(x)\sin x$. Then $F(-x) = h(-x)\sin(-x) = h(x)(-\sin x) = -h(x)\sin x = -F(x)$. Therefore, the function is odd.

(b) Let $u = -x$ so that $dx = -du$, and $x = 0 \Rightarrow u = 0$, $x = -a \Rightarrow u = a$.

Then $\int_{-a}^{0} h(x)\sin x\,dx = -\int_{0}^{a} h(x)\sin x\,dx = \int_{a}^{0} h(-u)\sin(-u)(-du)$

$= \int_{a}^{0} h(u)\sin(u)\,du = -\int_{0}^{a} h(x)\sin x\,dx.$

(c) $\int_{-a}^{a} h(x)\sin x\,dx = \int_{-a}^{0} h(x)\sin x\,dx + \int_{0}^{a} h(x)\sin x\,dx$

$= -\int_{0}^{a} h(x)\sin x\,dx + \int_{0}^{a} h(x)\sin x\,dx = 0.$

(d) $h(x) = \sec x$ is even, $a = \frac{\pi}{4}$, and $-a = -\frac{\pi}{4}$. By part (c)

$$\int_{-\frac{\pi}{4}}^{\frac{\pi}{4}} \sec x \sin x\,dx = 0.$$

24. $\int_{-a}^{a} h(x)\,dx = \int_{-a}^{0} h(x)\,dx + \int_{0}^{a} h(x)\,dx.$

Let $u = -x \Rightarrow du = -dx,\ x = -a \Rightarrow u = a,\ x = 0 \Rightarrow u = 0.$

If h is odd, then $\int_{-a}^{0} h(x)\,dx = \int_{a}^{0} h(-u)(-du) = \int_{a}^{0} -h(u)(-du)$

$= \int_{a}^{0} h(u)\,du = -\int_{0}^{a} h(u)\,du$, so $\int_{-a}^{0} h(x)\,dx + \int_{0}^{a} h(x)\,dx = 0.$

If h is even, then $\int_{-a}^{0} h(x)\,dx = \int_{a}^{0} h(-u)(-du) = \int_{a}^{0} h(u)(-du)$

$= \int_{0}^{a} h(u)\,du$, so $\int_{-a}^{0} h(x)\,dx + \int_{0}^{a} h(x)\,dx = 2\int_{0}^{a} h(x)\,dx.$

25. $\int_{0}^{1} x^2\,dx = \frac{1}{3}x^3\Big]_{0}^{1} = \frac{1}{3}$

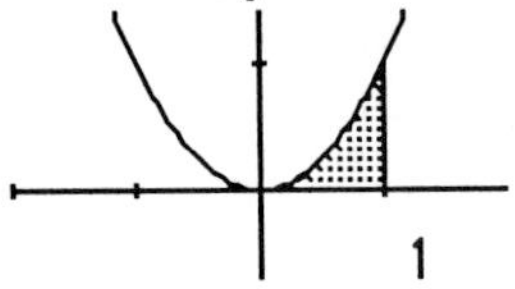

$\int_{-1}^{0} (x+1)^2\,dx = \frac{1}{3}(x+1)^3\Big]_{-1}^{0} = \frac{1}{3}$

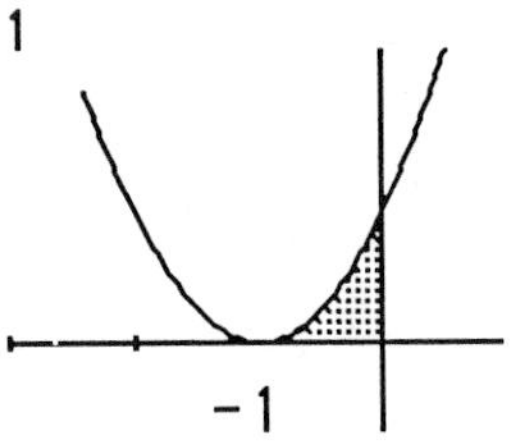

26. $\int_{0}^{\pi} \sin x\,dx = \cos x\Big]_{0}^{\pi} = 2$

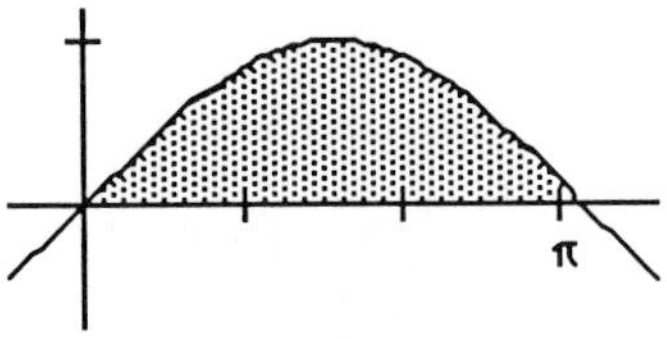

$\int_{-\pi/2}^{\pi/2} \sin\left(x + \frac{\pi}{2}\right)dx =$

$\int_{-\pi/2}^{\pi/2} \cos x\,dx = -\sin x\Big]_{-\pi/2}^{\pi/2} = 2$

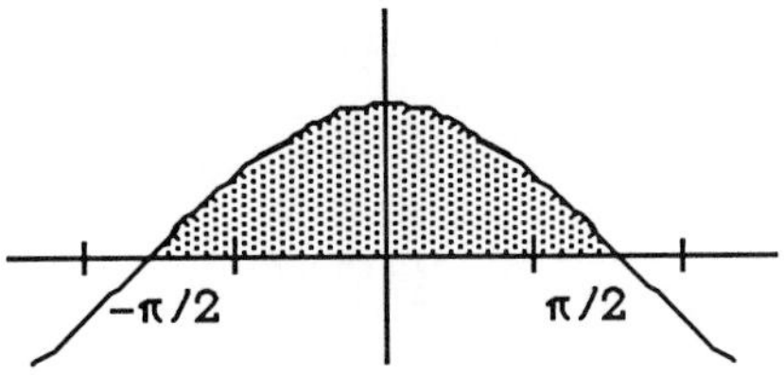

27. $\int_{4}^{8} \sqrt{x-4}\,dx = \frac{2}{3}(x-4)^{\frac{3}{2}}\Big]_{0}^{8} = \frac{16}{3}$

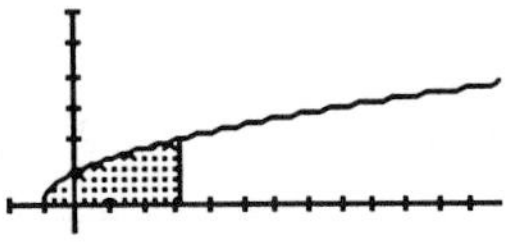

$\int_{-1}^{3} \sqrt{x+1}\,dx = \frac{2}{3}(x+1)^{\frac{3}{2}}\Big]_{-1}^{3} = \frac{16}{3}$

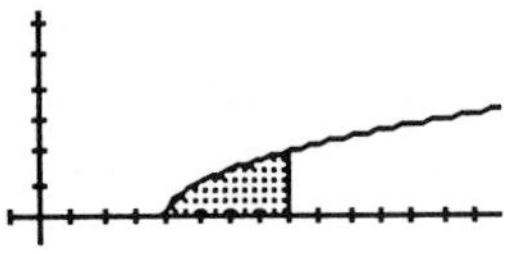

28. Let $u = x + c \Rightarrow du = dx,\ x = a - c \Rightarrow u = a,\ x = b - c \Rightarrow u = b.$

Then $\int_{a-c}^{b-c} f(x+c)\,dx = \int_{a}^{b} f(u)\,du = \int_{a}^{b} f(x)\,dx$

4.9 RULES FOR APPROXIMATING DEFINITE INTEGRALS

1.

i	0	1	2	3	4
x_i	0	0.5	1.0	1.5	2.0
y_i	0	0.5	1.0	1.5	2.0

(a) Trapezoidal Rule: $\frac{2-0}{2\cdot 4}(0 + 2(.5) + 2(1) + 2(1.5) + 2) = 2$

(b) Simpson's Rule: $\frac{2-0}{3\cdot 4}(0 + 4(.5) + 2(1) + 4(1.5) + 2) = 2$

(c) $\int_0^2 x\,dx = \frac{1}{2}x^2\Big]_0^2 = 2$

2.

i	0	1	2	3	4
x_i	0	0.5	1.0	1.5	2.0
y_i	0	0.25	1.0	2.25	4.0

(a) Trapezoidal Rule: $\frac{2-0}{2\cdot 4}(0 + 2(.25) + 2(1) + 2(2.25) + 4) = 2.75$

(b) Simpson's Rule: $\frac{2-0}{3\cdot 4}(0 + 4(.25) + 2(1) + 4(2.25) + 4) = 2.67$

(c) $\int_0^2 x^2\,dx = \frac{1}{3}x^3\Big]_0^2 = \frac{8}{3} \approx 2.67$

3.

i	0	1	2	3	4
x_i	0	0.5	1.0	1.5	2.0
y_i	0	0.125	1.0	3.375	8.0

(a) Trapezoidal Rule: $\frac{2-0}{2\cdot 4}(0 +2(.125) +2(1) +2(3.375) +8) = 4.25$

(b) Simpson's Rule: $\frac{2-0}{3\cdot 4}(0 + 4(.125) + 2(1) + 4(3.375) + 8) = 4$

(c) $\int_0^2 x^3\,dx = \frac{1}{4}x^4\Big]_0^2 = 4$

4.

i	0	1	2	3	4
x_i	1	1.25	1.5	1.75	2.0
y_i	1	0.64	0.44	.327	0.25

(a) Trapezoidal Rule: $\frac{2-1}{2\cdot 4}(1+2(.64)+2(.44)+2(.327)+.25) = 0.51$

(b) Simpson's Rule: $\frac{2-1}{3\cdot 4}(1+ 4(.64)+ 2(.44)+4(.327)+.25) = 0.499$

(c) $\int_1^2 \frac{1}{x^2}\,dx = -\frac{1}{x}\Big]_1^2 = -\frac{1}{2} + 1 = \frac{1}{2}$

5. (a) $\int_0^4 \sqrt{x}\,dx \approx \frac{1}{2}(0 + 2\sqrt{1} + 2\sqrt{2} + 2\sqrt{3} + \sqrt{4}) \approx 5.146$

(b) $\int_0^4 \sqrt{x}\,dx \approx \frac{1}{3}(0 + 4\sqrt{1} + 2\sqrt{2} + 4\sqrt{3} + \sqrt{4}) \approx 5.252$

(c) $\int_0^4 \sqrt{x}\,dx = \frac{2}{3}x^{\frac{3}{2}}\Big]_1^4 = \frac{16}{3}$

6. (a) $\int_0^{\pi} \sin x\,dx \approx \frac{\pi}{8}\left(\sin 0 + 2\sin\frac{\pi}{4} + 2\sin\frac{\pi}{2} + 2\sin\frac{3\pi}{4} + \sin\pi\right) \approx 1.8961$

(b) $\int_0^{\pi} \sin x\,dx \approx \frac{\pi}{12}\left(\sin 0 + 4\sin\frac{\pi}{4} + 2\sin\frac{\pi}{2} + 4\sin\frac{3\pi}{4} + \sin\pi\right) \approx 2.0045$

(c) $\int_0^{\pi} \sin x\,dx = -\cos x\Big]_0^{\pi} = 2$

7. (a) If $f(x) = \frac{1}{x}$, then $f''(x) = 2x^{-3}$ which is a decreasing function on $[1, 2]$. Therefore, $M = 2(1)^{-3} = 2$.

$$E_T \le \frac{b-a}{12}h^2 M = \frac{1}{12}\left(\frac{1}{10}\right)^2(2) = \frac{1}{600} \approx 0.0017$$

(b) $f^{(4)}(x) = 24x^{-5}$ takes its maximum M at $x = 1$.

$$E_S \le \frac{b-a}{180}h^4 M = \left(\frac{1}{180}\right)\left(\frac{1}{10^4}\right)(24) \approx 1.33 \times 10^{-5}.$$

(c) $E_T \le \left(\frac{1}{12}\right)\left(\frac{1}{4}\right)^2(2) = \frac{1}{96} \approx 0.0104$

$$E_S \le \;= \left(\frac{1}{180}\right)\left(\frac{1}{4}\right)^4(24) = \frac{1}{1920} \approx 0.0052$$

8. $f^{(4)}(x) = -\frac{24}{x^4}$ and $\left|-\frac{24}{x^4}\right| \le 24$ for $1 \le x \le 2$.

$$E_S \le \frac{b-a}{180}h^4 M = \frac{1}{180}\left(\frac{1}{n^4}\right)(24) = \frac{2}{15n^4} < 10^{-4} \Leftrightarrow n > 6.04.$$

Hence, $n \ge 8$ (since n must be even).

9. $f''(x) = 0$, so (a) the Trapezoidal Rule is exact for any n, and (b) Simpson's Rule is exact for any even n.

10. (a) $f''(x)=2$. $E_T \le \frac{2}{12}\left(\frac{2}{n}\right)^2(2) = \frac{4}{n^2} < 10^{-4} \Leftrightarrow n > 115.5$.

Hence, $n \ge 116$.

(b) $f^{(4)}(x)=0$, so Simpson's rule is exact for any even n.

11. (a) $\frac{2}{12}\left(\frac{2}{n}\right)^2(12) < 10^{-4} \Leftrightarrow \frac{8}{n^2} < 10^{-4} \Leftrightarrow n^2 > 8 \times 10^4$

$\Leftrightarrow n > 2\sqrt{2} \times 10^2 \approx 282.3$. Therefore, $n \ge 283$.

(b) Simpson's Rule is exact for any even n.

12. (a) $f''(x) = 12x^{-5} \le 12$. $E_T \le \frac{1}{12}\left(\frac{1}{n}\right)^2(12) = \frac{1}{n^2} < 10^{-4} \Leftrightarrow n > 100$.

(b) $f^{(4)}(x) = 360x^{-7} \le 360$. $E_S \le \frac{1}{180}\left(\frac{1}{n}\right)^4(360) = \frac{2}{n^4} < 10^{-4}$

$\Leftrightarrow n > 11.9$. Hence, take $n \ge 12$.

13. (a) $f''(x) = \frac{-1}{4x\sqrt{x}}$ is an increasing function, and $|f''(1)| = \frac{1}{4}$ is maximum.

$E_T \le \frac{3}{12}\left(\frac{3}{n}\right)^2\left(\frac{1}{4}\right) < 10^{-4} \Leftrightarrow \frac{9}{16n^2} < 10^{-4} \Leftrightarrow n > \sqrt{\frac{9}{16} \times 10^4} = 75..$

Hence, any $n \ge 75$.

(b) $|f^{(4)}(x)| = \left|-\frac{15}{16}x^{-\frac{7}{2}}\right| \le \frac{15}{16}$ on [1, 4].

$E_S \le \frac{3}{180}\left(\frac{3}{n}\right)^4\left(\frac{15}{16}\right) < 10^{-4} \Leftrightarrow < n^4 \ge \frac{3645}{2880} \times 10^4 \approx 10.6$.

Hence, any $n \ge 12$ (since n must be even).

14. (a) $|f''(x)| = |-\sin x| \le 1$. $E_T \le \frac{\pi}{12}\left(\frac{\pi}{n}\right)^2 = \frac{\pi^3}{12n^2} < 10^{-4} \Leftrightarrow n > 160.7$.

Hence, take $n \ge 161$.

(b) $|f^{(4)}(x)| = |\sin x| \le 1$. $E_S \le \frac{\pi}{180}\left(\frac{\pi}{n}\right)^4 = \frac{\pi^5}{180n^4} < 10^{-4}$

$\Leftrightarrow n > 11.4$. Hence, take $n \ge 12$.

15. $E_S \le \frac{1}{180}\left(\frac{1}{n^4}\right)(3) \le 10^{-5} \Rightarrow 60\,n^4 \ge 10^5$ or $n > 6$.

16. $S \approx \frac{200}{3}(0 + 4(520) + 2(800) + 4(1000) + 2(1140) + 4(1160)$

$+ 2(1110) + (860) = \frac{200}{3}(14080) \approx 938{,}666.67 \text{ ft}^2.$

$V = (938{,}666.67)(20) = 18{,}773{,}333.33 \text{ ft}^3$. You will start the season with 18,774 fish and plan to have 75% of these, or 14,080, fish, caught during the season. If each person licensed catches 20 fish, then 704 licenses may be sold.

17. $S \approx \frac{1}{3}(1.5 + 4(1.6) + 2(1.8) + 4(1.9) + 2(2.0) + 4(2.1) + 2.1) \approx 11.2 \text{ ft}^2.$

$V = \frac{5000 \text{ lb}}{\frac{42 \text{ lb}}{\text{ft}^3}} = 119.05 \text{ ft}^3.\quad l = \frac{V}{S} = \frac{119.05}{10.6} \approx 10.6 \text{ ft}.$

18. For a No. 22 flashbulb:

$A \approx \frac{5}{2}[4.2 + 2(3) + 2(1.7) + 2(.7) + 2(.35) + 2(.2) + 0] = 40.25$

For a No. 31 flashbulb:

$A \approx \frac{5}{2}[1 + 2(1.2) + 2(1) + 2(.9) + 2(1) + 2(1.1) + 2(1.3)$

$+ 2(1.4) + 2(1.3) + 2(1) + .8] = 55.5$

The No. 31 bulb is more efficient.

19. (a) $E_S \leq \frac{\pi}{180}\left(\frac{\pi}{4}\right)^4 \cdot 1 \approx 0.00664$

(b) $\frac{\pi}{12}\left(\frac{2}{\pi} + \frac{8\sqrt{2}}{\pi} + 2 + \frac{8\sqrt{2}}{\pi} + \frac{2}{\pi}\right) \approx 2.74$

(c) $\frac{.00664}{2.74} \cdot 100 = 0.24\ \%$

4.M MISCELLANEOUS

1. $\frac{dy}{dx} = xy^2 \Rightarrow y^{-2}\,dy = x\,dx \Rightarrow -y^{-1} = \frac{1}{2}x^2 + C \text{ or } y = \frac{-2}{C + x^2}.$

2. $\frac{dy}{dx} = \sqrt{1 + x + y + xy} = \sqrt{1+x}\,\sqrt{1+y} \Rightarrow (1+y)^{-1/2}\,dy = (1+x)^{1/2}dx$

$2(1+y)^{1/2} = \frac{2}{3}(1+x)^{3/2} + C$

3. $\frac{dy}{dx} = \frac{x^2 - 1}{y^2 + 1} \Rightarrow (y^2 + 1)\,dy = (x^2 - 1)\,dx \Rightarrow \frac{1}{3}y^3 + y = \frac{1}{3}x^3 - x + C$

4. $\frac{dy}{dx} = \frac{x - \sqrt{x}}{y\sqrt{y}} \Rightarrow y^{3/2}\,dy = (x - x^{1/2})\,dx \Rightarrow \frac{2}{5}y^{5/2} = \frac{1}{2}x^2 - \frac{2}{3}x^{3/2} + C$

5. $\frac{dr}{ds} = \left(\frac{2+r}{3-s}\right)^2 \Rightarrow (2+r)^{-2}\,dr = (3-s)^{-2}\,ds \Rightarrow \frac{-1}{2+r} = \frac{1}{3-s} + C$

6. $\frac{dr}{ds} = \frac{r^2}{s^2} + r^2 = r^2\left(\frac{1}{s^2} + 1\right) \Rightarrow r^{-2}\,dr = \left(\frac{1}{s^2} + 1\right)ds \Rightarrow -r^{-1} = -s^{-1} + s + C$

7. (a) $\frac{dy}{dx} = x\sqrt{x^2 - 4}$, $y = 3$ when $x = 2$. $y = \frac{1}{3}(x^2 - 4)^{\frac{3}{2}} + C$.

$3 = \frac{1}{3}(0) + C \Rightarrow C = 3$. Therefore $y = \frac{1}{3}(x^2 - 4)^{\frac{3}{2}} + 3$.

(b) $\frac{dy}{dx} = xy^3$, $y = 1$ when $x = 0$. $y^{-3}\,dy = x\,dx \Rightarrow -\frac{1}{2}y^{-2} = \frac{1}{2}x^2 + C$.

$-\frac{1}{2}(1) = 0 + C \Rightarrow C = \frac{1}{2}$. Therefore $-\frac{1}{2y^2} = \frac{1}{2}x^2 - \frac{1}{2}$ or $y = \frac{1}{\sqrt{1 - x^2}}$.

(c) $\frac{dy}{dx} = x^3y^2$, $y = 4$ when $x = 1$. $y^{-2}\,dy = x^3\,dx \Rightarrow -y^{-1} = \frac{1}{4}x^4 + C$.

$-\frac{1}{4} = \frac{1}{4} + C \Rightarrow C = -\frac{1}{2}$. $\therefore$ $-\frac{1}{y} = \frac{x^4}{4} - \frac{1}{2}$ or $y = \frac{4}{2 - x^4}$.

(d) $\sqrt{y + 1}\frac{dy}{dx} = \frac{1}{x^2}$, $y = 3$ when $x = -3$. $\sqrt{y + 1}\,dy = x^{-2}\,dx \Rightarrow$

$\frac{2}{3}(y + 1)^{\frac{3}{2}} = -x^{-1} + C$. $\frac{2}{3}(4)^{\frac{3}{2}} = \frac{1}{3} + C \Rightarrow C + 5$.

$\frac{2}{3}(y + 1)^{\frac{3}{2}} = -\frac{1}{x} + 5$ or $y = \left(\frac{15}{2} - \frac{3}{2x}\right)^{\frac{2}{3}} - 1$.

8. Yes, $f(x) = x$ passes through $(0,0)$, $f'(x) = 1$ and $f''(x) = 0$.

9. $\frac{dy}{dx} = 3x^2 + 2 \Rightarrow y = x^3 + 2x + C$. The point $(1,1)$ belongs to the curve, so $1 = 1 + 2 + C \Rightarrow C = -4$. The equation is $y = 3x^2 + 2x - 4$.

10. $a = -t^2 \Rightarrow v = -\frac{1}{3}t^3 + C_1$, where $v_0 = v(0) = C_1$. Then $x(t) = -\frac{1}{12}t^4 + v_0t + C_2$.

$x(0) = 0 \Rightarrow C_2 = 0$. $x(t) = b$ (a maximum) at the moment when $v(t) = 0$, or when $-\frac{1}{3}t^3 + v_0 = 0$ or $t = (3v_0)^{1/3}$. For this t, $x(t) = b$. Substituting,

$$-\frac{1}{12}[(3v_0)^{1/3}]^4 + v_0(3v_0)^{1/3} = b$$

$$(3)^{4/3}(v_0)^{4/3} - 12(3)^{1/3}(v_0)^{4/3} = -12b$$

$$(v_0)^{4/3}[-9(3)^{1/3}] = -12b$$

$$(v_0)^{4/3} = \frac{4}{3}(3)^{-1/3}b \Rightarrow v_0 = \left[\frac{4}{3}(3)^{-1/3}b\right]^{3/4} = \frac{2\sqrt{2}}{3}b^{3/4}.$$

11. (a) $a = \frac{dv}{dt} = \sqrt{t} - \frac{1}{\sqrt{t}} \Rightarrow v = \frac{2}{3}t^{\frac{3}{2}} - 2t^{\frac{1}{2}} + C$. $v = \frac{4}{3}$ when $t = 0$,

so $C = \frac{4}{3}$. $\therefore v(t) = \sqrt{t} - \frac{1}{\sqrt{t}} + \frac{4}{3}$.

(b) $v = \frac{ds}{dt} = \sqrt{t} - \frac{1}{\sqrt{t}} + \frac{4}{3} \Rightarrow s = \frac{4}{15}t^{\frac{5}{2}} - \frac{4}{3}t^{\frac{3}{2}} + \frac{4}{3}t + C$.

$S = -\frac{4}{15}$ when $t = 0$, so $C = -\frac{4}{15}$ and $s(t) = \frac{4}{15}t^{\frac{5}{2}} - \frac{4}{3}t^{\frac{3}{2}} + \frac{4}{3}t - \frac{4}{15}$.

12. $v(t) = \int (3 + 2t)\, dt = 3t + t^2 + C$. $v(0) = 4 \Rightarrow C = 4$

$s(t) = \int (3t + t^2 + 4)\, dt = \frac{3}{2}t^2 + \frac{1}{3}t^3 + 4t + C$.

$s(4) - s(0) = \left(24 + \frac{64}{3} + 16 + C - C\right) = \frac{184}{3}$

13. We are given $\frac{d^2x}{dt^2} = 4x$. We must express the derivative as a function of x.

Since $a = \frac{dv}{dt} = \frac{dv}{dx} \cdot \frac{dx}{dt} = v \cdot \frac{dv}{dx}$, we may write $v \cdot \frac{dv}{dx} = 4x$ or $v\, dv = 4x\, dx$.

$\therefore \frac{1}{2}v^2 = -2x^2 + C$. $v = 0$ when $x = 5$, so $C = 50$. $\therefore \frac{1}{2}v^2 = -2x^2 + 50$.

$\frac{1}{2}v^2 = -2(3)^2 + 50 \Rightarrow v^2 = 64$ or $v = \pm 8$. Since it is moving left, $v = -8$.

14. $v = \int -32\, dt = -32t + C$. $v(0) = 48 \Rightarrow C = 48$.

$s = \int (-32t + 48)\, dt = -16t^2 + 48t + C$. $s(0) = 0$.

$-16t^2 + 48t = 16 \Leftrightarrow t^2 - 3t + 1 = 0$ or $t \approx .4$ sec

$v(.4) = 35.2$ ft/sec.

15. $\frac{dy}{dx} = x\sqrt{1 + x^2}$, $y = -2$ when $x = 0$. $y = \frac{1}{3}(1 + x^2)^{\frac{3}{2}} + C$.

$-2 = \frac{1}{3} + C \Rightarrow C = -\frac{7}{3}$. $\therefore y = \frac{1}{3}(1 + x^2)^{\frac{3}{2}} - \frac{7}{3}$.

16. $\frac{dy}{dx} = \frac{1}{y\sqrt{x}} + \frac{\sec x \tan x}{y}$, $y = \sqrt{6}$ when $x = 0$

$y\, dy = (x^{-1/2} + \sec x \tan x)\, dx \Rightarrow \frac{1}{2}y^2 = 2\sqrt{x} + \sec x + C$

$\frac{1}{2}(6) = 0 + 1 + C \Rightarrow C = 2$. $\therefore \frac{1}{2}y^2 = 2\sqrt{x} + \sec x + 2$.

17. $\sqrt{x}\, y \frac{dy}{dx} = x + 1$, $y = 2$ when $x = 1$. $y\,dy = (x^{\frac{1}{2}} + x^{-\frac{1}{2}})\,dx \Rightarrow$

$\frac{1}{2}y^2 = \frac{2}{3}x^{\frac{3}{2}} + 2x^{\frac{1}{2}} + C$. $2 = \frac{2}{3} + 2 + C \Rightarrow C = -\frac{2}{3}$. $\frac{1}{2}y^2 = \frac{2}{3}x^{\frac{3}{2}} + 2x^{\frac{1}{2}} - \frac{2}{3}$ or

$y = 2\left(\frac{1}{3}x^{\frac{3}{2}} + x^{\frac{1}{2}} - \frac{1}{3}\right)^{\frac{1}{2}}$.

18. $\frac{du}{dv} = 2u^2(4v^3 + 4v^{-3})$, $u > 0$, $v > 0$, $u = 1$ when $v = 1$.

$u^{-2}\,du = 8(v^{-3} + v^3)\,dv \Rightarrow -u^{-1} = 8\left(-\frac{1}{2}v^{-2} + \frac{1}{4}v^4\right) + C$

$-1 = 8\left(-\frac{1}{2} + \frac{1}{4}\right) + C \Rightarrow C = 1$. $\therefore \frac{1}{u} = \frac{4}{v^2} - 2v^4 - 1$

19. $\frac{dy}{dx} = x\sqrt{9y + x^2 y} \Rightarrow y^{-\frac{1}{2}}\,dy = x\sqrt{9 + x^2}\,dx$ so $2y^{\frac{1}{2}} = \frac{1}{3}(9 + x^2)^{\frac{3}{2}} + C$.

$y = 36$ when $x = 0$ so $12 = \frac{1}{3}(9)^{\frac{3}{2}} + C \Rightarrow C = 3$. $2y^{\frac{1}{2}} = \frac{1}{3}(9 + x^2)^{\frac{3}{2}} + 3$ or

$y = \left(\frac{1}{6}(9 + x^2)^{\frac{3}{2}} + \frac{3}{2}\right)^2$.

20. $\frac{dy}{dx} = 27\csc^2 2y\sqrt{9x + 16}$, $y = 0$ when $x = 1$.

$\sin^2 2y\,dy = 27\sqrt{9x + 16}\,dx \Rightarrow \int\left(\frac{1}{2} - \frac{1}{2}\cos 4y\right)dy = \int 27(9x + 16)^{1/2}\,dx$

$\frac{1}{2}y - \frac{1}{8}\sin 4y = 2(9x + 16)^{3/2} + C$. $0 = 2(25)^{3/2} + C \Rightarrow C = -250$

$\therefore \frac{1}{2}y - \frac{1}{8}\sin 4y = 2(9x + 16)^{3/2} - 250$.

21. $a = -32$ ft/s^2 so $v = -32t + C$. $v_0 = 96$ when $t = 0$ so $C = 96$ and $v = -32t + 96$. It has reached its maximum height when $v = 0$ or $-32t + 96 = 0$ or when $t = 3$ seconds. $s = -16t^2 + 96t + C$. The initial height is 0 because it is thrown from the ground, so $C = 0$. Then $s(3) = -16(3)^2 + 96(3) = 144$ ft.

22. (a) $a = -k \Rightarrow v = -kt + C$. $v(0) = 88 \Rightarrow v = -kt + 88$.

$s = -\frac{1}{2}kt^2 + 88t + C$. $s(0) = 0 \Rightarrow C = 0$. $v = 0$ when $t = \frac{88}{k}$,

and at this moment, $100 = -\frac{1}{2}k\left(\frac{88}{k}\right)^2 + 88\left(\frac{88}{k}\right) \Rightarrow$

$200 = -\frac{1}{k}(88)^2 + \frac{2}{k}(88)^2 = \frac{1}{k}(88)^2$, or $k = 38.72$ ft/s^2.

(b) $a = -38.72 \Rightarrow v = -38.72t + C$. $v(0) = 44 \Rightarrow v = -38.72t + 44$.

$s = -19.36t^2 + 44t + C$. $s(0) = 0 \Rightarrow C = 0$. $v = 0$ when $t = \frac{44}{38.72}$.

$$-19.36\left(\frac{44}{38.72}\right)^2 + 44\left(\frac{44}{38.72}\right) = \frac{44^2}{38.72}\left(\frac{1}{2}\right) = 25 \text{ ft.}$$

23. $a = \frac{dv}{dt} = -K\sqrt{v} \Rightarrow \frac{1}{\sqrt{v}}\,dv = -K\,dt \Rightarrow 2\sqrt{v} = -Kt + C$. $v = 16$ when $t = 0$

so $2\sqrt{16} = C$ or $C = 8$ and $2\sqrt{v} = -Kt + 8$. $V = 0$ when $t = 4 \Rightarrow 0 = -4K + 8$ or

$K = -2$. $\therefore 2\sqrt{v} = -2t + 8$, or $v = (4 - t)^2$.

(a) $v(2) = 4$ ft/s.

(b) $s = \int_0^4 |4 - t|^2\,dt = -\frac{1}{3}(4 - 7)^3\Big]_0^4 = \frac{64}{3}$ ft.

24. $h(x) = f^2(x) + g^2(x) \Rightarrow h'(x) = 2f(x)f'(x) + 2g(x)g'(x)$

Now $f' = g \Rightarrow f'' = g'$. So if $f'' = -f$, then $g' = -f$. Therefore,

$h' = 2f(x)g(x) - 2f(x)g(x) = 0$. Then h is a constant function, and $h(0) = 5 \Rightarrow h(x) = 5$ for all x, so $h(10) = 5$.

25. $$\lim_{n\to\infty} \frac{1^5 + 2^5 + 3^5 + \ldots + n^5}{n^6} = \lim_{n\to\infty}\left[\left(\frac{1}{n}\right)^5 + \left(\frac{2}{n}\right)^5 + \ldots + \left(\frac{n}{n}\right)^5\right]\cdot\frac{1}{n}$$

Take $f(x) = x^5$. Identify $\frac{1}{n}$ with the needed partition of $[0, 1]$

since $\Delta x = \frac{1}{n} = \frac{1-0}{n}$. Since f is increasing on $[0, 1]$, the set

$\left\{\frac{1}{n}, \frac{2}{n}, \ldots, \frac{n}{n}\right\}$ is the set of the right endpoints of the partition.

Then $\sum_{j=1}^{n}\left(\frac{1}{j}\right)^5 \cdot \frac{1}{n}$ is an upper Riemann Sum for $f(x) = x^5$ on $[0, 1]$

and $\lim_{n\to\infty} \sum_{j=1}^{n}\left(\frac{1}{j}\right)^5 \cdot \frac{1}{n} = \int_0^1 x^5\,dx = \frac{1}{6}x^6\Big]_0^1 = \frac{1}{6}$.

26. $\lim_{n\to\infty} \frac{1}{n^4}[1^3 + 2^3 + \ldots + n^3] = \lim_{n\to\infty}\left[\left(\frac{1}{n}\right)^3 + \left(\frac{2}{n}\right)^3 + \ldots + \left(\frac{n}{n}\right)^3\right]\frac{1}{n}$

$$\lim_{n\to\infty} \sum_{j=1}^{n}\left(\frac{1}{j}\right)^3 \cdot \frac{1}{n} = \int_0^1 x^3\, dx = \frac{1}{4}x^4\Big]_0^1 = \frac{1}{4}$$

27. $\lim_{n\to\infty} \frac{1}{n}\left[f\left(\frac{1}{n}\right) + f\left(\frac{2}{n}\right) + \ldots + f\left(\frac{n}{n}\right)\right] = \int_0^1 f(x)\, dx$, where we have identified $\Delta x = \frac{1}{n}$ as the partition of $[0,1]$ into n equal parts.

28. (a) $\lim_{n\to\infty} \frac{1}{n^{16}}[1^{15} + 2^{15} + \ldots + n^{15}] = \int_0^1 x^{15}\, dx = \frac{1}{16}$

(b) $\lim_{n\to\infty} \frac{\sqrt{1} + \sqrt{2} + \sqrt{3} + \ldots + \sqrt{n}}{n^{3/2}} = \int_0^1 \sqrt{x}\, dx = \frac{2}{3}$

(c) $\lim_{n\to\infty} \frac{1}{n}\left[\sin\frac{\pi}{n} + \sin\frac{2\pi}{n} + \ldots + \sin\frac{n\pi}{n}\right] = \int_0^1 \sin \pi x\, dx = \frac{2}{\pi}$

(d) $\lim_{n\to\infty} \frac{1}{n^{17}}[1^{15} + 2^{15} + \ldots + n^{15}] = \left(\lim_{n\to\infty}\frac{1}{n}\right)\int_0^1 x^{15}\, dx = 0$

(e) $\lim_{n\to\infty} \frac{1}{n^{15}}[1^{15} + 2^{15} + \ldots + n^{15}] = \lim_{n\to\infty} \frac{n}{n^{16}}[1^{15} + 2^{15} + \ldots + n^{15}]$

$$= \left(\lim_{n\to\infty} n\right)\int_0^1 x^{15}\, dx = \infty$$

29. (a) The polygon can be divided into n isosceles triangles by joining the vertices to the center of the circle. The vertex angle of each triangle is $\theta_n = \frac{2\pi}{n}$, and the area of the triangle is $A = \frac{1}{2}r^2 \sin\theta_n$.

Then the area of the polygon $A_n = nA = \frac{nr^2}{2}\sin\theta_n$.

(b) Let $x = \frac{\pi}{n}$, so that $x \to 0$ as $n \to \infty$. Then

$$\lim_{n\to\infty} \frac{nr^2}{2}\sin\frac{2\pi}{n} = \lim_{x\to 0}\frac{r^2}{2}\left[\frac{\pi}{x}\sin 2x\right] = \pi r^2 \lim_{x\to 0}\frac{\sin 2x}{2x} = \pi r^2.$$

30. (a) We wish to show that $S_n^{(2)} = \sum_{j=1}^{n} \frac{j(j+1)}{2} = \frac{n(n+1)(n+2)}{2 \cdot 3}$.

If n = 1, then $\frac{1(1+1)}{2} = \frac{1(1+1)(1+2)}{2 \cdot 3}$, or 1 = 1.

$$\sum_{j=1}^{n+1} \frac{j(j+1)}{2} = \sum_{j=1}^{n} \frac{j(j+1)}{2} + \frac{(n+1)(n+2)}{2}$$

$$= \frac{n(n+1)(n+2)}{2 \cdot 3} + \frac{(n+1)(n+2)}{2}$$

$$= \frac{n(n+1)(n+2)}{2 \cdot 3} + \frac{3(n+1)(n+2)}{2 \cdot 3}$$

$$= \frac{(n+1)(n+2)(n+3)}{2 \cdot 3}$$

(b) We wish to show that $S_n^{(3)} = \sum_{j=1}^{n} \frac{j(j+1)(j+2)}{2 \cdot 3} = \frac{n(n+1)(n+2)(n+3)}{2 \cdot 3 \cdot 4}$.

If n = 1, then $\frac{1(1+1)(1+2)}{2 \cdot 3} = \frac{1(1+1)(1+2)(1+3)}{2 \cdot 3 \cdot 4}$, or 1 = 1.

$$\sum_{j=1}^{n+1} \frac{j(j+1)(j+2)}{2 \cdot 3} = \sum_{j=1}^{n} \frac{j(j+1)(j+2)}{2 \cdot 3} + \frac{(n+1)(n+2)(n+3)}{2 \cdot 3}$$

$$= \frac{n(n+1)(n+2)(n+3)}{2 \cdot 3 \cdot 4} + \frac{(n+1)(n+2)(n+3)}{2 \cdot 3}$$

$$= \frac{n(n+1)(n+2)(n+3)}{2 \cdot 3 \cdot 4} + \frac{4(n+1)(n+2)(n+3)}{2 \cdot 3 \cdot 4}$$

$$= \frac{(n+1)(n+2)(n+3)(n+4)}{2 \cdot 3 \cdot 4}$$

(c) $S_n^{(k)} = \frac{n(n+1)(n+2) \cdot \ldots \cdot (n+k)}{2 \cdot 3 \cdot \ldots \cdot (k+1)}$

31. $\int_0^{\pi} \cos 4x \sin 4x \, dx = -\frac{1}{8} \cos^2 4x \Big]_0^{\pi} = 0$

32. $\int_1^4 \frac{dt}{t\sqrt{2t}} = \frac{1}{\sqrt{2}} \int_1^4 t^{-3/2} \, dt = \frac{1}{\sqrt{2}}(-2 t^{-1/2}) \Big]_1^4 = -\sqrt{2}\left(\frac{1}{2} - 1\right) = \frac{\sqrt{2}}{2}$

33. $\int_{-1}^{0} \frac{12 \, dx}{(2-3x)^2} = 4(2-3x)^{-1} \Big]_{-1}^{0} = \frac{6}{5}$

34. $\int_{-1}^{1} x \cos(1-x^2) \, dx = -\frac{1}{2} \sin(1-x^2) \Big]_{-1}^{1} = 0$

35. $\int_0^{\frac{\pi}{2}} \frac{\sin x \cos x\, dx}{\sqrt{1+3\sin^2 x}} = \frac{1}{3}(1+3\sin^2 x)^{\frac{1}{2}}\Big]_0^{\frac{\pi}{2}} = \frac{1}{3}$

36. $\int_1^2 \frac{x^3+1}{x^2}\, dx = \int_1^2 (x + x^{-2})\, dx = \frac{1}{2}x^2 - \frac{1}{x}\Big]_1^2 = 2$

37. $\int_{-\frac{\pi}{2}}^{\frac{\pi}{2}} 15\sin^4 3x \cos 3x\, dx = \sin^5 3x\Big]_{-\frac{\pi}{2}}^{\frac{\pi}{2}} = -2$

38. $\int_1^4 \frac{(1+\sqrt{u})^{1/2}}{\sqrt{u}}\, du = \frac{4}{3}(1+\sqrt{u})^{3/2}\Big]_1^4 = \frac{4}{3}[3^{3/2} - 2^{3/2}]$

39. $\int_0^1 \frac{dr}{\sqrt[3]{(7-5r)^2}} = -\frac{3}{5}(7-5r)^{1/3}\Big]_0^1 = \frac{3}{5}(7^{1/3} - 2^{1/3})$

40. $\int_0^1 t^{1/3}(1+t^{4/3})^{-7}\, dt = -\frac{1}{8}(1+t^{4/3})^{-6}\Big]_0^1 = \frac{63}{512}$

41. $\int_0^1 \pi x^2 \sec^2\left(\frac{\pi x^3}{3}\right) dx = \tan \frac{\pi x^3}{3}\Big]_0^1 = \sqrt{3}$

42. $\int_0^{\frac{\pi}{4}} \cot^2\left(x+\frac{\pi}{4}\right)dx = \int_0^{\frac{\pi}{4}}\left[\csc^2\left(x+\frac{\pi}{4}\right) - 1\right]dx = -\cot\left(x+\frac{\pi}{4}\right) - x\Big]_0^{\frac{\pi}{4}} = 1 - \frac{\pi}{4}$

43. $\int_{-1}^3 f(x)\, dx = \int_{-1}^2 (3-x)\, dx + \int_2^3 \frac{x}{2}\, dx = 3x - \frac{1}{2}x^2\Big]_{-1}^2 + \frac{x^2}{4}\Big]_2^3 = \frac{35}{4}$

44. If $A(b) = \int_1^b f(x)\, dx = \sqrt{b^2+1} + \sqrt{2}$, Then $A'(b) = f(b)$.

So $f(b) = \frac{1}{2}(b^2+1)^{-1/2}(2b)$, or $f(x) = \frac{x}{\sqrt{x^2+1}}$.

45. (a) Let $F(x) = \int_0^x \frac{du}{u+\sqrt{u^2+1}}$. Then $F'(x) = \lim_{h\to 0}\frac{F(x+h)-F(x)}{h} =$

$$\lim_{h\to 0}\frac{\int_0^{x+h}\frac{du}{u+\sqrt{u^2+1}} - \int_0^x \frac{du}{u+\sqrt{u^2+1}}}{h} = \lim_{h\to 0}\frac{1}{h}\int_x^{x+h}\frac{du}{u+\sqrt{u^2+1}}$$

$= \frac{1}{1+\sqrt{x^2+1}}$ by the Fundamental Theorem for Calculus.

(b) If $F(x) = \int_a^x f(t)\,dt$, then $F'(2) = \lim_{x\to 2} \frac{f(x) - f(2)}{x - 2} =$

$$\lim_{x\to 2} \frac{\int_a^x f(t)\,dt - \int_a^2 f(t)\,dt}{x - 2} = \lim_{x\to 2} \frac{1}{x - 2} \int_2^x f(t)\,dt.$$

$$\therefore \lim_{x\to 2} \frac{x}{x - 2} \int_2^x f(t)\,dt = \lim_{x\to 2} x \cdot \lim_{x\to 2} \frac{x}{x - 2} \int_2^x f(t)\,dt = 2F'(2) = 2f(2).$$

(In this problem, we must assume that f is continuous)

46. If $x = \int_0^y \frac{1}{\sqrt{1 + 4t^2}}\,dt$, then $\frac{d}{dx}(x) = \frac{d}{dx}\left[\int_0^y \frac{1}{\sqrt{1 + 4t^2}}\,dt\right]$.

Thus $1 = \frac{1}{\sqrt{1 + 4y^2}} \cdot \frac{dy}{dx} \Rightarrow \frac{dy}{dx} = \sqrt{1 + 4y^2}$.

Then $\frac{d^2y}{dx^2} = \frac{1}{2}(1 + 4y^2)^{-1/2}\left(8y\,\frac{dy}{dx}\right) = 4y\left(\frac{1}{\sqrt{1 + 4y^2}}\right)\sqrt{1 + 4y^2}$.

Thus $\frac{d^2y}{dx^2} = 4y$, and the constant is 4.

47. The derivative of the left side of the equation is:

$$\frac{d}{dx}\int_0^x \left[\int_0^u f(t)\,dt\right] = \int_0^x f(t)\,dt.$$

The derivative of the right side of the equation is:

$$\frac{d}{dx}\left[\int_0^x f(u)\,(x - u)\,du\right] = \frac{d}{dx}\int_0^x x\,f(u)\,du - \frac{d}{dx}\int_0^x u\,f(u)\,du$$

$$= x\,\frac{d}{dx}\int_0^x f(u)\,du + \int_0^x f(u)\,du\,\frac{d}{dx}(x) - x\,f(x)$$

$$= x\,f(x) + \int_0^x f(u)\,du - x\,f(x) = \int_0^x f(u)\,du.$$

Since each side has the same derivative, they differ from each other by at most a constant. Since both sides equal zero when $x = 0$, the constant must be zero.

48. $y(x) = \frac{1}{a}\int_0^x f(t)\sin a(x-t)dt$. Using the hint,

$$y(x) = \frac{\sin ax}{a}\int_0^x f(t)\cos at\,dt - \frac{\cos ax}{a}\int_0^x f(t)\sin at\,dt$$

$$\frac{dy}{dx} = \cos ax\int_0^x f(t)\cos at\,dt + \frac{f(x)\sin ax\cos ax}{a} + \sin ax\int_0^x f(t)\sin at\,dt - \frac{f(x)\sin ax\cos ax}{a}$$

$$= \cos ax\int_0^x f(t)\cos at\,dt + \sin ax\int_0^x f(t)\sin at\,dt$$

$$\frac{d^2y}{dx^2} = -a\sin ax\int_0^x f(t)\cos at\,dt + f(x)\cos^2 ax + a\cos ax\int_0^x f(t)\sin at\,dt + f(x)\sin^2 ax$$

$$= -a\sin ax\int_0^x f(t)\cos at\,dt + a\cos ax\int_0^x f(t)\sin at\,dt + f(x)$$

It is now clear that $y'' + a^2 y = f(x)$.

49. $S \approx \frac{15}{3}(0 + 4(36) + 2(54) + 4(51) + 2(49.5) + 4(54)\ 2(64.4) + 4(67.5) + 42)$

$= 6{,}059\ \text{ft}^2$. The cost is then $(2.10)(6{,}059) = \$12{,}723.90$. No, the job cannot be done for \$11,000.

50. (a) $\text{erf}(1) \approx \frac{2}{30\sqrt{\pi}}(e^0 + 4e^{-.01} + 2e^{-.04} + .. + 4e^{-.81} + e^{-1}) \approx 0.844$

(b) $E_S \le \frac{1}{180}(.1)^4(12) \approx 6.7 \times 10^{-6}$

CHAPTER 5

APPLICATIONS OF DEFINITE INTEGRALS

5.1 DISTANCE TRAVELED BY A MOVING BODY

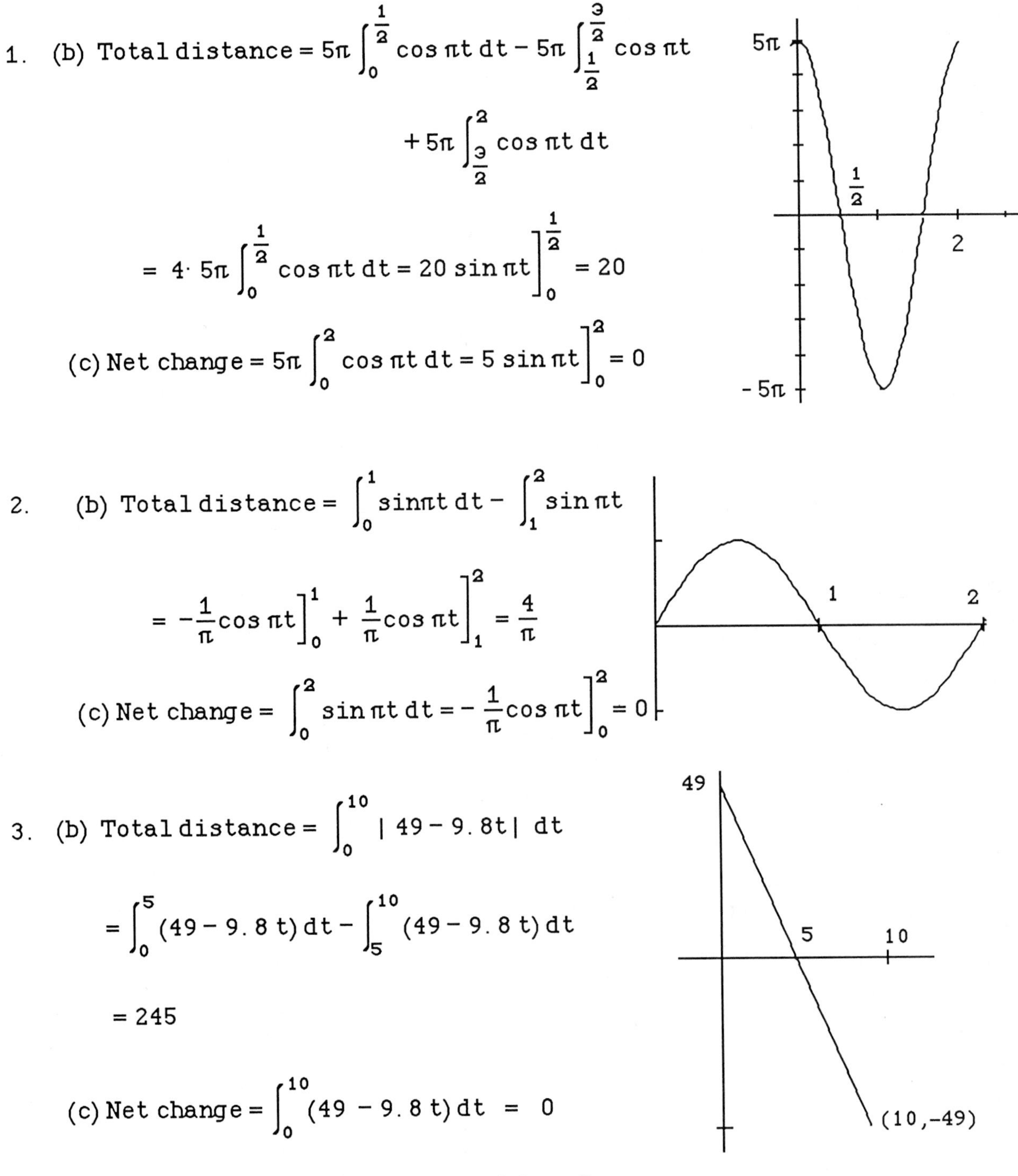

1. (b) $\text{Total distance} = 5\pi \int_0^{\frac{1}{2}} \cos \pi t \, dt - 5\pi \int_{\frac{1}{2}}^{\frac{3}{2}} \cos \pi t + 5\pi \int_{\frac{3}{2}}^{2} \cos \pi t \, dt$

$$= 4 \cdot 5\pi \int_0^{\frac{1}{2}} \cos \pi t \, dt = 20 \sin \pi t \Big]_0^{\frac{1}{2}} = 20$$

(c) $\text{Net change} = 5\pi \int_0^2 \cos \pi t \, dt = 5 \sin \pi t \Big]_0^2 = 0$

2. (b) $\text{Total distance} = \int_0^1 \sin \pi t \, dt - \int_1^2 \sin \pi t$

$$= -\frac{1}{\pi} \cos \pi t \Big]_0^1 + \frac{1}{\pi} \cos \pi t \Big]_1^2 = \frac{4}{\pi}$$

(c) $\text{Net change} = \int_0^2 \sin \pi t \, dt = -\frac{1}{\pi} \cos \pi t \Big]_0^2 = 0$

3. (b) $\text{Total distance} = \int_0^{10} |\, 49 - 9.8t \,| \, dt$

$$= \int_0^5 (49 - 9.8\,t) \, dt - \int_5^{10} (49 - 9.8\,t) \, dt$$

$$= 245$$

(c) $\text{Net change} = \int_0^{10} (49 - 9.8\,t) \, dt = 0$

4. (a) Graph is similar to Problem 3.

(b) Total distance $= \int_0^{10} |8 - 1.6t|\, dt$

$$= \int_0^{5} (8 - 1.6t)\, dt - \int_5^{10} (8 - 1.6t)\, dt = 40$$

(c) Net change $= \int_0^{10} (8 - 1.6t)\, dt = 0$

5. (b) Total distance $= \int_0^{2} |6(t-1)(t-2)|\, dt$

$$= \int_0^{1} 6(t-1)(t-2)\, dt - \int_1^{2} 6(t-1)(t-2)\, dt$$

$$= 2t^3 - 9t^2 + 12t\Big]_0^1 - (2t^3 - 9t^2 + 12t)\Big]_1^2$$

$= 6$ m.

(c) Net change $= \int_0^{2} 6(t-1)(t-2)\, dt$

$$= 2t^3 - 9t^2 + 12t\Big]_0^2$$

$= 4$ m.

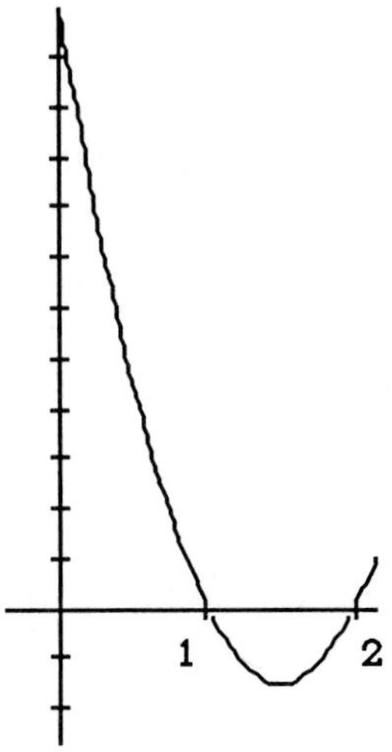

6. (b) Total distance $= \int_0^{3} |6(t-1)(t-2)|\, dt$

$$= 2\int_0^{1} 6(t-1)(t-2)\, dt - \int_1^{2} 6(t-1)(t-2)\, dt =$$

$$2(2t^3 - 9t^2 + 12t\Big]_0^1 - (2t^3 - 9t^2 + 12t)\Big]_1^2$$

$= 11$ m.

(c) Net change $= \int_0^{3} 6(t-1)(t-2)\, dt$

$$= 2t^3 - 9t^2 + 12t\Big]_0^2$$

$= 10$ m.

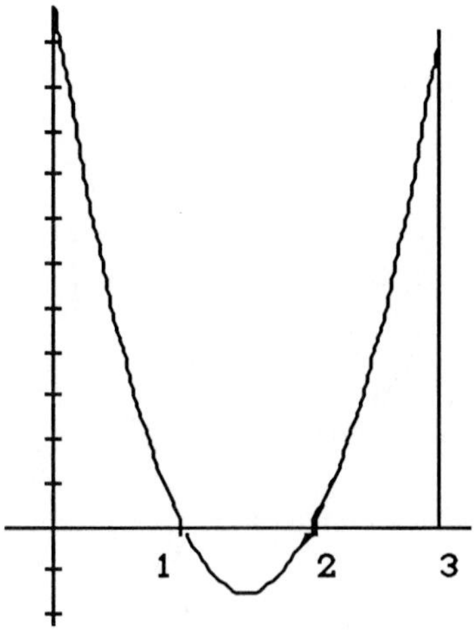

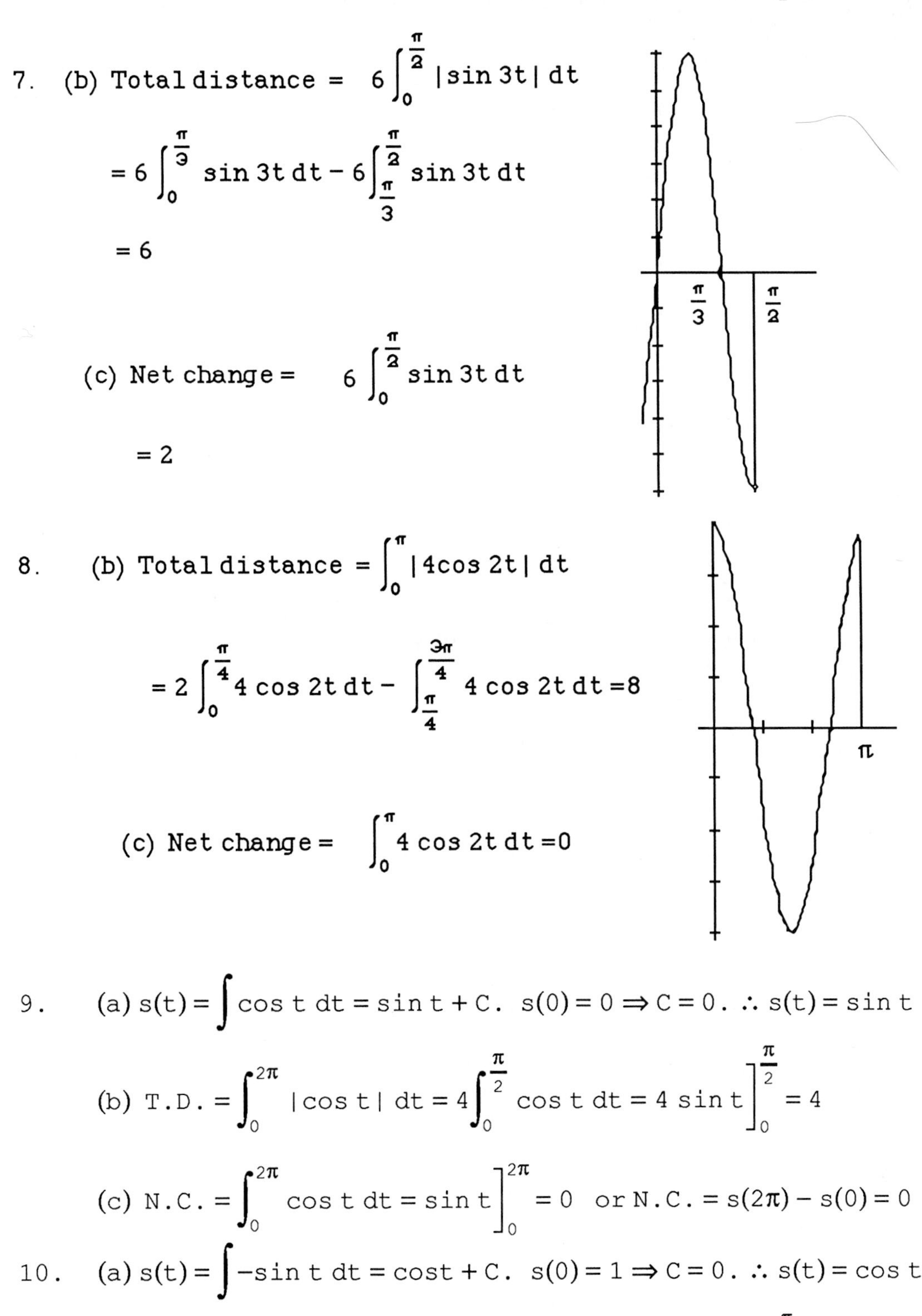

7. (b) Total distance $= 6\int_0^{\frac{\pi}{2}} |\sin 3t|\, dt$

$$= 6\int_0^{\frac{\pi}{3}} \sin 3t\, dt - 6\int_{\frac{\pi}{3}}^{\frac{\pi}{2}} \sin 3t\, dt$$

$$= 6$$

(c) Net change $= 6\int_0^{\frac{\pi}{2}} \sin 3t\, dt$

$$= 2$$

8. (b) Total distance $= \int_0^{\pi} |4\cos 2t|\, dt$

$$= 2\int_0^{\frac{\pi}{4}} 4\cos 2t\, dt - \int_{\frac{\pi}{4}}^{\frac{3\pi}{4}} 4\cos 2t\, dt = 8$$

(c) Net change $= \int_0^{\pi} 4\cos 2t\, dt = 0$

9. (a) $s(t) = \int \cos t\, dt = \sin t + C.\ \ s(0) = 0 \Rightarrow C = 0.\ \therefore s(t) = \sin t$

(b) $\text{T.D.} = \int_0^{2\pi} |\cos t|\, dt = 4\int_0^{\frac{\pi}{2}} \cos t\, dt = 4\sin t\Big]_0^{\frac{\pi}{2}} = 4$

(c) $\text{N.C.} = \int_0^{2\pi} \cos t\, dt = \sin t\Big]_0^{2\pi} = 0$ or $\text{N.C.} = s(2\pi) - s(0) = 0$

10. (a) $s(t) = \int -\sin t\, dt = \cos t + C.\ \ s(0) = 1 \Rightarrow C = 0.\ \therefore s(t) = \cos t$

(b) $\text{T.D.} = \int_0^{2\pi} |-\sin t|\, dt = 4\int_0^{\frac{\pi}{2}} \sin t\, dt = -4\cos t\Big]_0^{\frac{\pi}{2}} = 4$

(c) $\text{N.C.} = \int_0^{2\pi} -\sin t\, dt = \cos t\Big]_0^{2\pi} = 0$ or $\text{N.C.} = s(2\pi) - s(0) = 0$

11. (a) $s(t)=\int 5\pi \cos \pi t\, dt = 5 \sin \pi t + C$. $s(0)=5 \Rightarrow C=5$. $\therefore s(t)=5 \sin \pi t + 5$

(b) $T.D. = \int_0^{\frac{3}{2}} |5\pi \cos \pi t|\, dt = 5\pi \int_0^{\frac{1}{2}} \cos \pi t\, dt - 5\pi \int_{\frac{1}{2}}^{\frac{3}{2}} \cos \pi t\, dt = 15$

(c) $N.C. = \int_0^{\frac{3}{2}} 5\pi \cos \pi t\, dt = -5$ or $N.C. = s\left(\frac{3}{2}\right) - s(0) = -5$

12. (a) $s(t)=\int \sin \pi t\, dt = -\frac{1}{\pi}\cos \pi t + C$. $s(0)=0 \Rightarrow C=\frac{1}{\pi}$. $\therefore s(t) = -\frac{1}{\pi}\cos \pi t + \frac{1}{\pi}$

(b) $T.D. = \int_0^{\frac{3}{2}} |\sin \pi t|\, dt = 3\int_0^{\frac{1}{2}} \sin \pi t\, dt = -\frac{3}{\pi} \cos \pi t \Big]_0^{\frac{1}{2}} = \frac{3}{\pi}$

(c) $N.C. = \int_0^{\frac{3}{2}} \sin \pi t\, dt = -\frac{1}{\pi}\cos \pi t \Big]_0^{\frac{3}{2}} = \frac{1}{\pi}$ or $N.C. = s\left(\frac{3}{2}\right) - s(0) = \frac{1}{\pi}$

13. $a=-4\pi^2 \cos 2\pi t$, $v(0)=2$

$v=\int -4\pi^2 \cos 2\pi t\, dt = -2\pi \sin 2\pi t + C$. $v(0)=2 \Rightarrow C=2$.

$v(t) = -2\pi \sin 2\pi t + 2$

$N.C. = \int_0^2 (-2\pi \sin 2\pi t + 2)\, dt = 4$

14. $a = 9.8 + \sin \pi t$, $v(0)=0$

$v=\int (9.8 + \sin \pi t)\, dt = 9.8t - \frac{1}{\pi}\cos \pi t + C$. $v(0)=0 \Rightarrow C=\frac{1}{\pi}$

$v(t) = 9.8t - \frac{1}{\pi}\cos \pi t + \frac{1}{\pi}$

$N.C. = \int_0^2 \left(9.8t - \frac{1}{\pi}\cos \pi t + \frac{1}{\pi}\right) dt = 4.9t^2 - \frac{1}{\pi^2}\sin \pi t + \frac{t}{\pi}\Big]_0^2 = 19.6 + \frac{2}{\pi}$

15. $a=g$, $v(0)=0 \Rightarrow v = gt + C$. $v(0)=0 \Rightarrow C=0$ and $v(t) = gt$

$N.C. = \int_0^2 gt\, dt = \frac{1}{2}gt^2\Big]_0^2 = 2g$

16. $a = \sqrt{4t+1}$, $v(0) = -\frac{13}{3}$. $v = \int \sqrt{4t+1}\, dt$

$= \frac{1}{6}(4t+1)^{3/2} + C$. $v(0) = -\frac{13}{3} \Rightarrow C = -\frac{9}{2}$ $\therefore v(t) = \frac{1}{6}(4t+1)^{3/2} - \frac{9}{2}$

$\frac{1}{6}(4t+1)^{3/2} < \frac{9}{2} \Leftrightarrow (4t+1)^{3/2} < 27 \Leftrightarrow 4t+1 < 9 \Leftrightarrow t < 2$

$N.C. = \int_0^2 \left(\frac{9}{2} - \frac{1}{6}(4t+1)^{3/2}\right) dt = \frac{9}{2}t - \frac{1}{60}(4t+1)^{5/2}\Big]_0^2 = \frac{149}{30}$

17. (a) Total distance = 2; net change = 2

(b) Total distance = 4; net change = 0

(c) Total distance = 4; net change = 4

(d) Total distance = 2; net change = 2

18. $$\frac{120}{3\cdot 12}[0+4(32)+2(51)+4(57)+2(54)+4(64)+2(66)+4(66)$$
$$+2(66)+4(58)+2(40)+4(5)+0]=\frac{10}{3}(1682)=5606.6$$

$$\therefore \int_0^{120}[v(t)\ \text{m/hr}]\cdot\frac{1\text{hr}}{3600\text{ s}}\,dt \approx 1.56 \text{ miles}.$$

By the graph in Fig 1.80, the total distance ≈ 1.6 miles.

5.2 AREAS BETWEEN CURVES

1. The region is bounded by $y=x^2-2$ and $y=2$. The limits are where $x^2-2=2 \Leftrightarrow x=\pm 2$. Using symmetry, we have that

$$A=2\int_0^2[2-(x^2-2)]\,dx=2\int_0^2(-x^2+4)dx=-\frac{1}{3}x^3+4x\Big]=\frac{32}{3}$$

2. The region is bounded by $y=2x-x^2$ and $y=0$.
The limits are where $2x-x^2=0 \Leftrightarrow x=0, 2$.

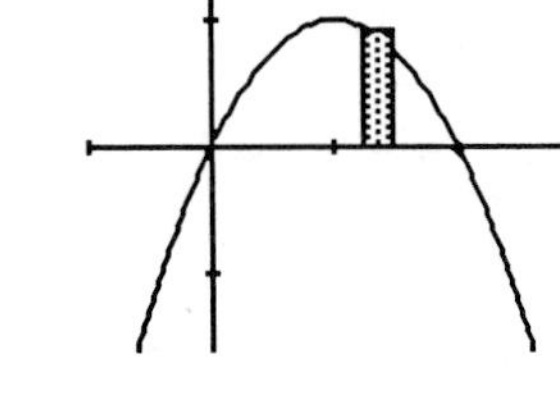

The area is:

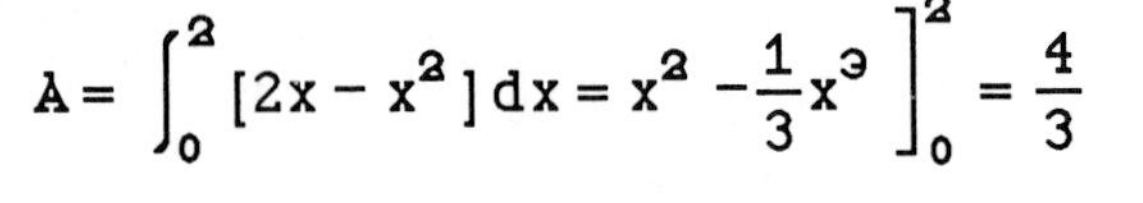

$$A=\int_0^2[2x-x^2]\,dx=x^2-\frac{1}{3}x^3\Big]_0^2=\frac{4}{3}$$

3. The region is bounded by $x=y^2-y^3$ and the y-axis.
The limits are the points where the graph crosses the y-axis: $y^2(1-y)=0 \Leftrightarrow y=0, 1$. Then

$$A=\int_0^1(y^2-y^3)\,dy=\frac{1}{3}y^3-\frac{1}{4}y^4\Big]=\frac{1}{12}$$

4. The region is bounded by $y^2=x$ and $x=4$.
The limits are where $y^2=4 \Leftrightarrow y=\pm 2$.

Using symmetry, the area is:

$$A=2\int_0^2[4-x]\,dy=2\int_0^2[4-y^2]\,dy=2\left(4y-\frac{1}{3}y^3\right]_0^2=\frac{32}{3}$$

5. The region is bounded by $y = 2x - x^2$ and $y = -3$.

They intersect where $2x - x^2 = -3$ or $x = 3, -1$.

The area is:

$$A = \int_{-1}^{3} [(2x - x^2) - (-3)]\,dx = x^2 - \frac{1}{3}x^3 + 3x \Big]_{-1}^{3} = \frac{32}{3}$$

6. The region is bounded by $y = x^2$ and $y = x$.

The limits are where $x^2 = x \Leftrightarrow x = 0, 1$.

The area is:

$$A = \int_0^1 (x - x^2)\,dx = \frac{1}{2}x^2 - \frac{1}{3}x^3 \Big]_0^1 = \frac{1}{6}$$

7. The region is bounded by $x = 3y - y^2$ and $x + y = 3$. They intersect where $3y - y^2 = 3 - y$ or $y = 3, 1$. The area is:

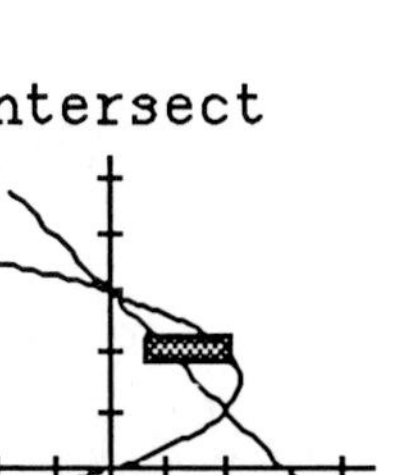

$$A = \int_1^2 [(3y - y^2) - (3 - y)]\,dy = 2y^2 - \frac{1}{3}y^3 - 3y \Big]_1^2 = \frac{4}{3}$$

8. The region is bounded by $y = x^4 - 2x^2$ and $y = 2x^2$.

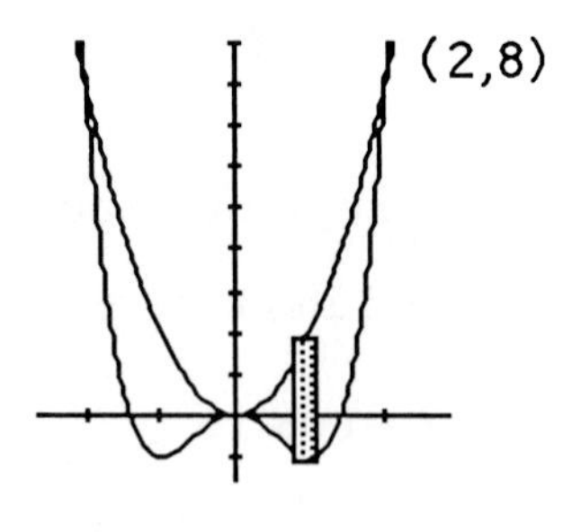

The limits are where $x^4 - 2x^2 = 2x^2 \Leftrightarrow x = 0, \pm 2$

Using symmetry, the area is:

$$A = 2\int_0^2 [2x^2 - (x^4 - 2x^2)]\,dx = 2\left(\frac{4}{3}x^3 - \frac{1}{5}x^5\right)\Big]_0^2 = \frac{128}{15}$$

9. The region is bounded by $x = y^2$ and $x = y + 2$.

They intersect where $y^2 - y - 2 = 0$ or $y = 2, -1$.

The area is:

$$A = \int_{-1}^{2} [(y + 2) - y^2]\,dy = \frac{1}{2}y^2 + 2y - \frac{1}{3}y^3 \Big]_{-1}^{2} = \frac{9}{2}$$

10. The region is bounded by $y = x^4$ and $y = 8x$.

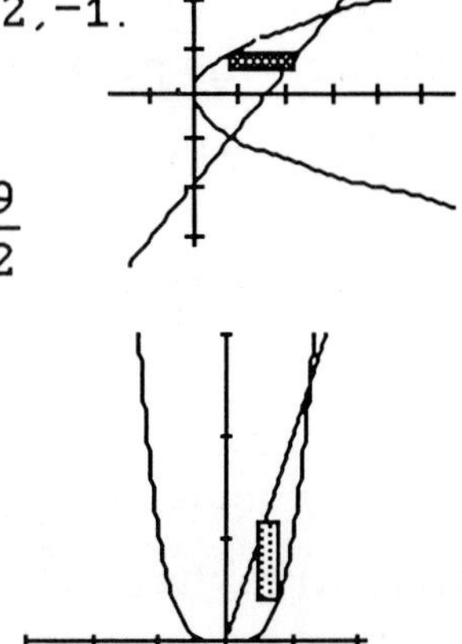

The limits are where $x^4 - 8x = 0 \Leftrightarrow x = 0, 2$

The area is:

$$A = \int_0^2 (8x - x^4)\,dx = 4x^2 - \frac{1}{5}x^5 \Big]_0^2 = \frac{48}{5}$$

11. The region is bounded by $x = y^3$ and $x = y^2$. They intersect where $y^3 = y^2 \Rightarrow y^3 - y^2 = 0$
$\Rightarrow y^2(y-1) = 0$ or $y = 0, 1$.
The area is:

$$A = \int_0^1 (y^3 - y^2)\,dy = \frac{1}{4}y^4 - \frac{1}{3}y^3\Big]_0^1 = \frac{1}{12}$$

12. The region is bounded by $y^3 = x$ and $y = x$.
The limits are where $y^3 - y = 0 \Leftrightarrow y = 0, \pm 1$

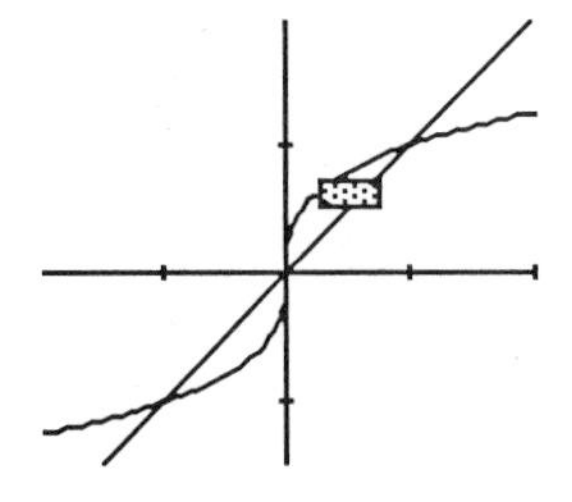

Using symmetry, the area is:

$$A = 2\int_0^1 (y - y^3)\,dy = 2\left(\frac{1}{2}y^2 - \frac{1}{4}y^4\right]_0^1 = \frac{1}{2}$$

13. The region is bounded by $y = x^2 - 2x$ and $y = x$.

They intersect where $x^2 - 2x = x$ or $x = 0, 3$.

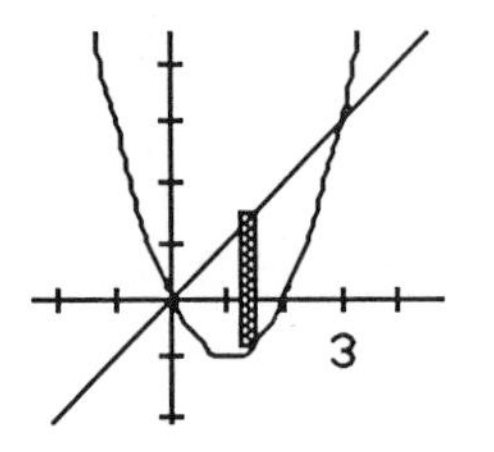

The area is:

$$A = \int_0^3 [x - (x^2 - 2x)]\,dx = \frac{3}{2}x^2 - \frac{1}{3}x^3\Big]_0^3 = \frac{9}{2}$$

14. The region is bounded by $x = 10 - y^2$ and $x = 1$.
The limits are where $10 - y^2 = 1 \Leftrightarrow y = \pm 3$

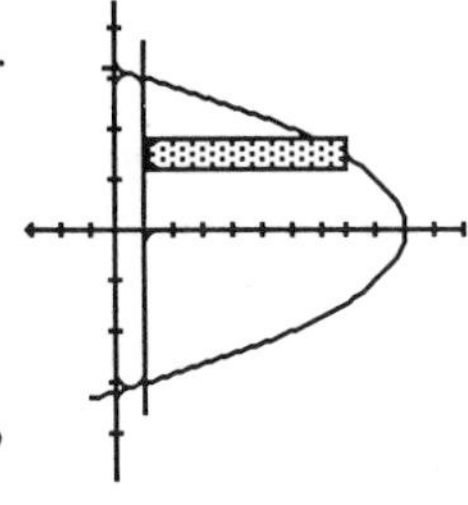

Using symmetry, the area is:

$$A = 2\int_0^3 [(10 - y^2) - 1]\,dy = 2\left(9y - \frac{1}{3}y^3\right]_0^3 = 36$$

15. The region is bounded by $x = -2y^2 + 3$ and $x = y^2$. They intersect where

$-2y^2 + 3 = y^2$ or $y = \pm 1$. Using symmetry,

$$A = 2\int_0^1 [(-2y^2 + 3) - y^2]\,dy = 2\left[-\frac{2}{3}y^3 + 3y - \frac{1}{2}y^2\right]_0^1 = 4.$$

16. The region is bounded by $y = x^2$ and $y = -x^2 + 4x$.
The limits are where $x^2 = -x^2 + 4x \Leftrightarrow x = 0, 2$
The area is:

$$A = \int_0^2 [(-x^2 + 4x) - x^2]\,dx = 2x^2 - \frac{2}{3}x^3\Big]_0^2 = \frac{8}{3}$$

17. The region is bounded by $y = x$ and $y = 2 - (x-2)^2$.

They intersect where $2 - (x-2)^2 = x$ or $x = 1, 2$.

The area is:

$$A = \int_1^2 ([2 - (x-2)^2] - x)\,dx = -\frac{1}{3}x^3 + \frac{3}{2}x^2 - 2x\Big]_1^2 = \frac{1}{6}$$

18. The region is bounded by $y = 7 - 2x^2$ and $y = x^2 + 4$.

The limits are where $7 - 2x^2 = x^2 + 4 \Leftrightarrow x = \pm 1$.

Using symmetry, the area is:

$$A = 2\int_0^1 [(7 - 2x^2) - (x^2 + 4)]\,dx = 2\left(3x - x^3\right)\Big]_0^1 = 4$$

19. The region is bounded by $y = 4 - 4x^2$ and $y = x^4 - 1$.

They intersect where $4 - 4x^2 = x^4 - 1$

or $x^4 + 4x^2 - 5 = 0 \Leftrightarrow x = \pm 1$. Using symmetry,

$$A = 2\int_0^1 [(4 - 4x^2) - (x^4 - 1)]\,dx = 2\left[5x - \frac{4}{3}x^3 - \frac{1}{5}x^5\right]_0^1 = \frac{104}{15}$$

20. The region is bounded by $y = \frac{1}{4}x^2$ and $y = \frac{1}{16}x^4$.

The limits are where $\frac{1}{4}x^2 = \frac{1}{16}x^4 \Leftrightarrow x = 0, \pm 2$.

Using symmetry, the area is:

$$A = 2\int_0^2 \left(\frac{1}{4}x^2 - \frac{1}{16}x^4\right)\Big]\,dx = 2\left(\frac{1}{2}x^3 - \frac{1}{80}x^5\right)\Big]_0^2 = \frac{8}{15}$$

21. Using symmetry, $A = 2\int_0^{\pi} (\cos x - (-1))\,dx = 2[\sin x + x]_0^{\pi} = 2\pi$

22. The region is bounded by $y = 1 - x^2$ and $y = \cos\frac{\pi x}{2}$

The limits are where $1 - x^2 = \cos\frac{\pi x}{2} \Leftrightarrow x = 0, \pm 1$.

Using symmetry, the area is:

$$A = 2\int_0^1 \left(1 - x^2 - \cos\frac{\pi x}{2}\right)\Big]\,dx = 2\left(x - \frac{1}{3}x^3 - \frac{2}{\pi}\sin\frac{\pi x}{2}\right)\Big]_0^1 = \frac{4(\pi - 3)}{3\pi}$$

23. The region is bounded by $y = \sin\left(\frac{\pi x}{2}\right)$ and $y = x$. They intersect where $\sin\left(\frac{\pi x}{2}\right)$ or $x = -1, 0,$ or 1. Using symmetry,

$$A = 2\int_0^1 \left(\sin\left(\frac{\pi x}{2}\right) - x\right) dx = -\frac{4}{\pi}\cos\frac{\pi x}{2} - x^2\Big]_0^1 = \frac{4}{\pi} - 1.$$

24. Since $1 + \tan^2 x = \sec^2 x$, the region is bounded by the line $y = 1$ and the two vertical lines $x = \pm\frac{\pi}{4}$. The area is that of a rectangle with base $\frac{\pi}{2}$ and height 1 and equals $\frac{\pi}{2}$

25. The graphs intersect when $\sin x = \cos x$ or $x = \frac{\pi}{4}$.

$$A = \int_0^{\frac{\pi}{4}} (\cos x - \sin x)\, dx = \sin x + \cos x\Big]_0^{\frac{\pi}{4}} = \sqrt{2} - 1$$

26. $A = \int_0^4 \sqrt{4 - x}\, dx = -\frac{2}{3}(4 - x)^{3/2}\Big]_0^4 = \frac{16}{3}$

27. The region is composed of two distinct parts, the left half bounded by $y = x^2$, $x = 1$ and x– axis with area given by $A = \int_0^1 x^2\, dx$, and the right piece bounded by $y = 2 - x$, x–axis and $x = 1$ with area given by $A = \int_1^2 (2 - x)\, dx$. The total area is:

$$A = \int_0^1 x^2\, dx + \int_1^2 (2 - x)\, dx = \frac{1}{3}x^3\Big]_0^1 + 2x - \frac{1}{2}x^2\Big]_1^2 = \frac{5}{6}$$

28. The points of intersection between $y = 6 - x$ and $y = \sqrt{x}$ are: $(6 - x)^2 = (\sqrt{x})^2 \Rightarrow x^2 - 13x + 36 = 0$, or where $x = 4$ and $y = 2$. (The root $x = 9$ is extraneous.)

$$A = \int_1^2 (6 - y - y^2)\, dy$$

$$= 6y - \frac{1}{2}y^2 - \frac{1}{3}y^3\Big]_1^2 = \frac{13}{6}$$

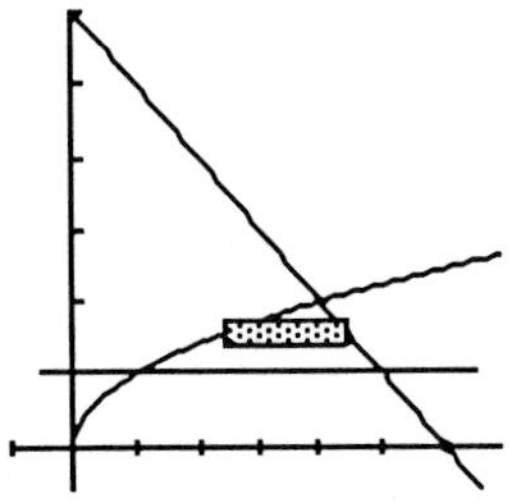

29. $y = 3 - x^2$ and $y = -1 \Rightarrow 3 - x^2 = -1 \Leftrightarrow x = \pm 2$

(a) $A = \int_{-2}^2 [3 - x^2 - (-1)]\, dx = 2\int_0^2 (4 - x^2)dx = 4x - \frac{1}{3}x^3\Big]_0^2 = \frac{32}{3}$

(b) $A = 3\int_{-1}^3 \sqrt{3 - y}\, dy = -\frac{4}{3}(3 - y)^{3/2}\Big]_{-1}^3 = \frac{32}{3}$

30. For $-\pi \le x \le 0$, $\sin|x| = \sin(-x) = -\sin x$.

$$A = \int_{-\pi}^{\pi} \sin|x|\, dx = \int_{-\pi}^{0} (-\sin x)\, dx + \int_{0}^{\pi} \sin\, dx$$

$$= 2\int_{0}^{\pi} \sin x\, dx = 2\,(-\cos x)\Big]_{0}^{\pi} = 4$$

31. $$A = \int_{\frac{\pi}{4}}^{\frac{3\pi}{4}} (\sin x - \cos x)dx = -\cos x - \sin x\ \Big]_{\frac{\pi}{4}}^{\frac{3\pi}{4}} = 2\sqrt{2}$$

32. (a) $$\int_{0}^{c} \sqrt{y}\, dy = \int_{c}^{4} \sqrt{y}\, dy \Rightarrow \frac{2}{3}y^{3/2}\Big]_{0}^{c} = \frac{2}{3}y^{3/2}\Big]_{c}^{4}$$

$$c^{3/2} = 8 - c^{3/2} \Rightarrow 2c^{3/2} = 8 \Rightarrow c^{3/2} = 4 \Rightarrow c = (4)^{2/3}$$

(b) $$\int_{0}^{\sqrt{c}} (c - x^2)\, dx = \frac{1}{2}\int_{0}^{2} (4 - x^2)\, dx \Rightarrow cx - \frac{1}{3}x^3\Big]_{0}^{\sqrt{c}} = \frac{1}{2}\left(4x - \frac{1}{3}x^3\right)\Big]_{0}^{2}$$

$$\frac{2}{3}c^{3/2} = \frac{8}{3} \Rightarrow c = (4)^{2/3}$$

33. Area of the parabolic region is:

$$2\int_{0}^{a} (a^2 - x^2)\, dx = 2\,a^2\,x - \frac{1}{3}x^3\Big]_{0}^{a} = \frac{4}{3}a^3$$

Area of the triangle is: $\frac{1}{2}[2a \cdot a^2] = a^3$.

The $$\lim_{a\to 0} \frac{a^3}{\frac{4a^3}{3}} = \frac{3}{4}.$$

34. Area of region: $R = 2\int_{0}^{k} (k^2 - x^2)\, dx = 2\left(k^2\,x - \frac{1}{3}x^3\right)\Big]_{0}^{k} = \frac{4k^3}{3}$

Area of triangle: $A = \frac{1}{2}(2k)y = k(k^2 - x^2)$ so $A' = -2kx$.

$-2kx = 0$ if $x = 0$. $A' = -2k \Rightarrow$ a maximum area. $A = \frac{1}{2}(2k)(k^2) = k^3$.

Observe that $\frac{3}{4}\left(\frac{4k^3}{3}\right) = k^3$.

5.3 CALCULATING VOLUMES BY SLICING. VOLUMES OF REVOLUTION

1. $V=\pi\int_0^2 y^2\,dx = \pi\int_0^2 (2-x)^2\,dx = \pi\int_0^2 (4-4x+x^2)\,dx$

$=\pi\left[4x-2x^2+\frac{1}{3}x^3\right]_0^2 = \frac{8\pi}{3}$

2. $V=\pi\int_0^\pi \sin^2 x\,dx = \pi\int_0^\pi\left(\frac{1}{2}-\frac{1}{2}\cos 2x\right)dx = \pi\left[\frac{1}{2}x-\frac{1}{4}\sin 2x\right]_0^\pi = \frac{\pi^2}{2}$

3. $x-x^2=0 \Leftrightarrow x=0$ or 1. Therefore, $V=\pi\int_0^1 y^2\,dx$

$=\pi\int_0^1 (x-x^2)^2\,dx = \pi\int_0^1 (x^2-2x^3+x^4)\,dx$

$=\pi\left[\frac{1}{3}x^3-\frac{1}{2}x^4+\frac{1}{5}x^5\right]_0^1 = \frac{\pi}{30}$

4. $-3x-x^2=0 \Leftrightarrow x=0$ or -3. Therefore, $V=\pi\int_{-3}^0 y^2\,dx$

$=\pi\int_{-3}^0 (-3x-x^2)^2\,dx = \pi\int_{-3}^0 (9x^2+6x^3+x^4)\,dx$

$=\pi\left[3x^3+\frac{3}{2}x^4+\frac{1}{5}x^5\right]_{-3}^0 = -\pi\left(-81+\frac{243}{2}-\frac{243}{5}\right)=\frac{81\pi}{10}$

5. $x^2-2x=0 \Leftrightarrow x=0$ or 2. Therefore, $V=\pi\int_0^2 y^2\,dx$

$=\pi\int_0^2 (x^2-2x)^2\,dx = \pi\int_0^2 (x^4-4x^3+4x^2)\,dx$

$=\pi\left[\frac{1}{5}x^5-x^4+\frac{4}{3}x^3\right]_0^2 = \frac{16\pi}{15}$

6. $V=\pi\int_0^2 x^6\,dx = \pi\left[\frac{1}{7}x^7\right]_0^2 = \frac{128\pi}{7}$

7. $V=\pi\int_0^1 y^2\,dx = \pi\int_0^1 (x^4)^2\,dx = \pi\int_0^1 x^8\,dx = \pi\frac{1}{9}x^9\Big]_0^1 = \frac{\pi}{9}$

8. $V=\pi\int_0^{\frac{\pi}{2}} (\sqrt{\cos x})^2\,dx = \pi\sin x\Big]_0^{\frac{\pi}{2}} = \pi$

9. $V=\pi\int_{-\frac{\pi}{4}}^{\frac{\pi}{4}} \sec^2 x\,dx = \pi\tan x\Big]_{-\frac{\pi}{4}}^{\frac{\pi}{4}} = 2\pi$

10. $y = x^3 + 1$ intersect the x–axis at $x = -1$. The volume is

$$V = \pi\int_{-1}^{2} (x^3 + 1)^2\, dx = \pi\int_{-1}^{2} (x^6 + 2x^3 + 1\,)dx = \pi\left[\frac{1}{7}x^7 + \frac{1}{2}x^4 + x\right]_{-1}^{2} = \frac{405\pi}{14}$$

11. $$V = \pi\int_{0}^{2} x^2\, dy = \pi\int_{0}^{2} (2y\,)^2 dy = \frac{4\pi}{3}\,y^3\Big]_{0}^{2} = \frac{32\pi}{3}$$

12. $$V = \pi\int_{0}^{4} (\sqrt{4 - y}\,)^2\, dy = \pi\left[\,4y = \frac{1}{2}y^2\,\right]_{0}^{4} = 8\pi$$

13. $$V = \pi\int_{-1}^{1} (1 - y^2\,)^2\, dy = 2\pi\int_{0}^{1} (1 - 2y^2 + y^4\,)\, dy = 2\pi\left[\,y - \frac{2}{3}y^3 + \frac{1}{5}\,y^5\,\right]_{0}^{1} = \frac{16\pi}{15}$$

14. $$V = \pi\int_{0}^{3} (y^{3/2}\,)^2\, dy = \pi\left[\frac{1}{4}y^4\right]_{0}^{3}\ \frac{81\pi}{4}$$

15. $$V = \pi\int_{1}^{2} \left(\frac{1}{y}\right)^2\, dy = -\frac{\pi}{y}\Big]_{1}^{2} = \frac{\pi}{2}$$

16. $$V = \pi\int_{0}^{1} \left(\frac{2}{y + 1}\right)^2\, dy = \frac{-4\pi}{y + 1}\Big]_{0}^{1} = 2\pi$$

17. $$V = \pi\int_{0}^{\frac{\pi}{2}} (2\,\sin 2x\,)^2\, dx = 4\pi\int_{0}^{\frac{\pi}{2}} \left(\frac{1}{2} - \frac{1}{2}\cos 4x\,\right)dx$$

$$= 2\pi\left[\,x - \frac{1}{4}\sin 4x\,\right]_{0}^{\frac{\pi}{2}} = \pi^2$$

18. $$V = \pi\int_{0}^{\frac{\pi}{3}} \tan^2 x\, dx = \pi\int_{0}^{\frac{\pi}{3}}(\sec^2 x - 1)\, dx = \pi\ (\tan x - x)\Big]_{0}^{\frac{\pi}{3}} = \pi\left(\sqrt{3} - \frac{\pi}{3}\right)$$

19. (a) The volume of the cylinder with radius $y = 2$ and height $x = 4$ is $V = \pi r^2\, h = \pi(2)^2 4 = 16\pi$. The volume formed by revolving the region bounded by $y = \sqrt{x}$, $x = 4$ and x–axis is:

$$V = \pi\int_{0}^{4} (\sqrt{x}\,)^2\, dx = \pi\left[\frac{1}{2}x^2\right]_{0}^{4} = 8\pi.$$

The required volume is the difference of these: $16\pi - 8\pi = 8\pi$.

(b) $$V = \pi\int_{0}^{4} (2 - \sqrt{x}\,)^2\, dx = \pi\int_{0}^{4} (4 - 4\sqrt{x} + x\,)\, dx = \pi\left[\,4x - \frac{8}{3}x^{3/2} + \frac{1}{2}x^2\,\right]_{0}^{4} = \frac{8\pi}{3}$$

20. The limits are the points where $3 - x^2 = -1 \Rightarrow x^2 = 4 \Rightarrow x = \pm\,2$

$$V = \pi\int_{-2}^{2} [(3 - x^2\,) - (-1)]^2\, dx = 2\pi\int_{0}^{2} (4 - x^2\,)^2\, dx$$

$$= 2\pi\int_{0}^{2} (16 - 8x^2 + x^4\,)\, dx = 2\pi\left[\,16x - \frac{8}{3}x^3 + \frac{1}{5}x^5\,\right]_{0}^{2} = \frac{512\pi}{15}$$

21. $V = \pi\int_0^1 (1-y)^2 dx = \pi\int_0^1 (1-x^2)^2 d = \pi\int_0^1 (1-x^2+x^4)\,dx$

$= \pi\left(x - \frac{1}{3}x^3 + \frac{1}{5}x^5\right)\Big]_0^1 = \frac{8\pi}{15}$

22. $V = \pi\int_0^1 (1-x)^2\,dy = \pi\int_0^1 (1-y^{2/3})^2\,dy = \pi\int_0^1 (1-2y^{2/3}+y^{4/3})\,dy$

$= \pi\left[y - \frac{6}{5}y^{5/3} + \frac{3}{7}y^{7/3}\right]_0^1 = \frac{8\pi}{35}$

23. $V = 2\pi\int_0^{\pi} (\cos x + 1)^2\,dx = 2\pi\int_0^{\pi} (\cos^2 x + 2\cos x + 1)dx$

$= 2\pi\int_0^{\pi}\left[\left(\frac{1}{2} + \frac{1}{2}\cos 2x\right) + 2\cos x + 1\right]dx$

$= 2\pi\left[\frac{3}{2}x + \frac{1}{4}\sin 2x \;\; 2\sin x\right]_0^{\pi} = 3\pi^2$

24. $V = \pi\int_0^1 (1-x)^2\,dy = \pi\int_0^1 (1-y^{3/2})^2\,dy = \pi\int_0^1 (1-2y^{3/2}+y^3)\,dy$

$= \pi\left[y - \frac{4}{5}y^{5/4} + \frac{1}{4}y^4\right]_0^1 = \frac{9\pi}{20}$

25. $V = \pi\int_{-1}^1 [4-(3x^2+1)]^2\,dx = 2\pi\int_0^1 9(1-2x^2+x^4)\,dx$

$= 18\pi\left[x - \frac{2}{3}x^3 + \frac{1}{5}x^5\right]_0^1 = \frac{144}{15}$

26. $V = \pi\int_0^{\pi} (2-y)^2\,dx = \pi\int_0^{\pi} (2-\sin x)^2\,dx = \pi\int_0^{\pi} (4 - 4\sin x + \sin^2 x)\,dx$

$= \pi\int_0^{\pi}\left(4 - 4\sin x + \frac{1}{2} - \frac{1}{2}\cos 2x\right)dx$

$= \pi\left[4x + 4\cos x + \frac{1}{2}x - \frac{1}{4}\sin 2x\right]_0^{\pi} = \frac{9\pi}{2} - 8$

27. $V = \pi\int_0^{\pi} (c - \sin x)^2\, dx = \pi\int_0^{\pi} (c^2 - 2c\sin x + \sin^2 x)\, dx$

$$= \pi\int_0^{\pi}\left(c^2 - 2c\sin x + \frac{1}{2} - \frac{1}{2}\cos 2x\right)dx$$

$$\pi\left[c^2 x + 2c\cos x + \frac{1}{2}x - \frac{1}{4}\sin 2x\right]_0^{\pi} = \pi\left(c^2\pi - 4c + \frac{\pi}{2}\right)$$

If $V(c) = \pi\left(c^2\pi - 4c + \frac{\pi}{2}\right)$ then $V'(c) = \pi(2c\pi - 4) = 0 \Leftrightarrow c = \frac{2}{\pi}$.

$V''(c) = 2\pi^2 > 0 \Rightarrow c = \frac{2}{\pi}$ minimizes the volume.

28. (a) $V = \pi\int_0^h \left(\frac{r}{h}x\right)^2 dx = \frac{\pi r^2}{h^2}\left[\frac{1}{3}x^3\right]_0^h = \frac{\pi r^2 h}{3}$

(b) Total volume of cylinder $= \pi r^2 h$. Volume generated by revolving the region above the line $y = \frac{r}{h}x$, $y = r$ about y-axis:

$$V = \pi\int_0^r x^2\, dy = \pi\int_0^r \left(\frac{h}{r}y\right)^2 dy = \frac{\pi h^2}{r^2}\left[\frac{1}{3}y^3\right]_0^r = \frac{\pi h^2 r}{3}.$$

Required volume is the difference $= \frac{2\pi h^2 r}{3}$.

29. (a) $V = \pi\int_0^h \left(\sqrt{a^2 - y^2}\right)^2 dy = \frac{\pi h^2}{3}(3a - h)$

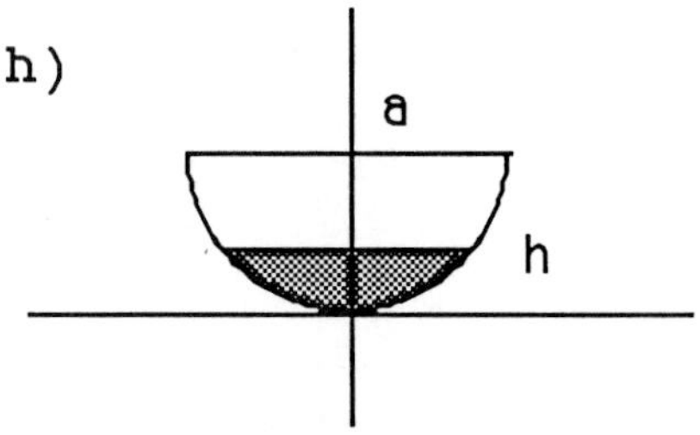

(b) From part (a), $V = \pi a h^2 - \frac{\pi}{3}h^3$

$$\frac{dV}{dt} = 2\pi a h\frac{dh}{dt} - \pi h^2\frac{dh}{dt}$$

$$(.2) = [2\pi(5)(4) - \pi(16)]\frac{dh}{dt}$$

$$\frac{dh}{dt} = \frac{1}{120\pi}\ \text{ft/s}$$

30. $V = \pi\int_{-a}^{a} y^2\, dx = 2\pi\int_0^a \left[b\sqrt{1 - \frac{x^2}{a^2}}\right]^2 dx = 2\pi b^2\left[x - \frac{1}{3a^2}x^3\right]_0^a = \frac{4\pi ab^2}{3}$

31. The volume of the pyramid is $V = Bh$, where B = base area. We use the formula $B = \frac{1}{2}d_1 d_2$, d_1 and d_2 diagonals. The diagonals of a square are equal, and $d = |y_1 - y_2| = 5x^2 - (-5x^2) = 10x^2$. Therefore,

$$V = \int_0^4 \frac{1}{2}(10x^2)(10x^2)\, dx = 10x^5\Big]_0^4 = 10{,}240$$

32. A diameter of the base = $|8 - x^2 - (x^2)| = 8 - 2x^2$. The base area is $B = \pi(4 - x^2)^2$. The limits are where $8 - x^2 = x^2$ or $x = \pm 2$. Therefore,

$$V = \int_{-2}^{2} \pi(4 - x^2)^2\, dx = 2\pi\int_0^2 (16 - 8x^2 + x^4)dx = 2\pi\left[16x - \frac{8}{3}x^3 + \frac{1}{5}x^5\right]_0^2 = \frac{512\pi}{15}$$

33. The base is a square with side a chord of the circle, running from a point on the top, $P\left(x, \sqrt{a^2 - x^2}\right)$, to a corresponding point on the bottom, $Q\left(x, -\sqrt{a^2 - x^2}\right)$. A side of the base is then $s = 2\sqrt{a^2 - x^2}$ and the base area is $B = s^2 = 4(a^2 - x^2)$. The volume is then:

$$V = 4\int_{-a}^{a} (a^2 - x^2)\, dx = 8\left[a^2x - \frac{1}{3}x^3\right]_0^a = \frac{16}{3}a^3$$

34. A side s of the base B is the hypotenuse of an isosceles right triangle whose leg is $\sqrt{a^2 - x^2}$. Then $s = \sqrt{2}\sqrt{a^2 - x^2}$ and the base area is $B = s^2 = 2(a^2 - x^2)$. The volume is then

$$V = \int_{-a}^{a} 2(a^2 - x^2)\, dx = 2\left[a^2x - \frac{1}{3}x^3\right]_{-a}^{a} = \frac{8a^3}{3}$$

35. The base is a leg of an isosceles right triangle with length, as in problem 33, equal to $2\sqrt{a^2 - y^2}$. The base area is given

$$B = \frac{1}{2}bh = \frac{1}{2}\left(2\sqrt{a^2 - y^2}\right)^2 = 2(a^2 - y^2).$$ The volume is

$$V = \int_{-a}^{a} 2(a^2 - y^2)\, dy = \frac{8a^3}{3}.$$

36. The base area $B = \frac{s^2\sqrt{3}}{4} = \frac{\sqrt{3}}{4}\sin^2 x$. The volume is

$$V = \int_0^{\frac{\pi}{2}} \frac{\sqrt{3}}{4}\sin^2 x\, dx = \frac{\sqrt{3}}{4}\int_0^{\frac{\pi}{2}} \left(\frac{1}{2} - \frac{1}{2}\cos 2x\right) dx = \frac{\sqrt{3}}{4}\left[\frac{1}{2}x - \frac{1}{4}\sin 2x\right]_0^{\frac{\pi}{2}} = \frac{\pi\sqrt{3}}{16}$$

37. $$V \approx \frac{50 - 0}{2(10)}\,[6+2(8.2)+2(9.1)+2(9.9)+2(10.5)+2(11.0)+2(11.5)+2(11.9)+2(12.3)+2(12.7)+13] = 15{,}990$$

5.4 VOLUMES MODELED WITH WASHERS AND CYLINDRICAL SHELLS

1. We use a disk, with radius $y = 2 - x$. The limits run from the origin to the x-intercept of the line, $x = 2$.

$$V = \pi\int_0^2 (2-x)^2\,dx = -\frac{\pi}{3}(2-x)^3\Big]_0^2 = \frac{8\pi}{3}$$

2. We use a shell with radius $r = y$ and height $h = x$. The limits are the points where $2y - y^2 = 0$, or $y = 0, 2$. The volume is $V = 2\pi\int rh\,dr$

$$= 2\pi\int_0^2 xy\,dy = 2\pi\int_0^2 y(2y - y^2)\,dy$$

$$= 2\pi\left[\frac{2}{3}y^3 - \frac{1}{4}y^4\right]_0^2 = \frac{8\pi}{3}$$

3. We use a washer, with outer radius $R = 3x - x^2$ and inner radius $r = x$. The limits are the points where $3x - x^2 = x$, or $x = 0, 2$. The volume is $V = \pi\int(R^2 - r^2)\,dx$

$$= \int_0^2 [(3x - x^2)^2 - x^2]\,dx = \pi\int_0^2 (8x^2 - 6x^3 + x^4)\,dx$$

$$= \pi\left[\frac{8}{3}x^3 - \frac{3}{2}x^4 + \frac{1}{5}x^5\right]_0^2 = \frac{56\pi}{15}$$

4. We use a washer with outer radius $R = 1$ and inner radius $r = y$. The limits are from origin to where $y = x$ intersects $y = 1$. The volume is $V = \pi\int(R^2 - r^2)\,dx$

$$= \pi\int_0^1 (1 - x^2)\,dx = \pi\left[x - \frac{1}{3}x^3\right]_0^1 = \frac{2\pi}{3}$$

5. We use a washer, with outer radius $R = 4$ and inner radius $r = x^2$. The limits are the points where $x^2 = 4$, or $x = \pm 2$. We also use the symmetry of the figure. The volume is $V = \pi\int(R^2 - r^2)\,dx$

$$= 2\pi\int_0^2 [(4)^2 - (x^2)^2]\,dx = 2\pi\int_0^2 (16 - x^4)\,dx$$

$$= 2\pi\left[16x - \frac{1}{5}x^5\right]_0^2 = \frac{256\pi}{5}$$

6. We use a washer, with outer radius $R = 4$ and inner radius $r = 3 + x^2$. The limits are the points where $3 + x^2 = 4$, or $x = \pm 1$. We also use the symmetry of the figure. The volume is $V = \pi \int (R^2 - r^2)\,dx$

$$= 2\pi \int_0^1 [(4)^2 - (3 + x^2)^2]\,dx = 2\pi \int_0^2 (7 - 6x^2 - x^4)\,dx$$

$$= 2\pi \left[7x - 2x^3 - \frac{1}{5}x^5 \right]_0^1 = \frac{48\pi}{5}$$

7. We use a washer, with outer radius $R = x + 3$ and inner radius $r = x^2 + 1$. The limits are the points where $x^2 + 1 = x + 3$, or $x = 2, -1$. The volume is $V = \pi \int (R^2 - r^2)\,dx$

$$= \pi \int_{-1}^2 [(x + 3)^2 - (x^2 + 1)^2]\,dx = \pi \int_{-1}^2 (-x^4 - x^2 + 6x + 8)\,dx$$

$$= \pi \left[-\frac{1}{5}x^5 - \frac{1}{3}x^3 + 3x^2 + 8x \right]_{-1}^2 = \frac{117\pi}{5}$$

8. We use a washer, with outer radius $R = 4 - x^2$ and inner radius $r = 2 - x$. The limits are the points where $4 - x^2 = 2 - x$ or $x = -1, 2$. The volume is $V = \pi \int (R^2 - r^2)\,dx$

$$= \pi \int_{-1}^2 [(4 - x^2)^2 - (2 - x)^2]\,dx = \pi \int_{-1}^2 (12 + 4x - 9x^2 + x^4)\,dx$$

$$= \pi \left[12x + 2x^2 - 3x^3 + \frac{1}{5}x^5 \right]_0^1 = \frac{108\pi}{5}$$

9. We use a shell, with height $h = x^4$ and radius $r = x$. The volume $V = \int 2\pi rh\,dr$

$$= 2\pi \int_0^1 x^5\,dx = 2\pi \left[\frac{1}{6}x^6 \right]_0^1 = \frac{\pi}{3}$$

10. We use ashell, with radius $r = x$ and height $= y$. The volume is $V = 2\pi \int rh\,dx$

$$= 2\pi \int_0^2 x\,y\,dx = 2\pi \int_0^2 x^4\,dx = 2\pi \left[\frac{1}{5}x^5 \right]_0^2 = \frac{64\pi}{5}$$

11. The equations of the sides of the triangle are $x = 1$, $y = 1$, and $y = x$.

(a) We use a shell, with radius $r = y$ and height $h = x - 1$.

$$V = 2\pi\int_1^2 y(1 - x)\,dy = 2\pi\int_1^2 y(1 - y)\,dy = \frac{5\pi}{3}$$

(b) We use a shell, with radius x and height $h = 2 - y$.

$$V = 2\pi\int_1^2 x(2 - y)\,dx = 2\pi\int_1^2 x(2 - x)\,dx = \frac{4\pi}{3}$$

12. (a) We use a shell with radius $r = y$ and height $h = x$.

$$V = 2\pi\int_0^1 xy\,dy = 2\pi\int_0^1 (y^2 - y^4)\,dy = 2\pi\left[\frac{1}{3}y^3 - \frac{1}{5}y^5\right]_0^1 = \frac{4\pi}{15}$$

(b) We use a disk with radius $r = x$.

$$V = \pi\int_0^1 x^2\,dy = \pi\int_0^1 (y^2 - 2y^4 + y^6)\,dy = \pi\left[\frac{1}{3}y^3 - \frac{2}{5}y^5 + \frac{1}{7}y^7\right] = \frac{8\pi}{105}$$

13. (a) We use a shell, with radius $r = 1 - x = 1 - (y - y^3)$ and height $h = y$. The curve $y - y^3$ intersects the $y-$axis at $y = 0, 1$.

$$V = 2\pi\int_0^1 y(1 - y + y^3)\,dy = 2\pi\left[\frac{1}{2}y^2 - \frac{1}{3}y^3 + \frac{1}{5}y^5\right]_0^1 = \frac{11\pi}{15}$$

(b) We use a washer, with outer radius $R = 1$ and inner radius $r = x = y - y^3$.

$$V = \pi\int_0^1 [(1)^2 - (y - y^3)^2]\,dy = \pi\int_0^1 (1 - y^2 + 2y^4 - y^6)\,dy$$

$$= \pi\left[y - \frac{1}{3}y^3 + \frac{2}{5}y^5 - \frac{1}{7}y^7\right]_0^1 = \frac{97\pi}{105}$$

(c) We use a disk, with radius $R = 1 - x = 1 - (y - y^3)$.

$$V = \pi\int_0^1 [(1 - y + y^3)^2]\,dy = \pi\int_0^1 (1 - 2y + y^2 + 2y^3 - 2y^4 + y^6)\,dy$$

$$= \pi\left[y - y^2 + \frac{1}{3}y^3 + \frac{1}{2}y^4 - \frac{2}{5}y^5 + \frac{1}{7}y^7\right]_0^1 = \frac{121\pi}{210}$$

(d) We use a shell, with radius $r = 1 - x = 1 - (y - y^3)$ and height $h = 1 - y$.

$$V = 2\pi\int_0^1 \Big[(1 - y)(1 - y + y^3)\,dy = 2\pi\int_0^1 (1 - 2y + y^2 + y^3 - y^4)\,dy$$

$$= 2\pi\left[y - y^2 + \frac{1}{3}y^3 + \frac{1}{4}y^4 - \frac{1}{5}y^5\right]_0^1 = \frac{23\pi}{30}$$

14. (a) We use a washer with outer radius $R = \frac{1}{2}x + 2$ and inner radius $r = x$.

$$V = \pi\int_0^4 \left[\left(\frac{1}{2}x + 2\right)^2 - x^2\right]dx = \pi\left[-\frac{1}{4}x^3 + x^2 + 4x\right]_0^4 = 16\pi$$

(b) We use a shell with radius $r = x$ and height $h = \left[\left(\frac{1}{2}x + 2\right) - x\right]$.

$$V = 2\pi\int_0^4 x\left(\frac{1}{2}x + 2 - x\right)dx = 2\pi\left[-\frac{1}{6}x^3 + x^2\right]_0^4 = \frac{32\pi}{3}$$

(c) We use a shell with radius $r = 4 - x$ and height

$$h = \left[\left(\frac{1}{2}x + 2\right) - x\right] = -\frac{1}{2}x + 2 = \frac{1}{2}(4 - x).$$

$$V = 2\pi\int_0^4 \frac{1}{2}(4 - x)^2\,dx = \pi\left[-\frac{1}{3}(4 - x)^3\right]_0^4 = \frac{64\pi}{3}$$

(d) We use a washer with outer radius $R = 4 - x$ and inner radius

$$r = \left[4 - \left(\frac{1}{2}x + 2\right)\right] = 2 - \frac{1}{2}x = \frac{1}{2}(4 - x).$$

$$V = \pi\int_0^4 \left[(4 - x)^2 - \frac{1}{4}(4 - x)^2\right]dx = \frac{3\pi}{4}\left[-\frac{1}{3}(4 - x)^3\right]_0^4 = 16\pi$$

15. The curve $y = x^3$ intersects $y = 4x$ in the point $(2, 8)$.

(a) We use a shell, with height h = horizontal distance to the cubic − the distance to the line $= y^{1/3} - \frac{y}{4}$, and radius $r = y$. Then

$$V = 2\pi\int_0^8 y\left(y^{1/3} - \frac{y}{4}\right)dy = 2\pi\left[\frac{3}{7}y^{7/3} - \frac{1}{12}y^3\right]_0^8 = \frac{512\pi}{21}$$

(b) We use a disk, with outer radius $R = 8 - x^3$ and inner radius $r = 8 - 4x$. Then

$$V = \pi\int_0^2 [(8 - x^3)^2 - (8 - 4x)^2]\,dx = \pi\left[-4x^4 - \frac{16}{3}x^3 + 32x^2 + \frac{1}{7}x^7\right]_0^2 = \frac{832\pi}{21}$$

16. The curves intersect where $\frac{x^2}{8} = \sqrt{x}$ or $x = 0, 4$.

(a) We use a washer with outer radius $R = \sqrt{x}$ and inner radius $r = \frac{x^2}{8}$.

$$V = \pi\int_0^4 \left[(\sqrt{x})^2 - \left(\frac{x^2}{8}\right)^2\right]dx = \pi\left[\frac{1}{2}x^2 - \frac{1}{320}x^5\right]_0^4 = \frac{24\pi}{5}$$

(b) We use a shell with radius $r = x$ and height $h = \sqrt{x} - \dfrac{x^2}{8}$.

$$V = 2\pi \int_0^4 x\left(\sqrt{x} - \frac{x^2}{8}\right)dx = 2\pi\left[\frac{2}{5}x^{5/2} - \frac{1}{32}x^4\right]_0^4 = \frac{48\pi}{5}$$

17. The curve $y = 2x - x^2$ intersects $y = x$ where $2x - x^2 = x$, or $x = 1, 0$.

(a) We use a shell with radius $r = x$ and height $h = x - x^2$.

$$V = 2\pi \int_0^1 x(x - x^2)\,dx = 2\pi\left[\frac{1}{3}x^3 - \frac{1}{4}x^4\right]_0^1 = \frac{\pi}{6}$$

(b) We use a shell with radius $r = 1 - x$ and height $h = x - x^2$.

$$V = 2\pi \int_0^1 (1 - x)(x - x^2)\,dx = 2\pi\int_0^1 (x - 2x^2 + x^3)\,dx$$

$$= 2\pi\left[\frac{1}{2}x^2 - \frac{2}{3}x^3 + \frac{1}{4}x^4\right]_0^1 = \frac{\pi}{6}$$

18. (a) We use washers with outer radius $R = 2$ and inner radius $r = \sqrt{x}$.

$$V = \pi\int_0^4 (4 - x)dx = \pi\left[4x - \frac{1}{2}x^2\right]_0^4 = 8\pi$$

(b) We use shell with radius $r = x$ and height $h = 2 - \sqrt{x}$.

$$V = 2\pi \int_0^4 x(2 - \sqrt{x})dx = 2\pi\left[x^2 - \frac{2}{5}x^{5/2}\right]_0^4 = \frac{32\pi}{5}$$

(c) We use a shell with radius $r = 4 - x$ and height $h = 2 - \sqrt{x}$.

$$V = 2\pi\int_0^4 (4 - x)(2 - \sqrt{x})dx = 2\pi\left[8x - x^2 + \frac{2}{5}x^{5/2} - \frac{8}{3}x^{3/2}\right]_0^4 = \frac{224\pi}{15}$$

(d) We use a washer with radius $r = 2 - \sqrt{x}$.

$$V = \pi \int_0^4 (2 - \sqrt{x})^2\,dx = \pi\left[4x - \frac{8}{3}x^{3/2} + \frac{1}{2}x^2\right]_0^4 = \frac{8\pi}{3}$$

19. $$V = \pi \int_0^{\frac{\pi}{4}} (\cos^2 x - \sin^2 x)\,dx = \pi \int_0^{\frac{\pi}{4}} \cos 2x\,dx = \frac{\pi}{2}\sin 2x\Big]_0^{\frac{\pi}{4}} = \frac{\pi}{2}$$

20. We use a shell with radius $r = x$ and height $h = 8x^2 - 8x^3$.

$$V = 2\pi\int_0^1 x(8x^2 - 8x^3)\,dx = 16\pi\left[\frac{1}{4}x^4 - \frac{1}{5}x^5\right]_0^1 = \frac{4\pi}{5}$$

21. We use a shell with radius $r = x$ and height $h = 2x^2 - (x^4 - 2x^2)$.

The curves intersect in $x = 0, \pm 2$.

$$V = 2\pi \int_0^2 x[2x^2 - (x^4 - 2x^2)]\,dx = 2\pi \int_0^2 (4x^3 - x^5)\,dx$$

$$= \left[x^4 - \frac{1}{6}x^6\right]_0^2 = \frac{32\pi}{3}$$

22. We use a shell with radius $r = y$ and height $h = (2 - y - \sqrt{y})$.

$$V = 2\pi \int_0^1 y(2 - y - \sqrt{y})\,dy = 2\pi\left[y^2 - \frac{1}{3}y^3 - \frac{2}{5}y^{5/2}\right]_0^1 = \frac{8\pi}{15}$$

23. $$V = 2\pi \int_0^{\pi} x \sin x\,dx = 2\pi\left[\sin x - x\cos x\right]_0^{\pi} = 2\pi^2$$

24. (a) We use a disk with radius $r = x$.

$$V = \pi \int_0^4 x^2\,dy = \pi \int_0^4 y\,dy = \pi\left[\frac{1}{2}y^2\right]_0^4 = 8\pi$$

(b) We use a disk with radius $r = 4 - y$

$$V = \pi \int_{-2}^2 (4 - y)^2\,dx = 2\pi \int_0^2 (4 - x^2)^2\,dx = 2\pi\left[16x - \frac{8}{3}x^3 + \frac{1}{5}x^5\right]_0^2 = \frac{512\pi}{15}$$

(c) We use a washer with outer radius $R = 4$ and inner radius $r = y$.

$$V = \pi \int_{-2}^2 [16 - (x^2)^2]\,dx = 2\pi\left[16x - \frac{1}{5}x^5\right]_0^2 = \frac{256\pi}{5}$$

(d) We use a washer with outer radius $R = 5$ and inner radius $r = y - (-1)$

$$V = \pi \int_{-2}^2 [25 - (x^2 + 1)^2]\,dx = 2\pi\left[24x - \frac{1}{5}x^5 - \frac{2}{3}x^3\right]_0^2 = \frac{1088\pi}{15}$$

(e) We use a shell with radius $r = 2 - x$ and height $h = 4 - y$.

$$V = 2\pi \int_{-2}^2 (2 - x)(4 - x^2)\,dx = 2\pi\left[8x - 2x^2 + \frac{1}{4}x^4 - \frac{2}{3}x^3\right]_{-2}^2 = \frac{128\pi}{3}$$

25. We use a shell of height $2\sqrt{a^2 - x^2}$ and radius $r = b - x$.

$$V = 2\pi \int_{-a}^a 2(b - x)\sqrt{a^2 - x^2}\,dx$$

$$= 4\pi b \int_{-a}^a \sqrt{a^2 - x^2}\,dx - 4\pi \int_{-a}^a x\sqrt{a^2 - x^2}\,dx$$

$$= 4\pi b\left(\frac{\pi a^2}{2}\right) - \frac{4\pi}{3}(a^2 - x^2)^{3/2}\Big]_{-a}^a = 2\pi^2 a^2 b$$

5.5 LENGTHS OF PLANE CURVES

1. $y = \frac{1}{3}(x^2+2)^{3/2}$, $0 \le x \le 3$. $\frac{dy}{dx} = x\sqrt{x^2+2}$.

$$s = \int_0^3 \sqrt{1+\left(\frac{dy}{dx}\right)^2} = \int_0^3 \sqrt{1+x^2(x^2+2)}\,dx = \int_0^3 \sqrt{(x^2+1)^2}\,dx$$

$$= \int_0^3 (x^2+1)\,dx = \frac{1}{3}x^3 + x\Big]_0^3 = 12$$

2. $y = x^{3/2}$, from $(0,0)$ to $(4,8)$. $\frac{dy}{dx} = \frac{3}{2}x^{1/2}$.

$$s = \int_0^4 \sqrt{1+\left(\frac{dy}{dx}\right)^2} = \int_0^4 \sqrt{1+\frac{9}{4}x}\,dx = \frac{8}{27}\left(1+\frac{9}{4}x\right)^{3/2}\Big]_0^4 = \frac{8}{27}[10\sqrt{10}-1]$$

3. $9x^2 = 4y^3$ from $(0,0)$ to $(2\sqrt{3}, 3)$. $x = \frac{2}{3}y^{3/2} \Rightarrow \frac{dx}{dy} = \sqrt{y}$.

$$s = \int_0^3 \sqrt{1+\left(\frac{dx}{dy}\right)^2}\,dy = \int_0^3 \sqrt{1+y}\,dy = \frac{2}{3}(1+y^{3/2}\Big]_0^3 = \frac{14}{3}$$

4. $y = \frac{1}{3}x^3 + \frac{1}{4x}$, $1 \le x \le 3$. $\frac{dy}{dx} = x^2 - \frac{1}{4x^2}$. $\left(\frac{dy}{dx}\right)^2 = x^4 - \frac{1}{2} + \frac{1}{16x^4}$.

$$s = \int_1^3 \sqrt{1+x^4-\frac{1}{2}+\frac{1}{16x^4}}\,dx = \int_1^3 \sqrt{x^4+\frac{1}{2}+\frac{1}{16x^4}}\,dx = \int_1^3 \sqrt{\left(x^2+\frac{1}{4x^2}\right)^2}\,dx$$

$$= \int_1^3 \left(x^2+\frac{1}{4x^2}\right)dx = \frac{1}{3}x^3 - \frac{1}{4x}\Big]_1^3 = \frac{53}{6}$$

5. $x = \frac{y^4}{4} + \frac{1}{8y^2}$, $1 \le y \le 2$. $\frac{dx}{dy} = y^3 - \frac{1}{4y^3}$. $\left(\frac{dx}{dy}\right)^2 = y^6 - \frac{1}{2} + \frac{1}{16y^6}$.

$$s = \int_1^2 \sqrt{1+y^6-\frac{1}{2}+\frac{1}{16y^6}}\,dy = \int_1^2 \sqrt{y^6+\frac{1}{2}+\frac{1}{16y^6}}\,dy = \int_1^2 \sqrt{\left(y^3+\frac{1}{4y^3}\right)^2}\,dy$$

$$= \int_1^2 \left(y^3+\frac{1}{4y^3}\right)dy = \frac{1}{4}y^4 - \frac{1}{8y^2}\Big]_1^2 = \frac{123}{32}$$

6. $(y+1)^2 = 4x^3 \Rightarrow y = \pm 2x^{3/2} - 1$. We will find the length of the top piece, $y = 2x^{3/2} - 1$, and double it.

$$s = 2\int_0^1 \sqrt{1 + (3x^{1/2})^2}\, dx$$

$$= 2\left[\frac{2}{27}(1+9x)^{3/2}\right]_0^1$$

$$= \frac{4}{27}[10\sqrt{10} - 1]$$

(1,1)

$y = + 2x^{3/2} - 1$

$y = - 2x^{3/2} - 1$

(1,-1)

7. $$x = a\cos^3 t \Rightarrow \frac{dx}{dt} = -3a\cos^2 t \sin t \Rightarrow \left(\frac{dx}{dt}\right)^2 = 9a^2\cos^4 t \sin^2 t$$

$$y = a\sin^3 t \Rightarrow \frac{dy}{dt} = 3a\sin^2 t\cos t \Rightarrow \left(\frac{dy}{dt}\right)^2 = 9a^2\sin^4 t\cos^2 t$$

$$ds = \sqrt{\left(\frac{dx}{dt}\right)^2 + \left(\frac{dy}{dt}\right)^2}\, dt = \sqrt{9a^2\cos^4 t\sin^2 t + 9a^2\sin^4 t\cos^2 t}\, dt$$

$$= 3a\,|\cos t\sin t|\, dt.$$

$$s = 4\int_0^{\frac{\pi}{2}} 3a\,|\cos t \sin t|\, dt = 4\int_0^{\frac{\pi}{2}} 3a\cos t\sin t\, dt = 12a\left(\frac{\sin^2 t}{2}\right)\Bigg]_0^{\frac{\pi}{2}} = 6a$$

8. $$y = \int_0^x \sqrt{\cos 2t}\, dt \Rightarrow \frac{dy}{dx} = \sqrt{\cos 2x}.$$

$$s = \int_0^{\frac{\pi}{4}} \sqrt{1+\cos 2t}\, dt = \int_0^{\frac{\pi}{4}} \sqrt{2}\sqrt{\frac{1+\cos 2t}{2}}\, dt = \sqrt{2}\int_0^{\frac{\pi}{4}} \sqrt{\cos^2 t}\, dt$$

$$= \sqrt{2}\int_0^{\frac{\pi}{4}} |\cos t|\, dt = \sqrt{2}\sin t\Big]_0^{\frac{\pi}{4}} = 1 \quad \left(\text{Note: } \cos t \geq 0 \text{ for } 0 \leq t \leq \frac{\pi}{4}\right)$$

9. $$s = \int_0^{\pi} \sqrt{(-\sin t)^2 + (1+\cos t)^2}\, dt = \int_0^{\pi} \sqrt{2 + 2\cos t}\, dt = 2\int_0^{\pi} \sqrt{\frac{1+\cos t}{2}}\, dt$$

$$= 2\int_0^{\pi} \cos\frac{t}{2}\, dt = 4\sin\frac{t}{2}\Big]_0^{\pi} = 4$$

10. $$x = t - \sin t \Rightarrow \frac{dx}{dt} = 1 - \cos t \Rightarrow \left(\frac{dx}{dt}\right)^2 = 1 - 2\cos t + \cos^2 t$$

$$y = 1 - \cos t \Rightarrow \frac{dy}{dt} = \sin t \Rightarrow \left(\frac{dy}{dt}\right)^2 = \sin^2 t$$

$$s = \int_0^{2\pi} \sqrt{2 - 2\cos t}\, dt = 2\int_0^{2\pi} \sqrt{\frac{1-\cos t}{2}}\, dt\ 2\int_0^{2\pi} \left|\sin\frac{t}{2}\right|\, dt$$

$$= -4\cos\frac{t}{2}\Big]_0^{2\pi} = 8. \quad \left(\text{Note: } \sin\frac{t}{2} \geq 0 \text{ since } 0 \leq t \leq 2\pi \Rightarrow 0 \leq \frac{t}{2} \leq \pi\right)$$

11. $x = a\cos t + at\sin t \Rightarrow \dfrac{dx}{dt} = -a\sin t + a\sin t + at\cos t$

$y = a\sin t - at\cos t \Rightarrow \dfrac{dy}{dt} = a\cos t - a\cos t + at\sin t$

$$s = \int_0^{\frac{\pi}{2}} \sqrt{a^2t^2\cos^2 t + a^2t^2\sin^2 t}\ dt = \int_0^{\frac{\pi}{2}} at\ dt = \frac{1}{2}at^2\Big]_0^{\frac{\pi}{2}} = \frac{a\pi^2}{8}$$

12. $x = \dfrac{t^2}{2} \Rightarrow \dfrac{dx}{dt} = t \Rightarrow \left(\dfrac{dx}{dt}\right)^2 = t^2$

$y = \dfrac{1}{3}(2t+1)^{3/2} \Rightarrow \dfrac{dy}{dt} = (2t+1)^{1/2} \Rightarrow \left(\dfrac{dy}{dt}\right)^2 = 2t+1$

$$s = \int_0^4 \sqrt{(t+1)^2}\ dt = \int_0^4 |t+1|\ dt = \frac{1}{2}t^2 + t\Big]_0^4 = 12$$

13. $x = \dfrac{1}{3}(2t+3)^{3/2} \Rightarrow \dfrac{dx}{dt} = (2t+3)^{1/2}$; $y = \dfrac{t^2}{2} + t \Rightarrow \dfrac{dy}{dt} = t+1.$

$$s = \int_0^3 \sqrt{2t+3+t^2+2t+1}\ dt = \int_0^3 \sqrt{(t+2)^2}\ dt = \int_0^3 (t+2)\ dt = \frac{21}{2}$$

14. $x = t^2 \Rightarrow \dfrac{dx}{dt} = 2t \Rightarrow \left(\dfrac{dx}{dt}\right)^2 = 4t^2$

$y = \dfrac{t^3}{3} - t \Rightarrow \dfrac{dy}{dt} = t^2 - 1 \Rightarrow \left(\dfrac{dy}{dt}\right)^2 = t^4 - 2t^2 + 1$

$$s = 2\int_0^{\sqrt{3}} \sqrt{(t^2+1)^2}\ dt = 2\int_0^{\sqrt{3}} (t^2+1)\ dt = 2\left[\frac{1}{3}t^3 + t\right]_0^{\sqrt{3}} = 4\sqrt{3}$$

15. $5y^3 = x^2$ intersects the circle $x^2 + y^2 = 6$ where $5y^3 = 6 - y^2 \Rightarrow$ $5y^3 + y^2 - 6 = 0$, which clearly has a root at $y = 1$.

$x = \sqrt{5}y^{3/2} \Rightarrow \dfrac{dx}{dt} = \dfrac{3\sqrt{5}}{2}y^{1/2}.$

$$s = 2\int_0^1 \sqrt{1 + \frac{45}{4}y}\ dy = \frac{16}{135}\left(1 + \frac{45}{4}y\right)^{3/2}\Big]_0^1 = \frac{134}{27}$$

16. If $c > 0$, $s = \displaystyle\int_0^c \sqrt{1+m^2}\ dx = \sqrt{1+m^2}\,\Big]_0^c = c\sqrt{1+m^2}$.

If $c < 0$, $s = \displaystyle\int_c^0 \sqrt{1+m^2}\ dx = -c\sqrt{1+m^2}$. $\therefore s = |c|\sqrt{1+m^2}$

17. If $y = f(x)$, then Equation 4 states that

$$L = \int_a^b \sqrt{1 + [f'(x)]^2}\, dx.$$

If we regard f a parametized by $x = x$, $y = f(x)$, then Equation 7 states that

$$L = \int_a^b \sqrt{\left(\frac{dx}{dx}\right)^2 + \left(\frac{dy}{dx}\right)^2}\, dx = \int_a^b \sqrt{1 + \left(\frac{dy}{dx}\right)^2}\, dx.$$

18. $s = \int_0^{20} \sqrt{1 + \frac{3\pi}{20} \cos^2 \frac{3\pi}{20} x}\, dx \approx 21.07$ inches. If

$F(x) = \sqrt{1 + \frac{3\pi}{20} \cos^2 \frac{3\pi}{20} x}$, then Simpson's Rule gives

$$s \approx \frac{2}{3} [F(0) + 4F(2) + 2F(4) + 4F(6) + 2F(8) + 4F(10) + 2F(12) + 4F(14)$$
$$+ 2F(16) + 4F(18) + F(20)]$$
$$\approx \frac{2}{3}(1.1055 + 4.152 + 2.022 + 4.384 + 2.14 + 4 +$$
$$2.14 + 4.384 + 2.022 + 4.152 + 1.1055) \approx 21.07$$

19. $y = 25 \cos \frac{\pi x}{50} \Rightarrow \frac{dy}{dx} = -\frac{\pi}{2} \sin \frac{\pi x}{50}$. Then $s = 2\int_0^{25} \sqrt{1 + \frac{\pi^2}{4} \sin^2 \frac{\pi x}{50}}\, dx$.

We approximate this integral using Simpson's Rule, with $n = 10$ and $h = 2.5$ to get $s \approx 73.17466440$. The cost is then approximately $73.1747 \times 300 \times 1.75 \approx \$38,400$.

5.6 THE AREA OF A SURFACE OF REVOLUTION

1. $$S = 2\pi \int_0^1 y \sqrt{1 + (3x^2)^2}\, dx = 2\pi \int_0^1 x^3 \sqrt{1 + 9x^4}\, dx$$
$$= \frac{\pi}{27}(1 + 9x^4)^{3/2} \Big]_0^1 = \frac{\pi}{27}[10\sqrt{10} - 1]$$

2. $$S = 2\pi \int_0^2 x\, ds = 2\pi \int_0^2 x\sqrt{1 + 4x^2}\, dx = 2\pi \left[\frac{1}{12}(1 + 4x^2)^{3/2}\right]_0^2 = \frac{\pi}{6}[17\sqrt{17} - 1]$$

3. $$S = 2\pi\int_1^3 (y+1)\sqrt{1+\left(x^2-\frac{1}{4}x^{-2}\right)^2}\,dx$$

$$= 2\pi\int_1^3 \left(1+\frac{x^3}{3}+\frac{1}{4x}\right)\sqrt{1+x^4-\frac{1}{2}+\frac{1}{16x^4}}\,dx$$

$$= 2\pi\int_1^3 \left(1+\frac{x^3}{3}+\frac{1}{4x}\right)\sqrt{x^4+\frac{1}{2}+\frac{1}{16x^4}}\,dx$$

$$= 2\pi\int_1^3 \left(1+\frac{x^3}{3}+\frac{1}{4x}\right)\left(x^2+\frac{1}{4x^2}\right)dx$$

$$= 2\pi\int_1^3 \left(x^2+\frac{x^5}{3}+\frac{x}{4}+\frac{1}{4}x^{-2}+\frac{x}{12}+\frac{1}{16}x^{-3}\right)dx$$

$$= 2\pi\left[\frac{x^3}{3}+\frac{x^6}{18}+\frac{x^2}{8}-\frac{1}{4x}+\frac{x^2}{24}-\frac{1}{32x^2}\right]_1^3 = \frac{1823\pi}{18}$$

4. $y = \frac{1}{6}x^3+\frac{1}{2x}$, $1 \le x \le 3$. $\left(\frac{dy}{dx}\right)^2 + 1 = \left(\frac{x^2}{2}-\frac{1}{2x^2}\right)^2 + 1 = \left(\frac{x^2}{2}+\frac{1}{2x^2}\right)^2$

$ds = \left(\frac{1}{2}x^2+\frac{1}{2x^2}\right)dx$. $S = 2\pi\int_1^3 y\,ds = 2\pi\int_1^3 \left(\frac{1}{6}x^3+\frac{1}{2x}\right)\left(\frac{1}{2}x^2+\frac{1}{2x^2}\right)dx$

$$= 2\pi\int_1^3 \left(\frac{1}{12}x^5+\frac{1}{3}x+\frac{1}{4x^3}\right)dx$$

$$= 2\pi\left[\frac{1}{60}x^5+\frac{1}{6}x^2-\frac{1}{8x^2}\right]_1^3 = \frac{463\pi}{45}$$

5. $$ds = \sqrt{1+\left(y^3-\frac{1}{4y^3}\right)^2}\,dy = \sqrt{1+y^6-\frac{1}{2}+\frac{1}{16y^6}}\,dy$$

$$= \sqrt{y^6+\frac{1}{2}+\frac{1}{16y^6}}\,dy = \sqrt{\left(y^3+\frac{1}{4y^3}\right)^2}\,dy.$$

$$S = 2\pi\int_1^2 y\,ds = 2\pi\int_1^2 y\left(y^3+\frac{1}{4y^3}\right)dy = 2\pi\left[\frac{y^5}{5}-\frac{1}{4y}\right]_0^{2\pi} = \frac{253\pi}{20}$$

6. $$S = 2\pi\int_0^1 x\sqrt{1+x^2}\,dx = \frac{2\pi}{3}(1+x^2)^{3/2}\Big]_0^1 = \frac{2\pi}{3}[2\sqrt{2}-1]$$

7. $y = \frac{1}{3}(x^2+2)^{3/2}$, $0 \le x \le 3$. $\frac{dy}{dx} = x\sqrt{x^2+2}$.

$$ds = \sqrt{1+\left(\frac{dy}{dx}\right)^2} = \sqrt{1+x^2(x^2+2)}\,dx = \sqrt{(x^2+1)^2}\,dx$$

$$S = \int 2\pi\rho\,ds = 2\pi\int_0^3 x(x^2+1)\,dx = 2\pi\left[\frac{x^4}{4}+\frac{x^2}{2}\right]_0^3 = \frac{99\pi}{2}$$

8. $y = 4 - \frac{3}{4}x \Rightarrow \frac{dy}{dx} = -\frac{3}{4}$ so $1+\left(\frac{dy}{dx}\right)^2 = \frac{25}{16}$

$$S = 2\pi\int_0^4 \frac{5}{4}\left(4-\frac{3}{4}x\right)dx = 2\pi\left[5x-\frac{15}{32}x^2\right]_0^4 = 25\pi$$

9. $\frac{y}{x} = \tan\theta \Rightarrow y = (\tan\theta)x \Rightarrow 1 = (\tan\theta)\frac{dx}{dy} \Rightarrow \frac{dx}{dy} = \cot\theta$.

$ds = \sqrt{1+\cot^2\theta}\,d\theta = \csc\theta$. Let L be the slant height of the frustrum.

$$S = 2\pi\int\rho\,ds = 2\pi\int_{r_1}^{r_2}\csc\theta\,y\,dy = \csc\theta\cdot\frac{1}{2}y^2\Big]_{r_1}^{r_2}$$

$$= 2\pi\,\frac{r_2^2-r_1^2}{2}\cdot\frac{L}{r_2-r_1} = \pi(r_2+r_1)L.$$

10. $y = 4x$ and $y = x^3$ intersect in the points $x = 0, \pm 2$

$$S_1 = 2\pi\int_0^2 x^3\sqrt{1+9x^4}\,dx = 2\pi\left[\frac{1}{54}(1+9x^4)^{3/2}\right]_0^2 = \frac{\pi}{27}[145\sqrt{145}-1]$$

$$S_2 = 2\pi\int_0^2 4\sqrt{17}\,x\,dx = 8\pi\sqrt{17}\left[\frac{1}{2}x^2\right]_0^2 = 16\sqrt{17}\pi$$

Total area is then $\frac{\pi}{27}[145\sqrt{145}-1] + 16\sqrt{17}\pi$

11. (a) $S = 2\pi\int_0^{2\pi}(1+\sin t)\sqrt{(-\sin t)^2+\cos^2 t}\,dt$

$$= 2\pi\int_0^{2\pi}(1+\sin t)\,dt = 2\pi(t-\cos t)\Big]_0^{2\pi} = 4\pi^2$$

(b) Example 4 found the general formuls to be $S = 4\pi^2a^2$.

If $a = 1$, $S = 4\pi^2$ as found above.

12. $x = t^2 \Rightarrow \frac{dx}{dt} = 2t$; $y = t \Rightarrow \frac{dy}{dt} = 1$

$$S = 2\pi \int_0^1 y\sqrt{\left(\frac{dx}{dt}\right)^2 + \left(\frac{dy}{dt}\right)^2}\, dt = 2\pi \int_0^1 t\sqrt{1 + 4t^2}\, dt$$

$$= 2\pi \left[\frac{1}{12}(1 + 4t^2)^{3/2}\right]_0^1 = \frac{\pi}{6}[5\sqrt{5} - 1]$$

13. $x = a\cos^3 t \Rightarrow \frac{dx}{dt} = -3a\cos^2 t \sin t \Rightarrow \left(\frac{dx}{dt}\right)^2 = 9a^2\cos^4 t \sin^2 t$

$y = a\sin^3 t \Rightarrow \frac{dy}{dt} = 3a\sin^2 t \cos t \Rightarrow \left(\frac{dy}{dt}\right)^2 = 9a^2 \sin^4 t \cos^2 t$

$$ds = \sqrt{\left(\frac{dx}{dt}\right)^2 + \left(\frac{dy}{dt}\right)^2}\, dt = \sqrt{9a^2\cos^4 t \sin^2 t + 9a^2 \sin^4 t \cos^2 t}\, dt$$

$= 3a \cos t \sin t\, dt$. $S = 2\pi\int \rho\, ds$. Therefore,

$$S = 2 \cdot 2\pi \int_0^{\frac{\pi}{2}} (a\sin^3 t)(3a\cos t \sin t)\, dt = 12\pi a^2 \left(\frac{\sin^5 t}{5}\right)\Bigg]_0^{\frac{\pi}{2}} = \frac{12\pi a^2}{5}$$

14. $x = t + 1 \Rightarrow \frac{dx}{dt} = 1$; $y = \frac{t^2}{2} + t \Rightarrow \frac{dy}{dt} = t + 1$

$$S = 2\pi \int_0^1 x\sqrt{\left(\frac{dx}{dt}\right)^2 + \left(\frac{dy}{dt}\right)^2}\, dt = 2\pi \int_0^1 (t + 1)\sqrt{1 + (t + 1)^2}\, dt$$

$$= \frac{2\pi}{3}\left[((1 + (t + 1)^2)^{3/2}\right]_0^1 = \frac{4\pi}{3}[13\sqrt{26} - \sqrt{2}]$$

15. The limits of integration will be from θ_1 to θ_2, where $\cos\theta_1 = \frac{a + h}{r}$ and $\cos\theta_2 = \frac{a}{r}$. We parametize the circle by $x = r\cos\theta$ and $y = r\sin\theta$. Then $ds = \sqrt{(-r\sin\theta)^2 + (r\cos\theta)^2}\, d\theta = r\, d\theta$.

$$S = 2\pi \int_{\theta_1}^{\theta_2} y\, ds = 2\pi \int_{\cos^{-1}\frac{a+h}{r}}^{\cos^{-1}\frac{a}{r}} r^2 \sin\theta\, d\theta = 2\pi r^2 [-\cos\theta]_{\cos^{-1}\frac{a+h}{r}}^{\cos^{-1}\frac{a}{r}} = 2\pi r h.$$

This is independent of a, the location of h.

5.7 THE AVERAGE VALUE OF A FUNCTION

1. (a) $y_{av} = \frac{1}{\frac{\pi}{2}} \int_0^{\frac{\pi}{2}} \sin x \, dx = -\frac{2}{\pi} \cos x \Big]_0^{\frac{\pi}{2}} = \frac{2}{\pi}$

(b) $y_{av} = \frac{1}{2\pi} \int_0^{2\pi} \sin x \, dx = -\frac{2}{\pi} \cos x \Big]_0^{2\pi} = 0$

2. (a) $y_{av} = \frac{1}{\frac{\pi}{2}} \int_0^{\frac{\pi}{2}} \sin^2 x \, dx = \frac{2}{\pi} \int_0^{\frac{\pi}{2}} \left(\frac{1}{2} - \frac{1}{2} \cos 2x\right) dx$

$= \frac{2}{\pi} \left[\frac{1}{2} x - \frac{1}{4} \sin 2x\right]_0^{\frac{\pi}{2}} = \frac{1}{2}$

(b) $y_{av} = \frac{1}{2\pi} \int_0^{2\pi} \sin^2 x \, dx = \frac{1}{2\pi} \int_0^{2\pi} \left(\frac{1}{2} - \frac{1}{2} \cos 2x\right) dx$

$= \frac{1}{2\pi} \left[\frac{1}{2} x - \frac{1}{4} \sin 2x\right]_0^{2\pi} = \frac{1}{2}$

3. $y_{av} = \frac{1}{8} \int_4^{12} \sqrt{2x+1} \, dx = \frac{1}{24} (2x+1)^{3/2} \Big]_4^{12} = \frac{49}{12}$

4. $y_{av} = \frac{1}{\pi} \int_0^{\pi} \left(\frac{1}{2} + \frac{1}{2} \cos 2x\right) dx = \frac{1}{\pi} \left[\frac{1}{2} x + \frac{1}{4} \sin 2x\right]_0^{\pi} = \frac{1}{2}$

5. (a) $y_{av} = \frac{\text{area}}{b - a} = \frac{1}{2}$ (b) $y_{av} = \frac{2}{4} = \frac{1}{2}$

6. $(i^2)_{av} = \frac{\omega}{2\pi} \int_0^{\frac{2\pi}{\omega}} I^2 \sin^2 \omega t \, dt = \frac{\omega}{2\pi} \int_0^{\frac{2\pi}{\omega}} I^2 \left(\frac{1}{2} - \frac{1}{2} \cos 2\omega t\right) dt$

$= \frac{I^2 \omega}{2\pi} \left[\frac{1}{2} t - \frac{1}{4\omega} \sin 2\omega t\right]_0^{\frac{2\pi}{\omega}} = \frac{I^2 \omega}{2\pi} \cdot \frac{\pi}{\omega} = \frac{I^2}{2}$

7. If $v = V \sin \omega t$ then $v^2 = V^2 \sin^2 \omega t$. Then

$(v^2)_{av} = \frac{\omega}{2\pi} \int_0^{2\pi} V^2 \sin^2 \omega t \, dt = \frac{V^2 \omega}{2\pi} \int_0^{2\pi} \left(\frac{1}{2} - \frac{1}{2} \cos 2\omega t\right) dt$

$= \frac{V^2 \omega}{2\pi} \left[\frac{1}{2} t - \frac{1}{4} \cos 2\omega t\right]_0^{2\pi} = \frac{V^2}{2}$. Therefore,

$V_{rms} = \sqrt{\frac{V^2}{2}} = \frac{V}{\sqrt{2}}$

8. $I_{rms} = \frac{I}{\sqrt{2}} \Rightarrow I = 20\sqrt{2} \approx 28.3$ amps.

9. Average daily inventory $= \frac{1}{30}\int_0^{30}\left(450 - \frac{x^2}{2}\right)dx = 300.$

Average daily holding cost = 300 × .02 = \$6.00.

10. $I_{av} = \frac{1}{60}\int_0^{60}(600 - 20\sqrt{15x})\,dx = \frac{1}{60}\left[600x - 20\sqrt{15}\left(\frac{2}{3}x^{3/2}\right)\right]_0^{60} = 200$ cases

The average daily holding cost = 200 (.005) = \$1.00 day

11. $f_{av} = \frac{1}{365}\int_0^{365} 37\sin\left[\frac{2\pi}{365}(x - 101) + 25\right]dx$

$= \frac{1}{365}\left[25x - \frac{37\cdot365}{2\pi}\cos\left(\frac{2\pi}{365}(x - 101)\right)\right]_0^{365} = 25$

12. (a) $\int_0^{60} L(t)\,dt \approx \frac{5}{2}[0 + 2(.2) + 2(.5) + 2(2.6) + 2(4.2) + 2(3.0)$

$+ 2(1.7) + 2(.7) + 2(.35) + 2(.2) + 0 + 0) = 67.25$ million lumens–msec.

Average lumen output $= \frac{1}{60}\int_0^{60} L(t)\,dt = 1.12$ million lumens–msec.

(b) $765\,t = 67.25 \times 10^6 \Rightarrow T = 87{,}900$ msec $= 87.9$ seconds.

13. (b) $v_{av} = \frac{1}{2}\int_0^2 32t\,dt = 8t^2\Big]_0^2 = 32$

(c) $v_{av} = \frac{1}{64}\int_0^{64} 8\sqrt{s}\,ds = \frac{1}{12}s^{3/2}\Big]_0^{64} = \frac{128}{3}$

14.

(b) $v_{av} = \frac{1}{2}\int_0^2 1.62t\,dt = \frac{1}{2}[0.81t^2]_0^2 = 1.62\ m/s^2$

(c) $v_{av} = \frac{1}{3.24}\int_0^{3.24}\sqrt{3.24s}\,ds = \frac{1}{\sqrt{3.24}}\left[\frac{2}{3}s^{3/2}\right]_0^{3.24} = 2.16\ m/s^2$

15. $f'_{av} = \frac{1}{b-a}\int_a^b f'(x)\,dx = \frac{1}{b-a}f(x)\Big]_a^b = \frac{f(b) - f(a)}{b-a}$

5.8 MOMENTS AND CENTERS OF MASS

1. $100x = 80(5) \Rightarrow x = 4$ feet from the fulcrum.

2. The coordinates of the centers of mass of the two pieces of the frame are $(\frac{L}{2}, 0)$ and $(0, \frac{L}{2})$. The center of mass of the frame lies at the midpoint between these two, which is $(\frac{L}{4}, \frac{L}{4})$.

3. $M_0 = \int_0^L x\,dx = \frac{1}{2}x^2\Big]_0^L = \frac{L^2}{2}$; $M = \int_0^L dx = L$; $\bar{x} = \frac{M_0}{M} = \frac{L}{2}$.

4. $M = \int_0^L \left(1 + \frac{x}{L}\right)dx = x + \frac{1}{2L}x^2\Big]_0^L = \frac{3L}{2}$

$$M_0 = \int_0^L x\left(1 + \frac{x}{L}\right)dx = \frac{1}{2}x^2 + \frac{1}{3L}x^3\Big]_0^L = \frac{5L^2}{6}$$

$$\bar{x} = \frac{M_0}{M} = \frac{5L^2}{6}\cdot\frac{2}{3L} = \frac{5L}{9}$$

5. $M_0 = \int_0^L \left(1 + \frac{x}{L}\right)^2 x\,dx = \int_0^L \left(x + \frac{2x^2}{L} + \frac{x^3}{L}\right)dx = \frac{1}{2}x^2 + \frac{2}{3L}x^3 + \frac{1}{4L}x^4\Big]_0^L = \frac{17}{12}L^2$

$$M = \int_0^L \left(1 + \frac{x}{L}\right)^2 dx = \int_0^L\left(1 + \frac{2x}{L} + \frac{x^2}{L^2}\right)dx = x + \frac{x^2}{L} + \frac{x^3}{3L^2}\Big]_0^L = \frac{7L}{3}$$

$$\bar{x} = \frac{M_0}{M} = \frac{17\,L^2}{12}\cdot\frac{3}{7L} = \frac{17\,L}{28}$$

6. $M = \int_0^{\frac{L}{2}} 2\,dx + \int_{\frac{L}{2}}^L dx = 2x\Big]_0^{\frac{L}{2}} + x\Big]_{\frac{L}{2}}^L = \frac{3L}{2}$

$$M_0 = \int_0^{\frac{L}{2}} 2x\,dx + \int_{\frac{L}{2}}^L x\,dx = x^2\Big]_0^{\frac{L}{2}} + \frac{1}{2}x^2\Big]_{\frac{L}{2}}^L = \frac{5L^2}{8}$$

$$\bar{x} = \frac{M_0}{M} = \frac{5L^2}{8}\cdot\frac{2}{3L} = \frac{5L}{12}$$

7. $M_x = \int_0^1 6x^2\,dx = 2x^3\Big]_0^1 = 2$; $\bar{y} = \frac{2}{3}$

8. $M = \int_{-2}^2 |3x|(4 - x^2)\,dx = 2\int_0^2 3x(4 - x^2)dx = 24$

$$M_y = \int_{-2}^2 x|3x|(4 - x^2)\,dx = 0;\quad \bar{x} = 0.$$

$$M_x = \int_{-2}^2 \frac{1}{2}|3x|(4 - x^2)^2\,dx = 3\int_0^2 (4 - x^2)^2\,x\,dx$$

$$= 3\left[-\frac{1}{6}(4 - x^2)^3\right]_0^2 = 32.\quad \bar{y} = \frac{32}{24} = \frac{4}{3}$$

9. $M = \int_0^1 (y - y^3)\,dy = \frac{1}{2}y^2 - \frac{1}{4}y^4\Big]_0^1 = \frac{1}{4}$

$M_x = \int_0^1 y\,dM = \int_0^1 y\,(y - y^3)\,dy = \frac{1}{3}y^3 - \frac{1}{5}y^5\Big]_0^1 = \frac{2}{15}$. $\bar{y} = \frac{2}{15}\cdot\frac{4}{1} = \frac{8}{15}$

$M_y = \int_0^1 \frac{1}{2}x\,dM = \int_0^1 \frac{1}{2}(y - y^3)^2\,dy = \frac{1}{2}\int_0^1 (y^2 - 2y^4 + y^6)\,dy$

$= \frac{1}{2}\left[\frac{1}{3}y^3 - \frac{2}{5}y^5 + \frac{1}{7}y^7\right]_0^1 = \frac{4}{105}$. $\bar{x} = \frac{4}{105}\cdot\frac{4}{1} = \frac{16}{105}$

$(\bar{x}, \bar{y}) = \left(\frac{16}{105}, \frac{8}{15}\right)$

10. $M = \int_{-2}^2 (4 - x^2)\,dx = \frac{32}{3}$; $\bar{x} = 0$ by symmetry.

$M_x = \int_{-2}^2 \frac{1}{2}(4 + x^2)(4 - x^2)\,dx = \frac{1}{2}\int_{-2}^2 (16 - x^4)\,dx = \frac{128}{5}$

$\bar{y} = \frac{128}{5} \div \frac{32}{3} = \frac{12}{5}$. $\therefore (\bar{x}, \bar{y}) = \left(0, \frac{12}{5}\right)$

11. $M = \int_0^2 [(x - x^2) - (-x)]\,dx = x^2 - \frac{1}{3}x^3\Big]_0^2 = \frac{4}{3}$.

$M_x = \int_0^2 \frac{1}{2}(x - x^2 + (-x))(2x - x^2)\,dx = -\frac{1}{2}\int_0^2 x^2(2x - x^2)\,dx$

$= -\frac{1}{2}\left[\frac{1}{2}x^4 - \frac{1}{5}x^5\right]_0^2 = -\frac{4}{5}$; $\bar{y} = \left(-\frac{4}{5}\right)\left(\frac{3}{4}\right) = -\frac{3}{5}$

$M_y = \int_0^2 x(2x - x^2)\,dx = \frac{2}{3}x^3 - \frac{1}{4}x^4\Big]_0^2 = \frac{4}{3}$. $\bar{x} = \frac{4}{3}\cdot\frac{3}{4} = 1$

$(\bar{x}, \bar{y}) = \left(1, -\frac{3}{5}\right)$

12. $M = \int_0^2 (2y - y^2)\,dy = \frac{4}{3}$

$M_x = \int_0^2 y(2y - y^2)\,dy = \frac{4}{3}$. $\bar{y} = \frac{4}{3} \div \frac{4}{3} = 1$

$M_y = \int_0^2 \frac{1}{2}y^2(2y - y^2)\,dy = \frac{4}{5}$. $\bar{x} = \frac{4}{5} \div \frac{4}{3} = \frac{3}{5}$

$\therefore (\bar{x}, \bar{y}) = \left(\frac{3}{5}, 1\right)$

13. $M = \frac{\pi a^2}{4}$; $M_x = \frac{1}{2}\int_0^a \left(\sqrt{a^2 - x^2}\right)^2 dx = \frac{1}{2}\left[a^2 x - \frac{x^3}{3}\right]_0^a = \frac{a^3}{3}$.

$\bar{y} = \frac{a^3}{3} \cdot \frac{4}{\pi a^2} = \frac{4a}{3\pi}$. $\bar{x} = \bar{y}$ by symmetry.

14. $M = \int_{-h}^{h} (h^2 - x^2)\, dx = 2\left[h^2 x - \frac{1}{3}x^3\right]_0^h = \frac{4h^3}{3}$

$M_x = \int_{-h}^{h} \frac{1}{2}(h^2 - x^2)^2\, dx = \frac{8\,h^5}{15}$. $\bar{y} = \frac{8\,h^5}{15} \div \frac{4h^3}{3} = \frac{2h^2}{5}$.

$\bar{x} = 0$ by symmetry. $\therefore$ $(\bar{x}, \bar{y}) = \left(0, \frac{2h^2}{5}\right)$

15. $M = a^2 - \frac{\pi a^2}{4}$; $M_x = \int_0^a \frac{a + \sqrt{a^2 - x^2}}{2}\left(a - \sqrt{a^2 - x^2}\right) dx$

$= \frac{1}{2}\int_0^a x^2\, dx = \frac{1}{6}x^3\Big]_0^a = \frac{a^3}{6}$. $\bar{y} = \frac{a^3}{6} \cdot \frac{4}{a^2 - \pi a^2} = \frac{2a}{3(4 - \pi)}$.

By symmetry, $\bar{x} = \bar{y}$.

16. $M = \int_0^{\pi} \sin x\, dx = -\cos x\Big]_0^{\pi} = 2$

$M_x = \int_0^{\pi} \frac{1}{2}\sin^2 x\, dx = \frac{1}{2}\int_0^{\pi}\left(\frac{1}{2} - \frac{1}{2}\cos 2x\right)dx = \frac{1}{2}\left[\frac{1}{2}x - \frac{1}{4}\sin 2x\right]_0^{\pi} = \frac{\pi}{4}$.

$\bar{y} = \frac{\pi}{4} \div 2 = \frac{\pi}{8}$. $\bar{x} = \frac{\pi}{2}$ by symmetry. $\therefore$ $(\bar{x}, \bar{y}) = \left(\frac{\pi}{2}, \frac{\pi}{8}\right)$

17. $M = \int_0^2 (2y - y^2)\, dy = y^2 - \frac{1}{3}y^3\Big]_0^2 = \frac{4}{3}$

$M_y = \frac{1}{2}\int_0^2 (2y - y^2)^2\, dy = \frac{2}{3}y^3 - \frac{1}{2}y^4 + \frac{1}{10}y^5\Big]_0^2 = \frac{8}{15}$

$\bar{x} = \frac{8}{15} \cdot \frac{3}{4} = \frac{2}{5}$. $\bar{y} = 1$ by symmetry.

18. $M_{xx} = \int_{-a}^{a} \frac{1}{2}\left(\sqrt{a^2 - x^2}\right)^2 dx = \frac{1}{2}\left[a^2 x - \frac{1}{3}x^3\right]_a^a = \frac{2a^3}{3}$. Area of semicircle $= \frac{\pi a^2}{2}$

$\bar{y} = \frac{2a^3}{3} \div \frac{\pi a^2}{2} = \frac{4a}{3\pi}$. $\bar{x} = 0$ by symmetry. $\therefore$ $(\bar{x}, \bar{y}) = \left(0, \frac{4a}{3\pi}\right)$

19. $y = x^3 - 3x^2 \Rightarrow y' = 3x^2 - 6x = 0 \Leftrightarrow x = 0, 2$. $y' < 0$ for $x < 0$, $y' > 0$ for $x > 0$ $\Rightarrow$ there is maximum at the point $(0,0)$. $y' < 0$ for $x < 2$ and $y' > 0$ for $x > 2 \Rightarrow$ there is minimum at the point $(2,-4)$.

$$A = \int_0^3 (3x^2 - x^3)\,dx = x^3 - \frac{1}{4}x^4\Big]_0^3 = \frac{27}{4}$$

20. $$M = \int_{-1}^{1} (1 - x^n)\,dx = 2\left[x - \frac{1}{n+1}x^{n+1}\right]_0^1 = \frac{2n}{n+1}$$

$$M_x = \int_{-1}^{1} \frac{1}{2}(1 - x^n)^2\,dx = \frac{1}{2}\left[x - \frac{2}{n+1}x^{n+1} + \frac{1}{2n+1}x^{2n+1}\right]_{-1}^{1} = \frac{2n^2}{(n+1)(2n+1)}.$$

$\bar{y} = \dfrac{2n^2}{(n+1)(2n+1)} \div \dfrac{2n}{n+1} = \dfrac{n}{2n+1}$. $\bar{x} = 0$ by symmetry.

$\therefore$ $(\bar{x}, \bar{y}) = \left(0, \dfrac{n}{2n+1}\right)$. Limiting position is $\left(0, \dfrac{1}{2}\right)$ since $\lim\limits_{n\to\infty} \dfrac{n}{2n+1} = \dfrac{1}{2}$.

21. A median lies along the y-axis, and the centroid lies $\frac{2}{3}$ of the distance from $(0,3)$ to $(0,0)$ at the point $(0,1)$.

22. The median from the vertex at the origin is $\frac{\sqrt{2}}{2}$ units long. The centroid is located $\frac{2}{3}$ of this length away from the origin, or $\frac{\sqrt{2}}{3}$ units along the median. The coordinates of this point are $(\frac{1}{3}, \frac{1}{3})$.

23. The median from the vertex at the origin is $\frac{3\sqrt{2}}{2}$ units long. The centroid is located $\frac{2}{3}$ of this length away from the origin, or $\sqrt{2}$ units along the median. The coordinates of this point are $(1,1)$.

24. Let the vertices be labeled $A(a,0)$, $B(b,0)$ and $C(0,c)$. The coordinates of the midpoint of AB are $Q(\frac{a+b}{2}, 0)$ and of the midpoint of BC are $R(\frac{b}{2}, \frac{c}{2})$. If one writes the parametric equations of the line from A to R as:

$$x = a + t\left(\frac{b}{2} - a\right) \text{ and } y = \frac{c}{2}t$$

then the answer is obtained quickly by letting $t = \frac{2}{3}$ to find the coordinates of the median as $(\frac{1}{3}(a + b), \frac{1}{3}c)$. An alternative solution is to write the equations of the line through A and R and the line through C and Q, and find the point of intersection, as follows:

Through CQ: $y = \dfrac{c}{b-2a}(x-a)$

Through AR: $y - c = -\dfrac{2c}{a+b}x$

$$\frac{c}{b-2a}(x-a) = c - \frac{2c}{a+b}x \Rightarrow \left(\frac{c}{b-2a} + \frac{2c}{a+b}\right)x = c + \frac{ac}{b-2a}$$

$$x = \frac{(bc-ac)(a+b)}{3bc-3ac} = \frac{1}{3}(a+b). \text{ Then } y = \frac{c}{b-2a}\left(\frac{1}{3}a + \frac{1}{3}b - a\right) = \frac{1}{3}c$$

25. $$M_x = \int_0^2 \sqrt{x}\left(\sqrt{1+\frac{1}{4x}}\right)dx = \int_0^2 \sqrt{x+\frac{1}{4}}\,dx = \left(x+\frac{1}{4}\right)^{3/2}\Bigg]_0^2 = \frac{13}{6}$$

This differs from the answer in Prob. 1, Art. 5.6 by a factor of 2π.

26. $$ds = \sqrt{1+9x^4}\,dx;\ M_x = \int y\,ds = \int_0^1 x^3\sqrt{1+9x^4}\,dx$$

$$= \frac{1}{54}(1+9x^4)^{3/2}\Bigg]_0^1 = \frac{1}{54}[10\sqrt{10}-1]$$

The integrand is the same, except for a factor of 2π.

27. Let the vertices of the triangle be O(0,0), B(b,0) and C(c,h).

The equation of side OC is $y = \frac{h}{c}x$ or $x = \frac{c}{h}y$. The equation of side BC is

$y = \dfrac{h}{c-b}(x-b)$ or $x = \dfrac{c-b}{h}y + b$. Then

$$M = \int_0^h k\sqrt{y}\left(\frac{c-b}{h}y + b - \frac{c}{h}y\right)dy = \frac{bk}{h}\int_0^h (h-y)\sqrt{y}\,dy = \frac{4bh^{3/2}}{15}$$

$$M_x = \frac{bk}{h}\int_0^h y(h-y)\sqrt{y}\,dy = \frac{4bh^{7/2}}{35}.\quad \bar{y} = \frac{4bh^{7/2}}{35}\cdot\frac{15}{4bh^{3/5}} = \frac{3h}{7}$$

28. Using the same notation as problem 27, we have:

$$M = \int_0^h ky^2\left(\frac{c-b}{h}y + b - \frac{c}{h}y\right)dy = \frac{bk}{h}\int_0^h (h-y)y^2\,dy = \frac{bkh^3}{12}$$

$$M_x = \frac{bk}{h}\int_0^h y(h-y)y^2\,dy = \frac{bkh^4}{20}.\quad \bar{y} = \frac{bkh^4}{20}\cdot\frac{12}{bkh^3} = \frac{3h}{5}$$

29. $M = \int_0^1 12x(x - x^2)\, dx = 12\left[\frac{x^3}{3} - \frac{x^4}{4}\right]_0^1 = 1$

$$M_x = \int_0^1 (12x)\left(\frac{x + x^2}{2}\right)(x - x^2)\, dx = 6\int_0^1 (x^3 - x^5)\, dx = \frac{1}{2}$$

$$M_y = \int_0^1 12x(x - x^2)\, dx = \frac{3}{5}. \quad \therefore (\bar{x}, \bar{y}) = \left(\frac{3}{5}, \frac{1}{2}\right)$$

30. $V = \pi\int_0^{100} y^2\, dx = \pi\int_0^{100} \left(\frac{1}{200}x + \frac{1}{2}\right)^2 dx = \frac{700\pi}{12}$

$$M_y = \pi\int_0^{100} x\left(\frac{1}{200}x + \frac{1}{2}\right)^2 dx = \frac{42500\pi}{12}. \quad \bar{y} = \frac{42500\pi}{12} \cdot \frac{12}{700\pi} = 60\frac{5}{7}$$

$\therefore$ The balance point is $39\frac{2}{7}$ cm from heavier end.

31. $M = ka\int_0^{\pi} a \sin\theta\, d\theta = -ak\cos\theta\Big]_0^{\pi} = 2ak$

$$M_y = ka\int_0^{\pi} \sin\theta\,(a\cos\theta)\, d\theta = ka^2\left(\frac{1}{2}\sin^2\theta\right]_0^{\pi} = 0$$

$$M_x = ka^2\int_0^{\pi} \sin^2\theta = ka^2\left[\frac{1}{2}\theta - \frac{1}{4}\sin 2\theta\right]_0^{\pi} = \frac{a^2k\pi}{2}.$$

$$\bar{x} = 0;\ \bar{y} = \frac{a^2k\pi}{2}\frac{1}{2ak} = \frac{\pi a}{4}$$

5.9 WORK

1. $6 = (0.4)k \Rightarrow k = 15;\ W = \int_0^{0.2} 15x\, dx = \frac{15}{2}x^2\Big]_0^{0.2} = 0.3$ Newtons

2. $90 = k(1) \Rightarrow k = 90;\ W = \int_0^5 90x\, dx = 45x^2\Big]_0^5 = 1125$ Newtons

3. (a) $800 = 4k \Rightarrow k = 200$

(b) $\int_0^2 200x\, dx = 400$ in–lbs

(c) $200x = 1600 \Rightarrow x = 8$ in

4. $10{,}000 = k(1) \Rightarrow k = 10{,}000$

(a) $W = \int_0^{0.5} 10000x\, dx = 5000x^2\Big]_0^{0.5} = 1250$ in–lbs

(b) $W = \int_{0.5}^{1} 10000x\, dx = 5000x^2\Big]_{0.5}^{1} = 3750$ in–lbs

5. $5k = 1 \Rightarrow k = \frac{1}{5}$; $W = \int_0^5 \frac{1}{5}x\,dx = \frac{x^2}{10}\Big]_0^5 = \frac{5}{2}$ ft-lbs

$\frac{1}{5}x = 2 \Rightarrow x = 10$. Total length is 12 ft.

6. $150 = k\left(\frac{1}{16}\right) \Rightarrow k = 2400$

$$W = \int_0^{\frac{1}{8}} 2400\,x\,dx = 1200x^2\Big]_0^{\frac{1}{8}} = 18.75 \text{ in-lbs}$$

Weight required to compress scales $= \frac{1}{8}(2400) = 300$ lbs.

7. (a) $W = \int_{-1}^{0} \frac{k}{(1-x)^2}dx = \frac{k}{1-x}\Big]_{-1}^{0} = \frac{k}{2}$

(b) $W = \int_3^5 \left[\frac{k}{(x+1)^2} + \frac{k}{(x-1)^2}\right]dx = \frac{-k}{x+1} + \frac{-k}{x-1}\Big]_3^5 = \frac{k}{3}$

8. $W = \int_0^R mg\left(\frac{r}{R}\right)dr = \frac{mg}{R}\left[\frac{1}{2}r^2\right]_0^R = \frac{mgR}{2}$

9. $18\frac{dw}{dx} = 72 \Rightarrow \frac{dw}{dx} = 4$ lbs/ft. $\therefore$ $w = 4x + C$. $x = 0 \Rightarrow w = 144$ so $C = 144$.

$$W = \int_0^{18} (144 - 4x)\,dx = 144x - 2x^2\Big]_0^{18} = 1,944 \text{ ft-lbs}$$

10. (a) $W = 42\int_0^{20} 25\pi\,(23 - y)\,dy = 1050\pi\left[23y - \frac{1}{2}y^2\right]_0^{20} = 273,000\,\pi$ ft-lbs

(b) $\bar{h} = 11$ ft; $wV = 42\pi\,(5)^2\,20 = 21,000\pi$ lbs.

$W = 13 \times 21,000\pi = 273,000$ ft-lbs. The answer is the same.

11. $W = 48\int_0^h \pi x^2 y\,(\pi + h - y)\,dy$

$= 48\int_0^h \pi\left(\frac{ry}{h}\right)^2(\pi + h - y)\,dy$

$= \frac{48r^2\pi}{h^2}\int_0^h (\pi y^2 + hy^2 - y^3)\,dy$

$= 4\pi r^2 h\,(4\pi + h)$

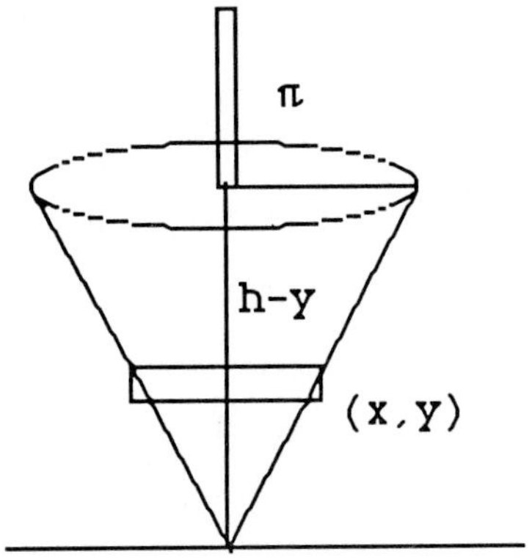

Note: If you know that the centroid of a right circular cone is located $\frac{3}{4}$ the distance from the vertex to the base, then you can compute

$$W = (48)\left(\frac{\pi r^2 h}{3}\right)\left(\frac{1}{4}h + \pi\right) = 4\pi r^2 h\,(4\pi + h)$$

12. $W = 51.2\int_0^{20} 100\pi\,(30 - y)\,dy = 5120\pi\left[30y - \frac{1}{2}y^2\right]_0^{20} = 2{,}048{,}000\pi$ ft-lbs.

13. $V = 9800\int_0^{16} \pi\,y\,(16 - y)\,dy = 9800\left[8y^2 - \frac{1}{3}y^3\right]_0^{16} = \frac{20{,}070{,}400\pi}{3}$ Newtons

14. $\bar{y} = \dfrac{\int_0^5 2y\sqrt{27 - y^2}\,dy}{\frac{25\pi}{2}} = \dfrac{20}{3\pi}$. $W = 42\left(11 + \frac{20}{3\pi}\right)\left(\frac{25\pi}{2}\right)20 \approx 432{,}853.9$ ft-lbs

15. The center of mass is 2 feet below the surface.

$$W = (62.5)\left(\frac{100\pi}{3}\right)(8)\,(2 + 6) = \frac{400{,}000\pi}{3}\text{ ft-lbs} = \frac{200\pi}{3}\text{ ft-tons}$$

16. The center of mass is $\frac{5}{4}$ feet below the surface. $\frac{r}{5} = \frac{5}{4} \Rightarrow r = \frac{25}{4}$ ft.

The distance is $\left(\frac{5}{4} + 3\right)$ ft. $W = 62.5\left(\frac{\pi}{3}\right)\left(\frac{25}{4}\right)^2 5\left(\frac{17}{4}\right) = 17{,}293.3$ ft-lbs

In this problem, it might be easier to use the following:

$$W = 62.5\int_0^5 \pi x^2\,(8 - y)\,dy = 62.5\,\pi\int_0^5 \frac{25}{16}y^2\,(8 - y)\,dy$$

17. $\frac{dw}{dh} = \frac{400\text{ gal}}{4750\text{ ft}}\cdot\frac{8\text{ lbx}}{\text{gal}} = \frac{64\text{lbs}}{95\text{ ft}}$.

$w = \frac{64}{95}h + C$. $C = 800\cdot 8 = 6400$ when $h = 0$.

$$W = \int_0^{4750}\left(6400 - \frac{64}{75}h\right)dh = 22{,}800{,}000\text{ ft-lbs} = 11.400\text{ ft-tons}$$

18. $W = 56\pi\int_0^{10}(100 - y^2)(12 - y)\,dy = 308{,}000\pi$ ft-lbs.

The cost is $308{,}000\pi \times 0.005 \approx \$4{,}838$.

19. Work to fill the pipe: $62.5\int_0^{360}\left(\frac{1}{3}\right)^2\pi\,dx = 450{,}000\pi$ ft-lbs

Work to fill tank: $62.5\int_0^{25}(100\pi)(360 + x)\,dx = 58{,}203{,}125\,\pi$ ft-lbs

$$\text{Time} = \frac{(450{,}000\pi + 58{,}203{,}125\pi)\text{ ft-lbs}}{1650\text{ ft-lbs/sec}} = 31.02\text{ hrs.}$$

20. $W = wV(\bar{x} + h) = w\bar{x}\,V + wh\,V = w\bar{x}\int dV + wh\int dV$

$$= w\int x\,dV + wh\int dV, \quad \text{since } \bar{x} = \frac{\int x\,dV}{\int dV}.$$

21. $W = \frac{1}{2}mv_2^2 - \frac{1}{2}mv_1^2 = \frac{0.3125 \text{ lb}\cdot(132)^2 \text{ ft}^2/\text{s}^2}{32 \text{ ft/s}^2} = 85.1 \text{ ft-lb}$

22. Weight = 1.6 oz = .1 lb. Mass $= \frac{.1 \text{ lb}}{32 \text{ ft/s}^2} = \frac{1}{320}$ slug.

$$\text{Work} = \frac{1}{2}\cdot\frac{.1 \text{ lb}}{32 \text{ ft/s}^2}(120 \text{ ft/s})^2 = 22.5 \text{ ft-lbs.}$$

5.10 HYDROSTATIC FORCE

1. $F = \int_0^3 w(2y)\,h\,dh$

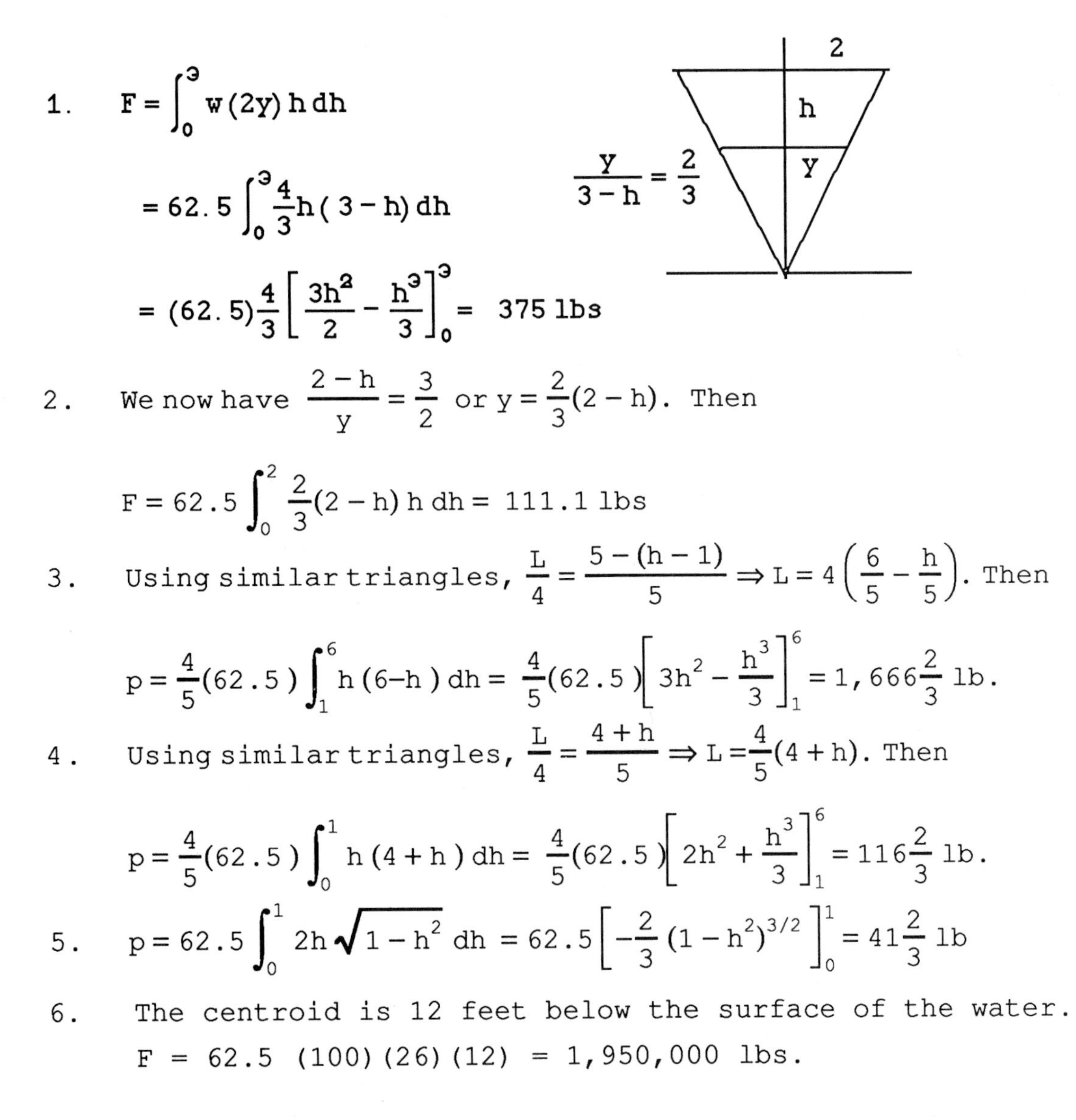

$$\frac{y}{3-h} = \frac{2}{3}$$

$$= 62.5\int_0^3 \frac{4}{3}h(3-h)\,dh$$

$$= (62.5)\frac{4}{3}\left[\frac{3h^2}{2} - \frac{h^3}{3}\right]_0^3 = 375 \text{ lbs}$$

2. We now have $\frac{2-h}{y} = \frac{3}{2}$ or $y = \frac{2}{3}(2-h)$. Then

$$F = 62.5\int_0^2 \frac{2}{3}(2-h)\,h\,dh = 111.1 \text{ lbs}$$

3. Using similar triangles, $\frac{L}{4} = \frac{5-(h-1)}{5} \Rightarrow L = 4\left(\frac{6}{5} - \frac{h}{5}\right)$. Then

$$p = \frac{4}{5}(62.5)\int_1^6 h(6-h)\,dh = \frac{4}{5}(62.5)\left[3h^2 - \frac{h^3}{3}\right]_1^6 = 1{,}666\frac{2}{3} \text{ lb.}$$

4. Using similar triangles, $\frac{L}{4} = \frac{4+h}{5} \Rightarrow L = \frac{4}{5}(4+h)$. Then

$$p = \frac{4}{5}(62.5)\int_0^1 h(4+h)\,dh = \frac{4}{5}(62.5)\left[2h^2 + \frac{h^3}{3}\right]_1^6 = 116\frac{2}{3} \text{ lb.}$$

5. $p = 62.5\int_0^1 2h\sqrt{1-h^2}\,dh = 62.5\left[-\frac{2}{3}(1-h^2)^{3/2}\right]_0^1 = 41\frac{2}{3} \text{ lb}$

6. The centroid is 12 feet below the surface of the water.

$F = 62.5\ (100)(26)(12) = 1{,}950{,}000$ lbs.

7. If d = the depth of the water, then the area $A = \frac{1}{2}bh$

$$= \left(\frac{1}{2}d\right)(2)\left(\frac{2d}{5}\right) = \frac{2d^2}{5}$$. Then, using the fact that the centroid is $\frac{d}{3}$ units below the base, we must have

$62.5\left(\frac{2d^2}{5}\right)\left(\frac{d}{3}\right) = 6667 \Rightarrow d \approx 9.3$ ft. Then $V = 30\left(\frac{2}{5}\right)(9.3)^2 \approx 1{,}033.4 \text{ ft}^3$

8. (a) $h + y = 2 \Rightarrow y = 2 - h$ and $y = x^2 \Rightarrow x = \sqrt{y}$. $dA = 2x\,dh = 2\sqrt{y}\,dh = 2\sqrt{2-h}\,dh$.

$$F = 50\int_1^2 2h\sqrt{2-h}\,dh = \frac{280}{3} \text{ lbs. (To integrate, let } u = 2-h)$$

(b) $F = 50\int_{d-1}^{d} 2h\sqrt{2-h}\,dh = \frac{200}{3}d - 40$

$\frac{200}{3}d - 40 = 160$ when $d = 3$ feet.

9. $F = \int_0^2 (62.5)\left(2\sqrt{4-h^2}\right)dy = 62.5\left(-\frac{2}{3}(4-h^2)^{3/2}\right]_0^2 = \frac{1000}{3}$ lbs.

$100x = 333.3 \Rightarrow x = 3.33$ ft. Yes, the trough will overflow because the spring will have moved only 3.33 ft by the time the the tank if full.

5.M MISCELLANEOUS PROBLEMS

1. $\text{T.D.} = \int_0^3 |3t^2 - 15t + 18|\,dt = 3\int_0^2 (t^2 - 5t + 6)\,dt - 3\int_2^3 (t^2 - 5t + 6)\,dt$

$$= 3\left[\frac{1}{3}t^3 - \frac{5}{2}t^2 + 6t\right]_0^2 - 3\left[\frac{1}{3}t^3 - \frac{5}{2}t^2 + 6t\right]_2^3 = \frac{29}{2}$$

$$\text{N.D.} = 3\int_0^3 (t^2 - 5t + 6)\,dt = 3\left[\frac{1}{3}t^3 - \frac{5}{2}t^2 + 6t\right]_0^3 = \frac{27}{2}$$

2. $\text{T.D.} = \int_0^2 |t^3 - 3t^2 + 2t|\,dt = \int_0^1 (t^3 - 3t^2 + 2t)\,dt - \int_1^2 (t^3 - 3t^2 + 2t)\,dt$

$$= \left[\frac{1}{4}t^4 - t^3 + t^2\right]_0^1 - \left[\frac{1}{4}t^4 - t^3 + t^2\right]_1^2 = \frac{1}{2}$$

$$\text{N.D.} = \int_0^2 (t^3 - 3t^2 + 2t)\,dt = \left[\frac{1}{4}t^4 - t^3 + t^2\right]_0^2 = 0$$

3. $y = 2 - x^2$ intersects $y = -x$ in the points $x = 2, -1$.

$$A = \int_{-1}^{2} (2 - x^2 + x)\,dx = 2x - \frac{1}{3}x^3 + \frac{1}{2}x^2 \Big]_{-1}^{2} = \frac{9}{2}$$

4. $y = \frac{1}{x^2}$ intersects $y = x$ in the points $x = 1$

$$A = \int_{1}^{2} \left(x - \frac{1}{x^2}\right) dx = \frac{1}{2}x^2 + \frac{1}{x}\Big]_{1}^{2} = 1$$

5. $y = x$ intersects $y = \frac{1}{\sqrt{x}}$ at the point $(1,1)$.

$$A = \int_{1}^{2} \left(x - \frac{1}{\sqrt{x}}\right) dx = \frac{1}{2}x^2 - 2\sqrt{x}\,\Big]_{1}^{2} = \frac{7}{2} - 2\sqrt{2}$$

6. $y = 3 - x^2$ intersects $y = x + 1$ in the points $x = 1, -2$

$$A = \int_{-2}^{1} [(3 - x^2) - (x + 1)]\,dx = 2x - \frac{1}{2}x^2 - \frac{1}{3}x^3\Big]_{-2}^{1} = \frac{9}{2}$$

7. $y = 2x^2$ intersects $y = x^2 + 2x + 3$ where $2x^2 = x^2 + 2x + 3$, or where $x = 3, -1$.

$$A = \int_{-1}^{3} [(x^2 + 2x + 3) - 2x^2]\,dx = \int_{-1}^{3} (-x^2 + 2x + 3)\,dx = -\frac{1}{3}x^3 + x^2 + 3x\,\Big]_{-1}^{3} = \frac{32}{3}$$

8. We will use a horizontal partition.

$$A = \int_{0}^{3} x\,dy = \int_{0}^{3} 2y^2\,dy = \frac{2}{3}y^3\Big]_{0}^{3} = 18$$

9. $4x = y^2 - 4$ intersects $4x = y + 16$ where $y^2 - 4 = y + 16$, or where $y = 5, -4$.

$$A = \int_{-4}^{5} \left(\frac{y}{4} + 4 - \frac{y^2}{4} + 1\right) dy = \frac{1}{8}y^2 + 5y - \frac{1}{12}y^3\Big]_{-4}^{5} = \frac{243}{8}$$

10. $y = x$ intersects $y = x^3$ when $x = 0$ or 1. Using symmetry,

$$A = 2\int_{0}^{1} (x - x^3)\,dx = 2\left(\frac{1}{2}x^2 - \frac{1}{4}x^4\right)\Big]_{0}^{1} = \frac{1}{2}$$

11. $y = \sin x$ intersects $y = \frac{\sqrt{2}}{2}x$ at the origin. To find the other point of intersection, we use Newton's Method on $f(x) = \sin x - \frac{\sqrt{2}}{2}x$ to find $x \approx 1.39$. Then

$$A = \int_{0}^{1.39} \left(\sin x - \frac{\sqrt{2}}{2}x\right) dx = -\cos x - \frac{\sqrt{2}}{4}x^2\Big]_{0}^{1.39} \approx 0.137$$

12. $$\int_{0}^{\frac{\pi}{4}} (x - \sin x)\,dx = \frac{1}{2}x^2 + \cos x\Big]_{0}^{\frac{\pi}{4}} = \frac{\pi^2}{32} + \frac{\sqrt{2}}{2} - 1$$

13. $y^2 = 9x$ intersects $y = \frac{3x^2}{8}$ where $9x = \left(\frac{3x^2}{8}\right)^2$, or $x = 0, 4$.

$$A = \int_0^4 \left(3\sqrt{x} - \frac{3}{8}x^2\right)dx = 2x^{3/2} - \frac{x^3}{8}\Bigg]_0^4 = 8$$

14. $\int_0^2 x\sqrt{2x^2+1}\,dx = \frac{1}{6}(2x^2+1)^{3/2}\Big]_0^2 = \frac{13}{3}$

15. $y^2 = 4x$ intersects $y = 4x - 2$ where $y = y^2 - 2$, or $y = 2, -1$.

$$A = \int_{-1}^2 \left(\frac{y}{4} + \frac{1}{2} - \frac{y^2}{4}\right)dy = \frac{y^2}{8} + \frac{y}{2} - \frac{y^3}{12}\Bigg]_{-1}^2 = \frac{9}{8}$$

16. $y = 2 - x^2$ intersects $y = x^2 - 6$ in the points $x = \pm 2$. Using symmetry,

$$2\int_0^2 [(2-x^2) - (x^2-6)]\,dx = 2\int_0^2 (8 - 2x^2)\,dx = 2\left[8x - \frac{2}{3}x^3\right]_0^2 = \frac{64}{3}$$

17. $A = \int_0^\pi (1 - |\cos x|)\,dx = \int_0^{\frac{\pi}{2}} (1 - \cos x)\,dx + \int_{\frac{\pi}{2}}^\pi (1 + \cos x)\,dx$

$$= x - \sin x\Big]_0^{\frac{\pi}{2}} + x + \sin x\Big]_{\frac{\pi}{2}}^{\pi} = \pi - 2$$

18. $2\int_0^\pi (2\sin x - \sin 2x)dx = 2\left[-2\cos x + \frac{1}{2}\cos 2x\right]_0^\pi = 8$

19. $y = x^3 - 3x^2 \Rightarrow y' = 3x^2 - 6x = 0 \Leftrightarrow x = 0, 2$. $y' < 0$ for $x < 0$, $y' > 0$ for $x > 0$ $\Rightarrow$ there is maximum at the point $(0, 0)$. $y' < 0$ for $x < 2$ and $y' > 0$ for $x > 2 \Rightarrow$ there is minimum at the point $(2, -4)$.

$$A = \int_0^3 (3x^2 - x^3)\,dx = x^3 - \frac{1}{4}x^4\Big]_0^3 = \frac{27}{4}$$

20. $x^{1/2} + y^{1/2} = a^{1/2} \Rightarrow y = (a^{1/2} - x^{1/2})^2$. $y = 0 \Rightarrow x = a$.

$$A = \int_0^a (a^{1/2} - x^{1/2})^2\,dx = \int_0^a (a - 2a^{1/2}x^{1/2} + x)dx$$

$$= ax - 2\sqrt{a}\left(\frac{2}{3}x^{3/2}\right) + \frac{1}{2}x^2\Big]_0^a = \frac{a^2}{6}$$

21. $V = 2\pi\int_0^2 x(2x - x^2)\,dx = 2\pi\left[\frac{2}{3}x^3 - \frac{1}{4}x^4\right]_0^2 = \frac{8\pi}{3}$

22. $V = \pi\int_{-\frac{\pi}{4}}^{\frac{\pi}{4}} y^2\,dx = 2\pi\int_0^{\frac{\pi}{4}} 4\tan^2 x\,dx = 8\pi\int_0^{\frac{\pi}{4}} (\sec^2 x - 1)dx =$

$$= 8\pi\,[\tan x - x\Big]_0^{\frac{\pi}{4}} = 8\pi\left(1 - \frac{\pi}{4}\right) = 2\pi(4 - \pi)$$

23. We write the volume as a funtion

$$V(x) = \int_a^x \pi[f(t)]^2\,dt = x^2 - ax. \text{ Then } V'(x) = \pi\,[f(x)]^2 = 2x - a.$$

Then $[f(x)]^2 = \dfrac{2x-a}{\pi}$ or $f(x) = \pm\sqrt{\dfrac{2x-a}{\pi}}$.

24. (a) $V = \pi\int_0^3 y^2\,dx = \pi\int_0^3 x^4\,dx = \pi\left[\frac{1}{5}x^5\right]_0^3 = \frac{243\pi}{5}$

(b) $V = 2\pi\int_0^3 y\,(x+3)dx = 2\pi\int_0^3 x^2\,(x+3)dx = 2\pi\left[\frac{1}{4}x^4 + x^3\right]_0^3 = \frac{189\pi}{2}$

(c) $V = 2\pi\int_0^3 xy\,dx = 2\pi\int_0^3 x^3\,dx = 2\pi\left[\frac{1}{4}x^4\right]_0^3 = \frac{81\pi}{2}$ or

$$V = \pi\int_0^9 [9 - x^2]\,dy = \pi\int_0^9 [9-y]dy = \pi\left[9y - \frac{1}{2}y^2\right]_0^9 = \frac{81\pi}{2}$$

(d) $V = \pi\int_0^4 x^2\,dy = \pi\int_0^4 (4y-y^2)^2\,dy = \pi\left[\frac{16}{3}y^5 - 2y^4 + \frac{1}{5}y^5\right]_0^4 = \frac{512\pi}{15}$

(e) $V = 2\pi\int_0^4 xy\,dy = 2\pi\int_0^4 (4y-y^2)y\,dy = 2\pi\left[\frac{4}{3}y^3 - \frac{1}{4}y^4\right]_0^4 = \frac{128\pi}{3}$

25. $V = 2\pi\int_0^4 y\left(y - \frac{y^2}{4}\right)dy = 2\pi\left[\frac{y^3}{3} - \frac{y^4}{16}\right]_0^4 = \frac{32\pi}{3}$

26. (a) $V = \pi\int_0^a y^2\,dx = \pi\int_0^a 4ax\,dx = 4a\pi\left[\frac{1}{2}x^2\right]_0^a = 2\pi a^3$

(b) $V = \pi\int_0^{2a} (a-x)^2\,dy = \pi\int_0^{2a}\left(a^2 - \frac{y^2}{2} + \frac{y^4}{16a^2}\right)dy$

$$= \pi\left(a^2y - \frac{1}{6}y^3 + \frac{1}{80a^2}y^5\right]_0^{2a} = \frac{16\pi a^3}{15}$$

(c) $V = \pi\int_0^{2a} (a^2 - x^2)\,dy = \pi\int_0^{2a}\left(a^2 - \frac{y^4}{16a^2}\right)dy = a^2\,y - \frac{1}{80a^2}y^5\Big]_0^{2a} = \frac{8\pi a^3}{5}$

27. We use a shell with radius $r = x$ and height $h = y = \dfrac{x}{\sqrt{x^3+8}}$.

$$V = 2\pi\int_0^2 x\left(\frac{x}{\sqrt{x^3+8}}\right)dx = 2\pi\int_0^2 \frac{x^2\,dx}{\sqrt{x^3+8}} = \frac{4\pi}{3}\sqrt{x^3+8}\,\Big]_0^2 = \frac{4\pi}{3}[4 - 2\sqrt{2}]$$

28. $V = \pi \int_0^1 (9 - x^2)\,dy = \pi \int_0^1 [9 - (y^2+1)^2]\,dy = \pi \int_0^1 (8 - 2y^2 - y^4)\,dy$

$= \pi \left[8y - \frac{2}{3}y^3 - \frac{1}{5}y^5 \right]_0^1 = \frac{107\pi}{15}$

29. We use a shell with radius $r = 2a - x$, and height $h = 2(2\sqrt{ax})$.

$V = 2\pi \int_0^a (2a - x)(4\sqrt{ax})\,dx = 8\pi\sqrt{a} \int_0^a (2a\sqrt{x} - x^{3/2})\,dx$

$= 16\pi\sqrt{a}\left(\frac{2}{3}x^{3/2}\right) - \frac{16\pi\sqrt{a}}{5}x^{5/2}\Big]_0^a = \frac{112\pi a^3}{15}$

30. A cross-sectional base area $B = s^2$. $V = \int_0^h s^2\,dy = s^2 h$.

This volume is independent of the number of turns since the cross-sectional base area would not change.

31. $V = \pi \int_0^{\frac{\pi}{2}} \sin^2 2x\,dx = \frac{\pi}{2}\int_0^{\frac{\pi}{2}} (1 - \cos 4x)\,dx = \frac{\pi}{2}\left[x - \frac{1}{4}\sin 4x \right]_0^{\frac{\pi}{2}} = \frac{\pi^2}{4}$

32. The volume is that of a cylinder with radius $r = \sqrt{3}$ and height 2 which equals $V_1 = 2(\sqrt{3})^2\pi = 6\pi$ plus two "caps". The volume of a cap is

$V = \pi \int_1^2 (4 - x^2)\,dx = \frac{5\pi}{3}$. The total volume $= \frac{28\pi}{3}$.

33. The curves $x^2 = 4y$ and $y^2 = 4x$ intersect where $x^4 = 16y^2 = 16(4x) \Rightarrow$ $x^4 - 64x = 0$ or $x = 0, 4$. A diameter in the base runs from $y = 2\sqrt{x}$ to $y = \frac{x^2}{4}$ so that a radius $r = \frac{1}{2}\left(2\sqrt{x} - \frac{x^2}{4}\right)$ and the base area is $B = \pi\left(\sqrt{x} - \frac{x^2}{8}\right)^2$. The volume of the solid is then

$V = \int_0^4 \pi\left(\sqrt{x} - \frac{x^2}{8}\right)^2 = \pi\int_0^4 \left(x - \frac{x^{5/2}}{4} + \frac{x^4}{64}\right)dx = \pi\left[\frac{x^2}{2} - \frac{x^{7/2}}{14} + \frac{x^5}{320}\right]_0^4 = \frac{72\pi}{35}$

34. The base area $B = \frac{s^2\sqrt{3}}{4} = \frac{(2y)^2\sqrt{3}}{4} = \frac{16ax\sqrt{3}}{4} = 4a\sqrt{3}\,x$

$V = 4a\sqrt{3}\int_0^a x\,dx = 4a\sqrt{3}\left[\frac{1}{2}x^2\right]_0^a = 2\sqrt{3}\,a^3$

35. If $V(a) = \int_0^a \pi [f(x)]^2 \, dx = a^2 + a$, then $V'(a) = 2a + 1$ and

$V'(x) = \pi [f(x)]^2$ also. Thus $\pi [f(x)]^2 = 2x + 1 \Rightarrow f(x) = \pm\sqrt{\dfrac{2x+1}{\pi}}$.

36. Define the function V as follows: $V(x) = \pi \int_0^x [f(t)]^2 \, dt$, $x > 0$.

If $V(x) = \pi x^3$ then $V'(x) = 3\pi x^2$. By the Fundamental Theorem of Integral

Calculus, $V'(v) = \pi [f(x)]^2$. $\therefore$ $[f(x)]^2 = 3x^2$ so $f(x) = \sqrt{3}\, x$.

37. (a) If $y = 2\sqrt{7}x^{3/2} - 1$, then $\dfrac{dy}{dx} = 3\sqrt{7x}$ and $\left(\dfrac{dy}{dx}\right)^2 = 63x$. Then

$$s = \int_0^1 \sqrt{1 + 63x} \, dx = \frac{2}{189}(1 + 63x)^{3/2} \Big]_0^1 = \frac{1022}{189}$$

(b) If $y = \dfrac{2}{3}x^{3/2} - \dfrac{1}{2}x^{1/2}$, then $\dfrac{dy}{dx} = x^{1/2} - \dfrac{1}{4}x^{-1/2}$ and

$$\left(\frac{dy}{dx}\right)^2 = x - \frac{1}{2} + \frac{1}{16}x^{-1}, \text{ so}$$

$$1 + \left(\frac{dy}{dx}\right)^2 = x + \frac{1}{2} + \frac{1}{16}x^{-1} = \left(x^{1/2} + \frac{1}{4}x^{-1/2}\right)^2. \text{ Then}$$

$$s = \int_0^4 \left(x^{1/2} + \frac{1}{4}x^{-1/2}\right) dx = \frac{2}{3}x^{3/2} + \frac{1}{2}x^{1/2} \Big]_0^4 = \frac{19}{3}$$

(c) If $x = \dfrac{3}{5}y^{5/3} - \dfrac{3}{4}y^{1/3}$, then $\dfrac{dx}{dy} = y^{2/3} - \dfrac{1}{4}y^{-2/3}$ and

$$\left(\frac{dx}{dy}\right)^2 = y^{4/3} - \frac{1}{2} + \frac{1}{16}y^{-4/3}, \text{ so}$$

$$1 + \left(\frac{dx}{dy}\right)^2 = y^{4/3} + \frac{1}{2} + \frac{1}{16}y^{-4/3} = \left(y^{2/3} + \frac{1}{4}y^{-2/3}\right)^2. \text{ Then}$$

$$s = \int_0^1 \left(y^{2/3} + \frac{1}{4}y^{-2/3}\right) dy = \frac{3}{5}y^{5/3} + \frac{3}{4}y^{1/3} \Big]_0^1 = \frac{27}{20}$$

38. (a) If $s(x) = Cx$ then $s'(x) = C$. Also, if $s(x) = \int_0^x \sqrt{1+[f'(t)]^2}\, dt$, then

$s'(x) = \sqrt{1+[f'(x)]^2}$. $\therefore$ $C = \sqrt{1+[f'(x)]^2} \Rightarrow f'(x) = \pm\sqrt{C^2-1}$

and hence $|C| \geq 1$.

(b) If $s(x) = x^n$ then $s'(x) = nx^{n-1}$ and $s'(0) = 0$.

But $s'(0) = \sqrt{1+[f'(0)]^2} \geq 1$. Therefore $s(x) \neq x^n$ for any $n > 1$.

39. (a) $S = 2\pi \int_0^4 x \left(x^{1/2} + \frac{1}{4}x^{-1/2}\right) dx = 2\pi \int_0^4 \left(x^{3/2} + \frac{1}{4}x^{1/2}\right) dx$

$$= 2\pi \left[\frac{2}{5}x^{5/2} + \frac{1}{6}x^{3/2}\right]_0^4 = \frac{424\pi}{15}$$

(b) $S = 2\pi \int_0^1 (y+1)\left(y^{2/3} + \frac{1}{4}y^{-2/3}\right) dy$

$$= 2\pi \int_0^1 \left(y^{5/3} + \frac{1}{4}y^{1/3} + y^{2/3} + \frac{1}{4}y^{-2/3}\right) dy$$

$$= 2\pi \left[\frac{3}{8}y^{8/3} + \frac{3}{16}y^{4/3} + \frac{3}{5}y^{5/3} + \frac{3}{4}y^{1/3}\right]_0^1 = \frac{153\pi}{40}$$

40. $A = 2\pi \int_0^2 \frac{t^2}{2}\sqrt{t^2 + \frac{4}{9}t^{-2/3}}\, dt = \pi \int_0^2 t^2 \sqrt{t^{-2/3}\left(t^{8/3} + \frac{4}{9}\right)}\, dt$

$$= \pi \int_0^2 t^{5/3}\sqrt{t^{8/3} + \frac{4}{9}}\, dt = \frac{\pi}{4}\left[t^{8/3} + \frac{4}{9}\right]_0^2 = \frac{2\pi\,[(9\sqrt[3]{4}+1)^{3/2} - 1]}{27}$$

or alternatively, $x = t^{2/3} \Rightarrow x^3 = t^2 \Rightarrow y = -\frac{1}{2}x^3$. Then

$$A = 2\pi \int_0^{4^{1/3}} \frac{x^3}{2}\sqrt{1 + \frac{9}{4}x^4}\, dx$$

41. Every continuous function over a closed interval must have both a maximum and a minimum value on that interval. Let $u \in [a,b]$ and $v \in [a,b]$ be such that $f(u)$ is the minimum value and $f(v)$ is the maximum value of f on $[a,b]$. Then

$$f(u)(b-a) \le \int_a^b f(x)\,dx \le f(v)(b-a).$$

By the Intermediate Value Theorem, there must exist a range value of f, say $f(c)$, where $c \in [a,b]$, such that

$$f(c)(b-a) = \int_a^b f(x)\,dx, \text{ or } f(c) = \frac{1}{b-a}\int_a^b f(x)\,dx.$$

42. $y_{ave} = \frac{1}{a}\int_0^a \sqrt{ax}\,dx = \frac{1}{\sqrt{a}}\left[\frac{2}{3}x^{3/2}\right]_0^a = \frac{2a}{3}$

43. Average length $= \frac{1}{2a}\int_{-a}^{a} 2\sqrt{a^2-x^2}\,dx = \frac{1}{a}\cdot\frac{\pi a^2}{2} = \frac{\pi a}{2}$

44. Average length $= \frac{1}{\pi}\int_0^{\pi} 2a\sin\theta\,d\theta = \frac{4a}{\pi}$

45. Average length $= \frac{1}{2a}\int_{-a}^{a}\left(2\sqrt{a^2-x^2}\right)^2 dx = \frac{2}{a}\left[a^2x - \frac{x^3}{3}\right]_{-a}^{a} = \frac{8a^2}{3}$

46. Average length $= \frac{1}{\pi}\int_0^{\pi}(2a\sin\theta)^2\,d\theta = \frac{4a^2}{\pi}\int_0^{\pi}\left(\frac{1}{2}-\frac{1}{2}\cos 2\theta\right)d\theta$

$$= \frac{4a^2}{\pi}\left[\frac{1}{2}\theta - \frac{1}{2}\sin 2\theta\right]_0^{\pi} = 2a^2$$

47. $s = 120t - 16t^2 \Rightarrow v = 120 - 32t$

$$v_{av} = \frac{1}{3}\int_0^3 (120-32t)\,dt = \frac{1}{3}\left[120t - 16t^2\right]_0^3 = 72$$

$s(3) - s(0) = 216$, $ds = (120-32t)\,dt$

$$v_{av} = \frac{1}{216}\int_0^{216} v(s)\,ds = \frac{1}{216}\int_0^3 v(t)(120-32t)\,dt = \frac{1}{216}\int_0^3 (120-32t)^2\,dt$$

$$= \frac{1}{216}\cdot\frac{-1}{96}(120-32t)^3\Big]_0^3 = 82\frac{2}{3}$$

48. (a) Average rate of change $= \dfrac{A(8) - A(1)}{7} = \dfrac{3}{7}$

(b) $A'(x) = \dfrac{3}{2\sqrt{1+3x}}$ so $A'(5) = \dfrac{3}{8}$

(c) $f(x) = A'(x) = \dfrac{3}{2\sqrt{1+3x}}$

(d) $f_{ave} = \dfrac{1}{7}\displaystyle\int_1^8 f(x)\,dx = \dfrac{A(8) - A(1)}{7} = \dfrac{3}{7}$

49. $A = \displaystyle\int_0^2 (2\sqrt{2}x^{1/2} - x^2)\,dx = \dfrac{4\sqrt{2}}{3}x^{3/2} - \dfrac{1}{3}x^3\Big]_0^2 = \dfrac{8}{3}$

$M_x = \displaystyle\int_0^2 \dfrac{1}{2}(2\sqrt{2}x^{1/2} + x^2)(2\sqrt{2}x^{1/2} - x^2)\,dx = \dfrac{1}{2}\int_0^2 (8x - x^4)\,dx$

$= \dfrac{1}{2}\left[4x^2 - \dfrac{1}{5}x^5\right]_0^2 = \dfrac{24}{5}$. $\therefore \bar{y} = \dfrac{24}{5}\cdot\dfrac{3}{8} = \dfrac{9}{5}$

$M_y = \displaystyle\int_0^2 x\,(2\sqrt{2}x^{1/2} - x^2)\,dx = \int_0^2 (2\sqrt{2}x^{3/2} - x^3)\,dx$

$= \dfrac{4\sqrt{2}}{5}x^{5/2} - \dfrac{1}{4}x^4\Big]_0^2 = \dfrac{12}{5}$. $\therefore \bar{x} = \dfrac{12}{5}\cdot\dfrac{3}{8} = \dfrac{9}{10}$

50. $M = \displaystyle\int_0^4 x\,dy = \int_0^4 2\sqrt{y}\,dy = \dfrac{32}{3}$; $M_y = \displaystyle\int_0^4 \dfrac{1}{2}x^2\,dy = \int_0^4 y\,dy = 16$

$\bar{x} = 16\left(\dfrac{3}{32}\right) = \dfrac{3}{2}$; $M_x = \displaystyle\int_0^4 y\,(2\sqrt{y})\,dy = 2\left(\dfrac{2}{5}y^{5/2}\right]_0^4 = \dfrac{128}{5}$

$\bar{y} = \dfrac{128}{5}\cdot\dfrac{3}{32} = \dfrac{12}{5}$. $\therefore (\bar{x}, \bar{y}) = \left(\dfrac{3}{2}, \dfrac{12}{5}\right)$

51. $y^2 = x$ intersects $x = 2y$ in the points $(4, 2)$ and $(0, 0)$.

$A = \displaystyle\int_0^4 \left(\sqrt{x} - \dfrac{x}{2}\right)dx = \dfrac{2}{3}x^{3/2} - \dfrac{x^2}{4}\Big]_0^4 = \dfrac{4}{3}$

$M_x = \displaystyle\int_0^4 \dfrac{1}{2}\left(\sqrt{x} + \dfrac{x}{2}\right)\left(\sqrt{x} - \dfrac{x}{2}\right)dx = \dfrac{1}{2}\int_0^4 \left(x - \dfrac{x^2}{4}\right)dx$

$= \dfrac{1}{2}\left[\dfrac{x^2}{2} - \dfrac{x^3}{12}\right]_0^4 = \dfrac{4}{3}$. $\therefore \bar{y} = \dfrac{4}{3}\cdot\dfrac{3}{4} = 1$

$M_y = \displaystyle\int_0^4 x\left(\sqrt{x} - \dfrac{x}{2}\right)dx = \int_0^4 \left(x^{3/2} - \dfrac{x^2}{2}\right)dx$

$= \dfrac{2}{5}x^{5/2} - \dfrac{1}{6}x^3\Big]_0^4 = \dfrac{32}{15}$. $\therefore \bar{x} = \dfrac{32}{15}\cdot\dfrac{3}{4} = \dfrac{8}{5}$

52. $M = \int_0^2 (2x - x^2)\,dx = \frac{4}{3}$; $M_y = \int_0^2 x(2x - x^2)\,dx = \frac{4}{3}$. $\therefore\ \bar{y} = 1$.

$$M_x = \int_0^2 \frac{1}{2}(6x - x^2)(2x - x^2)\,dx = \frac{1}{2}\int_0^2 (12x^2 - 8x^3 + x^4)\,dx = \frac{16}{5}.\quad \therefore\ \bar{x} = \frac{12}{5}$$

53. $A = \int_0^1 x^2\,dx = \frac{1}{3}x^3\Big]_0^1 = \frac{1}{3}$

$$M_x = \int_0^1 x^4\,dx = \frac{1}{10}x^5\Big]_0^1 = \frac{1}{10};\ \bar{y} = \frac{1}{10}\cdot\frac{3}{1} = \frac{3}{10}$$

$$M_y = \int_0^1 x^3\,dx = \frac{1}{4}x^4\Big]_0^1 = \frac{1}{4};\quad \bar{x} = \frac{1}{4}\cdot\frac{3}{1} = \frac{3}{4}$$

54. Let M and $\bar{x}$ denote the moment taken about the y–axis, and

M_b and $\bar{x}_b$ denote the moment taken about the line $x = b$. Then $M_b = \int (x - b)\,dA = \int x\,dA - \int b\,dA = M - bA$. Thus

$$\bar{x}_b = \frac{M_b}{A} = \frac{M - bA}{A} = \frac{M}{A} - b = \bar{x} - b,$$ and $\bar{x}$ is independent of any

translation of axes. A similar argument holds for $\bar{y}$.

55. (a) $M = 2\int_0^a 2\rho\sqrt{ax}\,dx = 4\sqrt{a}\int_0^a kx\sqrt{x}\,dx = \frac{8k\sqrt{a}}{5}x^{5/2}\Big]_0^a = \frac{8ka^3}{5}$

$$M_y = 4k\sqrt{a}\int_0^a x^{5/2}\,dx = \frac{8k\sqrt{a}}{7}x^{7/2}\Big]_0^a = \frac{8ka^4}{7}$$

$$\bar{x} = \frac{8ka^4}{7}\cdot\frac{5}{8ka^3} = \frac{5a}{7}.$$ $\bar{y} = 0$ by symmetry.

(b) $M = \int_{-2a}^{2a} |y|\left(a - \frac{y^2}{4a}\right)dy = 2\int_0^{2a}\left(ay - \frac{y^3}{4a}\right)dy = 2\left[\frac{ay^2}{2} - \frac{y^4}{16a}\right]_0^{2a} = 2a^3$

$$M_y = \frac{1}{2}\int_{-2a}^{2a}\left(a + \frac{y^2}{4a}\right)|y|\left(a - \frac{y^2}{4a}\right)dy = \frac{1}{2}\int_{-2a}^{2a}|y|\left(a^2 - \frac{y^4}{16a^2}\right)dy$$

$$= \int_0^{2a}\left(a^2y - \frac{y^5}{16a^2}\right)dy = \frac{a^2y^2}{2} - \frac{y^6}{96a^2}\Big]_0^{2a} = \frac{4a^4}{3}.$$

$$\bar{x} = \frac{4a^4}{3}\cdot\frac{1}{2a^3} = \frac{2a}{3}.$$ $\bar{y} = 0$ by symmetry.

56. $A = \int_0^b \sqrt{b^2 - x^2}\, dx - \int_0^a \sqrt{a^2 - x^2}\, dx = \text{(by geometry) } \frac{\pi}{4}(b^2 - a^2)$

$$M_y = \int x\, dA = \int_0^b x\sqrt{b^2 - x^2}\, dx - \int_0^a x\sqrt{a^2 - x^2}\, dx$$

$$= -\frac{1}{3}(b^2 - x^2)^{3/2}\Big]_0^b + \frac{1}{3}(a^2 - x^2)^{3/2}\Big]_0^a = \frac{1}{3}(b^3 - a^3)$$

$$\bar{x} = \bar{y} = \frac{(b-a)(b^2 + ab + a^2)}{3} \cdot \frac{4}{\pi(b-a)(b+a)} = \frac{4(b^2 + ab + a^2)}{\pi(b+a)}$$

$\lim_{a \to b} \frac{4(b^2 + ab + a^2)}{\pi(b+a)} = \frac{2b}{3\pi}$, where $\left(\frac{2b}{3\pi}, \frac{2b}{3\pi}\right)$ is the centroid of a quarter circle of radius b in the first quadrant.

57. $ds = \sqrt{\left(\frac{dx}{dt}\right)^2 + \left(\frac{dy}{dt}\right)^2}\, dt = \sqrt{(-3a\cos^2 t \sin t)^2 + (3a\sin^2 t \cos t)^2}\, dt$

$= 3a \sin t \cos t\, dt$. $\quad s = \int_0^{\frac{\pi}{2}} ds = \frac{3a}{2}\sin^2 t\Big]_0^{\frac{\pi}{2}} = \frac{3a}{2}$

$$M_x = \int_0^{\frac{\pi}{2}} (a\cos^3 t) 3a \sin t \cos t\, dt = -\frac{3a^2}{5}\cos^5 t\Big]_0^{\frac{\pi}{2}} = \frac{3a^2}{5}$$

$\bar{y} = \frac{3a^2}{5} \cdot \frac{2}{3a} = \frac{2a}{5}$. $\quad \therefore (\bar{x}, \bar{y}) = \left(\frac{2a}{5}, \frac{2a}{5}\right)$

58. Let the three vertices of the triangular region be (0,0), (a,0) and (0,b). Then the centroid of the triangular region is $\left(\frac{a}{3}, \frac{b}{3}\right) = \left(\frac{a}{3}, \frac{24}{a}\right)$,

since $ab = 72$. If $(\bar{x}, \bar{y})$ denotes the centroid of the remaining region, then $36\left(\frac{a}{3}\right) + 108\bar{x} = 6(144)$ and $36\left(\frac{24}{a}\right) + 108\bar{y} = 6(144)$. If $\bar{x} = 7$, then

$a = 8$ and $\bar{y} = \frac{64}{9} \approx 7.1$.

59. $W = 60\int_0^{10} \pi x^2 (10 - y)\, dy = 60\pi\int_0^{10} \left(3y^2 - \frac{1}{4}y^3\right) dy$

$$= 60\pi\left[y^3 - \frac{1}{16}y^4\right]_0^{10} = 22{,}500\pi \text{ ft-lbs}.$$

$22{,}500\pi$ ft-lbs) / 275 ft-lbs/s ≈ 257 s or 4.3 minutes.

60. $F = ma \Rightarrow M\dfrac{d^2x}{dt^2} = t^2 \Rightarrow \dfrac{dx}{dt} = \dfrac{1}{3M}t^3 + C_1$. $v(0) = 0 \Rightarrow C_1 = 0$. $x = \dfrac{1}{12M}t^4 + C_2$.

$x(0) = 0 \Rightarrow C_2 = 0$. Then $t^2 = \sqrt{12Mx}$. $\therefore W = \displaystyle\int_0^h \sqrt{12Mx}\,dx = \dfrac{4h\sqrt{3Mh}}{3}$

61. $W = \displaystyle\int_a^b \frac{k}{x^2}dx = -\frac{k}{x}\Big]_a^b = \frac{k(b-a)}{ab}$

62. If w_x is the weight when the object is x feet from the center.

Then $\dfrac{w_x}{w} = \dfrac{x}{R}$, where R is the radius of the earth. Therefore,

$$W = \int_{R-r}^{R} \frac{w}{R}x\,dx = \frac{(2rR - r^2)w}{2R} \text{ ft-lbs.}$$

63. $W = \displaystyle\int_0^4 57(10 + x)(20)2\sqrt{16 - x^2}\,dx$

$$= 22800\int_0^4 \sqrt{16 - x^2}\,dx + 2280\int_0^4 x\sqrt{16 - x^2}\,dx$$

$$= 22800\left(\text{area of } \frac{1}{4}\text{circle with } r = 4\right) + 2280\left[\frac{1}{3}(16 - x^2)^{3/2}\right]_0^4$$

$$= 22800(4\pi) + 2280\left(\frac{64}{3}\right) \approx 335{,}153.3 \text{ ft-lbs} \approx 167.6 \text{ ft-tons}$$

64. (a) $F = pA$ and $dV = A\,dx$. So $W = \displaystyle\int F\,dx = \int pA\,dx = \int_{(p_1,V_1)}^{(p_2,V_2)} p\,dV$

(b) $pv^{1.4} = C \Rightarrow p = Cv^{-1.4}$. Since $v = 243$ when $p = 50$, $C = 50(243)^{1.4} = 50(3^7)$.

$$W = 50(3^7)\int_{243}^{32} v^{-7/5}\,dV = 50(3^7)\left[-\frac{5}{2}v^{-2/5}\right]_{243}^{32} = -37{,}968\frac{3}{4} \text{ in-lbs.}$$

The negative sign indicates that the system is not doing, the work, but is having the work done on it.

65. $A = 2\displaystyle\int_0^1 (4 - 4x^2)\,dx = 2\left\{4x - \frac{4}{3}x^3\right]_0^1 = \frac{16}{3}$

$$M_x = \frac{1}{2}\int_{-1}^{1} (4 + 4x^2)(4 - 4x^2)\,dx = \frac{1}{2}\left[16x - \frac{16}{5}x^5\right]_{-1}^{1} = \frac{64}{5}$$

$\bar{y} = \dfrac{64}{5}\cdot\dfrac{3}{16} = \dfrac{12}{5}$. The depth to centroid is $\dfrac{33}{5}$ ft.

$$F = \left(\frac{33}{5}\text{ft}\right)\left(62.5\frac{\text{lb}}{\text{ft}^3}\right)\left(\frac{16}{3}\text{ft}^2\right) = 2200 \text{ lbs}$$

66. (a) After 9 hours, the pool is filled to a depth of 6 feet.

$$P = 62.5\int_0^1 (6-h)\,2h\,dh = 333\frac{1}{3}\text{ lbs.}$$

(b) $P = 62.5\int_0^1 (d-h)2h\,dh = 62.5\left(d-\frac{2}{3}\right)$

$$62.5\left(d-\frac{2}{3}\right) = 520 \text{ if } d \approx 8.987 \text{ or } 9.0 \text{ feet}$$

67. By similar triangle, $\frac{L}{4} = \frac{h-2}{4}$ or $L = h-2$.

$$F = 62.5\int_2^6 h(h-2)\,dh = 62.5\left[\frac{h^3}{3} - h^2\right]_2^6 = 2{,}333\frac{1}{3}\text{ lbs.}$$

68. If L is the length of a horizontal strip h feet from the surface, then, using similar triangles, $L = 200 - 5h$. The force is

$$F = 62.5\int_0^{20} h(200-5h)\,dh = \frac{5{,}000{,}000}{3}\text{ lbs} = 833\frac{1}{3}\text{ tons.}$$

69. (a) $M_x = \int_0^h y\,f(y)\,dy = \int_0^h w\,b\,y^2\,dy = \frac{wh^3}{3}$. The total force is

$$F = \int_0^h wby\,dy = \frac{wbh^2}{2}.\quad \therefore \left(\frac{wbh^2}{2}\right)\bar{y} = \frac{wbh^3}{3} \text{ or } \bar{y} = \frac{2h}{3}.$$

(b) $M_x = \int_a^{a+h} y\,f(y)\,dy = \int_a^{a+h} y\,(wy)\,l\,dy = \int_a^{a+h} wy^2\left(\frac{b}{h}(y-a)\right)dy$

and $F = \int_a^{a+h} wy\left(\frac{b}{h}(y-a)\right)dy$. Since $\bar{y}F = M_x$, we have

$$\int_a^{a+h} (y^3 - ay^2)\,dy = \left(\int_a^{a+h} (y^2 - ay)\,dy\right)\bar{y}$$

$$\bar{y}\left[\frac{1}{3}y^3 - \frac{a}{2}y^2\right]_a^{a+h} = \left[\frac{1}{4}y^4 - \frac{a}{3}y^3\right]_a^{a+h}$$

$$\bar{y} = \frac{3(a+h)^4 - 4a(a+h)^3 - 3a^4 + 4a^4}{4(a+h)^3 - 6a(a+h)^2 - 4a^3 + 6a^3} = \frac{6a^2 + 8ah + 3h^2}{2(3a+2h)}$$

70. The area of each of the triangular pieces is 36 ft^2. The centroid of the top triangle is 4 feet from A and of the bottom triangle is 8 feet from A. Then the force is $F = w_1(6)(36) + w_2(10)(36) = 216w_1 + 360w_2$.

71. $V = 2\pi(2)(8) = 32\pi$; $S = 2\pi(2)(8\sqrt{2}) = 32\sqrt{2}\pi$

72. The centroid is $\frac{2}{3}$ of the distance from the origin to the midpoint of the opposite side, which is $\left(\frac{3}{2}, 3\right)$. Therefore, the centroid is at (1,2), which is 4 units from the line $x = 5$. Then $V = 2\pi(4)(9) = 72\pi$.

73. $V = 2\pi(1)(\pi) = 2\pi^2$

74. (a) $S = 2\pi\left(\frac{r}{2}\right)\sqrt{r^2 + h^2}$

(b) $V = 2\pi\left(\frac{r}{3}\right)\left(\frac{rh}{2}\right) = \frac{1}{3}\pi r^2 h$

75. $A = 4\pi a^2$. $\therefore 2\pi(\pi a)\bar{y} = 4\pi a^2 \Rightarrow \bar{y} = \frac{2a}{\pi}$. $\bar{x} = 0$ by symmetry.

76. $V = 2\pi\left(a - \frac{2a}{\pi}\right)(\pi a) = 2\pi a^2(\pi - 2)$

77. $V = \frac{4}{3}\pi a^3$. $\therefore \frac{4}{3}\pi a^3 = 2\pi\left(\frac{\pi a^2}{2}\right)\bar{y} \Rightarrow \bar{y} = \frac{4a}{3\pi}$. $\bar{x} = 0$.

78. $V = 2\pi\left(\frac{4a}{\pi} + a\right)\left(\frac{\pi a^2}{2}\right) = \pi a^3(4 + \pi)$

79. $y = \frac{4a\sqrt{2}}{3\pi} + \frac{a - \frac{4a}{3\pi}}{\sqrt{2}} = \frac{2\sqrt{2}a}{3\pi} + \frac{a\sqrt{2}}{2}$.

$$V = 2\pi\left[\frac{2\sqrt{2}a}{3\pi} + \frac{a\sqrt{2}}{2}\right]\frac{\pi a^2}{2} = \frac{2\sqrt{2}a^3\pi}{3} + \frac{\pi^2\sqrt{2}a^3}{2} = \frac{\pi a^3(4 + 3\pi)}{3\sqrt{2}}$$

80. The distance from the point $\left(0, \frac{2\pi}{a}\right)$ to the line $y - x + a = 0$ is $d = \frac{\left|\frac{2a}{\pi} + a\right|}{\sqrt{2}} = \frac{2a + a\pi}{\pi\sqrt{2}}$. $S = 2\pi\left(\frac{2a + a\pi}{\pi\sqrt{2}}\right)\pi a = \sqrt{2}\pi a^2(2 + \pi)$

CHAPTER 6

TRANSCENDENTAL FUNCTIONS

6.1 INVERSE FUNCTIONS

1. $f(x)=2x+3$, and $f(1)=-1$. Interchanging and solving:

$x=2y+3 \Rightarrow y=\frac{1}{2}x-\frac{3}{2}=g(x)$.

$f'(x)=2$ and $g'(x)=\frac{1}{2}$. $\therefore f'(-1)=\frac{1}{g'(1)}$.

2. $f(x)=5-4x$, and $f\left(\frac{1}{2}\right)=3$. Interchanging and solving:

$x=5-4y \Rightarrow y=-\frac{1}{4}x+\frac{5}{4}=g(x)$.

$f'(x)=-4$ and $g'(x)=-\frac{1}{4}$. $\therefore f'(-1)=\frac{1}{g'(1)}$.

3. $f(x)=\frac{1}{5}x+7$ and $f(-1)=\frac{34}{5}$. Interchanging and solving:

$x=\frac{1}{5}y+7 \Rightarrow y=5x+35=g(x)$.

$f'(x)=\frac{1}{5}$ and $g'(x)=5$ $\therefore f'(-1)=\frac{1}{g'\left(\frac{34}{5}\right)}$.

4. $f(x)=2x^2$, $x\geq 0$, and $f(1)=2$. Interchanging and solving:

$x=2y^2 \Rightarrow y^2=\frac{x}{2}$ and $x\geq 0 \Rightarrow y=\sqrt{\frac{x}{2}}=g(x)$.

$f'(x)=4x$ and $g'(x)=\frac{1}{4}\sqrt{\frac{2}{x}}$. $\therefore f'(1)=4$ and $g'(2)=\frac{1}{4}$.

5. $f(x)=x^2+1$, $x\geq 0$ and $f(5)=26$. Interchanging and solving:

$x=y^2+1 \Rightarrow y=\sqrt{x-1}=g(x)$.

$f'(x)=2x$ and $g'(x)=\frac{1}{2\sqrt{x-1}}$. $\therefore f'(5)=10=\frac{1}{g'(26)}=\frac{1}{\frac{1}{10}}$.

6. $f(x)=(x-1)^{1/3}$, and $f(9)=2$. Interchanging and solving:

$x=(y-1)^{1/3} \Rightarrow x^3=y-1 \Rightarrow y=x^3+1=g(x)$.

$f'(x)=\frac{1}{3(x-1)^{2/3}}$ and $g'(x)=3x^2$. $\therefore f'(9)=\frac{1}{12}$ and $g'(2)=12$.

7. $f(x) = x^3 - 1$, and $f(2) = 7$. Interchanging and solving:

$x = y^3 - 1 \Rightarrow y^3 = x + 1 \Rightarrow y = (x+1)^{1/3} = g(x)$.

$f'(x) = 3x^2$ and $g'(x) = \dfrac{1}{3(x+1)^{2/3}}$. $\therefore f'(2) = 12$ and $g'(7) = \dfrac{1}{12}$.

8. $f(x) = x^2 - 2x + 1$, $x \ge 1$, and $f(4) = 9$. Interchanging and solving:

$x = y^2 - 2y + 1 = (y-1)^2 \Rightarrow y - 1 = \sqrt{x}$ or $g(x) = 1 + \sqrt{x}$.

$f'(x) = 2x - 2$ and $g'(x) = \dfrac{1}{2\sqrt{x}}$ $\therefore f'(4) = 6$ and $g'(9) = \dfrac{1}{6}$.

9. $f(x) = x^5$. Interchanging and solving: $x = y^5 \Rightarrow y = x^{\frac{1}{5}}$.

$f(f^{-1}(x)) = (x^{\frac{1}{5}})^5 = x$ and $f^{-1}(f(x)) = (x^5)^{\frac{1}{5}} = x$.

10. $f(x) = x^4$, $x \ge 0$. Interchanging and solving: $x = y^4 \Rightarrow y = x^{1/4}$.

$f(f^{-1}(x)) = (x^{1/4})^4 = x$ and $f^{-1}(f(x)) = (x^4)^{1/4} = x$

11. $f(x) = x^{\frac{2}{3}}$, $x \ge 0$. Interchanging and solving: $x = y^{\frac{2}{3}} \Rightarrow y = x^{\frac{3}{2}}$.

$f(f^{-1}(x)) = (x^{\frac{3}{2}})^{\frac{2}{3}} = x$ and $f^{-1}(f(x)) = (x^{\frac{2}{3}})^{\frac{3}{2}} = x$.

12. $f(x) = \frac{1}{2}x - \frac{7}{2}$. Interchanging and solving: $x = \frac{1}{2}y - \frac{7}{2}$ or

$f^{-1}(x) = 2x + 7$. $f(f^{-1}(x)) = \frac{1}{2}(2x+7) - \frac{7}{2} = x$ and

$f^{-1}(f(x)) = 2\left(\frac{1}{2}x - \frac{7}{2}\right) + 7 = x$.

13. $f(x) = (x-1)^2$, $x \ge 1$. Interchanging and solving: $x = (y-1)^2$

$\Rightarrow y = \sqrt{x} + 1$, $x \ge 0$. $f(f^{-1}(x)) = (\sqrt{x} + 1 - 1)^2 = x$

and $f^{-1}(f(x)) = \sqrt{(x-1)^2} + 1 = x$.

14. $f(x) = x^3 + 1$. Interchanging and solving: $x = y^3 + 1$

$\Rightarrow y = (x-1)^{1/3}$. $f(f^{-1}(x)) = ((x-1)^{1/3})^3 + 1 = x$

and $f^{-1}(f(x)) = (x^3 + 1 - 1)^{1/3} = x$.

15. $f(x) = x^{-2}$, $x > 0$. Interchanging and solving: $x = y^{-2} \Rightarrow y = x^{-\frac{1}{2}}$.

$f(f^{-1}(x)) = (x^{-\frac{1}{2}})^{-2} = x$ and $f^{-1}(f(x)) = (x^{-2})^{-\frac{1}{2}} = x$.

16. $f(x) = x^{-3}$, $x \neq 0$. Interchanging and solving: $x = y^{-3} \Rightarrow$

$y = x^{-1/3}$. $f(f^{-1}(x)) = (x^{-1/3})^3 = x$ and $f^{-1}(f(x)) = ((x^{-3})^{-1/3} = x$.

17.

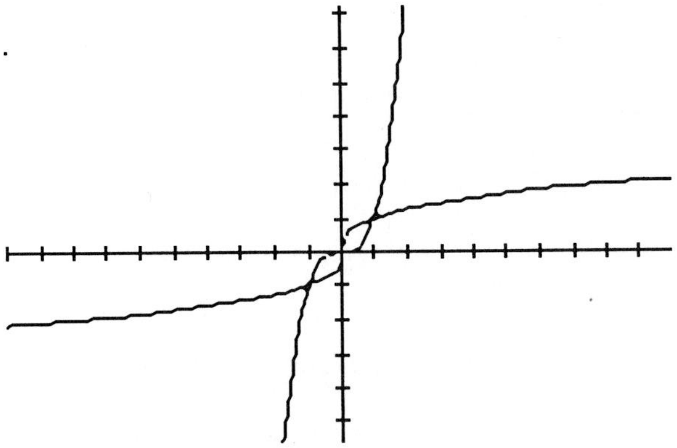

(b) $y = x^{1/3}$ fails to have a derivative at $x = 0$. The tangent is vertical here. $y = x^3$ has slope 0 and a horizontal tangent at $x = 0$.

18. (b) $y' = -\dfrac{1}{x^2}$ and $y'(a) = -\dfrac{1}{a^2}$. $y'\left(\dfrac{1}{a}\right) = -a^2$. The product of these slopes is 1.

(c) $f^{-1}(x) = \dfrac{1}{x} = f(x)$

19. $f(x) = x^2 - 4x - 3$, $x > 2$. $f(x) = 2 \Leftrightarrow x^2 - 4x - 3 = 2 \Rightarrow$

$(x-5)(x+1) = 0 \Rightarrow x = 5, -1$. $f'(x) = 2x - 4 \Rightarrow f'(5) = 6$.

$\therefore g'(2) = \dfrac{1}{f'(5)} = \dfrac{1}{6}$.

20. $f(x) = 1 + \frac{1}{x}$, $x \neq 0$. Interchanging, $x = 1 + \frac{1}{y} \Rightarrow \frac{1}{y} = x - 1$

or $y = \frac{1}{x-1} = g(x)$. $f(g(x)) = 1 + \frac{1}{\frac{1}{x-1}} = 1 + x - 1 = x$, and

$g(f(x)) = \frac{1}{1 + \frac{1}{x} - 1} = x$. $g'(x) = \frac{-1}{(x-1)^2}$ and $f'(x) = -\frac{1}{x^2}$.

$g'(f(x)) = \frac{-1}{\left(1 + \frac{1}{x} - 1\right)^2} = -x^2 = \frac{1}{f'(x)}$.

21. New volume $= \frac{4\pi}{3}(10)^3 + 1$. Since $r = \left(\frac{3V}{4\pi}\right)^{\frac{1}{3}}$, this change

in volume would be produced by a radius of $r = \left(1000 + \frac{3}{4\pi}\right)^{\frac{1}{3}} =$

10.0008 cm. This is a change of .0008 cm.

.1 mm/hr = .01 cm/hr. $\therefore$ $.01t = .0008 \Rightarrow t = .08$ hr or 4.8 min.

22. Let $x_1 \neq x_2$ be two points in the domain of an increasing function f. Then either $x_1 < x_2$ or $x_2 < x_1$, in which case either $f(x_1) < f(x_2)$ or $f(x_2) < f(x_1)$. In both cases we have $x_1 \neq x_2 \Rightarrow f(x_1) \neq f(x_2)$ so that f is one-to-one. A similar argument holds if f is decreasing.

6.2 THE INVERSE TRIGONOMETRIC FUNCTIONS

1. (a) $\frac{\pi}{4}$ (b) $\frac{\pi}{3}$ (c) $\frac{\pi}{6}$
2. (a) $-\frac{\pi}{4}$ (b) $-\frac{\pi}{3}$ (c) $-\frac{\pi}{6}$
3. (a) $\frac{\pi}{6}$ (b) $\frac{\pi}{4}$ (c) $\frac{\pi}{3}$
4. (a) $-\frac{\pi}{6}$ (b) $-\frac{\pi}{4}$ (c) $-\frac{\pi}{3}$
5. (a) $\frac{\pi}{3}$ (b) $\frac{\pi}{4}$ (c) $\frac{\pi}{6}$
6. (a) $\frac{2\pi}{3}$ (b) $\frac{3\pi}{4}$ (c) $\frac{5\pi}{6}$
7. (a) $\frac{\pi}{4}$ (b) $\frac{\pi}{6}$ (c) $\frac{\pi}{3}$
8. (a) $\frac{3\pi}{4}$ (b) $\frac{5\pi}{6}$ (c) $\frac{2\pi}{3}$
9. (a) $\frac{\pi}{4}$ (b) $\frac{\pi}{3}$ (c) $\frac{\pi}{6}$
10. (a) $-\frac{\pi}{4}$ (b) $-\frac{\pi}{3}$ (c) $-\frac{\pi}{6}$

11. (a) $\frac{\pi}{4}$ (b) $\frac{\pi}{6}$ (c) $\frac{\pi}{3}$ 12. (a) $\frac{3\pi}{4}$ (b) $\frac{5\pi}{6}$ (c) $\frac{2\pi}{3}$

13. $\alpha = \sin^{-1}\frac{1}{2} \Rightarrow \cos\alpha = \frac{\sqrt{3}}{2}$, $\tan\alpha = \frac{1}{\sqrt{3}}$, $\sec\alpha = \frac{2}{\sqrt{3}}$, $\csc\alpha = 2$

14. $\alpha = \cos^{-1}\left(-\frac{1}{2}\right) \Rightarrow \sin\alpha = \frac{\sqrt{3}}{2}$, $\tan\alpha = -\sqrt{3}$, $\sec\alpha = -2$, $\csc\alpha = \frac{2}{\sqrt{3}}$

15. $\sin\left(\cos^{-1}\frac{\sqrt{2}}{2}\right) = \frac{\sqrt{2}}{2}$ 16. $\tan\left(\sin^{-1}\left(-\frac{1}{2}\right)\right) = -\frac{1}{\sqrt{3}}$

17. $\sec\left(\cos^{-1}\frac{1}{2}\right) = 2$ 18. $\cot\left(\sin^{-1}\left(-\frac{1}{2}\right)\right) = -\sqrt{3}$

19. $\csc(\sec^{-1} 2) = \frac{2}{\sqrt{3}}$ 20. $\cos(\tan^{-1}(-\sqrt{3})) = \frac{1}{2}$

21. $\cos(\cot^{-1} 1) = \frac{\sqrt{2}}{2}$ 22. $\csc\left(\sin^{-1}\left(-\frac{\sqrt{2}}{2}\right)\right) = -\sqrt{2}$

23. $\cot(\cos^{-1} 0) = 0$ 24. $\sec\left(\tan^{-1}\left(-\frac{1}{2}\right)\right) = \frac{\sqrt{5}}{2}$

25. $\tan(\sec^{-1} 1) = 0$ 26. $\sin(\csc^{-1}(-1)) = -1$

27. $\sin^{-1} 1 - \sin^{-1}(-1) = \pi$ 28. $\tan^{-1}(1) - \tan^{-1}(-1) = \frac{\pi}{2}$

29. $\sec^{-1} 2 - \sec^{-1}(-2) = -\frac{\pi}{3}$ 30. $\sin(\sin^{-1}(0.735)) = 0.735$

31. $\cos(\sin^{-1} 0.8) = 0.6$ (a 3–4–5 right triangle)

32. $\tan^{-1}\left(\tan\frac{\pi}{3}\right) = \frac{\pi}{3}$ 33. $\cos^{-1}\left(-\sin\frac{\pi}{6}\right) = \frac{2\pi}{3}$

34. $\sec^{-1}(\sec(-30^\circ) = 30^\circ$

35. $\lim_{x\to 1^-} \sin^{-1} x = \sin^{-1} 1 = \frac{\pi}{2}$. 36. $\lim_{x\to -1^+} \cos^{-1} x = \pi$

37. $\lim_{x\to\infty} \tan^{-1} x = \frac{\pi}{2}$. 38. $\lim_{x\to -\infty} \tan^{-1} x = -\frac{\pi}{2}$

39. $\lim_{x\to\infty} \sec^{-1} x = \lim_{x\to\infty} \cos^{-1}\left(\frac{1}{x}\right) = \cos^{-1} 0 = \frac{\pi}{2}$.

40. $\lim_{x\to -\infty} \sec^{-1} x = \frac{\pi}{2}$

41. $\lim_{x\to\infty} \csc^{-1} x = \lim_{x\to\infty} \sin^{-1}\left(\frac{1}{x}\right) = \sin^{-1} 0 = 0$.

42. $\lim_{x\to -\infty} \csc^{-1} x = 0$

43. $65^{\circ} = \alpha + \beta$ and $\beta = \tan^{-1}\frac{21}{50}$. $\therefore \alpha = 65^{\circ} - \tan^{-1}\frac{21}{50} = 42.2^{\circ}$.

44. $\alpha = \theta_2 - \theta_1$

$$\cot\theta_2 = \frac{x}{a+b} \Rightarrow \theta_2 = \cot^{-1}\left(\frac{x}{a+b}\right)$$

$$\cot\theta_1 = \frac{x}{b} \Rightarrow \theta_1 = \cot^{-1}\frac{x}{b}$$

$$\alpha = \cot^{-1}\left(\frac{x}{a+b}\right) - \cot^{-1}\frac{x}{b}$$

45. $\frac{h}{3} = \cos\alpha$ and $\frac{r}{3} = \sin\alpha$. $V = \frac{1}{3}\pi r^2 h = \frac{\pi}{3}(9\sin^2\alpha)(3\cos\alpha)$

$V' = 9\pi(-\sin^3\alpha + 2\sin\alpha\cos^2\alpha)$. $V' = 0 \Leftrightarrow 9\pi\sin\alpha(2\cos^2\alpha - \sin^2\alpha) = 0$

$\Rightarrow 2\cos^2\alpha = \sin^2\alpha \Rightarrow \tan\alpha = \sqrt{2}$. $\alpha = \tan^{-1}\sqrt{2} = 54.7^{\circ}$.

$V'' = 9\pi(-3\sin^2\alpha\cos\alpha + 2\cos^3\alpha - 4\sin^2\alpha\cos\alpha) =$

$= 9\pi\cos\alpha(-7\sin^2\alpha + 2\cos^2\alpha) = 9\pi\left(\frac{1}{\sqrt{3}}\right)\left[-7\left(\frac{2}{3}\right) + 2\left(\frac{1}{3}\right)\right] < 0$

$\Rightarrow$ this angle gives maximum volume.

46. $V = \pi\int_0^{\frac{\pi}{4}}(1 - x^2)\,dy = \pi\int_0^{\frac{\pi}{4}}(1 - \tan^2 y)\,dy = \pi\int_0^{\frac{\pi}{4}}(2 - \sec^2 y)\,dy$

$= \pi(2y - \tan y)\Big]_0^{\pi/4} = \pi\left(\frac{\pi}{2} - 1\right)$

47. $\sec^{-1}(-x) = \cos^{-1}\left(-\frac{1}{x}\right) = \pi - \cos^{-1}\left(\frac{1}{x}\right) = \pi - \sec^{-1}x$

48. (a) $\sin^{-1}(1) + \cos^{-1}(1) = \frac{\pi}{2} + 0 = \frac{\pi}{2}$

$\sin^{-1}(0) + \cos^{-1}(0) = 0 + \frac{\pi}{2} = \frac{\pi}{2}$

$\sin^{-1}(-1) + \cos^{-1}(-1) = -\frac{\pi}{2} + \pi = \frac{\pi}{2}$

(b) $\sin^{-1}(-a) + \cos^{-1}(-a) = -\sin^{-1}a + \pi - \cos^{-1}a$

$= \pi - (\sin^{-1}a + \cos^{-1}a) = \pi - \frac{\pi}{2} = \frac{\pi}{2}$

49.

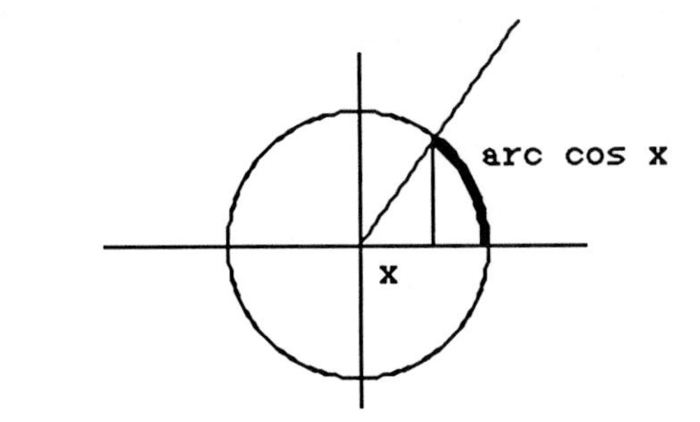

6.3 DERIVATIVES OF INVERSE TRIGONOMETRIC FUNCTIONS

1. $y = \cos^{-1} x^2 \Rightarrow \frac{dy}{dx} = \frac{-1}{\sqrt{1-(x^2)^2}} \frac{d}{dx}(x^2) = \frac{-2x}{\sqrt{1-x^4}}$.

2. $y = \cos^{-1}\left(\frac{1}{x}\right) \Rightarrow \frac{dy}{dx} = \frac{-1}{\sqrt{1-\left(\frac{1}{x}\right)^2}} \cdot \left(-\frac{1}{x^2}\right) = \frac{1}{|x|\sqrt{x^2-1}}$

3. $y = 5\tan^{-1} 3x \Rightarrow \frac{dy}{dx} = 5\left(\frac{1}{1+(3x)^2}\right)\frac{d}{dx}(3x) = \frac{15}{1+9x^2}$.

4. $y = \cot^{-1} \sqrt{x} \Rightarrow \frac{dy}{dx} = \frac{-1}{1+x} \cdot \frac{1}{2\sqrt{x}} = \frac{-1}{2\sqrt{x}\,(1+x)}$

5. $y = \sin^{-1} \frac{x}{2} \Rightarrow \frac{dy}{dx} = \frac{1}{\sqrt{1-\left(\frac{x}{2}\right)^2}} \frac{d}{dx}\left(\frac{x}{2}\right) = \frac{1}{\sqrt{4-x^2}}$.

6. $y = \sin^{-1}(1-x) \Rightarrow \frac{dy}{dx} = \frac{1}{\sqrt{1-(1-x)^2}}(-1) = \frac{-1}{\sqrt{2x-x^2}}$

7. $y = \sec^{-1} 5x \Rightarrow \frac{dy}{dx} = \frac{1}{|5x|\sqrt{(5x)^2-1}} \frac{d}{dx}(5x) = \frac{1}{|x|\sqrt{25x^2-1}}$.

8. $y = \frac{1}{3}\tan^{-1}\frac{x}{3} \Rightarrow \frac{dy}{dx} = \frac{1}{3} \cdot \frac{1}{1+\left(\frac{x}{3}\right)^2} \cdot \frac{1}{3} = \frac{1}{9+x^2}$

9. $y = \csc^{-1}(x^2+1) \Rightarrow \frac{dy}{dx} = \frac{-1}{|x^2+1|\sqrt{(x^2+1)^2-1}} \frac{d}{dx}(x^2+1) = \frac{-2x}{(x^2+1)\sqrt{x^4+2x^2}}$.

10. $y = \cos^{-1} 2x \Rightarrow \frac{dy}{dx} = \frac{-2}{\sqrt{1-4x^2}}$

11. $y = \csc^{-1}\sqrt{x} + \sec^{-1}\sqrt{x} = \frac{\pi}{2}$ since the secant and cosecant are cofunctions. $\therefore \frac{dy}{dx} = 0$.

12. $y = \csc^{-1}\sqrt{x+1} \Rightarrow \frac{dy}{dx} = \frac{-1}{\sqrt{x+1-1}\sqrt{x+1}} \cdot \frac{1}{2\sqrt{x+1}} = \frac{-1}{2|x+1|\sqrt{x}}$

13. $y = \cot^{-1}\sqrt{x-1} \Rightarrow \frac{dy}{dx} = \frac{-1}{1+(\sqrt{x-1})^2}\frac{d}{dx}(\sqrt{x-1}) = \frac{-1}{2x\sqrt{x-1}}$.

14. $y = x\sqrt{1-x^2} - \cos^{-1}x \Rightarrow$

$$\frac{dy}{dx} = \sqrt{1-x^2} + x\left(\frac{-x}{\sqrt{1-x^2}}\right) + \frac{1}{\sqrt{1-x^2}}$$

$$= \sqrt{1-x^2} + \frac{1-x^2}{\sqrt{1-x^2}} = 2\sqrt{1-x^2}$$

15. $y = \sqrt{x^2-4} - 2\sec^{-1}\frac{x}{2} \Rightarrow \frac{dy}{dx} = \frac{1}{2}(x^2-4)^{-\frac{1}{2}}(2x) - 2\left(\frac{\frac{1}{2}}{|\frac{x}{2}|\sqrt{\left(\frac{x}{2}\right)^2 - 1}}\right)$

$$= \frac{x}{\sqrt{x^2-4}} - \frac{1}{|\frac{x}{2}|\sqrt{\frac{x^2-4}{4}}} = \frac{x|x|-4}{|x|\sqrt{x^2-4}}.$$

If $x > 2$, $|x| = x$ and $\frac{dy}{dx} = \frac{\sqrt{x^2-4}}{x}$. If $x < -2$, $|x| = -x$ and $\frac{dy}{dx} = \frac{x^2+4}{x\sqrt{x^2-4}}$.

16. $y = \cot^{-1}\frac{2}{x} + \tan^{-1}\frac{x}{2} \Rightarrow \frac{dy}{dx} = \frac{\frac{2}{x^2}}{1+\frac{4}{x^2}} + \frac{\frac{1}{2}}{1+\frac{x^2}{4}} = \frac{4}{x^4+4}$

17. $y = \tan^{-1}\frac{x-1}{x+1} \Rightarrow \frac{dy}{dx} = \frac{1}{1+\left(\frac{x-1}{x+1}\right)^2}\frac{d}{dx}\left(\frac{x-1}{x+1}\right)$

$$= \left(\frac{(x+1)^2}{(x+1)^2+(x-1)^2}\right)\left(\frac{x+1-x+1}{(x+1)^2}\right) = \frac{1}{x^2+1}.$$

18. $y = x\sin^{-1}x + \sqrt{1-x^2} \Rightarrow \frac{dy}{dx} = \sin^{-1}x + \frac{x}{\sqrt{1-x^2}} - \frac{x}{\sqrt{1-x^2}} = \sin^{-1}x$

19. $y = x(\sin^{-1}x)^2 - 2x + 2\sqrt{1 - x^2}\sin^{-1}x$

$$\frac{dy}{dx} = (\sin^{-1}x)^2 + x(2\sin^{-1}x)\left(\frac{1}{\sqrt{1-x^2}}\right) - 2 + 2\left[\frac{1}{2}(1 - x^2)^{-\frac{1}{2}}(-2x)\sin^{-1}x\right.$$

$$+ 2\sqrt{1-x^2}\left(\frac{1}{\sqrt{1-x^2}}\right) =$$

$$(\sin^{-1}x)^2 + \frac{2x\sin^{-1}x}{\sqrt{1-x^2}} + \frac{-2x\sin^{-1}x}{\sqrt{1-x^2}} = (\sin^{-1}x)^2.$$

20. $y = x\cos^{-1}2x - \dfrac{\sqrt{1-4x^2}}{2} \Rightarrow$

$$\frac{dy}{dx} = \cos^{-1}2x - \frac{2x}{\sqrt{1-4x^2}} + \frac{2x}{\sqrt{1-4x^2}} = \cos^{-1}2x$$

21. $\displaystyle\int_0^{\frac{1}{2}} \frac{dx}{\sqrt{1-x^2}} = \sin^{-1}x \Big|_0^{\frac{1}{2}} = \sin^{-1}\frac{1}{2} - \sin^{-1}0 = \frac{\pi}{6}$

22. $\displaystyle\int_{-1}^{1} \frac{dx}{1+x^2} = \tan^{-1}x\Big]_{-1}^{1} = \frac{\pi}{4} - \left(-\frac{\pi}{4}\right) = \frac{\pi}{2}$

23. $\displaystyle\int_{\sqrt{2}}^{2} \frac{dx}{x\sqrt{x^2-1}} = \sec^{-1}|x|\Big]_{\sqrt{2}}^{2} = \sec^{-1}2 - \sec^{-1}\sqrt{2} = \frac{\pi}{3} - \frac{\pi}{4} = \frac{\pi}{12}$

24. $\displaystyle\int_{-2}^{-\sqrt{2}} \frac{dx}{x\sqrt{1-x^2}} = \sec^{-1}|x|\Big]_{-2}^{-\sqrt{2}} = \frac{\pi}{4} - \frac{\pi}{3} = -\frac{\pi}{12}$

25. $\displaystyle\int_{-1}^{0} \frac{4dx}{1+x^2} = 4\tan^{-1}x\Big]_{-1}^{0} = 0 - 4\tan^{-1}(-1) = \pi$

26. $\displaystyle\int_{\sqrt{3}/3}^{\sqrt{3}} \frac{6\,dx}{1+x^2} = 6\tan^{-1}x\Big]_{\sqrt{3}/3}^{\sqrt{3}} = 6\left(\frac{\pi}{3} - \frac{\pi}{6}\right) = \pi$

27. $$\int_0^{\frac{\sqrt{2}}{2}} \frac{x\,dx}{\sqrt{1-x^4}} = \int_0^{\frac{1}{2}} \frac{\frac{1}{2}du}{\sqrt{1-u^2}} = \frac{1}{2}\sin^{-1}u\Big]_0^{\frac{1}{2}} = \frac{\pi}{12}$$

Let $u = x^2 \Rightarrow du = 2x\,dx$. Then $x = \frac{\sqrt{2}}{2} \Rightarrow u = \frac{1}{2}$; $x = 0 \Rightarrow u = 0$.

28. $$\int_0^{1/4} \frac{dx}{\sqrt{1-4x^2}} = \frac{1}{2}\sin^{-1}2x\Big]_0^{1/4} = \frac{\pi}{12}$$

29. $$\int_{\frac{1}{\sqrt{3}}}^{1} \frac{dx}{x\sqrt{4x^2-1}} = \int_{\frac{2}{\sqrt{3}}}^{2} \frac{\frac{1}{2}du}{\frac{1}{2}u\sqrt{u^2-1}} = \sec^{-1}u\Big]_{\frac{2}{\sqrt{3}}}^{2} = \frac{\pi}{3} - \frac{\pi}{6} = \frac{\pi}{6}$$

Let $u = 2x \Rightarrow u^2 = 4x^2$ and $du = 2dx$. $x = \frac{1}{\sqrt{3}} \Rightarrow u = \frac{2}{\sqrt{3}}$ and $x = 1 \Rightarrow u = 2$

30. $$\int_0^1 \frac{x}{1+x^4}\,dx = \frac{1}{2}\int_0^1 \frac{du}{1+u^2} = \frac{1}{2}\tan^{-1}u\Big]_0^1 = \frac{\pi}{8}$$

Let $u = x^2 \Rightarrow du = 2x\,dx$, $x = 0 \Rightarrow u = 0$, $x = 1 \Rightarrow u = 1$

31. $$\int_0^{\sqrt{2}} \frac{4\,dx}{\sqrt{4-x^2}} = \int_0^{\frac{\pi}{4}} \frac{4\,(2\cos u\,du)}{\sqrt{4-4\sin^2 u}} = 4\int_0^{\frac{\pi}{4}} du = 4u\Big]_0^{\frac{\pi}{4}} = \pi$$

Let $x = 2\sin u \Rightarrow dx = 2\cos u\,du$. $x = 0 \Rightarrow u = 0$; $x = \sqrt{2} \Rightarrow u = \frac{\pi}{4}$

32. $$\int_0^1 \frac{dx}{\sqrt{4-x^2}} = \int_0^1 \frac{\frac{1}{2}dx}{\sqrt{1-\frac{x^2}{4}}} = \sin^{-1}\frac{x}{2}\Big]_0^1 = \frac{\pi}{6}$$

33. $$\int_{\sqrt{2}}^{\sqrt[4]{2}} \frac{x\,dx}{x^2\sqrt{x^4-1}} = \int_2^{\sqrt{2}} \frac{\frac{1}{2}du}{u\sqrt{u^2-1}} = \frac{1}{2}\sec^{-1}|u|\Big]_2^{\sqrt{2}} = -\frac{\pi}{24}$$

Let $u = x^2 \Rightarrow du = 2x\,dx$; $x = \sqrt{2} \Rightarrow u = 2$ and $x = \sqrt[4]{2} \Rightarrow u = \sqrt{2}$.

34. $$\int_2^4 \frac{dx}{2x\sqrt{x-1}} = \int_{\sqrt{2}}^{2} \frac{2u\,du}{2u^2\sqrt{u^2-1}} = \sec^{-1}|u|\Big]_{\sqrt{2}}^{2} = \frac{\pi}{3} - \frac{\pi}{4} = \frac{\pi}{12}$$

Let $x = u^2 \Rightarrow dx = 2u\,du$, $x = 2 \Rightarrow u = \sqrt{2}$, $x = 4 \Rightarrow u = 2$

35. $\displaystyle\int_0^2 \frac{dx}{1+(x-1)^2} = \tan^{-1}(x-1)\Big]_0^2 = \tan^{-1}1 - \tan^{-1}(-1) = \frac{\pi}{4} - \left(-\frac{\pi}{4}\right) = \frac{\pi}{2}$

36. $\displaystyle\int_1^3 \frac{2\,dx}{\sqrt{x}\,(1+x)} = \int_1^{\sqrt{3}} \frac{4\,u\,du}{u\,(1+u^2)} = 4\tan^{-1}u\Big]_1^{\sqrt{3}} = 4\left(\frac{\pi}{3} - \frac{\pi}{4}\right) = \frac{\pi}{3}$

Let $u^2 = x \Rightarrow 2\,u\,du = dx$, $x = 1 \Rightarrow u = 1$, $x = 3 \Rightarrow u = \sqrt{3}$

37. $\displaystyle\int_{\frac{1}{2}}^{\frac{3}{4}} \frac{dx}{\sqrt{x}\sqrt{1-x}} = \int_{\frac{1}{\sqrt{2}}}^{\frac{\sqrt{3}}{2}} \frac{2u\,du}{u\sqrt{1-u^2}} = 2\sin^{-1}u\Big]_{\frac{1}{\sqrt{2}}}^{\frac{\sqrt{3}}{2}} = \frac{\pi}{6}$

Let $u = \sqrt{x} \Rightarrow u^2 = x$ and $2u\,du = dx$. $x = \frac{1}{2} \Rightarrow u = \frac{1}{\sqrt{2}}$ and $x = \frac{3}{4} \Rightarrow u = \frac{\sqrt{3}}{2}$

38. $\displaystyle\int_{3/2}^{1+\sqrt{2}/2} \frac{dx}{\sqrt{1-(x-1)^2}} = \sin^{-1}(x-1)\Big]_{3/2}^{1+\sqrt{2}/2}$

$\displaystyle = \sin^{-1}\left(1 + \frac{\sqrt{2}}{2} - 1\right) - \sin^{-1}\left(\frac{1}{2}\right) = \sin^{-1}\left(\frac{\sqrt{2}}{2}\right) - \frac{\pi}{6} = \frac{\pi}{4} - \frac{\pi}{6} = \frac{\pi}{12}$

39. $\displaystyle\int_{-\frac{2}{3}}^{-\frac{\sqrt{2}}{3}} \frac{dx}{x\sqrt{9x^2-1}} = \int_{-2}^{-\sqrt{2}} \frac{\frac{1}{3}du}{\frac{1}{3}u\sqrt{u^2-1}} = \sec^{-1}|u|\Big]_{-2}^{-\sqrt{2}} = -\frac{\pi}{12}$

Let $u = 3x \Rightarrow u^2 = 9x^2$ and $du = 3dx$. $x = -\frac{2}{3} \Rightarrow u = -2$; $x = -\frac{\sqrt{2}}{3} \Rightarrow u = -\sqrt{2}$

40. $\displaystyle\int_{-\pi/2}^{\pi/2} \frac{2\cos x\,dx}{1+\sin^2 x} = 2\tan^{-1}(\sin x)\Big]_{-\pi/2}^{\pi/2} = 2\left(\frac{\pi}{4} - \left(-\frac{\pi}{4}\right)\right) = \pi$

41. $\displaystyle\lim_{x\to 0} \frac{\sin^{-1}2x}{x} = \lim_{x\to 0} \frac{\frac{2}{\sqrt{1-4x^2}}}{1} = 2$

42. $\displaystyle\lim_{x\to 0} \frac{2\tan^{-1}3x}{5x} = \lim_{x\to 0} \frac{\frac{6}{1+9x^2}}{5} = \frac{6}{5}$

43. $\lim_{x\to 0} x^{-3}(\sin^{-1}x - x) = \lim_{x\to 0} \dfrac{\dfrac{1}{\sqrt{1-x^2}} - 1}{3x^2} = \lim_{x\to 0} \dfrac{\dfrac{x}{\sqrt{1-x^2}}}{6x} = \dfrac{1}{6}$

44. $\lim_{x\to 0} x^{-3}(\tan^{-1}x - x) = \lim_{x\to 0} \dfrac{\dfrac{1}{1+x^2} - 1}{3x^2} = \lim_{x\to 0} \dfrac{\dfrac{-2x}{(1+x^2)^2}}{6x} = -\dfrac{1}{3}$

45. $f(x) = \sin^{-1}x + \cos^{-1}x \equiv \dfrac{\pi}{2}$. $\therefore f'(x) = 0$ and $f(.32) = \dfrac{\pi}{2}$.

46. $\dfrac{dy}{dx} = \dfrac{1}{\sqrt{1-x^2}} \Rightarrow y = \sin^{-1}x + C$. $1 = \sin^{-1}0 + C \Rightarrow C = 1$.

$\therefore\ y = \sin^{-1}x + 1$

47. $\tan\theta = x \Rightarrow \sec^2\theta\,\dfrac{d\theta}{dt} = \dfrac{dx}{dt}$. $x = 2 \Rightarrow \sec\theta = \sqrt{5}$.

$(\sqrt{5})^2\dfrac{d\theta}{dt} = 4 \Rightarrow \dfrac{d\theta}{dt} = \dfrac{4}{5}$ rad/hr

48. $V = \pi\int_0^1 \left[\dfrac{1}{1+x^2} - \dfrac{x^2}{2}\right]dx = \pi\left[\tan^{-1}x - \dfrac{x^3}{6}\right]_0^1 = \dfrac{\pi}{2}\left(\dfrac{\pi}{2} - \dfrac{1}{3}\right)$

49. Yes, $\sin^{-1}x = \dfrac{\pi}{2} - \cos^{-1}x \Rightarrow$ these functions differ by at most a constant.

50. (a) If $f(x) = \sin^{-1}\dfrac{x-1}{x+1}$, then $f'(x) = \dfrac{1}{\sqrt{1-\left(\dfrac{x-1}{x+1}\right)^2}} \cdot \dfrac{(x+1)-(x-1)}{(x+1)^2}$

$= \dfrac{1}{(x+1)\sqrt{x}}$. If $g(x) = 2\tan^{-1}\sqrt{x}$, then $g'(x) = \dfrac{\dfrac{1}{\sqrt{x}}}{1+x} = \dfrac{1}{(x+1)\sqrt{x}}$.

(b) $\sin^{-1}\dfrac{x-1}{x+1} = 2\tan^{-1}\sqrt{x} + C$ by part (a). Let $x = 1$:

$0 = 2\left(\dfrac{\pi}{4}\right) + C \Rightarrow C = -\dfrac{\pi}{2}$

51. Let $u = 1 - x^2$, $du = -2x\,dx$. Then $\displaystyle\int \dfrac{x\,dx}{\sqrt{1-x^2}} = -\dfrac{1}{2}\int u^{-\frac{1}{2}}du =$

$-\sqrt{u} + C = -\sqrt{1-x^2} + C$.

52. (a) If $f(x) = \int_0^x \frac{dt}{1+t^2}$, then $f'(x) = \frac{1}{1+x^2}$.

$$f'\left(\frac{1}{x}\right) = \int_0^{\frac{1}{x}} \frac{dt}{1+t^2} = \frac{-\frac{1}{x^2}}{1+\frac{1}{x^2}} = \frac{-1}{1+x^2}. \quad f'(x) = -f'\left(\frac{1}{x}\right) \Rightarrow$$

$$f(x) = f\left(\frac{1}{x}\right) + C.$$

(b) Let $x = 1$: $\int_0^1 \frac{dt}{1+t^2} + \int_0^1 \frac{dt}{1+t^2} = C \Rightarrow 2\tan^{-1} t\Big]_0^1 = C \Rightarrow C = \frac{\pi}{2}$.

53. $(x^2+1)\frac{dy}{dx} = -y^2$, $y = 1$ when $x = 0$

$$-\frac{dy}{y^2} = \frac{dx}{x^2+1} \Rightarrow \frac{1}{y} = \tan^{-1} x + C. \quad 1 = \tan^{-1} 0 + C \Rightarrow C = 1$$

$$\therefore \quad y = \frac{1}{\tan^{-1} x + 1}$$

54. $\sqrt{1-x^2}\,\frac{dy}{dx} = \sqrt{1-y^2}$, $y = 0$ when $x = 0 \Rightarrow \frac{dy}{\sqrt{1-y^2}} = \frac{dx}{\sqrt{1-x^2}}$

$$\sin^{-1} y = \sin^{-1} x + C. \quad \sin^{-1} 0 = \sin^{-1} 0 + C \Rightarrow C = 0. \therefore \sin^{-1} y = \sin^{-1} x.$$

55. $x\sqrt{x^2-1}\,\frac{dy}{dx} = \sqrt{1-y^2}$, $y = -\frac{1}{2}$ when $x = 2$.

$$\frac{dy}{\sqrt{1-y^2}} = \frac{dx}{x\sqrt{x^2-1}} \Rightarrow \sin^{-1} y = \sec^{-1}|x| + C$$

$$\sin^{-1}\left(-\frac{1}{2}\right) = \sec^{-1} 2 + C \Rightarrow C = -\frac{\pi}{6} - \frac{\pi}{3} = -\frac{\pi}{2}$$

$$\therefore \sin^{-1} y = \sec^{-1}|x| - \frac{\pi}{2}$$

56. $\frac{dy}{dx} = -\frac{\sqrt{1-y^2}}{x^2+1}$, $y = \frac{1}{2}$ when $x = 1 \Rightarrow \frac{dy}{\sqrt{1-y^2}} = -\frac{dx}{1+x^2}$

$\sin^{-1} y = -\tan^{-1} x + C$. $\sin^{-1}\frac{1}{2} = -\tan^{-1} 1 + C \Rightarrow C = \frac{5\pi}{12}$.

$\therefore \sin^{-1} y = -\tan^{-1} x + \frac{5\pi}{12}$.

57. (a) Let $y = \cos^{-1} u \Rightarrow \cos y = u \Rightarrow -\sin y \frac{dy}{du} = 1 \Rightarrow$

$\frac{dy}{du} = -\frac{1}{\sin y} = -\frac{1}{\sqrt{1-u^2}}$. Then $\frac{dy}{dx} = \frac{dy}{du}\frac{du}{dx} = -\frac{1}{\sqrt{1-u^2}}\frac{du}{dx}$

(b) Let $y = \tan^{-1} u \Rightarrow \tan y = u \Rightarrow \sec^2 y \frac{dy}{du} = 1 \Rightarrow$

$\frac{dy}{du} = \frac{1}{\sec^2 y} = \cos^2 y = \frac{1}{1+u^2}$. Then $\frac{dy}{dx} = \frac{1}{1+u^2}\frac{du}{dx}$.

(c) $\cot^{-1} u = \frac{\pi}{2} - \tan^{-1} u \Rightarrow \frac{d}{dx}(\cot^{-1} u) = -\frac{d}{dx}(\tan^{-1} u) = \frac{-1}{1+u^2}\frac{du}{dx}$

(d) $\frac{d}{dx}(\csc^{-1} u) = \frac{d}{dx}\left(\sin^{-1}\frac{1}{u}\right) = \frac{1}{\sqrt{1-\left(\frac{1}{u}\right)^2}}\left(\frac{-1}{u^2}\right)\frac{du}{dx} =$

$\frac{|u|}{\sqrt{u^2-1}}\left(\frac{-1}{u^2}\right)\frac{du}{dx} = \frac{-1}{|u|\sqrt{u^2-1}}\frac{du}{dx}$.

6.4 THE NATURAL LOGARITHM AND ITS DERIVATIVE

1. $y = \ln 2x \Rightarrow \frac{dy}{dx} = \frac{1}{2x}\frac{d}{dx}(2x) = \frac{2}{2x} = \frac{1}{x}$

2. $y = \ln 5x \Rightarrow \frac{dy}{dx} = \frac{1}{5x}\frac{d}{dx}(5x) = \frac{5}{5x} = \frac{1}{x}$

3. $y = \ln kx \Rightarrow \frac{dy}{dx} = \frac{1}{kx}\frac{d}{dx}(kx) = \frac{k}{kx} = \frac{1}{x}$

4. $y = (\ln x)^2 \Rightarrow \frac{dy}{dx} = 2 \ln x \frac{d}{dx}(\ln x) = \frac{2\ln x}{x}$

5. $y = \ln\left(\frac{10}{x}\right) = \ln(10x^{-1}) = -\ln 10x \Rightarrow \frac{dy}{dx} = -\frac{1}{x}$

6. $y = \ln(x^2 + 2x) \Rightarrow \frac{dy}{dx} = \frac{2x+2}{x^2 + 2x}$

7. $y = (\ln x)^3 \Rightarrow \frac{dy}{dx} = 3(\ln x)^2 \frac{1}{x} = \frac{3\ln^2 x}{x}$

8. $y = \ln \cos x \Rightarrow \frac{dy}{dx} = \frac{-\sin x}{\cos x} = -\tan x$

9. $y = \ln(\sec x + \tan x) \Rightarrow \frac{dy}{dx} = \frac{1}{\sec x + \tan x}(\sec x \tan x + \sec^2 x)$

10. $y = x \ln x - x \Rightarrow \frac{dy}{dx} = \ln x + 1 - 1 = \ln x$

$$= \frac{\sec x(\tan x + \sec x)}{\sec x + \tan x} = \sec x$$

11. $y = x^3 \ln 2x \Rightarrow \frac{dy}{dx} = x^3\left(\frac{2}{2x}\right) + 3x^2 \ln 2x = x^2(1 + 3\ln 2x)$

12. $y = \ln(\csc x) \Rightarrow \frac{dy}{dx} = \frac{-\csc x \cot x}{\csc x} = -\cot x$

13. $y = \tan^{-1}(\ln x) \Rightarrow \frac{dy}{dx} = \frac{1}{1 + \ln^2 x}\left(\frac{1}{x}\right) = \frac{1}{x(1 + \ln^2 x)}$

14. $y = \ln(\ln x) \Rightarrow \frac{dy}{dx} = \frac{1}{x \ln x}$

15. $y = x^2 \ln(x^2) \Rightarrow \frac{dy}{dx} = x^2\left(\frac{2x}{x^2}\right) + 2x \ln(x^2) = 2x[1 + \ln(x^2)]$

16. $y = \ln(x^2 + 4) - x\tan^{-1}\frac{x}{2} \Rightarrow \frac{dy}{dx} = \frac{2x}{x^2 + 4} - \tan^{-1}\frac{x}{2} - x\left(\frac{\frac{1}{2}}{1 + \frac{x^2}{4}}\right) = -\tan^{-1}\frac{x}{2}$

17. $y = \ln x - \frac{1}{2}\ln(1 + x^2) - \frac{\tan^{-1} x}{x}$

$$\frac{dy}{dx} = \frac{1}{x} - \frac{1}{2}\left(\frac{2x}{1 + x^2}\right) - \frac{1}{x}\left(\frac{1}{1 + x^2}\right) - (\tan^{-1} x)\left(-\frac{1}{x^2}\right)$$

$$= \frac{1}{x(1 + x^2)} - \frac{1}{x(1 + x^2)} + \frac{\tan^{-1} x}{x} = \frac{\tan^{-1} x}{x}$$

18. $y = x(\ln x)^3 \Rightarrow \frac{dy}{dx} = (\ln x)^3 + 3x(\ln x)^2 \cdot \frac{1}{x} = (\ln x)^3 + 3(\ln x)^2$

19. $y = x[\sin(\ln x) + \cos(\ln x)]$

$$\frac{dy}{dx} = [\sin(\ln x) + \cos(\ln x)] + x\left[\cos(\ln x)\left(\frac{1}{x}\right) - \sin(\ln x)\left(\frac{1}{x}\right)\right]$$

$$= 2\cos(\ln x)$$

20. $y = x \ln(a^2 + x^2) - 2x + 2a\tan^{-1}\frac{x}{a}$

$$\frac{dy}{dx} = \ln(a^2 + x^2) + \frac{2x^2}{a^2 + x^2} - 2 + 2a\left(\frac{\frac{1}{a}}{1 + \frac{x^2}{a^2}}\right)$$

$$= \ln(a^2 + x^2) - 2 + \frac{2x^2}{a^2 + x^2} + \frac{2a^2}{a^2 + x^2} = \ln(a^2 + x^2)$$

21. $\int \frac{dx}{x} = \ln|x| + C$

22. $\int \frac{2\,dx}{x} = 2\ln|x| + C$

23. $\int \frac{dx}{2x} = \frac{1}{2}\ln|x| + C$

24. $\int \frac{dx}{x + 2} = \ln|x + 2| + C$

25. $\int_0^1 \frac{dx}{x + 1} = \ln|x + 1|\Big]_0^1 = \ln 2 - \ln 1 = \ln 2$

26. $\int_{-1}^0 \frac{dx}{1 - x} = -\ln|1 - x|\Big]_{-1}^0 = -\ln 1 + \ln 2 = \ln 2$

27. $\int_{-1}^0 \frac{dx}{2x + 3} = \frac{1}{2}\ln|2x + 3|\Big]_{-1}^0 = \frac{1}{2}[\ln 3 - \ln 1] = \frac{1}{2}\ln 3$

28. $\int_{-1}^0 \frac{3\,dx}{2 - 3x} = -\ln|2 - 3x|\Big]_{-1}^0 = -(\ln 2 - \ln 5) = \ln\frac{5}{2}$

29. $\int_0^1 \frac{x\,dx}{4x^2 + 1} = \frac{1}{8}\ln(4x^2 + 1)\Big]_0^1 = \frac{1}{8}\ln 5$

30. $\int_0^{\pi} \frac{\sin x\,dx}{2 - \cos x} = \ln|2 - \cos x|\Big]_0^{\pi} = \ln 3$

31. $\int \tan 3x\,dx = \int \frac{\sin 3x}{\cos 3x}dx = -\frac{1}{3}\ln|\cos 3x| + C$

32. $\int \cot 5x\,dx = \int \frac{\cos 5x\,dx}{\sin 5x} = \frac{1}{5}\ln|\sin 5x| + C$

33. $\displaystyle\int \frac{x^2\,dx}{4-x^3} = -\frac{1}{3}\ln|4-x^3| + C$

34. $\displaystyle\int \frac{\sec^2 2x\,dx}{1+\tan 2x} = \frac{1}{2}\ln|1+\tan 2x| + C$

35. $\displaystyle\int \frac{dx}{x\ln x} = \int \frac{du}{u} = \ln|u| + C = \ln|\ln x| + C$

Let $u = \ln x \Rightarrow du = \frac{1}{x}dx$

36. $\displaystyle\int \frac{dx}{x(\ln x)^2} = -\frac{1}{\ln x} + C$

37. $\displaystyle\int_1^2 \frac{(\ln x)^2}{x}dx = \int_0^{\ln 2} u^2\,du = \frac{1}{3}u^3\Big]_0^{\ln 2} = \frac{1}{3}\ln^3 2$

Let $u = \ln x \Rightarrow du = \frac{1}{x}dx$; $x = 1 \Rightarrow u = \ln 1 = 0$; $x = 2 \Rightarrow u = \ln 2$

38. $\displaystyle\int_1^3 \frac{\cos(\ln x)\,dx}{x} = \sin(\ln x)\Big]_1^3 = \sin(\ln 3)$

39. $\displaystyle\int \frac{\sec^2 x + \sec x\tan x}{\sec x + \tan x}dx = \int u^{-1}\,du = \ln|u| + C = \ln|\sec x + \tan x| + C$

Let $u = \sec x + \tan x \Rightarrow du = \sec x\tan x + \sec^2 x\,dx$

40. $\displaystyle\int \frac{dx}{(1+x^2)\tan^{-1}x} = \ln|\tan^{-1} x| + C$

41. $\displaystyle\lim_{x\to\infty} \frac{\ln x}{x} = \lim_{x\to\infty}\left(\frac{\frac{1}{x}}{1}\right) = 0$

42. $\displaystyle\lim_{x\to\infty} \frac{\ln(\ln x)}{\ln x} = \lim_{x\to\infty}\frac{\frac{1}{x\ln x}}{\frac{1}{x}} = \lim_{x\to\infty}\frac{1}{\ln x} = 0$

43. $\displaystyle\lim_{t\to 0} \frac{\ln(1+2t) - 2t}{t^2} = \lim_{t\to 0}\left(\frac{\frac{2}{1+2t} - 2}{2t}\right) = \lim_{t\to 0}\left(\frac{\frac{-4}{(1+2t)^2}}{2}\right) = -2$

44. $\displaystyle\lim_{\theta\to 0^+} \frac{\ln(\sin\theta)}{\cot\theta} = \lim_{\theta\to 0^+} -\frac{\cot\theta}{\csc^2\theta} = \lim_{\theta\to 0^+} -\frac{\csc^2\theta}{2\csc^2\theta\cot\theta} = 0$

45. $\displaystyle A = \int_1^2 \left(\frac{2}{x} - 1\right)dx = 2\ln|x| - x\Big]_1^2 = 2\ln 2 - 1$

46. $A = \int_1^2 \frac{dx}{x} = \ln x\Big]_1^2 \ \ln 2$

$M_y = \int_1^2 x\left(\frac{1}{x}\right) dx = 1 \quad \therefore \ \bar{x} = \frac{1}{\ln 2}$

$M_x = \int_1^2 \left(\frac{y}{2}\right)\left(\frac{1}{x}\right) dx = \frac{1}{2}\int_1^2 \frac{dx}{x^2} = -\frac{1}{2x}\Big]_1^2 = \frac{1}{4}. \quad \therefore \ \bar{y} = \frac{1}{4 \ln 2}$

47. $A = \int_0^1 \frac{2}{1+x^2} dx = 2 \tan^{-1} x]_0^1 = \frac{\pi}{2}$

$\bar{x} = \frac{2}{\pi}\int_0^1 x\left(\frac{2}{1+x^2}\right) dx = \frac{2}{\pi} \ln|1+x^2|\Big]_0^1 = \frac{2 \ln 2}{\pi}$

$\bar{y} = 0$ by symmetry. $\therefore \ (\bar{x}, \bar{y}) = \left(\frac{2 \ln 2}{\pi}, 0\right)$.

48. $\frac{d^2y}{dx^2} = \sec^2 x$, $y = 0$ and $\frac{dy}{dx} = 1$ when $x = 0$.

$\frac{dy}{dx} = \int \sec^2 x \, dx = \tan x + C. \quad 1 = \tan 0 + C \Rightarrow C = 1.$

$y = \int (\tan x + 1) dx = -\ln|\cos x| + x + C. \quad 0 = 0 + C \Rightarrow C = 0.$

$\therefore \ y = -\ln|\cos x| + x$

49. $x = \ln(\sec t + \tan t) - \sin t \Rightarrow \frac{dx}{dt} = \frac{\sec t \tan t + \sec^2 t}{\sec t + \tan t} - \cos t$

$\left(\frac{dx}{dt}\right)^2 = (\sec t - \cos t)^2 = \sec^2 t - 2 + \cos^2 t.$

$y = \cos t \Rightarrow \frac{dy}{dt} = -\sin t \Rightarrow \left(\frac{dy}{dt}\right)^2 = \sin^2 t$

$s = \int_0^{\frac{\pi}{3}} \sqrt{\left(\frac{dx}{dt}\right)^2 + \left(\frac{dy}{dt}\right)^2} \, dt = \int_0^{\frac{\pi}{3}} \sqrt{\sec^2 t - 2 + \cos^2 t + \sin^2 t} \, dt$

$\int_0^{\frac{\pi}{3}} \sqrt{\sec^2 t - 1} \, dt = \int_0^{\frac{\pi}{3}} \tan t \, dt = \int_0^{\frac{\pi}{3}} \frac{\sin t}{\cos t} dt =$

$-\ln|\cos t|\Big]_0^{\frac{\pi}{3}} = -\left[\ln\frac{1}{2} - \ln 1\right] = -\ln\frac{1}{2} = \ln 2$

6.5 PROPERTIES OF THE NATURAL LOGARITHM

1. $\ln 16 = \ln 2^4 = 4 \ln 2$

2. $\ln \sqrt[3]{9} = \ln (3^2)^{1/3} = \frac{2}{3} \ln 3$

3. $\ln 2\sqrt{2} = \ln 2^{\frac{3}{2}} = \frac{3}{2} \ln 2$

4. $\ln 0.25 = \ln \frac{1}{4} = \ln (2)^{-2} = -2 \ln 2$

5. $\ln \frac{4}{9} = \ln 4 - \ln 9 = 2 \ln 2 - 2 \ln 3$

6. $\ln 12 = \ln 3 \cdot 2^2 = \ln 3 + 2 \ln 2$

7. $\ln \frac{9}{8} = \ln 9 - \ln 8 = 2 \ln 3 - 3 \ln 2$

8. $\ln 36 = \ln 2^2 \cdot 3^2 = 2 \ln 2 + 2 \ln 3$

9. $\ln 4.5 = \ln \frac{9}{2} = \ln 9 - \ln 2 = 2 \ln 3 - \ln 2$

10. $\ln \sqrt{13.5} = \frac{1}{2} \ln \frac{27}{2} = \frac{1}{2} (3 \ln 3 - \ln 2)$

11. $y = \ln \sqrt{x^2 + 5} = \frac{1}{2} \ln (x^2 + 5) \Rightarrow \frac{dy}{dx} = \frac{1}{2} \left(\frac{2x}{x^2 + 5} \right) = \frac{x}{x^2 + 5}$

12. $y = \ln x^{3/2} = \frac{3}{2} \ln x \Rightarrow \frac{dy}{dx} = \frac{3}{2x}$

13. $y = \ln \frac{1}{x\sqrt{x + 1}} = -\ln x\sqrt{x + 1} = -(\ln x + \frac{1}{2} \ln (x^2 + 5)$

$$\frac{dy}{dx} = -\left[\frac{1}{x} + \frac{1}{2(x + 1)}\right]$$

14. $y = \ln \sqrt[3]{\cos x} = \frac{1}{3} \ln \cos x \Rightarrow \frac{dy}{dx} = \frac{-\sin x}{3 \cos x} = -\frac{1}{3} \tan x$

15. $y = \ln(\sin x \sin 2x) \Rightarrow \frac{dy}{dx} = \frac{1}{\sin x \sin 2x} \cdot \frac{d}{dx}(\sin x \sin 2x)$

$$= \frac{\sin x(2\cos x) + (\sin 2x)\cos x}{\sin x \sin 2x}$$

$$= \frac{2\cos 2x + 2\cos^2 x}{\sin 2x}$$

16. $y = \ln \left(x\sqrt{x^2 + 1}\right) = \ln x + \frac{1}{2} \ln (x^2 + 1) \Rightarrow$

$$\frac{dy}{dx} = \frac{1}{x} + \frac{1}{2}\left(\frac{1}{x^2 + 1}\right)2x = \frac{2x^2 + 1}{x(x^2 + 1)}$$

17. $y = \ln (3x\sqrt{x + 2}) = \ln 3x + \frac{1}{2} \ln(x + 2)$

$$\frac{dy}{dx} = \frac{1}{x} + \frac{1}{2(x + 2)}$$

18. $y = \frac{1}{2} \ln \frac{1 + x}{1 - x} = \frac{1}{2}[\ln(1 + x) - \ln(1 - x)] \Rightarrow$

$$\frac{dy}{dx} = \frac{1}{2}\left[\frac{1}{1 + x} + \frac{1}{1 - x}\right] = \frac{1}{1 - x^2}$$

19. $y = \frac{1}{3} \ln \left(\frac{x^3}{1 + x^3}\right)$

$$= \frac{1}{3} [\ln x^3 - \ln(1 + x^3)]$$

$$\frac{dy}{dx} = \frac{1}{3}\left[\frac{3x^2}{x^3} - \frac{3x^2}{1 + x^3}\right]$$

20. $y = \ln \frac{x}{2 + 3x} = \ln x - \ln(2 + 3x) \Rightarrow \frac{dy}{dx} = \frac{1}{x} - \frac{3}{2 + 3x} = \frac{2}{x(2 + 3x)}$

21. $y = \ln \frac{(x^2 + 1)^5}{\sqrt{1 - x}} = 5\ln(x^2 + 1) - \frac{1}{2}\ln(1 - x)$

$$\frac{dy}{dx} = \frac{10x}{x^2 + 1} + \frac{1}{2(1 - x)}$$

22. $y = \int_{x^{1/2}}^{x^{1/3}} \ln t \, dt = \int_a^{x^{1/3}} \ln t \, dt - \int_a^{x^{1/2}} \ln t \, dt$

$$\frac{dy}{dx} = \ln x^{1/3}\left(\frac{1}{3}x^{-2/3}\right) - \ln x^{1/2}\left(\frac{1}{2}x^{-1/2}\right)$$

$$= \left(\frac{1}{9}x^{-2/3} - \frac{1}{4}x^{-1/2}\right)\ln x$$

23. $y^2 = x(x + 1), \; x > 0$

$$2\ln y = \ln x + \ln(x + 1)$$

$$\frac{2}{y}\frac{dy}{dx} = \frac{1}{x} + \frac{1}{x + 1} \Rightarrow \frac{dy}{dx} = \frac{y}{2}\left(\frac{1}{x} + \frac{1}{x + 1}\right)$$

24. $y = \sqrt[3]{\frac{x + 1}{x - 1}}, \; x > 1 \Rightarrow \ln y = \frac{1}{3}[\ln(x + 1) - \ln(x - 1)]$

$$\frac{1}{y}\frac{dy}{dx} = \frac{1}{3}\left[\frac{1}{x + 1} + \frac{1}{x - 1}\right] = \frac{-2}{3(x^2 - 1)}$$

$$\frac{dy}{dx} = \sqrt[3]{\frac{x + 1}{x - 1}}\left[\frac{-2}{3(x^2 - 1)}\right]$$

25. $y = \sqrt{x+2}\,\sin x \cos x,\ 0 < x < \frac{\pi}{2} \Rightarrow \ln y = \frac{1}{2}\ln(x+2) + \ln \sin x + \ln \cos x$

$$\frac{1}{y}\frac{dy}{dx} = \frac{1}{2(x+2)} + \frac{\cos x}{\sin x} - \frac{\sin x}{\cos x}$$

$$\frac{dy}{dx} = y\left[\frac{1}{2(x+2)} + \cot x - \tan x\right]$$

26. $y = \frac{x\sqrt{x^2+1}}{(x+1)^{2/3}},\ x > 0 \Rightarrow \ln y = \ln x + \frac{1}{2}\ln(x^2+1) - \frac{2}{3}\ln(x+1)$

$$\frac{1}{y}\frac{dy}{dx} = \frac{1}{x} + \frac{x}{x^2+1} - \frac{2}{3(x+1)}$$

$$\frac{dy}{dx} = \frac{x\sqrt{x^2+1}}{(x+1)^{2/3}}\left[\frac{1}{x} + \frac{x}{x^2+1} - \frac{2}{3(x+1)}\right]$$

27. $y = \sqrt[3]{\frac{x(x-2)}{x^2+1}},\ x > 2 \Rightarrow \ln y = \frac{1}{3}[\ln x + \ln(x-2) - \ln(x^2+1)]$

$$\frac{1}{y}\frac{dy}{dx} = \frac{1}{3}\left[\frac{1}{x} + \frac{1}{x+2} - \frac{2x}{x^2+1}\right] \Rightarrow \frac{dy}{dx} = \frac{y}{3}\left[\frac{1}{x} + \frac{1}{x+2} - \frac{2x}{x^2+1}\right]$$

28. $y^5 = \sqrt{\frac{(x+1)^5}{(x+2)^{10}}} \Rightarrow 5 \ln y = \frac{5}{2}\ln(x+1) - 5\ln(x+2)$

$$\frac{5}{y}\frac{dy}{dx} = \frac{5}{2(x+1)} - \frac{5}{x+2} \Rightarrow \frac{dy}{dx} = y\left[\frac{-x}{2(x+1)(x+2)}\right]$$

29. $y = \sqrt{\frac{x(x+1)(x-2)}{(x^2+1)(2x+3)}},\ x > 2$

$$\ln y = \frac{1}{3}[\ln x + \ln(x+1) + \ln(x-2) - \ln(x^2+1) - \ln(2x+3)$$

$$\frac{1}{y}\frac{dy}{dx} = \frac{1}{3}\left[\frac{1}{x} + \frac{1}{x+1} + \frac{1}{x-2} - \frac{2x}{x^2+1} - \frac{2}{2x+3}\right]$$

$$\frac{dy}{dx} = \frac{y}{3}\left[\frac{1}{x} + \frac{1}{x+1} + \frac{1}{x-2} - \frac{2x}{x^2+1} - \frac{2}{2x+3}\right]$$

30. $y^{4/5} = \frac{\sqrt{\sin x \cos x}}{1 + 2\ln x} \Rightarrow \frac{4}{5}\ln y = \frac{1}{2}(\ln \sin x + \ln \cos x) - \ln(1 + 2\ln x)$

$$\frac{4}{5y}\frac{dy}{dx} = \frac{1}{2}\left(\frac{\cos x}{\sin x} - \frac{\sin x}{\cos x}\right) - \left(\frac{1}{1+2\ln x}\right)\left(\frac{2}{x}\right)$$

$$\frac{dy}{dx} = \frac{5y}{4}\left[\cot 2x - \frac{2}{x(1+2\ln x)}\right]$$

31. $\sqrt{y} = \dfrac{x^5 \tan^{-1} x}{(3-2x)\sqrt[3]{x}} \Rightarrow$

$\frac{1}{2} y = 5 \ln x + \ln \tan^{-1} x - \ln(3-2x) - \frac{1}{3} \ln x$

$\dfrac{1}{2y}\dfrac{dy}{dx} = \dfrac{5}{x} + \dfrac{1}{\tan^{-1} x} \cdot \dfrac{1}{1+x^2} + \dfrac{2}{3-2x} - \dfrac{1}{3x}$

$\dfrac{dy}{dx} = 2y\left[\dfrac{14}{3x} + \dfrac{2}{3-2x} + \dfrac{1}{(1+x^2)\tan^{-1} x}\right]$

32. (a) $y = \sqrt{\dfrac{(x+1)(x+2)}{(3-x)(4-x)}}$; Largest domain is : $(-\infty,-2] \cup [-1,3) \cup (4,\infty)$

(b) $\ln y = \frac{1}{2}[\ln(x+1) + \ln(x+2) - \ln(3-x) - \ln(4-x)]$

$\dfrac{dy}{dx} = \dfrac{y}{2}\left[\dfrac{1}{x+1} + \dfrac{1}{x+2} + \dfrac{1}{3-x} + \dfrac{1}{4-x}\right]$

33. $\displaystyle\int_{-1}^{1} \frac{dx}{x+3} = \ln|x+3|\Big]_{-1}^{1} = \ln 4 - \ln 2 = \ln 2$

34. $\displaystyle\int_{0}^{6} \frac{dx}{x+2} = \ln|x+2|\Big]_{0}^{6} = \ln 8 - \ln 2 = \ln 4$

35. $\displaystyle\int_{\pi/4}^{\pi/2} \cot x \, dx = \int_{\pi/4}^{\pi/2} \frac{\cos x}{\sin x} dx = \ln|\sin x|\Big]_{\pi/4}^{\pi/2} = \ln\sqrt{2}$

36. (a) $\displaystyle\int_{0}^{\sqrt{3}} \frac{dx}{1+x^2} = \tan^{-1} x\Big]_{0}^{\sqrt{3}} = \frac{\pi}{3}$

(b) $\displaystyle\int_{0}^{\sqrt{3}} \frac{x\,dx}{1+x^2} = \frac{1}{2}\ln(1+x^2)\Big]_{0}^{\sqrt{3}} = \frac{1}{2}\ln 4 = \ln 2$

37. $\displaystyle\int_{2}^{4} \frac{2x-5}{x} dx = \int_{2}^{4}\left(2 - \frac{5}{x}\right)dx = 2x - 5\ln|x|\Big]_{2}^{4} = 4 - 5\ln 2$

38. $\displaystyle\int_{0}^{\pi/3} \frac{\sec s \tan s \, dx}{2 + \sec x} = \ln|2 + \sec x|\Big]_{0}^{\pi/3} = \ln 4 - \ln 3 = \ln\frac{4}{3}$

39. (a) $\displaystyle\int_{0}^{3/5} \frac{x\,dx}{1-x^2} = -\frac{1}{2}\int_{1}^{16/25} \frac{du}{u} = -\frac{1}{2}\ln|u|\Big]_{1}^{16/25} = \ln\left(\frac{16}{25}\right)^{-1/2} = \ln\frac{5}{4}$

Let $u = 1 - x^2 \Rightarrow du = -2x\,dx \Rightarrow x\,dx = -\frac{1}{2}u$;

$x = 0 \Rightarrow u = 1$; $x = \frac{3}{5} \Rightarrow u = \frac{16}{25}$

(b) $\displaystyle\int_0^{\frac{3}{5}} \frac{dx}{\sqrt{1-x^2}} = \sin^{-1} x \Big]_0^{\frac{3}{5}} = \sin^{-1}\frac{3}{5}$

(c) $\displaystyle\int_0^{\frac{3}{5}} \frac{x\,dx}{\sqrt{1-x^2}} = -\sqrt{1-x^2}\Big]_0^{\frac{3}{5}} = \frac{1}{5}$

40. (a) $\displaystyle\int_{-1}^{3} \frac{dx}{\sqrt{2x+3}} = \sqrt{2x+3}\Big]_{-1}^{3} = 3-1=2$

(b) $\displaystyle\int_{-1}^{3} \frac{dx}{2x+3} = \frac{1}{2}\ln|2x+3|\Big]_{-1}^{3} = \frac{1}{2}\ln 9 = \ln 3$

(c) $\displaystyle\int_{-1}^{3} \frac{dx}{(2x+3)^2} = -\frac{1}{2(2x+3)}\Big]_{-1}^{3} = \frac{4}{9}$

41. (a) $y = \log|x|$ (b) $y = |\ln x|$

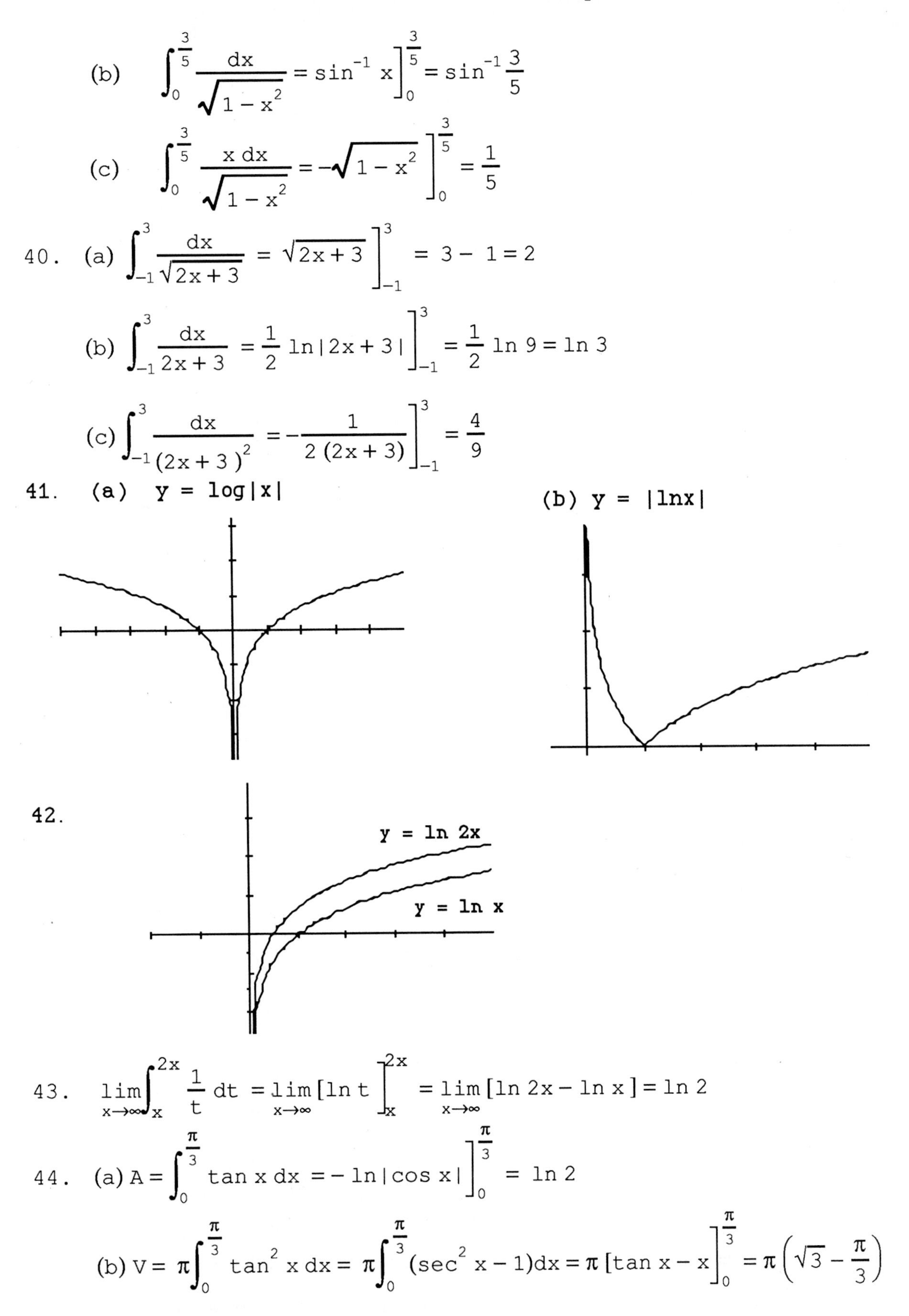

42.

43. $\displaystyle\lim_{x\to\infty}\int_x^{2x} \frac{1}{t}\,dt = \lim_{x\to\infty}[\ln t\Big]_x^{2x} = \lim_{x\to\infty}[\ln 2x - \ln x] = \ln 2$

44. (a) $\displaystyle A = \int_0^{\frac{\pi}{3}} \tan x\,dx = -\ln|\cos x|\Big]_0^{\frac{\pi}{3}} = \ln 2$

(b) $\displaystyle V = \pi\int_0^{\frac{\pi}{3}} \tan^2 x\,dx = \pi\int_0^{\frac{\pi}{3}} (\sec^2 x - 1)dx = \pi\,[\tan x - x\Big]_0^{\frac{\pi}{3}} = \pi\left(\sqrt{3} - \frac{\pi}{3}\right)$

45. The region is bounded by $y = \frac{4}{x}$ and $y = (x-3)^2$. These curves intersect where $\frac{4}{x} = (x-3)^2 \Leftrightarrow x^3 - 6x^2 + 9x - 4 = 0 \Leftrightarrow (x-1)^2(x-4) = 0$ or $x = 1, 4$. Then:

$$A = \int_1^4 \left[\frac{4}{x} - (x-3)^2\right]dx = 4\ \ln|x| - \frac{1}{3}(x-3)^3\Big]_1^4 = 4\ \ln 4 - 3$$

$$V = \pi\int_1^4 \left[\left(\frac{4}{x}\right)^2 - (x-3)^4\right]dx = \pi\left[-\frac{16}{x} - \frac{1}{5}(x-3)^5\right]_0^4 = \frac{27\pi}{5}$$

46. $V = \pi\int_{\frac{1}{2}}^4 \left(\frac{1}{\sqrt{x}}\right)^2 dx = \pi\ \ln x\Big]_{\frac{1}{2}}^4 = 3\pi\ \ln 2$

47. (a) If $f(x) = \ln(1+x)$, then $f'(x) = \frac{1}{1+x}$, $f''(x) = -\frac{1}{(1+x)^2}$ and $f'''(x) = \frac{2}{(1+x)^3}$. Then $L(x) \approx f(0) + f'(0)x = \ln 1 + (1)\,x = x$.

$$Q(x) \approx f(0) + f'(0)\,x + \frac{f''(0)}{2}x^2 = \ln 1 + (1)x - \frac{1}{2}x^2 = x - \frac{x^2}{2}.$$

(b) $|e_1(x)| \le \frac{1}{2}M_1x^2$, where $M_1 = \max\{|f''(x)| : 0 \le x \le .1\} = 1$

$\therefore\ |e_1(x)| \le \frac{1}{2}(1)(.1)^2 = 0.005$

$|e_2(x)| \le \frac{1}{6}M_2\ |x|^3$, where $M_2 = \max\{|f'''(x)| : 0 \le x \le .1\} = 2$.

$\therefore\ |e_2(x)| \le \frac{1}{6}(2)(.1)^3 = 0.000\bar{3}$

48. (a)

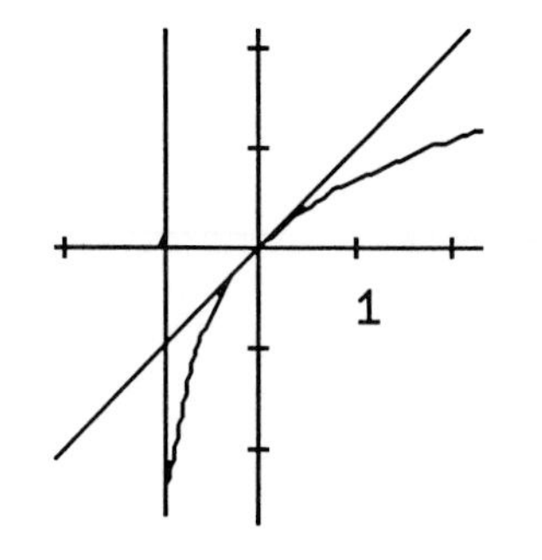

Let $F(x) = x - \ln(x+1)$. $F'(x) = \frac{x}{(1+x)^2} = 0$ if $x = 0$. $F' < 0$ if $-1 < x < 0$ and $F' > 0$ if $x > 0 \Rightarrow F(0) = 0$ is a minimum. There are no other critical points so F increases for $x > 0 \Rightarrow$ maximum difference occurs at $x = 0.1$.

48. (b) $\ln 1.1 - 0.1 = -0.00469$

49. (a) $\ln 1.2 = \ln(1+0.2) \approx 0.2$ by (16)

$$\approx 0.2 - \frac{(.2)^2}{2} = 0.1800 \text{ by } (17)$$

$$\ln 1.2 \approx \frac{.1}{3}\left[1 + 4\left(\frac{1}{1.1}\right) + \frac{1}{1.2}\right] \approx 0.18232 \text{ by Simpson's Rule.}$$

(b) $\ln .8 = \ln(1-0.2) \approx -0.2$ by (16)

$$\approx -0.2 - \frac{(-.2)^2}{2} = -0.2200 \text{ by } (17)$$

$$\ln .8 \approx -\frac{.1}{3}\left[\frac{1}{.8} + 4\left(\frac{1}{.9}\right) + 1\right] \approx -0.22315 \text{ by Simpson's Rule.}$$

50. $$\int_1^5 \frac{dx}{x} \approx \frac{1}{6}\left[1 + \frac{8}{3} + 1 + \frac{8}{5} + \frac{2}{3} + \frac{8}{7} + \frac{1}{2} + \frac{8}{9} + \frac{1}{5}\right] \approx 1.6108$$

By calculator, $\ln 5 \approx 1.6094$

6.6 THE EXPONENTIAL FUNCTION e^x

1. $e^{\ln x} = x$

2. $\ln e^{x} = x$

3. $e^{-\ln(x^2)} = e^{\ln(x^{-2})} = x^{-2}$

4. $\ln(e^{-x^2}) = -x^2$

5. $\ln e^{\frac{1}{x}} = \frac{1}{x}$

6. $\ln\left(\frac{1}{e^x}\right) = -x$

7. $e^{\ln 2 + \ln x} = e^{\ln 2x} = 2x$

8. $e^{2\ln x} = x^2$

9. $\ln e^{(x-x^2)} = x - x^2$

10. $\ln(x^2 e^{-2x}) = 2\ln x - 2x$

11. $e^{(x+\ln x)} = e^x e^{\ln x} = xe^x$

12. $e^{\ln x - 2\ln y} = \frac{x}{y^2}$

13. $e^{\sqrt{y}} = x^2 \Rightarrow \sqrt{y}\ln e = \ln x^2 \Rightarrow \sqrt{y} = 2\ln x \Rightarrow y = 4\ln^2 x$

14. $e^{2y} = x^2 \Rightarrow 2y = 2\ln x \Rightarrow y = \ln x$

15. $e^{(x^2)} e^{2x+1} = e^y \Leftrightarrow y = x^2 + 2x + 1$

16. $\ln(y-1) = x + \ln x \Rightarrow y - 1 = e^{x+\ln x} \Rightarrow y = 1 + xe^x$

17. $\ln(y-2) = \ln(\sin x) - x \Rightarrow \ln\frac{y-2}{\sin x} = -x \Rightarrow \frac{y-2}{\sin x} = e^{-x}$

$y = e^{-x}\sin x + 2.$

18. $\ln(y^2 - 1) - \ln(y+1) = \sin x \Rightarrow \ln(y-1) = \sin x$

$y - 1 = e^{\sin x} \Rightarrow y = 1 + e^{\sin x}$

19. $y = e^{3x} \Rightarrow \frac{dy}{dx} = 3e^{3x}$

20. $y = e^{x+1} \Rightarrow \frac{dy}{dx} = e^{x+1}$

21. $y = e^{5-7x} \Rightarrow \frac{dy}{dx} = -7e^{5-7x}$

22. $y = \cos e^{x} \Rightarrow \frac{dy}{dx} = -e^{x} \sin e^{x}$

23. $y = x^{2} e^{x} = \frac{dy}{dx} = x^{2} e^{x} + 2xe^{x} = xe^{x} (x + 2)$

24. $y = \sin e^{-x} \Rightarrow \frac{dy}{dx} = -e^{-x} \cos e^{-x}$

25. $y = e^{\sin x} \Rightarrow \frac{dy}{dx} = (\cos x)e^{\sin x}$

26. $y = e^{(x^2)} e^{-x} \Rightarrow \frac{dy}{dx} = -e^{(x^2)} e^{-x} + 2xe^{(x^2)} e^{-x} = e^{x^2 - x} (2x - 1)$

27. $y = \ln (3xe^{-x}) = \ln 3 + \ln x - x \Rightarrow \frac{dy}{dx} = \frac{1}{x} - 1 = \frac{1 - x}{x}$

28. $y = \ln \frac{e^{x}}{1 + e^{x}} = \ln e^{x} - \ln (1 + e^{x}) \Rightarrow x - \ln (1 + e^{x})$

$$\frac{dy}{dx} = 1 - \frac{e^{x}}{1 + e^{x}} = \frac{1}{1 + e^{x}}$$

29. $y = e^{\sin^{-1} x} \Rightarrow \frac{dy}{dx} = e^{\sin^{-1} x} \left(\frac{1}{\sqrt{1 - x^2}} \right)$

30. $y = (1 + 2x)e^{-2x} = \frac{dy}{dx} = 2e^{-2x} - 2(1 + 2x)e^{-2x} = -4xe^{-2x}$

31. $y = (9x^2 - 6x + 2)e^{3x} \Rightarrow \frac{dy}{dx} = 3(9x^2 - 6x + 2)e^{3x} + (18x - 6)e^{3x} = 27x^2 e^{3x}$

32. $y = \frac{ax - 1}{a^2} e^{ax} \Rightarrow \frac{dy}{dx} = \frac{ax - 1}{a^2} ae^{ax} + \frac{1}{a} e^{ax} = xe^{ax}$

33. $y = x^2 e^{-(x^2)} \Rightarrow \frac{dy}{dx} = x^2 (-2xe^{-(x^2)}) + 2xe^{-(x^2)} = 2xe^{-(x^2)} (1 - x^2)$

34. $y = e^{x} \ln x \Rightarrow \frac{dy}{dx} = \frac{e^{x}}{x} + e^{x} \ln x = e^{x} \left(\frac{1}{x} + \ln x \right)$

35. $y = \tan^{-1} (e^{x}) \Rightarrow \frac{dy}{dx} = \frac{e^{x}}{1 + e^{2x}}$

36. $y = \sec^{-1}(e^{2x}) \Rightarrow \dfrac{dy}{dx} = \dfrac{2e^{2x}}{e^{2x}\sqrt{e^{4x} - 1}} = \dfrac{2}{\sqrt{e^{4x} - 1}}$

37. $y = x^3 e^{-2x} \cos 5x \Rightarrow \ln y = 3 \ln x - 2x + \ln(\cos 5x)$

$$\frac{1}{y}\frac{dy}{dx} = \frac{3}{x} - 2 - \frac{5 \sin 5x}{\cos 5x} = \frac{3}{x} - 2 - 5 \tan 5x$$

$$\frac{dy}{dx} = y\left(\frac{3}{x} - 2 - 5 \tan 5x\right)$$

38. $y = \int_0^{\ln x} \sin e^t \, dt \Rightarrow \dfrac{dy}{dx} = \sin(e^{\ln x})\left(\dfrac{1}{x}\right) = \dfrac{\sin x}{x}$

39. $\ln y = x \sin x \Rightarrow \dfrac{1}{y}\dfrac{dy}{dx} = \sin x + x \cos x \Rightarrow \dfrac{dy}{dx} = y(\sin x + x \cos x)$

40. $\ln xy = e^{x+y} \Rightarrow \dfrac{1}{x} + \dfrac{1}{y}\dfrac{dy}{dx} = e^{x+y}\left(1 + \dfrac{dy}{dx}\right)$

$$\left(\frac{1}{y} - e^{x+y}\right)\frac{dy}{dx} = e^{x+y} - \frac{1}{x}$$

$$\left(\frac{1 - y e^{x+y}}{y}\right)\frac{dy}{dx} = \frac{x e^{x+y} - 1}{x} \Rightarrow \frac{dy}{dx} = \frac{y(x e^{x+y} - 1)}{x(1 - y e^{x+y})}$$

41. $e^{2x} = \sin(x + 3y) \Rightarrow 2e^{2x} = \cos(x + 3y)\left[1 + 3\dfrac{dy}{dx}\right]$

$$2e^{2x} = \cos(x + 3y) + 3\cos(x + 3y)\frac{dy}{dx}$$

$$\frac{dy}{dx} = \frac{2e^{2x} - \cos(x + 3y)}{3\cos(x + 3y)}$$

42. $\tan y = e^x + \ln x \Rightarrow \sec^2 y \dfrac{dy}{dx} = e^x + \dfrac{1}{x} \Rightarrow \dfrac{dy}{dx} = \cos^2 y\left(e^x + \dfrac{1}{x}\right)$

43. $\displaystyle\int_{\ln 3}^{\ln 5} e^{2x}\, dx = \frac{1}{2} e^{2x}\Big]_{\ln 3}^{\ln 5} = \frac{1}{2}[e^{2\ln 5} - e^{2\ln 3}] = \frac{1}{2}(25 - 9) = 8$

44. $\displaystyle\int_{-1}^{1} x e^{(x^2)}\, dx = \frac{1}{2} e^{(x^2)}\Big]_{-1}^{1} = \frac{1}{2}(e - e) = 0$

45. $\displaystyle\int_0^{\pi} e^{\sin x} \cos x \, dx = e^{\sin x}\Big]_0^{\pi} = 0$

46. $\displaystyle\int_0^{\ln 8} e^{x/3}\, dx = 3e^{x/3}\Big]_0^{\ln 8} = 3e^{\ln 2} - 3 = 3$

47. $\displaystyle\int_{-\ln(a+1)}^{0} e^{-x}\, dx = -e^{-x}\Big]_{-\ln(a+1)}^{0} = -[e^0 - e^{\ln(a+1)}] = a$

48. $\displaystyle\int_0^{2} e^{x/2}\, dx = 2e^{x/2}\Big]_0^{2} = 2e - 2$

49. $\int_0^1 e^{\ln\sqrt{x}}\,dx = \int_0^1 \sqrt{x}\,dx = \frac{2}{3}x^{3/2}\Big]_0^1 = \frac{2}{3}$

50. $\int_0^1 e^{-x}\,dx = -e^{-x}\Big]_0^1 = 1 - \frac{1}{e}$

51. $\int_0^{\ln 2} \frac{24\,dx}{e^{3x}} = -8\,e^{-3x}\Big]_0^{\ln 2} = -8\,(e^{-3\ln 2} - e^0) = -8\left(\frac{1}{8} - 1\right) = 7$

52. $\int_0^1 \frac{e^x}{1+e^x}\,dx = \ln(1+e^x)\Big]_0^1 = \ln(1+e) - \ln 2$

53. $\int_0^{\ln 13} \frac{e^x\,dx}{1+2e^x} = \frac{1}{2}\ln(1+2e^x)\Big]_0^{\ln 13} = \frac{1}{2}(\ln 27 - \ln 3) = \ln 3$

54. $\int_e^{e^2} \frac{dx}{x\ln x} = \ln|\ln x|\Big]_e^{e^2} = \ln 2$

55. $\int_0^{\ln 2} \frac{e^x}{1+e^{2x}}\,dx = \tan^{-1}e^x\Big]_0^{\ln 2} = \tan^{-1}2 - \frac{\pi}{4}$

56. $\int_1^4 \frac{e^{\sqrt{x}}\,dx}{\sqrt{x}} = 2e^{\sqrt{x}}\Big]_1^4 = 2e^2 - 2e$

57. $\lim\limits_{h\to 0}\frac{e^h - (1+h)}{h^2} = \lim\limits_{h\to 0}\frac{e^h - 1}{2h} = \lim\limits_{h\to 0}\frac{e^h}{2} = \frac{1}{2}$

58. $\lim\limits_{x\to 0}\frac{\sin x}{e^x - 1} = \lim\limits_{x\to 0}\frac{\cos x}{e^x} = 1$

59. $\lim\limits_{x\to\infty}\frac{x^2 + e^x}{x + e^x} = \lim\limits_{x\to\infty}\frac{2x + e^x}{1 + e^x} = \lim\limits_{x\to\infty}\frac{2 + e^x}{e^x} = \lim\limits_{x\to\infty}\frac{e^x}{e^x} = 1$

60. $\lim\limits_{x\to\infty} xe^{-x} = \lim\limits_{x\to\infty}\frac{x}{e^x} = \lim\limits_{x\to\infty}\frac{1}{e^x} = 0$

61. (a) $y = e^{\sin x}$, $-\pi \le x \le 2\pi$. $y'(x) = (\cos x)e^{\sin x} = 0 \Leftrightarrow \cos x = 0$.

$\therefore x = -\frac{\pi}{2}, \frac{\pi}{2}, \frac{3\pi}{2}$. $y\left(\frac{\pi}{2}\right) = e^{\sin\left(\frac{\pi}{2}\right)} = e$. $y\left(-\frac{\pi}{2}\right) = y\left(\frac{3\pi}{2}\right) = \frac{1}{e}$.

Testing endpoints: $y(\pi) = e^{\sin\pi} = 1$ and $y(2\pi) = 1$.

The absolute maximum $= e$ at $x = \frac{\pi}{2}$ and the

absolute minimum $= \frac{1}{e}$ at $x = -\frac{\pi}{2}$ or $\frac{3\pi}{2}$.

(b)

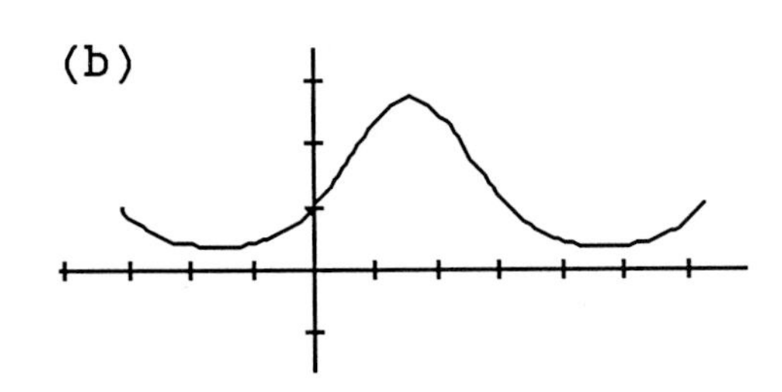

62. $f(x) = e^x - 2x \Rightarrow f'(x) = e^x - 2$. $f'(x) = 0$ if $x = \ln 2$. $f''(x) = e^x$, and $f'(\ln 2) > 0 \Rightarrow f(\ln 2) \approx 0.614$ is local minimum. $f(0) = 1$ and $f(1) = e - 2 \approx 0.718$. Therefore absolute maximum is 1 and absolute minimum is 0.614.

63. $f(x) = x^2 \ln \frac{1}{x} = -x^2 \ln x \Rightarrow f'(x) = x^2\left(\frac{1}{x}\right) - 2x \ln x = 0$ if $-x(1 + 2\ln x) = 0 \Leftrightarrow x = 0$ or $x = e^{-1/2}$. $f''(x) = -3 - 2\ln x$ and $f''(e^{-1/2}) = -2 \Rightarrow f(e^{-1/2}) = \frac{1}{2e}$ is a maximum.

64. $y = (x - 3)^2 e^x \Rightarrow$

$y' = 2(x - 3)e^x + (x - 3)^2 e^x$

$= (x - 3)(x - 1)e^x$

$y' < 0$ if $1 < x < 3$ and $y' > 0$ if $x > 3$ so $y(3)$ is local minimum value.

65. (a) $f(x) = f'(x) = f''(x) = f'''(x) = e^x$

Linear: $e^x \approx f(0) + f'(0)x = 1 + x$

Quadratic: $e^x \approx f(0) + f'(0)x + \frac{f''(0)}{2}x^2 = 1 + x + \frac{1}{2}x^2$

(b) $|e_1(x)| \le \frac{1}{2}Mx^2 = \frac{1}{2}(1)(0.1)^2 = 0.005$

$|e_2(x)| \le \frac{1}{6}Mx^3 = \frac{1}{6}(1)(0.1)^3 \approx 0.00017$

(c)

66. $V = \pi \int_1^{10} e^{-2x}\,dx = -\frac{\pi}{2}e^{-2x}\Big]_1^{10} = -\frac{\pi}{2}(e^{-20} - e^{-2}) = \frac{\pi}{2e^2}(1 - e^{-18})$

67. $A(t) = \int_0^t e^{-x}\,dx = -e^{-x}\Big]_0^t = -e^{-t} + 1$

$V(t) = \pi\int_0^t (e^{-x})^2\,dx = \pi\left[-\frac{1}{2}e^{-2x}\right]_0^t = \frac{\pi}{2}(1 - e^{-2t})$

(a) $\lim_{t\to\infty} A(t) = \lim_{t\to\infty} (-e^{-t} + 1) = 1$

(b) $\lim_{t\to\infty} \frac{V(t)}{A(t)} = \lim_{t\to\infty} \frac{\pi}{2}\left(\frac{1 - e^{-2t}}{-e^{-t} + 1}\right) = \frac{\pi}{2}$

(c) $\lim_{t\to 0^+} \frac{V(t)}{A(t)} = \lim_{t\to 0^+} \frac{\pi}{2}\left(\frac{1 - e^{-2t}}{-e^{-t} + 1}\right) = \lim_{t\to 0^+} \frac{\pi}{2}\left(\frac{2e^{-2t}}{e^{-t}}\right) = \pi$

68. $x = e^t \sin t \Rightarrow \frac{dx}{dt} = e^t \cos t + e^t \sin t$

$y = e^t \cos t \Rightarrow \frac{dx}{dt} = -e^t \sin t + e^t \cos t$

$s = \int_0^{\pi}\sqrt{\left(\frac{dx}{dt}\right)^2 + \left(\frac{dx}{dt}\right)^2}\,dt = \int_0^{\pi}\sqrt{2e^{2t}}\,dt = \sqrt{2}e^t\Big]_0^{\pi} = \sqrt{2}(e^{\pi} - 1)$

69. (a) $y = Ce^{ax} \Rightarrow \frac{dy}{dx} = aCe^{ax} = ay$

(b) $\frac{dy}{dt} = -2y \Rightarrow y = Ce^{-2t}$. $3 = Ce^0 \Rightarrow C = 3$. $\therefore y = 3e^{-2t}$

70. $y = e^{rx} \Rightarrow y' = re^{rx}$ and $y'' = r^2e^{rx}$. Substituting,

$r^2e^{rx} - 4re^{rx} + 4e^{rx} = 0 \Leftrightarrow e^{rx}(r^2 - 4r + 4) = 0$ or $r = 2$.

71. $\frac{dy}{dx} = e^{-x}$, $y = 0$ when $x = 4 \Rightarrow y = -e^{-x} + C$.

$0 = -e^{-4} + C \Rightarrow C = e^{-4}$. $\therefore\ y = -e^{-x} + e^{-4}$

72. $e^y \frac{dy}{dx} = 2x\,e^{x^2-1}$, $y = 0$ when $x = 1$.

$e^y = e^{x^2-1} + C$. $e^0 = e^0 + C \Rightarrow C = 0$. $\therefore\ e^y = e^{x^2-1}$ or $y = x^2 - 1$.

73. $\frac{1}{y+1}\frac{dy}{dx} = \frac{1}{2x}$, $x > 0$, $y = 1$ when $x = 2$

$\frac{dy}{y+1} = \frac{dx}{2x} \Rightarrow \ln|y + 1| = \frac{1}{2}\ln|x| + C$

$C = \ln 2 - \ln\sqrt{2} = \ln\frac{2}{\sqrt{2}} = \ln\sqrt{2}$

$\ln|1 + y| = \ln\sqrt{x} + \ln\sqrt{2} = \ln\sqrt{2x} \Rightarrow y + 1 = \sqrt{2x}$ or $(y + 1)^2 = 2x$

74. $\frac{1}{y+1}\frac{dy}{dx} = \frac{1}{x^2}$, $x > 0$, $y = 0$ when $x = 1$.

$\ln|y+1| = -\frac{1}{x} + C$. $0 = -1 + C \Rightarrow C = 1$. $\therefore \ln|y+1| = -\frac{1}{x} + 1$

$y + 1 = e^{(1-1/x)}$ or $y = e^{(1-1/x)} - 1$

75. $\frac{d}{dx}(\cosh x) = \frac{d}{dx}\left[\frac{1}{2}(e^x + e^{-x})\right] = \frac{1}{2}(e^x - e^{-x}) = \sinh x$

76. (a) $\cosh^2 x - \sinh^2 x = \left(\frac{e^x + e^{-x}}{2}\right)^2 - \left(\frac{e^x - e^{-x}}{2}\right)^2 =$

$$\frac{e^{2x} + 2 + e^{-2x}}{4} - \frac{e^{2x} - 2 + e^{-2x}}{4} = \frac{1}{2} - \left(-\frac{1}{2}\right) = 1$$

(b) $\cosh^2 x + \sinh^2 x = \left(\frac{e^x + e^{-x}}{2}\right)^2 + \left(\frac{e^x - e^{-x}}{2}\right)^2 =$

$$\frac{e^{2x} + 2 + e^{-2x}}{4} + \frac{e^{2x} - 2 + e^{-2x}}{4} = \frac{e^{2x} + e^{-2x}}{2} = \cosh 2x$$

77. $\cosh(-x) = \frac{1}{2}(e^{-x} + e^x) = \frac{1}{2}(e^x - e^{-x}) = \cosh x$

$\sinh(-x) = \frac{1}{2}(e^{-x} - e^x) = -\frac{1}{2}(e^x - e^{-x}) = -\sinh x$

78. $y = \cosh x = \frac{e^x + e^{-x}}{2} \Rightarrow y' = \frac{e^x - e^{-x}}{2}$ and $y'' = \frac{e^x + e^{-x}}{2}$

$$\sqrt{1 + \left(\frac{e^x - e^{-x}}{2}\right)^2} = \sqrt{1 + \frac{e^{2x} - 2 + e^{-2x}}{4}} = \sqrt{\frac{e^{2x} + 2 + e^{-2x}}{4}}$$

$$= \sqrt{\left(\frac{e^x + e^{-x}}{2}\right)^2} = \frac{e^x + e^{-x}}{2} = y''$$

6.7 THE FUNCTIONS a^x and a^u

1. If $y = 2^x = e^{\ln 2^x} = e^{x \ln 2}$, then $\frac{dy}{dx} = (\ln 2)\, e^{x \ln 2} = (\ln 2)2^x$

or $y = 2^x \Rightarrow \ln y = \ln 2^x = x \ln 2$, so $\frac{1}{y}\frac{dy}{dx} = \ln 2$, $\frac{dy}{dx} = y \ln 2 = (\ln 2)2^x$

2. $y = 2^{3x} \Rightarrow \frac{dy}{dx} = 2^{3x}(\ln 2)(3) = (3\ln 2)2^{3x}$

3. $y = 8^x = e^{\ln 8^x} = e^{x \ln 8} \Rightarrow \frac{dy}{dx} = (\ln 8)\, e^{x \ln 8} = (\ln 8)8^x$

4. $y = 3^{2x} \Rightarrow \frac{dy}{dx} = (2\ln 3)3^{2x}$

5. $y = 9^x = e^{\ln 9^x} = e^{x \ln 9} \Rightarrow \frac{dy}{dx} = (\ln 9)\, e^{x \ln 9} = (\ln 9)9^x$

6. $y = 2^x 3^x = 6^x \Rightarrow \frac{dy}{dx} = (\ln 6)6^x$

7. $y = (2^x)^2 = (2^2)^x = 4^x$. $\frac{dy}{dx} = (\ln 4)4^x$

8. $y = x^{\sin x},\ x > 0 \Rightarrow \ln y = \sin x \ln x \Rightarrow \frac{1}{y}\frac{dy}{dx} = \frac{\sin x}{x} + \ln x \cos x$

$$\frac{dy}{dx} = x^{\sin x}\left(\frac{\sin x}{x} + \ln x \cos x\right)$$

9. $y = (\sin x)^{\tan x},\ \sin x > 0 \Rightarrow \ln y = (\tan x)\ln(\sin x)$

$$\frac{1}{y}\frac{dy}{dx} = (\tan x)\left(\frac{\cos x}{\sin x}\right) + [\ln(\sin x)](\sec^2 x)$$

$$\frac{dy}{dx} = y\,[1 + (\sec^2 x)\ln(\sin x)]$$

10. $y = 2^{\sec x} \Rightarrow \frac{dy}{dx} = (\ln 2)(\sec x \tan x)2^{\sec x}$

11. $y = x^{\ln x},\ x > 0 \Rightarrow \ln y = (\ln x)(\ln x) = \ln^2 x$

$$\frac{1}{y}\frac{dy}{dx} = 2\ln x\left(\frac{1}{x}\right) \Rightarrow \frac{dy}{dx} = 2y\left(\frac{\ln x}{x}\right) = \frac{2\ln x\,(x^{\ln x})}{x}$$

12. $y = (\cos x)^x,\ \cos x > 0 \Rightarrow \ln y = x\ln(\cos x) \Rightarrow$

$$\frac{1}{y}\frac{dy}{dx} = \ln(\cos x) - \frac{x\sin x}{\cos x}$$

$$\frac{dy}{dx} = (\cos x)^x\,[\ln(\cos x) - x\tan x]$$

13. $y = (1-x)^x,\ x < 1 \Rightarrow \ln y = x\ln(1-x)$

$$\frac{1}{y}\frac{dy}{dx} = \frac{-x}{1-x} + \ln(1-x) \Rightarrow \frac{dy}{dx} = y\left(\frac{x}{x-1} + \ln(1-x)\right) \text{ or}$$

$$\frac{dy}{dx} = (1-x)^x\left(\frac{x}{x-1} + \ln(1-x)\right)$$

14. $y = x\,2^{(x^2)} \Rightarrow \ln y = \ln x + x^2\ln 2 \Rightarrow$

$$\frac{1}{y}\frac{dy}{dx} = \frac{1}{x} + 2x\ln 2$$

$$\frac{dy}{dx} = x\,2^{(x^2)}\left(\frac{1}{x} + 2x\ln 2\right) = 2^{(x^2)}(1 + 2x^2\ln 2)$$

15. $y = 2^x\ln x \Rightarrow \frac{dy}{dx} = 2^x\left(\frac{1}{x}\right) + \ln x(\ln 2)2^x = 2^x\left[\frac{1}{x} + \ln 2(\ln x)\right]$

16. $y = (\cos x)^{\sqrt{x}} \Rightarrow \ln y = \sqrt{x}\ln(\cos x) \Rightarrow$

$$\frac{1}{y}\frac{dy}{dx} = \frac{1}{2\sqrt{x}}\ln(\cos x) - \sqrt{x}\tan x$$

$$\frac{dy}{dx} = (\cos x)^{\sqrt{x}}\left(\frac{1}{2\sqrt{x}}\ln(\cos x) - \sqrt{x}\tan x\right)$$

17. $\int_0^1 5^x\,dx = \frac{1}{\ln 5}5^x\Big]_0^1 = \frac{1}{\ln 5}(5-1) = \frac{4}{\ln 5}$

18. $\int_{-1}^0 2^x\,dx = \frac{1}{\ln 2}2^x\Big]_{-1}^0 = \frac{1}{2\ln 2}$

19. $\int_0^1 \frac{1}{2^x}dx = \int_0^1 2^{-x}dx = -\frac{1}{\ln 2}2^{-x}\Big]_0^1 = -\frac{1}{\ln 2}\left[\frac{1}{2}-1\right] = \frac{1}{2\ln 2}$

20. $\int_{-1}^1 \left(\frac{1}{10}\right)^x dx = \int_{-1}^1 10^{-x}\,dx = -\frac{1}{\ln 10}10^{-x}\Big]_{-1}^1 = \frac{99}{10\ln 10}$

21. $\int_0^1 3^{2x}\,dx = \frac{1}{2\ln 3}3^{2x}\Big]_0^1 = \frac{1}{2\ln 3}[3^2-1] = \frac{4}{\ln 3}$

22. $\int_{-1}^1 2^{x+1}\,dx = \frac{1}{\ln 2}2^{x+1}\Big]_{-1}^1 = \frac{3}{\ln 2}$

23. $\int_{-1}^0 4^{-x}\ln 2\,dx = -\frac{\ln 2}{\ln 4}4^{-x}\Big]_{-1}^0 = -\frac{\ln 2}{\ln 4}[1-4] = \frac{3\ln 2}{\ln 4}$

24. $\int_{-2}^0 5^{-x}\,dx = -\frac{1}{\ln 5}5^{-x}\Big]_{-2}^0 = \frac{24}{\ln 5}$

25. $\int_1^2 5^{(2x-2)}\,dx = \frac{1}{2\ln 5}5^{(2x-2)}\Big]_1^2 = \frac{1}{2\ln 5}[5^2-5^0] = \frac{24}{\ln 25}$

26. $\int_1^{\sqrt{2}} x2^{(-x^2)}\,dx = -\frac{1}{2\ln 2}2^{(-x^2)}\Big]_1^{\sqrt{2}} = \frac{1}{8\ln 2}$

27. $\int_0^{\frac{\pi}{2}} 2^{\cos x}\sin x\,dx = \frac{-1}{\ln 2}2^{\cos x}\Big]_0^{\frac{\pi}{2}} = -\frac{1}{\ln 2}[2^0-2] = \frac{1}{\ln 2}$

28. $\int_0^{\frac{\pi}{3}} 2^{\sec x}\sec x\tan x\,dx = \frac{1}{\ln 2}2^{\sec x}\Big]_0^{\frac{\pi}{3}} = \frac{2}{\ln 2}$

29. (b), because $\int_0^1 2^{3x}\,dx = \int_0^1 8^x\,dx$, and $\int_0^1 3^{2x}\,dx = \int_0^1 9^x\,dx$

30. (a) $y = 2^{\ln x} \Rightarrow \frac{dy}{dx} = \left(\frac{\ln 2}{x}\right)2^{\ln x}$

(b) $y = \ln 2^x = x\ln 2 \Rightarrow \frac{dy}{dx} = \ln 2$

(c) $y = \ln x^2 = 2\ln x \Rightarrow \frac{dy}{dx} = \frac{2}{x}$

(d) $y = (\ln x)^2 \Rightarrow \frac{dy}{dx} = \frac{2\ln x}{x}$

31. $\lim_{x\to\infty} 2^{-x} = 0$

32. $\lim_{x\to-\infty} 3^{x} = 0$

33. $\lim_{x\to 0} \frac{3^{\sin x} - 1}{x} = \lim_{x\to 0} \frac{3^{\sin x}(\cos x)(\ln 3)}{1} = \ln 3$

34. Let $y = x^{1/(x-1)}$ so that $\ln y = \frac{\ln x}{x-1}$. Then $\lim_{x\to 1^+} \frac{\ln x}{x-1} = \lim_{x\to 1^+} \frac{1}{x} = 1$

so $\lim_{x\to 1^+} \ln y = 1 \Rightarrow \lim_{x\to 1^+} y = e$.

35. Let $y = (e^x + x)^{\frac{1}{x}}$ so that $\ln y = \frac{1}{x}\ln (e^x + x)$. We first find

$\lim_{x\to 0} \frac{\ln (e^x + x)}{x} = \lim_{x\to 0} \frac{e^x + 1}{e^x + x} = 2$. Thus $\lim_{x\to 0} \ln y = 2$, so

$\lim_{x\to 0} e^{\ln y} = \lim_{x\to 0} (e^x + x)^{\frac{1}{x}} = e^2$.

36. Let $y = x^{1/x}$ so that $\ln y = \frac{\ln x}{x}$. Then $\lim_{x\to\infty} \frac{\ln x}{x} = \lim_{x\to\infty} \frac{1}{x} = 0$

so $\lim_{x\to\infty} \ln y = 0 \Rightarrow \lim_{x\to\infty} y = 1$.

37. (a) $\lim_{x\to\infty} \frac{3^x - 5}{4(3^x + 2)} = \lim_{x\to\infty} \frac{1 - \frac{5}{3^x}}{4\left(1 + \frac{2}{3^x}\right)} = \frac{1}{4}$

(b) $\lim_{x\to-\infty} \frac{3^x - 5}{4(3^x + 2)} = \frac{0 - 5}{4(0 + 2)} = -\frac{5}{8}$

38. This problem is dependent on the type of calculator used.

39. Let $f(x) = 2^x - x^2$, so that $f'(x) = (\ln 2)\, 2^x - 2x$. Let $x_0 = -0.5$.

Using the iterative formula $x_n = x_{n-1} - \frac{f'(x_{n-1})}{f(x_{n-1})}$, we find

$x = -0.766664696$, $y = 0.587774756$.

40. (a) $y = x^{1/x} \Rightarrow \ln y = \frac{\ln x}{x} \Rightarrow \frac{1}{y}\frac{dy}{dx} = \frac{1 - \ln x}{x}$

$\frac{dy}{dx} = 0$ when $1 - \ln x = 0$ or when $x = e$. $\frac{dy}{dx}$ changes

positive to negative at $x = e \Rightarrow y = e^{1/e}$ is a maximum.

(b) $y = x^{1/x^2} \Rightarrow \ln y = \frac{\ln x}{x^2} \Rightarrow \frac{1}{y}\frac{dy}{dx} = \frac{x - 2x\ln x}{x^2} = \frac{1 - 2\ln x}{x^3}$

$\frac{dy}{dx} = 0$ when $1 - 2\ln x = 0$ or when $x = \sqrt{e}$. $\frac{dy}{dx}$ changes

positive to negative at $x = e \Rightarrow y = e^{1/2e}$ is a maximum.

(c) $y = x^{1/x^n} \Rightarrow \ln y = \frac{\ln x}{x^n} \Rightarrow \frac{1}{y}\frac{dy}{dx} = \frac{x^{n-1} - (\ln x)(nx^{n-1})}{x^{2n}}$

$\frac{dy}{dx} = 0$ when $1 - n\ln x = 0$ or when $x = e^{1/n}$. $\frac{dy}{dx}$ changes

positive to negative at $x = e \Rightarrow y = e^{1/ne}$ is a maximum.

41. Let $y = x^{(1/x^n)}$ and consider $\ln y = \frac{1}{x^n}\ln x$.

$\lim_{x\to\infty} \ln y = \lim_{x\to\infty} \frac{\ln x}{x^n} = \lim_{n\to\infty} \frac{\frac{1}{x}}{nx^{n-1}} = \lim_{n\to\infty} \frac{1}{nx^n} = 0$. Hence

$\lim_{x\to\infty} e^{\ln y} = \lim_{x\to\infty} x^{(1/x^n)} = e^0 = 1$

42. The expressions are equal when $x^x = x^2$, or when $x = 2$ or 1.

43. Equation 2 implies line (a), commutativity of multiplication implies line (b), Equaion 4 implies line (c), and Equation 2 implies line (d).

44. $(ab)^u = e^{\ln(ab)^u} = e^{u\ln(ab)} = e^{u(\ln a + \ln b)} = e^{(u\ln a + u\ln b)}$

$= e^{(\ln a^u + \ln b^u)} = (e^{\ln a^u})(e^{\ln b^u}) = a^u b^u$.

6.8 THE FUNCTIONS Y = $\log_a$ u. RATES OF GROWTH

1. $\log_4 16 = \frac{\ln 16}{\ln 4} = \frac{2\ln 4}{\ln 4} = 2$

2. $\log_8 32 = \frac{\ln 32}{\ln 8} = \frac{5\ln 2}{3\ln 2} = \frac{5}{3}$

3. $\log_5 0.04 = \frac{\ln 4 - \ln 100}{\ln 5} = \frac{\ln 4 - \ln 25 - \ln 4}{\ln 5} = -\frac{2\ln 5}{\ln 5} = -2$

4. $\log_{0.5} 4 = \frac{\ln 4}{\ln 0.5} = \frac{2\ln 2}{-\ln 2} = -2$

5. $\log_2 4 = \frac{\ln 4}{\ln 2} = \frac{2\ln 2}{\ln 2} = 2$

6. $\log_4 2 = \frac{\ln 2}{\ln 4} = \frac{\ln 2}{2\ln 2} = \frac{1}{2}$

7. $\log_8 16 = \frac{\ln 16}{\ln 8} = \frac{4\ln 2}{3\ln 2} = \frac{4}{3}$

8. $\log_{32} 4 = \frac{\ln 4}{\ln 32} = \frac{2\ln 2}{5\ln 2} = \frac{2}{5}$

9. $3^{\log_3 7} + 2^{\log_2 5} = 5^{\log_5 x} \Rightarrow x = 7 + 5 = 12$

10. $8^{\log_8 3} - e^{\ln 5} = x^2 - 7^{\log_7 3x}$

$3 - 5 = x^2 - 3x \Rightarrow x^2 - 3x + 2 = 0 \Leftrightarrow x = 1 \text{ or } 2$

11. $\lim_{x\to\infty} \frac{\log_2 x}{\log_3 x} = \lim_{x\to\infty} \frac{\frac{\ln x}{\ln 2}}{\frac{\ln x}{\ln 3}} = \frac{\ln 3}{\ln 2}$

12. $\lim_{x\to\infty} \frac{\log_2 x}{\log_8 x} = \lim_{x\to\infty} \frac{\frac{\ln x}{\ln 2}}{\frac{\ln x}{\ln 8}} = \frac{3\ln 2}{\ln 2} = 3$

13. $\lim_{x\to\infty} \frac{\log_9 x}{\log_3 x} = \lim_{x\to\infty} \frac{\frac{\ln x}{\ln 9}}{\frac{\ln x}{\ln 3}} = \frac{\ln 3}{2\ln 3} = \frac{1}{2}$

14. $\lim_{x\to\infty} \frac{\log_{\sqrt{10}} x}{\log_{\sqrt{2}} x} = \lim_{x\to\infty} \frac{\frac{\ln x}{\ln\sqrt{10}}}{\frac{\ln x}{\ln\sqrt{2}}} = \frac{\frac{1}{2}\ln 2}{\frac{1}{2}\ln 10} = \frac{\ln 2}{\ln 10}$

15. $y = \log_4 x = \frac{\ln x}{\ln 4} \Rightarrow \frac{dy}{dx} = \frac{1}{x\ln 4}$

16. $y = \log_4 x^2 \Rightarrow \frac{dy}{dx} = \frac{2}{x\ln 4} = \frac{1}{x\ln 2}$

17. $y = \log_{10} e^x = x\log_{10} e \Rightarrow \frac{dy}{dx} = \log_{10} e = \frac{\ln e}{\ln 10} = \frac{1}{\ln 10}$

18. $y = \log_5 \sqrt{x} = \frac{1}{2}\log_5 x \Rightarrow \frac{dy}{dx} = \frac{1}{2x\ln 5}$

19. $y = (\ln 2)\log_2 x = \frac{(\ln 2)(\ln x)}{\ln 2} = \ln x. \quad \therefore \frac{dy}{dx} = \frac{1}{x}$

20. $y = \log_2\left(\frac{1}{x}\right) = -\log_2 x \Rightarrow \frac{dy}{dx} = -\frac{1}{x\ln 2}$

21. $y = \log_{10}\sqrt{x+1} = \frac{1}{2}\log_{10}(x+1). \quad \therefore \frac{dy}{dx} = \frac{1}{2\ln 10\,(x+1)}$

22. $y = \log_2(3x+1) \Rightarrow \frac{dy}{dx} = \frac{3}{(3x+1)\ln 2}$

23. $y = \frac{1}{\log_2 x} = (\log_2 x)^{-1} \Rightarrow \frac{dy}{dx} = -(\log_2 x)^{-2}\frac{1}{x\ln 2} = -\frac{1}{x\log_2^2 x\ln 2}$

24. $y = \ln 10^x = x\ln 10 \Rightarrow \frac{dy}{dx} = \ln 10$

25. $y = \log_5 (x+1)^2 = \dfrac{\ln (x+1)^2}{\ln 5} = \dfrac{2 \ln (x+1)}{\ln 5}$. $\quad \dfrac{dy}{dx} = \dfrac{2}{(x+1) \ln 5}$

26. $y = \log_2 (\ln x) = \quad \dfrac{dy}{dx} = \dfrac{1}{\ln 2 \ln x} \cdot \dfrac{d}{dx}(\ln x) = \dfrac{1}{x \ln 2 \ln x}$

27. $y = \log_7 (\sin x) = \dfrac{\ln (\sin x)}{\ln 7}$. $\quad \dfrac{dy}{dx} = \dfrac{\cos x}{(\ln 7)\sin x} = \dfrac{\cot x}{\ln 7}$

28. $y = e^{\log_{10} x} \Rightarrow \dfrac{dy}{dx} = e^{\log_{10} x} \cdot \dfrac{d}{dx}(\log_{10} x) = \dfrac{e^{\log_{10} x}}{x \ln 10}$

29. If $y = \ln x$, then $\dfrac{dy}{dx} = \dfrac{1}{x}\Big|_{x=10} = \dfrac{1}{10}$. If $y = \log_2 x$, then

$\dfrac{dy}{dx} = \dfrac{1}{x \ln 2}\Big|_{x=10} = \dfrac{1}{10 \ln 2}$. Since $\dfrac{1}{10} < \dfrac{1}{10 \ln 2}$,

$\log_2 x$ is changing faster.

30. $\log_a u \cdot \log_b a = \dfrac{\ln u}{\ln a} \cdot \dfrac{\ln a}{\ln b} = \dfrac{\ln u}{\ln b} = \log_b u$

31. $\displaystyle\int_1^{10} \frac{\log_{10} x}{x} dx = \int_0^{10} \frac{\ln x}{(\ln 10)\, x} dx = \frac{1}{\ln 10}\left[\frac{1}{2} \ln^2 x\right]_1^{10} = \frac{\ln 10}{2}$

32. $\displaystyle\int_1^4 \frac{\log_2 x}{x} dx = \int_1^4 \frac{\ln x}{x \ln 2} dx = \frac{1}{\ln 2}\left(\frac{1}{2}\ln^2 x\right)\Bigg]_1^4 = \frac{(\ln 4)^2}{2\ln 2} = 2 \ln 2$

33. $\displaystyle\int_1^8 \frac{\log_4 (x^2)}{x} dx = \int_1^8 \frac{\ln x^2}{(\ln 4)\, x} dx = \frac{2}{\ln 4}\int_1^8 \frac{\ln x}{x} dx = \frac{2}{\ln 4}\left[\frac{\ln^2 x}{x}\right]_1^8 = \frac{\ln^2 8}{\ln 4}$

34. $\displaystyle\int_0^1 \frac{\log_2 (3x+1)\, dx}{3x+1} = \frac{1}{\ln 2}\int_0^1 \ln (3x+1) \frac{dx}{3x+1}$

Let $u = 3x+1 \Rightarrow du = 3\, dx$

$\displaystyle = \frac{1}{3 \ln 2}\int_1^4 \frac{\ln u\, du}{u} = \frac{1}{6 \ln 2} \ln^2 u\Bigg]_1^4 = \frac{1}{6 \ln 2} \cdot \ln^2 4 = \frac{2 \ln 2}{3}$

35. $\displaystyle\int_1^{125} \frac{(\log_5 x)^2}{x} dx = \int_1^{125} \frac{\ln^2 x}{(\ln^2 5)x} dx = \frac{1}{\ln^2 5}\left[\frac{\ln^3 x}{3}\right]_1^{125} = \frac{\ln^3 125}{3 \ln^2 5} = \frac{3^3 \ln^3 5}{3\ln^2 5} = 9 \ln 5$

36. $\displaystyle\int_e^{e^2} \frac{dx}{x \log_2 x} = \int_e^{e^2} \frac{\ln 2\, dx}{x \ln x} = \ln 2 (\ln|\ln x|)\Bigg]_e^{e^2} = \ln^2 2$

37. $\int_{\sqrt{e}}^{e} \frac{dx}{x \log_{10} x} = \int_{\sqrt{e}}^{e} \frac{\ln 10}{x \ln x}\, dx = \ln 10 \left[\ln(\ln x)\right]_{\sqrt{e}}^{e}$

$= \ln 10 \left[\ln(\ln e) - \ln(\ln\sqrt{e})\right] = \ln 10 \left[\ln 1 - \ln\left(\frac{1}{2}\right)\right] = (\ln 10)(\ln 2)$

38. $\int_{2}^{8} \frac{dx}{x(\log_8 x)^2} = \int_{2}^{8} \frac{\ln^2 8}{x \ln^2 x} = \ln^2 8\left(-\frac{1}{\ln x}\right)\Big]_2^8 = 2 \ln 8 = 6 \ln 2$

39. (a) $\lim_{x\to\infty} \frac{x+3}{e^x} = 0$; slower

(b) $\lim_{x\to\infty} \frac{x^3 - 3x + 1}{e^x} = 0$; slower

(c) $\lim_{x\to\infty} \frac{\sqrt{x}}{e^x} = \lim_{x\to\infty} \frac{1}{2\sqrt{x}e^x} = 0$; slower

(d) $\lim_{x\to\infty} \frac{4^x}{e^x} = \lim_{x\to\infty} \left(\frac{4}{e}\right)^x = \infty$; faster

(e) $\lim_{x\to\infty} \frac{(5/2)^x}{e^x} = \lim_{x\to\infty} \left(\frac{5}{2e}\right)^x = 0$; slower $\left(\frac{5}{2e} < 1\right)$

(f) $\lim_{x\to\infty} \frac{\ln x}{e^x} = \lim_{x\to\infty} \frac{1}{xe^x} = 0$; slower

40. (a) $\lim_{x\to\infty} \frac{x^2 - 1}{x^2 + 4x} = 1$, same

(b) $\lim_{x\to\infty} \frac{x^2 - 1}{x^3 + 3} = 0$, faster

(c) $\lim_{x\to\infty} \frac{x^2 - 1}{x^5} = 0$, faster

(d) $\lim_{x\to\infty} \frac{x^2 - 1}{15x + 3} = \infty$, slower

(e) $\lim_{x\to\infty} \frac{x^2 - 1}{(x^4 + 5x)^{1/2}} = 1$, same

(f) $\lim_{x\to\infty} \frac{x^2 - 1}{(x+1)^2} = 1$, same

(g) $\lim_{x\to\infty} \frac{x^2 - 1}{\ln x} = \infty$, slower

(h) $\lim_{x\to\infty} \frac{x^2 - 1}{\ln (x^2)} = \infty$, slower

(i) $\lim_{x\to\infty} \frac{x^2 - 1}{\ln (10^x)} = \infty$, slower

(j) $\lim_{x\to\infty} \frac{x^2 - 1}{2^x} = 0$, faster

41. (a) $\lim_{x\to\infty} \frac{\log_3 x}{\ln x} = \lim_{x\to\infty} \frac{\ln x}{(\ln 3)\ln x} = \frac{1}{\ln 3}$; same rate

(b) $\lim_{x\to\infty} \frac{\log_2 x^2}{\ln x} = \lim_{x\to\infty} \frac{2 \ln x}{(\ln 2)\ln x} = \frac{2}{\ln 2}$; same rate

(c) $\lim_{x\to\infty} \frac{\log_{10} \sqrt{x}}{\ln x} = \lim_{x\to\infty} \frac{\ln x}{(2 \ln 10) \ln x} = \frac{1}{2 \ln 10}$; same rate

(d) $\lim_{x\to\infty} \frac{\frac{1}{x}}{\ln x} = \lim_{x\to\infty} \frac{1}{x \ln x} = 0$; slower

(e) $\lim_{x\to\infty} \frac{\frac{1}{\sqrt{x}}}{\ln x} = \lim_{x\to\infty} \frac{1}{\sqrt{x} \ln x} = 0$; slower

(f) $\lim_{x\to\infty} \frac{e^{-x}}{\ln x} = 0$; slower

(g) $\lim_{x\to\infty} \frac{x}{\ln x} = \lim_{x\to\infty} \frac{1}{\frac{1}{x}} = \infty$; faster

(h) $\lim_{x\to\infty} \frac{5 \ln x}{\ln x} = 5$; same rate

(i) $\lim_{x\to\infty} \frac{2}{\ln x} = 0$; slower

(j) $\lim_{x\to\infty} \frac{\sin x}{\ln x} = 0$; slower

42. $\lim\limits_{x\to\infty} \frac{e^{x/2}}{e^x} = \lim\limits_{x\to\infty} \frac{1}{e^{x/2}} = 0$. so $e^{x/2}$ grows slower than e^x

$\lim\limits_{x\to\infty} \frac{e^x}{(\ln x)^x} = \lim\limits_{x\to\infty} \left(\frac{e}{\ln x}\right)^x = 0$ so e^x grows slower than $(\ln x)^x$

$\lim\limits_{x\to\infty} \frac{(\ln x)^x}{x^x} = \lim\limits_{x\to\infty} \left(\frac{\ln x}{x}\right)^x = 0$ so $(\ln x)^x$ grows slower than x^x

Therefore, from slowest to fastest: $e^{x/2}$, e^x, $(\ln x)^x$, x^x

43. $\ln x$ grows faster because $\lim\limits_{x\to\infty} \frac{\ln x}{\ln(\ln x)} = \lim\limits_{x\to\infty} \frac{\frac{1}{x}}{\frac{1}{x \ln x}} = \lim\limits_{x\to\infty} (\ln x) = \infty$

44. $\lim\limits_{x\to\infty} \frac{e^x}{x^n} = \lim\limits_{x\to\infty} \frac{e^x}{nx^{n-1}} = \ldots = \lim\limits_{x\to\infty} \frac{e^x}{n!} = \infty$

Therefore, e^x grows faster than x^n.

45. Let $p_1(x)$ and $p_2(x)$ be polynomials with degrees n_1 and n_2. Then

$n_1 > n_2 \Rightarrow p_1(x)$ grows faster than $p_2(x)$;

$n_1 < n_2 \Rightarrow p_1(x)$ grows slower than $p_2(x)$;

$n_1 = n_2 \Rightarrow p_1(x)$ grows at the same rate as $p_2(x)$.

46. $\lim\limits_{x\to\infty} \frac{\ln x}{x^{1/n}} = \lim\limits_{x\to\infty} \frac{\frac{1}{x}}{\frac{1}{nx^{1-1/n}}} = \lim\limits_{x\to\infty} \frac{n}{x^{1/n}} = 0$

Therefore, $\ln x$ grows slower than $x^{1/n}$.

47. Let $x = [H_3O^+]$ amd $S - x = [OH^-]$. Then $x(S - x) = 10^{-14} \Rightarrow S - x = \frac{10^{-14}}{x}$

(a) If $f(x) = x + \frac{10^{-14}}{x}$, then $f'(x) = 1 - \frac{10^{-14}}{x^2} = 0$ if $x = 10^{-7}$.

$f''(x) = \frac{10^{-14}}{x^3} > 0 \Rightarrow$ a minimum value.

(b) $pH = -\log_{10}[10^{-7}] = 7$

(c) $\frac{[OH^-]}{[H_3O^+]} = 1$

48. $10^{-mn} \approx e^{-n} \Rightarrow (10^m)^{-n} = e^{-n} \Rightarrow 10^m = e \Rightarrow m \ln 10 = 1$

$\Rightarrow m = \dfrac{1}{\ln 10} \approx 0.43429448$

49. (a) $\log_a uv = \dfrac{\ln uv}{\ln a} = \dfrac{\ln u}{\ln a} + \dfrac{\ln v}{\ln a} = \log_a u + \log_a u$

(b) $\log_a \dfrac{u}{v} = \dfrac{\ln (u/v)}{\ln a} = \dfrac{\ln u}{\ln a} - \dfrac{\ln v}{\ln a} = \log_a u - \log_a v$

6.9 APPLICATIONS OF EXPONENTIAL AND LOGARITHMIC FUNCTIONS

1. $y = y_0 e^{kt}$; when $t = 0$, $y_0 = 1 \Rightarrow y = e^{kt}$.

when $t = 30$ min $= \dfrac{1}{2}$hr, $2 = e^{.5k} \Rightarrow .5k = \ln 2 \Rightarrow k = 2 \ln 2$.

After 24 hrs, $y = e^{24(2 \ln 2)} = 2^{48} \approx 2.81 \times 10^{14}$.

2. $10000 = y_0 e^{3k}$ and $40000 = y_0 e^{5k}$. Dividing, $4 = e^{2k}$ or $k = \ln 2$.

Then $10000 = y_0 e^{3 \ln 2} \Rightarrow 8y_0 = 10000$ or $y_0 = 1250$.

3. $y = y_0 e^{kt}$; $t = 0 \Rightarrow y_0 = 10{,}000$ so $y = 10{,}000 e^{kt}$. When $t = 1$, there are 10% fewer cases or 9000 remaining, so $9000 = 10000 e^{k} \Rightarrow$

$k = \ln \dfrac{9}{10}$. Then $1000 = 10000e^{(\ln .9)t} \Rightarrow (0.9)^t = 0.1 \Rightarrow$

$t = \dfrac{\ln .1}{\ln .9} \approx 21.9$ years.

4. (a) $\dfrac{dp}{dh} = kh \Rightarrow dp = k\,h\,dh \Rightarrow p = \dfrac{1}{2}kh^2 + C$. $p = 1013$ when $h = 0 \Rightarrow C = 1013$.

$50 = \dfrac{1}{2}k(20)^2 + 1013 \Rightarrow k = -4.815$. $\therefore\ p = -\dfrac{4.815}{2}h^2 + 1013$

(b) $p = -\dfrac{4.815}{2}(50)^2 + 1013 = -5{,}005.7$ millibars

(c) $900 = -\dfrac{4.815}{2}h^2 + 1013 \Rightarrow h = 6.85$ km.

5. $\dfrac{dQ}{dt} = kQ \Rightarrow \dfrac{dQ}{Q} = kt \Rightarrow \ln Q = kt + C$. When $t = 0$, $C = \ln Q_0$ so

$\ln Q = kt + \ln Q_0 \Rightarrow \ln \dfrac{Q}{Q_0} = kt \Rightarrow \dfrac{Q}{Q_0} = e^{kt} \Rightarrow Q = Q_0 e^{kt}$.

6. $\dfrac{dy}{dt} = -0.6\,y \Rightarrow \ln y = -0.6\,t + C$. $y = 100$ when $t = 0 \Rightarrow C = \ln 100$

$\ln \dfrac{y}{100} = -.06t \Rightarrow y = 100\,e^{-0.6\,t}$. When $t = 1$, $y = 100e^{-0.6} \approx 54.88$ g.

7. $A = A_0 e^{rt}$, where $A_0 = 1000$ £. In 100 years, $A = 90{,}000$ £.

Therefore, $90000 = 1000\,e^{100\,r} \Rightarrow 100\,r = \ln 90$ or $r = 4.5$ %

8. $131 = e^{100r} \Rightarrow 100r = \ln 131$, or $r = 4.875\%$.

9. To double, we need $A = 2A_0$ in the formula $A = A_0 e^{rt}$. Thus $2A_0 = A_0 e^{rt} \Rightarrow 2 = e^{rt} \Rightarrow rt = \ln 2$. If the value $\ln 2 \approx 0.7$ is used, then $rt = 0.70$ or in percent, $rt = 70$.

10. (a) The formula becomes $P = P_o e^t$.

(b) $3P_o = P_o e^t \Rightarrow t = \ln 3 \approx 401$ days.

(c) $P \approx 2.718\ P_o$.

11. (a) To have a half-life of 5700 years means that $y = \frac{1}{2}y_0$ $\left(\text{the amount deteriorates by } \frac{1}{2}\right)$ in 5700 years, or $\frac{1}{2}y_0 = y_0 e^{5700k} \Rightarrow 5700k = \ln\frac{1}{2} \Rightarrow k = \frac{-\ln 2}{5700}$

(b) 90% decayed means 10% remaining, so

$$.1 = e^{\left(\frac{-\ln 2}{5700}\right)t} \Rightarrow t = \frac{(\ln 0.1)5700}{(-\ln 2)} \approx 18{,}935 \text{ years}$$

(c) $t = \frac{(\ln 0.445)\,5700}{(-\ln 2)} \approx 6{,}658$ years

12. Using the results in Problem 11:

(a) $t = \frac{(\ln 0.17)5700}{(-\ln 2)} \approx 12571$ BC

(b) $t = \frac{(\ln 0.18)5700}{(-\ln 2)} \approx 12101$ BC

(c) $t = \frac{(\ln 0.19)5700}{(-\ln 2)} \approx 13070$ BC

13. (a) To have a half-life of 140 days means that $y = \frac{1}{2}y_0$ $\left(\text{the amount deteriorates by } \frac{1}{2}\right)$ in 140 days, or $\frac{1}{2}y_0 = y_0 e^{140k} \Rightarrow 140\,k = \ln\frac{1}{2} \Rightarrow k = \frac{-\ln 2}{140}$.

(b) 90% decayed means 10% remaining, so

$$.1 = e^{\left(\frac{-\ln 2}{140}\right)t} \Rightarrow t = \frac{(\ln 0.1)140}{(-\ln 2)} \approx 465 \text{ days}$$

14. (a) In the formula $T - T_s = (T_0 - T_s)e^{kt}$, $T_0 = 90°$ and $T_s = 20°$.

When $t = 10$ minutes, $T = 60° \Rightarrow 60 - 20 = (90 - 20)e^{10k}$.

$$40 = 70e^{10k} \Rightarrow k = \frac{1}{10}\ln\frac{4}{7}. \therefore \quad 35 - 20 = 70e^{\left(\frac{1}{10}\ln\frac{4}{7}\right)t}$$

$$\Rightarrow \frac{3}{14} = \left(\frac{4}{7}\right)^{t/10} \Rightarrow t \approx 27.5 \text{ min, or } 17.5 \text{ minutes longer.}$$

(b) $T - T_s = (T_0 - T_s)e^{kt}$, $T_0 = 90°$ and $T_s = -15°$.

$35 + 15 = (90 + 15)e^{kt}$, where $k = \frac{1}{10}\ln\frac{4}{7}$.

$$\therefore \quad 50 = 105e^{\left(\frac{1}{10}\ln\frac{4}{7}\right)t} \Rightarrow t \approx 13.26 \text{ minutes.}$$

15. In the formula $T - T_s = (T_0 - T_s)e^{kt}$, $T_s = 30°$ is given.

When $t = 10$ minutes, $T = 0° \Rightarrow -30 = (T_0 - 30)e^{10k}$.

When $t = 20$ minutes, $T = 15° \Rightarrow -15 = (T_0 - 30)e^{20k}$.

$$\therefore (T_0 - 30)\left(\frac{-30}{T_0 - 30}\right)^2 = -15 \Rightarrow \frac{900}{T_0 - 30} = -15 \Rightarrow T_0 = -30°.$$

16. $T - T_s = (T_0 - T_s)e^{kt}$, $T_0 = 46°$. We have

$39 - T_s = (46 - T_s)e^{10k}$ and $33 - T_s = (46 - T_s)e^{20k}$.

$$\frac{39 - T_s}{46 - T_s} = e^{10k} \text{ and } \frac{33 - T_s}{46 - T_s} = e^{20k} = (e^{10k})^2.$$

$$\left(\frac{39 - T_s}{46 - T_s}\right)^2 = \frac{33 - T_s}{46 - T_s} \Rightarrow (39 - T_s)^2 = (33 - T_s)(46 - T_s) \text{ or } T_s = -3° \text{ C}.$$

17. $T_0 - T_s = 60$, so in the formula $T - T_s = (T_0 - T_s)e^{kt}$,

$T - T_s = 60e^{kt}$. When $t = -20$ minutes, $T - T_s = 70$.

$$\therefore 70 = 60e^{-20k} \Rightarrow k = -\frac{1}{20}\ln\frac{7}{6}.$$

(a) In 15 minutes, $T - T_s = 60e^{\left(-\frac{1}{20}\ln\frac{7}{6}\right)15} = 60\left(\frac{7}{6}\right)^{-3/4} \approx 53.4°$

(b) After 2 hours = 120 minutes, $T - T_s = 60\left(\frac{7}{6}\right)^{-6} \approx 23.8°$

(c) $60\left(\frac{7}{6}\right)^{-t/20} = 10 \Rightarrow -\frac{t}{20}\ln\frac{7}{6} = \ln\frac{1}{6} \Rightarrow t \approx 232.5 \text{ min} = 3.9 \text{ hr}$

18. In the formula $i = \frac{V}{R}(1 - e^{-Rt/L})$, when will $i = \frac{1}{2}\left(\frac{V}{R}\right)$?

$$\frac{1}{2} = 1 - e^{-Rt/L} \Rightarrow -\frac{Rt}{L} = -\ln 2 \text{ or } t = \frac{L}{R}\ln 2.$$

In Equation 8, $t = -\frac{\ln 2}{K}$ for $K < 0$.

19. $i = \frac{V}{R}(1 - e^{-\frac{R}{L}t})$ and $t = \frac{L}{R} \Rightarrow i = \frac{V}{R}\left(1 - \frac{1}{e}\right)$

20. (a) $L\frac{di}{dt} + Ri = 0 \Rightarrow L\frac{di}{dt} = -Ri \Rightarrow \frac{di}{i} = -\frac{R}{L}dt$

$\ln i = -\frac{R}{L}t + C$. Let $C = i_o$. Then $i = i_o e^{-(R/L)t}$

(b) $\frac{1}{2} = e^{-(R/L)t}$ when $t = \frac{L \ln 2}{R}$

(c) $i = i_o e^{-1}$

21. $F = -kv \Rightarrow m\frac{dv}{dt} = -kv \Rightarrow \frac{dv}{v} = -\frac{k}{m}\,dt \Rightarrow \ln v = -\frac{k}{m}t + C_1$.

$C_1 = \ln v_0 \Rightarrow \ln\frac{v}{v_0} = -\frac{k}{m}t \Rightarrow v = \frac{dx}{dt} = v_0 e^{-\frac{k}{m}t}$.

$x = -\frac{m}{k}v_0 e^{-\frac{k}{m}t} + C_2$. If $x_0 = 0$, then $C_2 = \frac{m}{k}v_0$ and $x = \frac{m}{k}v_0(1 - e^{-\frac{k}{m}t})$.

22. (a) $\frac{dc}{dt} = \frac{G}{100V} - kc \Rightarrow \frac{dc}{\frac{G}{100V} - kc} = dt \Rightarrow$

$-\frac{1}{k}\ln\left|\frac{G}{100V} - kc\right| = t + C$. When $t = 0$, $C = -\frac{1}{k}\ln\left|\frac{G}{100V} - kc_o\right|$

$t = -\frac{1}{k}\ln\left|\frac{G}{100V} - kc\right| + \frac{1}{k}\ln\left|\frac{G}{100V} - kc_o\right|$

$= \frac{1}{k}\ln\left|\frac{G - 100V(kc_o)}{G - 100V(kc)}\right| \Rightarrow \frac{G - 100V(kc_o)}{G - 100V(kc)} = e^{kt}$

$G - 100V(kc) = (G - 100V)(kc_o)e^{-kt}$

$100V(kc) = G - \frac{(G - 100V)(kc_o)}{}e^{-kt}$

$c = \frac{G}{100\,Vk} - e^{-kt}\left(\frac{(G - 100V)(kc_o)}{100Vk}\right)$

(b) $\lim_{t\to\infty} c(t) = \frac{G}{100\,Vk}$

23. $800 = 1000e^{10k} \Rightarrow 10\,k = \ln\frac{4}{5} \Rightarrow k = \frac{1}{10}\ln\frac{4}{5}$. Another 14 hours

means $t = 24$, so $y = 1000\,e^{(0.1\ln 0.8)24} = 1000\,(0.8)^{2.4} = 585.4$ kg

6.M MISCELLANEOUS EXERCISES

1. $\tan^{-1}x - \cot^{-1}x = \frac{\pi}{4} \Rightarrow \tan(\tan^{-1}x - \cot^{-1}x) = \tan\frac{\pi}{4} = 1.$

Using the formula $\tan(x-y) = \frac{\tan x - \tan y}{1 - \tan x \tan y}$ on the left,

$\frac{\tan(\tan^{-1}x) - \tan(\cot^{-1}x)}{1 - \tan(\tan^{-1}x)\tan(\cot^{-1}x)} = 1$, or $\frac{x - \frac{1}{x}}{2} = 1$. Thus,

$x^2 - 2x - 1 = 0$, or $x = 1 \pm \sqrt{2}$.

2. $\frac{dx}{dt} = \cos^2 \pi x \Rightarrow \sec^2 \pi x \, dx = dt$

$\frac{1}{\pi}\tan \pi x = t + C$. x=0 when $t = 0 \Rightarrow C = 0$. It reaches $\frac{1}{4}$ when

$\frac{1}{\pi}\tan\frac{\pi}{4} = t \Rightarrow t = \frac{1}{\pi}$. The particle will never reach $\frac{1}{2}$ however,

since $\lim_{x \to \frac{1}{2}} \frac{1}{\pi}\tan \pi x = \infty$.

3. $\lim_{b \to 1^-} \int_0^b \frac{dx}{\sqrt{1-x^2}} = \lim_{b \to 1^-} (\sin^{-1} x)\Big]_0^b \lim_{b \to 1^-} \sin^{-1} 1 = \frac{\pi}{2}$

4. $\lim_{x \to \infty} \frac{\int_0^x \tan^{-1} t \, dt}{x} = \lim_{x \to \infty} \frac{\tan^{-1} x}{1} = \frac{\pi}{2}$

5. $V = \pi \int_0^{\frac{\pi}{3}} \sec^2 y \, dy = \pi \tan y \Big]_0^{\frac{\pi}{3}} = \pi\sqrt{3}$

6.

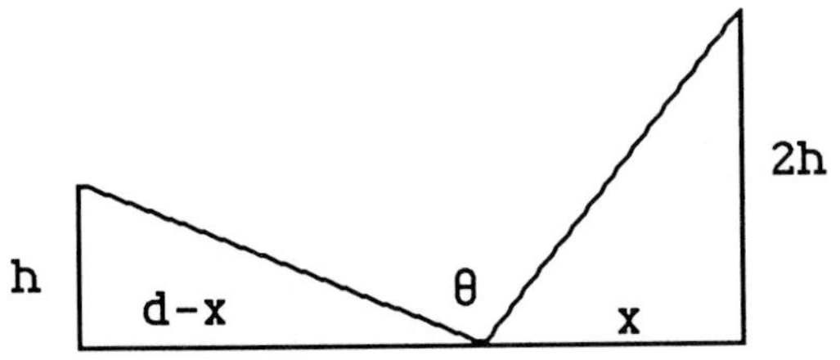

h d-x θ x 2h

$\theta = \pi - \tan^{-1}\frac{2h}{x} - \tan^{-1}\frac{h}{d-x} = \pi - \cot^{-1}\frac{x}{2h} - \cot^{-1}\frac{d-x}{h}$

$\frac{d\theta}{dx} = \frac{2h}{4h^2 + x^2} - \frac{h}{h^2 + (d-x)^2} = 0$ when

$2(h^2 + (d-x)^2) = 4h^2 + x^2$

$(x - 2d)^2 = 2(h^2 + d^2) \Rightarrow x = 2d - \sqrt{2(h^2 + d^2)}$ for $h \le x \le d$.

7. (a) $L = k\left(\frac{a - b\cot\theta}{R^4} + \frac{b\csc\theta}{r^4}\right) \Rightarrow \frac{dL}{d\theta} = k\left[\frac{-b}{R^4}(-\csc^2\theta) - \frac{b}{r^4}(\csc\theta\cot\theta)\right] = 0$

$\Leftrightarrow b\csc\theta\left(\frac{\csc\theta}{R^4} - \frac{\cot\theta}{r^4}\right) = 0 \Leftrightarrow \frac{r^4}{R^4} = \frac{\cot\theta}{\csc\theta} = \cos\theta \Leftrightarrow \theta = \cos^{-1}\frac{r^4}{R^4}.$

(b) $\frac{r}{R} = \frac{5}{6} \Rightarrow \frac{r^4}{r^4} = \left(\frac{5}{6}\right)^4 \Rightarrow \theta = \cos^{-1}\left(\frac{5}{6}\right)^4 \approx 61^\circ.$

8. (a) $\frac{\sin\theta_1}{c_1} = \frac{\sin\theta_2}{c_2} \Rightarrow \sin\theta_2 = \frac{c_2}{c_1}\sin\theta_1 \Rightarrow \theta_2 = \sin^{-1}\left(\frac{c_2}{c_1}\sin\theta_1\right)$

(b) $\frac{c_2}{c_1}\sin\theta_1 \le 1 \Rightarrow \sin\theta_1 \le \frac{c_1}{c_2} \Rightarrow \theta_1 \le \sin^{-1}\left(\frac{c_1}{c_2}\right)$

9. $\int_0^1 \frac{x^4(1-x)^4}{1+x^2}dx = \int_0^1 \frac{x^8 - 4x^7 + 6x^6 - 4x^5 + x^4}{x^2+1}dx =$

$\int_0^1 \left(x^6 - 4x^5 + 5x^4 - 4x^2 - 4 - \frac{4}{x^2+1}\right)dx =$

$\left.\frac{1}{7}x^7 - \frac{2}{3}x^6 + x^5 - \frac{4}{3}x^3 - 4x - 4\tan^{-1}x\right]_0^1 = \frac{22}{7} - \pi$

10. $y_1 = \ln 5x \Rightarrow \frac{dy_1}{dx} = \frac{1}{x}.\quad y_2 = \ln 3x \Rightarrow \frac{dy_2}{dx} = \frac{1}{x}.$

$\therefore \ln 5x = \ln 3x + C.\quad C = \ln 5x = \ln 3x = \ln\frac{5}{3}.$

11. $y = x\ln x \Rightarrow \frac{dy}{dx} = x\left(\frac{1}{x}\right) + \ln x = 1 + \ln x$

12. $y = \sqrt{x}\ln x \Rightarrow \frac{dy}{dx} = \frac{\sqrt{x}}{x} + \frac{\ln x}{2\sqrt{x}} = \frac{2 + \ln x}{2\sqrt{x}}$

13. $y = \frac{\ln x}{x} \Rightarrow \frac{dy}{dx} = \frac{x\left(\frac{1}{x}\right) - \ln x}{x^2} = \frac{1 - \ln x}{x^2}$

14. $y = \frac{\ln x}{\sqrt{x}} \Rightarrow \frac{dy}{dx} = \frac{\frac{\sqrt{x}}{x} - \frac{\ln x}{2\sqrt{x}}}{x} = \frac{2 - \ln x}{2x\sqrt{x}}$

15. $y = \frac{x}{\ln x} \Rightarrow \frac{dy}{dx} = \frac{\ln x - x\left(\frac{1}{x}\right)}{\ln^2 x} = \frac{\ln x - 1}{\ln^2 x}$

16. $y = x(\ln x)^3 \Rightarrow \frac{dy}{dx} = (\ln x)^3 + 3x(\ln x)^2\frac{1}{x} = (\ln x)^2(3 + \ln x)$

17. $y = x^3\ln x \Rightarrow \frac{dy}{dx} = x^3\left(\frac{1}{x}\right) + 3x^2\ln x = x^2(1 + 3\ln x)$

18. $y = \ln(\ln x) \Rightarrow \frac{dy}{dx} = \frac{1}{x\ln x}$

19. $y = \ln(3x^2) \Rightarrow \frac{dy}{dx} = \frac{6x}{3x^2} = \frac{2}{x}$

20. $y = \ln(ax^b) = \ln a + b \ln x,\ a > 0,\ b > 0 \Rightarrow \frac{dy}{dx} = \frac{b}{x}$

21. $y = \frac{1}{2}\ln\frac{1+x}{1-x} = \frac{1}{2}[\ln(1+x) - \ln(1-x)] \Rightarrow \frac{dy}{dx} = \frac{1}{2}\left[\frac{1}{1+x} + \frac{1}{1-x}\right] = \frac{1}{1-x^2}$

22. $y = \ln\sqrt{1+x^2} - \tan^{-1}x = \frac{1}{2}\ln(1+x^2) - \tan^{-1}x \Rightarrow$

$$\frac{dy}{dx} = \frac{x}{1+x^2} - \frac{1}{1+x^2} = \frac{x-1}{1+x^2}$$

23. $y = \ln\frac{x}{\sqrt{x^2+1}} = \ln x - \frac{1}{2}\ln(x^2+1) \Rightarrow \frac{dy}{dx} = \frac{1}{x} - \frac{x}{x^2+1} = \frac{1}{x(x^2+1)}$

24. $y = \ln\left(x - \sqrt{x^2-1}\right) \Rightarrow \frac{dy}{dx} = \frac{1}{x-\sqrt{x^2-1}}\left(1 - \frac{x}{\sqrt{x^2-1}}\right) = -\frac{1}{\sqrt{x^2-1}}$

25. $y = x\sec^{-1}x - \ln\left(x + \sqrt{x^2-1}\right),\ x > 1$

$$\frac{dy}{dx} = x\left(\frac{1}{x\sqrt{x^2-1}}\right) + \sec^{-1}x - \frac{1 + \frac{x}{\sqrt{x^2-1}}}{x + \sqrt{x^2-1}}$$

$$\sec^{-1}x + \frac{1}{\sqrt{x^2-1}} - \frac{\sqrt{x^2-1}+x}{\sqrt{x^2-1}\left(\sqrt{x^2-1}+x\right)} = \sec^{-1}x$$

26. $y = \left(\frac{2x}{\sqrt{x^2-1}}\right)^{-2} = \frac{x^2-1}{4x^2} = \frac{1}{4} - \frac{1}{4}x^{-2} \Rightarrow \frac{dy}{dx} = \frac{1}{2}x^{-3}$

27. $y = \frac{x(x-2)}{(x^2+1)^{1/3}} \Rightarrow \ln y = \ln x + \ln(x-2) - \frac{1}{3}\ln(x^2+1)$

$$\frac{1}{y}\frac{dy}{dx} = \frac{1}{x} + \frac{1}{x-2} - \frac{2x}{3(x^2+1)} \Rightarrow \frac{dy}{dx} = \frac{x(x-2)}{(x^2+1)^{1/3}}\left[\frac{2x-2}{x(x-2)} - \frac{2x}{3(x^2+1)}\right]$$

28. $y = (2x-5)(8x^2+1)^{1/2}/(x^3+2)^2$

$\ln y = \ln(2x-5) + \frac{1}{2}\ln(8x^2+1) - 2\ln(x^3+2)$

$$\frac{1}{y}\frac{dy}{dx} = \frac{2}{2x-5} + \frac{8x}{8x^2+1} - \frac{6x^2}{x^3+2} \Rightarrow \frac{dy}{dx} = y\left[\frac{2}{2x-5} + \frac{8x}{8x^2+1} - \frac{6x^2}{x^3+2}\right]$$

29. $\displaystyle\int_0^{\frac{8}{3}} \frac{dx}{4-3x} = -\frac{1}{3}\ln|4-3x|\Big]_0^{\frac{8}{3}} = -\frac{1}{3}[\ln 12 - \ln 4] = -\frac{1}{3}\ln 3$

30. $\displaystyle\int_0^5 \frac{x\,dx}{x^2+1} = \frac{1}{2}\ln(x^2+1)\Big]_0^5 = \frac{1}{2}\ln 26$

31. $\displaystyle\int_0^2 \frac{x\,dx}{x^2+2} = \frac{1}{2}\ln(x^2+2)\Big]_0^2 = \frac{1}{2}[\ln 6 - \ln 2] = \ln\sqrt{3}$

32. $\displaystyle\int_0^2 \frac{x\,dx}{(x^2+2)^2} = \frac{-1}{2(x^2+2)}\Big]_0^2 = \frac{1}{6}$

33. $\displaystyle\int_1^2 \frac{5\,dx}{x-3} = 5\ln|x-3|\Big]_1^2 = -\ln 32$

34. $\displaystyle\int_0^7 \frac{x\,dx}{2x+2} = \frac{1}{2}\int_0^7 \left(1-\frac{1}{x+1}\right)dx = \frac{1}{2}(x-\ln|x+1|)\Big]_0^7 = \frac{1}{2}(7-\ln 8)$

35. $\displaystyle\int \frac{x^3\,dx}{x^4+1} = \frac{1}{4}\ln(x^4+1) + C$

36. $\displaystyle\int \frac{\tan\sqrt{x}\,dx}{\sqrt{x}} = 2\ln|\sec\sqrt{x}| + C$

37. $\displaystyle\int x^2\cot(2+x^3)\,dx = \int \frac{x^2\cos(2+x^3)}{\sin(2+x^3)}dx = \frac{1}{3}\ln|\sin(2+x^3)| + C$

38. $\displaystyle\int \frac{\sin 3x\,dx}{5-2\cos 3x} = \frac{1}{6}\ln|5-2\cos 3x| + C$

39. $\displaystyle\int \frac{dx}{\sqrt{1-x^2}\,(3+\sin^{-1}x)} = \ln|3+\sin^{-1}x| + C$

40. $\displaystyle\int \frac{dx}{x\sec^{-1}x\sqrt{x^2-1}} = \ln|\sec^{-1}x| + C$

41. (a) $\displaystyle\lim_{h\to 0^+} h\ln h = \lim_{h\to 0^+}\frac{\ln h}{\frac{1}{h}} = \lim_{h\to 0^+}\frac{\frac{1}{h}}{-\frac{1}{h^2}} = 0$

(b) $\displaystyle\lim_{x\to 0^+} x^p\ln x.\ p>0 = \lim_{x\to 0^+}\frac{\ln x}{x^{-p}} = \lim_{x\to 0^+}\frac{\frac{1}{x}}{\frac{-p}{x^{p+1}}} = \lim_{x\to 0^+}\left(-\frac{x^p}{p}\right) = 0$

42. Show than $\lim_{x\to\infty}\frac{(\ln x)^n}{x}=0$. If $n=1$, $\lim_{x\to\infty}\frac{\ln x}{x}=\lim_{x\to\infty}\frac{1}{x}=0$.

If we assume that $\lim_{x\to\infty}\frac{(\ln x)^n}{x}=0$, then

$$\lim_{x\to\infty}\frac{(\ln x)^{n+1}}{x}=\lim_{x\to\infty}\frac{(n+1)(\ln x)^n\cdot\frac{1}{x}}{1}=(n+1)(0)=0.$$

43. $\lim_{n\to\infty}\frac{1}{n}\left(\frac{n}{n+1}+\frac{n}{n+2}+\ldots+\frac{n}{p\cdot n}\right)=\lim_{n\to\infty}\frac{1}{n}\left[\frac{1}{1+\frac{1}{n}}+\frac{1}{1+\frac{2}{n}}+\ldots+\frac{1}{1+p-1}\right]$

$$=\int_0^{p-1}\frac{dx}{1+x}=\ln|1+x|\Big]_0^{p-1}=\ln p,\ p\geq 2,\ p\text{ an integer.}$$

44. Let $f(x)=x-\ln(1+x)$ so that $f'(x)=1-\frac{1}{1+x}=\frac{x}{x+1}$.

If $0<x<1$, then $\frac{1}{2}x<f'(x)<x$ and thus

$$\int_0^x\frac{t}{2}\,dt<\int_0^x\frac{t}{t+1}\,dt<\int_0^x t\,dt\ \Rightarrow\ \frac{x^2}{4}<x-\ln(x+1)<\frac{x^2}{2}$$

45. (a) $f(x)=\ln(\sec x+\tan x)$; $f'(x)=\sec x$; $f''(x)=\sec x\tan x$.

$Q(x)=f(0)+f'(0)x+\frac{1}{2}f''(0)x^2=0+x+0=x$.

(b) $f(x)=\ln x$; $b'(x)=\frac{1}{x}$; $f''(x)=-\frac{1}{x^2}$.

$$Q(x)=f(1)+f'(1)(x-1)+\frac{1}{2}f''(1)(x-1)^2=x-1+\frac{1}{2}(x-1)^2=-\frac{3}{2}+2x-\frac{x^2}{2}$$

46. $\frac{x}{a}=\left(\frac{y}{b}\right)^2-\frac{1}{8}\left(\frac{b^2}{a^2}\right)\ln\left(\frac{y}{b}\right)\ \Rightarrow\ \frac{dx}{dy}=a\left[\frac{2y}{b^2}-\frac{1}{8}\left(\frac{b^2}{a^2}\right)\frac{1}{y}\right]$

$$1+\left(\frac{dx}{dy}\right)^2=1+a^2\left[\frac{16a^2y^2-b^4}{8a^2b^2y}\right]^2=\frac{(16a^2y^2+b^4)^2}{64a^2y^2b^4}$$

$$s=\int_b^{3b}\sqrt{1+\left(\frac{dx}{dy}\right)^2}\,dy=\int_b^{3b}\left(\frac{2a}{b^2}y+\frac{b^2}{8ay}\right)dy$$

$$=\frac{a}{b^2}y^2+\frac{b^2}{8a}\ln y\Big]_b^{3b}=8a+\frac{b^2}{8a}\ln 3.$$

47. $x = a\left(\cos t + \ln \tan \frac{t}{2}\right) \Rightarrow \frac{dx}{dt} = a\left(-\sin t + \frac{\frac{1}{2}\sec^2\frac{t}{2}}{\tan\frac{t}{2}}\right)$

$= a\left(-\sin t + \frac{1}{2\cos\frac{t}{2}\sin\frac{t}{2}}\right) = a\,(-\sin t + \csc t)$

$y = a\sin t \Rightarrow \frac{dy}{dt} = a\cos t$. $y = a = a\sin t \Rightarrow t = \frac{\pi}{2}$; $y_1 = a\sin t \Rightarrow$

$\sin t = \frac{y_1}{a} \Rightarrow t = \sin^{-1}\frac{y_1}{a}$. $\therefore\ s = \int_{\frac{\pi}{2}}^{\sin^{-1}\frac{y_1}{a}} \sqrt{\left(\frac{dx}{dt}\right)^2 + \left(\frac{dy}{dt}\right)^2}\, dt =$

$\int_{\frac{\pi}{2}}^{\sin^{-1}\frac{y_1}{a}} \sqrt{a^2 - 2a^2 + a^2\csc^2 t}\; dt = \int_{\frac{\pi}{2}}^{\sin^{-1}\frac{y_1}{a}} a\sqrt{\cot^2 t}\, dt =$

$a\ln|\sin t|\Big]_{\frac{\pi}{2}}^{\sin^{-1}\frac{y_1}{a}} = a\ln\left|\sin\left(\sin^{-1}\frac{y_1}{a}\right)\right| = a\ln\left|\frac{y_1}{a}\right|$

48. $a = \frac{4}{(4-t)^2} \Rightarrow v = \frac{4}{4-t} + C$. $v = 2$ when $t = 0 \Rightarrow C = 1$.

$s = \int_1^2 \left|\frac{4}{4-t} + 1\right| dt = -4\ln|4-t| + t\Big]_1^2 = 4\ln\frac{3}{2} + 1$

49. $\frac{dy}{dx} = \frac{1 + \frac{1}{x}}{1 + \frac{1}{y}}$, $x > 0$, $y > 0$, $x = 1$ when $y = 1$

$\left(1 + \frac{1}{y}\right)dy = \left(1 + \frac{1}{x}\right)dx \Rightarrow y + \ln y = x + \ln x + C$. $1 + \ln 1 = 1 + \ln 1 + C \Rightarrow C = 0$.

$\therefore\ \ln y - \ln x = x - y \Rightarrow \ln\frac{y}{x} = x - y \Rightarrow \frac{y}{x} = e^{x-y}$ or $y = xe^{x-y}$.

50. $\int_a^b \frac{1}{x}\, dx = \ln|x|\Big]_a^b = \ln\frac{b}{a}$ and

$\int_{ka}^{kb} \frac{1}{x}\, dx = \ln|x|\Big]_{ka}^{kb} = \ln kb - \ln ka = \ln\frac{kb}{ka} = \ln\frac{b}{a}$

51. $A = \int_0^x f(t)\,dt = \frac{1}{3}xy \Rightarrow f(x) = \frac{d}{dx}\left(\frac{1}{3}xy\right)$ or $y = \frac{1}{3}\left(y + x\frac{dy}{dx}\right)$.

$\frac{2}{3}y = \frac{1}{3}x\,\frac{dy}{dx} \Rightarrow \frac{2\,dx}{x} = \frac{dy}{y} \Rightarrow \ln x^2 = \ln y + C$. (a,b) belongs to the curve $\Rightarrow C = \ln\frac{a^2}{b}$. $\therefore \ln x^2 = \ln y + \ln\frac{a^2}{b}$, or $y = \frac{b}{a^2}x^2$.

52. $A_1 = \int_{x_1}^{x_2} \frac{R}{x}\,dx = R\ln x\Big]_{x_1}^{x_2} = R\ln\frac{x_2}{x_1}$. Using horizontal strips,

$$A_2 = \int_{y_1}^{y_2} \frac{R}{y}dy = R\ln y\Big]_{y_1}^{y_2} = R\ln\frac{y_2}{y_1} = R\ln\left(\frac{\frac{R}{x_1}}{\frac{R}{x_2}}\right) = R\ln\frac{x_2}{x_1}.$$

53. The slope of the tangent line between (x,y) and $(-x,0)$ is

$m = \frac{y-0}{x-(-x)} = \frac{y}{2x}$. Therefore, $\frac{dy}{dx} = \frac{y}{2x} \Rightarrow \ln y = \frac{1}{2}\ln x + C$.

$(1,2)$ belongs to the curve $\Rightarrow \ln 2 = \frac{1}{2}\ln 1 + C \Rightarrow C = \ln 2$.

Thus, $\ln y = \frac{1}{2}\ln x + \ln 2 \Rightarrow y = 2\sqrt{x}$ or $y^2 = 4x$.

54. If $n = 2$, $\ln(u_1u_2) = \ln u_1 + \ln u_2$. Assume that the formula is true for $n = k$ and consider the case for $n = k+1$:

$\ln(u_1u_2\cdot\ldots\cdot u_k\, u_{k+1}) = \ln(u_1u_2\cdot\ldots\cdot u_k) + \ln u_{k+1}$

$= \ln u_1 + \ln u_2 + \ldots + \ln u_k + \ln u_{k+1}$.

55. $y = e^{1/x} \Rightarrow \frac{dy}{dx} = -\frac{1}{x^2}e^{1/x}$

56. $y = \ln e^x \Rightarrow x\ln e = x \Rightarrow \frac{dy}{dx} = 1$

57. $y = xe^{-x} \Rightarrow \frac{dy}{dx} = e^{-x} - xe^{-x} = e^{-x}(1-x)$

58. $y = x^2e^x \Rightarrow \frac{dy}{dx} = x^2e^x + 2xe^x = e^x(x^2 + 2x)$

59. $y = \frac{\ln x}{e^x} \Rightarrow \frac{dy}{dx} = \frac{\frac{e^x}{x} - e^x\ln x}{(e^x)^2} = e^{-x}\left(\frac{1}{x} - \ln x\right)$

60. $x = \ln y \Rightarrow 1 = \frac{1}{y}\frac{dy}{dx} \Rightarrow \frac{dy}{dx} = y = e^x$

61. $y = \ln(2x\,e^{2x}) = \ln 2x + 2x \Rightarrow \frac{dy}{dx} \Rightarrow \frac{1}{x} + 2$

62. $y = e^{\sec x} \Rightarrow \frac{dy}{dx} \Rightarrow (\sec x\tan x)\,e^{\sec x}$

63. $y = e^{\sin^2 x} \Rightarrow \frac{dy}{dx} \Rightarrow (2\sin x\cos x)\,e^{\sin^2 x} = \sin 2x\,e^{\sin^2 x}$

64. $y = e^{\ln(\sin e^x)} = \sin(e^x) \Rightarrow \frac{dy}{dx} \Rightarrow e^x \cos(e^x)$

65. $y = \ln\left(\frac{e^x}{1+e^x}\right) = \ln e^x - \ln(1+e^x) \Rightarrow \frac{dy}{dx} = 1 - \frac{e^x}{1+e^x} = \frac{1}{1+e^x}$

66. $y = e^{-x}\sin 2x \Rightarrow \frac{dy}{dx} = 2e^{-x}\cos 2x - e^{-x}\sin 2x$

67. (a) $y = 2x - \frac{1}{2}e^{2x} \Rightarrow \frac{dy}{dx} = 2 - e^{2x}$

(b) $y = e^{\left(2x - \frac{1}{2}e^{2x}\right)} \Rightarrow \frac{dy}{dx} = (2 - e^{2x})e^{\left(2x - \frac{1}{2}e^{2x}\right)}$

68. (a) $y = x - e^x \Rightarrow \frac{dy}{dx} = 1 - e^x$

(b) $y = e^{x - e^x} \Rightarrow \frac{dy}{dx} = (1 - e^x)e^{x - e^x}$

69. $y = \frac{e^{2x} - e^{-2x}}{e^{2x} + e^{-2x}} \Rightarrow \frac{dy}{dx} = \frac{(e^{2x} + e^{-2x})(2e^{2x} + 2e^{-2x}) - (e^{2x} - e^{-2x})(2e^{2x} - 2e^{-2x})}{(e^{2x} + e^{-2x})^2}$

$= \frac{2[(e^{2x} + e^{-2x})^2 - (e^{2x} - e^{-2x})^2]}{(e^{2x} + e^{-2x})^2} = \frac{8}{(e^{2x} + e^{-2x})^2}$

70. $y = x^2 e^{2x}\sin 3x \Rightarrow \frac{dy}{dx} = 3x^2 e^{2x}\cos 3x + 2xe^{2x}\sin 3x + 2e^{2x}x^2\sin 3x$

71. $y = \sin^{-1}(x^2) - xe^{(x^2)} \Rightarrow \frac{dy}{dx} = \frac{2x}{\sqrt{1 - x^4}} - e^{(x^2)} - 2x^2 e^{(x^2)}$

72. $y = e^x(\sin 2x - 2\cos 2x) \Rightarrow$

$\frac{dy}{dx} = e^x(\sin 2x - 2\cos 2x) + 2e^x\cos 2x + 4e^x\sin 2x = 5e^x\sin 2x$

73. $y = e^{2x}(\sin 3x + \cos 3x)$

$\frac{dy}{dx} = e^{2x}(3\cos 3x - 3\sin 3x) + 2e^{2x}(\sin 3x + \cos 3x) = e^{2x}(5\cos 3x - \sin 3x)$

74. $\ln(x - y) = e^{xy} \Rightarrow \frac{1}{x-y}\left(1 - \frac{dy}{dx}\right) = e^{xy}\left(x\frac{dy}{dx} + y\right)$

$\left(-\frac{1}{x-y} - xe^{xy}\right)\frac{dy}{dx} = -\frac{1}{x-y} + ye^{xy}$

$\frac{1 + (x-y)xe^{xy}}{x-y}\frac{dy}{dx} = \frac{1 - (x-y)ye^{xy}}{x-y}$

$\frac{dy}{dx} = \frac{1 - (x-y)ye^{xy}}{1 + (x-y)xe^{xy}}$

75. $\int_1^e \frac{x+1}{x}dx = \int_1^e\left(1 + \frac{1}{x}\right)dx = x + \ln x\Big]_1^e = e$

76. $\int_0^1 (e^x + 1)\,dx = e^x + x\Big]_0^1 = e$

77. $\int_0^{\ln 2} e^{-2x}\,dx = -\frac{1}{2}e^{-2x}\Big]_0^{\ln 2} = \frac{3}{8}$

78. $\int_1^{e^2} \frac{2\ln x}{x}\,dx = (\ln x)^2\Big]_1^{e^2} = 4$

79. $\int_{-1}^{1} \frac{e^x - e^{-x}}{e^x + e^{-x}}\,dx = \ln(e^x + e^{-x})\Big]_{-1}^{1} = 0$

80. $\int_0^{\frac{\pi}{6}} \frac{\sec^3 x + e^{\sin x}}{\sec x}\,dx = \int_0^{\frac{\pi}{6}} (\sec^2 x + \cos x\, e^{\sin x})\,dx$

$= \tan x + e^{\sin x}\Big]_0^{\frac{\pi}{6}} = \frac{1}{\sqrt{3}} + \sqrt{e} - 1$

81. $\lim_{x\to\infty}\frac{x^5}{e^x} = \lim_{x\to\infty}\frac{5x^4}{e^x} = \lim_{x\to\infty}\frac{5\cdot 4x^3}{e^x} = \ldots = \lim_{x\to\infty}\frac{5!}{e^x} = 0$

82. $\lim_{x\to 0}\frac{xe^x}{4 - 4e^x} = \lim_{x\to 0}\frac{xe^x + e^x}{-4e^x} = -\frac{1}{4}$

83. $\lim_{x\to 4}\frac{e^{x-4} + 4 - x}{\cos^2(\pi x)} = \frac{e^0}{\cos^2(4\pi)} = 1$

84. Let $y = (e^x + x)^{1/x}$. Then $\lim_{x\to 0^+}\ln y = \lim_{x\to 0^+}\ln(e^x + x)^{1/x}$

$= \lim_{x\to 0^+}\frac{\ln(e^x + x)}{x} = \lim_{x\to 0^+}\frac{1 + e^x}{e^x + x} = 2.$

$\therefore \lim_{x\to 0^+}(e^x + x)^{1/x} = e^2.$

85. $f(x) = x + e^{4x}$ at $x = 0$; $f'(x) = 1 + 4e^{4x}$; $L(x) = f(0) + f'(0)x = 1 + 5x$

86. $\operatorname{erf}(x) = \frac{2}{\sqrt{\pi}}\int_0^x e^{-t^2}\,dt \Rightarrow \operatorname{erf}'(x) = \frac{2}{\sqrt{\pi}}e^{-x^2}$ and $\operatorname{erf}''(x) = \frac{-4x}{\sqrt{\pi}}e^{-x^2}$.

$\operatorname{erf}(0) = 0$, $\operatorname{erf}'(0) = \frac{2}{\sqrt{\pi}}$ and $\operatorname{erf}''(0) = 0$.

$\therefore \operatorname{erf}(x) \approx \frac{2}{\sqrt{\pi}}x$

87. (a) $y = \frac{\ln x}{\sqrt{x}}$; intercept (1, 0)

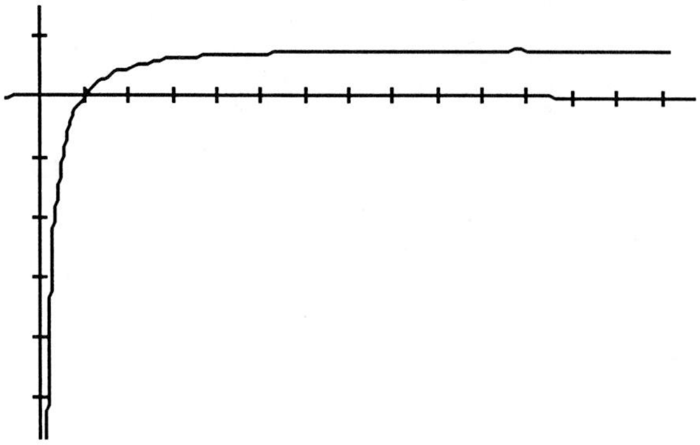

$y' = \frac{2 - \ln x}{2x^{3/2}} = 0$ if $x = e^2$

$\left(e^2, \frac{2}{e}\right)$ is maximum value

$y'' = \frac{-8 + 3\ln x}{x^{5/2}} = 0$ if $x = e^{8/3}$

concave down if $0 < x < e^{8/3}$;

concave up if $x > e^{8/3}$.

(b) $y = e^{-x^2}$; x-axis is asymptote

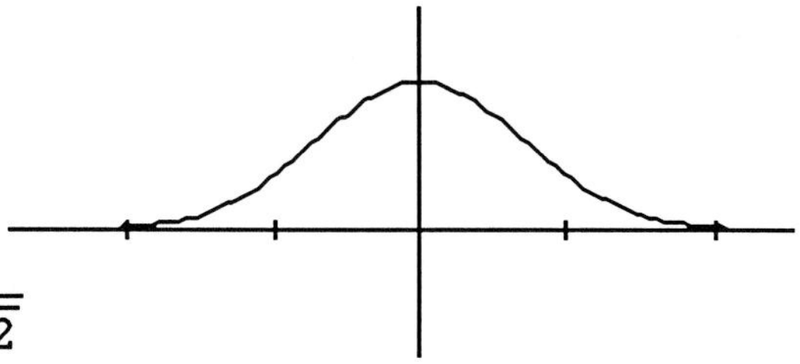

$y' = -2xe^{-x^2} = 0$ if $x = 0$

(0, 1) is maximum value

$y'' = 2e^{-x^2}(2x^2 - 1) = 0$ if $x = \pm \frac{1}{\sqrt{2}}$

$\left(\pm\frac{1}{\sqrt{2}}, e^{-1/2}\right)$ inflection points

symmetry to y-axis

(c) $y = (1 + x)e^{-x}$; x-axis is asymptote

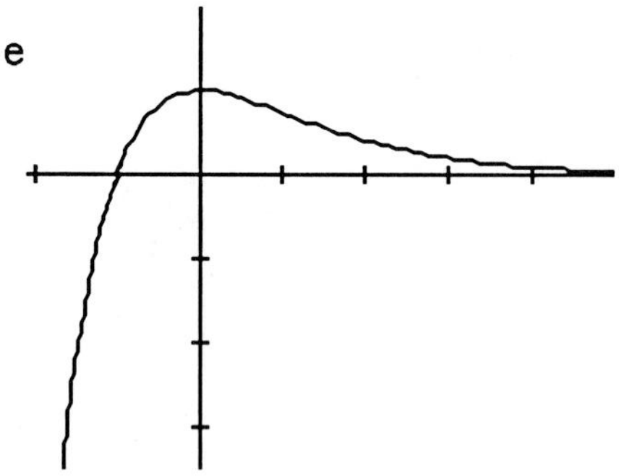

$y' = -xe^{-x} = 0$ if $x = 0$

(0, 1) is maximum value

$y'' = e^{-x}(x - 1) = 0$ if $x = 1$

$\left(1, \frac{2}{e}\right)$ inflection point

88. $g(x) = \int_2^x \frac{t}{1 + t^4}\, dt \Rightarrow g'(x) = \frac{x}{1 + x^4}$. $f(x) = e^{g(x)} \Rightarrow f'(x) = g'(x)\, e^{g(x)}$,

so $f'(2) = \frac{2}{17}e^0 = \frac{2}{17}$.

89. $S=\int_0^x \sqrt{1+\left(\frac{dy}{dx}\right)^2}\,dx = e^x + y - 1 \Rightarrow e^x + \frac{dy}{dx} = \sqrt{1+\left(\frac{dy}{dx}\right)^2}$

$\therefore e^{2x} + 2e^x\frac{dy}{dx} + \left(\frac{dy}{dx}\right)^2 = 1 + \left(\frac{dy}{dx}\right)^2 \Rightarrow 2e^x\frac{dy}{dx} = 1 - e^{2x}$

$\frac{dy}{dx} = \frac{1}{2}e^{-x} - \frac{1}{2}e^x \Rightarrow y = -\frac{1}{2}e^{-x} - \frac{1}{2}e^x + C$. (0,0) is on curve

so $C = 1$ and $y = -\frac{1}{2}e^{-x} - \frac{1}{2}e^x + 1$.

90. $y = \frac{e^{2x}-1}{e^{2x}+1} \Rightarrow \frac{dy}{dx} = \frac{2e^{2x}(e^{2x}+1) - 2e^{2x}(e^{2x}-1)}{(e^{2x}+1)^2} = \frac{4e^{2x}}{(e^{2x}+1)^2}$

$1 - y^2 = 1 - \left(\frac{e^{2x}-1}{e^{2x}+1}\right)^2 = \frac{(e^{2x}+1)^2 - (e^{2x}-1)^2}{(e^{2x}+1)^2} = \frac{4e^{2x}}{(e^{2x}+1)^2}$

91. $y = \frac{1}{2}(e^x + e^{-x}) \Rightarrow \frac{dy}{dx} = \frac{1}{2}(e^x - e^{-x}) \Rightarrow \left(\frac{dy}{dx}\right)^2 = \frac{1}{4}(e^{2x} - 2 + e^{-2x})$;

$ds = \sqrt{1 + \frac{1}{4}(e^{2x} - 2 + e^{-2x})}\,dx = \sqrt{\left(\frac{e^x + e^{-x}}{2}\right)^2}\,dx$.

$s = \int_0^{\frac{1}{2}\ln 2} 2\pi y\,ds = 2\pi\int_0^{\frac{1}{2}\ln 2} \frac{1}{2}(e^x + e^{-x})\frac{1}{2}(e^x + e^{-x})\,dx$

$= \frac{\pi}{2}\int_0^{\frac{1}{2}\ln 2} (e^{2x} + 2 + e^{-2x})\,dx = \frac{\pi}{2}\left[\frac{1}{2}e^{2x}n - \frac{1}{2}e^{-2x} + 2x\right]_0^{\frac{1}{2}\ln 2} = \frac{\pi}{2}\left(\frac{3}{4} + \ln 2\right)$

92. $V = \pi\int_0^2 e^{2x}\,dx = \frac{\pi}{2}e^{2x}\Big]_0^2 = \frac{\pi}{2}(e^4 - 1)$

93. $= \int_{-a}^{a} \frac{a}{2}(e^{x/a} + e^{-x/a})\,dx = \frac{a}{2}\left[a(e^{x/a} - ae^{-x/a}\right]_{-a}^{a} = a^2\left(e - \frac{1}{e}\right)$

94. $x = \ln t \Rightarrow t = e^x$. Then $y = t\sin(t-1) = e^x\sin(e^x - 1)$.

$A = \int_0^{\ln(\pi+1)} e^x \sin(e^x - 1)\,dx = -\cos(e^x - 1)\Big]_0^{\ln(\pi+1)} = 2$

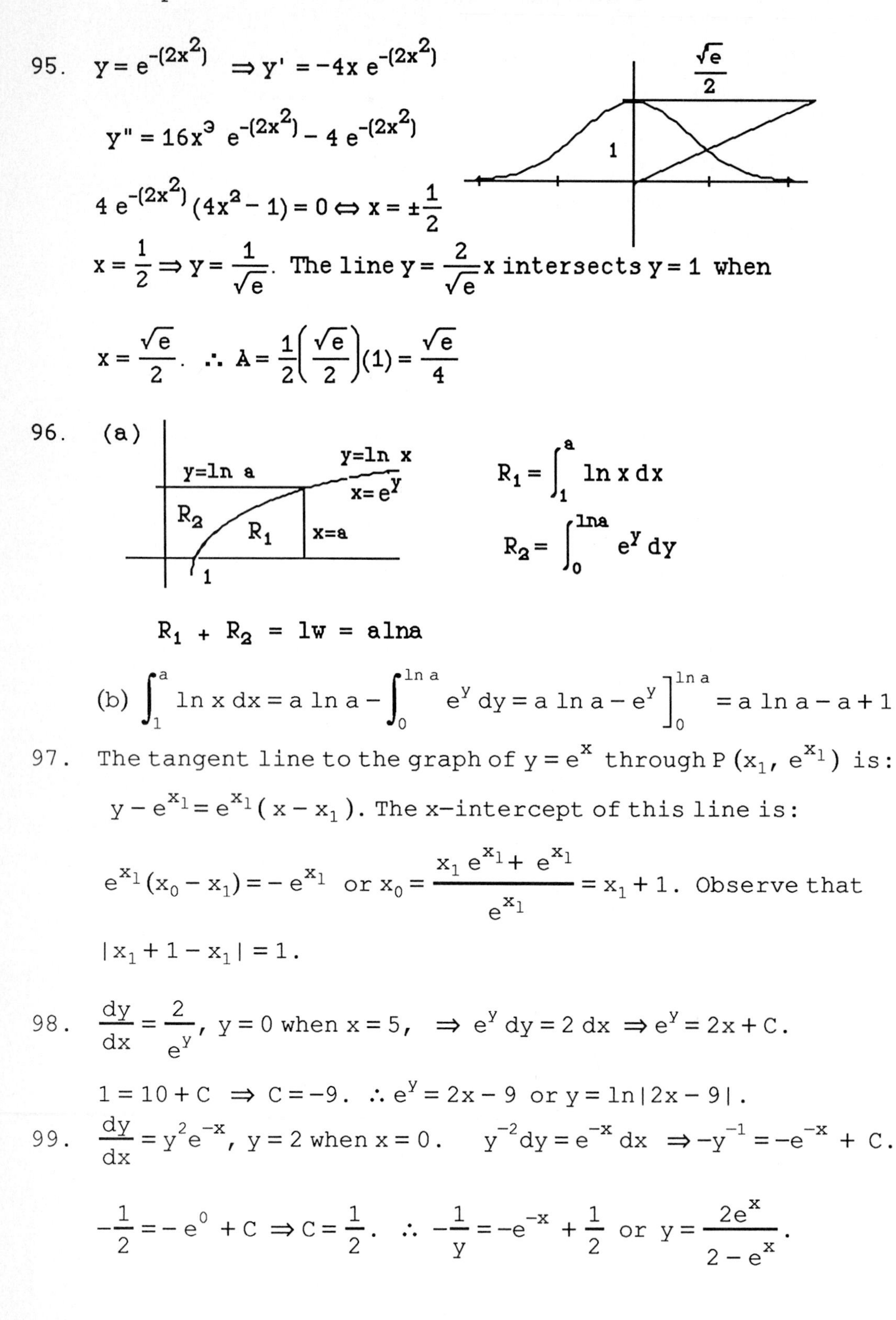

95. $y = e^{-(2x^2)} \Rightarrow y' = -4x\, e^{-(2x^2)}$

$y'' = 16x^3\, e^{-(2x^2)} - 4\, e^{-(2x^2)}$

$4\, e^{-(2x^2)}(4x^2 - 1) = 0 \Leftrightarrow x = \pm\frac{1}{2}$

$x = \frac{1}{2} \Rightarrow y = \frac{1}{\sqrt{e}}$. The line $y = \frac{2}{\sqrt{e}}x$ intersects $y = 1$ when

$x = \frac{\sqrt{e}}{2}$. $\therefore\ A = \frac{1}{2}\left(\frac{\sqrt{e}}{2}\right)(1) = \frac{\sqrt{e}}{4}$

96. (a)

$R_1 = \int_1^a \ln x\,dx$

$R_2 = \int_0^{\ln a} e^y\,dy$

$R_1 + R_2 = lw = a\ln a$

(b) $\int_1^a \ln x\,dx = a\ln a - \int_0^{\ln a} e^y\,dy = a\ln a - e^y\Big]_0^{\ln a} = a\ln a - a + 1$

97. The tangent line to the graph of $y = e^x$ through $P(x_1, e^{x_1})$ is:

$y - e^{x_1} = e^{x_1}(x - x_1)$. The x–intercept of this line is:

$e^{x_1}(x_0 - x_1) = -e^{x_1}$ or $x_0 = \dfrac{x_1 e^{x_1} + e^{x_1}}{e^{x_1}} = x_1 + 1$. Observe that

$|x_1 + 1 - x_1| = 1$.

98. $\frac{dy}{dx} = \frac{2}{e^y}$, $y = 0$ when $x = 5$, $\Rightarrow e^y\,dy = 2\,dx \Rightarrow e^y = 2x + C$.

$1 = 10 + C \Rightarrow C = -9$. $\therefore e^y = 2x - 9$ or $y = \ln|2x - 9|$.

99. $\frac{dy}{dx} = y^2 e^{-x}$, $y = 2$ when $x = 0$. $y^{-2}dy = e^{-x}\,dx \Rightarrow -y^{-1} = -e^{-x} + C$.

$-\frac{1}{2} = -e^0 + C \Rightarrow C = \frac{1}{2}$. $\therefore\ -\frac{1}{y} = -e^{-x} + \frac{1}{2}$ or $y = \dfrac{2e^x}{2 - e^x}$.

100. (a) $\frac{dx}{dt} = \frac{1}{t+2} \Rightarrow \ln(t+2) = x + C.$ $\ln 2 = \ln 2 + C \Rightarrow C = 0.$

$\therefore x = \ln(t+2)$

$\frac{dy}{dt} = 2t \Rightarrow y = t^2 + C.$ $1 = 0 + C \Rightarrow C = 1.$ $\therefore y = t^2 + 1.$

(b) $x = \ln(t+2) \Rightarrow t + 2 = e^x$ or $t = e^x - 2.$

$y = (e^x - 2)^2 + 1 = e^{2x} - 4e^x + 5$

(c) $t = \sqrt{y-1} \Rightarrow x = \ln(\sqrt{y-1} + 2)$

(d) $y_{ave} = \frac{y(2) - y(0)}{x(2) - x(0)} = \frac{5-1}{2\ln 2 - \ln 2} = \frac{4}{\ln 2}$

(e) $\frac{dy}{dx} = \frac{\frac{dy}{dt}}{\frac{dx}{dt}} = \frac{2t}{\frac{1}{t+2}} = 2t(t+2)\Big]_{t=1} = 6$

101. $x = ae^{\omega t} + be^{-\omega t} \Rightarrow v = \frac{dx}{dt} = a\omega e^{\omega t} - b\omega e^{-\omega t}$ and

$a = \frac{d^2x}{dt^2} = a\omega^2 e^{\omega t} + b\omega^2 e^{-\omega t} = \omega^2(ae^{\omega t} + be^{-\omega t}) = \omega^2 x.$

$\therefore F = ma = m\omega^2 x.$

102. (a) $\lim_{x\to\infty} \frac{\ln x}{x^n} = \lim_{x\to\infty} \frac{\frac{1}{x}}{n x^{n-1}} = \lim_{x\to\infty} \frac{1}{nx^n} = 0$

(b) Let $y = e^x \Rightarrow x = \ln y$, and $x \to \infty \Rightarrow y \to \infty$.

$\lim_{x\to\infty} \frac{x^n}{e^x} = \lim_{y\to\infty} \frac{(\ln y)^n}{y} = 0$ by Problem 42.

103. Show that $\frac{d^n}{dx^n}(xe^x) = (x+n)e^x$. If $n = 1$, then $\frac{d}{dx}(xe^x) = e^x + xe^x = (x+1)e^x.$

Assume that $\frac{d^k}{dx^k}(xe^x) = (x+k)e^x$. Then $\frac{d^{k+1}}{dx^{k+1}}(xe^x) = \frac{d}{dx}\left(\frac{d^k}{dx^k}(xe^x)\right) =$

$\frac{d}{dx}\left((x+k)e^x\right) = (x+k)e^x + e^x = e^x(x+k+1) = e^x[x + (k+1)].$

104. (a) No, if x = 4, then $\frac{\ln 4}{4} = \frac{2\ln 2}{4} = \frac{\ln 2}{2}$.

(b) Yes, if $y = \frac{\ln x}{x}$, then $y' = \frac{1 - \ln x}{x^2} > 0$ for $x < e$. Thus

y is one-to-one for $x < e$, and $y = -2\ln 2$ only once.

105. (a) $\lim_{h\to 0}\frac{e^h - 1}{h} = \lim_{h\to 0}\frac{e^h - e^0}{h} = f'(0) = 1$, where $f(x) = e^x$,

or L'Hopital's Rule: $\lim_{h\to 0}\frac{e^h - 1}{h} = \lim_{h\to 0}\frac{e^h}{1} = 1$

(b) Show that $\lim_{n\to\infty} n(\sqrt[n]{x} - 1) = \ln x$, for any $x > 0$.

Let $n = \frac{\ln x}{h}$, so that $\ln x = nh$ or $x = e^{nh}$. Observe that

$n \to \infty \Leftrightarrow h \to 0$. Then $\lim_{n\to\infty} n(\sqrt[n]{x} - 1) = \lim_{h\to 0}\left(\frac{\ln x}{h}(e^h - 1)\right) = \ln x$.

106. $\lim_{n\to\infty}\frac{1}{n}(e^{1/n} + e^{2/n} + ... + e^{n/n}) = \int_0^1 e^x\,dx = e^x\Big]_0^1 = e - 1$

107. (a) If $y = x^{\tan 3x}$, then $\ln y = \tan 3x \ln x$ and

$$\frac{1}{y}\frac{dy}{dx} = \tan 3x\left(\frac{1}{x}\right) + \ln x(3\sec^2 3x) \text{ or}$$

$$\frac{dy}{dx} = x^{\tan 3x}\left(\frac{\tan 3x + 3x\ln x \sec^2 3x}{x}\right)$$

(b) If $x^{\ln y} = 2$, then $\ln y \ln x = \ln 2$ and

$$\left(\frac{1}{y}\ln x + \frac{1}{x}\ln y\right)\frac{dy}{dx} = 0 \text{ so } \frac{dy}{dx} = -\frac{y\ln y}{x\ln x}$$

(c) If $y = (x^2 + 2)^{2-x}$, then $\ln y = (2 - x)\ln(x^2 + 2)$,

$$\frac{1}{y}\frac{dy}{dx} = \frac{2x(2 - x)}{x^2 + 2} - \ln(x^2 + 2) \text{ and}$$

$$\frac{dy}{dx} = (x^2 + 2)^{2-x}\left(\frac{4x - 2x^2 - (x^2 + 2)\ln(x^2 + 2)}{x^2 + 2}\right) =$$

$$= (x^2 + 2)^{1-x}[4x - 2x^2 - (x^2 + 2)\ln(x^2 + 2)]$$

(d) If $y = x^{1/x}$, then $\ln y = \frac{1}{x}\ln x$ and

$$\frac{1}{y}\frac{dy}{dx} = \frac{1}{x^2} - \frac{\ln x}{x^2} \text{ so } \frac{dy}{dx} = x^{1/x}\left(\frac{1}{x^2} - \frac{\ln x}{x^2}\right)$$

108. (a) $4^x = 2^x \Rightarrow 2^{2x} = 2^x \Rightarrow 2x = x$, or $x = 0$.

(b) $x^x = 2^x$, $x > 0$, $\Rightarrow x\ln x = x\ln 2 \Rightarrow \ln x = \ln 2$ or $x = 2$

(c) $3^x = 2^{x+1} \Rightarrow x\ln 3 = (x + 1)\ln 2 \Rightarrow x\ln 3 - x\ln 2 = \ln 2$

or $x = \frac{\ln 2}{\ln 3 - \ln 2}$.

(d) $4^{-x} = 3^{x+2} \Rightarrow -x\ln 4 = (x + 2)\ln 3 \Rightarrow x\ln 3 + x\ln 4 = -2\ln 3$

or $x = \frac{-2\ln 3}{\ln 3 + \ln 4}$.

109. (a) $\int_0^{\frac{\pi}{6}} (\cos x)4^{-\sin x}\,dx = -\frac{1}{\ln 4}4^{-\sin x}\Big]_0^{\frac{\pi}{6}} = \frac{1}{2\ln 4}$

(b) $\int_{\ln(\log_4(\ln 4))}^{\ln(\log_4(\ln 16))} e^x\, 4^{(e^x)}\,dx = \frac{1}{\ln 4}4^{(e^x)}\Big]_{\ln(\log_4(\ln 4))}^{\ln(\log_4(\ln 16))}$

$= \frac{1}{\ln 4}\left[4^{e^{\ln(\log_4(\ln 16))}} - 4^{e^{\ln(\log_4(\ln 4))}}\right]$

$= \frac{1}{\ln 4}\left[4^{\log_4(\ln 16)} - 4^{\log_4(\ln 4)}\right] = \frac{1}{\ln 4}[\ln 16 - \ln 4] = 1$

110. (a) $\frac{a^{x_1}}{a^{x_2}} = a^{(x_1-x_2)} > 1$, because $x_1 > x_2$ and $a > 1$.

(b) $y' = a^x \ln a \Rightarrow y'' = a^x(\ln a)^2 > 0$ for all x, so the graph is concave up for all x.

(c) Suppose $y = a^x < 0$ for some value of x. Since $y(0) = 1$, by the Intermediate Value Theorem there exists some value of x, say $x = c$, for which $a^c = 0$. But $c \ln a = \ln 0$, a contradiction since $\ln 0$ does not exist.

(d) $\frac{dy}{dx} = a^x \ln a = (\ln a)y = ky$, $k = \ln a$. At $x = 0$, $\frac{dy}{dx} = \ln a$.

(e) $\lim_{x\to-\infty} a^x = 0$, so x-axis is an asymptote.

111. (a) If $a^b = b^a$, then $\ln a^b = \ln b^a$, $b \ln a = a \ln b$, or $\frac{\ln a}{a} = \frac{\ln b}{b}$.

(b) $f(x) = \frac{\ln x}{x} \Rightarrow f'(x) = \frac{1-\ln x}{x^2}$

$1 - \ln x = 0$ if $x = e$. $f'(x) > 0$ if $x < e$ and $f'(x) < 0$ if $x < e \Rightarrow$ maximum at $x = e$. $f''(x) = \frac{2\ln x - 3}{x^3}$.

$2\ln x - 3 = 0$ if $x = e^{3/2}$. $f''(x) < 0$ if $x < e^{3/2}$ and $f''(x) > 0$ if $x > e^{3/2} \Rightarrow$ inflection point at $x = e^{3/2}$.

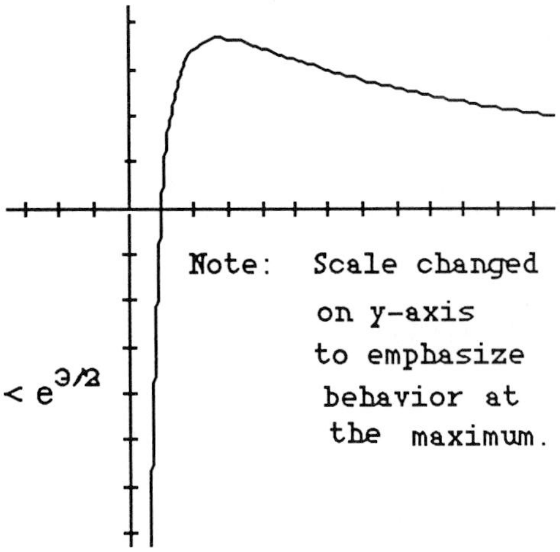

Note: Scale changed on y-axis to emphasize behavior at the maximum.

$\lim_{x\to\infty}\frac{\ln x}{x} = \lim_{x\to\infty}\frac{1}{x} = 0$; $\lim_{x\to 0^+}\frac{\ln x}{x} = \lim_{t\to\infty}\frac{\ln\frac{1}{t}}{\frac{1}{t}} = \lim_{t\to\infty}(-t\ln t) = -\infty$.

(c) (i) $f(x) = \frac{\ln x}{x}$ is increasing on $0 < x \le 1$, so that

if $\frac{\ln a}{a} = \frac{\ln b}{b}$ then $\ln a = \ln b$ so that $a = b$.

(ii) $f(x) = \frac{\ln x}{x}$ increases on $(1, e)$, decreases on (e, ∞)

and attains an absolute maximum at $x = e$ of $\frac{1}{e}$.

Therefore, for each y such that $0 < y < \frac{1}{e}$ such that

$\frac{\ln a}{a} = y$, there exists exactly one b for which $\frac{\ln b}{b} = y$.

112. $y = 1000\left(1 - 0.99^x + \frac{1}{x}\right) \Rightarrow y' = 1000\left[(-\ln 0.99)(0.99)^x - \frac{1}{x^2}\right] = 0$

if, using Newton's Method, $x \approx 10.57$ or 893.52. Let $a = -\ln 0.99 > 0$ and compare the graph of $y = a(0.99)^x$ with $y = \frac{1}{x^2}$ to see that y' cannot more than two zeros. $y(11) = 195.57$ is minimum and $y(894) = 1000.99$ is maximum.

113. $\frac{dN}{dt} = 0.02N \Rightarrow \ln N = 0.02t + C$. If $t = 0 \Rightarrow N = N_0$, then $C = N_0$ and $N = N_0 e^{0.02t}$. For the population to double, $N = 2N_0$ and $N_0 e^{0.02t} = 2N_0 \Leftrightarrow 0.02t = \ln 2$ or $t = 34.7$ years.

114. $\frac{dV}{dt} = -\frac{1}{40}V \Rightarrow V = V_0 e^{(-1/40)t}$

$.1 V_0 = V_0 e^{(-1/40)t} \Leftrightarrow t = -40 \ln 0.1 \approx 92.1$ seconds

115. $\frac{dx}{dt} = kx \Rightarrow x = x_0 e^{kt}$. If $t = 0$, then $x = 2$ so $x_0 = 2$ and $x = 2e^{kt}$. When $t = 10$, then $x = 4$ so $4 = 2e^{10k} \Rightarrow k = \frac{1}{10}\ln 2$.

Therefore, if $t = 5$, then $x = 2e^{\left(\frac{1}{10}\ln 2\right)5} = 2e^{\ln\sqrt{2}} = 2\sqrt{2}$.

116. (a) $\frac{dy}{dt} = k\frac{A}{V}(c - y) \Rightarrow \frac{dy}{c - y} = \frac{kA}{V}dt \Rightarrow -\ln|c - y| = \frac{kA}{V}t + C$.

$C = -\ln|c - y_0|$ so $\ln\left|\frac{c - y_0}{c - y}\right| = \frac{kA}{V}t \Rightarrow \frac{c - y_0}{c - y} = e^{kAt/V}$.

Then $y(t) = (y_0 - c)e^{-kAt/V} + c$

(b) $\lim_{t \to \infty} y(t) = c$

CHAPTER 7

INTEGRATION METHODS

7.1 BASIC INTEGRATION FORMULAS

1. Let $u = 3x^2 + 5 \Rightarrow du = 6x\,dx$

$$\int 6x\sqrt{3x^2+5}\,dx = \int \sqrt{u}\,du = \frac{2}{3}u^{3/2} + C = \frac{2}{3}(3x^2+5)^{3/2} + C$$

2. Let $u = 8x^2 + 2 \Rightarrow du = 16\,x\,dx$

$$\int \frac{16\,x\,dx}{8x^2+2} = \int \frac{du}{u} = \ln|u| + C = \ln(8x^2+2) + C$$

3. Let $u = x^2 \Rightarrow du = 2x\,dx \Rightarrow x\,dx = \frac{1}{2}du$

$$\int xe^{(x^2)}\,dx = \int \frac{1}{2}e^u\,du = \frac{1}{2}e^u + C$$

$$\int_0^{\sqrt{\ln 2}} xe^{(x^2)}\,dx = \frac{1}{2}e^{(x^2)}\Big]_0^{\sqrt{\ln 2}} = \frac{1}{2}e^{\ln 2} - \frac{1}{2} = \frac{1}{2}$$

4. Let $u = 1 + \sin x \Rightarrow du = \cos x\,dx$

$$\int \frac{\cos x\,dx}{\sqrt{1+\sin x}} = \int \frac{du}{\sqrt{u}} = 2\sqrt{u} + C = 2\sqrt{1+\sin x} + C$$

5. Let $u = 8x^2 + 1 \Rightarrow du = 16x\,dx \Rightarrow x\,dx = \frac{1}{16}du$

$$\int \frac{x\,dx}{\sqrt{8x^2+1}} = \int \frac{1}{16}u^{-1/2}\,du = \frac{1}{8}\sqrt{u} + C = \frac{1}{8}\sqrt{8x^2+1} + C$$

$$\int_0^1 \frac{x\,dx}{\sqrt{8x^2+1}} = \frac{1}{8}\sqrt{8x^2+1}\,\Big]_0^1 = \frac{1}{4}$$

6. Let $u = 3 + 4\cos x \Rightarrow du = -4\sin x\,dx \Rightarrow -\frac{1}{4}du = \sin x\,dx$

$$\int \frac{\sin x\,dx}{3+4\cos x} = -\frac{1}{4}\int \frac{du}{u} = -\frac{1}{4}\ln|u| + C = -\frac{1}{4}\ln|3+4\cos x| + C$$

7. Let $u = e^x \Rightarrow du = e^x\,dx$

$$\int e^x \sec^2(e^x)\,dx = \int \sec^2 u\,du = \tan u + C = \tan(e^x) + C$$

8. Let $u^2 = y \Rightarrow 2u\,du = dy$, $y = 1 \Rightarrow u = 1$, $y = 3 \Rightarrow u = \sqrt{3}$

$$\int_1^3 \frac{dy}{\sqrt{y}\,(1+y)} = \int_1^{\sqrt{3}} \frac{2u\,du}{u(1+u^2)} = 2\tan^{-1}u\Big]_1^{\sqrt{3}} = \frac{\pi}{6}$$

9. Let $u = 3 + 4e^x \Rightarrow du = 4e^x\,dx \Rightarrow e^x\,dx = \frac{1}{4}\,du$

$$\int e^x\sqrt{3 + 4e^x}\,dx = \int \frac{1}{4}\sqrt{u}\,du = \frac{1}{6}u^{3/2} + C = \frac{1}{6}(3 + 4e^x)^{3/2} + C$$

10. Let $u^2 = x \Rightarrow 2u\,du = dx$, $x = 4 \Rightarrow u = 2$, $x = 9 \Rightarrow u = 3$

$$\int_4^9 \frac{dx}{x - \sqrt{x}} = \int_2^3 \frac{2u\,du}{u^2 - u} = \int_2^3 \frac{2\,du}{u - 1} = 2\ln|u - 1|\Big]_2^3 = 2\ln 2$$

11. Let $u = \ln x \Rightarrow du = \frac{1}{x}\,dx$. $\int \frac{dx}{x\ln x} = \ln|\ln x| + C$

12. Let $u = 1 + e^x \Rightarrow du = e^x\,dx$. Then $\int \frac{e^x dx}{1 + e^x} = \int \frac{du}{u} = \ln|u| + C$.

Therefore $\int_0^2 \frac{e^x dx}{1 + e^x} = \ln|1 + e^x|\Big]_0^2 = \ln\left(\frac{1 + e^2}{2}\right)$.

13. Let $u = \sqrt{x} \Rightarrow du = \frac{1}{2\sqrt{x}}\,dx \Rightarrow dx = 2\sqrt{x}\,du = 2u\,du$

$$\int_0^1 e^{\sqrt{x}}\,dx = \int_0^1 2ue^u\,du = 2(ue^u - e^u)\Big]_0^1 = 2$$

Note: Although it is not difficult to guess that $\frac{d}{du}(ue^u - e^u) = ue^u$, it can be done by the technique of integration by parts taught in the next section.

14. Let $u = \sqrt{x} \Rightarrow du = \frac{1}{2\sqrt{x}}\,dx \Rightarrow 2\,du = \frac{1}{\sqrt{x}}dx$

$$\int \frac{\tan\sqrt{x}\,dx}{\sqrt{x}} = 2\int \tan u\,du = 2\ln|\sec u| + C = 2\ln|\sec\sqrt{x}| + C$$

15. Let $u = \tan x \Rightarrow du = \sec^2 x\,dx$.

$$\int \tan x\sec^2 x\,dx = \int u\,du = \frac{1}{2}u^2 + C = \frac{1}{2}\tan^2 x + C$$

16. $\int \tan x\sec^2 x\,dx = \frac{1}{2}\tan^2 x + C$

17. Let $u = \sin x \Rightarrow du = \cos x\,dx$

$$\int \cos^3 x\,dx = \int \cos^2 x\cos x\,dx = \int (1 - \sin^2 x)\cos x\,dx =$$

$$\int (1 - u^2)\,du = u - \frac{1}{3}u^3 + C = \sin x - \frac{1}{3}\sin^3 x + C$$

18. $\int \sin^4 x\cos^3 x\,dx = \int \sin^4 x\cos x\,(1 - \sin^2 x)\,dx$

$$= \int \sin^4 x\cos x\,dx - \int \sin^6 x\cos x\,dx = \frac{1}{5}\sin^5 x - \frac{1}{7}\sin^7 x + C$$

19. Let $u = \sec x \Rightarrow du = \sec x \tan x\, dx$. $\int \tan^3 x \sec x\, dx =$

$$\int (\sec^2 x - 1)\sec x \tan x\, dx = \int (u^2 - 1)\, du = \int \frac{1}{3}u^3 - u + C = \frac{1}{3}\sec^3 x - \sec x + C$$

20. $\int \tan^3 x \sec^3 x\, dx = \int \tan x(\sec^2 x - 1)\sec^3 x\, dx$

$$= \int \sec^4 x\,(\sec x \tan x)\, dx - \int \sec^2 x\,(\sec x \tan x)\, dx$$

$$= \frac{1}{5}\sec^5 x - \frac{1}{3}\sec^3 x + C$$

21. Let $u = 2x + 3 \Rightarrow du = 2\, dx \Rightarrow dx = \frac{1}{2}\, du$, $x = \frac{1}{2} \Rightarrow u = 3$, $x = 3 \Rightarrow u = 9$.

$$\int_{\frac{1}{2}}^{3} \sqrt{2x + 3}\, dx = \int_4^9 \frac{1}{2}\sqrt{u}\, du = \frac{1}{2}u^{3/2}\Big]_4^9 = \frac{19}{3}$$

22. $$\int_1^{40} \frac{dx}{3x + 5} = \frac{1}{3}\ln|3x + 5|\Big]_1^{40} = \frac{1}{3}\ln\frac{125}{8} = \ln\frac{5}{2}$$

23. Let $u = 2x - 7 \Rightarrow du = 2\, dx \Rightarrow dx = \frac{1}{2}\, du$.

$$\int \frac{dx}{(2x - 7)^2} = \int \frac{1}{2}u^{-2}\, du = -\frac{1}{2}u^{-1} + C = -\frac{1}{2}(2x - 7)^{-1} + C$$

24. $$\int \frac{(x + 1)\, dx}{x^2 + 2x + 3} = \frac{1}{2}\ln|x^2 + 2x + 3| + C$$

25. Let $u = \cos x \Rightarrow -du = \sin x\, dx$, $x = -\pi \Rightarrow u = -1$, $x = 0 \Rightarrow u = 1$

$$\int_{-\pi}^{0} \frac{\sin x\, dx}{2 + \cos x} = \int_{-1}^{1} \frac{-du}{2 + u} = -\ln|2 + u|\Big]_{-1}^{1} = -\ln 3$$

26. $$\int \tan^3 2x \sec^2 2x\, dx = \frac{1}{8}\tan^4 2x + C$$

27. Let $u = \sin x \Rightarrow du = \cos x\, dx$.

$$\int \sqrt{\sin x}\cos x\, dx = \int \sqrt{u}\, du = \frac{2}{3}u^{3/2} + C = \frac{2}{3}(\sin x)^{2/3} + C$$

28. $$\int \frac{\sec^2 x\, dx}{2 + \tan x} = \ln|2 + \tan x| + C$$

29. Let $u = \sin x \Rightarrow du = \cos x\, dx$.

$$\int \frac{\cos x\, dx}{(1 + \sin x)^2} = \int (1 + u)^{-2}\, du = -(1 + u)^{-1} + C = \frac{-1}{1 + \sin x} + C$$

30. $$\int_0^{\frac{\pi}{4}} 8\cos^3 2x \sin 2x\, dx = -\cos^4 2x\Big]_0^{\frac{\pi}{4}} = 1$$

31. $\int_{-\frac{\pi}{2}}^{\frac{\pi}{2}} \sin^2 2x \cos^3 2x\, dx = \int_{-\frac{\pi}{2}}^{\frac{\pi}{2}} \sin^2 2x\,(1 - \sin^2 2x)\cos 2x\, dx =$

$$\int_{-\frac{\pi}{2}}^{\frac{\pi}{2}} \sin^2 2x \cos 2x\, dx - \int_{-\frac{\pi}{2}}^{\frac{\pi}{2}} \sin^4 2x \cos 2x\, dx = \frac{1}{6}\sin^3 2x - \frac{1}{10}\sin^5 2x \Big]_{-\frac{\pi}{2}}^{\frac{\pi}{2}} = 0$$

32. $\int \csc^4 x\, dx = \int \csc^2 x\,(1 + \cot^2 x)\, dx = -\cot x - \frac{1}{3}\cot^3 x + C$

33. Let $u = 1 - 4x^2 \Rightarrow du = -8x\, dx \Rightarrow x\, dx = -\frac{1}{8}\, du$

$$\int \frac{x\, dx}{\sqrt{1 - 4x^2}} = -\frac{1}{8}\int \frac{du}{\sqrt{u}} = -\frac{1}{4}\sqrt{u} + C = -\frac{1}{4}\sqrt{1 - 4x^2} + C$$

34. $\int x^{1/3}\sqrt{x^{4/3} - 1}\, dx = \frac{1}{2}(x^{4/3} - 1)^{3/2} + C$

35. $\int_0^{\frac{\sqrt{2}}{2}} \frac{dx}{\sqrt{1 - x^2}} = \sin^{-1} x \Big]_0^{\frac{\sqrt{2}}{2}} = \frac{\pi}{4}$

36. $\int_0^{\frac{\pi}{2}} \sin 2x\, dx = -\frac{1}{2}\cos 2x \Big]_0^{\frac{\pi}{2}} = 1$

37. $\int_0^1 \frac{3x}{1 + x^2}\, dx = \frac{3}{2}\int_0^1 \frac{2x}{1 + x^2}\, dx = \frac{3}{2}\ln(1 + x^2)\Big]_0^1 = \frac{3}{2}\ln 2$

38. $\int_0^{\pi} x \sin(x^2)\, dx = -\frac{1}{2}\cos(x^2)\Big]_0^{\pi} = -\frac{1}{2}\cos(\pi^2) + \frac{1}{2}$

39. $\int_0^{\frac{\pi}{4}} \frac{\sin^2 2x\, dx}{1 + \cos 2x} = \int_0^{\frac{\pi}{4}} \frac{1 - \cos^2 2x}{1 + \cos 2x}\, dx = \int_0^{\frac{\pi}{4}} (1 - \cos 2x)\, dx =$

$$x - \frac{1}{2}\sin 2x \Big]_0^{\frac{\pi}{4}} = \frac{\pi - 2}{4}$$

40. $\int_{\sqrt{2}}^{2} \frac{dy}{y\sqrt{y^2 - 1}} = \sec^{-1}|y|\Big]_{\sqrt{2}}^{2} = \frac{\pi}{12}$

41. Let $u = 2x \Rightarrow du = 2\, dx$, $x = 0 \Rightarrow u = 0$, $x = \frac{1}{2} \Rightarrow u = 1$

$$\int_0^{\frac{1}{2}} \frac{2\, dx}{\sqrt{1 - 4x^2}} = \int_0^1 \frac{du}{\sqrt{1 - u^2}} = \sin^{-1} u \Big]_0^1 = \frac{\pi}{2}$$

42. $\int_0^{\frac{1}{\sqrt{2}}} \frac{2v\, dv}{\sqrt{1 - v^4}} = \sin^{-1} v^2 \Big]_0^{\frac{1}{\sqrt{2}}} = \frac{\pi}{6}$

43. Let $u = 3x^2 + 4 \Rightarrow du = 6x\,dx \Rightarrow x\,dx = \frac{1}{6}du$

$$\int \frac{x\,dx}{(3x^2+4)^3} = \frac{1}{6}\int u^{-3}\,du = -\frac{1}{12}u^{-2} + C = -\frac{1}{12}(3x^2+4)^{-2} + C$$

44. $\int x^2\sqrt{x^3+5}\,dx = \frac{2}{9}(x^3+5)^{3/2} + C$

45. Let $u = x^3 + 5 \Rightarrow du = 3x^2\,dx \Rightarrow x^2\,dx = \frac{1}{3}\,du$

$$\int \frac{x^2\,dx}{\sqrt{x^3+5}} = \frac{1}{3}\int \frac{1}{\sqrt{u}}\,du = \frac{2}{3}\sqrt{u} + C = \frac{2}{3}\sqrt{x^3+5} + C$$

46. $\int \frac{x\,dx}{4x^2+1} = \frac{1}{8}\ln(4x^2+1) + C$

47. $\int_0^{\ln 2} e^{2x}\,dx = \frac{1}{2}e^{2x}\Big]_0^{\ln 2} = \frac{3}{2}$

48. $\int e^{\cos x}\sin x\,dx = -e^{\cos x} + C$

49. $\int \frac{dx}{e^{3x}} = \int e^{-3x}\,dx = -\frac{1}{3}e^{-3x} + C$

50. $\int \frac{e^{\sqrt{x+1}}\,dx}{\sqrt{x+1}} = 2e^{\sqrt{x+1}} + C$

51. Let $u = e^x \Rightarrow du = e^x\,dx$. $\int \frac{e^x}{1+e^{2x}}\,dx = \int \frac{du}{1+u^2} = \tan^{-1}u + C = \tan^{-1}(e^x) + C$

52. $\int_0^{\frac{\sqrt{3}}{3}} \frac{dt}{1+9t^2} = \frac{1}{3}\tan^{-1}3t\Big]_0^{\frac{\sqrt{3}}{3}} = \frac{\pi}{9}$

53. Let $u = \cos x \Rightarrow du = -\sin x\,dx$. $\int \cos^2 x\sin x\,dx =$

$$\int -u^2\,du = -\frac{1}{3}u^3 + C = -\frac{1}{3}\cos^3 x + C$$

54. $\int \frac{\cos x\,dx}{\sin^3 x} = -\frac{1}{2\sin^2 x} + C = -\frac{1}{2}\csc^2 x + C$

55. $\int_{\frac{\pi}{6}}^{\frac{\pi}{2}} \cot^3 x\csc^2 x\,dx = -\frac{1}{4}\cot^4 x\Big]_{\frac{\pi}{6}}^{\frac{\pi}{2}} = \frac{9}{4}$

56. $\int_0^{\frac{\pi}{3}} \tan 3x\sec^2 3x\,dx = \frac{1}{6}\tan^2 3x\Big]_0^{\frac{\pi}{3}} = 0$

57. Let $u = e^{2x} - e^{-2x} \Rightarrow du = 2e^{2x} - 2e^{-2x} \Rightarrow \frac{1}{2}du = e^{2x} - e^{-2x}$.

$$\int \frac{e^{2x}+e^{-2x}}{e^{2x}-e^{-2x}}\,dx = \frac{1}{2}\int \frac{du}{u} = \frac{1}{2}\ln|u| + C = \frac{1}{2}\ln(e^{2x}-e^{-2x}) + C$$

58. $\int_0^{\pi} \sin 2x \cos^2 2x\, dx = -\frac{1}{6}\cos^3 2x \Big]_0^{\pi} = 0$

59. $\int_{-\frac{\pi}{2}}^{\frac{\pi}{2}} (1+\cos\theta)^3 \sin\theta\, d\theta = -\frac{1}{4}(1+\cos\theta)^4 \Big]_{-\frac{\pi}{2}}^{\frac{\pi}{2}} = 0$

60. $\int te^{-t^2}\, dt = -\frac{1}{2}e^{-t^2} + C$

61. Let $u = 2t \Rightarrow dt = \frac{1}{2}du$ and $t = \frac{1}{2}u$.

$$\int \frac{dt}{t\sqrt{4t^2-1}} = \int \frac{\frac{1}{2}du}{\frac{1}{2}u\sqrt{u^2-1}} = \sec^{-1}|u| + C = \sec^{-1}|2t| + C$$

62. $\int \frac{dx}{\sqrt{e^{2x}-1}} = \int \frac{e^x\, dx}{e^x\sqrt{e^{2x}-1}} = \sec^{-1}(e^x) + C$

63. $\int \frac{\cos x\, dx}{\sin x} = \ln|\sin x| + C$

64. $\int_0^{\frac{\pi}{2}} \frac{\cos x\, dx}{1+\sin x} = \ln|1+\sin x| \Big]_0^{\frac{\pi}{2}} = \ln 2$

65. $\int \sec^3 x \tan x\, dx = \int \sec^2 x(\sec x \tan x)\, dx = \frac{1}{3}\sec^3 x + C$

66. $\int \frac{\sin\theta\, d\theta}{\sqrt{1+\cos\theta}} = -2\sqrt{1+\cos\theta} + C$

67. Let $u = \tan 3x \Rightarrow du = 3\sec^2 3x\, dx$

$$\int e^{\tan 3x}\sec^2 3x\, dx = \int \frac{1}{3}e^u\, du = \frac{1}{3}e^u + C = \frac{1}{3}e^{\tan 3x} + C$$

68. $\int \cos 2t\sqrt{4-\sin 2t}\, dt = -\frac{1}{3}(4-\sin 2t)^{3/2} + C$

69. $\int_{\frac{\pi}{6}}^{\frac{\pi}{4}} \frac{1+\cos 2x}{\sin^2 2x}\, dx = \int_{\frac{\pi}{6}}^{\frac{\pi}{4}} \csc^2 2x\, dx + \int_{\frac{\pi}{6}}^{\frac{\pi}{4}} \cot 2x \csc 2x\, dx =$

$$-\frac{1}{2}\cot 2x - \frac{1}{2}\csc 2x \Big]_{\frac{\pi}{6}}^{\frac{\pi}{4}} = \frac{\sqrt{3-1}}{2}$$

70. $\int_{-\frac{\pi}{4}}^{\frac{\pi}{4}} \frac{\sin^2 2x\, dx}{1+\cos 2x} = \int_{-\frac{\pi}{4}}^{\frac{\pi}{4}} (1-\cos 2x)\, dx = x - \frac{1}{2}\sin 2x \Big]_{-\frac{\pi}{4}}^{\frac{\pi}{4}} = \frac{\pi}{2} - 1$

71. Let $u = \cot 2t \Rightarrow du = = -2\csc^2 2t\, dt$

$$\int \frac{\csc^2 2t}{\sqrt{1+\cot 2t}}\, dt = \int \frac{-\frac{1}{2}du}{\sqrt{1+u}} = = -\sqrt{1+u} + C = -\sqrt{1+\cot 2t} + C$$

72. $\int_0^{\ln 3} e^{3x}\,dx = \frac{1}{3}e^{3x}\Big]_0^{\ln 3} = \frac{26}{3}$

73. Let $u = \tan^{-1} 2t \Rightarrow du = \frac{2\,dt}{1+4t^2}$, $t = 0 \Rightarrow u = 0$, $t = \frac{1}{2} \Rightarrow u = \frac{\pi}{4}$

$$\int_0^{\frac{1}{2}} \frac{e^{\tan^{-1}2t}}{1+4t^2}\,dt = \int_0^{\frac{\pi}{4}} \frac{1}{2}e^u\,du = \frac{1}{2}e^u\Big]_0^{\frac{\pi}{4}} = \frac{1}{2}[e^{\frac{\pi}{4}} - 1]$$

74. $\int xe^{-x^2}\,dx = -\frac{1}{2}e^{-x^2} + C$

75. Let $u = \sqrt{x} \Rightarrow du = \frac{1}{2\sqrt{x}}\,dx$, $x = 1 \Rightarrow u = 1$, $x = 4 \Rightarrow u = 2$

$$\int_1^4 \frac{2^{\sqrt{x}}}{2\sqrt{x}}\,dx = \int_1^2 2^u\,du = \frac{1}{\ln 2}(2^u)\Big]_1^2 = \frac{2}{\ln 2}$$

76. $\int 10^{2x}\,dx = \frac{1}{2\ln 10}(10^{2x}) + C = \frac{100^x}{\ln 100} + C$

77. Let $u = \ln x \Rightarrow du = \frac{1}{x}\,dx$. $\int \frac{\ln x}{x}dx = \int u\,du = \frac{1}{2}u^2 + C = \frac{1}{2}\ln^2 x + C$

78. $\int \frac{\cos(\ln x)\,dx}{x} = \sin(\ln x) + C$

79. Let $u = \sqrt{x} \Rightarrow du = \frac{1}{2\sqrt{x}}\,dx \Rightarrow 2\,du = \frac{1}{\sqrt{x}}dx$, $x = 1 \Rightarrow u = 1$, $x = 9 \Rightarrow u = 3$.

$$\int_1^9 \frac{dx}{\sqrt{x}(1+\sqrt{x})} = \int_1^3 \frac{2\,du}{1+u} = 2\ln|1+u|\Big]_1^3 = 2\ln 2$$

80. $\int_0^{\sqrt{e-1}} \ln(x^2+1)\cdot 2x(x^2+1)^{-1}\,dx = \frac{\ln^2(x^2+1)}{2}\Big]_0^{\sqrt{e-1}} = \frac{1}{2}$

81. (a) Let $u = x^2 \Rightarrow du = 2x\,dx$. $\int xe^{(x^2)}\,dx = \int \frac{1}{2}e^u\,du = \frac{1}{2}e^u + C = \frac{1}{2}e^{(x^2)} + C$

(b) Let $u = e^{(x^2)} \Rightarrow du = 2xe^{(x^2)}\,dx$. $\int e^{(x^2)}\,dx = \int u\,du = \frac{1}{2}u^2 + C = \frac{1}{2}e^{(x^2)} + C$

7.2 INTEGRATION BY PARTS

1. Let $u = x$ and $dv = \sin x\,dx \Rightarrow du = dx$ and $v = -\cos x$

$$\int x\sin x\,dx = -x\cos x - \int(-\cos x)\,dx = -x\cos x + \sin x + C$$

2. $\int x \cos 2x\,dx = \frac{1}{2}x \sin 2x + \frac{1}{4}\cos 2x + C$

x		$\cos 2x$
1	$+$	$\frac{1}{2}\sin 2x$
0	$-$	$-\frac{1}{4}\cos 2x$

3. $\int x^2 \sin x\,dx = -x^2 \cos x + 2x \sin x + 2\cos x + C$

x^2		$\sin x$
$2x$	$+$	$-\cos x$
2	$-$	$-\sin x$
0	$+$	$\cos x$

4. $\int x^2 \cos x\,dx = x^2 \sin x + 2x \cos x - 2\sin x + C$

x^2		$\cos x$
$2x$	$+$	$\sin x$
2	$-$	$-\cos x$
0	$+$	$-\sin x$

5. Let $u = \ln x$ and $dv = x\,dx \Rightarrow du = \frac{1}{x}\,dx$ and $v = \frac{1}{2}x^2$

$$\int_1^2 \ln x\,dx = \frac{1}{2}x^2 \ln x\Big]_1^2 - \int_1^2 \frac{1}{2}x\,dx = \frac{1}{2}x^2 \ln x - \frac{1}{4}x^2\Big]_1^2 = 2\ln 2 - \frac{3}{4}.$$

6. $\int x^2 \ln x\,dx = \frac{1}{3}x^3 \ln|x| - \int \frac{1}{3}x^3\,dx$

$$= \frac{1}{3}x^3 \ln|x| - \frac{1}{9}x^3 + C = \frac{1}{9}x^3(3\ln|x| - 1) + C$$

Let $u = \ln x \Rightarrow du = \frac{1}{x}dx$; $dv = x^2\,dx = \frac{1}{3}x^3$

7. Let $u = \ln x$ and $dv = x^3\,dx \Rightarrow du = \frac{1}{x}\,dx$ and $v = \frac{1}{4}x^4$

$$\int x^3 \ln x\,dx = \frac{1}{4}x^4 \ln x - \int \frac{1}{4}x^3\,dx = \frac{1}{4}x^4 \ln x - \frac{1}{16}x^4 + C$$

8. $\int_0^1 \ln(x+1)\,dx = x\ln|x+1| - \int \frac{x}{x+1}\,dx$

Let $u = \ln(x+1) \Rightarrow du = \frac{dx}{x+1}$; $dv = dx \Rightarrow v = x$

$$= x\ln|x+1| - x + \ln|x+1|\Big]_0^1 = 2\ln 2 - 1$$

9. Let $u = \tan^{-1} x$ and $dv = dx \Rightarrow du = \frac{1}{1+x^2}\,dx$ and $v = x$

$$\int \tan^{-1} x\,dx = x\tan^{-1} x - \int \frac{x\,dx}{1+x^2} = x\tan^{-1} x - \frac{1}{2}\ln(1+x^2) + C$$

10. $$\int \tan^{-1} ax\,dx = x\tan^{-1} ax - \int \frac{ax\,dx}{1+a^2x^2} = x\tan^{-1} ax - \frac{1}{2a}\ln(1+a^2x^2) + C$$

Let $u = \tan^{-1} ax \Rightarrow du = \frac{a\,dx}{1+a^2x^2}$; $dv = dx \Rightarrow v = x$

11. Let $u = \sin^{-1} x$ and $dv = dx \Rightarrow du = \frac{dx}{\sqrt{1-x^2}}$ and $v = x$

$$\int \sin^{-1} x\,dx = x\sin^{-1} x - \int \frac{x\,dx}{\sqrt{1-x^2}} = x\sin^{-1} x + \sqrt{1-x^2} + C$$

12. $$\int \sin^{-1} ax\,dx = x\sin^{-1} ax - \int \frac{ax\,dx}{\sqrt{1-a^2x^2}} = x\sin^{-1} ax + \frac{1}{a}\sqrt{1-a^2x^2} + C$$

Let $u = \sin^{-1} ax \Rightarrow du = \frac{a\,dx}{\sqrt{1-a^2x^2}}$; $dv = dx \Rightarrow v = x$

13. Let $u = x$ and $dv = \sec^2 x\,dx \Rightarrow du = dx$ and $v = \tan x$

$$\int x\sec^2 x\,dx = x\tan x - \int \tan x\,dx = x\tan x + \ln|\cos x| + C$$

14. $$\int 4x\sec^2 2x\,dx = 2x\tan 2x + \ln|\cos 2x| + C$$

$4x$		$\sec^2 2x$
	$+$ ↘	
4		$\frac{1}{2}\tan 2x$
	$-$ ↘	
0		$-\frac{1}{4}\ln|\cos 2x|$

15. $$\int x^3e^x\,dx = x^3e^x - 3x^2e^x + 6xe^x - 6e^x + C = e^x(x^3 - 3x^2 + 6x - 6) + C$$

x^3		e^x
	$+$ ↘	
$3x^2$		e^x
	$-$ ↘	
$6x$		e^x
	$+$ ↘	
6		e^x
	$-$ ↘	
0		e^x

16. $\int x^4 e^{-x}\,dx = -e^{-x}(x^4 + 4x^3 + 12x^2 + 24x + 24) + C$

x^4		e^{-x}
	+	
$4x^3$		$-e^{-x}$
	−	
$12x^2$		e^{-x}
	+	
$24x$		$-e^{-x}$
	−	
24		e^{-x}
	+	
0		$-e^{-x}$

17. $\int (x^2 - 5x)e^x\,dx = (x^2 - 5x)e^x - (2x - 5)e^x + 2e^x - 2e^x + C$

$= e^x(x^2 - 7x + 7) + C$

$x^2 - 5x$		e^x
	+	
$2x - 5$		e^x
	−	
2		e^x
	+	
0		e^x

18. $\int (x^2 + x + 1)e^x\,dx = e^x(x^2 - x + 2) + C$

$x^2 + x + 1$		e^x
	+	
$2x + 1$		e^x
	−	
2		e^x
	+	
0		e^x

19. $\int x^5 e^x\,dx = x^5e^x - 5x^4e^x + 20x^3e^x - 60x^2e^x + 120xe^x - 120e^x + C$

$e^x(x^5 - 5x^4 + 20x^3 - 60x^2 + 120x - 120) + C$

x^5		e^x
	+	
$5x^4$		e^x
	−	
$20x^3$		e^x
	+	
$60x^2$		e^x
	−	
$120x$		e^x
	+	
120		e^x
	−	
0		e^x

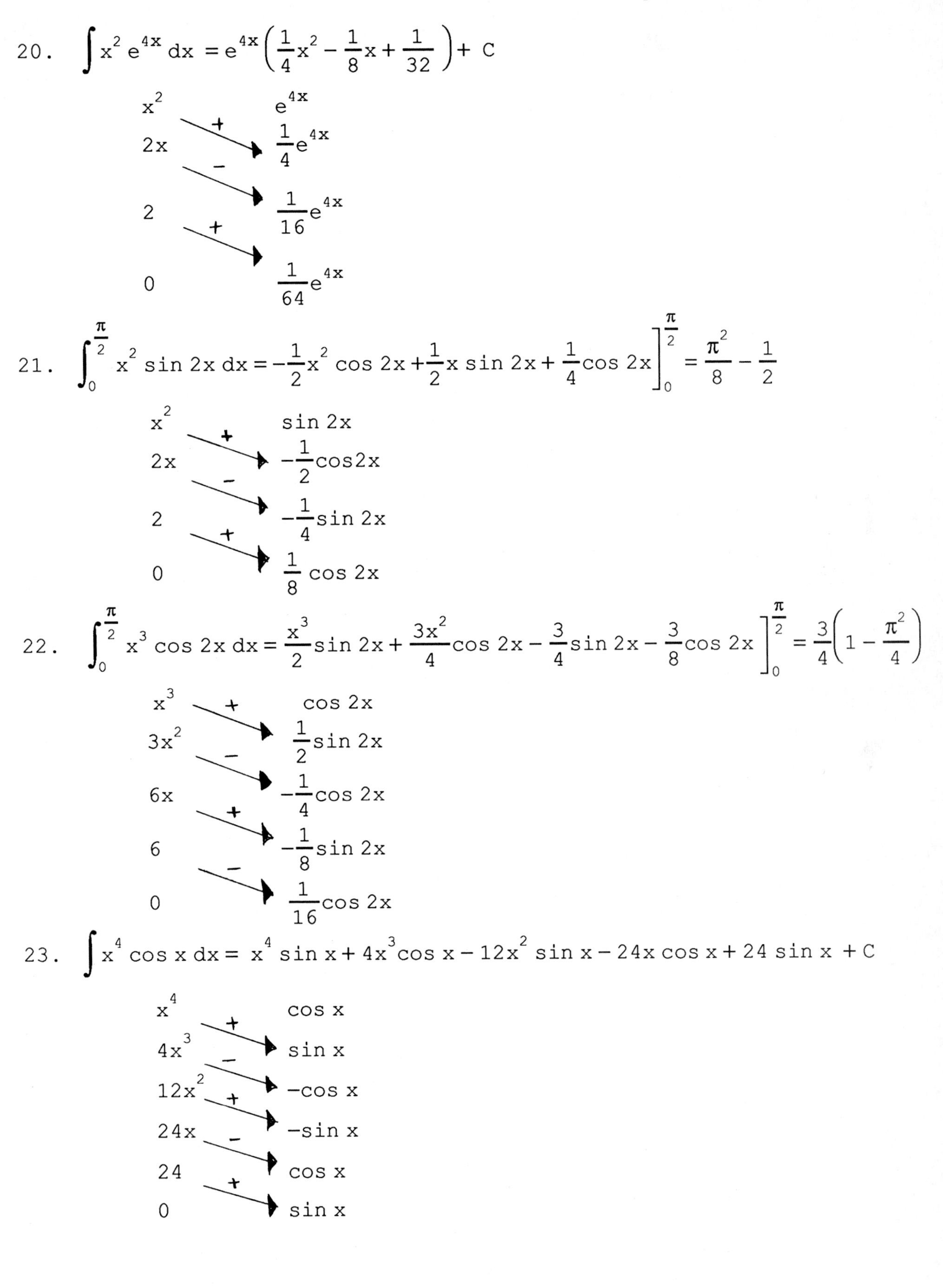

20. $\int x^2 e^{4x}\,dx = e^{4x}\left(\frac{1}{4}x^2 - \frac{1}{8}x + \frac{1}{32}\right) + C$

	sign	
x^2		e^{4x}
$2x$	+	$\frac{1}{4}e^{4x}$
2	−	$\frac{1}{16}e^{4x}$
0	+	$\frac{1}{64}e^{4x}$

21. $\int_0^{\frac{\pi}{2}} x^2 \sin 2x\,dx = -\frac{1}{2}x^2\cos 2x + \frac{1}{2}x\sin 2x + \frac{1}{4}\cos 2x\Big]_0^{\frac{\pi}{2}} = \frac{\pi^2}{8} - \frac{1}{2}$

	sign	
x^2		$\sin 2x$
$2x$	+	$-\frac{1}{2}\cos 2x$
2	−	$-\frac{1}{4}\sin 2x$
0	+	$\frac{1}{8}\cos 2x$

22. $\int_0^{\frac{\pi}{2}} x^3 \cos 2x\,dx = \frac{x^3}{2}\sin 2x + \frac{3x^2}{4}\cos 2x - \frac{3}{4}\sin 2x - \frac{3}{8}\cos 2x\Big]_0^{\frac{\pi}{2}} = \frac{3}{4}\left(1 - \frac{\pi^2}{4}\right)$

	sign	
x^3		$\cos 2x$
$3x^2$	+	$\frac{1}{2}\sin 2x$
$6x$	−	$-\frac{1}{4}\cos 2x$
6	+	$-\frac{1}{8}\sin 2x$
0	−	$\frac{1}{16}\cos 2x$

23. $\int x^4 \cos x\,dx = x^4\sin x + 4x^3\cos x - 12x^2\sin x - 24x\cos x + 24\sin x + C$

	sign	
x^4		$\cos x$
$4x^3$	+	$\sin x$
$12x^2$	−	$-\cos x$
$24x$	+	$-\sin x$
24	−	$\cos x$
0	+	$\sin x$

24. $\int x^5 \sin x\,dx =$

$-x^5 \cos x + 5x^4 \sin x + 20x^3 \cos x - 60x^2 \sin x - 120x \cos x + 120 \sin x + C$

x^5	$+$	$\sin x$
$5x^4$	$-$	$-\cos x$
$20x^3$	$+$	$-\sin x$
$60x^2$	$-$	$\cos x$
$120x$	$+$	$\sin x$
120	$-$	$-\cos x$
0		$-\sin x$

25. $\int x^2 \cos ax\,dx = \frac{x^2}{a}\sin ax + \frac{2x}{a^2}\cos ax - \frac{2}{a^3}\sin ax + C$

x^2	$+$	$\cos ax$
$2x$	$-$	$\frac{1}{a}\sin ax$
2	$+$	$-\frac{1}{a^2}\cos ax$
0		$-\frac{1}{a^3}\sin ax$

26. $\int x \cos(2x+1)\,dx = \frac{1}{2}x \sin(2x+1) + \frac{1}{4}\cos(2x+1) + C$

x	$+$	$\cos(2x+1)$
1	$-$	$\frac{1}{2}\sin(2x+1)$
0		$-\frac{1}{4}\cos(2x+1)$

27. Let $u = \sec^{-1} x$ and $dv = x\,dx \Rightarrow du = \frac{dx}{x\sqrt{x^2-1}}$ and $v = \frac{1}{2}x^2$

$$\int_1^2 x \sec^{-1} x\,dx = \frac{1}{2}x^2 \sec^{-1} x\Big]_1^2 - \frac{1}{2}\int_1^2 \frac{x}{\sqrt{x^2-1}}dx =$$

$$\frac{1}{2}x^2 \sec^{-1} x - \frac{1}{2}\sqrt{x^2-1}\Big]_1^2 = \frac{2\pi}{3} - \frac{\sqrt{3}}{2}$$

28. $\int_1^4 \sec^{-1}\sqrt{x}\,dx = x\sec^{-1}\sqrt{x}\Big]_1^4 - \int_1^4 \frac{dx}{2\sqrt{x-1}}$

Let $u = \sec^{-1}\sqrt{x} \Rightarrow du = \frac{dx}{2\sqrt{x-1}}$; $dv = dx \Rightarrow v = x$

$$= x\sec^{-1}\sqrt{x} - \sqrt{x-1}\Big]_1^4 = \frac{4\pi}{3} - \sqrt{3}$$

29. $\displaystyle\int_1^e \frac{\ln x}{x}dx = \frac{1}{2}\ln^2 x\Big]_1^e = \frac{1}{2}$

30. $\displaystyle\int_0^1 x\sqrt{1-x}\,dx = \int_1^0 (-2z^2 + 2z^4)\,dz = -\frac{2}{3}z^3 + \frac{2}{5}z^5\Big]_1^0 = \frac{4}{15}$

Let $z^2 = 1 - x \Rightarrow 2z\,dz = -dx$

31. Let $u = \sin^{-1}\left(\frac{1}{x}\right)$ and $dv = x\,dx \Rightarrow du = \dfrac{-dx}{x\sqrt{x^2-1}}$ and $v = \frac{1}{2}x^2$

$$\int x\sin^{-1}\left(\frac{1}{x}\right)dx = \frac{1}{2}x^2\sin^{-1}\left(\frac{1}{x}\right) + \int\frac{x\,dx}{\sqrt{x^2-1}} = \frac{1}{2}x^2\sin^{-1}\left(\frac{1}{x}\right) + \frac{1}{2}\sqrt{x^2-1} + C$$

32. $\displaystyle\int x\sin^{-1}\frac{a}{x}\,dx = \frac{x^2}{2}\sin^{-1}\frac{a}{x} + \frac{a}{2}\int\frac{dx}{\sqrt{1-\frac{a^2}{x^2}}}$

Let $u = \sin^{-1}\dfrac{a}{x} \Rightarrow du = \dfrac{1}{\sqrt{1-\frac{a^2}{x^2}}}\left(-\dfrac{a}{x^2}\right)dx$; $dv = x\,dx \Rightarrow v = \dfrac{x^2}{2}$

$$= \frac{x^2}{2}\sin^{-1}\frac{a}{x} - \frac{a}{2}\sqrt{x^2-a^2} + C$$

33. Let $u = e^x$ and $dv = \sin x\,dx \Rightarrow du = e^x\,dx$ and $v = -\cos x$.

$$\int e^x\sin x\,dx = -e^x\cos x + \int e^x\cos x\,dx$$

Now let $u = e^x$ and $dv = \cos x\,dx \Rightarrow du = e^x\,dx$ and $v = \sin x$.

$$\int e^x\sin x\,dx = -e^x\cos x + e^x\sin x - \int e^x\sin x\,dx$$

$$2\int e^x\sin x\,dx = e^x(\sin x - \cos x)$$

$$\int e^x\sin x\,dx = \frac{1}{2}e^x(\sin x - \cos x) + C$$

34. $\displaystyle\int e^{-x}\cos x\,dx = e^{-x}\sin x - e^{-x}\cos x - \int e^{-x}\cos x\,dx$

$$2\int e^{-x}\cos x\,dx = e^{-x}(\sin x - \cos x)$$

$$\int e^{-x}\cos x\,dx = \frac{e^{-x}}{2}(\sin x - \cos x)$$

e^{-x}	$+$	$\cos x$
$-e^{-x}$	$-$	$\sin x$
e^{-x}	$+$	$-\cos x$

35. Let $u = e^{2x}$ and $dv = \cos 3x\,dx \Rightarrow du = 2e^{2x}\,dx$ and $v = \frac{1}{3}\sin 3x$

$$\int e^{2x}\cos 3x\,dx = \frac{1}{3}e^{2x}\sin 3x - \frac{2}{3}\int e^{2x}\sin 3x\,dx$$

Now let $u = e^{2x}$ and $dv = \sin 3x\,dx \Rightarrow du = 2e^{2x}\,dx$ and $v = -\frac{1}{3}\cos 3x$.

$$\int e^{2x}\cos 3x\,dx = \frac{1}{3}e^{2x}\sin 3x + \frac{2}{9}e^{2x}\cos 3x - \frac{4}{9}\int e^{2x}\cos 3x\,dx$$

$$\frac{13}{9}\int e^{2x}\cos 3x\,dx = \frac{1}{9}e^{2x}(3\sin 3x + 2\cos 3x)$$

$$\int e^{2x}\cos 3x\,dx = \frac{1}{13}e^{2x}(3\sin 3x + 2\cos 3x) + C$$

36. $\int e^{-2x}\sin 2x\,dx = -\frac{1}{2}e^{-2x}\cos 2x - \frac{1}{8}e^{-2x}\sin 2x - \frac{1}{16}\int e^{-2x}\sin 2x\,dx$

$$\frac{17}{16}\int e^{-2x}\sin 2x\,dx = -\frac{1}{8}e^{-2x}(4\cos 2x + \sin 2x)$$

$$\int e^{-2x}\sin 2x\,dx = -\frac{2}{17}e^{-2x}(4\cos 2x + \sin 2x)$$

e^{-2x}		$\sin 2x$
$-\frac{1}{2}e^{-2x}$	$+$	$-\frac{1}{2}\cos 2x$
$\frac{1}{4}e^{-2x}$	$-$ / $+$	$-\frac{1}{4}\sin 2x$

37. Let $u = \sin(\ln x)$ and $dv = dx \Rightarrow du = \cos(\ln x)\frac{1}{x}dx$ and $v = x$

$$\int \sin(\ln x)dx = x\sin(\ln x) - \int \cos(\ln x)$$

Now let $u = \cos(\ln x)$ and $dv = dx \Rightarrow du = -\sin(\ln x)\frac{1}{x}dx$ and $v = x$

$$= x\sin(\ln x) - x\cos(\ln x) - \int \sin(\ln x)dx$$

$$2\int \sin(\ln x)dx = x\sin(\ln x) - x\cos(\ln x)$$

$$\int \sin(\ln x)dx = \frac{x}{2}(\sin(\ln x) - \cos(\ln x)) + C$$

38. $\int x(\ln x)^2\,dx = \frac{1}{2}x^2(\ln x)^2 - \int x \ln x\,dx$

Let $u = (\ln x)^2 \Rightarrow du = \frac{2\ln x\,dx}{x}$; $dv = x\,dx \Rightarrow v = \frac{1}{2}x^2$

$= \frac{1}{2}x^2(\ln x)^2 - \int x \ln x\,dx$

Let $u = \ln x \Rightarrow du = \frac{dx}{x}$; $dv = x\,dx \Rightarrow v = \frac{1}{2}x^2$

$\frac{1}{2}x^2(\ln x)^2 - \frac{1}{2}x^2(\ln x) + \int \frac{x}{2}\,dx$

$= \frac{1}{2}x^2(\ln x)^2 - \frac{1}{2}x^2(\ln x) + \frac{1}{4}x^2 + C$ or

$\frac{1}{2}x^2[(\ln x)^2 - \ln x + C']$

39. (a) $\int_0^{\pi} x\sin x\,dx = -x\cos x + \sin x\Big]_0^{\pi} = \pi$ (See problem 1)

(b) $\int_{\pi}^{2\pi} |x\sin x|\,dx = \int_{\pi}^{2\pi} (-x\sin x)\,dx = x\cos x - \sin x\Big]_{\pi}^{2\pi} = 3\pi$

40. $V = 2\pi\int_0^{\frac{\pi}{2}} x\cos x\,dx = 2\pi[x\sin x + \cos x\Big]_0^{\frac{\pi}{2}} = \pi(\pi - 2)$

41. $V = 2\pi\int_0^1 xe^{-x}\,dx = 2\pi(-xe^{-x} - e^{-x})\Big]_0^1 = 2\pi\left(\frac{e-2}{2}\right)$

42. $M = \int_0^{\pi} \sin x\,dx = 2$; $\bar{x} = \frac{\pi}{2}$ by symmetry.

$M_x = \int_0^{\pi} \frac{1}{2}\sin^2 x\,dx = \frac{1}{4}\int_0^{\pi}(1 - \cos 2x)\,dx = \frac{1}{4}\left[x - \frac{1}{2}\sin 2x\right]_0^{\pi} = \frac{\pi}{4}$; $\bar{y} = \frac{\pi}{8}$

43. $A = \int_0^1 x^2e^x\,dx = x^2e^x - 2xe^x + 2e^x\Big]_0^1 = e - 2$

$\bar{x} = \frac{1}{e-2}\int_0^1 x^3e^x\,dx = \frac{1}{e-2}[e^x(x^3 - 3x^2\ \ 6x - 6)\Big]_0^1 = \frac{6-2e}{2-e}$

$\bar{y} = \frac{1}{e-2}\int_0^1 \frac{1}{2}x^4e^{2x}\,dx = \frac{1}{2(e-2)}\left[e^{2x}\left(\frac{x^4}{2} - x^3 + \frac{3x^2}{2} - \frac{3x}{2} + \frac{3}{4}\right)\right]_0^1$

$= \frac{e^2 - 3}{8(e-2)}$

44. $M = \int_1^e (1 - \ln x)dx = x - x\ln x + x \Big]_1^e = e - 2$

$M_y = \int_1^e x(1 - \ln x)\,dx = \frac{x^2}{2} - \frac{x^2}{2}\ln x + \frac{x^2}{4}\Big]_1^e = \frac{1}{4}(e^2 - 3)$. $\therefore$ $\bar{x} = \frac{e^2 - 3}{4(e-2)}$

$M_x = \int_1^e \frac{1}{2}(1 + \ln x)(1 - \ln x)\,dx = \frac{1}{2}\int_1^e [1 - (\ln x)^2]\,dx$

$= \frac{1}{2}[x - x(\ln x)^2 + 2x\ln x - 2x\Big]_1^e = \frac{1}{2}$. $\therefore$ $\bar{y} = \frac{1}{2(e-2)}$

45. (a) $V = \pi\int_0^\pi x^2\sin^2 x\,dx = \frac{x^3}{2} - \frac{x^2\sin 2x}{4}\Big]_0^\pi - \int_0^\pi\left(x^2 - \frac{x\sin 2x}{2}\right)dx$

Let $u = x^2$ $\quad dv = \sin^2 x\,dx$ $\qquad$ Let $u = \frac{x}{2}$ $\quad dv = \sin 2x\,dx$

$du = 2x\,dx$ $\quad v = \frac{x}{2} - \frac{\sin 2x}{4}$ $\qquad$ $du = \frac{1}{2}dx$ $\quad v = -\frac{1}{2}\cos 2x\,dx$

$= \frac{x^3}{2} - \frac{x^2\sin 2x}{4} - \frac{x^3}{3} - \frac{x\cos 2x}{4} + \frac{\sin 2x}{8}\Big]_0^\pi = \frac{\pi^4}{6} - \frac{\pi^2}{4}$

(b) $V = 2\pi\int_0^\pi (\pi - x)\,x\sin x\,dx$

$= 2\pi^2[-x\cos x + \sin x\Big]_0^\pi - 2\pi[-x^2\cos x + 2x\sin x + 2\cos x\Big]_0^\pi = 8\pi$

46. $M = \int_1^2 \ln x\,dx = x\ln x + x\Big]_1^2 = 2\ln 2 - 1$

$M_y = \int_1^2 x\ln x\,dx = \frac{x^2}{2}\ln x - \frac{x^2}{4}\Big]_1^2 = 2\ln 2 - \frac{3}{4}$. $\therefore$ $\bar{x} = \frac{2\ln 2 - \frac{3}{4}}{2\ln 2 - 1}$

$M_x = \int_1^2 \frac{1}{2}(\ln x)^2 dx = \frac{1}{2}\Big[x(\ln x)^2 - 2x\ln x + 2x\Big]_1^2 = (\ln 2)^2 - 2\ln 2 + 1$

$\therefore$ $\bar{y} = \frac{(\ln 2 - 1)^2}{2\ln 2 - 1}$

47. $M_y = x\,\delta\,dA = \int_0^\pi x(1 + x)\sin x\,dx$

$= -(x + x^2)\cos x + (1 + 2x)\sin x + 2\cos x\Big]_0^\pi = \pi^2 + \pi - 4$

48. $V = 2\pi \int_0^1 x^2 \sqrt{1-x}\, dx = -4\pi \int_1^0 (z^2 - 2z^4 + z^6)\, dz$

$$= 4\pi \left[\frac{1}{3}z^3 - \frac{2}{5}z^5 + \frac{1}{7}z^7 \right]_0^1 = \frac{32\pi}{105}$$

Let $z^2 = 1 - x \Rightarrow 2z\, dz = -dx$, $x = 0 \Rightarrow z = 1$, $x = 1 \Rightarrow z = 0$

49. $x = e^t \sin t \Rightarrow \frac{dx}{dt} = e^t(\sin t + \cos t)$.

$y = e^t \cos t \Rightarrow \frac{dy}{dt} = e^t(-\sin t + \cos t)$. $ds = \sqrt{\left(\frac{dx}{dt}\right)^2 + \left(\frac{dy}{dt}\right)^2}\, dt$

$= e^t \sqrt{2}\, dt$. $S = \int 2\pi r\, ds \;\; = 2\pi\sqrt{2} \int_0^\pi e^{2t} \cos t\, dt$

$$= \frac{2\pi\sqrt{2}}{5} e^{2t} (\sin t + 2\cos t)\Big]_0^\pi = \frac{2\pi\sqrt{2}\,(e^\pi - 2)}{5}$$

50. $\int_0^1 e^{\sqrt{x}}\, dx = \int_0^1 2u\, e^u\, du = 2u\, e^u - 2e^u \Big]_0^1 = 2$

Let $u^2 = x \Rightarrow 2u\, du = dx$

$2u$	+	e^u
2	−	e^u
0		e^u

51. Let $u = \tan^{-1} x \Rightarrow du = \frac{dx}{1+x^2}$ and $dv = x\, dx \Rightarrow v = \frac{x^2}{2} + C$. Take $C = \frac{1}{2}$.

$$\int x \tan^{-1} x\, dx = \frac{x^2+1}{2}\tan^{-1} x - \int \frac{x^2+1}{2} \cdot \frac{dx}{1+x^2} = \frac{x^2+1}{2}\tan^{-1} x - \frac{x}{2} + C$$

7.3 PRODUCTS AND POWERS OF TRIGONOMETRIC FUNCTIONS

1. $\int \sin^5 x\, dx = \int (\sin^2 x)^2 \sin x\, dx = \int (1 - \cos^2 x)^2 \sin x\, dx$

$$= \int (1 - 2\cos^2 x + \cos^4 x) \sin x\, dx = -\cos x + \frac{2}{3}\cos^3 x - \frac{1}{5}\cos^5 x + C$$

2. $\int_0^\pi \sin^5 \frac{x}{2}\, dx = \int_0^\pi \left(\sin^2 \frac{x}{2}\right)^2 \sin \frac{x}{2}\, dx = \int_0^\pi \left(1 - \cos^2 \frac{x}{2}\right)^2 \sin \frac{x}{2}\, dx$

$$= \int_0^\pi \left(1 - 2\cos^2 \frac{x}{2} + \cos^4 \frac{x}{2}\right) \sin \frac{x}{2}\, dx =$$

$$= -2\cos \frac{x}{2} + \frac{4}{3}\cos^3 \frac{x}{2} - \frac{2}{5}\cos^5 \frac{x}{2}\Big]_0^\pi = \frac{16}{15}$$

3. $\int_{-\frac{\pi}{2}}^{\frac{\pi}{2}} \cos^3 x\,dx = \int_{-\frac{\pi}{2}}^{\frac{\pi}{2}} (1 - \sin^2 x)\cos x\,dx = \sin x - \frac{1}{3}\sin^3 x \Big]_{-\frac{\pi}{2}}^{\frac{\pi}{2}} = \frac{4}{3}$

4. $\int \cos^5 3x\,dx = \int (\cos^2 3x)^2 \cos 3x\,dx = \int (1 - \sin^2 3x)^2 \cos 3x\,dx$

$= \int (1 - 2\sin^2 3x + \sin^4 3x)\cos 3x\,dx$

$= \frac{1}{3}\sin 3x - \frac{2}{9}\sin^3 3x + \frac{1}{15}\sin^5 3x + C$

5. $\int \sin^7 x\,dx = \int (\sin^2 x)^3 \sin x\,dx = \int (1 - \cos^2 x)^3 \sin x\,dx$

$= \int (1 - 3\cos^2 x + 3\cos^4 x - \cos^6 x)\sin x\,dx$

$= -\cos x + \cos^3 x - \frac{3}{5}\cos^5 x + \frac{1}{7}\cos^7 x + C$

6. $\int \cos^7 x\,dx = \int (\cos^2 x)^3 \cos x\,dx = \int (1 - \sin^2 x)^3 \cos x\,dx$

$= \int (1 - 3\sin^2 x + 3\sin^4 x - \sin^6 x)\cos x\,dx$

$= \sin x - \sin^3 x + \frac{3}{5}\sin^5 x - \frac{1}{7}\sin^7 x + C$

7. $\int \cos^{\frac{2}{3}} x \sin^5 x\,dx = \int \cos^{\frac{2}{3}} x (1 - \cos^2 x)^2 \sin x\,dx$

$= \int (\cos^{\frac{2}{3}} x - 2\cos^{\frac{8}{3}} x + \cos^{\frac{14}{3}} x)\sin x\,dx$

$= -\frac{3}{5}\cos^{\frac{5}{3}} x + \frac{6}{11}\cos^{\frac{11}{3}} x - \frac{3}{17}\cos^{\frac{17}{3}} x + C$

8. $\int \sin^{3/2} x \cos^3 x\,dx = \int \sin^{3/2} x (1 - \sin^2 x)\cos x\,dx$

$= \int (\sin^{3/2} x - \sin^{7/2} x)\cos x\,dx = \frac{2}{5}(\sin x)^{5/2} - \frac{2}{9}(\sin x)^{9/2} + C$

9. $\int_0^{\frac{\pi}{3}} \sec x\,dx = \ln|\sec x + \tan x| \Big]_0^{\frac{\pi}{3}} = \ln(2 + \sqrt{3})$

10. $\int \sec 4t\,dt = \frac{1}{4}\ln|\sec 4t + \tan 4t| + C$

11. $\int_{-\frac{\pi}{3}}^{0} \sec^3 x\,dx = \frac{1}{2}\sec x \tan x + \frac{1}{2}\ln|\sec x + \tan x| \Big]_{-\frac{\pi}{3}}^{0}$

$= \sqrt{3} - \frac{1}{2}\ln(2 - \sqrt{3})$ (See Example 3 for integration)

12. $\int_0^{\frac{\pi}{6}} \frac{2\sin^2 x}{\cos x}\,dx = \int_0^{\frac{\pi}{6}} 2\sec x \tan x\,dx = 2\sec x \Big]_0^{\frac{\pi}{6}} = \frac{4\sqrt{3} - 6}{3}$

13. $\int e^x \sec^3 e^x \, dx = \int \sec^3 u \, du$, where $u = e^x$, $du = e^x dx$. By Example 3,

$$\int e^x \sec^3 e^x \, dx = \frac{1}{2} \sec e^x \tan e^x + \frac{1}{2} \ln |\sec e^x + \tan e^x| + C$$

14. $\int_0^{\frac{\pi}{4}} \sec^4 x \, dx = \int_0^{\frac{\pi}{4}} (1 + \tan^2 x) \sec^2 x \, dx = \tan x + \frac{1}{3}\tan^3 x \Big]_0^{\frac{\pi}{4}} = \frac{4}{3}$

15. $\int_{\frac{\pi}{4}}^{\frac{\pi}{2}} \frac{dx}{\sin^4 x} = \int_{\frac{\pi}{4}}^{\frac{\pi}{2}} \csc^4 x \, dx = \int_{\frac{\pi}{4}}^{\frac{\pi}{2}} (1 + \cot^2 x)\csc^2 x \, dx = -\cot x - \frac{1}{3}\cot^3 x \Big]_{\frac{\pi}{4}}^{\frac{\pi}{2}} = \frac{4}{3}$

16. $\int \sec^4 3x \, dx = \int (1 + \tan^2 3x) \sec^2 3x \, dx = \frac{1}{3}\tan 3x + \frac{1}{9}\tan^3 3x + C$

17. $\int_0^{\frac{\pi}{4}} \sec^8 x \, dx = \int_0^{\frac{\pi}{4}} (\sec^2 x)^3 \sec^2 x \, dx = \int_0^{\frac{\pi}{4}} (1 + \tan^2 x)^3 \sec^2 x \, dx$

$$= \int_0^{\frac{\pi}{4}} (1 + 3\tan^2 x + 3\tan^4 x + \tan^6 x)\sec^2 x \, dx$$

$$= \tan x + \tan^3 x + \frac{3}{5}\tan^5 x + \frac{1}{7}\tan^7 x \Big]_0^{\frac{\pi}{4}} = \frac{96}{35}$$

18. $\int \frac{2x \, dx}{\cos^3 (x^2)} = \int \sec^3 (x^2) \, 2x \, dx$

$$= \frac{1}{2}[\sec (x^2)\tan (x^2) + \ln|\sec (x^2) + \tan (x^2)|] + C$$

19. $\int_0^{\frac{\pi}{4}} \tan^3 dx = \int_0^{\frac{\pi}{4}} \tan^2 x \tan x \, dx = \int_0^{\frac{\pi}{4}} (\sec^2 x - 1) \tan x \, dx$

$$= \int_0^{\frac{\pi}{4}} \tan x \sec^2 x \, dx - \int_0^{\frac{\pi}{4}} \tan x \, dx = \frac{1}{2}\tan^2 x - \ln|\cos x| \Big]_0^{\frac{\pi}{4}} = \frac{1}{2} - \ln\frac{\sqrt{2}}{2}$$

20. $\int_{-\frac{\pi}{4}}^{\frac{\pi}{4}} \tan^4 x \, dx = \int_{-\frac{\pi}{4}}^{\frac{\pi}{4}} \tan^2 x (\sec^2 x - 1) \, dx$

$$= \int_{-\frac{\pi}{4}}^{\frac{\pi}{4}} \tan^2 x \sec^2 x \, dx - \int_{-\frac{\pi}{4}}^{\frac{\pi}{4}} (\sec^2 x - 1) \, dx$$

$$= \frac{1}{3}\tan^3 x - \tan x + x \Big]_{-\frac{\pi}{4}}^{\frac{\pi}{4}} = \frac{3\pi - 8}{6}$$

21. $\int \tan^6 x\,dx = \int (\tan^4 x)(\tan^2 x)\,dx = \int \tan^4 x(\sec^2 x - 1)\,dx$

$= \frac{1}{5}\tan^5 x - \int \tan^4 x\,dx = \frac{1}{5}\tan^5 x - \frac{1}{3}\tan^3 x + \tan x - x + C$

(See Example 4 for integration of $\int \tan^4 x\,dx$)

22. (a) $\int \cot^2 x\,dx = \int (\csc^2 x - 1)\,dx = -\cot x - x + C$

(b) $\int \cot^4 dx = \int \cot^2 x(\csc^2 x - 1)\,dx = -\frac{1}{3}\cot^3 x - \int \cot^2 x\,dx$

$= -\frac{1}{3}\cot^3 x + \cot x + x + C$

23. $\int \csc x\,dx = \int \frac{\csc x(\csc x + \cot x)}{\csc x + \cot x}\,dx = -\ln|\csc x + \cot x| + C$

24. Let $u = \csc x \Rightarrow du = -\csc x \cot x\,dx$; $dv = \csc^2 x \Rightarrow v = -\cot x$

$\int \csc^3 x\,dx = -\csc x \cot x - \int \csc x \cot^2 x\,dx$

$= -\csc x \cot x - \int \csc x(\csc^2 x - 1)\,dx$

$= -\csc x \cot x - \int \csc^3 x\,dx - \ln|\csc x + \cot x|$

$2\int \csc^3 x\,dx = -\csc x \cot x - \ln|\csc x + \cot x|$

$\int \csc^3 x\,dx = -\frac{1}{2}(\csc x \cot x + \ln|\csc x + \cot x|) + C$

25. (a) $\int_0^{\frac{\pi}{4}} \frac{dx}{\sqrt{1 - \sin^2 x}} = \int_0^{\frac{\pi}{4}} \sec x\,dx = \ln|\sec x + \tan x|\Big]_0^{\frac{\pi}{4}} = \ln(\sqrt{2} + 1)$

(b) $\int_{\frac{\pi}{3}}^{\frac{\pi}{2}} \frac{dx}{\sqrt{1 - \cos^2 x}} = \int_{\frac{\pi}{3}}^{\frac{\pi}{2}} \csc x\,dx = -\ln|\csc x + \cot x|\Big]_{\frac{\pi}{3}}^{\frac{\pi}{2}} = \ln\sqrt{3}$

26. $\int_0^{\frac{\pi}{3}} \frac{dx}{1 + \sin x} \cdot \frac{1 - \sin x}{1 - \sin x} = \int_0^{\frac{\pi}{3}} \frac{1 - \sin x}{\cos^2 x}\,dx = \int_0^{\frac{\pi}{3}} (\sec^2 x - \sec x \tan x)\,dx$

$= \tan x - \sec x\Big]_0^{\frac{\pi}{3}} = \sqrt{3} - 1$

27. $\int_{-\pi}^{0} \sin 3x \cos 2x\,dx = \frac{1}{2}\int_{-\pi}^{0} (\sin x + \sin 5x)\,dx = -\frac{1}{2}\cos x - \frac{1}{10}\cos 5x\Big]_{-\pi}^{0} = -\frac{6}{5}$

28. $\int_0^{\frac{\pi}{2}} \cos 3x \sin 2x\,dx = \frac{1}{2}\int_0^{\frac{\pi}{2}} (\sin 5x - \sin x)\,dx = -\frac{1}{10}\cos 5x + \frac{1}{2}\cos x\Big]_0^{\frac{\pi}{2}} = -\frac{2}{5}$

29. $\int_{-\pi}^{\pi} \sin^2 3x\,dx = \int_{-\pi}^{\pi}\left(\frac{1}{2} - \frac{1}{2}\cos 6x\right)dx = \frac{1}{2}x - \frac{1}{12}\sin 6x\Big]_{-\pi}^{\pi} = \pi$

30. $\int_0^{\frac{\pi}{2}} \sin x \cos x \, dx = \frac{1}{2} \sin^2 x \Big]_0^{\frac{\pi}{2}} = \frac{1}{2}$

31. $\int_0^{\pi} \cos 3x \cos 4x \, dx = \frac{1}{2}\int_0^{\pi} (\cos x + \cos 7x) \, dx = \frac{1}{2} \sin x + \frac{1}{7}\sin 7x \Big]_0^{\pi} = 0$

32. $\int_{-\frac{\pi}{2}}^{\frac{\pi}{2}} \cos x \cos 7x \, dx = \frac{1}{2}\int_{-\frac{\pi}{2}}^{\frac{\pi}{2}} (\cos 8x + \cos 6x) \, dx = \frac{1}{16}\sin 8x + \frac{1}{12}\sin 6x \Big]_{-\frac{\pi}{2}}^{\frac{\pi}{2}} = 0$

33. $\int \frac{\sec 2x \csc 2x}{2} \, dx = \int \frac{dx}{2 \cos 2x \sin 2x} = \int \frac{dx}{\sin 4x}$

$= \int \csc 4x \, dx = -\frac{1}{4}\ln|\csc 4x + \cot 4x| + C$

34. The integrands in (g), (k), (n), and (o) are even functions, so that the integrals are not zero. All of the other integrands are odd functions and the integrals are over a symmetric interval about zero, so that they are equal to zero.

35. $A = 2\int_0^{\frac{\pi}{4}} (2\cos x - \sec x) \, dx = 4 \sin x - 2\ln|\sec x + \tan x| \Big]_0^{\frac{\pi}{4}} = 2\sqrt{2} - 2\ln(\sqrt{2} + 1)$

36. $s = \int_0^{\frac{\pi}{3}} \sqrt{1 + \tan^2 x} \, dx = \int_0^{\frac{\pi}{3}} \sec x \, dx = \ln|\sec x + \tan x| \Big]_0^{\frac{\pi}{3}} = \ln(2 + \sqrt{3})$

37. $s = \int_0^{\frac{\pi}{4}} \sqrt{1 + \left(\frac{dy}{dx}\right)^2} \, dx = \int_0^{\frac{\pi}{4}} \sqrt{1 + \tan^2 x} \, dx = \ln|\sec x + \tan x| \Big]_0^{\frac{\pi}{4}} = \ln(\sqrt{2} + 1)$

38. $M = \int_{-\frac{\pi}{4}}^{\frac{\pi}{4}} \sec x \, dx = \ln|\sec x + \tan x| \Big]_{-\frac{\pi}{4}}^{\frac{\pi}{4}} = \ln|3 + 2\sqrt{2}|$

$M_x = \int_{-\frac{\pi}{4}}^{\frac{\pi}{4}} \frac{1}{2}\sec^2 x \, dx = \frac{1}{2}\tan x \Big]_{-\frac{\pi}{4}}^{\frac{\pi}{4}} = 1$

$\bar{y} = \frac{1}{\ln(3 + \sqrt{2})}$; $\bar{x} = 0$ by symmetry.

39. (a) $d = 25\int_{\frac{\pi}{6}}^{\frac{\pi}{4}} \sec x \, dx = 25 \ln|\sec x + \tan x| \Big]_{\frac{\pi}{6}}^{\frac{\pi}{4}} \approx 8.3$ cm

(b) $d = 25\int_{\frac{\pi}{4}}^{\frac{\pi}{3}} \sec x \, dx = 25 \ln|\sec x + \tan x| \Big]_{\frac{\pi}{4}}^{\frac{\pi}{3}} \approx 10.9$ cm

40. (a) $\int_0^{2\pi} \sin mx \sin nx\, dx = \frac{1}{2}\int_0^{2\pi} [\cos (m-n)x - \cos (m+n)x]\, dx$

$= \frac{1}{2(m-n)}\sin (m-n)x - \frac{1}{2(m+n)}\sin (m+n)x \Big]_0^{2\pi} = 0$ because

$m^2 \neq n^2 \Rightarrow m \neq \pm n$, and m, n integers $\Rightarrow m+n$ and $m-n$ are integers so

$\sin 2\pi(m+n) = 0$ and $\sin 2\pi(m-n) = 0$.

(b) $\int_0^{2\pi} \sin px \cos qx\, dx = \frac{1}{2}\int_0^{2\pi} [\sin (p+q)x + \sin (p-q)x]\, dx$

=, if $p \neq \pm q$, to $-\frac{1}{2(p+q)}\cos (p+q)x - \frac{1}{2(p-q)}\cos (p-q)x \Big]_0^{2\pi} = 0$ because

p, q integers $\Rightarrow p+q$ and $p-q$ are integers so

$\cos 2\pi(p+q) = 1$ and $\cos 2\pi(p-q) = 1$. If $p = \pm q$, the integral

becomes $\pm\frac{1}{2}\int_0^{2\pi} \sin 2px\, dx = \pm\frac{1}{4}\cos 2px\Big]_0^{2\pi} = 0$.

41. (a) $\int_k^{k+2\pi} \sin mx \sin nx\, dx = \frac{1}{2}\int_k^{k+2\pi} [\cos (m-n)x - \cos (m+n)x]\, dx$

$= \frac{\sin (m-n)x}{2(m-n)} - \frac{\sin (m+n)x}{2(m+n)},\ m^2 \neq n^2 \Big]_k^{k+2\pi} = 0$

since since $\sin k = \sin (k+2\pi)$

(b) $\int_k^{k+2\pi} \cos mx \cos nx\, dx = \frac{1}{2}\int_k^{k+2\pi} [\cos (m-n)x + \cos (m+n)x]\, dx$

$= \frac{\sin (m-n)x}{2(m-n)} - \frac{\sin (m+n)x}{2(m+n)},\ m^2 \neq n^2 \Big]_k^{k+2\pi} = 0$ as in part (a).

42. Let f be a continuous odd function.

$\int_{-a}^{a} f(x)\, dx = \int_{-a}^{0} f(x)\, dx + \int_0^a f(x)\, dx$. Let $u = -x$, $dx = -du$. Then

$\int_{-a}^{0} f(x)\, dx = \int_a^0 f(-u)(-du) = \int_a^0 -f(u)(-du) = \int_a^0 f(u)\, du = -\int_0^a f(u)\, du$.

Thus $\int_{-a}^{a} f(x)\, dx = -\int_0^a f(x)\, dx + \int_0^a f(x)\, dx = 0$.

7.4 EVEN POWERS OF SINES AND COSINES

1. $$\int_{-\pi}^{\pi} \sin^2 x\,dx = \int_{-\pi}^{\pi}\left(\frac{1}{2} - \frac{1}{2}\cos 2x\right)dx = \frac{1}{2}x - \frac{1}{4}\sin 2x\Big]_{-\pi}^{\pi} = \pi$$

2. $$\int_{-\pi}^{\pi} \cos^2 t\,dt = \frac{1}{2}\int_{-\pi}^{\pi}(1+\cos 2t)\,dt = \frac{1}{2}\left[t + \frac{1}{2}\sin 2t\right]_{-\pi}^{\pi} = \pi$$

3. $$\int \sin^2 2t\,dt = \int\left(\frac{1}{2} - \frac{1}{2}\cos 4t\right)dt = \frac{1}{2}t - \frac{1}{8}\sin 4t + C$$

4. $$\int \cos^2 3\theta\,d\theta = \frac{1}{2}\int(1+\cos 6\theta)\,d\theta = \frac{1}{2}\theta + \frac{1}{12}\sin 6\theta + C$$

5. $$\int_{-\frac{\pi}{4}}^{\frac{\pi}{4}} \sin^2 x\cos^2 x\,dx = \frac{1}{4}\int_{-\frac{\pi}{4}}^{\frac{\pi}{4}}(2\sin x\cos x)^2\,dx = \frac{1}{4}\int_{-\frac{\pi}{4}}^{\frac{\pi}{4}}\sin^2 2x\,dx$$

$$= \frac{1}{4}\int_{-\frac{\pi}{4}}^{\frac{\pi}{4}}\left(\frac{1}{2} - \frac{1}{2}\cos 4x\right)dx = \frac{1}{8}x - \frac{1}{32}\sin 4x\Big]_{\frac{-\pi}{4}}^{\frac{\pi}{4}} = \frac{\pi}{16}$$

6. $$\int_0^{\pi} \sin^4 x\,dx = \int_0^{\pi}\left(\frac{1}{2} - \frac{1}{2}\cos 2x\right)^2 dx = \int_0^{\pi}\left(\frac{1}{4} - \frac{1}{2}\cos 2x + \frac{1}{4}\cos^2 2x\right)dx$$

$$= \int_0^{\pi}\left(\frac{1}{4} - \frac{1}{2}\cos 2x + \frac{1}{4}\left(\frac{1}{2} + \frac{1}{2}\cos 4x\right)\right)dx = \int_0^{\pi}\left(\frac{3}{8} - \frac{1}{2}\cos 2x + \frac{1}{8}\cos 4x\right)dx$$

$$= \left[\frac{3}{8}x - \frac{1}{4}\sin 2x + \frac{1}{32}\sin 4x\right]_0^{\pi} = \frac{3}{8}\pi$$

7. $$\int_0^{\frac{\pi}{a}} \sin^4 ax\,dx = \int_0^{\frac{\pi}{a}}(\sin^2 ax)^2\,dx = \int_0^{\frac{\pi}{a}}\left(\frac{1}{2} - \frac{1}{2}\cos 2ax\right)^2 dx$$

$$= \int_0^{\frac{\pi}{a}}\left(\frac{1}{4} - \frac{1}{2}\cos 2ax + \frac{1}{4}\cos^2 2ax\right)dx$$

$$= \int_0^{\frac{\pi}{a}}\left[\left(\frac{1}{4} - \frac{1}{2}\cos 2ax + \frac{1}{4}\left(\frac{1}{2} + \frac{1}{2}\cos 4ax\right)\right)\right]dx$$

$$= \frac{3}{8}x - \frac{1}{4a}\sin 2ax + \frac{1}{32a}\sin 4ax\Big]_0^{\frac{\pi}{a}} = \frac{3\pi}{8a}$$

8. $$\int_0^1 \cos^4 2\pi t\,dt = \int_0^1\left(\frac{1}{2} + \frac{1}{2}\cos 4\pi t\right)^2 dt = \int_0^1\left(\frac{1}{4} + \frac{1}{2}\cos 4\pi t + \frac{1}{4}\cos^2 4\pi t\right)dt$$

$$= \int_0^1\left(\frac{1}{4} + \frac{1}{2}\cos 4\pi t + \frac{1}{4}\left(\frac{1}{2} + \frac{1}{2}\cos 8\pi t\right)\right)dt$$

$$= \left[\frac{3}{8}t + \frac{1}{8\pi}\sin 4\pi t + \frac{1}{64\pi}\sin 8\pi t\right]_0^1 = \frac{3}{8}$$

9. $$\int \frac{\sin^4 x}{\cos^2 x}\,dx = \int \frac{\sin^2 x(1-\cos^2 x)\,dx}{\cos^2 x} = \int (\tan^2 x - \sin^2 x)\,dx$$
$$= \int\left(\sec^2 x - 1 - \left(\frac{1}{2} - \frac{1}{2}\cos 2x\right)\right)dx = \tan x - \frac{3}{2}x + \frac{1}{4}\sin 2x + C$$

10. $$\int \frac{\cos^6 x\,dx}{\sin^2 x} = \int \frac{(1-\sin^2 x)^3\,dx}{\sin^2 x} = \int \frac{(1 - 3\sin^2 x + 3\sin^4 x - \sin^6 x)\,dx}{\sin^2 x}$$
$$= \int\left(\csc^2 x - 3 + 3\left(\frac{1}{2} - \frac{1}{2}\cos 2x\right) - \left(\frac{1}{2} - \frac{1}{2}\cos 2x\right)^2\right)dx$$
$$= -\cot x - \frac{3}{2}x - \frac{3}{4}\sin 2x - \int\left(\frac{1}{4} - \frac{1}{2}\cos 2x + \frac{1}{4}\left(\frac{1}{2} + \frac{1}{2}\cos 4x\right)\right)dx$$
$$= -\cot x - \frac{3}{4}\sin 2x - \frac{15}{8}x + \frac{1}{4}\sin 2x - \frac{1}{32}\sin 4x + C$$
$$= -\frac{15}{8}x - \cot x - \frac{1}{2}\sin 2x - \frac{1}{32}\sin 4x + C$$

11. $$\int_0^\pi \sin^4 y\cos^2 y\,dy = \int_0^\pi \sin^4 y(1-\sin^2 y)\,dy = I_1 - I_2, \text{ where}$$

$$I_1 = \int_0^\pi \sin^4 y\,dy = \int_0^\pi \left(\frac{1}{2} - \frac{1}{2}\cos 2y\right)^2 dy$$
$$= \int_0^\pi \left(\frac{1}{4} - \frac{1}{2}\cos 2y + \frac{1}{4}\cos^2 2y\right)dy$$
$$= \int_0^\pi \left(\frac{1}{4} - \frac{1}{2}\cos 2y + \frac{1}{4}\left(\frac{1}{2} + \frac{1}{2}\cos 4y\right)\right)dy$$
$$= \frac{3}{8}y - \frac{1}{4}\sin 2y + \frac{1}{32}\sin 4y\Big]_0^\pi = \frac{3\pi}{8}$$

and $$I_2 = \int_0^\pi \sin^6 y\,dy = \int_0^\pi \left(\frac{1}{2} - \frac{1}{2}\cos 2y\right)^3 dy$$
$$= \frac{1}{8}\int_0^\pi (1 - 3\cos 2y + 3\cos^2 2y - \cos^3 2y)\,dy$$
$$= \frac{1}{8}\int_0^\pi \left[1 - 3\cos 2y + 3\left(\frac{1}{2} + \frac{1}{2}\cos 4y\right) - (1-\sin^2 2y)\cos 2y\right]dy$$
$$= \frac{1}{8}\left[\frac{5}{2}y - 2\sin 2y + \frac{3}{8}\sin 4y + \frac{1}{6}\sin^3 y\right]_0^\pi = \frac{5\pi}{16}$$

Combining, $\frac{3\pi}{8} - \frac{5\pi}{16} = \frac{\pi}{16}$

12. $$\int_{-\frac{\pi}{4}}^{\frac{\pi}{4}} 4\sin^4 t\cos^4 t\,dt = \frac{1}{4}\int_{-\frac{\pi}{4}}^{\frac{\pi}{4}} (2\sin t\cos t)^4\,dt = \frac{1}{4}\int_{-\frac{\pi}{4}}^{\frac{\pi}{4}} \sin^4 2t$$

$$= \frac{1}{4}\left[\frac{3}{8}t - \frac{1}{8}\sin 4t + \frac{1}{64}\sin 8t\right]_{-\frac{\pi}{4}}^{\frac{\pi}{4}} \quad \text{(See problem 7)}$$

$$= \frac{1}{4}\left[\frac{3\pi}{32} - \left(-\frac{3\pi}{32}\right)\right] = \frac{3\pi}{64}$$

13. $$\int \frac{\sin^6\theta}{\cos^2\theta}\,d\theta = \int \frac{\sin^2\theta\,(1-\cos^2\theta)^2}{\cos^2\theta}\,d\theta = \int \tan^2\theta\,(1 - 2\cos^2\theta + \cos^4\theta)\,d\theta$$

$$= \int (\sec^2\theta - 1)\,d\theta - 2\int\left(\frac{1}{2} - \frac{1}{2}\cos 2\theta\right)d\theta + \frac{1}{4}\int (2\sin\theta\cos\theta)^2\,d\theta$$

$$= \tan\theta - 2\theta + \frac{1}{2}\sin 2\theta + \frac{1}{4}\int\left(\frac{1}{2} - \frac{1}{2}\cos 4\theta\right)d\theta$$

$$= \tan\theta + \frac{1}{2}\sin 2\theta - \frac{1}{32}\sin 4\theta - \frac{15}{8}\theta + C$$

14. $$\int_{-\pi}^{0} \sin^6 x\,dx = \frac{1}{8}\int_{-\pi}^{0} (1-\cos 2x)^3\,dx = \frac{1}{8}\int_{-\pi}^{0} (1 - 3\cos 2x + 3\cos^2 2x - \cos^3 2x)\,dx$$

$$= \frac{1}{8}\int_{-\pi}^{0}\left(1 - 3\cos 2x + \frac{3}{2}(1+\cos 4x) + (1-\sin^2 2x)\cos 2x\right)dx$$

$$= \left[\frac{1}{8}x - \frac{3}{16}\sin 2x + \frac{3}{16}x + \frac{3}{64}\sin 4x - \frac{1}{16}\sin 2x - \frac{1}{48}\sin^3 2x\right]_{-\pi}^{0} = \frac{5\pi}{16}$$

15. $$\int_0^{2\pi} \sqrt{\frac{1-\cos t}{2}}\,dt = \int_0^{2\pi} \left|\sin\frac{t}{2}\right|\,dt = \int_0^{2\pi} \sin\frac{t}{2}\,dt = -2\cos\frac{t}{2}\Big]_0^{2\pi} = 4$$

Note: $0 \le t \le 2\pi \Rightarrow 0 \le \frac{t}{2} \le \pi \Rightarrow \sin\frac{t}{2} \ge 0$ on this interval.

16. $$\int_0^{\pi} \sqrt{1-\cos 2x}\,dx = \int_0^{\pi} \sqrt{2\sin^2 x}\,dx = \sqrt{2}\int_0^{\pi} |\sin x|\,dx = \sqrt{2}\int_0^{\pi} \sin x\,dx$$

$$= -\sqrt{2}\cos x\Big]_0^{\pi} = 2\sqrt{2}. \quad \text{(Note: } 0 \le x \le \pi \Rightarrow \sin x \ge 0\text{)}$$

17. $$\int_0^{\frac{\pi}{10}} \sqrt{1+\cos 5\theta}\,d\theta = \sqrt{2}\int_0^{\frac{\pi}{10}} \sqrt{\frac{1+\cos 5\theta}{2}}\,d\theta = \sqrt{2}\int_0^{\frac{\pi}{10}} \cos\frac{5\theta}{2}\,d\theta$$

$$= \frac{2\sqrt{2}}{5}\sin\frac{5\theta}{2}\Big]_0^{\frac{\pi}{10}} = \frac{2}{5}$$

18. $\int_0^{2\pi}\sqrt{1+\cos\frac{y}{4}}\,dy = \sqrt{2}\int_0^{2\pi}\sqrt{\cos^2\frac{y}{8}}\,dy = \sqrt{2}\int_0^{2\pi}|\cos\frac{y}{8}|\,dy$

$= \sqrt{2}\left[8\sin\frac{y}{8}\right]_0^{2\pi} = 8\sqrt{2}\left(\frac{1}{\sqrt{2}}\right) = 8$

19. $\int_0^{\frac{\pi}{2}}\theta\sqrt{1-\cos\theta}\,d\theta = \sqrt{2}\int_0^{\frac{\pi}{2}}\theta\sin\frac{\theta}{2}\,d\theta = \sqrt{2}\left[-2\theta\cos\frac{\theta}{2} + \int_0^{\frac{\pi}{2}}2\cos\frac{\theta}{2}\,d\theta\right]$

$= \sqrt{2}\left(-2\theta\cos\frac{\theta}{2} + 4\sin\frac{\theta}{2}\Big]_0^{\frac{\pi}{2}}\right) = 4-\pi$

20. $\int_0^{\pi}\sqrt{1-\sin^2 t}\,dt = \int_0^{\pi}|\cos t|\,dt = 2\int_0^{\frac{\pi}{2}}\cos t\,dt = 2\sin t\Big]_0^{\frac{\pi}{2}} = 2$

21. $\int_{-\frac{\pi}{4}}^{\frac{\pi}{4}}\sqrt{1+\tan^2 x}\,dx = \int_{-\frac{\pi}{4}}^{\frac{\pi}{4}}|\sec x|\,dx = \int_{-\frac{\pi}{4}}^{\frac{\pi}{4}}\sec x\,dx$

$= 2\ln|\sec x+\tan x|\Big]_{-\frac{\pi}{4}}^{\frac{\pi}{4}} = 2\ln(\sqrt{2}+1)$

22. $\int_{-\frac{\pi}{4}}^{\frac{\pi}{4}}\sqrt{\sec^2 x-1}\,dx = \int_{-\frac{\pi}{4}}^{\frac{\pi}{4}}|\tan x|\,dx = 2\int_0^{\frac{\pi}{4}}\tan x\,dx = 2\ln|\sec x|\Big]_0^{\frac{\pi}{4}} = \ln 2$

23. $\int_0^{\pi}\sqrt{1-\cos^2\theta}\,d\theta = \int_0^{\pi}|\sin\theta|\,d\theta = -\cos\theta\Big]_0^{\pi} = 2$

24. $\int_0^{\pi}\sqrt{1-\cos^2 2x}\,dx = \int_0^{\pi}|\sin 2x|\,dx = 2\int_0^{\frac{\pi}{2}}\sin 2x\,dx = -\cos 2x\Big]_0^{\frac{\pi}{2}} = 2$

25. $\int_{\frac{\pi}{4}}^{\frac{3\pi}{4}}\sqrt{\cot^2\theta+1}\,d\theta = \int_{\frac{\pi}{4}}^{\frac{3\pi}{4}}|\csc\theta|\,d\theta = \int_{\frac{\pi}{4}}^{\frac{3\pi}{4}}\csc\theta\,d\theta$

$= -\ln|\csc\theta-\cot\theta|\Big]_{\frac{\pi}{4}}^{\frac{3\pi}{4}} = \ln\frac{\sqrt{2}+1}{\sqrt{2}-1} = \ln(3+2\sqrt{2}$

26. $\int_{-\pi}^{\pi}(1-\cos^2 t)^{3/2}\,dt = \int_{-\pi}^{\pi}(\sin^2 t)^{3/2}\,dt = \int_{-\pi}^{\pi}|\sin t|^3\,dt = 2\int_0^{\pi}\sin^3 t\,dt$

$= 2\int_0^{\pi}(1-\cos^2 t)\sin t\,dt = 2\left[-\cos t+\frac{1}{3}\cos^3 t\right]_0^{\pi} = \frac{8}{3}$

27. $\int_{-\pi}^{\pi}\sqrt{1-\cos^2 x}\sin x\,dx = 0$ because it the integral of an odd function over a symmetric interval about 0.

28. $\int\frac{1}{\cos^2 t}\,dt = \int\sec^2 t\,dt = \tan t + C$

29. $\int \frac{1}{\sin^4 x}\,dx = \int \csc^4 dx = \int (\cot^2 x + 1)\csc^2 x\,dx = -\frac{1}{3}\cot^3 x - \cot x + C$

30. $\int \frac{\sin^3\theta\,d\theta}{\cos^2\theta} = \int \frac{\sin\theta\,(1-\cos^2\theta)\,d\theta}{\cos^2\theta} = \int \tan\theta\sec\theta\,d\theta - \int \sin\theta\,d\theta$

$= \sec\theta + \cos\theta + C$

31. $\int_{-\frac{\pi}{4}}^{\frac{\pi}{4}} \frac{\sin^2 x}{\cos^2 x}\,dx = \int_{-\frac{\pi}{4}}^{\frac{\pi}{4}} \tan^2 x\,dx = \int_{-\frac{\pi}{4}}^{\frac{\pi}{4}} (\sec^2 x - 1)\,dx = \tan x - x\Big]_{-\frac{\pi}{4}}^{\frac{\pi}{4}} = 2 - \frac{\pi}{2}$

32. $\int \frac{\cos 2t\,dt}{\sin^4 2t} = \int \cot 2t \csc^3 2t\,dt = \int \csc^2 2t\,(\cot 2 \csc 2t\,dt) = -\frac{1}{6}\csc^3 2t + C$

33. $\int \frac{\sin^2 t}{\cos t}\,dt = \int \frac{1-\cos^2 t}{\cos t}\,dt = \int (\sec t - \cos t)\,dt = \ln|\sec t + \tan t| - \sin t +$

34. $\int \sin 2x\,(1-\cos 2x)^{3/2}\,dx = \frac{1}{5}(1-\cos 2x)^{5/2} + C$

35. $\int_0^{\pi} \sqrt{1+\cos 4x}\,dx = \sqrt{2}\int_0^{\pi} |\cos 2x|\,dx = 4\sqrt{2}\int_0^{\frac{\pi}{4}} \cos 2x\,dx = 2\sqrt{2}\sin 2x\Big]_0^{\frac{\pi}{4}} = 2\sqrt{2}$

36. $V = \pi\int_0^{\pi} \sin^2 x\,dx = \frac{\pi}{2}\int_0^{\pi} (1+\cos 2x)\,dx = \frac{\pi}{2}\left[x + \frac{1}{2}\sin 2x\right]_0^{\pi} = \frac{\pi^2}{2}$

37. $V = \pi\int_0^{\pi} x^2\sin^2 x\,dx = \pi\int_0^{\pi} x^2\left(\frac{1}{2} - \frac{1}{2}\cos 2x\right)dx = \frac{\pi}{2}\int_0^{\pi} (x^2 - x^2\cos 2x)\,dx$

$= \frac{\pi}{2}\left[\frac{x^3}{3} - \frac{x^2}{2}\sin 2x + \frac{x}{2}\cos 2x - \frac{1}{4}\sin 2x\right]_0^{\pi} = \frac{\pi^4}{6} - \frac{\pi^2}{4}$

38. $x = t - \sin t \Rightarrow \frac{dx}{dt} = 1 - \cos t \qquad y = 1 - \cos t \Rightarrow \frac{dy}{dt} = \sin t$

$ds = \sqrt{(1-\cos t)^2 + \sin^2 t}\,dt = \sqrt{2 - 2\cos t}\,dt$

$S = 2\pi\int_0^{2\pi} (1-\cos t)\sqrt{2-2\cos t}\,dt = 2\sqrt{2}\pi\int_0^{2\pi} (1-\cos t)^{3/2}\,dt$

$= 2\sqrt{2}\pi\int_0^{2\pi}\left(2\sin^2\frac{t}{2}\right)^{3/2} dt = 8\pi\int_0^{2\pi} \sin^3\frac{t}{2}\,dt = 8\pi\int_0^{2\pi}\left(1-\cos^2\frac{t}{2}\right)\sin\frac{t}{2}\,dt$

$= 8\pi\left[-2\cos\frac{t}{2} + \frac{2}{3}\cos^3\frac{t}{2}\right]_0^{2\pi} = \frac{64\pi}{3}$

7.5 TRIGONOMETRIC SUBSTITUTIONS

1. Let $x = 2\tan u \Rightarrow dx = 2\sec^2 u\,du$

$$\int_{-2}^{2} \frac{dx}{4 + x^2} = \int_{-\frac{\pi}{4}}^{\frac{\pi}{4}} \frac{2\sec^2 u\,du}{4 + 4\tan^2 u} = \int_{-\frac{\pi}{4}}^{\frac{\pi}{4}} \frac{1}{2}\,du = \frac{1}{2}\,u\,\Big]_{-\frac{\pi}{4}}^{\frac{\pi}{4}} = \frac{\pi}{4}$$

2. Let $2\tan u = x \Rightarrow dx = 2\sec^2 u\,du;\ x = 0 \Rightarrow u = 0,\ x = 2 \Rightarrow u = \frac{\pi}{4}$

$$\int_0^2 \frac{dx}{8 + 2x^2} = \int_0^{\frac{\pi}{4}} \frac{2\sec^2 u\,du}{8 + 8\tan^2 u} = \frac{1}{4}\int_0^{\frac{\pi}{4}} du = \frac{1}{4}u\Big]_0^{\frac{\pi}{4}} = \frac{\pi}{16}$$

3. $$\int \frac{dx}{1 + 4x^2} = \frac{1}{2}\int \frac{2\,dx}{1 + (2x)^2} = \frac{1}{2}\tan^{-1} 2x + C$$

4. Let $x = 3\sin u \Rightarrow dx = 3\cos u\,du;\ x = 0 \Rightarrow u = 0,\ x = \frac{3}{2} \Rightarrow u = \frac{\pi}{6}$

$$\int_0^{3/2} \frac{dx}{\sqrt{9 - x^2}} = \int_0^{\frac{\pi}{6}} \frac{\cos u\,du}{\cos u} = u\Big]_0^{\frac{\pi}{6}} = \frac{\pi}{6}$$

5. $$\int_0^{1/(2\sqrt{2})} \frac{2dx}{\sqrt{1 - 4x^2}} = \sin^{-1}(2x)\Big]_0^{1/(2\sqrt{2})} = \frac{\pi}{4} - 0 = \frac{\pi}{4}$$

6. Let $2x = 3\sin u \Rightarrow dx = \frac{3}{2}\cos u\,du$.

$$\int \frac{dx}{\sqrt{9 - 4x^2}} = \frac{3}{2}\int \frac{\cos u\,du}{3\cos u} = \frac{1}{2}u = \frac{1}{2}\sin^{-1}\frac{2x}{3}$$

$$\therefore \int_0^{\frac{3\sqrt{2}}{4}} \frac{dx}{\sqrt{9 - 4x^2}} = \frac{1}{2}\sin^{-1}\frac{2x}{3}\Big]_0^{\frac{3\sqrt{2}}{4}} = \frac{\pi}{8}$$

7. Let $5\tan u = y \Rightarrow 5\sec^2 u\,du = dy$. $\displaystyle\int \frac{dy}{\sqrt{25 + y^2}} = \int \frac{5\sec^2 u\,du}{\sqrt{25 + 25\tan^2 u}}$

$$= \int \sec u\,du == \ln|\sec u + \tan u| = \ln\left|\frac{\sqrt{25 + y^2}}{5} + \frac{y}{5}\right| + C$$

8. Let $3y = \tan u \Rightarrow 3\,dy = \sec^2 u\,du$

$$\int \frac{3\,dy}{\sqrt{1 + 9y^2}} = \int \frac{\sec^2 u\,du}{\sec u} = \ln|\sec u + \tan u| + C$$

$$= \ln|\sqrt{1 + 9y^2} + 3y| + C$$

9. Let $5\tan u = 3y \Rightarrow 5\sec^2 u\,du = 3\,dy$. $\int \frac{dy}{\sqrt{25+9y^2}} = \int \frac{\frac{5}{3}\sec^2 u\,du}{\sqrt{25+25\tan^2 u}}$

$$= \frac{1}{3}\int \sec u\,du = \frac{1}{3}\ln|\sec u + \tan u| = \frac{1}{3}\ln\left|\frac{\sqrt{25+9y^2}}{5} + \frac{3y}{5}\right| + C$$

(Note: the denominator may be absorbed into the constant)

10. Let $2\sec u = z \Rightarrow 2\sec u\tan u\,du = dz$

$$\int \frac{dz}{\sqrt{z^2-4}} = \int \frac{2\sec u\tan u\,du}{2\tan u} = \ln|\sec u + \tan u| + C$$

$$= \ln|z + \sqrt{z^2-4}| + C$$

11. Let $3z = \sec u \Rightarrow 3\,dz = \sec u\tan u\,du$. Then $\int \frac{3\,dz}{\sqrt{9z^2-1}} = \int \frac{\sec u\tan u\,du}{\sqrt{\sec^2 u - 1}}$

$$= \int \sec u\,du = \ln|\sec u + \tan u| = \ln|3z + \sqrt{9z^2-1}| + C$$

12. Let $3\sec u = 5z \Rightarrow 3\sec u\tan u\,du = 5\,dz$. Then $\int \frac{dz}{\sqrt{25z^2-9}} =$

$$\int \frac{\frac{3}{5}\sec u\tan u\,du}{\sqrt{9\sec^2 u - 9}} = \frac{1}{5}\int \sec u\,du = \frac{1}{5}\ln|\sec u + \tan u| + C$$

$$= \frac{1}{5}\ln|5z + \sqrt{25z^2-9}| + C$$

13. Let $x = 4\sec u \Rightarrow dx = 4\sec u\tan u\,du$. Then $\int_{8/\sqrt{3}}^{8} \frac{dx}{x\sqrt{x^2-16}}$

$$= \int_{\pi/6}^{\pi/3} \frac{4\sec u\tan u\,du}{4\sec u\sqrt{16\sec^2 u - 16}} = \frac{1}{4}\int_{\pi/6}^{\pi/3} du = \frac{1}{4}u\Big]_{\pi/6}^{\pi/3} = \frac{\pi}{24}$$

14. Let $x = \sqrt{3}\sec u \Rightarrow dx = \sqrt{3}\sec u\tan u\,du$; $x = 2 \Rightarrow u = \frac{\pi}{6}$, $x = \sqrt{6} \Rightarrow u = \frac{\pi}{4}$

$$\int_2^{\sqrt{6}} \frac{dx}{x\sqrt{x^2-3}} = \int_{\pi/6}^{\pi/4} \frac{\sqrt{3}\sec u\tan u\,du}{\sqrt{3}\sec u\sqrt{3}\tan u} = \frac{1}{\sqrt{3}}u\Big]_{\pi/6}^{\pi/4} = \frac{\pi}{12\sqrt{3}}$$

15. Let $x=\frac{1}{2}\sec u \Rightarrow dx=\frac{1}{2}\sec u\tan u\,du$. Then $\int_{\frac{\sqrt{2}}{2}}^{1}\frac{dx}{2x\sqrt{4x^2-1}}$

$$=\int_{\frac{\pi}{4}}^{\frac{\pi}{3}}\frac{\frac{1}{2}\sec u\tan u\,du}{\sec u\sqrt{\sec^2 u-1}}=\frac{1}{2}\int_{\frac{\pi}{4}}^{\frac{\pi}{3}}du=\frac{1}{2}u\Big]_{\frac{\pi}{4}}^{\frac{\pi}{3}}=\frac{\pi}{24}$$

16. Let $y=4\sec u \Rightarrow du=4\sec u\tan u\,du$

$$\int\frac{dy}{y^2\sqrt{y^2-16}}=\int\frac{4\sec u\tan u\,du}{16\sec^2 u\,(4\tan u)}=\frac{1}{16}\int\cos u\,du$$

$$=\frac{1}{16}\sin u + C=\frac{\sqrt{y^2-16}}{16y}+C$$

17. Let $x=2\sec w \Rightarrow dx=2\sec w\tan w dx$, $x=4\Rightarrow w=\frac{\pi}{3}$, $x=2\Rightarrow w=0$

$$\int_2^4\sqrt{x^2-4}\,dx=2\int_0^{\frac{\pi}{3}}\sqrt{4\sec^2 w-4}\,\sec w\tan w\,dw=4\int_0^{\frac{\pi}{3}}\tan^2 w\sec w\,dw$$

$$=4\int_0^{\frac{\pi}{3}}(\sec^2 w-1)\sec w\,dw=4\int_0^{\frac{\pi}{3}}(\sec^3 w-\sec w)\,dw$$

$$=4\left(\frac{1}{2}\sec w\tan w+\frac{1}{2}\ln|\sec w+\tan w|-\ln|\sec w+\tan w|\right)\Big]_0^{\frac{\pi}{3}}$$

$$=2\sec w\tan w-2\ln|\sec w+\tan w|\Big]_0^{\frac{\pi}{3}}=4\sqrt{3}-2\ln(2+\sqrt{3})$$

(For integration of $\int\sec^3 w\,dw$, see Sect. 7.3, Ex. 3)

18. Let $x=\cos u \Rightarrow dx=-\sin u\,du$; $x=0\Rightarrow u=\frac{\pi}{2}$, $x=\frac{4}{5}\Rightarrow u=\cos^{-1}\frac{4}{5}$

$$\int_0^{\frac{4}{5}}\frac{x^3\,dx}{\sqrt{1-x^2}}=\int_{\frac{\pi}{2}}^{\cos^{-1}\frac{4}{5}}\frac{\cos^3 u(-\sin u\,du)}{\sin u}=-\int_{\frac{\pi}{2}}^{\cos^{-1}\frac{4}{5}}\cos u(1-\sin^2 u)\,du$$

$$=-\sin u+\frac{1}{3}\sin^3 u\Big]_{\frac{\pi}{2}}^{\cos^{-1}\frac{4}{5}}=\left(-\frac{3}{5}+\frac{1}{3}\left(\frac{3}{5}\right)^3\right)-\left(-\frac{2}{3}\right)=\frac{52}{375}$$

19. Let $x=3\sin u \Rightarrow dx=3\cos u\,du$. Then $\int\frac{dx}{x^2\sqrt{9-x^2}}=$

$$\int\frac{3\cos u\,du}{9\sin^2 u\sqrt{9-9\sin^2 u}}=\frac{1}{9}\int\csc^2 u\,du=-\frac{1}{9}\left(\frac{\sqrt{9-x^2}}{x}\right)+C$$

20. Let $x = \tan u \Rightarrow dx = \sec u \tan u\, du$; $x = 0 \Rightarrow u = 0$, $x = \frac{1}{2} \Rightarrow u = \tan^{-1}\frac{1}{2}$

$$\int_0^{\frac{1}{2}} \frac{dx}{\sqrt{1+x^2}} = \int_0^{\tan^{-1}\frac{1}{2}} \frac{\sec^2 u\, du}{\sec u} = \ln|\sec u + \tan u|\Big]_0^{\tan^{-1}\frac{1}{2}} = \ln\left(\frac{\sqrt{5}+1}{2}\right)$$

21. Let $x = \csc u \Rightarrow dx = -\csc u \cot u\, du$. Then $\int_{\frac{5}{4}}^{\frac{5}{3}} \frac{dx}{x^2\sqrt{x^2-1}} =$

$$\int_{x=\frac{5}{4}}^{x=\frac{5}{3}} \frac{-\csc u \cot u\, du}{\csc^2 u\sqrt{\csc^2 u - 1}} = \int_{x=\frac{5}{4}}^{x=\frac{5}{3}} (-\sin u)\, du = \frac{\sqrt{x^2-1}}{x}\Big]_{\frac{5}{4}}^{\frac{5}{3}} = \frac{1}{5}$$

22. Let $x = \cos^2 u \Rightarrow dx = -2 \cos u \sin u\, du$; $x = \frac{1}{2} \Rightarrow u = \frac{\pi}{4}$, $x = 1 \Rightarrow u = 0$

$$\int_{\frac{1}{2}}^{1} \frac{\sqrt{1-x}}{x} dx = \int_{\frac{\pi}{4}}^{0} \frac{\sin u(-2\cos u \sin u\, du)}{\cos^2 u} = -2\int_{\frac{\pi}{4}}^{0} \frac{(1-\cos^2 u)du}{\cos u}$$

$$= -2\int_{\frac{\pi}{4}}^{0} (\sec u - \cos u)\, du = -2\left[\ln|\sec u + \tan u| - \sin u\right]_{\frac{\pi}{4}}^{0}$$

$$= 2\ln(\sqrt{2}+1) - \sqrt{2}$$

23. Let $x = 5 \sin u \Rightarrow dx = 5 \cos u\, du$, $x = 0 \Rightarrow u = 0$, $x = 5 \Rightarrow u = \frac{\pi}{2}$.

$$\int_0^5 \sqrt{25-x^2}\, dx = \int_0^{\frac{\pi}{2}} \sqrt{25 - 25\sin^2 u} \cdot 5\cos u\, du = 25\int_0^{\frac{\pi}{2}} \cos^2 u\, du$$

$$= 25\int_0^{\frac{\pi}{2}} \left(\frac{1}{2} + \frac{1}{2}\cos 2u\right) du = 25\left(\frac{1}{2}u + \frac{1}{4}\sin 2u\right)\Big]_0^{\frac{\pi}{2}} = \frac{25\pi}{4}$$

24. Let $2x = \sin u \Rightarrow 2\, dx = \cos u\, du$

$$\int \frac{dx}{\sqrt{1-4x^2}} = \frac{1}{2}\int \frac{\cos u\, du}{\cos u} = \frac{1}{2}u + C = \frac{1}{2}\sin^{-1} 2x + C$$

25. Let $x - 1 = 2 \sin u \Rightarrow dx = 2 \cos u\, du$, $x = 2 \Rightarrow u = \frac{\pi}{6}$, $x = 1 \Rightarrow u = 0$.

$$\int_1^2 \frac{dx}{\sqrt{4-(x-1)^2}} = \int_0^{\frac{\pi}{6}} \frac{2\cos u\, du}{\sqrt{4 - 4\sin^2 u}} = \int_0^{\frac{\pi}{6}} du = u\Big]_0^{\frac{\pi}{6}} = \frac{\pi}{6}$$

26. Let $x = 2\tan u \Rightarrow dx = 2\sec^2 u\, du$; $x = 0 \Rightarrow u = 0$, $x = 2 \Rightarrow u = \frac{\pi}{4}$

$$\int_0^2 \frac{dx}{\sqrt{4+x^2}} = \int_0^{\frac{\pi}{4}} \frac{2\sec^2 u\, du}{2\sec u} = \ln|\sec u + \tan u|\Big]_0^{\frac{\pi}{4}} = \ln(\sqrt{2}+1)$$

27. Let $x = 2\sin u \Rightarrow dx = 2\cos u\,du$, $x = 1 \Rightarrow u = \frac{\pi}{6}$, $x = 0 \Rightarrow u = 0$.

$$\int_0^1 \frac{12\,dx}{\sqrt{4 - x^2}} = \int_0^{\frac{\pi}{6}} \frac{24\cos u\,du}{\sqrt{4 - 4\sin^2 u}} = 12\int_0^{\frac{\pi}{6}} du = 12\,u\Big]_0^{\frac{\pi}{6}} = 2\pi$$

28. Let $x = 2\tan u \Rightarrow dx = 2\sec^2 du$; $x = 0 \Rightarrow u = 0$, $x = \frac{3}{2} \Rightarrow u = \tan^{-1}\frac{3}{4}$

$$\int_0^{\frac{3}{2}} \frac{x\,dx}{\sqrt{4 + x^2}} = \int_0^{\tan^{-1}\frac{3}{4}} \frac{2\tan u\,(2\sec^2 u)\,du}{2\sec u} = 2\int_0^{\tan^{-1}\frac{3}{4}} \tan u \sec u\,du$$

$$= 2\,[\sec u\Big]_0^{\tan^{-1}\frac{3}{4}} = 2\left(\frac{5}{4}\right) - 2 = \frac{1}{2}$$

29. Let $x = \tan u \Rightarrow dx = \sec^2 u\,du$, $x = 0 \Rightarrow u = 0$, $x = 1 \Rightarrow u = \frac{\pi}{4}$.

$$\int_0^1 \frac{x^3\,dx}{\sqrt{x^2 + 1}} = \int_0^{\frac{\pi}{4}} \frac{\tan^3 u \sec^2 u\,du}{\sqrt{\tan^2 u + 1}} = \int_0^{\frac{\pi}{4}} \tan^3 u \sec u\,du =$$

$$\frac{1}{3}\sec^3 u - \sec u\Big]_0^{\frac{\pi}{4}} = \frac{2 - \sqrt{3}}{3}$$

30. Let $x = 2\sin u \Rightarrow dx = 2\cos u\,du$. Then $\int \frac{x + 1}{\sqrt{4 - x^2}}\,dx$

$$= \int \frac{(2\sin u + 1)\,2\cos u\,du}{2\cos u} = -2\cos u + u + C = -\sqrt{4 - x^2} + \sin^{-1}\frac{x}{2} + C$$

31. Let $x = \frac{1}{2}\sec u \Rightarrow dx = \frac{1}{2}\sec u \tan u\,du$. Then

$$\int \frac{dx}{x\sqrt{x^2 - \frac{1}{4}}} = \int \frac{\frac{1}{2}\sec u \tan u\,du}{\frac{1}{2}\sec u\sqrt{\frac{1}{4}\sec^2 u - \frac{1}{4}}} = \int 2\,du = 2\sec^{-1} 2x + C$$

32. Let $x = \sqrt{\frac{2}{5}}\sin u \Rightarrow dx = \sqrt{\frac{2}{5}}\cos u\,du$

$$\int \frac{dx}{\sqrt{2 - 5x^2}} = \sqrt{\frac{2}{5}}\int \frac{\cos u\,du}{\sqrt{2}\cos u} = \frac{1}{\sqrt{5}}\int du = \frac{1}{\sqrt{5}}u + C = \frac{1}{\sqrt{5}}\sin^{-1}\sqrt{\frac{5}{2}}\,x + C$$

33. Let $x = \sin u \Rightarrow dx = \cos u\,du$. Then $\int \frac{\sqrt{1 - x^2}}{x^2}\,dx = \int \frac{\sqrt{1 - \sin^2 u}}{\sin^2 u}\cos u\,du$

$$= \int \cot^2 u\,du = -\cot u - u + C = -\frac{\sqrt{1 - x^2}}{x} - \sin^{-1} x + C$$

34. $\int_0^{\frac{1}{2}\ln 3} \frac{e^x\,dx}{1+e^{2x}} = \tan^{-1}(e^x)\Big]_0^{\frac{1}{2}\ln 3} = \tan^{-1}\sqrt{3} - \tan^{-1}1 = \frac{\pi}{12}$

35. $\int_{\frac{3}{4}}^{\frac{4}{5}} \frac{dx}{x^2\sqrt{1-x^2}} = \int_{x=\frac{3}{4}}^{x=\frac{4}{5}} \frac{\cos u\,du}{\sin^2 u\sqrt{1-\sin^2 u}} = \int_{x=\frac{3}{4}}^{x=\frac{4}{5}} \csc^2 u\,du$

$= -\cot u\Big]_{x=\frac{3}{4}}^{x=\frac{4}{5}} = -\frac{\sqrt{1-x^2}}{x}\Big]_{x=\frac{3}{4}}^{x=\frac{4}{5}} = -\left(\frac{3}{4} - \frac{\sqrt{7}}{3}\right)$

36. Let $x = \sin u \Rightarrow dx = \cos u\,du$

$\int \frac{4x^2\,dx}{(1-x^2)^{3/2}} = \int \frac{4\sin^2 u\cos u\,du}{\cos^3 u} = 4\int \tan^2 u\,du = 4\int(\sec^2 u - 1)\,du$

$= 4\tan u - 4u + C = \frac{4x}{\sqrt{1-x^2}} - 4\sin^{-1}x + C$

37. $\int \frac{dx}{(a^2-x^2)^{\frac{3}{2}}} = \int \frac{a\cos u\,du}{\left(\sqrt{a^2 - a^2\sin^2 u}\right)^3} = \frac{1}{a^2}\int \sec^2 u\,du = \frac{1}{a^2}\left(\frac{x}{\sqrt{a^2-x^2}}\right) + C$

38. Let $\cos\theta = \sqrt{2}\cos u \Rightarrow -\sin\theta\,d\theta = -\sqrt{2}\sin u\,du$

$\int \frac{\sin\theta\,d\theta}{\sqrt{2-\cos^2\theta}} = \int \frac{\sqrt{2}\sin u\,du}{\sqrt{2-2\cos^2 u}} = \int du = u + C = \cos^{-1}\left(\frac{1}{\sqrt{2}}\cos\theta\right) + C$

39. (a) Let $u^2 = 16 - y^2 \Rightarrow u\,du = -y\,dy$

$\int \frac{y\,dy}{\sqrt{16-y^2}} = -\int du = -u + C = -\sqrt{16-y^2} + C$

(b) Let $y = 4\sin u \Rightarrow dy = 4\cos u\,du$

$\int \frac{y\,dy}{\sqrt{16-y^2}} = \int \frac{16\sin u\cos u\,du}{\sqrt{16-16\sin^2 u}} = -4\cos u + C = -\sqrt{16-y^2} + C$

40. (a) $\int_0^2 \frac{x\,dx}{4+x^2} = \frac{1}{2}\ln(4+x^2)\Big]_0^2 = \frac{1}{2}(\ln 8 - \ln 4) = \frac{1}{2}\ln 2$

(b) $\int_0^2 \frac{dx}{4+x^2} = \frac{1}{2}\tan^{-1}\frac{x}{2}\Big]_0^2 = \frac{1}{2}\left(\frac{\pi}{4}\right) = \frac{\pi}{8}$

41. (a) Let $x^2 - 1 = u^2 \Rightarrow x\,dx = u\,du$. Then $\int \frac{x}{(x^2-1)^{\frac{3}{2}}}dx =$

$\int u^{-2} + C = -u^{-1} + C = -\frac{1}{\sqrt{x^2-1}} + C$

(b) Let $x = \sec u \Rightarrow dx = \sec u \tan u\, du$. Then $\int \frac{x}{(x^2-1)^{\frac{3}{2}}}dx =$

$$\int \frac{\sec u \cdot \sec u \tan u\, du}{(\sec^2 u - 1)^{\frac{3}{2}}} = \int \frac{\sec^2 u\, du}{\tan^2 u} = -\frac{1}{\tan u} + C = -\frac{1}{\sqrt{x^2-1}} + C$$

42. (a) $\int_0^{\frac{\sqrt{3}}{2}} \frac{x\, dx}{\sqrt{1-x^2}} = -\sqrt{1-x^2}\Big]_0^{\frac{\sqrt{3}}{2}} = \frac{1}{2}$

(b) $\int_0^{\frac{\sqrt{3}}{2}} \frac{dx}{\sqrt{1-x^2}} = \sin^{-1} x\Big]_0^{\frac{\sqrt{3}}{2}} = \frac{\pi}{3}$

43. (a) $\int \frac{du}{u^2+a^2} = \int \frac{a\, dz}{a^2z^2+a^2} = \frac{1}{a}\int \frac{dz}{z^2+1} = \frac{1}{a}\tan^{-1} z + C = \frac{1}{a}\tan^{-1}\frac{u}{a} + C$

(b) $\int \frac{du}{\sqrt{a^2-u^2}} = \int \frac{a\, dz}{\sqrt{a^2-a^2z^2}} = \int \frac{dz}{\sqrt{1-z^2}} = \sin^{-1} z + C = \sin^{-1}\frac{u}{a} + C$

44. If $\theta = \sin^{-1}\frac{u}{2} \Rightarrow \sin\theta = \frac{u}{2}$. Then $\cos\theta = \sqrt{1-\left(\frac{u}{2}\right)^2} = \frac{\sqrt{4-u^2}}{2}$

and $\tan\theta = \frac{u}{\sqrt{4-u^2}}$.

45. (a) $\sin\left(\tan^{-1}\frac{u}{a}\right) = \frac{u}{\sqrt{a^2+u^2}}$ (b) $\cos\left(\sec^{-1}\frac{u}{a}\right) = \frac{a}{u}$

46. $A = \int_0^3 \frac{1}{3}\sqrt{9-x^2}\, dx = \frac{1}{3}\int_0^{\frac{\pi}{2}} (3\cos u)(3\cos u)du$

$$= \frac{3}{2}\int_0^{\frac{\pi}{2}}(1+\cos 2u)\, du = \frac{3}{2}\left[u + \frac{1}{2}\sin 2u\right]_0^{\frac{\pi}{2}} = \frac{3\pi}{4}$$

47. $S = 2\pi y\, ds = 2\pi\int_0^{\pi} \sin t\sqrt{(-2\sin t)^2 + \cos^2 t}\, dt = 2\pi\int_0^{\pi}\sqrt{4-3\cos^2 t}\,\sin t\, dt$

Let $\frac{2}{\sqrt{3}}\sin\theta = \cos t \Rightarrow -\frac{2}{\sqrt{3}}\cos\theta\, d\theta = \sin t\, dt$

$$= 2\pi\int_{\frac{\pi}{3}}^{-\frac{\pi}{3}}\left(-\frac{2}{\sqrt{3}}\cos\theta\right)(2\cos\theta)\, d\theta = -\frac{8\pi}{\sqrt{3}}\int_{\frac{\pi}{3}}^{-\frac{\pi}{3}}\cos^2\theta\, d\theta =$$

$$= -\frac{4\pi}{\sqrt{3}}\int_{\frac{\pi}{3}}^{-\frac{\pi}{3}}(1+\cos 2\theta)\, d\theta = -\frac{4\pi}{\sqrt{3}}\left(\theta + \frac{1}{2}\sin 2\theta\right)\Big]_{\frac{\pi}{3}}^{-\frac{\pi}{3}} = \frac{3\pi^2 + 6\sqrt{3}}{3\sqrt{3}}$$

48. $s = \int_0^{\frac{\sqrt{3}}{2}} \sqrt{1 + 4x^2}\, dx = \int_0^{\frac{\pi}{3}} \sec^3 u\, du$

$= \sec u \tan u + \ln|\sec u + \tan u|\Big]_0^{\frac{\pi}{3}} = 2\sqrt{3} + \ln(2 + \sqrt{3})$

49. $\frac{dy}{dx} = y^2\left(1 - \frac{1}{\sqrt{4 - x^2}}\right) \Rightarrow \frac{dy}{y^2} = dx - \frac{dx}{\sqrt{4 - x^2}} \Rightarrow$

$-\frac{1}{y} = x - \sin^{-1}\frac{x}{2} + C$. $-\frac{\pi}{4} = \sqrt{2} - \sin^{-1}\frac{1}{\sqrt{2}} \Rightarrow C = -\sqrt{2}$. Therefore,

$$y = \frac{-1}{x - \sin^{-1}\frac{x}{2} - \sqrt{2}}$$

50. $y = \sqrt{x^2 + 2} \Rightarrow \frac{dy}{dx} = \frac{x}{\sqrt{x^2 + 2}}$; $ds = \sqrt{1 + \frac{x^2}{x^2 + 2}}\, dx = \sqrt{\frac{2x^2 + 2}{x^2 + 2}}\, dx$

$$S = 2\pi \int y\, ds = 2\pi \int_{-1}^{1} \sqrt{x^2 + 2}\sqrt{\frac{2x^2 + 2}{x^2 + 2}}\, dx = 2\sqrt{2}\,\pi \int_{-1}^{1} \sqrt{x^2 + 1}\, dx$$

$$= 2\sqrt{2}\,\pi \int_{-\frac{\pi}{4}}^{\frac{\pi}{4}} \sec^3 u\, du = \sqrt{2}\pi\,[\sec u \tan u + \ln|\sec u + \tan u|\Big]_{-\frac{\pi}{4}}^{\frac{\pi}{4}}$$

$$= \sqrt{2}\pi\,[(\sqrt{2} + \ln|\sqrt{2} + 1|) - (-\sqrt{2} + \ln|\sqrt{2} - 1)] = \sqrt{2}\pi\left(2\sqrt{2} + \ln\frac{\sqrt{2} + 1}{\sqrt{2} - 1}\right)$$

51. $M_x = \delta \int y\, ds = \int_0^{\ln\sqrt{3}} e^x \sqrt{1 + e^{2x}}\, dx = \int_{\frac{\pi}{4}}^{\frac{\pi}{3}} \sqrt{1 + \tan^2 u}\, \sec^2 u\, du$

$$= \int_{\frac{\pi}{4}}^{\frac{\pi}{3}} \sec^3 u\, du = \frac{1}{2}\sec u \tan u + \frac{1}{2}\ln|\sec u + \tan u|\Big]_{\frac{\pi}{4}}^{\frac{\pi}{3}}$$

$$= \frac{1}{2}\left(2\sqrt{3} - \sqrt{2} + \ln\frac{2 + \sqrt{3}}{1 + \sqrt{2}}\right)$$

7.6 INTEGRALS INVOLVING $ax^2 + bx + c$

1. $\int_1^3 \frac{dx}{x^2 - 2x + 5} = \int_1^3 \frac{dx}{(x - 1)^2 + 4} = \frac{1}{2}\tan^{-1}\left(\frac{x - 1}{2}\right)\Big]_1^3 = \frac{\pi}{8}$

2. Let $2\tan u = x - 1 \Rightarrow 2\sec^2 u\, du = dx$.

$$\int \frac{dx}{\sqrt{x^2 - 2x + 5}} = \int \frac{dx}{\sqrt{(x-1)^2 + 4}} = \int \frac{2\sec^2 u\, du}{2\sec u} = \ln|\sec u + \tan u| + C$$

$$= \ln|\sqrt{x^2 - 2x + 5} + (x-1)| + C$$

3. $$\int_1^3 \frac{x\,dx}{x^2 - 2x + 5} = \int_1^3 \frac{x\,dx}{(x-1)^2 + 4} = \int_1^3 \frac{(x-1)\,dx}{(x-1)^2 + 4} + \int_1^3 \frac{dx}{(x-1)^2 + 4} =$$

$$\frac{1}{2}\ln|(x-1)^2 + 4| + \frac{1}{2}\tan^{-1}\frac{x-1}{2}\Big]_1^3 = \frac{\pi}{8} - \ln\frac{\sqrt{2}}{2}$$

4. Let $2\tan u = x - 1 \Rightarrow 2\sec^2 u\, du = dx$.

$$\int \frac{x\,dx}{\sqrt{x^2 - 2x + 5}} = \int (2\tan u + 1)\sec u\, du = 2\sec u + \ln|\sec u + \tan u| + C$$

$$= \sqrt{x^2 - 2x + 5} + \ln|\sqrt{x^2 - 2x + 5} + x - 1| + C$$

$$\therefore \int_1^{\frac{5}{2}} \frac{x\,dx}{\sqrt{x^2 - 2x + 5}} = \frac{1}{2} + \ln 2$$

5. $$\int_1^2 \frac{dx}{x^2 - 2x + 4} = \int_1^2 \frac{dx}{(x-1)^2 + 3} = \frac{1}{\sqrt{3}}\tan^{-1}\frac{x-1}{\sqrt{3}}\Big]_1^2 = \frac{\pi}{6\sqrt{3}}$$

6. Let $2\tan u = 3x - 1 \Rightarrow 2\sec^2 u = 3\,dx$

$$\int \frac{3\,dx}{9x^2 - 6x + 5} = \int \frac{2\sec^2 u\, du}{4\sec^2 u} = \frac{1}{2}\int du = \frac{1}{2}\tan^{-1}\left(\frac{3x-1}{2}\right) + C$$

7. $$\int \frac{dx}{\sqrt{9x^2 - 6x + 5}} = \int \frac{dx}{\sqrt{(3x-1)^2 + 4}} = \int \frac{\frac{2}{3}\sec^2 u\, du}{\sqrt{4\tan^2 u + 4}} = \int \frac{1}{3}\sec u\, du$$

Let $3x - 1 = 2\tan u \Rightarrow dx = \frac{2}{3}\sec^2 u\, du$

$$= \frac{1}{3}\ln|\sec u + \tan u| + C = \frac{1}{3}\ln\left|\frac{\sqrt{9x^2 - 6x + 5}}{2} + \frac{3x-1}{2}\right| + C$$

8. Let $2\tan u = 3x - 1 \Rightarrow 2\sec^2 u = 3\,dx$

$$\int \frac{3x\,dx}{9x^2 - 6x + 5} = \int \frac{2\tan u + 1 \cdot \frac{2}{3}\sec^2 u\, du}{4\tan^2 u + 4} = \frac{1}{6}\int (2\tan u + 1)\, du$$

$$= \frac{1}{6}u + \frac{1}{3}\ln|\sec u| + C = \frac{1}{6}\tan^{-1}\left(\frac{3x-1}{2}\right) + \frac{1}{3}\ln\frac{\sqrt{9x^2 - 6x + 5}}{2} + C$$

9. $$\int \frac{x\,dx}{\sqrt{9x^2 - 6x + 5}} = \int \frac{x dx}{\sqrt{(3x-1)^2 + 4}} = \frac{1}{3}\int \frac{3(x-1+1)\,dx}{\sqrt{(3x-1)^2+4}} =$$

$$\frac{1}{3}\int \frac{(3x-1)\,dx}{\sqrt{(3x-1)^2+4}} + \frac{1}{3}\int \frac{dx}{\sqrt{(3x-1)^2+4}} =$$

$$\frac{1}{9}\sqrt{(3x-1)^2+4} + \frac{1}{9}\ln\left|\frac{\sqrt{(3x-1)^2+4}}{2} + \frac{3x-1}{2}\right| + C$$

10. Let $\sec u = x - 1 \Rightarrow \sec u \tan u\,du = dx$

$$\int \frac{dx}{\sqrt{x^2 - 2x}} = \int \frac{dx}{\sqrt{(x-1)^2 - 1}} = \int \frac{\sec u \tan u\,du}{\tan u}$$

$$\ln|\sec u + \tan u| + C = \ln\left|(x-1) + \sqrt{x^2 - 2x}\right| + C$$

11. $$\int \frac{dx}{\sqrt{x^2 + 2x}} = \int \frac{dx}{\sqrt{(x+1)^2 - 1}} = \int \frac{\sec u \tan u\,du}{\sqrt{\sec^2 u - 1}} =$$

$$\ln|\sec u + \tan u| = \ln|x + 1 + \sqrt{x^2 + 2x}| + C$$

12. Let $3\tan u = x + 2 \Rightarrow 3\sec^2 u\,du = dx$

$$\int \frac{dx}{\sqrt{x^2 + 4x + 13}} = \int \frac{dx}{\sqrt{(x+2)^2 + 9}} = \int \frac{3\sec^2 u\,du}{3\sec u} = \ln|\sec u + \tan u| + C$$

$$\therefore \int_{-2}^{1} \frac{dx}{\sqrt{x^2 + 4x + 13}} = \ln\left|\frac{x+2}{3} + \frac{\sqrt{x^2 + 4x + 13}}{3}\right|\Bigg]_{-2}^{1} = \ln(1 + \sqrt{2})$$

13. $$\int_{-2}^{2} \frac{x\,dx}{\sqrt{x^2 + 4x + 13}} = \int_{-2}^{2} \frac{x\,dx}{\sqrt{(x+2)^2 + 9}} = \int_{-2}^{2} \frac{(x+2)\,dx}{\sqrt{(x+2)^2 + 9}} - \int_{-2}^{2} \frac{2\,dx}{\sqrt{(x+2)^2 + 9}}$$

$$= \sqrt{(x+2)^2 + 9} - 2\ln\left|\sqrt{(x+2)^2 + 9}\right|\Bigg]_{-2}^{2} = 2 - \ln 9$$

14. Let $2\sin u = x + 1 \Rightarrow 2\cos u\,du = dx$

$$\int_{-1}^{0} \frac{dx}{\sqrt{3 - 2x - x^2}} = \int_{-1}^{0} \frac{dx}{\sqrt{4 - (x+1)^2}} = \int_{0}^{\frac{\pi}{6}} \frac{2\cos u\,du}{2\cos u} = u\Bigg]_{0}^{\frac{\pi}{6}} = \frac{\pi}{6}$$

15. $$\int \frac{dx}{\sqrt{x^2 + 4x + 13}} = \int \frac{dx}{\sqrt{(x-1)^2 - 4}} = \ln\left|x - 1 + \sqrt{(x-1)^2 - 4}\right| + C$$

16. Let $\sec u = x + 1 \Rightarrow \sec u \tan u \, du = dx$

$$\int \frac{dx}{(x+1)\sqrt{x^2+2x}} = \int \frac{dx}{(x+1)\sqrt{(x+1)^2-1}}$$

$$= \int \frac{\sec u \tan u \, du}{\sec u \tan u} = u + C = \sec^{-1} |x+1| + C$$

17. $$\int \frac{(x+1)\,dx}{\sqrt{2x-x^2}} = \int \frac{(x+1)^2\,dx}{\sqrt{1-(x-1)^2}} = -\sqrt{2x-x^2} + 2\sin^{-1}(x-1) + C$$

18. Let $\sec u = x - 2 \Rightarrow \sec u \tan u \, du = dx$

$$\int \frac{(x-1)\,dx}{\sqrt{x^2-4x+3}} = \int \frac{(x-1)\,dx}{\sqrt{(x-2)^2-1}} = \int \frac{(\sec u + 1)\sec u \tan u \, du}{\tan u}$$

$$= \tan u + \ln|\sec u + \tan u| + C = \sqrt{x^2-4x+3} + \ln|x-2+\sqrt{x^2-4x+3}\,| + C$$

19. $$\int \frac{x\,dx}{\sqrt{5+4x-x^2}} = \int \frac{x\,dx}{\sqrt{9-(x-2)^2}} = \int \frac{(x-2)\,dx}{\sqrt{9-(x-2)^2}} + \int \frac{2\,dx}{\sqrt{9-(x-2)^2}} =$$

$$-\sqrt{9-(x-2)^2} + 2\sin^{-1}\frac{x-2}{3} + C$$

20. Let $3\sec u = x - 1 \Rightarrow 3\sec u \tan u \, du = dx$

$$\int_5^6 \frac{dx}{\sqrt{x^2-2x-8}} = \int_5^6 \frac{dx}{\sqrt{(x-1)^2-9}} = \int_{x=5}^{x=6} \frac{3\sec u \tan u \, du}{3\tan u}$$

$$= \ln|\sec u + \tan u| = \ln\left|\frac{x-1}{3} + \frac{\sqrt{x^2-2x-8}}{3}\right|\Bigg]_5^6 = \ln\left(\frac{9}{4+\sqrt{7}}\right) = \ln(4-\sqrt{7})$$

21. $$\int_0^1 \frac{(1-x)\,dx}{\sqrt{8+2x-x^2}} = \int_0^1 \frac{(1-x)\,dx}{\sqrt{9-(1-x)^2}} = \sqrt{9-(1-x)^2}\Bigg]_0^1 = 3 - 2\sqrt{2}$$

22. Let $\tan u = x + 2 \Rightarrow \sec^2 u \, du = dx$

$$\int \frac{x\,dx}{\sqrt{x^2+4x+5}} = \int \frac{x\,dx}{\sqrt{(x+2)^2+1}} = \int \frac{(\tan u - 2)\sec^2 u \, du}{\sec u}$$

$$= \sec u - 2\ln|\sec u + \tan u| + C$$

$$= \sqrt{x^2+4x+5} - 2\ln|\sqrt{x^2+4x+5} + x + 2| + C$$

23. $$\int_{-2}^{-1} \frac{x\,dx}{x^2+4x+5} = \int_{-2}^{-1} \frac{x\,dx}{(x+2)^2+1} = \int_0^{\frac{\pi}{4}} \frac{(\tan u - 2)\sec^2 u \, du}{\sec^2 u} =$$

$$-\ln|\cos u| - 2u\Bigg]_0^{\frac{\pi}{4}} = \ln\sqrt{2} - \frac{\pi}{2}$$

24. Let $2\tan u = 2x+1 \Rightarrow 2\sec^2 u\, du = 2\, dx$

$$\int \frac{(2x+3)\,dx}{4x^2+4x+5} = \int \frac{(2x+3)\,dx}{(2x+1)^2+4} = \int \frac{(2\tan u+2)\sec^2 u\, du}{4\sec^2 u}$$

$$= \frac{1}{2}\int (\tan u + 1)\,du = \frac{1}{2}\ln|\sec u| + \frac{1}{2}u + C$$

$$= \frac{1}{4}\ln|4x^2+4x+5| + \frac{1}{2}\tan^{-1}\left(\frac{2x+1}{2}\right) + C$$

25. $$V = \pi\int_{-2}^{11}\left(\frac{20}{\sqrt{x^2-2x+17}}\right)^2 dx = 400\pi\int_{-2}^{11}\frac{dx}{(x-1)^2+16} =$$

$$100\pi\tan^{-1}\left(\frac{x-1}{4}\right)\Big]_{-2}^{11} = 100\pi\left[\tan^{-1}\frac{5}{2} - \tan^{-1}\left(-\frac{3}{4}\right)\right] \approx 183.3\pi$$

26. Let $2\tan u = x-2 \Rightarrow 2\sec^2 u\, du = dx$; $x = 2 \Rightarrow u = 0$, $x = 4 \Rightarrow u = \frac{\pi}{4}$

$$y_{ave} = \frac{1}{2}\int_2^4 \frac{4\,dx}{x^2-4x+8} = \frac{1}{2}\int_2^4 \frac{4\,dx}{(x-2)^2+4} = 2\int_0^{\frac{\pi}{4}} \frac{2\sec^2 u\, du}{4\sec^2 u} = u\Big]_0^{\frac{\pi}{4}} = \frac{\pi}{4}$$

27. $$S = 2\pi\int_{-1}^{0}\sqrt{x^2+2x+3}\sqrt{\frac{2x^2+4x+4}{x^2+2x+3}}\,dx = 2\sqrt{2}\,\pi\int_{-1}^{0}\sqrt{(x+1)^2+1}\,dx$$

$$= 2\sqrt{2}\,\pi\int_1^{\frac{\pi}{4}} \sec^3 u\, du = 2\pi + \sqrt{2}\,\pi\ln(\sqrt{2}+1)$$

28. (a) Let $\tan u = x-2 \Rightarrow \sec^2 u\, du = dx$; $x = 0 \Rightarrow u = \tan^{-1}(-2)$, $x = 1 \Rightarrow u = -\frac{\pi}{4}$

$$A = \int_0^1 \frac{2}{x^2-4x+5}\,dx = \int_0^1 \frac{2\,dx}{(x-2)^2+1} = \int_{\tan^{-1}(-2)}^{-\frac{\pi}{4}} \frac{2\sec^2 u\, du}{\sec^2 u}$$

$$= 2u\Big]_{\tan^{-1}(-2)}^{-\frac{\pi}{4}} = -\frac{\pi}{2} - 2u\tan^{-1}(-2) = 2\tan^{-1}2 - \frac{\pi}{2} \approx 0.644$$

(b) Let $\tan u = x-2 \Rightarrow \sec^2 u\, du = dx$; $x = 0 \Rightarrow u = \tan^{-1}(-2)$, $x = 1 \Rightarrow u = -\frac{\pi}{4}$

$$M_y = \int_0^1 \frac{2x\,dx}{x^2-4x+5}\,dx = \int_0^1 \frac{2x\,dx}{(x-2)^2+1} = \int_{\tan^{-1}(-2)}^{-\frac{\pi}{4}} \frac{2\sec^2 u(\tan u+2)\,du}{\sec^2 u}$$

$$= 2\ln|\sec u| + 4u\Big]_{\tan^{-1}(-2)}^{-\frac{\pi}{4}} = \ln\frac{2}{5} - \pi + 4\tan^{-1}2 \approx 0.3707$$

29. $A = \int_1^5 \frac{2}{\sqrt{x^2 - 2x + 10}}\,dx = \int_1^5 \frac{2\,dx}{\sqrt{(x-1)^2 + 9}} = \ln 9$

$\bar{x} = \frac{1}{\ln 9}\int_1^5 \frac{2x\,dx}{\sqrt{(x-1)^2+9}} = \frac{4 + 2\ln 3}{\ln 9}$

$\bar{y} = \frac{1}{\ln 9}\int_1^5 \frac{2\,dx}{\left(\sqrt{(x-1)^2+9}\right)^2} = \frac{2}{\ln 9}\int_1^5 \frac{dx}{(x-1)^2+9} = \frac{2}{3\ln 9}\tan^{-1}\frac{4}{3}$

30. $\lim_{a\to 1^+}\int_a^3 \frac{dx}{(x+1)\sqrt{x^2+2x-3}} = \lim_{b\to 0^+}\int_b^{\frac{\pi}{3}} \frac{2\sec u\tan u\,du}{4\sec u\tan u} = \lim_{b\to 0^+}\frac{1}{2}u\Big]_0^{\frac{\pi}{3}} = \frac{\pi}{6}$

31. $\lim_{a\to -5^+}\int_a^{-4} \frac{dx}{\sqrt{-x^2-8x-15}} = \lim_{a\to -5^+}\int_a^{-4}\frac{dx}{\sqrt{1-(x+4)^2}} = \lim_{a\to -5^+}\sin^{-1}(x+4)\,\Big]_a^{-4} = \frac{\pi}{2}$

7.7 THE INTEGRATION OF RATIONAL FUNCTIONS

1. $\frac{5x-13}{(x-3)(x-2)} = \frac{A}{x-3} + \frac{B}{x-2} = \frac{A(x-2)+B(x-3)}{(x-3)(x-2)} \Rightarrow$

$5x - 13 = A(x-2) + B(x-3)$. Let $x = 2 \Rightarrow -3 = -B \Rightarrow B = 3$.

Let $x = 3 \Rightarrow 2 = A$. $\therefore \frac{5x-13}{(x-3)(x-2)} = \frac{2}{x-3} + \frac{3}{x-2}$

2. $\frac{5x-7}{(x-2)(x-1)} = \frac{A}{x-2} + \frac{B}{x-1} = \frac{A(x-1)+B(x-2)}{(x-2)(x-1)} \Rightarrow$

$5x - 7 = A(x-1) + B(x-2)$. Let $x = 1 \Rightarrow -B = -2 \Rightarrow B = 2$.

Let $x = 2 \Rightarrow A = 3$. $\therefore \frac{5x-7}{(x-2)(x-1)} = \frac{3}{x-2} + \frac{2}{x-1}$

3. $\frac{x+4}{(x+1)^2} = \frac{A}{x+1} + \frac{B}{(x+1)^2} \Rightarrow x + 4 = A(x+1) + B$. $x = -1 \Rightarrow B = 3$.

Differentiating both sides $\Rightarrow A = 1$. $\therefore \frac{x+4}{(x+1)^2} = \frac{1}{x+1} + \frac{3}{(x+1)^2}$

4. $\dfrac{2(x+1)}{(x-1)^2} = \dfrac{A}{x-1} + \dfrac{B}{(x-1)^2} = \dfrac{A(x-1)+B}{(x-1)^2} \Rightarrow$

$A(x-1) + B = 2(x+1)$. $Ax = 2x \Rightarrow A = 2$. Let $x = 1 \Rightarrow B = 4$.

$$\therefore \frac{2(x+1)}{(x-1)^2} = \frac{2}{x-1} + \frac{4}{(x-1)^2}$$

5. $\dfrac{x+1}{x^2(x-1)} = \dfrac{A}{x} + \dfrac{B}{x^2} + \dfrac{C}{x-1} \Rightarrow x+1 = Ax(x-1) + B(x-1) + Cx^2$

$x = 0 \Rightarrow B = -1$. $x = 1 \Rightarrow C = 2$. If we let $x = 0$, then $A = -2$.

$$\therefore \frac{x+1}{x^2(x-1)} = -\frac{2}{x} - \frac{1}{x^2} + \frac{2}{x-1}$$

6. $\dfrac{z}{z^3 - z^2 - 6z} = \dfrac{1}{(z-3)(z+2)} = \dfrac{A}{z-3} + \dfrac{B}{z+2} = \dfrac{A(z+2)+B(z-3)}{(z-3)(z+2)} \Rightarrow$

$1 = A(z+2) + B(z-3)$. Let $z = -2 \Rightarrow -5B = 1$ or $B = -\dfrac{1}{5}$.

Let $z = 3 \Rightarrow 5A = 1$ or $A = \dfrac{1}{5}$. $\therefore \dfrac{z}{z^3 - z^2 - 6z} = \dfrac{1}{5(z-3)} - \dfrac{1}{5(z+2)}$

7. By long division, $\dfrac{x^2+8}{x^2-5x+6} = 1 + \dfrac{5x+2}{x^2-5x+6}$. Then

$\dfrac{5x+2}{x^2-5x+6} = \dfrac{A}{x-2} + \dfrac{B}{x-3} \Rightarrow 5x+2 = A(x-3) + B(x-2)$. If $x = 3$, $B = 17$

and if $x = 2$, $A = -12$. $\therefore \dfrac{x^2+8}{x^2-5x+6} = 1 + \dfrac{17}{x-3} - \dfrac{12}{x-2}$

8. $\dfrac{4}{x(x^2+4)} = \dfrac{A}{x} + \dfrac{Bx+C}{x^2+4} \Rightarrow 4 = A(x^2+4) + x(Bx+C)$. Then

$(A+B)x^2 + Cx + 4A = 4 \Rightarrow 4A = 4$ or $A = 1$, $C = 0$,

$A + B = 0 \Rightarrow B = -1$. $\therefore \dfrac{4}{x(x^2+4)} = \dfrac{1}{x} - \dfrac{x}{x^2+4}$

9. $\dfrac{3}{x^2(x^2+9)} = \dfrac{A}{x} + \dfrac{B}{x^2} + \dfrac{Cx+D}{x^2+9} \Rightarrow Ax(x^2+9) + B(x^2+9) + (Cx+D)x^2 = 3$

If $x = 0$, then $B = \dfrac{1}{3}$. Equating coefficients, we have

$(A+C)x^3 + (B+D)x^2 + 9Ax + 9B = 3$. $9A = 0 \Rightarrow A = 0$. $A + C = 0 \Rightarrow C = 0$.

$B + D = 0 \Rightarrow D = -\dfrac{1}{3}$. $\therefore \dfrac{3}{x^2(x^2+9)} = \dfrac{1}{3x^2} - \dfrac{1}{3(x^2+9)}$.

10. $\dfrac{x^3-1}{(x^2+x+1)^2} = \dfrac{(x-1)(x^2+x+1)}{(x^2+x+1)^2} = \dfrac{x-1}{x^2+x+1}$

11. $\displaystyle\int_0^{\frac{1}{2}} \frac{dx}{1-x^2} = \int_0^{\frac{1}{2}} \frac{\frac{1}{2}\,dx}{1-x} + \int_0^{\frac{1}{2}} \frac{\frac{1}{2}\,dx}{1+x} = -\frac{1}{2}\ln|1-x| + \frac{1}{2}\ln|1+x|\Big]_0^{\frac{1}{2}} = \ln\sqrt{3}$

12. $\displaystyle\int_1^2 \frac{dx}{x(x+2)} = \frac{1}{2}\int_1^2 \frac{dx}{x} - \frac{1}{2}\int_1^2 \frac{dx}{x+2} = \frac{1}{2}\ln|x| - \frac{1}{2}\ln|x+2|\Big]_1^2 = \frac{1}{2}\ln\frac{3}{2}$

13. $\displaystyle\int_0^{2\sqrt{2}} \frac{x^3}{x^2+1}\,dx = \int_0^{2\sqrt{2}} \left(x - \frac{x}{x^2+1}\right)dx = \frac{x^2}{2} - \frac{1}{2}\ln(x^2+1)\Big]_0^{2\sqrt{2}} = 4 - \ln 3$

14. $\displaystyle\int_1^2 \frac{dx}{x(x^2+1)} = \int_1^2 \frac{dx}{x} - \int_1^2 \frac{x\,dx}{x^2+1} = \ln|x| - \frac{1}{2}\ln|x^2+1|\Big]_1^2 = \frac{3}{2}\ln 2 - \frac{1}{2}\ln 5$

15. $\displaystyle\int_{\frac{1}{4}}^{\frac{3}{4}} \frac{dx}{x(1-x)} = \int_{\frac{1}{4}}^{\frac{3}{4}} \left(\frac{1}{x} + \frac{1}{1-x}\right)dx = \ln x - \ln|1-x|\Big]_{\frac{1}{4}}^{\frac{3}{4}} = 2\ln 3$

16. $\displaystyle\int_{-1}^0 \frac{x\,dx}{(x-2)(x-1)} = \int_{-1}^0 \frac{2\,dx}{x-2} - \int_{-1}^0 \frac{dx}{x-1}$

$\displaystyle = 2\ln|x-2| - \ln|x-1|\Big]_{-1}^0 = 3\ln 2 - 2\ln 3$

17. $\displaystyle\int \frac{(x+4)\,dx}{(x+6)(x-1)} = \frac{2}{7}\int \frac{dx}{x+6} + \frac{5}{7}\int \frac{dx}{x-1} = \frac{2}{7}\ln|x+6| + \frac{5}{7}\ln|x-1| + C$

18. $\displaystyle\int \frac{2x+1}{(x-4)(x-3)}dx = \int \frac{9\,dx}{x-4} - \int \frac{7\,dx}{x-3} = 9\ln|x-4| - 7\ln|x-3| + C$

19. $\displaystyle\int_0^1 \frac{3x^2\,dx}{x^2+2x+1} = \int_0^1 \left(3 + \frac{-6x+3}{(x+1)^2}\right)dx = \int_0^1 \left(3 - \frac{6}{x+1} + \frac{9}{(x+1)^2}\right)dx =$

$\displaystyle 3x - 6\ln|x+1| - \frac{3}{x+1}\Big]_0^1 = \frac{9}{2} - 6\ln 2$

20. $\displaystyle\int \frac{d\theta}{\theta(\theta^2+\theta-2)} = \int \frac{d\theta}{\theta(\theta+2)(\theta-1)} = -\frac{1}{2}\int \frac{d\theta}{\theta} + \frac{1}{6}\int \frac{d\theta}{\theta+2} + \frac{1}{3}\int \frac{d\theta}{\theta-1}$

$\displaystyle = -\frac{1}{2}\ln|\theta| + \frac{1}{6}\ln|\theta+2| + \frac{1}{3}\ln|\theta-1| + C$

21. $\displaystyle\int \frac{x\,dx}{(x+5)(x-1)} = \frac{5}{6}\int \frac{dx}{x+5} + \frac{1}{6}\int \frac{dx}{x-1} = \frac{5}{6}\ln|x+5| + \frac{1}{6}\ln|x-1| + C$

22. $\displaystyle\int_4^8 \frac{x\,dx}{(x-3)(x+1)} = \frac{3}{4}\int_4^8 \frac{dx}{x-3} + \frac{1}{4}\int_4^8 \frac{dx}{x+1} = \frac{3}{4}\ln|x-3| + \frac{1}{4}\ln|x+1|\Big]_4^8 = \ln\sqrt{15}$

23. $\displaystyle\int \frac{(x+1)dx}{(x+5)(x-1)} = \frac{2}{3}\int \frac{dx}{x+5} + \frac{1}{3}\int \frac{dx}{x-1} = \frac{2}{3}\ln|x+5| + \frac{1}{3}\ln|x-1| + C$

24. $$\int \frac{x^3\,dx}{x^2+2x+1} = \int\left(x-2+\frac{3x+2}{(x+1)^2}\right)dx = \int\left(x-2+\frac{3}{x+1}-\frac{1}{(x+1)^2}\right)dx$$

$$= \frac{x^2}{2} - 2x + 3\ln|x+1| + \frac{1}{x+1} + C$$

25. $$\int_1^3 \frac{dx}{x(x+1)^2} = \int_1^3\left(\frac{1}{x}-\frac{1}{x+1}-\frac{1}{(x+1)^2}\right)dx = \ln x - \ln|x+1| + \frac{1}{x+1}\Big]_1^3 = \ln\frac{3}{2}-\frac{1}{4}$$

26. $$\int_0^1 \frac{dx}{(x+1)(x^2+1)} = \frac{1}{2}\int_0^1\frac{dx}{x+1} - \frac{1}{2}\int\frac{x\,dx}{x^2+1} + \frac{1}{2}\int\frac{dx}{x^2+1} =$$

$$\frac{1}{2}\ln|x+1| - \frac{1}{4}\ln(x^2+1) + \frac{1}{2}\tan^{-1}x\Big]_0^1 = \frac{1}{4}\ln 2 + \frac{\pi}{8}$$

27. $$\int\frac{(x+3)\,dx}{2x(x-2)(x+2)} = -\frac{3}{4}\int\frac{dx}{2x} + \frac{5}{16}\int\frac{dx}{x-2} + \frac{1}{16}\int\frac{dx}{x+2} =$$

$$-\frac{3}{8}\ln|x| + \frac{5}{16}\ln|x-2| + \frac{1}{16}\ln|x+2| + C$$

28. $$\int\frac{\cos x\,dx}{(\sin x+3)(\sin x-2)} = \int\frac{dz}{(z+3)(z-2)}$$

Let $z = \sin x \Rightarrow dz = \cos x\,dx$

$$= -\frac{1}{5}\int\frac{dz}{z+3} + \frac{1}{5}\int\frac{dz}{z-2} = -\frac{1}{5}\ln|\sin x-2| + \frac{1}{5}\ln|\sin x+3| + C$$

29. $$\int_0^{\sqrt{3}}\frac{5x^2}{x^2+1} = \int_0^{\sqrt{3}}\left(5-\frac{5}{x^2+1}\right)dx = 5x + 5\tan^{-1}x\Big]_0^{\sqrt{3}} = 5\sqrt{3}-\frac{5\pi}{3}$$

30. $$\int_2^6\frac{x^3\,dx}{(x-1)^2} = \int_2^6\left(x+2+\frac{3x-2}{(x-1)^2}\right)dx = \int_2^6\left(x+2+\frac{3}{x-1}+\frac{1}{(x-1)^2}\right)dx$$

$$= \frac{1}{2}x^2 + 2x + 3\ln|x-1| - \frac{1}{x-1}\Big]_2^6 = \frac{124}{5} + 3\ln 5$$

31. $$\int_{-1}^1\frac{x^3+x}{x^2+1}\,dx = \int_{-1}^1 x\,dx = 0$$

32. $$\int_{\frac{\pi}{3}}^{\frac{\pi}{2}}\frac{\sin\theta\,d\theta}{\cos^2\theta+\cos\theta-2} = \int_{\frac{1}{2}}^0\frac{-dy}{y^2+y-2} = \int_0^{\frac{1}{2}}\frac{dy}{(y+2)(y-1)}$$

Let $y = \cos\theta \Rightarrow dy = -\sin\theta\,d\theta$

$$= \frac{1}{3}\int_0^{\frac{1}{2}}\left(\frac{1}{y-1}-\frac{1}{y+2}\right)dy = \frac{1}{3}(\ln|y-1| - \ln|y+2|\Big]_0^{\frac{1}{2}} = \frac{1}{3}\ln\frac{2}{5}$$

33. $$\int\frac{3x^2+x+4}{x(x^2+1)}dx = \int\left(\frac{4}{x}+\frac{-x+1}{x^2+1}\right)dx = 4\ln|x| - \frac{1}{2}\ln(x^2+1) + \tan^{-1}x + C$$

34. $$\int\frac{dx}{(x-1)^2(x+1)^2} = \frac{1}{4}\int\left(\frac{-1}{x-1}+\frac{1}{(x-1)^2}+\frac{1}{x+1}+\frac{1}{(x+1)^2}\right)dx$$

$$= -\frac{1}{4}\ln|x-1| - \frac{1}{4(x-1)} + \frac{1}{4}\ln|x+1| - \frac{1}{4(x+1)} + C$$

35. $\displaystyle\int \frac{x^3+4x^2}{x^2+4x+3}dx = \int\left(x - \frac{3x}{x^2+4x+3}\right)dx = \int\left(x + \frac{3}{2(x+1)} - \frac{9}{2(x+3)}\right)dx$

$\displaystyle\frac{x^2}{2} + \frac{3}{2}\ln|x+1| - \frac{9}{2}\ln|x+3| + C$

36. $\displaystyle\int \frac{4x+4}{x^2(x^2+2)}\,dx = 2\int\left(\frac{1}{x} + \frac{1}{x^2} + \frac{-x+1}{x^2+2}\right)dx =$

$\displaystyle 2\int\left(\frac{1}{x} + \frac{1}{x^2} - \frac{x}{x^2+2} + \frac{1}{x^2+2}\right)dx = 2\ln|x| - \frac{2}{x} - \ln(x^2+2) - \sqrt{2}\tan^{-1}\frac{x}{\sqrt{2}} + C$

37. $\displaystyle\int_0^1 \frac{x^2+2x+1}{(x^2+1)^2}\,dx \int_0^1\left(\frac{1}{x^2+1} + \frac{2x}{(x^2+1)^2}\right)dx = \tan^{-1}x - \frac{1}{x^2+1}\Big]_0^1 = \frac{\pi}{4} + \frac{1}{2}$

38. $\displaystyle\int_{-1}^0 \frac{x^3-x}{(x^2+1)(x-1)^2}\,dx = \int_{-1}^0\left(\frac{1}{x-1} + \frac{1}{x^2+1}\right)dx = \ln|x-1| + \tan^{-1}x\Big]_{-1}^0 = -\ln 2 + \frac{\pi}{4}$

$$\frac{x^3-x}{(x^2+1)(x-1)^2} = \frac{A}{x-1} + \frac{B}{(x-1)^2} + \frac{Cx+D}{x^2+1}$$

$x^3 - x = (A+C)x^3 + (-A+B-2C+D)x^2 + (A+C-2D)x + (-A+B+D)$

$A = 1,\ B = 0,\ C = 0,\ D = 1$

39. $\displaystyle\int_{-1}^0 \frac{2x\,dx}{(x^2+1)(x-1)^2} = \int_{-1}^0\left(\frac{-1}{x^2+1} + \frac{1}{(x-1)^2}\right)dx = -\tan^{-1}x - \frac{1}{x-1}\Big]_{-1}^0 = \frac{1}{2} - \frac{\pi}{4}$

40. $\displaystyle\int \frac{x^2\,dx}{(x-1)(x+1)^2} = \frac{1}{4}\int\frac{dx}{x-1} + \frac{3}{4}\int\frac{dx}{x+1} - \frac{1}{2}\int\frac{dx}{(x+1)^2}$

$\displaystyle = \frac{1}{4}\ln|x-1| + \frac{3}{4}\ln|x+1| + \frac{1}{2(x+1)} + C$

$$\frac{x^2}{(x-1)(x+1)^2} = \frac{A}{x-1} + \frac{B}{x+1} + \frac{C}{(x+1)^2}$$

$x^2 = (A+B)x^2 + (2A+C)x + (A-B-C)$

$A = \frac{1}{4},\ B = \frac{3}{4},\ C = -\frac{1}{2}$

41. Let $u = e^t \Rightarrow du = e^t\,dt$, $t = 0 \Rightarrow u = 1$, $t = \ln 2 \Rightarrow u = 2$

$$\int_0^{\ln 2} \frac{e^t\,dt}{e^{2t}+3e^t+2}dt = \int_1^2 \frac{du}{u^2+3u+2} = \int_1^2\left(\frac{1}{u+1} - \frac{1}{u+2}\right)du$$

$\displaystyle\ln|u+1| - \ln|u+2|\Big]_1^2 = 2\ln 3 - 3\ln 2$

42. Let $x = \tan u \Rightarrow dx = \sec^2 u\, du$, $x = 0 \Rightarrow u = 0$, $x = 1 \Rightarrow u = \frac{\pi}{4}$. Then

$$\int_0^1 \frac{dx}{(x^2+1)^2} = \int_0^{\frac{\pi}{4}} \frac{\sec^2 u\, du}{\sec^4 u} = \int_0^{\frac{\pi}{4}} \cos^2 u\, du = \frac{1}{2}\int_0^{\frac{\pi}{4}} (1 + \cos 2u)\, du$$

$$= \frac{1}{2}u + \frac{1}{4}\sin 2u \Big]_0^{\frac{\pi}{4}} = \frac{\pi}{8} + \frac{1}{4}$$

43. $$\int_0^1 \frac{x^4\, dx}{(x^2+1)^2} = \int_0^1 \left(1 - \frac{2x^2+1}{(x^2+1)^2}\right) dx = x\Big]_0^1 - \int_0^1 \frac{2x^2+1}{(x^2+1)^2}\, dx$$

Let $x = \tan u$, $dx = \sec^2 u\, du$, $x = 0 \Rightarrow u = 0$, $x = 1 \Rightarrow u = \frac{\pi}{4}$.

$$1 - \int_0^1 \frac{2x^2+1}{(x^2+1)^2}\, dx = 1 - \int_0^{\frac{\pi}{4}} \frac{(2\tan^2 u + 1)\sec^2 u\, du}{\sec^4 u} =$$

$$1 - \frac{3}{2}u + \frac{1}{4}\sin 2u \Big]_0^{\frac{\pi}{4}} = 1 - \frac{3\pi}{8} + \frac{1}{4} = \frac{5}{4} - \frac{3\pi}{8}$$

44. $$\int \frac{4x^3 - 20x}{x^4 - 10x^2 + 9} = \ln|x^4 - 10x^2 + 9| + C$$

45. Let $u = \sqrt{x} \Rightarrow u^2 = x$ and $2u\, du = dx$. Then $\int \frac{1-\sqrt{x}}{1+\sqrt{x}}\, dx = \int \frac{2u - 2u^2}{1+u}\, du$

$$= \int \left(-2u + 4 - \frac{4}{u+1}\right) du = -u^2 + 4u - 4\ln|u+1| = -x + 4\sqrt{x} - 4\ln(\sqrt{x}+1) + C$$

46. Let $z^2 = x \Rightarrow 2z\, dz = dx$. Then $\int \frac{dx}{1+\sqrt{x}} = \int \frac{2z\, dz}{1+z} = \int \left(2 - \frac{2}{z+1}\right) dz$

$$= 2z - 2\ln|z+1| + C = 2\sqrt{x} - 2\ln(\sqrt{x}+1) + C$$

47. Let $x = u^6 \Rightarrow dx = 6u^5\, du$. Then $\int \frac{dx}{\sqrt{x} + \sqrt[3]{x}} = \int \frac{6u^5\, du}{u^3 + u^2} = \int \frac{6u^3\, du}{u+1} =$

$$\int \left(6u^2 - 6u + 6 - \frac{6}{y+1}\right) dy = 2u^3 - 3u^2 + 6u - 6\ln|u+1| + C =$$

$$2x^{\frac{1}{2}} - 3x^{\frac{1}{3}} + 6x^{\frac{1}{6}} - 6\ln(x^{\frac{1}{6}} + 1) + C$$

48. $$\int x\ln(x+5)\, dx = \frac{x^2}{2}\ln|x+5| - \frac{1}{2}\int \frac{x^2}{x+5}\, dx$$

Let $u = \ln(x+5) \Rightarrow du = \frac{dx}{x+5}$; $dv = x\, dx \Rightarrow v = \frac{x^2}{2}$

$$= \frac{x^2}{2}\ln|x+5| - \frac{1}{2}\int \left(x - 5 + \frac{25}{x+5}\right) dx = \frac{x^2}{2}\ln|x+5| - \frac{x^2}{4} + \frac{5x}{2} - \frac{25}{2}\ln|x+5| + C$$

49. $\int_0^1 \ln(x^2+1)\,dx = x\ln(x^2+1) - \int \frac{2x^2\,dx}{x^2+1} = x\ln(x^2+1) - \int\left(2 - \frac{2}{x^2+1}\right)dx =$

$x\ln(x^2+1) - 2x + 2\tan^{-1}x\Big]_0^1 = \ln 2 - 2 + \frac{\pi}{2}$

50. One gets that A = B = 0

51. $V = \pi\int_{\frac{1}{2}}^{\frac{5}{2}} \frac{9}{3x - x^2}\,dx = \pi\int_{\frac{1}{2}}^{\frac{5}{2}}\left(\frac{3}{x} + \frac{3}{3-x}\right)dx = 3\pi(\ln x - \ln|3-x|)\Big]_{\frac{1}{2}}^{\frac{5}{2}} = 6\pi\ln 5$

52. $M = \int_0^{\sqrt{3}} \tan^{-1}x\,dx = x\tan^{-1}x - \frac{1}{2}\ln|1+x^2|\Big]_0^{\sqrt{3}} = \frac{\pi\sqrt{3} - 3\ln 2}{3}.$

$M_y = \int_0^{\frac{\pi}{3}} \frac{1}{2}(\sqrt{3}+x)(\sqrt{3}-x)\,dy = \frac{1}{2}\int_0^{\frac{\pi}{3}}(3 - \tan^2 y)\,dy$

$= \frac{1}{2}\int_0^{\frac{\pi}{3}}(4 - \sec^2 y)\,dy = \frac{1}{2}[4y - \tan y\Big]_0^{\frac{\pi}{3}} = \frac{4\pi - 3\sqrt{3}}{6}.\quad \bar{y} = \frac{4\pi - 3\sqrt{3}}{2\pi\sqrt{3} - 6\ln 2}$

53. $A = \int_3^5 \frac{4x^2 + 13x - 9}{x^3 + 2x^2 - 3x}dx = \int_3^5\left(\frac{3}{x} - \frac{1}{x+3} + \frac{2}{x-1}\right)dx = \ln\frac{125}{9}$

$M_y = \int_3^5 \frac{x(4x^2+13x-9)}{x^3+2x^2-3x}dx = \int_3^5\left(4 + \frac{1}{x-1} - \frac{1}{x+3}\right)dx = 8 + 8\ln 2 - 3\ln 3$

$\bar{y} = \frac{8 + 8\ln 2 - 3\ln 3}{3\ln 5 - 2\ln 3}.$

54. $s = \int_0^{\frac{1}{2}}\sqrt{1 + \frac{4x^2}{(1-x^2)^2}}\,dx = \int_0^{\frac{1}{2}}\frac{1+x^2}{1-x^2}\,dx = \int_0^{\frac{1}{2}}\left(\frac{2}{1-x^2} - 1\right)dx$

$= \int_0^{\frac{1}{2}}\left(\frac{1}{1-x} + \frac{1}{1+x} - 1\right)dx = \ln|x+1| - \ln|1-x| - x\Big]_0^{\frac{1}{2}} = \ln 3 - \frac{1}{2}$

55. $\frac{dx}{dt} = .004\,x(1000-x) \Rightarrow \int\frac{dx}{x(1000-x)} = .004\,dt \Rightarrow$

$\int\left(\frac{1}{x} + \frac{1}{1000-x}\right)dx = 4\,dt \Rightarrow \ln\frac{x}{1000-x} = 4t + C \Rightarrow \frac{x}{1000-x} = Ce^{4t}.$

$C = \frac{2}{1000-2} = \frac{1}{499}.$

(a) $\frac{x}{1000-x} = \frac{1}{499}e^{4t}$

(b) $\frac{500}{500} = \frac{1}{499}e^{4t} \Leftrightarrow t = \frac{\ln 499}{4} \approx 1.55$ days

56. (a) If $a = b$, then $\dfrac{dx}{(a-x)^2} = k\,dt \Rightarrow \dfrac{1}{a-x} = kt + C$. $x = 0$ when $t = 0 \Rightarrow c = \dfrac{1}{a}$.

$$\frac{1}{a-x} = kt + \frac{1}{a} \Rightarrow x = \frac{a^2 kt}{akt+1}$$

(b) If $a \neq b$, then $\dfrac{1}{(a-x)(b-x)} = \dfrac{\frac{1}{b-a}}{a-x} + \dfrac{\frac{1}{a-b}}{b-x}$, so

$$-\frac{1}{b-a}\ln|a-x| - \frac{1}{a-b}\ln|b-x| = kt + C. \quad C = \frac{1}{a-b}\ln\frac{a}{b}.$$

$$\therefore \ln\left|\frac{b-x}{a-x}\right| = (b-a)\,kt + \ln\frac{b}{a}.$$

57. $\dfrac{dx}{dt} = kx(a-x) \Rightarrow \dfrac{dx}{x(a-x)} = k\,dt$

$$\int\left(\frac{1}{ax} + \frac{1}{a(a-x)}\right)dx = \int k\,dt$$

$$\frac{1}{a}\ln|x| - \frac{1}{a}\ln|a-x| = kt + C$$

$$\ln\frac{x}{a-x} = akt + C \quad \text{or} \quad \frac{x}{a-x} = Ce^{akt}. \quad \text{Since } C = \frac{x_0}{a-x_0},$$

$$\frac{x}{a-x} = \left(\frac{x_0}{a-x_0}\right)e^{akt}$$

7.8 IMPROPER INTEGRALS

1. $\displaystyle\int_0^\infty \frac{dx}{x^2+1}$ converges, since $\displaystyle\lim_{b\to\infty}\int_0^b \frac{dx}{x^2+1} = \lim_{b\to\infty}\left[\tan^{-1}x\right]_0^b = \frac{\pi}{2}$.

2. $\displaystyle\int_0^1 \frac{dx}{\sqrt{x}}$ converges, since $\displaystyle\lim_{b\to 0^+}\int_b^1 \frac{dx}{\sqrt{x}} = \lim_{b\to 0^+} 2\sqrt{x}\Big]_b^1 = 2$

3. $\displaystyle\int_{-1}^1 \frac{dx}{x^{2/3}} = \lim_{b\to 0^-}\int_{-1}^b \frac{dx}{x^{2/3}} + \lim_{b\to 0+}\int_b^1 \frac{dx}{x^{2/3}} = \lim_{b\to 0^-} 3x^{1/3}\Big]_{-1}^b + \lim_{b\to 0^+} 3x^{1/3}\Big]_b^1 = 6$

Hence, $\displaystyle\int_{-1}^1 \frac{dx}{x^{2/3}}$ converges.

4. $\displaystyle\int_1^\infty \frac{dx}{x^{1.001}}$ converges, since $\displaystyle\lim_{b\to\infty}\int_1^b \frac{dx}{x^{1.001}} = \lim_{b\to\infty}\left[-\frac{1000}{x^{0.001}}\right]_1^b = 1000$

5. $\displaystyle\int_0^4 \frac{dx}{\sqrt{4-x}}$ converges, since $\displaystyle\lim_{b\to 4^-}\int_0^b \frac{dx}{\sqrt{4-x}} = \lim_{b\to 4^-}\left[-2\sqrt{4-x}\right]_0^b = 4$

6. $\displaystyle\int_0^1 \frac{dx}{\sqrt{1-x^2}}$ converges, since $\displaystyle\lim_{b\to 1^-}\int_0^b \frac{dx}{\sqrt{1-x^2}} = \lim_{b\to 1^-}\sin^{-1}x\Big]_0^b = \frac{\pi}{2}$

7. $\int_0^1 \frac{dx}{x^{.999}}$ converges, since $\lim_{b\to 0^+}\int_b^1 \frac{dx}{x^{.999}} = \lim_{b\to 0^+} 1000x^{.001}\Big]_b^1 = 1000$

8. $\int_{-\infty}^2 \frac{dx}{4-x}$ diverges, since $\lim_{b\to -\infty}\int_b^2 \frac{dx}{4-x} = \lim_{b\to -\infty}\left(-\ln|4-x|\right)\Big]_b^2 = \infty$

9. $\int_2^\infty \frac{dx}{x(x-1)}$ converges, since $\lim_{b\to\infty}\int_2^b \left(-\frac{1}{x}+\frac{1}{x-1}\right)dx$

$= \lim_{b\to\infty}\left[-\ln|x| + \ln|x-1|\right]_2^b = \ln 2$

10. Let $z^2 = x \Rightarrow 2z\,dz = dx$. Then $\int \frac{dx}{(1+x)\sqrt{x}} = \int \frac{2z\,dz}{z(1+z^2)} = 2\tan^{-1}z + C$.

$\int_0^\infty \frac{dx}{\sqrt{x}(1+x)} = \int_0^1 \frac{dx}{\sqrt{x}(1+x)} + \int_1^\infty \frac{dx}{\sqrt{x}(1+x)}$ converges, since

$= \lim_{a\to 0^+}\int_a^1 \frac{dx}{\sqrt{x}(1+x)} + \lim_{b\to\infty}\int_1^b \frac{dx}{\sqrt{x}(1+x)}$

$= \lim_{a\to 0^+}\left[2\tan^{-1}\sqrt{x}\right]_a^1 + \lim_{b\to\infty}\left[2\tan^{-1}\sqrt{x}\right]_1^b = \left(\frac{\pi}{2}-0\right) + \left(\pi - \frac{\pi}{2}\right) = \pi.$

11. $\int_1^\infty \frac{dx}{\sqrt{x}} = \lim_{b\to\infty}\int_1^b \frac{dx}{\sqrt{x}} = \lim_{b\to\infty} 2\sqrt{x}\Big]_1^b$ diverges

12. $\int_1^\infty \frac{dx}{x^3}$ converges since $\lim_{b\to\infty}\int_1^b \frac{dx}{x^3} = \lim_{b\to\infty}\left(-\frac{1}{x^2}\right)_1^b = \frac{1}{2}$

13. $\int_1^\infty \frac{dx}{x^3+1}$ converges, since $\frac{1}{x^3+1} \le \frac{1}{x^3}$, $x \ge 1$, and $\lim_{b\to\infty}\int_1^b \frac{dx}{x^3} = \lim_{b\to\infty} -x^{-2}\Big]_1^b = \frac{1}{2}$.

14. $\int_0^\infty \frac{dx}{x^3} = \int_0^1 \frac{dx}{x^3} + \int_1^\infty \frac{dx}{x^3}$ diverges, since $\lim_{a\to 0^+}\int_a^1 \frac{dx}{x^3} + \lim_{b\to\infty}\int_1^b \frac{dx}{x^3}$

$= \lim_{a\to 0^+}\left(-\frac{1}{2x^2}\right)_a^1 + \lim_{b\to\infty}\left(-\frac{1}{2x^2}\right)_1^b = \lim_{a\to 0^+}\left(-\frac{1}{2}+\frac{1}{2a^2}\right) - \lim_{b\to\infty}\left(\frac{1}{2b^2}+\frac{1}{2}\right) = \infty$

15. $\int_0^\infty \frac{dx}{x^{\frac{3}{2}}+1} = \int_0^1 \frac{dx}{x^{\frac{3}{2}}+1} + \int_1^\infty \frac{dx}{x^{\frac{3}{2}}+1}$. The first integral is finite, and the converges because $x^{\frac{3}{2}}+1 \ge x^{\frac{3}{2}} \Rightarrow \frac{1}{x^{3/2}+1} \le \frac{1}{x^{3/2}}$ and $\int_1^\infty \frac{dx}{x^{3/2}}$ converges.

16. $\int_0^\infty \frac{dx}{1+e^x} = \int_0^\infty \frac{e^{-x}\,dx}{e^{-x}+1}$ converges, since $\lim_{b\to\infty}\int_0^b \frac{e^{-x}\,dx}{e^{-x}+1}$

$= \lim_{b\to\infty}\left[-\ln(e^{-x}+1)\right]_0^b = \ln 2$

17. $\int_0^{\pi/2} \tan x\,dx$ diverges, since $\lim_{b\to\frac{\pi}{2}} (\ln|\sec x|)\Big]_0^b = \lim_{b\to\frac{\pi}{2}} (\ln|\sec b|) = \infty$.

18. $\int_{-1}^{1} \frac{dx}{x^2} = \int_{-1}^{0} \frac{dx}{x^2} + \int_{0}^{1} \frac{dx}{x^2}$ diverges, since $\lim_{b\to 0^-} \int_{-1}^{b} \frac{dx}{x^2}$

$= \lim_{b\to 0^-} \left(-\frac{1}{x}\right)_{-1}^{b}$ diverges (it is sufficient for one part to diverge).

19. $\int_{-1}^{1} \frac{dx}{x^{2/5}} = \lim_{b\to 0^-} \int_{-1}^{b} \frac{dx}{x^{2/5}} + \lim_{b\to 0^+} \int_{b}^{1} \frac{dx}{x^{2/5}} = \lim_{b\to 0^-} \frac{5}{3}x^{3/5}\Big]_{-1}^{b} + \lim_{b\to 0^+} \frac{5}{3}x^{3/5}\Big]_{b}^{1} = \frac{10}{3}$

Hence, $\int_{-1}^{1} \frac{dx}{x^{2/5}}$ converges.

20. $\int_0^{\infty} \frac{dx}{\sqrt{x}} = \int_0^{1} \frac{dx}{\sqrt{x}} + \int_1^{\infty} \frac{dx}{\sqrt{x}}$ diverges, since $\int_1^{\infty} \frac{dx}{\sqrt{x}} = \lim_{b\to\infty} \int_1^{b} \frac{dx}{\sqrt{x}}$

$= \lim_{b\to\infty} (2\sqrt{x})\Big]_1^b$ diverges.

21. $\int_2^{\infty} \frac{dx}{\sqrt{x-1}} = \lim_{b\to\infty} \int_2^{b} \frac{dx}{\sqrt{x-1}} = \lim_{b\to\infty} 2\sqrt{x-1}\,\Big]_2^b = \lim_{b\to\infty} 2\sqrt{b-1} - 2$, which diverges.

22. $\int_1^{\infty} \frac{5}{x}\,dx$ diverges, since $\lim_{b\to\infty} \int_1^{b} \frac{5}{x}\,dx = \lim_{b\to\infty} 5\ln|x|\,\Big]_1^b = \infty$

23. $\int_0^{2} \frac{dx}{1-x^2} = \lim_{b\to 1^+} \int_0^{b} \frac{dx}{1-x^2} + \lim_{b\to 1^-} \int_b^{2} \frac{dx}{1-x^2}$. Consider $\lim_{b\to 1^+} \int_0^{b} \frac{dx}{1-x^2}$

$= \lim_{b\to 1^+} \frac{1}{2}\left(\int_0^{b} \frac{dx}{1-x} + \int_0^{b} \frac{dx}{1+x} \right)$. Now $\lim_{b\to 1^+} \int_0^{b} \frac{dx}{1-x}$ diverges, since

$\lim_{b\to 1^+} \int_0^{b} \frac{dx}{1-x} = \lim_{b\to 1^+} (-\ln|1-x|)\Big]_0^b = -\lim_{b\to 1^+} \ln(1-b|)$. Thus $\int_0^{2} \frac{dx}{1-x^2}$ diverge

24. $\int_2^{\infty} \frac{dx}{(x+1)^2}$ converges, since $\lim_{b\to\infty} \int_2^{b} \frac{dx}{(x+1)^2} = \lim_{b\to\infty} \frac{-1}{x+1}\Big]_2^b = \frac{1}{3}$

25. $\int_0^{\infty} \frac{dx}{\sqrt{x^6+1}}$ converges since $\int_0^{\infty} \sqrt{\frac{1}{x^6}}\,dx = \int_0^{\infty} \frac{1}{x^3}\,dx$ converges, and

$\lim_{x\to\infty} \sqrt{\frac{1}{x^6+1}} \cdot \sqrt{\frac{x^6}{1}} = 1.$

26. $\int_{-1}^{1} \frac{dx}{\sqrt[3]{x}} = \int_{-1}^{0} \frac{dx}{\sqrt[3]{x}} + \int_{0}^{1} \frac{dx}{\sqrt[3]{x}}$ converges, since

$$\lim_{b\to 0^-} \int_{-1}^{b} \frac{dx}{\sqrt[3]{x}} + \lim_{a\to 0^+} \int_{a}^{1} \frac{dx}{\sqrt[3]{x}} = \lim_{b\to 0^-} \frac{3}{2}x^{2/3}\Big]_{-1}^{b} + \lim_{a\to 0^+} \frac{3}{2}x^{2/3}\Big]_{a}^{1} = 0$$

27. $\int_{0}^{\infty} x^2 e^{-x}\,dx = \lim_{b\to\infty} \int_{0}^{b} x^2 e^{-x}\,dx = \lim_{b\to\infty} [-e^{-x}(x^2 + 2x + 2)]_{0}^{b} = 2$, so converges.

28. $\int_{1}^{\infty} \frac{\sqrt{x+1}}{x^2}\,dx \le \int_{0}^{\infty} \frac{2\sqrt{x}}{x^2}\,dx = \int_{0}^{\infty} \frac{2}{x^{3/2}}dx$ converges by comparison

29. Since $2 + \cos x \ge 1$, and $\int_{\pi}^{\infty} \frac{dx}{x}$ diverges, $\int_{\pi}^{\infty} \frac{2 + \cos x}{x}dx$ diverges.

30. $\int_{1}^{\infty} \frac{\ln x}{x}dx$ diverges, since $\lim_{b\to\infty} \int_{0}^{b} \frac{\ln x}{x}dx = \lim_{b\to\infty} \frac{(\ln x)^2}{2}\Big]_{0}^{b} = \infty$

31. $\int_{6}^{\infty} \frac{1}{\sqrt{x+5}}dx = \lim_{b\to\infty} \int_{6}^{b} \frac{1}{\sqrt{x+5}}dx = \lim_{b\to\infty} 2\sqrt{x+5}\Big]_{6}^{b}$ which diverges.

32. $\int_{1}^{\infty} \frac{dx}{\sqrt{2x+10}}$ diverges, since $\lim_{b\to\infty} \int_{0}^{b} \frac{dx}{\sqrt{2x+10}} = \lim_{b\to\infty} \sqrt{2x+10}\Big]_{0}^{b} = \infty$

33. $\int_{2}^{\infty} \frac{2\,dx}{x^2 - 1}$ converges, since $\lim_{b\to\infty} \int_{2}^{b} \frac{2\,dx}{x^2 - 1} = \lim_{b\to\infty} \int_{2}^{b} \left(\frac{1}{x-1} - \frac{1}{x+1}\right)dx$

$$= \lim_{b\to\infty} [\ln|x-1| - \ln|x+1|]_{2}^{b} = \lim_{b\to\infty} \ln\left|\frac{b-1}{b+1}\right| + \ln 3 = \ln 3.$$

34. $\int_{1}^{\infty} \frac{dx}{e^{\ln x}} = \int_{1}^{\infty} \frac{dx}{x}$ diverges, since $\lim_{b\to\infty} \int_{0}^{b} \frac{dx}{x} = \lim_{b\to\infty} \ln x\Big]_{0}^{b} = \infty$

35. $\int_{2}^{\infty} \frac{dx}{\ln x}$ diverges, since $\ln x < x$ for $x \ge 2 \Rightarrow \frac{1}{\ln x} > \frac{1}{x}$ and $\int_{2}^{\infty} \frac{dx}{x}$ diverges.

36. $e^x \approx 1 + x + \frac{1}{2}e^x \Rightarrow e^x - x \ge \frac{1}{2}e^x$. $\therefore \int_{1}^{\infty} \frac{dx}{\sqrt{e^x - x}} \le \int_{1}^{\infty} \frac{\sqrt{2}\,dx}{e^{x/2}}$ which

converges since $\lim_{b\to\infty} \sqrt{2}(-2e^{x/2})\Big] = 2\sqrt{2}$.

37. $\int_{1}^{\infty} \frac{1}{e^x - 2^x}\,dx$ converges, by limit comparison test, since

$$\lim_{x\to\infty} \frac{e^x}{e^x - 2^x} = \lim_{x\to\infty} \frac{1}{1 - \left(\frac{2}{e}\right)^x} = 1 \ne 0 \text{ and } \int_{1}^{\infty} \frac{dx}{e^x} \text{ converges.}$$

38. For $x \geq 2$, $\dfrac{1}{x^3 - 5} \leq \dfrac{5}{x^3}$, so $\displaystyle\int_2^{\infty} \frac{1}{x^3 - 5}dx$ converges by comparison

to $\displaystyle\int_2^{\infty} \frac{5}{x^3}\,dx$, which converges to $\dfrac{5}{8}$.

39. $$\int_0^{\infty} \frac{dx}{\sqrt{x + x^4}} = \lim_{b\to 0^+} \int_b^1 \frac{dx}{\sqrt{x + x^4}} + \lim_{b\to\infty} \int_1^b \frac{dx}{\sqrt{x + x^4}}.$$

$\displaystyle\lim_{b\to 0^+} \int_b^1 \frac{dx}{\sqrt{x + x^4}}$ is finite, since $\dfrac{1}{\sqrt{x + x^4}} \leq \dfrac{1}{\sqrt{x}}$ and $\displaystyle\int_0^1 \frac{dx}{\sqrt{x}} = 2$.

$\displaystyle\lim_{b\to\infty} \int_1^b \frac{dx}{\sqrt{x + x^4}}$ is finite, since $\displaystyle\lim_{x\to\infty} \frac{\sqrt{x + x^4}}{x^2} = \lim_{x\to\infty} \sqrt{1 + \frac{1}{x^3}} = 1$

and $\displaystyle\int_1^{\infty} \frac{dx}{x^2} = 1$. Therefore, $\displaystyle\int_0^{\infty} \frac{dx}{\sqrt{x + x^4}}$ converges.

40. $\displaystyle\int_0^{\infty} e^{-x} \cos x\,dx$ converges by comparison, since

$$\int_0^{\infty} e^{-x} \cos x\,dx \leq \int_0^{\infty} e^{-x}\,|\cos x|\,dx \leq \int_0^{\infty} e^{-x}\,dx.$$

41. $$\int_3^{\infty} e^{-3x}dx = \lim_{b\to\infty} \int_3^b e^{-3x}dx = \lim_{b\to\infty} \left[-\frac{1}{3}e^{-3x}dx\right]_3^b = \frac{1}{3}e^{-9} \approx 0.0000041.$$

For $x \geq 3$, $x^2 \geq 3x \Rightarrow -x^2 \leq -3x \Rightarrow e^{(-x^2)} \leq e^{-3x}$.

So $\displaystyle\int_3^{\infty} e^{(-x^2)}dx \leq \int_3^{\infty} e^{-3x}dx < 0.000042$. Simpson's Rule with

$n = 6$ gives $\displaystyle\int_0^3 e^{(-x^2)}dx \approx 0.8862$.

42. $$V = \pi \int_1^{\infty} \frac{dx}{x^2} = \pi \lim_{b\to\infty} \int_1^b \frac{dx}{x^2} = \pi \lim_{b\to\infty} -\frac{1}{x}\Big]_1^b = \pi$$

43. $$\int_1^{\infty} \frac{dx}{x^p} = \lim_{b\to\infty} \int_1^b \frac{dx}{x^p} = \lim_{b\to\infty} \left[\frac{x^{-p+1}}{1 - p}\right]_1^b = \frac{1}{p - 1} + \lim_{b\to\infty} \frac{b^{1-p}}{1 - p}.$$

If $p > 1$, $1 - p < 0$ and $b^{1-p} \to 0$ as $b \to \infty$. If $p < 1$, $1 - p > 0$ and $b^{1-p} \to \infty$ as $b \to \infty$.

44. (a) $\int_1^2 \frac{dx}{x(\ln x)^p} = \lim_{b\to 1^+} \int_b^2 \frac{dx}{x(\ln x)^p} = \lim_{b\to 1^+} \frac{(\ln x)^{1-p}}{1-p}$

$= \lim_{b\to 1^+}\left[\frac{(\ln 2)^{1-p}}{1-p} - \frac{(\ln b)^{1-p}}{1-p}\right]$. If $p<1$, $1-p>0$ and

$(\ln a)^{1-p} \to 0$ as $p \to 1^+$. But if $p>1$, $1-p<0$ and

$(\ln a)^{1-p} \to \infty$ as $p \to 1^+$. $\therefore$ $\int_1^2 \frac{dx}{x(\ln x)^p}$ converges for $p<1$.

(b) $\int_2^\infty \frac{dx}{x(\ln x)^p} = \lim_{b\to\infty} \int_2^b \frac{dx}{x(\ln x)^p} = \lim_{b\to\infty} \frac{(\ln x)^{1-p}}{1-p}$

$= \lim_{b\to\infty}\left[\frac{(\ln b)^{1-p}}{1-p} - \frac{(\ln 2)^{1-p}}{1-p}\right]$. If $p<1$, $1-p>0$ and

$(\ln a)^{1-p} \to \infty$ as $p \to \infty$. But if $p>1$, $1-p<0$ and

$(\ln a)^{1-p} \to 0$ as $p \to \infty$. $\therefore$ $\int_2^\infty \frac{dx}{x(\ln x)^p}$ converges for $p>1$.

In both (a) and (b) $\ln(\ln b)$ diverges if $b \to 1^+$ or if $b \to \infty$.

45. $A = \int_0^\infty e^{-x}\,dx = \lim_{b\to\infty} \int_0^b e^{-x}\,dx = \lim_{b\to\infty} [e^{-x}\,dx]_0^b = 1$

46. $M_y = \int_0^\infty x e^{-x}\,dx = \lim_{b\to\infty}\left[-e^{-x} - xe^{-x}\right]_0^b = 1$. $\therefore$ $\bar{x} = 1$. (See Prob. 45)

$M_x = \int_0^\infty \frac{1}{2} e^{-2x}\,dx = \lim_{b\to\infty}\left[-\frac{1}{4} e^{-2x}\right]_0^b = \frac{1}{4}$. $\therefore$ $\bar{y} = \frac{1}{4}$.

47. $V = 2\pi \int_0^\infty xe^{-x}\,dx = \lim_{b\to\infty} 2\pi \int_0^b xe^{-x}\,dx = \lim_{b\to\infty} 2\pi\,[xe^{-x} - e^{-x}]_0^b = 2\pi$

48. $V = \pi \int_0^\infty e^{-2x}\,dx = \pi \lim_{b\to\infty}\left[-\frac{1}{2} e^{-2x}\right]_0^b = \frac{\pi}{2}$

49. $A = 2\int_0^1 \frac{dx}{\sqrt{1-x^2}} = \lim_{b\to 1^-} 2\int_0^b \frac{dx}{\sqrt{1-x^2}} = 2 \lim_{b\to 1^-} [\sin^{-1} x]_0^b = 2\left(\frac{\pi}{2}\right) = \pi$.

$\bar{y} = 0$ by symmetry. $\bar{x} = \frac{1}{\pi}\int_0^1 \frac{2x\,dx}{\sqrt{1-x^2}} = \frac{1}{\pi} \lim_{b\to 1^-} \int_0^b \frac{2x\,dx}{\sqrt{1-x^2}} =$

$\frac{1}{\pi} \lim_{b\to 1^-}\left[-2\sqrt{1-x^2}\right]_0^b = \frac{2}{\pi}$. $(\bar{x}, \bar{y}) = \left(\frac{2}{\pi}, 0\right)$.

50. $A = \int_0^{\frac{\pi}{2}} (\sec x - \tan x)\,dx = \lim_{b \to \frac{\pi}{2}^-} [\ln|\sec x + \tan x| - \ln|\sec x|\Big]_0^b$

$= \lim_{b \to \frac{\pi}{2}^-} \ln|1 + \sin x|\Big]_0^b = \ln 2$

51. $A = 2\int_1^{\infty} \frac{1}{1+x^2}dx = 2\lim_{b\to\infty}\int_1^b \frac{1}{1+x^2}dx = 2\lim_{b\to\infty}\tan^{-1}x\Big]_1^b = 2\left(\frac{\pi}{2}\right) = \pi,$

which is the area of a disk with radius = 1.

7.9 USING INTEGRAL TABLES

1. $\int_0^{\infty} e^{(-x^2)}\,dx = \frac{\sqrt{\pi}}{2}$ (Formula 140)

2. $\int x\cos^{-1}dx = \frac{x^2}{2}\cos^{-1}x + \frac{1}{2}\int\frac{x^2\,dx}{\sqrt{1-x^2}}$ (Formula 100)

$= \frac{x^2}{2}\cos^{-1}x + \frac{1}{2}\left(\frac{1}{2}\sin^{-1}x - \frac{1}{2}x\sqrt{1-x^2}\right)$ (Formula 33)

$= \frac{x^2}{2}\cos^{-1}x + \frac{1}{4}\sin^{-1}x - \frac{1}{4}x\sqrt{1-x^2} + C$

3. $\int_6^9 \frac{dx}{x\sqrt{x-3}} = \frac{2}{\sqrt{3}}\left[\tan^{-1}\sqrt{\frac{x-3}{3}}\right]_6^9 = \frac{2}{\sqrt{3}}\left(\tan^{-1}\sqrt{2} - \frac{\pi}{4}\right)$ (Formula 13a)

3. $\int_6^9 \frac{dx}{x\sqrt{x-3}} = \frac{2}{\sqrt{3}}\left[\tan^{-1}\sqrt{\frac{x-3}{3}}\right]_6^9 = \frac{2}{\sqrt{3}}\left(\tan^{-1}\sqrt{2} - \frac{\pi}{4}\right)$ (Formula 13a)

4. $\int x\tan^{-1}2x\,dx = \frac{x^2}{2}\tan^{-1}2x - \int\frac{x^2\,dx}{1+4x^2}$ (Formula 101)

$= \frac{x^2}{2}\tan^{-1}2x - \int\frac{1}{4}\,dx + \frac{1}{4}\int\frac{dx}{4x^2+1}$

$= \frac{x^2}{2}\tan^{-1}2x - \frac{1}{4}x + \frac{1}{8}\tan^{-1}2x$

$\therefore \int_0^{\frac{1}{2}} x\tan^{-1}2x\,dx = \frac{x^2}{2}\tan^{-1}2x - \frac{1}{4}x + \frac{1}{8}\tan^{-1}2x\Big]_0^{\frac{1}{2}} = \frac{\pi-2}{16}$

5. $\int\frac{dx}{(9-x^2)^2} = \frac{x}{18(9-x^2)} + \frac{1}{18}\int\frac{dx}{9-x^2}$ (Formula 19)

$= \frac{x}{18(9-x^2)} + \frac{1}{108}\ln\left|\frac{x+3}{x-3}\right| + C$ (Formula 18)

6. $$\int_4^{10} \frac{\sqrt{4x+9}}{x^2}\,dx = \left.\frac{-\sqrt{4x+9}}{x}\right]_4^{10} + 2\int_4^{10} \frac{dx}{x\sqrt{4x+9}} \quad \text{(Formula 14)}$$

$$= \frac{11}{20} + 2\left(\frac{1}{3}\ln\left|\frac{\sqrt{4x+9}-3}{\sqrt{4x+9}+3}\right|\right)_4^{10} \quad \text{(Formula 13b)}$$

$$= \frac{11}{20} + \frac{2}{3}\ln\frac{4}{10} - \frac{2}{3}\ln\frac{2}{8} = \frac{11}{20} + \frac{2}{3}\ln\frac{8}{5}$$

7. $$\int_3^{11} \frac{dx}{x^2\sqrt{7+x^2}} = -\left.\frac{\sqrt{7+x^2}}{7x}\right]_3^{11} = \frac{44-24\sqrt{2}}{231} \quad \text{(Formula 27)}$$

8. $$\int \frac{dx}{x^2\sqrt{7-x^2}} = \frac{-\sqrt{7-x^2}}{7x} + C \quad \text{(Formula 35)}$$

9. $$\int_{-2}^{-\sqrt{2}} \frac{\sqrt{x^2-2}}{x}\,dx = \sqrt{x^2-2} - \sqrt{2}\sec^{-1}\left|\frac{x}{\sqrt{2}}\right|\Bigg]_{-2}^{-\sqrt{2}} = \sqrt{2}\left(\frac{\pi}{4}-1\right) \quad \text{(Formula 42)}$$

10. $$\int_{-\frac{\pi}{12}}^{\frac{\pi}{4}} \frac{dx}{5+4\sin 2x} = \frac{-1}{3}\tan^{-1}\left[\frac{1}{3}\tan\left(\frac{\pi}{4}-x\right)\right]_{\frac{-\pi}{12}}^{\frac{\pi}{4}}$$

$$= -\frac{1}{3}\tan^{-1}\left[\frac{1}{3}\tan\frac{\pi}{3}\right] = \frac{1}{3}\tan^{-1}\frac{\sqrt{3}}{3} = \frac{\pi}{18} \quad \text{(Formula 35)}$$

11. $$\int \frac{dx}{4+5\sin 2x} = -\frac{1}{6}\ln\left|\frac{5+4\sin 2x+3\cos 2x}{4+5\sin 2x}\right| + C \quad \text{(Formula 71)}$$

12. $$\int_3^6 \frac{x\,dx}{\sqrt{x-2}} = (x-2)^{1/2}\left[\frac{2}{3}(x-2)+4\right]_3^6 = \frac{26}{3} \quad \text{(Formula 7)}$$

13. $$\int x\sqrt{2x-3}\,dx = \frac{(2x-3)^{3/2}}{4}\left[\frac{2}{5}(2x-3)+\frac{2}{9}\right] + C = \frac{(2x-3)^{3/2}(x+1)}{5} + C \quad \text{(Formula 7)}$$

14. $$\int \frac{\sqrt{3x-4}}{x}\,dx = 2\sqrt{3x-4} - 4\int \frac{dx}{x\sqrt{3x-4}} \quad \text{(Formula 12)}$$

$$2\sqrt{3x-4} - 4\tan^{-1}\sqrt{\frac{3x-4}{4}} + C \quad \text{(Formula 13a)}$$

15. $$\int_0^\infty x^{10}e^{-x}\,dx = \Gamma(11) = 10! \quad \text{(Formula 139)}$$

16. $$\int x^2\tan^{-1}x\,dx = \frac{x^3}{3}\tan^{-1}x - \frac{1}{3}\int \frac{x^3}{1+x^2}\,dx \quad \text{(Formula 101)}$$

$$= \frac{x^3}{3}\tan^{-1}x - \frac{1}{3}\int\left(x - \frac{x}{x^2+1}\right)dx = \frac{x^3}{3}\tan^{-1}x - \frac{1}{6}x^2 + \frac{1}{6}\ln(x^2+1) + C$$

$$\therefore \int_0^1 x^2\tan^{-1}x\,dx = \frac{\pi}{12} - \frac{1}{6} + \frac{1}{6}\ln 2$$

17. $\int_0^1 \sin^{-1}\sqrt{x}\,dx = 2\int_0^1 u\sin^{-1}u\,du = 2\left(\frac{u^2}{2}\sin^{-1}u - \frac{1}{2}\int_0^1 \frac{u^2\,du}{\sqrt{1-u^2}}\right)$ (Formula 99)

$= \left[u^2\sin^{-1}u - \left(\left[\frac{1}{2}\sin^{-1}u - \frac{1}{2}u\sqrt{1-u^2}\right)\right]_0^1 = \frac{\pi}{4}$ (Formula 33)

18. $\int_{\frac{3}{4}}^1 \frac{\cos^{-1}\sqrt{x}}{\sqrt{x}}\,dx = 2\int_{\frac{\sqrt{3}}{2}}^1 \cos^{-1}u\,du$ (Let $u = \sqrt{x}$)

$= 2\left[u\cos^{-1}u - \sqrt{1-u^2}\right]_{\frac{\sqrt{3}}{2}}^1 = 1 - \frac{\pi\sqrt{3}}{6}$ (Formula 97)

19. $\int_0^{\frac{1}{2}} \frac{\sqrt{x}}{\sqrt{1-x}}\,dx = \int_0^{\frac{1}{\sqrt{2}}} \frac{2u^2\,du}{\sqrt{1-u^2}} = 2\left[\frac{1}{2}\sin^{-1}u - \frac{1}{2}u\sqrt{1-u^2}\right]_0^{\frac{1}{\sqrt{2}}} = \frac{\pi}{4} - \frac{1}{2}$ (Formula 3

20. Let $u = \sin x \Rightarrow du = \cos x\,dx$; $x = \frac{\pi}{4} \Rightarrow u = \frac{1}{\sqrt{2}}$, $x = \frac{\pi}{2} \Rightarrow u = 1$

$\int_{\frac{\pi}{4}}^{\frac{\pi}{2}} \cot x\sqrt{1-\sin^2 x}\,dx = \int_{\frac{1}{\sqrt{2}}}^1 \frac{\sqrt{1-u^2}}{u}\,du$ (Formula 31)

$= \sqrt{1-u^2} - \ln\left|\frac{1+\sqrt{1-u^2}}{u}\right|\Bigg]_{\frac{1}{\sqrt{2}}}^1 = -\frac{1}{\sqrt{2}} + \ln(\sqrt{2}+1)$

21. $A = \int_0^3 \frac{dx}{\sqrt{x+1}} = 2\sqrt{x+1}\Big]_0^3 = 2$

$\bar{x} = \frac{1}{2}\int_0^3 \frac{x}{\sqrt{x+1}}\,dx = \frac{1}{2}\left(\sqrt{x+1}\left(\frac{2}{3}(x+1) - 2\right)\Big]_0^3\right) = \frac{4}{3}$

$\bar{y} = \frac{1}{2}\int_0^3 \frac{1}{2\sqrt{x+1}}\cdot\frac{1}{\sqrt{x+1}}\,dx = \frac{1}{4}\int_0^3 \frac{dx}{x+1} = \frac{1}{4}\ln(x+1)\Big]_0^3 = \frac{1}{4}\ln 4 = \frac{1}{2}\ln 2$

22. $M_y = \int_0^3 \frac{36x}{2x+3}\,dx = 36\left[\frac{x}{2} - \frac{3}{4}\ln|2x+3|\right]_0^3 = 54 - 27\ln 3$ (Formula 8)

23. $\frac{d}{dx}\left(-\frac{1}{a}\sqrt{\frac{2a-x}{x}}\right) = -\frac{1}{a}\left[\frac{1}{2}\left(\frac{2a-x}{x}\right)^{-1/2}\right]\cdot\frac{x(-1)-(2a-x)}{x^2} =$

$$-\frac{1}{2a}\sqrt{\frac{x}{2a-x}}\left(\frac{-2a}{x^2}\right) = \sqrt{\frac{x}{x^4(2a-x)}} = \frac{1}{x\sqrt{2ax-x^2}}.$$

Therefore, $\int \frac{1}{x\sqrt{2ax-x^2}}dx = -\frac{1}{a}\sqrt{\frac{2a-x}{x}} + C.$

24. Let $f(x) = \frac{1}{a}\tan\frac{ax}{2} + C$. Then $f'(x) = \frac{1}{2}\sec^2\frac{ax}{2} = \frac{1}{2\cos^2\frac{ax}{2}} = \frac{1}{1+\cos ax}$

since $2\cos^2\frac{ax}{2} - 1 = \cos ax$. $\therefore \int \frac{dx}{1+\cos ax} = \frac{1}{a}\tan\frac{ax}{2} + C$

25. $\int x(ax+b)^{-2}\,dx = \int\left(\frac{u-b}{a}\cdot\frac{1}{u^2}\cdot\frac{1}{a}\right)du = \frac{1}{a^2}\int\frac{u-b}{u^2}du$

$$= \frac{1}{a^2}(\ln|u|\ bu^{-1}) + C = \frac{1}{a^2}\left[\ln|ax+b| + \frac{b}{ax+b}\right] + C$$

26. $\int \frac{dx}{x^2\sqrt{x^2-a^2}} = \int \frac{a\sec u\tan u\,du}{a^2\sec^2 u\,(a\tan u)} = \frac{1}{a^2}\int \cos u\,du = \frac{1}{a^2}\sin u + C$

$$= \frac{\sqrt{x^2-a^2}}{a^2x} + C$$

7.10 REDUCTION FORMULAS

1. $\int_{-\pi}^{\pi}\cos^4 x\,dx = \frac{\cos^3 x\sin x}{4} + \frac{3}{4}\left(\frac{\cos x\sin x}{2} + \frac{x}{2}\right)\Bigg]_{-\pi}^{\pi} = \frac{3\pi}{4}$

2. $\int \cos^4 2x\,dx = \frac{\cos^3 2x\sin 2x}{8} + \frac{3}{4}\int\cos^2 2x\,dx$

$$= \frac{\cos^3 2x\sin 2x}{8} + \frac{3\cos 2x\sin 2x}{16} + \frac{3}{8}x + C$$

3. $\int\cos^6 x\,dx = \frac{\cos^5 x\sin x}{6} + \frac{5}{6}\int\cos^4 x\,dx =$

$$\frac{\cos^5 x\sin x}{6} + \frac{5}{6}\left[\frac{\cos^3 x\sin x}{4} + \frac{3}{4}\left(\frac{\cos x\sin x}{2} + \frac{x}{2}\right)\right] + C =$$

$$\frac{1}{6}\cos^5 x\sin x + \frac{5}{24}\cos^3 x\sin x + \frac{5}{16}(\cos x\sin x + x) + C$$

4. $$\int \cos^6 3x\,dx = \frac{\cos^5 3x \sin 3x}{18} + \frac{5}{6}\int \cos^4 3x\,dx$$

$$= \frac{\cos^5 3x \sin 3x}{18} + \frac{5\cos^3 3x \sin 3x}{72} + \frac{15}{24}\int \cos^2 3x\,dx$$

$$= \frac{\cos^5 3x \sin 3x}{18} + \frac{5\cos^3 3x \sin 3x}{72} + \frac{5\cos 3x \sin 3x}{48} + \frac{15}{48}x + C$$

5. $$\int_0^{\pi} \sin^4 x\,dx = -\frac{\sin^3 x \cos x}{4} + \frac{3}{4}\int_0^{\pi} \sin^2 x\,dx =$$

$$-\frac{\sin^3 x \cos x}{4} + \frac{3}{4}\left[-\frac{\sin x \cos x}{2} + \frac{x}{2}\right]_0^{\pi} = \frac{3\pi}{8}$$

6. $$\int \sin^4 \frac{x}{2}\,dx = -\frac{1}{2}\sin^3\frac{x}{2}\cos\frac{x}{2} + \frac{3}{4}\int \sin^2\frac{x}{2}\,dx$$

$$= -\frac{1}{2}\sin^3\frac{x}{2}\cos\frac{x}{2} - \frac{3}{4}\sin\frac{x}{2}\cos\frac{x}{2} + \frac{3}{8}x + C$$

7. $$\int_0^{\frac{\pi}{2}} \sin^5 x\,dx = -\frac{\sin^4 x \cos x}{5} + \frac{4}{5}\int_0^{\frac{\pi}{2}} \sin^3 x\,dx =$$

$$-\frac{\sin^4 x \cos x}{5} + \frac{4}{5}\left[-\frac{\sin^2 x \cos x}{3} + \frac{2}{3}\int_0^{\frac{\pi}{2}} \sin x\,dx\right] =$$

$$-\frac{\sin^4 x \cos x}{5} + \frac{4}{5}\left[-\frac{\sin^2 x \cos x}{3} - \frac{2}{3}\cos x\right]_0^{\frac{\pi}{2}} = \frac{8}{15}$$

8. $$\int_0^{\frac{\pi}{4}} \sin^5 2x\,dx = -\frac{\sin^4 2x \cos 2x}{10}\Big]_0^{\frac{\pi}{4}} + \frac{4}{5}\int_0^{\frac{\pi}{4}} \sin^3 2x\,dx$$

$$= 0 + \frac{4}{5}\left[-\frac{\sin^2 2x \cos 2x}{6}\right]_0^{\frac{\pi}{4}} + \frac{8}{15}\int_0^{\frac{\pi}{4}} \sin 2x\,dx$$

$$= 0 - \frac{4}{15}\cos 2x\Big]_0^{\frac{\pi}{4}} = \frac{4}{15}$$

9. $$\int \tan^3 2x\,dx = \frac{\tan^2 2x}{4} - \int \tan 2x\,dx = \frac{\tan^2 2x}{4} + \frac{1}{2}\ln|\cos 2x| + C$$

10. $$\int_0^{\frac{\pi}{2}} \tan^4\frac{x}{2}\,dx = \frac{2}{3}\tan^3\frac{x}{2} - 2\tan\frac{x}{2} + x\Big]_0^{\frac{\pi}{2}} = \frac{\pi}{2} - \frac{4}{3}$$

11. $\int \tan^5 x\,dx = \frac{\tan^4 x}{4} - \int \tan^3 x\,dx = \frac{\tan^4 x}{4} - \left[\frac{\tan^2 x}{2} - \int \tan x\,dx\right]$

$= \frac{\tan^4 x}{4} - \frac{\tan^2 x}{2} + \ln|\cos x| + C$

12. $\int \tan^5 2x\,dx = \frac{1}{8}\tan^4 2x\,dx - \int \tan^3 2x\,dx$

$= \frac{1}{8}\tan^4 2x\,dx - \frac{1}{4}\tan^2 2x + \int \tan 2x\,dx$

$= \frac{1}{8}\tan^4 2x\,dx - \frac{1}{4}\tan^2 2x + \frac{1}{2}\ln|\sec 2x| + C$

13. $\int \cot^3 x\,dx = -\frac{\cot^2 x}{2} - \int \cot x\,dx = -\frac{\cot^2 x}{2} - \ln|\sin x| + C$

14. $\int \cot^3 \frac{x}{3}\,dx = -\frac{3}{2}\cot^2 \frac{x}{3} = 3\ln|\sin \frac{x}{3}| + C$

15. $\int_{\frac{\pi}{4}}^{\frac{3\pi}{4}} \cot^4 x\,dx = -\frac{\cot^3 x}{3} - \int_{\frac{\pi}{4}}^{\frac{3\pi}{4}} \cot^2 x\,dx = -\frac{\cot^3 x}{3} + \cot x + x\Big]_{\frac{\pi}{4}}^{\frac{3\pi}{4}} = \frac{\pi}{2} - \frac{4}{3}$

16. $\int \cot^4 2x\,dx = -\frac{1}{6}\cos^3 2x + \frac{1}{2}\cos 2x + x + C$

17. $\int_{-\frac{\pi}{3}}^{\frac{\pi}{3}} \sec^4 x\,dx = \frac{\sec^2 x\tan x}{3} + \frac{2}{3}[\tan x\Big]_{-\frac{\pi}{3}}^{\frac{\pi}{3}} = 4\sqrt{3}$

18. $\int_0^{\frac{\pi}{16}} \sec^4 4x\,dx = \frac{1}{12}\sec^2 4x\tan 4x + \frac{1}{6}\tan 4x\Big]_0^{\frac{\pi}{16}} = \frac{7}{6}$

19. $\int \sec^5 x\,dx = \frac{\sec^3 x\tan x}{4} + \frac{3}{4}\int \sec^3 x\,dx =$

$\frac{\sec^3 x\tan x}{4} + \frac{3}{4}\left[\frac{\sec x\tan x}{2} + \frac{1}{2}\int \sec x\,dx\right] =$

$\frac{\sec^3 x\tan x}{4} + \frac{3}{8}\sec x\tan x + \frac{3}{8}\ln|\sec x + \tan x| + C$

20. $\int \sec^5 \frac{x}{2}\,dx = \frac{1}{2}\sec^3 \frac{x}{2}\tan \frac{x}{2} + \frac{3}{4}\int \sec^3 \frac{x}{2}\,dx$

$= \frac{1}{2}\sec^3 \frac{x}{2}\tan \frac{x}{2} + \frac{3}{4}\sec \frac{x}{2}\tan \frac{x}{2} + \frac{3}{8}\int \sec \frac{x}{2}\,dx$

$= \frac{1}{2}\sec^3 \frac{x}{2}\tan \frac{x}{2} + \frac{3}{4}\sec \frac{x}{2}\tan \frac{x}{2} + \frac{3}{4}\ln|\sec \frac{x}{2} + \tan \frac{x}{2}| + C$

21. $\int_{\frac{\pi}{4}}^{\frac{3\pi}{4}} \csc^3 x\,dx = -\frac{1}{2}\csc x\cot x - \frac{1}{2}\ln|\csc x + \cot x|\Big]_{\frac{\pi}{4}}^{\frac{3\pi}{4}} = \sqrt{2} + \frac{1}{2}\ln\frac{\sqrt{2}+1}{\sqrt{2}-1}$

22. $$\int_{\pi}^{2\pi} \csc^3 \frac{x}{3}\,dx = -\frac{3}{2}\csc\frac{x}{3}\cot\frac{x}{3} - \frac{3}{2}\ln\left|\csc\frac{x}{3} + \cot\frac{x}{3}\right|\Bigg]_{\pi}^{2\pi} = 2 + \frac{3}{2}\ln 3$$

23. $$\int \csc^4 x\,dx = -\frac{\csc^2 x\cot x}{3} - \frac{2}{3}\cot x + C$$

24. $$\int \csc^5 x\,dx = -\frac{1}{4}\csc^3 x\cot x + \frac{3}{4}\int \csc^3 x\,dx$$

$$= -\frac{1}{4}\csc^3 x\cot x - \frac{3}{8}\csc x\cot x - \frac{3}{8}\ln|\csc x + \cot x| + C$$

25. $$\int_0^1 (x^2+1)^{-3/2}\,dx = \int_0^{\frac{\pi}{4}} (\tan^2 u + 1)^{-3/2}\sec^2 u\,du = \cos u\Bigg]_0^{\frac{\pi}{4}} = \frac{1}{\sqrt{2}}$$

26. $$\int_0^1 (x^2+1)^{3/2}\,dx = \int_0^{\frac{\pi}{4}} (\tan^2 u + 1)^{3/2}\sec^2 u\,du = \int_0^{\frac{\pi}{4}} \sec^5 u\,du$$

$$= \frac{1}{4}\sec^3 u\tan u + \frac{3}{8}\sec u\tan u + \frac{3}{8}\ln|\sec u + \tan u|\Bigg]_0^{\frac{\pi}{4}}$$

$$= \frac{7\sqrt{2}}{8} + \frac{3}{8}\ln(\sqrt{2}+1)$$ (See Problem 19 for integration)

27. $$\int_0^{\frac{3}{5}} \frac{dx}{(1-x^2)^3} = \int_0^{\sin^{-1}\frac{3}{5}} \frac{\cos u\,du}{(1-\sin^2 u)^3} = \int_0^{\sin^{-1}\frac{3}{5}} \sec^5 u\,du =$$

$$\frac{1}{4}\sec^3 u\tan u + \frac{3}{8}\sec u\tan u + \frac{3}{8}\ln|\sec u + \tan u|\Bigg]_0^{\sin^{-1}\frac{3}{5}} = \frac{735}{1024} + \frac{3}{8}\ln 2\}$$

28. $$\int_1^2 \frac{(x^2-1)^{3/2}\,dx}{x} = \int_0^{\frac{\pi}{3}} \frac{(\sec^2 u - 1)^{3/2}\sec u\tan u\,du}{\sec u} = \int_0^{\frac{\pi}{3}} \tan^4 u\,du$$

$$= \frac{1}{3}\tan^3 u - \tan u + u\Bigg]_0^{\frac{\pi}{3}} = \frac{\pi}{3}$$

29. $$\frac{d}{dx}\left(-\frac{\sin^{n-1} x\cos x}{n}\right) = -\frac{1}{n}\sin^{n-1} x\,(-\sin x) - \left(\frac{1}{n}\cos x\right)(n-1)(\sin^{n-2} x)(\cos x)$$

$$= \frac{1}{n}\sin^n x - \frac{n-1}{n}\sin^{n-2} x\cos^2 x$$

$$\frac{d}{dx}\left(\frac{n-1}{n}\int \sin^{n-2} x\,dx\right) = \frac{n-1}{n}\sin^{n-2} x$$

$$\frac{1}{n}\sin^n x - \frac{n-1}{n}\sin^{n-2} x\cos^2 x + \frac{n-1}{n}\sin^{n-2} x =$$

$$\frac{1}{n}\sin^n x + \frac{n-1}{n}\sin^n x\left(\frac{1-\cos^2 x}{\sin^2 x}\right) = \sin^n x\left(\frac{1}{n} + \frac{n-1}{n}\right) = \sin^n x$$

30. $$\frac{d}{dx}\left(-\frac{\csc^{n-2} x \cot x}{n-1}\right) = -\frac{1}{n-1}\csc^{n-2} x\,(-\csc^2 x) - \frac{n-2}{n-1}\cot x \csc^{n-3} x\,(-\csc x \cot x)$$

$$= \frac{1}{n-1}\csc^n x + \frac{n-2}{n-1}\cot^2 x \csc^{n-2} x$$

$$\frac{d}{dx}\left(\frac{n-2}{n-1}\int \csc^{n-2} x\,dx\right) = \frac{n-2}{n-1}\csc^{n-2} x$$

$$\frac{1}{n-1}\csc^n x + \frac{n-2}{n-1}\cot^2 x \csc^{n-2} x + \frac{n-2}{n-1}\csc^{n-2} x =$$

$$\frac{1}{n-1}\csc^n x + \frac{n-2}{n-1}\csc^{n-2} x\,(\cot^2 x + 1) = \csc^n x\left(\frac{1}{n-1} + \frac{n-2}{n-1}\right) = \csc^n x$$

31. (a) Let $u = x^n \Rightarrow du = nx^{n-1}\,dx$, $dv = \sin x\,dx \Rightarrow v = -\cos x$

$$\int x^n \sin x\,dx = -x^n \cos x - \int nx^{n-1}(-\cos x)\,dx$$

$$= -x^n \cos x + n\int x^{n-1}\cos x\,dx$$

(b) $$\int x^n \sin ax\,dx = -\frac{x^n}{a}\cos ax + \frac{n}{a}\int x^{n-1}\cos ax\,dx$$

32. (a) Let $u = x^n \Rightarrow du = n\,x^{n-1}$, $dv = \cos x\,dx \Rightarrow v = \sin x$

Then $\int x^n \cos x\,dx = x^n \sin x - n\int x^{n-1}\sin x\,dx$

(b) $$\int x^n \cos ax\,dx = \frac{x^n}{a}\sin ax - \frac{n}{a}\int x^{n-1}\sin ax\,dx$$

33. (a) Let $dv = x^m\,dx \Rightarrow v = \frac{1}{m+1}x^{m+1}$, $v = (\ln x)^n \Rightarrow dv = \frac{n(\ln x)^{n-1}}{x}dx$

$$\int x^m(\ln x)^n\,dx = \frac{1}{m+1}x^{m+1}(\ln x)^n - \int \frac{1}{m+1}x^{m+1}\left(\frac{n(\ln x)^{n-1}}{x}\right)dx$$

$$= \frac{x^{m+1}(\ln x)^n}{m+1} - \frac{n}{m+1}\int x^m(\ln x)^{n-1}\,dx$$

(b) $$\int_1^e x^3(\ln x)^2\,dx = \frac{x^4(\ln x)^2}{4} - \frac{1}{2}\int x^3 \ln x\,dx$$

$$= \frac{x^4(\ln x)^2}{4} - \frac{1}{2}\left[\frac{x^4 \ln x}{4} - \frac{1}{4}\int x^3\,dx\right]$$

$$= \frac{x^4(\ln x)^2}{4} - \frac{x^4 \ln x}{8} + \frac{x^4}{32}\Bigg]_1^e = \frac{e^4 - 1}{16}$$

34. (a) Let $u = x^n \Rightarrow du = n x^{n-1}$, $dv = e^x\,dx \Rightarrow v = e^x$

Then $\int x^n e^x\,dx = x^n e^x - n\int x^{n-1} e^x\,dx$

(b) $\int_0^1 x^3 e^x\,dx = x^3 e^x - 3x^2 e^x + 6xe^x - 6e^x \Big]_0^1 = 6 - 2e$

7.M MISCELLANEOUS PROBLEMS

1. $\int \frac{\cos x\,dx}{\sqrt{1+\sin x}} = 2\sqrt{1+\sin x} + C$

2. $\int_0^{\frac{\sqrt{2}}{2}} \frac{\sin^{-1} x\,dx}{\sqrt{1-x^2}} = \frac{1}{2}(\sin^{-1} x)^2 \Big]_0^{\frac{\sqrt{2}}{2}} = \frac{1}{2}\left(\frac{\pi}{4}\right)^2 = \frac{\pi^2}{32}$

3. $\int \tan x \sec^2 x\,dx = \frac{1}{2}\tan^2 x + C$

4. $\int \frac{y\,dy}{1+y^4} = \frac{1}{2}\int \frac{du}{1+u^2} = \frac{1}{2}\tan^{-1} u + C = \frac{1}{2}\tan^{-1}(y^2) + C$

Let $u = y^2 \Rightarrow du = 2y\,dy \Rightarrow y\,dy = \frac{1}{2}du$

5. $\int_0^9 e^{\ln\sqrt{x}}\,dx = \int_0^9 \sqrt{x}\,dx = \frac{2}{3}x^{3/2}\Big]_0^9 = 18$

6. $\int \frac{\cos\sqrt{x}\,dx}{\sqrt{x}} = 2\int \cos u\,du = 2\sin u + C = 2\sin\sqrt{x} + C$

Let $u = \sqrt{x} \Rightarrow du = \frac{1}{2\sqrt{x}}\,dx \Rightarrow 2\,du = \frac{dx}{\sqrt{x}}$

7. Let $\tan u = x + 1 \Rightarrow \sec^2 u\,du = dx$. Then $\int \frac{dx}{\sqrt{x^2+2x+2}} = \int \frac{dx}{\sqrt{(x+1)^2+1}} =$

$$\int \frac{\sec^2 u\,du}{\sqrt{\tan^2 u + 1}} = \int \sec u\,du = \ln|\sec u + \tan u| + C =$$

$$\ln\left|\sqrt{x^2+2x+2} + x + 1\right| + C$$

8. $\int_4^5 \frac{(3x-7)\,dx}{(x-1)(x-2)(x-3)} = \int_4^5 \left(\frac{-2}{x-1} + \frac{1}{x-2} + \frac{1}{x-3}\right)dx$

$= -2\ln|x-1| + \ln|x-2| + \ln|x-3|\Big]_4^5$

$= -2\ln 4 + \ln 3 + \ln 2 + 2\ln 3 - \ln 2 - \ln 1$

$= 3\ln 3 - \ln 16 = \ln 27 - \ln 16$

9. $\int x^2 e^x\,dx = e^x(x^2 - 2x + 2) + C$

$$\begin{array}{ccc} x^2 & & e^x \\ & \searrow + & \\ 2x & & e^x \\ & \searrow - & \\ 2 & & e^x \\ & \searrow + & \\ 0 & & e^x \end{array}$$

10. $\int \sqrt{x^2+1}\,dx = \int \sec^3 u\,du = \frac{1}{2}(\sec u \tan u + \ln|\sec u + \tan u|) + C$

$$= \frac{1}{2}\left(x\sqrt{x^2+1} + \ln|x + \sqrt{x^2+1}|\right) + C$$

Let $x = \tan u \Rightarrow dx = \sec^2 u\,du$ (See Article 7.3, Ex. 3 for integration)

11. Let $u = e^t \Rightarrow du = e^t\,dt$. Then $\int \frac{e^t\,dt}{1+e^{2t}} = \int \frac{du}{1+u^2} = \tan^{-1} u = \tan^{-1}(e^t) + C$

12. $\int \frac{dx}{e^x + e^{-x}} = \int \frac{e^x\,dx}{e^{2x}+1} = \tan^{-1}(e^x) + C$

13. Let $u^2 = x \Rightarrow 2u\,du = dx$.

Then $\int \frac{dx}{(x+1)\sqrt{x}} = \int \frac{2u\,du}{u(u^2+1)} = 2\tan^{-1} u = 2\tan^{-1}\sqrt{x} + C$.

14. $\int_0^{64} \frac{dx}{\sqrt{1+\sqrt{x}}} = \int_1^3 \frac{4u(u^2-1)\,du}{u} = 4\left[\frac{1}{3}u^3 - u\right]_1^3 = \frac{80}{3}$

Let $u^2 = 1 + \sqrt{x} \Rightarrow 2u\,du = \frac{1}{2\sqrt{x}}\,dx \Rightarrow 4u\sqrt{x}\,du = dx \Rightarrow$

$4u(u^2-1)\,du = dx$; $x = 0 \Rightarrow u = 1$, $x = 64 \Rightarrow u = 3$

15. Let $u = t^{\frac{5}{3}} + 1 \Rightarrow du = \frac{5}{3}t^{\frac{2}{3}}\,dt \Rightarrow t^{\frac{2}{3}}\,dt = \frac{3}{5}\,du$

$$\int t^{\frac{2}{3}}(t^{\frac{5}{3}}+1)^{\frac{2}{3}}\,dt = \frac{3}{5}\int u^{\frac{2}{3}}\,du = \frac{3}{5}\left(\frac{3}{5}u^{\frac{5}{3}}\right) + C = \frac{9}{25}(t^{\frac{5}{3}}+1)^{\frac{5}{3}} + C$$

16. $\int_{\frac{\pi}{6}}^{\frac{\pi}{2}} \frac{\cot x\,dx}{\ln(e\sin x)} = \ln|\ln(e\sin x)|\Big]_{\frac{\pi}{6}}^{\frac{\pi}{2}}$

$\ln|\ln\left(e\sin\frac{\pi}{2}\right) - \ln\left(e\sin\frac{\pi}{6}\right)| = \ln|\ln e - \ln\frac{e}{2}| = \ln(\ln 2)$

17. Let $u^2 = e^t + 1 \Rightarrow 2u\,du = e^t\,dt \Rightarrow dt = \dfrac{2u\,du}{e^t} = \dfrac{2u\,du}{u^2 - 1}$.

$$\int \frac{dt}{\sqrt{e^t + 1}} = \int \frac{2u\,du}{u(u^2 - 1)} = \int \left(\frac{1}{u-1} - \frac{1}{u+1}\right) du = \ln|u-1| - \ln|u+1| + C$$

$$= \ln\left|\sqrt{e^t+1} - 1\right| - \ln\left|\sqrt{e^t+1} + 1\right| + C = \ln\left|\frac{\sqrt{e^t+1} - 1}{\sqrt{e^t+1} + 1}\right| + C$$

18. $\displaystyle\int (\tan x \sec x) e^{\sec x}\,dx = e^{\sec x} + C$

19. $\displaystyle\int_0^{\frac{\pi}{2}} \frac{\cos x\,dx}{1 + \sin^2 x} = \tan^{-1}(\sin x)\Big]_0^{\frac{\pi}{2}} = \frac{\pi}{4}$

20. $\displaystyle\int_{1/2}^{1+\sqrt{2}/2} \frac{dx}{\sqrt{2x - x^2}} = \int_{1/2}^{1+\sqrt{2}/2} \frac{dx}{\sqrt{1 - (x-1)^2}} = \sin^{-1}(x-1)\Big]_{1/2}^{1+\sqrt{2}/2}$

$$= \sin^{-1}\frac{\sqrt{2}}{2} - \sin^{-1}\frac{1}{2} = \frac{\pi}{4} - \frac{\pi}{6} = \frac{\pi}{12}$$

21. $\displaystyle\int_0^{\frac{\pi}{2}} \frac{\sin x\,dx}{1 + \cos^2 x} = -\tan^{-1}(\cos x)\Big]_0^{\frac{\pi}{2}} = \frac{\pi}{4}$

22. $\displaystyle\int_0^{\frac{\pi}{4}} \frac{\cos 2t\,dt}{1 + \sin 2t} = \frac{1}{2}\ln|1 + \sin 2t|\Big]_0^{\frac{\pi}{4}} = \frac{1}{2}\ln 2$

23. $\displaystyle\int_0^{\frac{\pi}{3}} \frac{dx}{\sin x \cos x} = \int_0^{\frac{\pi}{3}} \frac{2\,dx}{\sin 2x} = \int_0^{\frac{\pi}{3}} 2\csc 2x = -\ln|\csc 2x + \cot 2x|\Big]_0^{\frac{\pi}{3}} = \ln\sqrt{3}$

24. $\displaystyle\int \sqrt{1 + \sin x}\,dx = \int \sqrt{1 + \sin x} \cdot \frac{\sqrt{1 - \sin x}}{\sqrt{1 - \sin x}}\,dx = \int \frac{\cos x\,dx}{\sqrt{1 - \sin x}} = -2\sqrt{1 - \sin x} + C$

25. $\displaystyle\int_{-\frac{\pi}{2}}^{0} \sqrt{1 - \sin x}\,dx = \int_{-\frac{\pi}{2}}^{0} \frac{\sqrt{1 - \sin x}}{1} \cdot \frac{\sqrt{1 + \sin x}}{\sqrt{1 + \sin x}} = \int_{-\frac{\pi}{2}}^{0} \frac{\cos x\,dx}{\sqrt{1 + \sin x}}$

$$= 2\sqrt{1 + \sin x}\Big]_{-\frac{\pi}{2}}^{0} = 2$$

26. $\displaystyle\int \frac{dx}{(a^2 + x^2)^{1/2}} = \int \frac{a\sec^2\theta\,d\theta}{a^3\sec^3\theta} = \frac{1}{a^2}\int \cos\theta\,d\theta = \frac{1}{a^2}\sin\theta + C$

$$= \frac{x}{a^2\sqrt{x^2 + a^2}} + C \qquad (\text{Let } x = a\tan\theta)$$

27. Let $u = \sqrt[3]{1+e^x} \Rightarrow e^x = u^3 - 1 \Rightarrow e^x\,dx = 3u^2\,du$. Then

$$\int \frac{e^{2x}\,dx}{\sqrt[3]{1+e^x}} = \int \frac{(u^3-1)\,3u^2\,du}{u} = \int (3u^4 - 3u)\,du = \frac{3}{5}u^5 - \frac{3}{2}u^2 + C$$

$$= \frac{3}{5}(1+e^x)^{5/3} - \frac{3}{2}(1+e^x)^{2/3} + C$$

28. $\displaystyle\int_0^1 \ln\sqrt{1+x^2}\,dx = \frac{1}{2}\int_0^1 \ln(1+x^2)\,dx =$

Let $u = \ln(1+x^2) \Rightarrow du = \dfrac{2x}{1+x^2}$; $dv = dx \Rightarrow v = x$

$$\frac{1}{2}[x\ln(1+x^2)]_0^1 - \frac{1}{2}\int_0^1 \frac{2x^2\,dx}{1+x^2} = \frac{1}{2}[x\ln(1+x^2)]_0^1 - \frac{1}{2}\int_0^1\left(2 - \frac{2}{1+x^2}\right)dx$$

$$= \frac{1}{2}x\ln(1+x^2) - x + \tan^{-1}x\Big]_0^1 = \frac{1}{2}\ln 2 - 1 + \frac{\pi}{4}$$

29. Let $x = \sec u \Rightarrow dx = \sec u\tan u\,du$

$$\int_{\frac{5}{4}}^{\frac{5}{3}} \frac{dx}{(x^2-1)^{3/2}} = \int_{x=\frac{5}{4}}^{x=\frac{5}{3}} \frac{\sec u\tan u\,du}{(\tan^2 u)^{3/2}} = \int_{x=\frac{5}{4}}^{x=\frac{5}{3}} \sin^{-2}u\cos u\,du$$

$$= -\csc u = -\frac{x}{\sqrt{x^2-1}}\Bigg]_{\frac{5}{4}}^{\frac{5}{3}} = \frac{5}{12}$$

30. $$\int_0^{\frac{3}{5}} \frac{x^3}{\sqrt{1-x^2}}\,dx = \int_0^{\sin^{-1}\frac{3}{5}} \frac{\sin^3 u\cos u\,du}{\cos u} = \int_0^{\sin^{-1}\frac{3}{5}} \sin u(1-\cos^2 u)\,du$$

Let $x = \sin u \Rightarrow dx = \cos u\,du$, $x = 0 \Rightarrow u = 0$, $x = \dfrac{3}{5} \Rightarrow u = \cos^{-1}\dfrac{3}{5}$

$$-\cos u + \frac{\cos^3 u}{3}\Bigg]_0^{\sin^{-1}\frac{3}{5}} = -\frac{4}{5} + \frac{1}{3}\left(\frac{4}{5}\right)^3 + 1 - \frac{1}{3} = \frac{14}{375}$$

31. Let $u = 2 + \ln x \Rightarrow du = \dfrac{dx}{x}$. Then

$$\int \frac{dx}{x(2+\ln x)} = \int \frac{du}{u} = \ln|u| + C = \ln|2+\ln x| + C$$

32. $$\int \frac{\cos 2x - 1}{\cos 2x + 1}\,dx = \int \frac{(\cos 2x - 1)^2}{\cos^2 2x - 1}\,dx = \int \frac{\cos^2 2x - 2\cos 2x + 1}{-\sin^2 2x}\,dx$$

$$= -\int \cot^2 2x\,dx + \int 2\cot 2x\csc 2x\,dx - \int \csc^2 2x\,dx$$

$$= \int (1 - \csc^2 2x)\,dx + \int 2\cot 2x\csc 2x\,dx - \int \csc^2 2x\,dx$$

$$= x + \cot 2x - \csc 2x + C$$

33. Let $u = \sqrt[4]{e^x + 1} \Rightarrow u^4 = e^x + 1 \Rightarrow 4u^3\,du = e^x\,dx$,

$x = 0 \Rightarrow u = \sqrt[4]{2}$, $x = \ln 2 \Rightarrow u = \sqrt[4]{3}$.

$$\int_0^{\ln 2} \frac{e^{2x}\,dx}{\sqrt[4]{e^x + 1}} = \int_{\sqrt[4]{2}}^{\sqrt[4]{3}} \frac{(u^4 - 1)\,4u^3\,du}{u} = \int_{\sqrt[4]{2}}^{\sqrt[4]{3}} (4u^6 - 4u^2)\,du$$

$$\frac{4}{7}u^7 - \frac{4}{3}u^3 \Big]_{\sqrt[4]{2}}^{\sqrt[4]{3}} = \frac{4}{21}(\sqrt[4]{8} - 2\sqrt[4]{27})$$

34. $$\int \frac{2 \sin\sqrt{x}\cos\sqrt{x}\,dx}{\sqrt{x}} = \int \frac{\sin 2\sqrt{x}\,dx}{\sqrt{x}} = -\cos 2\sqrt{x} + C$$

35. $$\int_0^3 (16 + x^2)^{-3/2}\,dx = \int_0^{\tan^{-1}\frac{3}{4}} (16 + 16\tan^2 u)^{-3/2}\,4\sec^2 u\,du =$$

$$= \frac{1}{16}\int_0^{\tan^{-1}\frac{3}{4}} \cos u\,du = \frac{1}{16}\sin u\Big]_0^{\tan^{-1}\frac{3}{4}} = \frac{3}{80}$$

36. $$\int_0^{(e-1)^2} \frac{dx}{\sqrt{x+1}} = 2\sqrt{x+1}\Big]_0^{(e-1)^2} = 2\sqrt{(e-1)^2 + 1} - 2$$

37. Let $u^2 = x + 1 \Rightarrow 2u\,du = dx$. Then $\int \sin\sqrt{x+1}\,dx = \int 2u \sin u\,du$

$$= -2u\cos u + 2\sin u + C = -2\sqrt{x+1}\cos\sqrt{x+1} + 2\sin\sqrt{x+1} + C$$

38. $$\int \cos\sqrt{1-x}\,dx = \int -2u\cos u\,du = -2u\sin u - 2\cos u + C$$

Let $u^2 = 1 - x \Rightarrow 2u\,du = -\,dx$

$-2u$	$+$	$\cos u$
-2	$-$	$\sin u$
0		$-\cos u$

$$= -2\sqrt{1-x}\sin\sqrt{1-x} - 2\cos\sqrt{1-x} + C$$

39. $$\int_0^1 \frac{dx}{4 - x^2} = \frac{1}{4}\int_0^1 \frac{dx}{2+x} + \frac{1}{4}\int_0^1 \frac{dx}{2-x} = \frac{1}{4}\ln|2+x| - \frac{1}{4}\ln|2-x| = \frac{1}{4}\ln 3$$

40. $$\int_0^1 \frac{dx}{x^3+1} = \int_0^1 \frac{dx}{(x+1)(x^2-x+1)} = \frac{1}{3}\int_0^1 \frac{dx}{x+1} - \frac{1}{3}\int_0^1 \frac{x-2}{x^2-x+1}dx$$

$$= \frac{1}{3}\ln|x+1|\Big]_0^1 - \frac{1}{6}\int_0^1 \frac{2x-4}{x^2-x+1}\,dx$$

$$= \frac{1}{3}\ln 2 - \frac{1}{6}\int_0^1 \frac{2x-1}{x^2-x+1}\,dx - \frac{1}{6}\int_0^1 \frac{-3}{x^2-x+1}\,dx$$

$$= \frac{1}{3}\ln 2 - \frac{1}{6}\ln|x^2-x+1|\Big]_0^1 + \frac{1}{2}\int_0^1 \frac{1}{\left(x-\frac{1}{2}\right)^2+\frac{3}{4}}\,dx$$

$$\left(\text{Let } \frac{\sqrt{3}}{2}\tan u = x - \frac{1}{2} \Rightarrow dx = \frac{\sqrt{3}}{2}\sec^2 u\,du\right)$$

$$= \frac{1}{3}\ln 2 + \frac{1}{\sqrt{3}}\tan^{-1}\left[\frac{2}{\sqrt{3}}\left(x-\frac{1}{2}\right)\right]_0^1 = \frac{1}{3}\ln 2 + \frac{\pi}{3\sqrt{3}}$$

41. $$\frac{1}{y(2y^3+1)^2} = \frac{A}{y} + \frac{By^2+Cy+D}{2y^3+1} + \frac{Ey^2+Fy+G}{(2y^3+1)^2}$$

$A(2y^3+1)^2 + (By^2+Cy+D)(2y^3+1)y + (Ey^2+Fy+G)y = 1$

$(4A+2B)y^6 + 2Cy^5 + 2Dy^4 + (4A+B+E)y^3 + (C+F)y^2 + (D+G)y + A = 1$

$A = 1 \Rightarrow B = -2 \Rightarrow E = -2$. $C = D = F = G = 0$.

$$\int \frac{dy}{y(2y^3+1)^2} = \int\left(\frac{1}{y} - \frac{2y^2}{2y^3+1} - \frac{y^2}{(2y^3+1)^2}\right)dy$$

$$= \ln|y| - \frac{1}{3}\ln|2y^3+1| + \frac{1}{3}(2y^3+1)^{-1} + C$$

42. $\displaystyle\int \frac{x\,dx}{1+\sqrt{x}} = \int \frac{2u^3\,du}{1+u} = \int\left(u^2 - u + 1 - \frac{1}{u+1}\right)du$

Let $u^2 = x \Rightarrow dx = 2u\,du \Rightarrow x\,dx = 2u^3\,du$

$\displaystyle = 2\left(\frac{1}{3}u^3 - \frac{1}{2}u^2 + u - \ln|u+1|\right) + C$

$\displaystyle = \frac{2}{3}x^{3/2} - x + 2\sqrt{x} - 2\ln(\sqrt{x}+1) + C$

43. $\displaystyle\int \frac{dx}{x(x^2+1)^2} = \int \frac{\sec^2 u\,du}{\tan u(\sec^2 u)^2} = \int \frac{\cos^3 u}{\sin u}\,du$

$\displaystyle = \int \frac{\cos u\,du}{\sin u} - \int \sin u\cos u\,du = \ln|\sin u| + \frac{1}{2}\cos^2 u + C$

$\displaystyle = \ln\left|\frac{x}{\sqrt{x^2+1}}\right| + \frac{1}{2}(x^2+1)^{-1} + C$

44. $\displaystyle\int \ln\sqrt{x-1}\,dx = \frac{1}{2}\int \ln(x-1)\,dx = \frac{1}{2}\left(x\ln|x-1| - \int \frac{x\,dx}{x-1}\right)$

Let $u = \ln(x-1) \Rightarrow du = \dfrac{dx}{x-1}$, $dv = dx \Rightarrow v = x$

$\displaystyle = \frac{1}{2}\left(x\ln|x-1| - \int\left(1 + \frac{1}{x-1}\right)dx\right.$

$\displaystyle = \frac{1}{2}(x\ln|x-1| - x - \ln|x-1) + C$

45. Let $u = e^x \Rightarrow du = e^x\,dx \Rightarrow dx = \dfrac{du}{e^x} = \dfrac{du}{u}$. Then $\displaystyle\int \frac{dx}{e^x - 1} = \int \frac{du}{u(u-1)} =$

$\displaystyle\int\left(-\frac{1}{u} + \frac{1}{u-1}\right)du = -\ln|u| + \ln|u-1| + C = \ln|e^x - 1| - x + C$

46. $\displaystyle\int \frac{(x+1)dx}{x^2(x-1)} = -\int \frac{2}{x}\,dx - \int \frac{1}{x^2}\,dx + \int \frac{2}{x-1}\,dx$

$\displaystyle -2\ln|x| + \frac{1}{x} + 2\ln|x-1| + C$

47. $\displaystyle\int \frac{x\,dx}{x^2+4x+3} = \frac{3}{2}\int \frac{dx}{x+3} - \frac{1}{2}\int \frac{dx}{x+1} = \frac{3}{2}\ln|x+3| - \frac{1}{2}\ln|x+1| + C$

48. $\displaystyle\int_{\ln 2}^{\ln 3} \frac{15\,du}{(e^u - e^{-u})^2} = \int_{\ln 2}^{\ln 3} \frac{15e^{2u}\,du}{(e^{2u-1})^2} = -\frac{15}{2}(e^{2u-1})^{-1}\Big]_{\ln 2}^{\ln 3} = \frac{75}{48}$

49. $\displaystyle\int \frac{4\,dx}{x^3+4x} = \int \frac{1}{x}\,dx - \int \frac{x}{x^2+4}\,dx = \ln|x| - \frac{1}{2}\ln(x^2+4) + C = \ln\left|\frac{x}{\sqrt{x^2+4}}\right| + C$

50. $$\int \frac{dx}{5x^2+8x+5} = \frac{1}{5}\int \frac{dx}{x^2+\frac{8}{5}x+1} = \frac{1}{5}\int \frac{dx}{\left(x+\frac{4}{5}\right)^2+\frac{9}{25}}$$

$$= \frac{1}{5}\int \frac{\frac{3}{5}\sec^2 u\, du}{\frac{9}{25}\sec^2 u} = \frac{1}{3}\int du = \frac{1}{3}\tan^{-1}\left(\frac{5x+4}{3}\right) + C$$

Let $\frac{3}{5}\tan u = x + \frac{4}{5} \Rightarrow \frac{3}{5}\sec^2 u\, du = dx$

51. $$\int \frac{\sqrt{x^2-1}}{x}\, dx = \int \frac{\sqrt{\sec^2 u - 1}\ \sec u \tan u\, du}{\sec u} = \int (\sec^2 u - 1)\, du$$

$$= \tan u - u + C = \sqrt{x^2-1} - \tan^{-1}\sqrt{x^2-1} + C$$

52. $$\int e^x \cos 2x\, dx = \frac{1}{2}e^x \sin 2x - \frac{1}{2}\int e^x \sin 2x\, dx$$

Let $u = e^x \Rightarrow du = e^x dx$, $dv = \cos 2x\, dx \Rightarrow v = \frac{1}{2}\sin 2x$

$$= \frac{1}{2}e^x \sin 2x - \frac{1}{2}\left[-\frac{1}{2}e^x \cos 2x - \int -\frac{1}{2}e^x \cos 2x\, dx\right]$$

Let $u = e^x \Rightarrow du = e^x dx$, $dv = \sin 2x\, dx \Rightarrow v = -\frac{1}{2}\cos 2x$

$$\therefore \int e^x \cos 2x\, dx = \frac{1}{2}e^x \sin 2x + \frac{1}{4}e^x \cos 2x - \frac{1}{4}\int e^x \cos 2x\, dx$$

$$\frac{5}{4}\int e^x \cos 2x\, dx = \frac{1}{2}e^x \sin 2x + \frac{1}{4}e^x \cos 2x$$

$$\int e^x \cos 2x\, dx = \frac{2}{5}e^x \sin 2x + \frac{1}{5}e^x \cos 2x = \frac{e^x}{5}(2\sin 2x + \cos 2x) + C$$

53. Let $u = \sqrt{x} \Rightarrow u^2 = x \Rightarrow 2u\, du = dx$. Then $\int \frac{dx}{x(3\sqrt{x}+1)} =$

$$\int \frac{2u\, du}{u^2(3u+1)} = 2\int \frac{du}{u} - 6\int \frac{du}{3u+1} = 2\ln\sqrt{x} - 2\ln(3\sqrt{x}+1) + C$$

54. $$\int \frac{dx}{x(1+\sqrt[3]{x})} = \int \frac{3u^2\, du}{u^3(1+u)} = \int \frac{3\, du}{u(1+u)} = \int \left(\frac{3}{u} - \frac{3}{1+u}\right) du$$

Let $u^3 = x \Rightarrow 3u^2\, du = dx$

$$= 3\ln|u| - 3\ln|1+u| + C = \ln|x| - 3\ln|1+x^{1/3}| + C$$

55. Let $\tan u = \sin\theta \Rightarrow \sec^2 u\,du = \cos\theta\,d\theta$, $\theta = \frac{\pi}{6} \Rightarrow u = \tan^{-1}\frac{1}{2}$, $\theta = \frac{\pi}{2} \Rightarrow u = \frac{\pi}{4}$

$$\int_{\frac{\pi}{6}}^{\frac{\pi}{2}} \frac{\cot\theta\,d\theta}{1+\sin^2\theta} = \int_{\frac{\pi}{6}}^{\frac{\pi}{2}} \frac{\cos\theta\,d\theta}{\sin\theta\,(1+\sin^2\theta)} = \int_{\tan^{-1}\frac{1}{2}}^{\frac{\pi}{4}} \frac{\sec^2 u\,du}{\tan u \sec^2 u}$$

$$= \ln|\sin u|\Big]_{\tan^{-1}\frac{1}{2}}^{\frac{\pi}{4}} = \ln\frac{\sqrt{5}}{2} - \ln\frac{\sqrt{2}}{2} = \frac{1}{2}\ln\frac{5}{2}$$

56. $$\int \frac{z^5\,dz}{\sqrt{1+z^2}} = \int \tan^5 u \sec u\,du = \int (\sec^2 u - 1)^2 \tan u \sec u\,du$$

Let $z = \tan u \Rightarrow dz = \sec^2 u\,du$

$$= \int (\sec^4 u - 2\sec u + 1)\sec u \tan u\,du = \frac{1}{5}\sec^5 u - \frac{2}{3}\sec^3 u + \sec u + C$$

$$= \frac{1}{5}(1+z^2)^{5/2} - \frac{2}{3}(1+z^2)^{3/2} + (1+z^2)^{1/2} + C$$

57. Let $u^3 = 1+e^{2t} \Rightarrow 3u^2\,du = 2e^{2t}\,dt$

$$\int \frac{e^{4t}\,dt}{(1+e^{2t})^{2/3}} = \frac{3}{2}\int \frac{(u^3-1)\,u^2\,du}{(u^3)^{2/3}} = \frac{3}{2}\int (u^3-1)\,du = \frac{3}{8}u^4 - \frac{3}{2}u + C$$

$$= \frac{3}{8}(1+e^{2t})^{4/3} - \frac{3}{2}(1+e^{2t})^{1/3} + C$$

$$= \frac{3}{8}(1+e^{2t})^{1/3}(e^{2t} - 3) + C$$

58. $$\int \frac{dx}{x^{1/5}\sqrt{1+x^{4/5}}} = \frac{5}{4}\int \frac{du}{\sqrt{u}} = \frac{5}{2}\sqrt{u} + C = \frac{5}{2}\sqrt{1+x^{4/5}} + C$$

Let $u = 1 + x^{4/5} \Rightarrow \frac{5}{4}\,du = \frac{dx}{x^{1/5}}$

59. $$\int \frac{(x^3+x^2)\,dx}{x^2+x-2} = \int \left(x + \frac{2x}{x^2+x-2}\right)dx = \int x\,dx + \frac{4}{3}\int \frac{dx}{x+2} + \frac{2}{3}\int \frac{dx}{x-1}$$

$$= \frac{1}{2}x^2 + \frac{4}{3}\ln|x+2| + \frac{2}{3}\ln|x-1| + C$$

60. $$\int_2^3 \frac{x^3+1}{x^3-x}dx = \int_2^3 \left(1 + \frac{x+1}{x^3-x}\right)dx = \int_2^3 \left(1 - \frac{1}{x} + \frac{1}{x-1}\right)dx$$

$$x - \ln|x| + \ln|x+1|\Big]_2^3 = 1 + 2\ln 2 - \ln 3 = 1 + \ln\frac{4}{3}$$

61. $$\int \frac{x\,dx}{(x-1)^2} = \int \frac{dx}{x-1} + \int \frac{dx}{(x-1)^2} = \ln|x-1| - \frac{1}{x-1} + C$$

62. $$\int \frac{(x+1)\,dx}{(x^2+2x-3)^{2/3}} = \frac{3}{2}(x^2 + 2x - 3)^{1/3} + C$$

63. Let $\frac{1}{2}\sec u = y + \frac{1}{2} \Rightarrow \sec u = 2y + 1$ and $\frac{1}{2}\sec u \tan u\, du = dy$. Then

$$\int \frac{dy}{(2y+1)\sqrt{y^2+y}} = \int \frac{dy}{(2y+1)\sqrt{\left(y+\frac{1}{2}\right)^2 - \frac{1}{4}}} = \int \frac{\frac{1}{2}\sec u \tan u\, du}{\frac{1}{2}\sec u \tan u}$$

$$= u + C = \sec^{-1}(2y+1) + C \text{ or } \tan^{-1}\left(2\sqrt{y^2+y}\right) + C$$

64. $$\int \frac{dx}{x^2\sqrt{a^2-x^2}} = \int \frac{a\cos u\, du}{a^2\sin^2 u\, a\cos u} = \frac{1}{a^2}\int \csc^2 u\, du$$

Let $a\sin u = x \Rightarrow dx = a\cos u\, du$

$$= -\frac{1}{a^2}\cot u = -\frac{\sqrt{a^2-x^2}}{a^2 x} + C$$

65. Let $x = \sin u \Rightarrow dx = \cos u\, du$. Then $\int (1-x^2)^{3/2} = \int \cos^4 u\, du$

$$= \frac{1}{4}\int (1+\cos 2u)^2\, du = \frac{1}{4}\int \left(1 + 2\cos 2u + \frac{1}{2} + \frac{1}{2}\cos 4u\right) du$$

$$= \frac{3}{8}u + \frac{1}{4}\sin 2u + \frac{1}{32}\sin 4u$$

$$= \frac{3}{8}u + \frac{1}{2}\sin u\cos u + \frac{1}{8}\sin u\cos u\,(\cos^2 u - \sin^2 u)$$

$$= \frac{3}{8}\sin^{-1}x + \frac{1}{2}x\sqrt{1-x^2} + \frac{1}{8}x\sqrt{1-x^2}\,(1-2x^2) + C$$

66. $$\int \ln\left(x+\sqrt{1+x^2}\right)dx = x\ln\left(x+\sqrt{1+x^2}\right) - \int \frac{x\,dx}{\sqrt{1+x^2}}$$

Let $u = \ln\left(x+\sqrt{1+x^2}\right) \Rightarrow du = \frac{dx}{\sqrt{1+x^2}}$, $dv = dx \Rightarrow v = x$

$$= x\ln\left(x+\sqrt{1+x^2}\right) - \sqrt{1+x^2} + C$$

67. $$\int x\tan^2 x\, dx = \int x\sec^2 x\, dx - \int x\, dx = x\tan x + \ln|\cos x| - \frac{1}{2}x^2 + C$$

x	$+$	$\sec^2 x$
1	$-$	$\tan x$
0		$-\ln\lvert\cos x\rvert$

68. $\displaystyle\int x\cos^2 x\,dx = \frac{x}{2}\left(x + \frac{1}{2}\sin 2x\right) - \frac{x^2}{4} + \frac{1}{8}\cos 2x + C$

$$= \frac{x^2}{4} + \frac{x}{4}\sin 2x + \frac{1}{8}\cos 2x + C$$

$$\begin{array}{lcl}
x & & \frac{1}{2}(1+\cos 2x) \\
 & \xrightarrow{+} & \\
1 & & \frac{1}{2}\left(x + \frac{1}{2}\sin 2x\right) \\
 & \xrightarrow{-} & \\
0 & & \frac{1}{2}\left(\frac{x^2}{2} - \frac{1}{4}\cos 2x\right)
\end{array}$$

69. $\displaystyle\int_0^{\pi} x^2\sin x\,dx = -x^2\cos x + 2x\sin x + 2\cos x\Big]_0^{\pi} = \pi^2 - 4$

$$\begin{array}{lcl}
x^2 & \xrightarrow{+} & \sin x \\
2x & \xrightarrow{-} & -\cos x \\
2 & \xrightarrow{+} & -\sin x \\
0 & & \cos x
\end{array}$$

70. $\displaystyle\int x\sin^2 x\,dx = \frac{x}{2}\left(x - \frac{1}{2}\sin 2x\right) - \frac{x^2}{4} - \frac{1}{8}\cos 2x + C$

$$= \frac{x^2}{4} - \frac{x}{4}\sin 2x - \frac{1}{8}\cos 2x + C$$

$$\begin{array}{lcl}
x & & \frac{1}{2}(1-\cos 2x) \\
 & \xrightarrow{+} & \\
1 & & \frac{1}{2}\left(x - \frac{1}{2}\sin 2x\right) \\
 & \xrightarrow{-} & \\
0 & & \frac{1}{2}\left(\frac{x^2}{2} + \frac{1}{4}\cos 2x\right)
\end{array}$$

71. $\displaystyle\int_0^1 \frac{dt}{t^4 + 4t^2 + 3} = \frac{1}{2}\int_0^1 \frac{dt}{t^2+1} - \frac{1}{2}\int_0^1 \frac{dt}{t^2+3} = \frac{1}{2}\tan^{-1} t - \frac{\sqrt{3}}{6}\tan^{-1}\frac{t}{\sqrt{3}}\Big]_0^1 = \frac{(9 - 2\sqrt{3})\pi}{72}$

$$\frac{1}{(t^2+1)(t^2+3)} = \frac{At+B}{t^2+1} + \frac{Ct+D}{t^2+3}$$

$$At^3 + Bt^2 + 3At + 3B + Ct^3 + Dt^2 + Ct + D = 1$$

$$(A+C)t^3 + (B+D)t^2 + (3A+C)t + (3B+D) = 1$$

$$A = C = 0,\ B = -\frac{1}{2},\ D = \frac{1}{2}$$

72. $\displaystyle\int \frac{du}{e^{4u} + 4e^{2u} + 3} = \frac{1}{2}\int \frac{dz}{z(z+3)(z+1)}$

Let $z = e^{2u} \Rightarrow dz = 2e^{2u}\,du \Rightarrow du = \dfrac{dz}{2e^{2u}} = \dfrac{dz}{2x}$

$= \dfrac{1}{2}\left(\dfrac{1}{3}\displaystyle\int \frac{dz}{z} + \frac{1}{6}\int \frac{dz}{z+3} - \frac{1}{2}\int \frac{dz}{z+1}\right) = \dfrac{1}{2}\left(\dfrac{1}{3}\ln|z| + \dfrac{1}{6}\ln|z+3| - \dfrac{1}{2}\ln|z+1|\right)$

$= \dfrac{1}{3}u + \dfrac{1}{12}\ln|e^{2u} + 3| - \dfrac{1}{4}\ln|e^{2u} + 1| + C$

73. Let $u = \ln(x+2) \Rightarrow du = \dfrac{dx}{x+2}$, $dv = x\,dx \Rightarrow v = \dfrac{1}{2}x^2$. Then

$\displaystyle\int x\ln\sqrt{x+2}\,dx = \frac{1}{2}\left(\frac{1}{2}x^2\ln(x+2) - \frac{1}{2}\int_0^2 \frac{x^2\,dx}{x+2}\right)$

$= \dfrac{1}{4}x^2\ln(x+2) - \dfrac{1}{4}\displaystyle\int\left(x - 2 + \frac{4}{x+2}\right)dx$

$= \dfrac{1}{4}x^2\ln(x+2) - \dfrac{1}{8}x^2 + \dfrac{1}{2}x - \ln|x+2| + C$. Therefore

$\displaystyle\int_0^2 x\ln\sqrt{x+2}\,dx = \frac{1}{4}x^2\ln(x+2) - \frac{1}{8}x^2 + \frac{1}{2}x - \ln|x+2|\Big]_0^2 = \frac{1}{2} + \ln 2$

74. $\displaystyle\int (x+1)^2 e^x\,dx = (x+1)^2 e^x - 2(x+1)e^x + 2e^x + C$

$(x+1)^2$	+	e^x
$2(x+1)$	−	e^x
2	+	e^x
0		e^x

75. Let $u = \sec^{-1}x \Rightarrow du = \dfrac{dx}{x\sqrt{x^2-1}}$, $dv = dx \Rightarrow v = x$. Then

$\displaystyle\int \sec^{-1}x\,dx = x\sec^{-1}x - \int \frac{dx}{\sqrt{x^2-1}} = x\sec^{-1}x - \int \frac{\sec u\tan u\,du}{\tan u}$

$= x\sec^{-1}x - \ln|x + \sqrt{x^2-1}| + C$

76. $\displaystyle\int \frac{8\,dx}{x^3(x+2)} = \int\left(\frac{1}{x} - \frac{2}{x^2} + \frac{4}{x^3} - \frac{1}{x+2}\right)dx$

$= \ln|x| + \dfrac{2}{x} - \dfrac{2}{x^2} - \ln|x+2| + C$

77. $\int \frac{x\,dx}{x^4 - 16} = \frac{1}{16}\ln|x-2| + \frac{1}{16}\ln|x+2| - \frac{1}{16}\ln(x^2+4) + C = \frac{1}{16}\ln\left|\frac{x^2-4}{x^2+4}\right| + C$

$$\frac{x}{x^4-16} = \frac{A}{x-2} + \frac{B}{x+2} + \frac{Cx+D}{x^2+4}$$

$$A(x+2)(x^2+2) + B(x-2)(x^2+2) + (Cx+D)(x^2-4) = x$$

$$(A+B+C)x^3 + (2A-2B+D)x^2 + (4A+4B-4C)x + (8A-8B-4D) = x$$

$$A = B = \frac{1}{16},\ C = -\frac{1}{8},\ D = 0$$

78. $\int_0^{\frac{\pi}{2}} \frac{\cos x\,dx}{\sqrt{1+\cos x}} = \int_0^{\frac{\pi}{2}} \frac{2\cos^2\frac{x}{2} - 1}{\sqrt{2}\,|\cos\frac{x}{2}|} = \int_0^{\frac{\pi}{2}} \sqrt{2}\cos\frac{x}{2}\,dx - \int_0^{\frac{\pi}{2}} \frac{1}{\sqrt{2}}\sec\frac{x}{2}\,dx$

$\left(\text{Use: } 2\cos^2\frac{x}{2} - 1 = \cos x;\ \text{Note: for } 0 < x < \frac{\pi}{2},\ |\cos\frac{x}{2}| = \cos\frac{x}{2}\right)$

$$= 2\sqrt{2}\sin\frac{x}{2} - \sqrt{2}\ln\left|\sec\frac{x}{2} + \tan\frac{x}{2}\right|\Bigg]_0^{\frac{\pi}{2}} = 2 - \sqrt{2}\ln(\sqrt{2}+1)$$

79. $\int \frac{\cos x\,dx}{\sin^3 x - \sin x} = \int \frac{\cos x\,dx}{\sin x(-\cos^2 x)} = \int \frac{-2\,dx}{\sin 2x} = 2\ln|\csc 2x + \cot 2x| + C$

80. $\int_0^{\ln 2} \frac{du}{(e^u + e^{-u})^2} = \int_1^2 \frac{\frac{1}{z}dz}{\left(z + \frac{1}{z}\right)^2} = \int_1^2 \frac{z\,dz}{(z^2+1)^2} = -\frac{1}{2(x^2+1)^2}\Bigg]_1^2 = \frac{3}{20}$

Let $z = e^u = \frac{1}{z}dz = du;\ u = 0 \Rightarrow z = 1,\ u = \ln 2 \Rightarrow z = 2$

81. Let $u^2 = x \Rightarrow 2u\,du = dx,\ x = 0 \Rightarrow u = 0,\ x = 1 \Rightarrow u = 1$

$$\int_0^1 \frac{x\,dx}{1\ \sqrt{x} + x} = \int_0^1 \frac{2u^3\,du}{u^2+u+1} = 2\int_0^1 \left(u - 1 + \frac{1}{u^2+u+1}\right)dt$$

$$= u^2 - 2u\Big]_0^1 + \int_0^1 \frac{du}{\left(u + \frac{1}{2}\right)^2 + \frac{3}{4}}$$

$$= u^2 - 2u + \frac{4}{\sqrt{3}}\tan^{-1}\left(\frac{2u+1}{\sqrt{3}}\right)\Bigg]_0^1 = \frac{2\pi\sqrt{3} - 9}{9}$$

82. $\int \frac{\sec^2 t\,dt}{\sec^2 t - 3\tan t + 1} = \int \frac{\sec^2 t\,dt}{\tan^2 t - 3\tan t + 2} = \int \frac{dz}{z^2 - 3z + 2}$

Let $z = \tan t \Rightarrow dz = \sec^2 t\,dt$

$$= \int\left(\frac{1}{z-2} - \frac{1}{z-1}\right)dz = \ln|z-2| - \ln|z-1| = \ln\left|\frac{\tan t - 2}{\tan t - 1}\right| + C$$

83. Let $u = \tan t \Rightarrow du = \sec^2 t\, dt$. Then

$$\int \frac{dt}{\sec^2 t + \tan^2 t} = \int \frac{dt}{2\tan^2 t + 1} = \int \frac{dt}{2\tan^2 t + 1} \cdot \frac{\sec^2 t}{1 + \tan^2 t}$$

$$= \int \frac{du}{(2u^2 + 1)(u^2 + 1)} = 2\int \frac{du}{2u^2 + 1} - \int \frac{du}{u^2 + 1}$$

$$= \sqrt{2}\tan^{-1}(\sqrt{2}u) - \tan^{-1}u = \sqrt{2}\tan^{-1}(\sqrt{2}\tan t) - t + C$$

84. $$\int_0^{\tan^{-1}\sqrt{2}} \frac{dx}{1 + \cos^2 x} = \int_0^{\tan^{-1}\sqrt{2}} \frac{\sec^2 x\, dx}{\sec^2 x + 1} = \int_0^{\tan^{-1}\sqrt{2}} \frac{\sec^2 x\, dx}{\tan^2 x + 2}$$

$$\int_0^{\tan^{-1}\sqrt{2}} \frac{\frac{1}{2}\sec^2 x\, dx}{1 + \frac{1}{2}\tan^2 x} = \frac{1}{\sqrt{2}}\tan^{-1}\left(\frac{1}{\sqrt{2}} \tan x\right)\Bigg|_0^{\tan^{-1}\sqrt{2}} = \frac{\pi\sqrt{2}}{8}$$

85. Let $u = e^t \Rightarrow du = e^t dt$ and $dv = e^t \cos(e^t)\, dt \Rightarrow v = \sin(e^t)$. Then

$$\int e^{2t} \cos(e^t)\, dt = e^t \sin(e^t) - \int e^t \sin(e^t)\, dt$$

$$= e^t \sin(e^t) + \cos(e^t) + C$$

86. $$\int_0^1 \ln\sqrt{x^2 + 1}\, dx = \frac{1}{2}\int_0^1 \ln(x^2 + 1)\, dx = \frac{1}{2}\left(x \ln(x^2 + 1)\Big]_0^1 - \int_0^1 \frac{2x^2\, dx}{x^2 + 1}\right)$$

Let $u = \ln(x^2 + 1) \Rightarrow du = \frac{2x\, dx}{x^2 + 1}$; $dv = dx \Rightarrow v = x$

$$= \frac{1}{2}\left(x \ln(x^2 + 1)\right]_0^1 - \frac{1}{2}\int_0^1 \left(2 - \frac{2}{x^2 + 1}\right) dx$$

$$= \frac{1}{2}x \ln(x^2 + 1) - x + \tan^{-1}x\Big]_0^1 = \frac{1}{2}\ln 2 - 1 + \frac{\pi}{4}$$

87. Let $u = \ln(x^3 + x) \Rightarrow du = \frac{3x^2 + 1}{x^3 + x} dx$ $dv = x\, dx \Rightarrow v = \frac{1}{2}x^2$. Then

$$\int x \ln(x^3 + x)\, dx = \frac{1}{2}x^2 \ln(x^3 + x) - \int \frac{1}{2}x^2 \cdot \frac{3x^2 + 1}{x^3 + x}\, dx$$

$$= \frac{1}{2}x^2 \ln(x^3 + x) - \frac{1}{2}\int \left(3x - \frac{2x}{x^2 + 1}\right) dx$$

$$= \frac{1}{2}x^2 \ln(x^3 + x) - \frac{3}{4}x^2 + \frac{1}{2}\ln(x^2 + 1) + C$$

88. $$\int_0^1 x^3 e^{(x^2)}\, dx = \int_1^e \frac{1}{2} \ln z\, dz = \frac{1}{2}[z \ln z - z]_1^e = \frac{1}{2}$$

Let $z = e^{(x^2)} \Rightarrow \ln z = x^2 \Rightarrow \frac{dz}{z} = 2x\, dx$; $x = 0 \Rightarrow z = 1$; $x = 1 \Rightarrow z = e$

89. Let $\sin x = \sqrt{3}\tan u \Rightarrow \cos x\,dx = \sqrt{3}\sec^2 u\,du$

$$\int \frac{\cos x\,dx}{\sqrt{4-\cos^2 x}} = \int \frac{\cos x\,dx}{\sqrt{3+\sin^2 x}} = \int \frac{\sec^2 u\,du}{\sqrt{3+3\tan^2 u}} = \int \sec u\,du$$

$$= \ln|\sec u + \tan u| + C = \ln|\sqrt{3+\sin^2 x} + \sin x| + C$$

90. $$\int_0^{\frac{\pi}{4}} \frac{\sec^2 x\,dx}{\sqrt{4-\sec^2 x}} = \int_0^{\frac{\pi}{4}} \frac{\sec^2 x\,dx}{\sqrt{3-\tan^2 x}} = \int_0^{\frac{1}{\sqrt{3}}} \frac{\sqrt{3}\,du}{\sqrt{3-3u^2}} = \sin^{-1} u \Big]_0^{\frac{1}{\sqrt{3}}} = \sin^{-1}\frac{1}{\sqrt{3}}$$

Let $\tan x = \sqrt{3}\,u \Rightarrow \sec^2 x = \sqrt{3}\,du$; $x = 0 \Rightarrow u = 0$, $x = \frac{\pi}{4} \Rightarrow u = \Rightarrow \frac{1}{\sqrt{3}}$

91. $$\int x^2 \sin(1-x)\,dx = x^2\cos(1-x) + 2x\sin(1-x) - 2\cos(1-x) + C$$

x^2	$+$	$\sin(1-x)$
$2x$	$-$	$\cos(1-x)$
2	$+$	$-\sin(1-x)$
0		$-\cos(1-x)$

92. $$\int_0^1 \frac{dx}{(x^2+1)(2+\tan^{-1}x)} = \ln|2+\tan^{-1}x|\Big]_0^1 = \ln\left(\frac{8+\pi}{8}\right)$$

93. $$\int \frac{dx}{\cot^3 x} = \int \tan^3 x\,dx = \int \tan x(\sec^2 x - 1)\,dx$$

$$= \frac{1}{2}\tan^2 x + \ln|\cos x| + C$$

94. $$\int_0^{\frac{1}{3}} x\ln\sqrt[3]{3x+1}\,dx = \frac{1}{3}\int_0^{\frac{1}{3}} x\ln(3x+1)$$

Let $u = \frac{1}{3}\ln(3x+1) \Rightarrow du = \frac{dx}{3x+1}$; $dv = x\,dx \Rightarrow v = \frac{1}{2}x^2$.

$$= \frac{1}{6}x^2\ln(3x+1)\Big]_0^{\frac{1}{3}} - \frac{1}{2}\int_0^{\frac{1}{3}} \frac{x^2\,dx}{3x+1}$$

$$= \frac{1}{6}x^2\ln(3x+1)\Big]_0^{\frac{1}{3}} - \frac{1}{2}\int_0^{\frac{1}{3}}\left(\frac{1}{3}x - \frac{1}{9} + \frac{1}{9(3x+1)}\right)dx$$

$$= \frac{1}{6}x^2\ln(3x+1) - \frac{1}{12}x^2 + \frac{1}{18}x - \frac{1}{54}\ln|3x+1|\Big]_0^{\frac{1}{3}} = \frac{1}{108}$$

95. $$\int \frac{x^3\,dx}{(x^2+1)^2} = \int \frac{\tan^3 u \sec^2 u\,du}{(\tan^2 u+1)^2} = \int \frac{\sin^3 u\,du}{\cos u} = \int \frac{(1-\cos^2 u)\sin u\,du}{\cos u}$$

$$= \int \tan u\,du - \int \cos u \sin u\,du = \ln|\sec u| + \frac{1}{2}\cos^2 u + C$$

$$= \ln\sqrt{x^2+1} + \frac{1}{2(x^2+1)} + C$$

96. $$\int_0^{\frac{3}{4}} \frac{x\,dx}{\sqrt{1-x}} = \int_1^{\frac{1}{2}} \frac{(u^2-1)(2u\,du)}{u} = 2\left[\frac{1}{3}u^3 - u\right]_1^{\frac{1}{2}} = \frac{5}{12}$$

Let $u^2 = 1-x \Rightarrow 2u\,du = -\,dx$, $x = 0 \Rightarrow u = 1$, $x = \frac{3}{4} \Rightarrow u = \frac{1}{2}$

97. Let $u \Rightarrow u^2 = 2x+1 \Rightarrow 2u\,du = 2\,dx$, $x = 0 \Rightarrow u = 1$, $x = 4 \Rightarrow u = 3$. Then

$$\int_0^4 x\sqrt{2x+1}\,dx = \int_1^3 \frac{u^2-1}{2}\cdot u^2\,du = \frac{1}{2}\int_1^3 (u^4-u^2)\,du = \frac{1}{10}u^5 - \frac{1}{6}u^3\Big]_1^3 = \frac{298}{15}$$

98. $$\int \ln\left(x+\sqrt{x^2-1}\right)dx = x\ln\left(x+\sqrt{x^2-1}\right) - \int \frac{x\,dx}{\sqrt{x^2-1}}$$

Let $u = \ln\left(x+\sqrt{x^2-1}\right) \Rightarrow du = \frac{dx}{\sqrt{x^2-1}}$; $dv = dx \Rightarrow v = x$

$$= x\ln\left(x+\sqrt{x^2-1}\right) - \sqrt{x^2-1} + C$$

99. Let $u = \ln\left(x-\sqrt{x^2-1}\right) \Rightarrow du = -\frac{dx}{\sqrt{x^2-1}}$, $dv = dx \Rightarrow v = x$. Then

$$\int \ln\left(x-\sqrt{x^2-1}\right)dx = x\ln\left(x-\sqrt{x^2-1}\right) - \int \frac{x\,dx}{\sqrt{x^2-1}}$$

$$= \ln\left(x-\sqrt{x^2-1}\right) + \sqrt{x^2-1} + C$$

100. $\int_0^{\frac{1}{2}\ln 3} e^{-x}\tan^{-1}(e^x)\,dx = -e^{-x}\tan^{-1}(e^x)\Big]_0^{\frac{1}{2}\ln 3} + \int_0^{\frac{1}{2}\ln 3} \frac{dx}{1+e^{2x}}$

Let $u = \tan^{-1}(e^x) \Rightarrow du = \frac{e^x\,dx}{1+e^{2x}}$, $dv = e^{-x}\,dx \Rightarrow v = -e^{-x}$

Part I: $-e^{-x}\tan^{-1}(e^x)\Big]_0^{\frac{1}{2}\ln 3} = -\frac{\pi}{3\sqrt{3}} + \frac{\pi}{4}$

Part II: $\int_0^{\frac{1}{2}\ln 3} \frac{dx}{1+e^{2x}} = \frac{1}{2}\int_2^4 \frac{dz}{z(z-1)} = \frac{1}{2}\int_2^4 \left(\frac{1}{z-1} - \frac{1}{z}\right)dz$

Let $z = 1 + e^{2x} \Rightarrow dx = \frac{dz}{2(z-1)}$

$= \frac{1}{2}[\ln|z-1| - \ln|z|\Big]_2^4 = \frac{1}{2}\ln\frac{3}{2}$

$\therefore \int_0^{\frac{1}{2}\ln 3} e^{-x}\tan^{-1}(e^x)\,dx = -\frac{\pi}{3\sqrt{3}} + \frac{\pi}{4} + \frac{1}{2}\ln\frac{3}{2}$

101. Let $u = \ln(x+\sqrt{x}) \Rightarrow du = \frac{2\sqrt{x}+1}{2x\sqrt{x}+2x}dx$, $dv = dx \Rightarrow v = x$. Then

$\int \ln(x+\sqrt{x})\,dx = x\ln|x+\sqrt{x}| - \int \frac{2\sqrt{x}+1}{2x\sqrt{x}+2x}\cdot x\,dx$. Now

$\int \frac{2\sqrt{x}+1}{2x\sqrt{x}+2x}x\,dx = -\frac{1}{2}\int \frac{\sqrt{x}+\sqrt{x}+1}{\sqrt{x}+1}\,dx = -\frac{1}{2}\int dx - \frac{1}{2}\int \frac{\sqrt{x}\,dx}{\sqrt{x}+1}$.

Finally let $u^2 = x \Rightarrow 2u\,du = dx$. Then

$-\frac{1}{2}\int \frac{\sqrt{x}\,dx}{\sqrt{x}+1} = -\frac{1}{2}\int \frac{2u^2\,du}{u+1} = -\int\left(u - 1 + \frac{1}{u+1}\right)du = -\frac{1}{2}u^2 + u - \ln|u+1| =$
$-\frac{1}{2}x + \sqrt{x} - \ln(\sqrt{x}+1)$. Thus, putting the pieces together,

$\int \ln(x+\sqrt{x})\,dx = x\ln|x+\sqrt{x}| - x + \sqrt{x} - \ln|\sqrt{x}+1| + C.$

102. $\int \tan^{-1}\sqrt{x}\,dx = 2\int z\tan^{-1} z\,dz = z^2\tan^{-1} z - \int z^2 \cdot \frac{1}{1+z^2}\,dz$

Let $z = \sqrt{x} \Rightarrow dz = \frac{dx}{2\sqrt{x}} \Rightarrow 2z\;dz = dx$

Let $u = \tan^{-1} z \Rightarrow du = \frac{1}{1+z^2}\,dz$; $dv = 2\,z\,dz \Rightarrow v = z^2$

$= z^2\tan^{-1} z - \int\left[1 - \frac{1}{1+z^2}\right]dz = z^2\tan^{-1} z - z + \tan^{-1} z + C$

$= x\tan^{-1}\sqrt{x} - \sqrt{x} + \tan^{-1}\sqrt{x} + C$

103. $\int_1^2 \ln(x^2+x)\,dx = \int_1^2 \ln[x(x+1)]dx = \int_1^2 \ln x\,dx + \int_1^2 \ln(x+1)\,dx$

$= x\ln x - x + (x-1)\ln(x+1) - x = 3\ln 3 - 2$

104. $\int_0^{\pi^2} \cos\sqrt{x}\,dx = \int_0^{\pi} 2z\cos z\,dz = 2z\sin z + 2\cos z\Big]_0^{\pi} = -4$

Let $z^2 = x \Rightarrow 2z\,dz = dx$; $x = 0 \Rightarrow z = 0$, $x = \pi^2 \Rightarrow z = \pi$

$2z$	+	$\cos z$
2	−	$\sin z$
0		$-\cos z$

105. Let $u^2 = x \Rightarrow 2u\,du = dx$, $x = 0 \Rightarrow u = 0$, $x = \frac{\pi^2}{4} \Rightarrow u = \frac{\pi}{2}$. Then

$\int_0^{\frac{\pi^2}{4}} \sin\sqrt{x}\,dx = \int_0^{\frac{\pi}{2}} 2u\sin u\,du = -2u\cos u + 2\sin u\Big]_0^{\frac{\pi}{2}} = 2$

$2u$	+	$\sin u$
2	−	$-\cos u$
0		$-\sin u$

106. $\int_0^2 \tan^{-1}\sqrt{x+1}\,dx = \int_1^{\sqrt{3}} 2z\tan^{-1} z\,dz = z^2\tan^{-1} z - z + \tan^{-1} z\Big]_1^{\sqrt{3}} = \frac{5\pi}{6} + 1 - \sqrt{3}$

(See problem 102 for integration)

107. Let $u = \sin^{-1} x \Rightarrow du = \dfrac{dx}{\sqrt{1-x^2}}$

$dv = \sqrt{1-x^2}\,dx \Rightarrow v = \int \sqrt{1-x^2}\,dx = \frac{1}{2}\sin^{-1} x + \frac{1}{2}x\sqrt{1-x^2}$. Then

$$\int \sin^{-1} x\sqrt{1-x^2}\,dx = \sin^{-1} x\left(\frac{1}{2}\sin^{-1} x + \frac{1}{2}x\sqrt{1-x^2}\right) - \int\left(\frac{1}{2}\sin^{-1} x + \frac{1}{2}x\sqrt{1-x^2}\right)\frac{dx}{\sqrt{1-x^2}}$$

$$= \frac{1}{2}(\sin^{-1} x)^2 + \frac{1}{2}x\sin^{-1} x\sqrt{1-x^2} - \frac{1}{4}x^2 - \frac{1}{4}(\sin^{-1} x)^2$$

$$= \frac{1}{4}(\sin^{-1} x)^2 + \frac{1}{2}x\sin^{-1} x\sqrt{1-x^2} - \frac{1}{4}x^2 + C$$

108. $\displaystyle\int_0^\pi x\sin^2 2x\,dx = \frac{1}{2}\int_0^\pi x(1-\cos 4x)\,dx = \left.\frac{1}{4}x^2 - \frac{1}{8}x\sin 4x - \frac{1}{32}\cos 4x\right]_0^\pi = \frac{\pi^2}{4}$

x	$+$	$\cos 4x$
1	$-$	$\frac{1}{4}\sin 4x$
0		$-\frac{1}{16}\cos 4x$

109. $\displaystyle\int \frac{\tan x\,dx}{\tan x + \sec x}\cdot\frac{\tan x - \sec x}{\tan x - \sec x} = \int(-\tan^2 x + \tan x\sec x)\,dx$

$$= \int(1 - \sec^2 x + \tan x\sec x)\,dx = x - \tan x + \sec x + C$$

110. $\displaystyle\int \frac{dt}{\sqrt{e^{2t}+1}} = \int \frac{z\,dz}{z(z^2-1)} = \frac{1}{2}\int\frac{dz}{z-1} - \frac{1}{2}\int\frac{dz}{z+1}$

Let $z^2 = e^{2t} + 1 \Rightarrow 2z\,dz = 2e^{2t}\,dt \Rightarrow dt = \dfrac{z\,dz}{e^{2t}} = \dfrac{z\,dz}{z^2-1}$

$$= \frac{1}{2}\ln|z-1| - \frac{1}{2}\ln|z+1| + C = \frac{1}{2}\ln\left|\frac{\sqrt{e^{2t}+1}-1}{\sqrt{e^{2t}+1}+1}\right| + C$$

111. $\displaystyle\int \frac{dx}{(\cos^2 x + 4\sin x - 5)\cos x} = \int \frac{-\cos x\,dx}{(\sin^2 x - 4\sin x + 4)\cos^2 x}$

$$= \int \frac{-\cos x\,dx}{(\sin x - 2)^2(1 - \sin^2 x)}$$

Let $u = \sin x \Rightarrow du = \cos x\,dx$. Then

$$\int \frac{-\cos x\,dx}{(\sin x - 2)^2(1 - \sin^2 x)} = -\int \frac{du}{(u-2)^2(1-u^2)}$$

$$= \frac{1}{3}\int \frac{du}{(u-2)^2} - \frac{4}{9}\int \frac{du}{u-2} + \frac{1}{2}\int \frac{du}{u-1} - \frac{1}{18}\int \frac{du}{u+1}$$

$$= -\frac{1}{3}(u-2)^{-1} - \frac{4}{9}\ln|u-2| + \frac{1}{2}\ln|u-1| - \frac{1}{18}\ln|u+1| + C$$

$$= -\frac{1}{3}(\sin x - 2)^{-1} - \frac{4}{9}\ln|\sin x - 2| + \frac{1}{2}\ln|\sin x - 1| - \frac{1}{18}\ln|\sin x + 1| + C$$

112. $\displaystyle\int \frac{dt}{a + be^{ct}},\ a,b,c \neq 0 = \int \frac{dt}{a + be^{ct}} \cdot \frac{e^{-ct}}{e^{-ct}} = \int \frac{e^{-ct}\,dt}{ae^{-ct} + b} = -\frac{1}{ac}\ln|ae^{-ct} + b| + C$

113. $\displaystyle\int \sqrt{\frac{1-\cos x}{\cos\alpha - \cos x}}\,dx = \int \sqrt{\frac{2\sin^2(x/2)}{2\cos^2(\alpha/2) - 2\cos^2(x/2)}}\,dx$

$$= \frac{\sqrt{\sin^2(x/2)/\cos^2(\alpha/2)}}{\sqrt{1 - \cos^2(x/2)/\cos^2(\alpha/2)}}\,dx$$

Let $u = \dfrac{1}{\cos(\alpha/2)}\cos\dfrac{x}{2} \Rightarrow du = \left(\dfrac{1}{\cos(\alpha/2)}\right)\left(-\dfrac{1}{2}\sin\dfrac{x}{2}\right)$. Then

$$\frac{\sqrt{\sin^2(x/2)/\cos^2(\alpha/2)}}{\sqrt{1 - \cos^2(x/2)/\cos^2(\alpha/2)}}\,dx = \int \frac{-2\,du}{\sqrt{1-u^2}} = -2\sin^{-1}u + C$$

$$= -2\sin^{-1}\left(\frac{\cos(x/2)}{\cos(\alpha/2)}\right) + C$$

114. $\displaystyle\int \frac{dx}{9x^4 + x^2} = \int \left(\frac{1}{x^2} - \frac{9}{9x^2+1}\right)dx = -\frac{1}{x} - 3\tan^{-1}(3x) + C$

$$\frac{A}{x} + \frac{B}{x^2} + \frac{Cx + D}{9x^2 + 1} = \frac{1}{x^2(9x^2+1)} \Rightarrow A = 0,\ B = 1,\ C = 0,\ D = -9.$$

115. Let $u = \ln(2x^2+4) \Rightarrow du = \dfrac{2x\,dx}{x^2+2}$ and $dv = dx \Rightarrow v = x$. Then

$$\int_0^1 \ln(2x^2+4) = x\ln(2x^2+4)\Big]_0^1 - \int_0^1 \frac{2x^2\,dx}{x^2+2}$$

$$= x\ln(2x^2+4)\Big]_0^1 - \int_0^1\left(2 - \frac{4}{x^2+2}\right)dx$$

$$= x\ln(2x^2+4) - 2x + 2\sqrt{2}\tan^{-1}\frac{x}{\sqrt{2}}\Big]_0^1$$

$$= \ln 6 - 2 + 2\sqrt{2}\tan^{-1}\left(\frac{1}{\sqrt{2}}\right)$$

116. $$\int\frac{\sin x\,dx}{\cos^2 - 5\cos x + 4} = -\int\frac{dz}{z^2-5z+4} = -\frac{1}{3}\int\frac{dz}{z-4} + \frac{1}{3}\int\frac{dz}{z-1}$$

Let $z = \cos x \Rightarrow dz = -\sin x\,dx$

$$= -\frac{1}{3}\ln|z-4| + \frac{1}{3}\ln|z-1| + C = \frac{1}{3}\ln\left|\frac{\cos x - 1}{\cos x - 4}\right| + C$$

117. Let $u^2 = 1 - e^{-t} \Rightarrow 2u\,du = e^{-t}dt \Rightarrow dt = \dfrac{2u\,du}{e^{-t}} = \dfrac{2u\,du}{1-u^2}$. Then

$$\int\frac{dt}{\sqrt{1-e^{-t}}} = \int\frac{2u\,du}{u(1-u^2)} = \int\left(\frac{1}{1-u} + \frac{1}{1+u}\right)du$$

$$= -\ln|1-u| + \ln|1+u| + C$$

$$= \ln\left|\frac{1+\sqrt{1-e^{-t}}}{1-\sqrt{1-e^{-t}}}\right| + C$$

118. $$\int\frac{\tan^{-1}x\,dx}{x^2} = -\frac{1}{x}\tan^{-1}x + \int\frac{dx}{x(1+x^2)} = \int\left(\frac{1}{x} - \frac{x}{1+x^2}\right)dx$$

Let $u = \tan^{-1}x \Rightarrow du = \dfrac{1}{1+x^2}$; $dv = \dfrac{1}{x^2}dx \Rightarrow v = -\dfrac{1}{x}$

$$= -\frac{1}{x}\tan^{-1}x + \ln|x| - \frac{1}{2}\ln(1+x^2) + C$$

119. Let $u = x(\sin^{-1}x)^2 \Rightarrow du = \dfrac{2\sin^{-1}x\,dx}{\sqrt{1-x^2}}$, $dv = dx \Rightarrow v = x$. Then

$$\int (\sin^{-1}x)^2\,dx = x\,(\sin^{-1}x)^2 - \int \frac{2x\sin^{-1}x\,dx}{\sqrt{1-x^2}} + C$$

Let $u = \sin^{-1}x \Rightarrow du = \dfrac{dx}{\sqrt{1-x^2}}$, $dv = \dfrac{-2x\,dx}{\sqrt{1-x^2}} \Rightarrow v = 2\sqrt{1-x^2}$. Then

$$-\int \frac{2x\sin^{-1}x\,dx}{\sqrt{1-x^2}} = 2\sin^{-1}x\sqrt{1-x^2} - 2x + C.$$ Therefore,

$$\int (\sin^{-1}x)^2\,dx = x\,(\sin^{-1}x)^2 + 2\sin^{-1}x\sqrt{1-x^2} - 2x + C$$

120. Let $\dfrac{1}{x(x+1)(x+2)\ldots(x+m)} = \dfrac{A_0}{x} + \dfrac{A_1}{x+1} + \dfrac{A_2}{x+2} + \ldots + \dfrac{A_m}{x+m}$

To find a general coefficient, let $x = -k$ to force $A_i = 0$, $i \neq k$:

$$A_k\,x(x+1)\ldots(x+k-1)(x+k+1)\ldots(x+m) = 1$$

$$A_k(-k)(-k+1)\ldots(-1)(1)(2)\ldots(-k+m) = 1$$

$$(-1)^k A_k = k(1-k)(2-k)\ldots(1)(2)\ldots(m-k) = 1 \text{ or } A_k = \frac{(-1)^k}{k!\,(m-k)!}$$

$$\therefore \int \frac{1}{x(x+1)(x+2)\ldots(x+m)}\,dx = \sum_{k=0}^{m} \frac{(-1)^k}{k!\,(m-k)!} \ln|x+k| + C$$

121. Let $u = \sin^{-1}x \Rightarrow du = \dfrac{dx}{\sqrt{1-x^2}}$, $dv = x\,dx \Rightarrow v = \dfrac{1}{2}x^2$. Then

$$\int x\sin^{-1}x\,dx = \frac{1}{2}x^2\sin^{-1}x - \frac{1}{2}\int \frac{x^2\,dx}{\sqrt{1-x^2}}.$$

Let $x = \sin v \Rightarrow dx = \cos v\,dv$. Then $-\dfrac{1}{2}\displaystyle\int \frac{x^2\,dx}{\sqrt{1-x^2}} = -\dfrac{1}{2}\displaystyle\int \sin^2 v\,dv$

$$= -\frac{1}{2}\int\left(\frac{1}{2} - \frac{1}{2}\cos 2v\right)dv = -\frac{1}{4}v + \frac{1}{4}\sin v\cos v.$$ Therefore

$$\int x\sin^{-1}x\,dx = \frac{1}{2}x^2\sin^{-1}x - \frac{1}{4}\sin^{-1}x + \frac{1}{4}x\sqrt{1-x^2} + C$$

122. Let $z^2 = x \Rightarrow 2z\,dz = dx$. Then $\int \sin^{-1}\sqrt{x}\,dx = \int 2z \sin^{-1} z\,dz$

Let $u = \sin^{-1} z \Rightarrow du = \dfrac{dz}{\sqrt{1-z^2}}$; $dv = 2z\,dz \Rightarrow v = z^2$

$$\int 2z \sin^{-1} z\,dz = z^2 \sin^{-1} z - \int \frac{z^2\,dz}{\sqrt{1-z^2}}$$

Let $z = \sin\theta \Rightarrow dz = \cos\theta\,d\theta$

$$= z^2 \sin^{-1} z - \int \frac{\sin^2\theta\cos\theta\,d\theta}{\cos\theta} = z^2 \sin^{-1} z - \frac{1}{2}\int (1 - \cos 2\theta)\,d\theta$$

$$= z^2 \sin^{-1} z - \frac{1}{2}\theta + \frac{1}{4}\sin 2\theta = z^2 \sin^{-1} z - \frac{1}{2}\sin^{-1} z + \frac{z}{2}\sqrt{1-z^2} + C$$

$$= x \sin^{-1}\sqrt{x} - \frac{1}{2}\sin^{-1}\sqrt{x} + \frac{1}{2}\sqrt{x(1-x)} + C$$

123. $$\int \frac{d\theta}{1-\tan^2\theta} = \int \frac{\cos^2\theta\,d\theta}{\cos^2\theta - \sin^2\theta} = \frac{1}{2}\int \frac{1+\cos 2\theta\,d\theta}{\cos 2\theta}$$

$$= \frac{1}{2}\int \sec 2\theta\,d\theta + \frac{1}{2}\int d\theta$$

$$= \frac{1}{4}\ln|\sec 2\theta + \tan 2\theta| + \frac{1}{2}\theta + C$$

124. $$\int \ln(\sqrt{x} + \sqrt{1+x})\,dx = x\ln(\sqrt{x} + \sqrt{1+x}) - \frac{1}{2}\int \frac{x\,dx}{\sqrt{x}\sqrt{x+1}}$$

Let $u = \ln(\sqrt{x} + \sqrt{1+x}) \Rightarrow du = \dfrac{x\,dx}{\sqrt{x}\sqrt{x+1}}$; $dv = dx \Rightarrow v = x$

Now: $$\int \frac{x\,dx}{\sqrt{x}\sqrt{x+1}} = \int \frac{x\,dx}{\sqrt{\left(x+\frac{1}{2}\right)^2 - \frac{1}{4}}} = \int \frac{\left(\frac{1}{2}\sec u - \frac{1}{2}\right)\left(\frac{1}{2}\sec u \tan u\,du\right)}{\sqrt{\frac{1}{4}\sec^2 u - \frac{1}{4}}}$$

Let $\frac{1}{2}\sec u = x + \frac{1}{2} \Rightarrow \frac{1}{2}\sec u \tan u\,du = dx$

$$\frac{1}{2}\int (\sec^2 u - \sec u)\,du = \frac{1}{2}\tan u - \frac{1}{2}\ln|\sec u + \tan u| + C$$

$$\therefore \int \ln(\sqrt{x} + \sqrt{1+x})\,dx = x\ln(\sqrt{x} + \sqrt{1+x}) - \frac{1}{4}\tan u + \frac{1}{4}\ln|\sec u + \tan u| +$$

$$= x\ln(\sqrt{x} + \sqrt{1+x}) - \frac{1}{2}\sqrt{x^2+x} + \frac{1}{4}\ln|2x + 1 + 2\sqrt{x^2+x}| +$$

125. Let $t = \sin x \Rightarrow dt = \cos x\,dx$. Then $\int \frac{dt}{t - \sqrt{1 - t^2}}$

$$= \int \frac{\cos x\,dx}{\sin x - \cos x} \cdot \frac{\sin x + \cos x}{\sin x + \cos x} = \int \frac{\frac{1}{2}\sin 2x + \frac{1}{2}\cos 2x + \frac{1}{2}}{-\cos 2x}\,dx$$

$$= -\frac{1}{2}\int \tan 2x\,dx - \frac{1}{2}\int \sec 2x\,dx - \frac{1}{2}\int dx$$

$$= \frac{1}{4}\ln|\cos 2x| - \frac{1}{4}\ln|\sec 2x + \tan 2x| - \frac{1}{2}x + C$$

$$= \frac{1}{4}\ln|1 - 2t^2| - \frac{1}{4}\ln\left|\frac{1 + 2t\sqrt{1 - t^2}}{1 - 2t^2}\right| - \frac{1}{2}\sin^{-1}t + C$$

126. $\int \frac{(2e^{2x} - e^x)\,dx}{\sqrt{3e^{2x} - 6e^x - 1}} = \int \frac{(2e^x - 1)\,e^x dx}{\sqrt{3e^{2x} - 6e^x - 1}} = \int \frac{2u - 1}{\sqrt{3u^2 - 6u - 1}}\,du$

Let $u = e^x \Rightarrow du = e^x\,dx$

$$= \frac{1}{\sqrt{3}}\int \frac{(2u - 1)\,du}{\sqrt{(u - 1)^2 - \frac{4}{3}}} = \frac{1}{\sqrt{3}}\int \frac{\left(\frac{4}{\sqrt{3}}\sec z + 1\right)\left(\frac{2}{\sqrt{3}}\sec z \tan z\,dz\right)}{\frac{2}{\sqrt{3}}\tan z}$$

Let $u - 1 = \frac{2}{\sqrt{3}}\sec z \Rightarrow du = \frac{2}{\sqrt{3}}\sec z \tan z\,dz$

$$= \frac{1}{\sqrt{3}}\left(\frac{4}{\sqrt{3}}\tan z + \ln|\sec z + \tan z|\right) + C$$

$$= \frac{1}{\sqrt{3}}\left(2\sqrt{u^2 - 2u - \frac{1}{3}}\right) + 4\ln\left|u - 1 + \sqrt{u^2 - 2u - \frac{1}{3}}\right| + C$$

$$= \frac{1}{\sqrt{3}}\left(2\sqrt{e^{2x} - 2e^x - \frac{1}{3}} + 4\ln\left|e^x - 1 + \sqrt{e^{2x} - 2e^x - \frac{1}{3}}\right| + C\right.$$

127. $\int \frac{dx}{x^4+4} = \int \frac{dx}{(x^2+2)^2 - 4x^2} = \int \frac{dx}{(x^2+2x+2)(x^2-2x+2)}$

$$= \int \frac{\frac{1}{8}x + \frac{1}{4}}{x^2+2x+2}\,dx + \int \frac{-\frac{1}{8}x + \frac{1}{4}}{x^2-2x+2}\,dx$$

$$= \frac{1}{16}\int \frac{2x+4}{x^2+2x+2}\,dx - \frac{1}{16}\int \frac{2x-4}{x^2-2x+2}\,dx$$

$$= \frac{1}{16}\left(\int \frac{2x+2}{x^2+2x+2}\,dx + \int \frac{2\,dx}{(x+1)^2+1} - \int \frac{2x-2}{x^2-2x+2}\,dx + \int \frac{2\,dx}{(x-1)^2+1}\right)$$

$$= \frac{1}{16}\ln\left|\frac{x^2+2x+2}{x^2-2x+2}\right| + \frac{1}{8}[\tan^{-1}(x+1) + \tan^{-1}(x-1)] + C$$

128. $\int \frac{dx}{x^6-1} = \int \frac{dx}{(x-1)(x^2+x+1)(x-1)(x^2-x+1)}$

$$= \frac{1}{6}\int \frac{dx}{x-1} - \frac{1}{6}\int \frac{(x+2)\,dx}{x^2+x+1} + \frac{1}{6}\int \frac{(x-2)\,dx}{x^2-x+1} - \frac{1}{6}\int \frac{dx}{x+1}$$

Part 1: $\frac{1}{6}\int \frac{dx}{x-1} = \frac{1}{6}\ln|x-1|$

Part 2: $-\frac{1}{6}\int \frac{(x+2)\,dx}{x^2+x+1} = -\frac{1}{6}\int \frac{(x+2)\,dx}{\left(x+\frac{1}{2}\right)^2 + \frac{3}{4}}$

Let $\tan u = \frac{2x+1}{\sqrt{3}} \Rightarrow \frac{\sqrt{3}}{2}\sec^2 u\,du = dx$; $x = \frac{1}{2}(\sqrt{3}\tan u - 1)$

$$= -\frac{1}{6}\int \frac{\left(\frac{\sqrt{3}}{2}\tan u + \frac{3}{2}\right)\left(\frac{\sqrt{3}}{2}\sec^2 u\,du\right)}{\frac{3}{4}\tan^2 u + \frac{3}{4}} = -\frac{1}{6}\int (\tan u + \sqrt{3})\,du$$

$$= \frac{1}{6}\ln|\cos u| - \frac{\sqrt{3}}{6}u = \frac{1}{6}\ln\sqrt{x^2+x+1} - \frac{\sqrt{3}}{6}\tan^{-1}\left(\frac{2x+1}{\sqrt{3}}\right)$$

Part 3: $\frac{1}{6}\int \frac{(x-2)\,dx}{x^2-x+1} = \frac{1}{6}\int \frac{(x-2)\,dx}{\left(x-\frac{1}{2}\right)^2+\frac{3}{4}}$

Let $\tan u = \frac{2x-1}{\sqrt{3}} \Rightarrow \frac{\sqrt{3}}{2}\sec^2 u\,du = dx;\ x = \frac{1}{2}(\sqrt{3}\tan u + 1)$

$$= \frac{1}{6}\int \frac{\left(\frac{\sqrt{3}}{2}\tan u - \frac{3}{2}\right)\left(\frac{\sqrt{3}}{2}\sec^2 u\,du\right)}{\frac{3}{4}\tan^2 u + \frac{3}{4}} = \frac{1}{6}\int (\tan u - \sqrt{3})\,du$$

$$= -\frac{1}{6}\ln|\cos u| - \frac{\sqrt{3}}{6}u = -\frac{1}{6}\ln\sqrt{x^2-x+1} - \frac{\sqrt{3}}{6}\tan^{-1}\left(\frac{2x-1}{\sqrt{3}}\right)$$

Part 4: $-\frac{1}{6}\int \frac{dx}{x+1} = -\frac{1}{6}\ln|x+1|$

Final answer:

$$\frac{1}{6}\ln|x-1| + \frac{1}{6}\ln\sqrt{x^2+x+1} - \frac{\sqrt{3}}{6}\tan^{-1}\left(\frac{2x+1}{\sqrt{3}}\right) - \frac{1}{6}\ln\sqrt{x^2-x+1}$$

$$-\frac{\sqrt{3}}{6}\tan^{-1}\left(\frac{2x-1}{\sqrt{3}}\right) - \frac{1}{6}\ln|x+1| + C$$

129. $\lim_{n\to\infty}\left(\frac{n}{n^2+0^2} + \frac{n}{n^2+1^2} + \frac{n}{n^2+2^2} + \ldots + \frac{n}{n^2+(n+1)^2}\right) =$

$$\lim_{n\to\infty}\sum_{k=0}^{n+1}\frac{n}{n^2+k^2} = \lim_{n\to\infty}\left(\frac{1}{n}\sum_{k=0}^{n+1}\frac{n^2}{n^2+k^2}\right) = \lim_{n\to\infty}\left(\frac{1}{n}\sum_{k=0}^{n+1}\frac{1}{1+\left(\frac{k}{n}\right)^2}\right)$$

$$= \int_0^1 \frac{dx}{1+x^2} = \tan^{-1}x\Big]_0^1 = \frac{\pi}{4}$$

130. $\lim_{n\to\infty}\sum_{k=1}^{n}\ln\sqrt[n]{1+\frac{k}{n}} = \lim_{n\to\infty}\frac{1}{n}\sum_{k=1}^{n}\left(1+\frac{k}{n}\right) = \int_0^1 \ln(1+x)\,dx$

$$= (1+x)\ln(1+x) - x\Big]_0^1 = 2\ln 2 - 1$$

131. $\lim_{n\to\infty}\sum_{k=0}^{n-1}\frac{1}{\sqrt{n^2-k^2}} = \lim_{n\to\infty}\left(\frac{1}{n}\sum_{k=0}^{n-1}\frac{n}{\sqrt{n^2-k^2}}\right)$

$$= \lim_{n\to\infty}\left(\frac{1}{n}\sum_{k=0}^{n-1}\frac{1}{\sqrt{1-\left(\frac{k}{n}\right)^2}}\right) = \int_0^1 \frac{dx}{\sqrt{1-x^2}} = \sin^{-1}x\Big]_0^1 = \frac{\pi}{2}$$

132. $\int x^3 e^{(-x^2)}\,dx = -\frac{x^2}{2}e^{(-x^2)} + \int x\,e^{(-x^2)}\,dx = -\frac{x^2}{2}e^{(-x^2)} - \frac{1}{2}e^{(-x^2)}$

Let $u = x^2 \Rightarrow du = 2x\,dx \qquad dv = xe^{(-x^2)}\,dx \Rightarrow v = -\frac{1}{2}e^{(-x^2)}$

$$\therefore = \int_0^\infty x^3 e^{(-x^2)}\,dx = \lim_{b\to\infty}\int_0^b x^3 e^{(-x^2)}\,dx = \lim_{b\to\infty}\left[-\frac{x^2}{2}e^{(-x^2)} - \frac{1}{2}e^{(-x^2)}\right]_0^b = \frac{1}{2}$$

133. $\int_0^1 \ln x\,dx = \lim_{b\to0^+}\int_b^1 \ln x\,dx = \lim_{b\to0^+}(x\ln x - x)\Big]_b^1$

$$= \lim_{b\to0^+}(-1 - b\ln b + b) = -1$$

Note: $\lim_{b\to0^+} b\ln b = \lim_{b\to0^+}\frac{\ln b}{\frac{1}{b}} = \lim_{b\to0^+}\frac{\frac{1}{b}}{\frac{-1}{b^2}} = \lim_{b\to0^+}(-b) = 0$

134. $y = 2\sqrt{x} \Rightarrow \frac{dy}{dx} = \frac{1}{\sqrt{x}}$. $\quad ds = \sqrt{1 + \frac{1}{x}}\,dx$

$$A = \int y\,ds = \int_0^3 2\sqrt{x}\sqrt{1+\frac{1}{x}}\,dx = 2\int_0^3 \sqrt{1+x}\,dx = \frac{4}{3}(1+x)^{3/2}\Big]_0^3 = \frac{28}{3}$$

135. The line through $(a,0)$ and $(0,a)$ is: $y = -x + a$.

$$A = \int_0^a\left(\sqrt{a^2-x^2} - (a-x)\right)dx = \frac{a^2}{2}\left(\frac{\pi}{2} - 1\right)$$

$$M_y = \int_0^a x\left(\sqrt{a^2-x^2} - (a-x)\right)dx = \frac{a^3}{6}$$

$$\bar{x} = \left(\frac{a^3}{6}\right)\left(\frac{4}{a^2(\pi-2)}\right) = \frac{2a}{3(\pi-2)}. \qquad \bar{y} = \bar{x} \text{ by symmetry.}$$

136. $M = \int_0^1 (e^x - 1)\,dx = e^x - x\Big]_0^1 = e - 2$

$$M_x = \int_0^1 \frac{1}{2}(e^x+1)(e^x-1)\,dx = \frac{1}{2}\int_0^1 (e^{2x} - 1)\,dx = \frac{1}{4}e^{2x} - \frac{1}{2}x\Big]_0^1 = \frac{1}{4}e^2 - \frac{3}{4}$$

$$M_y = \int_0^1 x(e^x - 1)\,dx = xe^x - x - \frac{1}{2}x^2\Big]_0^1 = \frac{1}{2}$$

$$\therefore \quad (\bar{x}, \bar{y}) = \left(\frac{1}{2(e-2)}, \frac{e^2-3}{4(e-2)}\right)$$

137. $A = \int_0^{2\pi r} K\,s\,ds = \int_0^{2\pi} K(a\theta)\,a\,d\theta$ (since $s = a\theta$) $= Ka^2 \left.\frac{\theta^2}{2}\right]_0^{2\pi} = 2K\pi^2 a^2$.

Or, since if the figure is unwrapped, it forms a right triangle, just

$A = \frac{1}{2}bh = \frac{1}{2}(2\pi a)(2\pi K a) = 2K\pi^2 a^2$

138. Using the results in problem 136, the depth of the centroid

is $h = e - \frac{e^2 - 3}{4(e-2)} = \frac{3e^2 - 8e + 3}{4(e-2)}$ and the pressure is

$$P = 62.5(e-2)\left(\frac{3e^2 - 8e + 3}{4(e-2)}\right) = 62.5\left(\frac{3e^2 - 8e + 3}{4}\right) \text{ lbs} \approx 53.5 \text{ lbs}$$

139. $s = \int_1^e \sqrt{1 + \frac{1}{x^2}}\,dx = \int_1^e \frac{\sqrt{x^2+1}}{x}\,dx = \int_{\frac{\pi}{4}}^{\tan^{-1}e} \frac{\sec^3 u\,du}{\tan u}$

$$= \sec u - \ln|\csc u + \cot u| \Big]_{\frac{\pi}{4}}^{\tan^{-1}e}$$

$$= \sqrt{1+e^2} - \ln\left|\frac{\sqrt{1+e^2}}{e} + \frac{1}{e}\right| - \sqrt{2} + \ln(1+\sqrt{2})$$

140. From problem 139, $ds = \frac{\sqrt{1+x^2}}{x}\,dx$.

$$S = 2\pi\int_1^e x\,ds = 2\pi\int_1^e \sqrt{1+x^2}\,dx = 2\pi\int_{\frac{\pi}{4}}^{\tan^{-1}e} \sec^3 u\,du$$

Let $x = \tan u \Rightarrow dx = \sec^2 u\,du$; $x = 1 \Rightarrow u = \frac{\pi}{4}$, $x = e \Rightarrow u = \tan^{-1}e$

$$= 2\pi\,[\sec u \tan u + \ln|\sec u + \tan u|\Big]_{\frac{\pi}{4}}^{\tan^{-1}e} \quad \text{(Ex. 3, Sect. 7.3)}$$

$$= \pi\left[e\sqrt{e^2+1} + \ln\left(\sqrt{e^2+1} + e\right) - \sqrt{2} - \ln(\sqrt{2}+1)\right]$$

141. $S = 2\pi\int_0^2 e^x\sqrt{1+e^{2x}}\,dx = 2\pi\int_{\frac{\pi}{4}}^{\tan^{-1}e^2} \tan u\sqrt{1+\tan^2 u}\,\sec^2 u\,du$

$$= 2\pi\int_{\frac{\pi}{4}}^{\tan^{-1}e^2} \sec^3 u\,du$$

$$= 2\pi\left(\frac{\sec u \tan u}{2} + \frac{\ln|\sec u + \tan u|}{2}\right)\Bigg]_{\frac{\pi}{4}}^{\tan^{-1}e^2}$$

$$= \pi\left[e^2\sqrt{e^4+1} + \ln\left|\sqrt{e^4+1} + e^2\right| - \sqrt{2} - \ln(\sqrt{2}+1)\right]$$

142. $ds = \sqrt{1 + \left(\frac{dy}{dx}\right)^2}\, dx = \sqrt{1 + \sin^2 x}\, dx$

$$S = 2\pi\int y\, ds = 2\pi\int_{-\frac{\pi}{2}}^{\frac{\pi}{2}} \cos x \sqrt{1 + \sin^2 x}\, dx = 2\pi\int_{-\frac{\pi}{4}}^{\frac{\pi}{4}} \sec^3 u\, du$$

Let $\tan u = \sin x \Rightarrow \sec^2 u\, du = \cos x\, dx$; $x = \pm\frac{\pi}{2} \Rightarrow u = \pm\frac{\pi}{4}$

$$= 2\pi\left[\sec u \tan u + \ln|\sec u + \tan u|\right]_{-\frac{\pi}{4}}^{\frac{\pi}{4}} = 2\pi\left[\sqrt{2} + \ln(\sqrt{2} + 1)\right]$$

143. $\int_0^1 \pi(-\ln x)^2\, dx = \lim_{b\to 0^-} \int_b^1 \pi \ln^2 x\, dx$

$$= \lim_{b\to 0^-} (x\ln^2 x - 2x\ln x + 2x)\Big]_b^1 = 2\pi$$

144. $x = a\ln(\sec t + \tan t) - a\sin t \Rightarrow \frac{dx}{dt} = \frac{a(\sec^2 t + \sec t\tan t)}{\sec t + \tan t} - a\cos t$

$$= a\sec t - a\cos t = \frac{a\sin^2 t}{\cos t}$$

$$A = \int y\, dx = \int y(t)\left(\frac{dx}{dt}\right)dt = \int_{-\frac{\pi}{2}}^{\frac{\pi}{2}} (a\cos t)\left(\frac{a\sin^2 t}{\cos t}\right)dt = \int_{-\frac{\pi}{2}}^{\frac{\pi}{2}} a^2\sin^2 t\, dt = \frac{a^2\pi}{2}$$

145. $V = 2\pi\int_0^{\frac{\pi}{2}} y^2\, dx = 2\pi\int_0^{\frac{\pi}{2}} y^2\left(\frac{dx}{dt}\right)dt$

$$= 2\pi\int_0^{\frac{\pi}{2}} (a\cos t)^2 (a\sec t - a\cos t)\, dt$$

$$= 2\pi a^3\int_0^{\frac{\pi}{2}} (\cos t - \cos^3 t)\, dt = \frac{2\pi a^3}{3}\sin^3 t\Big]_0^{\frac{\pi}{2}} = \frac{2\pi a^3}{3}$$

146. From Problem 144, $\frac{dx}{dt} = = \frac{a\sin^2 t}{\cos t}$; $y = a\cos t \Rightarrow \frac{dy}{dt} = -a\sin t$

$$S = 2\pi\int y\, ds = 2\pi\int_{-\frac{\pi}{2}}^{\frac{\pi}{2}} (a\cos t)\sqrt{\frac{a^2\sin^4 t}{\cos^2 t} + a^2\sin^2 t}\, dt$$

$$= 2\pi a^2\int_{-\frac{\pi}{2}}^{\frac{\pi}{2}} |\sin t|\sqrt{1 + \cos^2 t}\, dt = 4\pi a^2\int_0^{\frac{\pi}{2}} \sin t\sqrt{1 + \cos^2 t}\, dt$$

Let $\cos t = \tan u \Rightarrow -\sin t\, dt = \sec^2 u\, du$

$$= -4\pi a^2\int_{\frac{\pi}{4}}^{0} \sec^3 u\, du = 2\pi a^2\left[\sec u\tan u + \ln|\sec u + \tan u|\right]_0^{\frac{\pi}{4}}$$

$$= 2\pi a^2(\sqrt{2} + \ln(\sqrt{2} + 1))$$

147. $\displaystyle\int \frac{\ln x\,dx}{x^2} = -\frac{1}{x}\ln x + \int \frac{1}{x^2}dx = -\frac{1}{x}\ln x - \frac{1}{x} + C$

$\displaystyle\therefore \int_1^\infty \frac{\ln x\,dx}{x^2} = \lim_{b\to\infty}\int_1^b \frac{\ln x\,dx}{x^2} = \lim_{b\to\infty}\left[-\frac{1}{x}\ln x - \frac{1}{x}\right]_1^b = 1$

148. (a) $y = x - e^x$ (b) $y = e^{x - e^x}$

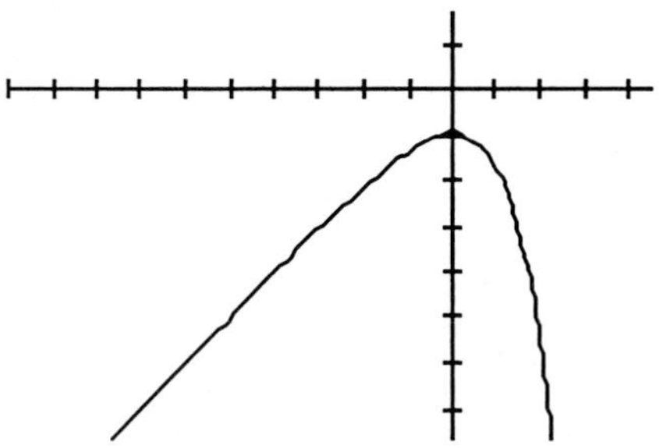

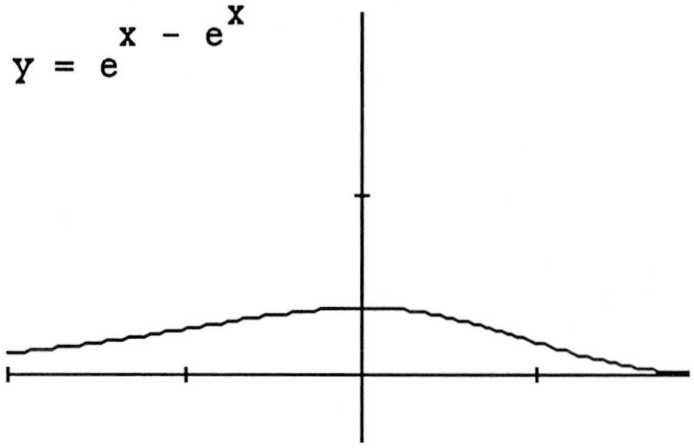

(c) $\displaystyle\int_{-\infty}^b e^{x - e^x}\,dx = \int_{-\infty}^b e^x e^{-e^x}\,dx = \lim_{a\to-\infty}\int_a^b e^x e^{-e^x}\,dx$

$\displaystyle= \lim_{a\to-\infty}\left(-e^{-e^x}\right)\Big]_a^b = 1 - e^{-e^b}$

(d) $\displaystyle\int_{-\infty}^\infty e^{x - e^x}\,dx = \int_{-\infty}^b e^{x-e^x}\,dx + \int_b^\infty e^{x-e^x}\,dx = 1 - e^{-e^b} + 0 + e^{-e^b} = 1.$

149. Let $u = \dfrac{1}{1+y} \Rightarrow du = -\dfrac{dy}{(1+y)^2}$, $dv = n\,y^{n-1}\,dy \Rightarrow v = y^n$. Then

$$\lim_{n\to\infty}\int_0^1 \frac{n\,y^{n-1}}{1+y}\,dy = \lim_{n\to\infty}\frac{y^n}{1+y}\Big]_0^1 + \lim_{n\to\infty}\int_0^1 \frac{y^n}{(1+y)^2}\,dy$$

$$= \frac{1}{2} + \lim_{n\to\infty}\int_0^1 \frac{y^n}{(1+y)^2}\,dy\,.$$

Since, for $0 \le y \le 1$, $\dfrac{y^n}{(1+y)^2} \le y^n$, and $\displaystyle\lim_{n\to\infty}\int_0^1 y^n\,dy = \lim_{n\to\infty}\frac{y^{n+1}}{n+1} = 0$,

$\displaystyle\lim_{n\to\infty}\int_0^1 \frac{y^n}{(1+y)^2}\,dy = 0$ and $\displaystyle\lim_{n\to\infty}\int_0^1 \frac{n\,y^{n-1}}{1+y}\,dy = \frac{1}{2}$.

150. By tabular integration:

$$\begin{array}{ccc} p(x) & \xrightarrow{+} & e^x \\ p'(x) & \xrightarrow{-} & e^x \\ p''(x) & \xrightarrow{+} & e^x \\ \cdot & & e^x \\ \cdot & & \cdot \\ p^{(n)}(x) & \xrightarrow{(-1)^n} & e^x \\ 0 & & e^x \end{array}$$

$$\therefore \int p(x)e^x\,dx = e^x[p(x) - p'(x) + p''(x) - \ldots + (-1)^n p^{(n)}(x)] + C$$

151. $$\int_0^{\pi} \frac{dx}{1+\sin x} = \int_0^{\infty} \frac{2\,dz}{1+z^2} \cdot \frac{1}{1+\frac{2z}{1+z^2}} = \int_0^{\infty} \frac{2\,dz}{(1+z)^2} = -\frac{2}{1+z}\Big]_0^{\infty} = -2$$

152. $$\int_{\frac{\pi}{2}}^{\pi} \frac{dx}{1-\cos x} = \int_1^{\infty} \frac{1}{1-\frac{1-z^2}{1+z^2}} \cdot \frac{2\,dz}{1+z^2} = \int_1^{\infty} \frac{dz}{z^2} = \lim_{b\to\infty} \int_1^b \frac{dz}{z^2} = \lim_{b\to\infty}\left[-\frac{1}{z}\right]_1^b = 1$$

153. $$\int \frac{dx}{1-\sin x} = \int \frac{2\,dz}{1+z^2} \cdot \frac{1}{1-\frac{2z}{1+z^2}} = \int \frac{2\,dz}{(1-z)^2} = \frac{2}{1-z} = \frac{2}{1-\tan\frac{x}{2}} + C$$

154. $$\int_0^{\frac{\pi}{2}} \frac{dx}{2+\cos x} = \int_0^1 \frac{1}{2+\frac{1-z^2}{1+z^2}} \cdot \frac{2\,dz}{1+z^2} = \int_0^1 \frac{2\,dz}{z^2+3} = \frac{2}{\sqrt{3}}\tan^{-1}\left(\frac{z}{\sqrt{3}}\right)\Big]_0^1 = \frac{\pi\sqrt{3}}{9}$$

155. $$\int \frac{\cos x\,dx}{1-\cos x} = \int \frac{1-z^2}{1+z^2} \cdot \frac{1}{1-\frac{1-z^2}{1+z^2}} \cdot \frac{2\,dz}{1+z^2} = \int \frac{1-z^2}{z^2(1+z^2)}dz$$

$$= \int\left(\frac{1}{z^2} - \frac{2}{1+z^2}\right)dz = -\frac{1}{z} - 2\tan^{-1}z + C = -\cot\frac{x}{2} - x + C$$

156. $$\int \frac{dx}{1+\sin x+\cos x} = \int \frac{1}{1+\frac{2z}{1+z^2}+\frac{1-z^2}{1+z^2}} \cdot \frac{2\,dz}{1+z^2} = \int \frac{dz}{1+z}$$

$$= \ln|1+z| = \ln|1+\tan\frac{x}{2}| + C$$

157. $\displaystyle\int \frac{dx}{\sin x - \cos x} = \int \frac{1}{\dfrac{2z}{1+z^2} - \dfrac{1-z^2}{1+z^2}} \cdot \frac{2\,dz}{1+z^2} = \int \frac{2}{z^2 + 2z - 1} dz$

Let $u = z + 1$, $du = dz$. Then $\displaystyle\int \frac{2\,dz}{(z+1)^2 - 2} = \int \frac{2\,du}{u^2 - 1}$

$$= \frac{1}{\sqrt{2}} \int \left(\frac{1}{u - \sqrt{2}} - \frac{1}{u + \sqrt{2}} \right) du = \frac{1}{\sqrt{2}} \ln \left| \frac{u - \sqrt{2}}{u\ \sqrt{2}} \right| + C$$

$$= \frac{1}{\sqrt{2}} \ln \left| \frac{\tan\frac{x}{2} + 1 - \sqrt{2}}{\tan\frac{x}{2} + 1 + \sqrt{2}} \right| + C$$

158. $\displaystyle\int_{\frac{\pi}{2}}^{\frac{2\pi}{3}} \frac{dx}{\sin x + \tan x} = \int_{\frac{\pi}{2}}^{\frac{2\pi}{3}} \frac{\cos x\,dx}{\sin x \cos x + \sin x} = \int_1^{\sqrt{3}} \frac{\dfrac{2\,dz}{1+z^2} \cdot \dfrac{1-z^2}{1+z^2}}{\dfrac{2z}{1+z^2} \cdot \dfrac{1-z^2}{1+z^2} + \dfrac{2z}{1+z^2}}$

$$\int_1^{\sqrt{3}} \frac{(1 - z^2)\,dz}{2z} = \frac{1}{2} \ln|z| - \frac{1}{4} z^2 \Big]_1^{\sqrt{3}} = \frac{1}{4} \ln 3 - \frac{1}{2}$$

CHAPTER 8

CONIC SECTIONS AND OTHER PLANE CURVES

8.1 EQUATIONS FROM THE DISTANCE FORMULA

1. $\sqrt{x^2+y^2} = |y-(-4)| \Rightarrow x^2+y^2 = (y+4)^2 \Rightarrow x^2 = 8y+16$

2. $\sqrt{x^2+(y-1)^2} = |y-(-1)| \Rightarrow x^2+(y-1)^2 = (y+1)^2 \Rightarrow$

   $x^2+y^2-2y+1 = y^2+2y+1 \Rightarrow x^2 = 4y$

3. $\sqrt{(x+2)^2+(y-1)^2} = \sqrt{(x-2)^2+(y+3)^2}$

   $x^2+4x+4+y^2-2y+1 = x^2-4x+4+y^2+6y+9$

   $8x-8y=8$ or $x-y=1$

4. $\sqrt{(x+1)^2+y^2} = 2\sqrt{(x-2)^2+y^2}$

   $x^2+2x+1+y^2 = 4(x^2-4x+4)+y^2$

   $3x^2+3y^2-18x+15=0$ or $(x-3)^2+y^2 = 4$

5. $\left(\sqrt{(x+2)^2+y^2}\right)\left(\sqrt{(x-2)^2+y^2}\right) = 4$

   $(x^2+4x+4+y^2)(x^2-4x+4+y^2) = 16$

   $[(x^2+4+y^2)+4x][(x^2+4+y^2)-4x] = 16$

   $(x^2+y^2+4)^2 - 16x^2 = 16$

   $(x^2+y^2)^2 + 8(y^2-x^2) = 0$

6. $\sqrt{x^2+(y-1)^2} + \sqrt{(x-1)^2+y^2} = C$. Since $(0,0)$ belongs to the curve, $C=2$.

   $x^2+(y-1)^2 = 4 - 4\sqrt{(x-1)^2+y^2} + (x-1)^2 + y^2$

   $x-y-2 = -2\sqrt{(x-1)^2+y^2}$

   $x^2-2xy+y^2-4x+4y+4 = 4(x^2-2x+1+y^2)$

   $3x^2+2xy+3y^2-4x-4y=0$

7. $|x-(-2)| = 2\sqrt{(x-2)^2+y^2} \Rightarrow x^2+4x+4 = 4(x^2-4x+4+y^2)$

   $3x^2-20x+4y^2+12=0$

8. $\sqrt{(x+\sqrt{2})^2+(y+\sqrt{2})^2} = \sqrt{(x-\sqrt{2})^2+(y-\sqrt{2})^2} + 2$

$$(x+\sqrt{2})^2 + (y+\sqrt{2})^2 = (x-\sqrt{2})^2 + (y-\sqrt{2})^2 + 4\sqrt{(x-\sqrt{2})^2+(y-\sqrt{2})^2} + 4$$

$$(\sqrt{2}\,x - \sqrt{2}\,y - 1)^2 = (x-\sqrt{2})^2 + (y-\sqrt{2})^2$$

$$2x^2 + 4xy + 2y^2 - 2\sqrt{2}x - 2\sqrt{2}y + 1 = x^2 - 2\sqrt{2}x + 2 + y^2 - 2\sqrt{2}y + 2$$

$$x^2 + 4xy + y^2 = 3$$

9. $\sqrt{(x+3)^2+y^2} = \sqrt{(x-3)^2+y^2} + 4$

$$(x+3)^2 + y^2 = (x-3)^2 + y^2 + 8\sqrt{(x-3)^2+y^2} + 16$$

$$x^2 + 6x + 9 + y^2 = x^2 - 6x + 9 + 8\sqrt{(x-3)^2+y^2} + 16$$

$$3x - 4 = 2\sqrt{(x-3)^2+y^2}$$

$$9x^2 - 24x + 16 = 4(x^2 - 6x + 9 + y^2)$$

$$5x^2 - 4y^2 = 20$$

10. $|y-1| + 3 = \sqrt{x^2+y^2}$. There are two cases:

If $y > 1$, then $y + 2 = \sqrt{x^2+y^2}$ or $x^2 = 4(y+1)$

If $y < 1$, then $4 - y = \sqrt{x^2+y^2}$ or $x^2 = -8(y-2)$

11. $\sqrt{(x-2)^2+(y-3)^2} = 3 \Rightarrow x^2 - 4x + 4 + y^2 - 6y + 9 = 9$

$$x^2 + y^2 - 4x - 6y + 4 = 0$$

12. Let $P(x, y)$ be such a point. The distance from P to point $(3, 0)$ is

$\sqrt{(x-3)^2+y^2} = 4$. Since P is on the line $x - y = 1$, we have

$\sqrt{(x-3)^2+(x-1)^2} = 4$, or $x^2 - 4x + 3 = 0$, or $x = 3, 1$. The points

are $(3, 2)$ and $(1, 0)$.

13. Let $P(x, y)$ be equidistant from each of $A(0, 1)$, $B(1, 0)$ and $C(4, 3)$.

Then $\sqrt{(x-0)^2+(y-1)^2} = \sqrt{(x-1)^2+(y-0)^2}$, and

$\sqrt{(x-0)^2+(y-1)^2} = \sqrt{(x-4)^2+(y-3)^2}$. Then

$x^2 + y^2 - 2y + 1 = x^2 - 2x + 1 + y^2$, and

$x^2 + y^2 - 2y + 1 = x^2 - 8x + 16 + y^2 - 6y + 9$. Simplifying,

we get $y = x$ and $2x + y = 6$. Hence the point is $P(2, 2)$.

The radius is $r = \sqrt{2^2 + 1^2} = \sqrt{5}$.

8.2 CIRCLES

1. $x^2 + (y-2)^2 = 4$ or $x^2 + y^2 - 4y = 0$

2. $(x+2)^2 + y^2 = 9$ or $x^2 + 4x + y^2 = 5$

3. $(x - 3)^2 + (y + 4)^2 = 25$ or $x^2 + y^2 - 6x + 8y = 0$

4. $(x-1)^2 + (y-1)^2 = 2$ or $x^2 - 2x + y^2 - 2y = 0$

5. $(x + 2)^2 + (y + 1)^2 < 6$ or $x^2 + y^2 + 4x + 2y < 1$

6. $(x+4)^2 + (y-2)^2 > 16$

7. $x2 + y2 = 16$ has $C(0,0)$ and radius $r = 4$.

8. $x^2 + y^2 + 6y = 0 \Rightarrow x^2 + y^2 + 6y + 9 = 9 \Rightarrow x^2 + (y+3)^2 = 9.$

   Center at $(0,-3)$, radius $= 3$

9. $x^2 + y^2 - 2y = 3 \Rightarrow x^2 + y^2 - 2y + 1 = 3 + 1 \Rightarrow x^2 + (y-1)^2 = 4$

   $C(0,1)$, $r = 2$

10. $x^2 + y^2 + 2x = 8 \Rightarrow x^2 + 2x + 1 + y^2 = 9 \Rightarrow (x+1)^2 + y^2 = 9.$

    Center at $(-1,0)$, radius $= 3$

11. $x^2 + 4x + y^2 = 12 \Rightarrow x^2 + 4x + 4 + y^2 = 12 + 4$

    $(x+2)^2 + y^2 = 16$ $C(-2,0)$, $r = 4$

12. $3x^2 + 3y^2 + 6x = 1 \Rightarrow x^2 + 2x + 1 + y^2 = \frac{1}{3} + 1 \Rightarrow (x+1)^2 + y^2 = \frac{4}{3}.$

    Center at $(-1,0)$, radius $= \frac{2}{\sqrt{3}}$

13. $x^2 + 2x + y^2 + 2y = -1 \Rightarrow x^2 + 2x + 1 + y^2 + 2y + 1 = -1 + 1 + 1$

    $(x+1)^2 + (y+1)^2 = 1$ $C(-1,-1)$, $r = 1$

14. $x^2 + y^2 - 6x + 2y + 1 = 0 \Rightarrow x^2 - 6x + 9 + y^2 + 2y + 1 = 9 \Rightarrow$

    $(x-3)^2 + (y+1)^2 = 9$. Center at $(3,-1)$, radius $= 3$.

15. $2x^2 + x + 2y^2 + y = 0 \Rightarrow x^2 + \frac{1}{2}x + y^2 + \frac{1}{2}y = 0$

    $x^2 + \frac{1}{2}x + \frac{1}{16} + y^2 + \frac{1}{2}y + \frac{1}{16} = \frac{1}{8} \Rightarrow \left(x + \frac{1}{4}\right)^2 + \left(y + \frac{1}{4}\right)^2 = \frac{1}{8}$

    $C\left(-\frac{1}{4}, -\frac{1}{4}\right)$, $r = \sqrt{\frac{1}{8}} = \frac{\sqrt{2}}{4}$

16. $2x^2 + 2y^2 - 28x + 12y + 114 = 0 \Rightarrow x^2 - 14x + 49 + y^2 + 6y + 9 = -57 + 49 + 9 \Rightarrow$

$(x - 7)^2 + (y + 3)^2 = 1$. Center at $(7, -3)$, radius $= 1$.

17. $x^2 + y^2 = 2x - 4y + 5 \leq 0 \Rightarrow x^2 - 2x + 1 + y^2 + 4y + 4 \leq -5 + 1 + 4$

$(x + 1)^2 + (y - 2)^2 \leq 0$. This is satisfied only by the point $(-1, 2)$.

18. $x^2 + y^2 + 4x + 4y + 9 \geq 0 \Rightarrow x^2 + 4x + 4 + y^2 + 4y + 4 = -9 + 4 + 4 = -1$

$(x + 2)^2 + (y + 2)^2 \geq -1$. True for all real x.

19. The circle with center $(2, 2)$ has the form $(x - 2)^2 + (y - 2)^2 = r^2$.
The point $(4, 5)$ belongs to the circle, and hence must satisfy this equation. Therefore, $(4 - 2)^2 + (5 - 2)^2 = r^2$, or $r^2 = 13$.
The equation is then $(x - 2)^2 + (y - 2)^2 = 13$ or $x^2 + y^2 - 4x - 4y = 5$.

20. The general equation of a circle is $(x - h)^2 + (y - k)^2 = r^2$.
The center lies on the $\perp$-bisector of the chord through $(0, 0)$ and $(6, 0)$, so $h = 3$. Substituting $(6, 0)$, we have $(6-3)^2 + (0-k)^2 = r^2$, or $9 + k^2 = r^2$. Also, $r = k + 1$, so $9 + k^2 = (k + 1)^2$, or $k = 4$ and $r = 5$. $\therefore$ the equation is $(x - 3)^2 + (y - 4)^2 = 25$.

21. The distance from the center to the line equals the radius.
Hence, $r = \dfrac{|-1 + 2 - 4|}{\sqrt{5}} = \dfrac{3}{\sqrt{5}}$. The equation is $(x + 1)^2 + (y - 1)^2 = \dfrac{9}{5}$
or $5x^2 + 5y^2 + 10x - 10y + 1 = 0$.

22. The general equation of a circle is $(x - h)^2 + (y - k)^2 = r^2$.
$(0, 0)$ belongs to the circle $\Rightarrow h^2 + k^2 = r^2$. Equating, $(x - h)^2 + (y - k)^2 = h^2 + k^2$ or $x^2 - 2xh - 2yk + y^2 = 0$. Substituting $(17, 7)$, we have $289 - 34h - 14k + 49 = 0$, or $34h + 14k = 338$.
Finally, (h, k) belongs to the line $12x - 5y = 0$, so $k = \dfrac{12}{5}h$
and $34h + 14\left(\dfrac{12}{5}h\right) = 338 \Rightarrow h = 5$ so $k = 12$ and $r^2 = 169$.
The required circle is: $(x - 5)^2 + (y - 12)^2 = 169$.

23. A general equation of a circle is $x^2 + y^2 + ax + by + c = 0$.

We substitute each of the three given points into this to obtain the system:

$$\begin{aligned} 2a + 3b + c &= -13 \\ 3a + 2b + c &= -13 \\ -4a + 3b + c &= -25, \end{aligned}$$

which has solution $a = 2$, $b = 2$, $c = -23$. The equation is

$$x^2 + y^2 + 2x + 2y - 23 = 0.$$

24. We will substitute the three given points into the equation $x^2 + y^2 + ax + by + c = 0$ and solve the resulting system.

$$\left.\begin{aligned} a \qquad + c &= -1 \\ b + c &= -1 \\ 2a + 2b + c &= -8 \end{aligned}\right\} \Rightarrow c = \frac{4}{3},\ a = b = -\frac{7}{3}$$

$$\therefore\ 3x^2 + 3y^2 - 7x - 7y + 4 = 0$$

25. A general equation of a circle is $x^2 + y^2 + ax + by + c = 0$.

We substitute each of the three given points into this to obtain the system:

$$\begin{aligned} 7a + b + c &= -50 \\ -a + 7b + c &= -50 \\ c &= 0, \end{aligned}$$

which has solution $a = -6$, $b = -8$, $c = 0$. The equation is

$x^2 + y^2 - 6x - 8y = 0$ or $(x - 3)^2 + (y - 4)^2 = 25$, with $C(3,4)$, $r = 5$.

26. $x^2 + y^2 - 2x - 4y + 3 = 0 \Rightarrow (x - 1)^2 + (y - 2)^2 = 2$.

Outside, since $(0.1 - 1)^2 + (3.1 - 2)^2 = 2.02 > 2$

27. $\sqrt{(x - 6)^2 + y^2} = 2\sqrt{x^2 + (y - 3)^2} \Rightarrow x^2 + y^2 + 4x - 8y = 0$ or

$(x + 2)^2 + (y - 4)^2 = 20$. $C(-2,4)$, $r = \sqrt{20} = 2\sqrt{5}$.

28. The midpoint of AB is $\left(\frac{-5 + 2}{2}, \frac{4 + 2}{2}\right) = (-2,3)$. The locus is

$(x + 5)^2 + (y - 2)^2 + (x - 1)^2 + (y - 4)^2 = 52 \Rightarrow x^2 + 4x + y^2 - 6y = 3 \Rightarrow$

$(x + 2)^2 + (y - 3)^2 = 16$. This is a circle with $C(-2,3)$ and radius $= 4$. The distance from $(-2,3)$ to A (and B) is

$\sqrt{(-2 -2)^2 + (3 - 4)^2} = \sqrt{10} < 4$, so A and B are inside the circle.

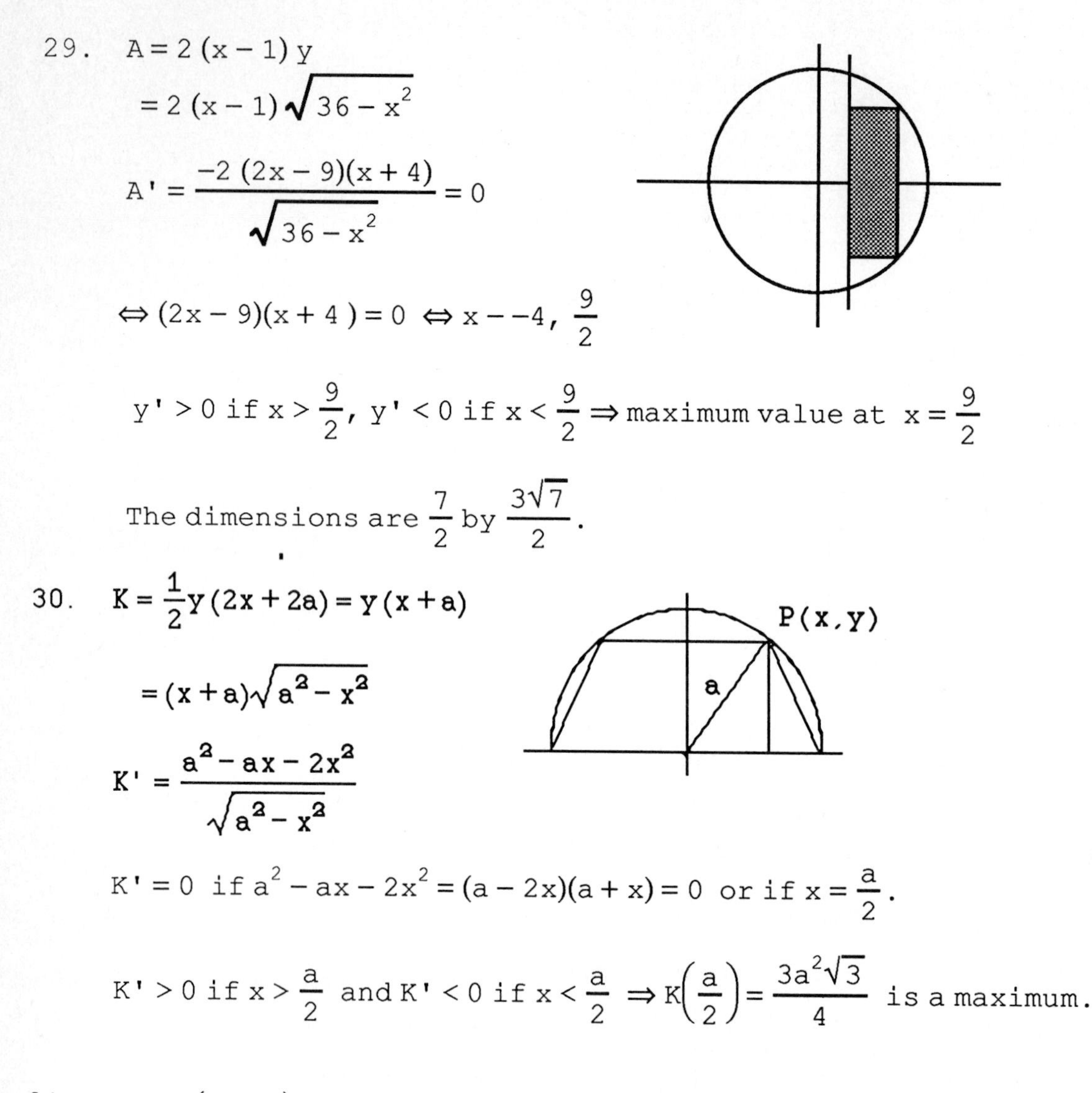

29. $A = 2(x-1)y$

$$= 2(x-1)\sqrt{36-x^2}$$

$$A' = \frac{-2(2x-9)(x+4)}{\sqrt{36-x^2}} = 0$$

$$\Leftrightarrow (2x-9)(x+4) = 0 \Leftrightarrow x - -4, \frac{9}{2}$$

$y' > 0$ if $x > \frac{9}{2}$, $y' < 0$ if $x < \frac{9}{2} \Rightarrow$ maximum value at $x = \frac{9}{2}$

The dimensions are $\frac{7}{2}$ by $\frac{3\sqrt{7}}{2}$.

30. $K = \frac{1}{2}y(2x+2a) = y(x+a)$

$$= (x+a)\sqrt{a^2-x^2}$$

$$K' = \frac{a^2-ax-2x^2}{\sqrt{a^2-x^2}}$$

$K' = 0$ if $a^2 - ax - 2x^2 = (a-2x)(a+x) = 0$ or if $x = \frac{a}{2}$.

$K' > 0$ if $x > \frac{a}{2}$ and $K' < 0$ if $x < \frac{a}{2} \Rightarrow K\left(\frac{a}{2}\right) = \frac{3a^2\sqrt{3}}{4}$ is a maximum.

31. Let $P(x_1, y_1)$ be the exterior point, and the center of the circle be $O(h, k)$. Let Q be either of the points of tangency from P to the circle and s be the length of PQ. $\triangle PQO$ is a right triangle with hypotenuse OP. Then $OP^2 = PQ^2 + OQ^2$, or $(x_1-h)^2 + (y_1-k)^2 = s^2 + a^2$.

32. If $x^2 + y^2 = a^2$, then $2x + 2y\frac{dy}{dx} = 0$ or $\frac{dy}{dx} = -\frac{x}{y}$. A normal to the circle at any point (x_1, y_1) would have equation

$y - y_1 = \frac{y_1}{x_1}(x - x_1)$ or $y = \frac{y_1}{x_1}x$ and hence passes through $(0, 0)$.

33. From a theorem in geometry, PT is the mean proportion between PM and PN. ($\triangle PTN \approx \triangle PTM$). Therefore, $\frac{PN}{PT} = \frac{PT}{PM}$, or $(PT)^2 = (PN)(PM)$.

34. Let O and A be positioned so that their coordinates are $O(-x_1, 0)$ and $A(x_1, 0)$, and let $P(x, y)$ be any point such that $\angle OPA$ is a right angle. Then the slope of OP is $\dfrac{y}{x + x_1}$, the slope of PA is $\dfrac{y}{x - x_1}$ and $\left(\dfrac{y}{x + x_1}\right)\left(\dfrac{y}{x - x_1}\right) = -1$. Then $y^2 = -(x^2 - x_1^2)$ or $x^2 + y^2 = x_1^2$. This is a circle with center at the origin and radius $= x_1$.

8.3 PARABOLAS

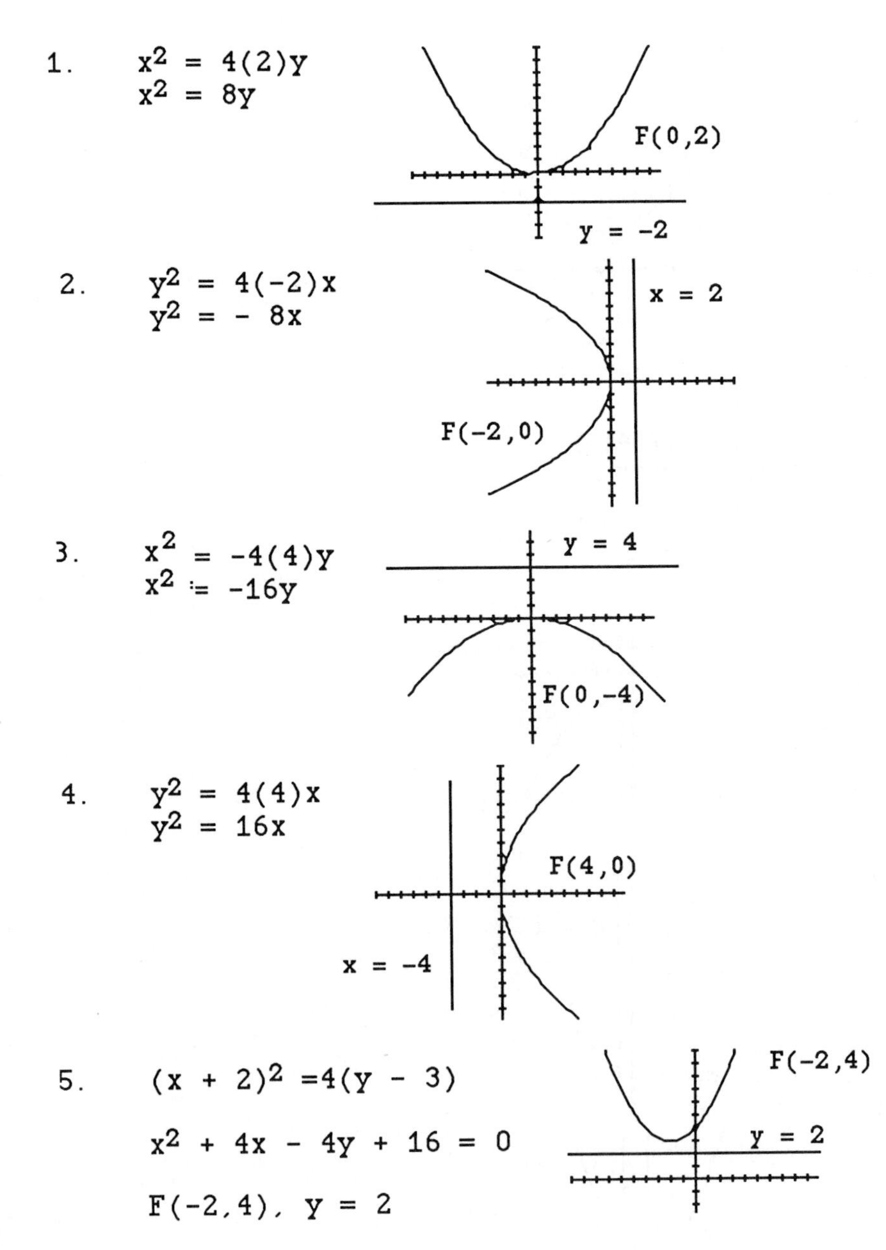

1. $x^2 = 4(2)y$
   $x^2 = 8y$

2. $y^2 = 4(-2)x$
   $y^2 = -8x$

3. $x^2 = -4(4)y$
   $x^2 = -16y$

4. $y^2 = 4(4)x$
   $y^2 = 16x$

5. $(x + 2)^2 = 4(y - 3)$

   $x^2 + 4x - 4y + 16 = 0$

   $F(-2, 4)$, $y = 2$

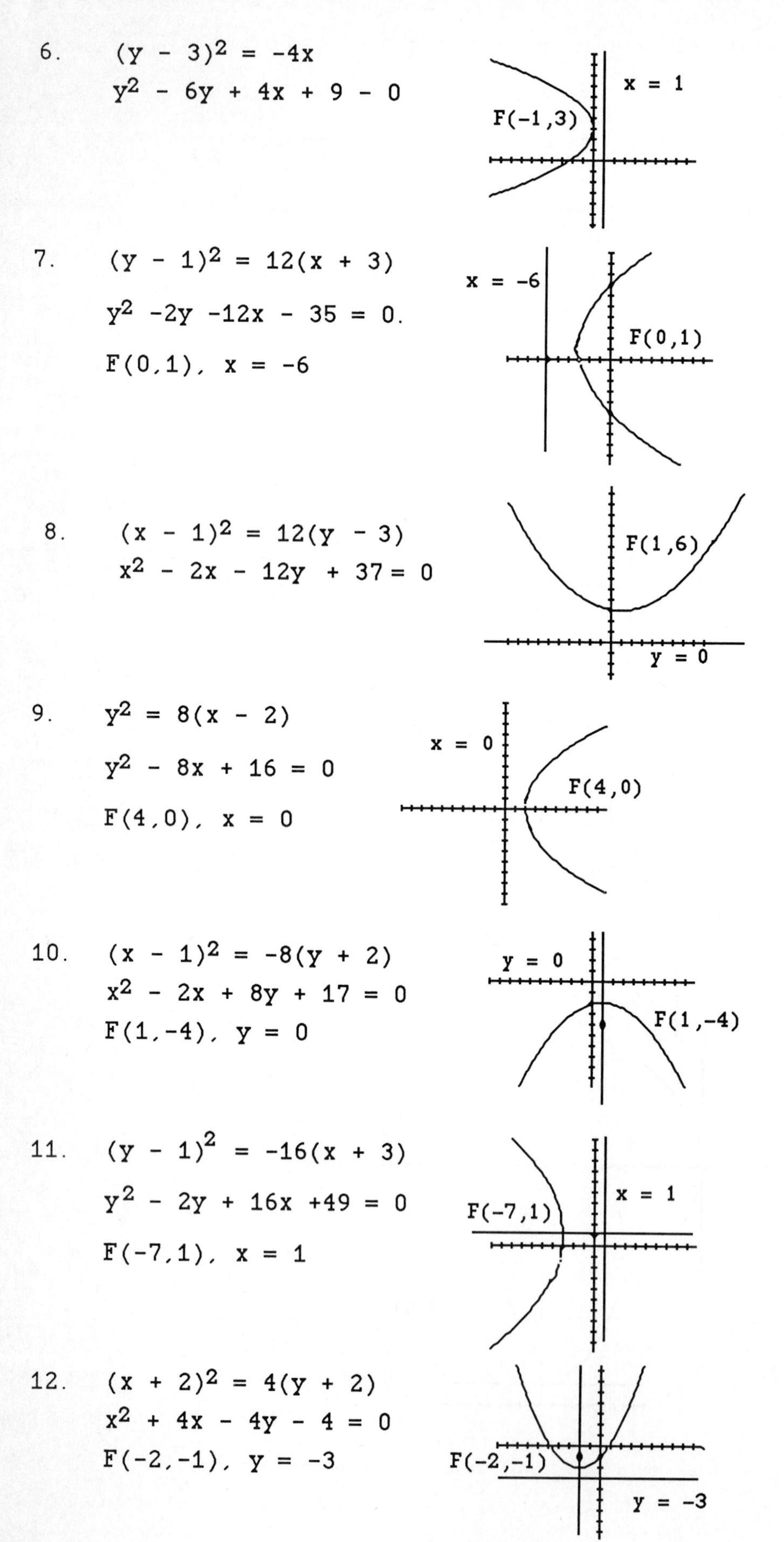

6. $(y - 3)^2 = -4x$

$y^2 - 6y + 4x + 9 - 0$

7. $(y - 1)^2 = 12(x + 3)$

$y^2 - 2y - 12x - 35 = 0.$

$F(0,1)$, $x = -6$

8. $(x - 1)^2 = 12(y - 3)$

$x^2 - 2x - 12y + 37 = 0$

9. $y^2 = 8(x - 2)$

$y^2 - 8x + 16 = 0$

$F(4,0)$, $x = 0$

10. $(x - 1)^2 = -8(y + 2)$

$x^2 - 2x + 8y + 17 = 0$

$F(1,-4)$, $y = 0$

11. $(y - 1)^2 = -16(x + 3)$

$y^2 - 2y + 16x + 49 = 0$

$F(-7,1)$, $x = 1$

12. $(x + 2)^2 = 4(y + 2)$

$x^2 + 4x - 4y - 4 = 0$

$F(-2,-1)$, $y = -3$

13. $(y - 1)^2 = 4x$

$y^2 - 2y - 4x + 1 = 0$

$F(1,1)$, $x = -1$

14. $x^2 = -4(y - 1)$

$x^2 + 4y - 4 = 0$

$F(0,0)$, $y = 2$

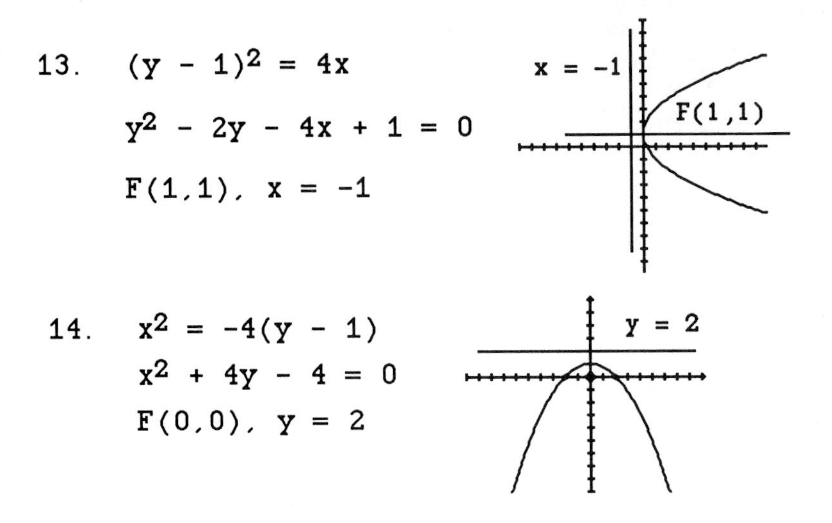

15. $y^2 = 8x$. $4p = 8 \Rightarrow p = 2$. Vertex is $V(0,0)$, focus is $F(2,0)$, directrix is $x = -2$, axis is $y = 0$.

16. $y^2 = -36x$. $4p = -36 \Rightarrow p = -9$. Vertex is $V(0,0)$, focus is $F(-9,0)$, directrix is $x = 9$, axis of symmetry is $y = 0$.

17. $x^2 = 100y$. $4p = 100 \Rightarrow p = 25$. $V(0,0)$, $F(0,25)$, directrix: $y = -25$, axis: $x = 0$.

18. $x^2 = -9y$. $4p = 9 \Rightarrow p = \frac{9}{4}$. Vertex is $V(0,0)$, focus is $F(0,-\frac{9}{4})$, directrix is $y = \frac{9}{4}$, axis is $x = 0$.

19. $x^2 - 2x + 8y - 7 = 0$
$x^2 - 2x + 1 = -8y + 7 + 1$
$(x - 1)^2 = -8(y - 1)$

$V(1,1)$ $F(1,-1)$
directrix: $y = 3$
axis: $x = 1$

20. $x^2 + 8x - 4y + 4 = 0$
$x^2 + 8x + 16 = 4y - 4 + 16$
$(x + 4)^2 = 4(y + 3)$

$V(-4,-3)$ $F(-4,-2)$
directrix: $y = -5$
axis: $x = -4$

21. $y^2 + 4x - 8 = 0$
$y^2 = -4x + 8$
$y^2 = -4(x - 2)$

$V(2,0)$ $F(1,0)$
directrix: $x = 3$
axis: $y = 0$

22. $x^2 + 8y - 4 = 0$

$x^2 = -8y + 4$

$x^2 = -8(y - \frac{1}{2})$

$V(0,\frac{1}{2})$ $F(0,-\frac{3}{2})$

directrix: $y = \frac{5}{2}$

axis: $x = 0$

23. $x^2 + 2x - 4y - 3 = 0$
$x^2 + 2x + 1 = 4y + 3 + 1$
$(x + 1)^2 = 4(y + 1)$

$V(-1,-1)$ $F(-1,0)$
directrix: $y = -2$
axis: $x = -1$

24. $x^2 + 2x + 4y - 3 = 0$ $\quad$ V(-1,1) $\quad$ F(-1,0)
$x^2 + 2x + 1 = -4y + 3 + 1$ $\quad$ directrix: $y = 2$
$(x + 1)^2 = -4(y - 1)$ $\quad$ axis: $x = -1$

25. $y^2 - 4y - 8x - 12 = 0$ $\quad$ V(-2,2) $\quad$ F(0,2)
$y^2 - 4y + 4 = 8x + 12 + 4$ $\quad$ directrix: $x = -4$
$(y - 2)^2 = 8(x + 2)$ $\quad$ axis: $y = 2$

26. $y^2 + 6y + 2x + 5 = 0$ $\quad$ V(2,-3) $\quad$ F$(\frac{3}{2},-3)$
$y^2 + 6y + 9 = -2x - 5 + 9$ $\quad$ directrix: $x = \frac{5}{2}$
$(y + 3)^2 = -2(x - 2)$ $\quad$ axis: $y = -3$

27. $y^2 < x$ is the region interior to the parabola $y^2 = x$, and $y^2 > x$ is the region exterior to the parabola.

28.

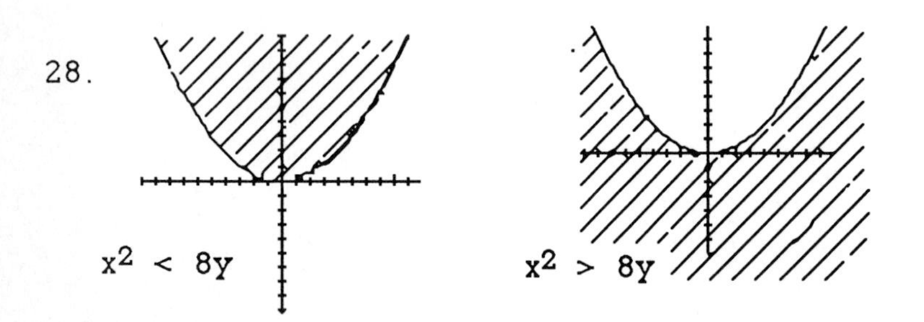

29. Let $P_1(-p, y_1)$ be any point on the line $x = -p$, and let $P(x, y)$be the point where the tangent intersects $y^2 = 4x$. Since $\frac{dy}{dx} = \frac{2p}{y}$, the slope of this tangent is: $\frac{y - y_1}{x + p} = \frac{2p}{y}$. We substitute for x and solve for y: $y(y - y_1) = 2p\left(\frac{y^2}{4p} + p\right) \Rightarrow y^2 - (2y_1)y - 4p^2 = 0 \Rightarrow$

$y = y_1 \pm \sqrt{y_1^2 + 4p^2}$. The slopes of the two tangents from P_1 to the curve are $m_1 = \frac{2p}{y_1 + \sqrt{y_1^2 + 4p^2}}$ and $m_2 = \frac{2p}{y_1 - \sqrt{y_1^2 + 4p^2}}$. Notice that $m_1 m_2 = -1$, so that the tangents are perpendicular.

30. (a) We start with $\left(x - \frac{b}{2}\right)^2 = -4p(y - h)$. Since (0,0) belongs to curve,

$$\left(-\frac{b}{2}\right)^2 = (-4p)(-h) \Rightarrow 4p = \frac{b^2}{4h}. \therefore \left(x - \frac{b}{2}\right)^2 = -\frac{b^2}{4h}(y - h).$$

(b) $$A = \int_0^b \left[-\frac{4h}{b^2}\left(x - \frac{b}{2}\right)^2 + h\right] dx = -\frac{4h}{b^2}\left(-\frac{1}{3}\left(x - \frac{b}{2}\right)^3\right) + hx\Bigg]_0^b = \frac{2bh}{3}$$

31. $V = \pi \int_0^h x^2\,dy = \pi \int_0^h \frac{b^2}{4h}\,y\,dy = \frac{\pi b^2}{4h}\left[\frac{y^2}{2}\right]_0^h = \frac{\pi b^2 h}{8}$

The volume of the cone $= \frac{1}{3}\pi r^2 h = \frac{1}{3}\pi\left(\frac{b}{2}\right)^2 h = \frac{\pi b^2 h}{12}$.

Notice that $\frac{3}{2}\left(\frac{\pi b^2 h}{12}\right) = \frac{\pi b^2 h}{8}$

32. $\frac{dy}{dx} = \frac{wx}{H} \Rightarrow y = \int \frac{w}{H}\,x\,dx = \frac{w}{2H}x^2 + C$. Since $(0, 0)$ is a point, $C = 0$ and we have the parabola $y = \frac{w}{2H}x^2$.

33. If $y^2 = 4px$, then $\frac{dy}{dx} = \frac{2p}{y}$. The slope of the tangent to the graph at $P(x_1, y_1)$ is $m = \frac{2p}{y_1}$, and the equation of this tangent is $y - y_1 = \frac{2p}{y_1}(x - x_1)$. Set $y = 0$ to find the x-intercept of this line:

$$-y_1 = \frac{2p}{y_1}(x - x_1) \text{ or } x = -\frac{y_1^2}{2p} + x_1 = -\frac{4px_1}{2p} + x_1 = -x_1.$$

34. $y^2 = 4px \Rightarrow \frac{dy}{dx} = \frac{2p}{y}$. At the point $P(x_0, y_0)$, $\frac{dy}{dx} = \tan\alpha = \frac{2p}{y_0}$. The angles are equal since they are corresponding angles. The focus is $F(p, 0)$ and the slope of PF is $\frac{y_0}{x_0 - p}$. $\tan\beta = \frac{\tan\beta - \tan\alpha}{1 + \tan\beta\tan\alpha} = \frac{\frac{y_0}{x_0 - p} - \frac{2p}{y_0}}{1 + \left(\frac{2p}{y_0}\right)\left(\frac{y_0}{x_0 - p}\right)}$

$$= \frac{-2px_0 + 2p^2 + y_0^2}{y_0x_0 - y_0p + 2py_0} = \frac{-2px_0 + 2p^2 + 4px_0}{y_0x_0 + py_0} = \frac{2p}{y_0}. \therefore \tan\alpha = \tan\beta \Rightarrow \alpha = \beta.$$

8.4 ELLIPSES

1. $c^2 = a^2 - b^2$

$4 = 16 - b^2 \Rightarrow b^2 = 12$

$\frac{y^2}{16} + \frac{x^2}{12} = 1$

$e = \frac{c}{a} = \frac{1}{2}$

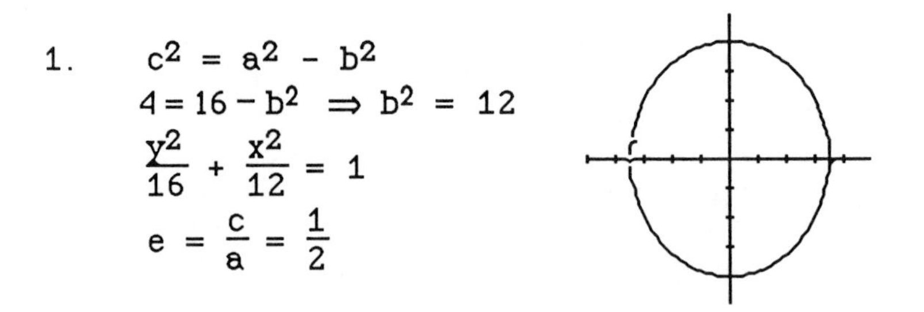

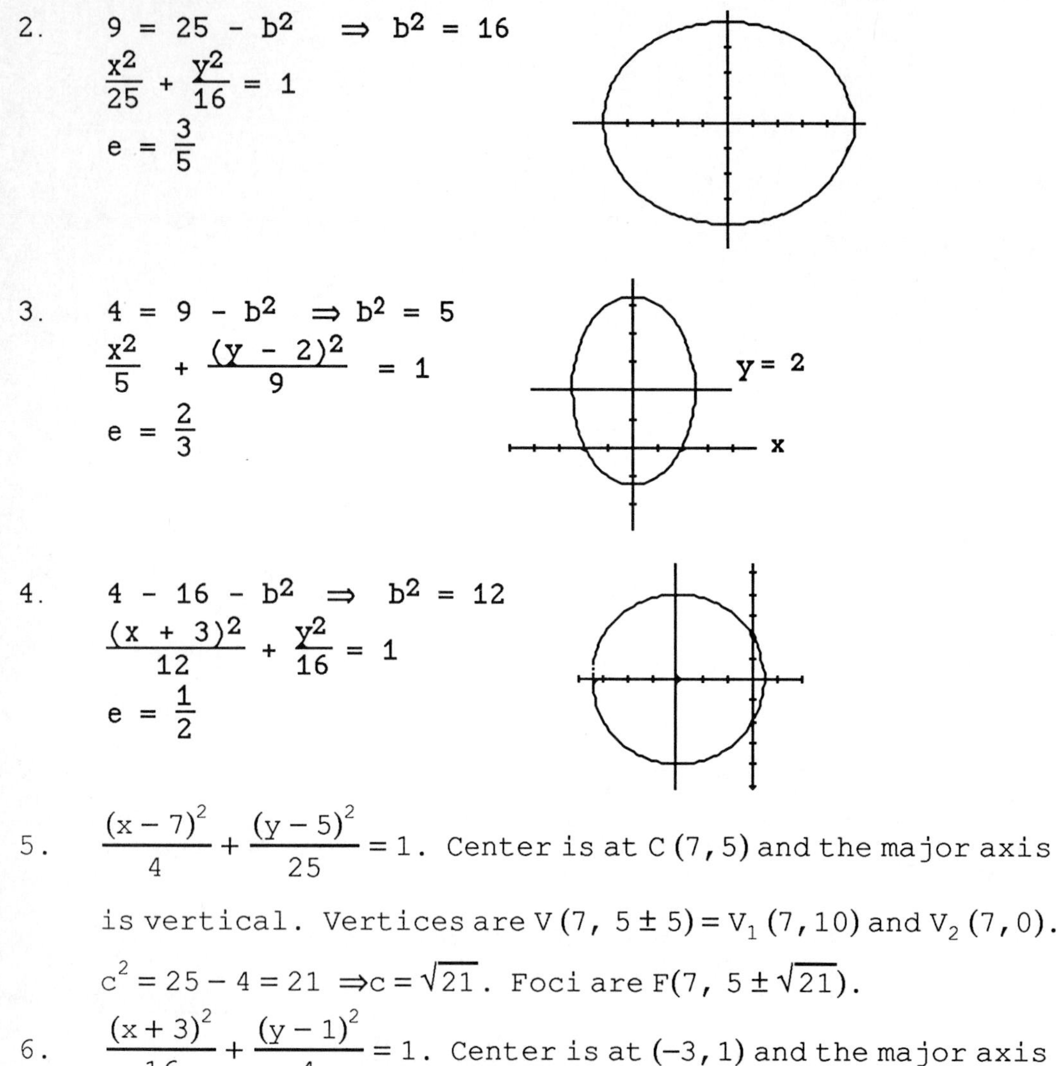

2. $9 = 25 - b^2 \Rightarrow b^2 = 16$

$\frac{x^2}{25} + \frac{y^2}{16} = 1$

$e = \frac{3}{5}$

3. $4 = 9 - b^2 \Rightarrow b^2 = 5$

$\frac{x^2}{5} + \frac{(y - 2)^2}{9} = 1$

$e = \frac{2}{3}$

4. $4 - 16 - b^2 \Rightarrow b^2 = 12$

$\frac{(x + 3)^2}{12} + \frac{y^2}{16} = 1$

$e = \frac{1}{2}$

5. $\frac{(x-7)^2}{4} + \frac{(y-5)^2}{25} = 1$. Center is at $C(7,5)$ and the major axis is vertical. Vertices are $V(7, 5 \pm 5) = V_1(7,10)$ and $V_2(7,0)$.

$c^2 = 25 - 4 = 21 \Rightarrow c = \sqrt{21}$. Foci are $F(7, 5 \pm \sqrt{21})$.

6. $\frac{(x+3)^2}{16} + \frac{(y-1)^2}{4} = 1$. Center is at $(-3,1)$ and the major axis is horizontal. Vertices are $V(-3 \pm 4, 1) = V_1(-7,1)$ and $V_2(1,1)$.

$c^2 = 16 - 4 = 12 \Rightarrow c = \sqrt{12}$. Foci are $(-3 \pm 2\sqrt{3}, 1)$.

7. $\frac{(x+1)^2}{9} + \frac{(y+4)^2}{25} = 1$. Center is at $(-1,-4)$ and the major axis is vertical. Vertices are $V_1(-1,-9)$ and $V_2(-1,1)$.

$c^2 = 25 - 9 = 16 \Rightarrow c = 4$. Foci are $(-1,0)$ and $(-1,-8)$.

8. $\frac{(x-8)^2}{25} + \frac{y^2}{81} = 1$. Center is at $(8,0)$ and the major axis is vertical. Vertices are $V_1(8,9)$ and $V_2(8,-9)$.

$c^2 = 81 - 25 = 56 \Rightarrow c = 2\sqrt{14}$. Foci are $(8, \pm 2\sqrt{14})$.

9. $25(x-3)^2 + 4(y-1)^2 = 100$

$\dfrac{(x-3)^2}{4} + \dfrac{(y-1)^2}{25} = 1$. Center is at $C(3,1)$ and the major axis is vertical. Vertices are $V(3, 1 \pm 5) = V_1(3,6)$ and $V_2(3,-4)$.

$c^2 = 25 - 4 = 21 \Rightarrow c = \sqrt{21}$. Foci are $F(3, 1 \pm \sqrt{21})$.

10. $9(x-4)^2 + 16(y-3)^2 = 144 \Rightarrow \dfrac{(x-4)^2}{16} + \dfrac{(y-3)^2}{9} = 1$.

Center is at $(4,3)$ and the major axis is horizontal.

Vertices are $V_1(8,3)$ and $V_2(0,3)$.

$c^2 = 16 - 9 = 7 \Rightarrow c = \sqrt{7}$. Foci are $(4 \pm \sqrt{7}, 3)$.

11. $x^2 + 10x + 25y^2 = 0 \Rightarrow x^2 + 10x + 100 + 25y^2 = 25$ or

$\dfrac{(x+5)^2}{25} + \dfrac{y^2}{1} = 1$. Center is at $C(-5,0)$ and the major axis is horizontal. Vertices are $V(5 \pm 5, 0) = V_1(10,0)$ and $V_2(0,0)$.

$c^2 = 25 - 1 = 24 \Rightarrow c = 2\sqrt{6}$. Foci are $F(-5 \pm 2\sqrt{6}, 0)$.

12. $x^2 + 16y^2 + 96y + 128 = 0 \Rightarrow x^2 + 16(y+3)^2 = -128 + 144 \Rightarrow$

$\dfrac{x^2}{16} + \dfrac{(y+3)^2}{1} = 1$. Center is at $(0,-3)$ and the major axis is horizontal.

Vertices are $V_1(4,-3)$ and $V_2(-4,-3)$.

$c^2 = 16 - 1 = 7 \Rightarrow c = \sqrt{15}$. Foci are $(\pm\sqrt{15}, -3)$.

13. $x^2 + 9y^2 - 4x + 18y + 4 = 0 \Rightarrow (x^2 - 4x + 4) + 9(y^2 + 2y + 1) = -4 + 4 + 9$ or

$\dfrac{(x-2)^2}{9} + \dfrac{(y+1)^2}{1} = 1$. Center is at $C(2,-1)$ and the major axis is horizontal. Vertices are $V(2 \pm 3, -1) = V_1(5,-1)$ and $V_2(-1,-1)$.

$c^2 = 9 - 1 = 8 \Rightarrow c = 2\sqrt{2}$. Foci are $F(2 \pm 2\sqrt{2}, -1)$.

14. $4x^2 + y^2 - 32x + 16y + 124 = 0 \Rightarrow 4(x-4)^2 + (y+8)^2 = -124 + 64 + 64 \Rightarrow$

$\dfrac{(x-4)^2}{1} + \dfrac{(y+8)^2}{4} = 1$. Center is at $(4, -8)$ and the major axis is ver

Vertices are $V_1(4,-10)$ and $V_2(4,-6)$.

$c^2 = 4 - 1 = 3 \Rightarrow c = \sqrt{3}$. Foci are $(4, -8 \pm \sqrt{3})$.

15. $4x^2 + y^2 - 16x + 4y + 16 = 0 \Rightarrow 4(x^2 - 4x + 4) + (y^2 + 4y + 4) = -16 + 16 + 4$ or

$\dfrac{(x-2)^2}{1} + \dfrac{(y+2)^2}{4} = 1$. Center is at $C(2,-2)$ and the major axis

is vertical. Vertices are $V(2, -2 \pm 2) = V_1(2,0)$ and $V_2(2,-4)$.

$c^2 = 4 - 1 = 3 \Rightarrow c = \sqrt{3}$. Foci are $F(2, -2 \pm \sqrt{3})$.

16. $x^2 + 4y^2 + 2x + 8y + 1 = 0 \Rightarrow (x+1)^2 + 4(y+1)^2 = -1 + 1 + 4 \Rightarrow$

$\dfrac{(x+1)^2}{4} + \dfrac{(y+1)^2}{1} = 1$. Center is at $(-1,-1)$ and the major

axis is horizontal. Vertices are $V_1(1,-1)$ and $V_2(-3,-1)$.

$c^2 = 4 - 1 = 3 \Rightarrow c = \sqrt{3}$. Foci are $(-1 \pm \sqrt{3}, -1)$.

17. $9x^2 + 16y^2 - 18x - 96y + 9 = 0 \Rightarrow 9(x^2 - 2x + 1) + 16(y^2 - 6y + 9) = -9 + 144 + 9$ or

$\dfrac{(x+1)^2}{16} + \dfrac{(y-3)^2}{9} = 1$. Center is at $C(-1,3)$ and the major axis

is horizontal. Vertices are $V(-1 \pm 4, 3) = V_1(-5,3)$ and $V_2(3,3)$.

$c^2 = 16 - 9 = 7 \Rightarrow c = \sqrt{7}$. Foci are $F(-1 \pm \sqrt{7}, 3)$.

18. $25x^2 + 9y^2 - 100x + 54y - 44 = 0 \Rightarrow 25(x-2)^2 + 9(y+3)^2 = 44 + 100 + 81 \Rightarrow$

$\dfrac{(x-2)^2}{9} + \dfrac{(y+3)^2}{25} = 1$. Center is at $(2,-3)$ and the major

axis is vertical. Vertices are $V_1(2,-8)$ and $V_2(2,2)$.

$c^2 = 25 - 9 = 16 \Rightarrow c = 4$. Foci are $(2,-7)$ and $(2,1)$

19. (a) (b)

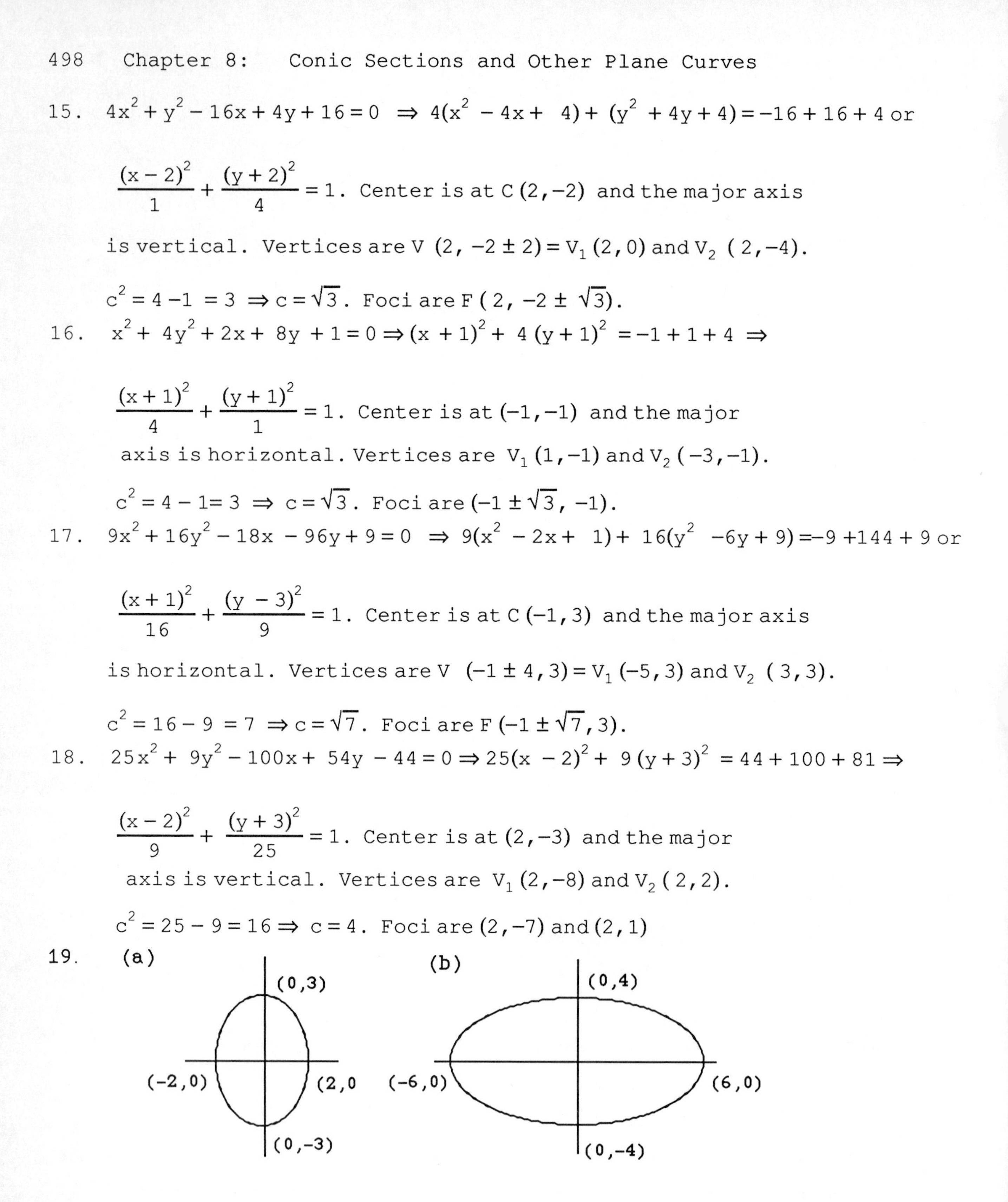

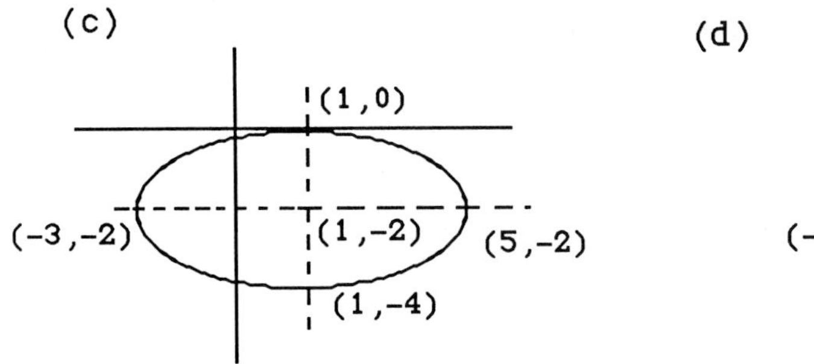

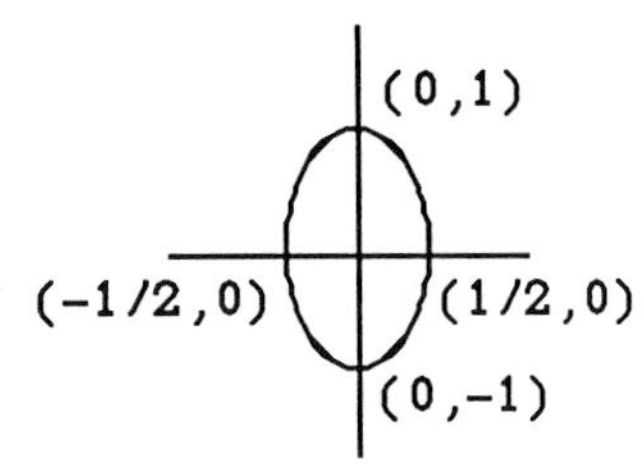

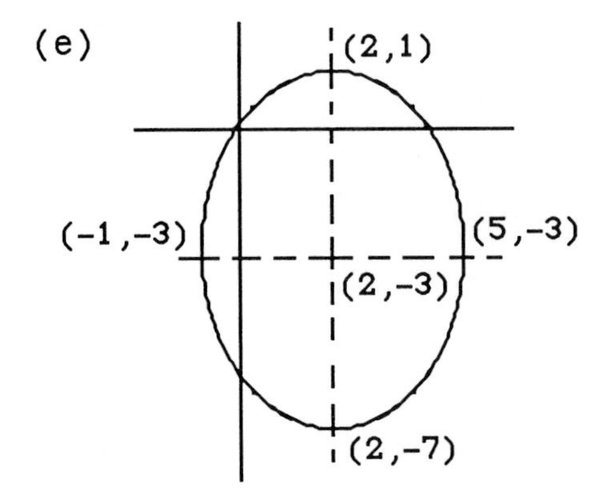

20. If the foci are $(-1,1)$ and $(1,1)$ then the center is $(0,1)$ and $c = 1$.

$\therefore\ \dfrac{x^2}{a^2} + \dfrac{(y-1)^2}{b^2} = 1$. Substituting $(0,0) \Rightarrow b^2 = 1$. Then $a^2 = 2$

and the equation is $\dfrac{x^2}{2} + \dfrac{(y-1)^2}{1} = 1$.

21. One axis is from A(1,1) to B(1,7) and is 6 units long. The other axis is from C(3,4) to D(-1,4) and is 4 units long. Therefore. $a = 3$, $b = 2$ and its major axis is vertical. The center is the point C(1,4). The ellipse is

$$\frac{(x-1)^2}{4} + \frac{(y-4)^2}{9} = 1.$$

The foci would be $F(1, 4 \pm \sqrt{5})$

22. Using $PF = e \cdot PD$, we have $\sqrt{(x-4)^2 + y^2} = \dfrac{2}{3}|x-9| \Rightarrow$

$$5x^2 + 9y^2 = 180 \text{ or } \frac{x^2}{36} + \frac{y^2}{20} = 1.$$

23. $9x^2 + 16y^2 \leq 144$

$\dfrac{x^2}{16} + \dfrac{y^2}{9} \leq 1$

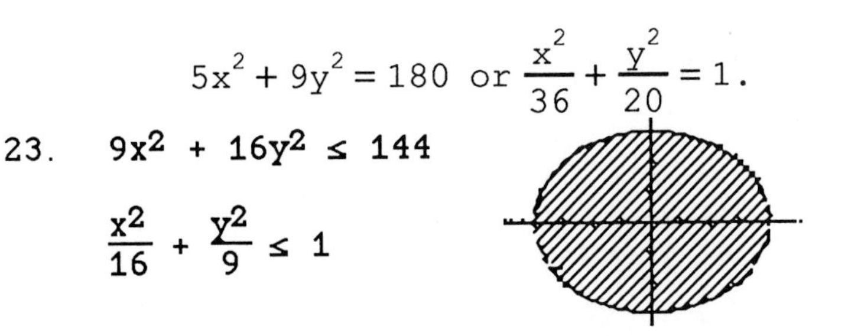

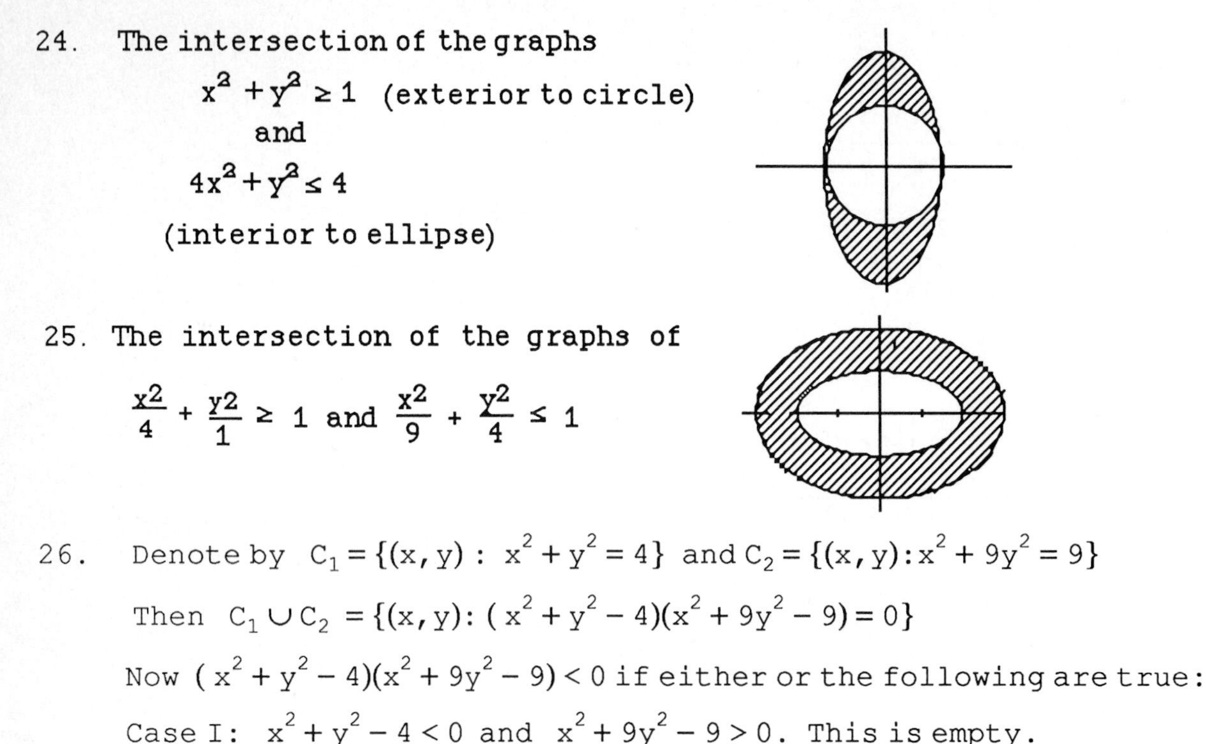

24. The intersection of the graphs

$x^2 + y^2 \geq 1$ (exterior to circle)

and

$4x^2 + y^2 \leq 4$

(interior to ellipse)

25. The intersection of the graphs of

$$\frac{x^2}{4} + \frac{y^2}{1} \geq 1 \text{ and } \frac{x^2}{9} + \frac{y^2}{4} \leq 1$$

26. Denote by $C_1 = \{(x, y) : x^2 + y^2 = 4\}$ and $C_2 = \{(x, y) : x^2 + 9y^2 = 9\}$

Then $C_1 \cup C_2 = \{(x, y) : (x^2 + y^2 - 4)(x^2 + 9y^2 - 9) = 0\}$

Now $(x^2 + y^2 - 4)(x^2 + 9y^2 - 9) < 0$ if either or the following are true:

Case I: $x^2 + y^2 - 4 < 0$ and $x^2 + 9y^2 - 9 > 0$. This is empty.

Case II: $x^2 + y^2 - 4 > 0$ and $x^2 + 9y^2 - 9 < 0$. These are the points exterior to C_1 and interior to C_2.

The graph is similar to problem 25.

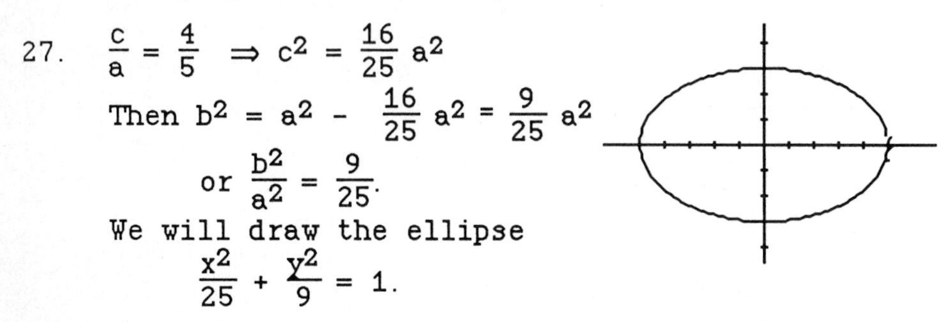

27. $\frac{c}{a} = \frac{4}{5} \Rightarrow c^2 = \frac{16}{25} a^2$

Then $b^2 = a^2 - \frac{16}{25} a^2 = \frac{9}{25} a^2$

or $\frac{b^2}{a^2} = \frac{9}{25}$.

We will draw the ellipse

$$\frac{x^2}{25} + \frac{y^2}{9} = 1.$$

28. The eccentricity of Pluto is $e = 0.25 = \frac{1}{4} = \frac{c}{a}$. Then we may take

$a = 4$, $c = 1 \Rightarrow b^2 = 16 - 1 = 15$. An equation is: $\frac{x^2}{16} + \frac{b^2}{15} = 1$.

29. (a) Using figures in the text, $a = \frac{36.18}{2} = 18.09$ AU; $b = \frac{9.12}{2} = 4.56$ AU;

$c = \sqrt{(18.09)^2 + (4.56)^2} = 17.50$. If the sun is at the origin, the center is $(c, 0)$ and the equation is

$$\frac{(x - 17.5)^2}{(18.09)^2} + \frac{y^2}{(4.56)^2} = 1.$$

(b) Minimum distance $= a - c = 0.5842$ AU $\approx 5.41 \times 10^7$ miles.

(c) Maximum distance $= a + c = 35.59$ AU $\approx 3.30 \times 10^9$ miles.

30. $A = (2x)(2y) = 2x\sqrt{4-x^2} \Rightarrow A' = \dfrac{16-8x^2}{\sqrt{4-x^2}} = 0$ if $x = \sqrt{2}$. $A' > 0$ if $x < \sqrt{2}$ and $A' < 0$ if $x > \sqrt{2} \Rightarrow$ maximum area, which is $(2\sqrt{2})(\sqrt{2}) = 4$.

31. $$A = 2\int_0^3 4\sqrt{1-\frac{x^2}{9}}\,dx = \frac{8}{3}\int_0^3 \sqrt{9-x^2}\,dx$$

$$= \frac{8}{3}\int_0^{\pi/2} \sqrt{9-9\sin^2 u}\;3\cos u\,du = 24\int_0^{\frac{\pi}{2}} \cos^2 u\,du = 24\left[\frac{1}{2}+\frac{1}{4}\sin 2u\right]_0^{\frac{\pi}{2}} = 6\pi$$

$$M_x = \int_{-3}^3 \frac{1}{2}\left(\frac{4\sqrt{9-x^2}}{3}\right)^2 dx = \frac{8}{9}\int_{-3}^3 (9-x^2)\,dx = \frac{8}{9}\left(9x-\frac{1}{3}x^3\right)]_{-3}^3 = 32.$$

$\bar{y} = \dfrac{32}{6\pi} = \dfrac{16}{3\pi}$. $\bar{x} = 0$ by symmetry.

32. (a) $V = \pi\displaystyle\int_{-2}^2 y^2\,dx = 2\pi\int_0^2 9\left(1-\frac{x^2}{4}\right)dx = 18\pi\left[x-\frac{1}{12}x^3\right]_0^2 = 24\pi$

(b) $V = \pi\displaystyle\int_{-3}^3 x^2\,dy = 2\pi\int_0^3 4\left(1-\frac{y^2}{4}\right)dy = 8\pi\left[y-\frac{1}{27}y^3\right]_0^3 = 16\pi$

33. The ellipse must pass through $(0,0) \Rightarrow c = 0$. $(-1,2)$ belongs $\Rightarrow -a+2b = -8$.

Tangent to x–axis $\Rightarrow$ center is on y–axis, so $a = 0$ and $b = -4$.

The equation is $4x^2+y^2-4y = 0$.

34. If $\dfrac{x^2}{a^2}+\dfrac{y^2}{b^2} = 1$, then $b^2x^2+a^2y^2 = a^2b^2$ and $y = \dfrac{b}{a}\sqrt{a^2-x^2}$. $y' = \dfrac{-bx}{a\sqrt{a^2-x^2}}$

Let $P(x_0, y_0)$ be any point on the ellipse. $y'(x_0) = \dfrac{-bx_0}{a\sqrt{a^2-x_0^2}} = \dfrac{-b^2x_0}{a^2y_0}$.

Let $F_1(c,0)$ and $F_2(-c,0)$ be the foci. Then $m_{PF_1} = \dfrac{y_0}{x_0-c}$ and $m_{PF_2} = \dfrac{y_0}{x_0+c}$.

Let α and β be the angles between the tangent line and PF_1 and PF_2

respectively. Then $\tan\alpha = \dfrac{-\dfrac{b^2x_0}{a^2y_0}-\dfrac{y_0}{x_0-c}}{1-\dfrac{b^2x_0y_0}{a^2y_0(x_0-c)}} = \dfrac{-b^2x_0^2+b^2x_0c-a^2y_0^2}{a^2y_0x_0-a^2y_0c-b^2x_0y_0}$

$$= \frac{b^2x_0c-(b^2x_0^2+a^2y_0^2)}{-a^2y_0c+(a^2-b^2)x_0y_0} = \frac{b^2x_0c-a^2b^2}{-a^2y_0c+c^2x_0y_0} = \frac{b^2}{cy_0}.$$ Similarly, $\tan\beta = \dfrac{b^2}{cy_0}$.

8.5 HYPERBOLAS

1. 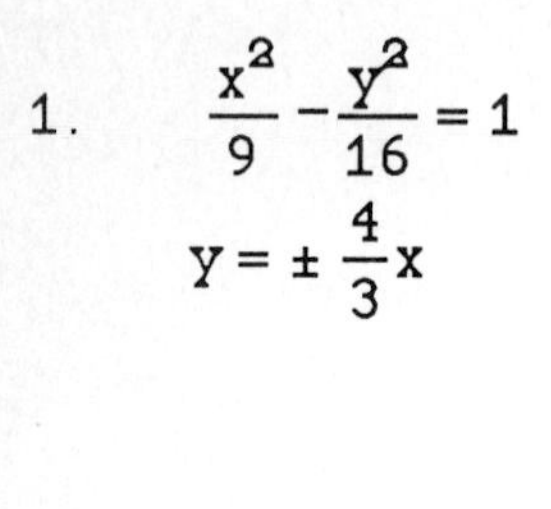

$$\frac{x^2}{9} - \frac{y^2}{16} = 1$$

$$y = \pm \frac{4}{3}x$$

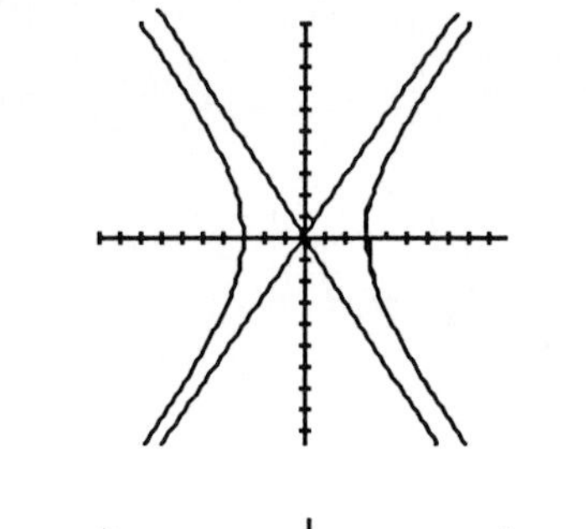

2. 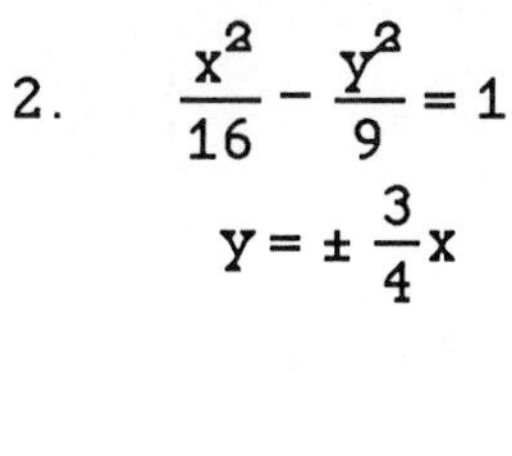

$$\frac{x^2}{16} - \frac{y^2}{9} = 1$$

$$y = \pm \frac{3}{4}x$$

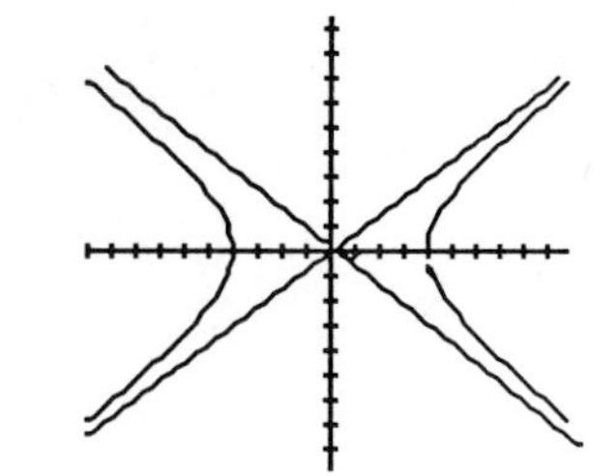

3. $$\frac{y^2}{9} - \frac{x^2}{16} = 1$$

$$y = \pm \frac{3}{4}x$$

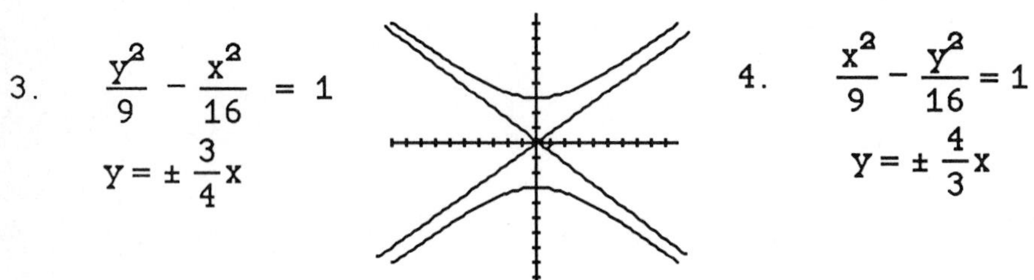

4. $$\frac{x^2}{9} - \frac{y^2}{16} = 1$$

$$y = \pm \frac{4}{3}x$$

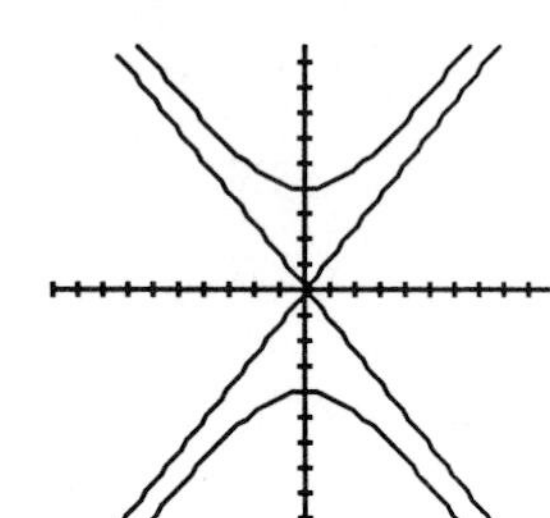

5. $$9(x-2)^2 - 4(y+3)^2 = 36$$

$$\frac{(x-2)^2}{4} - \frac{(y+3)^2}{9} = 1$$

Center: $C(2, -3)$

Vertices: $(4, -3)$ and $(0, -3)$

Foci: $(2 \pm \sqrt{13}, -3)$; $e = \frac{\sqrt{13}}{2}$

$$y + 3 = \pm \frac{4}{3}(x - 4)$$

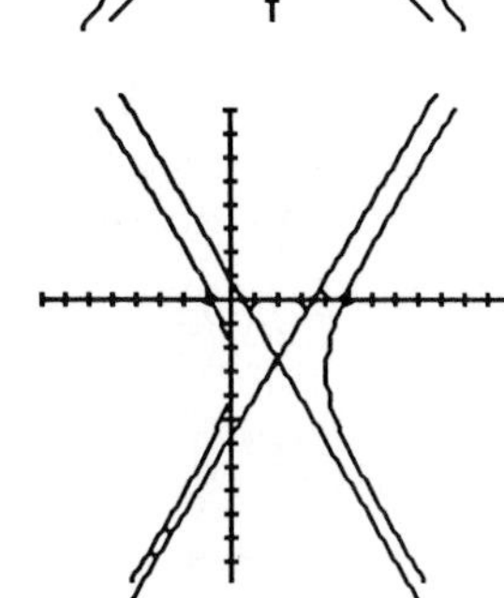

6. $$x^2 - 9(y-1)^2 = 9$$

$$\frac{x^2}{9} - \frac{(y-1)^2}{1} = 1$$

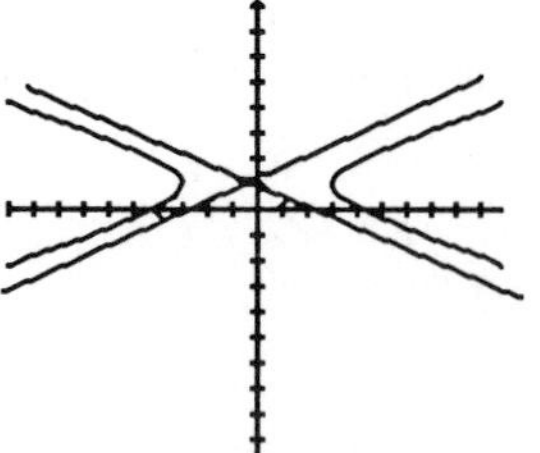

Center: $(0, 1)$

Vertices: $(3, 1)$ and $(-3, 1)$

Foci: $(\sqrt{10}, 1)$ and $(-\sqrt{10}, 1)$ $\quad y - 1 = \pm 3x$

7. $$4(x-2)^2 - 9(y+3)^2 = 36$$

$$\frac{(x-2)^2}{9} - \frac{(y+3)^2}{4} = 1$$

Center: $C(2, -3)$

Vertices: $(5, -3)$ and $(1, -3)$

Foci: $(2 \pm \sqrt{13}, -3)$; $e = \frac{\sqrt{13}}{3}$

$$y + 3 = \pm \frac{2}{3}(x - 2)$$

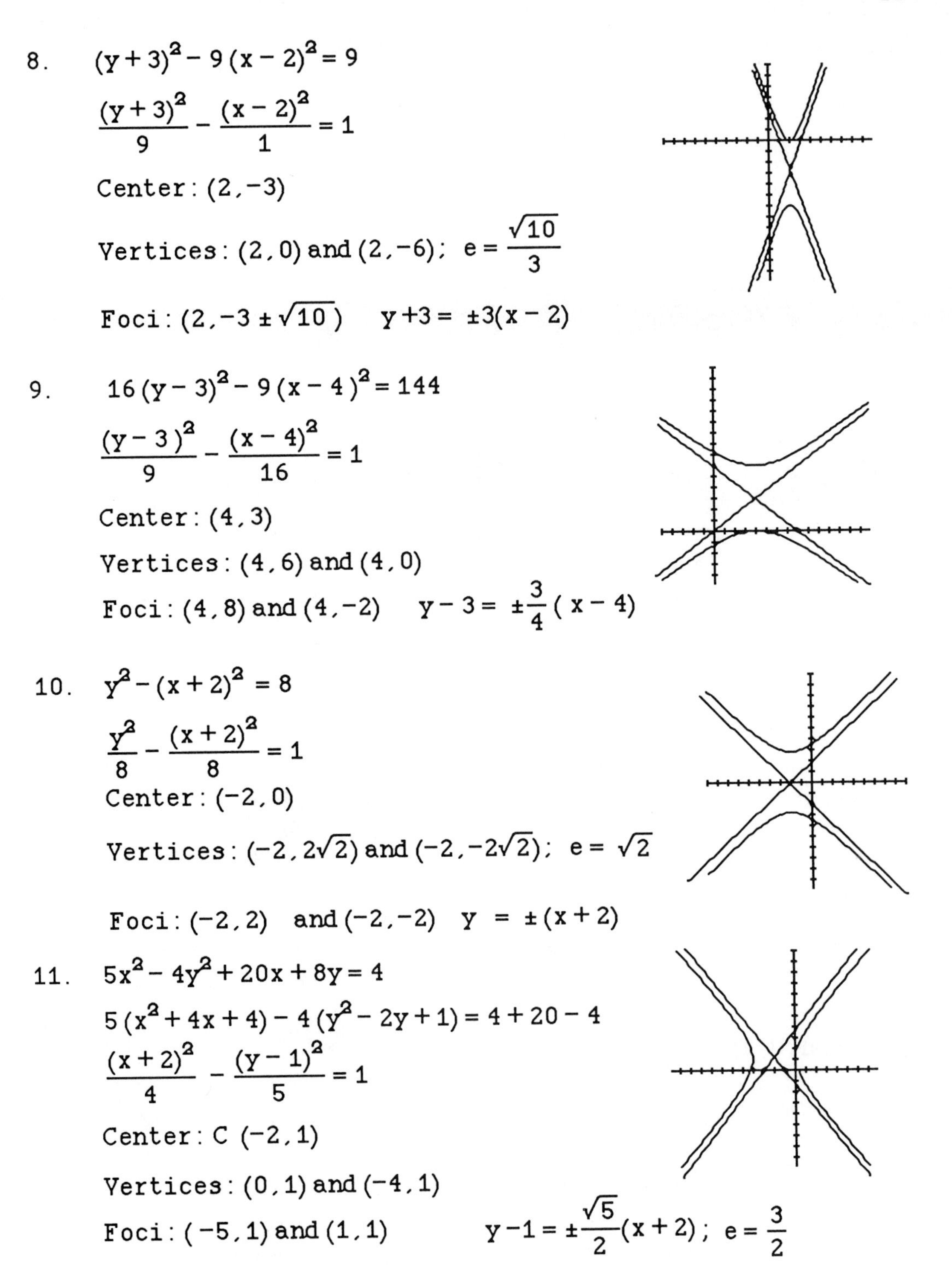

8. $(y+3)^2 - 9(x-2)^2 = 9$

$$\frac{(y+3)^2}{9} - \frac{(x-2)^2}{1} = 1$$

Center: $(2,-3)$

Vertices: $(2,0)$ and $(2,-6)$; $e = \dfrac{\sqrt{10}}{3}$

Foci: $(2, -3 \pm \sqrt{10})$ $\quad y+3 = \pm 3(x-2)$

9. $16(y-3)^2 - 9(x-4)^2 = 144$

$$\frac{(y-3)^2}{9} - \frac{(x-4)^2}{16} = 1$$

Center: $(4,3)$

Vertices: $(4,6)$ and $(4,0)$

Foci: $(4,8)$ and $(4,-2)$ $\quad y-3 = \pm\dfrac{3}{4}(x-4)$

10. $y^2 - (x+2)^2 = 8$

$$\frac{y^2}{8} - \frac{(x+2)^2}{8} = 1$$

Center: $(-2,0)$

Vertices: $(-2, 2\sqrt{2})$ and $(-2,-2\sqrt{2})$; $e = \sqrt{2}$

Foci: $(-2,2)$ and $(-2,-2)$ $\quad y = \pm(x+2)$

11. $5x^2 - 4y^2 + 20x + 8y = 4$

$5(x^2+4x+4) - 4(y^2-2y+1) = 4+20-4$

$$\frac{(x+2)^2}{4} - \frac{(y-1)^2}{5} = 1$$

Center: C $(-2,1)$

Vertices: $(0,1)$ and $(-4,1)$

Foci: $(-5,1)$ and $(1,1)$ $\quad y-1 = \pm\dfrac{\sqrt{5}}{2}(x+2)$; $e = \dfrac{3}{2}$

12. $4x^2 = y^2 - 4y + 8$

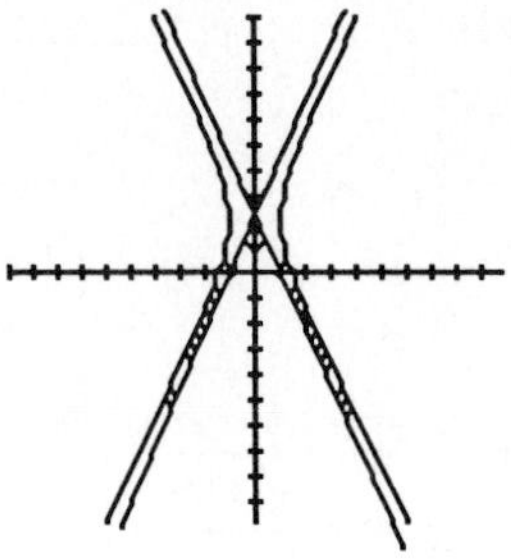

$4x^2 - (y^2 - 4y + 4) = 4$

$\frac{x^2}{1} - \frac{(y-2)^2}{4} = 1$

Center: (0, 2)

Vertices: (1, 2) and (−1, 2); $e = \sqrt{5}$

Foci: $(\pm\sqrt{5}, 2)$) $y - 2 = \pm 2x$

13. $4y^2 = x^2 - 4x$

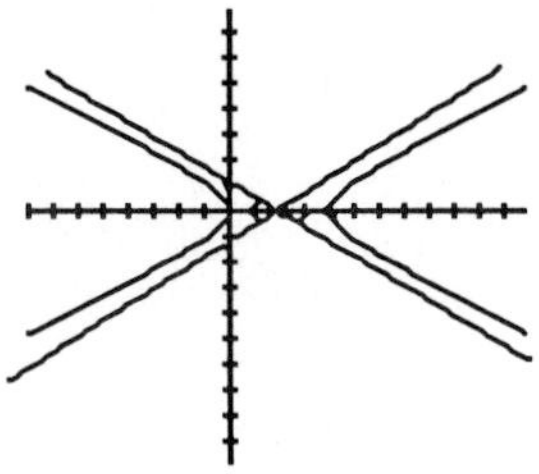

$4y^2 - (x^2 - 4x + 4) = -4$

$\frac{(x-2)^2}{4} - \frac{y^2}{1} = 1$

Center: C (2, 0)

Vertices: (0, 0) and (4, 0) Foci: $(2 \pm \sqrt{5}, 0)$; $e = \frac{\sqrt{5}}{2}$; $2y = \pm(x-2)$.

14. $4x^2 - 5y^2 - 16y + 10y + 31 = 0$

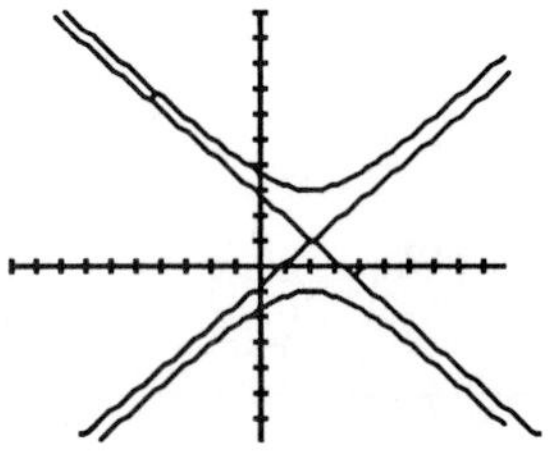

$4(x-2)^2 - 5(y-1)^2 = -31 + 16 - 5 = -20$

$\frac{(y-1)^2}{4} - \frac{(x-2)^2}{5} = 1$

Center: (2, 1)

Vertices: (2, 4) and (2, −1); $e = 3$

Foci: (2, 4) and (2, −2) $y - 1 = \pm\frac{2}{\sqrt{5}}(x-2)$

15. Foci at (0, 0) and (0, 4) ⇒ Center is (0, 2). Equation is:

$\frac{(y-2)^2}{a^2} - \frac{x^2}{b^2} = 1$. The point (12, 9) belongs to the hyperbola, giving

$\frac{49}{a^2} - \frac{144}{b^2} = 1$. Now $c = 2$, so $a^2 + b^2 = 4$, or $a^2 = 4 - b^2$. Substituting,

$\frac{49}{4-b^2} - \frac{144}{b^2} = 1 \Rightarrow b^4 + 189b^2 - 576 = 0 \Rightarrow (b^2 - 3)(b^2 + 192) = 0$.

Therefore, $b^2 = 3$, $a^2 = 1$ and $\frac{(y-2)^2}{1} - \frac{x^2}{3} = 1$ is required equation.

16. $\sqrt{(x-1)^2 + (y+3)^2} = \frac{3}{2}|y-2| \Rightarrow$

$x^2 - 2x + 1 + y^2 + 6y + 9 = \frac{9}{4}(y^2 - 4y + 4)$

$4x^2 - 5y^2 - 8x - 60y + 4 = 0$

17. (a) If the boat is at point P, then

PA - PB| = 1400 ms x 980 ft/s = 1.372 x 10^6 ft. = 259.8 miles.
The boat is on a hyperbola with foci A and B, and with
2a = 259.8 miles, or a = 129.9 miles.

18. This is a research question.

19. (a) $V = \pi \int_3^5 (x^2 - 9)\,dx = \pi \left[\frac{1}{3}x^3 - 9x \right]_3^5 = \frac{44\pi}{3}$

(b) $V = \pi \int_{-4}^4 (25 - x^2)\,dy = \pi \int_{-4}^4 (25 - (9 - y^2))\,dy$

$= 2\pi \int_0^4 (16 - y^2)\,dy = 2\pi \left[16y - \frac{1}{3}y^3 \right]_0^4 = \frac{256\pi}{3}$

20. (a) $V = 2\pi \int_0^3 2xy\,dy = 4\pi \int_0^3 y\sqrt{1 + y^2}\,dy = \frac{4\pi}{3}(1 + y^2)^{3/2} \Big]_0^3 = \frac{4\pi}{3}[10\sqrt{10} - 1]$

(b) $V = \pi \int_{-3}^3 x^2\,dy = 2\pi \int_0^3 (1 + y^2)\,dy = 2\pi \left[y + \frac{1}{3}y^3 \right]_0^3 = 24\pi$

21. $3x^2 - 4y^2 = 12$ and $x = 5 \Rightarrow y = \pm\frac{3\sqrt{7}}{2}$.

$V = 2\left(\pi \int_0^{\frac{3\sqrt{7}}{2}} (25 - x^2)\,dy \right) = 2\pi \int_0^{\frac{3\sqrt{7}}{2}} \left(25 - \left(4 + \frac{4}{3}y^2 \right) \right) dy$

$= 2\pi \left[21y - \frac{4}{9}y^3 \right]_0^{\frac{3\sqrt{7}}{2}} = 42\pi\sqrt{7}$

22. $A = \int_0^4 2x\,dy = 2\int_0^4 \sqrt{9 + y^2}\,dy = 2\int_0^{\tan^{-1}\frac{4}{3}} \sqrt{9 + 9\tan^2 u}\; 3\sec^2 u\,du$

$= 18 \int_0^{\tan^{-1}\frac{4}{3}} \sec^3 u\,du = 9\,[\sec x \tan x + \ln|\sec x + \tan x|\,\Big]_0^{\tan^{-1}\frac{4}{3}}$

$= 20 + 9\ln 3$. By symmetry, $\bar{x} = 0$. $M_y = \int_0^4 2xy\,dy$

$= 2\int_0^4 y\sqrt{9 + y^2}\,dy = \frac{2}{3}(9 + y^2)^{3/2} \Big]_0^4 = \frac{196}{3}$. $\bar{y} = \frac{196}{3\,(20 + 9\ln 3)} \approx 2.8$

23. The circles radii increase at the same rate, so their difference is constant.

24. $\frac{x^2}{a^2} - \frac{y^2}{b^2} = 1 \Rightarrow a^2y^2 = b^2x^2 - a^2b^2$ and $\frac{dy}{dx} = \frac{xb^2}{ya^2}$. Let $P(x_0, y_0)$ be a point of tangency. The slope from P to F(−c, 0) is $\frac{y_0}{x_0 + c}$ and from P to F_2 (c, 0) is $\frac{y_0}{x_0 - c}$. Let the tangent through P meet the x-axis in point A, $\angle F_1PA = \alpha$ and $\angle F_2PA = \beta$. We will show $\tan\alpha = \tan\beta$.

$$\tan\alpha = \frac{\frac{x_0b^2}{y_0a^2} - \frac{y_0}{x_0 + c}}{1 + \left(\frac{x_0b^2}{y_0a^2}\right)\left(\frac{y_0}{x_0 + c}\right)} = \frac{x_0^2b^2 + x_0b^2c - y_0^2a^2}{x_0y_0a^2 + y_0a^2c + x_0y_0b^2} = \frac{a^2b^2 + x_0b^2c}{x_0y_0c^2 + y_0a^2c} = \frac{b^2}{y_0c}$$

In a similar manner, $\tan\beta = \dfrac{\frac{y_0}{x_0 - c} - \frac{x_0b^2}{y_0a^2}}{1 + \left(\frac{y_0}{x_0 - c}\right)\left(\frac{x_0b^2}{y_0a^2}\right)} = \dfrac{b^2}{y_0c}$

8.6 THE GRAPHS OF QUADRATIC EQUATIONS

1. $\cot 2\alpha = 0 \Rightarrow 2\alpha = \frac{\pi}{2} \Rightarrow \alpha = \frac{\pi}{4}$.

$x = \frac{\sqrt{2}}{2}x' - \frac{\sqrt{2}}{2}y'$; $y = \frac{\sqrt{2}}{2}x' + \frac{\sqrt{2}}{2}y'$

$\left(\frac{\sqrt{2}}{2}x' - \frac{\sqrt{2}}{2}y'\right)\left(\frac{\sqrt{2}}{2}x' + \frac{\sqrt{2}}{2}y'\right) = 2$

$\frac{1}{2}x'^2 - \frac{1}{2}y'^2 = 2$ or $x'^2 - y'^2 = 4$

The graph is a hyperbola.

2. $x^2 + xy + y^2 = 1$; $A = B = C = 1$; $\cot 2\alpha = 0 \Rightarrow \alpha = \frac{\pi}{4}$.

$$A' = A\cos^2\alpha + B\sin\alpha\cos\alpha + C\sin^2\alpha = \left(\frac{1}{\sqrt{2}}\right)^2 + \left(\frac{1}{\sqrt{2}}\right)\left(\frac{1}{\sqrt{2}}\right) + \left(\frac{1}{\sqrt{2}}\right)^2 = \frac{3}{2}$$

$$C' = A\sin^2\alpha - B\sin\alpha\cos\alpha + C\cos^2\alpha = \left(\frac{1}{\sqrt{2}}\right)^2 - \left(\frac{1}{\sqrt{2}}\right)\left(\frac{1}{\sqrt{2}}\right) + \left(\frac{1}{\sqrt{2}}\right)^2 = \frac{1}{2}$$

$F' = F = 1$. $\therefore \frac{3}{2}x'^2 + \frac{1}{2}y'^2 = 1$ or $3x'^2 + y'^2 = 2$, an ellipse

3. $3x^2 + 2\sqrt{3}xy + y^2 - 8x + 8\sqrt{3}\,y = 0$; $A = 3$; $C = 1$; $B = 2\sqrt{3}$; $\cot 2\alpha = \sqrt{3} \Rightarrow \alpha = \frac{\pi}{4}$

$$A' = A\cos^2\alpha + B\sin\alpha\cos\alpha + C\sin^2\alpha = 3\left(\frac{\sqrt{3}}{2}\right)^2 + 2\sqrt{3}\left(\frac{1}{2}\right)\left(\frac{\sqrt{3}}{2}\right) + \left(\frac{1}{2}\right)^2 = 4$$

$$C' = A\sin^2\alpha - B\sin\alpha\cos\alpha + C\cos^2\alpha = 3\left(\frac{1}{2}\right)^2 - 2\sqrt{3}\left(\frac{1}{2}\right)\left(\frac{\sqrt{3}}{2}\right) + \left(\frac{\sqrt{3}}{2}\right)^2 = 0$$

$$D' = D\cos\alpha + E\sin\alpha = -8\left(\frac{\sqrt{3}}{2}\right) + 8\sqrt{3}\left(\frac{1}{2}\right) = 0$$

$$E' = -D\sin\alpha + E\cos\alpha = 8\left(\frac{1}{2}\right) + 8\sqrt{3}\left(\frac{\sqrt{3}}{2}\right) = 16$$

$F' = F = 0$. $\therefore\ 4x'^2 + 16y' = 0$ or $x^2 = -4y'$; a parabola

4. $x^2 - \sqrt{3}xy + 2y^2 = 1$; $A = 1$; $C = 2$; $B = -\sqrt{3}$; $\cot 2\alpha = \frac{1}{\sqrt{3}} \Rightarrow \alpha = \frac{\pi}{6}$.

$$A' = A\cos^2\alpha + B\sin\alpha\cos\alpha + C\sin^2\alpha = \left(\frac{\sqrt{3}}{2}\right)^2 - \sqrt{3}\left(\frac{1}{2}\right)\left(\frac{\sqrt{3}}{2}\right) + 2\left(\frac{1}{2}\right)^2 = \frac{1}{2}$$

$$C' = A\sin^2\alpha - B\sin\alpha\cos\alpha + C\cos^2\alpha = \left(\frac{1}{2}\right)^2 + \sqrt{3}\left(\frac{1}{2}\right)\left(\frac{\sqrt{3}}{2}\right) + 2\left(\frac{\sqrt{3}}{2}\right)^2 = \frac{5}{2}$$

$F' = F = 1$. $\therefore\ \frac{1}{2}x'^2 + \frac{5}{2}y'^2 = 1$ or $x'^2 + 5y'^2 = 2$, an ellipse

5. $x^2 - 2xy + y^2 = 2$; $A = C = 1$; $B = -2$; $\cot 2\alpha = 0 \Rightarrow \alpha = \frac{\pi}{4}$.

$$A' = A\cos^2\alpha + B\sin\alpha\cos\alpha + C\sin^2\alpha = \left(\frac{1}{\sqrt{2}}\right)^2 - 2\left(\frac{1}{\sqrt{2}}\right)\left(\frac{1}{\sqrt{2}}\right) + \left(\frac{1}{\sqrt{2}}\right)^2 = 0$$

$$C' = A\sin^2\alpha - B\sin\alpha\cos\alpha + C\cos^2\alpha = \left(\frac{1}{\sqrt{2}}\right)^2 + 2\left(\frac{1}{\sqrt{2}}\right)\left(\frac{1}{\sqrt{2}}\right) + \left(\frac{1}{\sqrt{2}}\right)^2 = 2$$

$F' = F = 2$. $\therefore\ 2y'^2 = 2$ or $y = \pm 1$, two parallel lines

6. $x^2 - 3xy + y^2 = 5$; $A = 1$; $C = 1$; $B = -3$; $\cot 2\alpha = 0 \Rightarrow \alpha = \frac{\pi}{4}$.

$$A' = A\cos^2\alpha + B\sin\alpha\cos\alpha + C\sin^2\alpha = \left(\frac{1}{\sqrt{2}}\right)^2 - 3\left(\frac{1}{\sqrt{2}}\right)\left(\frac{1}{\sqrt{2}}\right) + \left(\frac{1}{\sqrt{2}}\right)^2 = -\frac{1}{2}$$

$$C' = A\sin^2\alpha - B\sin\alpha\cos\alpha + C\cos^2\alpha = \left(\frac{1}{\sqrt{2}}\right)^2 + 3\left(\frac{1}{\sqrt{2}}\right)\frac{1}{\sqrt{2}}\Big) + \left(\frac{1}{\sqrt{2}}\right)^2 = \frac{5}{2}$$

$F' = F = 5$. $\therefore\ -\frac{1}{2}x'^2 + \frac{5}{2}y'^2 = 5$ or $5y'^2 - x'^2 = 10$, a hyperbola

7. $\sqrt{2}x^2 + 2\sqrt{2}xy + \sqrt{2}y^2 - 8x + 8y + 4\sqrt{2} = 0$; $\cot 2\alpha = 0 \Rightarrow \alpha = \frac{\pi}{4}$.

$A' = A\cos^2\alpha + B\sin\alpha\cos\alpha + C\sin^2\alpha = \left(\frac{1}{\sqrt{2}}\right)^2 + 2\left(\frac{1}{\sqrt{2}}\right)\left(\frac{1}{\sqrt{2}}\right) + \left(\frac{1}{\sqrt{2}}\right)^2 = 2$

$C' = A\sin^2\alpha - B\sin\alpha\cos\alpha + C\cos^2\alpha = 0$

$D' = D\cos\alpha + E\sin\alpha = -4\sqrt{2}\left(\frac{1}{\sqrt{2}}\right) + 4\sqrt{2}\left(\frac{1}{\sqrt{2}}\right) = 0$

$E' = -D\sin\alpha + E\cos\alpha = 8$; $F' = F = 4$

$\therefore\ 2x'^2 + 8y' + 4 = 0$ or $x'^2 = -4\left(y' + \frac{1}{2}\right)$, a parabola

8. $xy - x - y + 1 = 0$; $\cot 2\alpha = 0 \Rightarrow \alpha = \frac{\pi}{4}$.

$D' = D\cos\alpha + E\sin\alpha = -\left(\frac{1}{\sqrt{2}}\right) - \left(\frac{1}{\sqrt{2}}\right) = -\sqrt{2}$

$E' = -D\sin\alpha + E\cos\alpha = 0$; $F' = F = 1$

$\therefore\ -\sqrt{2}\,x' + 1 = 0$ or $x = \frac{1}{\sqrt{2}}$; a vertical line

9. $3x^2 + 2xy + 3y^2 = 19$; $A = C = 3$; $B = 2$; $\cot 2\alpha = 0 \Rightarrow \alpha = \frac{\pi}{4}$.

$A' = A\cos^2\alpha + B\sin\alpha\cos\alpha + C\sin^2\alpha = 3\left(\frac{1}{\sqrt{2}}\right)^2 + 2\left(\frac{1}{\sqrt{2}}\right)\left(\frac{1}{\sqrt{2}}\right) + 3\left(\frac{1}{\sqrt{2}}\right)^2 = 4$

$C' = A\sin^2\alpha - B\sin\alpha\cos\alpha + C\cos^2\alpha = 3\left(\frac{1}{\sqrt{2}}\right)^2 - 2\left(\frac{1}{\sqrt{2}}\right)\left(\frac{1}{\sqrt{2}}\right) + 3\left(\frac{1}{\sqrt{2}}\right)^2 = 2$

$F' = F = 19$

$\therefore\ 4x'^2 + 2y'^2 = 19$, an ellipse

10. $3x^2 + 4\sqrt{3}xy - y^2 = 7$; $A = 3$; $C = -1$; $B = 4\sqrt{3}$; $\cot 2\alpha = \frac{1}{\sqrt{3}} \Rightarrow \alpha = \frac{\pi}{6}$.

$A' = A\cos^2\alpha + B\sin\alpha\cos\alpha + C\sin^2\alpha = 3\left(\frac{\sqrt{3}}{2}\right)^2 + 4\sqrt{3}\left(\frac{1}{2}\right)\left(\frac{\sqrt{3}}{2}\right) - \left(\frac{1}{2}\right)^2 = 5$

$C' = A\sin^2\alpha - B\sin\alpha\cos\alpha + C\cos^2\alpha = 3\left(\frac{1}{2}\right)^2 - 4\sqrt{3}\left(\frac{1}{2}\right)\left(\frac{\sqrt{3}}{2}\right) - \left(\frac{\sqrt{3}}{2}\right)^2 = -3$

$F' = F = 7$. $\therefore\ 5x'^2 - 3y'^2 = 7$, a hyperbola

11. $\cot 2\alpha = \dfrac{14-2}{16} = \dfrac{3}{4}$. $\therefore \cos 2\alpha = \dfrac{3}{5}$.

$$\sin\alpha = \sqrt{\frac{1-\cos\alpha}{2}} = \sqrt{\frac{1-\frac{3}{5}}{2}} = \frac{1}{\sqrt{5}}$$

$$\cos\alpha = \sqrt{\frac{1+\cos\alpha}{2}} = \sqrt{\frac{1+\frac{3}{5}}{2}} = \frac{2}{\sqrt{5}}$$

12. $\sqrt{(x+1)^2+y^2} + \sqrt{x^2+(y-\sqrt{3})^2} = 2a$. Since (1, 0) satisfies this equation,

$2a = 4$. $\therefore \left(\sqrt{(x+1)^2+y^2}\right)^2 = \left(4 - \sqrt{x^2+(y-\sqrt{3})^2}\right)^2 \Rightarrow$

$4\sqrt{x^2+(y-\sqrt{3})^2} = 9-(x+\sqrt{3}y) \Rightarrow 15x^2 - 2\sqrt{3}xy + 13y^2 - 14\sqrt{3}y + 18x - 33 = 0.$

$\cot 2\alpha = \dfrac{15-13}{-2\sqrt{3}} = -\dfrac{1}{\sqrt{3}} \Rightarrow 2\alpha = \dfrac{2\pi}{3}$ and $\alpha = \dfrac{\pi}{3}$.

13. $a^2 = x^2 + y^2 = (x'\cos\alpha - y'\sin\alpha)^2 + (x'\sin\alpha + y'\cos\alpha)^2 =$

$x'^2\cos^2\alpha - 2x'y'\sin\alpha\cos\alpha + y'^2\sin^2\alpha + x'^2\sin^2\alpha$

$+ 2x'y'\sin\alpha\cos\alpha + y'^2\cos^2\alpha =$

$x'^2(\cos^2\alpha + \sin^2\alpha) + y'^2(\cos^2\alpha + \sin^2\alpha) = x'^2 + y'^2$

14. If $A = C$ then $\cot 2\alpha = \dfrac{A-C}{B} = 0$ and we may take $\alpha = \dfrac{\pi}{4}$. Then

$B' = B\cos 2\alpha + (C-A)\sin 2\alpha = B\cos\dfrac{\pi}{2} + 0 = 0$, regardless of B.

15. $\cot 2\alpha = 0 \Rightarrow \alpha = \dfrac{\pi}{4}$.

$A' = A\cos^2\alpha + B\sin\alpha\cos\alpha + C\sin^2\alpha = = \left(\dfrac{1}{\sqrt{2}}\right)^2 + 2\left(\dfrac{1}{\sqrt{2}}\right)\left(\dfrac{1}{\sqrt{2}}\right) + \left(\dfrac{1}{\sqrt{2}}\right)^2 = 2$

$C' = A\sin^2\alpha - B\sin\alpha\cos\alpha + C\cos^2\alpha = 0$; $F' = F = 1$

$\therefore 2x'^2 = 1$ or $x' = \pm\dfrac{1}{\sqrt{2}}$, two parallel lines

8.7 PARABOLA, ELLIPSE, OR HYPERBOLA?

1. $A = 1$, $B = 0$, $C = -1$; $B^2 - 4AC = 4$; hyperbola

2. $A = 25$, $B = 0$, $C = 9$; $B^2 - 4AC = -900$; ellipse

3. $A = 0$, $B = 0$, $C = 1$; $B^2 - 4AC = 0$; parabola

4. $A = 1$, $B = 0$, $C = 1$; $B^2 - 4AC = -4$; ellipse

5. $A = 1, B = 0, C = 4; B^2 - 4AC = -16$; ellipse

6. $A = 1; B = 1; C = 1; B^2 - 4AC = -3$; ellipse

7. $A = 2, B = 4, C = -1; B^2 - 4AC = 24$; hyperbola

8. $A = 1, B = 4, C = 4; B^2 - 4AC = 0$; parabola

9. $A = 1, B = 0, C = 1; B^2 - 4AC = -4$; ellipse

10. $A = 0, B = 1, C = 1; B^2 - 4AC = 1$; hyperbola

11. $A = 3, B = 6, C = 3; B^2 - 4AC = 0$; parabola

12. $A = 1, B = 0, C = -1; B^2 - 4AC = 4$; hyperbola

13. $A = 2, B = 0, C = 3; B^2 - 4AC = -24$; ellipse

14. $A = 1. B = -3, C = 3; B^2 - 4AC = -3$; ellipse

15. $A = 25, B = 0, C = -4; B^2 - 4AC = 400$; hyperbola

16. $A = 6, B = 3, D = 2; B^2 - 4AC = -39$; ellipse

17. $A = 3, B = 12, C = 12; B^2 - 4AC = 0$; parabola

18. We can rotate the equation $Ax^2 + Bxy + Cy^2 = 1$ to be of the form

$A'x'^2 + C'y'^2 = 1$. In standard form, $\dfrac{x'^2}{\frac{1}{A'}} + \dfrac{y'^2}{\frac{1}{C'}} = 1$ and the area

$A = \pi ab = \dfrac{\pi}{\sqrt{A'C'}}$. Since $B^2 - 4AC = B'^2 - 4A'C'$ and $B'=0$,

$$\frac{\pi}{\sqrt{A'C'}} = \frac{2\pi}{\sqrt{4A'C'}} = \frac{2\pi}{\sqrt{4AC - B^2}}.$$

19. $D'^2 + E'^2 = (D\cos\alpha + E\sin\alpha)^2 + (-D\sin\alpha + E\cos\alpha)^2$

$= D^2\cos^2\alpha + 2DE\cos\alpha\sin\alpha + E^2\sin^2\alpha + D^2\sin^2\alpha$

$\quad -2DE\cos\alpha\sin\alpha + E^2\cos\alpha\sin\alpha$

$= D^2(\cos^2\alpha + \sin^2\alpha) + E^2(\cos^2\alpha + \sin^2\alpha) = D^2 + E^2.$

20. To make $A' = 0$, we need $A\cos^2\alpha + B\cos\alpha\sin\alpha + C\sin^2\alpha = 0$.

If $A = -C$, then we can write this as:

$A(\cos^2\alpha - \sin^2\alpha) - \frac{B}{2}(2\sin\alpha\cos\alpha) = A\cos 2\alpha - \frac{B}{2}\sin 2\alpha = 0.$

This is equivalent to $\tan 2\alpha = \dfrac{2A}{B}$. Thus we can find α for which $A' = -C' = 0$.

21. $A' = A\cos^2\alpha + B\cos\alpha\sin\alpha + C\sin^2\alpha$

$C' = A\sin^2\alpha - B\cos\alpha\sin\alpha + C\cos^2\alpha$

$A' + C' = A(\sin^2\alpha + B\cos^2\alpha) + C(\sin^2\alpha + B\cos^2\alpha) = A + C$

$A' - C' = (A - C)\cos^2\alpha + (A - C)\sin^2\alpha + 2B\cos\alpha\sin\alpha$

$= (A - C)\cos 2\alpha + B\sin 2\alpha$

$(A' - C')^2 = (A - C)^2\cos^2 2\alpha + 2B(A - C)\sin 2\alpha\cos 2\alpha + B^2\sin^2 2\alpha$

$B'^2 = B^2\cos^2 2\alpha + 2B(C - A)\cos 2\alpha\sin 2\alpha + (C - A)^2\sin^2 2\alpha$

$(A' - C')^2 + B'^2 = (A - C)^2 + B^2(\cos^2 2\alpha + \sin^2 2\alpha) = (A - C)^2 + B^2$

$(A' + C')^2 = (A + C)^2$. Subtracting the last two, and simplifying,

we have that $B'^2 - 4A'B' = B^2 - 4AC$.

8.8 SECTIONS OF A CONE

1. $PQ = PA\cos\beta$ and $PQ = PD\cos\alpha \Rightarrow PA\cos\beta = PD\cos\alpha$, or

$\frac{PA}{PD} = \frac{\cos\alpha}{\cos\beta}$. Since $\alpha = \beta$, $PA = PD$ and hence $e = 1$. Therefore

we have a parabola.

2. As in Problem 1, $e = \frac{PA}{PD} = \frac{\cos\alpha}{\cos\beta}$. Since $\frac{\pi}{2} > \beta > \alpha > 0$,

$\cos\beta < \cos\alpha$, and hence $e > 1$. Therefore, we have a parabola.

3. The plane of the circle and the plane perpendicular to the axis of the cone are the same, so there is no line of intersecton on which to locate the point D.

4. Let $P(x, y)$ be a general point on the conic. Then $PF = e \cdot PD \Rightarrow$

$$e|x + p| = \sqrt{x^2 + y^2} \Rightarrow e^2(x^2 + 2xp + p^2) = x^2 + y^2 \Rightarrow$$

$$x^2(e^2 - 1) - 2e^2 p x + y^2 = e^2 p^2 \Rightarrow$$

$$(e^2 - 1)\left[x^2 - \frac{2e^2 p}{e^2 - 1}x + \left(\frac{e^2 p}{e^2 - 1}\right)^2\right] + y^2 = e^2 p^2 + \frac{e^4 p^2}{e^2 - 1} \Rightarrow$$

$$(e^2 - 1)\left[x - \frac{e^2 p}{e^2 - 1}\right]^2 + y^2 = e^2 p^2 + \frac{e^4 p^2}{e^2 - 1}.$$ Thus the

center is at the point $\left(\frac{e^2 p}{e^2 - 1}, 0\right)$

8.9 PARAMETRIC EQUATIONS FOR CONICS AND OTHER CURVES

1. $x = \cos t$ and $y = \sin t \Rightarrow x^2 = \cos^2 t$ and $y^2 = \sin^2 t$ so
$x^2 + y^2 = \sin^2 t + \cos^2 t = 1$.

2. $x = \cos 2t$ and $y = \sin 2t$, $0 \le t \le \pi \Rightarrow x^2 = \cos^2 2t$ and $y^2 = \sin^2 2t$.
$\therefore\ x^2 + y^2 = \cos^2 2t + \sin^2 2t = 1$.

3. $x = 4\cos t$ and $y = 2\sin t \Rightarrow \dfrac{x}{4} = \cos t$ and $\dfrac{y}{2} = \sin t \Rightarrow$
$\left(\dfrac{x}{4}\right)^2 = \cos^2 t$ and $\left(\dfrac{y}{2}\right)^2 = \sin^2 t$ so $\left(\dfrac{x}{4}\right)^2 + \left(\dfrac{y}{2}\right)^2 = \sin^2 t + \cos^2 t = 1$.

4. $x = 4\cos t$ and $y = 5\sin t$, $0 \le t \le 2\pi \Rightarrow \dfrac{x}{4} = \cos t$ and $\dfrac{y}{5} = \sin t$
so $\dfrac{x^2}{16} + \dfrac{y^2}{25} = \sin^2 t + \cos^2 t = 1$

5. $x = \cos 2t = 1 - 2\sin^2 t$ and $y = \sin t$, so $x = 1 - 2y^2$, $|x| \le 1$, $|y| \le 1$

6. $x = \cos t$ and $y = \sin 2t$, $0 \le t \le \pi$. $\cos t = x \Rightarrow \sin t = \sqrt{1 - x^2}$.
$y = 2\sin t \cos t = 2x\sqrt{1 - x^2} \Rightarrow y^2 = 4x^2(1 - x^2)$. If we complete the square, the nature of the curve becomes somewhat clearer:
$4\left(x^4 - x^2 + \dfrac{1}{4}\right) + y^2 = 1$ or $4\left(x^2 - \dfrac{1}{2}\right)^2 + y^2 = 1$.
The centers are $\left(\pm\dfrac{1}{\sqrt{2}}, 0\right)$. The graph is below.

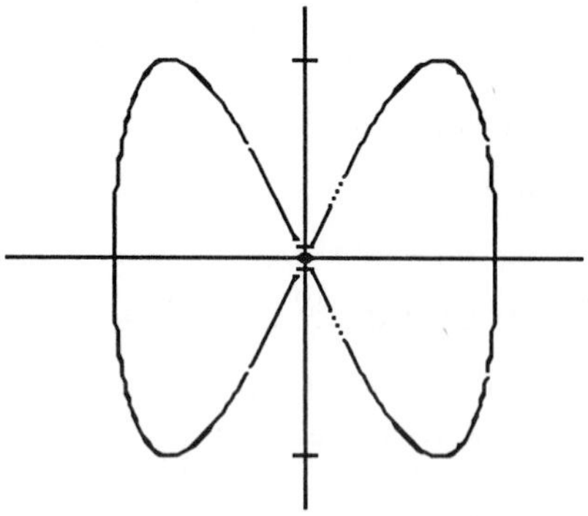

7. $x = -\sec t$ and $y = \tan t \Rightarrow x^2 = \sec^2 t$ and $y = \tan^2 t$ so
$x^2 - y^2 = \sec^2 t - \tan^2 t = 1$. Since $-\dfrac{\pi}{2} < t < \dfrac{\pi}{2}$, the curve includes only the left branch of the hyperbola.

8. $x = \csc t$ and $y = \cot t$, $0 < t < \pi \Rightarrow x^2 = \csc^2 t$ and $y^2 = \cot^2 t$
so $x^2 - y^2 = \csc^2 t - \cot^2 t = 1$. Since $0 < t < \pi$, $\csc t = x > 0$ and the graph only includes the right branch of the hyperbola.

9. $y = 1 - \cos t \Rightarrow \cos t = 1 - y \Rightarrow t = \cos^{-1}(1 - y)$. Therefore

$$x = t - \sin t = \cos^{-1}(1 - y) - \sin(\cos^{-1}(1 - y)) = \cos^{-1}(1 - y) - \sqrt{2y - y^2}.$$

10. $x = 2 + 4\sin t$ and $y = 3 - 2\cos t$, $0 \le t \le 2\pi$, $\Rightarrow$

$$\frac{x-2}{4} = \sin t \text{ and } \frac{y-3}{-2} = \cos t. \therefore \frac{(x-2)^2}{16} + \frac{(y-3)^2}{4} = 1.$$

11. $x = t^3 \Rightarrow t = x^{\frac{1}{3}}$ so $y = t^2 = x^{\frac{2}{3}}$.

12. $x = 2t + 3$ and $y = 4t^2 - 9$, $-\infty < t < \infty$. $t = \dfrac{x-3}{2}$ so

$$y = 4\left(\frac{x-3}{2}\right)^2 - 9 \text{ or } y = x^2 - 6x.$$

13. $x = \sec^2 t - 1 = \tan^2 t = y^2$. Therefore $x = y^2$.

14. $x = 2 + \dfrac{1}{t}$ and $y = 2 - t$, $0 < t < \infty$. $t = \dfrac{1}{x-2}$ so $y = 2 - \dfrac{1}{x-2}$

or $y = \dfrac{2x-5}{x-2}$. $t > 0 \Rightarrow x > 2$, so the graph consists of only

to portion to the right of the asymptote $x = 2$.

15. $x = t + 1 \Rightarrow t = x - 1$. Therefore, $y = t^2 + 4 = (x-1)^2 + 4$.

$t \ge 0 \Rightarrow x \ge 1$ so the curve consists of only the right half of the parabola.

16. $x = t^2 + t$, $y = t^2 - t$, $-\infty < t < \infty$. Subtracting, $x - y = 2t$ or $t = \dfrac{x-y}{2}$.

$$y = \left(\frac{x-y}{2}\right)^2 - \frac{x-y}{2} \Rightarrow x^2 - 2xy + y^2 - 2x - 2y = 0.$$ This is a parabola with

a 45° rotation of the axes $\left(x' = \dfrac{1}{\sqrt{2}}y'^2\right)$. The graph is below.

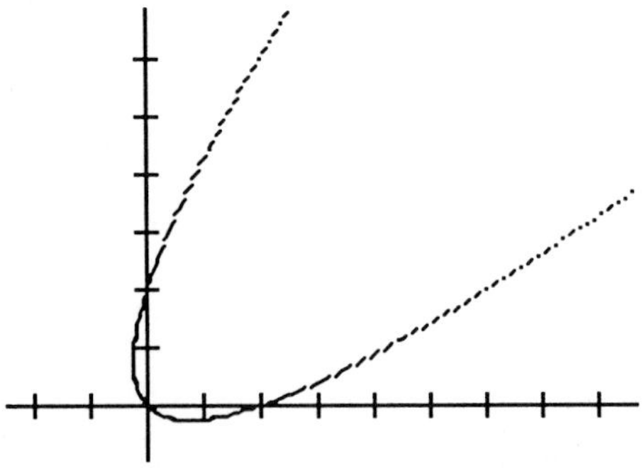

17. If $x^2 + y^2 = a^2$, then $2x + 2y\dfrac{dy}{dx} = 0$ or $\dfrac{dy}{dx} = -\dfrac{x}{y}$. Let $t = \dfrac{dy}{dx}$.

$$-\frac{x}{y} = t \Rightarrow x = -yt. \quad y^2t^2 + y^2 = a^2 \Rightarrow y = \frac{a}{\sqrt{1+t^2}} \text{ and } x = \frac{-at}{\sqrt{1+t^2}}.$$

18. In terms of θ, the circle is: $x = a\cos\theta$, $y = a\sin\theta$, $0 \le \theta < 2\pi$.

Since $\theta = \dfrac{s}{a}$, the parametizations are: $x = a\cos\dfrac{s}{a}$, $y = a\sin\dfrac{s}{a}$.

19. $\angle PTB = \angle AOT = t$. $PT = \text{arc}(AT) = at$

$$x = OB + BC = OB + DP$$
$$= a\cos t + at\sin t$$
$$= a(\cos t + t\sin t)$$
$$y = PC = TB - TD$$
$$= a\sin t - at\cos t$$
$$= a(\sin t - t\cos t)$$

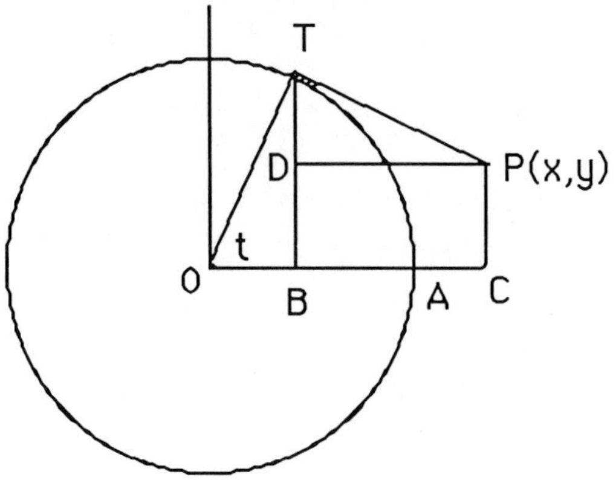

T
D
P(x,y)
t
O
B
A
C

20. $x = OD = OB + BD$; $y = PD = BC - CE$

$$\frac{BC}{a+b} = \sin\theta; \quad \frac{OB}{a+b} = \cos\theta$$

$$\frac{\text{arc}(PF)}{b} = \angle PCF; \quad \frac{\text{arc}(AF)}{a} = \theta$$

$\therefore \angle PCF = \dfrac{a\theta}{b}$. Since $\theta + \angle BCO = 90°$,

$$\theta + (\angle PCF - \alpha) = 90° \text{ or } \alpha = \left(\frac{a\theta}{b} + \theta\right) - 90°$$

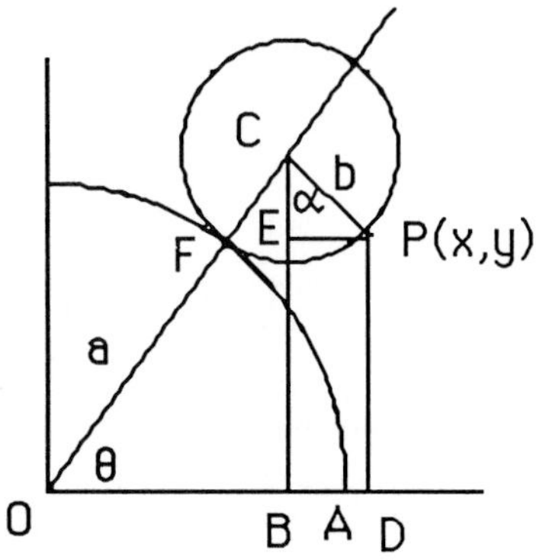

C
b
α
E
P(x,y)
F
a
θ
O
B
A
D

$$\cos\alpha = \cos\left[\left(\frac{a\theta}{b} + \theta\right) - 90°\right] = \cos\left[90° - \left(\theta + \frac{a\theta}{b}\right)\right] = \sin\left(\theta + \frac{a\theta}{b}\right).$$

$$\sin\alpha = -\sin\left[90° - \left(\theta + \frac{a\theta}{b}\right)\right] = -\cos\left(\theta + \frac{a\theta}{b}\right).$$

$$\therefore \quad x = (a+b)\cos\theta + b\sin\alpha = (a+b)\cos\theta - b\cos\left(\frac{a+b}{b}\right)\theta$$

$$y = (a+b)\sin\theta - b\cos\alpha = (a+b)\sin\theta - b\sin\left(\frac{a+b}{b}\right)\theta$$

22. (a) $x = OM = AQ = 2a\cot\theta$

$$y = AM - AP = 2a - AB\sin\theta$$

$$\frac{AB}{AQ} = \frac{AQ}{OA} \Rightarrow AB = (2a\cot\theta)(\cos\theta)$$

$$y = 2a - (2a\cot\theta)(\cos\theta)(\sin\theta)$$
$$= 2a - 2a\cos^2\theta = 2a\sin^2\theta$$

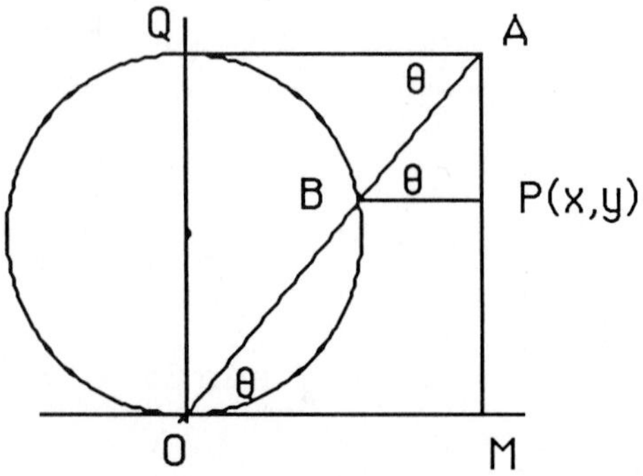

Q
A
θ
B
θ
P(x,y)
θ
O
M

(b) $\cot\theta = \dfrac{x}{2a} \Rightarrow \sin\theta = \dfrac{2a}{\sqrt{4a^2 + x^2}}$.

$$y = 2a\sin^2\theta = 2a\left(\frac{2a}{\sqrt{4a^2+x^2}}\right)^2 \Rightarrow y(4a^2 + x^2) = 8a^3$$

21. (a) The hypocycloid can be obtained from the equation of the epicycloid in problem 20 by replacing b with −b to obtain

$$x = (a-b)\cos\theta + b\cos\left(\frac{a-b}{b}\right)\theta$$

$$y = (a-b)\sin\theta - b\sin\left(\frac{a-b}{b}\right)\theta$$

(b) If $b = \dfrac{a}{4}$, then $x = \dfrac{3a}{4}\cos\theta + \dfrac{a}{4}\cos 3\theta$ and $y = \dfrac{3a}{4}\sin\theta - \dfrac{a}{4}\sin 3\theta$.

$$x = \frac{a}{4}[3\cos\theta + \cos(2\theta + \theta)]$$

$$= \frac{a}{4}(3\cos\theta + \cos 2\theta\cos\theta - \sin 2\theta\sin\theta)$$

$$= \frac{a}{4}[(3\cos\theta + (\cos^2\theta - \sin^2\theta)\cos\theta - 2\sin^2\theta\cos\theta]$$

$$= \frac{a}{4}[3\cos\theta + \cos^3\theta - 3\sin^2\theta\cos\theta]$$

$$= \frac{a}{4}[3\cos\theta + \cos^3\theta - 3(1 - \cos^2\theta)\cos\theta]$$

$$= \frac{a}{4}[3\cos\theta + \cos^3\theta - 3\cos\theta + 3\cos^3\theta]$$

$$= a\cos^3\theta$$

$$y = \frac{a}{4}[3\sin\theta - \sin(2\theta + \theta)]$$

$$= \frac{a}{4}(3\sin\theta - \sin 2\theta\cos\theta - \cos 2\theta\sin\theta)$$

$$= \frac{a}{4}[(3\sin\theta - (\cos^2\theta - \sin^2\theta)\sin\theta - 2\sin\theta\cos^2\theta]$$

$$= \frac{a}{4}[3\sin\theta + \sin^3\theta - 3\cos^2\theta\sin\theta]$$

$$= \frac{a}{4}[3\sin\theta + \sin^3\theta - 3(1 - \sin^2\theta)\sin\theta]$$

$$= \frac{a}{4}[3\sin\theta + \sin^3\theta - 3\sin\theta + 3\sin^3\theta]$$

$$= a\sin^3\theta$$

23. (a) $x = x_0 + (x_1 - x_0)t \Rightarrow t = \dfrac{x - x_0}{x_1 - x_0}$. $y = y_0 + (y_1 - y_0)t \Rightarrow t = \dfrac{y - y_0}{y_1 - y_0}$.

$$\frac{x - x_0}{x_1 - x_0} = \frac{y - y_0}{y_1 - y_0} \Rightarrow \frac{y - y_0}{x - x_0} = \frac{y_1 - y_0}{x_1 - x_0} = m.$$ Therefore, $y - y_0 = m(x - x_0)$.

(b) $x = tx_0$; $y = ty_0$;

(c) $x = -1 + t$; $y = t$ or $x = t$, $y = 1 + t$

24. Let r = radius of small circle and $3r$ = radius of large circle. Then the center of the small circle travels along the circumference of a circle of radius $4r$ for a distance of 8π units. Since the circumference of the small circle is 2π units, it takes 4 revolutions to return to its starting point.

25. $x = t$ and $y = t^2 \Rightarrow y = x^2$. $S = (x-2)^2 + \left(y - \frac{1}{2}\right)^2 = (x-2)^2 + \left(x^2 - \frac{1}{2}\right)^2$.

$S'(x) = 4x^3 - 4 = 0 \Leftrightarrow x = 1$. $S''(x) = 12x^2 \Rightarrow S(1)$ is a minimum.

The point closest to $\left(2, \frac{1}{2}\right)$ is $(1, 1)$.

26. Let s = distance of a point on $x = 2\cos t$, $y = \sin t$ to $\left(\frac{3}{4}, 0\right)$.

Then $S = s^2 = \left(x - \frac{3}{4}\right)^2 + y^2 = \left(2\cos t - \frac{3}{4}\right)^2 + \sin^2 t$.

$\dfrac{dS}{dt} = 2\left(2\cos t - \frac{3}{4}\right)(-2\sin t) + 2\sin t\cos t = 0$ if

$-6\cos t\sin t + 3\sin t = 0$, or if $t = 0$ or $\frac{\pi}{3}$. $S(0) = \frac{25}{16}$ and

$S\left(\frac{\pi}{3}\right) = \frac{13}{16}$. $\therefore$ The closest point is $\left(2\cos\frac{\pi}{3}, \sin\frac{\pi}{3}\right) = \left(1, \frac{\sqrt{3}}{2}\right)$.

27. $x = a(t - \sin t) \Rightarrow \frac{dx}{dt} = a(1 - \cos t) \Rightarrow \left(\frac{dx}{dt}\right)^2 = a^2(1 - 2\cos t + \cos^2 t)$

$y = a(1 - \cos t) \Rightarrow \frac{dy}{dx} = a \sin t \Rightarrow \left(\frac{dy}{dx}\right)^2 = a^2 \sin^2 t.$

$$s = \int_0^{2\pi} \sqrt{\left(\frac{dx}{dt}\right)^2 + \left(\frac{dy}{dt}\right)^2}\, dt = \int_0^{2\pi} \sqrt{2a^2(1 - \cos t)}\, dt$$

$$= a\sqrt{2}\int_0^{2\pi} \sqrt{2}\sqrt{\frac{1 - \cos t}{2}}\, dt = 2a\int_0^{2\pi} \left|\sin \frac{t}{2}\right| dt$$

$$= -4a\left[\cos \frac{t}{2}\right]_0^{2\pi} = 8a \quad \left(\text{Note: } \sin \frac{t}{2} \geq 0 \text{ for } 0 \leq t \leq 2\pi\right)$$

28. $x = t - \sin t,\ y = 1 - \cos t,\ 0 \leq t \leq 2\pi.$

$$ds = \sqrt{(1 - \cos t)^2 + \sin^2 t}\, dt = \sqrt{2 - 2\cos t}\, dt$$

$$S = \int 2\pi y\, ds = 2\sqrt{2}\int_0^{2\pi} (1 - \cos t)^{3/2}\, dt = 2\sqrt{2}\int_0^{2\pi} \left(\sqrt{2}\sin\frac{t}{2}\right)^3 dt$$

$$= 8\pi\int_0^{2\pi} \left(1 - \cos^2 \frac{t}{2}\right)\sin\frac{t}{2}\, dt = 8\pi\left[-2\cos\frac{t}{2} + \frac{2}{3}\cos^3\frac{t}{2}\right]_0^{2\pi} = \frac{64\pi}{3}$$

29. $V = \pi\int_0^{2\pi} y^2\, dx = \pi\int_0^{2\pi} y^2\left(\frac{dx}{dt}\right)dt = \pi\int_0^{2\pi} (1 - \cos t)^2(1 - \cos t)\, dt$

$$= \pi\int_0^{2\pi} (1 - 3\cos t + 3\cos^2 t - \cos^3 t)\, dt$$

$$I_1 = \pi\int_0^{2\pi} dt = 2\pi^2$$

$$I_2 = \pi\int_0^{2\pi} (-3\cos t)\, dt = -3\pi \sin t\Big]_0^{2\pi} = 0$$

$$I_3 = \pi\int_0^{2\pi} 3\cos^2 t\, dt = 3\pi\left[\frac{1}{2}t + \frac{1}{4}\sin 2t\right]_0^{2\pi} = 3\pi^2$$

$$I_4 = \pi\int_0^{2\pi} \cos^3 t\, dt = -\pi\int_0^{2\pi} (1 - \sin^2 t)\cos t\, dt = 0$$

$V = I_1 + I_2 + I_3 + I_4 = 5\pi^2$

30. $V = \pi \int_{-\frac{\pi}{2}}^{\frac{\pi}{2}} x^2 \left(\frac{dy}{dt}\right) dt = 2\pi \int_0^{\frac{\pi}{2}} (4\cos^2 t) \cos t \, dt$

$= 8\pi \int_0^{\frac{\pi}{2}} (1 - \sin^2 t) \text{dos } t \, dt = 8\pi \left[\sin t - \frac{1}{3} \sin^3 t \right]_0^{\frac{\pi}{2}} = \frac{16\pi}{3}$

31. From problem 27, $s = 8a$ for one arch. Therefore, the total length is $S = 8\left(\frac{5280}{2\pi}\right) = 6{,}723$.

32. (a) Deltoid:

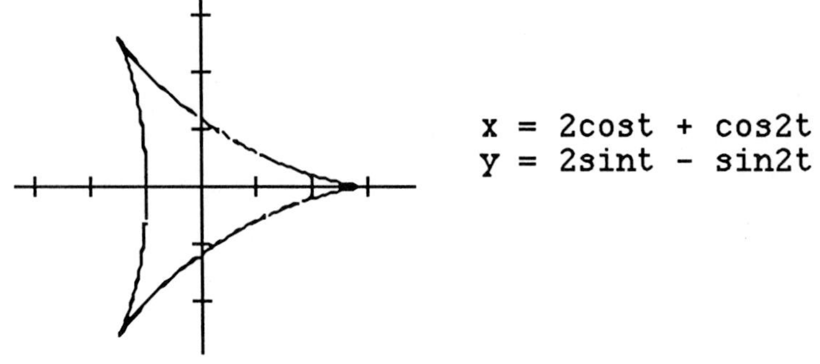

x = 2cost + cos2t
y = 2sint - sin2t

(b) Epicycloid

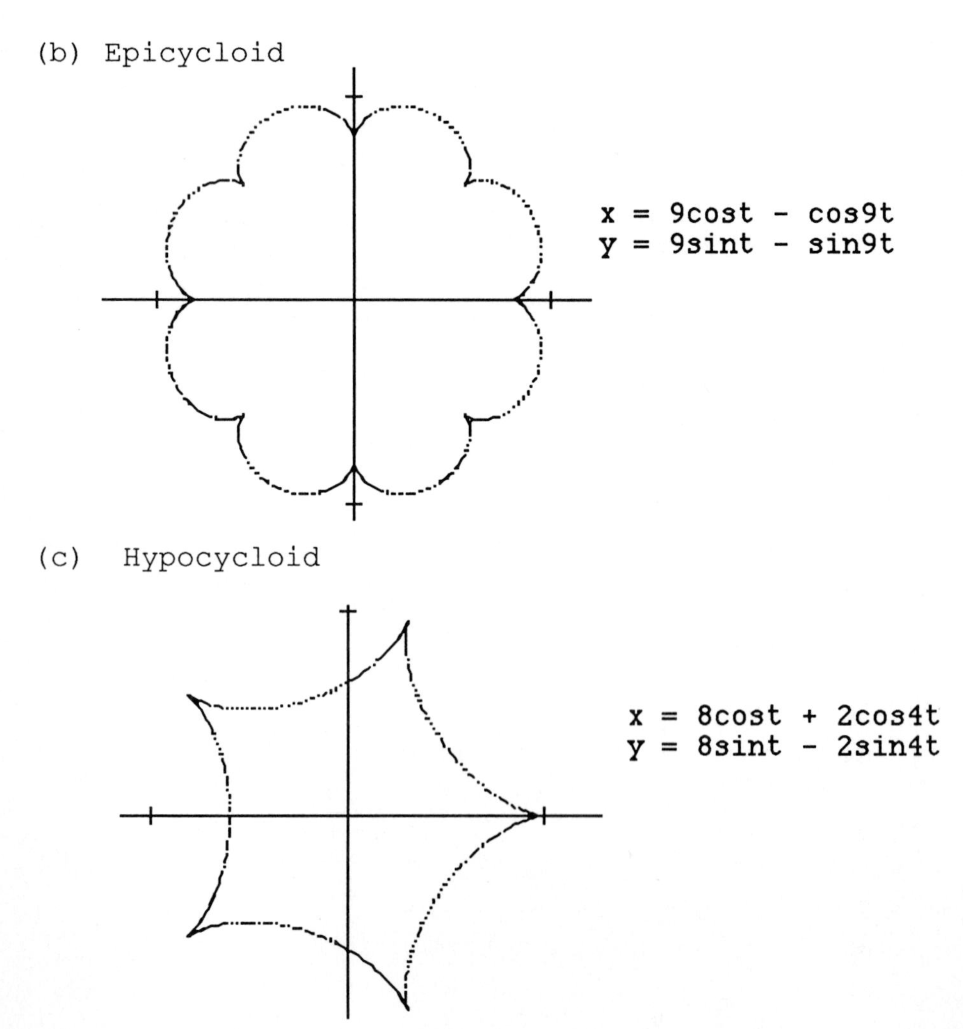

(d) Hypotrochoid

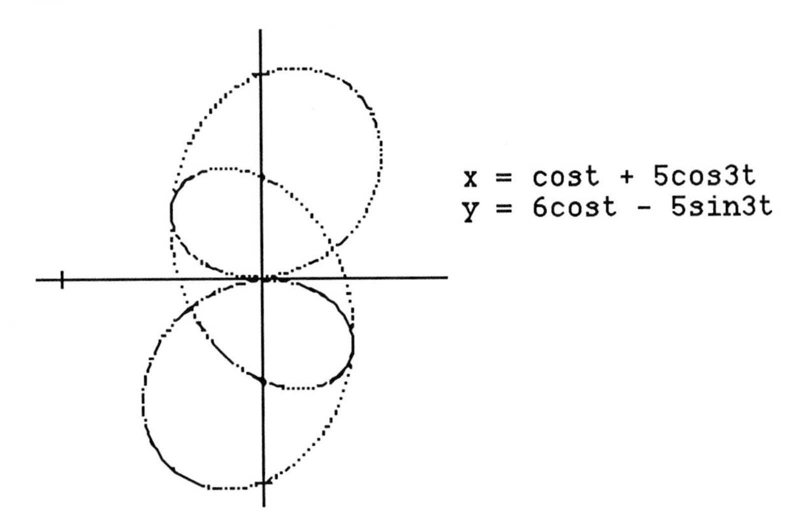

8.M MISCELLANEOUS PROBLEMS

1. Let $u = kx$ and $v = ky$, so that $x = \frac{u}{k}$ and $y = \frac{v}{k}$. Then

$$x^2 + xy + y^2 = 3 \Rightarrow \left(\frac{u}{k}\right)^2 + \left(\frac{u}{k}\right)\left(\frac{v}{k}\right) + \left(\frac{v}{k}\right)^2 = 3 \Rightarrow u^2 + uv + v^2 = 3k^2.$$

2. Let $Q(u, v)$ be on the line $x + 2y = 5$ and $P(x, y)$ be the point symmetric to Q with respect to $x^2 + y^2 = 4$. Then $y = mx$ and $v = mu$ for some slope m.

$u + 2v = 5 \Rightarrow u + 2mu = 5 \Rightarrow u = \frac{5}{1 + 2m}$. Also $\sqrt{x^2 + m^2x^2}\sqrt{u^2 + m^2u^2} = 4 \Rightarrow$

$xu(1 + m^2) = 4 \Rightarrow u = \frac{4}{x(1 + m^2)}$. Equating, $\frac{5}{1 + 2m} = \frac{4}{x(1 + m^2)} \Rightarrow$

$$5x(1 + m^2) = 4(1 + 2m) \Rightarrow 5xm^2 - 8m - 4 + 5x = 0 \Rightarrow m = \frac{8 \pm \sqrt{64 - 20x(5x - 4)}}{10x}.$$

$\therefore y = mx = \left(\frac{4 \pm \sqrt{16 + 20x - 25x^2}}{5x}\right)x \Rightarrow 5y - 4 = \pm\sqrt{16 + 20x - 25x^2}$. Then

$25\left(y - \frac{4}{5}\right)^2 + 25\left(x - \frac{2}{5}\right)^2 = 20$. The path is a circle with center $\left(\frac{2}{5}, \frac{4}{5}\right)$ and radius $= \frac{2}{\sqrt{5}}$.

3. $\sqrt{(x-x_1)^2+(y-y_1)^2} = k\sqrt{(x-x_0)^2+(y-y_0)^2} \Rightarrow$

$x^2 - 2xx_1 + x_1^2 + y^2 - 2yy_1 + y_1^2 = k^2[x^2 - 2xx_0 + x_0^2 + y^2 - 2yy_0 + y_0^2]$.

If $k = 1$, this reduces to $Ax + By = C$, where $A = 2x_0 - 2x_1$, $B = 2y_0 - 2y_1$,

and $C = x_0^2 + y_0^2 - x_1^2 - y_1^2$. If $k \neq 1$, this reduces to

$ax^2 + ay^2 + bx + cy = d$, where $a = 1 - k^2$, $b = 2k^2x_0 - 2x_1$, $c = 2k^2y_0 - 2y_1$,

and $d = kx_0^2 + ky_0^2 - x_1^2 - y_1^2$.

4. We see immediately that the center lies on the line $x = 4$. Let (u, v) be the point of tangency between the circle and parabola. We may write

(1) $(u-4)^2 + (v-k)^2 = r^2$

(2) $v = u^2$

The slope of the circle is $-\dfrac{x-4}{y-k}$ and of the parabola is $2x$. Thus

(3) $\dfrac{4-u}{k-u} = -2u$.

Finally, using the fact that $(2, 0)$ is on the circle, we have

(4) $4 + k^2 = r^2$

Substitute (2) and (4) into (1) and (3) to get the system

(1') $\dfrac{4-u}{k-u^2} = 2u \quad \Rightarrow \quad k = \dfrac{u-4+2u^3}{2u}$

(2') $(u-4)^2 + (u^2-k)^2 = 4 + k^2 \Rightarrow u^4 + u^2 - 2u^2k - 8u - 12 = 0$

Substituting (1') into (2') gives

$$u^4 + 4u - 12 = 0$$

Let $f(u) = u^4 + 4u - 12$. We test the rational possibilities:

$f(1) = -7$ and $f(2) = 4$. There is a root between 1 and 2, and DesCartes Rule of Signs tells us that this is the only positive root.

Using Newton's Method, with $x_1 = 1.5$, we get $x \approx 1.55$.

With this value, $k \approx 1.61$ making the center $(4, 1.61)$ and $r \approx 2.53$.

5. Let $(x-h)^2+(y-k)^2=r^2$ be the equation of the circle. Then

$\frac{dy}{dx}=-\frac{x-h}{y-k}$, and for $y=x^2$, $\frac{dy}{dx}=2x$. To be tangent at the

point $(2,4) \Rightarrow -\frac{2-h}{4-k}=4 \Rightarrow h=18-4k$. If the circle passes

through $(0,1)$, then $r^2=h^2+(k-1)^2$; similarly, $r^2=(h-2)^2+(4-k)^2$.

Thus $h^2+(k-1)^2=(h-2)^2+(4-k)^2 \Rightarrow 4h+6k=19$. Solving the two

linear equations together $\Rightarrow k=\frac{53}{10}$ and $h=-\frac{16}{5}$.

6. When $n=1$ the graph is the circle $x^2+y^2=a^2$ intersecting the line $y=x$ in the points $\left(\pm\frac{a}{\sqrt{2}}, \pm\frac{a}{\sqrt{2}}\right)$. For each successive value

of n the graph becomes more "boxlike", fitting in between the circle

and the square $|x|+|y|=a$. The points of intersection are

$\left(\pm\frac{a}{2^{1/2n}}, \pm\frac{a}{2^{1/2n}}\right)$ which converge to $(\pm a, \pm a)$ since $\lim_{n\to\infty} 2^{1/2n}=2^0=1$.

7. The vertex is the point $\left(\frac{7}{2}, 0\right)$.

$\therefore\ y^2=2\left(x-\frac{7}{2}\right)$.

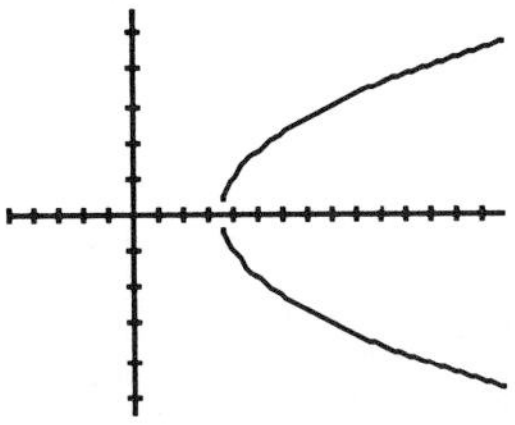

8. $x^2-6x-12y+9=0 \Rightarrow (x-3)^2=12y$. The vertex is $(3,0)$.

$4p=12 \Rightarrow p=3$. The focus is $(3,3)$ and directrix is $y=-3$.

9. Let $P(x_1, y_1)$ be any point not the origin on the curve $y^2=kx$.

$\frac{dy}{dx}=\frac{k}{2y}$ so the slope of the line through P and Q is $m=\frac{k}{2y_1}$.

Therefore, $\frac{y-y_1}{x-x_1}=\frac{k}{2y_1} \Rightarrow y-y_1=\frac{k}{2y_1}(x-x_1)$. At point A, $x=0$

so $y=y_1-\frac{kx_1}{2y_1}=y_1-\left(\frac{k}{2y_1}\right)\left(\frac{y_1^2}{k}\right)=y_1-\frac{1}{2}y_1=\frac{1}{2}y_1$.

Since $\triangle AQO \approx \triangle PQR$, $AQ=\frac{1}{2}PQ$ and A bisects PQ.

10. (a) $V(R_1)=\pi\int_0^{y_1} x^2\,dy=\pi\int_0^{y_1}\frac{y^4}{k^2}\,dy=\frac{\pi}{k^2}\left[\frac{1}{5}y^5\right]_0^{y_1}=\frac{\pi}{5}\left[\frac{y_1^5}{5}\right]$.

$$V(R_2)=\pi\int_0^{y_1}(x_1^2-x^2)\,dy=\pi\int_0^{y_1}\left(\frac{y_1^4}{k^2}-\frac{y^4}{k^2}\right)dy=\frac{\pi}{k^2}\left[y_1^4y-\frac{1}{5}y^5\right]_0^{y_1}=\frac{4\pi}{5}\left[\frac{y_1^5}{5}\right].$$

$$\therefore\ \frac{V(R_2)}{V(R_1)}=\frac{4}{1}$$

(b) $V(R_1) = \pi\int_0^{x_1} (y_1^2 - y^2)\,dx = \pi\int_0^{x_1} (kx_1 - kx)dx = \dfrac{k\pi x_1^2}{2}$

$V(R_2) = \pi\int_0^{x_1} y^2\,dx = \pi\int_0^{x_1} kx\,dx = \dfrac{k\pi x_1^2}{2}$

$\therefore \quad \dfrac{V(R_2)}{V(R_1)} = \dfrac{1}{1}$

11. Let $A(x_1, y_1)$ and $B(x_2, y_2)$ be any two pointson the parabola $x^2 = 4py$.

Then $m = \dfrac{y_1 - y_2}{x_1 - x_2} = \dfrac{\dfrac{x_1^2}{4p} - \dfrac{x_2^2}{4p}}{x_1 - x_2} = \dfrac{(x_1 + x_2)(x_1 - x_2)}{4p(x_1 - x_2)} = \dfrac{1}{4p}(x_1 + x_2)$

$= \dfrac{1}{2p}\left(\dfrac{x_1 + x_2}{2}\right) = \dfrac{1}{2p}x_m$ where x_m is the midpoint of the segment AB.

The equation is: $x = 2pm$

12. (a) The focus is the point $F(p, 0)$. The slope ofthe line through $P(x_1, y_1)$

is $m = \dfrac{y_1}{x_1 - p} = \dfrac{y_1}{\dfrac{y_1^2}{4p} - p} = \dfrac{4py_1}{y_1^2 - 4p^2}$. The equation of the line is

$y = \dfrac{4py_1}{y_1^2 - 4p^2}(x - p)$. This line intersects $x = \dfrac{y^2}{4p}$ where

$y = \dfrac{4py_1}{y_1^2 - 4p^2}\left[\dfrac{y^2}{4p} - p\right] \Rightarrow yy_1^2 - 4p^2y = y_1y^2 - 4p^2y_1 \Rightarrow$

$(y - y_1)(y_1y + 4p^2) = 0 \Rightarrow y = y_1$ or $y = -\dfrac{4p^2}{y_1}$. Then $x = \dfrac{y^2}{4p} = \dfrac{4p^3}{y_1^2}$.

(b) Let the coordinates of R be $(-p, y_2)$. Then $\dfrac{y_1 - y_2}{x_1 + p} = \dfrac{y_1}{x_1} \Rightarrow$

$y_2 = -\dfrac{p}{x_1}$. Then $y_2 = -\dfrac{p}{\dfrac{y_1^2}{4p}} = -\dfrac{4p^2}{y_1^2}$. Therefore R and Q lie on the

horizontal line $y = -\dfrac{4p^2}{y_1^2}$.

13. $S = x^2 + (y-4)^2 = y^3 + (y-4)^2$.

$$\frac{dS}{dy} = 3y^2 + 2(y-4) = 3y^2 + 2y - 8 = (3y-4)(y+2) = 0 \Leftrightarrow y = -2 \text{ or } \frac{4}{3}.$$

$$\frac{d^2S}{dy^2} = 6y + 2 > 0 \text{ if } y = \frac{4}{3} \Rightarrow \text{a minimum value}.$$

There are two points, $\left(\pm\frac{8\sqrt{3}}{9}, \frac{4}{3}\right)$.

14. **Position the parabola so that the focus is at the origin. Then**

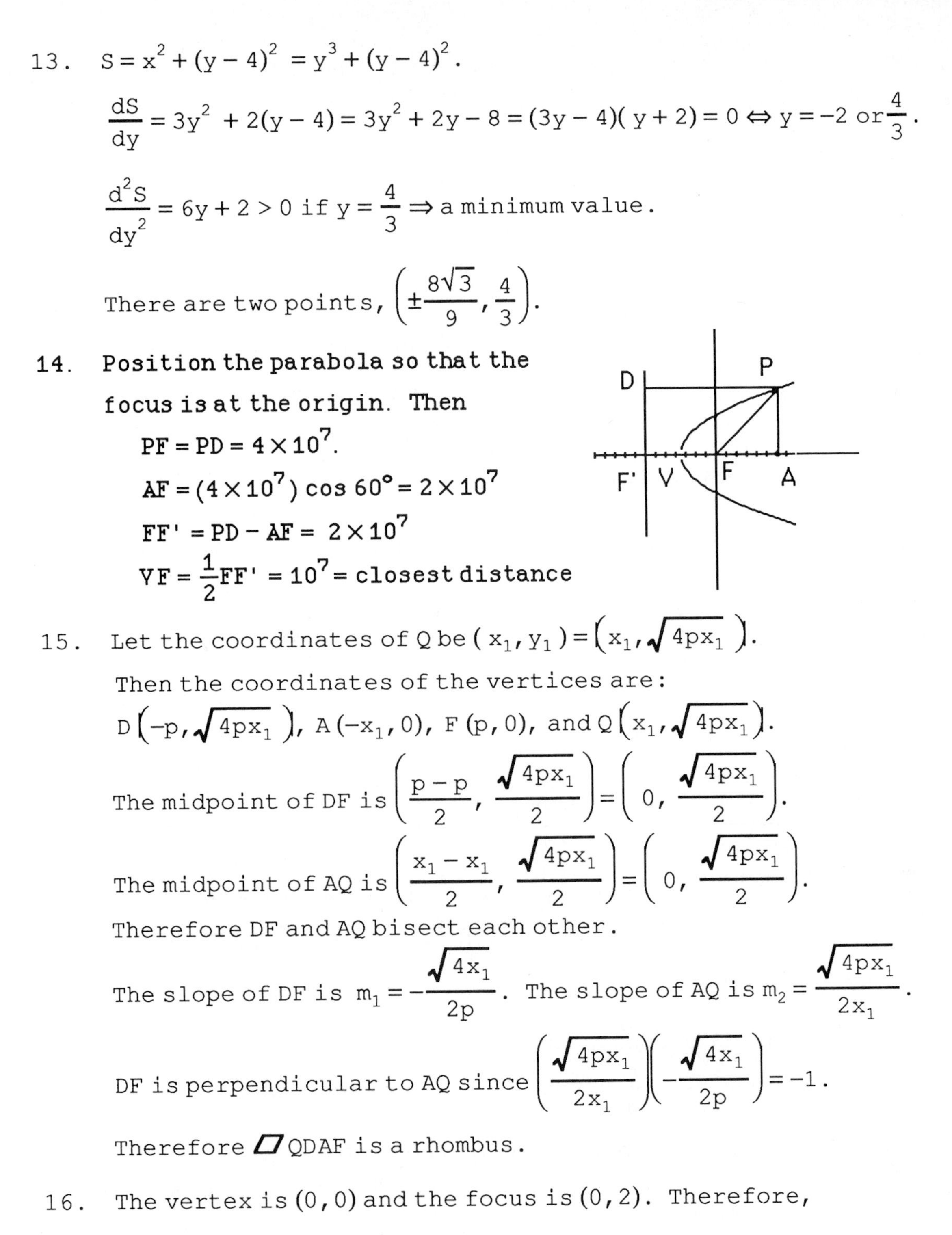

$PF = PD = 4 \times 10^7$.

$AF = (4 \times 10^7)\cos 60° = 2 \times 10^7$

$FF' = PD - AF = 2 \times 10^7$

$VF = \frac{1}{2}FF' = 10^7 =$ **closest distance**

15. Let the coordinates of Q be $(x_1, y_1) = \left(x_1, \sqrt{4px_1}\right)$.

Then the coordinates of the vertices are:

$D\left(-p, \sqrt{4px_1}\right)$, $A(-x_1, 0)$, $F(p, 0)$, and $Q\left(x_1, \sqrt{4px_1}\right)$.

The midpoint of DF is $\left(\frac{p-p}{2}, \frac{\sqrt{4px_1}}{2}\right) = \left(0, \frac{\sqrt{4px_1}}{2}\right)$.

The midpoint of AQ is $\left(\frac{x_1 - x_1}{2}, \frac{\sqrt{4px_1}}{2}\right) = \left(0, \frac{\sqrt{4px_1}}{2}\right)$.

Therefore DF and AQ bisect each other.

The slope of DF is $m_1 = -\frac{\sqrt{4x_1}}{2p}$. The slope of AQ is $m_2 = \frac{\sqrt{4px_1}}{2x_1}$.

DF is perpendicular to AQ since $\left(\frac{\sqrt{4px_1}}{2x_1}\right)\left(-\frac{\sqrt{4x_1}}{2p}\right) = -1$.

Therefore ▱QDAF is a rhombus.

16. The vertex is $(0,0)$ and the focus is $(0,2)$. Therefore,

$$\sqrt{x^2 + y^2} = 2\sqrt{x^2 + (y-2)^2} \Rightarrow 3x^2 + 3y^2 - 16y + 16 = 0, \text{ a circle}.$$

17. Let $y^2 = 4px$ be the parabola. Using the results in problem 9, $QM = MP$. Then $\triangle QMV \cong \triangle PTM \Rightarrow PT = QV$.

18. The center is $(3,0)$, which makes $c = 2$. Since a vertex is at the origin, $a = 3$. Then $b^2 = a^2 - c^2 = 5$. The equation is

$$\frac{(x-3)^2}{9} + \frac{y^2}{5} = 1$$

19. (a) $F_1P = \sqrt{4^2 + 3^2} = 5$. $F_2P = \sqrt{1^2 + 2^2} = \sqrt{5}$

(b) $OF_1 = 3$ and $Of_2 = 5$. $OF_1 + OF_2 = 8 > 5 + \sqrt{5} = 2a$. The point lies outside.

20. $x^2 + 12y^2 - 6x - 48y + 9 = 0 \Rightarrow x^2 - 6x + 9 + 12(y^2 - 4y + 4) = -9 + 9 + 48$

$\frac{(x-3)^2}{48} + \frac{(y-2)^2}{4} = 1$. Center is $(3,2)$; $e = \frac{\sqrt{44}}{\sqrt{48}} = \sqrt{\frac{11}{12}}$

21. $x^2 + 9y^2 - 6x - 36y = 99 = 0 \Rightarrow (x^2 - 6x + 9) + 9(y^2 - 4y + 4) = 99 + 9 + 36$.

$\frac{(x-3)^2}{144} + \frac{(y-2)^2}{16} = 1$. Center is $C(3,2)$, vertices are $(15,2)$ and $(-9,2)$,

the foci are $(3 \pm 8\sqrt{2}, 2)$, and the eccentricity is $\frac{2\sqrt{2}}{3}$.

22. The line $y = mx + c$ intersects $Ax^2 + y^2 - 1 = 0$ where $Ax^2 + (mx + c)^2 - 1 = 0 \Leftrightarrow (A + m^2)x^2 + 2cmx + c^2 - 1 = 0$. The solution is:

$x = \frac{-2cm \pm \sqrt{4c^2m^2 - 4(c^2-1)(A+m^2)}}{2(A+m^2)}$. If this is to be a point of tangency,

then we require a unique solution, i.e. that the discriminant be zero. $4c^2m^2 - 4(c^2-1)(A+m^2) = 0 \Leftrightarrow c^2m^2 - m^2(c^2-1) - A(c^2-1) = 0 \Leftrightarrow$ $m^2 = A(c^2 - 1)$.

23. If one vertex is $(3,1)$ and focus is $(1,1)$ then $a - c = 2$. Solving this equation with $e = \frac{2}{3} = \frac{c}{a}$ gives $\frac{c}{2+c} = \frac{2}{3}$ or $c = 4$. Then

$a = 6$, $b^2 = 36 - 16 = 20$, the center is $(-3,1)$ and the equation is

$$\frac{(x+3)^2}{36} + \frac{(y-1)^2}{20} = 1.$$

24. Let the segment $a + b$ intersect the y-axis in point A, the x-axis in point B so that $PB = b$ and $PA = a$. Let $\angle PBO = \theta$. Then

$\frac{x}{a} = \cos\theta$ and $\frac{y}{b} = \sin\theta$, so that $\frac{x^2}{a^2} + \frac{y^2}{b^2} = \cos^2\theta + \sin^2\theta = 1$.

25. $x^2 + 4y^2 - 4x - 8y + 4 = 0 \Rightarrow x^2 - 4x + 4 + 4(y^2 - 2y + 1) = 4$ or $(x-2)^2 + 4(y-1)^2 = 4$. The new center is $(2,1)$.

26. The reflective property of an ellipse states that the ripples must all intersect at the other focus.

27. (a) $K_{circle} = \int_0^a \sqrt{a^2 - x^2}\, dx$ (b) $K_{ellipse} = \int_0^a \frac{b}{a}\sqrt{a^2 - x^2}\, dx$.

Therefore $K_{ellipse} = \frac{b}{a} K_{circle} = \frac{b}{a}(\pi a^2) = \pi ab$.

28. (a) $L = 2x + 2c + y$

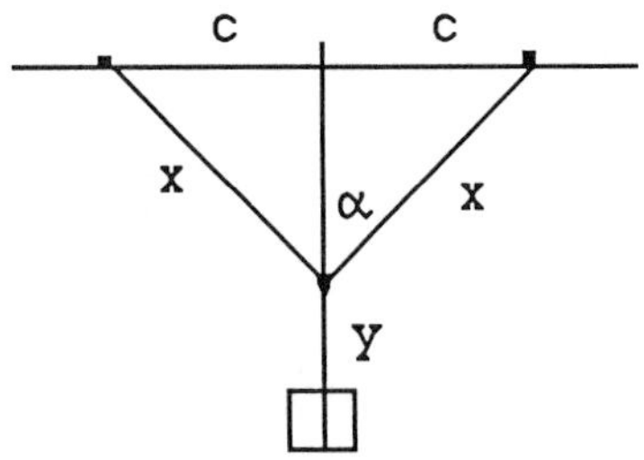

$d = \sqrt{x^2 - c^2} + y$

$= \sqrt{x^2 - c^2} + L - 2x - 2c$.

The weight will have descended as far as possible when d is maximal.

c c x α x y

$d' = \frac{x}{\sqrt{x^2 - c^2}} - 2 = 0$ when $x^2 = 4x^2 - 4c^2$ or when $\frac{c}{x} = \frac{\sqrt{3}}{2}$.

Since $\frac{c}{x} = \sin\alpha$, $\alpha = \frac{\pi}{3} \Rightarrow 2\alpha = \frac{2\pi}{3}$.

(b) For each fixed ring position, the sum of the distances from the ring to the pegs is constant. This defines an ellipse.

(c) Minimal potential energy will occur when the ring is at rest at its lowest point, which will be the vertex of the ellipse on the line of symmetry between the two foci.

29. $\frac{d_{11}}{c} + \frac{d_{12}}{c} = \frac{30}{c}$ and $\frac{d_{21}}{c} + \frac{d_{22}}{c} = \frac{30}{c} \Rightarrow$ that the locations P and Q lie on an ellipse with $2a = 30$ and $c = 10$. $b^2 = 225 - 100 = 125$ and the equation

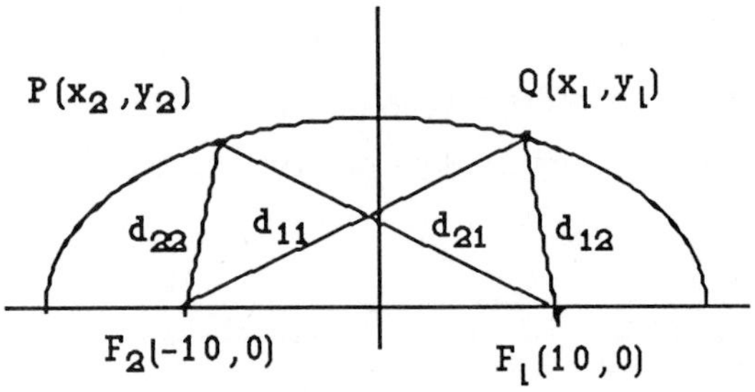

P(x_2, y_2) Q(x_1, y_1) d_{22} d_{11} d_{21} d_{12} $F_2(-10,0)$ $F_1(10,0)$

is $\frac{x^2}{225} + \frac{y^2}{125} = 1$. Moreover, $x_2 = x_1 + v_0 t = x_1 + 10$, and $x_2 = -x_1$,

so $x_2 = -5$. $y_2 = \sqrt{125\left(1 - \frac{1}{9}\right)} = \pm\frac{10\sqrt{10}}{3}$. Assuming $y_2 > 0$, the

plane is at the position $\left(-5, \frac{10\sqrt{10}}{3}\right)$.

30. $3x^2 - y^2 + 12x - 6y = 0 \Rightarrow 3(x^2 + 4x + 4) - (y^2 + 6y + 9) = 12 - 9$

or $\dfrac{(x+2)^2}{1} - \dfrac{(y+3)^2}{3} = 1$. The center is $(-2,-3)$; the vertices are $(-1,-3)$ and $(-3,-3)$; the foci are $(0,-3)$ and $(-4,-3)$. The asymptotes are $y + 3 = \pm\sqrt{3}\,(x+2)$.

31. $9x^2 - 4y^2 - 18x - 16y + 29 = 0 \Rightarrow 9(x^2 - 2x + 1) - 4(y^2 - 4y + 4) = -29 + 9 - 16$

$9(x-1)^2 - 4(y+2)^2 = -4$ or $\dfrac{(y+2)^2}{9} - \dfrac{(x-1)^2}{4} = 1$. The center is $C(1,-2)$, the vertices are $(1,-5)$ and $(1,1)$, the foci are $(1, -2 \pm\sqrt{13})$, amd the asymptotes are $y + 2 = \pm\dfrac{3}{2}(x-1)$.

32. If the vertices are $(2,0)$ and $(-2,0)$, then the center is the origin and $a = 2$. $e = \sqrt{2} = \dfrac{c}{a} \Rightarrow c^2 = 2a^2$. $\therefore$ $a^2 + b^2 = c^2 \Rightarrow 4 + b^2 = 8$ or $b^2 = 4$.

The hyperbola is: $\dfrac{x^2}{4} - \dfrac{y^2}{4} = 1$.

33. Let $\dfrac{x^2}{t^2} + \dfrac{y^2}{t^2 - c^2} = 1$ and $\dfrac{x^2}{u^2} - \dfrac{y^2}{c^2 - u^2} = 1$ be any members of the family of ellipses and hyperbolas. Then $\dfrac{dy_e}{dx} = -\dfrac{x}{y}\left(\dfrac{t^2 - c^2}{t^2}\right)$ and

$\dfrac{dy_h}{dx} = \dfrac{x}{y}\left(\dfrac{c^2 - u^2}{u^2}\right)$. At any point (x,y), $\left(\dfrac{dy_e}{dx}\right)\left(\dfrac{dy_h}{dx}\right) = -\dfrac{x^2}{y^2}\left(\dfrac{t^2 - c^2}{t^2}\right)\left(\dfrac{c^2 - u^2}{u^2}\right)$.

The curves intersect where $\dfrac{x^2}{t^2} + \dfrac{y^2}{t^2 - c^2} = \dfrac{x^2}{u^2} - \dfrac{y^2}{c^2 - u^2} \Rightarrow$

$$x^2\left(\frac{1}{u^2} - \frac{1}{t^2}\right) = y^2\left(\frac{1}{t^2 - c^2} + \frac{1}{c^2 - u^2}\right) \Rightarrow \frac{x^2}{y^2} = \frac{u^2 t^2}{(t^2 - c^2)(c^2 - u^2)}.$$ Thus

$$\left(\frac{dy_e}{dx}\right)\left(\frac{dy_h}{dx}\right) = -\left(\frac{u^2 t^2}{(t^2 - c^2)(c^2 - u^2)}\right)\left(\frac{t^2 - c^2}{t^2}\right)\left(\frac{c^2 - u^2}{u^2}\right) = -1.$$

34. The slope of a line through $P(x,y)$ and the origin is $\dfrac{dy}{dx} = \dfrac{y}{x}$.

The slope of $x^2 - y^2 = 1$ is $\dfrac{dy}{dx} = \dfrac{x}{y}$. If $\dfrac{y}{x} = \dfrac{x}{y}$ then $x^2 - y^2 = 0$.

Since $x^2 - y^2 = 1$, no tangent can pass through the origin.

35. $\angle A = 2\angle B$. $\dfrac{y}{x+c} = \tan A = \tan 2B$. Using the double-angle tangent formula,

$$\frac{y}{c-x} = \frac{2\left(\dfrac{y}{x+c}\right)}{1-\left(\dfrac{y}{x+c}\right)^2} = \frac{2y(x+c)}{(x+c)^2 - y^2}.$$ Simplifying, we get

$3x^2 - y^2 + 2cx - c^2 = 0$. The path is the right branch of this hyperbola.

36. Given that $\dfrac{x^2}{p-r} + \dfrac{y^2}{q-r} = 1$, $q < p$.

(a) If $r < q < p$, set $a^2 = p - r > 0$ and $b^2 = q - r > 0$. The equation is

$$\frac{x^2}{a^2} + \frac{y^2}{b^2} = 1 \text{ with } c = \sqrt{a^2 - b^2} = \sqrt{p-q}.$$

(b) If $q < r < p$, set $a^2 = p - r > 0$ and $b^2 = r - q > 0$. The equation is

$$\frac{x^2}{a^2} - \frac{y^2}{b^2} = 1 \text{ with } c = \sqrt{a^2 + b^2} = \sqrt{p-q}.$$

(c) If $p < r$ and $q < r$, then $\dfrac{x^2}{p-r} + \dfrac{y^2}{q-r} \le 0 \ne 1$.

37. The listener is on one branch of a hyperbola with foci the locations of the rifle and the target. Since the time for the bullet to hit the target remains constant, the difference between the distances from the listener to the rifle and to the target remains constant.

38. $xy = a^2 \Rightarrow \dfrac{dy}{dx} = -\dfrac{y}{x}$. Let $P(x_0, y_0)$ be a point on the curve. Then the

tangent line at P has equation $y - y_0 = -\dfrac{y_0}{x_0}(x - x_0)$. The asymptotes

are the coordinate axes, so we need the intercepts of the tangent line.

If $y = 0$, then $x = 2x_0$ and if $x = 0$, then $y = 2y_0$. The area is

$$A = \frac{1}{2}(2x_0)(2y_0) = 2x_0y_0 = 2a^2.$$

39. $\alpha = \dfrac{\pi}{4}$ so $x = \dfrac{x'}{\sqrt{2}} - \dfrac{y'}{\sqrt{2}}$ and $y = \dfrac{x'}{\sqrt{2}} + \dfrac{y'}{\sqrt{2}}$. Therefore

$$1 = xy = \left(\frac{x'}{\sqrt{2}} - \frac{y'}{\sqrt{2}}\right)\left(\frac{x'}{\sqrt{2}} + \frac{y'}{\sqrt{2}}\right) = \frac{x'^2}{2} - \frac{y'^2}{2}.$$ $a = \sqrt{2}$, $c = 2$ and $e = \sqrt{2}$.

40. $x^2 - 2xy - 3y^2 + 3 = 0$ is a hyperbola, since $(-2)^2 - 4(1)(-3) = 16 > 0$.

$2x - 2x\frac{dy}{dx} - 2y - 6y\frac{dy}{dx} = 0 \Rightarrow \frac{dy}{dx} = \frac{x-y}{x+3y}$. The line $x + y - 1$ has slope $m = -1$,

so we need $\frac{x-y}{x+3y} = 1 \Rightarrow x + 3y = x - y$ or $y = 0$. Then $x = \pm\sqrt{3}$. $\therefore (\pm\sqrt{3}, 0)$

41. $xy = x + y \Rightarrow x\frac{dy}{dx} + y = 1 + \frac{dy}{dx}$ or $\frac{dy}{dx} = \frac{1-y}{x-1}$.

$\left.\frac{dy}{dx}\right|_{\left(-2,\frac{2}{3}\right)} = -\frac{1}{9}$. The slope of the normal is then $m = 9$,

and one equation is $y - \frac{2}{3} = 9(x+2)$ or $3y - 2yx - 56 = 0$. We need to

find the other point where the slope to the curve is $-\frac{1}{9}$:

$\frac{1-y}{x-1} = -\frac{1}{9} \Rightarrow x = 1 + 9y - 9$. Substituting into the curve,

$y(1 + 9y - 9) = 1 + 9y - 9 + y \Rightarrow y = \frac{2}{3}$ or $\frac{4}{3}$. If $y = \frac{4}{3}$, then $x = 4$ and

the other normal is $y - \frac{4}{3} = 9(x-4)$ or $3y - 27x + 104 = 0$.

42. $x^2 - 2xy + y^2 + 2x + y - 6 = 0$ is a parabola, since $(-2)^2 - 4 = 0$.

$2x - 2x\frac{dy}{dx} - 2y + 2y\frac{dy}{dx} + 2 + \frac{dy}{dx} = 0$. At $(2,2)$, $\frac{dy}{dx} = -2$.

The tangent line is $y - 2 = -2(x-2)$ or $y + 2x = 6$.

43. (a) symmetric to the origin $\Rightarrow$

$Ax^2 + Bxy + Cy^2 + Dx + Ey + F = A(-x)^2 + B(-x)(-y) + C(-y)^2 + D(-x) + E(-y) + F$

$-Dx - Ey = Dx + Ey \Rightarrow D = E = 0$.

(b) If $Ax^2 + Bxy + Cy^2 + F = 0$ and $(1,0)$ belongs to the curve, then

$A + F = 0$ or $F = -A$. The point $(2,1)$ belongs to the curve, so

$4A - 2B + C + F = 0$ so $B = 4A$.

(c) $2Ax + B\left(x\frac{dy}{dx} + y\right) + 2Cy\frac{dy}{dx} = 0$ and we know that the

slope of the tangent at $(-2,1)$ is 0, so substituting we get $C = 5A$.

Let $A = 1$. Then $x^2 + 4xy + 5y^2 - 1 = 0$.

45. If we do not rotate the axes, we can reason as follows: $\sqrt{2}y - 2xy = 2 \Rightarrow$ $y = \dfrac{2}{\sqrt{2} - 2x}$. Since $\lim\limits_{x \to \frac{1}{\sqrt{2}}} \dfrac{2}{\sqrt{2} - 2x} = \infty$, $x = \dfrac{1}{\sqrt{2}}$ is vertical asymptote.

$\lim\limits_{x \to \infty} \dfrac{2}{\sqrt{2} - 2x} = 0 \Rightarrow y = 0$ is horizontal asymptote. Hence the center is $\left(\dfrac{1}{\sqrt{2}}, 0\right)$. One axis passes through the center with slope $= -1$, and has equation $2y + 2x = \sqrt{2}$. This intersects the curve at the vertices $\left(1 + \dfrac{1}{\sqrt{2}}, -1\right)$ and $\left(-1 + \dfrac{1}{\sqrt{2}}, 1\right)$. The other axis has slope $= 1$ and equation $2x - 2y = \sqrt{2}$. The distance from the center to a vertex $= \sqrt{2} = a$. The hyperbolar is rectangular, so $e = \sqrt{2}$, hence $c = 2$ The foci are then $\left(\sqrt{2} + \dfrac{1}{\sqrt{2}}, -\sqrt{2}\right)$ and $\left(-\sqrt{2} + \dfrac{1}{\sqrt{2}}, \sqrt{2}\right)$.

Alternatively, we rotate the axes. Then $\cot 2\alpha = 0 \Rightarrow \alpha = \dfrac{\pi}{4}$.

$$A' = A\cos^2\alpha + B\sin\alpha\cos\alpha + C\sin^2\alpha = -2\left(\frac{1}{\sqrt{2}}\right)\left(\frac{1}{\sqrt{2}}\right) = -1$$

$$C' = A\cos^2\alpha - B\sin\alpha\cos\alpha + C\sin^2\alpha = 1$$

$$D' = D\cos\alpha + E\sin\alpha = \sqrt{2}\left(\frac{1}{\sqrt{2}}\right) = 1$$

$$E' = -D\cos\alpha + E\sin\alpha = 1; \quad F' = F = -2$$

$$\therefore\ -x'^2 + y'^2 \quad x' + y' = 2, \text{ or } \frac{\left(y' + \frac{1}{2}\right)^2}{2} - \frac{\left(x' - \frac{1}{2}\right)^2}{2} = 1.$$

With reference to these axes, we have $C\left(\frac{1}{2}, -\frac{1}{2}\right)$, $V\left(\frac{1}{2}, -\frac{1}{2} \pm \sqrt{2}\right)$, $F\left(\frac{1}{2}, -\frac{1}{2} \pm 2\right)$, $e = \sqrt{2}$, $y + \frac{1}{2} = \pm\left(x - \frac{1}{2}\right)$.

46. (a) $b^2x^2 + a^2y^2 = a^2b^2 \Rightarrow \dfrac{dy}{dx} = -\dfrac{b^2x}{a^2y}$. At (x_1, y_1) the tangent line is

$$y - y_1 = -\frac{b^2x_1}{a^2y_1}(x - x_1) \Rightarrow a^2yy_1 + b^2xx_1 = b^2x_1^2 + a^2y_1^2 = a^2b^2.$$

(b) $b^2x^2 - a^2y^2 = a^2b^2 \Rightarrow \dfrac{dy}{dx} = \dfrac{b^2x}{a^2y}$. At (x_1, y_1) the tangent line is

$$y - y_1 = \frac{b^2x_1}{a^2y_1}(x - x_1) \Rightarrow b^2xx_1 - a^2yy_1 = b^2x_1^2 - a^2y_1^2 = a^2b^2.$$

(c) $Ax^2 + Bxy + Cy^2 + Dx + Ey + F = 0$ has derivative $\frac{dy}{dx} = \frac{-2Ax - By - D}{Bx + 2Cy + E}$.

Equation of tangent: $y - y_1 = \frac{-2Ax_1 - By_1 - D}{Bx_1 + 2Cy_1 + E}(x - x_1)$

$Byx_1 + 2Cyy_1 + Ey - By_1x_1 - 2Cy_1^2 - Ey_1 = -2Axx_1 - Bxy_1 - Dx + 2Ax_1^2 + Bx_1y_1 + Dx_1$

$2Axx_1 + B(yx_1 + xy_1) + 2Cyy_1 + Dx - Dx_1 + Ey - Ey_1 = 2ax_1^2 + 2Bx_1y_1 + 2Cy_1^2$.

Add $2Dx_1 + 2Ey_1$ to both sides, divide by 2, and let the constant value on the right be represented by F, to get:

$$Axx_1 + B\left(\frac{yx_1 + xy_1}{2}\right) + Cyy_1 + D\left(\frac{x + x_1}{2}\right) + E\left(\frac{y + y_1}{2}\right) = F$$

47. $\left(\frac{x'}{\sqrt{2}} - \frac{y'}{\sqrt{2}}\right)^{1/2} + \left(\frac{x'}{\sqrt{2}} + \frac{y'}{\sqrt{2}}\right)^{1/2} = a^{1/2}$

$$\left[\left(\frac{x'}{\sqrt{2}} - \frac{y'}{\sqrt{2}}\right)^{1/2}\right]^2 = \left[a^{1/2} - \left(\frac{x'}{\sqrt{2}} + \frac{y'}{\sqrt{2}}\right)^{1/2}\right]^2$$

$$\frac{x'}{\sqrt{2}} - \frac{y'}{\sqrt{2}} = a - 2a^{1/2}\left(\frac{x'}{\sqrt{2}} + \frac{y'}{\sqrt{2}}\right)^{1/2} + \frac{x'}{\sqrt{2}} + \frac{y'}{\sqrt{2}}$$

$$\left[-\frac{2y'}{\sqrt{2}} - a\right]^2 = \left[-2a^{1/2}\left(\frac{x'}{\sqrt{2}} + \frac{y'}{\sqrt{2}}\right)^{1/2}\right]^2$$

$2y'^2 + 2a\sqrt{2}y' + a^2 = 2a\sqrt{2}x' + 2a\sqrt{2}y'$ or $2y'^2 = 2a\sqrt{2}x' - a^2$.

This is a part of a parabola in the first quadrant $(x > 0, y > 0)$.

48. $dx = dx'\cos\alpha - dy'\sin\alpha \Rightarrow$

$$dx^2 = dx'^2\cos^2\alpha - 2dx'dy'\cos\alpha\sin\alpha + dy'^2\sin^2\alpha$$

$dy = dx'\sin\alpha + dy'\cos\alpha \Rightarrow$

$$dy^2 = dx'^2\sin^2\alpha + 2dx'dy'\cos\alpha\sin\alpha + dy'^2\cos^2\alpha$$

$dx^2 + dy^2 = dx'^2(\cos^2\alpha + \sin^2\alpha) + dy'^2(\cos^2\alpha + \sin^2\alpha) = dx'^2 + dy'^2$.

$y\,dx = (x'\sin\alpha + y'\cos\alpha)(dx'\cos\alpha - dy'\sin\alpha) =$

$$x'\sin\alpha\, dx'\cos\alpha - x'dy'\sin^2\alpha + y'dx'\cos^2\alpha - y'\cos\alpha\, dy'\sin\alpha$$

$x\,dy = (x'\cos\alpha - y'\sin\alpha)(dx'\sin\alpha + dy'\cos\alpha) =$

$$x'\cos\alpha\, dx'\sin\alpha + x'dy'\cos^2\alpha - y'\sin\alpha\, dy'\cos\alpha - y'dx'\sin^2\alpha$$

$x\,dy - y\,dx = x'dy'\cos^2\alpha + x'dy'\sin^2\alpha - y'dx'\cos^2\alpha - y'dx'\sin^2\alpha$

$= x'dy' - y'dy'$

49. The solution set is the union of points which belong to the circle, line or parabola.

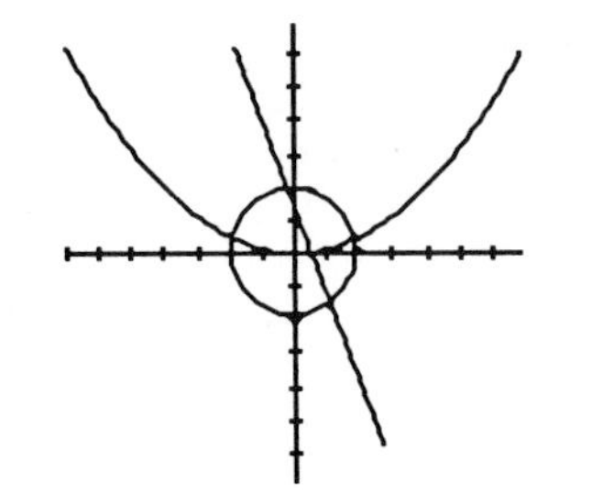

50. The solution set is the union of points which belong to the circle, ellipse, parabola or hyperbola.

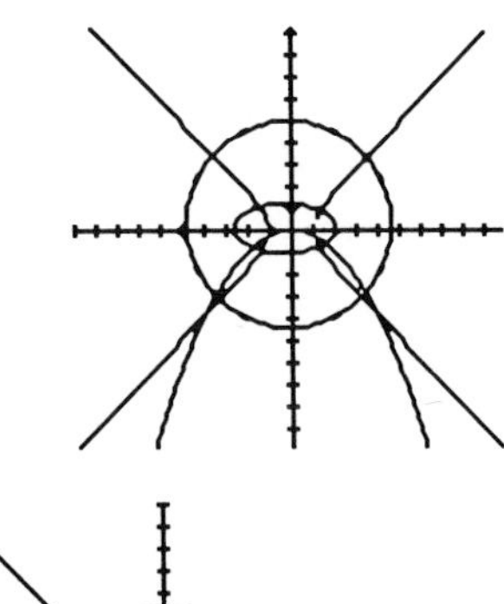

51. The solution set is the union of points which belong to the circle or line.

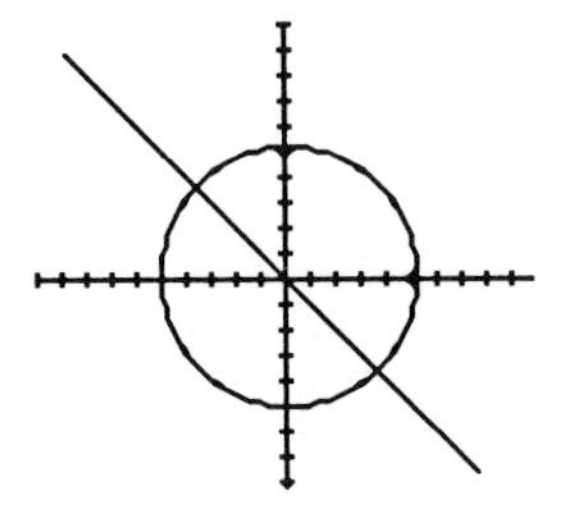

52. The solution set is the union of points on the two lines.

53. The solution set is the ellipse and the points interior to it.

54.

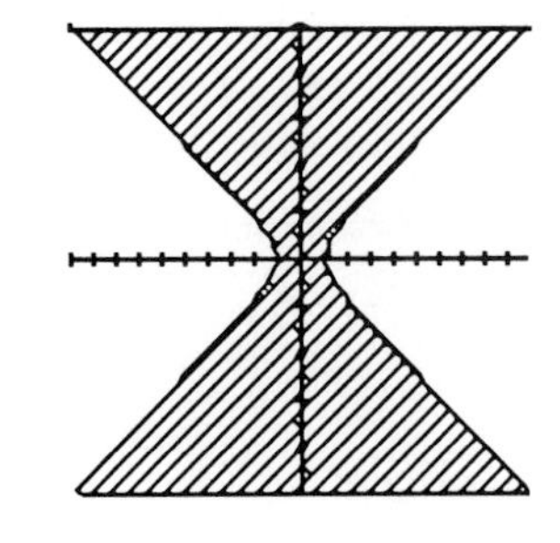

55.

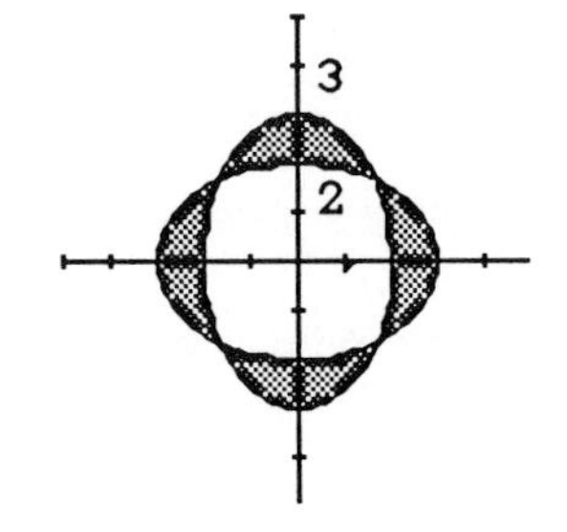

56.

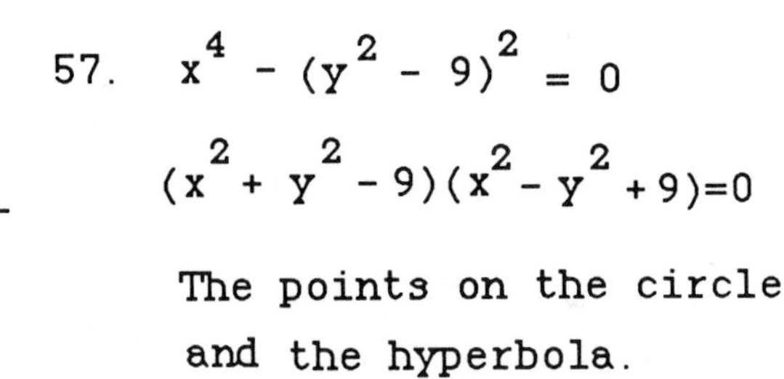

57. $x^4 - (y^2 - 9)^2 = 0$

$(x^2 + y^2 - 9)(x^2 - y^2 + 9) = 0$

The points on the circle and the hyperbola.

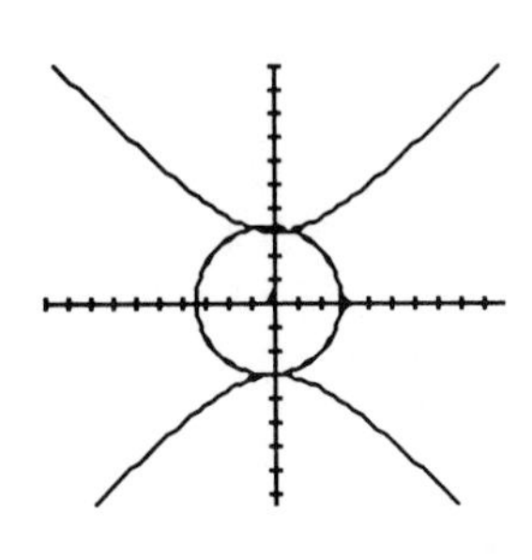

58.

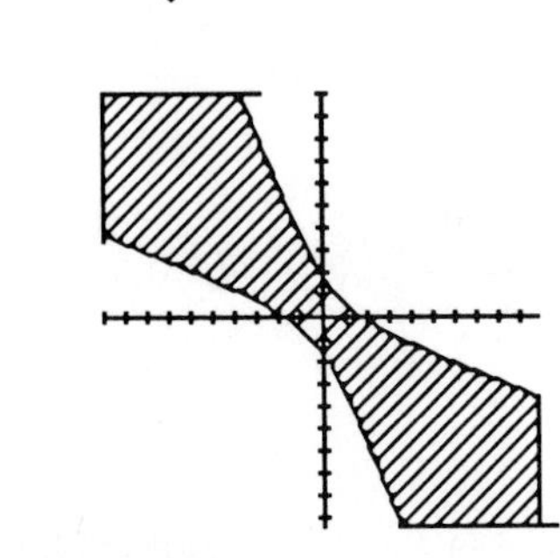

59. $|OA| = a$. $\frac{|AN|}{a} = \tan t$ and $\frac{|AM|}{a} = \sin t$. $MN = OP$, so

$|OP|^2 = |AN|^2 - |AM|^2 = a^2 \tan^2 t - a^2 \sin^2 t \Rightarrow$

$|OP| = \sqrt{a^2 \tan^2 t - a^2 \sin^2 t} = \frac{a \sin^2 t}{\cos t}$. $\frac{x}{|OP|} = \cos\left(\frac{\pi}{2} - t\right)$ and

$\frac{y}{|OP|} = \sin\left(\frac{\pi}{2} - t\right) = \cos t$. $\therefore x = \frac{a \sin^3 t}{\cos t}$ and $y = a \sin^2 t$.

60. The point P traces the diameter of the larger circle.

61. Use the equations for a trochoid derived in Section 8.9.

$x = a\phi - b \sin \phi$ and $y = a - b \cos \phi$, where $a = 4$, $b = 2$ and $\omega = 2$ rad/s $\Rightarrow$

$\frac{d\phi}{dt} = 2 \Rightarrow \phi = 2t$. Therefore, $x = 8t - 2 \sin 2t$ and $y = 4 - 2 \cos 2t$.

62. $x = a(t - \sin t) \Rightarrow \frac{dx}{dt} = a - a \cos t$ $\quad y = a(1 - \cos t) \Rightarrow \frac{dy}{dt} = a \sin t$

$\frac{dy}{dx} = \frac{a \sin t}{a - a \cos t} = \frac{2 \sin \frac{t}{2} \cos \frac{t}{2}}{1 - \left(1 - 2\sin^2 \frac{t}{2}\right)} = \cot \frac{t}{2}$. If $t = 0$ or π, then

$\cot \frac{t}{2} = 0$, so the tangent is undefined or vertical.

63. $x = at - b \sin t \Rightarrow \frac{dx}{dt} = a - b \cos t$ $\quad y = a \ - b \cos t) \Rightarrow \frac{dy}{dt} = b \sin t$

$\frac{dy}{dx} = \frac{b \sin t}{a - b \cos t} = \frac{\sin t}{\frac{a}{b} - \cos t}$. If $b < a$, $\frac{a}{b} > 1 \Rightarrow \frac{a}{b} - \cos t > 0$

so $\frac{dy}{dx}$ is always finite.

64. $\frac{dy}{dt} = \cos t \Rightarrow y = -\sin t + C$. $y = 0$ when $t = 0 \Rightarrow C = 0$.

$\frac{dx}{dt} = -2y = 2 \sin t \Rightarrow x = 2 \cos t + C$. $x = 3$ when $t = 0 \Rightarrow C = 1$.

$\therefore x = 2 \cos t + 1$, $y = -\sin t$. Also, $\frac{x - 1}{2} = \cos t \Rightarrow$

$\frac{(x-1)^2}{4} + y^2 = \sin^2 t + \cos^2 t = 1$. It is an ellipse.

65. (a) $s = 4\int_0^{\frac{\pi}{2}} \sqrt{a^2 \sin^2 t + b^2 \cos^2 t}\, dt = 4\int_0^{\frac{\pi}{2}} \sqrt{a^2(1-\cos^2 t) + b^2 \cos^2 t}\, dt$

$$= 4\int_0^{\frac{\pi}{2}} \sqrt{a^2 - (a^2 - b^2)\cos^2 t}\, dt = 4\int_0^{\frac{\pi}{2}} \sqrt{a^2 - c^2\cos^2 t}\, dt$$

$$= 4\int_0^{\frac{\pi}{2}} \sqrt{a^2\left(1 - \frac{c^2}{a^2}\cos^2 t\right)}\, dt = 4a\int_0^{\frac{\pi}{2}} \sqrt{1 - e^2\cos^2 t}\, dt$$

(b) $L = 4\int_0^{\frac{\pi}{2}} \sqrt{1 - \frac{1}{4}\cos^2 t}\, dt \approx 5.868$, with $h = \frac{\pi}{20}$ and $n = 10$

(c) $|E| \le \frac{\pi}{24}\left(\frac{\pi}{20}\right)^2 (1) \approx 0.003$

66. $A = \int_0^{2\pi} y\, dx = \int_0^{2\pi} a^2(1-\cos t)^2 = a^2\int_0^{2\pi}\left(1 - 2\cos t + \frac{1}{2} + \frac{1}{2}\cos 2t\right)dt$

$$= a^2\left[\frac{3}{2}t - 2\sin t - \frac{1}{4}\sin 2t\right]_0^{2\pi} = 3\pi a^2$$

$$M_x = \int_0^{2\pi} \frac{1}{2}y^2\, dx = \frac{a^3}{2}\int_0^{2\pi} (1-\cos t)^3\, dt = \frac{a^3}{2}\int_0^{2\pi} (1 - 3\cos t + 3\cos^2 t - \cos^3 t)dt$$

$$= \frac{a^3}{2}\int_0^{2\pi} dt - \frac{3a^3}{2}\int_0^{2\pi} \cos t\, dt + \frac{3a^3}{2}\int_0^{2\pi}\left(\frac{1}{2} + \frac{1}{2}\cos 2t\right)dt$$

$$- \frac{a^3}{2}\int_0^{2\pi} (1-\sin^2 t)\cos t\, dt = \frac{5\pi a^3}{2}.$$

$$\bar{y} = \frac{5\pi a^3}{2} \div 3\pi a^2 = \frac{5a}{6}.$$

$$M_y = \int_0^{2\pi} xy\, dx = \int_0^{2\pi} a(t - \sin t)\, a^2(1-\cos t)^2\, dt$$

$$= a^3\int_0^{2\pi} t - 2t\cos t + t\cos^2 t - \sin t + 2\sin t\cos t - \sin t\cos^2 t\,)\, dt$$

$$= 3\pi^2 a^3. \quad \bar{x} = \frac{3\pi^2 a^3}{3\pi a^2} = \pi a$$

67. $xy = 2 \Rightarrow x\frac{dy}{dx} + y = 0 \Rightarrow \frac{dy}{dx} = -\frac{y}{x}$.

$x^2 - y^2 = 3 \Rightarrow 2x - 2y\frac{dx}{dy} = 0 \Rightarrow \frac{dy}{dx} = \frac{x}{y}$.

If (x_0, y_0) is a point of intersection,

the product of the slopes $\left(\frac{x_0}{y_0}\right)\left(-\frac{y_0}{x_0}\right) = -1$ so

the curves are orthogonal.

68. $y^2 = 4x + 4$ and $y^2 = 64 - 16x$ intersect in the points $(3, \pm 4)$.

The slopes of the curves are $m_1 = \frac{dy}{dx} = \frac{2}{y}$ and $m_2 = \frac{dy}{dx} = -\frac{8}{y}$.

At the point $(3, 4)$, $m_1m_2 = \left(\frac{2}{4}\right)\left(-\frac{8}{4}\right) = -1$ and at the point $(3, -4)$

$m_1m_2 = \left(-\frac{2}{4}\right)\left(\frac{8}{4}\right) = -1$.

69. $2x^2 + 3y^2 = a^2 \Rightarrow \frac{dy}{dx} = -\frac{2x}{3y}$.

$Ky^2 = x^3 \Rightarrow \frac{dy}{dx} = \frac{3x^2}{2Ky} = \frac{3x^2y}{2Ky^2} = \frac{3x^2y}{2x^3} = \frac{3y}{2x}$.

$\left(-\frac{2x}{3y}\right)\left(\frac{3y}{2x}\right) = -1$ independently of a and K.

70. $y^2 = 4a(a - x) = -4a(x - a)$ has Vertex $(a, 0)$. $p = -a \Rightarrow$ the focus is located at the origin. Similarly $y^2 = 4b(x + b)$ has vertex $(-b, 0)$ and focus at the origin. They intersect where $4a(a - x) = 4b(b + x)$ or $a^2 - b^2 = (b + a)x \Rightarrow x = a - b$. Then $y^2 = 4ab \Rightarrow y = \pm 2\sqrt{ab}$.

The slopes of the curves are $\frac{dy}{dx} = -\frac{2a}{y}$ and $\frac{dy}{dx} = \frac{2b}{y}$. The product of these slopes is $P = -\frac{4ab}{y^2}$. At the points of intersection,

$P = -\frac{4ab}{4ab} = -1$, so that the parabolas are orthogonal.

CHAPTER 9

HYPERBOLIC FUNCTIONS

9.1 DEFINITIONS AND IDENTITIES

1. $\sinh u = -\frac{3}{4}$

(a) $\cosh^2 u - \sinh^2 u = 1 \Rightarrow \cosh^2 u = 1 + \left(-\frac{3}{4}\right)^2 \Rightarrow \cosh u = \frac{5}{4}$

(b) $\tanh u = \frac{\sinh u}{\cosh u} = -\frac{3}{5}$ (c) $\coth u = \frac{1}{\tanh u} = -\frac{5}{3}$

(d) $\operatorname{sech} u = \frac{1}{\cosh u} = \frac{4}{5}$ (e) $\operatorname{csch} u = \frac{1}{\sinh u} = -\frac{4}{5}$

2. $\cosh u = \frac{17}{15}$, $u > 0$

(a) $\cosh^2 u - \sinh^2 u = 1 \Rightarrow \sinh^2 u = \left(\frac{17}{15}\right)^2 - 1 \Rightarrow \sinh u = \pm\frac{8}{15}$

(b) $\tanh u = \pm\frac{8}{17}$ (c) $\coth u = \pm\frac{17}{8}$

(d) $\operatorname{sech} u = \frac{15}{17}$ (e) $\operatorname{csch} u = \pm\frac{15}{8}$

3. $\tanh u = -\frac{7}{25}$

(a) $1 - \tanh^2 u = \operatorname{sech}^2 u \Rightarrow 1 - \left(-\frac{7}{25}\right)^2 = \operatorname{sech}^2 u \Rightarrow \operatorname{sech} u = \frac{24}{25}$

(b) $\cosh u = \frac{1}{\operatorname{sech} u} = \frac{25}{24}$

(c) $\coth u = \frac{1}{\tanh u} = -\frac{25}{7}$ (d) $\frac{\sinh u}{\frac{25}{24}} = -\frac{7}{25} \Rightarrow \sinh u = -\frac{7}{24}$

(e) $\operatorname{csch} u = \frac{1}{\sinh u} = -\frac{24}{7}$

4. $\coth u = \frac{13}{12}$

(a) $\coth^2 u - 1 = \operatorname{csch}^2 u \Rightarrow \left(\frac{13}{12}\right)^2 - 1 = \operatorname{csch}^2 u \Rightarrow \operatorname{csch} u = \frac{5}{12}$

(b) $\tanh u = \frac{12}{13}$ (c) $\cosh u = \frac{13}{5}$

(d) $\operatorname{sech} u = \frac{5}{13}$ (e) $\sinh u = \frac{12}{5}$

5. $\operatorname{sech} u = \frac{3}{5}$ (a) $\cosh u = \frac{5}{3}$

(b) $\cosh^2 u - \sinh^2 u = 1 \Rightarrow \frac{25}{9} - \sinh^2 u = 1 \Rightarrow \sinh u = \pm \frac{4}{3}$

(c) $\operatorname{csch} u = \frac{1}{\sinh u = \pm\frac{3}{4}}$ (d) $\tanh u = \frac{\sinh u}{\cosh u} = \frac{\pm\frac{4}{3}}{\pm\frac{5}{3}} = \pm\frac{4}{5}$

(e) $\coth u = \frac{1}{\tanh u} = \pm\frac{5}{4}$

6. $\operatorname{csch} u = \frac{5}{12}$

(a) $\coth^2 u - 1 = \operatorname{csch}^2 u \Rightarrow \left(\frac{5}{12}\right)^2 + 1 = \coth^2 u \Rightarrow \coth u = \frac{13}{12}$

(b) $\tanh u = \frac{12}{13}$ (c) $\cosh u = \frac{13}{5}$

(d) $\operatorname{sech} u = \frac{5}{13}$ (e) $\sinh u = \frac{12}{5}$

7. $2\cosh(\ln x) = 2\left[\frac{e^{\ln x} + e^{-\ln x}}{2}\right] = x + \frac{1}{x}$

8. $\sinh(2\ln x) = \frac{1}{2}(e^{2\ln x} - e^{-2\ln x}) = \frac{1}{2}(x^2 - x^{-2}) = \frac{x^4 - 1}{2x^2}$

9. $\tanh(\ln x) = \frac{e^{\ln x} - e^{-\ln x}}{e^{\ln x} + e^{-\ln x}} = \frac{x - \frac{1}{x}}{x + \frac{1}{x}} = \frac{x^2 - 1}{x^2 + 1}$

10. $\frac{1}{\cosh x - \sinh x} \cdot \frac{\cosh x + \sinh x}{\cosh x + \sinh x} = \frac{\cosh x + \sinh x}{\operatorname{cosxh}^2 x - \sinh^2 x} = \frac{e^x}{1} = e^x$

11. $\cosh 5x + \sinh 5x = e^{5x}$

12. $(\sinh x + \cosh x)^4 = e^{4x}$

13. $\cosh 3x - \sinh 3x = e^{-3x}$

14. $\ln|\cosh x + \sinh x| + \ln|\cosh x - \sinh x| = \ln(e^x) + \ln(e^{-x}) = x - x = 0.$

15. $\tanh(-x) = \frac{\sinh(-x)}{\cosh(-x)} = \frac{-\sinh x}{\cosh x} = -\tanh x \Rightarrow$ odd

16. $\coth(-x) = \frac{1}{\tanh(-x)} = -\frac{1}{\tanh x} = -\coth x \Rightarrow$ odd

17. $\operatorname{sech}(-x) = \frac{1}{\cosh(-x)} = \frac{1}{\cosh x} = \operatorname{sech} x \Rightarrow$ even

18. $\operatorname{csch}(-x) = \frac{1}{\sinh(-x)} = -\frac{1}{\sinh x} = -\operatorname{csch} x \Rightarrow$ odd

19. $\cosh(-3x) = \cosh 3x \Rightarrow$ even

20. $\sinh(-2x) = -\sinh 2x \Rightarrow$ odd

21. $\sinh(-x)\cosh(-x) = (-\sinh x)(\cosh x) = -\sinh x\cosh x \Rightarrow$ odd

22. $(\sinh x)^2$ is even

23. $\operatorname{sech}(-x) + \cosh(-x) = \operatorname{sech}x + \cosh x \Rightarrow$ even

24. $\sinh x + \cosh x = e^x$ is neither even nor odd

25. $\cosh x = \sinh x + \frac{1}{2} \Rightarrow e^{-x} = \frac{1}{2} \Rightarrow x = -\ln\frac{1}{2}$

26. $\tanh x = \frac{3}{5} \Rightarrow \dfrac{e^x - e^{-x}}{e^x + e^{-x}} = \frac{3}{5} \Rightarrow 5e^x - 5e^{-x} = 3e^x + 3e^{-x}$

$2e^x = 8e^{-x} \Rightarrow e^{2x} = 4 \Rightarrow 2x = \ln 4 \Rightarrow x = \frac{1}{2}\ln 4 = \ln 2$

27. $\sinh u \cosh v + \cosh u \sinh v = \left(\dfrac{e^u - e^{-u}}{2}\right)\left(\dfrac{e^v + e^{-v}}{2}\right) + \left(\dfrac{e^u + e^{-u}}{2}\right)\left(\dfrac{e^v - e^{-v}}{2}\right)$

$= \frac{1}{4}(e^{u+v} - e^{-u+v} + e^{u-v} - e^{-u-v} + e^{u+v} + e^{-u+v} - e^{u-v} - e^{-u-v})$

$= \frac{1}{4}(2e^{u+v} - 2e^{-u-v}) = \dfrac{e^{u+v} - e^{-(u+v)}}{2} = \sinh(u+v)$

28. $\cosh u \cosh v + \sinh u \sinh v = \left(\dfrac{e^u + e^{-u}}{2}\right)\left(\dfrac{e^v + e^{-v}}{2}\right) + \left(\dfrac{e^u - e^{-u}}{2}\right)\left(\dfrac{e^v - e^{-v}}{2}\right)$

$= \frac{1}{4}(e^{u+v} + e^{-u+v} + e^{u-v} + e^{-u-v} + e^{u+v} - e^{-u+v} - e^{u-v} + e^{-u-v})$

$= \frac{1}{4}(2e^{u+v} + 2e^{-u-v}) = \dfrac{e^{u+v} + e^{-u-v}}{2} = \cosh(u+v)$

29. $\sinh(u - v) = \sinh(u + (-v)) = \sinh u \cosh(-v) + \cosh u \sinh(-v)$

$= \sinh u \cosh v - \cosh u \sinh v$

30. $\cosh(u - v) = \cosh(u + (-v)) = \cosh u \cosh(-v) + \sinh u \sinh(-v)$

$= \cosh u \cosh v - \sinh u$ sihn v

31. $\sinh(u + v) + \sinh(u - v)$

$= (\sinh u \cosh v + \cosh u \sinh v) + (\sinh u \cosh v - \cosh u \sinh v)$

$= 2 \sinh u \cosh v$

$\therefore \sinh u \cosh v = \frac{1}{2}\sinh(u + v) + \frac{1}{2}\sinh(u - v)$

32. $\sinh(u + v) - \sinh(u - v)$

$= (\sinh u \cosh v + \cosh u \sinh v) - (\sinh u \cosh v - \cosh u \sinh v)$

$= 2$ coshh $u \sinh v$

$\therefore \cosh u \sinh v = \frac{1}{2}\sinh(u + v) - \frac{1}{2}\sinh(u - v)$

33. $\cosh(u + v) + \cosh(u - v)$

$= (\cosh u \cosh v + \sinh u \sinh v) + (\cosh u \cosh v - \sinh u \sinh v)$

$= 2 \cosh u \cosh v$

$\therefore \cosh u \cosh v = \frac{1}{2}\cosh(u + v) + \frac{1}{2}\cosh(u - v)$

34. $\cosh(u + v) - \cosh(u - v)$

$= (\cosh u \cosh v + \sinh u \sinh v) - (\cosh u \cosh v - \sinh u \sinh v)$

$= 2 \sinh u \sinh v$

$\therefore \sinh u \sinh v = \frac{1}{2} \cosh (u + v) + \frac{1}{2} \cosh (u - v)$

35. $\sinh 3u = \sinh (2u + u) = \sinh 2u \cosh u + \sinh u \cosh 2u$

$= (2\sinh u \cosh u) \cosh u + \sinh u (\cosh^2 u + \sinh^2 u)$

$= 2 \sinh u \cosh^2 u + \sinh u \cosh^2 u + \sinh^3 u$

$= \sinh^3 u + 3 \sinh u \cosh^2 u$

or $= 3\sinh(1 + \sinh^2 x) + \sinh^3 u$

$= 3\sinh u + 4\sinh^3 u$

36. $\cosh 3u = \cosh(2u + u) = \cosh 2u \cosh u + \sinh 2u \sinh u$

$= (1 + 2\sinh^2 u)\cosh u + (2 \sinh u \cosh u)\sinh u$

$= \cosh u + 4\sinh^2 u \cosh u$

or $= (2 \cosh^2 u - 1)\cosh u + (2 \sinh u \cosh u)\sinh u$

$= 2\cosh^3 u - \cosh u + 2\cosh u(\cosh^2 u - 1)$

$= 4\cosh^3 u - 3\cosh u$

37. $\cosh^2 u - \cosh^2 v = (1 + \sinh^2 u) - (1 + \sinh^2 v) = \sinh^2 u - \sinh^2 v$

38. $(\cosh x + \sinh x)^n = (e^x)^n = e^{nx} = \cosh nx + \sinh nx$

39. $x = -\cosh u,\ y = \sinh u,\ -\infty < u < \infty$

$\left.\begin{array}{l} x^2 = \cosh^2 u \\ y^2 = \sinh^2 u \end{array}\right\} \Rightarrow x^2 - y^2 = \cosh^2 u - \sinh^2 u = 1$

$\cosh u > 0 \Rightarrow -\cosh u < 0 \Rightarrow x < 0 \Rightarrow$ left-hand branch

40. $x^2 - y^2 = 1 \Rightarrow 2x - 2y \frac{dy}{dx} = 0 \Rightarrow \frac{dy}{dx} = \frac{x}{y}\Big]_{(\cosh u,\ \sinh u)} = \frac{\cosh u}{\sinh u} = \coth u$

Tangent line: $y - \sinh u = \coth u (x - \cosh u)$

y-intercept: $-\sinh u = \frac{\cosh u}{\sinh u}(x - \cosh u)$

$\cosh^2 u - \sinh^2 u = x \cosh u \Rightarrow 1 = x \cosh u$ or $x = \operatorname{sech} u$

x-intercept: $y - \sinh u = -\frac{\cosh^2 u}{\sinh u} \Rightarrow y \sinh u = -1$ or $y = -\operatorname{csch} u$

41. $r = \sqrt{\cosh^2 u + \sinh^2 u} = \sqrt{\left(\dfrac{e^u + e^{-u}}{2}\right)^2 + \left(\dfrac{e^u - e^{-u}}{2}\right)^2}$

$= \sqrt{\dfrac{e^{2u} + 2 + e^{-2u}}{4} + \dfrac{e^{2u} - 2 + e^{-2u}}{4}} = \sqrt{\dfrac{e^{2u} + e^{-2u}}{2}} = \sqrt{\cosh 2u}$

42. $x^2 - y^2 = 1 \Rightarrow 2x - 2y\dfrac{dy}{dx} = 0 \Rightarrow \dfrac{dy}{dx} = \dfrac{x}{y}$. At (1,0), the slope of the tangent line is undefined, and the equation is $x = 1$.

This intersects $y = \tan u$ in the point $(1, \tanh u)$.

43. $-\dfrac{\pi}{2} < \theta < \dfrac{\pi}{2} \Rightarrow \cos\theta > 0$.

Then $\sec\theta = \sqrt{1 + \tan^2\theta} = \sqrt{1 + \sinh^2 x} = \sqrt{\cosh^2 x} = |\cosh x| = \cosh x$

$\cos\theta = \dfrac{1}{\sec\theta} = \dfrac{1}{\cosh x} = \operatorname{sech} x$

$\dfrac{\sin\theta}{\cos\theta} = \tan\theta \Rightarrow \sin\theta = \tan\theta\cos\theta = \sinh x \operatorname{sech} x = \dfrac{\sinh x}{\cosh x} = \tanh x$

$\cot\theta = \dfrac{1}{\tan\theta} = \dfrac{1}{\sinh x} = \operatorname{csch} x$

$\csc\theta = \dfrac{1}{\sin\theta} = \dfrac{1}{\tanh x} = \coth x$

9.2 DERIVATIVES AND INTEGRALS

1. $y = \sinh 3x \Rightarrow \dfrac{dy}{dx} = 3\cosh 3x$

2. $y = \cosh^2 5x \Rightarrow \dfrac{dy}{dx} = 2\cosh 5x \sinh 5x(5) = 5\sinh 10x$

3. $y = \cosh^2 5x - \sinh^2 5x = 1 \Rightarrow \dfrac{dy}{dx} = 0$

4. $y = \tanh 2x \Rightarrow \dfrac{dy}{dx} = 2 \operatorname{sech}^2 2x$

5. $y = \coth(\tan x) \Rightarrow \dfrac{dy}{dx} = -\operatorname{csch}^2(\tan x)\sec^2 x$

6. $y = \operatorname{sech}^3 x \Rightarrow \dfrac{dy}{dx} = 3\operatorname{sech}^2 x\,(-\operatorname{sech} x \tanh x) = -3\operatorname{sech}^3 x \tanh x$

7. $y = 4\operatorname{csch}\left(\dfrac{x}{4}\right)$

$\dfrac{dy}{dx} = -4\operatorname{csch}\left(\dfrac{x}{4}\right)\coth\left(\dfrac{x}{4}\right)\left(\dfrac{1}{4}\right) = -\operatorname{csch}\left(\dfrac{x}{4}\right)\coth\left(\dfrac{x}{4}\right)$

8. $\sinh y = \tan x \Rightarrow \cosh y\dfrac{dy}{dx} = \sec^2 x \Rightarrow \dfrac{dy}{dx} = \operatorname{sech} y \sec^2 x$

9. $y = \operatorname{sech}^2 x + \tanh^2 x = 1 \Rightarrow \dfrac{dy}{dx} = 0$

10. $y = \operatorname{csch}^2 x \Rightarrow \dfrac{dy}{dx} = 2\operatorname{csch} x(-\operatorname{csch} x \coth x) = -2\operatorname{csch}^2 x \coth x$

11. $y = \sin^{-1}(\tanh x)$

$$\frac{dy}{dx} = \sqrt{\frac{1}{1-\tanh^2 x}} \cdot \frac{d}{dx}(\tanh x) = \sqrt{\frac{1}{1-\tanh^2 x}} \cdot \operatorname{sech}^2 x$$

$$= \frac{1.}{\operatorname{sech} x} \cdot \operatorname{sech}^2 x = \operatorname{sech} x$$

12. $y = x - \frac{1}{4}\coth 4x \quad \Rightarrow \quad \frac{dy}{dx} = 1 + \operatorname{csch}^2 4x$

13. $y = \ln|\tanh\left(\frac{x}{2}\right)|$

$$\frac{dy}{dx} = \frac{1}{|\tanh\left(\frac{x}{2}\right)|} \cdot \operatorname{sech}^2\left(\frac{x}{2}\right)\cdot\left(\frac{1}{2}\right) = \frac{1}{2} \cdot \frac{\cosh\left(\frac{x}{2}\right)}{\sinh\left(\frac{x}{2}\right)} \cdot \frac{1}{\cosh^2\left(\frac{x}{2}\right)}$$

$$= \frac{1}{2\sinh\left(\frac{x}{2}\right)\left(\cosh\left(\frac{x}{2}\right)\right)} = \frac{1}{\sinh x} = \operatorname{csch} x$$

14. $y = x^4 \sinh x \Rightarrow \frac{dy}{dx} = x^4 \cosh x + 4x^3 \sinh x$

15. $y = x \sinh 2x - \left(\frac{1}{2}\right)\cosh 2x$

$$\frac{dy}{dx} = \sinh 2x + 2x\cosh 2x - 2\left(\frac{1}{2}\right)\sinh 2x = 2x \cosh 2x$$

16. $y = x \sinh x - \cosh x \Rightarrow \frac{dy}{dx} = \sinh x + x\cosh x - \sinh x = x \cosh x$

17. $\int \operatorname{sech} x\, dx = \sin^{-1}(\tanh x) + C$ because

$$\frac{d}{dx}(\sin^{-1}(\tanh x)) = \frac{1}{\sqrt{1-\tanh^2 x}} \cdot \operatorname{sech}^2 x = \operatorname{sech} x$$

18. $$\frac{d}{dx}\left(\ln|\tanh\frac{x}{2}|\right) = \frac{1}{2} \cdot \frac{\operatorname{sech}^2\frac{x}{2}}{\tanh\frac{x}{2}} = \frac{\cosh\frac{x}{2}}{2\cosh^2\frac{x}{2}\sinh\frac{x}{2}} = \frac{1}{\sinh x} = \operatorname{csch} x.$$

$$\therefore \int \operatorname{csch} x\, dx = \ln|\tanh\frac{x}{2}| + C$$

19. $\int_{-1}^{1} \cosh 5x\, dx = \frac{1}{5}\sinh 5x\Big]_{-1}^{1} = \frac{1}{5}(\sinh 5 - \sinh(-5)) = \frac{2}{5}\sinh 5$

20. $\int_{-1}^{0} \cosh(2x+1)\, dx = \frac{1}{2}\sinh(2x+1)\Big]_{-1}^{0} = \frac{1}{2}(\sinh 1 - \sinh(-1)) = \sinh 1$

21. $\int_{-3}^{3} \sinh x\, dx = 0$ since $\sinh x$ is an odd function.

22. $\int_{-\pi}^{\pi} \tan 2x\, dx = 0$ (odd function across symmetric interval)

or $\int_{-\pi}^{\pi} \tan 2x\, dx = \int_{-\pi}^{\pi} \frac{\sinh 2x\, dx}{\cosh 2x} = \frac{1}{2}\ln|\cosh 2x|\Big]_{-\pi}^{\pi} =$

$= \frac{1}{2}\ln|\cosh 2\pi| - \frac{1}{2}\ln|\cosh(-2\pi)| = 0.$

23. $\int_0^1 x\cosh x\, dx = x\sinh x\Big]_0^1 - \int_0^1 \sinh x\, dx = \sinh 1 - \cosh 1 + 1 = 1 - e^{-1}$

Let $u = x \Rightarrow du = dx$, $dv = \cosh x\, dx \Rightarrow v = \sinh x$

24. $\int_{\ln 2}^{\ln 4} \coth x\, dx = \int_{\ln 2}^{\ln 4} \frac{\cosh x\, dx}{\sinh x} = \ln|\sinh x|\Big]_{\ln 2}^{\ln 4}$

$= \ln|\sinh(\ln 4)| - \ln|\sinh(\ln 2)|$

$= \ln\left[\frac{e^{\ln 4} - e^{-\ln 4}}{2}\right] - \ln\left[\frac{e^{\ln 2} - e^{-\ln 2}}{2}\right] = \ln\left[\frac{4 - \frac{1}{4}}{2}\right] - \ln\left[\frac{2 - \frac{1}{2}}{2}\right]$

$= \ln\frac{15}{8} - \ln\frac{3}{4} = \ln\frac{5}{2}$

25. $\int_0^{\frac{1}{2}} \frac{\sinh x}{e^x}\, dx = \int_0^{\frac{1}{2}} e^{-x}\left(\frac{e^x - e^{-x}}{2}\right)dx = \int_0^{\frac{1}{2}} \left(\frac{1}{2} - \frac{1}{2}e^{-2x}\right)dx$

$= \frac{1}{2}x + \frac{1}{4}e^{-2x}\Big]_0^{\frac{1}{2}} = \frac{1}{4} + \frac{1}{4e} - \frac{1}{4} = \frac{1}{4e}$

26. $\int_0^{\ln 2} 4e^x \cosh x\, dx = \int_0^{\ln 2} 2e^x(e^x + e^{-x})\, dx = \int_0^{\ln 2} (2e^{2x} + 2)\, dx$

$= e^{2x} + 2x\Big]_0^{\ln 2} = 3 + \ln 2$

27. $\int_0^1 \sinh\sqrt{x}\, dx = \int_0^1 2y\sinh y\, dy = 2y\cosh y - 2\int_0^1 \cosh y\, dy$

Let $y = \sqrt{x} \Rightarrow dy = \frac{1}{2\sqrt{x}}dx \Rightarrow dx = 2\sqrt{x}dy = 2y\, dy$

Limits: $x = 0 \Rightarrow y = \sqrt{0} = 0$; $x = 1 \Rightarrow y = \sqrt{1} = 1$

Let $u = 2y$ $dv = \sinh y\, dy$

$du = 2\, dy$ $v = \cosh y$

$= 2y\cosh y - 2\sinh y\Big]_0^1 = 2\cosh 1 - 2\sinh 1 = 2e^{-1}$

28. $\int_1^2 \frac{\cosh(\ln x)\, dx}{x} = \sinh(\ln x)\Big]_1^2 = \sinh(\ln 2) - \sinh(\ln 1) = \frac{3}{4}$

29. $\int \cosh(2x+1)\,dx = \frac{1}{2}\sinh(2x+1) + C$

30. $\int \tan x\,dx = \int \frac{\sinh x\,dx}{\cosh x} = \ln|\cosh x| + C$

31. $\int \frac{\sinh x\,dx}{\cosh^4 x} = \int \cosh^{-4}x \sinh x\,dx = -\frac{1}{3}\cosh^{-3}x + C = -\frac{1}{3}\text{sech}^3 x + C$

32. $\int \frac{4}{(e^x + e^{-x})^2}\,dx = \int \left(\frac{2}{e^x + e^{-x}}\right)^2 dx = \int \text{sech}^2 x\,dx = \tanh x + C$

33. $\int \frac{e^x - e^{-x}}{e^x + e^{-x}}\,dx = \int \frac{\sinh x}{\cosh x}\,dx = \ln|\cosh x| + C = \ln(\cosh x) + C$

34. $\int \tanh^2 x\,dx = \int (1 - \text{sech}^2 x)\,dx = x - \tanh x + C$

35. $\int \frac{\sinh\sqrt{x}}{\sqrt{x}}\,dx = 2\cosh\sqrt{x} + C$

Let $u = \sqrt{x} \Rightarrow du = \frac{1}{2\sqrt{x}}\,dx \Rightarrow 2\,du = \frac{1}{\sqrt{x}}\,dx$

$\int 2\sinh u\,du = 2\cosh u + C$

36. $\int \cosh^2 3x\,dx = \int \frac{1}{2}(\cosh 6x + 1)\,dx = \frac{1}{12}\sinh 6x + \frac{1}{2}x + C$

37. $\int \sqrt{\cosh x - 1}\,dx = \int \sqrt{\left(2\cosh^2\frac{x}{2} - 1\right) - 1}\,dx$

$= \sqrt{2}\int \sqrt{\cosh^2\frac{x}{2} - 1}\,dx = \sqrt{2}\int \sinh\frac{x}{2}\,dx = 2\sqrt{2}\cosh\frac{x}{2} + C$

38. $\int \cosh^2 5x\,dx = \int \frac{1}{2}(\cosh 10x + 1)\,dx = \frac{1}{20}\sinh 10x + \frac{1}{2}x + C$

39. There are three possibilities:

(1) $\int 2\cosh x \sinh x\,dx = \cosh^2 x + C$

(2) $\int 2\cosh x \sinh x\,dx = \sinh^2 x + C$

(3) $\int 2\cosh x \sinh x\,dx = \int \sinh 2x\,dx = \frac{1}{2}\cosh 2x + C$

40. $\int \cosh^3 x\,dx = \int (1 + \sinh^2 x)\cosh x\,dx = \sinh x + \frac{1}{3}\sinh^3 x + C$

41. $\int \frac{\sinh x}{1 + \cosh x}\,dx = \ln(1 + \cosh x) + C$

42. $\int x^2 \sinh x\,dx = x^2\cosh x - 2x \sinh x + 2\cosh x + C$

x^2	$+$	$\sinh x$
$2x$	$-$	$\cosh x$
2	$+$	$\sinh x$
0		$\cosh x$

43. $\int x^2 \cosh x\,dx = x^2\sinh x - 2\int x \sinh x\,dx$

Let $u = x^2 \Rightarrow du = 2x\,dx$, $dv = \cosh x\,dx \Rightarrow v = \sinh x$

$= x^2\sinh x - 2\left(x\cosh x - \int \cosh x\,dx\right)$

Let $u = x \Rightarrow du = dx$, $dv = \sinh x\,dx \Rightarrow v = \cosh x$

$= x^2\sinh x - 2x\cosh x + 2\sinh x + C$

44. $\int_0^{\ln 2} \frac{1-e^{-2x}}{1+e^{-2x}}\,dx = \int_0^{\ln 2} \frac{e^x - e^{-x}}{e^x + e^{-x}}\,dx = \ln|e^x + e^{-x}|\Big]_0^{\ln 2} = \ln\frac{3}{4}$

45. $\int \operatorname{sech}^3 5x \tanh 5x\,dx = \int \operatorname{sech}^2 5x(\operatorname{sech} 5x \tanh 5x)\,dx = -\frac{1}{15}\operatorname{sech}^3 x + C$

46. $\int \operatorname{csch}^2 x \coth x\,dx = -\frac{1}{2}\operatorname{csch}^2 x + C$

47. $\int \sinh^4 3x\,dx = \frac{1}{12}\sinh^3 3x \cosh 3x - \frac{3}{4}\int \sinh^2 3x\,dx$

$= \frac{1}{12}\sinh^3 3x\cosh 3x - \frac{1}{16}\sinh 6x + \frac{3}{8}x + C$

48. $\int \operatorname{sech} 7x\,dx = \frac{1}{7}\sin^{-1}(\tanh 7x) + C$

49. $\int e^{3x}\cosh 2x\,dx = \frac{e^{3x}}{2}\left[\frac{e^{2x}}{5} + \frac{e^{-2x}}{1}\right] + C = \frac{e^{5x}}{10} + \frac{e^x}{2} + C$

50. $\int \tanh^3 x\,dx = \int \tanh x(1 - \operatorname{sech}^2 x)\,dx = \ln(\cosh x) - \frac{1}{2}\tanh^2 x + C$

51. (a) $\int \operatorname{csch} x\,dx = \int \operatorname{csch} x\left(\frac{\operatorname{csch} x + \coth x}{\operatorname{csch} x + \coth x}\right)dx$

$= \int \frac{\operatorname{csch}^2 x + \operatorname{csch} x \coth x}{\operatorname{csch} x + \coth x}\,dx = -\ln|\operatorname{csch} x + \coth x| + C$

(b) $-\ln|\operatorname{csch} x + \coth x| + C = \ln\left|\tanh\frac{x}{2}\right| + C$

$= \ln\left|\frac{\sinh\frac{x}{2}}{\cosh\frac{x}{2}}\right| + C = \ln\left|\sinh\frac{x}{2}\right| - \ln\left|\cosh\frac{x}{2}\right| + C$

52. $\int_0^{\infty}(\cosh x - \sinh x)\,dx = \lim_{b\to\infty}\int_0^b (\cosh x - \sinh x)\,dx$

$= \lim_{b\to\infty}[\sinh x - \cosh x]_0^b = \lim_{b\to\infty}[-e^{-b} + 1] = 1$

53. $V = \pi\int_0^3 (\cosh^2 x - \sinh^2 x)\,dx$

$= \pi\int_0^3 dx = \pi x\Big]_0^3 = 3\pi$

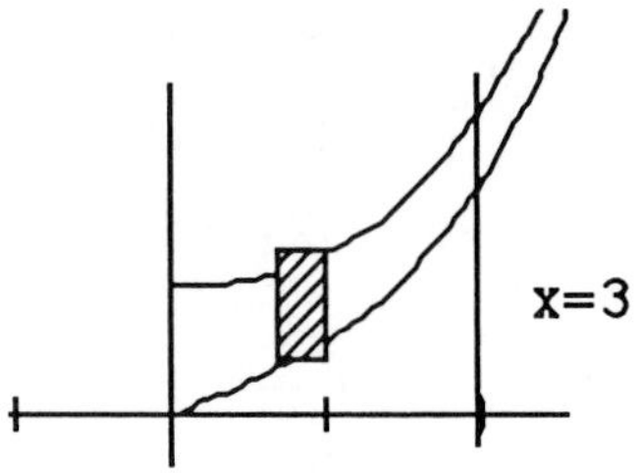

x=3

54. $\int_0^1 \sqrt{1 + \sinh^2 x}\,dx = \int_0^1 \cosh x\,dx = \sinh x\Big]_0^1 = \sinh 1$

55. $S = 2\pi\int_0^{\ln 2} \cosh x\sqrt{1 + \sinh^2 x}\,dx$

$= 2\pi\int_0^{\ln 2} \cosh^2 x\,dx = 2\pi\int_0^{\ln 2} \frac{\cosh 2x + 1}{2}\,dx$

$= \pi\left[\frac{\sinh 2x}{2} + x\right]_0^{\ln 2} = \pi\left[\frac{e^{2\ln 2} - e^{-2\ln 2}}{4} + \ln 2\right]$

$= \frac{15}{16}\pi + \pi\ln 2$

56. $V = 2\pi\int_0^{\infty} \operatorname{sech}^2 x\,dx = 2\pi\lim_{b\to\infty}\int_0^b \operatorname{sech}^2 x\,dx = 2\pi\lim_{b\to\infty}\Big[\tanh x\Big]_0^b = 2\pi$

57. $V = \pi\int_{\ln 2}^{\infty} \operatorname{csch}^2 x\,dx = \lim_{t\to\infty}\int_{\ln 2}^{t} \operatorname{csch}^2 x\,dx$

$= \pi\lim_{t\to\infty}(-\coth^2 x)\Big]_{\ln 2}^{t} = \pi[-1 + \coth(\ln 2)]$

$= \pi\left[-1 + \frac{e^{\ln 2} + e^{-\ln 2}}{e^{\ln 2} - e^{-\ln 2}}\right] = \frac{2}{3}\pi$

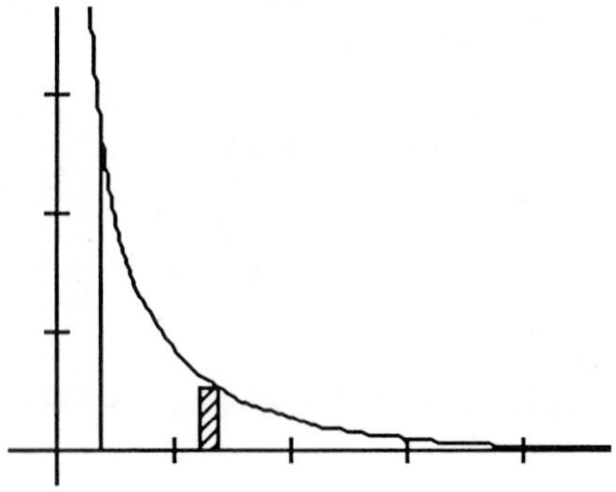

58. (a) $\int_0^{\infty} 2\pi x(\cosh x - \sinh x)\,dx = 2\pi\lim_{b\to\infty}\int_0^b xe^{-x}\,dx = 2\pi\lim_{b\to\infty}[-xe^{-x} - e^{-x}]_0^b = 2\pi$

(b) $\int_0^{\infty} \pi x(\cosh^2 x - \sinh^2 x)\,dx = \pi\lim_{b\to\infty}\int_0^b dx = \pi\lim_{b\to\infty} x\Big]_0^b = \infty$

59. $\bar{x} = 0$ by symmetry.

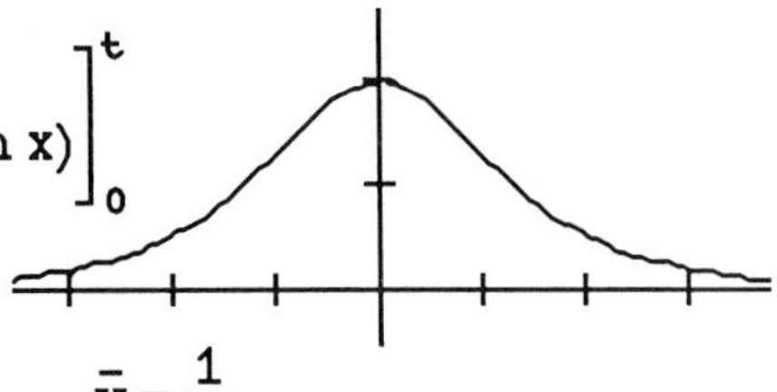

$$m = \lim_{t\to\infty} 2\int_0^t \operatorname{sech} x\,dx = 2\lim_{t\to\infty} \sin^{-1}(\tanh x)\Big]_0^t$$

$$= 2(\sin^{-1} 1 - 0) = \pi$$

$$M_x = \lim_{t\to\infty} \int_0^t \frac{\operatorname{sech}^2 x}{2}\,dx = \lim_{t\to\infty} \tanh x\Big]_0^t = 1. \quad \bar{y} = \frac{1}{\pi}$$

60. $$M = \int_0^{\ln 2} \delta\,ds = \int_0^{\ln 2} \delta\sqrt{1+\sinh^2 x}\,dx = \int_0^{\ln 2} \delta\cosh x\,dx = \delta\sinh x\Big]_0^{\ln 2} = \frac{3}{4}\delta$$

$$M_y = \int_0^{\ln 2} \delta x\sqrt{1+\sinh^2 x}\,dx = \int_0^{\ln 2} \delta x\cosh x\,dx = \delta(x\sinh x - \cosh x)\Big]_0^{\ln 2}$$

$$= \frac{1}{4}\delta(3\ln 2 - 1). \quad \therefore \quad \bar{x} = \frac{3\ln 2 - 1}{3}$$

$$M_x = \int_0^{\ln 2} \delta\cosh x\sqrt{1+\sinh^2 x}\,dx = \int_0^{\ln 2} \delta\cosh^2 x\,dx = \frac{1}{2}\delta\int_0^{\ln 2} (\cosh 2x + 1)\,dx$$

$$= \frac{1}{2}\delta\left[\frac{1}{2}\sinh 2x + x\right]_0^{\ln 2} = \frac{1}{2}\delta\left[\frac{15}{16} + \ln 2\right]. \quad \therefore \bar{y} = \frac{16\ln 2 + 15}{24}$$

61. $$V = \pi\int_0^\infty (1 - \tanh^2 x)\,dx$$

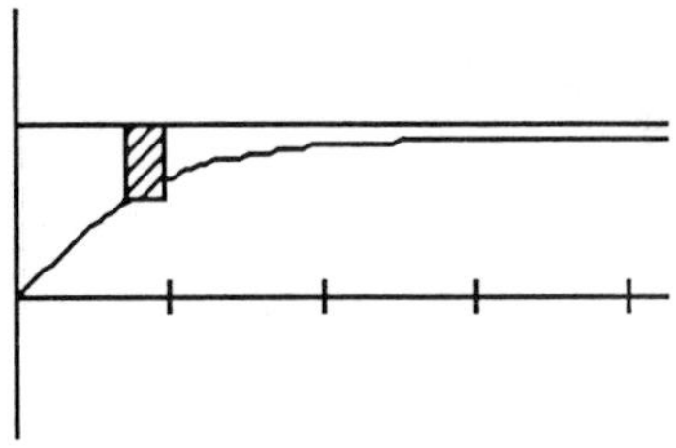

$$= \pi\lim_{t\to\infty} \int_0^t \operatorname{sech}^2 x\,dx = \pi\lim_{t\to\infty} [\tanh x]_0^t$$

$$= \pi(1 - 0) = \pi$$

62. (a) The region consists of a triangle with $A_1 = \frac{1}{2}bh = \frac{1}{2}\cosh u\sinh u$

minus the part whose area is given by $\int_1^{\cosh u} y\,dx$, where $y = \sqrt{x^2 - 1}$.

$$\therefore \quad A(u) = \frac{1}{2}\cosh u\sinh u - \int_1^{\cosh u} \sqrt{x^2 - 1}\,dx$$

(b) $$\frac{dA}{du} = \frac{1}{2}\cosh^2 u + \frac{1}{2}\sinh^2 u - \sinh u\sqrt{\cosh^2 u - 1}$$

$$= \frac{1}{2}(\cosh^2 u - \sinh^2 u) = \frac{1}{2}$$

(c) $\frac{dA}{du} = \frac{1}{2} \Rightarrow dA = \frac{1}{2}du \Rightarrow A = \frac{1}{2}u + C$. $A(0) = 0 \Rightarrow C = 0$. $\therefore 2A = u$.

63. (a) $y = A\cosh x + B\sinh x + C\cos x + D\sin x$

$y' = A\sinh x + B\cosh x - C\sin x + D\cos x$

$y'' = A\cosh x + B\sinh x - C\cos x - D\sin x$

$y^{(3)}(x) = A\sinh x + B\cosh x + C\sin x - D\cos x$

$y^{(4)}(x) = A\cosh x + B\sinh x + C\cos x + D\sin x$

$y^{(4)} - y = 0$

(b) $y^{(4)} = y \Rightarrow y^{(4)} - y = 0$

This yields the system

$$\begin{aligned} A + C &= 0 \\ B + D &= 0 \\ A - C &= 2 \\ B - D &= 2, \end{aligned}$$

which has solution $A = 1,\ B = 1,\ C = -1,\ D = -1$

64. (a) An infinite number of solutions

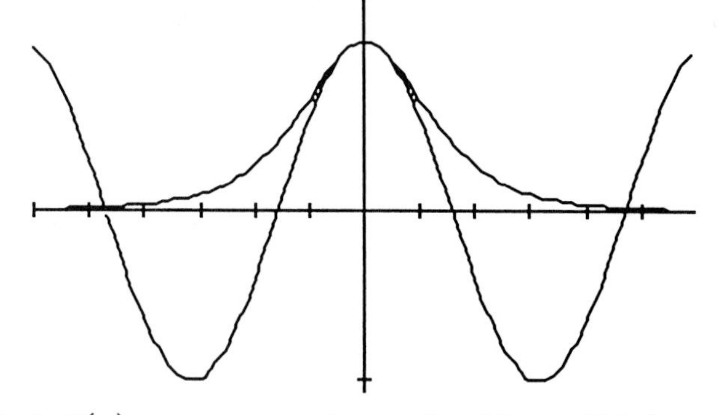

(b) Let $f(x) = \cos x \cosh x - 1$. Then $f'(x) = \cosh x(\cos x - \sin x)$.

Using Newton's Method, with $x_0 = 6$, we find the root to be

$x \approx 4.730040745$.

65. $x = -\frac{2}{\sqrt{3}}\sinh\frac{t}{\sqrt{3}}$ $\qquad \frac{dx}{dt} = -\frac{2}{\sqrt{3}}\cdot\frac{1}{\sqrt{3}}\cosh\frac{t}{\sqrt{3}}$

$y = \frac{1}{\sqrt{3}}\sinh\frac{t}{\sqrt{3}} + \cosh\frac{t}{\sqrt{3}}$ $\qquad \frac{dy}{dt} = \frac{1}{\sqrt{3}}\cdot\frac{1}{\sqrt{3}}\cosh\frac{t}{\sqrt{3}} + \frac{1}{\sqrt{3}}\sinh t$

$$\frac{dx}{dt} + 2\frac{dy}{dt} + x = -\frac{2}{3}\cosh\frac{t}{\sqrt{3}} + 2\left(\frac{1}{3}\cosh\frac{t}{\sqrt{3}} + \frac{1}{\sqrt{3}}\sinh\frac{1}{\sqrt{3}}\right) - \frac{2}{\sqrt{3}}\sinh\frac{t}{\sqrt{3}} = 0$$

$$\frac{dx}{dt} - \frac{dy}{dt} + y = -\frac{2}{3}\cosh\frac{t}{\sqrt{3}} - \frac{1}{3}\cosh\frac{t}{\sqrt{3}} - \frac{1}{\sqrt{3}}\sinh\frac{1}{\sqrt{3}} + \frac{1}{\sqrt{3}}\sinh\frac{t}{\sqrt{3}} + \cosh\frac{t}{\sqrt{3}} = 0$$

$x(0) = -\frac{2}{\sqrt{3}}\sinh 0 = 0$ $\quad y(0) = \frac{1}{\sqrt{3}}\sinh 0 + \cosh 0 = 1$

9.3 HANGING CABLES

1. $$s = \int_0^{x_1} \sqrt{1 + \sinh^2\left(\frac{x}{a}\right)}\, dx = \int_0^{x_1} \cosh \frac{x}{a}\, dx = a \sinh \frac{x}{a}\Big]_0^{x_1} = a \sinh \frac{x_1}{a}$$

2. If $y = a \cosh \frac{x}{a}$, then $\frac{dy}{dx} = a \sinh \frac{x}{a} \cdot \frac{1}{a} = \sinh \frac{x}{a}$.

$$s = \int_0^{x} \sqrt{1 + \sinh^2 \frac{t}{a}}\, dt = \int_0^{x} \cosh \frac{t}{a}\, dt = a \sinh \frac{t}{a}\Big]_0^{x} = a \sinh \frac{x}{a}$$

$$\therefore \frac{s}{a} = \frac{dy}{dx}$$

3. By problem 1, the arc length is $a \sinh \frac{x_1}{a}$, so the area of the rectangle is $A = a\left(a \sinh \frac{x_1}{a}\right) = a^2 \sinh \frac{x_1}{a}$.

4. If $y = a \cosh \frac{x}{a}$, then $\frac{dy}{dx} = \sinh \frac{x}{a}$.

$$S = 2\pi \int_0^{x_1} a \cosh \frac{x}{a} \sqrt{1 + \sinh^2 \frac{x}{a}}\, dt = 2\pi a \int_0^{x_1} \cosh^2 \frac{x}{a}\, dx$$

$$= 2\pi a \int_0^{x_1} \left(\frac{1}{2} + \frac{1}{2} \cosh \frac{2x}{a}\right) dx = \pi a \left[x + \frac{a}{2} \sinh \frac{2x}{a}\right]_0^{x_1}$$

$$= \pi a \left[x_1 + \frac{a}{2} \sinh \frac{2x_1}{a}\right]$$

5. $\bar{x} = 0$ by symmetry.

$$s = \int_{-x_1}^{x_1} \sqrt{1 + \sinh^2 \frac{x}{a}}\, dx = \cosh \frac{x}{a}\Big]_{-x_1}^{x_1} = 2 \sinh \frac{x_1}{a}$$

$$M_x = \int_{-x_1}^{x_1} a \cosh^2 \frac{x}{a}\, dx = \frac{a}{2} \int_{-x_1}^{x_1} \left(\cosh \frac{2x}{a} + 1\right) dx = \frac{1}{2}\left[x + \frac{a}{2} \sinh \frac{2x}{a}\right]_{-x_1}^{x_1}$$

$$= x_1 + \frac{a}{2} \sinh \frac{2x_1}{a}. \quad \bar{y} = \frac{M_x}{s} = \frac{x_1}{2} \operatorname{csch} \frac{x_1}{a} + \frac{a}{2} \cosh \frac{x_1}{a} = \frac{x_1}{2} \operatorname{csch} \frac{x_1}{a} + \frac{y_1}{2}$$

6. $$V = \pi \int_0^{x_1} a^2 \cosh^2 \frac{x}{a}\, dx = \pi a^2 \int_0^{x_1} \left(\frac{1}{2} + \frac{1}{2}\cosh \frac{2x}{a}\right) dx$$

$$= \frac{\pi a^2}{2}\left[x + \frac{a}{2}\sinh \frac{2x}{a}\right]_0^{x_1} = \frac{\pi a^2}{2}\left[x_1 + \frac{a}{2}\sinh \frac{2x_1}{a}\right]$$

$$= \frac{\pi a^2}{2}\left[x_1 + \frac{a}{2}\sinh \frac{2x_1}{a}\right] = \frac{\pi a^2}{2}\left[x_1 + a \sinh\frac{x}{2}\cosh\frac{x}{2}\right]$$

$$= \frac{\pi a^2}{2}\left[x_1 + \frac{y_1}{a}\sqrt{y_1^2 - a^2}\right]$$

7. (a) If $s = a \sinh \frac{x}{a}$ then $\sinh \frac{x}{a} = \frac{x}{a}$ and $x = a \sinh^{-1}\left(\frac{x}{a}\right)$.

$$y = a \cosh \frac{x}{a} = \sqrt{a^2 + a^2 \sinh^2 \frac{x}{a}} = \sqrt{s^2 + a^2}$$

(b) $\dfrac{dx}{ds} = \dfrac{a}{\sqrt{1 + \frac{s^2}{a^2}}} \cdot \dfrac{1}{a} = \dfrac{a}{\sqrt{a^2 + s^2}}$ $\qquad \dfrac{dy}{ds} = \dfrac{s}{\sqrt{s^2 + a^2}}$

$$\left(\frac{dx}{ds}\right)^2 + \left(\frac{dy}{ds}\right)^2 = \frac{a^2}{a^2 + s^2} + \frac{s^2}{a^2 + s^2} = 1$$

8. (a) $x = a \sinh^{-1} \frac{s}{a} \Rightarrow 15 = a \sinh^{-1} \frac{16}{a} \Rightarrow \frac{15}{a} = \sinh^{-1} \frac{16}{a}$.

Let $u = \frac{15}{a}$ so that $\frac{16}{a} = \frac{16}{15}u$. Then $u = \sinh^{-1}\left(\frac{16}{15}u\right)$ or $\sinh u = \frac{16}{15}u$.

(b) $\sinh 0.6 \approx 0.63665$, and $\frac{16}{15}(0.6) = 0.64$.

(c) $a = \frac{15}{u} = \frac{15}{0.6} = 25$ feet. $\therefore y = 25 \cosh\left(\frac{x}{25}\right)$. If $x = 0$, $y = 25$.

If $x = 15$, $y = 25 \cosh(0.6) \approx 29.6$. The dip is approximately 4.6 feet.

(d) $T = 2\,\frac{\text{lb}}{\text{ft}} \cdot 25 \text{ ft} = 50 \text{ lbs}$.

9. (a) We will use Newton's Method on the function $f(x) = \cosh x - \frac{x}{2} - 1$.

$$x_{n+1} = x_n - \frac{f(x_n)}{f'(x_n)} = x_n - \frac{2 \cosh x_n - x_n + 2}{2 \sinh x_n - 1}. \text{ Take } x_1 = 1.$$

$x_2 = 0.9362$, $x_3 = 0.9309$ and $F(0.9309) = 0.00002$. The curves cross at approximately $(0.9309, 1.4654)$

(b) From part (a), $\frac{50}{a} \approx 0.930$ or $a \approx 53.8$.

$$s = \int_{-50}^{50} \sqrt{1 + \sinh^2 \frac{x}{a}}\, dx = \int_{-50}^{50} \cosh \frac{x}{a}\, dx = a \sinh \frac{x}{a} \Big]_{-50}^{50} = 115 \text{ ft}$$

(c) $T = wy = wa \cosh \frac{x}{a} \approx (0.3)(53.8) \approx 16.1$ lbs.

9.4 INVERSE HYPERBOLIC FUNCTIONS

1. $\sinh^{-1}(0) = \ln(0 + \sqrt{0+1}) = \ln 1 = 0$

2. $\sinh^{-1}\left(\frac{3}{4}\right) = \ln\left(\frac{3}{4} + \sqrt{\frac{9}{16} + 1}\right) = \ln\left(\frac{3}{4} + \frac{5}{4}\right) = \ln 2$

3. $\sinh^{-1}\left(-\frac{4}{3}\right) = \ln\left(-\frac{4}{3} + \sqrt{\frac{16}{9} + 1}\right) = \ln\left(-\frac{4}{3} + \frac{5}{3}\right) = \ln \frac{1}{3}$

4. $\sinh^{-1}\left(-\frac{5}{12}\right) = \ln\left(-\frac{5}{12} + \sqrt{\frac{25}{144} + 1}\right) = \ln\left(-\frac{5}{12} + \frac{13}{12}\right) = \ln \frac{2}{3}$

5. $\cosh^{-1}\left(\frac{5}{4}\right) = \ln\left(\frac{5}{4} + \sqrt{\frac{25}{16} - 1}\right) = \ln\left(\frac{5}{4} + \frac{3}{4}\right) = \ln 2$

6. $\cosh^{-1}\left(\frac{5}{3}\right) = \ln\left(\frac{5}{3} + \sqrt{\frac{25}{9} - 1}\right) = \ln\left(\frac{5}{3} + \frac{4}{3}\right) = \ln 3$

7. $\cosh^{-1}\left(\frac{2}{\sqrt{3}}\right) = \ln\left(\frac{2}{\sqrt{3}} + \sqrt{\frac{4}{3} - 1}\right) = \ln\left(\frac{2}{\sqrt{3}} + \frac{1}{\sqrt{3}}\right) = \frac{1}{2} \ln 3$

8. $\cosh^{-1}\left(\frac{13}{12}\right) = \ln\left(\frac{13}{12} + \sqrt{\frac{169}{144} - 1}\right) = \ln\left(\frac{13}{12} + \frac{5}{12}\right) = \ln \frac{3}{2}$

9. $\tanh^{-1}\left(\frac{1}{2}\right) = \frac{1}{2} \ln\left(\frac{1 + \frac{1}{2}}{1 - \frac{1}{2}}\right) = \frac{1}{2} \ln 3$

10. $\coth^{-1}\left(\frac{5}{4}\right) = \frac{1}{2} \ln\left(\frac{\frac{5}{4} + 1}{\frac{5}{4} - 1}\right) = \frac{1}{2} \ln 9 = \ln 3$

11. $\coth^{-1}(-2) = \frac{1}{2} \ln\left(\frac{-2+1}{-2-1}\right) = \frac{1}{2} \ln \frac{1}{3} = -\frac{1}{2} \ln 3$

12. $\tanh^{-1}\left(-\frac{3}{5}\right) = \frac{1}{2} \ln\left(\frac{1 - \frac{3}{5}}{1 + \frac{3}{5}}\right) = \frac{1}{2} \ln \frac{1}{4} = \ln \frac{1}{2} = -\ln 2$

13. $\operatorname{csch}^{-1} \frac{5}{12} = \ln\left(\frac{12}{5} + \sqrt{1 + \frac{25}{144} \cdot \frac{12}{5}}\right) = \ln 5$

14. $\operatorname{sech}^{-1} \frac{4}{5} = \ln\left(\frac{5}{4} + \sqrt{1 - \frac{16}{15} \cdot \frac{5}{4}}\right) = \ln 2$

15. $\operatorname{csch}^{-1}\left(\frac{5}{12}\right) = \ln\left(\frac{12}{5} + \sqrt{1 + \frac{25}{144} \cdot \frac{12}{5}}\right) = \ln 5$

16. $\operatorname{csch}^{-1}\left(-\frac{1}{\sqrt{3}}\right) = \sinh^{-1}(-\sqrt{3}) = \ln(-\sqrt{3} + 2)$

17. $y = \sinh^{-1}(2x) \qquad \frac{dy}{dx} = \frac{2}{\sqrt{1 + 4x^2}}$

18. $y = \tanh^{-1}(\cos x) \Rightarrow \frac{dy}{dx} = \frac{1}{1 - \cos^2 x}(-\sin x) = -\frac{1}{\sin x} = -\csc x$

19. $y = \cosh^{-1}(\sec x) \qquad \frac{dy}{dx} = \frac{\sec x \tan x}{\sqrt{\sec^2 x - 1}} = \frac{\sec x \tan x}{\tan x} = \sec x$

20. $y = \coth^{-1}(\sec x) \Rightarrow \frac{dy}{dx} = \frac{1}{1 - \sec^2 x}(\sec x \tan x) = \frac{\sec x \tan x}{-\tan^2 x} = -\csc x$

21. $y = \operatorname{sech}^{-1}(\sin 2x) \qquad \frac{dy}{dx} = \frac{-2\cos 2x}{\sin 2x\sqrt{1 - \sin^2 2x}} = -2\csc 2x$

22. $y = \cosh^{-1}(x^2) \Rightarrow \frac{dy}{dx} = \frac{2x}{\sqrt{x^4 - 1}}$

23. $y = \sinh^{-1}\sqrt{x - 1} \qquad \frac{dy}{dx} = \frac{1}{\sqrt{1 + x - 1}} \cdot \frac{1}{2\sqrt{x - 1}} = \frac{1}{2\sqrt{x(x - 1)}}$

24. $y = \operatorname{csch}^{-1}(\tan x) \Rightarrow \frac{dy}{dx} = \frac{-\sec^2 x}{|\tan x|\sqrt{1 + \tan^2 x}} = -\frac{\sec x}{|\tan x|} = -|\csc x|$

25. $y = \sinh^{-1}\frac{1}{x} \qquad \frac{dy}{dx} = -\frac{1}{x^2}\frac{1}{\sqrt{1 + \frac{1}{x^2}}} = -\frac{1}{x^2} \cdot \frac{|x|}{\sqrt{x^2 + 1}} = -\frac{1}{|x|\sqrt{x^2 + 1}}$

26. $y = \cosh^{-1}\sqrt{x + 1} \Rightarrow \frac{dy}{dx} = \frac{1}{\sqrt{(x + 1) - 1}} \cdot \frac{1}{2\sqrt{x + 1}} = \frac{1}{2\sqrt{x^2 + x}}$

27. $y = \sinh^{-1}(\tan x) \qquad \frac{dy}{dx} = \frac{\sec^2 x}{\sqrt{1 + \tan^2 x}} = \sec x$

28. $y = \coth^{-1}(\csc x) \Rightarrow \frac{dy}{dx} = \frac{1}{1 - \csc^2 x}(-\csc x \cot x) = \frac{\csc x}{\cot x} = \sec x$

29. $y = \sqrt{1 + x^2} - \sinh^{-1}\frac{1}{x} = \sqrt{1 + x^2} + \operatorname{csch}^{-1} x$

$$\frac{dy}{dx} = \frac{2x}{2\sqrt{1 + x^2}} + \frac{1}{|x|\sqrt{x^2 + 1}}$$

30. $y = \frac{x}{2}\sqrt{x^2 - 1} - \frac{1}{2}\cosh^{-1} x$

$$\frac{dy}{dx} = \left(\frac{x}{2}\right)\left(\frac{x}{\sqrt{x^2 - 1}}\right) + \frac{\sqrt{x^2 - 1}}{2} - \frac{1}{2\sqrt{x^2 - 1}} = \frac{x^2 + x^2 - 1 - 1}{2\sqrt{x^2 - 1}} = \sqrt{x^2 - 1}$$

31. $y = 2\cosh^{-1}\left(\frac{x}{2}\right) + \frac{x}{2}\sqrt{x^2 - 4}$

$$\frac{dy}{dx} = \frac{2\cdot\frac{1}{2}}{\sqrt{\frac{x^2}{4} - 1}} + \frac{1}{2}\sqrt{x^2 - 4} + \left(\frac{x}{2}\right)\left(\frac{1}{2}\right)\left(\frac{2x}{\sqrt{x^2 - 4}}\right)$$

$$= \frac{2}{\sqrt{x^2 - 4}} + \frac{\sqrt{x^2 - 4}}{2} + \frac{x^2}{2\sqrt{x^2 - 4}} = \frac{x^2}{\sqrt{x^2 - 4}}$$

32. $y = x^2 \operatorname{sech}^{-1} x - \sqrt{1 - x^2}$

$$\frac{dy}{dx} = \frac{-x^2}{x\sqrt{1 - x^2}} + 2x \operatorname{sech}^{-1} x - \frac{(-2x)}{2\sqrt{1 - x^2}} = 2x \operatorname{sech}^{-1} x$$

33. $\displaystyle\int_0^{\frac{4}{3}} \frac{dx}{\sqrt{1 + 4x^2}} = \frac{1}{2}\sinh^{-1} 2x\Big]_0^{\frac{4}{3}} = \frac{1}{2}\left[\sinh^{-1}\frac{8}{3} - \sinh^{-1} 0\right]$

$$= \frac{1}{2}\left[\ln\left(\frac{8}{3} + \sqrt{\frac{64}{9} + 1}\right) - \ln(0 + 1)\right] = \frac{1}{2}\ln\left(\frac{8}{3} + \frac{\sqrt{73}}{3}\right)$$

34. $\displaystyle\int_0^{2\sqrt{3}} \frac{dx}{\sqrt{4 + x^2}} = \int_0^{2\sqrt{3}} \frac{\frac{1}{2}dx}{\sqrt{1 + \left(\frac{x}{2}\right)^2}} = \sinh^{-1}\frac{x}{2}\Big]_0^{2\sqrt{3}} = \ln(\sqrt{3} + 2)$

35. $\displaystyle\int_0^{.5} \frac{dx}{1 - x^2} = \tanh^{-1} x\Big]_0^{.5} = \frac{1}{2}\ln\left|\frac{\frac{3}{2}}{\frac{1}{2}}\right| - \frac{1}{2}\ln 1 = \frac{1}{2}\ln 3$

36. $\displaystyle\int_{\frac{5}{4}}^{2} \frac{dx}{1 - x^2} = \coth^{-1} x\Big]_{\frac{5}{4}}^{2} = \frac{1}{2}\ln 3 - \frac{1}{2}\ln 9 = -\frac{1}{2}\ln 3$

37. $\displaystyle\int_1^2 \frac{dx}{x\sqrt{4 + x^2}} = \int_1^2 \frac{dx}{2x\sqrt{1 + \left(\frac{x}{2}\right)^2}} = -\frac{1}{2}\operatorname{csch}^{-1}\frac{x}{2}\Big]_1^2$

$$= -\frac{1}{2}\left[\operatorname{csch}^{-1} 1 - \operatorname{csch}^{-1}\frac{1}{2}\right] = -\frac{1}{2}\left[\ln(1 + \sqrt{2}) - \ln\left(2 + \frac{\sqrt{\frac{5}{4}}}{\frac{1}{2}}\right)\right]$$

$$= -\frac{1}{2}[\ln(1 + \sqrt{2}) - \ln(2 + \sqrt{5})]$$

38. $\displaystyle\int_0^{\pi} \frac{\cos x\, dx}{\sqrt{1 + \sin^2 x}} = \sinh^{-1}(\sin x)\Big]_0^{\pi} = 0$

39. $$\int_{-1}^{1} \sinh^{-1} x\, dx = x \sinh^{-1} x \Big]_{-1}^{1} - \int_{-1}^{1} \frac{x}{\sqrt{1+x^2}}\, dx$$

$$= x \sinh^{-1} x - \sqrt{1+x^2} \Big]_{-1}^{1} = \sinh^{-1} 1 + \sinh^{-1}(-1) - \sqrt{2.} + \sqrt{2} = 0$$

40. $$\int_0^{\frac{1}{2}} \tanh^{-1} x\, dx = x\tanh^{-1} x \Big]_0^{\frac{1}{2}} - \int_0^{\frac{1}{2}} \frac{x\, dx}{1-x^2}$$

Let $u = \tanh^{-1} x \Rightarrow du = \dfrac{dx}{1-x^2}$; $dv = dx \Rightarrow v = x$

$$= x\tanh^{-1} x + \frac{1}{2} \ln(1-x^2) \Big]_0^{\frac{1}{2}} = \frac{3}{4} \ln 3 - \ln 2$$

41. $$\int \sqrt{x^2+1}\, dx = \int \frac{x^2+1}{\sqrt{x^2+1}}\, dx = \int \frac{x^2}{\sqrt{x^2+1}}\, dx + \int \frac{1}{\sqrt{x^2+1}}\, dx$$

$$\int \sqrt{x^2} + 1 = x\sqrt{x^2+1} - \int \sqrt{x^2+1}\, dx + \sinh^{-1} x + C$$

$$2 \int \sqrt{x^2+1}\, dx = x\sqrt{x^2+1} + \sinh^{-1} x + C$$

$$\int \sqrt{x^2+1}\, dx = \frac{x}{2}\sqrt{x^2+1} + \frac{1}{2} \sinh^{-1} x + C$$

42. $$\int (x^2+1)^{3/2}\, dx = \int (\tan^2 u + 1)^{3/2} \sec^2 u\, du = \int \sec^5 u\ du$$

Let $x = \tan u \Rightarrow dx = \sec^2 u\, du$. (We now use Formula 92.)

$$= \frac{\sec^3 u \tan u}{4} + \frac{3}{4} \int \sec^3 u\, du = \frac{\sec^3 u \tan u}{4} + \frac{3}{4}\left(\frac{\sec u \tan u}{2} + \frac{1}{2} \int \sec x\, dx\right)$$

$$= \frac{\sec^3 u \tan u}{4} + \frac{3}{4}\left(\frac{\sec u \tan u}{2}\right) + \frac{3}{8} \ln|\sec u + \tan u| + C$$

$$= \frac{1}{4} x (x^2+1)^{3/2} + \frac{3}{8} x\sqrt{x^2+1} + \frac{3}{8} \ln|\sqrt{x^2+1} + x| + C$$

43. $$\int_2^5 4x \coth^{-1} x\, dx = 2x^2 \coth^{-1} x \Big]_2^5 - \int_2^5 \frac{2x^2}{1-x^2}\, dx$$

$$= 2x^2 \coth^{-1} x \Big]_2^5 + \int_2^5 \left(2 - \frac{2}{1-x^2}\right) dx$$

$$= (2x^2 - 2) \coth^{-1} x + 2x \Big]_2^5 = 24 \ln \frac{3}{2} - 3 \ln 3 + 6$$

44. $\int_{\frac{3}{5}}^{\frac{4}{5}} 2x \operatorname{sech}^{-1}x\,dx = x^2 \operatorname{sech}^{-1}x \Big]_{\frac{3}{5}}^{\frac{4}{5}} + \int_{\frac{3}{5}}^{\frac{4}{5}} \frac{x\,dx}{\sqrt{1-x^2}}$

Let $u = \operatorname{sech}^{-1}x \Rightarrow du = \frac{-1}{x\sqrt{1-x^2}}$; $dv = 2x\,dx \Rightarrow v = x^2$

$= x^2 \operatorname{sech}^{-1}x - \sqrt{1-x^2}\Big]_{\frac{3}{5}}^{\frac{4}{5}} = \frac{16}{25}\ln 2 - \frac{9}{25}\ln 3 + \frac{1}{5}$

45. $\int \frac{dx}{\sqrt{x^2-4x+3}} = \int \frac{dx}{\sqrt{(x-2)^2-1}} = \cosh^{-1}(x-2) + C$, if $x > 3$

$= \ln(x - 2 + \sqrt{x^2 - 4x + 3}) + C$

46. $\int \frac{(x-1)\,dx}{\sqrt{x^2-4x+3}} = \int \frac{(x-2)+1}{\sqrt{(x-2)^2-1}}\,dx = \int \frac{(x-2)\,dx}{\sqrt{(x-2)^2-1}} + \int \frac{dx}{\sqrt{(x-2)^2-1}}$

$= \sqrt{(x-2)^2-1} + \cosh^{-1}(x-2) + C$

$= \sqrt{(x-2)^2-1} + \ln|x-2+\sqrt{(x-2)^2-1}| + C$

47. $\int \frac{du}{\sqrt{u^2-1}} = \int \frac{\sec\theta\tan\theta\,d\theta}{\tan\theta} = \int \sec\theta\,d\theta = \ln|\sec\theta + \tan\theta|$

$= \ln|u^2 + \sqrt{u^2-1}| + C$

48. $\int \frac{du}{u\sqrt{u^2-1}} = \int \frac{\sec x\tan x\,dx}{\sec x\tan x} = x + C = \sec^{-1}u + C$

Let $u = \sec x \Rightarrow du = \sec x\tan x\,dx$

49. $\int \frac{du}{u\sqrt{u^2-1}} = \int \frac{\sec^2\theta\,d\theta}{\tan\theta\sec\theta} = \int \csc\theta\,d\theta = \ln|\csc\theta - \cot\theta| + C$

$= \ln\left|\frac{\sqrt{u^2+1}}{u} - \frac{1}{u}\right| + C$

50. $\int \frac{du}{1-u^2} = \frac{1}{2}\int \frac{du}{1+u} + \frac{1}{2}\int \frac{du}{1-u} = \frac{1}{2}\ln\left|\frac{1+u}{1-u}\right| + C$

51. Use Formula # 42 in the textbook. Then

$$\int \frac{\sqrt{x^2-25}}{x}\,dx = \sqrt{x^2-25} - 5\sec^{-1}\left|\frac{x}{5}\right| + C$$

52. Use Formula # 42 in the textbook. Then

$$\int \frac{\sqrt{x^2 - 25}}{x^2}\, dx = \cosh^{-1}\frac{x}{5} - \frac{\sqrt{x^2 - 25}}{x} + C$$

53. Use Formula # 44 in the textbook. Then

$$\int \frac{x^2}{\sqrt{x^2 - 25}}\, dx = \frac{25}{2}\cosh^{-1}\frac{x}{5} + \frac{x}{2}\sqrt{x^2 - 25} + C$$

54. Use Formula # 22 in the textbook. Then

$$\int x^2\sqrt{x^2 + 3}\, dx = \frac{x(3 + 2x^2)\sqrt{3 + x^2}}{8} - \frac{9}{8}\sinh^{-1}\frac{x}{\sqrt{3}} + C$$

55. Use Formula #37 in the textbook. Then

$$\int \sqrt{x^2 - 4}\, dx = \frac{x}{2}\sqrt{x^2 - 4} - 2\cosh^{-1}\frac{x}{2} + C$$

56. Use Formula # 41 in the textbook. Then

$$\int x^2\sqrt{x^2 - 4}\, dx = \frac{x}{8}(2x^2 - 4)\sqrt{x^2 - 4} - 2\cosh^{-1}\frac{x}{2} + C$$

57. $$s = \int_0^1 \sqrt{1 + 4x^2}\, dx = \int_0^1 2\sqrt{\frac{1}{4} + x^2}\, dx = 2\left(\frac{x}{2}\sqrt{\frac{1}{4} + x^2} + \frac{\frac{1}{4}}{2}\sinh^{-1}\frac{x}{\frac{1}{2}}\right)_0^1$$

$$= \frac{\sqrt{5}}{2} + \frac{1}{4}\ln(2 + \sqrt{5})$$

58. $$S = 2\pi\int_0^1 x^2\sqrt{1 + 4x^2}\, dx = 2\pi\int_0^2 \left(\frac{u^2}{4}\right)\sqrt{1 + u^2}\left(\frac{1}{2}du\right)$$

Let $u = 2x \Rightarrow du = 2\, dx$; $x = 0 \Rightarrow u = 0$, $x = 1 \Rightarrow u = 2$

$$= \frac{\pi}{4}\int_0^2 u^2\sqrt{1 + u^2}\, du = \frac{\pi}{4}\left[\frac{u(1 + 2u^2)\sqrt{1 + u^2}}{8} - \frac{1}{8}\sinh^{-1}u\right]_0^2$$

$$= \frac{\pi}{4}\left[\frac{9\sqrt{5}}{4} - \frac{\sinh^{-1}2}{8}\right] = \frac{\pi}{4}\left[\frac{9\sqrt{5}}{4} - \frac{1}{8}\ln(2 + \sqrt{5})\right]$$

59. $$\int_{\frac{3}{4}}^1 \sqrt{1 + \left(\frac{1}{x}\right)^2}\, dx = \int_{\frac{3}{4}}^1 \frac{\sqrt{x^2 + 1}}{x}\, dx = \sqrt{x^2 + 1} - \sinh^{-1}\left|\frac{1}{x}\right|\Bigg]_{\frac{3}{4}}^1$$

$$= \sqrt{2} - \ln(1 + \sqrt{2}) - \frac{5}{4} + \ln 3$$

60. (a) The slope of the tangent to the curve at the point (x, (f(x))

is $\frac{dy}{dx} = -\frac{\sqrt{a^2 - x^2}}{x}$.

(b) $y = \int -\frac{\sqrt{a^2 - x^2}}{x}\, dx = \sqrt{a^2 - x^2} - \ln\left|\frac{a + \sqrt{a^2 - x^2}}{x}\right| + C$

$0 = -\ln\frac{a}{a} + C \Rightarrow C = 0.$ $\therefore$ $y = \sqrt{a^2 - x^2} - \ln\left|\frac{a + \sqrt{a^2 - x^2}}{x}\right|$

61. Solve $x\frac{d^2y}{dx^2} = \sqrt{1 + \left(\frac{dy}{dx}\right)^2}$, $y = 0$, $\frac{dy}{dx} = 0$ when $x = 1$.

Let $\frac{dy}{dx} = p$, $\frac{dp}{dx} = \frac{d^2y}{dx^2}$. Then $x\frac{dp}{dx} = \sqrt{1 + p^2} \Rightarrow \frac{dp}{\sqrt{1 + p^2}} = \frac{dx}{x}$ or

$\sinh^{-1}p = \ln|x| + C$. $p = o$ when $x = 1$, so $C = 0$ and thus $p = \sinh(\ln x)$.

$y = \int \sinh(\ln x)\, dx = \int \frac{e^{\ln x} - e^{-\ln x}}{2}\, dx = \frac{1}{2}\int\left(x - \frac{1}{x}\right) dx.$

$y = \frac{x^2}{4} - \frac{1}{2}\ln|x| + C$. Since $0 = \frac{1}{4} - 0$, $C = -\frac{1}{4}$. Therefore, $y = \frac{x^2}{4} - \frac{1}{2}\ln|x|$.

62. $m\left(\frac{dv}{dt}\right) = mg - kv^2 \Rightarrow \int \frac{dv}{g - \frac{k}{m}v^2} = \int dt$. Let $u = \sqrt{\frac{k}{mg}}\, v$. Then

$$\int \frac{dv}{g - \frac{k}{m}v^2} = \frac{1}{g}\int \frac{dv}{1 - \left(\sqrt{\frac{k}{mg}}\right)^2 v^2} = \frac{1}{g}\sqrt{\frac{mg}{k}}\int \frac{du}{1 - u^2} = \sqrt{\frac{m}{kg}}\tanh^{-1}\left(\sqrt{\frac{k}{mg}}\, v\right)$$

$$\therefore\ \tanh^{-1}\left(\sqrt{\frac{k}{mg}}\, v\right) = \sqrt{\frac{kg}{m}}\, t \Rightarrow v = \sqrt{\frac{mg}{k}}\tanh\left(\sqrt{\frac{kg}{m}}\, t\right).$$

$$\lim_{t\to\infty} \sqrt{\frac{mg}{k}}\tanh\left(\sqrt{\frac{kg}{m}}\, t\right) = \sqrt{\frac{mg}{k}}.$$

63. Solve $x = \sinh y = \frac{1}{2}(e^y - e^{-y})$ for y. Multiply both sides of $2x = e^y - e^{-y}$ by e^y to form an equation quadratic in e^y.

Then, $e^{2y} - 2xe^y - 1 = 0 \Leftrightarrow y = \frac{-(-2x) \pm \sqrt{4x^2 + 4}}{2}$

$= x + \sqrt{x^2 + 1}$ (since we need the positive root). Therefore, $y = \ln(x + \sqrt{x^2 + 1})$ or $\sinh^{-1} x = x + \sqrt{x^2 + 1}$.

64. $y = \cosh^{-1} x \Rightarrow x = \cosh y = \frac{1}{2}(e^y + e^{-y})$. Let $w = e^y$.

$$x = \left(w + \frac{1}{w}\right) \Rightarrow w^2 - 2wx + 0 = 0 \Rightarrow w = \frac{2x \pm \sqrt{4x^2 - 4}}{2} = -x \pm \sqrt{x^2 - 1}.$$

Choose the positive root, so that $y = \ln w = \ln \left| x + \sqrt{x^2 - 1} \right|$, $|x| \geq 1$.

65. Prove: $\frac{d}{dx}(\sinh^{-1} u) = \frac{1}{\sqrt{1+u^2}} \frac{du}{dx}$.

If $\sinh y = x$ then $\frac{d}{dx}\sinh y = 1$ or $\cosh y \frac{dy}{dx} = 1$. Therefore,
$\frac{dy}{dx} = \frac{1}{\cosh y} = \frac{1}{\sqrt{1 + \sinh^2 y}} = \frac{1}{\sqrt{1 + x^2}}$. Applying the Chain Rule,
$\frac{dy}{dx} = \frac{dy}{du} \cdot \frac{du}{dx}$, to this equation gives the desired result.

66. Prove: $\frac{d}{dx}(\tanh^{-1} u) = \frac{1}{1-u^2} \cdot \frac{du}{dx}$, $|u| < 1$

If $\tanh y = x$, then $\frac{d}{dx}(\tanh y) = 1 \Rightarrow \operatorname{sech}^2 y \frac{dy}{dx} = 1$

$\frac{dy}{dx} = \frac{1}{\operatorname{sech}^2 y} = \frac{1}{\sqrt{1 - \tanh^2 y}} = \frac{1}{1 - x^2}$. Since $\frac{dy}{dx} = \frac{dy}{du} \cdot \frac{du}{dx}$,
$\frac{d}{dx}(\tanh^{-1} u) = \frac{1}{\sqrt{1 - u^2}} \cdot \frac{du}{dx}$.

9.M MISCELLANEOUS

1. Prove: $\cosh x\, 2x = \cosh^2 x + \sinh^2 x$

$\cosh^2 x + \sinh^2 x = \frac{1}{2}(e^x + e^{-x})^2 + \frac{1}{2}(e^x + e^{-x})^2$

$= \frac{1}{2}(e^{2x} + 2 + e^{-2x}) + \frac{1}{2}(e^{2x} - 2 + e^{-2x}) = \frac{1}{2}(e^{2x} + e^{-2x}) = \cosh 2x$.

2. $\tanh x = \frac{\sinh 2x}{1 + \cosh 2x} = \frac{2 \sinh x \cosh x}{2 \cosh^2 x} = \frac{\sinh x}{\cosh x} = \tanh x$

3. $\lim_{x \to \infty} (\cosh x - \sinh x) = \lim_{x \to \infty} \left(\frac{1}{2}(e^x + e^{-x}) - \frac{1}{2}(e^x + e^{-x}) \right) = \lim_{x \to \infty} e^{-x} = 0$.

4. $\cosh x = \frac{5}{4} \Rightarrow \sinh^2 x = \left(\frac{5}{4}\right)^2 - 1 = \frac{9}{16} \Rightarrow \sinh x = \pm \frac{3}{4}$, so $\tanh x = \pm \frac{3}{5}$.

5. If $\operatorname{csch} x = -\frac{9}{40}$, then $\sinh x = -\frac{40}{9}$ and $\cosh^2 x = \sqrt{1 + \frac{1600}{81}} = \frac{41}{9}$.

$\tanh x = \frac{\sinh x}{\cosh x} = -\frac{40}{41}$.

6. $\frac{d}{dx}(\tanh^{-1} x) = \frac{1}{1 - x^2} > 0$ for $|x| < 1 \Rightarrow \tanh^{-1} x$ is a strictly increasing function, so $\tanh x > \frac{5}{13} \Rightarrow \tanh^{-1}(\tanh x) > \tanh^{-1}\frac{5}{13}$ or

$x > \frac{1}{2}\ln\frac{1 + \frac{5}{13}}{1 - \frac{5}{13}} = \frac{1}{2}\ln\frac{9}{4} \approx 0.40$. $\frac{d}{dx}\sinh x = \cosh x \Rightarrow \sinh x$ is also increasing, so $x > 0.40 \Rightarrow \sinh x > \sinh 0.40 \approx 0.41$.

$\frac{d}{dx}\operatorname{sech} x = -\operatorname{sech}x \tanh x < 0$ for $x > 0$ so sech x is decreasing.

If $x > 0.4$, $\operatorname{sech} x < \operatorname{sech} 0.4 \approx 0.925 < 0.95$

7. Since the radius = 1, $RP^2 + PQ^2 = RQ^2 = 1$. RP is equal to tanh x, so $\tanh^2 x + PQ^2 = 1$, $PQ = \sqrt{1 - \tanh^2 x} = \operatorname{sech} x$.

8. $x^2 + y^2 = a^2$ and $x = a \tanh t \Rightarrow a^2 \tanh^2 t + y^2 = a^2 \Rightarrow y^2 = a^2(1 - \tanh^2 t)$

$\therefore y^2 = a^2 \operatorname{sech}^2 t$ so $y = a \operatorname{sech} t$.

9. $y = \tanh\left(\frac{1}{2}\ln x\right) = \tanh(\ln\sqrt{x}) = \frac{e^{\ln\sqrt{x}} - e^{-\ln\sqrt{x}}}{e^{\ln\sqrt{x}} + e^{\ln\sqrt{x}}} = \frac{\sqrt{x} - \frac{1}{\sqrt{x}}}{\sqrt{x} + \frac{1}{\sqrt{x}}} = \frac{x - 1}{x + 1}$.

Vertical asymptote is at $x = -1$.

As the $\lim_{x\to\infty} \frac{x - 1}{x + 1} = 1$, the horizontal asymptote is $y = 1$.

10. (a) $x = a\cos kt + b\sin kt \Rightarrow v = \frac{dx}{dt} = -ak\sin kt + bk\cos kt$ and

$a = \frac{d^2x}{dt^2} = -ak^2\cos kt - bk^2\sin kt = -k^2 x$. The acceleration is opposite in sign to the position, hence directed towards the origin.

(b) $x = a\cosh kt + b\sinh kt \Rightarrow v = \frac{dx}{dt} = ak\sinh kt + bk\cosh kt$ and

$a = \frac{d^2x}{dt^2} = ak^2\cosh t + bk^2\sinh t = k^2 x$. The acceleration has the same sign as x, hence is directed away from the origin.

11. $y = \cosh 2x$ $\quad$ $y = \sinh 2x$ $\quad$ $y = \cos 2x$

$\frac{dy}{dx} = 2 \sinh 2x$ $\quad$ $\frac{dy}{dx} = 2 \cosh 2x$ $\quad$ $\frac{dy}{dx} = -2 \sin 2x$

$\frac{d^2y}{dx^2} = 4 \cosh 2x$ $\quad$ $\frac{d^2y}{dx^2} = 4 \sinh 2x$ $\quad$ $\frac{d^2y}{dx^2} = -4 \cos 2x$

$\frac{dy^3}{dx^3} = 8 \sinh 2x$ $\quad$ $\frac{dy^3}{dx^3} = 8 \cosh 2x$ $\quad$ $\frac{dy^3}{dx^3} = 8 \sin 2x$

$\frac{dy^4}{dx^4} = 16 \cosh 2x$ $\quad$ $\frac{dy^4}{dx^4} = 16 \sinh 2x$ $\quad$ $\frac{dy^4}{dx^4} = 16 \cos 2x$

$\frac{dy^4}{dx^4} = y$ $\quad$ $\frac{dy^4}{dx^4} = y$ $\quad$ $\frac{dy^4}{dx^4} = y$

12. $y = \frac{1}{2} \ln \frac{1 + \tan x}{1 - \tanh x} = \tanh^{-1} (\tanh x) = x.$

13. If $y = \sinh^2 3x$, then $\frac{dy}{dx} = 6 \sinh 3x \cosh 3x$

14. $\tan x = \tanh^2 x \Rightarrow \sec^2 x = 2 \tanh y \operatorname{sech}^2 y \frac{dy}{dx} \Rightarrow \frac{dy}{dx} = \frac{\sec^2 x}{2 \tanh y \operatorname{sech}^2 y}.$

15. $\sin^{-1} x = \operatorname{sech} y$

$$\frac{1}{\sqrt{1 - x^2}} = -\operatorname{sech} y \tanh y \frac{dy}{dx} \text{ or } \frac{dy}{dx} = \frac{-1}{\operatorname{sech} y \tanh y \sqrt{1 - x^2}}$$

16. $\sinh y = \sec x \Rightarrow \cosh y \frac{dy}{dx} = \sec x \tan x \Rightarrow \frac{dy}{dx} = \sec x \operatorname{sech} y \tan x$

17. $\tan^{-1} y = \tanh^{-1} x$

$$\frac{1}{1 + y^2} \frac{dy}{dx} = \frac{1}{1 - x^2} \text{ or } \frac{dy}{dx} = \frac{1 + y^2}{1 - x^2} = \frac{1 + \tan^2(\tanh^{-1} x)}{1 - x^2} = \frac{\sec^2(\tanh^{-1} x)}{1 - x^2}$$

18. $y = \tanh (\ln x) \Rightarrow \frac{dy}{dx} = \frac{\operatorname{sech}^2 (\ln x)}{x} = \frac{4x}{(x^2 + 1)^2}$

19. $x = \cosh (\ln y) = \frac{e^{\ln y} + e^{-\ln y}}{2} = \frac{y + \frac{1}{y}}{2} = \frac{y^2 + 1}{2y}$

$$1 = \frac{(2y)^2 \frac{dy}{dx} - 2 (y^2 + 1) \frac{dy}{dx}}{4y^2} \text{ or } \frac{dy}{dx} = \frac{2y^2}{y^2 - 1}.$$

20. $y = \sinh (\tan^{-1} e^{3x}) \Rightarrow \frac{dy}{dx} = \cosh (\tan^{-1} e^{3x}) \left[\frac{3e^x}{1 - e^{6x}} \right].$

21. If $y = \sinh^{-1}(\tan x)$ then $\dfrac{dy}{dx} = \dfrac{\sec^2 x}{\sqrt{1+\tan^2 x}} = \sec x$.

22. $y^2 + x\cosh y + \sinh^2 x = 50 \Rightarrow$

$$2y\frac{dy}{dx} + x\sinh y\,\frac{dy}{dx} + \cosh y + 2\sinh x\cosh x = 0$$

$$\frac{dy}{dx} = -\frac{\sinh 2x + \cosh y}{2y + x\sinh y}$$

23. $$\int_{-\ln 2}^{0} \frac{d\theta}{\sinh\theta + \cosh\theta} = \int_{-\ln 2}^{0} \frac{d\theta}{\sinh\theta + \cosh\theta}\cdot\frac{\cosh\theta - \sinh\theta}{\cosh\theta - \sinh\theta}$$

$$= \int_{-\ln 2}^{0} (\cosh\theta - \sinh\theta)\,d\theta = \sinh\theta - \cosh\theta\Big]_{-\ln 2}^{0}$$

$$= -1 - \left[\frac{e^{\ln 2} + e^{\ln 2}}{2}\right] + \left[\frac{e^{\ln 2} - e^{\ln 2}}{2}\right] = 1$$

24. $$\int_{-\ln 2}^{\ln 2} \frac{\cosh\theta\,d\theta}{\sinh\theta + \cosh\theta} = \frac{1}{2}\int_{-\ln 2}^{\ln 2} \frac{e^{\theta} + e^{-\theta}}{e^{\theta}}\,d\theta$$

$$= \frac{1}{2}\int_{-\ln 2}^{\ln 2} (1 + e^{-2\theta})\,d\theta = \frac{1}{2}\left[\theta - \frac{1}{2}e^{-2\theta}\right]_{-\ln 2}^{\ln 2} = \ln 2 + \frac{15}{16}$$

25. $$\int_{0}^{\frac{\ln 3}{2}} \sinh^3 x\,dx = \int_{0}^{\frac{\ln 3}{2}} (\cosh^2 x - 1)\sinh x\,dx = \frac{1}{3}\cosh^3 x - \cosh x\Big]_{0}^{\frac{\ln 3}{2}}$$

$$= \frac{1}{3}\left(\frac{e^{\frac{\ln 3}{2}} + e^{-\frac{\ln 3}{2}}}{2}\right)^3 - \frac{e^{\frac{\ln 3}{2}} + e^{-\frac{\ln 3}{2}}}{2} + \frac{2}{3}$$

$$= \frac{1}{24}\left(\frac{4}{3}\sqrt{3}\right)^3 - \frac{2}{3}\sqrt{3} + \frac{2}{3} = \frac{-10\sqrt{3} + 18}{27}.$$

26. $$\int_{-\ln 2}^{0} e^{x}\sinh 2x\,dx = \int_{-\ln 2}^{0} e^{x}\left(\frac{e^{2x} - e^{-2x}}{2}\right)dx$$

$$= \frac{1}{2}\int_{-\ln 2}^{0} (e^{3x} - e^{-x})\,dx = \frac{1}{6}e^{3x} + \frac{1}{2}e^{-x}\Big]_{-\ln 2}^{0} = -\frac{17}{48}$$

27. $$\int_{1}^{\sqrt{2}} \frac{e^{2x} - 1}{e^{2x} + 1}\,dx = \int_{1}^{\sqrt{2}} \frac{e^{2x} - 1}{e^{2x} + 1}\cdot\frac{e^{-x}}{e^{-x}}\,dx = \int_{1}^{\sqrt{2}} \frac{\sinh x}{\cosh x}\,dx = \int_{1}^{\sqrt{2}} \tanh x\,dx$$

$$= \ln|\cosh x|\Big]_{1}^{\sqrt{2}} = \ln|\cosh\sqrt{2} - \cosh 1|.$$

28. $$\int_{0}^{1} \frac{dx}{4 - x^2} = \frac{1}{4}\int_{0}^{1} \frac{dx}{1 - \frac{x^2}{4}} = \frac{1}{2}\tanh^{-1}\frac{x}{2}\Big]_{0}^{1} = \frac{1}{4}\ln 3$$

29. $\int_0^1 \frac{dx}{\sqrt{x} - x\sqrt{x}} = \lim_{t\to 0^+} \int_t^k \frac{dx}{\sqrt{x} - x\sqrt{x}} + \lim_{t\to 1^-} \int_k^t \frac{dx}{\sqrt{x} - x\sqrt{x}}$

$$\lim_{t\to 1^-} \int_k^t \frac{dx}{\sqrt{x} - x\sqrt{x}} = \lim_{t\to 1^-} \int_k^t \frac{2du}{1-u^2} = \lim_{t\to 1^-} (\tanh^{-1} u)\Big]_k^t = \infty.$$

Since both parts must converge for the integral to converge, $\int_0^1 \frac{dx}{\sqrt{x} - x\sqrt{x}}$ diverges.

30. $\int_0^{\ln\frac{3}{4}} \frac{e^t dt}{\sqrt{2+e^{2t}}} = \int_0^{\ln\frac{3}{4}} \frac{\frac{1}{\sqrt{2}} e^t\, dt}{\sqrt{1 + \frac{e^{2t}}{2}}} = \sinh^{-1} \frac{e^t}{\sqrt{2}}\Big]_0^{\ln\frac{3}{4}} = \sinh^{-1} \frac{3}{4\sqrt{2}} - \sinh^{-1} \frac{1}{\sqrt{2}}$

31. $\int_{\frac{\pi}{3}}^{\frac{\pi}{2}} \frac{\sin x\, dx}{1 - \cos^2 x} = -\tanh^{-1} (\cos x)\Big]_{\frac{\pi}{3}}^{\frac{\pi}{2}} = -\tanh^{-1} 0 + \tanh^{-1}\left(\frac{1}{2}\right) = \ln\sqrt{3}.$

32. $\int_{\frac{\pi}{4}}^{\frac{\pi}{3}} \frac{\sec^2 \theta\, d\theta}{\sqrt{\tan^2\theta - 1}} = \cosh^{-1}(\tan\theta)\Big]_{\frac{\pi}{4}}^{\frac{\pi}{3}} = \cosh^{-1}\sqrt{3} = \cosh^{-1} 1 = \ln(\sqrt{3} + \sqrt{2})$

33. $\lim_{x\to\infty} (\cosh^{-1} x - \ln x) = \lim_{x\to\infty} \left[\left(x + \sqrt{x^2 - 1}\right) - \ln x\right]$

$$= \lim_{x\to\infty} \ln \left|\frac{x + \sqrt{x^2-1}}{x}\right| = \lim_{x\to\infty} \left|1 + \frac{\sqrt{x^2-1}}{x}\right| = \ln 2$$

34. $\lim_{x\to\infty} \int_1^x \left(\frac{1}{\sqrt{1+t^2}} - \frac{1}{t}\right) dt = \lim_{x\to\infty} [\sinh^{-1} t - \ln t\Big]_1^x$

$$= \lim_{x\to\infty} \Big[\sinh^{-1} x - \ln x - \ln(1+\sqrt{2}) = \lim_{x\to\infty} \ln\left(\frac{x + \sqrt{x^2+1}}{x}\right) - \ln(1+\sqrt{2})$$

$$= \lim_{x\to\infty} \ln\left(1 + \sqrt{1 + \frac{1}{x^2}}\right) - \ln(1+\sqrt{2}) = \ln\left(\frac{2}{1+\sqrt{2}}\right)$$

CHAPTER 10

POLAR COORDINATES

10.1 THE POLAR COORDINATE SYSTEM

1. The following groups represent the same points:
   a,c; b,d; e,j,k; f,i,l; m,o; n,p

2. (a) $x = r\cos\theta = 3\cos 0 = 3$ $\quad y = r\sin\theta = 3\sin 0 = 0$
   (b) $x = -3\cos 0 = -3$ $\quad y = 0\sin 0 = 0$
   (c) $x = -3\cos\pi = 3$ $\quad y = -3\sin\pi = 0$
   (d) $x = -3\cos 2\pi = -3$ $\quad y = -3\sin 2\pi = 0$
   (e) $x = 2\cos\frac{2\pi}{3} = -1$ $\quad y = 2\sin\frac{2\pi}{3} = \sqrt{3}$
   (f) $x = 2\cos(-\frac{\pi}{3}) = 1$ $\quad y = 2\sin(-\frac{\pi}{3}) = -\sqrt{3}$
   (g) $x = 2\cos(\frac{7\pi}{3}) = 1$ $\quad y = 2\sin(\frac{7\pi}{3}) = \sqrt{3}$
   (h) $x = -2\cos\frac{\pi}{3} = -1$ $\quad y = -2\sin\frac{\pi}{3} = -\sqrt{3}$
   (i) $x = 2\cos(-\frac{\pi}{3}) = 1$ $\quad y = 2\sin(-\frac{\pi}{3}) = -\sqrt{3}$
   (j) $x = 2\cos(-\frac{4\pi}{3}) = -1$ $\quad y = 2\sin(-\frac{4\pi}{3}) = \sqrt{3}$
   (k) $x = -2\cos(-\frac{\pi}{3}) = -1$ $\quad y = 2\sin(-\frac{\pi}{3}) = \sqrt{3}$
   (l) $x = -2\cos\frac{2\pi}{3} = 1$ $\quad y = 2\sin\frac{2\pi}{3} = -\sqrt{3}$

3. (a) $(2, \frac{\pi}{2} + 2k\pi)$ or $(-2, -\frac{\pi}{2} + 2k\pi)$, k an integer.
   (b) $(2, 2k\pi)$ or $(-2, (2k+1)\pi)$, k an integer.
   (c) $(-2, \frac{\pi}{2} + 2k\pi)$ or $(2, \frac{3\pi}{2} + 2k\pi)$, k an integer.
   (d) $(2, (2k+1)\pi)$ or $(-2, 2k\pi)$, k an integer.

4. (a) $(3, \frac{\pi}{4} + 2k\pi)$ or $(-3, -\frac{3\pi}{4} + 2k\pi)$, k an integer.
   (b) $(-3, \frac{\pi}{4} + 2k\pi)$ or $(3, \frac{5\pi}{4} + 2k\pi)$, k an integer.
   (c) $(3, -\frac{\pi}{4} + 2k\pi)$ or $(-3, \frac{3\pi}{4} + 2k\pi)$, k an integer.
   (d) $(-3, -\frac{\pi}{4} + 2k\pi)$ or $(3, \frac{3\pi}{4} + 2k\pi)$, k an integer.

5. (a) $x = r\cos\theta = \sqrt{2}\cos\frac{\pi}{4} = 1$ $\quad y = r\sin\theta = \sqrt{2}\sin\frac{\pi}{4} = 1$
   (b) $x = 1\cos 0 = 1$ $\quad y = 1\sin 0 = 0$
   (c) $r = 0 \Rightarrow x = 0$ and $y = 0$

(d) $x = -\sqrt{2}\cos\frac{\pi}{4} = -1$ $\qquad y = -\sqrt{2}\sin\frac{\pi}{4} = -1$

(e) $x = -3\cos\frac{5\pi}{6} = \frac{3\sqrt{3}}{2}$ $\qquad y = -3\sin\frac{5\pi}{6} = -\frac{3}{2}$

(f) $x = 5\cos(\tan^{-1}\frac{4}{3}) = 5(\frac{3}{5}) = 3$ $\qquad y = 5\sin(\tan^{-1}\frac{4}{3}) = 5(\frac{4}{5})$ 4

(g) $x = -1\cos 7\pi = 1$ $\qquad y = -1\sin 7\pi = 0$

(h) $x = 2\sqrt{3}\cos\frac{2\pi}{3} = -\sqrt{3}$ $\qquad y = 2\sqrt{3}\sin\frac{2\pi}{3} = 3$

6. $(0,\theta)$, for any real θ.

7. $r = 2$ 8. $0 \le r \le 2$

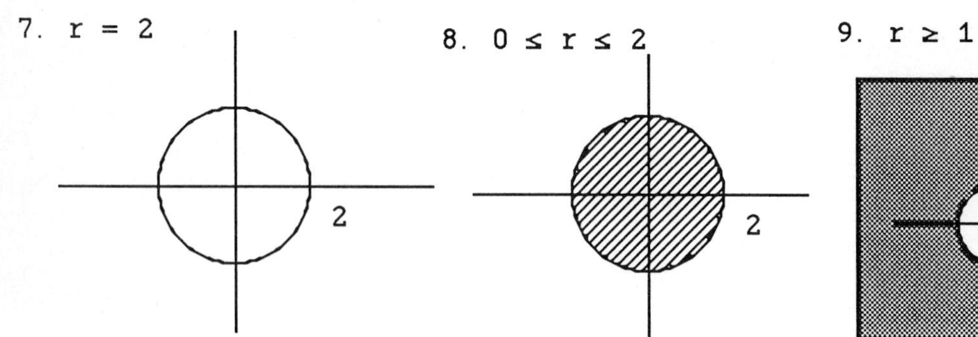

9. $r \ge 1$

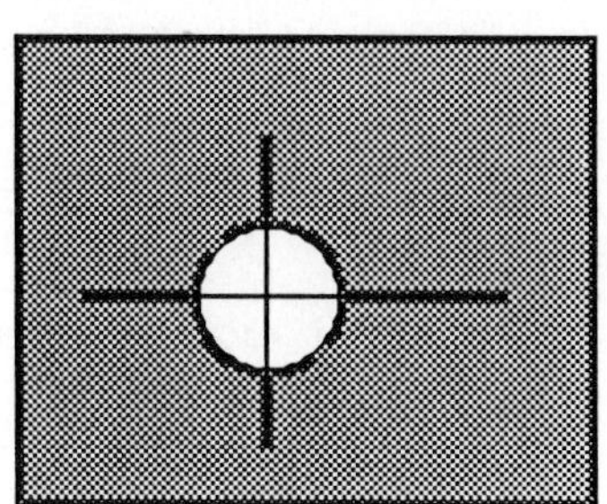

11. $0 \le \theta \le \frac{\pi}{6}$, $r \ge 0$ 12. $\theta = \frac{2\pi}{3}$, $r \le -2$ 13. $\theta = \frac{\pi}{3}$, $-1 \le r \le 3$

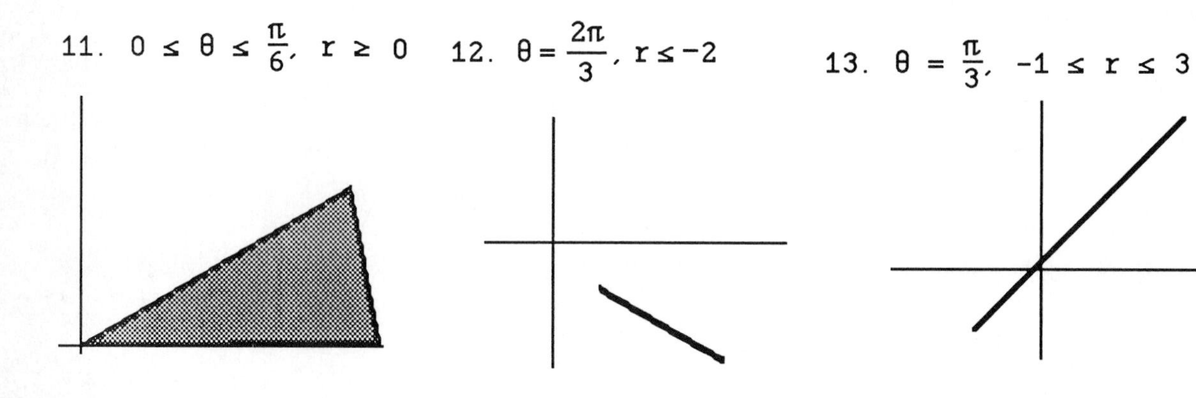

14. $\theta = \frac{11\pi}{4}$, $r \ge -1$ 15. $\theta = \frac{\pi}{2}$, $r \ge 0$ 16. $\theta = \frac{\pi}{2}$, $r \le 0$

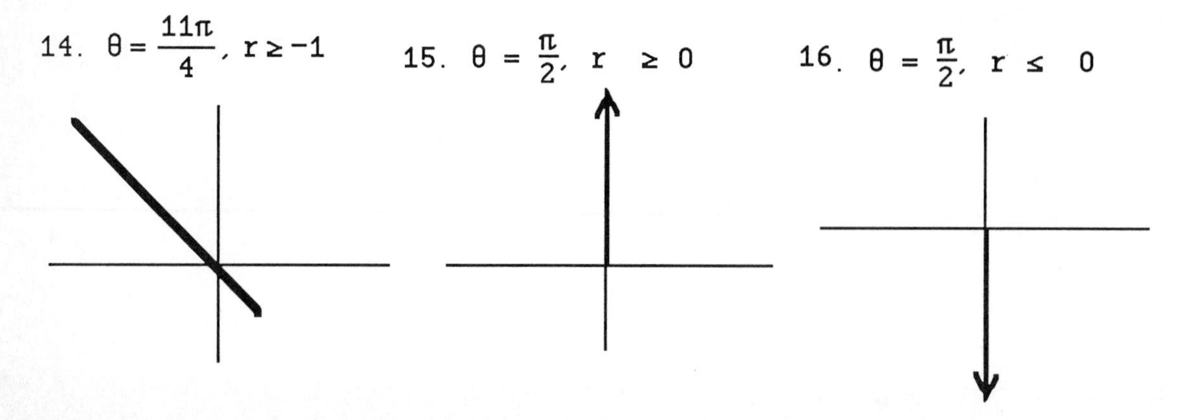

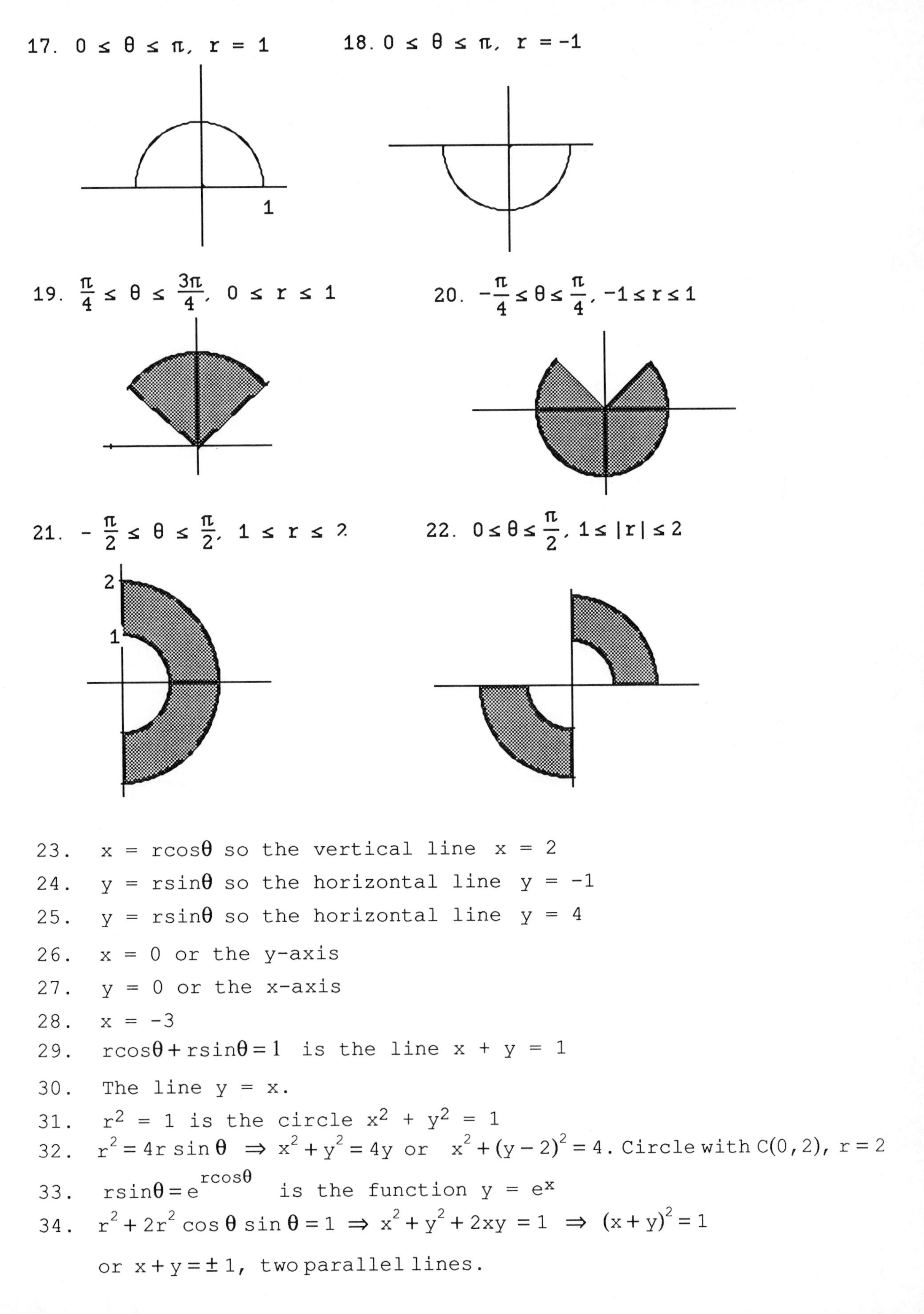

17. $0 \le \theta \le \pi$, $r = 1$

18. $0 \le \theta \le \pi$, $r = -1$

19. $\frac{\pi}{4} \le \theta \le \frac{3\pi}{4}$, $0 \le r \le 1$

20. $-\frac{\pi}{4} \le \theta \le \frac{\pi}{4}$, $-1 \le r \le 1$

21. $-\frac{\pi}{2} \le \theta \le \frac{\pi}{2}$, $1 \le r \le 2$

22. $0 \le \theta \le \frac{\pi}{2}$, $1 \le |r| \le 2$

23. $x = r\cos\theta$ so the vertical line $x = 2$

24. $y = r\sin\theta$ so the horizontal line $y = -1$

25. $y = r\sin\theta$ so the horizontal line $y = 4$

26. $x = 0$ or the y-axis

27. $y = 0$ or the x-axis

28. $x = -3$

29. $r\cos\theta + r\sin\theta = 1$ is the line $x + y = 1$

30. The line $y = x$.

31. $r^2 = 1$ is the circle $x^2 + y^2 = 1$

32. $r^2 = 4r\sin\theta \Rightarrow x^2 + y^2 = 4y$ or $x^2 + (y-2)^2 = 4$. Circle with $C(0,2)$, $r = 2$

33. $r\sin\theta = e^{r\cos\theta}$ is the function $y = e^x$

34. $r^2 + 2r^2\cos\theta\sin\theta = 1 \Rightarrow x^2 + y^2 + 2xy = 1 \Rightarrow (x+y)^2 = 1$

or $x + y = \pm 1$, two parallel lines.

35. $r = \dfrac{5}{\sin\theta - 2\cos\theta} \Leftrightarrow r\sin\theta - 2r\cos\theta = 5$ or $y - 2x = 5$

36. $r = 4\cos\theta \Rightarrow \sqrt{x^2+y^2} = \dfrac{4x}{\sqrt{x^2+y^2}} \Rightarrow x^2+y^2 = 4x$

$x^2 - 4x + 4 + y^2 = 4$ or $(x-2)^2 + y^2 = 4$.

37. $r = 4\sin\theta \Leftrightarrow \sqrt{x^2+y^2} = \dfrac{4y}{\sqrt{x^2+y^2}}$

$x^2 + y^2 - 4y = 0$ or $x^2 + (y-2)^2 = 4$

38. $r = 2\cos\theta + 2\sin\theta \Rightarrow \sqrt{x^2+y^2} = \dfrac{2x}{\sqrt{x^2+y^2}} + \dfrac{2y}{\sqrt{x^2+y^2}}$

$x^2+y^2 = 2x+2y \Rightarrow (x-1)^2 + (y-1)^2 = 2$

39. $r = 4\tan\theta\sec\theta = \dfrac{4\sin\theta}{\cos\theta} \cdot \dfrac{1}{\cos\theta} \cdot \dfrac{r}{r}$

$r\cos\theta = \dfrac{4r\sin\theta}{r\cos\theta}$ or $x = \dfrac{4y}{x}$ or $x^2 = 4y$

40. $r + \sin\theta = 2\cos\theta \Rightarrow \sqrt{x^2+y^2} + \dfrac{y}{\sqrt{x^2+y^2}} = \dfrac{2x}{\sqrt{x^2+y^2}}$

$x^2+y^2+y-2x = 0 \Rightarrow (x-1)^2 + \left(y+\dfrac{1}{2}\right)^2 = \dfrac{5}{4}$

41. $r\cos\theta = 7$

42. $r\sin\theta = 1$

43. $r\cos\theta = r\sin\theta \Rightarrow \tan\theta = 1$ or $\theta = \dfrac{\pi}{4}$.

44. $r\cos\theta - r\sin\theta = 3 \Rightarrow r = \dfrac{3}{\cos\theta - \sin\theta}$

45. A circle centered at origin with radius 2: $r = 2$

46. $x^2 - y^2 = 1 \Rightarrow r^2\cos^2\theta - r^2\sin^2\theta = 1 \Rightarrow r^2\cos 2\theta = 1$

47. $\dfrac{x^2}{9} + \dfrac{y^2}{4} = 1 \Leftrightarrow \dfrac{r^2\cos^2\theta}{9} + \dfrac{r^2\sin^2\theta}{4} = 1$

48. $xy = 2 \Rightarrow r\cos\theta\, r\sin\theta = 2 \Rightarrow \dfrac{r^2}{2}(2\cos\theta\sin\theta) = 2 \Rightarrow r^2 = \dfrac{4}{\sin 2\theta}$

49. $y^2 = 4x \Leftrightarrow r^2\sin^2\theta = 4r\cos\theta \Leftrightarrow r = \dfrac{4\cos\theta}{\sin^2\theta} = 4\cot\theta\csc\theta$

50. $x^2 - y^2 = 25\sqrt{x^2+y^2} \Rightarrow r^2\cos^2\theta - r^2\sin^2\theta = 25r$

$r^2\cos 2\theta = 25r \Rightarrow r\cos 2\theta = 25$

51. $3 = r\cos(\theta - \frac{\pi}{3}) = r(\cos\theta\cos\frac{\pi}{3} + \sin\theta\sin\frac{\pi}{3})$

$= r\cos\theta\cdot\frac{1}{2} + r\sin\theta\cdot\frac{\sqrt{3}}{2}$ $\therefore\ x + \sqrt{3}\,y = 6$

52. $r\sin\left(\theta+\frac{\pi}{4}\right)=4 \Rightarrow r\left[\sin\theta\cos\frac{\pi}{4}+\cos\theta\sin\frac{\pi}{4}\right]=4$

$r\sin\theta+r\cos\theta=4\sqrt{2} \Rightarrow y+x=4\sqrt{2}$

53. $\sqrt{2} = r\sin(\frac{\pi}{4} - \theta)=r(\sin\frac{\pi}{4}\cos\theta-\cos\frac{\pi}{4}\sin\theta)$

$= r\cos\theta\cdot\frac{1}{\sqrt{2}} - r\sin\theta\cdot\frac{1}{\sqrt{2}}$ $\qquad \therefore x - y = 2$

54. $r\cos\left(\frac{\pi}{6}-\theta\right)=0 \Rightarrow r\left[\cos\theta\cos\frac{\pi}{6}+\sin\theta\sin\frac{\pi}{6}\right]=0$

$r\sqrt{3}\cos\theta+r\sin\theta=0 \Rightarrow x\sqrt{3}+y=0$

10.2 GRAPHING IN POLAR COORDINATES

1. $\cos\theta = \cos(-\theta) \Rightarrow$ symmetry to x=axis.
$|\cos\theta| \leq 1 \Rightarrow 0 \leq r \leq 2a$

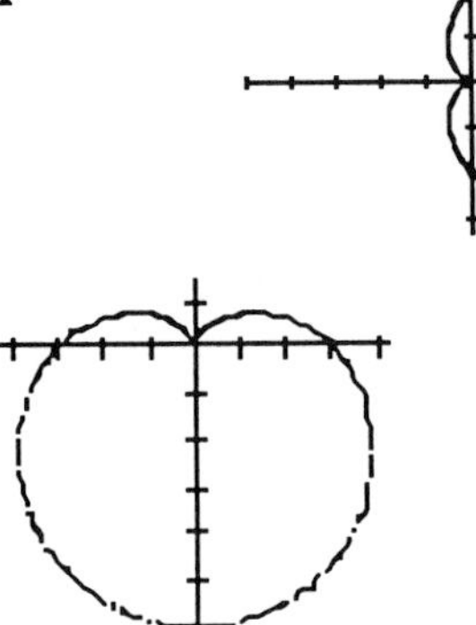

2. Replacing θ by $\pi-\theta$:
$r=a(1-\sin(\pi-\theta)$
$=a(1-\cos\theta) \Rightarrow$
symmetry to y-axis.

3. Replacing (r,θ) by $(-r,-\theta)$:
$-r = \sin2(-\theta) = -\sin2\theta$ or
$r = \sin2\theta$. $\therefore$ The graph has symmetry to y-axis.
$\theta = \frac{\pi}{4} \Rightarrow r = a$

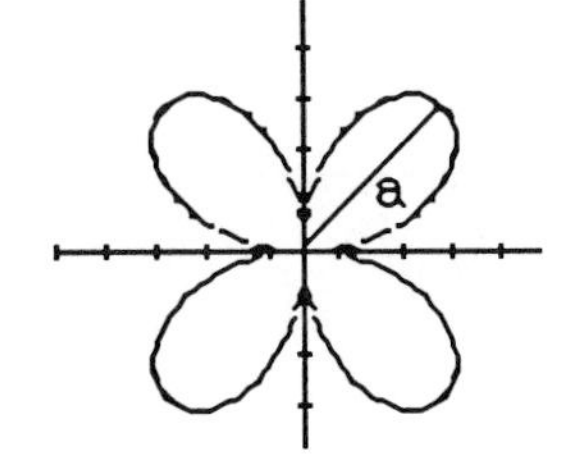

4. $r^2=2a^2\cos2\theta$
Has all symmetry

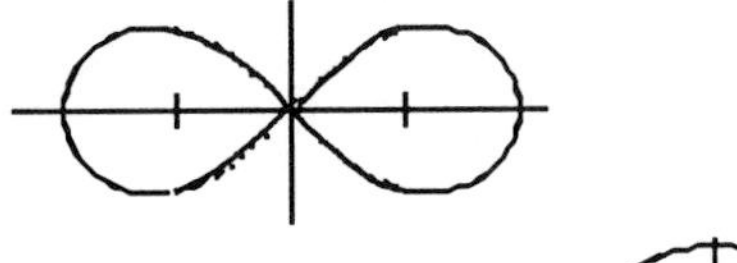

5. Replacing θ by $\pi-\theta$:
$r = a(2 + \sin(\pi-\theta))$
$= a(2 + \sin\theta) \Rightarrow$
symmetry to y-axis

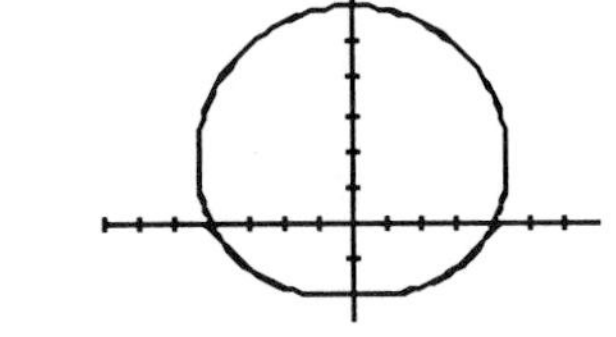

6. $r = a(1 + 2\sin(\pi-\theta)$
$= a(1 + 2\sin\theta)$
Symmetry to y-axis

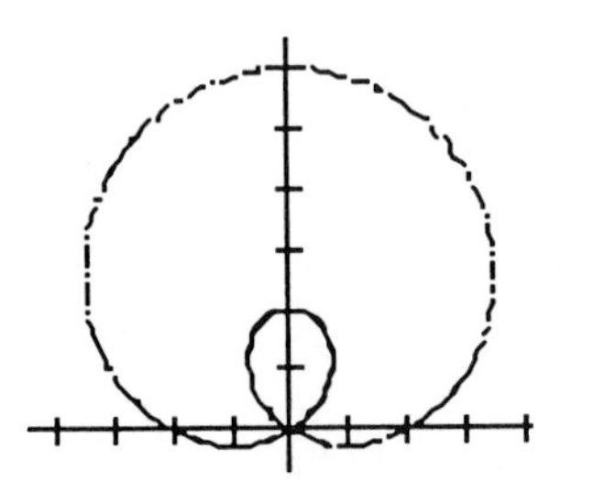

7. **Spiral of Archimedes**
$(r,\theta) = (-r,-\theta) \Rightarrow$ symmetry to y-axis.

8. $r = a \sin \frac{\theta}{2}$

9. (a) $r = \frac{1}{2} + \cos\theta$ (b) $r = \frac{1}{2} + \sin\theta$

10. (a) $r = 1 - \cos\theta$ (b) $r = -1 + \sin\theta$

11. (a) $r = \frac{3}{2} + \cos\theta$ (b) $r = \frac{3}{2} - \sin\theta$

12. (a) $r = 2 + \cos\theta$ (b) $r = -2 + \sin\theta$

13. Region: $0 \le r \le 2 - 2\cos\theta$

14. $0 \le r^2 \le \cos\theta$

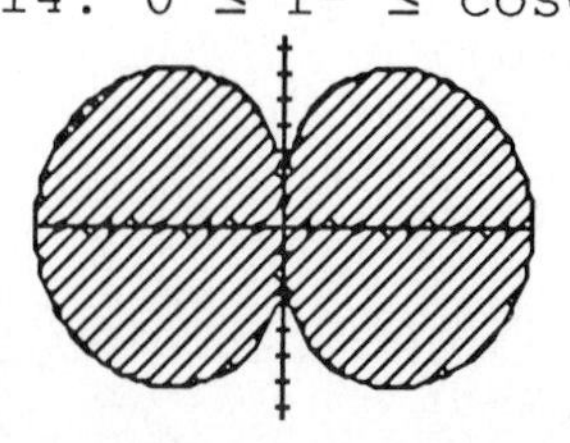

15. When named by $(2,\frac{3\pi}{4})$, the point does not satisfy the equation $r = 2\sin2\theta$, since $2\sin2(\frac{3\pi}{4}) = 2\sin\frac{3\pi}{2} = -2$. If the point is renamed as $(-2,-\frac{\pi}{4})$, then it will satisfy the equation.

16. Another name for the point $\left(\frac{1}{2},\frac{3\pi}{2}\right)$ is $\left(\frac{1}{2},-\frac{\pi}{2}\right)$. For this,

$r=-\sin\left(-\frac{\pi}{6}\right)=-\left(-\frac{1}{2}\right)=\frac{1}{2}$, so the point lies on the curve.

17. $1+\cos\theta = 1-\sin\theta$

$\cos\theta = -\sin\theta$

$\tan\theta = -1$

$\theta = \frac{3\pi}{4}$ or $\frac{7\pi}{4}$

∴ The points are

$(a(1-\frac{1}{\sqrt{2}}),\frac{3\pi}{4})$, $(a(1+\frac{1}{\sqrt{2}}),\frac{7\pi}{4})$

Also $(0,0)$ is a point of intersection.

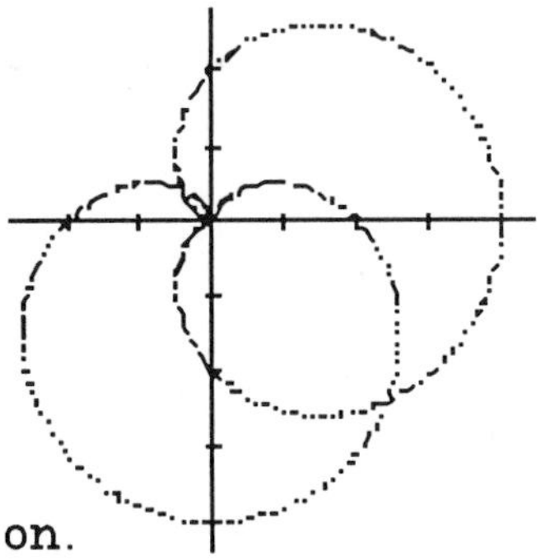

18. $\sin 2\theta=\cos 2\theta$ if $\tan 2\theta=1 \Rightarrow 2\theta=\frac{\pi}{4}$ or $\frac{5\pi}{4} \Rightarrow \theta=\frac{\pi}{8}$ or $\frac{5\pi}{8}$.

$r^2=\sin\frac{\pi}{4} \Rightarrow 2^{1/4}$. The curves intersect in the points $\left(2^{1/4},\frac{\pi}{8}\right)$ and

$\left(2^{1/4},\frac{5\pi}{8}\right)$. They also intersect at $(0,0)$.

19. $r=1-\cos\theta$ and $r^2=\cos\theta \Rightarrow (1-\cos\theta)^2=\cos\theta$

$1-2\cos\theta+\cos^2\theta=\cos\theta \Rightarrow \cos^2\theta-3\cos\theta+1=0$

$\cos\theta=\frac{3-\sqrt{5}}{2}$. $r=1-\frac{3-\sqrt{5}}{2}=\frac{-1+\sqrt{5}}{2}$. The points of intersection are

$(0,0)$, $\left(\frac{-1+\sqrt{5}}{2},\cos^{-1}\left(\frac{3-\sqrt{5}}{2}\right)\right)$ and $\left(\frac{-1+\sqrt{5}}{2},2\pi-\cos^{-1}\left(\frac{3-\sqrt{5}}{2}\right)\right)$

20. $\sin\theta=\cos\theta$ when $\theta=\frac{\pi}{4}$ (r^2 cannot be negative).

This gives two points $\left(\pm 2^{1/4},\frac{\pi}{4}\right)$.

The curves also intersect

at $\left(\pm 2^{1/4},\frac{3\pi}{4}\right)$ and the pole.

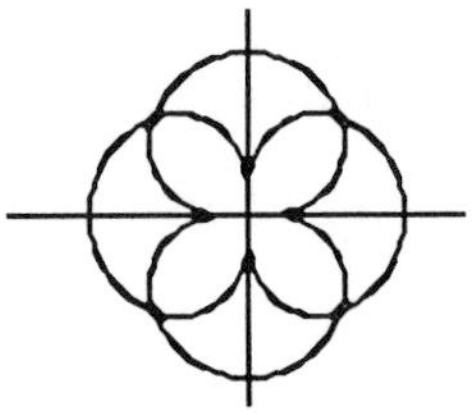

21. $2\sin 2\theta=1 \Leftrightarrow \sin 2\theta=\frac{1}{2} \Rightarrow 2\theta=\frac{\pi}{6} \Rightarrow \theta=\frac{\pi}{12}$, etc.

There are 8 points of intersection between the circle and

the four-leafed rose. These are

$\left(1,\pm\frac{\pi}{12}\right),\left(1,\pm\frac{5\pi}{12}\right),\left(1,\pm\frac{13\pi}{12}\right)$ and $\left(1,\pm\frac{17\pi}{12}\right)$.

22. $\sin 2\theta = \cos 2\theta$ when $2\theta = \dfrac{\pi}{4}$ or $\theta = \dfrac{\pi}{8}$.

There are nine points of intersection:

$\left(\pm\dfrac{a}{\sqrt{2}}, \dfrac{\pi}{8}\right), \left(\pm\dfrac{a}{\sqrt{2}}, \dfrac{3\pi}{8}\right), \left(\pm\dfrac{a}{\sqrt{2}}, \dfrac{5\pi}{8}\right),$

$\left(\pm\dfrac{a}{\sqrt{2}}, \dfrac{7\pi}{8}\right)$ and the pole.

23. $1 + \cos\dfrac{\theta}{2} = 1 - \sin\dfrac{\theta}{2}$

$\tan\dfrac{\theta}{2} = -1$

$\dfrac{\theta}{2} = \dfrac{3\pi}{4}$ or $\dfrac{7\pi}{2} \Rightarrow \theta = \dfrac{3\pi}{2}$ or $\dfrac{\pi}{2}$

$r = 1 \pm \dfrac{\sqrt{2}}{2}$

There are 5 points of intersection in all.

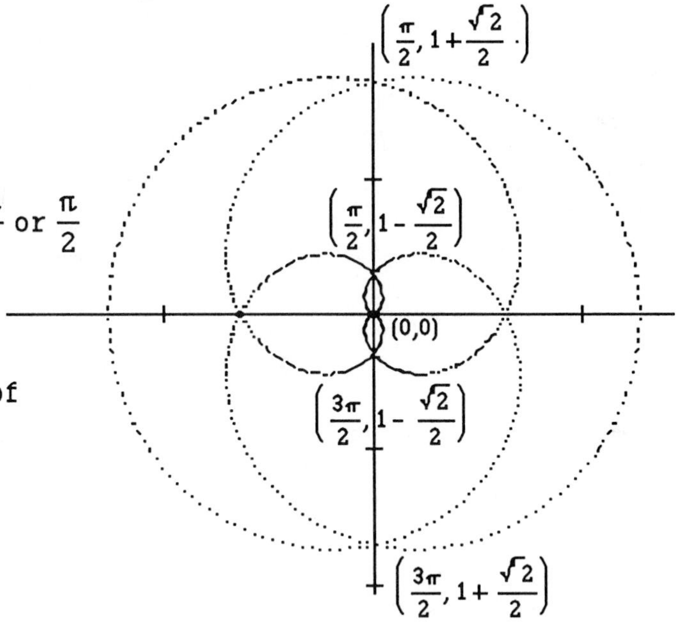

$\left(\dfrac{\pi}{2}, 1+\dfrac{\sqrt{2}}{2}\right)$

$\left(\dfrac{\pi}{2}, 1-\dfrac{\sqrt{2}}{2}\right)$

(0,0)

$\left(\dfrac{3\pi}{2}, 1-\dfrac{\sqrt{2}}{2}\right)$

$\left(\dfrac{3\pi}{2}, 1+\dfrac{\sqrt{2}}{2}\right)$

24. $a^2 = 2a^2 \sin 2\theta \Rightarrow \sin 2\theta = \dfrac{1}{2} \Rightarrow 2\theta = \dfrac{\pi}{6}, \dfrac{5\pi}{6}$ and $\theta = \dfrac{\pi}{12}, \dfrac{5\pi}{12}$.

There are four points: $\left(\pm a, \dfrac{\pi}{12}\right), \left(\pm a, \dfrac{5\pi}{12}\right)$

25. We shall show that whenever (r, θ) satisfies one equation, then $(-r, \cos(\pi + \theta))$ satisfies the other. Since these are different names for the same point, the equations must represent the same curve. If (r_1, θ_1) satisfies $r = 1 + \cos\theta$, then $r = -1 + \cos(\pi + \theta_1) = -1 - \cos\theta_1 = -(1 + \cos\theta_1) = -r_1$ satisfies $r = -1 + \cos\theta$. Conversely, if (r_1, θ_1) satisfies $r = -1 + \cos\theta$, then $r = 1 + \cos(\pi + \theta_1) = 1 - \cos\theta_1 = -(-1 + \cos\theta_1) = -r_1$ satisfies $r = 1 + \cos\theta$.

26. (a) $a^2(1-\cos\theta)^2 = -4a^2\cos\theta$

$1-2\cos\theta+\cos^2\theta = -4\cos\theta \Rightarrow (\cos\theta+1)^2 = 0 \Rightarrow \theta = \pi$

$\therefore$ $(2a,\pi)$ is a common solution.

(b) $4a^2\cos\theta = 0$ when $\theta = \frac{\pi}{2}$. $a(1-\cos\theta) = 0$ when $\theta = 0$. The pole belongs to both curves.

27. arc OT = arc DP $\Rightarrow \angle OBC = \angle PAD$. Then $\Delta ABC \cong \Delta PAD \Rightarrow OT = DP$. $\therefore OP \parallel AB$

$\Rightarrow \theta = \angle OBC$. $TB = \frac{1}{2}(2a-r)$. Thus $\dfrac{a-\frac{1}{2}r}{a} = \cos\theta \Rightarrow r = 2a(1-\cos\theta)$.

28. (a) $r = 1 + 2\sin\frac{\theta}{2}$ (b) $r = \cos(\frac{\theta}{3})$

(c) $r = \cos 2\theta$ (d) $r = \cos 3\theta$ (e) $r = \cos 7\theta$

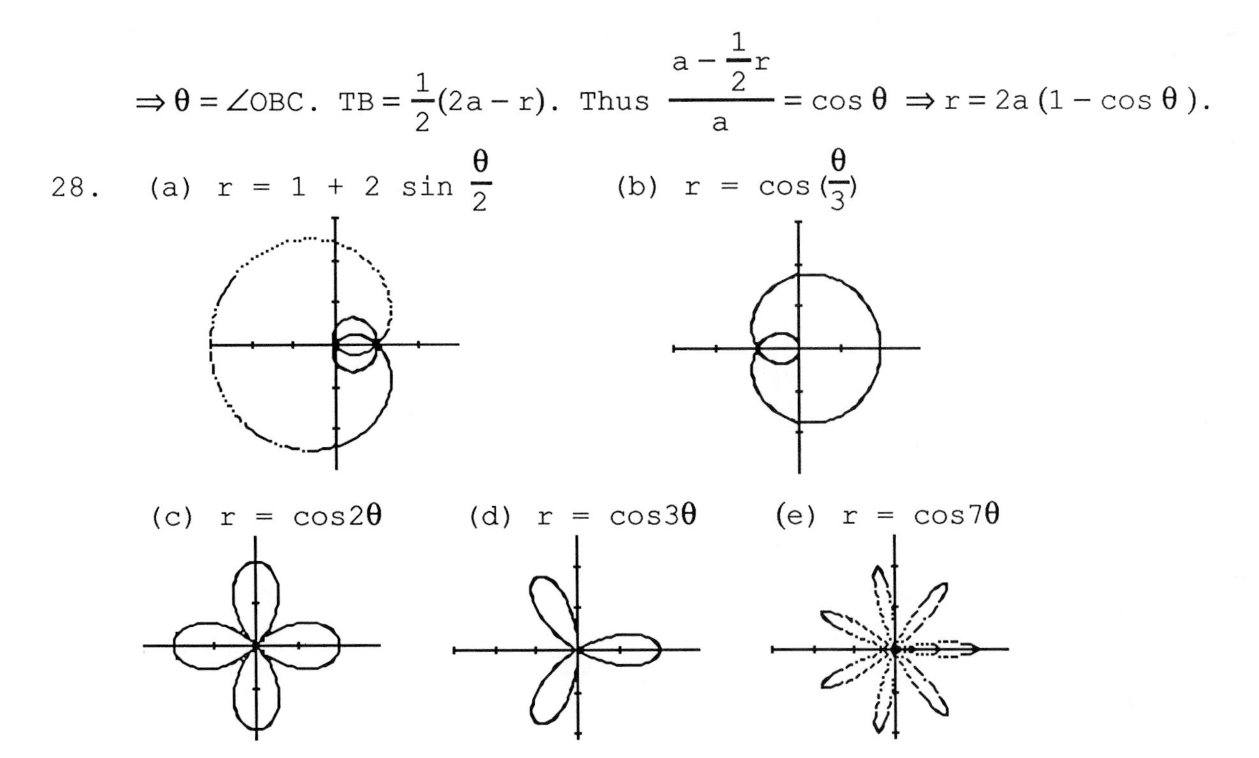

10.3 POLAR EQUATIONS OF CONIC SECTIONS AND OTHER CURVES

1. $r = 4\cos\theta \Rightarrow \sqrt{x^2+y^2} = \dfrac{4x}{\sqrt{x^2+y^2}} \Rightarrow x^2+y^2 = 4x$ or $(x-2)^2+y^2 = 4$

2. $r = 6\sin\theta \Rightarrow \sqrt{x^2+y^2} = \dfrac{6y}{\sqrt{x^2+y^2}} \Rightarrow x^2+y^2-6y = 0$ or $x^2+(y-3)^2 = 9$

3. $r = -2\cos\theta \Rightarrow \sqrt{x^2+y^2} = \dfrac{-2x}{\sqrt{x^2+y^2}} \Rightarrow x^2+y^2 = -2x$ or $(x+1)^2+y^2 = 1$

4. $r = -2\sin\theta \Rightarrow \sqrt{x^2+y^2} = \dfrac{-2y}{\sqrt{x^2+y^2}} \Rightarrow x^2+y^2+2y = 0$ or $x^2+(y+1)^2 = 1$

5. $r = \sin 2\theta = 2\sin\theta\cos\theta \Leftrightarrow \sqrt{x^2+y^2} = \dfrac{2xy}{x^2+y^2} \Rightarrow (x^2+y^2)^{\frac{3}{2}} = 2xy$

$\therefore$ $(x^2+y^2)^3 = 4x^2y^2$

6. $r = \sin 3\theta = \sin(2\theta + \theta) = \sin 2\theta \cos\theta + \cos 2\theta \sin\theta$

$= 2\sin\theta\cos^2\theta + (2\cos^2\theta - 1)\sin\theta$

$$\sqrt{x^2 + y^2} = 4\left(\frac{y}{\sqrt{x^2 + y^2}}\right)\left(\frac{x^2}{x^2 + y^2}\right) - \frac{y}{\sqrt{x^2 + y^2}}$$

$$x^2 + y^2 = y\left(\frac{4x^2 - x^2 - y^2}{x^2 + y^2}\right) \text{ or } (x^2 + y^2)^2 = y(3x^2 - y^2)$$

7. $r^2 = 8\cos 2\theta = 8(2\cos^2\theta - 1) \Leftrightarrow x^2 + y^2 = \dfrac{16x^2}{x^2 + y^2} - 8$

$(x^2 + y^2)^2 = 8(x^2 - y^2)$

8. $r^2 = 4\sin 2\theta = 8\sin\theta\cos\theta \Rightarrow x^2 + y^2 = \dfrac{8xy}{x^2 + y^2}$ or $(x^2 + y^2)^2 = 8xy$

9. $r = 8(1 - 2\cos\theta) \Rightarrow \sqrt{x^2 + y^2} = 8\left(1 - \dfrac{2x}{\sqrt{x^2 + y^2}}\right)$

$$x^2 + y^2 = 8\left(\sqrt{x^2 + y^2} - 2x\right) \text{ or } (x^2 + y^2 + 16x)^2 = 64(x^2 + y^2).$$

10. $r = \dfrac{1}{2 - \cos\theta} \Rightarrow \sqrt{x^2 + y^2} = \dfrac{1}{2 - \dfrac{x}{\sqrt{x^2 + y^2}}} \Rightarrow 2\sqrt{x^2 + y^2} = x + 1 \Rightarrow$

$3x^2 + 4y^2 - 2x = 1$

11. $r = 4(1 - \cos\theta) \Rightarrow \sqrt{x^2 + y^2} = 4 - \dfrac{4x}{\sqrt{x^2 + y^2}} \Rightarrow (x^2 + y^2 + 4x)^2 = 16(x^2 + y^2).$

12. $r(2 - 2\cos\theta) = 4 \Rightarrow \sqrt{x^2 + y^2}\left(1 - \dfrac{x}{\sqrt{x^2 + y^2}}\right) = 2$

$$\sqrt{x^2 + y^2} - x = 2 \Rightarrow x^2 + y^2 = 4 + 4x + x^2 \text{ or } y^2 = 4(x + 1)$$

13. $r(3 - 6\cos\theta) = 12 \Rightarrow \sqrt{x^2 + y^2}\left(1 - \dfrac{2x}{\sqrt{x^2 + y^2}}\right) = 4 \Rightarrow$

$$\sqrt{x^2 + y^2} = 2x + 4 \Rightarrow x^2 + y^2 = 4x^2 + 16x + 16 \Rightarrow 3x^2 - y^2 + 16x + 16 = 0.$$

14. $r(10 - 5\cos\theta) = 25 \Rightarrow \sqrt{x^2 + y^2}\left(2 - \dfrac{x}{\sqrt{x^2 + y^2}}\right) = 5$

$$2\sqrt{x^2 + y^2} - x = 5 \Rightarrow 4x^2 + 4y^2 = 25 + 10x + x^2 \text{ or } 3x^2 + 4y^2 - 10x = 25$$

15. $r(2 + \cos\theta) = 4 \Rightarrow 2\sqrt{x^2 + y^2} + x = 4 \Rightarrow 4(x^2 + y^2) = 16 - 8x + x^2 \Rightarrow$

$3x^2 + 4y^2 + 8x = 16.$

16. $r(2+3\cos\theta)=1 \Rightarrow \sqrt{x^2+y^2}\left(2+\frac{3x}{\sqrt{x^2+y^2}}\right)=1$

$2\sqrt{x^2+y^2}+3x=1 \Rightarrow 4x^2+4y^2=1-6x+9x^2$ or $5x^2-4y^2-6x+1=0$

17. $r(3+3\cos\theta)=2 \Rightarrow 3\sqrt{x^2+y^2}=2-3x \Rightarrow 9(x^2+y^2)=4-12x+9x^2 \Rightarrow$

$9y^2=4-12x$.

18. $r(16+8\cos\theta)=416 \Rightarrow \sqrt{x^2+y^2}\left(16+\frac{8x}{\sqrt{x^2+y^2}}\right)=416$

$2\sqrt{x^2+y^2}+x=52 \Rightarrow 4x^2+4y^2=2704-104x+x^2$ or $3x^2+4y^2+104x=2704$

19. $r=2\cos\left(\theta+\frac{\pi}{4}\right)$

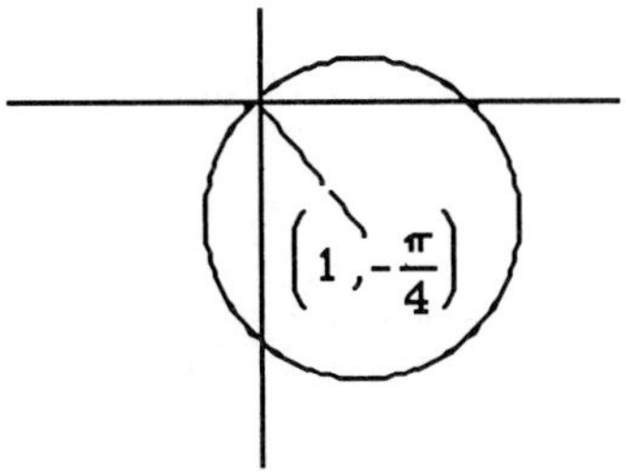

$\left(1,-\frac{\pi}{4}\right)$

20. $r=4\csc\left(\theta-\frac{\pi}{6}\right)=\frac{8}{\sqrt{3}\sin\theta-\cos\theta}$ is a line with intercepts

$(-8,0)$ and $\left(\frac{8}{\sqrt{3}},\frac{\theta}{2}\right)$.

21. $r=5\sec\left(\frac{\pi}{3}-\theta\right)$ or

$r\cos\left(\theta-\frac{\pi}{3}\right)=5$

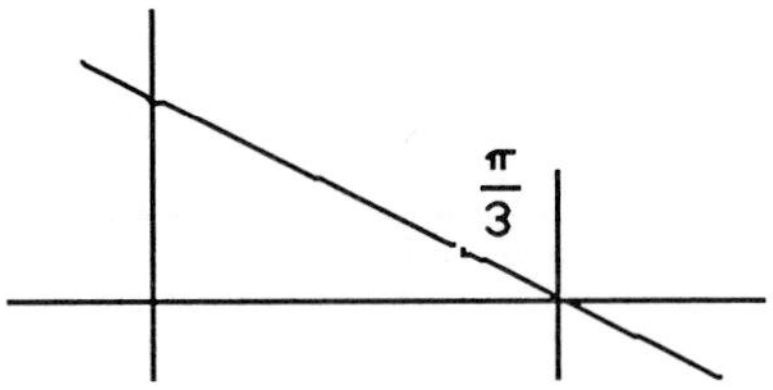

$\frac{\pi}{3}$

22. $r=3\sin\left(\theta+\frac{\pi}{6}\right)$ is a circle with radius $r=\frac{3}{2}$, and center

rotated clockwise $\frac{\pi}{6}$ from the point $\left(0,\frac{3}{2}\right)$ to the point $\left(\frac{3}{4},\frac{3\sqrt{3}}{4}\right)$.

23. A cardioid with its axis of symmetry rotated counterclockwise through and angle of $\frac{\pi}{6}$ radians.

24. The circle with center (1,0) and radius r = 1, and its interior.

25.	(d)	26.	(e)	27.	(l)	28.	(f)
29.	(k)	30.	(h)	31.	(i)	32.	(j)

33. Consider any ray $\theta=k$. This ray will intersect the spiral $r=a\theta$ in two successive points $(a(k+2n\pi), k+2n\pi)$ and $(a(k+2(n+1)\pi), k+2(n+1)\pi)$. Then $a(k+2(n+1)\pi)-a(k+2n\pi)=$ $ak+2an\pi+2a\pi-ak-2an\pi=2a\pi$, a constant width.

34. $r = 1 - 2\sin 3\theta$

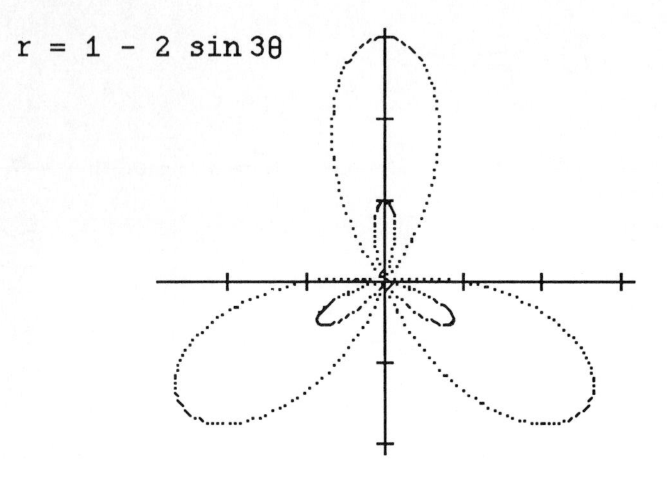

35. Mercury: $r = \dfrac{0.3871(1-(0.2056)^2)}{1-(0.2056)\cos\theta} = \dfrac{0.3707}{1-(0.2056)\cos\theta}$

Venus: $r = \dfrac{0.7233(1-(0.0068)^2)}{1-(0.0068)\cos\theta} = \dfrac{0.7233}{1-(0.0068)\cos\theta}$

Earth: $r = \dfrac{1.0000(1-(0.0167)^2)}{1-(0.0167)\cos\theta} = \dfrac{0.9997}{1-(0.0167)\cos\theta}$

Mars: $r = \dfrac{1.524(1-(0.0934)^2)}{1-(0.0934)\cos\theta} = \dfrac{1.5107}{1-(0.0934)\cos\theta}$

Jupiter: $r = \dfrac{5.203(1-(0.0484)^2)}{1-(0.0484)\cos\theta} = \dfrac{5.1908}{1-(0.0484)\cos\theta}$

Saturn: $r = \dfrac{9.539(1-(0.0543)^2)}{1-(0.0543)\cos\theta} = \dfrac{9.5109}{1-(0.0543)\cos\theta}$

Uranus: $r = \dfrac{19.18(1-(0.0460)^2)}{1-(0.0460)\cos\theta} = \dfrac{19.139}{1-(0.0460)\cos\theta}$

Neptune: $r = \dfrac{30.06(1-(0.0082)^2)}{1-(0.0082)\cos\theta} = \dfrac{30.0580}{1-(0.0082)\cos\theta}$

36. The planet is closest when $\theta = \pi$ and farthest when $\theta = 0$ in the equation $r = \dfrac{a(1-e^2)}{1-e\cos\theta}$. Then $\theta = 0 \Rightarrow r = \dfrac{a(1-e^2)}{1-e} = a(1+e)$ and $\theta = \pi \Rightarrow r = \dfrac{a(1-e^2)}{1+e} = a(1+e)$.

Mercury	Closest:	0.3871(1 - 0.2056) =	0.3075 AU
	Farthest:	0.3871(1 + 0.2056) =	0.4667 AU
Venus	Closest:	0.7233(1 - 0.0068) =	0.7184 AU

	Farthest:	0.7233(1 + 0.0068) =	0.7282 AU
Earth	Closest:	1.0000(1 - 0.0167) =	0.9833 AU
	Farthest:	1.0000(1 + 0.0167) =	1.0167 AU
Mars	Closest:	1.524(1 - 0.0934) =	1.3817 AU
	Farthest:	1.524(1 + 0.0934) =	1.6663 AU
Jupiter	Closest:	5.203(1 - 0.0484) =	4.9512 AU
	Farthest:	5.203(1 + 0.0484) =	5.4548 AU
Saturn	Closest:	9.539(1 - 0.0543) =	9.021 AU
	Farthest:	9.539(1 + 0.0543) =	10.057 AU
Uranus	Closest:	19.18(1 - 0.0460) =	18.298 AU
	Farthest:	19.18(1 + 0.0460) =	20.062 AU
Neptune	Closest:	30.06(1 - 0.0082) =	29.814 AU
	Farthest:	30.06(1 + 0.0082) =	30.306 AU
Pluto	Closest:	39.44(1 - 0.2481) =	29.655 AU
	Farthest:	39.44(1 + 0.2481) =	49.225 AU

37. $r = 2\sin\theta \Rightarrow \sqrt{x^2+y^2} = \dfrac{2y}{\sqrt{x^2+y^2}} \Rightarrow x^2+y^2 = 2y$

or $x^2 + (y-1)^2 = 1$ is a circle with center $(0,1)$ and radius $= 1$.

$r = \csc\theta \Rightarrow r\sin\theta = 1 \Rightarrow y = 1$ is ahorizontal line intersecting

the circle n the points $(1,1)$ or $\left(\sqrt{2}, \frac{\pi}{4}\right)$ and $(-1,1)$ or $\left(\sqrt{2}, \frac{3\pi}{4}\right)$.

38. $r = 2\cos\theta \Rightarrow \sqrt{x^2+y^2} = \dfrac{2x}{\sqrt{x^2+y^2}} \Rightarrow x^2+y^2 = 2x$

or $(x-1)^2 + y^2 = 1$ is a circle with center $(1,0)$ and radius $= 1$.

$r = \sec\theta \Rightarrow r\cos\theta = 1 \Rightarrow x = 1$ is a vertical line intersecting

the circle n the points $(1,1)$ or $\left(\sqrt{2}, \frac{\pi}{4}\right)$ and $(1,-1)$ or $\left(\sqrt{2}, -\frac{\pi}{4}\right)$.

39. In the equation $r = \dfrac{ke}{1 - e\cos\theta}$, $k = 4$ and $e = 1$. Therefore, $r = \dfrac{4}{1-\cos\theta}$

40. $r = \dfrac{2}{2-\cos\theta} = \dfrac{1}{1-\frac{1}{2}\cos\theta}$. $\therefore$ $e = \frac{1}{2}$ and $k = 1$. Since $ke = a(1-e^2)$,

$\frac{1}{2} = a\left(1 - \frac{1}{4}\right)$ or $a = \frac{2}{3}$. The center is $\left(\frac{2}{3}, 0\right)$.

41. $k=-9$, so $r=\dfrac{-9\left(\frac{5}{4}\right)}{1-\frac{5}{4}\cos\theta}=\dfrac{-45}{4-5\cos\theta}$. The vertices are at $(5,0)$ and $(-45,\pi)=(45,0)$. The other focus is at $(50,0)$

42. Since $\cos\left(\theta-\frac{\pi}{2}\right)=\sin\theta$, the directrix is $r\sin\theta=2$ or $y=2$. Therefore, $k=2$ and the equation is $r=\dfrac{2}{1+\sin\theta}$.

10.4 INTEGRALS IN POLAR COORDINATES

1. $A=\frac{1}{2}\int r^2\,d\theta=\frac{1}{2}\int_0^{\frac{\pi}{4}}\cos^2\theta\,d\theta=\frac{1}{2}\int_0^{\frac{\pi}{4}}\frac{1}{2}(1+\cos 2\theta)\,d\theta=\frac{1}{4}+\frac{1}{8}\sin 2\theta\Big]_0^{\frac{\pi}{4}}=\frac{\pi+2}{16}$

2. $A_1=\int_{-\frac{\pi}{2}}^{\frac{\pi}{2}}\frac{1}{2}\left[a(1-\cos\theta)\right]^2 d\theta=a^2\int_0^{\frac{\pi}{2}}(1-2\cos\theta+\cos^2\theta)\,d\theta$

$$=a^2\int_0^{\frac{\pi}{2}}\left(1-2\cos\theta+\frac{1}{2}+\frac{1}{2}\cos 2\theta\right)d\theta=a^2\left[\frac{3}{2}\theta-2\sin\theta+\frac{1}{4}\sin 2\theta\right]_0^{\frac{\pi}{2}}$$

$=\dfrac{3\pi a^2}{4}-2a^2$. $A_2=$ semicircle $=\dfrac{\pi a^2}{2}$. Total area $=\dfrac{5\pi a^2}{4}-2a^2$.

3. $A=\int_0^{2\pi}\frac{1}{2}(4+2\cos\theta)^2\,d\theta=\int_0^{\pi}(16+16\cos\theta+4\cos^2\theta)\,d\theta$

$$=4\int_0^{\pi}\left(4+4\cos\theta+\frac{1}{2}(1+\cos 2\theta)\right)d\theta=18\,\theta+16\sin\theta+\sin 2\theta\Big]_0^{\pi}=18\pi$$

4. $A=\int_0^{2\pi}\frac{1}{2}\left[a(1+\cos\theta)\right]^2 d\theta=a^2\int_0^{\pi}(1+2\cos\theta+\cos^2\theta)\,d\theta$

$$=a^2\int_0^{\pi}\left(1+2\cos\theta+\frac{1}{2}+\frac{1}{2}\cos 2\theta\right)d\theta=a^2\left[\frac{3}{2}\theta+2\sin\theta+\frac{1}{4}\sin 2\theta\right]_0^{\frac{\pi}{2}}=\frac{3\pi a^2}{2}$$

5. $A=\int_0^{\pi}\frac{1}{2}(2a\sin\theta)^2 d\theta=2a^2\int_0^{\pi}\left(\frac{1}{2}-\frac{1}{2}\cos 2\theta\right)d\theta=2a^2\left[\frac{1}{2}-\frac{1}{4}\sin 2\theta\right]_0^{\pi}=\pi a^2$

6. $A=4\int_0^{\frac{\pi}{4}}\frac{1}{2}(2a^2\cos 2\theta)\,d\theta=4a^2\left[\sin 2\theta\right]_0^{\frac{\pi}{4}}=2a^2$

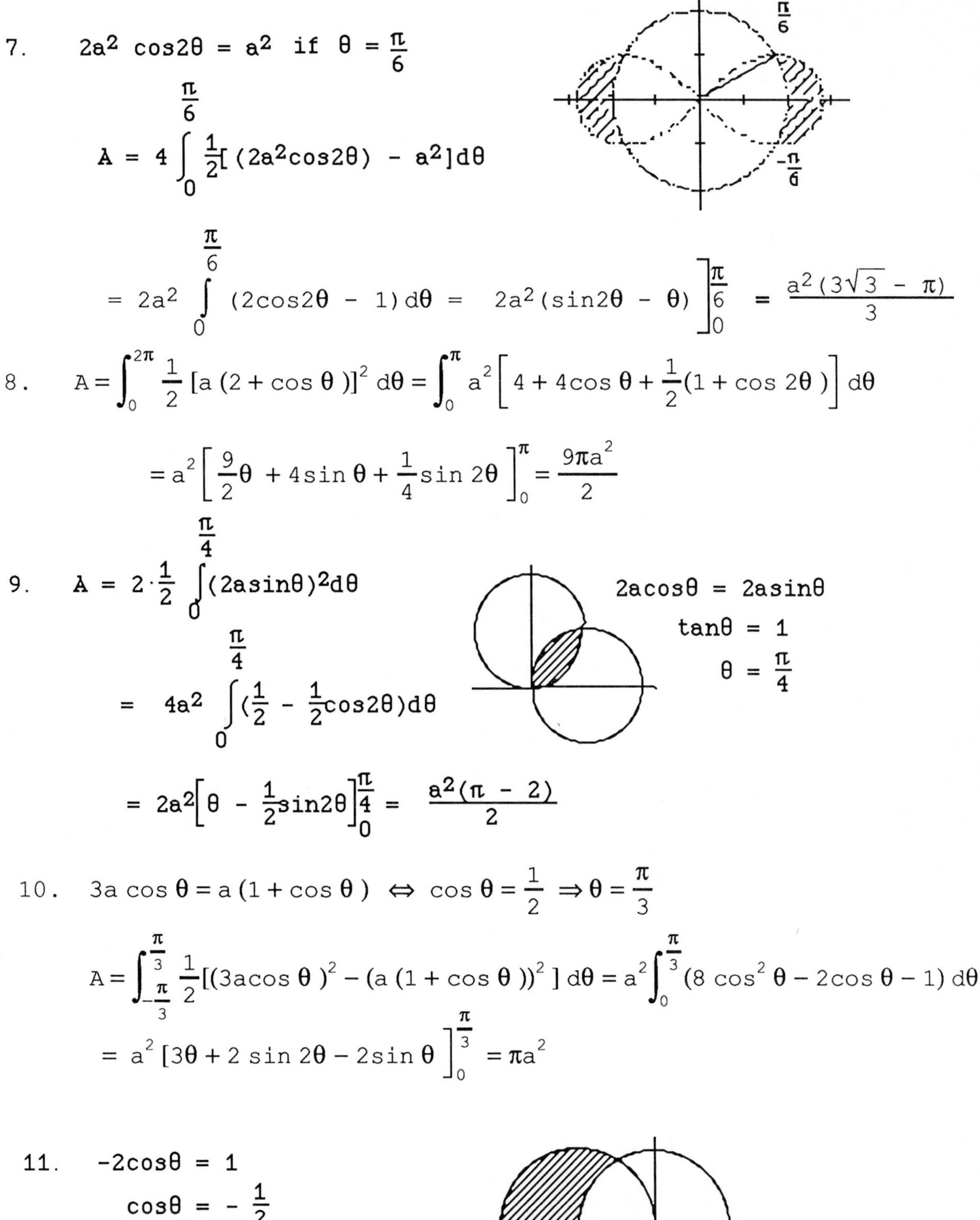

7. $2a^2\cos 2\theta = a^2$ if $\theta = \frac{\pi}{6}$

$$A = 4\int_0^{\frac{\pi}{6}} \frac{1}{2}[(2a^2\cos 2\theta) - a^2]d\theta$$

$$= 2a^2\int_0^{\frac{\pi}{6}} (2\cos 2\theta - 1)d\theta = 2a^2(\sin 2\theta - \theta)\Big]_0^{\frac{\pi}{6}} = \frac{a^2(3\sqrt{3} - \pi)}{3}$$

8. $$A = \int_0^{2\pi} \frac{1}{2}[a(2+\cos\theta)]^2 d\theta = \int_0^{\pi} a^2\left[4 + 4\cos\theta + \frac{1}{2}(1+\cos 2\theta)\right]d\theta$$

$$= a^2\left[\frac{9}{2}\theta + 4\sin\theta + \frac{1}{4}\sin 2\theta\right]_0^{\pi} = \frac{9\pi a^2}{2}$$

9. $$A = 2\cdot\frac{1}{2}\int_0^{\frac{\pi}{4}}(2a\sin\theta)^2 d\theta$$

$2a\cos\theta = 2a\sin\theta$

$\tan\theta = 1$

$\theta = \frac{\pi}{4}$

$$= 4a^2\int_0^{\frac{\pi}{4}}\left(\frac{1}{2} - \frac{1}{2}\cos 2\theta\right)d\theta$$

$$= 2a^2\left[\theta - \frac{1}{2}\sin 2\theta\right]_0^{\frac{\pi}{4}} = \frac{a^2(\pi - 2)}{2}$$

10. $3a\cos\theta = a(1+\cos\theta) \Leftrightarrow \cos\theta = \frac{1}{2} \Rightarrow \theta = \frac{\pi}{3}$

$$A = \int_{-\frac{\pi}{3}}^{\frac{\pi}{3}} \frac{1}{2}[(3a\cos\theta)^2 - (a(1+\cos\theta))^2]\,d\theta = a^2\int_0^{\frac{\pi}{3}}(8\cos^2\theta - 2\cos\theta - 1)\,d\theta$$

$$= a^2[3\theta + 2\sin 2\theta - 2\sin\theta\,]_0^{\frac{\pi}{3}} = \pi a^2$$

11. $-2\cos\theta = 1$

$\cos\theta = -\frac{1}{2}$

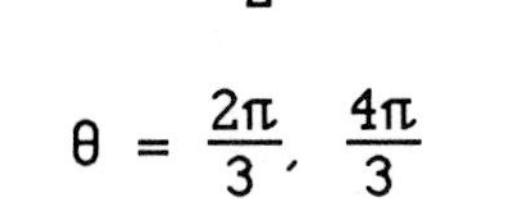

$\theta = \frac{2\pi}{3}, \frac{4\pi}{3}$

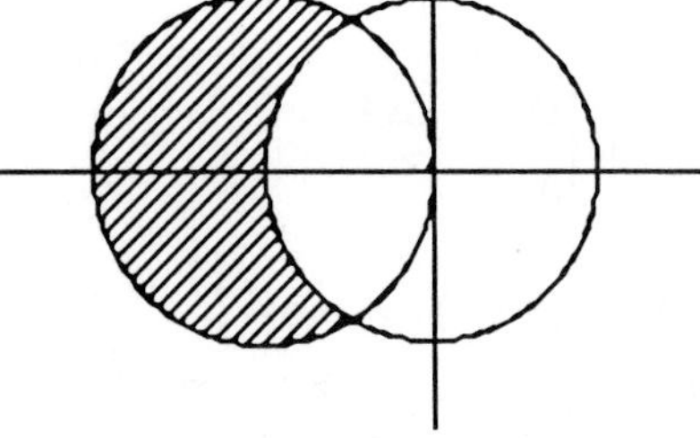

$$A = \int_{\frac{2\pi}{3}}^{\frac{4\pi}{3}} \frac{1}{2}[(-2\cos\theta)^2 - 1]\,d\theta = \frac{1}{2}\int_{\frac{2\pi}{3}}^{\frac{4\pi}{3}} (4\cos^2\theta - 1)\,d\theta$$

$$= \frac{1}{2}\int_{\frac{2\pi}{3}}^{\frac{4\pi}{3}} [2(1 + \cos2\theta) - 1]\,d\theta \quad = \frac{1}{2}\,[\theta + \sin2\theta\,]_{\frac{2\pi}{3}}^{\frac{4\pi}{3}}$$

$$= \frac{1}{2}\,(\frac{4\pi}{3} - \frac{2\pi}{3} + \frac{\sqrt{3}}{2} - (-\frac{\sqrt{3}}{2})) \quad = \frac{1}{2}\,(\frac{2\pi}{3} + \sqrt{3}\,) = \frac{2\pi + 3\sqrt{3}}{6}$$

12. $a = 2a\sin\theta \Leftrightarrow \theta = \frac{\pi}{6}$ or $\frac{5\pi}{6}$

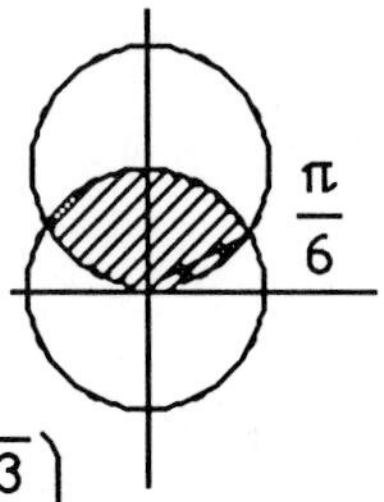

$$A = 2\int_0^{\frac{\pi}{6}} \frac{1}{2}(4a^2\sin^2\theta)\,d\theta + 2\int_{\frac{\pi}{6}}^{\frac{\pi}{2}} \frac{1}{2}a^2\,d\theta$$

$$= a^2\int_0^{\frac{\pi}{6}} (2 + 2\cos2\theta)\,d\theta + \frac{\pi a^2}{3} = a^2\left(\frac{2\pi}{3} - \frac{\sqrt{3}}{2}\right)$$

$\frac{\pi}{6}$

14. $A = 8\int_0^{\frac{\pi}{4}} \frac{1}{2}(\cos^2 2\theta)\,d\theta = 4\int_0^{\frac{\pi}{4}} \frac{1}{2}(1 + \cos4\theta)\,d\theta = \frac{\pi}{2}$

15. $A = 2\int_0^{\frac{\pi}{4}} \frac{1}{2}(4\sin2\theta)\,d\theta = 4\left[-\frac{1}{2}\cos2\theta\right]_0^{\frac{\pi}{4}} = 2$

16. $A = 2\int_0^{\pi} \frac{1}{2}(2\cos\theta - 4)^2\,d\theta = 4\int_0^{\pi} (\cos^2\theta - 4\cos\theta + 4)\,d\theta$

$$= 4\left[\frac{9}{2}\theta + \frac{1}{4}\sin2\theta - 4\sin\theta\right]_0^{\pi} = 18\pi$$

17. In one loop,

$$A = \frac{1}{2}\int_0^{\frac{\pi}{3}} (2a^2\sin3\theta)\,d\theta$$

$$= a^2\left[-\frac{1}{3}\cos3\theta\right]_0^{\frac{\pi}{3}} = \frac{2a^2}{3}$$

In six loops, $6(\frac{2a^2}{3}) = 4a^2$

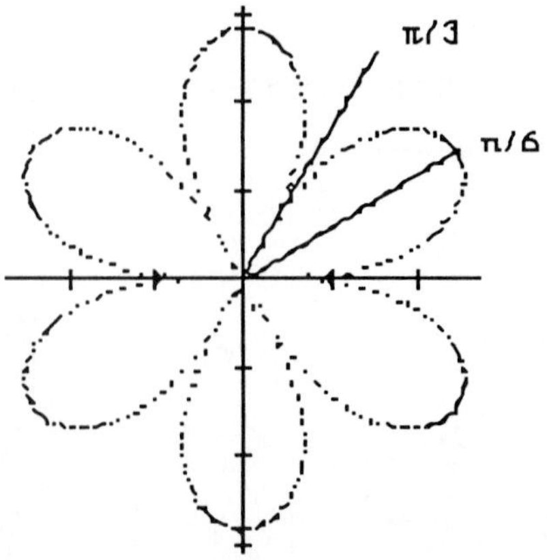

$\pi/3$

$\pi/6$

18. (a) $$A = 2\int_0^{\frac{2\pi}{3}} \frac{1}{2}(2\cos\theta + 1)^2\, d\theta = \int_0^{\frac{2\pi}{3}} \left[4\left(\frac{1}{2} + \frac{1}{2}\cos 2\theta\right) + 4\cos\theta + 1 \right] d\theta$$

$$= 3\theta + \sin 2\theta + 4\sin\theta \Big]_0^{\frac{2\pi}{3}} = 2\pi + \frac{3\sqrt{3}}{2}$$

(b) $$2\int_{\frac{2\pi}{3}}^{\pi} \frac{1}{2}(2\cos\theta + 1)^2\, d\theta = \pi - \frac{3\sqrt{3}}{2}.$$ The difference is $\pi + 3\sqrt{3}$.

19. $$A = \frac{1}{2}\int_0^{\pi} [\sqrt{\theta}e^{\theta}]^2 d\theta = \frac{1}{2}\int_0^{\pi} \theta e^{2\theta} d\theta =$$

$$= \frac{1}{2}\left[\frac{\theta}{2}e^{2\theta} - \frac{1}{4}e^{2\theta}\right]_0^{\pi} = \frac{\pi e^{2\pi}}{4} - \frac{e^{2\pi}}{8} + \frac{1}{8}$$

20. $$A = 2\int_{\frac{\pi}{6}}^{\frac{\pi}{2}} \frac{1}{2}\left[36 - \frac{9}{\sin^2\theta}\right] d\theta = \int_{\frac{\pi}{6}}^{\frac{\pi}{2}} (36 - 9\csc^2\theta)\, d\theta = 36 + 9\cot\theta \Big]_{\frac{\pi}{6}}^{\frac{\pi}{2}} = 12\pi - 9\sqrt{3}$$

21. (a) $r = a \Rightarrow dr = 0$. $\therefore\ ds^2 = r^2 d\theta^2 + dr^2 = a^2 d\theta^2$

$$L = \int ds = \int_0^{2\pi} a\, d\theta = [a\theta]_0^{2\pi} = 2\pi a$$

(b) $r = a\cos\theta \Rightarrow dr = -a\sin\theta\, d\theta$

$$ds^2 = r^2 d\theta^2 + dr^2$$
$$= a^2\cos^2\theta\, d\theta^2 + a^2\sin^2\theta\, d\theta^2 = a^2 d\theta^2$$

$$L = \int_{-\frac{\pi}{2}}^{\frac{\pi}{2}} a\, d\theta = [a\theta]_{-\frac{\pi}{2}}^{\frac{\pi}{2}} = \pi a$$

(c) $r = a\sin\theta \Rightarrow dr = a\cos\theta\, d\theta$

$$ds^2 = r^2 d\theta^2 + dr^2$$
$$= a^2\cos^2\theta\, d\theta^2 + a^2\sin^2\theta\, d\theta^2 = a^2 d\theta^2$$

$$L = \int_0^{\pi} a\, d\theta = [a\theta]_0^{\pi} = \pi a$$

22. $r = a(1 + \cos\theta) \Rightarrow dr = -a\sin\theta\, d\theta$

$ds^2 = r^2\, d\theta^2 + dr^2 = [a^2(1 + 2\cos\theta + \cos^2\theta)]d\theta^2 + a^2\sin^2\theta\, d\theta^2$

$= a^2(2 + 2\cos\theta)\, d\theta^2 \Rightarrow ds = a\sqrt{2}\,(\sqrt{1+\cos\theta})\, d\theta$

$$s = 2\int_0^{\pi} a\sqrt{2}\,(\sqrt{1+\cos\theta})\, d\theta = 2a\sqrt{2}\int_0^{\pi}\sqrt{2}\sqrt{\frac{1+\cos\theta}{2}}\, d\theta$$

$$= 4a\int_0^{\pi}\left|\cos\frac{\theta}{2}\right| d\theta = 8a\sin\frac{\theta}{2}\Big]_0^{\pi} = 8a.$$

23. $r = a\sin^2\frac{\theta}{2},\ 0 \le \theta \le \pi, \Rightarrow dr = a\sin\frac{\theta}{2}\cos\frac{\theta}{2}\, d\theta$

$ds^2 = r^2d\theta^2 + dr^2 = a^2\sin^4\frac{\theta}{2}d\theta^2 + a^2\sin^2\frac{\theta}{2}\cos^2\frac{\theta}{2}d\theta^2$

$a^2\sin^2\frac{\theta}{2}d\theta^2(\sin^2\frac{\theta}{2} + \cos^2\frac{\theta}{2}) = a^2\sin^2\frac{\theta}{2}d\theta^2$

NOTE: $ds = a|\sin\frac{\theta}{2}|d\theta$ but that $\sin\frac{\theta}{2} \ge 0$ for $0 \le \theta \le \pi$.

$$L = a\int_0^{\pi}\sin\frac{\theta}{2}d\theta = \left[-2a\cos\frac{\theta}{2}\right]_0^{\pi} = 2a$$

24. $r = a\theta^2 \Rightarrow dr = 2a\theta\, d\theta$

$ds^2 = r^2\, d\theta^2 + dr^2 = a^2\theta^4 d\theta^2 + 4a^2\theta^2\, d\theta^2$; $ds = a\theta\sqrt{\theta^2 + 4}\, d\theta$

$$s = \int_0^{\pi} a\theta\sqrt{\theta^2+4}\, d\theta = \frac{a}{3}(\theta^2 + 4)^{3/2}\Big]_0^{\pi} = \frac{a}{3}[(\pi^2 + 4)^{3/2} - 8]$$

25. $r = a\sin^3\frac{\theta}{3},\ 0 \le \theta \le 3\pi, \Rightarrow dr = 3a\sin^2\frac{\theta}{3}\cos\frac{\theta}{3}(\frac{1}{3})\, d\theta$

$ds^2 = r^2d\theta^2 + dr^2 = a^2\sin^6\frac{\theta}{3}\, d\theta^2 + a^2\sin^4\frac{\theta}{3}\cos^2\frac{\theta}{3}\, d\theta^2$

$= a^2\sin^4\frac{\theta}{3}(\sin^2\frac{\theta}{3} + \cos^2\frac{\theta}{3})\, d\theta^2 = a^2\sin^4\frac{\theta}{3}\, d\theta^2$

$$s = \int_0^{3\pi} a\sin^2\frac{\theta}{3}\, d\theta = \frac{a}{2}\int_0^{3\pi}\left(1 - \cos\frac{2\theta}{3}\right)d\theta = \frac{a}{2}\left[\theta - \frac{3}{2}\sin\frac{2\theta}{3}\right]_0^{3\pi} = \frac{3a\pi}{2}$$

26. (a) $A = \frac{1}{2}\int r^2\, d\theta = \frac{1}{2}\int_0^{\frac{\pi}{6}} e^{4t}(3\, dt) = \frac{3}{8}e^{4t}\Big]_0^{\frac{\pi}{6}} = \frac{3}{8}[e^{2\pi/3} - 1]$

(b) $s = \int_0^{\frac{\pi}{6}}\sqrt{e^{4t} + \frac{4}{9}e^{4t}}\,(3\, dt) = \sqrt{13}\int_0^{\frac{\pi}{6}} e^{2t}\, dt = \frac{\sqrt{13}}{2}(e^{2\pi/3} - 1)$

27. $r^2 = 2a^2\cos 2\theta \Rightarrow 2r\,dr = -2(2a^2\sin 2\theta)d\theta \Rightarrow r^2dr^2 = 4a^4\sin^2 2\theta\, d\theta^2$

Then $y ds^2 = r\sin\theta ds^2 = r\sin\theta(r^2d\theta^2 + dr^2)$

$$S = \int 2\pi y ds = 2\pi\int_0^{\frac{\pi}{4}} r\sin\theta\sqrt{r^2d\theta^2 + dr^2} = 2\pi\int_0^{\frac{\pi}{4}} \sin\theta\sqrt{r^4d\theta^2 + r^2dr^2}$$

$$= 2\pi\int_0^{\frac{\pi}{4}} \sin\theta\sqrt{4a^4\cos^2 2\theta d\theta^2 + 4a^4\sin^2 2\theta d\theta^2}$$

$$= 2\pi\int_0^{\frac{\pi}{4}} 2a^2 \sin\theta\, d\theta = 4\pi a^2 \Big[-\cos\theta\Big]_0^{\frac{\pi}{4}} = 2\pi a^2 (2 - \sqrt{2}).$$ Total $= 4\pi a^2 (2 - \sqrt{2})$

28. $$A = \int 2\pi x\, ds = 2\pi\int_{-\frac{\pi}{2}}^{\frac{\pi}{2}} (r\cos\theta)\sqrt{4a^2\cos^2\theta + 4a^2\sin^2\theta}\, d\theta$$

$$= 4\pi\int_0^{\frac{\pi}{2}} (2a\cos\theta)(\cos\theta)(2a\, d\theta) = 16\pi a^2\left[\frac{1}{2}\theta + \frac{1}{4}\sin 2\theta\right]_0^{\frac{\pi}{2}} = 4\pi a^2$$

29. $r = 1 + \cos\theta \Rightarrow dr = -\sin\theta d\theta \quad \Rightarrow dr^2 = \sin^2\theta d\theta^2$

$\therefore ds^2 = r^2d\theta^2 + dr^2 = (1 + \cos\theta)^2d\theta^2 + \sin^2\theta d\theta^2$

$= 1 + 2\cos\theta + (\sin^2\theta + \cos^2\theta)\, d\theta^2 = (2 + 2\cos\theta)d\theta^2$

$$S = 2\pi\int_0^{\frac{\pi}{2}} y ds = 2\pi\int_0^{\frac{\pi}{2}} r\sin\theta\sqrt{2 + 2\cos\theta}\, d\theta$$

$$= 2\pi\int_0^{\frac{\pi}{2}} r\sin\theta\sqrt{2(2\cos^2\frac{\theta}{2})}\, d\theta = 4\pi\int_0^{\frac{\pi}{2}} r\left|\cos\frac{\theta}{2}\right|\sin\theta d\theta$$

$$= 4\pi\int_0^{\frac{\pi}{2}} (1 + \cos\theta)\cos\frac{\theta}{2}\sin\theta d\theta = 4\pi\int_0^{\frac{\pi}{2}} 2\cos^2\frac{\theta}{2}\cos\frac{\theta}{2} 2\sin\frac{\theta}{2}\cos\frac{\theta}{2} d\theta$$

$$= 16\pi\int_0^{\frac{\pi}{2}} 2\cos^4\frac{\theta}{2}\sin\frac{\theta}{2} d\theta = 16\pi\left[-\frac{2}{5}\cos^5\frac{\theta}{2}\right]_0^{\frac{\pi}{2}} = \frac{4\pi(8 - \sqrt{2})}{5}$$

30. (a) $r_{av} = \frac{1}{2\pi}\int_0^{2\pi} a(1 - \cos\theta)\, d\theta = \frac{a}{2\pi}[\theta - \sin\theta\Big]_0^{2\pi} = a$

(b) $r_{av} = \frac{1}{2\pi}\int_0^{2\pi} a\, d\theta = \frac{a}{2\pi}[\theta\Big]_0^{2\pi} = a$

(c) $r_{av} = \frac{1}{\pi}\int_{-\frac{\pi}{2}}^{\frac{\pi}{2}} a\cos\theta\, d\theta = \frac{a}{\pi}[\sin\theta\Big]_{-\frac{\pi}{2}}^{\frac{\pi}{2}} = \frac{2a}{\pi}$

10.M MISCELLANEOUS

1. $r = a\theta$ is the Spiral of Archimedes. See Problem 7, Article 10.2.

2. $r = a(1 + \cos 2\theta)$

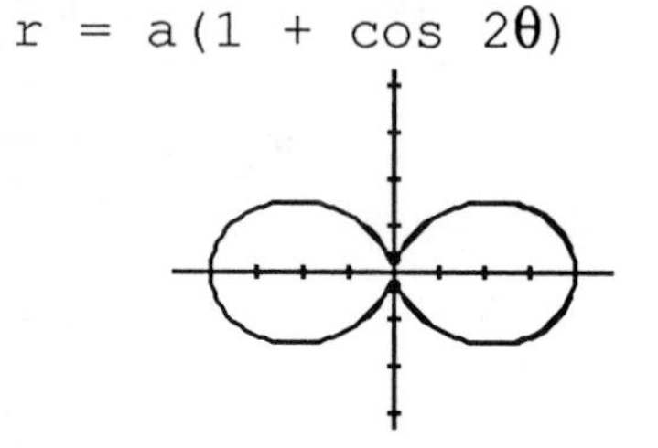

3. (a) $r = a\sec\theta = a(\frac{1}{\cos\theta}) \Rightarrow r\cos\theta = a$. $\therefore$ The graph is the vertical line $x = a$.

(b) $r = a\csc\theta = a(\frac{1}{\sin\theta}) \Rightarrow r\sin\theta = a$. $\therefore$ The graph is the horizontal line $y = a$.

(c) $r = a\sec\theta + a\csc\theta =$

$= a(\frac{1}{\cos\theta} + \frac{1}{\sin\theta})$

$1 = \frac{a}{r}(\frac{1}{\cos\theta} + \frac{1}{\sin\theta})$

$= a(\frac{1}{x} + \frac{1}{y})$

$xy = a(y + x) \Rightarrow y = \frac{ax}{x - a}$

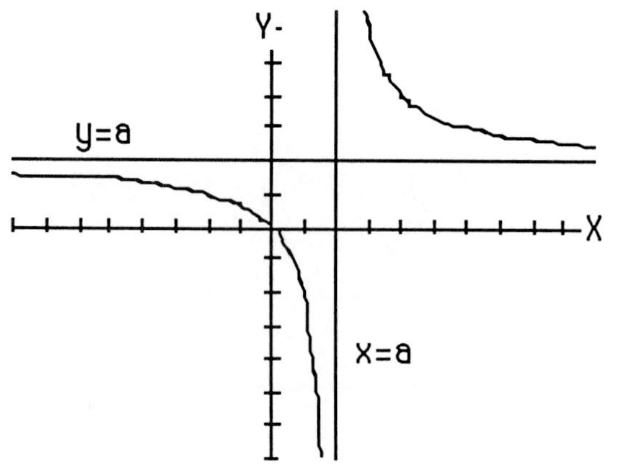

4. $r = a\sin\left(\theta + \frac{\pi}{3}\right)$

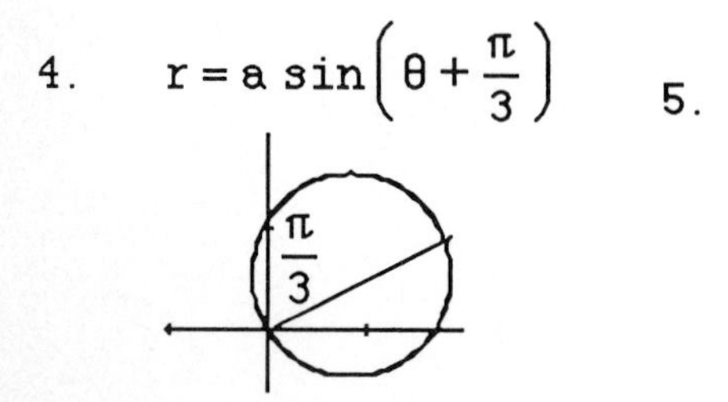

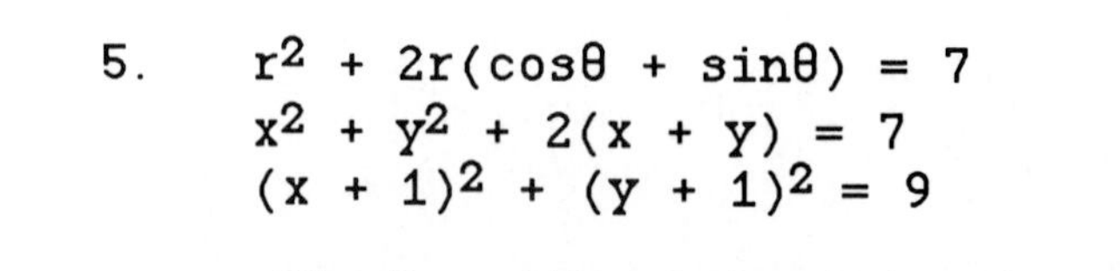

5. $r^2 + 2r(\cos\theta + \sin\theta) = 7$

$x^2 + y^2 + 2(x + y) = 7$

$(x + 1)^2 + (y + 1)^2 = 9$

Circle with center$(-1,-1)$, radius $= 3$

6. $r = a(\cos\theta + \sin\theta) \Rightarrow \sqrt{x^2+y^2} = a\left(\dfrac{x}{\sqrt{x^2+y^2}} + \dfrac{y}{\sqrt{x^2+y^2}}\right)$

$x^2 + y^2 = ax + ay \quad \Rightarrow \left(x - \dfrac{a}{2}\right)^2 + \left(y - \dfrac{a}{2}\right)^2 = \dfrac{a^2}{2}$

7. $r\cos\dfrac{\theta}{2} = a$

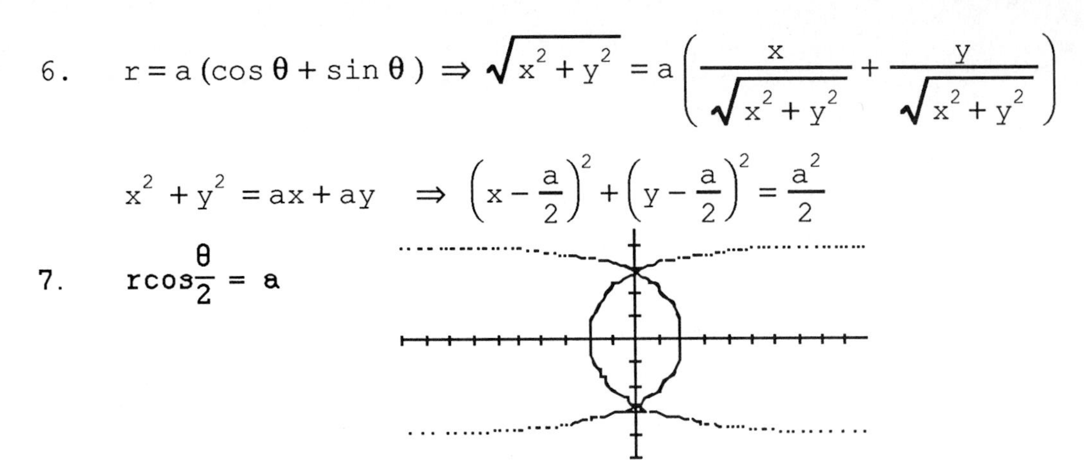

8. $r^2 = a^2 \sin\theta$

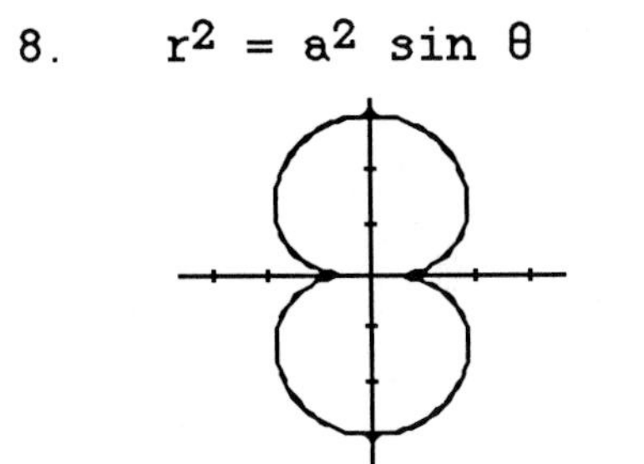

9. $r^2 = 2a^2 \sin 2\theta$

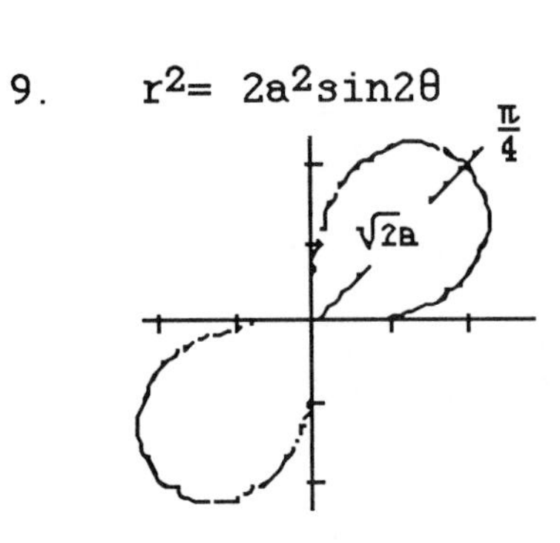

10. $r = a(1 - 2\sin 3\theta)$

11. (a) $r = \cos 2\theta$

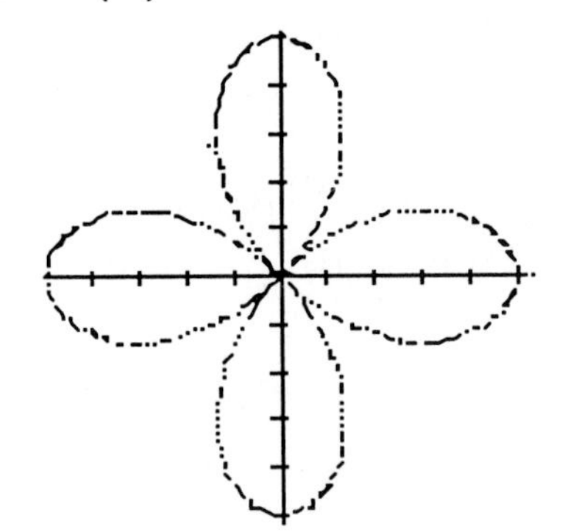

(b) $r^2 = \cos 2\theta$

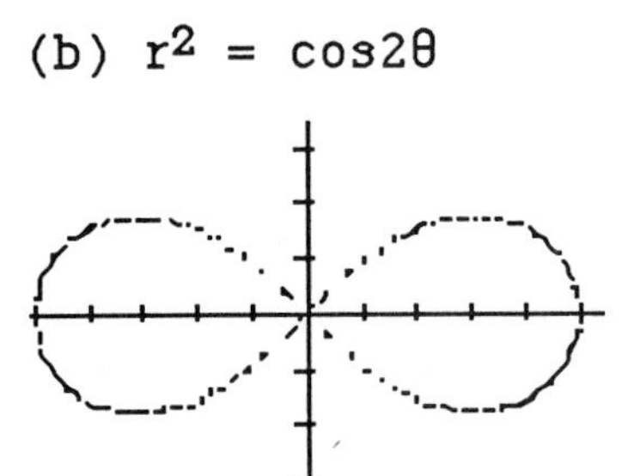

12. (a) $r = 1 + \cos\theta$

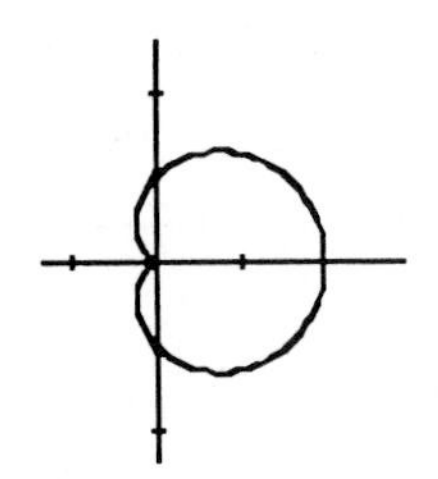

(b) $r = \dfrac{1}{1 + \cos\theta}$

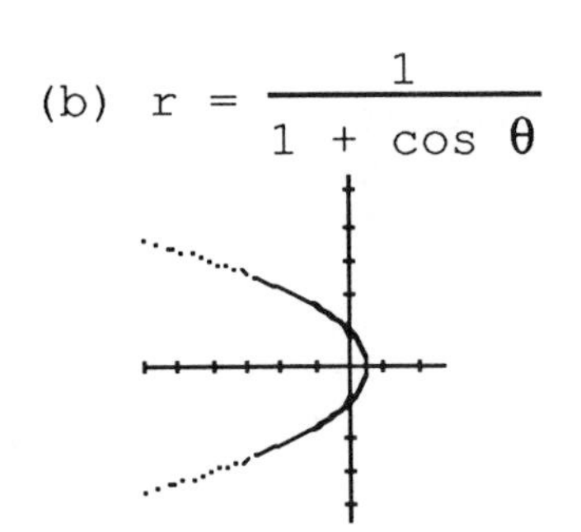

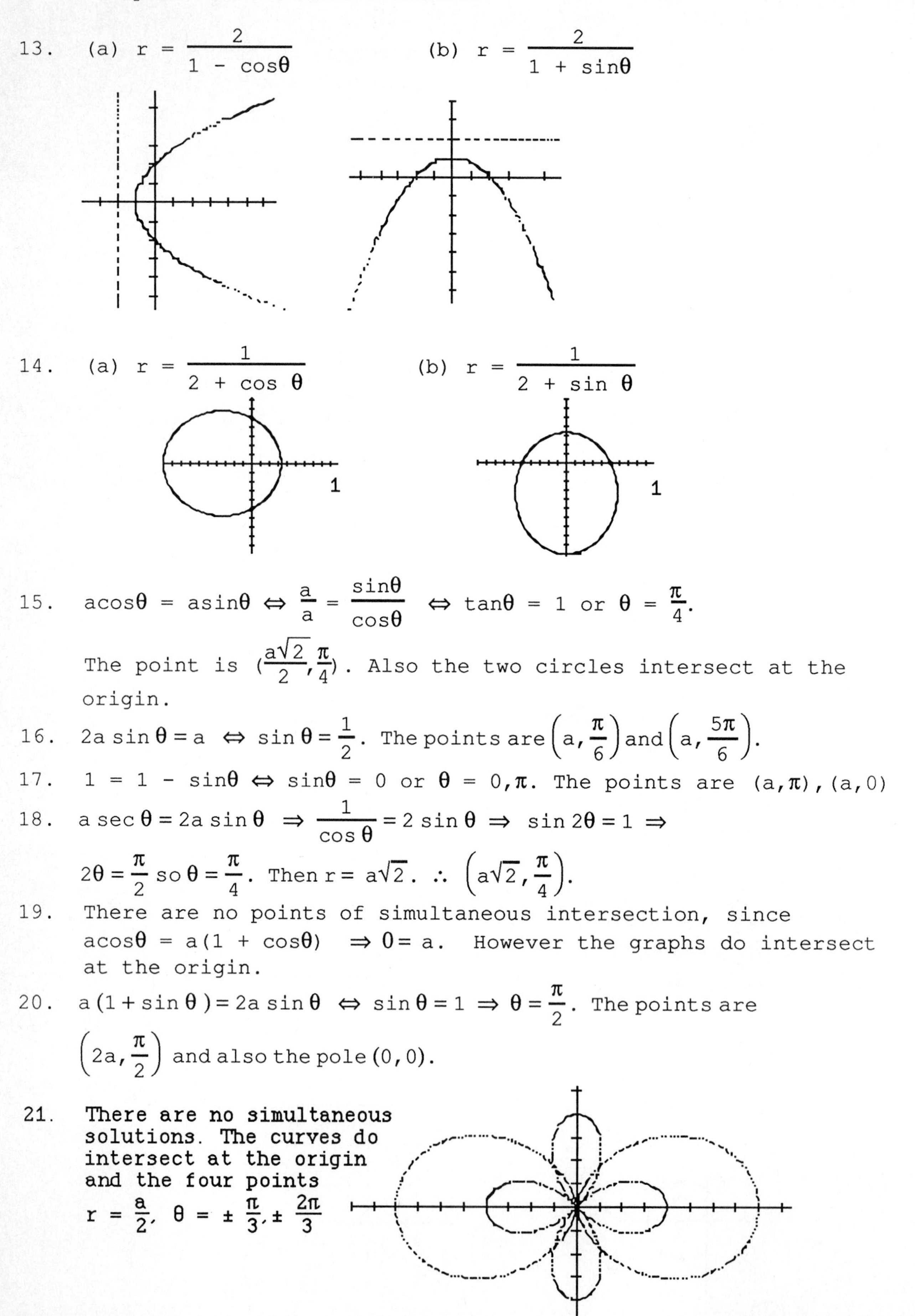

13. (a) $r = \dfrac{2}{1 - \cos\theta}$ (b) $r = \dfrac{2}{1 + \sin\theta}$

14. (a) $r = \dfrac{1}{2 + \cos\theta}$ (b) $r = \dfrac{1}{2 + \sin\theta}$

15. $a\cos\theta = a\sin\theta \Leftrightarrow \dfrac{a}{a} = \dfrac{\sin\theta}{\cos\theta} \Leftrightarrow \tan\theta = 1$ or $\theta = \dfrac{\pi}{4}$.

The point is $(\frac{a\sqrt{2}}{2}, \frac{\pi}{4})$. Also the two circles intersect at the origin.

16. $2a\sin\theta = a \Leftrightarrow \sin\theta = \dfrac{1}{2}$. The points are $\left(a, \dfrac{\pi}{6}\right)$ and $\left(a, \dfrac{5\pi}{6}\right)$.

17. $1 = 1 - \sin\theta \Leftrightarrow \sin\theta = 0$ or $\theta = 0, \pi$. The points are $(a, \pi), (a, 0)$

18. $a\sec\theta = 2a\sin\theta \Rightarrow \dfrac{1}{\cos\theta} = 2\sin\theta \Rightarrow \sin 2\theta = 1 \Rightarrow$

$2\theta = \dfrac{\pi}{2}$ so $\theta = \dfrac{\pi}{4}$. Then $r = a\sqrt{2}$. $\therefore$ $\left(a\sqrt{2}, \dfrac{\pi}{4}\right)$.

19. There are no points of simultaneous intersection, since $a\cos\theta = a(1 + \cos\theta) \Rightarrow 0 = a$. However the graphs do intersect at the origin.

20. $a(1 + \sin\theta) = 2a\sin\theta \Leftrightarrow \sin\theta = 1 \Rightarrow \theta = \dfrac{\pi}{2}$. The points are $\left(2a, \dfrac{\pi}{2}\right)$ and also the pole $(0, 0)$.

21. There are no simultaneous solutions. The curves do intersect at the origin and the four points $r = \frac{a}{2}$, $\theta = \pm\frac{\pi}{3}, \pm\frac{2\pi}{3}$

22. $4\cos 2\theta = \sec 2\theta \Rightarrow 4\cos^2 2\theta = 1 \Rightarrow \cos 2\theta = \pm\frac{1}{2} \Rightarrow \theta = \pm\frac{\pi}{6}, \pm\frac{5\pi}{6}.$

$r^2 = 2 \Rightarrow r = \pm\sqrt{2}. \therefore \left(\sqrt{2}, \pm\frac{\pi}{6}\right)$ and $\left(\sqrt{2}, \pm\frac{5\pi}{6}\right).$

23. (a) $r = \dfrac{1}{1 - \cos\theta}$

$r - r\cos\theta = 1$

$\sqrt{x^2 + y^2} = 1 + x$

$x^2 + y^2 = 1 + 2x + x^2$

$y^2 - 2x = 1$

(b) $r = \dfrac{1}{1 + \cos\theta}$

$r + r\cos\theta = 1$

$\sqrt{x^2 + y^2} = 1 - x$

$x^2 + y^2 = 1 - 2x + x^2$

$y^2 + 2x = 1$

24. (a) $r = \dfrac{1}{1 - \sin\theta}$

$r - r\sin\theta = 1$

$\sqrt{x^2 + y^2} - y = 1$

$x^2 + y^2 = 1 + 2y + y^2$

$x^2 = 2\left(y + \frac{1}{2}\right)$

(b) $r = \dfrac{1}{1 + \sin\theta}$

$r + r\sin\theta = 1$

$\sqrt{x^2 + y^2} + y = 1$

$x^2 + y^2 = 1 - 2y + y^2$

$x^2 = -2\left(y - \frac{1}{2}\right)$

25. (a) $r = \dfrac{1}{1 - 2\cos\theta}$

$r - 2r\cos\theta = 1$

$\sqrt{x^2 + y^2} = 1 + 2x$

$x^2 + y^2 = 1 + 4x + 4x^2$

$3x^2 - y^2 + 4x + 1 = 0$

(b) $r = \dfrac{1}{1 + 2\cos\theta}$

$r + 2r\cos\theta = 1$

$\sqrt{x^2 + y^2} = 1 - 2x$

$x^2 + y^2 = 1 - 4x + 4x^2$

$3x^2 - y^2 - 4x + 1 = 0$

26. (a) $r = \dfrac{2}{2 - \cos\theta}$

$2r - r\cos\theta = 2$

$2\sqrt{x^2 + y^2} - x = 2$

$4(x^2 + y^2) = 4 + 4x + x^2$

$3x^2 + 4y^2 - 4x = 4$

(b) $r = \dfrac{2}{2 + \cos\theta}$

$2r + r\cos\theta = 2$

$2\sqrt{x^2 + y^2} + x = 2$

$4(x^2 + y^2) = 4 - 4x + x^2$

$3x^2 + 4y^2 + 4x = 4$

27. The directrix is the line $x = 2$. $\therefore r = \dfrac{2}{1 + \cos\theta}$

28. The line has rectangular equation $y = -\frac{b}{a}x + b$.

$\therefore r\sin\theta = -\frac{b}{a}(r\cos\theta) + b$ or $r = \dfrac{ab}{a\sin\theta + b\cos\theta}$.

29. The diameter is $2a$. $\therefore r = -2a\cos\theta$

30. The equation of a parabola with focus $(0,0)$ and vertex $(a,0)$ is

$r = \dfrac{2a}{1 + \cos\theta}$. To rotate this 45°: $r = \dfrac{2a}{1 + \cos\left(\theta - \frac{\pi}{4}\right)}$.

31. The eccentricity is $\frac{1}{3}$, since a = 3 and c = 1. Using equation 16 in Section 10.3, we have

$$r = \frac{3(1 - \frac{1}{9})}{1 - \frac{1}{3}\cos\theta} = \frac{8}{3 - \cos\theta}$$

32. $a = 1,\ c = 2 \Rightarrow e = \frac{c}{a} = 2.\ \ k = ae - \frac{a}{e} = \frac{3}{2}.$

$$r = \frac{ke}{1 - e\cos\theta} = \frac{3}{1 - 2\cos\left(\theta + \frac{\pi}{2}\right)} = \frac{3}{1 + 2\sin\theta}.$$

33. $A = 4\cdot\frac{1}{2}\int_0^{\frac{\pi}{4}} a^2\cos 2\theta\,d\theta = 2a^2\left[\frac{1}{2}\sin 2\theta\right]_0^{\frac{\pi}{4}} = a^2$

34. $A = 2\int_0^{\pi}\frac{1}{2}a^2(2 - \cos\theta)^2\,d\theta = a^2\int_0^{\pi}\left(4 - 4\cos\theta + \frac{1}{2} + \frac{1}{2}\cos 2\theta\right)d\theta$

$$= a^2\left[\frac{9}{2}\theta - 4\sin\theta + \frac{1}{4}\sin 2\theta\right]_0^{\pi} = \frac{9\pi a^2}{2}$$

35. $A = 4\cdot\frac{1}{2}\int_0^{\frac{\pi}{2}} a^2(1 + \cos 2\theta)^2 d\theta = 2\int_0^{\frac{\pi}{2}} a^2(1 + 2\cos 2\theta + \cos^2 2\theta)\,d\theta$

$$= 2a^2\int_0^{\frac{\pi}{2}} 1 + 2\cos 2\theta + \frac{1}{2}(1 + \cos 4\theta)\,d\theta$$

$$= 2a^2\left[\frac{3\theta}{2} + \frac{\sin 2\theta}{4} + \frac{\sin 4\theta}{8}\right]_0^{\frac{\pi}{2}} = \frac{3a^2\pi}{2}$$

36. $A = 3\int_0^{\frac{\pi}{3}}\frac{1}{2}(4a^2\sin^2 3\theta)\,d\theta = 6a^2\int_0^{\frac{\pi}{3}}\left(\frac{1}{2} - \frac{1}{2}\cos 6\theta\right)d\theta$

$$= 3a^2\left[\theta - \frac{1}{6}\sin 6\theta\right]_0^{\frac{\pi}{3}} = \pi a^2$$

37. $A = 6\cdot\frac{1}{2}\int_0^{\frac{\pi}{3}} 2a^2\sin 3\theta\,d\theta = 6a^2\left[-\frac{1}{3}\cos 3\theta\right]_0^{\frac{\pi}{3}} = 4a^2$

38. $A = 4\int_0^{\frac{\pi}{2}}\frac{1}{2}\left(2a^2\cos^2\frac{\theta}{2}\right)d\theta$

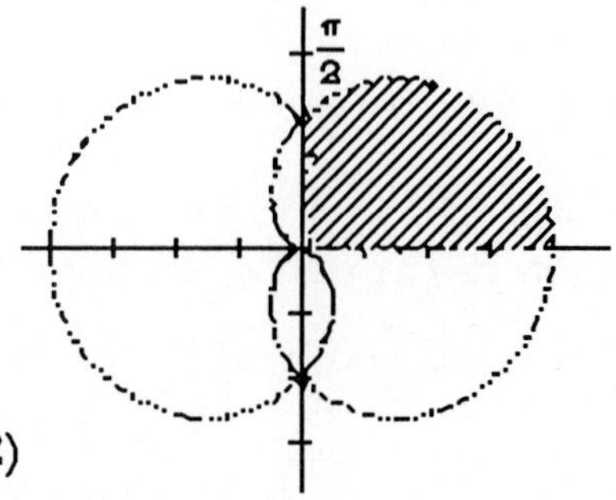

$$= 4a^2\int_0^{\frac{\pi}{2}}\frac{1 + \cos\theta}{2}\,d\theta$$

$$= 2a^2\left[\theta + \sin\theta\right]_0^{\frac{\pi}{2}} = a^2(\pi + 2)$$

$\frac{\pi}{2}$

39. $A = R_1 + R_2$, where the regions are above and below the x-axis.

$$R_1 = \frac{a^2}{2}\int_0^{\pi}(1 + \sin\theta)^2 - (\sin\theta)^2 d\theta$$

$$= \frac{a^2}{2}\int_0^{\pi}(1 + 2\sin\theta)d\theta$$

$$= \frac{a^2}{2}\Big[\theta - 2\cos\theta\Big]_0^{\pi} = \frac{a^2\pi}{2}$$

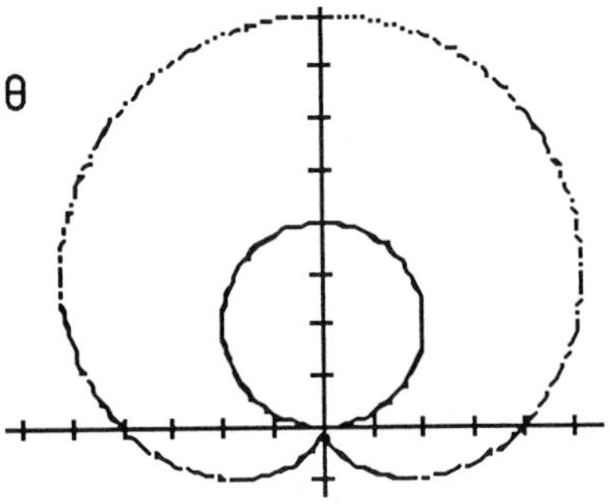

$$R_2 = 2\cdot\frac{1}{2}\int_{-\frac{\pi}{2}}^{0} a^2(1 + \sin\theta)^2 d\theta = \int_{-\frac{\pi}{2}}^{0} a^2(1 + 2\sin\theta + \frac{1}{2}(1 - \cos 2\theta))\,d\theta$$

$$= a^2\left[\frac{3\theta}{2} - 2\cos\theta - \frac{\sin 2\theta}{4}\right]_0^{\frac{\pi}{2}} = \frac{3a^2\pi}{4}.$$ The total area is then $\frac{5a^2\pi}{4}$

40. $$A = 8\cdot\frac{1}{2}\int_0^{\frac{\pi}{8}} (4a^2\cos^2 2\theta - 2a^2)\,d\theta = 4a^2\int_0^{\frac{\pi}{8}}(2 + 2\cos 4\theta - 2)\,d\theta$$

$$= 2a^2 \sin 4\theta\Big]_0^{\frac{\pi}{8}} = 2a^2$$

41. $$A = 4\cdot\frac{1}{2}\int_0^{\frac{\pi}{2}}[2a\sin^2\frac{\theta}{2}]^2 d\theta = 8a^2\int_0^{\frac{\pi}{2}}\left(\frac{1 - \cos\theta}{2}\right)^2 d\theta$$

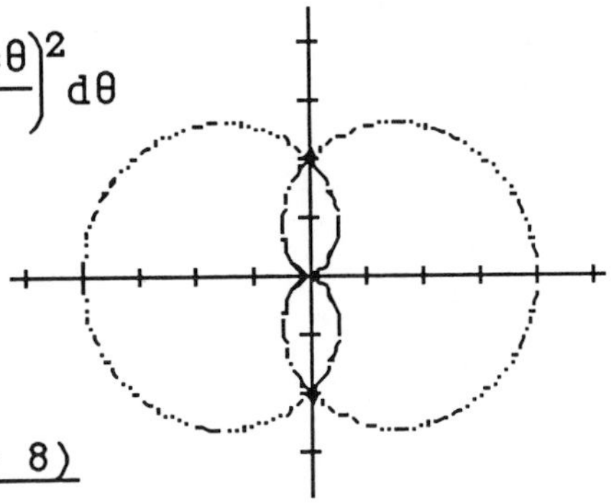

$$= 2a^2\int_0^{\frac{\pi}{2}}(1 - 2\cos\theta + \frac{1}{2}(1 + \cos 2\theta))d\theta$$

$$= 2a^2\left[\frac{3\theta}{2} - 2\sin\theta + \frac{\sin 2\theta}{4}\right]_0^{\frac{\pi}{2}} = \frac{a^2(3\pi - 8)}{2}$$

42. $$A = 4\cdot\frac{1}{2}\int_0^{\frac{\pi}{6}}(2a^2\cos 2\theta - a^2)\,d\theta = 2a^2[\sin 2\theta - \theta\Big]_0^{\frac{\pi}{6}} = a^2\left[\sqrt{3} - \frac{\pi}{3}\right]$$

43. $$r = a\cos^3\frac{\theta}{3} \Rightarrow dr = 3a\cos^2\frac{\theta}{3}(-\sin\frac{\theta}{3})\frac{1}{3}d\theta$$

$$ds^2 = r^2 d\theta^2 + dr^2 = a^2(\cos^3\frac{\theta}{3})^2 d\theta^2 + a^2(\cos^2\frac{\theta}{3}(-\sin\frac{\theta}{3}))^2 d\theta^2$$

$$= a^2\cos^4\frac{\theta}{3}d\theta^2(\cos^2\frac{\theta}{3} + \sin^2\frac{\theta}{3})$$

$\therefore \quad ds = a(\cos^2\frac{\theta}{3})\,d\theta$

$$\rho = 2\int_0^{\frac{3\pi}{2}} a\cos^2\frac{\theta}{3}d\theta = 2a\int_0^{\frac{3\pi}{2}}\left(\frac{1}{2}+\frac{1}{2}\cos\frac{2\theta}{3}\right)d\theta$$

$$= 2a\left[\frac{1}{2}\theta + \frac{3}{4}\sin\frac{2\theta}{3}\right]_0^{\frac{3\pi}{2}} = \frac{3a\pi}{2}$$

44. $r = a(1-\cos\theta) \Rightarrow dr = a\sin\theta\,d\theta;\ ds = \sqrt{dr^2 + (rd\theta)^2} =$

$$\sqrt{a^2\sin^2\theta\,d\theta^2 + a^2(1-2\cos\theta+\cos^2\theta)\,d\theta^2} = \sqrt{2a^2(1-\cos\theta)}\,d\theta$$

$$S = \int 2\pi\,y\,ds = \int_0^{\pi} 2\pi(r\sin\theta) = 2\pi\int_0^{\pi} a(1-\cos\theta)(\sin\theta)\,a\sqrt{2}(1-\cos\theta)^{1/2}\,d\theta$$

$$= 2\pi a^2\sqrt{2}\int_0^{\pi}\left(2\sin\frac{\theta}{2}\cos\frac{\theta}{2}\right)\left(2\sin^2\frac{\theta}{2}\right)^{3/2}d\theta$$

$$= 2\pi a^2\sqrt{2}\int_0^{\pi} 4\sqrt{2}\sin^4\frac{\theta}{2}\cos\frac{\theta}{2}\,d\theta = 16\pi a^2\left[\frac{2}{5}\sin^5\frac{\theta}{2}\right]_0^{\pi} = \frac{32\pi a^2}{5}$$

45. $\beta = \psi_2 - \psi_1$

$\tan\beta = \tan(\psi_2 - \psi_1)$

$$= \frac{\tan\psi_2 - \tan\psi_1}{1 + \tan\psi_2\tan\psi_1}$$

The curves will be orthogonal when $\tan\beta$ is undefined, or when

$$\tan\psi_2 = \frac{-1}{\tan\psi_1}$$

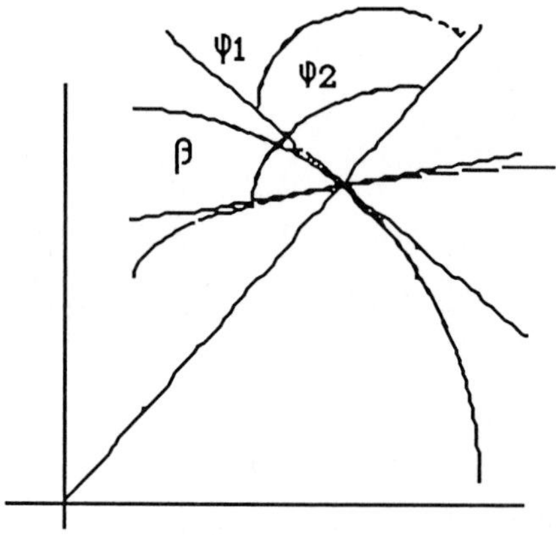

ψ_1 ψ_2 β

46. $r = \sin^4\frac{\theta}{4} \Rightarrow \frac{dr}{d\theta} = \sin^3\frac{\theta}{4}\cos\frac{\theta}{4}.\ \therefore \tan\varphi = \dfrac{\sin^4\frac{\theta}{4}}{\sin^3\frac{\theta}{4}\cos\frac{\theta}{4}} = \tan\frac{\theta}{4}$

47. $\tan\varphi = \dfrac{r}{\frac{dr}{d\theta}} = \dfrac{2a\sin3\theta}{6a\cos3\theta} = \frac{1}{3}\tan3\theta$

When $\theta = \frac{\pi}{3}$, $\tan\varphi = \frac{1}{3}\tan\pi = 0$ so $\varphi = 0$.

48. $r\theta = a \Rightarrow r = a\theta^{-1} \Rightarrow \dfrac{dr}{d\theta} = -a\theta^{-2}$.

$$\tan\varphi = \frac{a\theta^{-1}}{-a\theta^{-2}} = -\theta\Bigg]_{\theta=1} = -1,\ \text{so } \varphi = \frac{3\pi}{4}.$$

$\lim_{\theta\to\infty}\tan\varphi = -\infty$ so $\varphi \to \frac{\pi}{2}$.

49. $\tan\varphi_1 = \dfrac{\sqrt{3}\cos\theta}{-\sqrt{3}\sin\theta} = -\cot\theta = -\dfrac{1}{\sqrt{3}}$ at $\theta = \dfrac{\pi}{3}$

$\tan\varphi_2 = \dfrac{\sin\theta}{\cos\theta} = \tan\theta = \sqrt{3}$ at $\theta = \dfrac{\pi}{3}$. Since these values are negative reciprocals, the tangents are perpendicular.

50. $a(1 + \cos\theta) = 3a\cos\theta \Leftrightarrow \cos\theta = \dfrac{1}{2}$ or $\theta = \dfrac{\pi}{3}$.

$$\tan\varphi_2 = \left.\frac{a(1+\cos\theta)}{-a\sin\theta}\right]_{\theta=\frac{\pi}{3}} = -\sqrt{3}$$

$$\tan\varphi_1 = \left.\frac{3\cos\theta}{-3\sin\theta}\right]_{\theta=\frac{\pi}{3}} = -\frac{1}{\sqrt{3}}$$

$$\tan\beta = \frac{-\sqrt{3} + \frac{1}{\sqrt{3}}}{1-1} \text{ is undefined. } \therefore \beta = \frac{\pi}{2}$$

51. $r_1 = \dfrac{1}{1 - \cos\theta} \Rightarrow \dfrac{dr_1}{d\theta} = -\dfrac{\sin\theta}{(1-\cos\theta)^2}$

$r_2 = \dfrac{3}{1 + \cos\theta} \Rightarrow \dfrac{dr_2}{d\theta} = \dfrac{3\sin\theta}{(1+\cos\theta)^2}$

$\dfrac{1}{1-\cos\theta} = \dfrac{3}{1+\cos\theta} \Leftrightarrow 1 + \cos\theta = 3 - 3\cos\theta \Leftrightarrow 4\cos\theta = 2$

$\Leftrightarrow \cos\theta = \dfrac{1}{2}$ or $\theta = \pm\dfrac{\pi}{3}$. Intersection is at points $(2, \pm\frac{\pi}{3})$

$$\tan\varphi_1 = \frac{\frac{1}{1-\cos\theta}}{\frac{-\sin\theta}{(1-\cos\theta)^2}} = -\frac{1-\cos\theta}{\sin\theta} = -\frac{1}{\sqrt{3}} \text{ at } \theta = \frac{\pi}{3}$$

$$\tan\varphi_2 = \frac{\frac{3}{1+\cos\theta}}{\frac{3\sin\theta}{(1+\cos\theta)^2}} = \frac{1+\cos\theta}{\sin\theta} = \sqrt{3} \text{ at } \theta = \frac{\pi}{3}$$

$\tan\beta$ is undefined at $\theta = \dfrac{\pi}{3}$ since $1 + \left(\dfrac{-1}{\sqrt{3}}\right)(\sqrt{3}) = 1 - 1 = 0$

52. (a) We need $\varphi + \theta = \pi$, so that $\tan\varphi = \tan(\pi - \theta) = -\tan\theta$.

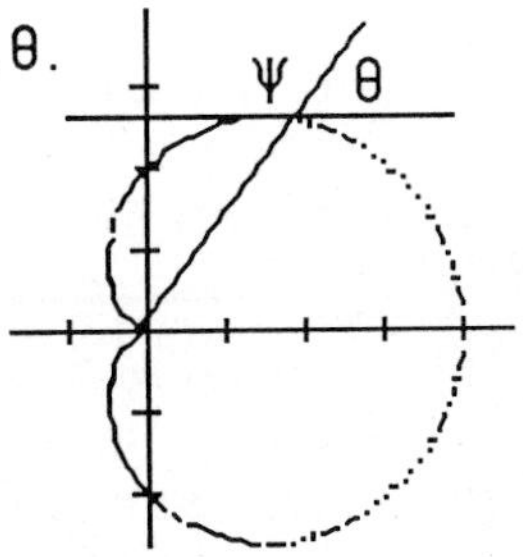

$\dfrac{1+\cos\theta}{-\sin\theta} = -\dfrac{\sin\theta}{\cos\theta} \Rightarrow \cos\theta + \cos^2\theta = \sin^2\theta$

$2\cos^2\theta + \cos\theta - 1 = 0 \Rightarrow \cos\theta = \dfrac{1}{2}$ or $\cos\theta = -1$.

The points are $\left(\dfrac{3a}{2}, \pm\dfrac{\pi}{3}\right)$ and $(0, \pi)$

ψ θ

(b) We need $\varphi+\theta = \frac{\pi}{2}$, so that $\tan\varphi = \tan\left(\frac{\pi}{2}-\theta\right) = \cot\theta$.

$$\frac{1+\cos\theta}{-\sin\theta} = \frac{\cos\theta}{\sin\theta} \Rightarrow \sin\theta(1+2\cos\theta)=0$$

$$\cos\theta = -\frac{1}{2} \text{ or } \sin\theta = 0$$

The points are $\left(\frac{a}{2}, \pm\frac{2\pi}{3}\right)$ and $(2a, 0)$

53. $$r_1 = \frac{a}{1+\cos\theta} \Rightarrow \frac{dr_1}{d\theta} = \frac{a\sin\theta}{(1+\cos\theta)^2}$$

$$r_2 = \frac{b}{1-\cos\theta} \Rightarrow \frac{dr_2}{d\theta} = -\frac{b\sin\theta}{(1-\cos\theta)^2}$$

$$\tan\varphi_1 = \frac{\dfrac{a}{1+\cos\theta}}{\dfrac{a\sin\theta}{(1+\cos\theta)^2}} = \frac{1+\cos\theta}{\sin\theta}$$

$$\tan\varphi_2 = \frac{\dfrac{b}{1-\cos\theta}}{\dfrac{-b\sin\theta}{(1-\cos\theta)^2}} = \frac{1-\cos\theta}{-\sin\theta}$$

$$1+\tan\varphi_1\tan\varphi_2 = 1+\left(\frac{1+\cos\theta}{\sin\theta}\right)\left(\frac{1-\cos\theta}{-\sin\theta}\right) = 1-\frac{1-\cos^2\theta}{\sin^2\theta} = 0$$

54. $$\tan\varphi = \left.\frac{a(1-\cos\theta)}{a\sin\theta}\right]_{\theta=\frac{\pi}{2}} = 1 \Rightarrow \varphi = \frac{\pi}{4}.$$

55. $$r = 3\sec\theta \Rightarrow r = \frac{3}{\cos\theta}$$

$$\frac{3}{\cos\theta} = 4+4\cos\theta \Leftrightarrow 3 = 4\cos\theta+4\cos^2\theta \Leftrightarrow (2\cos\theta+3)(2\cos\theta-1)=0$$

$$\cos\theta = \frac{1}{2} \text{ or } \theta = \frac{\pi}{3}, \frac{5\pi}{3}.$$

$$\tan\varphi_2 = \frac{4(1+\cos\theta)}{-4\sin\theta} = -\frac{1+\cos\theta}{\sin\theta} = -\sqrt{3} \text{ at } \frac{\pi}{3}$$

$$\tan\varphi_1 = \frac{3\sec\theta}{3\sec\theta\tan\theta} = \cot\theta = \frac{1}{\sqrt{3}} \text{ at } \frac{\pi}{3}.$$

$\tan\beta$ is undefined and $\beta = \frac{\pi}{2}$

56. $$\tan\varphi = \left.\frac{a\tan\dfrac{\theta}{2}}{\dfrac{a}{2}\sec^2\dfrac{\theta}{2}}\right]_{\theta=\frac{\pi}{2}} = 1 \Rightarrow \varphi = \frac{\pi}{4}.\ \Phi = \theta+\varphi = \frac{3\pi}{4}, \text{ so } \tan\Phi = -1.$$

57. $$\frac{1}{1-\cos\theta} = \frac{1}{1-\sin\theta} \Leftrightarrow 1-\cos\theta = 1-\sin\theta$$

$$\Leftrightarrow \cos\theta = \sin\theta \text{ or } \theta = \frac{\pi}{4}$$

$$\tan\varphi_1 = \frac{\dfrac{1}{1-\cos\theta}}{\dfrac{-\sin\theta}{(1-\cos\theta)^2}} = \frac{1-\cos\theta}{-\sin\theta}, \quad \tan\varphi_2 = \frac{\dfrac{1}{1-\sin\theta}}{\dfrac{\cos\theta}{(1-\sin\theta)^2}} = \frac{1-\sin\theta}{\cos\theta}$$

At $\theta = \frac{\pi}{4}$, $\tan\varphi_1 = 1 - \sqrt{2}$ and $\tan\varphi_2 = \sqrt{2} - 1$

$$\tan\beta = \frac{(\sqrt{2}-1) - (1-\sqrt{2})}{1 + (\sqrt{2}-1)(1-\sqrt{2})}) = \frac{2\sqrt{2}-2}{2\sqrt{2}-2} = 1 \quad \therefore\ \beta = \frac{\pi}{4}$$

58. (b) $r^2 = 2\csc 2\theta = \dfrac{2}{2\sin\theta\cos\theta} \Rightarrow r^2\sin\theta\cos\theta = 1 \Rightarrow xy = 1$

(c) At $\theta = \frac{\pi}{4}$, $x = y = 1$. Then $\dfrac{dy}{dx} = -\dfrac{1}{x^2} = -1$ so $\Phi = \dfrac{3\pi}{4} \Rightarrow \varphi = \dfrac{\pi}{2}$.

59. (a) $\tan a = \dfrac{r}{\frac{dr}{d\theta}} \Rightarrow \dfrac{dr}{r} = \dfrac{d\theta}{\tan a}$

$$\ln r = \frac{1}{\tan a}\theta + C \quad \text{or } r = Ae^{\frac{\theta}{\tan a}}$$

$$A = \frac{1}{2}\int_{\theta_1}^{\theta_2} A^2 e^{\frac{2\theta}{\tan a}}d\theta =$$

$$= \left[\frac{1}{4}A^2 \tan a\, e^{\frac{2\theta}{\tan a}}\right]_{\theta_2}^{\theta_1} = \frac{\tan a}{4}(r_2^2 - r_1^2) \text{ since}$$

$$r_2^2 = A^2 e^{\frac{2\theta_2}{\tan a}} \text{ and } r_1^2 = A^2 e^{\frac{2\theta_1}{\tan a}}. \quad K = \frac{\tan a}{4}$$

(b) $\tan a = \dfrac{r}{\frac{dr}{d\theta}} \Rightarrow dr = \dfrac{r\,d\theta}{\tan a} \Rightarrow dr^2 = \dfrac{r^2 d\theta^2}{\tan^2 a}$

$$ds^2 = r^2\,d\theta^2 + dr^2 = r^2\,d\theta^2 + \frac{r^2 d\theta^2}{\tan^2 a} = r^2\,d\theta^2\left(\frac{\sec^2 a}{\tan^2 a}\right)$$

$$s = \int_{\theta_1}^{\theta_2} Ae^{\frac{\theta}{\tan a}}\frac{\sec a}{\tan a}d\theta = A\sec a\, e^{\frac{\theta}{\tan a}}\Big]_{\theta_1}^{\theta_2}$$

$= K(r_2 - r_1)$, constant $K = \sec a$.

60. (b) $r^2 \sin 2\theta = 2a^2 \Rightarrow r^2 \sin\theta\cos\theta = a^2 \Rightarrow xy = a^2$. $\frac{dy}{dx} = -\frac{a^2}{x^2}$.

If $P(x_1, y_1)$ is a point on the curve, the tangent line is

$y - y_1 = -\frac{a^2}{x_1^2}(x - x_1)$. Its x-intercept is $x = \frac{x_1^2 y_1}{a^2} + x_1 = 2x_1$.

But then $PQ^2 = x_1^2 + y_1^2 = OP^2$ so $\triangle$ OPQ is isosceles.

61. By Prob. 1, Art. 10.4, the area is $\frac{3\pi a^2}{2}$. $\bar{y} = 0$ by symmetry.

$$M_y = \frac{1}{3}\int_0^{2\pi}[a(1 + \cos\theta)]^3\cos\theta d\theta$$

$$= \frac{a^3}{3}\int_0^{2\pi}[(\cos\theta + 3\cos^2\theta + 3\cos^3\theta + \cos^4\theta)d\theta$$

$$I_1 = \int_0^{2\pi}\cos\theta d\theta = [\sin\theta]_0^{2\pi} = 0$$

$$I_2 = \int_0^{2\pi}3\cos^2\theta d\theta = \frac{3}{2}\int_0^{2\pi}(1 + \cos 2\theta)d\theta = \frac{3}{2}(\theta + \frac{\sin 2\theta}{2})_0^{2\pi} = 3\pi$$

$$I_3 = \int_0^{2\pi}3\cos^3\theta d\theta = 3\int_0^{2\pi}(1 - \sin^2\theta)\cos\theta d\theta = 3\sin\theta - \sin^3\theta]_0^{2\pi} = 0$$

$$I_4 = \int_0^{2\pi}\cos^4\theta d\theta = \frac{1}{4}\int_0^{2\pi}(1 + 2\cos 2\theta + \cos^2 2\theta)\, d\theta$$

$$= \frac{1}{4}\left[\theta + \sin 2\theta + \frac{\theta}{2} + \frac{\sin 4\theta}{8}\right]_0^{2\pi} = \frac{3\pi}{4}$$

$$My = \frac{a^3}{3}(3\pi + \frac{3\pi}{4}) = \frac{5\pi a^3}{4}\ ;\ \bar{x} = \frac{\frac{5\pi a^3}{4}}{\frac{3\pi a^2}{2}} = \frac{5a}{6}$$

62. $\bar{x} = 0$ by symmetry. $A = \frac{\pi a^2}{2}$. $M_y = \frac{1}{3}\int_0^{\pi} a^3 \sin\theta\, d\theta = -\frac{a^3}{3}\cos\theta\Big]_0^{\pi} = \frac{2a^3}{3}$.

$\bar{y} = \frac{4a}{3\pi}$. $\therefore \left(0, \frac{4a}{3\pi}\right)$ in rectangular or $\left(\frac{4a}{3\pi}, \frac{\pi}{2}\right)$ in polar.

63. $r = a(1 + \cos\theta) \Rightarrow dr = -a\sin\theta d\theta \Rightarrow dr^2 = a^2\sin^2\theta d\theta^2$

$\therefore ds^2 = r^2 d\theta^2 + dr^2 = a^2(1 + \cos\theta)^2 d\theta^2 + a^2\sin^2\theta d\theta^2$

$= a^2(1 + 2\cos\theta + (\sin^2\theta + \cos^2\theta))\, d\theta^2 = 2a^2(1 + \cos\theta)d\theta^2$

$$L = \int_0^{2\pi} \sqrt{2a^2(2\cos^2\frac{\theta}{2})}\, d\theta = 2a\int_0^{2\pi} |\cos\frac{\theta}{2}| d\theta = 4a\int_0^{\pi} \cos\frac{\theta}{2} d\theta = 8a\sin\frac{\theta}{2}]_0^{\pi} = 8a$$

$\bar{y} = 0$ by symmetry. $\int_0^{2\pi} r\cos\theta ds = \int_0^{2\pi} a(1 + \cos\theta)(\cos\theta)(2a|\cos\frac{\theta}{2}|)\, d\theta$

$$= 2\int_0^{\pi} a(2\cos^2\frac{\theta}{2})(\cos\theta)(2a|\cos\frac{\theta}{2}|)\, d\theta = 8a^2\int_0^{\pi} (\cos^3\frac{\theta}{2})(\cos\theta) d\theta$$

$$= 8a^2\int_0^{\pi} (\cos^3\frac{\theta}{2})(2\cos^2\frac{\theta}{2} - 1)\, d\theta = 8a^2\int_0^{\pi} (2\cos^4\frac{\theta}{2} - \cos^2\frac{\theta}{2}) \cos\frac{\theta}{2} d\theta$$

$$= 8a^2\int_0^{\pi} [2(1-\sin^2\frac{\theta}{2})^2 - (1 - \sin^2\frac{\theta}{2})] \cos\frac{\theta}{2} d\theta$$

$$= 8a^2\int_0^{\pi} (1-3\sin^2\frac{\theta}{2} + 2\sin^4\frac{\theta}{2}) \cos\frac{\theta}{2} d\theta$$

$$= 8a^2\left[2\sin\frac{\theta}{2} - 2\sin^3\frac{\theta}{2} + \frac{4}{5}\sin^5\frac{\theta}{2}\right]_0^{\pi} = \frac{32a^2}{5};\quad \bar{x} = \frac{32a^2}{5}\cdot\frac{1}{8a} = \frac{4a}{5}.$$

CHAPTER 11

INFINITE SEQUENCES AND INFINITE SERIES

11.1 SEQUENCES OF NUMBERS

1. $a_1 = \frac{2}{3}$; $a_2 = \frac{3}{5}$; $a_3 = \frac{4}{7}$; $a_4 = \frac{5}{9}$; $\lim\limits_{x \to \infty} \frac{n+1}{2n+1} = \frac{1}{2}$

2. $a_1 = \frac{1}{2}$; $a_2 = 1$; $a_3 = \frac{5}{4}$; $a_4 = \frac{7}{5}$; $\lim\limits_{n \to \infty} \frac{2n-1}{n+1} = 2$

3. $a_1 = -\frac{1}{3}$; $a_2 = -\frac{3}{5}$; $a_3 = -\frac{5}{7}$; $a_4 = -\frac{7}{9}$; $\lim\limits_{x \to \infty} \frac{1-2n}{1+2n} = -1$

4. $a_1 = \frac{1}{2}$.; $a_2 = \frac{3}{4}$; $a_3 = \frac{7}{8}$; $a_4 = \frac{15}{16}$; $\lim\limits_{n \to \infty} \frac{2^n - 1}{2^n} = 1$

5. $a_1 = \frac{1}{2}$; $a_2 = \frac{1}{2}$; $a_3 = \frac{1}{2}$; $a_4 = \frac{1}{2}$; $\lim\limits_{x \to \infty} \frac{2^n}{2^{n+1}} = \frac{1}{2}$

6. $a_1 = \frac{1}{2}$; $a_2 = \frac{5}{4}$; $a_3 = \frac{7}{8}$; $a_4 = \frac{17}{16}$; $\lim\limits_{n \to \infty} 1 + \frac{(-1)^n}{2^n} = 1$

7. $x_1 = 1$; $x_{n+1} = x_n + \left(\frac{1}{2}\right)^n$; $x_2 = 1 + \frac{1}{2} = \frac{3}{2}$; $x_3 = \frac{3}{2} + \left(\frac{1}{2}\right)^2 = \frac{7}{4}$;

$$x_4 = \frac{7}{4} + \left(\frac{1}{2}\right)^3 = \frac{15}{8};\ x^5 = \frac{15}{8} + \left(\frac{1}{2}\right)^4 = \frac{31}{16};\ x_6 = \frac{31}{16} + \left(\frac{1}{2}\right)^5 = \frac{63}{32}$$

8. $x_1 = 1$; $x_{n+1} = \frac{x_n}{n+1}$; $x_2 = \frac{1}{3}$; $x_3 = \frac{\frac{1}{3}}{3+1} = \frac{1}{12}$; $x_4 = \frac{\frac{1}{12}}{4+1} = \frac{1}{60}$;

$$x_5 = \frac{\frac{1}{60}}{5+1} = \frac{1}{360};\ x_6 = \frac{\frac{1}{360}}{6+1} = \frac{1}{2520}$$

9. $x_1 = 2$; $x_{n+1} = \frac{x_n}{2}$; $x_2 = \frac{2}{2} = 1$; $x_3 = \frac{1}{2}$; $x_4 = \frac{\frac{1}{2}}{2} = \frac{1}{4}$;

$$x_5 = \frac{\frac{1}{4}}{2} = \frac{1}{8};\ x_6 = \frac{\frac{1}{8}}{2} = \frac{1}{16}$$

10. $x_1 = -2$; $x_{n+1} = \frac{n}{n+1} x_n$; $x_2 = \frac{2}{3}(-2) = -\frac{4}{3}$; $x_3 = \frac{3}{4}\left(-\frac{4}{3}\right) = -1$;

$$x_4 = \frac{4}{5}(-1) = -\frac{4}{5};\ x_5 = \frac{5}{6}\left(-\frac{4}{5}\right) = -\frac{2}{3};\ x_6 = \frac{6}{7}\left(-\frac{2}{3}\right) = -\frac{4}{7}$$

11. $x_1 = x_2 = 1$; $x_{n+2} = x_{n+1} + x_n$; $x_3 = 1+1 = 2$; $x_4 = 2+1 = 3$;

$x_5 = 3+2 = 5$; $x_6 = 5+3 = 8$

12. $x_1 = 1$; $x_{n+1} = x_1 + x_2 + \ldots + x_n$; $x_2 = x_1 = 1$; $x_3 = x_1 + x_2 = 2$;

$x_4 = x_1 + x_2 + x_3 = 4$; $x_5 = x_1 + x_2 + x_3 + x_4 = 8$;

$x_6 = x_1 + x_2 + x_3 + x_4 + x_5 = 16$; $x_{n+1} = 1 + \sum_{k=0}^{n} 2^k$

13. (a) $(1)^2 - 2(1)+2 = -1$; $(3)^2 - 2(2)^2 = 1$; If $a^2 - 2b^2 = 1$, then

$(a + 2b)^2 - 2(a + b)^2 = a^2 - 4ab + 4b^2 - 2a^2 - 4ab - 2b^2 =$

$2b^2 - a^2 = -1$. If $a^2 - 2b^2 = -1$, then $(a + 2b)^2 - 2(a + b)^2$

$2b^2 - a^2 = -(a^2 - 2b^2) = -(-1) = 1$

(b) $\left(\dfrac{a+2b}{a+b}\right)^2 - 2 = \dfrac{a^2+4ab+4b^2}{a^2+2ab+b^2} - 2 = \dfrac{2b^2-a^2}{(a+b)^2} = \dfrac{\pm 1}{(y_n)^2}$

$= \lim_{n\to\infty} r_n = \lim_{n\to\infty} \sqrt{2 \pm \left(\dfrac{1}{y_n}\right)^2} = \sqrt{2}$

14. Computer Exercise

15. Let $f(x) = \cos x - x$. $f'(x) = -\sin x - 1$ and using the formula $x_{n+1} = x_n - \dfrac{f(x_n)}{f'(x_n)}$, we have $x_1 = 0.755222417$, $x_2 = 0.739141666$, $x_3 = 0.739085134$, $x_4 = 0.739085133$.

16. $x_0 = 1$; $x_{n+1} = \cos(x_n)$; $x_1 - \cos 1$; $x_2 = \cos(x_1) = \cos(\cos 1)$;

$x_3 = \cos(\cos(\cos 1))$; $x_4 = \cos(\cos(\cos(\cos(1)))$

Converges (slowly) to the value in Problem 15.

17. 0.876726216; $x^2 - \sin x = 0$

18. Define $f(x) = x - 0.1 \sin x - \dfrac{\pi}{3}$ so that $f'(x) = 1 - 0.1 \cos x$;

With $x_1 = \dfrac{\pi}{3}$, Newton's Method gives $x \approx 1.3976209$.

19. (a) Using $y = \tan x - 2x$, the root is $x = 1.65561185$

(b) Yes, $\dfrac{\pi}{3} \approx 1.05 < 1.66$

(c) If $x < \tan x < 2x$ for all $0 < x < b$,

then $\int x\,dx < \int \tan x\,dx < \int 2x\,dx$ or $\dfrac{x^2}{2} < \ln|\sec x| < x^2$

11.2 LIMIT THEOREMS

1. $0, -\dfrac{1}{4}, -\dfrac{2}{9}, -\dfrac{3}{16}$; converges to 0

2. $\dfrac{1}{2}, \dfrac{2}{4}, \dfrac{3}{8}, \dfrac{4}{16}$; converges to 0

3. $\frac{1}{3}, \frac{1}{9}, \frac{1}{27}, \frac{1}{81}$; converges to 0

4. $1, \frac{1}{2}, \frac{1}{6}, \frac{1}{24}$; converges to 0

5. $1, -\frac{1}{3}, \frac{1}{5}, -\frac{1}{7}$; converges to 0

6. 1,3,1,3, diverges

7. 0,-1,0,1,0; diverges

8. $8, 2\sqrt{2}, 2, \sqrt{2}$; converges to 1

9. $1, -\frac{1}{\sqrt{2}}, \frac{1}{\sqrt{3}}, -\frac{1}{2}$; converges to 0

10. 1,1,1,1; converges to 1

11. converges to 0

12. $\lim_{n\to\infty} \frac{n}{10} = \frac{1}{10} \lim_{n\to\infty} n = \infty$, diverges

13. converges to 1

14. $\lim_{n\to\infty} \frac{1+(-1)^n}{n} \le \lim_{n\to\infty} \frac{2}{n} = 0$

15. diverges because the terms oscillate between ±1.

16. $\lim_{n\to\infty} (1+(-1)^n)$ diverges by oscillation

17. converges to $-\frac{2}{3}$

18. $\lim_{n\to\infty} \frac{n^2 - n}{2n^2 + n} = \lim_{n\to\infty} \frac{1 - \frac{1}{n}}{2 + \frac{1}{n}} = \frac{1}{2}$

19. $\sqrt{\frac{2n}{n+1}} = \sqrt{\frac{2}{1+\frac{1}{n}}}$ converges to $\sqrt{2}$

20. $\lim_{n\to\infty} \frac{\sin n}{n} \le \lim_{n\to\infty} \frac{|\sin n|}{n} \le \lim_{n\to\infty} \frac{1}{n} = 0$

21. converges to 0

22. $\lim_{n\to\infty} \sin\left(\frac{\pi}{2} + \frac{1}{n}\right) = \sin\frac{\pi}{2} = 1$

23. diverges, terms oscillate between 1 and -1

24. $\lim_{n\to\infty} \frac{\sin^2 n}{2^n} \le \lim_{n\to\infty} \frac{1}{2^n} = 0$

25. $\frac{n^2}{(n+1)^2} = \left(\frac{n}{n+1}\right)^2$ converges to 1

26. $\lim_{n\to\infty} \frac{\sqrt{n-1}}{\sqrt{n}} = \lim_{n\to\infty} \sqrt{\frac{n-1}{n}} = 1$

27 $\lim \frac{1 - 5n^4}{n^4 + 8n^3} = \frac{\frac{1}{n^4} - 5}{1 + \frac{8}{n}} = -5$

28. $\lim_{n\to\infty} (3^{2n+1})^{1/n} = \lim_{n\to\infty} 3^{(2+1/n)} = 9$

29. $\lim_{n\to\infty} \tanh n = \lim_{n\to\infty} \frac{e^n - e^{-n}}{e^n + e^{-n}} = \lim_{n\to\infty} \frac{1 - \frac{1}{e^{2n}}}{1 + \frac{1}{e^{2n}}} = 1$

30. $\lim_{n\to\infty} \frac{\ln n}{\sqrt{n}} = \lim_{n\to\infty} \frac{\frac{1}{n}}{\frac{1}{2\sqrt{n}}} = \lim_{n\to\infty} \frac{2}{\sqrt{n}} = 0$

31. $\lim_{n\to\infty} \frac{2(n+1)+1}{2n+1} = \lim_{n\to\infty} \frac{2n+3}{2n+1} = \lim_{n\to\infty} \frac{2+\frac{3}{n}}{2+\frac{1}{n}} = 1$

32. $\lim_{n\to\infty} \frac{(n+1)!}{n!} = \lim_{n\to\infty} (n+1) = \infty$

33. $\lim_{n\to\infty} 5 = 5$

34. $\lim_{n\to\infty} 5^n = \infty$

35. $\lim_{n\to\infty} (.5)^n = \lim_{n\to\infty} \left(\frac{1}{2}\right)^n = 0$

36. $\lim_{n\to\infty} \frac{10^{n+1}}{10^n} = 10$

37. $\lim_{n\to\infty} \frac{n^n}{(n+1)^{n+1}} = \lim_{n\to\infty} \left(\frac{n}{n+1}\right)^n \left(\frac{1}{n+1}\right) = (1)(0) = 0$

38. $\lim_{n\to\infty} (0.03)^{1/n} = 1$

39. $\lim_{n\to\infty} \sqrt{2 - \frac{1}{n}} = \sqrt{2}$

40. $\lim_{n\to\infty} [2 + (0.1)^n] = 2$

41. $\lim_{n\to\infty} \frac{3^n}{n^3} = \lim_{n\to\infty} \frac{(\ln 3)3^n}{3n^2} = \lim_{n\to\infty} \frac{(\ln 3)^2 3^n}{6n} = \lim_{n\to\infty} \frac{(\ln 3)^3 3^n}{6} = \infty$

42. $\lim_{n\to\infty} \frac{\ln(n+1)}{n+1} = \lim_{n\to\infty} \frac{1}{n+1} = 0$

43. $\lim_{n\to\infty} (\ln n - \ln(n+1)) = \lim_{n\to\infty} \ln\left(\frac{n}{n+1}\right) = \ln \lim_{n\to\infty} \left(\frac{n}{n+1}\right) = \ln 1 = 0$

44. $\lim_{n\to\infty} \frac{1-2^n}{2^n} = \lim_{n\to\infty} \left[\frac{1}{2^n} - 1\right] = -1$

45. $\lim_{n\to\infty} \frac{n^2 - 2n + 1}{n-1} = \lim_{n\to\infty} \frac{1 - \frac{2}{n} + \frac{1}{n^2}}{\frac{1}{n} - \frac{1}{n^2}} = \frac{1}{0} = \infty$

46. $\lim_{n\to\infty} \frac{n + (-1)^n}{n} = \lim_{n\to\infty} \left[1 + \frac{(-1)^n}{n}\right] = 1$

47. $\lim\limits_{n\to\infty}\left(-\frac{1}{2}\right)^n = 0$

48. $\lim\limits_{n\to\infty}\frac{\ln n}{\ln 2n} = \lim\limits_{n\to\infty}\frac{\frac{1}{n}}{\frac{2}{2n}} = 1$

49. $\lim\limits_{n\to\infty}\tan^{-1} n = \frac{\pi}{2}$

50. $\lim\limits_{n\to\infty}\sinh(\ln n) = \lim\limits_{n\to\infty}\frac{e^{\ln n} - e^{-\ln n}}{2} = \lim\limits_{n\to\infty}\frac{n - \frac{1}{n}}{2} = \infty$

51. $\lim\limits_{n\to\infty} n\sin\frac{1}{n} = \lim\limits_{n\to\infty}\frac{\sin\frac{1}{n}}{\frac{1}{n}} = \lim\limits_{n\to\infty}\frac{\cos\frac{1}{n}\left(-\frac{1}{n^2}\right)}{-\frac{1}{n^2}} = \cos 0 = 1$

52. $\lim\limits_{n\to\infty}\frac{2n + \sin n}{n + \cos 5n} = \lim\limits_{n\to\infty}\frac{2 + \frac{\sin n}{n}}{1 + \frac{\cos 5n}{n}} = 2$

53. $\lim\limits_{n\to\infty}\frac{n^2}{2n-1}\sin\frac{1}{n} = \lim\limits_{n\to\infty}\left(\frac{n}{2n-1}\right)\left(n\sin\frac{1}{n}\right) = \left(\frac{1}{2}\right)(1) = \frac{1}{2}$

54. $\lim\limits_{n\to\infty} n\left(1 - \cos\frac{1}{n}\right) = \lim\limits_{n\to\infty}\frac{1 - \cos\frac{1}{n}}{\frac{1}{n}} = \lim\limits_{n\to\infty}\frac{\sin\frac{1}{n}\left(-\frac{1}{n^2}\right)}{-\frac{1}{n^2}} = 0$

55. Note that $\frac{n!}{n^n} = \frac{1\cdot 2\cdot 3\cdot \ldots \cdot n}{n\cdot n\cdot n \ldots \cdot n} < \frac{1}{n}$ since $\frac{2\cdot 3\cdot \ldots \cdot n}{n\cdot n\cdot \ldots \cdot n} < 1$

$\therefore\ 0 < \lim\limits_{n\to\infty}\frac{n!}{n^n} < \lim\limits_{n\to\infty}\frac{1}{n} = 0$

56. $a = 3;\ x_1 = 1;\ x_2 = 2;\ x_3 = 1.75;\ x_4 = 1.732142857;\ x_5 = 1.73205081$

57. $\lim\limits_{n\to\infty}(x)^{1/n} = 1$ for all $x > 0$. Fix $x > 0$ and consider $a_n = x^{1/n}$.

$\lim\limits_{n\to\infty}(\ln a_n) = \lim\limits_{n\to\infty}\frac{1}{n}\ln x = \ln x \lim\limits_{n\to\infty}\frac{1}{n} = 0$. Therefore,

$\lim\limits_{n\to\infty}(x)^{1/n} = \lim\limits_{n\to\infty} e^{\frac{1}{n}\ln x} = e^0 = 1$

58. $x_1 = 1;\ x_2 = 1 + \cos 1 = 1.5403023;\ x_3 = x_2 + \cos x_2 = 1.5707916$

$x_4 = x_3 + \cos x_3 = 1.5707963;$ if $x_1 = 5$, then $x_2 = 5.2836622$,

$x_3 = 5.8243657$, .., converges to $\frac{5\pi}{2}$.

59. $\lim\limits_{n\to\infty} nf\left(\frac{1}{n}\right) = \lim\limits_{n\to\infty}\frac{f\left(\frac{1}{n}\right)}{\frac{1}{n}} = \lim\limits_{n\to\infty}\frac{f'\left(\frac{1}{n}\right)\left(-\frac{1}{n^2}\right)}{-\frac{1}{n^2}} = \lim\limits_{n\to\infty} f'\left(\frac{1}{n}\right) = f'(0)$

60. If $f(x) = \tan^{-1} x$ then $f(0) = 0$, $f'(x) = \dfrac{1}{1 + x^2}$ and $f'(0) = 1$.

By Problem 59, $\lim\limits_{n\to\infty} n \tan^{-1} n = 1$.

61. Let $f(\frac{1}{n}) = e^{\frac{1}{n}} - 1$. Then $f(x) = e^x - 1$ and $f'(x) = e^x$.

$\lim\limits_{n\to\infty} (e^{\frac{1}{n}} - 1) = 1$ since $f'(0) = 1$

62. If $f(x) = \ln(1 + 2x)$ then $f(0) = 0$, $f'(x) = \dfrac{2}{1 + 2x}$ and $f'(0) = 2$.

By Problem 59, $\lim\limits_{n\to\infty} n \ln(1 + 2x) = 2$.

63. Suppose that $\{a_n\}$ converges to some finite value L. Let $\varepsilon = 1$ be given. There exists $N_1 > 0$ for which

(1) $|a_n - L| < 1$ or $a_n < L + 1$ for all $n > N_1$.

There also exists $N_2 > 0$ for which

(2) $f(n) = a_n > L + 1$ for all $n > N_2$.

Let $N > \max\{N_1, N_2\}$. For all $n > N$, both equations (1) and (2) are true, which cannot be. Thus the sequence $\{a_n\}$ cannot converge, and hence must diverge.

64. Please see Theorem 1, Appendix A1.

65. The conclusion is that $|f(a_n) - f(L)| < \varepsilon$, so that the sequence $\{f(a_n)\}$ converges to $f(L)$.

66. Let $\{a_n\}$ and $\{b_n\}$ be sequences both converging to L. Define $\{c_n\}$ by

$$c_{2n} = a_n \text{ and } c_{2n+1} = b_n,\ n = 1, 2, 3, ..$$

Let $\varepsilon > 0$ be given. There exists N_1 for which $|a_n - L| < \varepsilon$ for $n > N_1$ and there exists N_2 for which $|b_n - L| < \varepsilon$ for all $n > N_2$.

Choose $N = \max\{N_1, N_2\}$ so that both inequalities hold for all $n > N$.

For this N, we must then have $|c_n - L| < \varepsilon$ so $\{c_n\}$ also converges to L.

11.3 LIMITS THAT ARISE FREQUENTLY

1. $\lim\limits_{n\to\infty} \dfrac{1 + \ln n}{n} = \lim\limits_{n\to\infty} \left(\dfrac{1}{n} + \dfrac{\ln n}{n}\right) = 0 + 0 = 0$

2. $\lim\limits_{n\to\infty} \dfrac{\ln n}{3n} = \dfrac{1}{3} \lim\limits_{n\to\infty} \dfrac{\ln n}{n} = 0$

3. $\lim\limits_{n\to\infty} \dfrac{(-4)^n}{n!} = 0$ by Formula 6 with $x = -4$.

3. $\lim_{n\to\infty} \frac{(-4)^n}{n!} = 0$ by Formula 6 with $x = -4$.

4. $\lim_{n\to\infty} (10n)^{1/n} = \lim_{n\to\infty} (10)^{1/n} \lim_{n\to\infty} n^{1/n} = 1$ By Formulas 2 and 3

5. $\lim_{n\to\infty} (.5)^n = 0$ by Formula 4 for $x = 0.5$.

6. $\lim_{n\to\infty} \frac{1}{(0.9)^n} = \lim_{n\to\infty} \left(\frac{10}{9}\right)^n$ diverges since $\frac{10}{9} > 1$.

7. $\lim_{n\to\infty} \left(1 + \frac{7}{n}\right)^n = e^7$, by Formula 5, for $x = 7$

8. $\lim_{n\to\infty} \left(\frac{n+5}{n}\right)^n = \lim_{n\to\infty} \left(1 + \frac{5}{n}\right)^n = e^5$, by Formula 5, for $x = 5$.

9. $\lim_{n\to\infty} \frac{\ln(n+1)}{n} = \lim_{n\to\infty} \frac{\frac{1}{n+1}}{1} = 0$

10. $\lim_{n\to\infty} \ln a_n = \lim_{n\to\infty} \ln (n+1)^{1/n} = \lim_{n\to\infty} \frac{\ln (n+1)}{n} = \lim_{n\to\infty} \frac{1}{n+1} = 0.$

$\therefore \lim_{n\to\infty} e^{a_n} = e^0 = 1$

11. $\lim_{n\to\infty} \frac{n!}{10^{6n}} = \lim_{n\to\infty} \frac{1}{\frac{10^{6n}}{n!}} = \infty.$

12. $\lim_{n\to\infty} \frac{1}{\sqrt{2^n}} = \lim_{n\to\infty} \left(\sqrt{\frac{1}{2}}\right)^n = 0$

13. $\lim_{n\to\infty} \sqrt[2n]{n} = \lim_{n\to\infty} \left(n^{\frac{1}{n}}\right)^{\frac{1}{2}} = 1$

14. $\lim_{n\to\infty} \ln (n+4)^{1/(n+4)} = \lim_{n\to\infty} \frac{\ln (n+4)}{n+4} = \lim_{n\to\infty} \frac{1}{n+4} = 0$

$\therefore \lim_{n\to\infty} (n+4)^{1/(n+4)} = e^0 = 1$

15. $\lim_{n\to\infty} \frac{1}{3^{2n-1}} = 0$

16. $\lim_{n\to\infty} \ln \left(1 + \frac{1}{n}\right)^n = \ln \left(\lim_{n\to\infty} \left(1 + \frac{1}{n}\right)^n\right) = \ln e = 1$

17. $\lim_{n\to\infty} \left(\frac{n}{n+1}\right)^n = \lim_{n\to\infty} \left(\frac{n+1}{n}\right)^{-n} = \lim_{n\to\infty} \left[\left(1 + \frac{1}{n}\right)^n\right]^{-1} = e^{-1}$

18. $\lim_{n\to\infty} \left(1 + \frac{1}{n}\right)^{-n} = \lim_{n\to\infty} \left[\left(1 + \frac{1}{n}\right)^n\right]^{-1} = e^{-1}$

19. $\lim_{n\to\infty} \frac{\ln (2n+1)}{n} = \lim_{n\to\infty} \frac{\frac{2}{2n+1}}{1} = 0$

20. $\lim_{n\to\infty} \ln(2n+1)^{1/n} = \lim_{n\to\infty} \frac{\ln(2n+1)}{n} = \lim_{n\to\infty} \frac{1}{2n+1} = 0$

$\therefore \lim_{n\to\infty} (2n+1)^{1/n} = e^0 = 1$

21. $\lim_{n\to\infty} \sqrt[n]{\frac{x^n}{2n+1}}$, $x > 0$, $= x\left(\lim_{n\to\infty} \sqrt[n]{\frac{1}{2n+1}}\right) = x$

22. $\lim_{n\to\infty} (n^2)^{1/n} = \lim_{n\to\infty} (n^{1/n})^2 = 1$

23. Consider $a_n = \ln(n^2+n)^{1/n}$. $\lim_{n\to\infty} \ln(n^2+n)^{1/n} = \lim_{n\to\infty} \frac{1}{n}\ln(n^2+n)^{1/n} =$

$\lim_{n\to\infty} \frac{2n+1}{n^2+n} = 0$. $\therefore \lim_{n\to\infty} e^{\frac{1}{n}\ln(n^2+n)} = e^0 = 1$.

24. $\lim_{n\to\infty} \frac{3^n \cdot 6^n}{2^{-n} \cdot n!} = \lim_{n\to\infty} \frac{6^{2n}}{n!} = 0$

25. $\lim_{n\to\infty} \left(\frac{3}{n}\right)^{\frac{1}{n}} = \lim_{n\to\infty} \frac{3^{1/n}}{n^{1/n}} = 1$

26. $\lim_{n\to\infty} (4^n n)^{1/n} = 4 \lim_{n\to\infty} n^{1/n} = 4$

27. $\lim_{n\to\infty} \left(1 - \frac{1}{n}\right)^n = e^{-1}$

28. $\lim_{n\to\infty} \left(1 - \frac{1}{n^2}\right)^n = \lim_{n\to\infty} \left(1 - \frac{1}{n}\right)^n \left(1 + \frac{1}{n}\right)^n = e^{-1} e = 1$

29. $\lim_{n\to\infty} \frac{\ln(n^2)}{n} = \lim_{n\to\infty} \frac{2\ln n}{n} = 2\lim_{n\to\infty} \frac{\ln n}{n} = 0$

30. $\lim_{n\to\infty} \frac{(\ln n)^{200}}{n} = \lim_{n\to\infty} \frac{200(\ln n)^{199}}{n} = \ldots = \lim_{n\to\infty} \frac{200!\ln n}{n} = 0$

31. Diverges, since $\lim_{n\to\infty} \ln n = \infty$ and $\lim_{n\to\infty} n^{1/n} = 1$.

32. $\lim_{n\to\infty} \frac{1}{n} \int_1^n \frac{1}{x} dx = \lim_{n\to\infty} \frac{\frac{d}{dn}\int_1^n \frac{1}{x} dx}{\frac{dn}{dn}} = \lim_{n\to\infty} \frac{1}{n} = 0$

33. $\int_1^n \frac{1}{x^p} dx = \left.\frac{x^{-p+1}}{-p+1}\right]_1^n = \frac{1}{-p+1}[n^{-p+1} - 1]$. For $p > 1$,

$\frac{1}{-p+1} \lim_{n\to\infty} [n^{-p+1} - 1] = (-1)\frac{1}{-p+1} = \frac{1}{p-1}$.

34. $N \geq 693$

35. $N \geq 9124$

36. $\frac{2^n}{n!} < 10^{-9}$ if $n \geq 17$ since $\frac{2^{17}}{17!} \approx 3.685 \times 10^{-10}$

37. $|\frac{1}{n^c} - 1| < \varepsilon \Leftrightarrow \frac{1}{n^c} < \varepsilon \Leftrightarrow n^c > \frac{1}{\varepsilon}$ or $n > \sqrt[c]{\frac{1}{\varepsilon}}$

$\therefore$ Let $N = \varepsilon^{-\frac{1}{c}}$. For $n > N$, $0 < \frac{1}{n^c} < \varepsilon$ so $\frac{1}{n^c}$ converges to 0.

About the hint: $\frac{1}{n^{0.04}} < .001 \Leftrightarrow n^{0.04} > 10^3 \Leftrightarrow n > (10^3)^{25} = 10^{75}$

11.4 INFINITE SERIES

1. $S_n = \frac{2\left(1-\left(\frac{1}{3}\right)^n\right)}{1-\frac{1}{3}} = 3\left(1-\left(\frac{1}{3}\right)^n\right)$. $r = \frac{1}{3} < 1$, so $S = \frac{2}{1-\frac{1}{3}} = 3$

2. $S_n = \frac{\frac{9}{100}\left(1-\left(\frac{1}{100}\right)^n\right)}{1-\frac{1}{100}} = \frac{1}{11}\left(1-\left(\frac{1}{100}\right)^n\right)$. $r = \frac{1}{100}$ so $S = \frac{1}{11}$

3. $S_n = \frac{1(1-e^{-n})}{1-e^{-1}}$. $r = \frac{1}{e} < 1$ so $S = \frac{1}{1-\frac{1}{e}} = \frac{e}{e-1}$

4. $S_n = \frac{2}{3}\left[1-(-1)^{n-1}2^{n-1}\right]$; $S = \frac{1}{1+\frac{1}{2}} = \frac{2}{3}$

5. $S_n = \frac{1(1-(-2)^n)}{1-(-2)} = \frac{1-(-2)^n}{3}$. $r = 2 > 1$ so series diverges.

6. Using partial fractions, $\frac{1}{(n+1)(n+2)} = \frac{1}{n+1} - \frac{1}{n+2}$.

$$\sum_{n=1}^{\infty}\frac{1}{(n+1)(n+2)} = \sum_{n=1}^{\infty}\left(\frac{1}{n+1} - \frac{1}{n+2}\right) = \lim_{n\to\infty}\left(\frac{1}{2} - \frac{1}{n+2}\right) = \frac{1}{2}$$

7. $\ln\frac{1}{2} + \ln\frac{2}{3} + \ln\frac{3}{4} + \ldots + \ln\frac{n}{n+1} =$

$\ln 1 - \ln 2 + \ln 2 - \ln 3 + \ln 3 - \ln 4 + \ldots + \ln n - \ln(n+1)$

$\therefore \lim_{n\to\infty} S_n = \lim_{n\to\infty}(-\ln(n+1)) = -\infty$. so series diverges

8. $S_n = 1 + 2 + 3 + \ldots + n = \frac{n(n+1)}{2}$; diverges

9. (a) $\sum_{n=-2}^{\infty}\frac{1}{(n+4)(n+5)}$ (b) $\sum_{n=0}^{\infty}\frac{1}{(n+2)(n+3)}$ (c) $\sum_{n=5}^{\infty}\frac{1}{(n-3)(n-2)}$

10. (a) Down: $4 + \frac{3}{4}(4) + \left(\frac{3}{4}\right)^2 4 + \ldots = \dfrac{4}{1 - \frac{3}{4}} = 16$

Up: $\frac{3}{4}(4) + \left(\frac{3}{4}\right)^2 4 + \ldots = \dfrac{3}{1 - \frac{3}{4}} = 12$. Total $= 28$

(b) $t = \sqrt{\dfrac{4}{4.9}} + 2\sqrt{\dfrac{3}{4}\cdot\dfrac{4}{4.9}} + 2\sqrt{\left(\dfrac{3}{4}\right)^2 \dfrac{4}{4.9}} + \ldots$

$= \sqrt{\dfrac{4}{4.9}} + \dfrac{4}{\sqrt{4.9}}\left(\dfrac{1}{1 - \sqrt{\frac{3}{4}}}\right) \approx 12.58$ sec

11. $S = \dfrac{1}{1 - \frac{1}{4}} = \dfrac{4}{3}$

12. $S = \dfrac{\frac{1}{16}}{1 - \frac{3}{4}} = \dfrac{1}{12}$

13. $S = \dfrac{\frac{7}{4}}{1 - \frac{1}{4}} = \dfrac{7}{3}$

14. $S = \dfrac{5}{1 + \frac{1}{4}} = 4$

15. $S = \dfrac{5}{1 - \frac{1}{2}} + \dfrac{1}{1 - \frac{1}{3}} = 10 + \dfrac{3}{2} = \dfrac{23}{2}$

16. $S = \dfrac{5}{1 - \frac{1}{2}} + \dfrac{1}{1 - \frac{1}{3}} = \dfrac{17}{2}$

17. $S = \dfrac{1}{1 - \frac{2}{5}} = \dfrac{5}{3}$

18. $S = \dfrac{2}{1 - \frac{2}{5}} = \dfrac{10}{3}$

19. $\displaystyle\sum_{n=1}^{\infty} \frac{4}{(4n-3)(4n+1)} = \sum_{n=1}^{\infty}\left(\frac{1}{4n-3} - \frac{1}{4n+1}\right) =$

$\left(1 - \frac{1}{5}\right) + \left(\frac{1}{5} - \frac{1}{9}\right) + \left(\frac{1}{9} - \frac{1}{13}\right) + \ldots + \left(\frac{1}{4n-3} - \frac{1}{4n+1}\right) + \ldots$

$\therefore \lim\limits_{n\to\infty} S_n = \lim\limits_{n\to\infty}\left(1 - \dfrac{1}{4n+1}\right) = 1$

20. $\displaystyle\sum_{n=1}^{\infty} \frac{1}{(4n-3)(4n+1)} = \sum_{n=1}^{\infty}\left(\frac{1}{4n-3} - \frac{1}{4n+1}\right) = \lim_{n\to\infty}\frac{1}{4}\left(1 - \frac{1}{4n+1}\right) = \frac{1}{4}$

21. $\sum_{n=3}^{\infty} \frac{4}{(4n-3)(4n+1)} = \sum_{n=3}^{\infty} \left(\frac{1}{4n-3} - \frac{1}{4n+1}\right) =$

$\left(\frac{1}{9} - \frac{1}{13}\right) + \left(\frac{1}{13} - \frac{1}{17}\right) + \ldots + \left(\frac{1}{4n-3} - \frac{1}{4n+1}\right) + \ldots$

$\therefore \lim_{n\to\infty} S_n = \lim_{n\to\infty} \left(\frac{1}{9} - \frac{1}{4n+1}\right) = \frac{1}{9}$

22. $\sum_{n=1}^{\infty} \frac{2n+1}{n^2(n+1)^2} = \sum_{n=1}^{\infty} \left(\frac{1}{n^2} - \frac{1}{(n+1)^2}\right) = \lim_{n\to\infty} \left(1 - \frac{1}{(n+1)^2}\right) = 1$

23. (a) $0.234234234\ldots = \frac{234}{10^3} + \frac{234}{10^6} + \ldots$

$$S = \frac{\frac{234}{10^3}}{1 - \frac{1}{10^3}} = \frac{234}{999} = \frac{26}{111}$$

(b) Yes, every repeating decimal is a geometric series, with ratio $= 10^{-n}$, where n is the number of repeating digits.

24. $1.24\,123\,123\ldots = \frac{124}{100} + \frac{123}{10^5} + \frac{123}{10^8} + \ldots = \frac{124}{100} + \frac{\frac{123}{10^5}}{1 - \frac{1}{10^3}}$

$= \frac{124}{100} + \frac{123}{99900} = \frac{41333}{333000}$

25. $\sum_{n=0}^{\infty} \left(\frac{1}{\sqrt{2}}\right)^n = \frac{1}{1 - \frac{1}{\sqrt{2}}} = \frac{\sqrt{2}}{\sqrt{2} - 1} = 2 + \sqrt{2}$

26. $\sum_{n=1}^{\infty} \ln\frac{1}{n}$ diverges, since $\lim_{n\to\infty} \ln\frac{1}{n} \neq 0$

27. $\sum_{n=1}^{\infty} (-1)^{n+1} \frac{3}{2^n} = \frac{\frac{3}{2}}{1 - \left(-\frac{1}{2}\right)} = 1$

28. $\sum_{n=1}^{\infty} (\sqrt{2})^n$ diverges, geometric series with $r = \sqrt{2} > 1$

29. $\sum_{n=0}^{\infty} \cos n\pi = 1 - 1 + 1 - 1 + 1\ldots$ diverges because $\lim_{n\to\infty} (-1)^n \neq 0$

30. $\sum_{n=0}^{\infty} \frac{\cos n\pi}{5^n} = \sum_{n=0}^{\infty} (-1)^n \left(\frac{1}{5}\right)^n$ converges to $S = \frac{1}{1 + \frac{1}{5}} = \frac{5}{6}$

31. $\sum_{n=0}^{\infty} e^{-2n} = \frac{1}{1-e^{-2}} = \frac{e^2}{e^2-1}$

32. $\sum_{n=1}^{\infty} \frac{n^2+1}{n}$ diverges, since $\lim_{n\to\infty} \frac{n^2+1}{n} \neq 1$

33. $\sum_{n=1}^{\infty} (-1)^{n+1} n$ diverges because $\lim_{n\to\infty} (-1)^{n+1} n \neq 0$

34. $\sum_{n=1}^{\infty} \frac{2}{10^n} = \frac{\frac{2}{10}}{1-\frac{1}{10}} = \frac{2}{9}$

35. $\sum_{n=0}^{\infty} \frac{2^n-1}{3^n} = \sum_{n=0}^{\infty} \left(\frac{2}{3}\right)^n - \sum_{n=0}^{\infty} \left(\frac{1}{3}\right)^n = \frac{1}{1-\frac{2}{3}} - \frac{1}{1-\frac{1}{3}} = \frac{3}{2}$

36. $\sum_{n=1}^{\infty} \left(1-\frac{1}{n}\right)^n$ diverges, since $\lim_{n\to\infty} \left(1-\frac{1}{n}\right)^n = e \neq 1$

37. $\sum_{n=0}^{\infty} \frac{n!}{1000^n}$ diverges because $\lim_{n\to\infty} \frac{n!}{1000^n} = \infty$

38. $\sum_{n=0}^{\infty} \frac{1}{x^n} = \frac{1}{1-\frac{1}{x}} = \frac{x}{x-1}$, since $|x| > 1 \Rightarrow \frac{1}{|x|} < 1$

39. $a = 1$ and $r = -x$, since $\frac{1}{1+x} = \frac{1}{1-(-x)} = \sum_{n=0}^{\infty} (-1)^n x^n$, $|x| < 1$.

40. $a = 1$ and $r = -x^2$

41. The area of each square is one-half that of the preceding square. Thererore, the sum of the areas is $S = 4 + 2 + \frac{1}{2} + \ldots = \frac{4}{1-\frac{1}{2}} = 8$.

42. If n is odd, $S_n = 1$ and if n is even, $S_n = 0$. Therefore, $S_n = \frac{1+(-1)^n}{2}$.

43. Let $\sum_{n=1}^{\infty} n$ and $\sum_{n=1}^{\infty} (-n)$ be the two divergent series. But the sum $\sum_{n=1}^{\infty} (n+(-n)) = \sum_{n=0}^{\infty} 0$ converges.

44. $\sum_{n=0}^{\infty} \left(\frac{1}{2}\right)^n = 2$, $\sum_{n=0}^{\infty} \left(\frac{1}{3}\right)^n = \frac{3}{2}$, but $\sum_{n=0}^{\infty} \left(\frac{1}{2}\right)^n \left(\frac{1}{3}\right)^n = \sum_{n=0}^{\infty} \left(\frac{1}{6}\right)^n = \frac{6}{5} \neq 2 \cdot \frac{3}{2}$

45. Let $\sum_{n=1}^{\infty} \frac{1}{2^n} = \frac{1}{2}$ and $\sum_{n=1}^{\infty} \frac{1}{3^n} = \frac{1}{3}$ be the two convergent series.

Then $\sum_{n=1}^{\infty} \frac{\frac{1}{2^n}}{\frac{1}{3^n}} = \sum_{n=1}^{\infty} \left(\frac{3}{2}\right)^n$ diverges.

46. $\sum_{n=0}^{\infty} \left(\frac{1}{2}\right)^n = 2$, $\sum_{n=0}^{\infty} \left(\frac{1}{3}\right)^n = \frac{3}{2}$, but $\sum_{n=0}^{\infty} \frac{\frac{1}{3^n}}{\frac{1}{2^n}} = \sum_{n=0}^{\infty} \left(\frac{2}{3}\right)^n = 3 \neq \frac{\frac{3}{2}}{2} = \frac{3}{4}$

47. If $\sum_{n=1}^{\infty} a_n$ converges, then $\lim_{n\to\infty} a_n = 0$. Therefore, $\lim_{n\to\infty} \left(\frac{1}{a_n}\right) \neq 0$

and $\sum_{n=1}^{\infty} \left(\frac{1}{a_n}\right)$ diverges.

48. (b) $\int_0^x \frac{1}{1+t}\,dt = \int_0^x \left(1 - t + t^2 + \ldots + (-1)^n t^n + \frac{(-1)^{n+1} t^{n+1}}{1+t}\right) dt$

$$\ln|1+t|\Big]_0^x = t - \frac{1}{2}t^2 + \frac{1}{3}t^3 + \ldots + \frac{(-1)^n}{n+1} t^{n+1}\Big]_0^x + \int_0^x \frac{(-1)^{n+1} t^{n+1}}{n+1}$$

$$\ln|1+x| = x - \frac{1}{2}x^2 + \frac{1}{3}x^3 + \ldots + \frac{(-1)^{n+1}}{n+1} + R, \text{ where } R = \int_0^x \frac{(-1)^{n+1} t^{n+1}}{n+1}.$$

(c) If $x > 0$, $|R| = \int_0^x \frac{(-1)^{n+1} t^{n+1}}{n+1} < \int_0^x t^{n+1}\,dt = \frac{t^{n+2}}{n+2}\Big]_0^x = \frac{x^{n+2}}{n+2}$

(d) $\frac{1}{n+2}\left(\frac{1}{2}\right)^{n+2} < 0.001 \Leftrightarrow 2^{n+2}(n+2) > 1000$ or if $n \geq 6$.

$$\ln(1+x) \approx x - \frac{1}{2}x^2 + \frac{1}{3}x^3 - \frac{1}{4}x^4 + \frac{1}{5}x^5$$

(e) $\frac{1}{n+2} < 0.001 \Leftrightarrow n > 998$

11.5 TESTS FOR CONVERGENCE OF SERIES WITH NONNEGATIVE TERMS

Note: The reasons given for convergence may not be the only ones that apply.

1. $\sum_{n=1}^{\infty} \frac{1}{10^n}$ converges. Geometric series with $r = \frac{1}{10} < 1$.

2. $\sum_{n=1}^{\infty} \frac{n}{n+2}$ diverges, because $\lim_{n\to\infty} \frac{n}{n+2} = 1 \neq 0$

3. $\sum_{n=1}^{\infty} \frac{\sin^2 n}{2^n}$ converges, since $\sin^2 n \leq 1 \Rightarrow \frac{\sin^2 n}{2^n} \leq \frac{1}{2^n}$ and $\sum_{n=1}^{\infty} \frac{1}{2^n}$ converges.

4. $\sum_{n=1}^{\infty} \frac{5}{n} = 5\sum_{n=1}^{\infty} \frac{1}{n}$ diverges, multiple of the harmonic series.

5. $\sum_{n=1}^{\infty} \frac{1+\cos n}{n^2}$ converges by comparison with $\sum_{n=1}^{\infty} \frac{2}{n^2} =$

$2\sum_{n=1}^{\infty} \frac{1}{n^2}$ which is a multiple of a p-series with $p = 2 > 1$.

6. $\sum_{n=1}^{\infty} -\frac{1}{8^n} = -\frac{1}{7}$, geometric series with $r = \frac{1}{8}$.

7. $\sum_{n=1}^{\infty} \frac{\ln n}{n}$ diverges since $\ln n > 1$ for $n > e \Rightarrow \frac{\ln n}{n} > \frac{1}{n}$ and $\sum_{n=1}^{\infty} \frac{1}{n}$ diverges.

8. $\sum_{n=1}^{\infty} \frac{1}{n^{3/2}}$ converges, p – series with $p = \frac{3}{2}$.

9. $\sum_{n=1}^{\infty} \frac{2^n}{3^n}$ converges, geometric series with $r = \frac{2}{3} < 1$.

10. $\sum_{n=0}^{\infty} \frac{-2}{n+1} = -2\sum_{n=1}^{\infty} \frac{1}{n}$ diverges, multiple of harmonic series.

11. $\sum_{n=1}^{\infty} \frac{1}{1+\ln n}$ diverges by comparison with $\sum_{n=1}^{\infty} \frac{1}{1+n}$, since

$\ln n < n$ for $n > 1 \Rightarrow 1 + \ln n < 1 + n \Rightarrow \frac{1}{1+\ln n} > \frac{1}{1+n}$.

12. $\sum_{n=2}^{\infty} \frac{\ln n}{n\sqrt{n+1}} < \sum_{n=2}^{\infty} \frac{\ln n}{n^{3/2}}$ which converges by integral test:

$$\int_2^{\infty} \frac{\ln x}{x^{3/2}}\,dx = \lim_{b\to\infty}\left[-\frac{2\ln x}{x^{1/2}} - \frac{4}{x^{1/2}}\right]_2^b = \sqrt{2}\,(\ln 2 + 2)$$

13. $\sum_{n=1}^{\infty} \frac{2^n}{n+1}$ diverges, since $\lim_{n\to\infty} \frac{2^n}{n+1} \neq 0$.

14. $\sum_{n=1}^{\infty} \left(\frac{n}{3n+1}\right)^n$ converges by comparison to $\sum_{n=1}^{\infty} \left(\frac{n}{3n}\right)^n$

15. $\sum_{n=1}^{\infty} \frac{1}{\sqrt{n^3+1}}$ converges, since $\sum_{n=1}^{\infty} \frac{1}{n^{3/2}}$ converges and

$$\lim_{n\to\infty} \frac{\frac{1}{\sqrt{n^3+1}}}{\frac{1}{\sqrt{n^3}}} = \lim_{n\to\infty} \sqrt{\frac{n^3}{n^3+1}} = 1.$$

16. $\sum_{n=1}^{\infty} \frac{1}{\sqrt{n}} \frac{(\ln n)^{10}}{n^{2/3}} = \sum_{n=1}^{\infty} \frac{(\ln n)^{10}}{n^{7/6}} = \sum_{n=1}^{\infty} \frac{1}{n^{13/12}} \frac{(\ln n)^{10}}{n^{1/12}}$

$= \sum_{n=1}^{\infty} \frac{1}{n^{13/12}} \left(\frac{\ln n}{n^{1/120}}\right)^{10}$ converges by comparison to $\sum_{n=1}^{\infty} \frac{1}{n^{13/12}}$ $\left(p = \frac{13}{12} > 1\right)$

since $\frac{\ln n}{n^{1/120}} \to 0$ (See Example 8, Sect. 11.3)

17. $\sum_{n=1}^{\infty} \frac{n}{n^2+1}$ diverges by comparison with $\sum_{n=1}^{\infty} \frac{1}{n}$, since

$$\lim_{n\to\infty} \frac{\frac{n}{n^2+1}}{\frac{1}{n}} = \lim_{n\to\infty} \frac{n^2}{n^2+1} = 1.$$

18. $\sum_{n=1}^{\infty} \frac{1}{2^{1/n}}$ diverges, since $\lim_{n\to\infty} \frac{1}{2^{1/n}} = 1 \neq 0$

19. $\sum_{n=1}^{\infty} \left(1+\frac{1}{n}\right)^n$ diverges, since $\lim_{n\to\infty} \left(1+\frac{1}{n}\right)^n = e \neq 0$.

20. $\sum_{n=1}^{\infty} \frac{\sqrt{n}}{n^2+1} \le \sum_{n=1}^{\infty} \frac{1}{n^{3/2}}$ converges by comparison with p-series

21. $\sum_{n=1}^{\infty} \frac{1-n}{n\cdot 2^n}$ converges, because it is the difference of

$\sum_{n=1}^{\infty} \frac{1}{n\cdot 2^n}$ which converges because $\frac{1}{n\cdot 2^n} < \frac{1}{2^n}$ and $\sum_{n=1}^{\infty} \frac{1}{2^n}$.

22. $\sum_{n=1}^{\infty} \frac{1}{(\ln 2)^n}$ diverges, geometric series with $r = \frac{1}{\ln 2} > 1$.

23. $\sum_{n=1}^{\infty} \frac{1}{3^{n-1}+1}$ converges by comparison to $\sum_{n=1}^{\infty} \frac{1}{3^{n-1}} = \frac{3}{2}$.

24. $\sum_{n=1}^{\infty} \frac{10n+1}{n(n+1)(n+2)}$ converges, limit comparison test with $\sum_{n=1}^{\infty} \frac{1}{n^2}$

25. $\sum_{n=1}^{\infty} \frac{1}{2n-1}$ diverges since $\int_1^{\infty} \frac{dx}{2x-1} = \lim_{t\to\infty} \int_1^t \frac{dx}{2x-1} =$

$\lim_{t\to\infty} \frac{1}{2} \ln|2x-1| \Big]_1^t = \lim_{t\to\infty} \frac{1}{2}[2t-1] = \infty$.

26. $\int_2^{\infty} \frac{dx}{x(\ln x)^p} = \lim_{b\to\infty} \int_2^b \frac{dx}{x(\ln x)^p} = \lim_{b\to\infty} \left[\frac{(\ln x)^{1-p}}{1-p} \right]_0^b = \lim_{b\to\infty} \frac{(\ln b)^{1-p}}{1-p} - \frac{(\ln 2)^{1-p}}{1-p}$

$\lim_{b\to\infty} \frac{(\ln b)^{1-p}}{1-p} = \infty$ if $1-p>0$ or $p<1$ but converges if $1-p<0$ or $p>1$.

If $p=1$, $\int_2^{\infty} \frac{dx}{x \ln x} = \lim_{b\to\infty} (\ln(\ln b) - \ln(\ln 2)) = \infty$

(a) $\sum_{n=2}^{\infty} \frac{1}{n \ln n}$ diverges, $p=1$

(b) $\sum_{n=2}^{\infty} \frac{1}{n(\ln n)^{1.01}}$ converges, $p = 1.01 > 1$

(c) $\sum_{n=5}^{\infty} \frac{n^{1/2}}{(\ln n)^3}$ diverges, since $\lim_{n\to\infty} \left[\frac{n^{1/2}}{(\ln n)^3} \right]^2 = \lim_{n\to\infty} \frac{n}{(\ln n)^6} = \infty$

(d) $\sum_{n=3}^{\infty} \frac{1}{n \ln(n^3)} = \frac{1}{3} \sum_{n=3}^{\infty} \frac{1}{n \ln n}$ diverges

(e) $\sum_{n=2}^{\infty} \frac{1}{n(\ln n)^{(n+1)/n}}$ diverges, limit comparison test with $\sum_{n=2}^{\infty} \frac{1}{n \ln n}$

$\lim_{n\to\infty} \left(\frac{1}{n(\ln n)^{(n+1)/n}} \div \frac{1}{n \ln n} \right) = \lim_{n\to\infty} \frac{1}{(\ln n)^{1/n}} = 1$

27. $S_n \le 1 + \ln(365 \cdot 24 \cdot 60 \cdot 60 \cdot 13 \cdot 10^9) \approx 41.55$

28. $\sum_{n=1}^{\infty} \frac{1}{nx} = \frac{1}{x} \sum_{n=1}^{\infty} \frac{1}{n}$, which diverges, so $\sum_{n=1}^{\infty} \frac{1}{nx}$ diverges.

29. For $n \ge 1$, $\frac{1}{n} \le 1$ so $\frac{a_n}{n} \le a_n$. $\therefore \sum_{n=1}^{\infty} \frac{a_n}{n}$ converges if $\sum_{n=1}^{\infty} a_n$ converges.

30. $\sum_{n=1}^{\infty} a_n$ converges $\Rightarrow \lim_{n\to\infty} a_n = 0$. There is $N > 0$ for which $a_n < 1$ for $n > N$,

hence $a_n b_n < b_n$ for $n > N$. $\sum_{n=1}^{\infty} a_n b_n = \sum_{n=1}^{N} a_n b_n + \sum_{n=N+1}^{\infty} a_n b_n$

$\le \sum_{n=1}^{N} a_n b_n + \sum_{n=N+1}^{\infty} b_n < \infty$, since $\sum_{n=1}^{\infty} b_n$ converges

31. If $\{S_n\}$ is nonincreasing with lower bound M, then $\{-S_n\}$ is a nondecreasing sequence with upper bound -M. By Theorem 1, $\{-S_n\}$ converges, and hence $\{S_n\}$ converges. If $\{S_n\}$ has no lower bound, then $\{-S_n\}$ has no upper bound and diverges. Hence $\{S_n\}$ also diverges.

32. Let $\{a_n\}$ be a decreasing sequence of positive terms that converges to 0.

Let $A_n = \sum_{k=1}^{n} a_k$ and $B_k = \sum_{k=1}^{n} 2^k a_{2^k}$.

(i) $B_n = 2a_2 + 4a_4 + 8a_8 + \ldots + 2^n a_{2^n}$

$= 2a_2 + (2a_4 + 2a_4) + (4a_8 + 4a_8) + \ldots + (2^{n-1} a_{2^{n-1}} + (2^{n-1} a_{2^{n-1}})$

$\le 2a_1 + (2a_2 + 2a_3) + \ldots . + (2a_{2^{n-1}} + 2a_{2^{n-1}+1} + \ldots + 2a_{2^n - 1})$

$= 2A_{2^n - 1} \le \sum_{k=1}^{\infty} a_k$. $\therefore$ If $\sum_{k=1}^{n} a_k$ converges, then $\sum_{k=1}^{n} 2^k a_{2^k}$ converges.

(ii) $A_n = a_1 + (a_2 + a_3) + (a_4 + a_5 + a_6 + a_7) + \ldots + a_n$

$= a_1 + B_n \le a_1 + \sum_{k=1}^{\infty} 2^k a_{2^k}$.

$\therefore$ if $\sum_{k=1}^{\infty} 2^k a_{2^k}$ converges then $\sum_{k=1}^{\infty} a_k$ converges.

33. (a) $\sum_{n=2}^{\infty} \frac{1}{n \ln n}$ diverges, since $\sum_{n=2}^{\infty} 2^n \cdot \frac{1}{2^n \ln 2^n} = \sum_{n=2}^{\infty} \frac{1}{n \ln 2}$

$= \frac{1}{\ln 2} \sum_{n=2}^{\infty} \frac{1}{n}$ diverges.

(b) $\sum_{n=1}^{\infty} 2^n \cdot \frac{1}{(2^n)^p} = \sum_{n=1}^{\infty} 2^{n(1-p)}$ converges if $p > 1$ or $1 - p < 0$ and

diverges if $p \le 1$ or $1 - p \ge 0$.

34. (a) Let $f(x) = \frac{1}{x}$. We have

$$\ln n < \ln(n+1) = \int_0^{n+1} \frac{1}{x}\,dx \le 1 + \frac{1}{2} + \frac{1}{3} + \ldots + \frac{1}{n} \le 1 + \int_1^n \frac{1}{x}dx = 1 + \ln n,$$

or $0 < 1 + \frac{1}{2} + \frac{1}{3} + \ldots + \frac{1}{n} - \ln n < 1$

(b) Let $a_n = 1 + \frac{1}{2} + \frac{1}{3} + \ldots + \frac{1}{n} - \ln n$. Then $a_{n+1} - a_n = \frac{1}{n+1} - [\ln(n+1) - \ln n]$.

From the graph of $f(x) = \frac{1}{x}$, it is clear that

$$\frac{1}{n+1} \cdot 1 < \int_n^{n+1} \frac{1}{x}dx = \ln(n+1) - \ln n < 0, \text{ or } \frac{1}{n+1} - [\ln(n+1) - \ln n] < 0.$$

$\therefore \{a_n\}$ is decreasing and bounded below by 0.

Let $\lim_{n\to\infty} a_n = \gamma$. Then γ is Euler's Constant.

35. Since $\sum_{n=2}^{\infty} \frac{1}{n \ln n}$ diverges, the limit comparison test and the

fact that $\lim_{n\to\infty} \frac{n \ln n}{p_n} = 1$ states that $\sum_{n=1}^{\infty} \frac{1}{p_n}$ diverges.

11.6 SERIES WITH NONNEGATIVE TERMS: RATIO AND ROOT TESTS

Note: The reasons given for convergence may not be the only ones that apply.

1. $\sum_{n=1}^{\infty} \frac{n^2}{2^n}$ converges, since $\lim_{n\to\infty} \left| \frac{(n+1)^2}{2^{n+1}} \cdot \frac{2^n}{n^2} \right| = \lim_{n\to\infty} \frac{1}{2} \cdot \left(\frac{n+1}{n}\right)^2 = \frac{1}{2} < 1$.

2. $\sum_{n=1}^{\infty} \frac{n!}{10^n}$ diverges, since $\lim_{n\to\infty} \frac{(n+1)!}{10^{n+1}} \cdot \frac{10^n}{n!} = \lim_{n\to\infty} \frac{n+1}{10} = \infty$

3. $\sum_{n=1}^{\infty} \frac{n^{10}}{10^n}$ converges, since $\lim_{n\to\infty} \left(\frac{n^{10}}{10^n}\right)^{\frac{1}{n}} = \frac{1}{10}(1)^{10} = \frac{1}{10} < 1$.

4. $\sum_{n=1}^{\infty} n^2 e^{-n}$ converges, since $\lim_{n\to\infty} \frac{(n+1)^2}{e^{n+1}} \cdot \frac{e^n}{n^2} = \lim_{n\to\infty} \left(\frac{n+1}{n}\right)^2 \frac{1}{e} = \frac{1}{e} < 1$.

5. $\sum_{n=1}^{\infty}\left(\frac{n-2}{n}\right)^n$ diverges since $\lim_{n\to\infty}\left(\frac{n-2}{n}\right)^n = e^{-2} \neq 0$.

6. $\sum_{n=1}^{\infty}\frac{2+(-1)^n}{1.25^n} = \sum_{n=1}^{\infty}\left(\frac{4}{5}\right)^n(2+(-1)^n) \leq 3\sum_{n=1}^{\infty}\left(\frac{4}{5}\right)^n$ converges by comparison.

7. $\sum_{n=1}^{\infty} n!e^{-n}$ diverges since $\lim_{n\to\infty}\left|\frac{(n+1)!}{e^{n+1}}\cdot\frac{e^n}{n!}\right| = \lim_{n\to\infty}\frac{n+1}{e} = \infty$.

8. $\sum_{n=1}^{\infty}\frac{(-2)^n}{3^n} = -\frac{2}{5}$ converges, geometric with $r = -\frac{2}{3}$.

9. $\sum_{n=1}^{\infty}\left(\frac{n-3}{n}\right)^n$ diverges since $\lim_{n\to\infty}\left(1-\frac{3}{n}\right)^n = e^{-3} \neq 0$.

10. $\sum_{n=1}^{\infty}\left(1-\frac{1}{n^2}\right)$ diverges, $\lim_{n\to\infty}\left(1-\frac{1}{n^2}\right) = 1 \neq 0$.

11. $\sum_{n=1}^{\infty}\sin\frac{1}{n}$ diverges, since $\lim_{n\to\infty}\frac{\sin\frac{1}{n}}{\frac{1}{n}} = \lim_{n\to\infty}\frac{\left(-\frac{1}{n^2}\right)\cos\frac{1}{n}}{-\frac{1}{n^2}} = \cos 0 = 1$.

12. $\sum_{n=1}^{\infty}\sin\left(\frac{2}{n^2}\right)$ converges, since $\sin\left(\frac{2}{n^2}\right) \leq \frac{2}{n^2}$ and $\sum_{n=1}^{\infty}\frac{2}{n^2}$ converges

13. $\sum_{n=1}^{\infty}\left(1-\cos\frac{1}{n}\right)$ converges, since $\lim_{n\to\infty}\frac{1-\cos\frac{1}{n}}{\frac{1}{n^2}} = \lim_{n\to\infty}\frac{\left(-\frac{1}{n^2}\right)\sin\frac{1}{n}}{-\frac{2}{n^3}}$

$$= \lim_{n\to\infty}\frac{n\sin\frac{1}{n}}{2} = \frac{1}{2}\lim_{n\to\infty}\frac{\sin\frac{1}{n}}{\frac{1}{n}} = \frac{1}{2}.$$

14. $\sum_{n=1}^{\infty}\sin^2\frac{1}{n}$ converges, since $\lim_{n\to\infty}\frac{\sin^2\frac{1}{n}}{\frac{1}{n^2}} = \lim_{n\to\infty}\left(\frac{\sin\frac{1}{n}}{\frac{1}{n}}\right)^2 = 1$.

15. $\sum_{n=1}^{\infty}\tan\left(\frac{\ln n}{n}\right)$ diverges, since $\lim_{n\to\infty}\frac{\tan\left(\frac{\ln n}{n}\right)}{\frac{\ln n}{n}}$

$$= \lim_{n\to\infty}\frac{\sec^2\left(\frac{\ln n}{n}\right)D\left(\frac{\ln n}{n}\right)}{D\left(\frac{\ln n}{n}\right)} = \sec^2 0 = 1 \text{ and } \sum_{n=1}^{\infty}\frac{\ln n}{n} \text{ diverges.}$$

16. $\sum_{n=1}^{\infty} \frac{\ln n}{2^n}$ converges, since $\lim_{n\to\infty} \frac{\ln(n+1)}{2^{n+1}} \cdot \frac{2^n}{\ln n} = \frac{1}{2} < 1$.

Then $\sum_{n=1}^{\infty} \tan(2^{-n} \ln n)$ converges by comparison, since

$$\lim_{n\to\infty} \frac{\tan(2^{-n} \ln n)}{2^{-n} \ln n} = \lim_{n\to\infty} \frac{\sin(2^{-n} \ln n) \sec(2^{-n} \ln n)}{2^{-n} \ln n} = 1$$

17. $\sum_{n=1}^{\infty} \ln \frac{n+2}{n+1} = \sum_{n=1}^{\infty} [\ln(n+2) - \ln(n+1)]$ diverges since

$\ln 3 - \ln 2 + \ln 4 - \ln 3 + \ln 5 - \ln 4 + ... + \ln(n+1) - \ln n + \ln(n+2) - \ln(n+1)$

$= -\ln 2 + \ln(n+2) = \infty$

18. $$\lim_{n\to\infty} \frac{\ln\left(1 + \frac{1}{n^2}\right)}{\frac{1}{n^2}} = \lim_{n\to\infty} \frac{\frac{n^2}{n^2+1} \cdot D_n\left(1 + \frac{1}{n^2}\right)}{D_n\left(\frac{1}{n^2}\right)} = 1.$$

$\therefore \sum_{n=1}^{\infty} \ln\left(\frac{n^2+1}{n^2}\right)$ converges by comparison with $\sum_{n=1}^{\infty} \frac{1}{n^2}$.

19. $\sum_{n=1}^{\infty} n \sin\left(\frac{1}{n^2}\right)$ diverges, because $\lim_{n\to\infty} \frac{n \sin\left(\frac{1}{n^2}\right)}{\frac{1}{n}}$

$$= \lim_{n\to\infty} \frac{\sin\left(\frac{1}{n^2}\right)}{\frac{1}{n^2}} = \lim_{n\to\infty} \frac{\cos\left(\frac{1}{n^2}\right) D_n(n^{-2})}{D_n(n^{-2})} = \cos 0 = 1$$

20. $\sum_{n=1}^{\infty} \frac{n+2}{n^2+5}$ diverges by comparison with $\sum_{n=1}^{\infty} \frac{1}{n}$.

Then $\sum_{n=1}^{\infty} n^2 \tan\left(\frac{n+2}{n^2+5}\right)$ diverges, since $\lim_{n\to\infty} \frac{n^2 \tan\left(\frac{n+2}{n^2+5}\right)}{\frac{n+2}{n^2+5}} = \infty$

21. $\sum_{n=1}^{\infty} \frac{(n+1)(n+2)}{n!}$ converges because

$$\lim_{n\to\infty} \frac{(n+2)(n+3)}{(n+1)!} \cdot \frac{n!}{(n+1)(n+2)} = \lim_{n\to\infty} \frac{n+3}{(n+1)^2} = 0 < 1$$

22. $\sum_{n=1}^{\infty} e^{-n} n^3$ converges by Ratio test, since $\lim_{n\to\infty} \frac{(n+1)^3}{e^{n+1}} \cdot \frac{e^n}{n^3} = \frac{1}{e} < 1$.

23. $\sum_{n=1}^{\infty} \frac{(n+3)!}{3!n!3^n}$ converges because

$$\lim_{n\to\infty} \frac{(n+4)!}{3!(n+1)!3^{n+1}} \cdot \frac{3!n!3^n}{(n+3)!} = \lim_{n\to\infty} \frac{n+4}{3(n+1)} = \frac{1}{3} < 1$$

24. $\sum_{n=1}^{\infty} -\frac{n^2}{2^n} = -\sum_{n=1}^{\infty} \frac{n^2}{2^n}$ converges by Ratio test, since $\lim_{n\to\infty} \frac{(n+1)^2}{2^{n+1}} \cdot \frac{2^n}{n^2} = \frac{1}{2} < 1$.

25. $\sum_{n=1}^{\infty} \frac{1}{(2n+1)!}$ converges because $\lim_{n\to\infty} \frac{(2n+1)!}{(2n+3)!} =$

$\lim_{n\to\infty} \frac{1}{(2n+2)(2n+3)} = 0 < 1$

26. $\sum_{n=1}^{\infty} \frac{n!}{n^n}$ converges by Ratio test, since $\lim_{n\to\infty} \frac{(n+1)!}{(n+1)^{n+1}} \cdot \frac{n^n}{n!}$

$$= \lim_{n\to\infty} \frac{(n+1)\,n!}{(n+1)(n+1)^n} \cdot \frac{n^n}{n!} = \lim_{n\to\infty} \left(\frac{n}{n+1}\right)^n = \frac{1}{e} < 1$$

27. $\sum_{n=1}^{\infty} \frac{|nx^n|}{2^n}$ converges for $-2 < x < 2$, because:

$$\lim_{n\to\infty} \left| \frac{(n+1)\,x^{n+1}}{2^{n+1}} \cdot \frac{2^n}{nx^n} \right| = \lim_{n\to\infty} \frac{n+1}{n} \cdot \frac{1}{2} \cdot |x| < 1 \Leftrightarrow |x| < 2$$

If $x = \pm 2$, $\sum_{n=1}^{\infty} |n|$ diverges because $\lim_{n\to\infty} |n| = \infty$.

28. $\sum_{n=1}^{\infty} \frac{(n+1)\,x^{2n-1}}{4^n}$ converges for $-2 < x < 2$ because:

$$\lim_{n\to\infty} \frac{(n+2)\,x^{2n+1}}{4^{n+1}} \cdot \frac{4^n}{(n+1)\,x^{2n-1}} = \lim_{n\to\infty} \frac{n+2}{n+1} \cdot \frac{1}{4} |x|^2 < 1 \text{ if } x^2 < 4 \text{ or } |x| < 2.$$

Let $x = \pm 2$: $\sum_{n=1}^{\infty} \frac{(n+1)\,(\pm 2)^{2n-1}}{2^{2n}} = \pm \sum_{n=1}^{\infty} \frac{n+1}{2}$ diverges

29. $\sum_{n=1}^{\infty} \left(\frac{x^2+1}{3}\right)^n$ converges for $-\sqrt{2} < x < \sqrt{2}$, because a geometric series

converges for $|r| < 1$. $\frac{x^2+1}{3} < 1 \Leftrightarrow x^2 + 1 < 3 \Leftrightarrow x^2 < 2$ or $|x| < \sqrt{2}$

30. $\sum_{n=1}^{\infty}\left(\frac{1}{|x|}\right)^n$ converges for $|x|>1$, since it is a geometric series with $r=\frac{1}{|x|}<1 \Leftrightarrow |x|>1$.

31. $\sum_{n=1}^{\infty}\frac{x^{2n+1}}{n^2}$ converges for $-1 \le x \le 1$ because:

$$\lim_{n\to\infty}\frac{x^{2n+3}}{(n+1)^2}\cdot\frac{n^2}{x^{2n+1}}=\lim_{n\to\infty}\left(\frac{n}{n+1}\right)^2\cdot x^2<1 \Leftrightarrow |x|<1$$

If $x=1$, $\sum_{n=1}^{\infty}\frac{1}{n^2}$ converges, and if $x=-1$, $\sum_{n=1}^{\infty}\frac{(-1)^{2n+1}}{n^2}$ converges.

32. $$\lim_{n\to\infty}\frac{(n+1)!\,(n+1)!\,|2x|^{n+1}}{(2n+2)!}\cdot\frac{(2n)!}{n!\,n!\,|2x|^n}$$

$$=\lim_{n\to\infty}\frac{(n+1)n!\,(n+1)n!}{(2n+2)(2n+1)(2n)!}\cdot\frac{(2n)!}{n!\,n!}|2x|=\frac{1}{4}|2x|<1 \text{ if } -2<x<2$$

33. Converges, because $\lim_{n\to\infty}\left|\frac{a_{n+1}}{a_n}\right|=\lim_{n\to\infty}\left|\frac{\frac{(1+\sin n)a_n}{n}}{a_n}\right|=\lim_{n\to\infty}\frac{1+\sin n}{n}=0<1$

34. $\lim_{n\to\infty}\frac{\frac{3n-1}{2n+5}a_n}{a_n}=\frac{3}{2}>1$. The series diverges by ratio test.

35. Diverges, because $a_1=3$, $a_2=\frac{3}{2}$, $a_3=1$, $a_4=\frac{3}{4}$, ...is the series $\sum_{n=1}^{\infty}\frac{3}{n}$.

36. $\lim_{n\to\infty}\frac{\frac{2}{n}a_n}{a_n}=\lim_{n\to\infty}\frac{2}{n}=0$. The series converges by ratio test.

37. Converges, because $\lim_{n\to\infty}\left|\frac{a_{n+1}}{a_n}\right|=\lim_{n\to\infty}\left|\frac{(1+\ln n)a_n}{na_n}\right|=\lim_{n\to\infty}\frac{1+\ln n}{n}=\lim_{n\to\infty}\frac{\frac{1}{n}}{1}=0<1$

38. For $n\ge 22{,}027$, $\ln n>10$ so $\frac{n+\ln n}{n+10}>1$. Then for all such n,

$a_{n+1}=\frac{n+\ln n}{n+10}a_n>a_n$ so $\lim_{n\to\infty}a_n\ne 0$. The series diverges.

39. $\sum_{n=1}^{\infty}\frac{2^n n!\,n!}{(2n)!}$ converges, because $\lim_{n\to\infty}\frac{2^{n+1}(n+1)!(n+1)!}{(2n+2)!}\cdot\frac{(2n)!}{2^n n!\,n!}$

$$=\lim_{n\to\infty}\frac{2(n+1)^2}{(2n+1)(2n+2)}=\frac{1}{2}<1.$$

40. $\sum_{n=1}^{\infty} \frac{(3n)!}{n!\,(n+1)!\,(n+2)!}$ diverges because

$$\lim_{n\to\infty} \frac{(3n+3)!}{(n+1)!(n+2)!(n+3)!} \cdot \frac{n!\,(n+1)!(n+2)!}{(3n)!} =$$

$$\lim_{n\to\infty} \frac{(3n+3)(3n+2)(3n+1)(3n)!}{(n+1)n!\,(n+2)(n+1)!(n+3)(n+2)!} \cdot \frac{n!\,(n+1)!(n+2)!}{(3n)!} = 27 > 1$$

41. $a_1 = 1;\ a_2 = \frac{1\cdot 2}{3\cdot 4};\ a_3 = \frac{2\cdot 3}{4\cdot 5}\,\frac{1\cdot 2}{3\cdot 4};\ a_4 = \frac{3\cdot 4}{5\cdot 6}\cdot\frac{2\cdot 3}{4\cdot 5}\,\frac{1\cdot 2}{3\cdot 4};$

$a_5 = \frac{4\cdot 5}{6\cdot 7}\,\frac{3\cdot 4}{5\cdot 6}\cdot\frac{2\cdot 3}{4\cdot 5}\,\frac{1\cdot 2}{3\cdot 4};\ a_n = \frac{12}{(n+1)(n+3)(n+2)^2}$

$\sum_{n=1}^{\infty} \frac{12}{(n+1)(n+3)(n+2)^2}$ converges by comparison with $\sum_{n=1}^{\infty} \frac{12}{n^4}$

11.7 ABSOLUTE CONVERGENCE

1. $\sum_{n=1}^{\infty} \frac{1}{n^2}$ converges absolutely, p-series with $p = 2 > 1$.

2. $\sum_{n=1}^{\infty} \frac{1}{(-n)^3}$ converges absolutely, since $\sum_{n=1}^{\infty} \frac{1}{n^3}$ is a convergent p-series.

3. $\sum_{n=1}^{\infty} \frac{1-n}{n^2}$ diverges, since is the sum of $\sum_{n=1}^{\infty} \frac{1}{n^2}$ which converges,

and $\left(-\sum_{n=1}^{\infty} \frac{1}{n}\right)$ which diverges.

4. $\sum_{n=1}^{\infty} \left(-\frac{1}{5}\right)^n$ converges absolutely, since $\sum_{n=1}^{\infty} \frac{1}{5^n}$ converges.

5. $\sum_{n=1}^{\infty} \frac{-1}{n^2+2n+1}$ converges absolutely, since $\sum_{n=1}^{\infty} \frac{1}{(n+1)^2}$

converges by comparison to $\sum_{n=1}^{\infty} \frac{1}{n^2}$.

6. $\sum_{n=1}^{\infty} \frac{(-1)^n}{2n}$ does not converge absolutely, since

$\sum_{n=1}^{\infty} \frac{1}{2n}$ is a multiple of the harmonic series and diverges.

7. $\sum_{n=1}^{\infty} \frac{|\cos n\pi|}{n\sqrt{n}} = \sum_{n=1}^{\infty} \frac{1}{n^{3/2}}$ is a p-series for $p = \frac{3}{2} > 1$ and hence

converges. Therefore $\sum_{n=1}^{\infty} \frac{\cos n\pi}{n\sqrt{n}}$ converges absolutely.

8. $\sum_{n=1}^{\infty} \frac{-10}{n}$ does not converge absolutely, since

$\sum_{n=1}^{\infty} \frac{10}{n}$ is a multiple of the harmonic series and diverges.

9. $\sum_{n=1}^{\infty} \frac{(-1)^n}{(2n)!}$ converges absolutely, since $\lim_{n\to\infty} \left| \frac{(-1)^{n+1}}{(2n+2)!} \cdot \frac{(2n)!}{(-1)^n} \right| =$

$\lim_{n\to\infty} \frac{1}{(2n+2)(2n+1)} = 0 < 1.$

10. $\sum_{n=0}^{\infty} \frac{(-1)^n}{(2n+1)!}$ converges absolutely, because

$$\lim_{n\to\infty} \frac{(2n+1)!}{(2n+3)!} = \lim_{n\to\infty} \frac{1}{(2n+3)(2n+2)} = 0$$

11. $\sum_{n=1}^{\infty} \left| (-1)^n \frac{n}{n+1} \right|$ diverges, since $\lim_{n\to\infty} \frac{n}{n+1} \neq 0$

12. $\sum_{n=0}^{\infty} \frac{-n}{2^n}$ converges absolutely, because $\lim_{n\to\infty} \frac{n+1}{2^{n+1}} \cdot \frac{2^n}{n} = \lim_{n\to\infty} \frac{1}{2} \cdot \frac{n+1}{n} = \frac{1}{2}$

13. $\sum_{n=1}^{\infty} (5)^{-n}$ converges, geometric series with $r = \frac{1}{5} < 1$

14. $\sum_{n=0}^{\infty} \left(\frac{1}{2^n} - 1 \right)$ diverges, because $\lim_{n\to\infty} \left(\frac{1}{2^n} - 1 \right) = -1 \neq 0$

15. $\sum_{n=1}^{\infty} \left| \frac{(-100)^n}{n!} \right|$ converges, since $\lim_{n\to\infty} \left| \frac{(-100)^{n+1}}{(n+1)!} \cdot \frac{n!}{(-100)^n} \right| = \lim_{n\to\infty} 100 \cdot \frac{1}{n+1} = 0$

16. $\sum_{n=2}^{\infty}(-1)^n \frac{\ln n}{\ln n^2} = \sum_{n=2}^{\infty}(-1)^n \frac{1}{2}$ diverges, because $\lim_{n\to\infty}\left((-1)^n \frac{1}{2}\right)$ does not exist.

17. $\sum_{n=1}^{\infty}\frac{2-n}{n^3}$ converges absolutely, because $\sum_{n=1}^{\infty}\frac{1}{n^2}$ is a

p-series, $p = 2 > 1$, and $-2\sum_{n=2}^{\infty}\frac{1}{n^3}$ is a multiple of a p-series, $p=3 > 1$.

18. $\sum_{n=1}^{\infty}\left(\frac{1}{2^n} - \frac{1}{3^n}\right) = \frac{\frac{1}{2}}{1-\frac{1}{2}} - \frac{\frac{1}{3}}{1-\frac{1}{3}} = \frac{1}{2}$ converges absolutely.

19. Since $|a_n| \geq a_n$, if $\sum_1^{\infty} a_n$ diverges then $\sum_1^{\infty}|a_n|$ must diverge.

20. For each n, $\left|\sum_{k=1}^{n} a_k\right| \leq \sum_{k=1}^{n}|a_k|$.

Hence $\left|\sum_{k=1}^{\infty} a_k\right| = \lim_{n\to\infty}\left|\sum_{k=1}^{n} a_k\right| \leq \lim_{n\to\infty}\sum_{k=1}^{n}|a_k| = \lim_{n\to\infty}\sum_{k=1}^{\infty}|a_k|$

21. Let $\sum_1^{\infty} a_n$ and $\sum_1^{\infty} b_n$ converge absolutely. Then

(a) $|a_n + b_n| \leq |a_n| + |b_n| \Rightarrow \sum_1^{\infty}|a_n + b_n| \leq \sum_1^{\infty}|a_n| + \sum_1^{\infty}|b_n|$

and hence $\sum_1^{\infty}(a_n + b_n)$ converges absolutely.

(b) $|a_n - b_n| = |a_n + (-b_n)| \leq |a_n| + |-b_n| = |a_n| + |b_n|$.

Hence $\sum_1^{\infty}|a_n - b_n|$ converges and $\sum_1^{\infty}(a_n - b_n)$ converges absolutely.

(c) $|ka_n| = |k||a_n| \Rightarrow \sum_1^{\infty}|ka_n| = |k|\sum_1^{\infty}|a_n|$ converges. Hence

$\sum_1^{\infty} ka_n$ converges absolutely.

22. Let $\sum a_n$ converge absolutely, and $\{b_n\}$ be any rearrangement of $\{a_n\}$.

Let $S_n = \sum_{k=1}^{n} a_k$ and $\lim_{n\to\infty} S_n = L$. We show $\sum b_n = L$. Let $\varepsilon > 0$ be given. There is

$N_1 > 0$ fof which $\sum_{k=N_1}^{\infty} |a_k| < \frac{\varepsilon}{2}$. There is $N_2 > N_1$ for which $|S_{N_2} - L| < \frac{\varepsilon}{2}$.

Let N_3 be such that $\{a_1, a_2, ..., a_{N_2}\} \subseteq \{b_1, b_2, ..., b_{N_3}\}$. Then, for $n > N_3$,

$$\left|\sum_{k=1}^{n} b_k - \sum_{k=1}^{N_2} a_k\right| \le \sum_{k=N_2+1}^{\infty} |a_k| \le \sum_{k=N_1}^{\infty} |a_k| < \frac{\varepsilon}{2}.$$ Therefore,

$$\left|\sum_{k=1}^{n} b_k - L\right| \le \left|\sum_{k=1}^{n} b_k - S_{N_2}\right| + \left|S_{N_2} - L\right| \le \sum_{k=N_1}^{\infty} |a_k| \; \left|S_{N_2} - L\right| < \varepsilon.$$

23. Since $b_n = a_n$ if $a_n \ge 0$ and $b_n = 0$ when $a_n < 0$, for each n $|b_n| \le |a_n|$.

$\therefore \sum |b_n|$ converges. Then $\sum b_n$ converges. Similarly, $|c_n| \le |a_n|$

so $\sum c_n$ converges absolutely and hence converges. Hence

$$\sum b_n - \sum c_n = \sum \frac{1}{2}(a_n + |a_n|) - \sum \frac{1}{2}(-a_n + |a_n|) = \sum a_n$$

24. Since $a_k b_{n-k} = \frac{1}{2^k 3^{n-k}} \le \frac{1}{2^n}$, $c_n = \sum_{k=0}^{n} a_k b_{n-k} \le \frac{n+1}{2^n}$. Then

$$\lim_{n\to\infty} \frac{c_{n+1}}{c_n} \le \lim_{n\to\infty} \frac{n+2}{2^{n+1}} \cdot \frac{2^n}{n+1} = \frac{1}{2} < 1, \quad \sum_{n=1}^{\infty} c_n \text{ converges.}$$

Since $|c_n| = c_n$, the convergence is absolute.

11.8 ALTERNATING SERIES AND CONDITIONAL CONVERGENCE

1. $\sum_{n=1}^{\infty} (-1)^{n+1} \frac{1}{n^2}$ converges because it converges absolutely, since

$\sum_{n=1}^{\infty} \frac{1}{n^2}$ converges (p-series for $p = 2 > 1$).

2. $\sum_{n=2}^{\infty}(-1)^{n+1}\frac{1}{\ln n}$ converges, because $\lim_{n\to\infty}\frac{1}{\ln n}=0$ and $\left\{\frac{1}{\ln n}\right\}$ is a decreasing sequence.

3. $\sum_{n=1}^{\infty}(-1)^{n-1}=\sum_{n=1}^{\infty}(-1)^{n-1}(1)$ diverges, since $\lim_{n\to\infty}(1)=1\neq 0$.

4. $\sum_{n=1}^{\infty}(-1)^{n+1}\frac{10^n}{n^{10}}$ diverges because $\lim_{n\to\infty}\frac{10^n}{n^{10}}=\infty\ (\neq 0)$

5. $\sum_{n=1}^{\infty}(-1)^{n+1}\frac{\sqrt{n}+1}{n+1}$ converges since $\lim_{n\to\infty}\frac{\sqrt{n}+1}{n+1}=\lim_{n\to\infty}\frac{\frac{1}{\sqrt{n}}+\frac{1}{n}}{1+\frac{1}{\sqrt{n}}}=0$

and $\left\{\frac{\sqrt{n}+1}{n+1}\right\}$ is a decreasing sequence.

6. $\sum_{n=2}^{\infty}(-1)^{n+1}\frac{\ln n}{n}$ converges, because $\lim_{n\to\infty}\frac{\ln n}{n}=0$ and $\left\{\frac{\ln n}{n}\right\}$ is a decreasing sequence. If $f(x)=\frac{\ln x}{x}$, then $f'(x)=\frac{1-\ln x}{x^2}<0$ for $x>e$.

7. $\sum_{n=1}^{\infty}(-1)^{n+1}\frac{1}{n^{3/2}}$ converges since it converges absolutely.

8. $\sum_{n=1}^{\infty}(-1)^{n+1}\frac{\ln n}{\ln n^2}$ diverges because $\lim_{n\to\infty}\frac{\ln n}{2\ln n}=\frac{1}{2}\ (\neq 0)$

9. $\sum_{n=1}^{\infty}(-1)^{n}\ln\left(1+\frac{1}{n}\right)$ converges because $\lim_{n\to\infty}\ln\left(1+\frac{1}{n}\right)=\ln 1=0$.

If $f(x)=\ln\left(1+\frac{1}{x}\right)$ then $f'(x)=\frac{x}{x+1}\cdot\frac{x(1)-(x+1)(1)}{x^2}=$

$\frac{-1}{x(x+1)}<0$ for $x>1$. Hence $\left\{\ln\left(1+\frac{1}{n}\right)\right\}$ is decreasing.

10. $\sum_{n=1}^{\infty}(-1)^{n+1}\frac{3\sqrt{n}+1}{\sqrt{n}+1}$ diverges because $\lim_{n\to\infty}\frac{3\sqrt{n}+1}{\sqrt{n}+1}=3\ (\neq 0)$

11. $\sum_{n=1}^{\infty}(-1)^{n-1}(0.1)^{n}$ converges absolutely because it is a geometric series with $r = .1 < 1$.

12. $\sum_{n=1}^{\infty}(-1)^{n+1}\frac{1}{\sqrt{n}}$ converges conditionally. $\sum_{n=1}^{\infty}\frac{1}{\sqrt{n}}$ diverges because it is a p-series for $p = \frac{1}{2}$. But $\left\{\frac{1}{\sqrt{n}}\right\}$ is a decreasing sequence with limit zero.

13. $\sum_{n=1}^{\infty}(-1)^{n+1}\frac{n}{n^3+1}$ converges absolutely by comparison with $\sum_{n=1}^{\infty}\frac{1}{n^2}$, since $n^3 \le n^3 + 1 \Rightarrow \frac{1}{n^3+1} \le \frac{1}{n^3} \Rightarrow \frac{n}{n^3+1} \le \frac{n}{n^3} = \frac{1}{n^2}$

14. $\sum_{n=1}^{\infty}\frac{n!}{2^n}$ diverges, since $\lim_{n\to\infty}\frac{(n+1)!}{2^{n+1}}\cdot\frac{2^n}{n!} = \infty$

15. $\sum_{n=1}^{\infty}(-1)^{n+1}\frac{1}{n+3}$ converges conditionally, since $\left\{\frac{1}{n+3}\right\}$ is a decreasing sequence with limit 0, but $\sum_{n=1}^{\infty}\frac{1}{n+3}$ diverges.

16. $\sum_{n=1}^{\infty}(-1)^n\frac{\sin n}{n^2}$ converges absolutely, since $\frac{|\sin n|}{n^2} \le \frac{1}{n^2}$ and $\sum_{n=1}^{\infty}\frac{1}{n^2}$ converges (p-series for $p = 2 > 1$).

17. $\sum_{n=1}^{\infty}(-1)^{n+1}\frac{3+n}{5+n}$ diverges since $\lim_{n\to\infty}\frac{3+n}{5+n} = 1 \ne 0$.

18. $\sum_{n=2}^{\infty}(-1)^n\frac{1}{\ln n^3}$ converges conditionally. $\sum_{n=2}^{\infty}\frac{1}{\ln n^3} = \sum_{n=2}^{\infty}\frac{1}{3\ln n}$ diverges, but $\left\{\frac{1}{3\ln n}\right\}$ decreases and has limit 0.

19. $\sum_{n=1}^{\infty}(-1)^{n+1}\frac{1+n}{n^2}$ converges conditionally, since $\left\{\frac{1+n}{n^2}\right\}$ is a decreasing sequence converging to 0. But the series $\sum_{n=1}^{\infty}\frac{1+n}{n^2}$ diverges by comparison to $\sum_{n=1}^{\infty}\frac{1}{n}$ since $\lim_{n\to\infty}\frac{\frac{1+n}{n^2}}{\frac{1}{n}} = \lim_{n\to\infty}\frac{1+n}{n} = 1$.

20. $\sum_{n=1}^{\infty} \frac{(-2)^{n+1}}{n+5^n}$ converges absolutely. $\sum_{n=2}^{\infty} \frac{2^{n+1}}{n+5^n}$ converges by comparison to $2\sum_{n=1}^{\infty}\left(\frac{2}{5}\right)^n$.

21. $\sum_{n=1}^{\infty} n^2\left(\frac{2}{3}\right)^n$ converges absolutely since $\lim_{n\to\infty} \frac{(n+1)^2\left(\frac{2}{3}\right)^{n+1}}{n^2\left(\frac{2}{3}\right)^n} = 1$

22. $\sum_{n=1}^{\infty} (-1)^{n+1} 10^{1/n}$ diverges, because $\lim_{n\to\infty} 10^{1/n} = 1 \neq 0$

23. $\sum_{n=1}^{\infty} (-1)^n \frac{\tan^{-1} n}{n^2+1}$ converges absolutely since $|\tan^{-1} n| < \frac{\pi}{2} \Rightarrow$

$$\sum_{n=1}^{\infty} \left|\frac{\tan^{-1} n}{n^2+1}\right| \le \frac{\pi}{2}\sum_{n=1}^{\infty} \frac{1}{n^2+1} \le \frac{\pi}{2}\sum_{n=1}^{\infty} \frac{1}{n^2}$$

24. $\sum_{n=2}^{\infty} (-1)^{n+1} \frac{1}{n \ln n}$ converges conditionally. $\sum_{n=2}^{\infty} \frac{1}{n \ln n}$ diverges, but $\left\{\frac{1}{n \ln n}\right\}$ decreases and has limit 0.

25. $\sum_{n=1}^{\infty} \left(\frac{1}{n} - \frac{1}{2n}\right) = \frac{1}{2}\sum_{n=1}^{\infty} \frac{1}{n}$ diverges.

26. $\sum_{n=1}^{\infty} (-1)^{n+1} \frac{(0.1)^n}{n}$ converges absolutely. $\sum_{n=1}^{\infty} \frac{(0.1)^n}{n} \le \sum_{n=1}^{\infty} (0.1)^n = \frac{1}{9}$

27. $\sum_{n=1}^{\infty} (-1)^{n+1}(\sqrt{n+1} - \sqrt{n})$ converges conditionally since:

$\frac{\sqrt{n+1} - \sqrt{n}}{1} \cdot \frac{\sqrt{n+1} + \sqrt{n}}{\sqrt{n+1} + \sqrt{n}} = \frac{1}{\sqrt{n+1} + \sqrt{n}}$ and $\left\{\frac{1}{\sqrt{n+1} + \sqrt{n}}\right\}$ is a decreasing sequence which converges to 0. But $\frac{1}{\sqrt{n+1} + \sqrt{n}} \ge \frac{1}{3\sqrt{n}}$

so $\sum_{n=1}^{\infty} \frac{1}{\sqrt{n+1} + \sqrt{n}}$ diverges.

28. $\sum_{n=1}^{\infty}(-1)^{n+1}\frac{(n!)^2}{(2n)!}$ converges absolutely.

$$\lim_{n\to\infty}\frac{(n+1)!^2}{(2n+2)!}\cdot\frac{(2n)!}{(n!)^2} = \lim_{n\to\infty}\frac{[(n+1)(n!)]^2(2n)!}{(2n+2)(2n+1)(2n)!(n!)^2} = \frac{1}{4}.$$

29. $a_5 = \frac{1}{5}$; error ≤ 0.2

30. $a_5 = \frac{1}{10^5}$; error $\leq 10^{-5}$

31. $a_5 = \frac{(10^{-10})}{5}$; error $\leq 2 \times 10^{-11}$

32. $a_5 = -t^4$; error $\leq t^5 < 1$

33. Since $\frac{1}{9!} = .0000028 = 2.8 \times 10^{-6}$, the sum of the first 4 terms is sufficiently accurate.
$1 - \frac{1}{2!} + \frac{1}{4!} - \frac{1}{4!} + \frac{1}{8!} = 0.540302579.$

34. $\frac{1}{n!} < 0.000005$ if $n! > 20{,}000$. Since $9! = 362{,}880$, the first 10 terms are needed. $S_{10} = 0.3678792.$

35. (a) The condition $a_n \geq a_{n+1}$ is not met.

(b) $S = \dfrac{\frac{1}{3}}{1-\frac{1}{3}} - \dfrac{\frac{1}{2}}{1-\frac{1}{2}} = \frac{1}{2} - 1 = -\frac{1}{2}$

36. $S_{20} = 0.6687714$; $s_{20} + .5(\frac{1}{21}) = 0.692580927.$

37. $$\sum_{j=n+1}^{\infty}(-1)^{j+1}a_j = (-1)^{n+1}(a_{n+1} - a_{n+2}) + (-1)^{n+3}(a_{n+3} - a_{n+4}) + \ldots$$
$$= (-1)^{n+1}(a_{n+1} - a_{n+2}) + (a_{n+3} - a_{n+4}) + \ldots$$
Each grouped term is positive, so the remainder has the same sign as $(-1)^{n+1}$, which is the sign of the first unused term.

38. $$1 - \frac{1}{2} + \frac{1}{2} - \frac{1}{3} + \frac{1}{3} - \ldots = \sum_{n=1}^{\infty}\left(\frac{1}{n} - \frac{1}{n+1}\right) = \sum_{n=1}^{\infty}\frac{1}{n(n+1)}$$
$$= \frac{1}{1\cdot 2} + \frac{1}{2\cdot 3} + \ldots + \frac{1}{n(n+1)}.$$ $\sum_{n=1}^{\infty}\frac{1}{n^2+n}$ converges by comparison to $\sum_{n=1}^{\infty}\frac{1}{n^2}$. $S_n = \sum_{k=1}^{n}\left(\frac{1}{k} - \frac{1}{k+1}\right) = 1 - \frac{1}{n+1}$, so $\lim_{n\to\infty} S_n = 1$.
$S_{2n+1} = 1 - \frac{1}{2n+2}.$

39. Let $a_n = b_n = (-1)^n\frac{1}{\sqrt{n}}$. Then $\sum_1^\infty (-1)^n\frac{1}{\sqrt{n}}$ converges but

$\sum_1^\infty a_nb_n = \sum_1^\infty \frac{1}{n}$ diverges.

40. $$\frac{(-1)^n}{\sqrt{n}} - \frac{1}{n+(-1)^n\sqrt{n}} = \frac{(-1)^n[n+(-1)^n\sqrt{n}]-\sqrt{n}}{\sqrt{n}[n+(-1)^n\sqrt{n}]} = \frac{(-1)^n n}{\sqrt{n}[n+(-1)^n\sqrt{n}]} = \frac{(-1)^n}{\sqrt{n}+(-1)^n}.$$

$\sum_{n=1}^\infty \frac{(-1)^n}{\sqrt{n}}$ converges conditionally. $\sum_{n=2}^\infty \frac{1}{n+(-1)^n\sqrt{n}}$ diverges by comparisor

with $\sum_{n=2}^\infty \frac{1}{n}$, since $\lim_{n\to\infty} \frac{n}{n+(-1)^n\sqrt{n}} = 1 > 0$. $\therefore \sum_{n=2}^\infty \frac{(-1)^n}{\sqrt{n}+(-1)^n}$ diverges.

$\lim_{n\to\infty} \frac{(-1)^n}{\sqrt{n}+(-1)^n} \neq 0$.

41. The rearranged sequences of partial sums would be:

$-\frac{1}{2}$ with $S_1 = -\frac{1}{2}$

$-\frac{1}{2} + 1$ with $S_2 = \frac{1}{2}$

$-\frac{1}{2}+1-\frac{1}{4}-\frac{1}{6}-\frac{1}{8}$ with $S_5 = -\frac{1}{24}$

$-\frac{1}{2}+1-\frac{1}{4}-\frac{1}{6}-\frac{1}{8}+\frac{1}{3}+\frac{1}{5}+\frac{1}{7}$ with $S_8 = \frac{498}{840}$

11.9 RECAPITULATION

1. $\sum_{n=1}^\infty (-1)^{n-1}\frac{1}{\ln(n+1)}$ converges since $\lim_{n\to\infty}\frac{1}{\ln(n+1)} = 0$ and

$\frac{1}{\ln(n+2)} \le \frac{1}{\ln(n+1)}$ for all n.

2. $$\lim_{n\to\infty}\frac{4^n\,n!\,n!}{(2n)!} = \lim_{n\to\infty} 4^n \cdot \frac{n(n-1)(n-2)\cdot\ldots\cdot 3\cdot 2\cdot 1}{(2n)(2n-2)(2n-4)\cdot\ldots\cdot 4\cdot 2\cdot 1}\cdot\frac{n(n-1)n-2)\cdot\ldots\cdot 3\cdot 2\cdot 1}{(2n-1)(2n-3)\cdot\ldots\cdot 5\cdot 3\cdot 1}$$

$$= 4^n\left(\frac{1}{2^n}\right)\left(\frac{1}{2^n}\right) = 1 \neq 0.$$ $\sum_{n=1}^\infty \frac{4^n\,n!\,n!}{(2n)!}$ diverges.

3. This is the series $\sum_{n+1}^\infty (-1)^{n+1}\frac{1}{n}$ which converges.

4. $\lim_{n\to\infty} \frac{(n+1)!}{(n+1)^{n+1}} \cdot \frac{n^n}{n!} = \lim_{n\to\infty} \frac{(n+1)n!}{(n+1)(n+1)^n} \cdot \frac{n^n}{n!} = \lim_{n\to\infty}\left(\frac{n}{n+1}\right)^n = \frac{1}{e}$

$\therefore \sum_{n=1}^{\infty} \frac{n^n}{n!}$ diverges by the Ratio test.

5. Diverges, because $\lim_{n\to\infty} \frac{(n+1)^{n+1}}{(n+1)!} \cdot \frac{n!}{n^n} = \lim_{n\to\infty} \frac{(n+1)^n(n+1)}{(n+1)n!} \cdot \frac{n!}{n^n}$

$= \lim_{n\to\infty}\left(\frac{n+1}{n}\right)^n = e > 1$

6. Converges, since $\lim_{n\to\infty} \frac{a_{n+1}}{a_n} = \lim_{n\to\infty} \frac{(a_n)^{1/n}}{a_n} = 0.$

7. Converges, because $\lim_{n\to\infty} \frac{(n+1)^2}{2^{n+1}} \cdot \frac{2^n}{n^2} = \frac{1}{2} < 1.$

8. Diverges, since $\lim_{n\to\infty} \frac{a_{n+1}}{a_n} = \lim_{n\to\infty} \frac{2^{n+1}}{(n+1)^2} \cdot \frac{n^2}{2^n} = 2 > 1.$

9. Converges; it is the geometric series $\sum_{n=1}^{\infty}\left(\frac{1}{2}\right)^n.$

10. Diverges, since $\lim_{n\to\infty} \frac{a_{n+1}}{a_n} = \lim_{n\to\infty} \frac{2a_n}{a_n} = 2 > 1.$

11. Diverges; it is the series $2\sum_{n=1}^{\infty} \frac{1}{n}.$

12. Diverges, since $a_n > 1$ for $n > 3 \Rightarrow \lim_{n\to\infty} a_n > 1.$

13. Diverges; $a_n \le 1 \Rightarrow 1 + a_n \le 2 \Rightarrow \frac{1}{1+a_n} \ge \frac{1}{2}$. Thus $\lim_{n\to\infty} a_{n+1} \ne 0.$

14. Converges to 0, $a_n = 0$ for all n.

15. Diverges; $\lim_{n\to\infty} na_n = \infty \ne 0.$

16. Converges, since $\lim_{n\to\infty} \frac{a_{n+1}}{a_n} = \frac{1}{n} = 0$

17. Diverges; $\lim_{n\to\infty} a_n \ne 0$ since $a_n =$ either $+1$ or -1.

18. $\sum_{n=1}^{\infty} \frac{1}{3^{2n-1}}$ converges, geometric series with $r = \frac{1}{9}.$

$\sum_{n=1}^{\infty} \frac{2n}{3^{2n}}$ converges, since $\lim_{n\to\infty} \frac{2n+2}{3^{2n+2}} \cdot \frac{3^{3n}}{2n} = \frac{1}{9}$. $\therefore \sum a_n$ converges.

19. Converges by comparison to $\sum_{n=1}^{\infty} \frac{1}{n^2}$ since $|\sin n| \le 1.$

20. $\sum_{n=1}^{\infty} \frac{2n+3}{n^3+2}$ converges by comparison with $\sum_{n=1}^{\infty} \frac{1}{n^2}$, since

$\lim_{n\to\infty} \frac{2n+3}{n^3+2} \cdot \frac{n^2}{1} = 2 > 0.$

21. (a) Let $t_1 = c_1$, $t_2 = c_1 + c_2 \Rightarrow c_2 = t_2 - t_1$, $t_3 = c_1 + c_2 + c_3 \Rightarrow$

$c_3 = t_3 - (c_1 + c_2) = t_3 - t_2$, and in general, $t_n - t_{n-1} = \sum_{k=1}^{n} c_k$.

$$s_{2n+1} = \sum_{k=1}^{2n+1} \frac{c_k}{k} = c_1(1) + c_2\left(\frac{1}{2}\right) + \ldots + c_{2n+1}\left(\frac{1}{2n+1}\right)$$

$$= t_1(1) + \frac{1}{2}(t_2 - t_1) + \ldots + t_{2n}\left(\frac{1}{2n} - \frac{1}{2n+1}\right) + t_{2n+1}\left(\frac{1}{2n+1}\right)$$

$$= \sum_{k=1}^{2n} \frac{t_k}{k(k+1)} + \frac{t_{2n+1}}{2n+1}$$

$\sum_{k=1}^{2n} \left| \frac{t_k}{k(k+1)} \right| \le M \sum_{k=1}^{2n} \frac{1}{k(k+1)}$ converges absolutely, and $\lim_{n\to\infty} \frac{t_{2n+1}}{2n+1} = ($

so $\lim_{n\to\infty} s_{2n+1}$ exists. If $s_{2n} = \sum_{k=1}^{2n} \frac{c_k}{k}$, then $\lim_{n\to\infty} (s_{2n+1} - s_{2n})$

$= \lim_{n\to\infty} \frac{c_{2n+1}}{2n+1} = 0$, so $\sum_{k=1}^{\infty} \frac{c_k}{k}$ converges to $\sum_{k=1}^{\infty} \frac{t_k}{k(k+1)}$.

$$= t_1(1) + \frac{1}{2}(t_2 - t_1) + \ldots + t_{2n}\left(\frac{1}{2n} - \frac{1}{2n+1}\right) + t_{2n+1}\left(\frac{1}{2n+1}\right)$$

$$= \sum_{k=1}^{2n} \frac{t_k}{k(k+1)} + \frac{t_{2n+1}}{2n+1}$$

(b) In $\sum_{n=1}^{\infty} (-1)^{n+1} \frac{1}{n}$, take $\{c_k\} = \{1, -1, 1, -1, ..\}$ so that

$\sum_{k=1}^{n} c_k \le 1$, so that the alternating harmonic series converges.

(c) If $\{c_k\} = \{1, -1, -1, 1, 1, -1, -1, 1, 1, \ldots\}$ then $\sum_{k=1}^{n} c_k \le 1$, so

the series converges.

11.10 ESTIMATING THE SUM OF A SERIES

3. The ratios $\frac{a_{n+1}}{a_n} = \frac{n+1}{3n}$ form a decreasing sequence which converges to $\frac{1}{3}$. Take $r_1 = \frac{1}{3}$ and $r_2 = \frac{N+1}{3N}$.

(a) $\frac{10}{3^{10}} \cdot \frac{\frac{1}{3}}{1 - \frac{1}{3}} \le R_{10} \le \frac{10}{3^{10}} \cdot \frac{\frac{11}{30}}{1 - \frac{11}{30}}$; $8.47 \times 10^{-5} \le R_{10} \le 1.07 \times 10^{-5}$

(b) $\frac{100}{3^{100}} \cdot \frac{\frac{1}{3}}{1 - \frac{1}{3}} \le R_{100} \le \frac{100}{3^{100}} \cdot \frac{\frac{101}{300}}{1 - \frac{101}{300}}$; $9.70 \times 10^{-47} \le R_{100} \le 9.85 \times 10^{-47}$

11.M MISCELLANEOUS

1. $\sum_{k=2}^{n} \ln\left(1 - \frac{1}{k^2}\right) = \sum_{k=2}^{n}\left[\ln\left(1 + \frac{1}{k}\right) + \ln\left(1 - \frac{1}{k}\right)\right] =$

$\sum_{k=2}^{n} [\ln (k+1) - \ln k + \ln (k-1) - \ln k] = \ln (n+1) - \ln n - \ln 2$

$= \ln \frac{n+1}{2n}$. $\therefore \lim_{n\to\infty} \ln \frac{n+1}{2n} = \ln \frac{1}{2}$.

2. $\sum_{k=2}^{\infty} \frac{1}{k^2 - 1} = \frac{1}{2} \sum_{k=2}^{\infty} \left(\frac{1}{k-1} - \frac{1}{k+1}\right)$, so $\lim_{n\to\infty} S_n = \lim_{n\to\infty} \frac{1}{2}\left(\frac{3}{2} - \frac{1}{n+1}\right) = \frac{3}{4}$.

3. $\sum_{n=1}^{\infty} (x_{n+1} - x_n) = \lim_{n\to\infty} \sum_{j=1}^{n} (x_{j+1} - x_j) = \lim_{n\to\infty} (x_{n+1} - x_1) =$

$\left(\lim_{n\to\infty} x_{n+1}\right) - x_1$. Therefore, the series and the sequence either both converge or both diverge.

4. Converges conditionally, since $\sum_{n=1}^{\infty} \frac{1}{\sqrt{n}}$ diverges $\left(p = \frac{1}{2}\right)$ but $\left\{\frac{1}{\sqrt{n}}\right\}$ decreases and has limit 0.

5. $\frac{1}{1-x} = -\frac{\frac{1}{x}}{1 - \frac{1}{x}}$. Using $a = r = \frac{1}{x}$, this equals

$-\left(\frac{1}{x} + \frac{1}{x^2} + \frac{1}{x^3} + \ldots + \frac{1}{x^n} + \ldots\right)$ for $\frac{1}{|x|} < 1$ or $|x| > 1$.

6. $\sum_{n=1}^{\infty} \operatorname{sech} n$ converges, since $\sum_{n=1}^{\infty} \frac{2}{e^n + e^{-n}} < \sum_{n=1}^{\infty} \frac{2}{e^n}$ which converges.

7. $\sum_{n=1}^{\infty} (-1)^n \tanh n$ diverges because:

$$\lim_{n\to\infty} \tanh n = \lim_{n\to\infty} \frac{\sinh n}{\cosh n} = \lim_{n\to\infty} \frac{e^x - e^{-x}}{e^x + e^{-x}} = \lim_{n\to\infty} \frac{e^{2x} - 1}{e^{2x} + 1} = \lim_{n\to\infty} \frac{2e^{2x}}{2e^{2x}} = 1 \neq 0$$

8. $\frac{1}{\ln(n+1)} > \frac{1}{n+1}$, so $\sum_{n=1}^{\infty} \frac{1}{\ln(n+1)}$ diverges in comparison with $\sum_{n=1}^{\infty} \frac{1}{n+1}$.

9. $\sum_{n=1}^{\infty} \frac{n}{2(n+1)(n+2)}$ diverges because $\sum_{n=1}^{\infty} \frac{1}{n}$ diverges and

$$\lim_{n\to\infty} \frac{\frac{n}{2(n+1)(n+2)}}{\frac{1}{n}} = \lim_{n\to\infty} \frac{n^2}{2(n^2 + 3n + 2)} = \frac{1}{2}$$

10. $\sum_{n=1}^{\infty} \frac{\sqrt{n+1} - \sqrt{n}}{\sqrt{n}} \cdot \frac{\sqrt{n+1} + \sqrt{n}}{\sqrt{n+1} + \sqrt{n}} = \sum_{n=1}^{\infty} \frac{1}{\sqrt{n}\,(\sqrt{n+1} + \sqrt{n})} \geq \sum_{n=1}^{\infty} \frac{1}{2(n+1)} = \infty.$

11. $\sum_{n=2}^{\infty} \frac{1}{n(\ln n)^2}$ converges because $\int_2^{\infty} \frac{dx}{x(\ln x)^2} = \lim_{t\to\infty} \int_2^t \frac{dx}{x(\ln x)^2}$

$$= \lim_{t\to\infty} \left[-\frac{1}{\ln x}\right]_2^t = \lim_{t\to\infty} \left[-\frac{1}{\ln t} + \frac{1}{\ln 2}\right] = \frac{1}{\ln 2}$$

12. Diverges, because $\lim_{n\to\infty} \frac{1 + (-2)^{n-1}}{2^n} \neq 0$.

13. $\sum_{n=1}^{\infty} \frac{n}{1000n^2 + 1}$ diverges by comparison to $\sum_{n=1}^{\infty} \frac{1}{n}$, since

$$\lim_{n\to\infty} \frac{n}{1000n^2 + 1} \cdot \frac{n}{1} = \frac{1}{1000}$$

14. $\sum_{n=1}^{\infty} \frac{e^n}{n!}$ converges, since $\lim_{n\to\infty} \frac{e^{n+1}}{(n+1)!} \cdot \frac{n!}{e^n} = \frac{e}{n+1} = 0 < 1$.

15. $\sum_{n=1}^{\infty} \frac{1}{n\sqrt{n^2 + 1}}$ converges by comparison to $\sum_{n=1}^{\infty} \frac{1}{n^2}$ because $\lim_{n\to\infty} \frac{1}{n\sqrt{n^2 + 1}} \cdot \frac{n^2}{1} =$

16. $\sum_{n=1}^{\infty} \frac{1}{n^{1+1/n}}$ diverges by comparison with $\sum_{n=1}^{\infty} \frac{1}{n}$, since

$$\lim_{n\to\infty} \frac{n^{1+1/n}}{n} = \lim_{n\to\infty} n^{1/n} = 1.$$

17. Diverges, because $\frac{1\cdot3\cdot5\cdot\ldots\cdot(2n-1)}{2\cdot4\cdot6\cdot\ldots\cdot(2n)} \ge \frac{1\cdot2\cdot4\cdot\ldots\cdot(2n-2)}{2\cdot4\cdot6\cdot\ldots\cdot(2n)} = \frac{1}{2n}$

and $\frac{1}{2}\sum_{n=1}^{\infty}\frac{1}{n}$ diverges.

18. $\sum_{n=1}^{\infty}\frac{n^2}{n^3+1}$ diverges by comparison with $\sum_{n=1}^{\infty}\frac{1}{n}$, since $\lim_{n\to\infty}\frac{n^2}{n^3+1}\cdot\frac{n}{1} = 1$

19. $\sum_{n=1}^{\infty}\frac{n+1}{n!}$ converges because $\lim_{n\to\infty}\frac{n+2}{(n+1)!}\cdot\frac{n!}{n+1} = 0 < 1$

20. $\sum_{n=1}^{\infty}\frac{1}{(n+1)(n+2)} = \sum_{n=1}^{\infty}\left(\frac{1}{n+1} - \frac{1}{n+2}\right) = \lim_{n\to\infty}\left(\frac{1}{2} - \frac{1}{n+2}\right) = \frac{1}{2}$

21. (a) $\sum_{n=1}^{\infty}\frac{a_n}{n} = a_1 + \frac{1}{2}a_2 + \frac{1}{3}a_3 + \frac{1}{4}a_4 + \frac{1}{5}a_5 + \frac{1}{6}a_6 + \ldots + \frac{1}{n}a_n + \ldots$

$\ge a_1 + \frac{1}{2}a_2 + \frac{1}{3}a_4 + \frac{1}{4}a_4 + \frac{1}{5}a_8 + \frac{1}{6}a_8 + \frac{1}{7}a_8 + \frac{1}{8}a_8 + \ldots + \frac{1}{n}a_n + \ldots$

$= a_1 + \frac{1}{2}a_2 + \left(\frac{1}{3} + \frac{1}{4}\right)a_4 + \left(\frac{1}{5} + \frac{1}{6} + \frac{1}{7} + \frac{1}{8}\right)a_8 + \left(\frac{1}{9} + \frac{1}{10} + \ldots + \frac{1}{16}\right)a_{16} + \ldots$

$\ge \frac{1}{2}(a_2 + a_4 + a_8 + a_{16} + \ldots)$ which diverges.

(b) Let $a_n = \frac{1}{\ln n}$, $n \ge 2$. Then

(i) $a_2 \ge a_3 \ge a_4 \ge \ldots$ and

(ii) $\frac{1}{\ln 2} + \frac{1}{\ln 4} + \frac{1}{\ln 8} + \frac{1}{\ln 16} + \ldots = \frac{1}{\ln 2} + \frac{1}{2\ln 2} + \frac{1}{3\ln 2} + \frac{1}{4\ln 4} + \ldots$

$= \frac{1}{\ln 2}\left(1 + \frac{1}{2} + \frac{1}{3} + \frac{1}{4} + \ldots\right)$ which diverges.

By part (a), $1 + \sum_{n=2}^{\infty}\frac{1}{n\ln n}$ diverges.

22. (a) Let $\sum a_n = M$. Then $a_n^2 = a_n \cdot a_n \le a_n \sum a_n = M a_n$.

Therefore, $\sum a_n^2 \le M\sum a_n \le M^2 < \infty$.

(b) $\sum\frac{a_n}{1-a_n}$ converges by comparison with $\sum a_n$, since

$\lim_{n\to\infty}\frac{a_n}{1-a_n}\cdot\frac{1}{a_n} = 1$, and $\sum a_n$ converges.

23. $\sum_{n=3}^{\infty} \frac{1}{n\ln n(\ln(\ln n))^p}$ converges since $\int_3^{\infty} \frac{dx}{x\ln x(\ln(\ln x))^p} =$

$\frac{1}{-p+1}(\ln(\ln x))^{-p+1}\Big]_3^{\infty}$ converges only for $p < 1$.

24. (a) Follow the outline for Prob. 21. Sect 11.9:

$\sum_{k=1}^{2n} \frac{|t_k|}{k(k+1)}$ converges absolutely, because:

$\frac{|t_k|}{k(k+1)} \le \frac{Mk^h}{k(k+1)} \le \frac{Mk^h}{k^2} = \frac{M}{k^{2-h}}$, and $2 - h > 1$ since $h < 1$.

$s_{2n+1} - S_{2n} = \frac{c_{2n+1}}{2n+1} = \frac{t_{2n+1}}{2n+1} + \frac{t_{2n}}{2n+1} \to 0$ since $|t^n|$ are bounded.

(b) $\{c_n\} = 1, -1, -1, 1, 1, 1, 1, 1, 1, 1, \ldots,$ so that

$\{t_n\} = 1, 0, -1, 0, 1, 2, 1, 0, -1, -2, \ldots.$ It eventually becomes

apparent that $t_{\frac{n(n+1)}{2}} \le \frac{n(n+1)}{2}$ so that for sufficiently large

k, $t_k < 2\sqrt{k}$. Take $h = \frac{1}{2}$ and $M = 2$.

CHAPTER 12

POWER SERIES

12.2 TAYLOR POLYNOMIALS

1.

n	$f^n(x)$	$f^n(0)$
0	e^{-x}	1
1	$-e^{-x}$	-1
2	e^{-x}	1
3	$-e^{-x}$	-1
4	e^{-x}	1

$$P_3(x) = 1 - x + \frac{x^2}{2} - \frac{x^3}{6}$$

$$P_4(x) = 1 - x + \frac{x^2}{2} - \frac{x^3}{6} + \frac{x^4}{24}$$

2.

n	$f^n(x)$	$f^n(0)$
0	sinx	0
1	cosx	1
2	-sinx	0
3	-cosx	-1
4	sinx	0

$$P_3(x) = x - \frac{x^3}{6}$$

$$P_4(x) = x - \frac{x^3}{6}$$

3.

n	$f^n(x)$	$f^n(0)$
0	cosx	1
1	-sinx	0
2	-cosx	-1
3	sinx	0
4	cosx	1

$$P_3(x) = 1 - \frac{x^2}{2}$$

$$P_4(x) = 1 - \frac{x^2}{2} + \frac{x^4}{24}$$

4.

n	$f^n(x)$	$f^n(0)$
0	$\sin(x+\pi/2)$	1
1	$\cos(x+\pi/2)$	0
2	$-\sin(x+\pi/2)$	-1
3	$-\cos(x+\pi/2)$	0
4	$\sin(x+\pi/2)$	1

$$P_3(x) = 1 - \frac{x^2}{2}$$

$$P_4(x) = 1 - \frac{x^2}{2} + \frac{x^4}{24}$$

5.

n	$f^n(x)$	$f^n(0)$
0	sinhx	0
1	coshx	1
2	sinhx	0
3	coshx	1
4	sinhx	0

$$P_3(x) = x + \frac{x^3}{6}$$

$$P_4(x) = x + \frac{x^3}{6}$$

6.

n	$f^n(x)$	$f^n(0)$
0	coshx	1
1	sinhx	0
2	coshx	1
3	sinhx	0
4	coshx	1

$$P_3(x) = 1 + \frac{x^2}{2}$$

$$P_4(x) = 1 + \frac{x^2}{2} + \frac{x^4}{24}$$

7.

n	$f^n(x)$	$f^n(0)$
0	$x^4 - 2x + 1$	1
1	$4x^3 - 2$	-2
2	$12x^2$	0
3	$24x$	0
4	24	24

$P_3(x) = 1 - 2x$

$P_4(x) = 1 - 2x + x^4$

8.

n	$f^n(x)$	$f^n(0)$
0	$x^3 - 2x + 1$	1
1	$3x^2 - 2$	-2
2	$6x$	0
3	6	6
4	0	0

$P_3(x) = 1 - 2x + x^3$

$P_4(x) = 1 - 2x + x^3$

9.

n	$f^n(x)$	$f^n(0)$
0	$x^2 - 2x + 1$	1
1	$2x - 2$	-2
2	2	2
3	0	0
4	0	0

$P_3(x) = 1 - 2x + x^2$

$P_4(x) = P_3(x)$

10. $f(x) = (1 + x)^{-1}$ $\quad f(0) = 1$

$f'(x) = -(1 + x)^{-2}$ $\quad f'(0) = -1$

$f''(x) = 2(1 + x)^{-3}$ $\quad f''(0) = 2$

$f'''(x) = -3\cdot 2\ (1 + x)^{-4}$ $\quad f'''(0) = -3!$

$f^{(4)}(x) = -4\cdot -3\cdot 2(1 + x)^{-5}$ $\quad f^{(4)}(0) = 4!$

$$\frac{1}{1+x} = \sum_{n=0}^{\infty} (-1)^2\, x^n$$

11. $f(x) = x^2;\ f'(x) = 2x; f''(x) = 2;\ f^n(x) = 0$ for $n > 2$
$f(0) = 0; f'(0) = 0; f''(0) = 2$

$x^2 = 0 + 0x + \frac{2}{2}x^2 + 0 + \ldots = x^2$

12. $f(x) = (1 + x)^2$ $\quad f(0) = 1$

$f'(x) = 2(1 + x)$ $\quad f'(0) = 2$

$f''(x) = 2$ $\quad f''(0) = 2$

$f'''(x) = 0$ $\quad f'''(0) = 0$

$(1 + x)^2 = 1 + 2x + x^2$

13. $f(x) = (1+x)^{\frac{3}{2}}$ $\qquad f(0) = 1$

$f'(x) = \frac{3}{2}(1+x)^{\frac{1}{2}}$ $\qquad f'(0) = \frac{3}{2}$

$f''(x) = \frac{1}{2}\cdot\frac{3}{2}(1+x)^{-\frac{1}{2}}$ $\qquad f''(0) = \frac{1\cdot 3}{2^2}$

$f'''(x) = -\frac{1}{2}\cdot\frac{1}{2}\cdot\frac{3}{2}(1+x)^{-\frac{3}{2}}$ $\qquad f'''(0) = \frac{(-1)\cdot 1\cdot 3}{2^3}$

$f^4(x) = \frac{3\cdot 1\cdot(-1)(-3)}{2^4}(1+x)^{-\frac{5}{2}}$ $\qquad f^4(x) = \frac{3\cdot 1\cdot(-1)(-3)}{2^4}$

$$f(x) = 1 + \sum_{n=1}^{\infty} \frac{(5-2n)}{n!2^n} x^n$$

14. $f(x) = (1-x)^{-1}$ $\qquad f(0) = 1$

$f'(x) = (1-x)^{-2}$ $\qquad f'(0) = 1$

$f''(x) = 2(1-x)^{-3}$ $\qquad f''(0) = 2$

$f'''(x) = 3!(1-x)^{-4}$ $\qquad f'''(0) = 3!$

$\frac{1}{1-x} = \sum_{n=0}^{\infty} x^n$ is a geometric series with $r = x$, hence converges for $|x| < 1$ and diverges for $|x| \geq 1$.

15. $f(x) = e^{10} + e^{10}(x-10) + \frac{e^{10}}{2!}(x-10)^2 + \ldots$

$$= \sum_{n=0}^{\infty} \frac{e^{10}}{n!}(x-10)^n$$

16. $f(x) = x^2$ $\qquad f\left(\frac{1}{2}\right) = \frac{1}{4}$

$f'(x) = 2x$ $\qquad f'\left(\frac{1}{2}\right) = 1$

$f''(x) = 2$ $\qquad f''\left(\frac{1}{2}\right) = 2$

$f'''(x) = 0$ $\qquad f'''\left(\frac{1}{2}\right) = 0$

$$x^2 = \frac{1}{4} + \left(x - \frac{1}{2}\right) + \left(x - \frac{1}{2}\right)^2$$

17.

n	$f^n(x)$	$f^n(1)$
0	$\ln x$	0
1	x^{-1}	1
2	$-x^{-2}$	-1
3	$2x^{-3}$	2
4	$-3\cdot 2x^{-4}$	-6

$$\ln x = \ln 1 + \frac{1}{1}(x-1) - \frac{1}{1^2\cdot 2}(x-1)^2 + \frac{2}{1^3\cdot 3!}(x-1)^3 - \ldots$$

$$= \sum_{n=1}^{\infty}(-1)^{n-1}\frac{(x-1)^n}{n}$$

18. $f(x) = \sqrt{x}$ $\quad f(4) = 2$

$f'(x) = \frac{1}{2}x^{-1/2}$ $\quad f'(4) = \frac{1}{2^2}$

$f''(x) = -\frac{1}{2^2}x^{-3/2}$ $\quad f''(4) = -\frac{1}{2^5}$

$f'''(x) = \frac{3}{2^3}x^{-5/2}$ $\quad f'''(4) = \frac{3}{2^8}$

$$\sqrt{x} = 2 + \frac{(x-4)}{2^2} - \frac{(x-4)^2}{2!\,2^5} + \frac{3\,(x-4)^3}{3!\,2^8} - \frac{3\cdot 5\,(x-4)^4}{4!\,2^{11}} + \ldots$$

19.

n	$f^n(x)$	$f^n(-1)$
0	x^{-1}	-1
1	$-x^{-2}$	-1
2	$2x^{-3}$	-2
3	$-3\cdot 2x^{-4}$	-6
4	$4\cdot 3\cdot 2x^{-5}$	-24

$$f(x) = -\sum_{n=0}^{\infty}(x+1)^n$$

20. $f(x) = \cos x$ $\quad f\left(\frac{\pi}{4}\right) = \frac{1}{\sqrt{2}}$

$f'(x) = -\sin x$ $\quad f'\left(\frac{\pi}{4}\right) = -\frac{1}{\sqrt{2}}$

$f''(x) = -\cos x$ $\quad f''\left(\frac{\pi}{4}\right) = -\frac{1}{\sqrt{2}}$

$f'''(x) = \sin x$ $\quad f'''\left(\frac{\pi}{4}\right) = \frac{1}{\sqrt{2}}$

$$\cos x = \frac{1}{\sqrt{2}}\left[1 - \left(x-\frac{\pi}{4}\right) - \frac{\left(x-\frac{\pi}{4}\right)^2}{2!} + \frac{\left(x-\frac{\pi}{4}\right)^3}{3!} + \frac{\left(x-\frac{\pi}{4}\right)^4}{4!} - \ldots\right]$$

21. $f(x) = \tan x$ $\quad f\left(\frac{\pi}{4}\right) = 1$

$f'(x) = \sec^2 x$ $\quad f'\left(\frac{\pi}{4}\right) = 2$

$f''(x) = 2\sec^2 x \tan x$ $\quad f''\left(\frac{\pi}{4}\right) = 4$

$$\tan x = 1 + 2\left(x - \frac{\pi}{4}\right) + 2\left(x - \frac{\pi}{4}\right)^2 + \ldots$$

22. $f(x) = \ln \cos x \qquad f\left(\frac{\pi}{3}\right) = \ln \frac{1}{2}$

$f'(x) = -\tan x \qquad f'\left(\frac{\pi}{3}\right) = -\sqrt{3}$

$f''(x) = -\sec^2 x \qquad f''\left(\frac{\pi}{3}\right) = -4$

$f'''(x) = -2\sec^2 x \tan x \qquad f'''\left(\frac{\pi}{3}\right) = -8\sqrt{3}$

$$\ln \cos x = \ln\frac{1}{2} - \sqrt{3}\left(x - \frac{\pi}{3}\right) - 2\left(x - \frac{\pi}{3}\right)^2 - \frac{8\sqrt{3}}{3!}\left(x - \frac{\pi}{3}\right)^3 - \ldots$$

12.3 TAYLOR'S THEOREM WITH REMAINDER: SINES, COSINES, AND e^x

1. $e^{\frac{x}{2}} = \sum_{n=0}^{\infty}\left(\frac{x}{2}\right)^n \cdot \frac{1}{n!} = \sum_{n=0}^{\infty} \frac{x^n}{2^n n!}$

2. $\sin 3x = \sum_{n=0}^{\infty} (-1)^n \frac{(3x)^{2n+1}}{(2n+1)!}$

3. $5\cos\frac{x}{\pi} = 5\sum_{n=0}^{\infty}(-1)^n\left(\frac{x}{\pi}\right)^{2n}\frac{1}{(2n)!} = 5\sum_{n=0}^{\infty}(-1)^n\frac{x^{2n}}{\pi^{2n}(2n)!}$

4. $\sinh x = \frac{1}{2}(e^x - e^{-x}) = \frac{1}{2}\left(\sum_{n=0}^{\infty}\frac{x^n}{n!} + \sum_{n=0}^{\infty}(-1)^{n+1}\frac{x^n}{n!}\right) =$

$$\frac{1}{2}\sum_{n=0}^{\infty} 2\left(\frac{x^{2n+1}}{(2n+1)!}\right) = \sum_{n=0}^{\infty}\frac{x^{2n+1}}{(2n+1)!}$$

5. $\frac{x^2}{2} - 1 + \cos x = \frac{x^2}{2} - 1 + 1 - \frac{x^2}{2} + \frac{x^4}{4!} - \ldots = \sum_{n=2}^{\infty}(-1)^n\frac{x^{2n}}{(2n)!}$

6. $\cos^2 x = \frac{1}{2}(1 + \cos 2x) = \frac{1}{2}\left(1 + \sum_{n=0}^{\infty}(-1)^{2n}\frac{(2x)^{2n}}{(2n)!}\right)$

$$= \frac{1}{2}\left(1 + 1 - \frac{(2x)^2}{2!} + \frac{(2x)^4}{4!} + \ldots\right) = 1 - x^2 + \frac{x^4}{3} - \frac{2x^6}{45} + \ldots$$

7. (a) $\cos(-x) = \sum_{n=0}^{\infty}(-1)^n\frac{(-x)^{2n}}{(2n)!} = \sum_{n=0}^{\infty}(-1)^n\frac{x^{2n}}{(2n)!} = \cos x$

(b) $\sin(-x) = \sum_{n=0}^{\infty}(-1)^n\frac{(-x)^{2n+1}}{(2n+1)!} = -\sum_{n=0}^{\infty}(-1)^n\frac{x^{2n+1}}{(2n+1)!} = -\sin x$

8. $e^x = f(a) + f'(a)(x-a) + \frac{f''(a)}{2!}(x-a)^2 + \ldots.$

$= e^a + e^a(x-a) + \frac{e^a}{2!}(x-a)^2 + \ldots = e^a\left[1 + (x-a) + \frac{(x-a)^2}{2!} + \ldots\right]$

9. Using the formula for a geometric series with a = 1 and r = -x:

$\frac{1}{1+x} = 1 - x + x^2 + R_n(x)$

10. $\int_0^{0.1} e^{(-x^2)}\,dx = \int_0^{0.1}\left(1 - x^2 + \frac{x^4}{2} - \ldots\right)dx$

$= x - \frac{1}{3}x^3 + \ldots\Big]_0^{0.1} \approx 0.100$ with error $|R_3(x)| \le \frac{(0.1)^5}{10} < 0.000001$

11. $f(x) = (1+x)^{\frac{1}{2}}$; $f(0) = 1$; $f'(x) = \frac{1}{2}(1+x)^{-\frac{1}{2}}$; $f'(0) = \frac{1}{2}$

$f''(x) = -\frac{1}{4}(1+x)^{-\frac{3}{2}}$; $f''(0) = -\frac{1}{4}$

$(1+x)^{\frac{1}{2}} \approx 1 + \frac{1}{2}x - \frac{1}{8}x^2 + R_n(x)$

12. $e^x = e + e(x-1) + \frac{e}{2!}(x-1)^2 + \frac{e}{3!}(x-1)^3 + \ldots$

$= e\left[1 + (x-1) + \frac{(x-1)^2}{2!} + \frac{(x-1)^3}{3!} + \ldots\right]$

13. $\left|\frac{x^5}{5!}\right| < 5\times 10^{-4} \Leftrightarrow |x^5| < 120\cdot 5\times 10^{-4} = .06 \Leftrightarrow |x| < 0.5697$

14. $|R_3(\ )| = \frac{\cos c}{4!}x^4 \le \frac{|x|^4}{4!}$. If $|x| < 0.5$,

then $|R_3(x)| \le \frac{(0.5)^4}{4!} < 0.0026$. It tends to be too small.

15. (a) $R_2(x) = \frac{-\cos c}{3!}x^3$. $\therefore$ $|R_2(x)| = \frac{\cos c}{6}|x|^3$. If $|x| < 10^{-3}$,

then $|R_2(x)| \le \frac{1}{6}(10^{-3})^3 < 1.67 \times 10^{-10}$.

(b) $-10^{-3} < x < 10^{-3} \Rightarrow \cos c > 0 \Rightarrow -\cos c < 0$.

If $-10^{-3} < x < 0$, $\frac{-\cos c}{3!}x^3 < 0 \Rightarrow x > \sin x$

If $10^{-3} > x > 0$, $\frac{-\cos c}{3!}x^3 > 0 \Rightarrow \sin x > x$

16. $f''(x) = \frac{-1}{4(1+x)^{3/2}}$. $R_2(x) = \frac{-1}{4(1+c)^{3/2}}\cdot\frac{x^2}{2!}$. For $|x| < 0.01$,

$|R_2(x)| \le \frac{(0.01)^2}{8} = 0.0000125$

17. If $|x| < 0.1$, then $e^c < e^{.1}$. Therefore,

$$|R_2(x)| \le \frac{e^{.1}(.1)^3}{3!} < 0.000184.$$

18. $\text{Error} \le \frac{|x^3|}{3!} = \frac{(0.1)^3}{3!} < 0.0001\bar{6}$. The third term in the series is negative if $x < 0$, and so the approximation is too large.

19. $|R_4(x)| \le \frac{|\sinh c||x^5|}{5!} = \frac{.521(0.5)^5}{5!} < 0.0003$

20. $R_2(x) = \frac{e^c}{2!}x^2 \le \frac{e^{0.1}(.01)h}{2} \approx \frac{(1.105)(0.01)h}{2} < 0.005525h.$

Since 0.6% of $h = 0.006h$, $R_2(x) < 0.6\%$ of h.

21. $(f+g)(x) = \sum_{n=0}^{\infty} \frac{(f+g)^n(0)}{n!}x^n = \sum_{n=0}^{\infty} \frac{f^n(0)+g^n(0)}{n!}x^n.$

22. (a) $\sin(0.1)$

(b) $\cos\frac{\pi}{4}$

(c) $\cosh 1$

23. (a) $e^{i\pi} = \cos\pi + i\sin\pi = -1 + 0i$

(b) $e^{\frac{i\pi}{4}} = \cos\frac{\pi}{4} + i\sin\frac{\pi}{4} = \frac{\sqrt{2}}{2} + \frac{\sqrt{2}}{2}i$

(c) $e^{-\frac{i\pi}{2}} = \cos\left(-\frac{\pi}{2}\right) + i\sin\left(-\frac{\pi}{2}\right) = 0 - i$

(d) $e^{i\pi} \cdot e^{-\frac{i\pi}{2}} = e^{\frac{i\pi}{2}} = \cos\frac{\pi}{2} + i\sin\frac{\pi}{2} = 0 + i$

24. $$\frac{e^{i\theta} + e^{-i\theta}}{2} = \frac{\cos\theta + i\sin\theta + \cos(-\theta) + i\sin(-\theta)}{2}$$

$$= \frac{2\cos\theta}{2} = \cos\theta$$

$$\frac{e^{i\theta} - e^{-i\theta}}{2i} = \frac{\cos\theta + i\sin\theta - \cos(-\theta) - i\sin(-\theta)}{2i}$$

$$= \frac{2i\sin\theta}{2i} = \sin\theta$$

25. $$\cos^3\theta = \left(\frac{e^{i\theta} + e^{-i\theta}}{2}\right)^3 = \frac{1}{8}(e^{3i\theta} + 3e^{2i\theta}e^{-i\theta} + 3e^{i\theta}e^{-2i\theta} + e^{-3i\theta})$$

$$= \frac{1}{8}(\cos3\theta + i\sin3\theta + 3[\cos\theta + i\sin\theta] + 3[\cos(-\theta) + i\sin(-\theta)] + \cos(-3\theta) + i\sin(-3\theta))$$

$$= \frac{1}{8}(2\cos3\theta + 6\cos\theta) = \frac{1}{4}\cos3\theta + \frac{3}{4}\cos\theta$$

$$\sin^3\theta = \left(\frac{e^{i\theta} - e^{-i\theta}}{2i}\right)^3 = \frac{1}{8i^3}(e^{3i\theta} - 3e^{2i\theta}e^{-i\theta} + 3e^{i\theta}e^{-2i\theta} - e^{-3i\theta})$$

$$= -\frac{1}{8i}\left(\cos 3\theta + i\sin 3\theta - 3[\cos\theta + i\sin\theta] + 3[\cos(-\theta) + i\sin(-\theta)] - \cos(-3\theta) - i\sin(-3\theta)\right)$$

$$= -\frac{1}{8i}(2i\sin 3\theta - 6i\sin\theta) = -\frac{1}{4}\sin 3\theta + \frac{3}{4}\sin\theta$$

26. $\frac{d}{dx}(e^{(a+ib)x}) = \frac{d}{dx}[e^{ax}(\cos bx + i\sin bx)]$

$$= e^{ax}(-b\sin x + ib\cos x) + ae^{ax}(\cos bx + i\sin bx)$$

$$= ib(e^{ax})(\cos bx + i\sin bx) + ae^{ax}(\cos bx + i\sin bx)$$

$$= (a + ib)e^{ax}(\cos bx + i\sin bx) = (a + ib)e^{(a+ib)x}$$

27. $\int e^{(a+ib)x}dx = \frac{1}{a+ib}e^{(a+ib)x} + C = \frac{a-ib}{a^2+b^2}e^{(a+ib)x} + C$

$$= \frac{a}{a^2+b^2}e^{(a+ib)x} + \frac{-ib}{a^2+b^2}e^{(a+ib)x}$$

$$= \frac{ae^{ax}}{a^2+b^2}\cos bx - \frac{ib\,e^{ax}}{a^2+b^2}\cos bx + \frac{iae^{ax}}{a^2+b^2}\sin bx + \frac{be^{ax}}{a^2+b^2}\sin bx$$

$$= \frac{1}{a^2+b^2}e^{ax}(a\cos bx + b\sin bx) + \frac{i}{a^2+b^2}e^{ax}(a\sin bx - b\cos bx)$$

$$\int e^{(a+ib)x}dx = \int e^{ax}(\cos bx + i\sin bx)dx = \int e^{ax}\cos bx\,dx + i\int e^{ax}\sin bx\,dx$$

Equating real part to real part and imaginary part to imaginary part in the two expressions for the integral, we have:

$$\int e^{ax}\cos bx\,dx = \frac{1}{a^2+b^2}e^{ax}(a\cos bx + b\sin bx)$$

$$\int e^{ax}\sin bx\,dx = \frac{1}{a^2+b^2}e^{ax}(a\sin bx - b\cos bx)$$

12.4 EXPANSION POINTS, THE BINOMIAL THEOREM, ARCTANGENTS & Π

1. $31° = \frac{31\pi}{180} \approx 0.5411$ radians.

$\cos 31° = 1 - \frac{(.5411)^2}{2} + \frac{(.5411)^4}{24} \approx 0.857$ with error

$|R_5(x)| \le \frac{(.5411)^6}{6!} < 0.00003533$

2. $46^\circ = \frac{23\pi}{90} = 0.80285$ radians.

$$\sin 46^\circ = 0.80285 - \frac{(0.80285)^3}{3!} + \frac{(0.80285)^5}{5!} \approx 0.7194$$

$$\text{with error } |R_5(x)| \le \frac{(0.80285)^7}{7!} < 0.00004$$

$$\cos 46^\circ = 1 - \frac{(0.80285)^2}{2!} + \frac{(0.80285)^4}{4!} - \frac{(0.80285)^6}{6!} \approx 0.6946$$

$$\text{with error } |R_4(x)| \le \frac{(0.80285)^8}{8!} < 0.000004$$

$$\text{Tan } 45^\circ = \frac{\sin 46^\circ}{\cos 46^0} = \frac{0.7194}{0.6946} \approx 1.036$$

(The tangent series converges too slowly to be practical)

3. Using $\sin(2\pi + x) = \sin x$, $\sin 6.3 = \sin(2\pi + 0.0168) = \sin 0.0168$

We need only the first term $\sin 0.0168 = 0.0168$ with error $|R_2(x)| \le \frac{(0.0168)^3}{6} < 7.9 \times 10^{-7}$

4. 69 radians is close to 11 revolutions or 22π.

$$\cos 69 = \cos(22\pi - 69) \approx \cos 0.1150 = 1 - \frac{(0.1150)^2}{2} \approx 0.993$$

$$\text{with } |R_3(x)| \le \frac{(0.1150)^4}{4!} < 0.000007$$

5. $\ln 1.25 = \ln(1 + .25) = .25 - \frac{(.25)^2}{2} + \frac{(.25)^3}{3} - \frac{(.25)^4}{4} = .223$

with error $|R_5(x)| \le \frac{(.25)^5}{5} < 0.0002$

6. The radius of convergence for $\tan^{-1} x$ is $|x| \le 1$.
Let $\tan^{-1}(1.02) = y$ so $1.02 = \tan y = \tan\left(\frac{\pi}{4} + x\right)$.

$$\tan(x+y) = \frac{\tan x + \tan y}{1 - \tan x \tan y} \Rightarrow \tan\left(\frac{\pi}{4} + x\right) = \frac{1 + \tan x}{1 - \tan x} \Rightarrow$$

$$\frac{1 + \tan x}{1 - \tan x} = 1.02 \text{ or } \tan x = 0.0099.$$

$$\tan^{-1}(0.0099) = (0.0099) - \frac{(0.0099)^3}{3} \approx 0.0099 \text{ with}$$

$$|R_3(x)| \le \frac{(0.0099)^5}{5} \approx 1.97 \times 10^{-11}. \quad \tan^{-1}(1.01) = \frac{\pi}{4} - 0.0099 \approx 0.795$$

7. $\ln(1+2x) = 2x - \frac{(2x)^2}{2} + \frac{(2x)^3}{3} - \ldots = \sum_{n=1}^{\infty}(-1)^{n-1}\frac{2^n x^n}{n}$ converges

for all $-1 < 2x \le 1$ or $-\frac{1}{2} < x \le \frac{1}{2}$.

8. $|R_1(x)| \le \frac{x^2}{2} < 0.01\,|x|$ if $|x| < 0.02$.

9. $\int_0^{0.1} \frac{\sin x}{x}dx = \int_0^{0.1} \frac{1}{x}\left(x - \frac{x^3}{3!} + \frac{x^5}{5!} - \ldots\right)dx = \int_0^{0.1}\left(1 - \frac{x^2}{3!} + \frac{x^4}{5!} - \frac{x^6}{7!} + ..\right)dx$

$= x - \frac{x^3}{3 \cdot 3!} + \frac{x^5}{5 \cdot 5!} - ..\Big]_0^{0.1} = 0.1$ with error $|R_2(x)| \le \frac{(0.1)^3}{18} = 0.00006$

10. $\int_0^{0.1} e^{(-x^2)}\,dx = \int_0^{0.1}\left(1 - x^2 + \frac{x^4}{2} - \ldots\right)dx$

$= x - \frac{1}{3}x^3 + ..\Big]_0^{0.1} \approx 0.100$ with error $|R_3(x)| \le \frac{(0.1)^5}{10} < 0.000001$

11. The parabola $x^2 = 2a(y - a)$ solved for y is $y = a + \frac{x^2}{2a}$
These are the first two terms of the Maclaurin's Series for $y = \cosh x$. The remainder is:

$$|R_3(x)| \le \frac{|a|\,|\cosh c|}{4!\,3^4} = 0.0005|a|$$

12. (a) $\ln\left(\frac{1+x}{1-x}\right) = \ln(1+x) - \ln(1-x)$

$= \left[x - \frac{x^2}{2} + \frac{x^3}{3} - \frac{x^5}{5} + \ldots\right] - \left[-x - \frac{x^2}{2} - \frac{x^3}{3} - \frac{x^5}{5} - \ldots\right]$

$= 2\left[x + \frac{x^3}{3} + \frac{x^5}{5} + \ldots\right]$ for $|x| < 1$.

(b) $\frac{1+x}{1-x} = 2$ if $x = \frac{1}{3}$. $\ln 2 = 2\left[\frac{1}{3} + \frac{1}{3}\left(\frac{1}{3}\right)^3 + \frac{1}{5}\left(\frac{1}{3}\right)^5 + \frac{1}{7}\left(\frac{1}{3}\right)^7\right] \approx 0.6931$

$\therefore \ln 2 \approx 0.693$

13. This is the series for $\ln(1 + x)$ evaluated at $x = \frac{1}{2}$, which converges to $\ln(\frac{3}{2})$

14. We must have $\frac{1}{2n-1} < 0.005 \Rightarrow 2n - 1 > 200 \Rightarrow 2n > 201$ or $n \ge 101$.

15. $\pi = 48\tan^{-1}\frac{1}{18} + 32\tan^{-1}\frac{1}{57} - 20\tan^{-1}\frac{1}{239} =$

$= 48\left[.0556 - \frac{(.0556)^3}{3}\right] + 32\left[.0175 - \frac{(.0175)^3}{3}\right] - 20\left[.0042 - \frac{(.0042)^3}{3}\right]$
$= 2.66604 + 0.55994 - 0.0839 = 3.142$

16. (a) $\pi = 4\left[\frac{2}{3}\cdot\frac{4}{3}\cdot\frac{4}{5}\cdot\frac{6}{5}\right] \approx 3.413$

17. $a_0 = 1$ $\qquad b_0 = \frac{1}{\sqrt{2}} \approx 0.707107$

$a_1 = \frac{1 + \frac{1}{\sqrt{2}}}{2} = 0.853553$ $\qquad b_1 = \sqrt{\frac{1}{\sqrt{2}}} = 0.840896$

$a_2 = \frac{a_1 + b_1}{2} = 0.847225$ $\qquad b_2 = \sqrt{a_1 b_1} = 0.847201$

$a_3 = \frac{a_2 + b_2}{2} = 0.847213$ $\qquad b_3 = \sqrt{a_2 b_2} = 0.847213$

$$c_3 = \frac{4a_3b_3}{1 - 4(a_1^2 - b_1^2) - 8(a_2^2 - b_2^2) - 16(a_3^2 - b_3^2)}$$

$$= \frac{2.871079}{1 - .085788 - .000325 - 0} = 3.1416127$$

18. $\lim_{n\to\infty}\left|\frac{x^{2n+1}}{2n+1}\cdot\frac{2n-1}{x^{2n-1}}\right| = x^2 < 1$ if $|x| < 1$. If $x = \pm 1$,

$\sum_{n=0}^{\infty}\frac{(-1)^n x^{2n+1}}{2n+1} = \sum_{n=0}^{\infty}(\pm 1)^n\frac{1}{2n+1}$ converge by alternating series test.

∴ The series converges for $|x| \le 1$ or diverges for $|x| > 1$.

19. By dividing $1 - t^2$ into 1, and expressing the answer as quotient plus remainder over divisor, we obtain the identity

$$\frac{1}{1 - t^2} = 1 + t^2 + t^4 + \ldots + t^{2n} + \frac{t^{2n+2}}{1 - t^2}$$

Another way of obtaining this identity is to use the formula for the nth partial sum of a geometric series

$$1 + t^2 + t^4 + \ldots + t^{2n} = \frac{1 - (t^2)^{n+1}}{1 - t^2}$$

Then

$$\int_0^x \frac{dt}{1-t^2} = \int_0^x\left[1 + t^2 + t^4 + \ldots + t^{2n} + \frac{t^{2n+2}}{1-t^2}\right]dt$$

$$= t + \frac{t^3}{3} + \frac{t^5}{5} + \ldots + \frac{t^{2n+1}}{2n+1}\Bigg]_0^x + \int_0^x \frac{t^{2n+2}}{1-t^2}dt$$

Thus $\tanh^{-1}x = x + \frac{x^3}{3} + \frac{x^5}{5} + \ldots + \frac{x^{2n+1}}{2n+1} + R$, with

$$R = \int_0^x \frac{t^{2n+2}}{1-t^2}dt$$

20. $R_2(x) = \frac{e^c}{2!}x^2 \le \frac{e^{0.1}(.01)h}{2} \approx \frac{(1.105)(0.01)h}{2} < 0.005525h.$

Since 0.6% of $h = 0.006h$, $R_2(x) <$ 0.6% of h.

21. (a) $\frac{d}{dx}(1 - x)^{-1} = \frac{d}{dx}\left(1 + x + x^2 + \ldots + x^n + \frac{x^{n+1}}{1 - x}\right)$

$$(1 - x)^{-2} = 1 + 2x + 3x^2 + \ldots + nx^{n-1} + R, \text{ where}$$

$$R = \frac{(1 - x)(n + 1)x^n + x^{n+1}}{(1 - x)^2}$$

(b) $\lim_{n\to\infty} x^{n+1} = 0$ for $|x| < 1$. We consider $\lim_{n\to\infty} (n + 1)x^n =$

$$\lim_{n\to\infty} \frac{n+1}{x^{-n}} = \lim_{n\to\infty} \frac{1}{-nx^{-n-1}} = \lim_{n\to\infty} \frac{x^{n+1}}{-n} = 0$$

(c) $\sum_{n=1}^{\infty} n\left(\frac{5}{6}\right)^{n-1}\left(\frac{1}{6}\right) = \frac{1}{6}\left(\frac{1}{1-\left(\frac{5}{6}\right)^2}\right) = 6$

(d) $\sum_{n=1}^{\infty} np^{n-1}q = \frac{q}{(1-p)^2} = \frac{q}{q^2} = \frac{1}{q}$

22. (a) $\sum_{k=1}^{\infty} p_k = \sum_{k=1}^{\infty} 2^{-k} = \frac{\frac{1}{2}}{1-\frac{1}{2}} = 1$

$$E = \sum_{k=1}^{\infty} kp_k = \sum_{k=1}^{\infty} k2^{-k} = 2^{-1}\sum_{k=1}^{\infty} k2^{-k+1} = \frac{1}{2}\left(\frac{1}{\left(1-\frac{1}{2}\right)^2}\right) = 2$$

(b) $\sum_{k=1}^{\infty} p_k = \sum_{k=1}^{\infty} \frac{5^{k-1}}{6^k} = \frac{1}{5}\sum_{k=1}^{\infty}\left(\frac{5}{6}\right)^k = \frac{1}{5}\left(\frac{\frac{5}{6}}{1-\frac{5}{6}}\right) = 1$

$$E = \sum_{k=1}^{\infty} kp_k = \sum_{k=1}^{\infty} k\frac{5^{k-1}}{6^k} = \frac{1}{6}\sum_{k=1}^{\infty} k\left(\frac{5}{6}\right)^{k-1} = \frac{1}{6}\left(\frac{1}{\left(1-\frac{5}{6}\right)^2}\right) = 6$$

c) $\sum_{k=1}^{\infty} p_k = \sum_{k=1}^{\infty} \frac{1}{k(k+1)}$. $S_n = \left(1-\frac{1}{2}\right)+\left(\frac{1}{2}-\frac{1}{3}\right)+\ldots+\left(\frac{1}{n}-\frac{1}{n+1}\right)$

$= 1 - \frac{1}{n+1}$ so $\lim_{n\to\infty} S_n = 1$

$$E = \sum_{k=1}^{\infty} kp_k = \sum_{k=1}^{\infty} k\left(\frac{1}{k(k+1)}\right) = \sum_{k=1}^{\infty}\frac{1}{k+1} \text{ diverges.}$$

12.5 CONVERGENCE OF POWER SERIES, INTEGRATION, DIFFERENTIATION, MULTIPLICATION AND DIVISION

1. $\sum_{n=0}^{\infty} x^n$ converges for $-1 < x < 1$ because $\lim_{n\to\infty} \frac{|x^{n+1}|}{|x^n|} = \lim_{n\to\infty} |x| < 1$

   for all x such that $|x| < 1$. If $x = 1$, then $\sum_{n=0}^{\infty} (1)^n$ diverges, and

   if $x = -1$, $\sum_{n=0}^{\infty} (-1)^n$ diverges.

2. $\sum_{n=0}^{\infty} n^2 x^n$ converges for $-1 < x < 1$ because $\lim_{n\to\infty} \left| \frac{(n+1)^2 x^{n+1}}{n^2 x^n} \right| = \lim_{n\to\infty} |x| < 1$

   for all x such that $|x| < 1$. If $x = 1$, $\sum_{n=0}^{\infty} n^2$ diverges and

   if $x = -1$, $\sum_{n=0}^{\infty} (-1)^n n^2$ diverges.

3. $\sum_{n=0}^{\infty} \frac{nx^n}{2^n}$ converges for $-2 < x < 2$ because $\lim_{n\to\infty} \left| \frac{(n+1)x^{n+1}}{2^{n+1}} \cdot \frac{2^n}{nx^n} \right| =$

   $\lim_{n\to\infty} \left| \frac{n+1}{n} \cdot \frac{1}{2} x \right| = \frac{1}{2} |x| < 1$ for all x such that $|x| < 2$. If $x = \pm 2$, then

   $\sum_{n=0}^{\infty} \frac{n2^n}{2^n} = \sum_{n=0}^{\infty} n$ diverges, and $\sum_{n=0}^{\infty} \frac{n(-2)^n}{2^n} = \sum_{n=0}^{\infty} (-1)^n n$ diverges.

4. $\sum_{n=0}^{\infty} \frac{(2x)^n}{n!}$ converges for all x because $\lim_{n\to\infty} \left| \frac{(2x)^{n+1}}{(n+1)!} \cdot \frac{n!}{(2x)^n} \right|$

   $= \lim_{n\to\infty} \frac{1}{n+1} |2x| = 0.$

5. $\sum_{n=0}^{\infty} \frac{(-1)^n x^{2n+1}}{(2n+1)!}$ converges for all x because $\lim_{n\to\infty} \left| \frac{(n+1)x^{n+1}}{2^{n+1}} \cdot \frac{2^n}{nx^n} \right| =$

   $\lim_{n\to\infty} \left| \frac{x^{2n+3}}{(2n+3)!} \cdot \frac{(2n+1)!}{x^{2n+1}} \right| = \lim_{n\to\infty} \frac{1}{(2n+3)(2n+1)} x^2 = 0 < 1$ for all x.

6. $\sum_{n=0}^{\infty} (-1)^{n-1} \frac{(x-1)^n}{n}$ converges for $0 < x < 2$ because $\lim_{n\to\infty} \left| \frac{(x-1)^{n+1}}{n+1} \cdot \frac{n}{(x-1)^n} \right|$

   $= \lim_{n\to\infty} \frac{n}{n+1} |x-1| < 1$ if $|x-1| < 1$ or if $0 < x < 2$.

   If $x = 2$, $\sum_{n=0}^{\infty} (-1)^{n-1} \left(\frac{1}{n}\right)$ converges. If $x = 0$, $\sum_{n=1}^{\infty} \frac{1}{n}$ diverges.

7. $\sum_{n=0}^{\infty} \frac{n^2 (x+2)^n}{2^n}$ converges for $-4 < x < 0$ because $\lim_{n\to\infty} \left| \frac{(n+1)^2 (x+2)^{n+1}}{2^{n+1}} \cdot \frac{2^n}{n^2 (x+2)^n} \right| =$

$\lim_{n\to\infty} \left| \left(\frac{n+1}{n}\right)^2 \cdot \frac{1}{2}(x+2) \right| < 1$ if $|x+2| < 2$ or $-4 < x < 0$.

$\sum_{n=0}^{\infty} \frac{n^2}{2^n} \cdot 2^n = \sum_{n=0}^{\infty} n^2$ diverges and $\sum_{n=0}^{\infty} \frac{n^2}{2^n}(-2)^n = \sum_{n=0}^{\infty} (-1)n^2$ diverges

8. $\sum_{n=0}^{\infty} \frac{x^{2n+1}}{2n+1}$ converges for $-1 < x < 1$ because $\lim_{n\to\infty} \left| \frac{x^{2n+3}}{2n+3} \cdot \frac{2n+1}{x^{2n+1}} \right|$

$= \lim_{n\to\infty} \frac{2n+1}{2n+3} |x^2| < 1$ if $|x| < 1$.

If $x = 1$, $\sum_{n=0}^{\infty} \frac{1}{2n+1}$ diverges. If $x = -1$, $-\sum_{n=1}^{\infty} \frac{1}{2n+1}$ diverges.

9. $\sum_{n=0}^{\infty} \frac{(-1)^n x^{2n+1}}{2n+1}$ converges for $-1 < x < 1$ because

$\lim_{n\to\infty} \left| \frac{x^{2n+3}}{2n+3} \cdot \frac{2n+1}{x^{2n+1}} \right| = \lim_{n\to\infty} \left| \left(\frac{2n+3}{2n+1}\right) x^2 \right| < 1$ if $|x| < 1$.

$\sum_{n=0}^{\infty} (-1)^n \frac{1}{2n+1}$ converges by alternating series test.

$\sum_{n=0}^{\infty} (-1)^n \frac{(-1)^{2n+1}}{2n+1} = \sum_{n=0}^{\infty} (-1)^{n+1} \frac{1}{2n+1}$ also converges.

10. $\sum_{n=1}^{\infty} \frac{(x-2)^n}{n^2}$ converges for $1 < x < 3$ because

$\lim_{n\to\infty} \left| \frac{(x-2)^{n+1}}{(n+1)^2} \cdot \frac{n^2}{(x-2)^n} \right| = \lim_{n\to\infty} \left(\frac{n}{n+1}\right)^2 |x-2| < 1$ if $1 < x < 3$.

If $x = 3$, $\sum_{n=1}^{\infty} \frac{1}{n^2}$ converges. If $x = 1$, $\sum_{n=1}^{\infty} \frac{(-1)^n}{n^2}$ converges.

11. $\sum_{n=0}^{\infty} \frac{\cos nx}{2^n}$ converges absolutely for all x since

$\frac{|\cos nx|}{2^n} \le \frac{1}{2^n}$ and $\sum_{n=0}^{\infty} \frac{1}{2^n}$ converges.

12. $\sum_{n=1}^{\infty} \frac{2^n x^n}{n^5}$ converges for $-\frac{1}{2} < x < \frac{1}{2}$ because

$$\lim_{n\to\infty} \left| \frac{2^{n+1} x^{n+1}}{(n+1)^5} \cdot \frac{n^5}{2^n x^n} \right| = \lim_{n\to\infty} \left(\frac{n}{n+1} \right)^5 2\,|x| < 1 \text{ if } -\frac{1}{2} < x < \frac{1}{2}.$$

If $x = \frac{1}{2}$, $\sum_{n=1}^{\infty} \frac{1}{n^5}$ converges. If $x = -\frac{1}{2}$, $\sum_{n=1}^{\infty} \frac{(-1)^n}{n^5}$ converges.

13. $\sum_{n=0}^{\infty} \frac{x^n e^n}{n+1}$ converges for $-\frac{1}{e} \le x < \frac{1}{e}$ because $\lim_{n\to\infty} \left| \frac{x^{n+1} e^{n+1}}{n+2} \cdot \frac{n+1}{x^n e^n} \right| =$

$\lim_{n\to\infty} \left(\frac{n+1}{n+2} \right) |x|\, e < 1$ if $|x| < \frac{1}{e}$. If $x = \frac{1}{e}$, $\sum_{n=0}^{\infty} \frac{1}{n+1}$ diverges,

and if $x = -\frac{1}{e}$, $\sum_{n=0}^{\infty} (-1)^n \frac{1}{n+1}$ converges.

14. $\sum_{n=1}^{\infty} \frac{(\cos x)^n}{n^n}$ converges for all x because

$$\lim_{n\to\infty} \sqrt[n]{\frac{(\cos x)^n}{n^n}} = \lim_{n\to\infty} \frac{\cos x}{n} = 0$$

15. $\sum_{n=0}^{\infty} n^n x^n$ converges for $x = 0$ only because

$\lim_{n\to\infty} \sqrt[n]{n^n x^n} = \lim_{n\to\infty} |nx| = \infty$ for all x except $x = 0$.

16. $\sum_{n=0}^{\infty} \frac{(3x+6)^n}{n!}$ converges for all x because

$$\lim_{n\to\infty} \left| \frac{(3x+6)^{n+1}}{(n+1)!} \cdot \frac{n!}{(3x+6)^n} \right| = \lim_{n\to\infty} \frac{1}{n+1} \,|\, 3x+6 \,| = 0 .$$

17. $\sum_{n=0}^{\infty}(-2)^n (n+1)(x-1)^n$ converges for $\frac{1}{2} < x < \frac{3}{2}$ because

$$\lim_{n\to\infty}\left|\frac{(-2)^{n+1}(n+2)(x-1)^{n+1}}{(-2)^n(n+1)(x-1)^n}\right| = \lim_{n\to\infty} |-2|\left(\frac{n+2}{n+1}\right)|x-1| < 1 \text{ if}$$

$|x-1| < \frac{1}{2}$. At $x = \frac{3}{2}$ and $\frac{1}{2}$, $\sum_{n=0}^{\infty}(-1)^n (n+1)$ and $\sum_{n=0}^{\infty}(n+1)$ both diverge.

18. $\sum_{n=1}^{\infty}\frac{(-1)^{n+1}(x-2)^n}{n\cdot 2^n}$ converges for $0 < x < 4$ because

$$\lim_{n\to\infty}\left|\frac{(x-2)^{n+1}}{(n+1)\,2^{n+1}}\cdot\frac{n\cdot 2^n}{(x-2)^n}\right| = \lim_{n\to\infty}\frac{n}{n+1}\cdot\frac{1}{2}|x-2| < 1 \text{ if } |x-2| < 2.$$

If $x = 4$, $\sum_{n=1}^{\infty}\frac{(-1)^{n+1}}{n}$ converges but if $x = 1$, $-\sum_{n=1}^{\infty}\frac{1}{n}$ diverges.

19. $\sum_{n=0}^{\infty}\left(\frac{x^2-1}{2}\right)^n$ converges for $-\sqrt{3} < x < \sqrt{3}$ because $\lim_{n\to\infty}\left|\frac{(x^2-1)^{n+1}}{2^{n+1}}\cdot\frac{2^n}{(x^2-1)^n}\right| =$

$\lim_{n\to\infty}\frac{1}{2}|x^2-1| < 1$ if $|x^2-1| < 3$ or if $|x| < \sqrt{3}$.

At $x = \pm\sqrt{3}$, $\sum_{n=0}^{\infty}(1)^n$ diverges.

20. $\sum_{n=1}^{\infty}\frac{(x+3)^{n-1}}{n}$ converges for $-4 < x < -2$ because

$$\lim_{n\to\infty}\left|\frac{(x+3)^n}{n+1}\cdot\frac{n}{(x+3)^{n-1}}\right| = \lim_{n\to\infty}\frac{n}{n+1}\cdot|x+3| < 1 \text{ if } -4 < x < -2$$

If $x = -4$, $\sum_{n=1}^{\infty}\frac{(-1)^{n-1}}{n}$ converges but if $x = -2$, $\sum_{n=1}^{\infty}\frac{1}{n}$ diverges.

21. The series converges to e^{3x+6}

22. It is a geometric series and converges to $\dfrac{1}{1-\dfrac{x^2-1}{2}} = \dfrac{2}{3-x^2}$

23 (a) $\cos x = 1 - \frac{x^2}{2!} + \frac{x^4}{4!} + \ldots (-1)^n\frac{x^{2n}}{(2n)!}$

$$\frac{d}{dx}(\cos x) = -\frac{2x}{2!} + \frac{4x^3}{4!} + \ldots (-1)^n(2n\frac{x^{2n-1}}{(2n-1)!}$$

$$= -1 + \frac{x^3}{3!} - \frac{x^5}{5!} + \ldots (-1)\frac{x^{2n-1}}{(2n-1)!} = -\sin x$$

(b) $$\int_0^x \cos t\,dt = \int_0^x \left(1 - \frac{t^2}{2!} + \frac{t^4}{4!} - \ldots + (1)^n \frac{t^{2n}}{(2n)!}\right) dt$$

$$= t - \frac{1}{3}\cdot\frac{t^3}{2!} + \frac{1}{5}\cdot\frac{t^5}{4!} - \ldots + (-1)^n \frac{1}{2n+1}\cdot\frac{t^{2n+1}}{(2n)!}\Bigg]_0^x$$

$$= x - \frac{x^3}{3!} + \frac{x^5}{5!} - \ldots + (-1)^n \frac{x^{2n+1}}{(2n+1)!} = \sin x$$

(c) $y = e^x = 1 + x + \dfrac{x^2}{2!} + \dfrac{x^3}{3!} + \ldots + \dfrac{x^n}{n!} + \ldots$

$$y' = 1 + \frac{2x}{2!} + \frac{3x^2}{3!} + \ldots + \frac{nx^{n-1}}{n!} + \ldots$$

$$= 1 + x + \frac{x^2}{2!} + \frac{x^3}{3!} + \ldots + \frac{x^n}{n!} + \ldots = e^x$$

24. $\dfrac{d}{dx}\left(\dfrac{-1}{1+x}\right) = \dfrac{1}{(1+x)^2}$ so if

$\dfrac{-1}{1+x} = -1 + x - x^2 + x^3 - \ldots.$ then

$$\frac{1}{(1+x)^2} = 1 - 2x + 3x^2 - 4x^3 + .. = \sum_{n=0}^{\infty} (-1)^n (n+1)x^n$$

25. $\dfrac{1}{1-x^2} = 1 + x^2 + x^4 + x^6 + \ldots + (x^{2n}) + \ldots = \displaystyle\sum_{n=0}^{\infty} x^{2n}$, $|x| < 1$.

Note that $\dfrac{d}{dx}(1-x^2)^{-1} = \dfrac{2x}{(1-x^2)^2}$. So, for $|x| < 1$

$$\frac{2x}{(1-x^2)^2} = 2x + 4x^3 + 6x^5 + \ldots + 2nx^{2n-1} = \sum_{n=1}^{\infty} (2n)x^{2n-1}$$

26. $\sin^2 x = \dfrac{1}{2}(1 - \cos 2x) = \dfrac{1}{2}\left[1 - \left(1 - \dfrac{(2x)^2}{2!} + \dfrac{(2x)^4}{4!} - \dfrac{(2x)^6}{6!} + ..\right)\right]$

$$\frac{d}{dx}(\sin^2 x) = \frac{1}{2}\cdot\frac{d}{dx}\left[\frac{2^2x^2}{2!} - \frac{2^4x^4}{4!} + \frac{2^6x^6}{6!} - \ldots\right]$$

$$2\sin x\cos x = \frac{1}{2}\left[2^2 x - \frac{2^4x^3}{3!} + \frac{2^6x^5}{5!} - ..\right] = 2x - \frac{(2x)^3}{3!} + \frac{(2x)^5}{5!} - \ldots$$

This is the series for $\sin 2x$.

27. $\int_0^{.2} \sin x^2 dx = \int_0^{.2}\left(x^2 - \frac{x^6}{3!} + \frac{x^{10}}{5!} - \ldots\right)dx = \frac{1}{3}x^3 - \frac{1}{7\cdot 3!}x^7 - \ldots\Big]_0^{.2}$

$= 0.0027$ with error $|E| \le \frac{1}{7\cdot 3!}(.2)^7 = 3\times 10^{-7}$

28. $\int_0^{0.1} \tan^{-1} x\, dx = \int_0^{0.1}\left(x - \frac{x^3}{3} + \frac{x^5}{5} - \frac{x^7}{7} + \ldots\right)dx$

$= \frac{1}{2}x^2 - \frac{1}{12}x^4 + \ldots\Big]_0^{0.1} = 0.005$ with error $|E| < \frac{(0.1)^4}{12} = 0.0000008\overline{3}$

29. $\int_0^{.1} x^2 e^{-x^2} dx = \int_0^{.1} x^2\left(1 - x^2 + \frac{x^4}{2!} - \frac{x^6}{3!} + \ldots\right)dx = \int_0^{.1}\left(x^2 - x^4 + \frac{x^6}{2!} - \ldots\right)dx$

$= \frac{1}{3}x^3 - \frac{1}{5}x^5 + \frac{1}{7\cdot 2!}x^7 - \ldots\Big]_0^{.1} = \frac{1}{3}(.1)^3 = 0.00033$

with error $|E| \le \frac{1}{5}(.1)^5 = 2\times 10^{-6}$

30. $\int_0^{0.1} \frac{\tan^{-1} x}{x} dx = \int_0^{0.1} \frac{1}{x}\left(x - \frac{x^3}{3} + \frac{x^5}{5} - \ldots\right)dx = \int_0^{0.1}\left(1 - \frac{x^2}{3} + \frac{x^4}{5} - \ldots\right)dx$

$= x - \frac{1}{9}x^3 + \ldots\Big]_0^{0.1} \approx 0.1$ with error $|E| < \frac{(0.1)^3}{9} \approx 0.0001$

31. $\int_0^{.4} \frac{1 - e^{-x}}{x} dx = \int_0^{.4} \frac{1}{x}\left[1 - \left(1 - x + \frac{x^2}{2} - \frac{x^3}{3!} + \ldots\right)\right]dx$

$= \int_0^{.4}\left(1 - \frac{x}{2!} + \frac{x^2}{3!} - \frac{x^3}{4!} + \ldots\right)dx = 1 - \frac{1}{2\cdot 2!}x^2 + \frac{1}{3\cdot 3!}x^3 - \frac{1}{4\cdot 4!}x^4 + \ldots\Big]_0^{.4}$

$= 0.3636$ with error $|E| \le \frac{(.4)^4}{4\cdot 4!} < 0.0003$

32. $\int_0^{0.1} \frac{\ln(1+x)}{x} dx = \int_0^{0.1} \frac{1}{x}\left(x - \frac{x^2}{2} + \frac{x^3}{3} - \ldots\right)dx = \int_0^{0.1}\left(1 - \frac{x}{2} + \frac{x^2}{3} - \ldots\right)dx$

$= x - \frac{1}{4}x^2 + \frac{1}{9}x^3 \ldots\Big]_0^{0.1} \approx 0.0975$ with error $|E| < \frac{(0.1)^3}{9} \approx 0.0001$

33. $\int_0^{.1} \frac{1}{\sqrt{1+x^4}} dx = \int_0^{.1}\left(1 - \frac{1}{2}x^4 + \frac{\left(-\frac{1}{2}\right)\left(-\frac{3}{2}\right)}{2}x^8 \ldots\right)dx$

$= \int_0^{.1}\left(1 - \frac{1}{2}x^4 + \frac{3}{8}x^8 - \ldots\right)dx = x - \frac{1}{10}x^5 + \frac{3}{72}x^9 - \ldots\Big]_0^{.1}$

$= 0.1$ with error $|E| \le 1\times 10^{-6}$

34. $\int_0^{0.25} \sqrt[3]{1+x^2}\, dx = \int_0^{0.25} \left(1 + \frac{1}{3}x^2 - \frac{1}{9}x^4 + ..\right)dx$

$= x + \frac{1}{9}x^3 - \frac{1}{45}x^5 \; ...\Big]_0^{0.25} \approx 0.2517$ with error $|E| < \frac{(0.25)^5}{45} \approx 0.00002$

35. (a) $\sinh^{-1}x = \int_0^x \frac{dt}{\sqrt{1+t^2}} = \int_0^x \left(1 - \frac{1}{2}t^2 + \frac{3}{8}t^4 - \frac{5}{16}t^6 + ...\right)dt$

$= t - \frac{1}{6}t^3 + \frac{3}{40}t^5 - \frac{5}{112}t^7 + ...\Big]_0^x = x - \frac{1}{6}x^3 + \frac{3}{40}x^5 - \frac{5}{112}x^7 + ...$

(b) $\sinh^{-1}.25 = .25 - \frac{(.25)^3}{6} = 0.247$

with error $|E| \le \frac{3(.25)^5}{40} = 0.00007$

36. $\int_0^1 \cos x^2\, dx = \int_0^1 \left(1 - \frac{(x^2)^2}{2} + \frac{(x^2)^4}{4!} - \frac{(x^2)^6}{6!} + \frac{(x^2)^8}{8!} - ...\right)dx$

$= x - \frac{x^5}{10} + \frac{x^9}{216} - \frac{x^{13}}{9360} + \frac{x^{17}}{685440} \approx 0.904524$

37. Problem 15 of this section is an example of a series which converges only for $x = 0$.

38. See Problem 6 for conditional convergence at an endpoint, and Problem 12 for absolute convergence at an endpoint.

39. We are given that $\sum a_n$ converges for $-r < x < r$. Let a be any point such that $-r < a < r$. There exists r_1 such that $-r < -r_1 < a < r_1 < r$. The $\sum a_n$ converges for r_1 and hence absolutely for a, by Theorem 1. But a was any point between $-r$ and r, and hence the series converges absolutely for all x such that $-r < x < r$.

40. $(1+x)^m = 1 + \sum_{n=1}^{\infty} \frac{m(m-1)m-2)\cdot...\cdot(m-n+1)}{n!}x^n$. Therefore

$\lim_{n\to\infty}\left|\frac{a_{n+1}x^{n+1}}{a_nx^n}\right| = \lim_{n\to\infty}\left|\frac{m(m-1)(m-2)\cdot...\cdot(m-n)}{(n+1)!}\cdot\frac{n!}{m(m-1)\cdot...\cdot(m-n+1)}\right|$

$= \lim_{n\to\infty}\left|\frac{m-n}{n+1}\right| |x| = |x|$, so the binomial series converges for $|x| < 1$.

41. $e^x \sin x = (1 + x + \frac{x^2}{2!} + \frac{x^3}{3!} + .+\frac{x^n}{n!})(x - \frac{x^3}{3!} + \frac{x^5}{5!} -.+(-1)^n\frac{x^{2n+1}}{(2n+1)!})$

$=1(x - \frac{x^3}{3!} + \frac{x^5}{5!} - ...) + x(x - \frac{x^3}{3!} + \frac{x^5}{5!} - ...) +$

$\frac{x^2}{2}(x - \frac{x^3}{3!} + \frac{x^5}{5!} - ...) + \frac{x^3}{3!}(x - \frac{x^3}{3!} + ..) + \frac{x^4}{4!}(x - \frac{x^3}{3!} +..)$

$$= \left(x - \frac{x^3}{3!} + \frac{x^5}{5!} - ..\right) + \left(x^2 - \frac{x^4}{3!} + ..\right) + \left(\frac{x^3}{2} - \frac{x^5}{2\cdot 3!} + ...\right)$$

$$+ \left(\frac{x^4}{3!} + ..\right) + \left(\frac{x^5}{4!} - ..\right)$$

$$= x + x^2 + \frac{1}{3}x^3 - \frac{1}{30}x^5 \; ...$$

Check: $(e^x)(e^{ix}) = e^{(1+i)x} = 1 + (1+i)x + \frac{(1+i)^2x^2}{2} + \frac{(1+i)^3x^3}{3!}$

$$+ \frac{(1+i)^4x^4}{4!} + \frac{(1+i)^5x^5}{5!} + \;....$$

$$= 1 + (1+i)x + \frac{2ix^2}{2} + \frac{(2i-2)x^3}{3!} - \frac{4x^4}{4!} + \frac{(-4-4i)x^5}{5!} + ..$$

The imaginary part of this series is the same as the one obtained in the first part of the problem.

42.

$$\begin{array}{r|l} & 1 + \frac{x^2}{2} + \frac{5x^4}{24} + ... \\ \hline 1 - \frac{x^2}{2} + \frac{x^4}{24} - \frac{x^3}{720} + ... & 1 \\ & 1 - \frac{x^2}{2} + \frac{x^4}{24} - ... \\ \cline{2-2} & \frac{x^2}{2} - \frac{x^4}{24} + .. \\ & \frac{x^2}{2} - \frac{x^4}{4} \\ \cline{2-2} & \frac{5x^4}{24} + ... \end{array}$$

For $|x| < \frac{\pi}{2}$.

43. $\int_0^x \tan t\,dt = \int_0^x \left(t + \frac{t^3}{3} + \frac{2t^5}{15} + ...\right)dt = \frac{1}{2}t^2 + \frac{1}{12}t^4 + \frac{2}{90}t^6 + ...\Big]_0^x$

$\ln|\sec x| = \frac{1}{2}x^2 + \frac{1}{2}x^4 + \frac{1}{45}x^6 + ..$

44. $y^2 = \left(\frac{x^2}{2} + \frac{5x^4}{24} + ...\right)\left(\frac{x^2}{2} + \frac{5x^4}{24} + ...\right) = \frac{x^4}{4} + \; ...$

So, $\ln \sec x = y - \frac{y^2}{2} = \frac{x^2}{2} + \frac{5x^4}{24} - \frac{x^4}{8} + ... = \frac{x^2}{2} + \frac{x^4}{12} + ...$

45. (a) $\frac{r_2}{r_1} = \sec\frac{\pi}{3}$

$\frac{r_3}{r_2} = \sec\frac{\pi}{4}$

$\frac{r_4}{r_3} = \sec\frac{\pi}{5}$

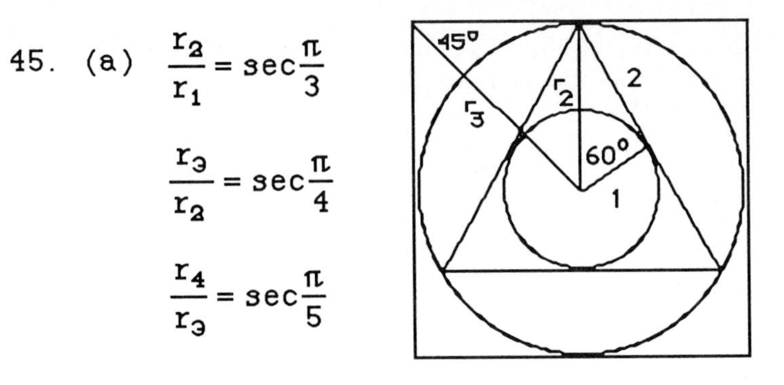

In general, if a (n+1)-sided polygon is inscribed in a circle, the central angle is $\frac{2\pi}{n+1}$ and the ratio is $\frac{r_n}{r_{n-1}} = \sec\frac{1}{2}\left(\frac{2\pi}{n+1}\right)$

(b) $r_n = r_{n-1}\sec\frac{\pi}{n+1} = \sec\frac{\pi}{n+1}\left(r_{n-2}\sec\frac{\pi}{n}\right) = \sec\frac{\pi}{n+1}\sec\frac{\pi}{n}\left(r_{n-3}\sec\frac{\pi}{n-1}\right)$

$= \sec\frac{\pi}{n+1}\sec\frac{\pi}{n}\sec\frac{\pi}{n-1}\ldots\sec\frac{\pi}{4}\left(r_1\sec\frac{\pi}{3}\right)$

$\ln r_n = \ln r_1 + \ln\sec\frac{\pi}{3} + \ln\sec\frac{\pi}{4} + \ldots + \ln\sec\frac{\pi}{n+1}$

(c) $\lim_{n\to\infty} \frac{\ln\sec\frac{\pi}{n}}{\frac{1}{n^2}} = \lim_{n\to\infty} n^2\left(\frac{\pi^2}{2n^2} + \frac{\pi^4}{12n^4} + \ldots\right) = \frac{\pi^2}{2}.$

$\sum_{n=3}^{\infty} \ln\sec\frac{\pi}{n}$ converges by comparison to $\sum_{n=1}^{\infty} \frac{1}{n^2}$.

46. (a) $\frac{u_{n+1}}{u^n} = \frac{n+1}{n} = 1 + \frac{1}{n} + \frac{0}{n^2}$; $C = 1$ so $\sum\frac{1}{n}$ diverges.

(b) $\frac{u_{n+1}}{u^n} = \frac{(n+1)^2}{n^2} = 1 + \frac{2}{n} + \frac{1}{n^2}$; $C = 2$ so $\sum\frac{1}{n^2}$ converges.

(c) $\frac{u_{n+1}}{u^n} = \frac{4n^2 - 4n + 1}{4n^2 + 2n} = 1 - \frac{3}{2n} + \frac{2n}{(2n+1)n^2}$; $C = -\frac{3}{2}$ so $\sum u_n$ diverges.

12.6 INDETERMINATE FORMS

1. $\lim_{h\to 0} \frac{\sinh}{h} = \lim_{h\to 0} \frac{h - \frac{h^3}{3!} + \frac{h^5}{5!} - \ldots}{h} = \lim_{h\to 0}\left(1 - \frac{h^2}{3!} - \frac{h^4}{5!} - \ldots\right) = 1$

2. $\lim_{x\to 0} \frac{e^x - (1+x)}{x^2} = \lim_{x\to 0} \frac{1}{x^2}\left[\left(1 + x + \frac{x^2}{2} + \frac{x^3}{3!} + \ldots\right) - 1 - x\right] = \frac{1}{2}$

3. $$\lim_{t\to 0}\frac{1-\cos t-\frac{t^2}{2}}{t^4}=\lim_{t\to 0}\frac{1}{t^4}\left[1-\frac{t^2}{2}-\left(1-\frac{t^2}{2}+\frac{t^4}{4!}-\frac{t^6}{6!}+..\right)\right]$$

$$=\lim_{t\to 0}\left[-\frac{1}{4!}+\frac{t^2}{6!}-..\right]=-\frac{1}{24}$$

4. $$\lim_{x\to\infty}x\sin\frac{1}{x}=\lim_{x\to\infty}x\left[\frac{1}{x}-\frac{1}{3!}\left(\frac{1}{x^3}\right)+\ ...\right]=1$$

5. $$\lim_{x\to 0}\frac{x^2}{1-\cosh x}=\lim_{x\to 0}\frac{x^2}{1-\left(1+\frac{x^2}{2!}+\frac{x^4}{4!}+..\right)}=\lim_{x\to 0}\frac{1}{-\frac{1}{2}-\frac{x^2}{4!}-\ ..}=-2$$

6. $$\lim_{h\to 0}\frac{\frac{\sinh}{h}-\cos h}{h^2}=\lim_{h\to 0}\frac{1}{h^2}\left[\frac{1}{h}\left(h-\frac{h^3}{3!}+\frac{h^5}{5!}-..\right)-\left(1-\frac{h^2}{2!}+\frac{h^4}{4!}-...\right)\right]$$

$$=\lim_{h\to 0}\frac{1}{h^2}\left[1-\frac{h^2}{6}+\ ...-1+\frac{h^2}{2}-..\right]=\frac{1}{3}$$

7. $$\lim_{x\to 0}\frac{1-\cos x}{\sin x}-\lim_{x\to 0}\frac{1-\left(1-\frac{x^2}{2}+\frac{x^4}{4!}-...\right)}{x-\frac{x^3}{3!}+\frac{x^5}{5!}-...}=\lim_{x\to 0}\frac{x^2\left(\frac{1}{2}-\frac{x^2}{4!}+..\right)}{x\left(1-\frac{x^2}{3!}+..\right)}=0$$

8. $$\lim_{x\to 0}\frac{\sin x}{e^x-1}=\lim_{x\to 0}\frac{x-\frac{x^3}{3!}+\frac{x^5}{5!}-\ ...}{x+\frac{x^2}{2}+\frac{x^3}{3!}+\ ...}=1$$

9. $$\lim_{z\to 0}\frac{\sin(z^2)-\sinh(z^2)}{z^6}=\lim_{z\to 0}\frac{\left(z^2-\frac{z^6}{3!}+\frac{z^{10}}{5!}-...\right)-\left(z^2+\frac{z^6}{3!}+\frac{z^{10}}{5!}+..\right)}{z^6}$$

$$=\lim_{z\to 0}\frac{-\frac{2z^6}{3!}-\frac{2z^{10}}{5!}-..}{z^6}=-\frac{1}{3}$$

10. $$\lim_{t\to 0}\frac{\cos t-\cosh t}{t^2}=\lim_{t\to 0}\frac{1}{t^2}\left[\left(1-\frac{t^2}{2}+\frac{t^4}{24}-..\right)-\left(1+\frac{t^2}{2}+\frac{t^4}{24}+..\right)\right]$$

$$\lim_{t\to 0}\frac{1}{t^2}\left[-\frac{2t^2}{2}-...\right]=-1$$

11. $$\lim_{x\to 0}\frac{\sin x-x+\frac{x^3}{6}}{x^5}=\lim_{x\to 0}\frac{-x+\frac{x^3}{6}+\left(x-\frac{x^3}{3!}+\frac{x^5}{5!}-\frac{x^7}{7!}..\right)}{x^5}=\frac{1}{120}$$

12. $$\lim_{x\to 0} \frac{e^x - e^{-x} - 2x}{x - \sin x} = \lim_{x\to 0} \frac{\left(1 + x + \frac{x^2}{2} + \frac{x^3}{6} + ..\right) - \left(1 - x + \frac{x^2}{2} - \frac{x^3}{6} + ..\right) - 2x}{x - \left(x - \frac{x^3}{6} + \frac{x^5}{120} - \ldots\right)}$$

$$= \lim_{x\to 0} \frac{\frac{2x^3}{6} + \ldots}{\frac{x^3}{6} - \ldots} = 2$$

13. $$\lim_{x\to 0} \frac{x - \tan^{-1} x}{x^3} = \lim_{x\to 0} \frac{x - \left(x - \frac{x^3}{3} + \frac{x^5}{5} - \ldots\right)}{x^3} = \frac{1}{3}$$

14. $$\lim_{x\to\infty} \frac{\tan x - \sin x}{x^3 \cos x} = \lim_{x\to\infty} \frac{\left(x + \frac{x^3}{3} + \frac{2x^5}{15} + \ldots\right) - \left(x - \frac{x^3}{6} + \frac{x^5}{120} - \ldots\right)}{x^3\left(1 - \frac{x^2}{2} + \frac{x^4}{24} - \ldots\right)}$$

$$= \lim_{x\to\infty} \frac{\frac{x^3}{2} + \frac{x^5}{8} + \ldots}{x^3 - \frac{x^5}{2} + \ldots} = \frac{1}{2}$$

15. $$\lim_{x\to\infty} x^2(e^{-1/x^2} - 1) = \lim_{x\to\infty} x^2\left[\left(1 - \frac{1}{x^2} + \frac{1}{2x^4} - \frac{1}{6x^6} + \ldots\right) - 1\right] = -1$$

16. $$\lim_{x\to 0} \frac{\ln(1 + x^2)}{1 - \cos x} = \lim_{x\to 0} \frac{x^2 - \frac{x^4}{2} + \frac{x^6}{3} - \ldots}{1 - \left(1 - \frac{x^2}{2} + \frac{x^4}{24} - \ldots\right)} = 2$$

17. $$\lim_{x\to 0} \frac{\tan 3x}{x} = \lim_{x0} \frac{3x + \frac{(3x)^3}{3} + \frac{2(3x)^5}{15} + \ldots}{x} = 3$$

18. $$\lim_{x\to 1} \frac{2 \ln x}{x - 1} = \lim_{x\to 1} \frac{2\left[(x - 1) + \frac{(x-1)^2}{2} + \frac{(x-1)^3}{3} + \ldots\right]}{x - 1} = 2$$

19. $$\lim_{x\to\infty} \frac{x^{100}}{e^x} = \lim_{x\to\infty} \frac{x^{100}}{1 + x + \frac{x^2}{2!} + \ldots + \frac{x^{101}}{101!} + \ldots} = 0$$

20. $$\lim_{x\to 0}\left(\frac{1}{2-2\cos x}-\frac{1}{x^2}\right)=\lim_{x\to 0}\frac{x^2-2+2\left(1-\frac{x^2}{2}+\frac{x^4}{24}-\frac{x^6}{720}+..\right)}{x^2\left[2-2\left(1-\frac{x^2}{2}+\frac{x^4}{24}-...0\right]\right.}$$

$$=\lim_{x\to 0}\frac{\frac{x^4}{12}-\frac{x^6}{360}+...}{x^4-\frac{x^6}{12}+...}=\frac{1}{12}$$

21. (a) For $x \geq 0$, $e^{x^2} \geq 1$. Therefore, $\int_0^x e^{t^2}dt \geq \int_0^x dt = x$

and $\int_0^x e^{t^2}dt$ diverges.

(b) $$\lim_{x\to\infty} x\int_0^x e^{t^2-x^2}dt = \lim_{x\to\infty} x\int_0^x e^{t^2}e^{-x^2}dt = \lim_{x\to\infty} xe^{-x^2}\int_0^x e^{t^2}dt$$

$$=\lim_{x\to\infty}\frac{x\int_0^x e^{t^2}dt}{e^{x^2}}=\lim_{x\to\infty}\frac{\int_0^x e^{t^2}dt+xe^{x^2}}{2xe^{x^2}}=\lim_{x\to\infty}\frac{e^{x^2}+e^{x^2}+2x^2e^{x^2}}{4x^2e^{x^2}+2e^{x^2}}$$

$$=\lim_{x\to\infty}\frac{2+2x^2}{2+4x^2}=\frac{1}{2}$$

22. $$\lim_{x\to 0}(x^{-3}\sin 3x+rx^{-2}+s)=\lim_{x\to 0}\left[\frac{3x-\frac{(3x)^3}{6}+\frac{(3x)^5}{120}...}{x^3}+\frac{r}{x^2}+s\right\}$$

$$=\lim_{x\to 0}\left[\frac{3}{x^2}-\frac{9}{2}+\frac{81x^2}{40}+...+\frac{r}{x^2}+s\right]=0 \text{ if } r=-3 \text{ and } s=\frac{9}{2}.$$

23.

x	$\sin x$	$\frac{6x}{6+x^2}$
± 1.0	± 0.84147	± 0.85714
± 0.1	± 0.09983	± 0.09983
± 0.01	± 0.00999	± 0.00999

$\operatorname{Sin} x \approx \frac{6x}{6+x^2}$ is better

12.M MISCELLANEOUS

1. (a) $\frac{x^2}{1+x^2} = x^2\left(\frac{1}{1-(-x)}\right) = x^2(1 - x + x^2 - x^3 + .. + (-1)^n x^n) = \sum_{n=0}^{\infty}(-1)^n x^{n+2}$.

   (b) No, the radius of convergence for the series is $-1 < x < 1$.

2. $$\sin^{-1} x = \int_0^x \frac{dt}{\sqrt{1-t^2}} = \int_0^x \sum_{n=0}^{\infty} \frac{\left(-\frac{1}{2}\right)\left(-\frac{3}{2}\right)..\left(-\frac{1}{2}-(n-1)\right)}{n!}(-1)^n t^{2n}\, dt$$

   $$= \sum_{n=1}^{\infty} \frac{1\cdot 2\cdot 3\cdot ..\cdot(2n-1)}{2^n n!(2n+1)} x^{2n+1}.$$ The binomial series converges for $|t| < 1$

3. $$e^{\sin x} = 1 + \left(x - \frac{x^3}{3!} + \frac{x^5}{5!} - ...\right) + \frac{1}{2}\left(x - \frac{x^3}{3!} + \frac{x^5}{5!} - ...\right)^2 + \frac{1}{6}\left(x - \frac{x^3}{3!} + \frac{x^5}{5!} - ...\right)^3 + \frac{1}{24}\left(x - \frac{x^3}{3!} + \frac{x^5}{5!} - ...\right)^4 + ..$$

   $$= 1 + \left(x - \frac{x^3}{3!} + \frac{x^5}{5!} - ...\right) + \frac{1}{2}\left(x^2 - \frac{x^4}{3} + \frac{x^6}{36} - ..\right) + \frac{1}{6}\left(x^3 + 3x^2\cdot\frac{x^3}{3!} + .. \right) + \frac{1}{24}(x^4 + ...) + ...$$

   $$= 1 + x + \frac{1}{2}x^2 - \frac{1}{8}x^4 + ...$$

4. (a) Assume first that $x > 1$. Then $\int_x^{\infty} \frac{dt}{1+t^2} = \lim_{b\to\infty}\int_x^b \frac{dt}{1+t^2}$

   $= \lim_{b\to\infty}[\tan^{-1} b - \tan^{-1} x] = \frac{\pi}{2} - \tan^{-1} x$. Using the series,

   $$\int_x^{\infty} \frac{dt}{1+t^2} = \int_x^{\infty}\left(\frac{1}{t^2} - \frac{1}{t^4} + \frac{1}{t^6} - ...\right)dt = \left[-\frac{1}{t} + \frac{1}{3t^2} - \frac{1}{5t^5} + ...\right]_x^{\infty}$$

   $= \frac{1}{x} - \frac{1}{3x^2} + \frac{1}{5x^5} - ....$ Equating the two expressions, we have

   $$\tan^{-1} x = \frac{\pi}{2} - \frac{1}{x} + \frac{1}{3x^2} - \frac{1}{5x^5} + ...$$

(b) Now let $x < -1$. Then $\int_{-\infty}^{x} \frac{dt}{1+t^2} = \lim_{b \to -\infty} \int_{b}^{x} \frac{dt}{1+t^2}$

$= \lim_{b \to -\infty} [\tan^{-1} x - \tan^{-1} b] = \tan^{-1} x + \frac{\pi}{2}$. Using the series,

$$\int_{-\infty}^{x} \frac{dt}{1+t^2} = \int_{-\infty}^{x} \left(\frac{1}{t^2} - \frac{1}{t^4} + \frac{1}{t^6} - \cdots\right) dt = -\frac{1}{t} + \frac{1}{3t^2} - \frac{1}{5t^5} + \ldots \Big]_{-\infty}^{x}$$

$= -\frac{1}{x} + \frac{1}{3x^2} - \frac{1}{5x^5} + \ldots$. Equating the two expressions, we have

$$\tan^{-1} x = -\frac{\pi}{2} - \frac{1}{x} + \frac{1}{3x^2} - \frac{1}{5x^5} + \ldots.$$

5 (a) $\ln(\cos x) = \ln[1 - (1 - \cos x)]$

$$= -\left(\frac{x^2}{2} - \frac{x^4}{24} + \frac{x^6}{720} - \ldots\right) - \frac{1}{2}\left(\frac{x^2}{2} - \frac{x^4}{24} + \ldots\right)^2 - \frac{1}{3}\left(\frac{x^2}{2} - \frac{x^4}{24} + \ldots\right)^3 - \ldots$$

$$= -\frac{x^2}{2} + \frac{x^4}{24} - \frac{x^6}{720} + \ldots - \frac{x^4}{8} + \frac{x^6}{48} - \ldots - \frac{x^6}{24} - \ldots$$

$$= -\frac{x^2}{2} - \frac{x^4}{12} - \frac{x^6}{45} - \ldots$$

(b) $\int_0^{.1} \ln(\cos x)\, dx = \int_0^{.1} \left(-\frac{x^2}{2} - \frac{x^4}{12} - \frac{x^6}{45} - \ldots\right) dx$

$$= -\frac{1}{6}x^3 - \frac{1}{60}x^5 - \frac{1}{315}x^7 \Big]_0^{.1} = -0.00017$$

6. $\int_0^1 \frac{\sin x}{x}\, dx = \int_0^1 \frac{1}{x}\left[x - \frac{x^3}{6} + \frac{x^5}{120} - \frac{x^7}{5040} + \ldots\right] dx$

$= x - \frac{x^3}{18} + \frac{x^5}{600} - \frac{x^7}{35280} + \ldots \Big]_0^1 \approx 0.946$ with error $E < \frac{1}{35280} \approx 0.000003$

7. $\int_0^1 e^{-(x^2)}\, dx = \int_0^1 \left(1 - x^2 + \frac{x^4}{2} - \frac{x^6}{6} + \frac{x^8}{24} - \ldots\right) dx$

$$= x - \frac{1}{3}x^3 + \frac{1}{10}x^5 - \frac{1}{42}x^7 + \frac{1}{216}x^9 - \ldots \Big]_0^1 = 0.747$$

8. $f(x)=\sqrt{1+x^2} \Rightarrow f(1)=\sqrt{2}$; $f'(x)=\dfrac{x}{\sqrt{1+x^2}} \Rightarrow f'(1)=\dfrac{1}{\sqrt{2}}$

$f''(x)=(1+x^2)^{-3/2} \Rightarrow f''(1)=\dfrac{1}{2\sqrt{2}}$.

$$\therefore \sqrt{1+x^2} = \sqrt{2} + \frac{1}{\sqrt{2}}(x-1) + \frac{1}{2!\,2\sqrt{2}}(x-1)^2 + \ldots$$
$$= \sqrt{2}\left[1+\frac{1}{2}(x-1) + \frac{1}{8}(x-1)^2 + \ldots\right]$$

9. $f(x)=\dfrac{1}{1-x}$ $\qquad f(2)=-1$

$f'(x)=\dfrac{1}{(1-x)^2}$ $\qquad f'(2)=1$

$f''(x)=2(1-x)^3$ $\qquad f''(2)=-2$

$f^{(n)}(x)=\dfrac{n!}{(1-x)^n}$ $\qquad f^{(n)}(2)=(-1)^{n+1}n!$

$f(x)=\sum_{n=0}^{\infty}(-1)^{n+1}(x-2)^n$ converges for $1<x<3$ since

$$\lim_{n\to\infty}\left|\frac{(x-2)^{n+1}}{(x-2)^n}\right| < 1 \Leftrightarrow |x-2|<1$$

10. $f(x)=(x+1)^{-1} \Rightarrow f(3)=\dfrac{1}{4}$; $f'(x)=-(1+x)^{-2} \Rightarrow f'(3)=-\dfrac{1}{4^2}$

$f''(x)=2(1+x)^{-3} \Rightarrow f''(1)=\dfrac{2}{4^3}$; $f'''(x)=-3!\,(1+x)^{-4} \Rightarrow f'''(3)=\dfrac{4!}{4^5}$.

$$\therefore (x+1)^{-1} = \frac{1}{4} - \frac{1}{4^2}(x-3) + \frac{1}{4^3}(x-3)^2 - \frac{1}{4^4}(x-3)^3 + \ldots = \sum_{n=0}^{\infty}\frac{(-1)^n(x-3)^n}{4^{n+1}}$$

Note: The results of Problem 9 could be used by writing

$$\frac{1}{x+1} = \frac{1}{4+(x-3)} = \frac{1}{4}\left[\frac{1}{1+\left(\frac{x-3}{4}\right)}\right] = \frac{1}{4}\sum_{n=0}^{\infty}(-1)^n\left(\frac{x-3}{4}\right)^n$$

11. $f(x)=\cos x$ $\qquad f\left(\dfrac{\pi}{3}\right)=\dfrac{1}{2}$

$f'(x)=-\sin x$ $\qquad f\left(\dfrac{\pi}{3}\right)=-\dfrac{\sqrt{3}}{2}$

$f''(x)=-\cos x$ $\qquad f''\left(\dfrac{\pi}{3}\right)=-\dfrac{1}{2}$

$f'''(x)=\sin x$ $\qquad f'''\left(\dfrac{\pi}{3}\right)=\dfrac{\sqrt{3}}{2}$

$$\cos x = \frac{1}{2} - \frac{\sqrt{3}}{2}\left(x - \frac{\pi}{3}\right) - \frac{1}{2}\cdot\frac{1}{2}\left(x - \frac{\pi}{3}\right)^2 + \frac{1}{3!}\cdot\frac{\sqrt{3}}{2}\left(x - \frac{\pi}{3}\right)^3 + \ldots$$

$$= \frac{1}{2}\left(1 - \frac{1}{2}\left(x - \frac{\pi}{3}\right)^2 - \ldots\right) + \frac{\sqrt{3}}{2}\left(-\left(x - \frac{\pi}{3}\right) + \left(x - \frac{\pi}{3}\right)^3 - \ldots\right)$$

$$= \frac{1}{2}\sum_{n=0}^{\infty}\frac{(-1)^n}{(2n)!}\left(x - \frac{\pi}{3}\right)^n + \frac{\sqrt{3}}{2}\sum_{n=0}^{\infty}\frac{(-1)^{n+1}}{(2n+1)!}\left(x - \frac{\pi}{3}\right)^{2n+1}$$

12. $f(x) = x^{-1} \Rightarrow f(\pi) = \frac{1}{\pi}$; $f'(x) = -x^{-2} \Rightarrow f'(\pi) = -\frac{1}{\pi^2}$

$f''(x) = 2x^{-3} \Rightarrow f''(1) = \frac{2}{\pi^3}$; $f'''(x) = -3!x^{-4} \Rightarrow f'''(\pi) = -\frac{3!}{\pi^4}$.

$$\therefore \frac{1}{x} = \frac{1}{\pi} - \frac{1}{\pi^2}(x - \pi) + \frac{2}{\pi^3 2!}(x - \pi)^2 - \ldots = \sum_{n=0}^{\infty}\frac{(-1)^n (x-\pi)^n}{\pi^{n+1}}$$

13. $f'(x) = g(x) \Rightarrow f''(x) = g'(x) = f(x)$. Then $f'''(x) = f'(x) = g(x)$. In general, $f^{(2n+1)}(x) = g(x)$ and $f^{(2n)}(x) = f(x)$. Therefore,

$$f(x) = f(0) + f'(0)x + \frac{f''(0)}{2!}x^2 + \frac{f'''(0)}{3!}x^3 + \ldots.$$

$$= f(0) + g(0)x + \frac{f(0)}{2!}x^2 + \frac{g(0)}{3!}x^3 = 1 + \frac{1}{2}x^2 + \frac{1}{4!}x^4 + \frac{1}{6!}x^6 +$$

$f(1) = 1.543$

14. Note the following facts: (i) f odd $\Rightarrow f'$ is even; (ii) f even $\Rightarrow f'$ is odd; (iii) f odd $\Rightarrow f(0) = 0$; (iv) If $f(x) = \sum a_n x^n$, then $a_n = \frac{f^{(n)}(0)}{n!}$.

(a) If f is even, then $f^{(1)}, f^{(3)}, f^{(5)}, \ldots$ must all be odd, so that $f^{(1)}(0) = f^{(3)}(0) = f^{(5)}(0) = \ldots = 0$ or $a_1 = a_3 = a_5 = \ldots = 0$.

(b) If f is odd, then $f^{(2)}, f^{(4)}, f^{(6)}, \ldots$ must be odd, so that $f^{(2)}(0) = f^{(4)}(0) = f^{(6)}(0) = \ldots = 0$, or $a_2 = a_4 = a_6 = \ldots = 0$.

15. $f(x) = e^{(e^x)}$ $\qquad f(0) = e$

$f'(x) = e^x e^{(e^x)} = e^{(x+e^x)}$ $\qquad f'(0) = e$

$f''(x) = (1 + e^x)\, e^{(x+e^x)}$ $\qquad f''(0) = 2e$

$f'''(x) = e^x e^{(x+e^x)} + (1 + e^x)^2 e^{(x+e^x)}$ $\qquad f'''(0) = 5e$

$f(x) = e + ex + ex^2 + \frac{5e}{6}x^3 + \ldots$

16. (a) $e^h = 1 + h + R_1(x)$, where $|R_1(x)| \le \frac{e^c}{2}x^2 \le \frac{2(0.001)^2}{2} = (0.001)^2$.

(b) Computer or calculator exercise.

(c) $\exp\left(\frac{1}{n}\ln n\right) \approx 1 + \frac{1}{n}\ln n = 1 + \frac{1}{10^m}\ln 10^m = 10^{-m}(m \ln 10)$.

If $m = 10$, and $\ln 10 = 2.30258509299404$ then

$$n^{1/n} \approx 1 + 10^{-10}(10)(2.30258509299404) \approx 1.00000\ 00023\ 02585$$

(d) We will use a quadratic instead of a linear approximation, which mean

we need to add the next term $= \frac{h^2}{2} = \frac{1}{2 \cdot 10^{10}}(10 \ln 10)^2$ to the

linear approximation in (c) to get $n^{1/n} \approx 1.00000\ 00023\ 02585\ 092645$

17. $(1+x)^{\frac{1}{3}} = 1 + \frac{1}{3}x + \frac{\left(\frac{1}{3}\right)\left(-\frac{2}{3}\right)}{2}x^2 - \ldots$ begins alternating after the first

term, and the error $E \le \left|-\frac{1}{9}\left(\frac{1}{10}\right)^2\right| = 0.0011$

18. $\cos^2 x = \left(1 - \frac{x^2}{2} + \frac{x^4}{24} - \ldots\right)^2 = 1 - x^2 + \frac{x^4}{3} - \ldots$

$$\lim_{x \to 0} \frac{\ln(1-x) - \sin x}{1 - \cos^2 x} = \lim_{x \to 0}\left[\frac{\left(-x - \frac{x^2}{2} - \frac{x^3}{3} - ..\right)}{1 - \left(1 - x^2 + \frac{x^4}{3} - ..\right)} - 1\right] = \infty$$

19. $\lim_{x\to 0}\left(\frac{\sin x}{x}\right)^{\frac{1}{x^2}} = e^{-1/6}$. To see this, consider $\lim_{x\to 0}\left[\ln\left(\frac{\sin x}{x}\right)^{\frac{1}{x^2}}\right]$

$$= \lim_{x\to 0}\left[\frac{1}{x^2}\ln\left(\frac{\sin x}{x}\right)\right] = \lim_{x\to 0}\left[\frac{\ln\left(\frac{\sin x}{x}\right)}{x^2}\right] = \lim_{x\to 0}\frac{\left(\frac{x}{\sin x}\right)\left(\frac{x\cos x - \sin x}{x^2}\right)}{2x}$$

$$= \lim_{x\to 0}\frac{x\cos x - \sin x}{2x^2 \sin x} = \lim_{x\to 0}\frac{\cos x - x\sin x - \cos x}{4x\sin x + 2x^2\cos x}$$

$$= \lim_{x\to 0}\frac{-\sin x}{4\sin x + 2x\cos x} = \lim_{x\to 0}\frac{-\cos x}{4\cos x - 2x\sin x + 2\cos x} = -\frac{1}{6}$$

20. $\ln(1 + a_n) \approx a_n - \frac{1}{2}a_n^2 \Rightarrow \ln(1 + a_n) < a_n$. Since $\sum a_n$ converges,

$\sum \ln(1 + a_n)$ must converge by the Comparison Test.

21. $\lim_{n\to\infty}\left|\frac{(x+2)^{n+1}}{3^{n+1}(n+1)}\cdot\frac{3^n n}{(x+2)^n}\right| = \lim_{n\to\infty}\left(\frac{n}{n+1}\right)\left(\frac{1}{3}\right)|x+2| < 1$

if $\frac{1}{3}|x+2| < 1$ or $-5 < x < 1$. At $x = 1$, $\sum_{n=1}^{\infty}\frac{1}{n}$ diverges, and

at $x = -5$, $\sum_{n=1}^{\infty}(-1)^n\frac{1}{n}$ converges. The convergenge is for $-5 \le x < 1$.

22. $\lim_{n\to\infty}\left|\frac{(x-1)^{2n}}{(2n)!}\cdot\frac{(2n-2)!}{(x-1)^{2n-2}}\right| = \lim_{n\to\infty}\frac{(x-1)^2}{2n(2n-1)} = 0$

The series converges absolutely for all x.

23. $\sum_{n=1}^{\infty}\frac{x^n}{n^n}$ converges for all x, since $\lim_{n\to\infty}\sqrt[n]{\left|\frac{x^n}{n^n}\right|} = 0$

24. $\lim_{n\to\infty}\left|\frac{(n+1)!\,x^{n+1}}{(n+1)^{n+1}}\cdot\frac{n^n}{n!\,x^n}\right| = \lim_{n\to\infty}\left(\frac{n}{n+1}\right)^n |x| = \frac{x}{e} < 1$ if $|x| < e$

Stirling's Formula states that $\lim_{n\to\infty}\frac{n!}{n^n e^{-n}\sqrt{2\pi n}} = 1$. $\therefore$ $n! \approx n^n e^{-n}\sqrt{2\pi n}$

for large n. Hence $\frac{n!\,e^n}{n^n} \approx \sqrt{2\pi n} \to \infty$ and $n \to \infty$, and the series

diverges at $x = \pm e$.

25. $\sum_{n=0}^{\infty}\frac{n+1}{2n+1}\frac{(x-3)^n}{2^n}$ converges absolutely for $1 < x < 5$ because

$\lim_{n\to\infty}\left|\frac{(n+2)(x-3)^{n+1}}{(2n+3)\,2^{n+1}}\cdot\frac{(2n+1)\,2^n}{(n+1)(x-3)^n}\right| = \lim_{n\to\infty}\left(\frac{n+2}{n+1}\right)\left(\frac{2n+1}{2n+3}\right)\left(\frac{1}{2}\right)|x-3| < 1$

if $|x-3| < 1$ or is $1 < x < 5$. Since $\lim_{n\to\infty}\frac{n+1}{2n+1} = \frac{1}{2} \ne 0$, the

series diverges at both endpoints.

26. $\lim_{n\to\infty}\left|\frac{(n+2)(x-2)^{n+1}}{(2n+3)\,3^{n+1}}\cdot\frac{(2n+1)\,3^n}{(n+1)(x-2)^n}\right| < 1$ if $\frac{1}{3}|x-2| < 1$ or $-1 < x < 5$

Since $\lim_{n\to\infty}\frac{n+1}{2n+1} = \frac{1}{2} \ne 0$, the series diverges at $x = -1$ and $x = 5$.

27. $\sum_{n=1}^{\infty}\frac{(-1)^{n-1}(x-1)^n}{n^2}$ converges for $0 \le x \le 2$.

$\lim_{n\to\infty}\left|\frac{(x-1)^{n+1}}{(n+1)^2}\cdot\frac{n^2}{(x-1)^n}\right| = \lim_{n\to\infty}\left(\frac{n+1}{n}\right)^2|x-1| < 1$ if $0 < x < 2$.

At $x = 0$, $\sum_{n=1}^{\infty} \frac{(-1)^{n-1}(-1)^n}{n^2} = \sum_{n=1}^{\infty} \frac{1}{n^2}$ converges (p-series, $p = 2$).

At $x = 2$, $\sum_{n=1}^{\infty} \frac{(-1)^{n-1}}{n^2}$ converges (alternating series test).

28. $\lim_{n\to\infty} \left| \frac{x^{n+1}}{\sqrt{n+1}} \cdot \frac{\sqrt{n}}{x^n} \right| < 1$ if $|x| < 1$, so series converges absolutely

for $-1 < x < 1$. If $x = 1$, $\sum_{n=1}^{\infty} \frac{1}{\sqrt{n}}$ diverges; if $x = -1$, $\sum_{n=1}^{\infty} (-1)^n \frac{1}{\sqrt{n}}$ converges

$\therefore \sum_{n=1}^{\infty} \frac{x^n}{\sqrt{n}}$ converges for $-1 \le x < 1$.

29. $\sum_{n=1}^{\infty} \frac{(x-2)^{3n}}{n!}$ converges for all x.

$\lim_{n\to\infty} \left| \frac{(x-2)^{3n+3}}{(n+1)!} \cdot \frac{n!}{(x-2)^{3n}} \right| = \lim_{n\to\infty} \frac{1}{n+1} |x-2|^3 = 0$ for all x.

30. $\lim_{n\to\infty} \left| \frac{2^{n+1}(\sin x)^{n+1}}{(n+1)^2} \cdot \frac{n^2}{2^n(\sin x)^n} \right| < 1$ if $2|\sin x| < 1$, so series converges

for $-\frac{1}{2} < \sin x < \frac{1}{2}$. If $x = \frac{1}{2}$, $\sum_{n=1}^{\infty} \frac{1}{n^2}$ converges; if $x = -\frac{1}{2}$,

$\sum_{n=1}^{\infty} (-1)^n \frac{1}{n^2}$ converges. $\therefore \sum_{n=1}^{\infty} \frac{2^n(\sin x)^n}{n^2}$ converges for

all x for which $-\frac{1}{2} \le \sin x \le \frac{1}{2}$.

31. $\sum_{n=1}^{\infty} \frac{1}{n}\left(\frac{x-1}{x}\right)^n$ converges for all $x \ge \frac{1}{2}$.

$$\lim_{n\to\infty} \left| \frac{\left(\frac{x-1}{x}\right)^{n+1} \frac{1}{n+1}}{\left(\frac{x-1}{x}\right)^n \frac{1}{n}} \right| \lim_{n\to\infty} \left(\frac{n}{n+1}\right) \left| \frac{x-1}{x} \right| < 1 \Leftrightarrow -1 < \frac{x-1}{x} < 1.$$

Case I: $\frac{x-1}{x} < 1 \Leftrightarrow \frac{x-1}{x} - 1 < 0 \Leftrightarrow -\frac{1}{x} < 0 \Leftrightarrow x > 0$

Case II: $\frac{x-1}{x} > -1 \Leftrightarrow \frac{x-1}{x} + 1 > 0 \Leftrightarrow \frac{2x-1}{x} > 0 \Leftrightarrow x < 0 \text{ or } x > \frac{1}{2}$.

The intersection of these solutions sets is $x > \frac{1}{2}$.

At $x = \frac{1}{2}$, $\sum_{n=1}^{\infty} (-1)^n \frac{1}{n}$ converges.

32. (a) $\lim_{n\to\infty} \left| \frac{1\cdot4\cdot7\cdot\ldots\cdot(3n+1)\,x^{3n+3}}{(3n+3)!} \cdot \frac{(3n)!}{1\cdot4\cdot7\cdot\ldots\cdot(3n-2)\,x^{3n}} \right|$

$= \lim_{n\to\infty} \left| \frac{(3n+1)\,x^3}{(3n+3)(3n+2)(3n+1)} \right| = 0$. The series converges absolutely for all x.

(b) $y' = \frac{1}{2}x^2 + \frac{1}{30}x^5 + \ldots + \frac{1\cdot4\cdot7\cdot\ldots\cdot(3n-2)}{(3n-1)!}x^{3n-1} + \ldots$

$y'' = x + \frac{1}{6}x^4 + \ldots + \frac{1\cdot4\cdot7\cdot\ldots\cdot(3n-2)}{(3n-2)!}x^{3n-2} + \ldots$

$= x\left(1 + \frac{1}{6}x^3 + \ldots + \frac{1\cdot4\cdot7\cdot\ldots\cdot(3n-5)}{(3n-3)!}x^{3n-3} + \ldots\right)$

$= xy$. $\quad\therefore$ a = 1 and b = 0.

33. If $\sum_{n=1}^{\infty} a_n$ converges and $a_n > 0$, show that $\sum_{n=1}^{\infty} \frac{a_n}{1+a_n}$ converges.

$\lim_{n\to\infty} \frac{\frac{a_n}{1+a_n}}{a_n} = \lim_{n\to\infty} \frac{1}{1+a_n} = 1$ since $\lim_{n\to\infty} a_n = 0$. By the Limit Comparison Test, $\sum_{n=1}^{\infty} \frac{a_n}{1+a_n}$ since $\sum_{n=1}^{\infty} a_n$ does.

34. If $0 < a_n < 1$, then $|\ln(1-a_n)| = -\ln(1-a_n) = a_n + \frac{a_n^2}{2} + \frac{a_n^3}{3} + \ldots$

$< a_n + a_n^2 + a_n^3 + \ldots = \frac{a_n}{1-a_n}$. By Problem 22 (b), Chapter 11 Miscellaneous

$\sum \frac{a_n}{1-a_n}$ converges if $\sum a_n$ converges, so $\sum \ln(1-a_n)$ converges.

35. If $\sum_{n=1}^{\infty} |a_n|$ converges, and $a_n > -1$, prove $\prod_{n=1}^{\infty}(1+a_n)$ converges.

The convergence of $\sum_{n=1}^{\infty} |a_n|$ means that $\lim_{n\to\infty} |a_n| = 0$. Let $N > 0$ be such

that $|a_n| < \frac{1}{2}$ for all $n > N$ and consider $\sum_{n=N}^{\infty} \ln(1+a_n)$.

$$|\ln(1+a_n)| = \left|a_n - \frac{a_n^2}{2} + \frac{a_n^3}{3} - \frac{a_n^4}{4} + \ldots\right| \le |a_n| + \left|\frac{a_n^2}{2}\right| + \left|\frac{a_n^3}{3}\right| + \left|\frac{a_n^4}{4}\right| + .$$

$$< |a_n| + |a_n|^2 + |a_n|^3 + |a_n|^4 + \ldots.$$

$$= \frac{|a_n|}{1-|a_n|} < 2|a_n| \text{ since, for } n > N,\ 1-|a_n| \ge \frac{1}{2}.$$

Therefore, $\sum_{n=N}^{\infty} \ln(1+a_n) \le \left|\sum_{n=N}^{\infty} \ln(a_n)\right| \le \sum_{n=N}^{\infty} 2|a_n|$

$\le 2\sum_{n=1} |a_n|$ which is convergent. Hence $\prod_{n=1}^{\infty}(1+a_n)$ converges.

36. $\ln(1+x)\tan^{-1} x = \left(x - \frac{x^2}{2} + \frac{x^3}{3} - \frac{x^4}{4} + ..\right)\left(x - \frac{x^3}{3} + \frac{x^5}{5} - \ldots\right)$

$$= x\left(x - \frac{x^3}{3} + ..\right) - \frac{x^2}{2}\left(x - \frac{x^3}{3} + ..\right) + \frac{x^3}{3}(x - ..) - \frac{x^4}{4}(x - ..)$$

$$= x^2 - \frac{x^3}{2} - \frac{x^5}{12} + \ldots$$

37. $\frac{\tan^{-1} x}{1-x} = \frac{1}{1-x} \cdot \tan^{-1} x = (1 + x + x^2 + x^3 + x^4 + x^5 + \ldots)\left(x - \frac{x^3}{3} + \frac{x^5}{5} - \ldots\right)$

$$= x + x^2 + x^3 + x^4 + x^5 - \frac{x^3}{3} - \frac{x^4}{3} - \frac{x^5}{3} + \frac{x^5}{5} + \ldots$$

$$= x + x^2 + \frac{2}{3}x^3 + \frac{2}{3}x^4 + \frac{13}{15}x^5 + \ldots$$

38. Long division produces $\frac{x}{e^x - 1} = 1 - \frac{1}{2}x - \frac{1}{12}x^2 + \ldots$, so $c_0 = 1$, $c_1 = -\frac{1}{2}$, and $c_2 = \frac{1}{12}$.

CHAPTER 13

VECTORS

13.1 VECTORS IN THE PLANE

1. See the sketches in the answer section of the textbook.

2. $\overrightarrow{P_1P_2} = (2-1)\mathbf{i} + (-1-1)\mathbf{j} = \mathbf{i} - 4\mathbf{j}$

3. $P_3 = \left(\frac{-4+2}{2}, \frac{3-1}{2}\right) = (-1, 1);\ \overrightarrow{OP_3} = -\mathbf{i} + \mathbf{j}$

4. $\overrightarrow{AO} = -2\mathbf{i} - 3\mathbf{j}$

5. $\overrightarrow{AB} = (2-1)\mathbf{i} + (0+1)\mathbf{j} = \mathbf{i} + \mathbf{j};$

   $\overrightarrow{CD} = (-2+1)\mathbf{i} + (3-2)\mathbf{j} = -\mathbf{i} - \mathbf{j};$

   $\overrightarrow{AB} + \overrightarrow{CD} = 0\mathbf{i} + 0\mathbf{j}.$

6. $\mathbf{u} = \left(\cos\frac{\pi}{6}\right)\mathbf{i} + \left(\sin\frac{\pi}{6}\right)\mathbf{j} = \frac{\sqrt{3}}{2}\mathbf{i} + \frac{1}{2}\mathbf{j}$

7. $\mathbf{u} = \cos(-30^\circ)\mathbf{i} + \sin(-30^\circ)\mathbf{j} = \frac{\sqrt{3}}{2}\mathbf{i} - \frac{1}{2}\mathbf{j}$

8. $|3\mathbf{i} - 4\mathbf{j}| = \sqrt{9+16} = 5;\ \mathbf{u} = \frac{3}{5}\mathbf{i} - \frac{4}{5}\mathbf{j}$

9. $y = x^2 \Rightarrow y' = 2x.\ y'(2) = 4 = \frac{4}{1}.\ \mathbf{v} = \mathbf{i} + 4\mathbf{j}$ is tangent to the curve.

   $|\mathbf{v}| = \sqrt{1+16} = \sqrt{17}.\ \therefore\ \mathbf{u} = \frac{1}{\sqrt{17}}\mathbf{i} + \frac{4}{\sqrt{17}}\mathbf{j}$ is the required unit vector.

10. Using the tangent found in problem 9, the required normal is

    $\mathbf{n} = -\frac{4}{\sqrt{17}}\mathbf{i} + \frac{1}{\sqrt{17}}\mathbf{j}$

11. (a) $y = x^2 + 2x \Rightarrow y' = 2x + 2.\ y'(1) = 4 = \frac{4}{1}.\ \mathbf{v} = -\mathbf{i} - 4\mathbf{j}$

    is tangent to the curve. $|\mathbf{v}| = \sqrt{1+16} = \sqrt{17}.$

    $\therefore\ \mathbf{u} = -\frac{1}{\sqrt{17}}\mathbf{i} - \frac{4}{\sqrt{17}}\mathbf{j}$ is the required unit vector.

    (b) $\mathbf{w} = -4\mathbf{i} + \mathbf{j}$ is orthogonal to $\mathbf{u}$, hence the normal is

    $\mathbf{n} = -\frac{4}{\sqrt{17}}\mathbf{i} + \frac{1}{\sqrt{17}}\mathbf{j}.$

12. $\theta = 0$: $\mathbf{u} = \mathbf{i}$ $\quad \theta = \frac{\pi}{4}$: $\mathbf{u} = \frac{1}{\sqrt{2}}\mathbf{i} + \frac{1}{\sqrt{2}}\mathbf{j}$

$\theta = \frac{\pi}{2}$: $\mathbf{u} = \mathbf{j}$ $\quad \theta = \frac{2\pi}{3}$: $\mathbf{u} = -\frac{1}{2}\mathbf{i} + \frac{\sqrt{3}}{2}\mathbf{j}$

$\theta = \frac{5\pi}{4}$: $\mathbf{u} = -\frac{1}{\sqrt{2}}\mathbf{i} - \frac{1}{\sqrt{2}}\mathbf{j}$ $\quad \theta = \frac{5\pi}{3}$: $\mathbf{u} = \frac{1}{2}\mathbf{i} - \frac{\sqrt{3}}{2}\mathbf{j}$

13. $|\mathbf{i} + \mathbf{j}| = \sqrt{2}$. $\mathbf{u} = \frac{1}{\sqrt{2}}\mathbf{i} + \frac{1}{\sqrt{2}}\mathbf{j}$. $\cos\theta = \frac{1}{\sqrt{2}} \Rightarrow \theta = \frac{\pi}{4}$.

14. $|2\mathbf{i} - 3\mathbf{j}| = \sqrt{13}$. $\mathbf{u} = \frac{2}{\sqrt{13}}\mathbf{i} - \frac{3}{\sqrt{13}}\mathbf{j}$. $\tan\theta = -\frac{3}{2} \Rightarrow \theta = \tan^{-1}\left(-\frac{3}{2}\right)$.

15. $|\sqrt{3}\mathbf{i} + \mathbf{j}| = 2$. $\mathbf{u} = \frac{\sqrt{3}}{2}\mathbf{i} + \frac{1}{2}\mathbf{j}$. $\cos\theta = \frac{\sqrt{3}}{2} \Rightarrow \theta = \frac{\pi}{6}$.

16. $|-2\mathbf{i} + 3\mathbf{j}| = \sqrt{13}$. $\mathbf{u} = -\frac{2}{\sqrt{13}}\mathbf{i} + \frac{3}{\sqrt{13}}\mathbf{j}$. $\theta = \cos^{-1}\left(-\frac{2}{\sqrt{13}}\right)$.

17. $|5\mathbf{i} + 12\mathbf{j}| = 13$. $\mathbf{u} = \frac{5}{13}\mathbf{i} + \frac{12}{13}\mathbf{j}$. $\theta = \cos^{-1}\left(\frac{5}{13}\right)$.

18. $|-5\mathbf{i} - 12\mathbf{j}| = 13$. $\mathbf{u} = -\frac{5}{13}\mathbf{i} - \frac{12}{13}\mathbf{j}$. $\theta = \pi + \cos^{-1}\left(\frac{5}{13}\right)$.

19. $\mathbf{v} = -4\mathbf{i} + 2\mathbf{j}$. $|\mathbf{v}| = \sqrt{16 + 4} = 2\sqrt{5}$.

20. $\mathbf{A} = 3\mathbf{i} + 6\mathbf{j}$ has $|\mathbf{A}| = \sqrt{45} = 3\sqrt{5}$ and direction $\mathbf{u} = \frac{1}{\sqrt{5}}\mathbf{i} + \frac{2}{\sqrt{5}}\mathbf{j}$.

$\mathbf{B} = -\mathbf{i} - 2\mathbf{j}$ has $|\mathbf{B}| = \sqrt{5}$ and direction $\mathbf{v} = -\frac{1}{\sqrt{5}}\mathbf{i} - \frac{2}{\sqrt{5}}\mathbf{j}$.

Note that $\mathbf{v} = -\mathbf{u}$.

21. $\mathbf{C} = 3\mathbf{i} + 6\mathbf{j}$ has $|\mathbf{C}| = \sqrt{45} = 3\sqrt{5}$ and direction $\mathbf{u} = \frac{1}{\sqrt{5}}\mathbf{i} + \frac{2}{\sqrt{5}}\mathbf{j}$.

$\mathbf{D} = \frac{1}{2}\mathbf{i} - 2\mathbf{j}$ has $|\mathbf{D}| = \frac{\sqrt{5}}{2}$ and direction $\mathbf{v} = \frac{1}{\sqrt{5}}\mathbf{i} + \frac{2}{\sqrt{5}}\mathbf{j}$.

22. The slopes will be the same, because the vectors are collinear.

23. By definition, $\mathbf{A}$ and $\mathbf{B}$ have opposite directions if and only if $\frac{\mathbf{A}}{|\mathbf{A}|} = -\frac{\mathbf{B}}{|\mathbf{B}|}$. Then $\mathbf{A} = -\frac{|\mathbf{A}|}{|\mathbf{B}|}\mathbf{B} = -k\mathbf{B}$.

24. $\mathbf{A'B'} = \mathbf{A'B} + \mathbf{BB'} = \frac{1}{2}\mathbf{AB} + \frac{1}{2}\mathbf{BC} = \frac{1}{2}\mathbf{AC}$

$\mathbf{D'C'} = \mathbf{D'D} + \mathbf{DC'} = \frac{1}{2}\mathbf{AD} + \frac{1}{2}\mathbf{DC} = \frac{1}{2}\mathbf{AC}$. $\therefore \mathbf{A'B'} = \mathbf{D'C'}$

In exactly the same manner, $\mathbf{A'D'} = \mathbf{B'C'}$. Hence A'B'C'D' is a parallelogram, since both pairs of opposite sides are equal.

25. In ▱ ABCD, let N be the midpoint of AC, M be the midpoint of BD.

$$\mathbf{AN} = \frac{1}{2}\mathbf{AC} = \frac{1}{2}(\mathbf{AB} + \mathbf{BC}) = \frac{1}{2}\mathbf{AB} + \frac{1}{2}\mathbf{BC} = \frac{1}{2}\mathbf{AB} + \frac{1}{2}\mathbf{AD}.$$

$$\mathbf{AB} + \mathbf{BD} + \mathbf{DA} = 0 \Rightarrow \mathbf{BD} = -\mathbf{DA} - \mathbf{AB} = \mathbf{AD} - \mathbf{AB}.$$

$$\mathbf{AM} = \mathbf{AB} + \mathbf{BM} = \mathbf{AB} + \frac{1}{2}\mathbf{BD} = \mathbf{AB} + \frac{1}{2}(\mathbf{AD} - \mathbf{AB}) = \frac{1}{2}\mathbf{AB} + \frac{1}{2}\mathbf{AD} = \mathbf{AN}$$

Hence, $\mathbf{AM} = \mathbf{AN} \Rightarrow M = N$ so the diagonals bisect each other.

13.2 MODELING PROJECTILE MOTION

1. $x = (v_0 \cos\alpha)\,t$. $\therefore$ $(840\text{ m/s})(\cos 60^\circ) = (21\text{ km})\left(\frac{1000\text{ m}}{1\text{ km}}\right) \Rightarrow t = 50$ seconds.

2. $R_{max} = \dfrac{v_0^2 \sin 2(45^\circ)}{g}$. $\therefore$ $v_0 = \sqrt{24.5\text{ km} \times \dfrac{1000\text{ m}}{1\text{ km}} \times \dfrac{9.8\text{ m}}{s^2}} = 490\text{ m/s}$

3. (a) $t = \dfrac{2 v_0 \sin\alpha}{g} = \dfrac{2(500\text{ m/sec})(\sin 45^\circ)}{9.8\text{ m/sec}^2} \approx 72.2\text{ sec}$

$R = v_0 \cos\alpha\, t = (500\text{ m/sec})(\cos 45^\circ)(72.2\text{ sec}) \approx 25{,}510.2\text{ m}$

(b) $v_0 \cos\alpha\, t = R$, so $(500\text{ m/sec})(\cos 45^\circ)\,t = 5000\text{ m} \Rightarrow t = 10\sqrt{2}\text{ sec}$

$y = v_0 \sin\alpha\, t - \frac{1}{2}gt^2$

$= (500\text{ m})\left(\frac{1}{\sqrt{2}}\right)(10\sqrt{2}\text{ sec}) - 4.9\text{ m/sec}^2\,(10\sqrt{2}\text{ sec})^2 = 4020\text{ m}$

(c) $y_{max} = \dfrac{(v_0 \sin\alpha)^2}{2g} = \dfrac{\left(500 \cdot \frac{1}{\sqrt{2}}\right)^2}{2(9.8)} = 6{,}377.6\text{ m}$

4. We need $v_0 \sin\alpha\, t + y_0 - \frac{1}{2}gt^2 = 0$, where $y_0 = 32$ ft.

$32\left(\frac{1}{2}\right)t + 32 - 16t^2 = 0$ if $t^2 - t - 2 = 0$ or if $t = 2$ sec

$R = v_0 \cos\alpha\, t = (32\text{ ft/sec})\left(\frac{\sqrt{3}}{2}\right)(2\text{ sec}) \approx 55.4\text{ ft}$

5. Let $\beta = 90^0 - \alpha$. Then $R = \dfrac{v_0^2}{g}\sin 2\beta = \dfrac{v_0^2}{g}\sin 2(90^0 - \alpha)$

$= \dfrac{v_0^2}{g}\sin(180^\circ - 2\alpha) = \dfrac{v_0^2}{g}\sin 2\alpha.$

6. $R = \dfrac{v_0^2}{g}\sin 2\alpha$. Then $\sin 2\alpha\,(400\text{ m/sec})^2 = (16000\text{ m})(9.8\text{ m/sec}^2)$

$\sin 2\alpha = 0.98 \Rightarrow 2\alpha = 78.5^\circ$, so $\alpha = 39.3^\circ$ or $90^\circ - 39.3^\circ = 50.7^\circ$

7. $R = \frac{v_0^2}{g}\sin 2\alpha$. Then $v_0^2 \sin 90° = (10\text{ m})(9.8\text{ m/sec}^2) \Rightarrow v_0 = 9.9\text{ m/sec}$

$(9.9\text{ m/sec})^2 \sin 2\alpha = (6\text{m})(9.8\text{ m/sec}^2) \Rightarrow \sin 2\alpha = 0.5999 \Rightarrow 2\alpha = 39.6°$,

so $\alpha = 18.5°$ or $90° - 18.5° = 71.6°$.

8. $R = v_0 \cos\alpha\, t$. Then $.4\text{ m} = (5\times 10^6\text{ m/s})\,t \Rightarrow t = 8\times 10^{-8}$ sec.

$y = -\frac{1}{2}gt^2 = (-9.8\text{ m/sec}^2)(8\times 10^{-8}\text{ sec})^2 = 3.1\times 10^{-14}$ m.

9. $\frac{v_0^2}{32\text{ ft/sec}^2}(\sin 18°) = 248.8\text{ yd}\left(\frac{3\text{ft}}{1\text{ yd}}\right) \Rightarrow v_0 = 278\text{ ft/sec} = 18936\text{ mph}$

10. $R_{old} = \frac{v_0^2}{g}\sin 2\alpha$. Let $v_1 = 2v_0$. Then $R_{new} = \frac{v_1^2}{g}\sin 2\alpha$

$= \frac{(2v_0)^2}{g}\sin 2\alpha = \frac{4v_0^2}{g}\sin 2\alpha = 2\left(\frac{v_0^2}{g}\sin 2\alpha\right) = 4R_{old}$.

$y_{new} = \frac{(2v_0\sin\alpha)^2}{2g} = \frac{4(v_0\sin\alpha)^2}{2g} = 4y_{old}$. To double the height and range, $v_1 = \sqrt{2}\,v_0$, or increase by a factor of ≈ 41%.

11. The maximum height $y_{max} = \frac{(v_0\sin\alpha)^2}{g}$ is reached in $t_{max} = \frac{v_0\sin\alpha}{g}$ sec.

The time required to reach $\frac{3}{4}$ the maximum height is:

$(v_0\sin\alpha)t - \frac{1}{2}gt^2 = \frac{3}{4}\frac{(v_0\sin\alpha)^2}{g} \Rightarrow 4g^2t^2 - 8gv_0\sin\alpha\, t + 3(v_0\sin\alpha)^2 = 0$

$(2gt - v_0\sin\alpha)(2gt - 3v_0\sin\alpha\, t) = 0 \Rightarrow t = \frac{v_0\sin\alpha}{2g}$ or $\frac{3v_0\sin\alpha}{2g}$

$\therefore\ t = \frac{1}{2}t_{max}$ (going up) or $\frac{3}{2}t_{max}$ (going down)

12. The angle required to hit the cushion is:

$\sin 2\alpha = \frac{Rg}{v_0^2} = \frac{(200)(32)}{\left(\frac{80\sqrt{10}}{3}\right)^2} = \frac{9}{10} \Rightarrow 2\alpha = 64.2°$ or $\alpha = 32.1°$.

For this angle, the maximum height is: $y = \frac{(v_0\sin\alpha)^2}{2g} = 31.4$ feet.

So the performer hits the cushion comfortably.

13. The time required to travel 135 feet is: $t = \frac{x}{v_0\cos\alpha} = \frac{135}{45\sqrt{3}} = \sqrt{3}$ sec.

$y = v_0\sin\alpha\, t - \frac{1}{2}gt^2 = 90\left(\frac{1}{2}\right)\sqrt{3} - \frac{1}{2}(32)(\sqrt{3})^2 = 29.9$ ft.

The ball barely clears the 30 ft tree.

14. The time required to travel 369feet is:

$$t = \frac{x}{v_0 \cos \alpha} = \frac{369}{116\left(\frac{1}{\sqrt{2}}\right)} = 4.5 \text{ sec.}$$

$$y = v_0 \sin \alpha\, t - \frac{1}{2}gt^2 = 116\left(\frac{1}{\sqrt{2}}\right)4.5 - \frac{1}{2}(32)(4.5)^2 = 45.1\text{ft.}$$

The ball will reach the pin but it is not a hole in one.

15. The time required to travel 315 feet is $t = \dfrac{315}{v_0 \cos 20^\circ}$

During this time, the ball rose to a height of 37 feet, i.e..

$$y = v_0 \sin \alpha\, t + y_0 - \frac{1}{2}gt^2 \quad \text{or}$$

$$v_0 \sin 20^\circ \left(\frac{315}{v_0 \cos 20^\circ}\right) + 3 - 16\left(\frac{315}{v_0 \cos 20^\circ}\right)^2 = 37 \Rightarrow v_0 = 149.3 \text{ ft/sec}$$

The time $t = \dfrac{315}{v_0 \cos 20^\circ} = 2.2$ sec

16. $t_{max} = \dfrac{v_0 \sin \alpha}{g}$. By protractor, $\alpha \approx 65^\circ$ and $t = \dfrac{1}{2}$ sec.

$$v_0 = \frac{(9.8)(.5)}{\sin 65^\circ} = 5.4 \text{ m/sec.} \quad y_{max} = \frac{(5.4 \sin 65^\circ)^2}{2\,(9.8)} \approx 1.2 \text{ m}$$

17. For B: $y = R \tan \alpha - \frac{1}{2}gt^2$. For A: $y = v_0 \sin \alpha\, t - \frac{1}{2}gt^2$.

Since $t = \dfrac{R}{v_0 \cos \alpha}$, for A: $y = v_0 \sin \alpha \left(\dfrac{R}{v_0 \cos \alpha}\right) - \dfrac{1}{2}gt^2$

$= R \tan \alpha - \frac{1}{2}gt^2$. $\therefore$ A and B will collide regardless of v_0.

18.

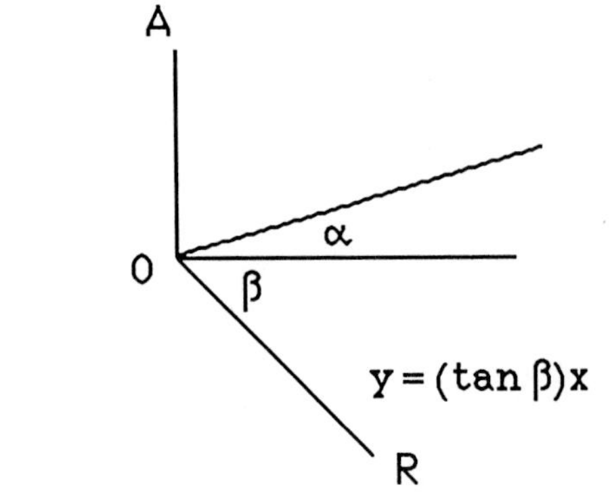

$y = (v_0 \sin\alpha)t - \frac{1}{2}gt^2$, $x = (v_0 \cos\alpha)t$ and $y = (\tan\beta)x \Rightarrow$

$$\frac{(v_0 \sin\alpha)t - \frac{1}{2}gt^2}{(v_0 \cos\alpha)t} = \tan\beta \Rightarrow t = \frac{2v_0(\sin\alpha - \cos\alpha\tan\beta)}{g}.$$

This is the moment when the projectile strikes the plane. At this moment,

$x = \frac{2v_0^2}{g}\left(\frac{1}{2}\sin 2\alpha - \cos^2\alpha\tan\beta\right)$. $\frac{dx}{d\alpha} = \frac{2v_0^2}{g}(\cos 2\alpha - \sin 2\alpha\tan\beta) = 0$

when $\cot 2\alpha = \tan\beta \Rightarrow 2\alpha = \frac{\pi}{2} - \beta$. Then $\angle AOR = \frac{\pi}{2} + \beta = 2\alpha + 2\beta$.

19. The distance to be traveled is $R = b + at$. $\therefore$ $\frac{v_0^2 \sin 2\alpha}{g} = b + at$.

$t = \frac{2v_0 \sin\alpha}{g}$, so $\frac{v_0^2 \sin 2\alpha}{g} = b + a\left(\frac{2v_0 \sin\alpha}{g}\right)$, or

$v_0^2 \sin 2\alpha - bg - 2av_0 \sin\alpha = 0$.

13.3 VECTOR FUNCTIONS AND MOTION

1. $\mathbf{R}(t) = (2\cos t)\mathbf{i} + (3\sin t)\mathbf{j}$

$\mathbf{v}(t) = (-2\sin t)\mathbf{i} + (3\cos t)\mathbf{j}$

$\mathbf{a}(t) = (-2\cos t)\mathbf{i} + (-3\sin t)\mathbf{j}$

$\mathbf{v}\left(\frac{\pi}{4}\right) = -\sqrt{2}\,\mathbf{i} + \frac{3\sqrt{2}}{2}\mathbf{j}$; $\mathbf{a}\left(\frac{\pi}{4}\right) = -\sqrt{2}\mathbf{i} - \frac{3\sqrt{2}}{2}\mathbf{j}$; $\left|\mathbf{v}\left(\frac{\pi}{4}\right)\right| = \frac{\sqrt{26}}{2}$

2. $\mathbf{R}(t) = (t+1)\mathbf{i} + (t^2 - 1)\mathbf{j}$

$\mathbf{v}(t) = \mathbf{i} + (2t)\mathbf{j}$

$\mathbf{a}(t) = 2\mathbf{j}$

$\mathbf{v}(2) = \mathbf{i} + 4\mathbf{j}$; $\mathbf{a}(2) = 2\mathbf{j}$; $|\mathbf{v}(2)| = \sqrt{17}$

3. $\mathbf{R}(t) = (\cos 2t)\mathbf{i} + (2\sin t)\mathbf{j}$

$\mathbf{v}(t) = (-2\sin 2t)\mathbf{i} + (2\cos t)\mathbf{j}$

$\mathbf{a}(t) = (-4\cos 2t)\mathbf{i} + (-2\sin t)\mathbf{j}$

$\mathbf{v}(0) = 2\mathbf{j}$; $\mathbf{a}(0) = -4\mathbf{i}$; $|\mathbf{v}(0)| = 2$

4. $\mathbf{R}(t) = e^{t}\,\mathbf{i} + \frac{2}{9}e^{2t}\,\mathbf{j}$

$\mathbf{v}(t) = e^{t}\,\mathbf{i} + \frac{4}{9}e^{2t}\,\mathbf{j}$

$\mathbf{a}(t) = e^{t}\,\mathbf{i} + \frac{8}{9}e^{2t}\,\mathbf{j}$

$\mathbf{v}(\ln 3) = 3\mathbf{i} + 4\mathbf{j}$; $\mathbf{a}(\ln 3) = 3\mathbf{i} + 8\,\mathbf{j}$; $|\mathbf{v}(\ln 3)| = 5$

5. $\mathbf{R}(t) = (\sec t)\mathbf{i} + (\tan t)\mathbf{j}$

$\mathbf{v}(t) = (\sec t \tan t)\mathbf{i} + (\sec^2 t)\mathbf{j}$

$\mathbf{a}(t) = (\sec^3 t + \tan^2 t \sec t)\mathbf{i} + (2\sec^2 t \tan t)\mathbf{j}$

$\mathbf{v}\left(\frac{\pi}{6}\right) = \frac{2}{3}\mathbf{i} + \frac{4}{3}\mathbf{j}$; $\mathbf{a}\left(\frac{\pi}{6}\right) = \frac{10\sqrt{3}}{9}\mathbf{i} + \frac{8\sqrt{3}}{9}\mathbf{j}$; $\left|\mathbf{v}\left(\frac{\pi}{6}\right)\right| = \frac{2\sqrt{5}}{3}$

6. $\mathbf{R}(t) = \ln(t+1)\mathbf{i} + t^2\mathbf{j}$

$\mathbf{v}(t) = \frac{1}{t+1}\mathbf{i} + 2t\,\mathbf{j}$

$\mathbf{a}(t) = -\frac{1}{(t+1)^2}\mathbf{i} + 2\,\mathbf{j}$

$\mathbf{v}(1) = \frac{1}{2}\mathbf{i} + 2\mathbf{j}$; $\mathbf{a}(1) = -\frac{1}{4}\mathbf{i} + 2\mathbf{j}$; $|\mathbf{v}(1)| = \frac{\sqrt{17}}{2}$

7. $\mathbf{R}(t) = (a\cos\omega t)\mathbf{i} + (a\sin\omega t)\mathbf{j}$

$\mathbf{v}(t) = (-a\omega\sin\omega t)\mathbf{i} + (a\omega\cos\omega t)\mathbf{j}$

$\mathbf{a}(t) = (-a\omega^2\cos\omega t)\mathbf{i} + (-a\omega^2\sin\omega t)\mathbf{j}$

$\mathbf{v}\left(\frac{\pi}{3\omega}\right) = -\frac{a\omega\sqrt{3}}{2}\mathbf{i} + \frac{a\omega}{2}\mathbf{j}$; $\mathbf{a}\left(\frac{\pi}{3\omega}\right) = -\frac{a\omega^2}{2}\mathbf{i} - \frac{a\omega^2\sqrt{3}}{2}\mathbf{j}$; $\left|\mathbf{v}\left(\frac{\pi}{3\omega}\right)\right| = a\omega$

8. $\mathbf{R}(t) = (\cosh 3t)\mathbf{i} + (2\sinh t)\mathbf{j}$

$\mathbf{v}(t) = (3\sinh 3t)\mathbf{i} + (2\cosh t)\mathbf{j}$

$\mathbf{a}(t) = (9\cosh 3t)\mathbf{i} + (2\sinh t)\mathbf{j}$

$\mathbf{v}(0) = 2\mathbf{j}$; $\mathbf{a}(0) = 9\mathbf{i}$; $|\mathbf{v}(0)| = 2$

9. $\mathbf{v}(t) = \int (-3t)\, dt\, \mathbf{i} = \left(-\frac{3}{2}t^2 + C_1\right)\mathbf{i} + C_2\,\mathbf{j}.$

$\mathbf{v}(0) = 2\mathbf{j} \Rightarrow C_1\mathbf{i} + C_2\,\mathbf{j} = 2\mathbf{j} \Rightarrow C_1 = 0$ and $C_2 = 2$

$\mathbf{R}(t) = \int -\frac{3}{2}t^2\, dt\, \mathbf{i} + \int 2\, dt\, \mathbf{j} = \left(-\frac{1}{2}t^3 + C_3\right)\mathbf{i} + (2t + C_4)\,\mathbf{j}$

$\mathbf{R}(0) = 4\mathbf{i} \Rightarrow C_3\,\mathbf{i} + C_4\,\mathbf{j} = 4\mathbf{i} \Rightarrow C_3 = 4$ and $C_4 = 0$.

$\mathbf{R}(t) = \left(-\frac{1}{2}t^3 + 4\right)\mathbf{i} + (2t)\,\mathbf{j}$

10. $\mathbf{v}(t) = \int (3t)\, dt\, \mathbf{i} + \int 4\, dt\, \mathbf{j} = \left(\frac{3}{2}t^2 + C_1\right)\mathbf{i} + (4t + C_2)\mathbf{j}.$

$\mathbf{v}(0) = 4\mathbf{i} \Rightarrow C_1\mathbf{i} + C_2\,\mathbf{j} = 4\mathbf{i} \Rightarrow C_1 = 4$ and $C_2 = 0$.

$\mathbf{R}(t) = \int \left(\frac{3}{2}t^2 + 4\right)dt\, \mathbf{i} + \int 4dt\, \mathbf{j}$

$= \left(\frac{1}{2}t^3 + 4t + C_3\right)\mathbf{i} + (2t^2 + C_4)\,\mathbf{j}$

$\mathbf{R}(0) = 5\mathbf{j} \Rightarrow C_3\,\mathbf{i} + C_4\,\mathbf{j} = 5\mathbf{j} \Rightarrow C_4 = 5$ and $C_3 = 0$

$\mathbf{R}(t) = \left(\frac{1}{2}t^3 + 4t\right)\mathbf{i} + (2t^2 + 5)\,\mathbf{j}$

11. $\mathbf{v}(t) = \int (1+t)^{-1/2}\, dt\, \mathbf{i} - \int e^{-t}\, dt\, \mathbf{j} = (2\sqrt{1+t} + C_1)\mathbf{i} + (e^{-t} + C_2)\mathbf{j}.$

$\mathbf{v}(0) = -\mathbf{i} + \mathbf{j} \Rightarrow (2 + C_1)\mathbf{i} + (1 + C_2)\mathbf{j} = -\mathbf{i} + \mathbf{j} \Rightarrow C_1 = -3$ and $C_2 = 0$

$\mathbf{R}(t) = \int (2\sqrt{1+t} - 3)dt\, \mathbf{i} + \int e^{-t}\, dt\, \mathbf{j} = \left(\frac{4}{3}(1+t)^{3/2} - 3t + C_3\right)\mathbf{i} - (e^{-t} + C_4)\,\mathbf{j}$

$\mathbf{R}(0) = \frac{1}{3}\mathbf{i} - \mathbf{j} = \left(\frac{4}{3} + C_3\right)\mathbf{i} + (-1 + C_4)\mathbf{j} \Rightarrow C_3 = -1, C_4 = 0.$

$\mathbf{R}(t) = \left(\frac{4}{3}(1+t)^{3/2} - 3t - 1\right)\mathbf{i} - e^{-t}\,\mathbf{j}$

12. $\mathbf{v}(t) = \int -9.8\, dt\, \mathbf{j} = C_1\mathbf{i} + (-9.8t + C_2)\mathbf{j}.$

$\mathbf{v}(0) = v_0 \cos\alpha\, \mathbf{i} + v_0 \sin\alpha\, \mathbf{j} \Rightarrow C_1 = v_0 \cos\alpha,\ C_2 = v_0 \sin\alpha$

$\mathbf{R}(t) = \int (v_0 \cos\alpha)\, dt\, \mathbf{i} + \int (v_0 \sin\alpha - 9.8t)\, dt\, \mathbf{j}$

$= (v_0 \cos\alpha\, t + C_3)\mathbf{i} + (v_0 \sin\alpha\, t - 4.9t^2 + C_4)\mathbf{j}$

$\mathbf{R}(0) = x_0\,\mathbf{i} + y_0\,\mathbf{j} = C_3\,\mathbf{i} + C_4\,\mathbf{j} \Rightarrow C_3 = x_0, C_4 = y_0$

$\mathbf{R}(t) = (v_0 \cos\alpha\, t + x_0)\mathbf{i} + (v_0 \sin\alpha\, t - 4.9t^2 + y_0)\mathbf{j}$

13. (a) $\mathbf{R}(t) = t\mathbf{i} + t^2\mathbf{j} \Rightarrow \mathbf{v}(t) = \mathbf{i} + 2t\,\mathbf{j}$ and $\mathbf{a}(t) = 2\mathbf{j}$

(b) $\mathbf{v}(2) = \mathbf{i} + 4\mathbf{j}$, $\mathbf{a}(2) = 2\mathbf{j}$

(See graph in Answer section of textbook)

14. $\dfrac{d}{dt}\left(\dfrac{d\mathbf{R}}{dt} + \dfrac{k}{m}\mathbf{R}\right) = \dfrac{d}{dt}(v(0) - gt\mathbf{j}) \Rightarrow \dfrac{d^2\mathbf{R}}{dt^2} + \dfrac{k}{m}\dfrac{d\mathbf{R}}{dt} = -g\mathbf{j}$

$m\dfrac{d^2\mathbf{R}}{dt^2} = -mg\mathbf{j} - k\dfrac{d\mathbf{R}}{dt}$. $\therefore$ The second equation is the integral of the first.

To solve: $e^{(k/m)t}\dfrac{d\mathbf{R}}{dt} + \dfrac{k}{m}e^{(k/m)t} = v(0)e^{(k/m)t} - gte^{(k/m)t}\,\mathbf{j}$

$$e^{(k/m)t}\mathbf{R} = \frac{k}{m}v(0)e^{(k/m)t} - g\left[\frac{m}{k}te^{(k/m)t} - \frac{m^2}{k^2}e^{(k/m)t}\right]\mathbf{j} + \mathbf{C}$$

$$\mathbf{R} = \frac{k}{m}v(0) - \left[\frac{gm}{k}t + \frac{gm^2}{k^2}\right]\mathbf{j} + \mathbf{C}e^{-(k/m)t}$$

15. (a) $\mathbf{R}(t) = 20t\mathbf{i} + (-4.9t^2 + 100)\mathbf{j} \Rightarrow \mathbf{v}(t) = 20\mathbf{i} - 9.8\mathbf{j}$

(b) $\mathbf{v}(2) = 20\mathbf{i} - 19.6\mathbf{j}$; $|\mathbf{v}(2)| = \sqrt{20^2 + 19.6^2} \approx 28.0$

13.M MISCELLANEOUS

1. Extend $\overrightarrow{CD}$ to $\overrightarrow{CG}$ so that $\overrightarrow{CD} = \overrightarrow{DG}$. Then $\overrightarrow{CG} = \overrightarrow{CA} + \overrightarrow{AG} = \overrightarrow{CA} + \overrightarrow{CB}$. $\overrightarrow{CB} = 3\overrightarrow{CE}$. Let $\overrightarrow{CG} = x\,\overrightarrow{CF}$. Then $x\,\overrightarrow{CF} - 3\,\overrightarrow{CB} - \overrightarrow{CA} = 0$. Since A, E and F are collinear, $x - 3 - 1 = 0$ or $x = 4$. Then $\overrightarrow{CG} = 4\overrightarrow{CF} \Rightarrow \overrightarrow{CD} = 2\overrightarrow{CF}$.
$\therefore$ F is the midpoint of $\overrightarrow{CD}$.

2. The equation of the line through (2, 3) and (4, 1) is $x = 2 + 2t$, $y = 3 - 2t$. If (5, y) is to lie on this line, then $5 = 2 + 2t \Rightarrow t = \dfrac{3}{2}$. Then $y = 3 - 2\left(\dfrac{3}{2}\right) = 0$.

3. $x + y = 1 \Rightarrow y = 1 - x$. $\mathbf{P} = \overrightarrow{OP} = x\mathbf{A} + y\mathbf{B} = x\mathbf{A} + (1 - x)\mathbf{B} \Rightarrow$ $\mathbf{P} = \mathbf{B} + x(\mathbf{A} - \mathbf{B})$. $\therefore$ P is on the line AB. Since $x < 1$, P is actually on the segment AB.

4. (a) The equation of CM is: $\mathbf{v} = \overrightarrow{OC} + t(\overrightarrow{OM} - \overrightarrow{OC})$. Since P is $\frac{2}{3}$ of the way from C to M, we have that $\overrightarrow{OP} = \overrightarrow{OC} + \frac{2}{3}(\overrightarrow{OM} - \overrightarrow{OC})$
$= \frac{1}{3}\overrightarrow{OC} + \frac{2}{3}\overrightarrow{OM}$. But $\overrightarrow{OM} = \frac{1}{2}(\overrightarrow{OA} + \overrightarrow{OB})$. $\therefore$ $\overrightarrow{OP} = \frac{1}{3}\overrightarrow{OC} + \frac{2}{3}\left[\frac{1}{2}(\overrightarrow{OA} + \overrightarrow{OB})\right]$
or $\overrightarrow{OP} = \frac{1}{3}(\overrightarrow{OA} + \overrightarrow{OB} + \overrightarrow{OC})$

(b) Let P' and P" be the points which are two-thirds of the way from A and B to the midpoints of the opposite sides. The same argument would show that $\overrightarrow{OP'} = \frac{1}{3}(\overrightarrow{OA} + \overrightarrow{OB} + \overrightarrow{OC})$. Hence $\overrightarrow{OP} = \overrightarrow{OP'}$ $(= \overrightarrow{OP''})$ so that P, P', and P" are the same point.

5. Let P be the point of intersection of $\overrightarrow{Aa}$, $\overrightarrow{Bb}$ and $\overrightarrow{Cc}$. By Problem 4 if O is any point, then $\overrightarrow{OP} = \frac{1}{3}(\overrightarrow{OA} + \overrightarrow{OB} + \overrightarrow{OC})$. In particular, let O = P. Then $\overrightarrow{PP} = \vec{0} = \frac{1}{3}(\overrightarrow{PA} + \overrightarrow{PB} + \overrightarrow{PC})$. Since $\overrightarrow{PA} = 3\overrightarrow{Aa}$, $\overrightarrow{PB} = 3\overrightarrow{Bb}$ and $\overrightarrow{PC} = 3\overrightarrow{Cc}$, we have that $\overrightarrow{Aa} + \overrightarrow{Bb} + \overrightarrow{Cc} = 0$.

6. Let $V_1V_2V_3...V_n$ be the vertices of a regular n-gon, and let $\mathbf{v}_i$ be the vector from 0 to V_i, $i = 1, 2, ..., n$. Let $\mathbf{S} = \sum_{i=1}^{n} \mathbf{v}_i$. If the polygon is rotated through an angle of $\frac{2\pi}{n}$, $\mathbf{S}$ remains the same. Hence $\mathbf{S} = \mathbf{0}$, since the $\mathbf{0}$-vector is the only vector invariant under rotations

7. The height of the ball: $y = (v_0 \sin\alpha)t - \frac{1}{2}gt^2$

Let h = height of hill: $h = x\tan\phi = (v_0\cos\alpha)t\cdot\frac{\sin\phi}{\cos\phi}$.

When h = y, the ball has reached the ground, i.e. when

$$(v_0\cos\alpha)t\cdot\frac{\sin\phi}{\cos\phi} = (v_0\sin\alpha)t - \frac{1}{2}gt^2$$

$$\frac{(v_0\sin\alpha)(\cos\phi)t - \frac{1}{2}gt^2\cos\phi - v_0\cos\alpha\sin\phi}{\cos\phi} = 0$$

$$v_0\sin(\alpha-\phi)\,t - \frac{1}{2}gt^2\cos\phi = 0$$

$$t = \frac{2v_0\sin(\alpha-\phi)}{g\cos\phi}.$$

$$s = \frac{x}{\cos\phi} = \frac{v_0\cos\alpha\, t}{\cos\phi} = \frac{v_0\cos\alpha}{\cos\phi}\cdot\frac{2v_0\sin(\alpha-\phi)}{g\cos\phi} = \frac{2v_0^2\cos\alpha\sin(\alpha-\phi)}{g\cos^2\phi}$$

$$\frac{ds}{d\alpha} = \frac{2v_0^2}{g\cos^2\phi}[-\sin\alpha\sin(\alpha-\phi) + \cos\alpha\cos(\alpha-\phi)] = 0$$

when $\cos(\alpha+\alpha-\phi) = 0 \Rightarrow 2\alpha-\phi = \frac{\pi}{2} \Rightarrow \alpha = \frac{\phi}{2}+\frac{\pi}{4}$.

8. (a) If **A**, **B**, and **C** are collinear, then C divides AB in some ratio $\frac{x}{y}$.

Thus $\mathbf{C} = \frac{x}{x+y}\mathbf{A} + \frac{y}{x+y}\mathbf{B}$. Let $z = -(x+y)$ so that

$x\mathbf{A} + y\mathbf{B} + z\mathbf{C} = \mathbf{0}$.

(b) Conversely, if $x+y+z=0$ and $x\mathbf{A} + y\mathbf{B} + z\mathbf{C} = \mathbf{0}$ then

$\mathbf{C} = \frac{x}{z}\mathbf{A} + \frac{y}{z}\mathbf{B}$, where $z = -(x+y) \neq 0$ so C is collinear with A and B.

9. (a) $\mathbf{v}(t) = (\pi - \pi\cos\pi t)\mathbf{i} + (1-\cos\pi t)\mathbf{j}$

$\mathbf{a}(t) = \pi^2\sin\pi t\,\mathbf{i} + \pi^2\cos\pi t\,\mathbf{j}$

(b) Draw PA ⊥ QC. $m_{PC} = \tan\angle CPA = \cot\pi t$

$\angle PQA = \frac{1}{2}(\angle PCA)$ so $m_{PQ} = \tan\angle PQA = \cot\frac{\pi t}{2}$

(c) $$m_{\mathbf{v}} = \frac{\pi\sin\pi t}{\pi - \pi\cos\pi t} = \frac{2\sin\frac{\pi t}{2}\cos\frac{\pi t}{2}}{1-\left(1-2\sin^2\frac{\pi t}{2}\right)} = \cot\frac{\pi t}{2} = m_{PQ}$$

$$m_{\mathbf{a}} = \frac{\pi^2\cos\pi t}{\pi^2\sin\pi t} = \cot\pi t = m_{PC}$$

10. $x(t) = (1+t^2)^{-1/2} \Rightarrow x'(t) = -t(1+t^2)^{-3/2}$

$y(t) = t(1+t^2)^{-1/2} \Rightarrow y'(t) = (1+t^2)^{-3/2}$

$\mathbf{v}(t) = \left[-t(1+t^2)^{-3/2}\right]\mathbf{i} + \left[(1+t^2)^{-3/2}\right]\mathbf{j}$

$s(t) = |\mathbf{v}(t)| = (1+t^2)^{-1}$; $s'(t) = -2t(1+t^2)^{-2} = 0$ if $t = 0$.

$s''(t) = (6t^2 - 2)(1+t^2)^{-3}$; $s''(0) = -2 \Rightarrow s(0) = 1$ is maximum.

CHAPTER 14

DIFFERENTIAL EQUATIONS

14.1 INTRODUCTION

1. (a) $y = x^2 + C \Rightarrow y' = 2x$ and $y'' = 2$. $\therefore\ xy'' - y' = x(2) - 2x = 0$

   (b) $y = C_1 x^2 + C_2 \Rightarrow y' = 2C_1 x$ and $y'' = 2C_1$. $\therefore\ xy'' - y' = x(2C_1) - 2C_1 x = 0$

2. $y = \frac{1}{2}x \Rightarrow y' = \frac{1}{2}$ and $y'' = y''' = 0$. $\therefore\ x^3 y''' + 4x^2 y'' + xy' + y =$

   $x^3(0) + 4x^2(0) + x\left(\frac{1}{2}\right) + \frac{1}{2}x = x$

3. (a) $y = C \Rightarrow y' = y'' = 0$. $\therefore$ $(y)(0) = 2(0)^2 - 2(0)$ or $0 = 0$

   (b) $C_1 y = \tan(C_1 x + C_2) \Rightarrow y' = \sec^2(C_1 x + C_2)$ and

   $y'' = 2C_1 \sec^2(C_1 x + C_2)\tan(C_1 x + C_2)$.

   $$y y'' = \left(\frac{1}{C_1}\tan(C_1 x + C_2)\right)\left(2C_1 \sec^2(C_1 x + C_2)\tan(C_1 x + C_2)\right)$$

   $$= 2\sec^2(C_1 x + C_2)\tan^2(C_1 x + C_2)$$

   $$2(y')^2 - 2y' = 2\left(\sec^2(C_1 x + C_2)\right)^2 - 2\sec^2(C_1 x + C_2)$$

   $$= 2\sec^2(C_1 x + C_2)(\sec^2(C_1 x + C_2) - 1)$$

   $$= 2\sec^2(C_1 x + C_2)\tan^2(C_1 x + C_2)$$

4. $y = \frac{C}{x} + \frac{x}{2} \Rightarrow y' = -\frac{C}{x^2} + \frac{1}{2}$. $\therefore\ y' + \frac{1}{x}y = -\frac{C}{x^2} + \frac{1}{2} + \frac{1}{x}\left(\frac{C}{x} + \frac{x}{2}\right) = 1$

5. $y = e^{-x} + Ce^{-(3/2)x} \Rightarrow y' = -e^{-x} - \frac{3}{2}Ce^{-(3/2)x}$.

   $\therefore\ 2y' + 3y = 2\left(-e^{-x} - \frac{3}{2}Ce^{-(3/2)x}\right) + 3\left(e^{-x} + Ce^{-(3/2)x}\right) = e^{-x}$.

6. $y = \frac{1}{x \sin x}\int_1^x \frac{e^t}{t}\,dt$

$$y' = \left(\int_1^x \frac{e^t}{t}\,dt\right)(-x \sin x)^{-2}(\sin x + x \cos x) + \frac{1}{x \sin x}\left(\frac{e^x}{x}\right)$$

$$\therefore\ (x \sin x)\left(\left(\int_1^x \frac{e^t}{t}\,dt\right)(-x \sin x)^{-2}(\sin x + x \cos x) + \frac{1}{x \sin x}\left(\frac{e^x}{x}\right)\right)$$

$$+ (\sin x + x \cos x)\left(\frac{1}{x \sin x}\int_1^x \frac{e^t}{t}\,dt\right)$$

$$= \frac{\sin x + x \cos x}{x \sin x}\left(\int_1^x \frac{e^t}{t}\,dt - \int_1^x \frac{e^t}{t}\,dt\right) + \frac{e^x}{x} = \frac{e^x}{x}$$

14.2 FIRST ORDER DIFFERENTIAL EQUATIONS OF FIRST DEGREE

Separable

1. $x(2y-3)\,dx + (x^2+1)\,dy = 0 \Rightarrow (x^2+1)\,dy = -x(2y-3)\,dx$

$$\int \frac{dy}{2y-3} = \int \frac{-x\,dx}{x^2+1} \Rightarrow \frac{1}{2}\ln|2y-3| = -\frac{1}{2}\ln|x^2+1| + C'$$

$$\ln|2y-3| = \ln\frac{1}{x^2+1} + \ln C' \quad \text{or} \quad y = \frac{C}{x^2+1}$$

2. $x^2(y^2+1)\,dx + y\sqrt{x^3+1}\,dy = 0 \Rightarrow \frac{y\,dy}{y^2+1} = \frac{-x^2\,dx}{\sqrt{x^3+1}}$

$$\frac{1}{2}\ln(y^2+1) = -\frac{2}{3}(x^3+1)^{1/2} + C \Rightarrow \ln(y^2+1) = C - \frac{4}{3}\sqrt{x^3+1}$$

3. $\frac{dy}{dx} = e^{x-y} = e^x e^{-y} \Rightarrow \int e^y\,dy = \int e^x\,dx \Rightarrow e^y = e^x + C$

4. $\sqrt{2xy}\,\frac{dy}{dx} = 1 \Rightarrow \sqrt{2y}\,dy = \frac{dx}{\sqrt{x}} \Rightarrow \frac{2\sqrt{2}}{3}y^{3/2} = 2x^{1/2} + C'$

$$y = \left(\frac{3}{\sqrt{2}}x^{1/2} + C\right)^{2/3}$$

5. $\sin x\,\frac{dx}{dy} + \cosh 2y = 0 \Rightarrow \int \sin x\,dx = \int -\cosh 2y\,dy \Rightarrow$

$$-\cos x = -\frac{1}{2}\sinh 2y + C' \quad \text{or} \quad \sinh 2y - 2\cos x = C$$

6. $\ln x\,\frac{dx}{dy} = \frac{x}{y} \Rightarrow \frac{\ln x\,dx}{x} = \frac{dy}{y} \Rightarrow \frac{1}{2}\ln^2 x = \ln|y| + C$

7. $xe^y\,dy + \dfrac{x^2+1}{y}\,dx = 0 \Rightarrow \dfrac{x^2+1}{y}\,dx = -x\,e^y\,dy \Rightarrow \int\left(x+\dfrac{1}{x}\right)dx = -\int ye^y\,dy \Rightarrow$

$\ln|x| + \frac{1}{2}x^2 = -ye^y + e^y + C$

8. $y\sqrt{2x^2+3}\,dy + x\sqrt{4-y^2}\,dx = 0 \Rightarrow x\sqrt{4-y^2}\,dx = -y\sqrt{2x^2+3}\,dy$

$\dfrac{y\,dy}{\sqrt{4-y^2}} = \dfrac{-x\,dx}{\sqrt{2x^2+3}} \Rightarrow -(4-y^2)^{1/2} = -\frac{1}{2}(2x^2+3)^{1/2} + C$

9. $\sqrt{1+x^2}\,dy + \sqrt{y^2-1}\,dx = 0 \Rightarrow \int\dfrac{dy}{\sqrt{y^2-1}} = -\int\dfrac{dx}{\sqrt{1+x^2}} \Rightarrow$

$\cosh^{-1}y = -\sinh^{-1}x + C.$

10. $x^2y\dfrac{dy}{dx} = (1+x)\csc y \Rightarrow \dfrac{y\,dy}{\csc y} = \dfrac{(1+x)\,dx}{x^2}$

$\int y\sin y\,dy = \int(x^{-2}+x^{-1})dx \Rightarrow \sin y - y\cos y = -\dfrac{1}{x} + \ln|x| + C$

11. $\dfrac{dx}{dt} = 1000 + 0.1x \Rightarrow \dfrac{dx}{1000+0.1x} = dt \Rightarrow 10\ln(1000+0.1x) = t + C$

$1000 + 0.1x = Ae^{t/10} \quad (A = e^{C/10})$

$x(t) = Be^{t/10} - 10{,}000 \quad (B = 10A)$. Since $x(0) = 1000$, $B = 11{,}000$

$\therefore x(t) = 1000(11e^{t/10} - 10).$

$100{,}000 = 1000(11e^{t/10} - 10)$ in $(10\ln 10) \approx 23.03$ years

12. Define: F in/hr = rate at which snow is falling

R in^3/hr = rate at which plow removes snow

w in = width of the plow

$t_0 = 12$ noon, for convenience

If the plow moves Δx inches in Δt hours, then it clears a volume of $wF(t-t_0)\Delta x$ in^3.

$\therefore \quad R\Delta t = wF(t-t_0)\Delta x$ or $\dfrac{\Delta x}{\Delta t} = \dfrac{R}{wF(t-t_0)}$. If $\Delta t \to 0$, we have

$\dfrac{dx}{dt} = \dfrac{R}{wF(t-t_0)} \Rightarrow x(t) = \dfrac{R}{wF}\ln(t-t_0) + C$

$x(0) = 0 \Rightarrow C = -\dfrac{R}{wF}\ln(-t_0) \Rightarrow x(t) = \dfrac{R}{wF}\ln\dfrac{t_0-t}{t_0}$

We are given that $x(2) - x(1) = \frac{1}{2}\left[x(1) - x(0)\right]$, so

$$2\ln\frac{t_0-2}{t_0-1} = \ln\frac{t_0-1}{t_0} \Rightarrow \left(\frac{t_0-2}{t_0-1}\right)^2 = \frac{t_0-1}{t_0} \Rightarrow t_0^2 - t_0 - 1 = 0$$

or $t_0 = \dfrac{1 \pm \sqrt{5}}{2}$. Since t_0 must be negative, it started snowing

$\dfrac{\sqrt{5}-1}{2} \approx .62$ hours before noon, or at 11:23 a.m.

13. $\dfrac{dT}{dt} = k(T - T_a) \Rightarrow \ln(T - T_a) = kt + C_1 \Rightarrow T - T_a = Ce^{kt} \quad (C = e^{C_1})$

$T(0) = 100 \Rightarrow 100 - 20 = C$, so $T = 20 + 80e^{kt}$

$T(20) = 80 \Rightarrow 80 = 20 + 80e^{20k}$ or $k = \frac{1}{20}\ln\frac{3}{4}$.

$T = 60$: $40 = 80\,e^{kt}$ or $\left(\frac{1}{20}\ln\frac{3}{4}\right)t = \ln\frac{1}{2} \Rightarrow t = \dfrac{20\ln 0.5}{\ln 0.75} \approx 48.2$ minutes

Homogeneous

14. $(x^2 + y^2)\,dx + xy\,dy = 0 \Rightarrow \dfrac{dy}{dx} = \dfrac{-(x^2+y^2)}{xy} = -\left(\dfrac{x}{y} + \dfrac{y}{x}\right)$ or

$\dfrac{dy}{dx} = -\left(\dfrac{1}{\frac{y}{x}} + \dfrac{y}{x}\right)$. The equation is homogeneous with

$F(v) = -\left(\frac{1}{v} + v\right)$, $v = \frac{y}{x}$. $\therefore \dfrac{dx}{x} + \dfrac{dv}{v - F(v)} = 0 \Rightarrow \dfrac{dx}{x} + \dfrac{dv}{v + \frac{1}{v} + v} = 0$

$$\frac{dx}{x} = -\frac{v\,dv}{2v^2+1} \Rightarrow \ln|x| = -\frac{1}{4}\ln(2v^2+1) + C \Rightarrow \ln|x| = -\frac{1}{4}\ln\left(\frac{2y^2}{x^2} + 1\right) + C$$

15. $x^2\,dy + (y^2 - xy)\,dx = 0 \Rightarrow \dfrac{dy}{dx} = -\dfrac{y^2 - xy}{x^2} = -\left(\dfrac{y}{x}\right)^2 + \dfrac{y}{x}$.

$F(v) = v - v^2$ with $v = \frac{y}{x}$. Then $\dfrac{dx}{x} + \dfrac{dv}{v - v + v^2} = 0$.

$\ln|x| - \dfrac{1}{v} = C \Rightarrow \ln|x| - \dfrac{x}{y} = C$ or $y = \dfrac{x}{\ln|x| + C}$.

16. $(xe^{y/x} + y)\,dx - x\,dy = 0 \Rightarrow x\,dy = (xe^{y/x} + y)\,dx \Rightarrow \dfrac{dy}{dx} = e^{y/x} + \dfrac{y}{x}$.

$\therefore F(v) = e^v + v$, and $\dfrac{dx}{x} + \dfrac{dv}{v - e^v - v} = 0 \Rightarrow \dfrac{dx}{x} - e^{-v}\,dv = 0$.

$\ln|x| + e^{-v} = C \Rightarrow \ln|x| + e^{-(y/x)} = C$

17. $(x+y)\,dy + (x-y)\,dx = 0 \Rightarrow (x+y)\,dy = (y-x)\,dx \Rightarrow \dfrac{dy}{dx} = \dfrac{y-x}{x+y} = \dfrac{\frac{y}{x}-1}{1+\frac{y}{x}}$.

$F(v) = \dfrac{v-1}{v+1}$ so $\dfrac{dx}{x} + \dfrac{dv}{v - \frac{v-1}{v+1}} = 0 \Rightarrow \dfrac{dx}{x} + \dfrac{v+1}{v^2+1}\,dv = 0$.

$\ln|x| + \frac{1}{2}\ln(v^2+1) + \tan^{-1} v = C \Rightarrow \ln|x| + \frac{1}{2}\ln\left(\frac{y^2}{x^2}+1\right) + \tan^{-1}\frac{y}{x} = C$

or $\frac{1}{2}\ln(x^2+y^2) + \tan^{-1}\frac{y}{x} = C$

18. $\dfrac{dy}{dx} = \dfrac{y}{x} + \cos\dfrac{y-x}{x} = \dfrac{y}{x} + \cos\left(\dfrac{y}{x}-1\right)$. $\therefore F(v) = v + \cos(v-1)$, so

$\dfrac{dx}{x} + \dfrac{dv}{v - v - \cos(v-1)} = 0 \Rightarrow \dfrac{dx}{x} = \sec(v-1)\,dv$

$\ln|x| = \ln|\sec(v-1) + \tan(v-1)| + C$

$\ln|x| = \ln\left|\sec\dfrac{y-x}{x} + \tan\dfrac{y-x}{x}\right| + C$

19. $\left(x\sin\frac{y}{x} - y\cos\frac{y}{x}\right)dx + \left(x\cos\frac{y}{x}\right)dy = 0 \Rightarrow \dfrac{dy}{dx} = \dfrac{y}{x} - \tan\dfrac{y}{x}$.

$F(v) = v - \tan v$ and $\dfrac{dx}{x} + \dfrac{dv}{v - v + \tan v} = 0 \Rightarrow \dfrac{dx}{x} + \cot v\,dv = 0$

$\ln|x| + \ln|\sin v| = C \Rightarrow \ln\left|\sin\frac{y}{x}\right| = \ln C - \ln|x| \Rightarrow \sin\frac{y}{x} = \frac{C}{x}$.

20. Let $x = r + a$ and $y = s + b \Rightarrow dx = dr$ and $dy = ds$. Thus

$x + y + 1 = r + a + s + b + s = (r+s) + (a+b+1)$ and

$y - x - 3 = s + b - r - a - 3 = (s-r) + (-a+b-3)$

$\therefore a + b = -1$ and $-a + b = 3 \Rightarrow a = -2$ and $b = 1$. The transformed

equation is $(r+s)dr + (s-r)\,ds = 0 \Rightarrow \dfrac{ds}{dr} = \dfrac{r+s}{r-s} = \dfrac{1+\frac{s}{r}}{1-\frac{s}{r}}$.

$\dfrac{dr}{r} - \dfrac{dv}{v - \left(\frac{1+v}{1-v}\right)} = 0 \Rightarrow \displaystyle\int\frac{dr}{r} - \int\frac{1}{1+v^2}\,dv + \int\frac{v}{1+v^2}\,dv = 0$

$\ln|r| - \tan^{-1} v + \frac{1}{2}\ln(1+v^2) = C$ or

$\ln|x+2| - \tan^{-1}\dfrac{y-1}{x+2} + \dfrac{1}{2}\ln\left[1 + \dfrac{(y-1)^2}{(x+2)^2}\right] = C$ or

$\ln\left[(x+2)^2 + (y-1)^2\right] - 2\tan^{-1}\dfrac{y-1}{x+2} = C$

21. $x\,dy - 2y\,dx = 0 \Rightarrow \frac{dy}{y} = \frac{2\,dx}{x} \Rightarrow \ln|y| = 2\ln|x| + C$ or $y = C_1 x^2$,

a family of parabolas. The orthogonal trajectories are:

$2y\,dy + x\,dx = 0 \Rightarrow y^2 + \frac{1}{2}x^2 = C$, a family of ellipses.

22. $2xy\,dy + (x^2 - y^2)\,dx = 0 \Rightarrow \frac{dy}{dx} = \frac{y^2 - x^2}{2xy} = \frac{1}{2}\left(\frac{y}{x}\right) - \frac{1}{2\left(\frac{y}{x}\right)}$.

$F(v) = \frac{1}{2}v - \frac{1}{2v}$, and $\frac{dx}{x} + \frac{dv}{v - \frac{1}{2}v + \frac{1}{2v}} = 0$

$\frac{dx}{x} + \frac{2v\,dv}{v^2+1} = 0 \Rightarrow \ln|x| + \ln|v^2 + 1| = C$ or $\ln|x| + \ln\left(\frac{y^2 + x^2}{x^2}\right) = C$

$\ln(x^2 + y^2) - \ln|x| = \ln C \Rightarrow x^2 + y^2 = Cx$ (a family of circles)

Orthogonal trajectories: $(y^2 - x^2)dx - 2xy\,dy = 0 \Rightarrow \frac{dy}{dx} = \frac{y^2 - x^2}{2xy}$.

This leads to the same family of solutions.

23. $xy = C \Rightarrow x\,dy + y\,dx = 0$. $\therefore$ $y\,dy - x\,dx = 0 \Rightarrow \frac{1}{2}y^2 - \frac{1}{2}x^2 = C$

or $y^2 - x^2 = C'$.

Linear

24. $\frac{dy}{dx} + 2y = e^{-x}$; $\int P(x)\,dx = \int 2\,dx = 2x$. Let $\rho = e^{2x}$.

Then $e^{2x}\frac{dy}{dx} + 2ye^{2x} = e^{x} \Rightarrow ye^{2x} = \int e^{x}\,dx$.

$\therefore$ $ye^{2x} = e^{x} + C$ or $y = e^{-x} + Ce^{-2x}$.

25. $2\frac{dy}{dx} - y = e^{x/2} \Rightarrow \frac{dy}{dx} - \frac{1}{2}y = \frac{1}{2}e^{x/2}$; $\int P(x)\,dx = \int -\frac{1}{2}dx = -\frac{1}{2}x$. Let $\rho = e^{-x/2}$.

Then $e^{-x/2}\frac{dy}{dx} - \frac{1}{2}e^{-x/2}y = \frac{1}{2} \Rightarrow e^{-x/2}y = \int \frac{1}{2}dx$.

$\therefore$ $e^{-x/2}y = \frac{1}{2}x + C$ or $y = \frac{1}{2}xe^{x/2} + Ce^{x/2} = \frac{1}{2}e^{x/2}(x + C')$.

26. $x\frac{dy}{dx} + 3y = \frac{\sin x}{x^2} \Rightarrow \frac{dy}{dx} + \frac{3}{x}y = \frac{\sin x}{x^3}$

$\int P(x)\,dx = \int \frac{3}{x}\,dx = 3\ln x$. Let $\rho = e^{3\ln x} = x^3$

Then $x^3\frac{dy}{dx} + 3x^3 y = \sin x \Rightarrow x^3 y = \int \sin x\,dx$.

$\therefore$ $x^3 y = -\cos x + C$ or $y = \frac{1}{x^3}(C - \cos x)$.

27. $x\,dy + y\,dx = \sin x\,dx \Rightarrow \dfrac{dy}{dx} + \dfrac{1}{x}y = \dfrac{\sin x}{x}$

$\int P(x)\,dx = \int \dfrac{1}{x}\,dx = \ln x$. Let $\rho = e^{\ln x} = x$

Then $x\dfrac{dy}{dx} + y = \sin x \Rightarrow xy = \int \sin x\,dx$.

$\therefore\ xy = -\cos x + C$ or $y = \dfrac{1}{x}(C - \cos x)$.

28. $x\,dy + y\,dx = y\,dy \Rightarrow y\,dx = (y - x)\,dy \Rightarrow \dfrac{dx}{dy} + \dfrac{1}{y}x = 1$

$\int P(y)\,dy = \int \dfrac{1}{y}\,dy = \ln y$. Let $\rho = e^{\ln y} = y$

Then $y\dfrac{dx}{dy} + x = y \Rightarrow xy = \int y\,dy$.

$\therefore\ xy = \dfrac{1}{2}y^2 + C$ or $x = \dfrac{y}{2} + \dfrac{C}{y}$

29. $(x-1)^3\dfrac{dy}{dx} + 4(x-1)^2 y = x + 1 \Rightarrow \dfrac{dy}{dx} + \dfrac{4}{x-1}y = \dfrac{x+1}{(x-1)^3}$

$\int P(x)\,dx = \int \dfrac{4}{x-1}\,dx = 4\ln(x-1)$. Let $\rho = (x-1)^4$

Then $(x-1)^4\dfrac{dy}{dx} + 4(x-1)^3 = x^2 - 1 \Rightarrow (x-1)^4 y = \int (x^2 - 1)dx$.

$\therefore\ (x-1)^4 y = \dfrac{1}{3}x^3 - x + C$ or $y = \dfrac{1}{(x-1)^4}\left(\dfrac{1}{3}x^3 - x + C\right)$

30. $\cosh x\,dy + (y\sinh x + e^x)\,dx = 0 \Rightarrow \dfrac{dy}{dx} + (\tanh x)\,y = -\dfrac{e^x}{\cosh x}$

$\int P(x)\,dx = \int \tanh x\,dx = \ln(\cosh x)$. Let $\rho = \cosh x$

Then $\cosh x\dfrac{dy}{dx} + \sinh x = -e^x \Rightarrow y\cosh x = \int -e^x\,dx$.

$\therefore\ y\cosh x = -e^x + C$ or $y = \operatorname{sech} x\,(C - e^x)$

31. $e^{2y}\,dx + 2(xe^{2y} - y)\,dy = 0 \Rightarrow \dfrac{dx}{dy} + 2x = 2y\,e^{-2y}$

$\int P(y)\,dy = \int 2\,dy = 2y$. Let $\rho = e^{2y}$

Then $e^{2y}\dfrac{dx}{dy} + 2xe^{2y} = 2y \Rightarrow xe^{2y} = \int 2y\,dy$.

$\therefore\ xe^{2y} = y^2 + C$ or $x = e^{-2y}(y^2 + C)$

32. $(x - 2y)dy + y\,dx = 0 \Rightarrow \frac{dx}{dy} + \frac{1}{y}x = 2$

$\int P(y)\,dy = \int \frac{1}{y}dy = \ln y$. Let $\rho = y$

Then $y\frac{dx}{dy} + x = 2y \Rightarrow xy = \int 2y\,dy$.

$\therefore xy = y^2 + C$ or $x = y + \frac{C}{y}$

33. $(y^2 + 1)\,dx + (2xy + 1)\,dy = 0 \Rightarrow \frac{dx}{dy} + \frac{2y}{y^2+1}x = -\frac{1}{y^2+1}$

$\int P(y)\,dy = \int \frac{2y}{y^2+1}\,dy = \ln(y^2+1)$. Let $\rho = y^2 + 1$

Then $(y^2+1)\frac{dx}{dy} + x = -1 \Rightarrow (y^2+1)x = \int -dy$.

$\therefore (y^2+1)x = -y + C$ or $x = \frac{1}{y^2+1}(C - y)$

34. (a) $\frac{dc}{dt} = \frac{G}{100V} - kc \Rightarrow \frac{dc}{dt} + kc = \frac{G}{100V}$. Let $\rho = e^{kt}$. Then

$ce^{kt} = \frac{G}{100k\,V}e^{kt} + C$. If $c(0) = c_0$, $C = c_0 - \frac{G}{100k\,V}$

$$c = e^{-kt}\left(c_0 - \frac{G}{100k\,V}\right) + \frac{G}{100k\,V}$$

(b) $\lim_{t\to\infty} c(t) = \frac{G}{100k\,V}$

35. $\frac{dx}{dt} = 1000 + 0.08x + 50t \Rightarrow \frac{dx}{dt} - 0.08x = 1000 + 50t$. Let $\rho = e^{-0.08t}$.

$e^{-0.08t}\frac{dx}{dt} - 0.08xe^{-0.08t} = 1000e^{-0.08t} + 50te^{-0.08t}$

$xe^{-0.08t} = -12{,}500e^{-0.08t} + 50(-12.5te^{-0.08t} - 156.25e^{-0.08t}) + C$

$$x = -12{,}500 - 625t - 7{,}812.5 + Ce^{-0.08t}$$

$x(0) = 1000 \Rightarrow C = 21{,}312.5$. Therefore,

$$x = -20{,}312.5 - 625t + 21{,}312.5e^{-0.08t}$$

36. (a) $(\cos x + y\cos x)\,dx + dy = 0 \Rightarrow \frac{dy}{1+y} = -\cos x\,dx$

$\ln(1+y) = -\sin x + C$

(b) $y\left(\frac{\pi}{2}\right) = 0 \Rightarrow C = 1$. $\therefore \ln(1+y) = 1 - \sin x$ or $y = e^{1-\sin x} - 1$

37. (a) $\frac{dy}{dx} + 2y = x$; let $\rho = e^{2x}$. Then $ye^{2x} = \int xe^{2x}\,dx = \frac{1}{2}xe^{2x} - \frac{1}{4}e^{2x} + C$

$y = \frac{1}{2}x - \frac{1}{4} + Ce^{-2x}$

(b) $y(0) = 1 \Rightarrow C = \frac{5}{4}$ $\therefore y = \frac{1}{2}x - \frac{1}{4} + \frac{5}{4}e^{-2x}$

38. (a) $(x + xy^2)\,dx + (y - x^2 y)\,dy = 0 \Rightarrow \dfrac{y\,dy}{1+y^2} = \dfrac{-x\,dx}{1-x^2}$

$\frac{1}{2}\ln(1+y^2) = \frac{1}{2}\ln(1-x^2) + C$

(b) $y(0) = 1 \Rightarrow C = \ln 2$. $\therefore\ \frac{1}{2}\ln(1+y^2) = \frac{1}{2}\ln(1-x^2) + \ln 2$

$1 + y^2 = 2(1 - x^2)$ or $y = \pm\sqrt{1 - 2x^2}$

39. (a) $(1 + y^2)\,dx + e^{-x}\,dy = 0 \Rightarrow \dfrac{dy}{1+y^2} = -e^x\,dx$

$\tan^{-1} y = -e^x + C$

(b) $y(0) = 1 \Rightarrow C = 1 + \frac{\pi}{4}$. $\therefore\ \tan^{-1} y = -e^x + 1 + \frac{\pi}{4}$

$y = \tan\left(1 + \frac{\pi}{4} - e^x\right)$

40. (a) $x\dfrac{dy}{dx} + 2y = x^3 \Rightarrow \dfrac{dy}{dx} + \dfrac{2}{x}y = x^2$. Let $\rho = x^2$. Then

$x^2 y = \int x^4\,dx = \frac{1}{5}x^5 + C \Rightarrow y = \frac{1}{5}x^3 + \dfrac{C}{x^2}$

(b) $y(2) = 1 \Rightarrow C = -12$ $\therefore\ y = \frac{1}{5}x^3 - \dfrac{12}{x^2}$

41. (a) $(x + 2y)\,dx + (y + 2x)\,dy = 0 \Rightarrow x\,dx + (2y\,dx + 2x\,dy) + y\,dy = 0$

$\frac{1}{2}x^2 + 2xy + \frac{1}{2}y^2 = C$ or $x^2 + 4xy + y^2 = C$

(b) $y(1) = 1 \Rightarrow C = 6$. $\therefore\ x^2 + 4xy + y^2 = 6$

42. (a) $(x + 2y)\,dx + (y - 2x)\,dy = 0 \Rightarrow \dfrac{dy}{dx} = \dfrac{x + 2y}{2x - y} = \dfrac{1 + 2\left(\frac{y}{x}\right)}{2 - \frac{y}{x}}$

$$\frac{dx}{x} + \frac{dv}{v - \dfrac{1+2v}{2-v}} = 0 \Rightarrow \frac{dx}{x} + \frac{v-2}{v^2+1}\,dv = 0$$

$\ln|x| + \frac{1}{2}\ln(v^2 + 1) - 2\tan^{-1} v = C$

$\ln|x| + \frac{1}{2}\ln\left(\dfrac{y^2}{x^2} + 1\right) - 2\tan^{-1}\dfrac{y}{x} = C$

$\ln(y^2 + x^2) - 4\tan^{-1}\dfrac{y}{x} = C$

(b) $y(1) = 1 \Rightarrow C = \ln 2 - \pi$. $\therefore\ \ln(y^2 + x^2) - 4\tan^{-1}\dfrac{y}{x} = \ln 2 - \pi$

14.3 SECOND ORDER EQUATIONS REDUCIBLE TO FIRST ORDER

1. Let $p = \frac{dy}{dx}$ and $\frac{dp}{dx} = \frac{d^2y}{dx^2}$. Then $\frac{dp}{dx} + p = 0 \Rightarrow \frac{dp}{p} = -\,dx$

   $\ln p = -x + C \Rightarrow p = e^{-x+C} = C_1 e^{-x}$. $\therefore \frac{dy}{dx} = C_1 e^{-x} \Rightarrow y = -C_1 e^{-x} + C_2$

2. Let $p = \frac{dy}{dx}$ and $\frac{d^2y}{dx^2} = \frac{dp}{dx} = \frac{dp}{dy}\frac{dy}{dx} = p\frac{dp}{dy}$.

   Then $p\frac{dp}{dy} + yp = 0 \Rightarrow dp = -y\,dy \Rightarrow p = -\frac{1}{2}y^2 + C$

   $$\frac{dy}{dx} = -\frac{1}{2}y^2 + C = \frac{2C - y^2}{2} \Rightarrow \frac{dy}{2C - y^2} = \frac{1}{2}dx$$

   Case I: $2C < 0$. Then $\frac{dy}{2C + y^2} = -\frac{1}{2}dx$. Let $B^2 = 2C$. We have

   $$\frac{1}{B}\tan^{-1}\frac{y}{B} = -\frac{1}{2}x + C_1 \quad \text{or } y = B\tan\left[B\left(C_1 - \frac{x}{2}\right)\right]$$

   Case 2: $C = 0$. Then $\frac{dy}{y^2} = -\frac{1}{2}dx \Rightarrow -\frac{1}{y} = -\frac{1}{2}x + C_1$ or $y = \frac{2}{x - 2C_1}$

   Case 3: $C > 0$. Then $\frac{dy}{2C - y^2} = \frac{1}{2}dx$. Let $B^2 = 2C$. Then

   $$\frac{1}{2B}\int\left(\frac{1}{B+y} + \frac{1}{B-y}\right)dy = \int\frac{1}{2}dx \Rightarrow \frac{1}{2B}\ln\frac{B+y}{B-y} = \frac{1}{2}x + C_1$$

3. Let $p = \frac{dy}{dx}$ and $\frac{dp}{dx} = \frac{d^2y}{dx^2}$. Then $\frac{dp}{dx} + xp = 0 \Rightarrow \frac{dp}{p} = -x\,dx$

   $\ln p = -\frac{x^2}{2} + C \Rightarrow p = C_1 e^{(-x^2/2)}$. $\therefore \frac{dy}{dx} = C_1 e^{(-x^2/2)} \Rightarrow$

   $y = C_1\int e^{(-x^2/2)}\,dx + C_2$, which cannot be evaluated as a

   finite combination of elementary functions.

4. Let $p = \frac{dy}{dx}$ and $\frac{dp}{dx} = \frac{d^2y}{dx^2}$. Then $x\frac{dp}{dx} + p = 0 \Rightarrow \frac{dp}{p} = -\frac{dx}{x}$

   $\ln|p| = -\ln|x| + C \Rightarrow p = C_1 x^{-1}$. $\therefore \frac{dy}{dx} = C_1 x^{-1} \Rightarrow y = C_1 \ln|x| + C_2$

5. Let $p = \frac{dy}{dx}$ and $\frac{d^2y}{dx^2} = \frac{dp}{dx} = \frac{dp}{dy}\frac{dy}{dx} = p\frac{dp}{dy}$.

Then $p\frac{dp}{dy} - y = 0 \Rightarrow p\,dp = y\,dy \Rightarrow \frac{1}{2}p^2 = \frac{1}{2}y^2 + C$

$p = \pm\sqrt{y^2 + 2C} \Rightarrow \frac{dy}{dx} = \pm\sqrt{y^2 + 2C}$

Case I: $2C < 0$. Then $\frac{dy}{\sqrt{y^2 - 2C}} = \pm dx$. Let $B^2 = 2C$. We have

$$\cosh^{-1}\frac{y}{B} = \pm x + C_1 \text{ or } y = B\cosh(C_1 \pm x)$$

Case 2: $C = 0$. Then $\frac{dy}{dx} = \pm y \Rightarrow \ln y = \pm x + C_1$ or $y = C_2 e^{\pm x}$

Case 3: $C > 0$. Then $\frac{dy}{\sqrt{y^2 + 2C}} = \pm dx$. Let $B^2 = 2C$. Then

$\sinh^{-1}\frac{y}{B} = C_2 \pm x$ or $y = B\sinh(C_2 \pm x)$

6. Let $p = \frac{dy}{dx}$ and $\frac{d^2y}{dx^2} = \frac{dp}{dx} = \frac{dp}{dy}\frac{dy}{dx} = p\frac{dp}{dy}$.

Then $p\frac{dp}{dy} + \omega^2 y = 0 \Rightarrow p\,dp = -\omega^2 y\,dy \Rightarrow \frac{1}{2}p^2 = -\frac{1}{2}\omega^2 y^2 + C$

$p = \pm\sqrt{2C - \omega^2 y^2} \Rightarrow \frac{dy}{dx} = \pm\sqrt{2C - \omega^2 y^2}$. $p^2 + \omega^2 y^2 = 2C \Rightarrow 2C \geq 0$.

Let $B^2 = 2C$. Then $\frac{dy}{\sqrt{\left(\frac{B}{\omega}\right)^2 - y^2}} = \pm\omega x \Rightarrow \sin^{-1}\frac{\omega y}{B} = \pm\omega x + C_1$

or $y = \frac{B}{\omega}\sin(C_1 \pm \omega x)$

7. Let $\frac{d^2y}{dx^2} = q \Rightarrow \frac{d^3y}{dx^3} = \frac{dq}{dx}$

Then $x\frac{dq}{dx} - 2q = 0 \Rightarrow \frac{dq}{q} = \frac{2}{x}dx \Rightarrow \ln q = \ln x^2 + C$

$q = C_1x^2 \Rightarrow \frac{d^2y}{dx^2} = C_1x^2 \Rightarrow \frac{dy}{dx} = \frac{1}{3}C_1x^3 + C_2 \Rightarrow y = \frac{1}{12}C_1x^4 + C_2x + C_3$

8. Let $p = \frac{dy}{dx} \Rightarrow \frac{dp}{dx} = \frac{d^2y}{dx^2}$

Then $\frac{dp}{dx} + p^2 + 1 = 0 \Rightarrow \frac{dp}{p^2 + 1} = -dx \Rightarrow \tan^{-1}p = C - x$

$p = \tan(C - x) \Rightarrow \frac{dy}{dx} = \tan(C - x) \Rightarrow y = -\ln|\cos(C - x)| + C_1$

9. (a) $y = C_1 \sin(x + C_2)$; $y(0) = 0 \Rightarrow 0 = C_1 \sin C_2 \Rightarrow C_2 = 0$

$$y\left(\frac{\pi}{2}\right) = 5 \Rightarrow 5 = C_1 \sin\frac{\pi}{2} \Rightarrow C_1 = 5 \text{ and } y = 5 \sin x$$

(b) $y' = C_1 \cos(x + C_2)$; $y'(0) = 2 \Rightarrow 2 = C_1 \cos 0 \Rightarrow C_1 = 3$ and $y = 2 \sin x$

10. $m\dfrac{d^2x}{dt^2} = -kx$. Let $p = \dfrac{dx}{dt}$ and $\dfrac{d^2x}{dt^2} = \dfrac{dp}{dt} = \dfrac{dp}{dx}\cdot\dfrac{dx}{dt} = p\dfrac{dp}{dx}$

Then $mp\dfrac{dp}{dx} + kx = 0 \Rightarrow \dfrac{1}{2}mp^2 = -\dfrac{1}{2}kx^2 + C \Rightarrow p = \pm\sqrt{\dfrac{2C - kx^2}{m}}$

$\dfrac{1}{2}mp^2 + \dfrac{1}{2}kx^2 = C \Rightarrow C \geq 0$. Hence $\dfrac{dx}{dt} = \pm\sqrt{\dfrac{2C - kx^2}{m}} \Rightarrow$

$$\frac{dx}{\sqrt{2C - kx^2}} = \pm\frac{dt}{\sqrt{m}} \Rightarrow \frac{1}{\sqrt{k}}\sin^{-1}\sqrt{\frac{2C}{k}}\,x = \pm\frac{1}{\sqrt{m}}t + C$$

$$\sin^{-1}\sqrt{\frac{2C}{k}}\,x = \pm\sqrt{\frac{k}{m}}\,t + B \Rightarrow x = A \sin\left(\pm\sqrt{\frac{k}{m}}\,t + B\right).$$

11. We have $m\dfrac{d^2x}{dt^2} = mg - k\dfrac{dx}{dt}$. Let $p = \dfrac{dx}{dt}$ and $\dfrac{d^2x}{dt^2} = \dfrac{dp}{dt}$

Then $m\dfrac{dp}{dx} + kp = 0 = mg \Rightarrow \dfrac{dp}{dx} + \dfrac{k}{m}p = g$. Let $\rho = e^{(k/m)t}$ so that

$$pe^{(k/m)t} = \int ge^{(k/m)t}\,dt = \frac{mg}{k}e^{(k/m)t} + C \Rightarrow p = \frac{mg}{k} + Ce^{-(k/m)t}$$

$\dfrac{dx}{dt} = \dfrac{mg}{k} + Ce^{-(k/m)t} \Rightarrow x = \dfrac{mg}{k}t - \dfrac{mC}{k}e^{-(k/m)t} + C_1$. $t = 0 \Rightarrow x = 0$

and $\dfrac{dx}{dt} = 0$, so $C = -\dfrac{mg}{k}$ and $C_1 = -\dfrac{m^2g}{k^2}$. Thus $x = \dfrac{mg}{k}t + \dfrac{m^2g}{k^2}[e^{-(k/m)t} - 1]$.

12. $u = \cos x \Rightarrow u' = -\sin x$ and $u'' = -\cos x$. $\therefore u'' + u = -\cos x + \cos x = 0$.

Let $y = uv = v\cos x$. Then $y' = -v\sin x + v'\cos x$ and

$y'' = -v\cos x - v'\sin x + v''\cos x - v'\sin x$. Substituting,

$v''\cos x - 2v'\sin x = 0$. Let $v'p$ and $v'' = \dfrac{dp}{dx}$. Then

$\cos x\dfrac{dp}{dx} - 2p\sin x = 0 \Rightarrow \dfrac{dp}{p} = 2\tan x\,dx \Rightarrow \ln p = 2\ln(\sec x) + C$

$\therefore p = C_1\sec^2 x \Rightarrow \dfrac{dv}{dx} = C_1\sec^2 x \Rightarrow V = C_1\tan x + C_2$. The general

solution is $y = C_1\sin x + C_2\cos x$.

13. $u = x^2 \Rightarrow u' = 2x$ and $u'' = 2$. $\therefore$ $x^2 y'' - 2y = 2x^2 - 2x^2 = 0$

Let $y = uv = vx^2$. Then $y' = 2xv + x^2 v'$ and

$y'' = 2xv' + 2v + x^2 v'' + 2xv'$. Substituting,

$2x^3 v' - 2vx^2 + x^4 v'' + 2x^3 v' - 2x^2 v = 0$ or $x^4 v'' + 4x^3 v' = 0$

Let $v' = p$ and $v'' = \frac{dp}{dx} \Rightarrow x^4 \frac{dp}{dx} + 4x^3 p = 0 \Rightarrow \frac{dp}{p} = -\frac{4}{x} dx$

$\therefore \ln p = -4 \ln x + C \Rightarrow p = Cx^{-4} \Rightarrow \frac{dv}{dx} = Cx^{-4} \Rightarrow v = -\frac{1}{3} C_1 x^{-3} + C_2$.

The general solution is $y = \frac{A}{x} + Bx^2$

14. $u = e^{-x} \Rightarrow u' = -e^{-x}$ and $u'' = e^{-x}$. $\therefore$ $y'' - y' - 2y = e^{-x} + e^{-x} - 2e^{-x} = 0$

Let $y = uv = ve^{-x}$. Then $y' = v'e^{-x} - ve^{-x}$ and

$y'' = v''e^{-x} - 2v'e^{-x} + ve^{-x}$. Substituting,

$v''e^{-x} - 2v'e^{-x} + ve^{-x} - v'e^{-x} + ve^{-x} - 2ve^{-x} = 0$ or $v'' - 3v' = 0$

Let $v' = p$ and $v'' = \frac{dp}{dx} \Rightarrow \frac{dp}{dx} - 3p = 0 \Rightarrow \frac{dp}{p} = 3\,dx$

$\therefore p = Ce^{3x} \Rightarrow \frac{dv}{dx} = Ce^{3x} \Rightarrow v = Ce^{3x} + C_2$. The general

solution is $y = Ce^{2x} + C_2 e^{-x}$.

15. $u = x^{1/2} \Rightarrow u' = \frac{1}{2} x^{-1/2}$ and $u'' = -\frac{1}{4} x^{-3/2}$. $\therefore$ $y'' + \frac{y}{4x^2} = -\frac{1}{4} x^{-3/2} + \frac{x^{1/2}}{4x^2} = 0$

Let $y = uv = vx^{1/2}$. Then $y' = \frac{1}{2} x^{-1/2} v + x^{1/2} v'$ and

$y'' = -\frac{1}{4} x^{-3/2} + x^{-1/2} v' + x^{1/2} v''$. Substituting,

we get $x^{1/2} v'' + x^{-1/2} v' = 0$ or $v'' + \frac{1}{x} v' = 0$.

Let $v' = p$ and $v'' = \frac{dp}{dx} \Rightarrow \frac{dp}{dx} + \frac{1}{x} p = 0 \Rightarrow \frac{dp}{p} = -\frac{dx}{x} \Rightarrow p = \frac{C}{x}$

$\therefore \frac{dv}{dx} = \frac{C}{x} \Rightarrow v = C \ln |x| + C_2$. The general

solution is $y = x^{1/2} (C \ln |x| + C_2)$

16. $u = x \Rightarrow u' = 1$ and $u'' = 0$. $\therefore\ x^2 y'' + xy' - y = x - x = 0$

Let $y = uv = vx$. Then $y' = v + xv'$ and

$y'' = v' + xv'' + v''$. Substituting,

we get $x^2(x+1)v'' + 2x^2 v' = 0$ or $v'' + \dfrac{2}{x+1} v' = 0$.

Let $v' = p$ and $v'' = \dfrac{dp}{dx} \Rightarrow \dfrac{dp}{dx} + \dfrac{2}{x+1} p = 0 \Rightarrow \dfrac{dp}{p} = -\dfrac{2\,dx}{x+1} \Rightarrow p = \dfrac{C_1}{(x+1)^2}$

$\therefore\ v = -\dfrac{C_1}{x+1} + C_2$. The general solution is $y = x\left(C_2 - \dfrac{C_1}{x+1}\right)$

17. Let $y = uv$. Then $y' = uv' + vu'$ and $y'' = uv'' + 2v'u' + vu''$

Substituting into $y'' + Py' + Qy = F$ gives

$(u'' + Pu' + Qu)v + uv'' + (Pu + 2u')v' = F$ or $v'' + \left(P + \dfrac{2u'}{u}\right)v' = F$

Let $w = v'$ and $w' = v''$. Then $w' + \left(P + \dfrac{2u'}{u}\right)w = \dfrac{F}{u}$

Let $y = ve^x \Rightarrow y' = ve^x + v'e^x$ and $y'' = ve^x + 2v'e^x + v''e^x$.

Then $y'' - 2y' + y = e^x \Rightarrow ve^x + 2v'e^x + v''e^x - 2ve^x - 2v'e^x + ve^x = e^x$.

$v''e^x = e^x \Rightarrow v'' = 1$. Let $w = v'$ and $w' = v''$. Then $w' = 1 \Rightarrow$

$w = x + C_1 = v' \Rightarrow v = \dfrac{1}{2}x^2 + C_1 x + C_2 \Rightarrow y = e^x\left(\dfrac{1}{2}x^2 + C_1 x + C_2\right)$.

14.4 LINEAR SECOND ORDER HOMOGENEOUS EQUATIONS WITH CONSTANT COEFFICIENTS

1. $\dfrac{d^2y}{dx^2} + 2\dfrac{dy}{dx} = 0 \qquad r^2 + 2r = 0 \Rightarrow r(r+2) = 0$ or $r = 0$ or -2

$\therefore\ y = C_1 + C_2 e^{-2x}$

2. $\dfrac{d^2y}{dx^2} + 5\dfrac{dy}{dx} + 6y = 0 \qquad r^2 + 5r + 6 = 0 \Rightarrow (r+2)(r+3) = 0$ or $r = -2$ or -3

$\therefore\ y = C_1 e^{-3x} + C_2 e^{-2x}$

3. $\dfrac{d^2y}{dx^2} + 6\dfrac{dy}{dx} + 5y = 0 \qquad r^2 + 6r + 5 = 0 \Rightarrow (r+1)(r+5) = 0$ or $r = -1$ or -5

$\therefore\ y = C_1 e^{-x} + C_2 e^{-5x}$

4. $\dfrac{d^2y}{dx^2} - 2\dfrac{dy}{dx} - 3y = 0 \qquad r^2 - 2r - 3 = 0 \Rightarrow (r+1)(r-3) = 0$

or $r = -1$ or 3 $\quad\therefore\ y = C_1 e^{-x} + C_2 e^{3x}$

5. $\dfrac{d^2y}{dx^2} + \dfrac{dy}{dx} + y = 0 \qquad r^2 + r + 1 = 0 \Rightarrow r = \dfrac{-1 \pm \sqrt{1-4}}{2}$

or $r = -\dfrac{1}{2} \pm i\dfrac{\sqrt{3}}{2} \quad \therefore \quad y = e^{-(x/2)}\left(C_1 \cos\dfrac{\sqrt{3}}{2} + C_2 \sin\dfrac{\sqrt{3}}{2}\right)$

6. $\dfrac{d^2y}{dx^2} - 4\dfrac{dy}{dx} + 4y = 0 \qquad r^2 - 4r + 4 = 0 \Rightarrow r = 2, 2$

$\therefore \quad y = (C_1 + C_2 x)e^{2x}$

7. $\dfrac{d^2y}{dx^2} + 6\dfrac{dy}{dx} + 9y = 0 \qquad r^2 + 6r + 9 = 0 \Rightarrow r = -3, -3$

$\therefore \quad y = (C_1 + C_2 x)e^{-3x}$

8. $\dfrac{d^2y}{dx^2} - 6\dfrac{dy}{dx} + 10y = 0 \qquad r^2 - 6r + 10 = 0 \Rightarrow r = \dfrac{6 \pm \sqrt{36-40}}{2}$

or $r = 3 \pm i \quad \therefore \quad y = e^{3x}(C_1 \cos x + C_2 \sin x)$

9. $\dfrac{d^2y}{dx^2} - 2\dfrac{dy}{dx} + 4y = 0 \qquad r^2 - 2r + 4 = 0 \Rightarrow r = \dfrac{2 \pm \sqrt{4-16}}{2}$

or $r = 1 \pm \sqrt{3}\, i \quad \therefore \quad y = e^{x}(C_1 \cos\sqrt{3}\,x + C_2 \sin\sqrt{3}\,x)$

10. $\dfrac{d^2y}{dx^2} - 10\dfrac{dy}{dx} + 16y = 0 \qquad r^2 - 10r + 16 = 0 \Rightarrow (r-2)(r-8) = 0$

or $r = 2, 8 \quad \therefore \quad y = C_1 e^{2x} + C_2 e^{8x}$

11. $y'' - y = 0 \qquad r^2 - 1 = 0 \Rightarrow r = \pm 1$

$\therefore\ y = C_1 e^{x} + C_2 e^{-x}; \quad y' = C_1 e^{x} - C_2 e^{-x}$

$y(0) = 1 \Rightarrow 1 = C_1 + C_2. \quad y'(0) = -2 \Rightarrow -2 = C_1 - C_2 \Rightarrow C_1 = -\dfrac{1}{2}$ and $C_2 = \dfrac{3}{2}$.

$\therefore\ y = \dfrac{3}{2}e^{-x} - \dfrac{1}{2}e^{x}.$

12. $y'' + 2y' + y = 0 \qquad r^2 + 2r + 1 = 0 \Rightarrow (r+1)^2 = 0 \quad r = -1, -1$

$\therefore\ y = C_1 x e^{-x} + C_2 e^{-x}; \quad y' = C_1 e^{-x} - C_1 x e^{-x} - C_2 e^{-x}$

$y(0) = 0 \Rightarrow 0 = C_2. \quad y'(0) = 1 \Rightarrow 1 = -C_2 + C_1 \Rightarrow C_1 = 1. \quad \therefore\ y = xe^{-x}.$

13. $2y'' - y' - y = 0 \qquad 2r^2 - r - 1 = 0 \Rightarrow (2r+1)(r-1) = 0 \quad r = 1, -\dfrac{1}{2}$

$\therefore\ y = C_1 e^{x} + C_2 e^{-x/2}; \quad y' = C_1 e^{x} - \dfrac{1}{2} C_2 e^{-x/2}$

$y(0) = -1 \Rightarrow -1 = C_1 + C_2. \quad y'(0) = 0 \Rightarrow 0 = C_1 - \dfrac{1}{2} C_2 \Rightarrow C_2 = -\dfrac{2}{3},\ C_1 = -\dfrac{1}{3}.$

$\therefore\ y = -\dfrac{2}{3}e^{-x/2} - \dfrac{1}{3}e^{x}$

14. $y'' - 2y' + 3y = 0 \quad r^2 - 2r + 3 = 0 \Rightarrow r = \dfrac{2 \pm \sqrt{4-12}}{2} = 1 \pm \sqrt{2}i$

$y = e^x(C_1 \cos \sqrt{2}\,x + C_2 \sin \sqrt{2}x)$

$y' = e^x(C_1 \cos \sqrt{2}\,x + C_2 \sin \sqrt{2}x) + e^x(-\sqrt{2}\,C_1 \sin \sqrt{2}x + \sqrt{2}C_2 \cos \sqrt{2}x)$

$y(0) = 0 \Rightarrow 0 = C_1.\ y'(0) = 1 \Rightarrow C_2 \Rightarrow \dfrac{1}{\sqrt{2}}.\ \therefore y = \dfrac{1}{\sqrt{2}}e^x \sin \sqrt{2}\,x$

15. $y'' - 4y = 0 \quad r^2 - 4 = 0 \Rightarrow r = \pm 2$

$y = C_1 e^{2x} + C_2 e^{-2x}$ and $y' = 2C_1e^{2x} - 2C_2e^{-2x}$

$y(0) = 0 \Rightarrow 0 = C_1 + C_2.\ y'(0) = 3 \Rightarrow 3 = 2C_1 - 2C_2$

$C_1 = \dfrac{3}{4}$ and $C_2 = -\dfrac{3}{4} \quad \therefore y = \dfrac{3}{4}e^{2x} - \dfrac{3}{4}e^{-2x}$

16. $y'' - 4y = 0 \quad r^2 - 4 = 0 \Rightarrow r = \pm 2$

$y = C_1e^{2x} + C_2 e^{-2x}$ and $y' = 2C_1e^{2x} - 2C_2e^{-2x}$

$y(0) = 0 \Rightarrow 0 = C_1 + C_2.\ y'(0) = 2 \Rightarrow 2 = 2C_1 - 2C_2$

$C_1 = \dfrac{1}{2}$ and $C_2 = -\dfrac{1}{2} \quad \therefore y = \dfrac{1}{2}e^{2x} - \dfrac{1}{2}e^{-2x}$

17. $y'' + 4y = 0 \quad r^2 + 4 = 0 \Rightarrow r = \pm 2i$

$y = C_1\cos 2x + C_2 \sin 2x$ and $y' = -2\sin 2x + 2C_2\cos 2x$

$y(0) = 0 \Rightarrow 0 = C_1.\ y'(0) = 2 \Rightarrow 2 = 2C_2 \Rightarrow C_2 = 1$

$\therefore y = \sin 2x$

14.5 LINEAR SECOND ORDER NONHOMOGENEOUS EQUATIONS WITH CONSTANT COEFFICIENTS

1. $\dfrac{d^2y}{dx^2} + \dfrac{dy}{dx} = x \qquad r^2 + r = 0 \Rightarrow r(r+1) = 0 \Rightarrow r = 0$ or -1

Let $u_1 = 1$ and $u_2 = e^{-x}$. $D = \begin{vmatrix} 1 & e^{-x} \\ 0 & -e^{-x} \end{vmatrix} = -e^{-x}$

$v_1' = \dfrac{-xe^{-x}}{-e^{-x}} = x \Rightarrow v_1 = \dfrac{1}{2}x^2 + C_1$

$v_2' = \dfrac{x}{-e^{-x}} = -xe^x \Rightarrow v_2 = e^x(1-x) + C_2$

Then $y = \dfrac{1}{2}x^2 + C_1 + e^{-x}\left[\, e^x(1-x) + C_2 \,\right] = 1 - x + \dfrac{1}{2}x^2 + C_2 e^{-x} + C_1$

2. $\dfrac{d^2y}{dx^2} + y = \tan x,\ -\dfrac{\pi}{2} < x < \dfrac{\pi}{2}$ $\qquad r^2 + 1 = 0 \Rightarrow r = \pm i$

Let $u_1 = \cos x$ and $u_2 = \sin x$. $D = \begin{vmatrix} \cos x & \sin x \\ -\sin x & \cos x \end{vmatrix} = 1$

$$v_1' = -\sin x \tan x \Rightarrow v_1 = \int -\frac{\sin^2 x}{\cos x}dx$$

$$= \int (\cos x - \sec x)dx = \sin x - \ln|\sec x + \tan x| + C_1$$

$v_2' = \cos x \tan x = \sin x \Rightarrow v_2 = -\cos x + C_2$

Then $y = \cos x\left(\sin x - \ln|\sec x + \tan x| + C_1\right) + \sin x(-\cos x + C_2)$

$$= -\cos x \ln|\sec x + \tan x| + C_1 \cos x + C_2 \sin x$$

3. $\dfrac{d^2y}{dx^2} + y = \sin x$ $\qquad r^2 + 1 = 0 \Rightarrow r = \pm i$

Let $u_1 = \cos x$ and $u_2 = \sin x$. $D = \begin{vmatrix} \cos x & \sin x \\ -\sin x & \cos x \end{vmatrix} = 1$

$$v_1' = -\sin^2 x \Rightarrow v_1 = \int -\sin^2 x dx = -\frac{1}{2}x + \frac{1}{4}\sin 2x + C_1$$

$$v_2' = \cos x \sin x \Rightarrow v_2 = \int \cos x \sin x\, dx = \frac{1}{2}\sin^2 x + C_2$$

Then $y = \sin x\left(\dfrac{1}{2}\sin^2 x + C_2\right) + \cos x\left(-\dfrac{1}{2}x + \dfrac{1}{4}\sin 2x + C_1\right)$

$$= \frac{1}{2}\sin^3 x - \frac{1}{2}x\cos x + \frac{1}{4}\cos x \sin 2x + C_1 \cos x + C_2 \sin x$$

$$= C_1 \cos x + C_2 \sin x - \frac{1}{2}x\cos x + \frac{1}{2}\sin x(\cos^2 x + \sin^2 x)$$

$$= C_1 \cos x + C_3 \sin x - \frac{1}{2}x\cos x$$

4. $\dfrac{d^2y}{dx^2} + 2\dfrac{dy}{dx} + y = e^x$ $\qquad r^2 + 2r + 1 = 0 \Rightarrow r = -1, -1$

Let $u_1 = e^{-x}$ and $u_2 = xe^{-x}$. $D = \begin{vmatrix} e^{-x} & xe^{-x} \\ -e^{-x} & -xe^{-x} + e^{-x} \end{vmatrix} = e^{-2x}$

$$v_1' = -xe^{2x} \Rightarrow v_1 = \int -xe^{2x}dx = -\frac{1}{2}xe^{2x} + \frac{1}{4}e^{2x} + C_1$$

$$v_2' = e^{2x} \Rightarrow v_2 = \int e^{2x}dx = \frac{1}{2}e^{2x} + C_2$$

Then $y = xe^{-x}\left(\dfrac{1}{2}e^{2x} + C_2\right) + e^{-x}\left(-\dfrac{1}{2}xe^{2x} + \dfrac{1}{4}e^{2x} + C_1\right) = C_1 e^{-x} + C_2 xe^{-x} + \dfrac{1}{4}e^x$

5. $\dfrac{d^2y}{dx^2} + 2\dfrac{dy}{dx} + y = e^{-x}$ $\quad r^2 + 2r + 1 = 0 \Rightarrow r = -1, -1$

Let $u_1 = e^{-x}$ and $u_2 = xe^{-x}$ $\quad D = \begin{vmatrix} e^{-x} & xe^{-x} \\ -e^{-x} & -xe^{-x} + e^{-x} \end{vmatrix} = e^{-2x}$

$v_1' = -x \Rightarrow v_1 = \int -x\,dx = -\dfrac{1}{2}x^2 + C_1$

$v_2' = 1 \Rightarrow v_2 = \int dx = x + C_2$

Then $y = xe^{-x}\left(x + C_2\right) + e^{-x}\left(-\dfrac{1}{2}x^2 + C_1\right) = C_1 e^{-x} + C_2 xe^{-x} + \dfrac{1}{2}x^2 e^{x}$

6. $\dfrac{d^2y}{dx^2} - y = x$ $\quad r^2 - 1 = 0 \Rightarrow r = \pm 1$

Let $u_1 = e^x$ and $u_2 = e^{-x}$. $\quad D = \begin{vmatrix} e^x & e^{-x} \\ e^x & -e^{-x} \end{vmatrix} = -2$

$v_1' = \dfrac{1}{2}xe^{-x} \Rightarrow v_1 = \int \dfrac{1}{2}xe^{-x}\,dx = -\dfrac{1}{2}e^{-x}(x + 1) + C_1$

$v_2' = -\dfrac{1}{2}xe^{x} \Rightarrow v_2 = \int -\dfrac{1}{2}xe^{x}\,dx = -\dfrac{1}{2}e^{x}(x - 1) + C_2$

Then $y = e^x\left(-\dfrac{1}{2}e^{-x}(x + 1) + C_1\right) + e^{-x}\left(-\dfrac{1}{2}e^{x}(x - 1) + C_2\right) = C_1e^x + C_2e^{-x} - x$

7. $\dfrac{d^2y}{dx^2} - y = e^x$ $\quad r^2 - 1 = 0 \Rightarrow r = \pm 1$

Let $u_1 = e^x$ and $u_2 = e^{-x}$. $\quad D = \begin{vmatrix} e^x & e^{-x} \\ e^x & -e^{-x} \end{vmatrix} = -2$

$v_1' = \dfrac{1}{2} \Rightarrow v_1 = \int \dfrac{1}{2}\,dx = \dfrac{1}{2}x + C_1$

$v_2' = -\dfrac{1}{2}e^xe^x \Rightarrow v_2 = \int -\dfrac{1}{2}e^{2x}\,dx = -\dfrac{1}{4}e^{2x} + C_2$

Then $y = e^x\left(\dfrac{1}{2}x + C_1\right) + e^{-x}\left(-\dfrac{1}{4}e^{2x} + C_2\right)$

$= C_1 e^x + C_2 e^{-x} - \dfrac{1}{4}e^x + \dfrac{1}{2}xe^x = C_3e^x + C_2 e^{-x} + \dfrac{1}{2}xe^x$

8. $\frac{d^2y}{dx^2} - y = \sin x \qquad r^2 - 1 = 0 \Rightarrow r = \pm 1$

Let $u_1 = e^x$ and $u_2 = e^{-x}$. $D = \begin{vmatrix} e^x & e^{-x} \\ e^x & -e^{-x} \end{vmatrix} = -2$

$$v_1' = \frac{1}{2}e^{-x}\sin x \Rightarrow v_1 = \int \frac{1}{2}e^{-x}\sin x\, dx = -\frac{1}{4}e^{-x}(\sin x + \cos x) + C_1$$

$$v_2' = -\frac{1}{2}e^{x}\sin x \Rightarrow v_2 = \int -\frac{1}{2}e^{x}\sin x\, dx = -\frac{1}{4}e^{x}(\sin x - \cos x) + C_2$$

Then $y = e^x\left(-\frac{1}{4}e^{-x}(\sin x + \cos x) + C_1\right) + e^{-x}\left(-\frac{1}{4}e^{x}(\sin x - \cos x) + C_2\right)$

$$= C_1 e^x + C_2 e^{-x} - \frac{1}{2}\sin x$$

9. $\frac{d^2y}{dx^2} + 4\frac{dy}{dx} + 5y = 10 \qquad r^2 + 4r + 5 = 0 \Rightarrow r = -2 \pm i$

Let $u_1 = e^{-2x}\cos x$ and $u_2 = e^{-2x}\sin x$

$$D = \begin{vmatrix} e^{-2x}\cos x & e^{-2x}\sin x \\ -e^{-2x}(2\cos x + \sin x) & e^{-2x}(\cos x - 2\sin x) \end{vmatrix} = e^{-4x} \qquad v_1' = -10\, e^{2x}\sin x$$

$$v_1 = \int -10\, e^{2x}\sin x\, dx = -2e^{2x}(2\sin x - \cos x) + C_1$$

$$v_2' = 10\, e^{2x}\cos x \Rightarrow v_2 = \int 10\, e^{2x}\cos x\, dx = 2e^{2x}(2\cos x + \sin x) + C_2$$

$$y = e^{-2x}\cos x\,(-2e^{2x}(2\sin x - \cos x) + C_1) + e^{-2x}\sin x\,(2e^{2x}(2\cos x + \sin x) +$$

$$= e^{-2x}(C_1\cos x + C_2\sin x) + 2$$

10. $\frac{d^2y}{dx^2} - \frac{dy}{dx} = 2^x \qquad r^2 - r = 0 \Rightarrow r = 0, 1$

Let $u_1 = 1$ and $u_2 = e^x$. $D = \begin{vmatrix} 1 & e^x \\ 0 & e^x \end{vmatrix} = e^x$

$$v_1' = -2^x \Rightarrow v_1 = \int -2^x\, dx = -\frac{1}{\ln 2}2^x + C_1$$

$$v_2' = \left(\frac{2}{e}\right)^x \Rightarrow v_2 = \int \left(\frac{2}{e}\right)^x dx = \frac{1}{\ln 2 - 1}\left(\frac{2}{e}\right)^x + C_2$$

Then $y = \left(-\frac{1}{\ln 2}2^x + C_1\right) + e^x\left(\frac{1}{\ln 2 - 1}\left(\frac{2}{e}\right)^x + C_2\right)$

$$= C_1 + C_2 e^x + 2^x\left(\frac{1}{\ln 2 - 1} - \frac{1}{\ln 2}\right)$$

11. $\frac{d^2y}{dx^2} + y = \sec x, -\frac{\pi}{2} < x < \frac{\pi}{2}$ $\quad r^2 + 1 = 0 \Rightarrow r = \pm i$

Let $u_1 = \cos x$ and $u_2 = \sin x$ $\quad D = \begin{vmatrix} \cos x & \sin x \\ -\sin x & \cos x \end{vmatrix} = 1$

$v_1' = -\sin x \sec x = -\tan x \Rightarrow v_1 = \int -\tan x \, dx = \ln(\cos x) + C_1$

$v_2' = \cos x \sec x = 1 \Rightarrow v_2 = \int dx = x + C_2$

Then $y = \cos x(\ln(\cos x) + C_1) + \sin x(x + C_2)$

$= C_1 \cos x + C_2 \sin x + \cos x \ln(\cos x) + x \sin x$

12. $\frac{d^2y}{dx^2} - \frac{dy}{dx} = e^x \cos x, x > 0$ $\quad r^2 - r = 0 \Rightarrow r = 0, 1$

Let $u_1 = 1$ and $u_2 = e^x$. $\quad D = \begin{vmatrix} 1 & e^x \\ 0 & e^x \end{vmatrix} = e^x$

$v_1' = -e^x \cos x \Rightarrow v_1 = \int -e^x \cos x \, dx = -\frac{1}{2}e^x(\cos x + \sin x) + C_1$

$v_2' = \cos x \Rightarrow v_2 = \int \cos x \, dx = \sin x + C_2$

Then $y = -\frac{1}{2}e^x(\cos x + \sin x) + C_1 + e^x(\sin x + C_2)$

$= C_1 + C_2 e^x + \frac{1}{2}e^x(\sin x - \cos x)$

13. $\frac{d^2y}{dx^2} - 3\frac{dy}{dx} - 10y = -3$ $\quad r^2 - 3r - 10 = 0 \Rightarrow r = 5, -2$

$\therefore y_h = C_1 e^{5x} + C_2 e^{-2x}$. Guess $y_p = A$. Then $y_p' = y_p'' = 0$

$y_p'' - 3y_p' - 10y_p = -3 \Rightarrow -10A = -3 \Rightarrow A = \frac{3}{10}$

Then $y = y_h + y_p = C_1 e^{5x} + C_2 e^{-2x} + \frac{3}{10}$

14. $\frac{d^2y}{dx^2} - 3\frac{dy}{dx} - 10y = 2x - 3$ $\quad r^2 - 3r - 10 = 0 \Rightarrow r = 5, -2$

$\therefore y_h = C_1 e^{5x} + C_2 e^{-2x}$. Guess $y_p = Ax + B$. Then $y_p' = A$, $y_p'' = 0$

$y_p'' - 3y_p' - 10y_p = -3 \Rightarrow -3A - 10(Ax + B) = 2x - 3 \Rightarrow$

$-10Ax - (3A + 10B) = 2x - 3 \Rightarrow -10A = 2$ so $A = -\frac{1}{5}$; $3A + 10B = 3$ so $B = \frac{9}{25}$

Then $y = y_h + y_p = C_1 e^{5x} + C_2 e^{-2x} - \frac{1}{5}x + \frac{9}{25}$

15. $\dfrac{d^2y}{dx^2} - \dfrac{dy}{dx} = \sin x \qquad r^2 - r = 0 \Rightarrow r = 0, 1$

$\therefore y_h = C_1 + C_2 e^x$. Guess $y_p = A\cos x + B\sin x$.

Then $y_p' = -A \sin x + B \cos x$, $y_p'' = -A\cos x - B \sin x$

$y_p'' - y_p' = \sin x \Rightarrow -A\cos x - B \sin x + A \sin x - B \cos x = \sin x$

$(A - B) \sin x - (A + B) \cos x = \sin x$; $A - B = 1$ and $A + B = 0 \Rightarrow A = \dfrac{1}{2}$ and $B = -\dfrac{1}{2}$

Then $y = y_h + y_p = C_1 + C_2 e^x + \dfrac{1}{2}(\cos x - \sin x)$

16. $\dfrac{d^2y}{dx^2} + 2\dfrac{dy}{dx} + y = x^2 \qquad r^2 + 2r + 1 = 0 \Rightarrow r = -1, -1$

$\therefore y_h = C_1 e^{-x} + C_2 xe^{-x}$. Guess $y_p = Ax^2 + Bx + C$

Then $y_p' = 2A x + B$, $y_p'' = 2A$

$y_p'' + 2 y_p' + y_p = x^2 \Rightarrow Ax^2 + Bx + C + 4Ax + 4B + 2A = x^2$

$Ax^2 = x^2 \Rightarrow A = 1$; $4A + B = 0 \Rightarrow B = -4$; $2A + 4B + C = 0 \Rightarrow C = 6$

Then $y = y_h + y_p = C_1 e^{-x} + C_2 xe^{-x} + x^2 - 4x + 6$

17. $\dfrac{d^2y}{dx^2} + y = \cos 3x \qquad r^2 + 1 = 0 \Rightarrow r = \pm i$

$\therefore y_h = C_1 \cos x + C_2 \sin x$. Guess $y_p = A \cos 3x + B\sin 3x$.

Then $y_p' = -3A \sin 3x + 3B \cos 3x$, $y_p'' = -9A\cos 3x - 9B \sin 3x$

$y_p'' + y_p = \cos 3x \Rightarrow -8A \cos 3x - 8B \sin 3x = \cos 3x$

$-8A \cos 3x = \cos 3x \Rightarrow A = -\dfrac{1}{8}$; $B = 0$

Then $y = y_h + y_p = C_1 \cos x + C_2 \sin x - \dfrac{1}{8} \cos 3x$

18. $\dfrac{d^2y}{dx^2} + y = e^{2x} \qquad r^2 + 1 = 0 \Rightarrow r = \pm i$

$\therefore y_h = C_1 \cos x + C_2 \sin x$. Guess $y_p = A e^{2x}$.

Then $y_p' = 2A e^{2x}$, $y_p'' = 4A e^{2x}$

$y_p'' + y_p = e^{2x} \Rightarrow 4 A e^{2x} + A e^{2x} = e^{2x}$

$5A e^{2x} = e^{2x} \Rightarrow A = \dfrac{1}{5}$

Then $y = y_h + y_p = C_1 \cos x + C_2 \sin x + \dfrac{1}{5} e^{2x}$

19. $\frac{d^2y}{dx^2} - \frac{dy}{dx} - 2y = 20\cos x \quad r^2 - r - 2 = 0 \Rightarrow r = 2, -1$

$\therefore y_h = C_1e^{2x} + C_2e^{-x}$. Guess $y_p = A\cos x + B\sin x$.

Then $y_p' = -A\sin x + B\cos x$, $y_p'' = -A\cos x - B\sin x$

$-A\cos x - B\sin x + A\sin x - B\cos x - 2A\cos x - 2B\sin x = 20\cos x$

$(A - 3B)\sin x + (-3A - B)\cos x = 20\cos x$; $A = -6$, $B = -2$

Then $y = y_h + y_p = C_1e^{2x} + C_2e^{-x} - 6\cos x - 2\sin x$

20. $\frac{d^2y}{dx^2} + y = 2x + 3e^x \quad r^2 + 1 = 0 \Rightarrow r = \pm i$

$\therefore y_h = C_1\cos x + C_2\sin x$. Guess $y_p = Ax + B + Ce^x$.

Then $y_p' = A + Ce^x$, $y_p'' = Ce^x$

$Ce^x + Ax + B + Ce^x = 2x + 3e^x$

$2C = 3 \Rightarrow C = \frac{3}{2}$, $A = 2$, $B = 0$

Then $y = y_h + y_p = C_1\cos x + C_2\sin x + \frac{3}{2}e^x + 2x$

21. $\frac{d^2y}{dx^2} - y = e^x + x^2 \quad r^2 - 1 = 0 \Rightarrow r = \pm 1$

$\therefore y_h = C_1e^x + C_2e^{-x}$. Guess $y_p = Axe^x + Bx^2 + Cx + D$.

Then $y_p' = Ae^x + Axe^x + 2Bx + C$, $y_p'' = 2Ae^x + Axe^x + 2B$

$2Ae^x + Axe^x + 2B - Axe^x - Bx^2 - Cx - D = e^x + x^2$

$2Ae^x = e^x \Rightarrow A = \frac{1}{2}$, $B = -1$, $C = 0$, $D = -2$

Then $y = y_h + y_p = C_1e^x + C_2e^{-x} + \frac{1}{2}xe^x - x^2 - 2$

22. $\frac{d^2y}{dx^2} + 2\frac{dy}{dx} + y = 6\sin 2x \quad r^2 + 2r + 1 = 0 \Rightarrow r = -1, -1$

$\therefore y_h = C_1e^{-x} + C_2xe^{-x}$. Guess $y_p = A\sin 2x + B\cos 2x$.

Then $y_p' = 2A\cos 2x - 2B\sin 2x$, $y_p'' = -4A\sin 2x - 4B\cos 2x$

$-4A\sin 2x - 4B\cos 2x + 4A\cos 2x - 4B\sin 2x + A\sin 2x + B\cos 2x = 6\sin 2x$

$(-3A - 4B)\sin 2x + (-3B + 4A)\cos 2x = 6\sin 2x \Rightarrow A = -\frac{24}{25}$, $B = -\frac{18}{25}$

Then $y = y_h + y_p = C_1e^{-x} + C_2xe^{-x} - \frac{24}{25}\sin 2x - \frac{18}{25}\cos 2x$

23. $\frac{d^2y}{dx^2} - \frac{dy}{dx} - 6y = e^{-x} - 7\cos x \quad r^2 - r - 6 = 0 \Rightarrow r = -2, 3$

$\therefore y_h = C_1e^{-2x} + C_2e^{3x}$. Guess $y_p = Ae^{-x} + B\cos x + C\sin x$

Then $y_p' = -Ae^{-x} - B\sin x + C\cos x$, $y_p'' = Ae^{-x} - B\cos x - C\sin x$

$Ae^{-x} - B\cos x - C\sin x + Ae^{-x} + B\cos x - C\sin x - 6Ae^{-x}$

$\quad - 6B\cos x - 6A\sin x = e^{-x} - 7\cos x$

$-4Ae^{-x} = e^{-x} \Rightarrow A = -\frac{1}{4}$; $7B + C = 7$, $7C - B = 0 \Rightarrow B = \frac{49}{50}$, $C = \frac{7}{50}$

Then $y = y_h + y_p = C_1e^{-2x} + C_2e^{3x} - \frac{1}{4}e^{-x} + \frac{49}{50}\cos x + \frac{7}{50}\sin x$

24. $\frac{d^2y}{dx^2} + 3\frac{dy}{dx} + 2y = e^{-x} + e^{-2x} - x; \quad r^2 + 3r + 2 = 0 \Rightarrow r = -2, -1$

$\therefore y_h = C_1e^{-2x} + C_2e^{-x}$. Guess $y_p = Axe^{-x} + Bxe^{-2x} + Cx + D$

Then $y_p' = Ae^{-x} - Axe^{-x} + Be^{-2x} - 2Bxe^{-2x} + C$

$y_p'' = -2Ae^{-x} + Axe^{-x} - 4Be^{-2x} + 4Bxe^{-2x}$

$Ae^{-x} - Be^{-2x} + 2Cx + 2D + 3C = e^{-x} + e^{-2x} - x$

$A = 1$; $B = -1$, $C = -\frac{1}{2}$, $D = \frac{3}{4}$

Then $y = y_h + y_p = C_1e^{-2x} + C_2e^{-x} + xe^{-x} - xe^{-2x} - \frac{1}{2}x + \frac{3}{4}$

25. $\frac{d^2y}{dx^2} + 5\frac{dy}{dx} = 15x^2; \quad r^2 + 5r = 0 \Rightarrow r = 0, -5$

$\therefore y_h = C_1 + C_2e^{-5x}$. Guess $y_p = Ax^3 + Bx^2 + Cx$

Then $y_p' = 3Ax^2 + 2Bx + C$; $y_p'' = 6Ax + 2B$

$6Ax + 2B + 15Ax^2 + 10Bx + 5C = 15x^2$; $A = 1, B = -\frac{6}{10}, C = \frac{6}{25}$

Then $y = y_h + y_p = C_1 + C_2e^{-5x} + x^3 - \frac{3}{5}x^2 + \frac{6}{25}x$

26. $\frac{d^2y}{dx^2} - \frac{dy}{dx} = -8x + 3; \quad r^2 - r = 0 \Rightarrow r = 0, 1$

$\therefore y_h = C_1 + C_2e^{x}$. Guess $y_p = Ax^2 + Bx$

Then $y_p' = 2Ax + B$; $y_p'' = 2A$

$2A - 2Ax - B = -8x + 3$; $A = 4, B = 5$

Then $y = y_h + y_p = C_1 + C_2e^{x} + 4x^2 + 5x$

27. $\dfrac{d^2y}{dx^2} - 3\dfrac{dy}{dx} = e^{3x} - 12x$; $r^2 - 3r = 0 \Rightarrow r = 0, 3$

$\therefore y_h = C_1 + C_2 e^{3x}$. Guess $y_p = Axe^{3x} + Bx^2 + Cx$

Then $y_p' = Ae^{3x} + 3Axe^{3x} + 2Bx + C$; $y_p'' = 6Ae^{3x} + 9Axe^{3x} + 2B$

$3ae^{3x} - 6Bx + 2B - 3C = e^{3x} - 12x$; $A = \dfrac{1}{3}, B = 2, C = \dfrac{4}{3}$

Then $y = y_h + y_p = C_1 + C_2 e^{3x} + \dfrac{1}{3}xe^{3x} + 2x^2 + \dfrac{4}{3}x$

28. $\dfrac{d^2y}{dx^2} + 7\dfrac{dy}{dx} = 42x^2 + 5x + 1$; $r^2 + 7r = 0 \Rightarrow r = 0, -7$

$\therefore y_h = C_1 + C_2 e^{-7x}$. Guess $y_p = Ax^3 + Bx^2 + Cx$

Then $y_p' = 3Ax^2 + 2Bx + C$; $y_p'' = 6Ax + 2B$

$6Ax + 2B + 21Ax^2 + 14Bx + 7C = 42x^2 + 5x + 1$; $21A = 42 \Rightarrow A = 2$

$6A + 14B = 5 \Rightarrow B = -\dfrac{1}{2}$; $2B + 7C = 1 \Rightarrow C = \dfrac{2}{7}$

Then $y = y_h + y_p = C_1 + C_2 e^{-7x} + 2x^3 - \dfrac{1}{2}x^2 + \dfrac{2}{7}x$

29. $\dfrac{d^2y}{dx^2} - 5\dfrac{dy}{dx} = xe^{5x}$; $r^2 - 5r = 0 \Rightarrow r = 0, 5$

$\therefore y_h = C_1 + C_2 e^{5x}$. $y_p = Ax^2e^{5x} + Bxe^{5x}$

Then $y_p' = 2Axe^{5x} + 5Ax^2 e^{5x} + Be^{5x} + 5Bxe^{5x}$

$y_p'' = 2Ae^{5x} + 20Axe^{5x} + 25Ax^2 e^{5x} + 10Be^{5x} + 25Bxe^{5x}$

$10Axe^{5x} + 5Be^{5x} + 2Ae^{5x} = xe^{5x}$; $A = \dfrac{1}{10}$

$2A + 5B = 0 \Rightarrow B = -\dfrac{1}{25}$

Then $y = y_h + y_p = C_1 + C_2 e^{5x} + \left(\dfrac{1}{10}x^2 - \dfrac{1}{25}x\right)e^{5x}$

30. $\dfrac{d^2y}{dx^2} - \dfrac{dy}{dx} = \cos x + \sin x$; $r^2 - r = 0 \Rightarrow r = 0, 1$

$\therefore y_h = C_1 + C_2 e^{x}$. $y_p = A\cos x + B\sin x$

Then $y_p' = -A\sin x + B\cos x$; $y_p'' = -A\cos x - B\sin x$

$-(A + B)\cos x - (B - A)\sin x = \cos x + \sin x \Rightarrow A = 0$ and $B = -1$

Then $y = y_h + y_p = C_1 + C_2 e^{x} - \sin x$

31. $\dfrac{d^2y}{dx^2} + y = 2\cos x + \sin x;\quad r^2 + 1 = 0 \Rightarrow r = \pm i$

$\therefore\ y_h = C_1\cos x + C_2 \sin x. \quad y_p = x(A\cos x + B\sin x)$

Then $y_p' = (A\cos x + B\sin x) + x(-A\sin x + B\cos x)$

$y_p'' = 2(-A\sin x + B\cos x) - x(A\cos x + B\sin x)$

$-2A\sin x + 2B\cos x = 2\cos x + \sin x \Rightarrow A = -\dfrac{1}{2}$ and $B = 1$

Then $y = y_h + y_p = C_1\cos x + C_2\sin x + x\left(\sin x - \dfrac{1}{2}\cos x\right)$

32. $\dfrac{d^2y}{dx^2} - 4\dfrac{dy}{dx} + 4y = 2e^{2x};\quad r^2 - 4r + 4 = 0 \Rightarrow r = 2, 2$

$\therefore\ y_h = C_1e^{2x} + C_2\, xe^{2x}.$

(a) $u_1 = e^{2x},\ u_2 = xe^{2x},\ F(x) = 2e^{2x}$

$$D = \begin{vmatrix} e^{2x} & xe^{2x} \\ 2e^{2x} & e^{2x} + 2xe^{2x} \end{vmatrix} = e^{4x};\quad v_1' = -2x \Rightarrow v_1 = -x^2$$

$v_2' = 2 \Rightarrow v_2 = 2x.$ Thus $y_p = -x^2e^{2x} + 2x^2e^{2x} = x^2e^{2x}$

(b) Let $y_p = Ax^2e^{2x}$. Then $y_p' = (2Ax + 2Ax^2)e^{2x}$ and

$y_p'' = (2A + 4Ax)e^{2x} + 4(Ax + x^2)e^{2x}$

$y_p'' - 4y_p' + 4y_p = 2e^{2x} \Rightarrow 2Ae^{2x} = 2e^{2x} \Rightarrow A = 1$ and $y_p = x^2e^{2x}$

$\therefore\ y = (C_1 + C_2\,x)\,e^{2x} + x^2\,e^{2x}$

33. $\dfrac{d^2y}{dx^2} - \dfrac{dy}{dx} = e^x + e^{-x};\quad r^2 - r = 0 \Rightarrow r = 0, 1$

$\therefore\ y_h = C_1 + C_2\,e^x.$

(a) $u_1 = 1,\ u_2 = e^x,\ F(x) = e^x + e^{-x}$

$$D = \begin{vmatrix} 1 & e^x \\ 0 & e^x \end{vmatrix} = e^x;\quad v_1' = -(e^x + e^{-x}) \Rightarrow v_1 = e^{-x} - e^x$$

$v_2' = 1 + e^{-2x} \Rightarrow v_2 = x - \dfrac{1}{2}e^{-2x}.$ Thus $y_p = (x-1)e^x + \dfrac{1}{2}e^{-x}$

(b) Let $y_p = Axe^x + Be^{-x}$. Then $y_p' = Axe^x + Ae^x - Be^x$ and

$y_p'' = 2Ae^x + Axe^x + Be^{-x}$

$y_p'' - 4y_p' + 4y_p = 2e^{2x} \Rightarrow Ae^x + 2Be^{-x} = e^x + e^{-x} \Rightarrow A = 1$ and $B = \dfrac{1}{2}$

$\therefore\ y = (C_1 + C_2\,e^x) + xe^x + \dfrac{1}{2}e^{-x}$

34. $\frac{d^2y}{dx^2} - 9\frac{dy}{dx} = 9e^{9x}$; $r^2 - 9r = 0 \Rightarrow r = 0, 9$

$\therefore y_h = C_1 + C_2 e^{9x}$.

(a) $u_1 = 1$, $u_2 = e^{9x}$, $F(x) = 9e^{9x}$

$$D = \begin{vmatrix} 1 & e^{9x} \\ 0 & 9e^{9x} \end{vmatrix} = 9e^{9x}; \quad v_1' = -e^{9x} \Rightarrow v_1 = -\frac{1}{9}e^{9x}$$

$v_2' = 1 \Rightarrow v_2 = x$. Thus $y_p = -\frac{1}{9}e^{9x} + xe^{9x}$

(b) Let $y_p = Axe^{9x}$. Then $y_p' = Ae^{9x} + 9Axe^{9x}$ and

$y_p'' = 18Ae^{9x} + 81Axe^{9x}$

$9Ae^{9x} = 9e^{9x} \Rightarrow A = 1$. Thus $y_p = xe^{9x}$

$$\therefore y = (C_1 + C_2 e^{9x}) + xe^{9x}$$

35. $\frac{d^2y}{dx^2} - 4\frac{dy}{dx} - 5y = e^x + 4$; $r^2 - 4r - 5 = 0 \Rightarrow r = 5, -1$

$\therefore y_h = C_1e^{5x} + C_2 e^{-x}$

(a) $u_1 = e^{5x}$, $u_2 = e^{-x}$, $F(x) = e^x + 4$

$$D = \begin{vmatrix} e^{5x} & e^{-x} \\ 5e^{5x} & -e^{-x} \end{vmatrix} = -6e^{4x}; \quad v_1' = \frac{1}{6}e^{-4x} + \frac{2}{3}e^{-5x} \Rightarrow v_1 = -\frac{1}{24}e^{-4x} - \frac{2}{15}e^{-5x}$$

$v_2' = -\frac{1}{6}e^{2x} - \frac{2}{3}e^x \Rightarrow v_2 = -\frac{1}{12}e^{2x} - \frac{2}{3}e^x$. Thus $y_p = -\frac{1}{8}e^x - \frac{4}{5}$

(b) Let $y_p = Ae^x + B$. Then $y_p' = Ae^x$ and $y_p'' = Ae^x$

$Ae^x - 4Ae^x - 5Ae^x - 5B = e^x + 4 \Rightarrow A = -\frac{1}{8}$ and $B = -\frac{4}{5}$. Thus $y_p = xe^{9x}$

$$\therefore y = C_1e^{5x} + C_2e^{-x} - \frac{1}{8}e^x - \frac{4}{5}$$

36. $\frac{d^2y}{dx^2} + y = \csc x$, $0 < x < \pi$ $\quad r^2 + 1 = 0 \Rightarrow r = \pm i$

Let $u_1 = \cos x$, $u_2 = \sin x$. $D = \begin{vmatrix} \cos x & \sin x \\ -\sin x & -\cos x \end{vmatrix} = 1$

$v_1' = -\sin x \csc x = -1 \Rightarrow v_1 = -x + C_1$

$v_2' = \cos x \csc x = \cot x \Rightarrow v_2 = \ln|\sin x| + C_2$

$\therefore y = C_1 \cos x + C_2 \sin x - x\cos x + \sin x \ln|\sin x|$

37. $\frac{d^2y}{dx^2} + y = \cot x,\ 0 < x < \pi \qquad r^2 + 1 = 0 \Rightarrow r = \pm i$

Let $u_1 = \cos x,\ u_2 = \sin x.\quad D = \begin{vmatrix} \cos x & \sin x \\ -\sin x & -\cos x \end{vmatrix} = 1$

$v_1' = -\sin x \cot x = -\cos x \Rightarrow v_1 = -\sin x + C_1$

$v_2' = \cos x \cot x = \csc x - \sin x \Rightarrow v_2 = -\ln|\csc x + \cot x| + \cos x + C_2$

$\therefore\ y = C_1 \cos x + C_2 \sin x - \sin x \ln|\csc x + \cot x|$

38. $\frac{d^2y}{dx^2} + 4y = \sin x \qquad r^2 + 4 = 0 \Rightarrow r = \pm 2i$

$y_h = C_1 \cos 2x + C_2 \sin 2x \qquad \text{Let } y_p = A \sin x + B \cos x$

Then $y_p' = A \cos x - B \sin x$ and $y_p'' = -A \sin x - B \cos x$

$-A \sin x - B \cos x + 4A \sin x + 4B \cos x = \sin x \Rightarrow A = \frac{1}{3},\ B = 0$

$\therefore\ y = C_1 \cos 2x + C_2 \sin 2x + \frac{1}{3} \sin x$

39. $\frac{d^2y}{dx^2} - 8\frac{dy}{dx} = e^{8x} \qquad r^2 - 8r = 0 \Rightarrow r = 0, 8$

$y_h = C_1 + C_2 e^{8x} \qquad \text{Let } y_p = A x e^{8x}$

Then $y_p' = A e^{8x} + 8 x e^{8x}$ and $y_p'' = 16 Ae^{8x} + 64 Axe^{8x}$

$16 Ae^{8x} + 64 Axe^{8x} - 8A e^{8x} - 64x e^{8x} = e^{8x} \Rightarrow A = \frac{1}{8}$

$\therefore\ y = C_1 + C_2 e^{8x} + \frac{1}{8} xe^{8x}$

40. $\frac{d^2y}{dx^2} + 4\frac{dy}{dx} + 5y = x + 2 \qquad r^2 + 4r + 5 = 0 \Rightarrow r = -2 \pm i$

$y_h = e^{-2x}(C_1 \cos x + C_2 \sin x) \qquad \text{Let } y_p = Ax + B$

Then $y_p' = A$ and $y_p'' = 0$

$4A + 5Ax + 5B = x + 2 = A = \frac{1}{5}$ and $B = \frac{6}{25}$

$\therefore\ y = e^{-2x}(C_1 \cos x + C_2 \sin x) + \frac{1}{5}x + \frac{6}{25}$

41. $\frac{d^2y}{dx^2} - \frac{dy}{dx} = x^3 \qquad r^2 - r = 0 \Rightarrow r = 0, 1$

$y_h = C_1 + C_2 e^x \qquad \text{Let } y_p = Ax^4 + Bx^3 + Cx^2 + Dx$

Then $y_p' = 4Ax^3 + 3Bx^2 + 2Cx + D$ and $y_p'' = 12Ax^2 + 6Bx + 2C$

$4Ax^3 + 3Bx^2 + 2Cx + D - 12Ax^2 - 6Bx - 2C = x^3 \Rightarrow A = -\frac{1}{4},\ B = -1,\ C = -3,\ D = -6$

$\therefore\ y = C_1 + C_2 e^x - \frac{1}{4}x^4 - x^3 - 3x^2 - 6$

42. $\dfrac{d^2y}{dx^2} + 9y = 9x - \cos x \qquad r^2 + 9 = 0 \Rightarrow r = \pm 3i$

$y_h = C_1 \cos 3x + C_2 \sin 3x$. Let $y_p = Ax + B + C\cos x + D\sin x$

Then $y_p' = A + D\cos x + C\sin x$ and $y_p'' = -D\sin x - C\cos x$

$-D\sin x - C\cos x + 9Ax + 9B + 9C\cos x + 9D\sin x = 9x - \cos x$

$9Ax + 9B + 8C\cos x + 8D\sin x = 9x - \cos x \Rightarrow A = 1,\ B = 0,\ C = -\dfrac{1}{8},\ D = 0$

$\therefore\ y = C_1 \cos 3x + C_2 \sin 3x + x - \dfrac{1}{8}\cos x + x$

43. $\dfrac{d^2y}{dx^2} + 2\dfrac{dy}{dx} = x^2 - e^x \qquad r^2 + 2r = 0 \Rightarrow r = 0, -2$

$y_h = C_1 + C_2 e^{-2x}$. Let $y_p = Ax^3 + Bx^2 + Cx + De^x$

Then $y_p' = 3Ax^2 + 2Bx + C + De^x$ and $y_p'' = 6Ax + 2B + De^x$

$6Ax + 2B + De^x + 2Ax^3 + 2Bx^2 + 2Cx + 2De^x = x^2 - e^x$

$6Ax^2 + (6A + 4B)x + (2B + 2C) + 3De^x = x^2 - e^x \Rightarrow A = \dfrac{1}{6},\ B = -\dfrac{1}{4},\ C = \dfrac{1}{4},\ D = -\dfrac{1}{3}$

$\therefore\ y = C_1 + C_2 e^{-2x} + \dfrac{1}{6}x^3 - \dfrac{1}{4}x^2 + \dfrac{1}{4}x - \dfrac{1}{3}e^x$

44. $\dfrac{d^2y}{dx^2} - 3\dfrac{dy}{dx} + 2y = e^x - e^{2x} \qquad r^2 - 3r + 2 = 0 \Rightarrow r = 2, 1$

$y_h = C_1 e^x + C_2 e^{2x}$. Let $y_p = Axe^x + Bxe^{2x}$

Then $y_p' = (A + Ax)e^x + (B + 2Bx)e^{2x}$ and

$y_p'' = Ae^x + (A + Ax)e^x + 2Be^{2x} + 2(B + 2Bx)e^{2x}$

$-Ae^x + Be^{2x} = e^x - e^{2x} \Rightarrow A = -1$ and $B = -1$

$\therefore\ y = C_1 e^x + C_2 e^{2x} - xe^x - xe^{2x}$

45. $\dfrac{d^2y}{dx^2} + y = \sec x \tan x,\ -\dfrac{\pi}{2} < x < \dfrac{\pi}{2} \qquad r^2 + 1 = 0 \Rightarrow r = \pm i$

$u_1 = \cos x \qquad u_2 = \sin x \quad F = \sec x \tan x$

$$D = \begin{vmatrix} \cos x & \sin x \\ -\sin x & \cos x \end{vmatrix} = 1$$

$v_1' = -\sin x \sec x \tan x \Rightarrow v_1 = -\int \tan^2 x\, dx = x - \tan x + C_1$

$v_2' = \cos x \sec x \tan x \Rightarrow v_2 = \int \tan x\, dx = \ln(\sec x) + C_2$

$\therefore\ y = C_1 \cos x + C_2 \sin x + s\cos x - \sin x + \sin x \ln(\sec x)$

46. $\dfrac{dy}{dx} + 4y = x$ $\qquad r + 4 = 0 \Rightarrow r = -4$

$y_h = Ce^{-4x}$ Let $y_p = Ax + B$. Then $y_p' = A$

$A + 4Ax + 4B = x \Rightarrow A = \dfrac{1}{4}$ and $B = -\dfrac{1}{16}$

$\therefore\ y = Ce^{-4x} + \dfrac{1}{4}x - \dfrac{1}{16}$

47. $\dfrac{dy}{dx} - 3y = e^x$ $\qquad r - 3 = 0 \Rightarrow r = 3$

$y_h = Ce^{3x}$ Let $y_p = Ae^x$. Then $y_p' = Ae^x$

$Ae^x - 3Ae^x = e^x \Rightarrow A = -\dfrac{1}{2}$ $\quad \therefore\ y = Ce^{3x} - \dfrac{1}{2}e^x$

48. $\dfrac{dy}{dx} + y = \sin x$ $\qquad r + 1 = 0 \Rightarrow r = -1$

$y_h = Ce^{-x}$ Let $y_p = A\cos x + B\sin x$. Then

$y_p' = -A\sin x + B\cos x$

$-A\sin x + B\cos x + A\cos x + B\sin x = \sin x \Rightarrow A = -\dfrac{1}{2}$ and $B = \dfrac{1}{2}$

$\therefore\ y = Ce^{-x} - \dfrac{1}{2}\sin x + \dfrac{1}{2}\cos x$

49. $\dfrac{dy}{dx} - 3y = 5e^{3x}$ $\qquad r - 3 = 0 \Rightarrow r = 3$

$y_h = Ce^{3x}$ Let $y_p = Axe^{3x}$. Then $y_p' = 3Axe^{3x} + Ae^{3x}$

$3Axe^{3x} + Ae^{3x} - 3Axe^{3x} = 5e^{3x} \Rightarrow A = 5$ $\quad \therefore\ y = Ce^{3x} + 5xe^{3x}$

50. From Problem 18, we know that $y = C_1\cos x + C_2\sin x + \dfrac{1}{5}e^{2x}$

$y(0) = 0 \Rightarrow 0 = C_1 + \dfrac{1}{5} \Rightarrow C_1 = -\dfrac{1}{5}$. $y'(0) = \dfrac{2}{5} \Rightarrow C_2 = 0$

$\therefore\ y = -\dfrac{1}{5}\cos x + \dfrac{1}{5}e^{2x}$

51. $\dfrac{d^2y}{dx^2} + y = \sec^2 x,\ -\dfrac{\pi}{2} < x < \dfrac{\pi}{2}$ $\qquad r^2 + 1 = 0 \Rightarrow r = \pm i$

Let $u_1 = \cos x$ and $u_2 = \sin x$

$D = \begin{vmatrix} \cos x & \sin x \\ -\sin x & \cos x \end{vmatrix} = 1$ $\qquad v_1' = -\sin x\sec^2 x = -\sec x\tan x$

$v_1 = \displaystyle\int -\sec x\tan x\,dx = -\sec x + C_1$

$v_2' = \cos x\sec^2 x = \sec x \Rightarrow v_2 = \displaystyle\int \sec x\,dx = \ln|\sec x + \tan x| + C_2$

Then $y = C_1\cos x + C_2\sin x - 1 + \sin x\ln|\sec x + \tan x|$

$y(0) = 1 \Rightarrow C_1 = 2$; $y'(0) = 1 \Rightarrow C_2 = 1$

$y = 2\cos x + \sin x - 1 + \sin x\ln|\sec x + \tan x|$

52. $\frac{dy}{dx} + y = (xy)^2 \Rightarrow \frac{1}{y^2}\frac{dy}{dx} + \frac{1}{y} = x^2$. Let $u = \frac{1}{y}$, $\frac{du}{dx} = -\frac{1}{y^2}\frac{dy}{dx}$

Then $\frac{du}{dx} - u = -x^2$. $y_h = Ce^x$. Let $y_p = Ax^2 + Bx + C$

$y_p' = 2Ax + B$ and $y_p'' = 2A$. $-Ax^2 + (2A - B)x + (B - C) = -x^2 \Rightarrow A = 1, B = C = 2$

$\therefore u = Ce^x + x^2 + 2x + 2 \Rightarrow y = \dfrac{1}{Ce^x + x^2 + 2x + 2}$

53. $y(x) + \int_0^x y(t)\,dt = x \Rightarrow \frac{d}{dx}\left[y(x) + \int_0^x y(t)\,dt\right] = 1$

$\frac{dy}{dx} + y(x) = 1 \quad \Rightarrow y_h = Ce^{-x}$. Let $y_p = A = 1$. $\therefore y = Ce^{-x} + 1$

$y(0) = 1 \Rightarrow C = -1$. Thus $y = -e^{-x} + 1$

14.6 VIBRATIONS

1. From Equation 5, $x = C_1 \cos \omega t + C_2 \sin \omega t$. $x(0) = x_0 \Rightarrow C_1 = x_0$.

$x'(0) = v_0 \Rightarrow C_2 = \frac{v_0}{\omega}$. $\therefore x = x_0 \cos \omega t + \frac{v_0}{\omega} \sin \omega t$.

Also, $x = C \sin(\omega t + \phi)$ with $C = \sqrt{x_0^2 + \left(\frac{v_0}{\omega}\right)^2}$ and $\phi = \tan^{-1}\left(\frac{\omega x_0}{v_0}\right)$

2. $k = \frac{F}{s} = \dfrac{5\text{ lb}}{\frac{1}{6}\text{ ft}} = 30\text{ lb/ft}$. $\omega = \sqrt{\frac{k}{m}} = \sqrt{\dfrac{30\text{ lb/ft}}{5\text{ lb}/32\text{ ft/s}^2}} = 13.856\text{ sec}$

$v_0 = 4\text{ ft/s}$, $x_0 = 0$; $x(t) = \frac{v_0}{\omega} \sin \omega t = 0.288 \sin(13.856\,t)$

3. (a) v a constant $\Rightarrow \frac{dV}{dt} = 0$. We have $\frac{d^2 i}{dt^2} + \omega^2 i = 0$

$\therefore i = C_1 \cos \omega t + C_2 \sin \omega t$

(b) $i_h = C_1 \cos \omega t + C_2 \sin \omega t$ from part (a).

$v = V \sin \alpha t \Rightarrow \frac{dv}{dt} = \alpha V \cos \alpha t$. $\frac{d^2 i}{dt^2} + \omega^2 i = \frac{\alpha V}{L} \cos \alpha t$

Guess $i_p = A \cos \alpha t + B \sin \alpha t$. We get $B = 0$, $A = \dfrac{\alpha V}{L(\omega^2 - \alpha^2)}$

$\therefore i = C_1 \cos \omega t + C_2 \sin \omega t + \dfrac{\alpha V}{L(\omega^2 - \alpha^2)} \cos \alpha t$

(c) $i_h = C_1 \cos \omega t + C_2 \sin \omega t$ from part (a).

$$v = V \sin \omega t \Rightarrow \frac{dv}{dt} = \omega V \cos \omega t. \quad \frac{d^2 i}{dt^2} + \omega^2 i = \frac{V\omega}{L} \cos \omega t$$

Guess $i_p = A t \cos \omega t + B t \sin \omega t$. We get $B = 0,\ A = \frac{V}{2L}$

$$\therefore i = C_1 \cos \omega t + C_2 \sin \omega t + \frac{V}{2L} t \sin \omega t$$

(d) $5\frac{d^2 i}{dt^2} + 50\frac{di}{dt} + \frac{10^6}{9} i = 0 \Rightarrow r = -5 \pm 149\,i$

$$\therefore i = e^{-5t}(C_1 \cos 149t + C_2 \sin 149t$$

4. $\frac{d^2\theta}{dt^2} + \frac{g}{l}\theta = 0 \Rightarrow r = \pm\sqrt{\frac{g}{l}}\,i. \quad \theta = C_1 \cos\sqrt{\frac{g}{l}}\,t + C_2 \sin\sqrt{\frac{g}{l}}\,t.$

$$\theta(0) = 0 \Rightarrow C_1 = \theta_0. \quad \frac{d\theta}{dt} = 0 \text{ at } t = 0 \Rightarrow C_2 = 0. \quad \therefore \theta = \theta_0 \cos\left(\sqrt{\frac{g}{l}}\,t\right)$$

5. $\frac{d^2\theta}{dt^2} + \omega^2\theta = 0$, where $\omega = \sqrt{\frac{2k}{mr^2}} \Rightarrow r = \pm\omega i. \quad \theta = C_1 \cos \omega t + C_2 \sin \omega t.$

$$\theta(0) = 0 \Rightarrow C_1 = \theta_0. \quad \frac{d\theta}{dt} = v_0 \text{ at } t = 0 \Rightarrow C_2 = \frac{v_0}{\omega}.$$

$$\therefore \theta = \theta_0 \cos \omega t + \frac{v_0}{\omega} \sin \omega t, \quad \omega = \sqrt{\frac{2k}{mr^2}}$$

6. $\frac{d^2x}{dt^2} + \frac{gc}{100}\frac{dx}{dt} + \frac{16\pi g}{100} x = 0 \Rightarrow 100 r^2 + gc\,r + 16\pi g = 0$

$$25r^2 + 8c\,r + 128\pi = 0 \Rightarrow r = -\frac{4c}{25} \pm \frac{4\sqrt{200\pi - c^2}}{25}\,i.$$

$$\text{Period} = \frac{2\pi}{\omega} \text{ where } \omega = \frac{4\sqrt{200\pi - c^2}}{25}. \quad \therefore 1.6 = \frac{4\sqrt{200\pi - c^2}}{25} \quad c = 5.09$$

7. $m\dfrac{d^2x}{dt^2} + kx = k\,f(t)$ $\quad r^2 + \dfrac{k}{m} = 0 \Rightarrow r = \pm i\sqrt{\dfrac{k}{m}}$. Let $\omega^2 = \dfrac{k}{m}$

Then $x_h = C_1\cos\omega t + C_2\sin\omega t$

(a) $f(t) = A\sin\alpha t,\ \alpha \neq \omega$. Guess $x_p = B\cos\alpha t + C\sin\alpha t$

Then one finds $B = 0,\ C = \dfrac{A\omega^2}{\omega^2 - \alpha^2} \Rightarrow$

$$x = C_1\cos\omega t + C_2\sin\omega t + \frac{A\omega^2}{\omega^2 - \alpha^2}\sin\alpha t$$

$x = x_0$ and $\dfrac{dx}{dt} = 0$ when $t = 0 \Rightarrow C_1 = x_0$ and $C_2 = -\dfrac{\alpha\omega A}{\omega^2 - \alpha^2}$

(b) $f(t) = A\sin\alpha t,\ \alpha = \omega$. Guess $x_p = t\,(B\cos\alpha t + C\sin\alpha t)$

Then one finds $C = 0,\ B = -\dfrac{\omega A}{2} \Rightarrow$

$$x = C_1\cos\omega t + C_2\sin\omega t - \frac{\omega A}{2}\cos\alpha t$$

$x = x_0$ and $\dfrac{dx}{dt} = 0$ when $t = 0 \Rightarrow C_1 = x_0$ and $C_2 = \dfrac{A}{2}$

14.7 HIGHER ORDER LINEAR EQUATIONS WITH CONSTANT COEFFICIENTS

1. $\dfrac{d^3y}{dx^3} - 3\dfrac{d^2y}{dx^2} + 2\dfrac{dy}{dx} = 0$ $\quad r^3 - 3r^2 + 2r = r(r-2)(r-1) = 0$

$y = C_1e^x + C_2e^{2x} + C_3$

2. $\dfrac{d^3y}{dx^3} - y = 0$ $\quad r^3 - 1 \Rightarrow r = 1,\ -\dfrac{1}{2} \pm \dfrac{\sqrt{3}}{2}i$

$$y = C_1e^x + e^{-x/2}\left(C_2\cos\frac{\sqrt{3}}{2}x + C_3\sin\frac{\sqrt{3}}{2}\right)$$

3. $\dfrac{d^4y}{dx^4} - 4\dfrac{d^2y}{dx^2} + 4y = 0$ $\quad (r^2 - 2)^2 = 0 \Rightarrow r = \pm\sqrt{2}, \pm\sqrt{2}$

$$y = e^{\sqrt{2}x}(C_1 + C_2x) + e^{-\sqrt{2}x}(C_3 + C_4x)$$

4. $\dfrac{d^4y}{dx^4} - 16y = 0$ $\quad r = \pm 2,\ \pm 2i$

$$y = C_1e^{2x} + C_2e^{-2x} + C_3\cos 2x + C_4\sin 2x$$

5. $\frac{d^4y}{dx^4} + 16y = 0 \qquad r = \sqrt{2} \pm i\sqrt{2}, -\sqrt{2} \pm i\sqrt{2}$ (See Ex. 5, Page A-56)

$$y = e^{\sqrt{2}x}(C_1 \cos\sqrt{2}x + C_2 \sin\sqrt{2}x) + e^{-\sqrt{2}x}(C_3 \cos\sqrt{2}x + C_4 \sin\sqrt{2}x)$$

6. $\frac{d^3y}{dx^3} - 3\frac{dy}{dx} + 2y = e^x \qquad r^3 - 3r + 2 = (r-1)(r-1)(r+2) \quad r = 1, 1, -2$

$y_h = C_1e^x + C_2xe^x + C_3e^{-2x}$; Try $y_p = Ax^2e^x$. Then

$$(Ax^2e^x + 6Axe^x + 6Ae^{2x}) - 3(2Axe^{2x} + Ax^2e^x) + 2Ax^2e^x = e^x \Rightarrow A = \frac{1}{6}$$

$$\therefore\ y = C_1e^x + C_2xe^x + C_3e^{-2x} + \frac{1}{6}x^2e^x$$

7. $\frac{d^4y}{dx^4} - 4\frac{d^3y}{dx^3} + 6\frac{d^2y}{dx^2} - 4\frac{dy}{dx} + y = 7 \qquad r^4 - 4r^3 + 6r^2 - 4r + 1 = (r-1)^4$

$y_h = e^x(C_1 + C_2x + C_3x^2 + C_4x^3)$; Try $y_p = 7$. Then

$$\therefore\ y = e^x(C_1 + C_2x + C_3x^2 + C_4x^3) + 7$$

8. $\frac{d^4y}{dx^4} + y = x + 1 \qquad r^4 + 1 = 0 \Rightarrow r = \frac{1}{\sqrt{2}} \pm \frac{1}{\sqrt{2}}i, -\frac{1}{\sqrt{2}} \pm \frac{1}{\sqrt{2}}i$

(See Appendix A-56); $y_p = x + 1$ since $y^{(4)} = 0$

$$y_h = e^{x/\sqrt{2}}\left(C_1\cos\frac{1}{\sqrt{2}}x + \sin\frac{1}{\sqrt{2}}x\right) + e^{-x/\sqrt{2}}\left(C_3\cos\frac{1}{\sqrt{2}}x + \sin\frac{1}{\sqrt{2}}x\right) + x + 1$$

14.8 APPROXIMATION METHODS: POWER SERIES

1. $y = 2e^{x-1} - 2 - (x-1) \Rightarrow y' = 2e^{x-1} - 1$

$x + y = x + 2e^{x-1} - 2 - (x-1) = 2e^{x-1} - 1$. Also $y(1) = 0$

2. $y(x) = y(0) + y'(0)x + \frac{y''(0)}{2!}x^2 + \ldots$

$y' + y = 0 \Rightarrow y' = y. \quad \therefore\ y'(0) = y(0) = 1$

$y'' = y' \Rightarrow y''(0) = y'(0) = 1$

$$\therefore\ y = 1 + x + \frac{1}{2}x^2 + \ldots = \sum_{n=0}^{\infty}\frac{x^n}{n!}$$

3. $y(x) = y(0) + y'(0)x + \frac{y''(0)}{2!}x^2 + \ldots$

$y' + y = 0 \Rightarrow y' = -y. \therefore y'(0) = -y(0) = -1$

$y'' = -y' \Rightarrow y''(0) = -y'(0) = 1$

$\therefore y = 1 + x - \frac{1}{2}x^2 + \ldots = \sum_{n=0}^{\infty} (-1)^n \frac{x^n}{n!}$

4. $y(x) = y(0) + y'(0)x + \frac{y''(0)}{2!}x^2 + \ldots$

$y' = 2y. \therefore y'(0) = 2y(0) = 2^2$

$y'' = 2y' \Rightarrow y''(0) = 2y'(0) = 2^3$

$\therefore y = 2 + 2^2 x + \frac{2^3}{2!}x^2 + \frac{2^4}{3!}x^3 \ldots = 2\sum_{n=0}^{\infty} \frac{(2x)^n}{n!}$

5. $y(x) = y(0) + y'(0)(x-1) + \frac{y''(0)}{2!}(x-1)^2 + \ldots$

$y' = -2y. \therefore y'(1) = -2y(1) = 2$

$y'' = -2y' \Rightarrow y''(1) = 2y'(1) = -2^2$

$\therefore y = -(x-1) + 2(x-1) - \frac{2^2}{2!}(x-1)^2 \ldots = \sum_{n=0}^{\infty} (-1)^{n+1} \frac{2^n}{n!}(x-1)^n$

6. $y(x) = y(0) + y'(0)x + \frac{y''(0)}{2!}x^2 + \ldots$

$y' = y. \quad y'(0) = 1$ and $y(0) = 0$

$y'' = y' \Rightarrow y''(0) = y'(0) = 1$

$\therefore y = x + \frac{1}{2}x^2 + \frac{1}{3!}x^3 + \ldots = \sum_{n=1}^{\infty} \frac{1}{n!}x^n$

7. $y(x) = y(0) + y'(0)x + \frac{y''(0)}{2!}x^2 + \ldots; y'(0) = 0$ and $y(0) = 1$

$y'' = -y \Rightarrow y''(0) = -1.$

$y''' = -y' \Rightarrow y'''(0) = y'(0) = 0; \; y^{iv} = -y'' = 1$

$\therefore y = 1 - \frac{1}{2}x^2 + \frac{1}{4!}x^4 - \ldots = \sum_{n=0}^{\infty} (-1)^n \frac{x^{2n}}{(2n)!}$

8. $y(x) = y(0) + y'(0)x + \dfrac{y''(0)}{2!}x^2 + \ldots$

$y'' = -y + x$. $y'(0) = 1$ and $y(0) = 2 \Rightarrow y''(0) = -2$

$y''' = -y' + 1 \Rightarrow y'''(0) = -1 + 1 = 0$

$y^{iv} = -y'' = 2$; $y^{v} = -y''' = 0$; $y^{vi} = -y^{iv} = -2$

$$\therefore y = 2 + x - \frac{2}{2!}x^2 + 0 + \frac{2}{4!}x^4 + 0 + \ldots = 2 + x - 2\sum_{n=1}^{\infty}(-1)^{n+1}\frac{x^{2n}}{(2n)!}$$

9. $y(x) = y(0) + y'(0)x + \dfrac{y''(0)}{2!}x^2 + \ldots$

$y'' = y + x$. $y'(0) = 2$ and $y(0) = -1 \Rightarrow y''(0) = -1$

$y''' = y' + 1 \Rightarrow y'''(0) = 2 + 1 = 3$

$y^{iv} = y'' = -1$; $y^{v} = y''' = 3$; $y^{vi} = y^{iv} = -1$

$$\therefore y = -1 + 2x - \frac{1}{2!}x^2 + \frac{3}{3!}x^3 - \frac{1}{4!}x^4 + \frac{3}{5!} + \ldots$$

$$= 3\sum_{n=0}^{\infty}\frac{x^{2n+1}}{(2n+1)!} - \sum_{n=0}^{\infty}\frac{x^{2n}}{(2n)!} - x$$

10. $y(x) = y(0) + y'(0)(x-2) + \dfrac{y''(0)}{2!}(x-2)^2 + \ldots$

$y'' = y - x$. $y'(2) = -2$ and $y(2) = 0 \Rightarrow y''(2) = -2$

$y''' = y' - 1 \Rightarrow y'''(2) = -2 - 1 = -3$

$y^{iv} = y'' = -2$; $y^{v} = y''' = -3$

$$\therefore y = -2(x-2) - 2\sum_{n=1}^{\infty}\frac{(x-2)^{2n}}{(2n)!} - 3\sum_{n=1}^{\infty}\frac{(x-2)^{2n+1}}{(2n+1)!}$$

11. $y(x) = y(0) + y'(0)x + \dfrac{y''(0)}{2!}x^2 + \ldots$

$y'' = x^2 y$. $y' = y_1$ and $y = y_0$; $y'' = 0$

$y''' = 2xy + x^2 y' \Rightarrow y''' = 0$

$y^{iv} = 2xy' + 2y + 2xy' + x^2 y'' = 2y_0$

$y^{v} = 2xy'' + 2y' + 2y' + 2xy'' + 2y' + 2xy'' + x^2 y''' = 6y_1$

$y^{vi} = y^{vii} = 0$; $y^{viii} = 60y_0$

$$\therefore y = y_0 + y_1 x + \frac{2y_0}{4!}x^4 + \frac{6y_1}{5!} + \ldots$$

$$= \sum_{n=0}^{\infty} a_n x^n, \text{ where } a_0 = y_0, a_1 = y_1, a_2 = a_3 = 0, a_n = \frac{1}{n(n-1)}a_{n-4} \text{ for } n \geq 4.$$

14.9 DIRECTION FIELDS AND PICARD'S THEOREM

1. The isoclines are the vertical lines x = constant

   (See graph in Answer section of the textbook)

2. The isoclines are the horizontal lines y = constant.

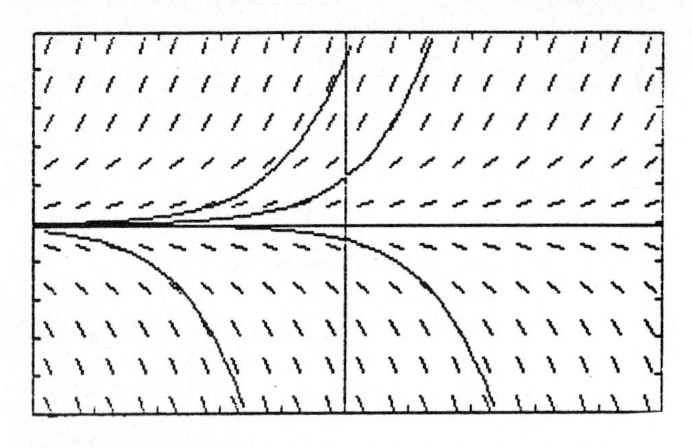

3. If $\frac{1}{x} = C$, then $x = \frac{1}{C} = C_1$. The isoclines are the vertical lines x = constant. (See graph in Answer section of the textbook.)

4. The isoclines are the horizontal lines y = constant.

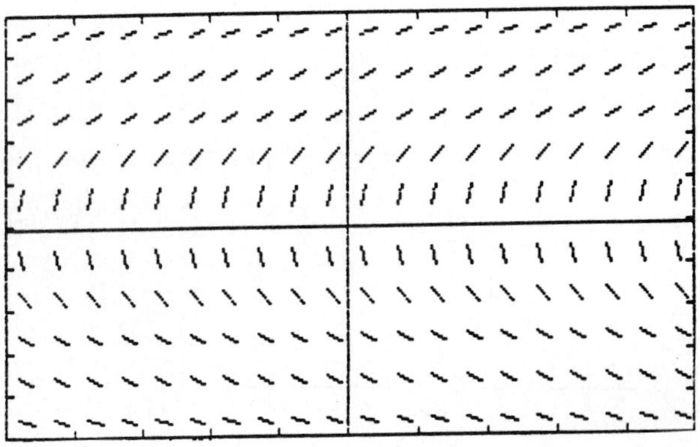

5. The isoclines are the curves xy = constant.
   (See graph in answer section of the textbook.)

6. The isoclines are the curves $x^2 + y^2 = \text{constant}$

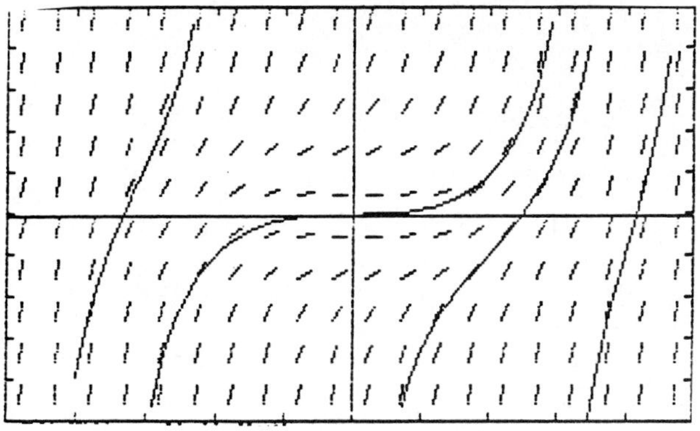

7. Let $u = x + y \Rightarrow \dfrac{du}{dx} = 1 + \dfrac{dy}{dx}$. Hence $y' = (x + y)^2$ becomes

$\dfrac{du}{dx} = 1 + u^2 \Rightarrow \dfrac{du}{1 + u^2} = dx$ or $\tan^{-1} u = x + C$.

$\therefore\ y = \tan(x + C) - x$. This passes through $(0, 0)$ when $C = 0$

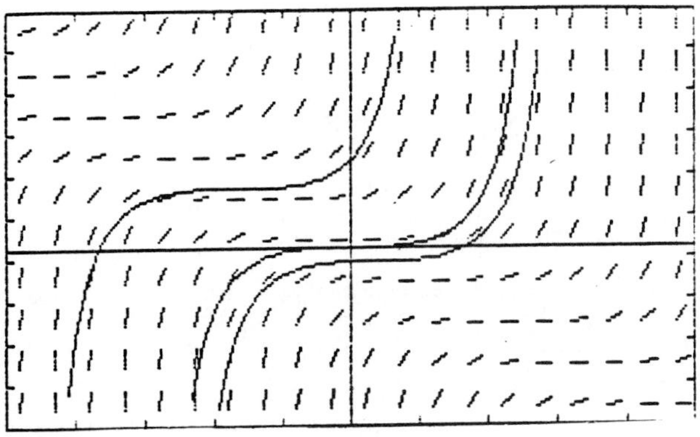

8. $y = \tan(x + C) - x \Rightarrow \dfrac{dy}{dx} = \sec^2(x + C) - 1 \ge 0$ since $|\sec\theta| \ge 1$.

Since $\dfrac{dy}{dx}$ cannot change sign, there are no extrema.

$\dfrac{d^2y}{dx^2} = 2\sec^2(x + C)\tan(x + C) = 0$ if $\tan(x + C) = 0$ or if $x = -C$.

Since $\dfrac{d^2y}{dx^2} < 0$ if $x < -C$ and $\dfrac{d^2y}{dx^2} > 0$ if $x > -C$, there is a point

of inflection at $(-C, C)$.

9. $\frac{dy}{dx} + y = x$. Let $\rho = e^{\int dx} = e^x$. Then $e^x y = \int xe^x\,dx$

$e^x y = xe^x - e^x + C \Rightarrow y = x - 1 + Ce^{-x}$

(a) If $C = 0$, then $y = x - 1$ is a solution.

(b) If $y' = x - y$ then $y'' = 1 - y' = 1 - (x - y)$

Concave up ($y'' > 0$) if $y > x - 1$ and concave down ($y'' < 0$) if $y < x - 1$

(See graph in Answer section of the textbook.)

10. $y = 1 + \int_0^x y(t)\,dt \Rightarrow y' = y,\ y(0) = 1$

11. $y = -1 + \int_1^x t - y(t)\,dt \Rightarrow y' = x - y,\ y(1) = -1$

12. $y = \int_1^x \frac{1}{t}\,dt \Rightarrow y' = \frac{1}{x},\ y(1) = 0$

13. $y = 2 - \int_0^x (1 + y(t))\sin t\,dt \Rightarrow y' = -(1 + y)\sin x,\ y(0) = 2$

14. $y' = f(x), y(x_0) = y_0$ is $y = y_0 + \int_{x_0}^x f(t)\,dt$

15. $y_0 = 2,\ y_1 = 2 + \int_1^x t\,dt = 2 + \frac{1}{2}x^2 - \frac{1}{2} = \frac{1}{2}x^2 + \frac{3}{2}$

$y_2 = y_3 = 2 + \int_1^x t\,dt = \frac{1}{2}x^2 + \frac{3}{2}$

16. $y_0 = 1,\ y_1 = 1 + \int_0^x y_0(t)\,dt = 1 + x;\ y_2 = 1 + \int_0^x (1 + t)dt = 1 + x + \frac{1}{2}x^2$

$y_3 = 1 + \int_0^x \left(1 + t + \frac{1}{2}t^2\right)dt = 1 + x + \frac{1}{2}x^2 + \frac{1}{6}x^3$

17. $y_0 = 1,\ y_1 = 1 + \int_1^x t\,dt = \frac{1}{2}(1 + x^2)$

$y_2 = 1 + \int_1^x \frac{1}{2}(1 + t^2)\,t\,dt = \frac{5}{8} + \frac{1}{4}x^2 + \frac{1}{8}x^4$

$y_3 = 1 + \int_1^x \left(\frac{5}{8} + \frac{1}{4}t^2 + \frac{1}{8}t^4\right)t\,dt = \frac{29}{48} + \frac{5}{16}x^2 + \frac{1}{16}x^4 + \frac{1}{48}x^6$

18. $y_0 = 0,\ y_1 = \int_0^x t\,dt = \frac{1}{2}x^2$

$$y_2 = \int_0^x \left(\frac{1}{2}t^2 + t\right) dt = \frac{1}{2}x^2 + \frac{1}{6}x^3$$

$$y_3 = \int_0^x \left(t + \frac{1}{2}t^2 + \frac{1}{6}t^3\right)t\,dt = \frac{1}{2}x^2 + \frac{1}{6}x^3 + \frac{1}{24}x^4$$

19. $y_0 = 1,\ y_1 = 1 + \int_0^x (t+1)\,dt = 1 + x + \frac{1}{2}x^2$

$$y_2 = 1 + \int_0^x \left[t + \left(1 + t + \frac{1}{2}t^2\right)\right] dt = 1 + x + x^2 + \frac{1}{6}x^3$$

$$y_3 = 1 + \int_0^x \left[t + \left(1 + t + t^2 + \frac{1}{6}t^3\right)t\,dt = 1 + x + x^2 + \frac{1}{3}x^3 + \frac{1}{24}x^4$$

20. $y_0 = 1,\ y_1 = 1 + \int_{-1}^x (2t - 1)\,dt = -1 - x + x^2$

$$y_2 = 1 + \int_{-1}^x [2t - (-1 - t + t^2)]\,dt = \frac{1}{6} + x + \frac{3}{2}x^2 - \frac{1}{3}x^3$$

$$y_3 = 1 + \int_{-1}^x \left[2t - \left(\frac{1}{6} + t + \frac{3}{2}t^2 - \frac{1}{3}t^3\right)t\,dt = -\frac{1}{4} - \frac{1}{6}x + \frac{1}{2}x^2 - \frac{1}{2}x^3 + \frac{1}{12}x^4$$

21. $y' - y = x$. Let $\rho = e^{-x}$. Then $e^{-x}y = \int xe^{-x} = -xe^{-x} - e^{-x} + C$

$y = -x - 1 + Ce^x$. $y(x_0) = y_0 \Rightarrow y_0 = Ce^{x_0} - x_0 - 1$ or $C = x_0 + y_0 + 1$

$\therefore\ y = (x_0 + y_0 + 1)e^{x - x_0} - (x + 1)$

22. $$y_3 = \int_0^x \left[t^2 + \left(\frac{t^3}{3} + \frac{t^7}{63}\right)^2\right] dt = \int_0^x \left(t^2 + \frac{t^6}{9} + \frac{2t^{10}}{189} + \frac{t^{14}}{3969}\right)dt$$

$$= \frac{1}{3}x^3 + \frac{x^7}{63} + \frac{2x^{11}}{2079} + \frac{x^{15}}{59535}$$

14.10 NUMERICAL METHODS

1.

i	x_i	y_i	$y_{i+1} = y_i(h+1)$
0	0	1	1.2
0	0	1	1.
1	0.2	1.2	1.44
2	0.4	1.44	1.728
3	0.6	1.728	2.0736
4	0.8	2.0736	2.48832

The exact value is e^x

2. $y_1 = y_0\left(1+\frac{1}{n}\right) = 1+\frac{1}{n}$

$y_2 = \left(1+\frac{1}{n}\right)\left(1+\frac{1}{n}\right) = \left(1+\frac{1}{n}\right)^2; \; y_n = \left(1+\frac{1}{n}\right)^n$

$\lim_{n\to\infty}\left(1+\frac{1}{n}\right)^n = e$

3.

i	x_i	y_i	$z_i = y_i(1+h)$	$y_{i+1} = y_i + 0.1(y_i + z_{i+1})$
0	0	1	1.2	1.22
1	0.2	1.22	1.464	1.4884
2	0.4	1.4884	1.78608	1.815848
3	0.6	1.815848	2.1790176	2.2153346
4	0.8	2.2153346	2.6584015	2.7027082

4.

i	x_i	y_i
0	1	1
1	0.2	1.2214
2	0.4	1.49181796
3	0.6	1.82210646
4	0.8	2.22552083
5	1.0	2.71825114

5. $\frac{dy}{dx} = a^2 + y^2 \Rightarrow \frac{dy}{a^2+y^2} = dx \Rightarrow \frac{1}{a}\tan^{-1}\frac{y}{a} = x + C$

$y(a) = f(a) \Rightarrow C = \frac{1}{a}\tan^{-1}\frac{f(a)}{a} - a. \;\therefore\; y = a\tan\left[a\left(x + \frac{1}{a}\tan^{-1}\frac{f(a)}{a} - a\right)\right].$

$a\left[x + \frac{1}{a}\tan^{-1}\frac{f(a)}{a} - a\right] = \frac{\pi}{2} \Rightarrow x = a + \frac{1}{a}\left[\frac{\pi}{2} - \tan^{-1}\frac{f(a)}{a}\right]$

For $a = 2.0$ and $f(a) = 317.2244$, $x^* = 2.0031523$

6. $\frac{dy}{dx} = y^2 \Rightarrow \frac{dy}{y^2} = dx \Rightarrow -\frac{1}{y} = x + C.$ $y(0) = 1 \Rightarrow C = -1$

$\therefore\; y = \frac{1}{x-1}$ is the solution. Since $x^2 + y^2 \geq y^2$, the solution to $y' = x^2 + y^2$ grows faster than that of $y' = y^2$, which grows infinite as $x \to 1$.

7. $y(0)=1 \Rightarrow a_0 = 1$

$c_0 = a_0^2 = 1 \qquad a_1 = c_0 = 1$

$c_1 = 2a_0 a_1 = 2 \qquad a_2 = \frac{1}{2}c_1 = 1$

$c_2 = 2a_0 a_2 + a_1^2 = 3 \qquad a_3 = \frac{1}{3}(1 + c_2) = \frac{4}{3}$

$c_3 = 2a_0 a_3 + 2a_1 a_2 = \frac{14}{3} \qquad a_4 = \frac{14}{12} = \frac{7}{6}$

8. (a) $\frac{dy}{dx} = 1 + y^2 \Rightarrow \frac{dy}{1+y^2} = dx \Rightarrow \tan^{-1} y = x + C$. $y(0) = 0 \Rightarrow C = 0$.

$\therefore \quad y = \tan x$

(b) $y = -\frac{u'}{u} \Rightarrow y' = -\frac{uu'' - (u')^2}{u^2}$. So $-\frac{uu'' - (u')^2}{u^2} = 1 + \left(\frac{u'}{u}\right)^2$

or $\frac{u''}{u} = -1$. The solution to $u'' + u = 0$ is $u = C_1 \cos x + C_2 \sin x$.

$u'(0) = 0 \Rightarrow C_2 = 0$, so $u = C_1 \cos x$ and $y = -\frac{-C_1 \sin x}{C_1 \cos x} = \tan x$.

14.M MISCELLANEOUS

1. $y \ln y \, dx + (1 + x^2)\, dy \Rightarrow (1 + x^2)\, dy = -y \ln y \, dx \Rightarrow$

$\frac{dy}{y \ln y} = -\frac{dx}{1+x^2} \Rightarrow \ln|\ln y| = -\tan^{-1} x + C$

2. $\frac{dy}{dx} = \frac{y^2 - y - 2}{x^2 + x} \Rightarrow \frac{dy}{(y-2)(y+1)} = \frac{dx}{x(x+1)}$

$\frac{1}{3}\left(\frac{1}{y-2} - \frac{1}{y+1}\right)dy = \left(\frac{1}{x} - \frac{1}{x+1}\right)dx \Rightarrow \frac{1}{3}\ln\frac{y-2}{y+1} = \ln\frac{x}{x+1} + C$

$\frac{y-2}{y+1} = C\left(\frac{x}{x+1}\right)^3$

3. $e^{x+2y}\, dy - e^{y-2}\, dx = 0 \Rightarrow e^{x+2y}\, dy = e^{y-2}\, dx$

$e^{y+2}\, dy = e^{-x}\, dx \Rightarrow e^{y+2} = -e^{-x} + C$ or $y = -2 + \ln(C - e^{-x})$

4. $\sqrt{1 + \left(\frac{dy}{dx}\right)^2} = ky \Rightarrow \frac{dy}{dx} = \pm\sqrt{k^2 y^2 - 1} \Rightarrow \frac{dy}{\sqrt{k^2 y^2 - 1}} = \pm\, dx$

$\frac{1}{k}\cosh^{-1}(ky) = \pm x + C \Rightarrow y = \frac{1}{k}\cosh(kx + C)$

5. $y\,dy = \sqrt{1+y^4}\,dx \Rightarrow \dfrac{y\,dy}{\sqrt{1+y^4}} = dx \Rightarrow \dfrac{1}{2}\sinh^{-1}(y^2) = x + C$

6. $(2x + y)dx + (x - 2y)dy = 0 \quad \Rightarrow \quad 2x\,dx + (x\,dy + y\,dx) - 2y\,dy = 0$

$\therefore \quad x^2 + xy - y^2 = C$

7. Let $v = \dfrac{y}{x}$, $\dfrac{dy}{dx} = v + x\dfrac{dv}{dx}$. Then $\dfrac{dy}{dx} = \dfrac{x^2+y^2}{2xy} \Rightarrow 2xy\dfrac{dy}{dx} = x^2 + y^2$

$2\left(\dfrac{y}{x}\right)\dfrac{dy}{dx} = 1 + \left(\dfrac{y}{x}\right)^2$ so $2v\left(v + x\dfrac{dv}{dx}\right) = 1 - v^2 \Rightarrow \dfrac{2v\,dv}{1-v^2} = \dfrac{dx}{x}$

$\ln|1 - v^2| = -\ln|x| + C \Rightarrow 1 - v^2 = \dfrac{1}{x} + C \Rightarrow y^2 = x^2 - Cx$

8. $x\dfrac{dy}{dx} = y + \sqrt{x^2+y^2} \Rightarrow \dfrac{dy}{dx} = \dfrac{y}{x} + \sqrt{1 + \left(\dfrac{y}{x}\right)^2}$

$v + x\dfrac{dv}{dx} = v + \sqrt{1+v^2} \Rightarrow \dfrac{dv}{\sqrt{1+v^2}} = \dfrac{dx}{x} \Rightarrow \ln|v + \sqrt{1+v^2}| = \ln|x| + C$

$\dfrac{y}{x} + \sqrt{1 + \left(\dfrac{y}{x}\right)^2} = Cx \Rightarrow y + \sqrt{x^2+y^2} = Cx^2$

9. $x\,dy = \left(y + x\cos^2\dfrac{y}{x}\right)dx \Rightarrow x\,dy - y\,dx = x\cos^2\dfrac{y}{x}\,dx$

$(x\,dy - y\,dx)\sec^2\dfrac{y}{x} = x\,dx \Rightarrow \dfrac{(x\,dy - y\,dx)}{x^2}\sec^2\dfrac{y}{x} = \dfrac{dx}{x}$

$\therefore \tan\dfrac{y}{x} = \ln|x| + C$ or $y = x\tan^{-1}(\ln|x| + C)$

10. $x(\ln y - \ln x)\,dy = y(1 + \ln y - \ln x)\,dx$

$\dfrac{dy}{dx}\left(\ln\dfrac{y}{x}\right) = \dfrac{y}{x}\left(1 + \ln\dfrac{y}{x}\right)$; Let $v = \dfrac{y}{x}$, $\dfrac{dy}{dx} = v + x\dfrac{dv}{dx}$

$\left(v + x\dfrac{dv}{dx}\right)\ln v = v(1 + \ln v) \Rightarrow \dfrac{\ln v\,dv}{v} = \dfrac{dx}{x}$

$\dfrac{1}{2}(\ln v)^2 = \ln|x| + C \Rightarrow (\ln|y| - \ln|x|)^2 = 2\ln|x| + C$

11. $x\,dy + (2y - x^2 - 1)\,dx = 0 \Rightarrow \dfrac{dy}{dx} + \dfrac{2}{x}y = x + \dfrac{1}{x}$.

Then $\rho = e^{\int 2/x\,dx} = x^2$, so $x^2 y = \displaystyle\int (x^3 + x)dx = \dfrac{1}{4}x^4 + \dfrac{1}{2}x^2 + C$

$y = \dfrac{1}{4}x^2 + \dfrac{1}{2} + Cx^{-2}$

12. $\cos y\,dx + (x\sin y - \cos^2 y)\,dy = 0$

$\cos y\dfrac{dx}{dy} + (\sin y)x = \cos^2 y \Rightarrow \dfrac{dx}{dy} + (\tan y)x = \cos y$

$\rho = e^{\ln(\sec y)} = \sec y$, so $x\sec y = \displaystyle\int dy = y + C$, or $x\sec y - y = C$

13. $\cosh x\, dy - (y + \cosh x)\sinh x\, dx = 0$

$$\cosh x \frac{dy}{dx} - (\sinh x)\, y = \cosh x \sinh x \Rightarrow \frac{dy}{dx} - (\tanh x)\, y = \sinh x$$

$$\rho = e^{-\ln(\cosh x)} = \text{sech}\, x, \text{ so } \; y\, \text{sech}\, x = \int \tanh x\, dx = \ln(\cosh x) + C$$

$$y = \cosh x\, [\ln(\cosh x) + C]$$

14. $(x+1)dy + (2y - x)\, dx = 0 \Rightarrow (x+1)\frac{dy}{dx} + 2y = x \Rightarrow \frac{dy}{dx} + \frac{2}{x+1}\, y = \frac{x}{x+1}$

$$\rho = e^{2\ln(x+1)} = (x+1)^2, \text{ so } \; y\,(x+1)^2 = \int x\,(x+1)\, dx = \frac{1}{3}x^3 + \frac{1}{2}x^2 + C$$

$$y = (x+1)^{-2}\left(\frac{1}{3}x^3 + \frac{1}{2}x^2 + C\right)$$

15. $(1 + y^2)dx + (2xy + y^2 + 1)dy = 0 \Rightarrow \frac{dx}{dy} + \frac{2y}{1+y^2}\, x = -1$

$$\rho = 1 + y^2 \; \text{ so } \; x\,(1 + y^2) = -\int (1 + y^2)\, dy = -y - \frac{1}{3}y^3 + C$$

$$3x\,(1 + y^2) + 3y + y^3 = C$$

16. $(x^2 + y)\, dx + (e^y + x)\, dy = 0 \Rightarrow x^2\, dx + (y\, dx + x\, dy) + e^y\, dy = 0$

$$\therefore \; \frac{1}{3}x^3 + xy + e^y = C$$

17. $(x^2 + y^2)\, dx + (2xy + \cosh y)\, dy = 0 \Rightarrow x^2\, dx + (2xy\, dy + y^2\, dx) + \cosh y\, dy = 0$

$$\frac{1}{3}x^3 + xy^2 + \sinh y = C$$

18. $(e^x + \ln y)\, dx + \frac{x+y}{y}\, dy = 0 \Rightarrow e^x\, dx + \left(\ln y\, dx + \frac{x}{y}\, dy\right) + dy = 0$

$$e^x + x\ln y + y = C$$

19. $x\,(1 + e^y)\, dx + \frac{1}{2}(x^2 + y^2)\, e^y\, dy = 0$

$$x\, dx + \left(xe^y\, dx + \frac{1}{2}x^2\, e^y\, dy\right) + \frac{1}{2}y^2\, e^y\, dy = 0.$$

$$\frac{1}{2}x^2 + \frac{1}{2}x^2\, e^y + \left(\frac{1}{2}y^2\, e^y - y\, e^y + e^y\right) = C$$

$$x^2 + e^y\,(x^2 + y^2 - 2y + 2) = C$$

20. $\left(\sin x + \tan^{-1}\frac{y}{x}\right)dx - \left(y - \ln\sqrt{x^2+y^2}\right)dy = 0$

Let $M = \sin x + \tan^{-1}\frac{y}{x}$ and $N = \ln\sqrt{x^2+y^2} - y$. Then $\frac{\partial M}{\partial y} = \frac{\partial N}{\partial x}$.

$\int\left(\sin x + \tan^{-1}\frac{y}{x}\right)dx = -\cos x + x\tan^{-1}\frac{y}{x} + y\ln\sqrt{x^2+y^2} + g(y)$

$\therefore \ln\sqrt{x^2+y^2} + 1 + g'(y) = \ln\sqrt{x^2+y^2} - y \Rightarrow g(y) = -\frac{1}{2}y^2 - y$

$-\cos x + x\tan^{-1}\frac{y}{x} + y\ln\sqrt{x^2+y^2} - \frac{1}{2}y^2 - y = C$

21. $\frac{d^2y}{dx^2} - 2y\frac{dy}{dx} = 0$. Let $p = \frac{dy}{dx}$ so $\frac{d^2y}{dx^2} = p\frac{dp}{dy}$. Then $p\frac{dp}{dy} - 2yp = 0 \Rightarrow$

$p = 0$ or $dp = 2y\,dy \Rightarrow p = C$ or $p = y^2 + C \Rightarrow \frac{dy}{dx} = y^2 + C$ or $y = C$.

For $\frac{dy}{dx} = y^2 + C$ there are three cases to consider.

$C = 0$: $\frac{dy}{y^2} = dx \Rightarrow -y^{-1} = x + K$ or $y = -\frac{1}{x+K}$

$C = B^2 > 0$: $\frac{dy}{B^2+y^2} = dx \Rightarrow \frac{1}{B}\tan^{-1}\frac{y}{B} = x + K \Rightarrow y = B\tan(Bx + K')$

$C < 0$, $C = -B^2$: $\frac{dy}{y^2-B^2} = dx \Rightarrow y = \frac{1}{2B}\ln\left|\frac{y-B}{y+B}\right| = x + K$

22. $\frac{d^2x}{dy^2} + 4x = 0$ $\qquad r^2 + 4 = 0 \Rightarrow r = \pm 2i$

$x = C_1\cos 2y + C_2\sin 2y$

23. $\frac{d^2y}{dx^2} = 1 + \left(\frac{dy}{dx}\right)^2$. Let $p = \frac{dy}{dx}$. Then $\frac{dp}{dx} = 1 + p^2 \Rightarrow \frac{dp}{1+p^2} = dx$

$\tan^{-1}p = x + C \Rightarrow p = \frac{dy}{dx} = \tan(x+C) \Rightarrow y = \ln|\sec(x+C)| + K$

24. $\frac{d^2x}{dy^2} = 1 - \left(\frac{dx}{dy}\right)^2$. Let $p = \frac{dx}{dy}$. Then $\frac{dp}{dy} = 1 - p^2 \Rightarrow \frac{dp}{1-p^2} = dy$

$\tanh^{-1}p = y + C \Rightarrow p = \frac{dx}{dy} = \tanh(y+C) \Rightarrow x = \ln|\cosh(y+C)| + K$

25. $x^2\frac{d^2y}{dx^2} + x\frac{dy}{dx} = 1$. Let $p = \frac{dy}{dx}$. Then $x^2\frac{dp}{dx} + xp = 1$

$\frac{dp}{dx} + \frac{1}{x}p = x^{-2} \Rightarrow xp = \int x^{-1}\,dx = \ln x + C$.

$\frac{dy}{dx} = \frac{\ln x}{x} + \frac{C}{x} \Rightarrow y = \frac{1}{2}(\ln x)^2 + C\ln x + K$

26. $\frac{d^2y}{dx^2} - 4\frac{dy}{dx} + 3y = 0.$ $r^2 - 4r + 3 = 0 \Rightarrow r = 1, 3$

$y = C_1e^x + c_2e^{3x}$

27. $\frac{d^3y}{dx^3} - 2\frac{d^2y}{dx^2} + \frac{dy}{dx} = 0$ $r^3 - 2r^2 + r = 0 \Rightarrow r = 0, 1, 1$

$y = C_1 + C_2e^x + C_3\, x\, e^x$

28. $\frac{d^2y}{dx^2} + 4y = \sec 2x.$ $r^2 + 4 = 0 \Rightarrow r = \pm 2i$

$y_h = C_1\cos 2x + C_2 \sin 2x$. Let $u_1 = \cos 2x$ and $u_2 = \sin 2x$.

$D = 2$, so $v_1{}' = -\frac{1}{2}\tan 2x \Rightarrow v_1 = \frac{1}{4}\ln|\cos 2x|$

$v_2{}' = \frac{1}{2}$ so $v_2 = \frac{1}{2}x$. Then $y_p = \frac{1}{4}\cos 2x \ln|\cos 2x| + \frac{1}{2}x \sin 2x$ and

$y = C_1\cos 2x + C_2 \sin 2x + \frac{1}{4}\cos 2x \ln|\cos 2x| + \frac{1}{2}x \sin 2x$

29. $\frac{d^2y}{dx^2} - \frac{dy}{dx} - 2y = e^{2x}$ $r^2 - r - 2 = 0 \Rightarrow r = 2, -1$

$y_h = C_1e^{2x} + C_2e^{-x}$. Try $y_p = Axe^{2x}$. Then $3Ae^{2x} = e^{2x} \Rightarrow A = \frac{1}{3}$

$y = C_1e^{2x} + C_2e^{-x} + \frac{1}{3}xe^{2x}$

30. $\frac{d^2y}{dx^2} - 2\frac{dy}{dx} + 5y = e^{-x}$ $r^2 - 2r + 5 = 0 \Rightarrow r = 1 \pm 2i$

$y_h = e^x(C_1\cos 2x + C_2 \sin 2x)$. Try $y_p = Ae^{-x}$. Then $A = \frac{1}{8}$

$y = e^x(C_1\cos 2x + C_2 \sin 2x) + \frac{1}{8}e^{-x}$

31. $4x^2\frac{d^2y}{dx^2} + 4x\frac{dy}{dx} - y = 0.$ If $y = x^c$ is a solution then

$\frac{dy}{dx} = cx^{c-1}$ and $\frac{d^2y}{dx^2} = c(c-1)x^{c-2}$ satisfy the equation.

$4c(c-1)x^2\, x^{c-2} + 4cx\, x^{c-1} - x^c = 4c(c-1)\, x^c + 4cx^c - x^c = 0$

$x^c(4c^2 - 1) = 0$ or $c = \pm\frac{1}{2} \Rightarrow y = C_1x^{1/2} + C_2\, x^{-1/2}$

32. We need $\dfrac{\dfrac{d^2y}{dx^2}}{\left[1+\left(\dfrac{dy}{dx}\right)^2\right]^{3/2}} = A$. There are two cases:

$A = 0$: $\dfrac{d^2y}{dx^2} = 0 \Rightarrow y = mx + b$, a line

$A \neq 0$: Let $p = \dfrac{dy}{dx}$. Then $(1+p^2)^{-3/2}\,dp = A\,dx$

$$\frac{p}{\sqrt{1+p^2}} = Ax + B \Rightarrow p = \frac{dy}{dx} = \frac{Ax+B}{\sqrt{1-(Ax+B)^2}}$$

$$y = \frac{1}{A}\sqrt{1-(Ax+B)^2} + C \Rightarrow A^2(y-C)^2 + A^2\left(x+\frac{B}{A}\right)^2 = 1, \text{ a circle}$$

33. $x^2 = Cy^3 \Rightarrow 3Cy^2\dfrac{dy}{dx} = 2x \Rightarrow 3\left(\dfrac{x^2}{y^3}\right)y^2\dfrac{dy}{dx} = 2x \Rightarrow \dfrac{dy}{dx} = \dfrac{2y}{3x}$.

The orthogonal trajectories should have slope $\dfrac{dy}{dx} = -\dfrac{3x}{2y}$

Then $y^2 = -\dfrac{3}{2}x^2 + A$ or $2y^2 + 3x^2 = B$

34. $(x-C)^2 + y^2 = C^2 \Rightarrow x^2 - 2xC + C^2 + y^2 = C^2 \Rightarrow 2x - 2C + 2y\dfrac{dy}{dx} = 0$

$x - \left(\dfrac{x^2+y^2}{2x}\right) + y\dfrac{dy}{dx} = 0 \Rightarrow \dfrac{dy}{dx} = -\dfrac{x^2-y^2}{2xy}$. The orthogonal

trajectories satisfy $\dfrac{dy}{dx} = \dfrac{2xy}{x^2-y^2} = \dfrac{2\left(\dfrac{y}{x}\right)}{1-\left(\dfrac{y}{x}\right)^2}$.

Let $v = \dfrac{y}{x}$, so that $x\dfrac{dv}{dx} + v = \dfrac{2v}{1-v^2} \Rightarrow x\dfrac{dv}{dx} = \dfrac{v+v^3}{1-v^2}$

$$\frac{1-v^2}{v+v^3}\,dv = \frac{dx}{x} \Rightarrow \left(\frac{1}{v} - \frac{2v}{1+v^2}\right)dv = \frac{dx}{x} \Rightarrow \ln|v| - \ln(1+v^2) = \ln|x| + A$$

$\dfrac{v}{1+v^2} = Bx$. $\therefore$ $\dfrac{xy}{x^2+y^2} = Bx$ or $x^2 + y^2 = By$.

35. $y^2 = 4C(C - x) \Rightarrow 2y\frac{dy}{dx} = -4C \Rightarrow y^2\left(\frac{dy}{dx}\right)^2 = 4C^2$

$$y^2\left(\frac{dy}{dx}\right)^2 = y^2 + 4Cx = y^2 - x\left(2y\frac{dy}{dx}\right).$$

$$y^2\left(\frac{dy}{dx}\right)^2 + 2xy\frac{dy}{dx} - y^2 = 0 \Rightarrow \left(\frac{dy}{dx}\right)^2 + \frac{2x}{y}\frac{dy}{dx} - 1 = 0$$

$$\frac{dy}{dx} = \frac{-\frac{2x}{y} \pm \sqrt{\frac{4x^2}{y^2} + 4}}{2} = -\frac{x}{y} \pm \sqrt{\left(\frac{x}{y}\right)^2 + 1}$$. The orthogonal trajectories

satisfy $\frac{dx}{dy} = -\frac{x}{y} \pm \sqrt{\left(\frac{x}{y}\right)^2 + 1}$ also. Let $v = \frac{x}{y}$, so $\frac{dx}{dy} = v + y\frac{dy}{dy}$.

$$v + y\frac{dv}{dy} = -v \pm \sqrt{v^2 + 1} \Rightarrow \frac{dv}{\pm\sqrt{v^2 + 1}} = \frac{dy}{y} \Rightarrow \pm \ln|v + \sqrt{v^2 + 1}| = \ln y + B$$

$$v \pm \sqrt{v^2 + 1} = By \Rightarrow \frac{x}{y} \pm \sqrt{\left(\frac{x}{y}\right)^2 + 1} = By \Rightarrow x \pm \sqrt{x^2 + y^2} = B$$

$x^2 - 2Bx + B^2 = x^2 + y^2$ or $y^2 = B^2 - 2Bx$.

36. $\frac{d^2y}{dt^2} + 100y = 0$ $\qquad r^2 + 100 = 0 \Rightarrow r = \pm 10i$

$y = C_1 \cos 10t + C_2 \sin 10t$. $y(0) = 10$, $y'(0) = 50 \Rightarrow C_1 = 10$, $C_2 = 5$

$y = 10 \cos 10t + 5 \sin 10t$. The amplitude $= 5\sqrt{5}$ and

period $= \frac{2\pi}{10} \approx 0.63$.

37. $\frac{dy}{dx} - y = x$. Let $\rho = e^{-x}$. Then $ye^{-x} = \int xe^{-x}\,dx = -xe^{-x} - e^{-x} + C$.

$y = Ce^x - x - 1$. $y(0) = 0 \Rightarrow C = 1$. $\therefore y = e^x - x - 1$. The series is

$$y = \left(1 + x + \frac{1}{2}x^2 + \ldots\right) - x - 1 = \sum_{n=2}^{\infty} \frac{x^n}{n!}$$

38. $y' = x + \sin y$ $\qquad y(0) = 0,\ y'(0) = 0$

$y'' = 1 + (\cos y)y'$ $\qquad y''(0) = 1$

$y''' = (-\sin y)y' + (\cos y)y''$ $\qquad y'''(0) = 1$

$y^{iv} = (-2\sin y)y'' + (-\sin y)y' + (\cos y)y'''$ $\qquad y^{iv}(0) = 1$

$$y = \frac{1}{2}x^2 + \frac{1}{3!}x^3 + \frac{1}{4!}x^4 + \ldots$$

39. (a) $y' = x + \sin y$ $\qquad y(0) = \frac{\pi}{2},\ y'(0) = 1$

$y'' = 1 + (\cos y)y'$ $\qquad y''(0) = 1$

$y''' = (-\sin y)\, y' + (\cos y)\, y''$ $\qquad y'''(0) = -1$

$y^{iv} = (-2\sin y)y'' + (-\sin y)y' + (\cos y)\, y'''$ $\qquad y^{iv}(0) = -3$

$y = \frac{\pi}{2} + x - \frac{1}{2}x^2 - \frac{1}{6}x^3 - \frac{3}{8}x^4 + \ldots$

(b) $y' = x + \sin y$ $\qquad y(0) = -\frac{\pi}{2},\ y'(0) = -1$

$y'' = 1 + (\cos y)y'$ $\qquad y''(0) = 1$

$y''' = (-\sin y)\, y' + (\cos y)\, y''$ $\qquad y'''(0) = 1$

$y^{iv} = (-2\sin y)y'' + (-\sin y)y' + (\cos y)\, y'''$ $\qquad y^{iv}(0) = -3$

$y = -\frac{\pi}{2} - x + \frac{1}{2}x^2 + \frac{1}{6}x^3 - \frac{3}{8}x^4 + \ldots$